P S Y C H O L O G Y
Themes & Variations
Briefer Version 3rd Edition

Wayne Weiten
Santa Clara University

Brooks/Cole Publishing Company
I(T)P® An International Thomson Publishing Company

Pacific Grove • Albany • Belmont, CA • Bonn • Boston • Cincinnati • Detroit • Johannesburg • London • Madrid •
Melbourne • Mexico City • New York • Paris • Singapore • Tokyo • Toronto • Washington

⚡ A CLAIREMONT BOOK

Sponsoring Editor: Eileen Murphy
Marketing Team: Margaret Parks, Lauren Harp
Editorial Associates: Patricia Vinneau, Lisa Blanton
Production Coordinator: Marjorie Sanders
Production: Nancy Sjoberg, Del Mar Associates
Manuscript Editor: Jackie Estrada
Interior and Cover Design: John Odam
Cover and Chapter Opening Illustrator: JoAnn Koppany
Interior Illustration: John Odam, Kim Fraley, Jonathan Parker
Permissions and Photo Research: Linda L. Rill
Digital Typography: John Odam Design Associates and Del Mar Associates
Color Separation: Thompson Type
Printing and Binding: Von Hoffman

Credits continue on page 551.

For more information, contact:

BROOKS/COLE PUBLISHING COMPANY
511 Forest Lodge Rd.
Pacific Grove, CA 93950
USA

International Thomson Editores
Campos Eliseos 385, Piso 7
Col. Polanco
11560 México D.F. México

International Thomson Publishing Europe
Berkshire House 168-173
High Holborn
London, WC1V 7AA
England

International Thomson Publishing GmbH
Königswinterer Strasse 418
53227 Bonn
Germany

Thomas Nelson Australia
102 Dodds Street
South Melbourne 3205
Victoria, Australia

International Thomson Publishing Asia
221 Henderson Road
#05-10 Henderson Building
Singapore 0315

Nelson Canada
1120 Birchmount Road
Scarborough, Ontario
Canada M1K 5G4

International Thomson Publishing Japan
Hirakawacho Kyowa Building, 3F
2-2-1 Hirakawacho
Chiyoda-ku, Tokyo 102
Japan

Printed in the United States of America

1 2 3 4 5 6 7 8 9 10—02 01 00 99 96 96

Library of Congress Cataloging-in-Publication Data
Weiten, Wayne, [date]
    Psychology: themes and variations / Wayne Weiten. — 3rd ed., briefer version.
        p.   cm.
    Includes bibliographical references and index.
    ISBN 0-534-33926-3 (pbk.)
    1. Psychology. I. Title
BF121.W38 1996
150—dc20

96-6003
CIP

To the Instructor

sychology is an exciting, dynamic discipline that has grown by leaps and bounds in recent decades. This progress has been reflected in the field's introductory texts, which have grown longer and longer. However, the length of the introductory psychology course generally has not changed. Hence, an increasing number of professors are reporting that they find it difficult to cover the wealth of material found in the typical introductory text. With this reality in mind, I decided to write a briefer version of *Psychology: Themes and Variations* to help meet the needs of those teachers who would like a challenging, but concise, introductory text.

If I had to sum up in a single sentence what I hope will distinguish this text, the sentence would be this: I have set out to create a *paradox* instead of a *compromise*.

Let me elaborate. An introductory psychology text must satisfy two disparate audiences: professors and students. Because of the tension between the divergent needs and preferences of these audiences, textbook authors usually indicate that they have attempted to strike a compromise between being theoretical versus practical, comprehensive versus comprehensible, research oriented versus applied, rigorous versus accessible, and so forth. However, I believe that many of these dichotomies are false. As Kurt Lewin once remarked, "What could be more practical than a good theory?" Similarly, is rigorous really the opposite of accessible? Not in my dictionary. I maintain that many of the antagonistic goals that we strive for in our textbooks only seem incompatible, and that we may not need to make compromises as often as we assume.

In my estimation, a good introductory textbook is a paradox in that it integrates characteristics and goals that appear contradictory. With this in mind, I have endeavored to write a text that is paradoxical in three ways. First, in surveying psychology's broad range of content, I have tried to show that our interests are characterized by diversity *and* unity. Second, I have emphasized both research *and* application and how they work in harmony. Finally, I have aspired to write a book that is challenging to think about *and* easy to learn from. Let's take a closer look at these goals.

Goals

1. *To show both the unity and the diversity of psychology's subject matter.* Students entering an introductory psychology course often are unaware of the immense diversity of subjects studied by psychologists. I find this diversity to be part of psychology's charm, and throughout the book I highlight the enormous range of questions and issues addressed by psychology. Of course, our diversity proves disconcerting for some students who see little continuity between such disparate areas of research as physiology, motivation, cognition, and abnormal behavior. Indeed, in this era of specialization, even some psychologists express concern about the fragmentation of the field.

However, I believe that there is considerable overlap among the subfields of psychology and that we should emphasize their common core by accenting the connections and similarities among them. Consequently, I portray psychology as an integrated whole rather than as a mosaic of loosely related parts. A principal goal of this text, then, is to highlight the unity in psychology's intellectual heritage (the themes), as well as the diversity of psychology's interests and uses (the variations).

2. *To illuminate the process of research and its intimate link to application.* For me, a research-oriented book is not one that bulges with summaries of many studies but one that enhances students' appreciation of the logic and excitement of empirical inquiry. I want students to appreciate the strengths of the empirical approach and to see scientific psychology as a creative effort to solve intriguing behavioral puzzles. For this reason, the text emphasizes not only *what* we know (and don't know) but *how* we attempt to find out. Methods are examined in some detail, and students are encouraged to adopt the skeptical attitude of a scientist and to think critically about claims regarding behavior.

Learning the virtues of research should not mean that students cannot also satisfy their desire for concrete, personally useful information about the challenges of everyday life. Most researchers believe that psychology has a great deal to offer those outside the field and that we should share the practical implications of our work. In this text, practical insights are carefully qualified and closely tied to data, so that students can see the interdependence of research and application. I find that students come to appreciate the science of psychology more when they see that worthwhile practical applications are derived from careful research and sound theory.

3. *To make the text challenging to think about and easy to learn from.* Perhaps most of all, I have sought to create a *book of ideas* rather than a compendium of studies. I consistently emphasize concepts and theories over facts, and I focus on major issues and tough questions that cut across the subfields of psychology (for example, the extent to which behavior is governed by nature, nurture, and their interaction), as opposed to parochial debates (such as the merits of averaging versus adding in impression formation). Challenging students to think also means urging them to confront the complexity and ambiguity of our knowledge. Hence, the text doesn't skirt gray areas, unresolved questions, and theoretical controversies. Instead, readers are encouraged to contemplate open-ended questions, to examine their assumptions about behavior, and to apply psychological concepts to their own lives. My goal is not simply to describe psychology but to stimulate students' intellectual growth.

However, students can grapple with "the big issues and tough questions" only if they first master the basic concepts and principles of psychology—ideally, with as little struggle as possible. In my writing, I never let myself forget that a textbook is a tool for teaching. Accordingly, great care has been taken to ensure that the book's content, organization, writing, illustrations, and pedagogical aids work in harmony to facilitate instruction and learning.

Admittedly, these goals are ambitious. If you're skeptical, you have every right to be. Let me explain how I have tried to realize the objectives I have outlined.

Special Features

This text has a variety of unusual features, each contributing in its own way to the book's paradoxical nature. These special features include unifying themes, application sections, a didactic illustration program, an integrated running glossary, and concept checks.

Unifying Themes

Chapter 1 introduces seven key ideas that serve as unifying themes throughout the text. The themes serve several purposes. First, they provide threads of continuity across chapters that help students to see the connections among different areas of research in psychology. Second, as the themes evolve over the course of the book, they provide a forum for a relatively sophisticated discussion of enduring issues in psychology, thus helping to make this a "book of ideas." Third, the themes focus a spotlight on a number of basic insights about psychology and its subject matter that should leave lasting impressions on your students.

In selecting the themes, the question I asked myself (and other professors) was "What do I really want students to remember five years from now?" The resulting themes are grouped into two sets.

THEMES RELATED TO
PSYCHOLOGY AS A FIELD OF STUDY
Theme 1: Psychology is empirical. This theme is used to enhance the student's appreciation of psychology's scientific nature and to demonstrate the advantages of empiricism over uncritical common sense and speculation. I also use this theme to encourage the reader to adopt a scientist's skeptical attitude and to engage in more critical thinking about information of all kinds.

Theme 2: Psychology is theoretically diverse. Students are often confused by psychology's theoretical pluralism and view it as a weakness. I don't downplay or apologize for our theoretical diversity, because I honestly believe that it is one of our greatest strengths. Throughout the book, I provide concrete examples of how clashing theories have stimulated productive research, how converging on a question from several perspectives can yield increased understanding, and how competing theories are sometimes reconciled in the end.

Theme 3: Psychology evolves in a sociohistorical context. This theme emphasizes that psychology is embedded in the ebb and flow of everyday life. The text shows how the spirit of the times has often shaped psychology's evolution and how progress in psychology leaves its mark on our society.

THEMES RELATED TO PSYCHOLOGY'S
SUBJECT MATTER
Theme 4: Behavior is determined by multiple causes. Throughout the book, I emphasize, and repeatedly illustrate, that behavioral processes are complex and that multifactorial causation is the rule. This theme is used to discourage simplistic, single-cause thinking and to encourage more critical reasoning.

Theme 5: Our behavior is shaped by our cultural heritage. This theme, which is new to this edition, is intended to enhance students' appreciation of

Unifying Themes Highlighted in Each Chapter

Chapter	Theme 1 Empiricism	2 Theoretical Diversity	3 Sociohistorical Context	4 Multifactorial Causation	5 Cultural Heritage	6 Heredity and Environment	7 Subjectivity of Experience
1. The Evolution of Psychology	●	●	●	●	●	●	●
2. The Research Enterprise in Psychology	●						●
3. The Biological Bases of Behavior	●			●		●	
4. Sensation and Perception		●			●		●
5. Variations in Consciousness		●	●		●		●
6. Learning Through Conditioning			●			●	
7. Human Memory				●			●
8. Language and Thought	●				●	●	●
9. Intelligence and Psychological Testing			●		●	●	
10. Motivation and Emotion		●	●	●	●		
11. Development Across the Life Span		●	●	●	●	●	
12. Personality: Theory, Research, and Assessment		●	●		●		
13. Stress, Coping, and Health				●			●
14. Psychological Disorders			●	●	●	●	
15. Psychotherapy		●			●		
16. Social Behavior	●				●		●

how cultural factors moderate psychological processes and how the viewpoint of one's own culture can distort one's interpretation of the behavior of people from other cultures. The discussions that elaborate on this theme do not simply celebrate diversity. They strike a careful balance—that accurately reflect the research in this area—highlighting both cultural variations *and* similarities in behavior.

Theme 6: Heredity and environment jointly influence behavior. Repeatedly discussing this theme permits me to air out the nature versus nurture issue in all its complexity. Over a series of chapters, students gradually learn how biology shapes behavior, how experience shapes behavior, and how scientists estimate the relative importance of each. Along the way, students will gain an in-depth appreciation of what we mean when we say that heredity and environment interact.

Theme 7: Our experience of the world is highly subjective. All of us tend to forget the extent to which we view the world through our own personal lens. This theme is used to explain the principles that underlie the subjectivity of human experience, to clarify its implications, and to repeatedly remind the readers that their view of the world is not the only legitimate view.

After all seven themes have been introduced in Chapter 1, different sets of themes are discussed in each chapter, as they are relevant to the subject matter. The connections between a chapter's content and the unifying themes are highlighted in a standard section near the end of the chapter, in which I reflect on the "lessons to be learned" from the chapter. The discussions of the unifying themes are largely confined to these sections, titled "Putting It in Perspective." No effort was made to force every chapter to illustrate a certain number of themes. The themes were allowed to emerge naturally, and I found that two to four surfaced in any given chapter. The accompanying chart shows which themes are highlighted in each chapter.

Application Sections
To reinforce the pragmatic implications of theory and research that are stressed throughout the text, each chapter closes with an Application section

that highlights the personal, practical side of psychology. Each Application devotes three to six *pages* of text (rather than the usual box) to a single issue that should be of special interest to many of your students. Although most of the Application sections have a "how to" character, they continue to review studies and summarize data in much the same way as the main body of each chapter. Thus, they portray research and application not as incompatible polarities but as two sides of the same coin. Many of the Applications—such as those on finding and reading journal articles and understanding art and illusion—provide topical coverage unusual for an introductory text.

A Didactic Illustration Program

When I first outlined my plans for this text, I indicated that I wanted every aspect of the illustration program to have a genuine didactic purpose and that I wanted to be deeply involved in its development. In retrospect, I had no idea what I was getting myself into, but it has been a rewarding learning experience. I was intimately involved in planning every detail of the illustration program, along with another psychologist with experience in these matters (Alastair McLeod) and an editor who was familiar with every nuance of the book (John Bergez). Together, we have worked to create a program of figures, diagrams, photos, and tables that work hand in hand with the prose to strengthen and clarify the main points in the text. As part of this effort, we have designed many original illustrations and revised many old standbys that you have seen before.

The most obvious results of our didactic approach to illustration are the three summary spreads that combine tabular information, photos, diagrams, and sketches to provide exciting overviews of key ideas in learning, development, and personality theory. But I hope you will also notice the subtleties of the illustration program. For instance, diagrams of important concepts (conditioning, synaptic transmission, EEGs, experimental design, and so forth) are often repeated in several chapters (with variations) to highlight connections among research areas and to enhance students' mastery of key ideas. Numerous easy-to-understand graphs of research results underscore psychology's foundation in research, and we often use photos and diagrams to bolster each other (for example, see the treatment of classical conditioning in Chapter 6). Color is used carefully as an organizational device (see the figures showing psychology's areas of specialization in Chapter 1), and visual schematics are used to simplify hard-to-

visualize concepts (see the figure explaining reaction range for intelligence in Chapter 9). All of these efforts were made in the service of one master: the desire to make this an inviting book that is easy to learn from.

Integrated Running Glossary

An introductory text should place great emphasis on acquainting students with psychology's technical language—not for the sake of jargon, but because a great many of our key terms are also our cornerstone concepts (for example, independent variable, reliability, and cognitive dissonance). This text handles terminology with a running glossary embedded in the prose itself. The terms are set off in boldface italics, and the definitions follow in boldface roman type. This approach retains the two advantages of a conventional running glossary: vocabulary items are made salient, and their definitions are readily accessible. However, it does so without interrupting the flow of discourse, while eliminating redundancy between text matter and marginal entries.

Concept Checks

To help students assess their mastery of important ideas, Concept Checks are sprinkled throughout the book. In keeping with my goal of making this a book of ideas, the Concept Checks challenge students to apply ideas instead of testing rote memory. For example, in Chapter 6 the reader is asked to analyze realistic examples of conditioning and identify conditioned stimuli and responses, reinforcers, and schedules of reinforcement. Many of the Concept Checks require the reader to put together ideas introduced in different sections of the chapter. For instance, in Chapter 4 students are asked to identify parallels between vision and hearing. Some of the Concept Checks are quite challenging, but students find them engaging, and they report that the answers (available in the back of the book) are illuminating.

In addition to the special features just described, the text includes a variety of more conventional, "tried and true" features as well. The back of the book contains a standard *alphabetical glossary*. Opening *outlines* preview each chapter, and a thorough *summary* of key ideas appears at the end of each chapter, along with lists of *key terms* and *key people* (important theorists and researchers). I make frequent use of *italics for emphasis*, and I depend on *frequent headings* to maximize organizational clarity. The preface for students describes these pedagogical devices in more detail.

Content

The text is divided into 16 chapters, which follow a traditional ordering. The chapters are not grouped into sections or parts, primarily because such groupings can limit your options if you want to reorganize the order of topics. The chapters are written in a way that facilitates organizational flexibility, as I always assumed that some chapters might be omitted or presented in a different order.

The topical coverage in the text is relatively conventional, but there are some subtle departures from the norm. For instance, Chapter 1 presents a relatively "meaty" discussion of the evolution of ideas in psychology. This coverage of history lays the foundation for many of the crucial ideas emphasized in subsequent chapters. The historical perspective is also my way of reaching out to the students who find that psychology just isn't what they expected it to be. If we want students to contemplate the mysteries of behavior, we must begin by clearing up the biggest mysteries of them all: "Where did these rats, statistics, synapses, and JNDs come from; what could they possibly have in common; and why doesn't this course bear any resemblance to what I anticipated?" I use history as a vehicle to explain how psychology evolved into its modern form and why misconceptions about its nature are so common.

I also devote an entire chapter (Chapter 2) to the scientific enterprise—not just the mechanics of research methods but the logic behind them. I believe that an appreciation of the nature of empirical evidence can contribute greatly to improving students' critical thinking skills. Ten years from now, many of the "facts" reported in this book will have changed, but an understanding of the methods of science will remain invaluable. An introductory psychology course, by itself, isn't going to make a student think like a scientist, but I can't think of a better place to start the process.

Overall, I trust you'll find the coverage up to date, although I do not believe in the common practice of piling up gratuitous references to recent studies to create an impression of currency. I think that an obsession with this year's references derogates our intellectual heritage and suggests to students that the studies we cite today will be written off tomorrow. I often chose to cite an older source over a newer one to give students an accurate feel for when an idea first surfaced or when an issue generated heated debate.

As for changes in content, the most significant change is the incorporation of the new theme, which emphasizes both the variance and invariance of behavior across cultures. This theme seems particularly pertinent for students given the way our society is evolving into an increasingly diverse multicultural mosaic.

Writing Style

I strive for a down-to-earth, conversational writing style; effective communication is always the paramount goal. My intent is to talk *with* the reader rather than throw information *at* the reader. To clarify concepts and maintain students' interest, I frequently provide concrete examples that students can relate to. As much as possible, I avoid the use of technical jargon when ordinary language serves just as well.

Making learning easier depends, above all else, on clear, well-organized writing. For this reason, I've worked hard to ensure that chapters, sections, and paragraphs are organized in a logical manner, so that key ideas stand out in sharp relief against supportive information.

To keep myself on the path of clarity, I submit my chapters to the ultimate authority: my students, who take great delight in grading *me* for a change. They're given first drafts of chapters and are urged to slash away at pompous language and to flag sources of confusion. They are merciless—and enormously helpful.

Changes in the Briefer Version

As its title indicates, this book is a condensed version of my introductory text, *Psychology: Themes and Variations*. I have reduced the length of the book from 326,000 words to 220,000 words. A recent study of brief introductory psychology texts (Griggs, Jackson, & Napolitano, 1994) estimated the average length of such texts to be 242,000 words, so the present volume is shorter than the typical brief text. Indeed, based on the data from the Griggs et al. study, it appears that this book is the third shortest of the brief editions currently available.

How was this reduction in size accomplished? It required a great many difficult decisions, but fortunately, I had excellent advice from a team of 14 professors who served as consultants. About one-third of the reduction came from deleting entire topics, such as psychophysics, mental retardation, blocking in classical conditioning, the biochemistry of memory, sexual behavior, and so forth. However, the bulk of the reduction was achieved by compressing and simplifying coverage throughout the book. I carefully scrutinized the parent book sentence by sentence and forced myself to justify the existence of every study, every example, every citation, every phrase. The result is a thoroughly *rewritten* text, rather than one that was *reassembled* through "cut and paste" techniques.

Although the briefer verion has been shortened considerably, the overall organization is the same as in the parent book. Sixteen chapters on the same topics are presented in the same order. I did not feel a compelling need to reduce the number of chapters in the condensed edition because I had held the number of chapters in the parent book reasonably low.

I had originally planned to add some new pedagogical devices to the briefer version, but feedback from our consultants dissuaded me from doing so. Many of them pointed out that the parent book already included an abundance of learning aids. Moreover, several of them argued convincingly that an "essentials" book should be a simpler, more streamlined, less cluttered book, with fewer rather than more ancillary features. Based on their advice, I restrained myself and made only one small change in pedagogy. This change involved a modest increase in the number of concept checks, which have proven to be a popular learning aid in the parent book.

Supplementary Materials

The introductory course in psychology presents inherent difficulties for student and teacher alike. The teaching/learning package that has been developed to supplement *Psychology: Themes and Variations, Briefer Version*, was designed with these difficulties in mind. The development of all its parts was carefully coordinated so that they are mutually supported.

Study Guide (by Richard Stalling and Ronald Wasden)

For your students, there is an exceptionally thorough *Study Guide* available to help them master the information in the text. It was written by two of my former professors, Richard Stalling and Ronald Wasden of Bradley University. They have 25 years of experience, as a team, writing study guides for introductory psychology texts, and their experience is readily apparent in the high-quality materials that they have developed. They have carefully revised the Study Guide to reflect the myriad changes in the *Briefer Version*.

The review of key ideas for each chapter is made up of an engaging mixture of matching exercises, fill-in-the-blank items, free-response questions, and programmed learning. Each review is organized around learning objectives written by myself. The *Study Guide* is closely coordinated with the *Test Bank*, as the same learning objectives guided the construction of the questions in the *Test Bank*. The *Study Guide* also includes a review of key terms, a review of key people, and a self-test for each chapter in the text. An interactive *Electronic Study Guide* is available for Mac, DOS, and Windows. For U.S. customers, the text and study guide can be packaged together for a discount, ISBN: 0-534-33730-9.

Instructor's Resource Book

A talented roster of professors, whose efforts were coordinated by Randolph Smith, made contributions to the *Instructor's Resource Book (IRB)* in their respective areas of expertise. The *IRB* contains a diverse array of materials designed to facilitate efforts to teach the introductory course and includes the following six sections.

• *Strategies for Effective Teaching*, by Joseph Lowman (University of North Carolina), discusses practical issues such as what to put in a course syllabus, how to handle the first class meeting, how to cope with large classes, and how to train and organize teaching assistants.
• *Films and Videos for Introductory Psychology*, by Russ Watson (College of DuPage), provides a comprehensive, up-to-date critical overview of educational films relevant to the introductory course.
• *Computer Simulations for Introductory Psychology*, by Bernard Beins (Ithaca College), offers a thorough listing of the computer simulations that are germane to the introductory course and analyzes their strengths and weaknesses.
• *Integrating Writing into Introductory Psychology*, by Jane Jegerski (Elmhurst College), examines the writing across the curriculum movement and provides suggestions and materials for specific writing assignments chapter by chapter.
• *Integrating Cross-Cultural Topics into Introductory Psychology*, by William Hill (Kennesaw State College), discusses the movement toward "internationalizing" the curriculum and provides suggestions for lectures, exercises, and assignments that can add a cross-cultural flavor to the introductory course.
• The *Instructor's Manual*, by Randolph Smith (Ouachita Baptist University), contains a wealth of detailed suggestions for lecture topics, class

demonstrations, exercises, discussion questions, and suggested readings, organized around the content of each chapter in the text.

Brooks/Cole has received a great deal of positive feedback about the *Instructor's Resource Package for Psychology: Themes and Variations*, and I am sure that you will find the condensed version just as valuable.

Test Bank (by Gary G. Bothe, Susan Jones Bothe, Robin Lashley, and William Addison)
Several outstanding professors have contributed to the development of the *Test Bank* that accompanies this text. Robin Lashley (Kent State University) and William Addison (Eastern Illinois University) originally wrote the test questions for the parent book, and Gary Bothe and Susan Bothe (Pensacola Junior College) made the revisions necessitated by content changes in the *Briefer Version*.

The questions are closely tied to the chapter learning objectives and to the lists of key terms and key people found in both the text and the *Study Guide*. Most of the questions are categorized as either factual or conceptual. However, for each chapter there are also a few integrative questions that require students to link, synthesize, and interrelate information from different sections of the chapter. Computerized versions of the *Test Bank* are availabe for Mac, DOS, and Windows. The *Computerized Test Bank* is user-friendly and allows teachers to insert their own questions and to customize the over 1800 provided.

Other Teaching Aids
Transparencies: A set of 100 text-specific, full-color transparencies is available.

Psychology: Careers for the Twenty-First Century: Brooks/Cole has an exclusive agreement to offer this 13-minute video produced by the APA free to adopters of this text.

Psychology: Careers for the Twenty-First Century: This 30-page booklet produced by the APA is offered exclusively by APA and Brooks/Cole. It describes the field of psychology and discusses career preparation in the many areas of psychology. This booklet can be shrink-wrapped with the text at no additional cost.

The Integrator CD-ROM: Authored by Arthur J. and Wendy Kohn and a development team at Pacific University, this CD-ROM provides stu-

dents with dramatic new ways to learn psychology. Exceptionally easy to use, it enables students to independently explore important concepts via interactive experiments, animations, video clips, and images. All materials include page references to the textbook. The Faculty Version allows professors to readily assemble and present impressive multimedia lectures. The Student Version can be shrink-wrapped with the text for a discount.

Psych Lab I and II: Created by Roger Harnish of the Rochester Institute of Technology, these interactive software programs provide psychology demonstrations and simulations, available for DOS and Mac.

Animations Plus! Videodisc: Produced by Brooks/Cole, this videodisc includes a collection of animations with still frame review and quizzing, diagrams, and video segments. The videodisc comes with an Instructor's Guide that includes bar codes.

Technical Support: ITP Technology Services provides technical support and customer service for Brooks/Cole software, multimedia, and computerized testing. For assistance, call 800-327-0325.

Brooks/Cole Film and Video Library for Psychology: Adopters can choose from a variety of film and video options. Call Brooks/Cole Marketing to request videos, 800-354-0092. The library includes:

• *The Pennsylvania State University's PCR: Films and Videos in the Behavioral Sciences*—adopters can choose from the world's largest collection of films and videos on human behavior.

• *The Brain* videotapes—30 video modules and a faculty guide prepared by Frank Vattano of Colorado State University in conjuction with the Annenberg/CPB Project Video Collection.

• *The Mind* videotapes—38 brief video modules offering examples of important concepts in introductory psychology and a faculty guide prepared by Frank Vattano of Colorado State University in cooperation with WNET, New York.

• *Seeing Beyond the Obvious: Understanding Perception in Everyday and Novel Environments*—a videotape that provides an introduction to basic concepts of visual perception, created by NASA Ames Research Center in conjunction with the University of Virginia.

• *Discovering Psychology* videotapes—a series of 26 programs from the Annenberg/CPB Collection.

Acknowledgments

Creating an introductory psychology text is a complicated challenge, and a small army of people have contributed to the evolution of this book. Foremost among them are the psychology editors I have worked with at Brooks/Cole—Claire Verduin, C. Deborah Laughton, Phil Curson, and Eileen Murphy—and the developmental editor for this book, John Bergez. They have helped me immeasurably, and each has become a treasured friend along the way. I am especially indebted to Claire, who educated me in the intricacies of textbook publishing, and to John, who has left an enduring imprint on my writing.

I also want to thank Brooks/Cole's editor-in-chief, Craig Barth, and the president of Brooks/Cole, Bill Roberts, for giving me the freedom to pursue my personal vision of what an introductory text should be like. They have let me take some chances and have allowed me extensive input regarding every aspect of the book's production. I have never felt constrained by a conservative corporate mentality.

The challenge of meeting a difficult schedule in producing this book was undertaken by a talented team of people coordinated by Nancy Sjöberg at Del Mar Associates. The color scheme for the book and the page layouts were designed by John Odam, who showed remarkable ingenuity and creativity (not to mention patience) in juggling the conflicting demands of the illustration program. Chris Davis provided assistance in laying out the book. Kim Fraley provided excellent anatomical and vignette drawings, Linda Rill handled permissions and photo research with efficiency and enthusiasm, Jackie Estrada did an excellent job in copy editing the manuscript, and Martha Ghent was meticulous in her proofreading. Finally, Nancy Sjoberg provided the organizational glue that held these efforts together.

A host of psychologists deserve thanks for the contributions they made to this book. I am grateful to Rick Stalling and Ron Wasden for their work on the *Study Guide;* to Robin Lashley, Bill Addison, Gary Bothe, and Susan Bothe for their work on the *Test Bank;* to Randy Smith, Joseph Lowman, Russ Watson, Barney Beins, Jane Jegerski, and Bill Hill for their work on the *Instructor's Resource Book;* to Charles Brewer for allowing us to reprint his "Ten Commandments" in the *Instructor's Manual;* to Harry Upshaw, Larry Wrightsman, Shari Diamond, Rick Stalling, and Claire Etaugh for their help and guidance over the years; and to the consultants listed on page xi and the reviewers listed on page xii, who provided insightful and constructive critiques of various portions of the manuscript.

Many other people have also contributed to this project, and I am grateful to all of them for their efforts. At Brooks/Cole, Marjorie Sanders monitored the production process, and Vernon Boes, Bill Bokermann, Margaret Parks, Jim Brace-Thompson, Patricia Vienneau, Lisa Blanton, and Jean Vevers Thompson helped with varied aspects of the book's development and production. At the College of DuPage, where I taught until 1991, all of my colleagues in psychology provided support and information at one time or another, but I am especially indebted to Barb Lemme and Don Green. I also want to thank my colleagues at Santa Clara University, who have been a fertile source of new ideas, the great many students from my classes who critiqued chapters, and Rosanna Guadagno, who helped complete the reference entries.

Last, but not least, I am grateful to many friends for their support, especially Jerry Mueller, Sam Auster, Michael Block, Bruce Krattenmaker, Carol Ricks, Cheryl Kasel, Tom Braden, and Katie Konradt. My greatest debt is to my wife, Beth Traylor, who has been a steady source of emotional sustenance while enduring the grueling rigors of her medical career. Beth, thanks for the patience. This one's for you.

Wayne Weiten

Chapter Consultants

Chapter 1

Charles L. Brewer
Furman University

E. R. Hilgard
Stanford University

Chapter 2

Larry Christensen
Texas A & M University

Francis Durso
University of Oklahoma

Chapter 3

Nelson Freedman
Queen's University at Kingston

Michael W. Levine
University of Illinois at Chicago

Chapter 4

Nelson Freedman
Queen's University at Kingston

Kevin Jordan
San Jose State University

Michael W. Levine
University of Illinois at Chicago

John N. Park
Mankato State University

Chapter 5

Frank Etscorn
New Mexico Institute of Mining and Technology

Wilse Webb
University of Florida

Chapter 6

Michael Domjan
University of Texas, Austin

William C. Gordon
University of New Mexico

Chapter 7

Tracey L. Kahan
Santa Clara University

Stephen K. Reed
San Diego State University

Patricia Tenpenny
Loyola University, Chicago

Chapter 8

John Best
Eastern Illinois University

David Carroll
University of Wisconsin-Superior

Stephen K. Reed
San Diego State University

Chapter 9

Charles Davidshofer
Colorado State University

Shalynn Ford
Teikyo Marycrest University

Chapter 10

Robert Franken
University of Calgary

Douglas Mook
University of Virginia

Chapter 11

Ruth L. Ault
Davidson College

Claire Etaugh
Bradley University

Chapter 12

Caroline Collins
University of Victoria

Christopher F. Monte
Manhattanville College

Chapter 13

Robin M. DiMatteo
University of California, Riverside

Jess Feist
McNeese State University

Chapter 14

Chris L. Kleinke
University of Alaska, Anchorage

Elliot A. Weiner
Pacific University

Chapter 15

Gerald Corey
California State University, Fullerton

Jane S. Halonen
Alverno College

Chapter 16

Donelson R. Forsyth
Virginia Commonwealth University

Consultants for the Briefer Version

Bart Bare
Caldwell Community College

Charles B. Blose
MacMurray College

Edward Brady
Belleville Area College

Thomas Collins
Mankato State University

Linda Gibbons
Westark College

Richard Griggs
University of Florida

Jane Halonen
Alverno College

Stephen Hoyer
Pittsburg State University

Nancy Jackson
Johnson & Wales University

Deborah R. McDonald
New Mexico State University

Jack J. Mino
Holyoke Community College

Joel Morogovsky
Brookdale Community College

Dirk W. Mosig
University of Nebraska at Kearney

David R. Murphy
Waubonsee College

Edward I. Pollack
West Chester University of Pennsylvania

Elizabeth A. Rider
Elizabethtown College

Jayne Rose
Augustana College

Heide Sedwick
Mount Aloysius College

Randolph A. Smith
Ouachita Baptist University

Thomas Smith
Vincennes University

Iva Trottier
Concordia College

Doris C. Vaughn
Alabama State University

Randall Wight
Ouachita Baptist University

Reviewers

Lyn Y. Abramson
University of Wisconsin

Ruth L. Ault
Davidson College

Elaine Baker
Marshall University

Daniel R. Bellack
Trident Technical College

Robert Bornstein
Miami University

Bette L. Bottoms
University of Illinois at
Chicago

Allen Branum
South Dakota State
University

Robert G. Bringle
Indiana University-Purdue
University at Indianapolis

Dan W. Brunworth
Kishwaukee College

James Butler
James Madison University

Mary M. Cail
University of Virginia

James F. Calhoun
University of Georgia

William Calhoun
University of Tennessee

Francis B. Colavita
University of Pittsburgh

Thomas B. Collins
Mankato State University

Stan Coren
University of British
Columbia

Norman Culbertson
Yakima Valley College

Betty M. Davenport
Campbell University

Stephen F. Davis
Emporia State University

Kenneth Deffenbacher
University of Nebraska

Roger Dominowski
University of Illinois,
Chicago

Robert J. Douglas
University of Washington

James Eison
Southeast Missouri State
University

Robert G. Elliott II
Florida State University

M. Jeffrey Farrar
University of Florida

Thomas P. Fitzpatrick
Rockland Community
College

Karen E. Ford
Mesa State College

Donelson R. Forsyth
Virginia Commonwealth
University

Jim Friedrich
Willamette University

Barry Fritz
Quinnipiac College

William J. Froming
University of Florida

Mary Ellen Fromuth
Middle Tennessee State
University

Dean E. Frost
Portland State University

Peter Gram
Pensacola Junior College

Richard Griggs
University of Florida

Arthur Gutman
Florida Institute of
Technology

Jane S. Halonen
Alverno College

Roger Harnish
Rochester Institute of
Technology

Philip L. Hartley
Chaffey College

Glenn R. Hawkes
Virginia Commonwealth
University

Myra D. Heinrich
Mesa State College

Lyllian B. Hix
Houston Community
College

John P. Hostetler
Albion College

Robert A. Johnston
College of William and
Mary

Andrea M. Karkowksi
Dickinson College

Margaret Karolyi
Kent State University

Alan R. King
University of North Dakota

Melvyn B. King
State University of New
York, Cortland

James Knight
Humboldt State University

Mike Knight
Central State University

Ronald Kopcho
Mercer Community
College

Barry J. Krikstone
Saint Michael's College

Jerry N. Lackey
Stephen F. Austin State
University

Robin L. Lashley
Kent State University,
Tuscarawas

Curtis K. Leech
Anderson University

Peter Leppman
University of Guelph

Charles F. Levinthal
Hofstra University

Wolfgang Linden
University of British
Columbia

Donald McBurney
University of Pittsburgh

Ronald K. McLaughlin
Juniata College

Sheryll Mennicke
University of Minnesota

Ken Merrell
Utah State University

James M. Murphy
Indiana University-Purdue
University at Indianapolis

Michael Murphy
Henderson State
University

David L. Novak
Lansing Community
College

Richard Page
Wright State University

Joseph J. Palladino
University of Southern
Indiana

Leanne Parker
University of Montana

Bobby J. Poe
Belleville Area College

Terry Polinskey
Westark Community
College

Maureen K. Powers
Vanderbilt University

Janet Proctor
Purdue University

Jacqueline Ralston
University of Dayton

Robin Raygor
Anoka-Ramsey
Community College

Celia Reaves
Monroe Community
College

Daniel W. Richards
Houston Community
College

Alysia D. Ritter
Murray State University

Michelle Ceynar Rosell
University of Montana

Michael Schuller
Fresno City College

Fred Shima
California State University,
Dominguez Hills

Susan A. Shodahl
San Bernardino Valley
College

Steven M. Smith
Texas A & M University

Marjorie Taylor
University of Oregon

Frank R. Terrant, Jr.
Appalachian State
University

Jim Turcott
Kalamazoo Valley
Community College

Donald Tyrrell
Franklin and Marshall
College

Frank J. Vattano
Colorado State University

Wayne Viney
Colorado State University

Benjamin Wallace
Cleveland State University

Keith D. White
University of Florida

Randall D. Wight
Ouachita Baptist
University

Cecilia Yoder
Oklahoma City
Community College

Brief Contents

Contents

2 The Research Enterprise in Psychology

Population:
The complete set

Inference

Sample:
A subset of the
population

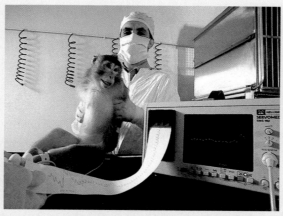

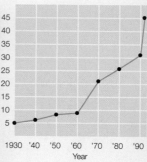

3 **The Biological Bases of Behavior**

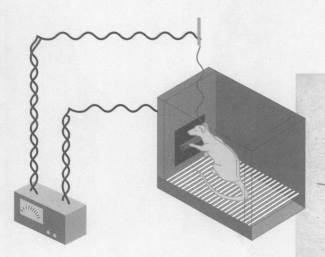

4 Sensation and Perception

Short-wavelength "blue" cones   Medium-wavelength "green" cones   Long-wavelength "red" cones

Sensitivity (% of maximum response)

100
75
50
25
0

400   450   500   550   600   650

Wavelength (nanometers)

5 Variations in Consciousness

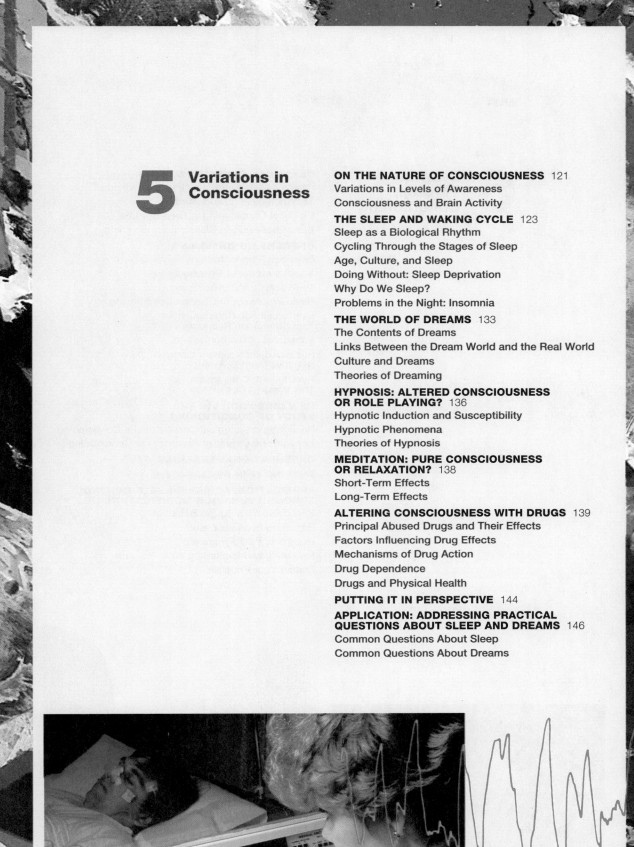

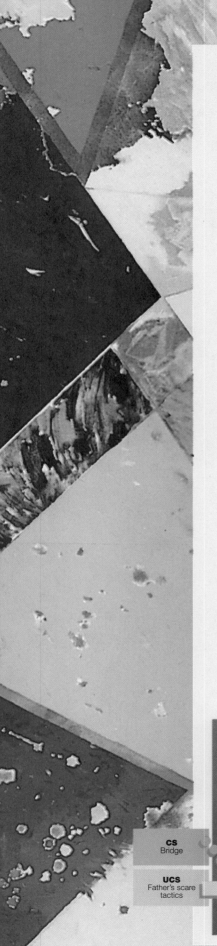

6 Learning Through Conditioning

CS
Bridge

UCS
Father's scare
tactics

CR
Fear
UCR

7 Human Memory

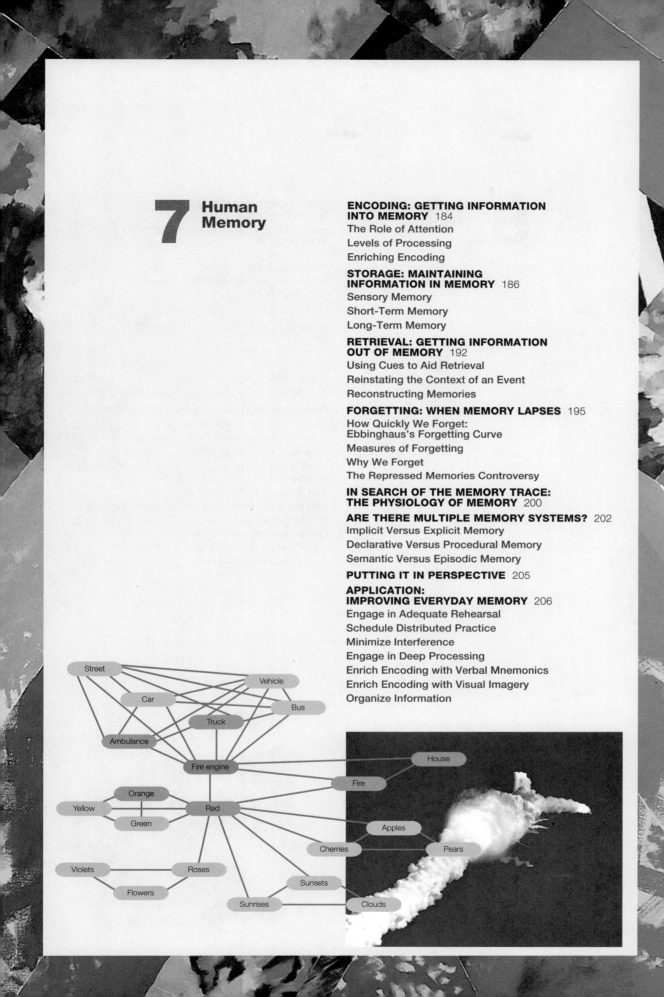

8 Language and Thought

9 Intelligence and Psychological Testing

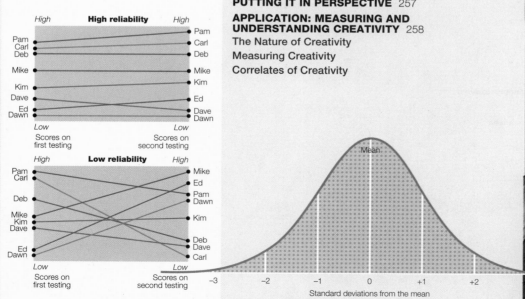

10 Motivation and Emotion

Need for self-actualization:

Aesthetic needs:

Cognitive needs:

Esteem needs:

Belongingness and love needs:

Safety and security needs:

Physiological needs:

Progression if lower needs are satisfied

Regression if lower needs are not being satisfied

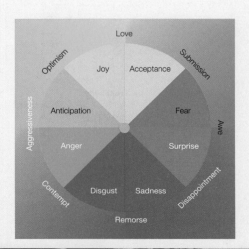

Love
Submission
Optimism
Joy
Acceptance
Anticipation
Fear
Aggressiveness
Awe
Anger
Surprise
Contempt
Disgust
Sadness
Disappointment
Remorse

11 Human Development Across the Life Span

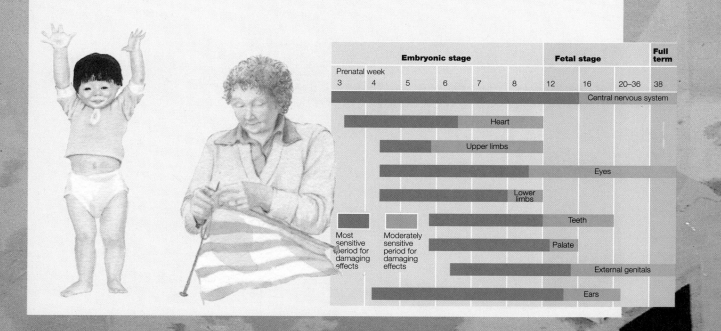

	Embryonic stage						Fetal stage			Full term
Prenatal week										
3	4	5	6	7	8	12	16	20–36	38	
									Central nervous system	
	Heart									
	Upper limbs									
		Eyes								
		Lower limbs								
		Teeth								
Most sensitive period for damaging effects	Moderately sensitive period for damaging effects	Palate								
		External genitals								
		Ears								

12 Personality: Theory, Research, and Assessment

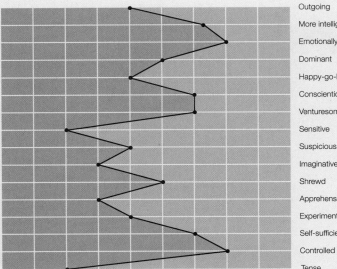

Reserved				Outgoing
Less intelligent				More intelligent
Affected by feelings				Emotionally stable
Submissive				Dominant
Serious				Happy-go-lucky
Expedient				Conscientious
Timid				Venturesome
Tough-minded				Sensitive
Trusting				Suspicious
Practical				Imaginative
Forthright				Shrewd
Self-assured				Apprehensive
Conservative				Experimenting
Group-dependent				Self-sufficient
Uncontrolled				Controlled
Relaxed				Tense

13 Stress, Coping, and Health

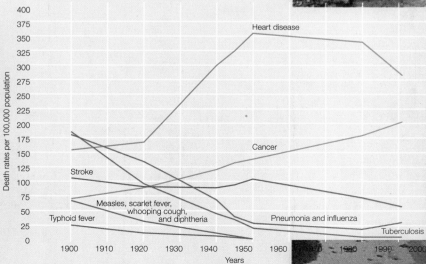

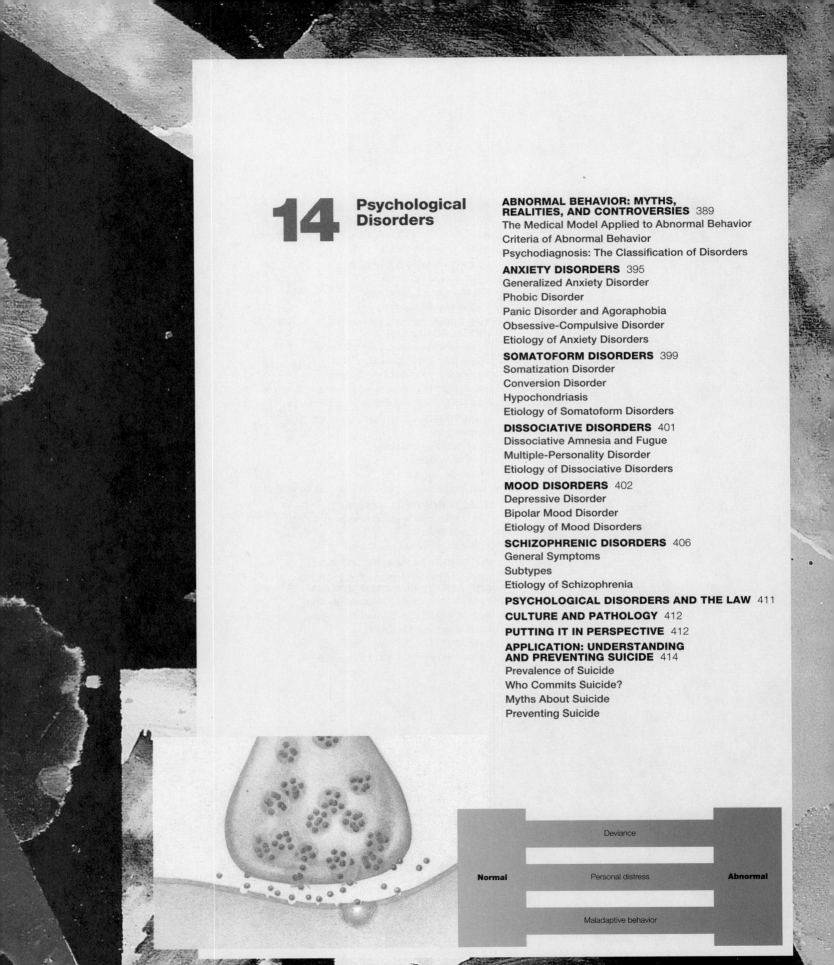

14 Psychological Disorders

Deviance

Normal   Personal distress   Abnormal

Maladaptive behavior

15 Psychotherapy

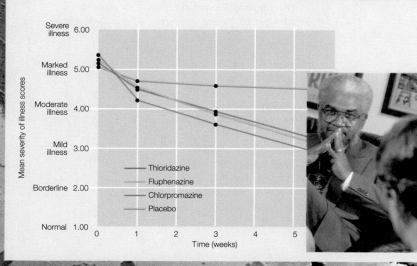

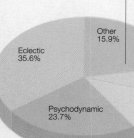

16 Social Behavior

Who	What	By what means	To whom
Source factors	*Message factors*	*Channel factors*	*Receiver factors*
Credibility	Fear appeal versus logic	In person	Personality
Expertise	One-sided versus two-sided argument	On television	Expectations (e.g., forewarning)
Trustworthiness		Via audiotape	Preexisting attitudes
Likability	Repetition		Intelligence
Attractiveness			
Similarity			

To the Student

Welcome to your introductory psychology textbook. In most college courses, students spend more time with their textbooks than with their professors, so it helps if students *like* their textbooks. Making textbooks likable, however, is a tricky proposition. By its very nature, a textbook must introduce students to many complicated concepts, ideas, and theories. If it doesn't, it isn't much of a textbook, and instructors won't choose to use it. Nevertheless, in writing this book I've tried to make it as likable as possible without compromising the academic content that your instructor demands. I've especially tried to keep in mind your need for a clear, well-organized presentation that makes the important material stand out and yet is interesting to read. Above all else, I hope you find this book challenging to think about and easy to learn from.

Before you plunge into your first chapter, let me introduce you to the book's key features. Becoming familiar with how the book works will help you to get more out of it.

Key Features

You're about to embark on a journey into a new domain of ideas. Your text includes some important features that are intended to highlight certain aspects of psychology's landscape.

Unifying Themes

To help you make sense of a complex and diverse field of study, I introduce seven themes in Chapter 1 that will reappear in a number of variations as we move from chapter to chapter. These unifying themes are meant to provoke thought about important issues and to highlight the connections between chapters. They are discussed at the end of each chapter in a section called "Putting It in Perspective."

Application Sections

At the end of each chapter you'll find an Application section that shows how psychology is relevant to everyday life. Some of these sections provide concrete advice that could be helpful to you in school, such as those on improving academic per-

formance, improving everyday memory, and achieving self-control. So, you may want to jump ahead and read some of these Applications early.

Learning Aids

This text contains a great deal of information. A number of learning aids have been incorporated into the book to help you digest it all.

An *outline* at the beginning of each chapter provides you with an overview of the topics covered in that chapter. Think of the outlines as road maps, and bear in mind that it's easier to reach a destination if you know where you're going.

Headings serve as road signs in your journey through each chapter. Four levels of headings are used to make it easy to see the organization of each chapter.

Italics (without boldface) are used liberally throughout the text to emphasize crucial points.

Key terms are identified with ***italicized boldface*** type to alert you that these are important vocabulary items that are part of psychology's technical language. The key terms are also listed at the end of the chapter.

An *integrated running glossary* provides an on-the-spot definition of each key term as it's introduced in the text. These formal definitions are printed in **boldface** type. Becoming familiar with psychology's terminology is an essential part of learning about the field. The integrated running glossary should make this learning process easier.

Concept Checks are sprinkled throughout the chapters to let you test your mastery of important ideas. Generally, they ask you to integrate or organize a number of key ideas, or to apply ideas to real-world situations. Although they're meant to be engaging and fun, they do check conceptual *understanding*, and some are challenging. But if you get stuck, don't worry; the answers (and explanations, where they're needed) are in the back of the book in Appendix A.

Illustrations in the text are important elements in your complete learning package. Some illustrations provide enlightening diagrams of complicated concepts; others furnish examples that help to flesh out ideas or provide concise overviews of research results. Careful attention to the tables and figures in the book will help you understand the material discussed in the text.

A *Chapter Review* at the end of each chapter provides a thorough summary of the chapter's *key ideas*, a list of *key terms*, and a list of *key people* (important theorists and researchers). It's wise to read over these review materials to make sure you've digested the information in the chapter.

An *alphabetical glossary* is provided in the back of the book. Most key terms are formally defined in the integrated running glossary only when they are first introduced. So, if you run into a technical term a second time and can't remember its meaning, it may be easier to look it up in the alphabetical glossary than to backtrack to find the definition where the term was originally introduced.

A Few Footnotes

Psychology textbooks customarily identify the studies, theoretical treatises, books, and articles that information comes from. These *citations* occur (1) when names are followed by a date in parentheses, as in "Smith (1972) found that . . ." or (2) when names and dates are provided together within parentheses, as in "In one study (Smith, Miller, & Jones, 1987), the researchers attempted to . . .." All of the cited publications are listed by author in the alphabetized *References* section in the back of the book. The citations and references are a necessary part of a book's scholarly and scientific foundation. Practically speaking, however, you'll probably want to glide right over them as you read. You definitely don't need to memorize the names and dates. The only names you may need to know are the handful listed under Key People in each Chapter Review (unless your instructor mentions a personal favorite that you should know).

In addition to the references, you'll find a *Name Index* and a *Subject Index* in the back of the book.

The name index tells you the pages on which various names were cited. It's very helpful if you're looking for the discussion of a particular study and you know the name(s) of the author(s). And, if the need arises, the subject index allows you to look up the pages on which a specific topic is covered.

A Word About the Study Guide

A *Study Guide* is available to accompany this text. It was written by two of my former professors, who introduced me to psychology years ago. They have done a great job of organizing review materials to help you master the information in the book. I suggest that you seriously consider using it to help you study. An interactive version of the *Study Guide* is available for Mac, DOS, and Windows.

The Integrator CD-ROM— Student Version

A CD-ROM also accompanies this text. It allows you to independently explore important psychological concepts via a wide range of multimedia, including interactive experiments, tutorials, activities, and animations. You can purchase a copy at your campus bookstore.

A Final Word

I'm very pleased to be a part of your first journey into the world of psychology, and I sincerely hope that you'll find the book as thought provoking and as easy to learn from as I've tried to make it. If you have any comments or advice on the book, please write to me in care of the publisher (Brooks/Cole Publishing Company, 511 Forest Lodge Road, Pacific Grove, California, 93950). You can be sure I'll pay careful attention to your feedback. Finally, let me wish you good luck. I hope you enjoy your course and learn a great deal.

Wayne Weiten

PSYCHOLOGY
Themes & Variations
Briefer Version 3rd Edition

1 The Evolution of Psychology

What is psychology?

Your initial answer to this question is likely to bear little resemblance to the picture of psychology that will emerge as you work your way through this book. I know that when I ambled into my introductory psychology course about 20 years ago, I had no idea what psychology involved. I was a pre-law/political science major fulfilling a general education requirement with what I thought would be my one and only psychology course. I encountered two things I didn't expect. The first was to learn that psychology is about a great many things besides abnormal behavior and ways to win friends and influence people. I was surprised to discover that psychology is also about how we are able to perceive color, how hunger is actually regulated by the brain, whether chimpanzees can use language to communicate, and a multitude of other topics I'd never thought to wonder about. The second thing I didn't expect was that I would be so completely seduced by the subject. Before long I changed majors and embarked on a career in psychology—a decision I never regretted.

Why has psychology continued to fascinate me? One reason is that *psychology is practical*. It offers a vast store of information about issues that concern everyone. These issues range from broad social questions, such as how to reduce the incidence of mental illness, to highly personal questions, such as how to improve your self-control. In a sense, psychology is about you and me. It's about life in our modern world. The practical side of psychology will be apparent throughout this text, especially in the end-of-chapter Applications. The

Applications focus on everyday problems, such as coping more effectively with stress, improving memory, enhancing performance in school, and dealing with sleep difficulties.

Another element of psychology's appeal for me is that it represents *a way of thinking*. We are all exposed to claims about psychological issues. For instance, we hear assertions that men and women have different abilities or that violence on television has a harmful effect on children. As a science, psychology demands that researchers ask precise questions about such issues and that they test their ideas through systematic observation. Psychology's commitment to testing ideas encourages a healthy brand of critical thinking. In the long run, this means that psychology provides a way of building knowledge that is relatively accurate and dependable.

Of course, psychological research cannot discover an answer for every interesting question about the mind and behavior. You won't find the meaning of life or the secret of happiness in this text. But you will find an approach to investigating questions that has proven very fruitful. The more you learn about psychology as a way of thinking, the better equipped you will be to evaluate the psychological assertions you encounter in daily life.

There is still another reason for my fascination with psychology. As you proceed through this text, you will find that psychologists study an enormous diversity of subjects, from acrophobia (fear of heights) to zoophobia (fear of animals), from problem solving in apes to the symbolic language of dreams. Psychologists look at all the

The rich diversity of contemporary psychology embraces a wide range of topics, including psychotherapy with clients of all ages, perceptual processes in infants, and brain studies involving sophisticated equipment such as CT scanners.

seasons of human life, from development in the womb to the emotional stages that people go through in the process of dying. Psychologists study observable behaviors such as eating, fighting, and mating. But they also dig beneath the surface to investigate how hormones affect emotions and how the brain registers pain. They probe the behavior of any number of species, from humans to house cats, from monkeys to moths. This rich diversity is, for me, perhaps psychology's most appealing aspect.

Mental illness, rats running in mazes, the physiology of hunger, the mysteries of love, creativity, and prejudice—what ties all these subjects together in a single discipline? How did psychology come to be such a diverse field of study? Why is it so different from what most people expect? If psychology is a social science, why do psychologists study subjects such as brain chemistry and the physiological basis of vision? To answer these questions, we begin our introduction to psychology by retracing its development. By seeing how psychology grew and changed, you will discover why it has the shape it does today.

Physiology informs us about those life phenomena that we perceive by our external senses. In psychology, the person looks upon himself as from within and tries to explain the interrelations of those processes that this internal observation discloses.
WILHELM WUNDT 1832–1920

After our journey into psychology's past, we will examine a formal definition of psychology. We'll also look at psychology as it is today—a sprawling, multifaceted science and profession. To help keep psychology's diversity in perspective, the chapter concludes with a discussion of seven unifying themes that will serve as connecting threads in the chapters to come. Finally, in the chapter's Application, we'll return to psychology's practical side, as we review research that gives insights on how to be an effective student.

FROM SPECULATION TO SCIENCE: HOW PSYCHOLOGY DEVELOPED

Psychology's story is one of people groping toward a better understanding of themselves. As psychology has evolved, its focus, methods, and explanatory models have changed. Let's look at how psychology has developed from philosophical speculations about the mind into a modern behavioral science.

The term *psychology* comes from two Greek words, *psyche*, meaning the soul, and *logos*, referring to the study of a subject. These two Greek roots were first put together to define a topic of study in the 16th century, when *psyche* was used to refer to the soul, spirit, or mind, as distinguished from the body (Boring, 1966). Not until the early 18th century did the term *psychology* gain more than rare usage among scholars. By that time it had acquired its literal meaning, "the study of the mind."

Of course, people have always wondered about the mysteries of the mind. To take just one example, in ancient Greece the philosopher Aristotle engaged in intriguing conjecture about thinking, intelligence, motives, and emotions in his work *Peri Psyches (About the Soul)*. Philosophical speculation about psychological issues is as old as the human race. But it was only a little over a hundred years ago that psychology emerged as a scientific discipline.

A New Science Is Born

Psychology's intellectual parents were the disciplines of *philosophy* and *physiology*. By the 1870s a small number of scholars in both fields were actively exploring questions about the mind. How are bodily sensations turned into a mental awareness of the outside world? Are our perceptions of the world accurate reflections of reality? How do mind and body interact? The philosophers and physiologists who were interested in the mind viewed such questions as fascinating issues *within* their respective fields. It was a German professor, Wilhelm Wundt (1832–1920), who eventually changed this view. Wundt mounted a campaign to make psychology an independent discipline rather than a stepchild of philosophy or physiology.

The time and place were right for Wundt's appeal. German universities were in a healthy period of expansion, so resources were available for new disciplines. Furthermore, the intellectual climate favored the scientific approach that Wundt advocated. Hence, his proposals were well received by the academic community. In 1879 Wundt succeeded in establishing the first formal laboratory for research in psychology at the University of Leipzig. In deference to this landmark event, historians have christened 1879 as psychology's "date of birth." Soon afterward, in 1881, Wundt established the first journal devoted to publishing research on psychology. All in all, Wundt's campaign was so successful that today he is widely characterized as the founder of psychology.

Wundt's conception of psychology dominated the field for two decades and was influential for several more. Borrowing from his training in physiology, Wundt (1874) declared that the new psychology should be a science modeled after fields such as physics and chemistry. What was the subject matter of the new science? According to Wundt, it was *consciousness*—the awareness of immediate experience. *Thus, psychology became the scientific study of conscious experience.* This orientation kept psychology focused squarely on the mind. But it demanded that the methods used to investigate the mind be as scientific as those of chemists or physicists.

Wundt was a tireless, dedicated scholar who generated an estimated 54,000 pages of books and articles in his career (Bringmann & Balk, 1992). His hard work and provocative ideas soon attracted attention. Many outstanding young scholars came to Leipzig to study under Wundt and do research on vision, hearing, touch, taste, attention, and emotion. Many of his students then fanned out across Germany and America, establishing laboratories that formed the basis for the new, independent science of psychology.

Indeed, it was in North America that Wundt's new science grew by leaps and bounds. Between 1883 and 1893, some 24 new psychological research laboratories sprang up in the United States and Canada, at the schools shown in Figure 1.1 (Garvey, 1929). Many of the laboratories were started by Wundt's students, or by his students' students.

Exactly why Americans took to psychology so quickly is hard to say. Perhaps it was because America's relatively young universities were more open to new disciplines than were the older, more tradition-bound universities elsewhere in the world. In any case, although psychology was born in Germany, it blossomed into adolescence in America. Like many adolescents, however, the young science was about to enter a period of turbulence and turmoil.

The Battle of the "Schools" Begins: Structuralism Versus Functionalism

When you read about how psychology became a science, you might have imagined that psychologists became a unified group of scholars who busily added new discoveries to an uncontested store of "facts." In reality, no science works that way. Competing schools of thought exist in most scientific disciplines. Sometimes the disagreements among these schools are sharp. Such diversity in thought is natural and often stimulates enlightening debate. In psychology, the first two major schools of thought, *structuralism* and *functionalism*, were entangled in the first great intellectual battle in the field.

Structuralism was shaped by Wundt's ideas, under the leadership of his student Edward Titchener, an Englishman who emigrated to the United States in 1892. **Structuralism was based on the notion that the task of psychology is to analyze consciousness into its basic ele-**

Figure 1.1. Early research laboratories in North America. This map highlights the location and year of founding for the first 24 psychological research labs established in North American colleges and universities. (Based on Garvey, 1929; Hilgard, 1987)

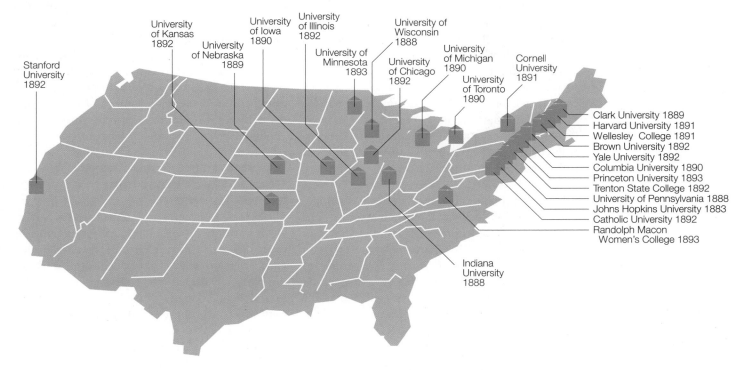

Stanford University 1892

University of Kansas 1892

University of Nebraska 1889

University of Iowa 1890

University of Illinois 1892

University of Minnesota 1893

University of Wisconsin 1888

University of Chicago 1892

University of Michigan 1890

University of Toronto 1890

Cornell University 1891

Clark University 1889
Harvard University 1891
Wellesley College 1891
Brown University 1892
Yale University 1892
Columbia University 1890
Princeton University 1893
Trenton State College 1892
University of Pennsylvania 1888
Johns Hopkins University 1883
Catholic University 1892
Randolph Macon Women's College 1893

Indiana University 1888

It is just this free water of consciousness that psychologists resolutely overlook.
WILLIAM JAMES 1842–1910

ments and investigate how these elements are related. Just as physicists were studying how matter is made up of basic particles, the structuralists wanted to identify and examine the fundamental components of conscious experience, such as sensations, feelings, and images.

Although the structuralists explored many questions, most of their work concerned sensation and perception in vision, hearing, and touch. To examine the contents of consciousness, the structuralists depended on the method of **introspection, or the careful, systematic self-observation of one's own conscious experience**. As practiced by the structuralists, introspection required training to make the subject—the person being studied—more objective and more aware. Once trained, subjects were typically exposed to auditory tones, optical illusions, and visual stimuli such as pieces of fruit and were asked to analyze what they experienced.

The functionalists took a different view of psychology's task. *Functionalism* **was based on the belief that psychology should investigate the function or purpose of consciousness, rather than its structure.** The chief architect of functionalism was William James (1842–1910), a brilliant American scholar (and brother of novelist Henry James). James's formal training was in medicine. However, he was too sickly to pursue a medical practice (he couldn't imagine standing all day long), so he joined the faculty of Harvard University to pursue a less arduous career (Ross, 1991). Medicine's loss proved to be a boon for psychology, as James quickly became an intellectual giant in the field. James's landmark book, *Principles of Psychology* (1890), became standard reading for generations of psychologists and is perhaps the most influential text in the history of psychology (Weiten & Wight, 1992).

James's thinking illustrates how psychology, like any field, is deeply embedded in a network of cultural and intellectual influences. James had been impressed with Charles Darwin's (1859, 1871) theory of *natural selection*. According to Darwin, the characteristics that give a species a survival advantage come to be "selected" over time. That is, these characteristics are more likely to be passed on to subsequent generations. This cornerstone notion of Darwin's evolutionary theory suggested that all characteristics of a spe-

cies must serve some purpose. Applying this idea to humans, James (1890) noted that consciousness obviously is an important characteristic of our species. Hence, he contended that psychology should investigate the *functions* rather than the *structure* of consciousness.

James also argued that the structuralists' approach missed the real nature of conscious experience. Consciousness, he argued, consists of a continuous *flow* of thoughts. In analyzing consciousness into its "elements," the structuralists were looking at static points in that flow. James wanted to understand the flow itself, which he called the "stream of consciousness."

Whereas structuralists naturally gravitated to the laboratory, functionalists were more interested in how people adapt their behavior to the demands of the real world around them. This practical slant led them to introduce new subjects into psychology. Instead of focusing on sensation and perception, functionalists such as G. Stanley Hall, James McKeen Cattell, and John Dewey began to investigate mental testing, patterns of development in children, the effectiveness of educational practices, and behavioral differences between the sexes. These new topics may have played a role in attracting the first women into the field of psychology (see Figure 1.2).

The impassioned advocates of structuralism and functionalism saw themselves as fighting for high stakes: the definition and future direction of the new science of psychology. Their war of ideas continued energetically for many years. Who won? Neither camp scored a decisive victory, and in time the influence of both began to fade. However, functionalism left a more enduring imprint on psychology (Buxton, 1985). Its practical orientation fostered the development of two descendants that have dominated modern psychology: applied psychology and behaviorism.

Watson Alters Psychology's Course as Behaviorism Makes Its Debut

The debate between structuralism and functionalism was only the prelude to other fundamental controversies in psychology. In the early 1900s, another major school of thought appeared that dramatically altered the course of psychology. Founded by John B. Watson (1878–1958), *behaviorism* **is a theoretical orientation based on the premise that scientific psychology should study only observable behavior.** It is important to understand what a radical change

Mary Whiton Calkins
(1863–1930)

Margaret Floy Washburn
(1871–1939)

Leta Stetter Hollingworth
(1886–1939)

Mary Calkins, who studied under William James, founded one of the first dozen psychology laboratories in America at Wellesley College in 1891, invented a widely used technique for studying memory, and became the first woman to serve as president of the American Psychological Association in 1905. Ironically, however, she never received her Ph.D. in psychology. Because she was a woman, Harvard University only reluctantly allowed her to take graduate classes as a "guest student." When she completed the requirements for her Ph.D., Harvard would only offer her a doctorate from its undergraduate sister school, Radcliffe. Calkins felt that this decision perpetuated unequal treatment of the sexes, so she refused the Radcliffe degree.

Margaret Washburn was the first woman to receive a Ph.D. in psychology. She wrote an influential book, *The Animal Mind* (1908), which served as an impetus to the subsequent emergence of behaviorism and was standard reading for several generations of psychologists. In 1921 she became the second woman to serve as president of the American Psychological Association. Washburn studied under James McKeen Cattell at Columbia University, but like Mary Calkins, she was only permitted to take graduate classes unofficially, as a "hearer." Hence, she transferred to Cornell University, which was more hospitable toward women, and completed her doctorate in 1894. Like Calkins, Washburn spent most of her career at a college for women (Vassar).

Leta Hollingworth did pioneering work on adolescent development, mental retardation, and gifted children. Indeed, she was the first person to use the term *gifted* to refer to youngsters who scored exceptionally high on intelligence tests. Hollingworth (1914, 1916) also played a major role in debunking popular theories of her era that purported to explain why women were "inferior" to men. For instance, she conducted a study refuting the myth that phases of the menstrual cycle are reliably associated with performance decrements in women. Her careful collection of objective data on gender differences forced other scientists to subject popular, untested beliefs about the sexes to skeptical, empirical inquiry.

Figure 1.2. Women pioneers in the history of psychology. Women have long made major contributions to the development of psychology (Russo & Denmark, 1987), and today roughly one-third of all psychologists are female. As in other fields, however, women have often been overlooked in histories of psychology (Furumoto & Scarborough, 1986). The three psychologists profiled here demonstrate that women have been making significant contributions to psychology almost from its beginning—despite formidable barriers to pursuing their academic careers.

this definition represents. Watson (1913) was proposing that psychologists *abandon the study of consciousness altogether* and focus exclusively on behaviors that they could observe directly. In essence, he was redefining what scientific psychology should be about.

Why did Watson argue for such a fundamental shift in direction? Because to him, the power of the scientific method rested on the idea of *verifiability*. In principle, scientific claims can always be verified (or disproved) by anyone who is able and willing to make the required observations. However, this power depends on studying things that can be observed objectively. Otherwise, the advantage of using the scientific approach—replacing vague speculation and personal opinion with reliable, exact knowledge—is lost. For Watson, mental processes were not a proper subject for scientific study because they are ultimately private events. After all, no one can see or touch another's thoughts. Consequently, if psychology was to be a science, it would have to give up consciousness as its subject matter and become instead the *science of behavior*.

***Behavior* refers to any overt (observable) response or activity by an organism.** Watson asserted that psychologists could study anything that people do or say—shopping, playing chess, eating, complimenting a friend—but they could *not* study scientifically the thoughts, wishes, and feelings that might accompany these observable behaviors.

Watson's radical reorientation of psychology did not end with his redefinition of its subject matter. He also took an extreme position on one of psychology's oldest and most fundamental questions: the issue of nature versus nurture. This age-old debate is concerned with whether behavior is determined mainly by genetic inheritance ("nature") or by environment and experience ("nurture"). To oversimplify, the question is this: Is a great concert pianist or a master criminal born, or made?

Watson argued that each is made, not born. In other words, he discounted the importance of heredity, maintaining that behavior is governed entirely by the environment. Indeed, he boldly claimed:

Give me a dozen healthy infants, well-formed, and my own special world to bring them up in and I'll guarantee to take any one at random and train him to become any type of specialist I might select—doctor, lawyer, artist, merchant-chief, and yes, even beggar-man and thief, regardless of his talents, penchants, tendencies, abilities, vocations and race of his ancestors. I am going beyond my facts and I admit it, but so have the advocates of the contrary and they have been doing it for many thousands of years. (1924, p. 82)

The time seems to have come when psychology must discard all references to consciousness.
JOHN B. WATSON
1878–1958

For obvious reasons, Watson's tongue-in-cheek challenge was never put to a test. Although this widely cited quote overstated and oversimplified Watson's views on the nature-nurture issue (Todd & Morris, 1992), his writings contributed to the environmental slant that became associated with behaviorism (Horowitz, 1992).

The behaviorists came to view psychology's mission as an attempt to relate overt behaviors ("responses") to observable events in the environment ("stimuli"). **A *stimulus* is any detectable input from the environment.** Stimuli can range from light and sound waves to such complex inputs as the words on this page, advertisements on TV, or sarcastic remarks from a friend. Because the behaviorists investigated stimulus-response relationships, the behavioral approach is often referred to as *stimulus-response (S-R) psychology.*

Although it met resistance and skepticism in some quarters, Watson's behavioral point of view gradually took hold (Samelson, 1981). Among other things, the growth of behaviorism contributed to the rise of animal research in psychology. Having deleted consciousness from their scope of concern, behaviorists no longer needed to study human subjects who could report on their mental processes. Many psychologists thought that animals would make better research subjects anyway. One key reason was that experimental research is often more productive if experimenters can exert considerable *control* over their subjects. Otherwise, too many complicating factors enter into the picture and contaminate the experiment. Obviously, a researcher can exert much more control over a laboratory rat or pigeon than over a human subject, who arrives at a lab with years of uncontrolled experience and who will probably insist on going home at night. Thus, the discipline that had begun its life a few decades earlier as the study of the mind now found itself heavily involved in the study of simple responses made by laboratory animals.

Although Watson's views shaped the evolution of psychology for many decades, his ideas did not go unchallenged. In Germany opposition came from an emerging school of thought called *Gestalt psychology.* The Gestalt theorists, who were primarily concerned with perception (we'll discuss their ideas in Chapter 4), argued that psychology should continue to study conscious experience rather than overt behavior. Another alternative

CONCEPT CHECK 1.1

Understanding the Implications of Major Theories: Wundt, James, and Watson

Check your understanding of the implications of some of the major theories reviewed in this chapter by indicating who is likely to have made each of the statements quoted below. Choose from the following theorists: (a) Wilhelm Wundt, (b) William James, and (c) John B. Watson. You'll find the answers in Appendix A at the back of the book.

_____ 1. "Our conclusion is that we have no real evidence of the inheritance of traits. I would feel perfectly confident in the ultimately favorable outcome of careful upbringing of a healthy, well-formed baby born of a long line of crooks, murderers and thieves, and prostitutes."

_____ 2. "The book which I present to the public is an attempt to mark out a new domain of science. . . . The new discipline rests upon anatomical and physiological foundations. . . . The experimental treatment of psychological problems must be pronounced from every point of view to be in its first beginnings."

_____ 3. "Consciousness, then, does not appear to itself chopped up in bits. Such words as 'chain' or 'train' do not describe it fitly. . . . It is nothing jointed; it flows. A 'river' or 'stream' are the metaphors by which it is most naturally described."

conception of psychology emerged from Austria, where an obscure physician named Sigmund Freud had been contemplating the mysteries of unconscious mental processes. We'll look at Freud's ideas next.

Freud Brings the Unconscious into the Picture

Long before he turned his attention to psychology, Sigmund Freud (1856–1939) dreamed of achieving fame by making an important discovery. His determination was such that in medical school he dissected 400 male eels to prove for the first time that they had testes. His work with eels did not make him famous, but his subsequent work with people did. Indeed, his theories made him one of the most influential—and controversial—intellectual figures of modern times.

Freud's (1900, 1933) approach to psychology grew out of his efforts to treat mental disorders. In his medical practice, Freud treated people troubled by psychological problems such as irrational fears, obsessions, and anxieties with an innovative procedure he called *psychoanalysis* (described in detail in Chapter 15). Decades of experience probing into his patients' lives provided much of the inspiration for Freud's theory. He also gathered material by looking inward and examining his own anxieties, conflicts, and desires.

His work with patients and his own self-exploration persuaded Freud of the existence of what he called the unconscious. According to Freud, **the *unconscious* contains thoughts, memories, and desires that are well below the surface of conscious awareness but that nonetheless exert great influence on behavior.** Freud based his concept of the unconscious on a variety of observations. For instance, he noticed that seemingly meaningless slips of the tongue (such as "I decided to take a summer school curse") often appeared to reveal a person's true feelings. He also noted that his patients' dreams often seemed to express important feelings that they were unaware of. Knitting these and other observations together, Freud eventually concluded that psychological disturbances are largely caused by personal conflicts existing at an unconscious level. More generally, his *psychoanalytic theory* **attempts to explain personality, motivation, and mental disorders by focusing on unconscious determinants of behavior.**

Freud's concept of the unconscious was not entirely new (it was anticipated by a few earlier theorists). However, it was a major departure from the prevailing belief that people are fully aware of the forces governing their behavior. In arguing that behavior is governed by unconscious forces, Freud made the disconcerting suggestion that people are not masters of their own minds. Other aspects of Freud's theory also stirred up debate. For instance, he proposed that behavior is greatly influenced by how people cope with their sexual urges. At a time when people were far less comfortable discussing sexual issues than they are today, even scientists were offended and scandalized by Freud's emphasis on sex. Small wonder, then, that Freud was soon engulfed in controversy.

In part because of their controversial nature, Freud's ideas gained influence only very slowly. By 1920 psychoanalytic theory was widely known around the world, but it continued to meet with considerable resistance in psychology. Why? The main reason was that it conflicted with the spirit of the times in psychology. Many psychologists were becoming uncomfortable with their earlier focus on conscious experience and were turning to the less murky subject of observable behavior. If they felt that *conscious* experience was inaccessible to scientific observation, you can imagine how they felt about trying to study *unconscious* experience. Most psychologists contemptuously viewed psychoanalytic theory as unscientific speculation that would eventually fade away (Hornstein, 1992).

They turned out to be wrong. Psychoanalytic ideas steadily gained acceptance in the culture at large, influencing thought in medicine, the arts, and literature. Then, in the 1930s and 1940s, more and more psychologists found themselves becoming interested in areas Freud had studied: personality, motivation, and abnormal behavior. As they turned to these topics, many of them saw merit in some of Freud's notions (Rosenzweig, 1985). Although psychoanalytic theory continued to generate heated debate, it survived to become an influential theoretical perspective. Today, many psychoanalytic concepts have filtered into the mainstream of psychology (Hillner, 1984).

Skinner Questions Free Will as Behaviorism Flourishes

While psychoanalytic thought was slowly gaining a foothold within psychology, the behaviorists were temporarily softening their stance on the

The unconscious is the true psychical reality; in its innermost nature it is as much unknown to us as the reality of the external world.
SIGMUND FREUD 1856–1939

I submit that what we call the behavior of the human organism is no more free than its digestion.
B. F. SKINNER 1904–1990

acceptability of studying internal mental events. Under the leadership of Clark Hull, this modified behavioral approach still emphasized the study of observable behavior, but it permitted careful inferences to be drawn about an organism's internal states, such as drives, needs, and habits. For example, Hull (1943) argued that if an animal ate eagerly when offered food, it was not farfetched to infer the existence of an internal hunger drive.

This movement toward the consideration of internal states was dramatically reversed in the 1950s by the work of B. F. Skinner (1904–1990), one of the most influential of all American psychologists. In response to the softening in the behaviorist position, Skinner (1953) championed a return to Watson's strict stimulus-response approach. Skinner did not deny the existence of internal mental events. However, he insisted that they could not be studied scientifically. Moreover, he maintained, there was no need to study them. According to Skinner, if the stimulus of food is followed by the response of eating, we can fully describe what is happening without making any guesses about whether the animal is experiencing hunger. He asserted that finding out how stimuli and responses are associated is all we need in order to understand and predict behavior.

The fundamental principle of behavior documented by Skinner is deceptively simple: *Organisms tend to repeat responses that lead to positive outcomes, and they tend not to repeat responses that lead to neutral or negative outcomes*. Despite its simplicity, this principle turns out to be quite powerful. Working primarily with laboratory rats and pigeons, Skinner showed that he could exert remarkable control over the behavior of animals by

It seems to me that at bottom each person is asking, "Who am I, really? How can I get in touch with this real self, underlying all my surface behavior? How can I become myself?"
CARL ROGERS 1905–1987

manipulating the outcomes of their responses. He was even able to train animals to perform unnatural behaviors. For example, he once trained some pigeons to play Ping-Pong! Skinner's followers eventually showed that the principles uncovered in their animal research could be applied to complex human behaviors as well. Behavioral principles are now widely used in factories, schools, prisons, mental hospitals, and a variety of other settings.

Skinner's ideas had repercussions that went far beyond the debate among psychologists about what they should study.

Skinner spelled out the full implications of his findings in his book *Beyond Freedom and Dignity* (1971). There he asserted that all behavior is fully governed by external stimuli. In other words, your behavior is determined in predictable ways by lawful principles, just as the flight of an arrow is governed by the laws of physics. Thus, if you believe that your actions are the result of conscious decisions, you're wrong. According to Skinner, we are all controlled by our environment, not by ourselves. In short, Skinner arrived at the conclusion that *free will is an illusion*.

As you can readily imagine, such a disconcerting view of human nature was not universally acclaimed. Like Freud, Skinner was the target of harsh criticism. Despite the controversy, however, behaviorism flourished as the dominant school of thought in psychology during the 1950s and 1960s (Gilgen, 1982).

The Humanists Revolt

By the 1950s behaviorism and psychoanalytic theory had become the most influential schools of thought in psychology. However, many psychologists found these theoretical orientations unappealing. The principal charge hurled at both schools was that they were "dehumanizing." Psychoanalytic theory was attacked for its belief that behavior is dominated by primitive, sexual urges. Behaviorism was criticized for its preoccupation with the study of simple animal behavior. Both theories were criticized because they suggested that people are not masters of their own destinies. Above all, many people argued, both schools of thought failed to recognize the unique qualities of *human* behavior.

Beginning in the 1950s, the diverse opposition to behaviorism and psychoanalytic theory blended into a loose alliance that eventually became a new school of thought called "humanism" (Buhler & Allen, 1972). In psychology, **humanism is a theoretical orientation that emphasizes the unique qualities of humans, especially their freedom and their potential for personal growth**. Some of the key differences between the humanistic, psychoanalytic, and behavioral viewpoints are summarized in Table 1.1, which compares five contemporary theoretical perspectives in psychology.

Humanists take an *optimistic* view of human nature. They maintain that people are not pawns of either their animal heritage or environmental circumstances. Furthermore, they say, because humans are fundamentally different from other animals, research on animals has little relevance to the understanding of human behavior. The most

Table 1.1 Overview of Five Contemporary Theoretical Perspectives in Psychology

Perspective and Its Influential Period	Principal Contributors	Subject Matter	Basic Premise
Behavioral (1913–present)	John B. Watson Ivan Pavlov B. F. Skinner	Effects of environment on the overt behavior of humans and animals	Only observable events (stimulus-response relations) can be studied scientifically.
Psychoanalytic (1900–present)	Sigmund Freud Carl Jung Alfred Adler	Unconscious determinants of behavior	Unconscious motives and experiences in early childhood govern personality and mental disorders.
Humanistic (1950s–present)	Carl Rogers Abraham Maslow	Unique aspects of human experience	Humans are free, rational beings with the potential for personal growth, and they are fundamentally different from animals.
Cognitive (1950s–present)	Jean Piaget Noam Chomsky Herbert Simon	Thoughts; mental processes	Human behavior cannot be fully understood without examining how people acquire, store, and process information.
Biological (1950s–present)	James Olds Roger Sperry	Physiological bases of behavior in humans and animals	An organism's functioning can be explained in terms of the bodily structures and biochemical processes that underlie behavior.

prominent architects of the humanistic movement have been Carl Rogers (1902–1987) and Abraham Maslow (1908–1970). Rogers (1951) argued that human behavior is governed primarily by each individual's sense of self, or "self-concept"—which animals presumably lack. Both he and Maslow (1954) maintained that to fully understand people's behavior, psychologists must take into account the fundamental human drive toward personal growth. They asserted that people have a basic need to continue to evolve as human beings and to fulfill their potentials.

The humanists' greatest contribution to psychology has been their innovative treatments for psychological problems and disorders. The humanistic movement has provided a fertile breeding ground for the development of creative approaches to psychotherapy (see Chapter 15). More generally, the humanists have argued eloquently for a different picture of

---

CONCEPT CHECK 1.2

Understanding the Implications of Major Theories: Freud, Skinner, and Rogers

Check your understanding of the implications of some of the major theories reviewed in this chapter by indicating who is likely to have made each of the statements quoted below. Choose from the following: (a) Sigmund Freud, (b) B. F. Skinner, and (c) Carl Rogers. You'll find the answers in Appendix A at the back of the book.

_____ 1. "In the traditional view, a person is free. . . . He can therefore be held responsible for what he does and justly punished if he offends. That view, together with its associated practices, must be reexamined when a scientific analysis reveals unsuspected controlling relations between behavior and environment."

_____ 2. "He that has eyes to see and ears to hear may convince himself that no mortal can keep a secret. If the lips are silent, he chatters with his fingertips; betrayal oozes out of him at every pore. And thus the task of making conscious the most hidden recesses of the mind is one which it is quite possible to accomplish."

_____ 3. "I do not have a Pollyanna view of human nature. . . . Yet one of the most refreshing and invigorating parts of my experience is to work with [my clients] and to discover the strongly positive directional tendencies which exist in them, as in all of us, at the deepest levels."

human nature than those implied by psychoanalysis and behaviorism.

Psychology Comes of Age as a Profession

The 1950s also saw psychology come of age as a profession. As you know, psychology is not all pure science. It has a highly practical side. Many psychologists provide a variety of professional services to the public. Their work falls within the domain of *applied psychology*, **the branch of psychology concerned with everyday, practical problems.**

This branch of psychology, which is so prominent today, was actually slow to develop. Although the first psychological clinic was established as early as 1896, few psychologists were concerned with applications of their science until World War I (1914–1918). The war created a huge demand for mental testing of military personnel so that recruits could be assigned to jobs according to their abilities. The war thus brought many psychologists into the applied arena for the first time and established mental testing as a routine professional activity conducted by psychologists.

After World War I, psychology continued to grow as a profession, but only very slowly. The principal professional arm of psychology was *clinical psychology*. As practiced today, *clinical psychology* **is the branch of psychology concerned with the diagnosis and treatment of psychological problems and disorders.** In its early days, however, the emphasis was almost exclusively on psychological testing, and few psychologists were involved in clinical work. As late as 1937 only about one in five psychologists reported an interest in clinical psychology (Goldenberg, 1983).

That picture was about to change with dramatic swiftness. Once again the impetus was a world war. During World War II (1941–1945), many academic psychologists were pressed into service as clinicians. They were needed to screen military recruits and to treat soldiers suffering from trauma. Many of these psychologists (often to their surprise) found the clinical work to be challenging and rewarding, and a substantial portion continued to do clinical work after the war. More significantly, some 40,000 American veterans, many with severe psychological scars, returned to seek postwar treatment in Veterans Administration (VA) hospitals. With the demand for clinicians far greater than the supply, the VA stepped in to finance many new training programs in clinical psychology. These programs, emphasizing training in the treatment of psychological disorders as well as in psychological testing, proved attractive. Within a few years, about half of the new Ph.D.'s in psychology were specializing in clinical psychology (Goldenberg, 1983). Thus, during the 1950s the prewar orphan of applied/professional psychology rapidly matured into a robust, powerful adult.

Since the 1950s, the professionalization of psychology has continued at a steady pace. In fact, the trend has spread into additional areas of psychology. Today the broad umbrella of applied psychology covers a variety of professional specialties, including school psychology, industrial and organizational psychology, and counseling psychology. Whereas psychologists were once almost exclusively research scientists, roughly two-thirds of today's psychologists devote some of their time to providing professional services.

Psychology Returns to Its Roots: Renewed Interest in Cognition and Physiology

While applied psychology has blossomed in recent years, scientific research has continued to progress. Ironically, two of the latest trends in research hark back a century to psychology's beginning, when psychologists were principally interested in consciousness and physiology. Today psychologists are showing renewed interest in consciousness (now called "cognition") and the physiological bases of behavior.

Cognition **refers to the mental processes involved in acquiring knowledge.** In other words, cognition involves thinking or conscious experience. For many decades, the dominance of behaviorism discouraged investigation of "unobservable" mental processes, and most psychologists showed little interest in cognition. During the 1950s and 1960s, however, this situation slowly began to change. Major progress in the study of children's cognitive development (Piaget, 1954), memory (Miller, 1956), language (Chomsky, 1957), and problem solving (Newell, Shaw, & Simon, 1958) sparked a surge of interest in cognitive psychology.

Cognitive theorists argue that psychology must study internal mental events to fully understand human behavior (Gardner, 1985; Neisser, 1967). Advocates of the *cognitive perspective* point out that our manipulations of mental images surely influence how we behave. Consequently, focusing exclusively on overt behavior yields an incomplete picture of why we behave as we do. Equally important, psychologists investigating decision making, reasoning, and problem solving have shown that methods *can* be devised to study cognitive processes scientifically. Although the methods are different from those used in psychology's early days, recent research on the inner workings of the mind has put the *psyche* back in contemporary psychology.

The 1950s and 1960s also saw many discoveries that highlighted the interrelations among mind, body, and behavior. For example, psychologists demonstrated that electrical stimulation of the brain could evoke emotional responses such as pleasure and rage in animals (Olds, 1956). Other work showed that the right and left halves of the brain are specialized to handle different types of mental tasks (Gazzaniga, Bogen, & Sperry, 1965). These and many other findings stimulated an increase in research on the biological bases of behavior. Advocates of the *biological perspective* maintain that much of human and animal behavior can be explained in terms of the bodily structures and biochemical processes that allow organisms to behave. As you know, in the 19th century the young science of psychology had a heavy physiological emphasis. Thus, the recent interest in the biological bases of behavior represents another return to psychology's heritage.

Although adherents of the cognitive and biological perspectives haven't done as much organized campaigning for their viewpoint as proponents of the older, traditional schools of thought, these newer perspectives have become important theoretical orientations in modern psychology. They are increasingly influential viewpoints regarding what psychology should study and how. The cognitive and biological perspectives are compared to other contemporary theoretical perspectives (the behavioral, psychoanalytic, and humanistic viewpoints) in Table 1.1.

Psychology Broadens Its Horizons: Increased Interest in Cultural Diversity

Throughout psychology's history, most researchers have worked under the assumption that they were seeking to identify general principles of behavior that would be applicable to all of humanity. In reality, however, psychology has largely been a Western (North American and European) enterprise with a remarkably provincial slant. The vast preponderance of research has been conducted in the United States by middle- and upper-class white psychologists who have used mostly middle- and upper-class white males as subjects (Segall et al., 1990). Traditionally, Western psychologists have paid scant attention to how well

their theories and research might apply to non-Western cultures, to ethnic minorities in Western societies, or even to women as opposed to men.

However, in recent years Western psychologists have begun to recognize that their neglect of cultural variables has diminished the value of their work, and they are devoting increased attention to culture as a determinant of behavior. What brought about this shift? The new interest in culture appears mainly attributable to two recent trends: (1) advances in communication, travel, and international trade have "shrunk" the world and increased global interdependence, bringing more and more Americans and Europeans into contact with people from non-Western cultures, and (2) the ethnic makeup of the Western world has become an increasingly diverse multicultural mosaic, as the data in Figure 1.3 show for the United States (Brislin, 1993; Locke, 1992).

These realities have prompted more and more Western psychologists to broaden their horizons and incorporate cultural factors into their theories and research (Shweder & Sullivan, 1993). These psychologists are striving to study previously underrepresented groups of subjects to test the generality of earlier findings and to catalog both the differences and similarities among cultural groups. They are working to increase knowledge of how culture is transmitted through socialization practices and how culture colors one's view of the world. They are seeking to learn how people cope with cultural change and to find ways to reduce misunderstandings and conflicts in intercultural interactions. In addi-

Figure 1.3. Increased cultural diversity in the United States. The 1980s brought significant changes in the ethnic makeup of the United States. The nation's Hispanic population grew by 53% during the decade, and its Asian American population more than doubled (a 108% increase), while the white population increased by only 6%. Experts project that ethnic minorities will account for over one-third of the U.S. population early in the 21st century (Sue, 1991). Perhaps more important than sheer numbers has been the rise in ethnic identity. Today, many ethnic minorities strive to maintain their distinctive cultural heritages rather than to be assimilated into the dominant North American culture (Moghaddam, Taylor, & Wright, 1993). These realities have contributed to psychologists' increased interest in cultural factors as determinants of behavior. (Data from U.S. Bureau of the Census)

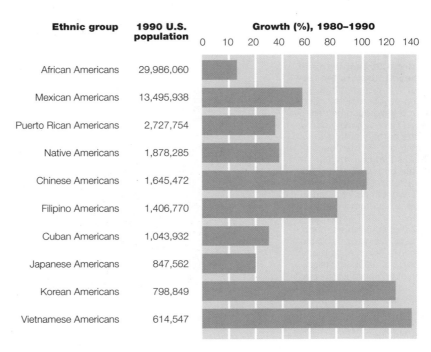

Ethnic group	1990 U.S. population	Growth (%), 1980–1990
African Americans	29,986,060	
Mexican Americans	13,495,938	
Puerto Rican Americans	2,727,754	
Native Americans	1,878,285	
Chinese Americans	1,645,472	
Filipino Americans	1,406,770	
Cuban Americans	1,043,932	
Japanese Americans	847,562	
Korean Americans	798,849	
Vietnamese Americans	614,547	

tion, they are trying to enhance understanding of how cultural groups are affected by prejudice, discrimination, and racism. In all these efforts, they are striving to understand the unique experiences of culturally diverse people *from the point of view of those people*. These efforts to ask new questions, study new groups, and apply new perspectives promise to enrich the discipline of psychology as it moves into the 21st century (Betancourt & Lopez, 1993).

Our review of psychology's past has shown how the field has evolved. We have seen psychology develop from philosophical speculation into a rigorous science committed to research. We have seen how a highly visible professional arm involved in mental health services emerged from this science. We have seen how psychology's focus on physiology is rooted in its 19th-century origins. We have seen how and why psychologists began conducting research on lower animals. We have seen how psychology has evolved from the study of mind and body to the study of behavior. And we have seen how the investigation of mind and body has been welcomed back into the mainstream of modern psychology. We have seen how different theoretical schools have defined the scope and mission of psychology in different ways. We have seen how psychology's interests have expanded and become increasingly diverse. Above all else, we have seen that psychology is a growing, evolving intellectual enterprise.

Psychology's history is already rich, but its story has barely begun. The century or so that has elapsed since Wilhelm Wundt put psychology on a scientific footing is only an eyeblink of time in human history. What has been discovered during those years, and what remains unknown, is the subject of the rest of this book.

PSYCHOLOGY TODAY: VIGOROUS AND DIVERSIFIED

We began this chapter with an informal description of what psychology is about. Now that you have a feel for how psychology has developed, you can better appreciate a definition that does justice to the field's modern diversity: ***Psychology* is the science that studies behavior and the physiological and cognitive processes that underlie behavior, and it is the profession that applies the accumulated knowledge of this science to practical problems.**

Contemporary psychology is a thriving science and profession. Its growth has been remarkable. One simple index of this growth is the dramatic rise in membership in the American Psychological Association (APA), a national organization devoted to the advancement of psychology. The APA was founded in 1892 with just 26 members. Today, the APA has over 132,000 members (counting student affiliates). Moreover, as Figure 1.4 shows, APA membership has increased sevenfold since 1950. In the United States, psychology now accounts for about 10% of all doctoral degrees awarded in the sciences and humanities. The comparable figure in 1945 was only 4% (Howard et al., 1986). Of course, psychology is an international enterprise. Today, over 1100 technical journals from all over the world publish research articles on psychology. Thus, by any standard of measurement—the number of people involved, the number of degrees granted, the number of studies conducted, the number of journals published—psychology is a healthy, growing field.

Psychology's vigorous presence in modern so-

Figure 1.4. Membership in the American Psychological Association, 1900—1993. The steep rise in the number of psychologists in the APA since 1950 testifies to psychology's remarkable growth as a science and a profession. If student affiliates are also counted, the APA has over 132,000 members.

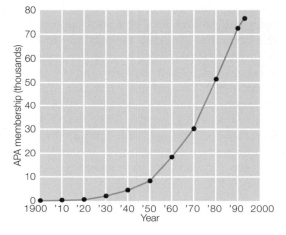

Figure 1.5. Employment of psychologists by setting. The work settings in which psychologists are employed have become very diverse. Recent survey data on the primary employment setting of APA members indicates that one-third are in private practice (compared to 12% in 1976) and only 27% work in colleges and universities (compared to 47% in 1976). These data may slightly underestimate the percentage of psychologists in academia, as many research psychologists are now joining another, newer organization (founded in 1988), called the American Psychological Society (APS). (Data based on *Profile of All APA Members: 1993*)

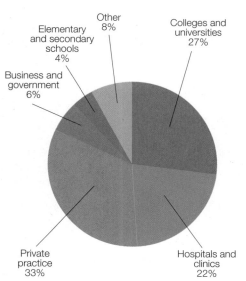

ciety is also demonstrated by the great variety of settings in which psychologists work. The distribution of psychologists employed in various categories of settings can be seen in Figure 1.5. Psychologists were once found almost exclusively in the halls of academia. However, today only about one-fourth of American psychologists work in colleges and universities. The remaining three-fourths work in hospitals, clinics, police departments, research institutes, government agencies, business and industry, schools, nursing homes, counseling centers, and private practice.

Clearly, contemporary psychology is a multifaceted field, a fact that is especially apparent when we consider the many areas of specialization within psychology today. Let's look at the current areas of specialization in both the science and the profession of psychology.

Research Areas in Psychology

Although most psychologists receive broad training that provides them with knowledge about many areas of psychology, they usually specialize when it comes to doing research. Such specialization is necessary because the subject matter of psychology has become so vast over the years. Today it is virtually impossible for anyone to stay abreast of the new research in all specialties. Specialization is also necessary because specific skills and training are required to do research in some areas.

The seven major research areas in modern psychology are (1) developmental psychology, (2) social psychology, (3) experimental psychology, (4) physiological psychology, (5) cognitive psychology, (6) personality, and (7) psychometrics. Figure 1.6 (on page 16) describes these areas briefly and shows the percentage of research psychologists who identify each area as their primary interest (American Psychological Association, 1993). As you can see, social psychology and developmental psychology have become especially popular areas of specialization.

Professional Specialties in Psychology

Within applied psychology there are four clearly identified areas of specialization: (1) clinical psychology, (2) counseling psychology, (3) educational and school psychology, and (4) industrial and organizational psychology. Descriptions of these specialties can be found in Figure 1.7 (on page 16), along with the percentage of professional psychologists specializing in each area (American Psychological Association, 1993). As

Although psychology is broken down into research areas and specialties for our convenience, in reality a single psychologist may be classified in a number of subfields. (Top) Here we see a counseling psychologist working with and testing a patient recuperating from brain surgery. (Bottom) A psychologist observes behavior of children in a day-care center.

the figure indicates, clinical psychology is currently the most widely practiced professional specialty.

The data in Figures 1.6 and 1.7 are based on psychologists' reports of their single, principal area of specialization. However, many psychologists work on both research and application. Some academic psychologists work as consultants, therapists, and counselors on a part-time basis. Similarly, some applied psychologists conduct basic research on issues related to their specialty. For example, many clinical psychologists are involved in research on the nature and causes of abnormal behavior.

PUTTING IT IN PERSPECTIVE: SEVEN KEY THEMES

The enormous breadth and diversity of psychology make it a challenging subject for the beginning student. In the pages ahead you will be introduced to many areas of research and a multitude of new ideas, concepts, and principles. Fortunately, all ideas are not created equal. Some are far more important than others. In this section, I will highlight seven fundamental themes that will reappear in a number of variations as we move from

Figure 1.6. Major research areas in contemporary psychology. Most research psychologists specialize in one of the seven broad areas described here. The figures in the pie chart reflect the percentage of research psychologists belonging to APA who identify each area as their primary interest. (Data based on *Profile of All APA Members: 1993*)

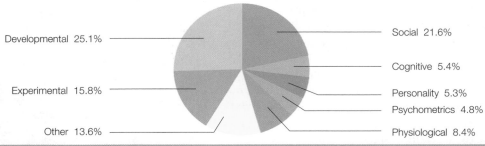

Area	Focus of research
Developmental psychology	Looks at human development across the life span. Developmental psychology once focused primarily on child development but today devotes a great deal of research to adolescence, adulthood, and old age.
Social psychology	Focuses on interpersonal behavior and the role of social forces in governing behavior. Typical topics include attitude formation, attitude change, prejudice, conformity, attraction, aggression, intimate relationships, and behavior in groups.
Experimental psychology	Encompasses the traditional core of topics that psychology focused on heavily in its first half-century as a science: sensation, perception, learning, conditioning, motivation, and emotion. The name *experimental psychology* is somewhat misleading, as this is not the only area in which experiments are done. Psychologists working in all the areas listed here conduct experiments.
Physiological psychology	Examines the influence of genetic factors on behavior and the role of the brain, nervous system, endocrine system, and bodily chemicals in the regulation of behavior.
Cognitive psychology	Focuses on "higher" mental processes, such as memory, reasoning, information processing, language, problem solving, decision making, and creativity.
Personality	Is interested in describing and understanding individuals' consistency in behavior, which represents their personality. This area of interest is also concerned with the factors that shape personality and with personality assessment.
Psychometrics	Is concerned with the measurement of behavior and capacities, usually through the development of psychological tests. Psychometrics is involved with the design of tests to assess personality, intelligence, and a wide range of abilities. It is also concerned with the development of new techniques for statistical analysis.

Figure 1.7. Principal professional specialties in contemporary psychology. Most psychologists who deliver professional services to the public specialize in one of the four areas described here. The figures in the pie chart reflect the percentage of those psychologists belonging to APA who identify each area as their chief specialty. (Data based on *Profile of All APA Members: 1993*)

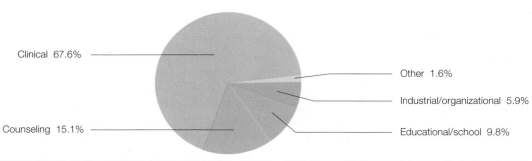

Specialty	Focus of professional practice
Clinical psychology	Clinical psychologists are concerned with the evaluation, diagnosis, and treatment of individuals with psychological disorders, as well as treatment of less severe behavioral and emotional problems. Principal activities include interviewing clients, psychological testing, and providing group or individual psychotherapy.
Counseling psychology	Counseling psychology overlaps with clinical psychology in that specialists in both areas engage in similar activities — interviewing, testing, and providing therapy. However, counseling psychologists usually work with a somewhat different clientele, providing assistance to people struggling with everyday problems of moderate severity. Thus, they often specialize in family, marital, or career counseling.
Educational and school psychology	Educational psychologists work to improve curriculum design, achievement testing, teacher training, and other aspects of the educational process. School psychologists usually work in elementary or secondary schools, where they test and counsel children having difficulties in school, and aid parents and teachers in solving school-related problems.
Industrial and organizational psychology	Psychologists in this area perform a wide variety of tasks in the world of business and industry. These tasks include running human resources departments, working to improve staff morale and attitudes, striving to increase job satisfaction and productivity, examining organizational structures and procedures, and making recommendations for improvements.

Check your understanding of the various research areas in psychology reviewed in this chapter by indicating which type of psychologist would be most likely to perform each of the investigations described below. Choose from the following: (a) physiological psychology, (b) cognitive psychology, (c) developmental psychology, (d) psychometrics, and (e) personality. You'll find the answers in Appendix A at the back of the book.

_____ 1. Researchers interviewed the parents of 141 children (all born in 1956) every few months throughout childhood. Questions dealt with various aspects of the children's temperaments. The conclusion was that most children fall into one of three temperamental categories: "easy," "difficult," or "slow to warm up."

_____ 2. It was discovered that rats will work extremely hard (pressing a lever, for instance) to earn small amounts of electrical stimulation directed to specific areas of their brains. Research indicates that the human brain may also contain similar "pleasure centers."

_____ 3. The Sensation Seeking Scale (SSS) was developed to measure individual differences in the extent to which people prefer high or low levels of sensory stimulation. People such as skydivers tend to score high on the SSS, while someone whose idea of a good time is settling down with a good book would tend to score low.

one area of psychology to another in this text. You have already met some of these key ideas in our review of psychology's past and present. Now we will isolate them and highlight their significance. In the remainder of the book these ideas serve as organizing themes to provide threads of continuity across chapters and to help you see the connections among the various areas of research in psychology.

In studying psychology, you are learning about both behavior and the scientific discipline that investigates it. Accordingly, our seven themes come in two sets. The first set consists of statements highlighting crucial aspects of psychology as a way of thinking and as a field of study. The second set consists of broad generalizations about psychology's subject matter: behavior and the cognitive and physiological processes that underlie it.

Themes Related to Psychology as a Field of Study

Looking at psychology as a field of study, we see three crucial ideas: (1) psychology is empirical; (2) psychology is theoretically diverse; (3) psychology evolves in a sociohistorical context. Let's look at each of these ideas in more detail.

Theme 1: Psychology Is Empirical

Everyone tries to understand behavior. Most of us have our own personal answers to questions such as why some people are hard workers, why some are overweight, and why others stay in demeaning relationships. If all of us are amateur psychologists, what makes scientific psychology different? The critical difference is that psychology is *empirical*.

What do we mean by empirical? **Empiricism is the premise that knowledge should be acquired through observation.** This premise is crucial to the scientific method that psychology embraced in the late 19th century. To say that psychology is empirical means that its conclusions are based on direct observation rather than on reasoning, speculation, traditional beliefs, or common sense. Psychologists are not content with having ideas that sound plausible. They conduct research to *test* their ideas. Is intelligence higher on the average in some social classes than in others? Are men more aggressive than women? Psychologists find a way to make direct, objective, and precise observations to answer such questions.

The empirical approach requires a certain attitude—a healthy brand of *skepticism*. Empiricism is a tough taskmaster. It demands data and documentation. Psychologists' commitment to empiricism means that they must learn to think critically about generalizations concerning behavior. If someone asserts that people tend to get depressed around Christmas, a psychologist is likely to ask, "How many people get depressed? In what population? In comparison to what baseline rate of depression? How is depression defined and measured?" Their skeptical attitude means that psychologists are trained to ask, "Where's the evidence? How do you know?" If psychology's empirical orientation rubs off on you (and I hope it does), you will be asking similar questions by the time you finish this book.

Theme 2: Psychology Is Theoretically Diverse

Although psychology is based on observation, a string of unrelated observations would not be terribly enlightening. Psychologists do not set out to just collect isolated facts; they seek to explain and understand what they observe. To achieve these goals they must construct theories. **A *theory* is a system of interrelated ideas used to explain a set of observations.** In other words, a theory links apparently unrelated observations and tries to explain them. As an example, consider Sigmund Freud's observations about slips of the tongue, dreams, and psychological disturbances. On the surface, these observations appear unrelated. By devising the concept of the *unconscious*, Freud created a theory that links and explains these seemingly unrelated aspects of behavior.

Our review of psychology's past should have made one thing abundantly clear: psychology is marked by theoretical diversity. Why do we have so many competing points of view? One reason is that no single theory can adequately explain everything that is known about behavior. Sometimes different theories focus on different aspects of behavior—that is, different collections of observations. Sometimes there is simply more than one way to look at something. Is the glass half empty or half full? Obviously, it is both. To take an example from another science, physicists wrestled for years with the nature of light. Is it a wave, or is it a particle? In the end, it proved useful to think of light sometimes as a wave and sometimes as a particle. Similarly, if a business executive lashes out at her employees with stinging criticism, is she releasing pent-up aggressive urges (a psychoanalytic view)? Is she making a habitual response to the stimulus of incompetent work (a behavioral view)? Or is she scheming to motivate her employees with "mind games" (a cognitive view)? In some cases, all three of these explanations might have some validity. In short, it is an oversimplification to expect that one view has to be right while all others are wrong. Life is rarely that simple.

Students are often troubled by psychology's many conflicting theories, which they view as a weakness. However, contemporary psychologists increasingly recognize that theoretical diversity is a strength rather than a weakness (Hilgard, 1987). As we proceed through this text, you will see how clashing theories have stimulated productive research and how several theoretical perspectives often provide a more complete understanding of behavior than could be achieved by any one perspective alone.

Theme 3: Psychology Evolves in a Sociohistorical Context

Science is often seen as an "ivory tower" undertaking, isolated from the ebb and flow of everyday life. In reality, however, psychology and other sciences do not exist in a cultural vacuum. Dense interconnections exist between what happens in psychology and what happens in society at large (Altman, 1990; Danziger, 1990). Trends, issues, and values in society influence psychology's evolution. Similarly, progress in psychology affects trends, issues, and values in society. To put it briefly, psychology develops in a *sociohistorical* (social and historical) context.

Our review of psychology's past is filled with examples of how social trends have left their imprint on psychology. In the late 19th century, psychology's rapid growth as a laboratory science was due, in part, to its fascination with physics as the model discipline. Thus, the spirit of the times fostered a scientific approach rather than a philosophical approach to the investigation of the mind. Similarly, Freud's groundbreaking ideas emerged out of a specific sociohistorical context. Cultural values in Freud's era encouraged the suppression of sexuality. Hence, people tended to feel guilty about their sexual urges to a much greater extent than is common today. This situation clearly contributed to Freud's emphasis on unconscious sexual conflicts. As a final example, consider how World War II sparked the rapid growth of psychology as a profession.

If we reverse our viewpoint, we can see that psychology has in turn left its mark on society. Consider, for instance, the pervasive role of mental testing in modern society. Your own career success may depend in part on how well you weave your way through a complex maze of intelligence and achievement tests made possible (to the regret of some) by research in psychology. As another example of psychology's impact on society, consider the influence that various theorists have had on parenting styles. Trends in child-rearing practices have been shaped by the ideas of John B. Watson, Sigmund Freud, B. F. Skinner, and Carl Rogers—not to mention a host of additional psychologists yet to be discussed. In short, society and psychology influence each other in complex ways. In the chapters to come, we will frequently have occasion to notice this dynamic relationship.

Themes Related to Psychology's Subject Matter

Looking at psychology's subject matter, we see three additional crucial ideas: (4) behavior is determined by multiple causes; (5) our behavior is shaped by our cultural heritage; (6) heredity and environment jointly influence behavior; (7) our experience of the world is highly subjective.

Theme 4: Behavior Is Determined by Multiple Causes

As psychology has matured, it has provided more and more information about the forces that govern behavior. This growing knowledge has led to a deeper appreciation of a simple but important fact: Behavior is exceedingly complex and most aspects of behavior are determined by multiple causes.

Although the complexity of behavior may seem self-evident, people usually think in terms of single causes. Thus, they offer explanations such as "Andrea flunked out of school because she is lazy." Or they assert that "teenage pregnancies are increasing because of all the sex in the media." Single-cause explanations are sometimes accurate insofar as they go, but they usually are incomplete. In general, psychologists find that behavior is governed by a complex network of interacting factors, an idea referred to as the *multifactorial causation of behavior*.

As a simple illustration, consider the multiple factors that might influence your performance in your introductory psychology course. Relevant personal factors might include your overall intelligence, your reading ability, your memory skills, your motivation, and your study skills. In addition, your grade could be affected by numerous situational factors, including whether you like your psychology professor, whether you like your assigned text, whether the class meets at a good time for you, whether your work schedule is light or heavy, and whether you're having any personal problems. As you proceed through this book, you will learn that complexity of causation is the rule rather than the exception. If we expect to understand behavior, we usually have to take into account multiple determinants.

Theme 5: Our Behavior Is Shaped by Our Cultural Heritage

Among the multiple determinants of human behavior, cultural factors are particularly prominent. Just as psychology evolves in a sociohistorical context, so, too, do individuals. Our cultural backgrounds exert considerable influence over our behavior. What is *culture*? It's the human-made part of our environment. More specifically, **culture refers to the widely shared customs, beliefs, values, norms, institutions, and other products of a community that are transmitted socially across generations.** Culture is a very broad construct, encompassing everything from a society's legal system to its assumptions about family roles, from its dietary habits to its political ideals, from its technology to its attitudes about time, from its modes of dress to its spiritual beliefs, and from its art and music to its unspoken rules about sexual liaisons. We tend to think of culture as belonging to entire societies or broad ethnic groups within societies—which it does—but the concept can also be applied to small groups (a tiny Aboriginal tribe in Australia, for example) and to nonethnic groups (gay/homosexual culture, for instance).

Much of one's cultural heritage is invisible (Brislin, 1993). Assumptions, ideals, attitudes, beliefs, and unspoken rules exist in people's minds and may not be readily apparent to outsiders. Moreover, because our cultural background is widely shared, we feel little need to discuss it with others, and we often take it for granted. For example, you probably don't spend much time thinking about the importance of living in rectangular rooms, trying to minimize body odor, limiting yourself to one spouse at a time, or using credit cards to obtain material goods and services. Although we generally fail to appreciate its influence, our cultural heritage has a pervasive impact on our thoughts, feelings, and behavior.

Let's look at a couple examples of this influence. In North America, when people are invited to dinner in someone's home they generally show their appreciation of their host's cooking efforts by eating all of the food they are served. In India, this behavior would be insulting to the host, as guests are expected to leave some food on their plates. The leftover food acknowledges the generosity of the host, implying that he or she provided so much food the guest could not eat it all (Moghaddam, Taylor, & Wright, 1993). Cultures also vary in their emphasis on punctuality. In North America, we expect people to show up for meetings on time; if someone is more than 10 to 15 minutes late, we begin to get upset. We generally strive to be on time, and many of us are quite proud of our precise and dependable punctuality. However, in many Asian and Latin American countries, social obligations that arise at the last minute are given just as much priority as scheduled commitments. Hence, people often show up for important meetings an hour or two late with little remorse, and they may be quite puzzled by the consternation of their Western visitors (Brislin, 1993). These examples may seem trivial, but culture can also influence crucial matters, such as educational success, physical health, and a host of other things, as you will see throughout this book.

In discussing the importance of culture, Segall and his colleagues (1990) go so far as to assert that "it is rare (perhaps even impossible) for any human being ever to behave without responding to some aspect of culture" (p. 5). Although the influence of culture is everywhere, generalizations about cultural groups must always be tempered by the realization that there is great diversity within any society or ethnic group. Researchers may be able to pinpoint genuinely useful insights about Ethiopian, Korean American, or Ukrainian culture, for example, but it would be foolish to assume that all Ethiopians, Korean Americans, or Ukrainians exhibit identical behavior. It is also important to realize that *there are both differences and similarities across cultures in behavior*. As we will see repeatedly, psychological processes are characterized by both cultural variance and invariance. Caveats aside, if we hope to achieve a sound understanding of human behavior, we need to consider cultural determinants.

Theme 6: Heredity and Environment Jointly Influence Behavior

Are we who we are—athletic or artistic, quick-tempered or calm, shy or outgoing, energetic or laid back—because of our genetic inheritance or because of our upbringing? This question about the importance of nature versus nurture, or heredity versus environment, has been asked in one form or another since ancient times. Historically, the nature versus nurture question was framed as an all-or-none proposition. In other words, theorists argued that personal traits and abilities are governed entirely by heredity or entirely by environment. John B. Watson, for instance, asserted that personality and ability depend exclusively on an individual's environment. In contrast, Sir Francis Galton, a pioneer in mental testing, maintained that personality and ability depend almost entirely on genetic inheritance.

Today, most psychologists agree that heredity and environment are both important. A century of research has shown that genetics and experience jointly influence an individual's intelligence, temperament, personality, and susceptibility to many psychological disorders (Plomin & Rende, 1991; Scarr & Kidd, 1983; Schlesinger, 1985). If we ask whether people are born or made, psychology's answer is "Both." This does not mean that nature versus nurture is a dead issue. Lively debate about the *relative influence* of genetics and experience continues unabated. Furthermore, psychologists are actively seeking to understand the complex

Check your understanding of the seven key themes introduced in the chapter by matching the vignettes with the themes they exemplify. You'll find the answers in Appendix A.

Themes

1. Psychology is empirical.
2. Psychology is theoretically diverse.
3. Psychology evolves in a sociohistorical context.
4. Behavior is determined by multiple causes.
5. Our behavior is shaped by our cultural heritage.
6. Heredity and environment jointly influence behavior.
7. Our experience of the world is highly subjective.

Vignettes

_____ a. Several or more theoretical models of emotion have contributed to our overall understanding of the dynamics of emotion.

_____ b. According to the stress-vulnerability model, some people are at greater risk for developing certain psychological disorders for genetic reasons. Whether these people actually develop the disorders depends on how much stress they experience in their work, families, or other areas of their lives.

_____ c. Physical health and illness seem to be influenced by a complex constellation of psychological, biological, and social system variables.

_____ d. One of the difficulties in investigating the effects of drugs on consciousness is that individuals tend to have different experiences with a given drug because of their different expectations.

ways in which genetic inheritance and experience interact to mold behavior.

Theme 7: Our Experience of the World Is Highly Subjective

People's experience of the world is highly subjective. Even elementary perception—for example, of sights and sounds—is not a passive process. We actively process incoming stimulation, selectively focusing on some aspects of that stimulation while ignoring others. Moreover, we impose organization on the stimuli that we pay attention to. These tendencies combine to make perception personalized and subjective.

The subjectivity of perception was demonstrated nicely in a study by Hastorf and Cantril (1954). They showed students at Princeton and Dartmouth universities a film of a recent football game between the two schools. The students were told to watch for rules infractions. Both groups saw the same film, but the Princeton students "saw" the Dartmouth players engage in twice as many infractions as the Dartmouth students "saw." The investigators concluded that the game "actually was many different games and that each version of the events that tran-

spired was just as 'real' to a particular person as other versions were to other people" (Hastorf & Cantril, 1954). This study showed how people sometimes see what they *want* to see. Other studies have demonstrated that people also tend to see what they *expect* to see (Kelley, 1950). Thus, it is clear that motives and expectations color our experiences.

Human subjectivity is precisely what the scientific method is designed to counteract. In using the scientific approach, psychologists strive to make their observations as objective as possible. In some respects, overcoming subjectivity is what science is all about. Left to their own subjective experience, people might still believe that the earth is flat and that the sun revolves around it. Thus, psychologists are committed to the scientific approach because they believe it is the most reliable route to accurate knowledge.

Now that you have been introduced to the text's organizing themes, let's turn to an example of how psychological research can be applied to the challenges of everyday life. In our first Application, we'll focus on a subject that should be highly relevant to you: how to be a successful student.

Improving Academic Performance

Answer the following "true" or "false."

___ **1** If you have a professor who delivers chaotic, hard-to-follow lectures, there is little point in attending class.

___ **2** Cramming the night before an exam is an efficient method of study.

___ **3** In taking lecture notes, you should try to be a "human tape recorder" (that is, write down everything your professor says).

___ **4** You should never change your answers to multiple-choice questions, because your first hunch is your best hunch.

All of the above statements are false. If you answered them all correctly, you may have already acquired the kinds of skills and habits that facilitate academic success. If so, however, you are *not* typi-cal. Today, many students enter college with poor study skills and habits—and it's not entirely their fault. Our educa-tional system generally provides mini-mal instruction on good study techniques. In this first Application, I will try to remedy this situation to some extent by reviewing some insights that psychology offers on how to improve academic per-formance. We will discuss how to pro-mote better study habits, how to enhance reading efforts, how to get more out of lectures, and how to improve test-taking strategies. You may also want to jump ahead and read the Application for Chap-ter 7, which focuses on how to improve everyday memory.

Developing Sound Study Habits

Effective study is crucial to success in college. Although you may run into a few classmates who boast about getting good grades without studying, you can be sure that if they perform well on exams, they *do* study. Students who claim otherwise simply want to be viewed as extremely bright rather than as studious.

Learning can be immensely gratifying, but studying usually involves hard work. The first step toward effective study hab-its is to face up to this reality. You don't have to feel guilty if you don't look for-ward to studying. Most students don't. Once you accept the premise that study-ing doesn't come naturally, it should be apparent that you need to set up an orga-nized program to promote adequate study. According to Walter and Siebert (1990), such a program should include the following considerations:

1. *Set up a schedule for studying.* If you wait until the urge to study strikes you, you may still be waiting when the exam rolls around. Thus, it is important to allocate definite times to studying. Re-view your various time obligations (work, chores, and so on) and figure out in advance when you can study. When al-lotting certain times to studying, keep in mind that you need to be wide awake and alert. Be realistic about how long you can study at one time before you wear down from fatigue. Allow time for study breaks—they can revive sagging concentration.

It's important to write down your study schedule. A written schedule serves as a reminder and increases your commit-ment to following it. You should begin by setting up a general schedule for the quarter or semester, like the one in Fig-ure 1.8. Then, at the beginning of each week, plan the specific assignments that you intend to work on during each study session. This approach to scheduling should help you avoid cramming for ex-ams at the last minute. Cramming is an ineffective study strategy for most stu-

Where you study can be an important factor in whether your study efforts pay off. Some locations, such as the one shown here, are far more conducive to effective studying than others.

Figure 1.8. One student's general activity schedule for a semester. Each week the student fills in the specific assignments to work on during each study period.

Weekly activity schedule

	Monday	Tuesday	Wednesday	Thursday	Friday	Saturday	Sunday
8 A.M.						Work	
9 A.M.	History	Study	History	Study	History	Work	
10 A.M.	Psychology	French	Psychology	French	Psychology	Work	
11 A.M.	Study	French	Study	French	Study	Work	
Noon	Math	Study	Math	Study	Math	Work	Study
1 P.M.							Study
2 P.M.	Study	English	Study	English	Study		Study
3 P.M.	Study	English	Study	English	Study		Study
4 P.M.							
5 P.M.							
6 P.M.	Work	Study	Study	Work			Study
7 P.M.	Work	Study	Study	Work			Study
8 P.M.	Work	Study	Study	Work			Study
9 P.M.	Work	Study	Study	Work			Study
10 P.M.	Work			Work			

dents (Underwood, 1961; Zechmeister & Nyberg, 1982). It will strain your memorization capabilities, can tax your energy level, and may stoke the fires of test anxiety.

In planning your weekly schedule, try to avoid the tendency to put off working on major tasks such as term papers and reports. Time-management experts, such as Alan Lakein (1973), point out that many of us tend to tackle simple, routine tasks first, saving larger tasks for later when we supposedly will have more time. This common tendency leads many of us to repeatedly delay working on major assignments until it's too late to do a good job. You can avoid this trap by breaking major assignments down into smaller component tasks that can be scheduled individually. Some additional guidelines that promote efficient time management are listed in Figure 1.9.

Figure 1.9. Managing time more effectively. Johnson, Springer, and Sternglanz (1982) offer these hints for improving time management.

1	Set aside times and places for work.
2	Set priorities and then *do* things in priority order.
3	Break large tasks into much smaller ones.
4	Keep the tasks planned for a day down to a reasonable number.
5	Work on one thing (an important task) at a time.
6	Define all tasks specifically (in terms of what you want to have written or want to be able to recall, and so forth).
7	Check your progress often.

2. *Find a place to study where you can concentrate.* Where you study is also important. The key is to find a place where distractions are likely to be minimal. Most people cannot study effectively while the TV or stereo is on or while other people are talking. Don't depend on willpower to carry you through such distractions. It's much easier to plan ahead and avoid the distractions altogether. In fact, you would be wise to set up one or two specific places used solely for study (Hettich, 1992).

3. *Reward your studying.* One reason that it is so difficult to be motivated to study regularly is that the payoffs often lie in the distant future. The ultimate reward, a degree, may be years away. Even more short-term rewards, such as an A in the course, may be weeks or months away. To combat this problem, it helps to give yourself immediate, tangible rewards for studying, such as a snack, TV show, or phone call to a friend. Thus, you should set realistic study goals for yourself and then reward yourself when you meet them. The systematic manipulation of rewards involves harnessing the principles of *behavior modification* described by B. F. Skinner and other behavioral psychologists. These principles are covered in the Chapter 6 Application.

Improving Your Reading

Much of your study time is spent reading and absorbing information. *These efforts must be active.* Many students deceive themselves into thinking that they are studying by running a marker through a few sentences here and there in their book. If they do so without thoughtful selectivity, they are simply turning a textbook into a coloring book.

You can use a number of methods to actively attack your reading assignments. One of the more worthwhile strategies is Robinson's (1970) SQ3R method. **SQ3R is a study system designed to promote effective reading by means of five steps: survey, question, read, recite, and review.** Its name is an acronym for the five steps in the procedure.

Step 1: Survey. Before you plunge into the reading itself, glance over the topic headings in the chapter. Try to get a general overview of the material. If you know where the chapter is going, you can better appreciate and organize the information you are about to read.

Step 2: Question. Once you have an overview of your reading assignment, you should proceed through it one section at a time. Take a look at the heading of the first section and convert it into a question. This is usually quite simple. If the heading is "Prenatal Risk Factors," your question should be "What are sources of risk during prenatal development?" If the heading is "Stereotyping," your question should be "What is stereotyping?" Asking these questions gets you actively involved in your reading and helps you identify the main ideas.

Step 3: Read. Only now, in the third step, are you ready to sink your teeth into the reading. Read only the specific section that you have decided to tackle. Read it with an eye toward answering the question you have just formulated. If necessary, reread the section until you can answer that question. Decide whether the segment addresses any other important questions and answer them as well.

Step 4: Recite. Now that you can answer the key question for the section, recite the answer out loud to yourself in your own words. Don't move on to the next section until you understand the main ideas of the current section. You may want to write down these ideas for review later. When you have fully digested the first section, you may go on to the next. Repeat steps 2 through 4 with the next section. Once you have mastered the crucial points there, you can go on again. Keep repeating steps 2 through 4, section by section, until you finish the chapter.

Step 5: Review. When you have read the entire chapter, refresh your memory by going back over the key points. Repeat your questions and try to answer them without consulting your book or notes. This review should fortify your retention of the main ideas. It should also help you see how the main ideas are related.

The SQ3R method should probably be applied to many texts on a paragraph-by-paragraph basis. Obviously, this will require you to formulate some questions without the benefit of topic headings. If you don't have enough headings, you can simply reverse steps 2 and 3. Read the paragraph first and then formulate a question that addresses the basic idea of the paragraph. Then work at answering the question in your own words. The point is that you can be flexible in your use of the SQ3R technique. *What makes SQ3R effective is that it breaks a reading assignment into manageable parts and requires understanding before you move on.* Any method that accomplishes these goals should enhance your reading.

Besides topic headings, your textbooks may contain various other learning aids you can use to improve your reading. If a book provides a chapter outline, chapter summary, or learning objectives, don't ignore them. They can help you recognize the important points in the chapter. Good learning objectives practically create the questions for you in the SQ3R process (learning objectives for this text can be found in the separate Study Guide). A lot of thought goes into formulating these and other learning aids. It is wise to take advantage of them.

Getting More out of Lectures

Although lectures are sometimes boring and tedious, it is a simple fact that poor class attendance is associated with poor grades. For example, in one study, Lindgren (1969) found that absences from class were much more common among "unsuccessful" students (grade average C– or below) than among "successful"

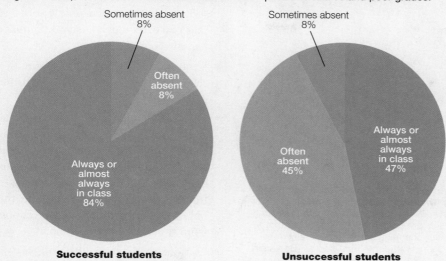

Figure 1.10. Attendance and grades. When Lindgren (1969) compared the class attendance of successful students (B average or above) and unsuccessful students (C– average or below), he found a clear association between poor attendance and poor grades.

Successful students

Sometimes absent 8%

Often absent 8%

Always or almost always in class 84%

Unsuccessful students

Sometimes absent 8%

Often absent 45%

Always or almost always in class 47%

students (grade average B or above), as shown in Figure 1.10. Even when you have an instructor who delivers hard-to-follow lectures, it is still important to go to class. If nothing else, you can get a feel for how the instructor thinks, which can help you anticipate the content of exams and respond in the manner expected by your professor.

Fortunately, most lectures are reasonably coherent. Research indicates that attentive note taking helps students identify and remember the most important points from a lecture, while weeding out ideas of lesser importance (Einstein, Morris, & Smith, 1985). Books on study skills (Longman & Atkinson, 1991; Sotiriou, 1993) offer a number of suggestions on how to take good lecture notes, some of which are summarized here:

- Extracting information from lectures requires active listening. Focus full attention on the speaker. Try to anticipate what's coming and search for deeper meanings.

- When course material is especially complex, it is a good idea to prepare for the lecture by reading ahead on the scheduled subject in your text. Then you have less brand-new information to digest.

- You are not supposed to be a human tape recorder. Insofar as possible, try to write down the lecturer's thoughts in your own words. Doing so forces you to organize the ideas in a way that makes sense to you. In taking notes, pay attention to clues about what is most important. These clues may range from subtle hints, such as an instructor repeating a point, to not-so-subtle hints, such as an instructor saying "You'll run into this again."

- Asking questions during lectures can be helpful. Doing so keeps you actively involved in the lecture and allows you to clarify points that you may have misunderstood. Many students are more bashful about asking questions than they should be. They don't realize that most professors welcome questions.

Improving Test-Taking Strategies

Let's face it—some students are better than others at taking tests. *Testwiseness* **is the ability to use the characteristics and format of a cognitive test to maximize one's score.** Students clearly vary in testwiseness, and such variations are reflected in performance on exams (Fagley, 1987; Sarnacki, 1979). Testwiseness is *not* a substitute for knowledge of the subject matter. However, skill in tak-

ing tests can help you show what you know when it is critical to do so.

A number of myths exist about the best way to take tests. For instance, it is widely believed that students shouldn't go back and change their answers to multiple-choice questions. Benjamin, Cavell, and Shallenberger (1984) found this to be the dominant belief among college *faculty* as well as students (see Figure 1.11 on the next page). However, the old adage that "your first hunch is your best hunch on tests" has been shown to be wrong. Empirical studies clearly and consistently indicate that, over the long run, changing answers pays off. Benjamin and his colleagues reviewed 20 studies on this issue; their findings are presented in Figure 1.12 on the next page. As you can see, answer changes that go from a wrong answer to a right answer outnumber changes that go from a right answer to a wrong one by a sizable margin. The popular belief that answer changing is harmful is probably attributable to painful memories of right-to-wrong changes. In any case, you can see how it pays to be familiar with sound test-taking strategies.

General Tips

The principles of testwiseness were first described by Millman, Bishop, and Ebel (1965). Let's look at some of their general ideas.

- If efficient time use appears crucial, set up a mental schedule for progressing through the test. Make a mental note to check whether you're one-third finished when a third of your time is gone.

- Don't waste time pondering difficult-to-answer questions excessively. If you have no idea at all, just guess and go on. If you need to devote a good deal of time to the question, skip it and mark it so you can return to it later if time permits.

- Adopt the appropriate level of sophistication for the test. Don't read things into questions. Sometimes students make things more complex than they

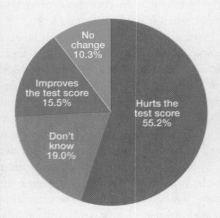

Figure 1.11. Beliefs about the effects of answer changing on tests. Benjamin et al. (1984) asked 58 college faculty whether changing answers on tests is a good idea. Like most students, the majority of the faculty felt that answer changing usually hurts a student's test score, even though the evidence contradicts this belief (see Figure 1.12).

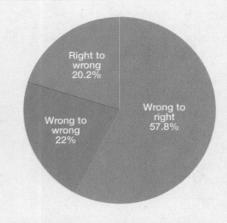

Figure 1.12. Actual effects of changing answers on multiple-choice tests. When the data from all the relevant studies are combined, they indicate that answer changing on tests generally does not reduce students' test scores (Benjamin et al., 1984). As you can see, wrong-to-right changes outnumber right-to-wrong changes by almost three to one. It is interesting to note the contrast between beliefs about answer changing (see Figure 1.11) and the actual results of this practice, as determined by empirical research.

were intended to be. Often, simple-looking questions are just what they appear to be.

- If you complete all of the questions and still have some time remaining, review the test. Make sure that you have recorded your answers correctly. If you were unsure of some answers, go back and reconsider them.

Tips for Multiple-Choice Exams

Sound test-taking strategies are especially important with multiple-choice (and true-false) questions. These types of questions often include clues that may help you converge on the correct answer (Mentzer, 1982; Weiten, 1984). You may be able to improve your performance on such tests by considering the following points:

- As you read the stem of each multiple-choice question, *anticipate* the answer if you can, before looking at the options. If the answer you anticipated is among the options, it is likely to be the correct one.

- Always read each question completely. Continue reading even if you find your anticipated answer among the options. There may be a more complete option farther down the list.

- Learn how to quickly eliminate options that are highly implausible. Many questions have only two plausible options, accompanied by "throwaway" options for filler. You should work at spotting these implausible options so that you can quickly discard them and narrow your choices.

- Be alert to the fact that information relevant to one question is sometimes given away in another test item.

- On items that have "all of the above" as an option, if you know that just two of the options are correct, you should choose "all of the above." If you are confident that one of the options is incorrect, you should eliminate this option and "all of the above" and choose from the remaining options.

- Options that represent broad, sweeping generalizations tend to be incorrect. You should be vigilant for words such as *always, never, necessarily, only, must, completely, totally,* and so forth that create these improbable assertions.

- In contrast, options that represent carefully qualified statements tend to be correct. Words such as *often, sometimes, perhaps, may,* and *generally* tend to show up in these well-qualified statements.

In summary, sound study skills and habits are crucial to academic success. Intelligence alone won't do the job (although it certainly helps). Good academic skills do not develop overnight. They are acquired gradually, so be patient with yourself. Fortunately, tasks such as reading textbooks, writing papers, and taking tests get easier with practice. Ultimately, I think you'll find that the rewards—knowledge, a sense of accomplishment, and progress toward a degree—are worth the effort.

Chapter 1 Review

KEY IDEAS

From Speculation to Science: How Psychology Developed

♦ Psychology's intellectual parents were 19th-century philosophy and physiology, which shared an interest in the mysteries of the mind. Psychology was born as an independent discipline when Wilhelm Wundt established the first psychological research laboratory in 1879 at Leipzig, Germany. He argued that psychology should be the scientific study of consciousness. The new discipline grew rapidly in North America in the late 19th century.

♦ The structuralists believed that psychology should use introspection to analyze consciousness into its basic elements. Functionalists, such as William James, believed that psychology should focus on the purpose and adaptive functions of consciousness. Functionalism left a more enduring imprint on psychology.

♦ Behaviorists, led by John B. Watson, argued that psychology should study only observable behavior. Thus, they campaigned to redefine psychology as the science of behavior. Emphasizing the importance of the environment over heredity, they began to explore stimulus-response relationships, often using laboratory animals as subjects.

♦ Sigmund Freud's psychoanalytic theory emphasized the unconscious determinants of behavior and the importance of sexuality. Freud's ideas were controversial, and they met with resistance in academic psychology. However, as more psychologists developed an interest in personality, motivation, and abnormal behavior, psychoanalytic concepts were incorporated into mainstream psychology.

♦ Behaviorism continued as a powerful force in psychology, boosted greatly by B. F. Skinner's research. Like Watson before him, Skinner asserted that psychology should study only observable behavior, and he generated controversy by arguing that free will is an illusion.

♦ Finding both behaviorism and psychoanalysis unsatisfactory, advocates of humanism, such as Carl Rogers and Abraham Maslow, became influential in the 1950s. Humanism emphasizes the unique qualities of human behavior and humans' freedom and potential for personal growth.

♦ Stimulated by the demands of World War II, clinical psychology grew rapidly in the 1950s. Thus, psychology became a profession as well as a science. This movement toward professionalization eventually spread to other areas in psychology. During the 1950s and 1960s advances in the study of cognitive processes and the physiological bases of behavior led to renewed interest in cognition and physiology.

♦ In the 1980s, Western psychologists, who had previously been rather provincial, developed a greater interest in how cultural factors influence thoughts, feelings, and behavior. This trend was sparked in large part by growing global interdependence and by increased cultural diversity in Western societies.

Psychology Today: Vigorous and Diversified

♦ Contemporary psychology is a diversified science and profession that has grown rapidly in recent decades. Major areas of research in modern psychology include developmental psychology, social psychology, experimental psychology, physiological psychology, cognitive psychology, personality, and psychometrics. Applied psychology encompasses four professional specialties: clinical psychology, counseling psychology, educational and school psychology, and industrial and organizational psychology.

Putting It in Perspective: Seven Key Themes

♦ As we examine psychology in all its many variations, we will emphasize seven key ideas as unifying themes. Looking at psychology as a field of study, our three key themes are (1) psychology is empirical, (2) psychology is theoretically diverse, and (3) psychology evolves in a sociohistorical context.

♦ Looking at psychology's subject matter, the remaining four themes are (4) behavior is determined by multiple causes, (5) our behavior is shaped by our cultural heritage, (6) heredity and environment jointly influence behavior, and (7) our experience of the world is highly subjective.

Application: Improving Academic Performance

♦ To foster sound study habits, you should devise a written study schedule and reward yourself for following it. You should also try to find one or two specific places for studying that are relatively free of distractions.

♦ You should use active reading techniques to select the most important ideas from the material you read. SQ3R, one approach to active reading, breaks a reading assignment into manageable segments and requires that you understand each segment before you move on.

♦ Good note taking can help you get more out of lectures. It's important to use active listening techniques and to record lecturers' ideas in your own words. It also helps if you read ahead to prepare for lectures and ask questions as needed.

♦ Being an effective student also requires sound test-taking skills. In general, it's a good idea to devise a schedule for progressing through an exam, to adopt the appropriate level of sophistication, to avoid wasting time on troublesome questions, and to review your answers whenever time permits.

KEY TERMS

Applied psychology	Introspection
Behavior	Psychoanalytic theory
Behaviorism	Psychology
Clinical psychology	SQ3R
Cognition	Stimulus
Culture	Structuralism
Empiricism	Testwiseness
Functionalism	Theory
Humanism	Unconscious

KEY PEOPLE

Sigmund Freud	B. F. Skinner
William James	John B. Watson
Carl Rogers	Wilhelm Wundt

2 The Research Enterprise in Psychology

- Can stress lead to physical disease? If so, what kinds of experiences make people more vulnerable to illness?

- How does anxiety affect people's desire to be with others? Does misery love company?

- Can hypnosis improve the accuracy of eyewitness testimony in court?

- Are there differences between young girls and young boys in their willingness to take risks?

- What are the psychological characteristics of people who receive the death penalty?

- How common is it for college men to force women into sexual acts against their will?

Questions, questions, questions—everyone has questions about behavior. The most basic question is: How should these questions be investigated? As noted in Chapter 1, *psychology is empirical.* Psychologists rely on formal, systematic observations to address their questions about behavior. This methodology is what makes psychology a scientific endeavor.

The scientific enterprise is an exercise in creative problem solving. Scientists have to figure out how to make observations that will shed light on the puzzles they want to solve. To make these observations, psychologists use a variety of research methods because different questions call for different strategies of study. In this chapter, you will see how researchers have used such methods as experiments, case studies, surveys, and naturalistic observation to investigate the questions listed at the beginning of this chapter. Psychology's methods are worth a close look for at least two reasons. First, a better appreciation of the empirical approach will enhance your understanding of the research-based information you will be reading about in the remainder of this book. Second, familiarity with the logic of the empirical approach should improve your ability to think critically about research. This skepticism is important because you hear about research findings nearly every day. The news media constantly report on studies that yield conclusions about how you should raise your children, improve your health, and enhance your interpersonal relationships. Learning how to evaluate these reports with more sophistication can help you use such information wisely.

In this chapter, we will examine the scientific approach to the study of behavior and then look at the specific research methods that psychologists use most frequently. We'll also see why psychologists use statistics in their research. After you learn how research is done, you'll also learn how *not* to do it. That is, we'll review some common flaws in doing research. Finally, we will take a look at ethical issues in behavioral research. In the Application, you'll learn how to find and read journal articles that report on research.

LOOKING FOR LAWS: THE SCIENTIFIC APPROACH TO BEHAVIOR

Whether the object of study is gravitational forces or people's behavior under stress, *the scientific approach assumes that events are governed by some lawful order.* As scientists, psychologists assume that behavior is governed by discernible laws or principles, just as the movement of the earth around the sun is governed by the laws of gravity. The behavior of living creatures may not seem as lawful and predictable as the "behavior" of planets. However, the scientific enterprise is based on the belief that there *are* consistencies or laws that can be uncovered. Fortunately, the plausibility of applying this fundamental assumption to psychology has been supported by the discovery of a great many such consistencies in behavior, some of which provide the subject matter for this text.

Goals of the Scientific Enterprise

Psychologists and other scientists share three sets of interrelated goals: measurement and description, understanding and prediction, and application and control.

1. *Measurement and Description.* Science's commitment to observation requires that an investigator figure out a way to measure the phenomenon under study. For example, a psychologist could not investigate whether men are more or less sociable than women without first developing some means of measuring sociability. Thus, the first goal of psychology is to develop measurement techniques that make it possible to describe behavior clearly and precisely.

2. *Understanding and Prediction.* A higher-level goal of science is understanding. Scientists believe that they understand events when they can

explain the reasons for their occurrence. To evaluate their understanding, scientists make and test predictions about relationships between variables. *Variables* **are any measurable conditions, events, characteristics, or behaviors that are controlled or observed in a study.** If we predicted that putting people under time pressure would lower the accuracy of their time perception, the variables in our study would be time pressure and accuracy of time perception. If our prediction were verified in the study, this finding would increase our confidence that we understand the relationship between time pressure and time perception.

3. *Application and Control.* Ultimately, most scientists hope that the information they gather will be of some practical value in helping to solve everyday problems. Once people understand a phenomenon, they often can exert more control over it. Today, the profession of psychology attempts to apply research findings to practical problems in schools, businesses, factories, and mental hospitals. For example, a school psychologist might use findings about the causes of math anxiety to devise a program to help students control their math phobias.

Steps in a Scientific Investigation

Curiosity about a question provides the point of departure for any kind of investigation, scientific or otherwise. Scientific investigations, however, are *systematic*. They follow an orderly pattern, which is outlined in Figure 2.1. Let's look at how this standard series of steps was followed in a study of stress by Thomas Holmes and his colleagues (Wyler, Masuda, & Holmes, 1971). Holmes wanted to know two things: Can stress lead to physical disease? Is stress due mostly to changes that take place in people's lives? To investigate these matters, Holmes and his co-workers interviewed thousands of medical patients to find out whether significant life changes preceded the onset of their diseases.

Step 1: Formulate a Testable Hypothesis

The cornerstone of the scientific method is its commitment to putting ideas to an empirical test. Thus, the first step in a scientific investigation is to translate a general idea into a testable hypothesis. **A** *hypothesis* **is a tentative statement about the relationship between two or more variables.** Normally, hypotheses are expressed as predictions. They spell out how changes in one variable will be related to changes in another variable. Thus, Holmes hypothesized that an increase in life changes would be associated with increased physical illness.

To be testable, scientific hypotheses must be formulated precisely, and the variables under study must be clearly defined. Researchers achieve these clear formulations by providing operational definitions of the relevant variables. **An** *operational definition* **describes the actions or operations that will be made to measure or control a variable**. Operational definitions establish precisely what is meant by each variable in the context of a study.

To illustrate, let's examine the operational definitions used by Wyler, Masuda, and Holmes (1971). They measured life change with the Social Readjustment Rating Scale (SRRS), a questionnaire that tabulates the occurrence of 43

Figure 2.1. Flowchart of steps in a scientific investigation. As illustrated by a study by Wyler, Masuda, and Holmes (1971), a scientific investigation consists of a sequence of carefully planned steps, beginning with the formulation of a testable hypothesis and ending with the publication of the study, if its results are worthy of examination by other researchers.

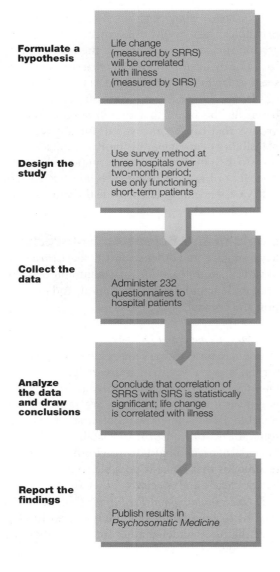

Formulate a hypothesis — Life change (measured by SRRS) will be correlated with illness (measured by SIRS)

Design the study — Use survey method at three hospitals over two-month period; use only functioning short-term patients

Collect the data — Administer 232 questionnaires to hospital patients

Analyze the data and draw conclusions — Conclude that correlation of SRRS with SIRS is statistically significant; life change is correlated with illness

Report the findings — Publish results in *Psychosomatic Medicine*

major life changes. They measured the extent of participants' physical illness with the Seriousness of Illness Rating Scale (SIRS), a checklist of 126 common illnesses, with numerical values reflecting the severity of each illness. Thus, in this study the variable of life change was operationally defined as an individual's score on the SRRS, while the variable of physical illness was operationally defined as his or her score on the SIRS.

Step 2: Select the Research Method and Design the Study

The second step in a scientific investigation is to figure out how to put the hypothesis to an empirical test. The research method chosen depends to a large degree on the nature of the question under study. The various methods—experiments, case studies, surveys, naturalistic observation—each have advantages and disadvantages. The researcher has to ponder the pros and cons and then select the strategy that appears to be the most appropriate and practical. In this case, Wyler, Masuda, and Holmes decided that their question called for a *survey*. This method involves administering questionnaires to a large number of people.

Once researchers have chosen a general method, they must make detailed plans for executing their study. Thus, Wyler, Masuda, and Holmes had to decide when they would conduct their survey, how many people they needed to survey, and where they would get their subjects. *Subjects* **are the persons or animals whose behavior is systematically observed in a study.** For example, Wyler, Masuda, and Holmes chose patients seen at three local hospitals during a specified two-month period.

Step 3: Collect the Data

The third step in the research enterprise is to collect the data. Thus, Wyler, Masuda, and Holmes spent two months administering their questionnaires to 232 patients who served as subjects in their study. Psychologists use a variety of *data collection techniques,* **which are procedures for making empirical observations and measurements.** Commonly used techniques include direct observation, questionnaires, interviews, psychological tests, physiological recordings, and examination of archival records (see Table 2.1). The data collection techniques used in a study depend largely on what is being investigated. For example, questionnaires are well suited for studying attitudes, psychological tests for studying personality, and physiological recordings for studying brain function.

Step 4: Analyze the Data and Draw Conclusions

The observations made in a study are usually converted into numbers, which constitute the raw data of the study. In this instance, the subjects' responses to the two questionnaires were tabu-

Table 2.1 Key Data Collection Techniques in Psychology

Technique	Description
Direct observation	Observers are trained to watch and record behavior as objectively and precisely as possible. They may use some instrumentation, such as a stopwatch or video recorder.
Questionnaire	Subjects are administered a series of written questions designed to obtain information about attitudes, opinions, and specific aspects of their behavior.
Interview	A face-to-face dialogue is conducted to obtain information about specific aspects of a subject's behavior.
Psychological test	Subjects are administered a standardized measure to obtain a sample of their behavior. Tests are usually used to assess mental abilities or personality traits.
Physiological recording	An instrument is used to monitor and record a specific physiological process in a subject. Examples include measures of blood pressure, heart rate, muscle tension, and brain activity.
Examination of archival records	The researcher analyzes existing institutional records (the archives), such as census, economic, medical, legal, educational, and business records.

lated. This yielded two scores for each subject, one for the amount of life change the person had experienced and another for the amount of his or her physical illness.

Researchers use *statistics* to analyze their data and to decide whether their hypotheses have been supported. **Statistics is the use of mathematics to organize, summarize, and interpret numerical data.** Based on their statistical analyses, Wyler, Masuda, and Holmes concluded that their data supported their hypothesis. As predicted, they found that high scores on the measure of life change were associated with high scores on the index of physical illness. Statistics play an essential role in the scientific enterprise. The basic principles of statistical analysis are discussed in Appendix B in the back of the book.

Step 5: Report the Findings

Scientific progress can be achieved only if researchers share their findings with one another and with the general public. Therefore, the final step in a scientific investigation is to write up a concise summary of the study and its findings. Typically, researchers prepare a report that is delivered at a scientific meeting and submitted to a journal for publication. A **journal is a periodical that publishes technical and scholarly material, usually in a narrowly defined area of inquiry.** The study by Wyler, Masuda, and Holmes (1971) was accepted for publication in a journal called *Psychosomatic Medicine*. It was one of several ground-breaking studies by Holmes and his colleagues linking life stress to physical illness that set a precedent for hundreds of follow-up studies by other researchers all over the world.

The process of publishing scientific studies allows other experts to evaluate and critique new research findings. Sometimes this process of critical evaluation discloses flaws in a study. If the flaws are serious enough, the results may be discounted or discarded. This evaluation process is a major strength of the scientific approach because it gradually weeds out erroneous findings. This self-correcting aspect of science emerged to some extent in the research that followed up on Holmes's original findings. His most basic conclusion—that there is a relationship between stress and vulnerability to physical illness—has been supported in hundreds of studies. However, subsequent research has revealed that (1) the association between stress and physical illness is not as strong as

---

CONCEPT CHECK 2.1
Recognizing the Steps in a Scientific Investigation

Check your understanding of the steps in a scientific investigation reviewed in this chapter by matching each of the following activities with the step that it best illustrates. Choose from the following: (a) formulate a testable hypothesis, (b) select the research method and design the study, (c) collect the data, (d) analyze the data and draw conclusions, and (e) report the findings. You'll find the answers in Appendix A at the back of the book.

_____ 1. James J. Gibson believed that humans are not passive receivers of sensory information, but instead active seekers of information who try to find patterns in the environmental stimuli that they take in through the senses. He theorized that active perception of a tactile (touch) stimulus would result in more accurate recognition of the stimulus than passive perception would.

_____ 2. Subjects were tested individually and the experimenter recorded the number of times that each subject correctly identified the picture of a cookie cutter that they were currently feeling.

_____ 3. Gibson found that the "passive" group was correct 29% of the time. In comparison, the "active" group was correct 95% of the time. Analyses indicated that this difference was statistically significant. It was concluded that perception of the shapes depended on active exploration, not just passive reception of stimulation.

_____ 4. To investigate his ideas, Gibson planned an experiment in which subjects would either passively or actively experience tactile sensations. He decided that his subjects would sit at a table across from the experimenter with a curtain between them and the experimenter. For the "passive" group of subjects, six differently shaped cookie cutters would be pressed against their palms, out of their sight. The "active" group would be told to run their fingers over the surfaces of the cookie cutters. Afterward, subjects would be asked to identify pictures of the cookie cutters they had felt.

_____ 5. Gibson's article, "Observations on Active Touch," was published in *Psychological Bulletin* in 1962.

Holmes concluded, and (2) stress is not exclusively a function of change in a person's life (Perkins, 1982; Smith, 1993). We'll discuss these issues in more detail in Chapter 13.

Advantages of the Scientific Approach

Science is certainly not the only method that can be used to draw conclusions about behavior. We all use logic, casual observation, and good old-fashioned common sense. Because the scientific method often requires painstaking effort, it seems reasonable to ask what advantages make it worth the trouble.

Basically, the scientific approach offers two major advantages. The first is its clarity and precision. Commonsense notions about behavior tend to be vague and ambiguous. Consider the old adage "Spare the rod and spoil the child." What exactly does this generalization about child rearing amount to? How severely should children be punished if parents are not to "spare the rod"? How do we assess whether a child qualifies as "spoiled"? A fundamental problem is that such statements have different meanings, depending on the person. In contrast, the scientific approach requires that people specify *exactly* what they are talking about when they formulate hypotheses. This clarity and precision enhance communication about important ideas.

The second and perhaps greatest advantage offered by the scientific approach is its relative intolerance of error. Scientists are trained to be skeptical. They subject their ideas to empirical tests. They also scrutinize one another's findings with a critical eye. They demand objective data and thorough documentation before they accept ideas. When the findings of two studies conflict, the scientist tries to figure out why, usually by conducting additional research. In contrast, commonsense analyses involve little effort to verify ideas or detect errors.

All this is not to say that science has an exclusive copyright on truth. However, the scientific approach does tend to yield more accurate and dependable information than casual analyses and armchair speculation do. Knowledge of scientific data can thus provide a useful benchmark against which to judge claims and information from other kinds of sources.

Now that we have had an overview of how the scientific enterprise works, we can focus on how specific research methods are used. *Research meth-*ods consist of differing approaches to the observation, measurement, manipulation, and control of variables in empirical studies. In other words, they are general strategies for conducting studies. No single research method is ideal for all purposes and situations. Much of the ingenuity in research involves selecting and tailoring the method to the question at hand. The next two sections of this chapter discuss the two basic types of methods used in psychology: *experimental research methods* and *descriptive/correlational research methods*.

LOOKING FOR CAUSES: EXPERIMENTAL RESEARCH

Does misery love company? This question intrigued social psychologist Stanley Schachter. When people feel anxious, he wondered, do they want to be left alone, or do they prefer to have others around? Schachter's review of relevant theories suggested that in times of anxiety people would want others around to help them sort out their feelings. Thus, his hypothesis was that increases in anxiety would cause increases in the desire to be with others, which psychologists call the *need for affiliation*. To test this hypothesis, Schachter (1959) designed a clever experiment.

The *experiment* **is a research method in which the investigator manipulates a variable under carefully controlled conditions and observes whether any changes occur in a second variable as a result.** The experiment is a relatively powerful procedure that allows researchers to detect cause-and-effect relationships. Psychologists depend on this method more than any other. To see how an experiment is designed, let's use Schachter's study as an example.

Independent and Dependent Variables

The purpose of an experiment is to find out whether changes in one variable (let's call it X) cause changes in another variable (let's call it Y). To put it more concisely, we want to find out *how X affects Y*. In this formulation, we refer to X as the *independent variable* and to Y as the *dependent variable*.

An *independent variable* **is a condition or event that an experimenter varies in order to see its impact on another variable.** The independent variable is the variable that the experimenter controls or manipulates. It is hypothesized to have some effect on the dependent variable, and the experiment is conducted to verify this effect. **The *dependent variable* is the variable that is thought to be affected by manipulation of the independent variable.** In psychology studies, the dependent variable usually is a measurement of some aspect of the subjects' behavior. The independent variable is called *independent* because it is *free* to be varied by the experimenter. The dependent variable is called *dependent* because it is thought to *depend* (at least in part) on manipulations of the independent variable.

In Schachter's experiment, *the independent variable was the subjects' anxiety level.* He manipulated anxiety level in a clever way. Subjects assembled in his laboratory were told by a "Dr. Zilstein" that they would be participating in a study on the physiological effects of electric shock. They were further informed that during the experiment they would receive a series of electric shocks while their pulse and blood pressure were being monitored. Half of the subjects were warned that the shocks would be very painful. They made up the *high-anxiety* group. The other half of the subjects (the *low-anxiety* group) were told that the shocks would be mild and painless. In reality, there was no plan to shock anyone at any time. These orientation procedures were simply intended to evoke different levels of anxiety. After the orientation,

the experimenter indicated that there would be a delay while he prepared the shock apparatus for use. The subjects were asked whether they would prefer to wait alone or in the company of others. *The subjects' desire to affiliate with others was the dependent variable.*

Experimental and Control Groups

In an experiment the investigator typically assembles two groups of subjects who are treated differently in regard to the independent variable. These two groups are referred to as the experimental group and the control group. **The *experimental group* consists of the subjects who receive some special treatment in regard to the independent variable. The *control group* consists of similar subjects who do *not* receive the special treatment given to the experimental group.**

In the Schachter study, the subjects in the high-anxiety condition constituted the experimental group. They received a special treatment designed to create an unusually high level of anxiety. The subjects in the low-anxiety condition constituted the control group. They were not exposed to the special anxiety-arousing procedure.

It is crucial that the experimental and control groups in a study be very similar, except for the different treatment that they receive in regard to the independent variable. This stipulation brings us to the logic that underlies the experimental method. If the two groups are alike in all respects *except for the variation created by the manipulation of the independent variable*, then any differences between the two groups on the dependent variable *must be due to the manipulation of the independent variable*. In this way researchers isolate the effect of the independent variable on the dependent variable. Schachter, for example, isolated the impact of anxiety on the need for affiliation. As predicted, he found that increased anxiety led to increased affiliation. As Figure 2.2 indicates, the percentage of subjects in the high-anxiety group who wanted to wait with others was nearly twice that of the low-anxiety group.

Extraneous Variables

As we have seen, the logic of the experimental method rests on the assumption that the experimental and control groups are alike except for their treatment in regard to the independent variable. Any other differences between the two groups can cloud the situation and

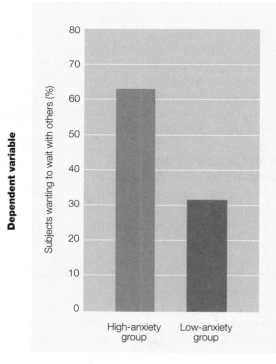

Figure 2.2. Results of Schachter's (1959) study of affiliation. The percentage of people wanting to wait with others was higher in the high-anxiety (experimental) group than in the low-anxiety (control) group, consistent with Schachter's hypothesis that anxiety would increase the desire for affiliation. The graphic portrayal of these results allows us to see at a glance the effects of the experimental manipulation on the dependent variable.

make it difficult to draw conclusions about how the independent variable affects the dependent variable.

In practical terms, of course, it is impossible to ensure that two groups of subjects are exactly alike in *every* respect. The experimental and control groups only have to be alike on dimensions that are relevant to the dependent variable. Thus, Schachter did not need to worry about whether his two groups were similar in hair color, height, or interest in ballet. Obviously, these variables weren't likely to influence the dependent variable of affiliation behavior.

Instead, experimenters concentrate on making sure that the experimental and control groups are alike on a limited number of variables that could have a bearing on the results of the study. These variables are called extraneous, secondary, or nuisance variables. *Extraneous variables* **are any variables other than the independent variable that seem likely to influence the dependent variable in a specific study.**

In Schachter's study, one extraneous variable would have been the subjects' tendency to be sociable. Why? Because subjects' sociability could affect their desire to be with others (the dependent variable). If the subjects in one group had hap-pened to be more sociable (on the average) than those in the other group, the variables of anxiety and sociability would have been confounded. **A** *confounding of variables* **occurs when two variables are linked together in a way that makes it difficult to sort out their specific effects.** When an extraneous variable is confounded with an independent variable, a researcher cannot tell which is having what effect on the dependent variable.

Unanticipated confoundings of variables have wrecked innumerable experiments. That is why so much care, planning, and forethought must go into designing an experiment. A key quality that separates a talented experimenter from a mediocre one is the ability to foresee troublesome extraneous variables and control them to avoid confoundings.

Experimenters use a variety of safeguards to control for extraneous variables. For instance, subjects are usually assigned to the experimental and control groups randomly. *Random assignment* **of subjects occurs when all subjects have an equal chance of being assigned to any group or condition in the study.** When experimenters distribute subjects into groups through some random procedure, they can be

---

CONCEPT CHECK 2.2
Recognizing Independent and Dependent Variables

Check your understanding of the experimental method by identifying the independent variable (IV) and dependent variable (DV) in the following investigations. Note that one study has two IVs and another has two DVs. You'll find the answers in Appendix A at the back of the book.

1. A researcher is interested in how heart rate and blood pressure are affected by viewing a violent film sequence as opposed to a nonviolent film sequence.

    IV _____

    DV _____

2. An organizational psychologist develops a new training program to improve clerks' courtesy to customers in a large chain of retail stores. She conducts an experiment to see whether the training program leads to a reduction in the number of customer complaints.

    IV _____

    DV _____

3. A researcher wants to find out how stimulus complexity and stimulus contrast (light/dark variation) affect infants' attention to stimuli. He manipulates stimulus complexity and stimulus contrast and measures how long infants stare at various stimuli.

    IV _____

    DV _____

4. A social psychologist investigates the impact of group size on subjects' conformity in response to group pressure.

    IV _____

    DV _____

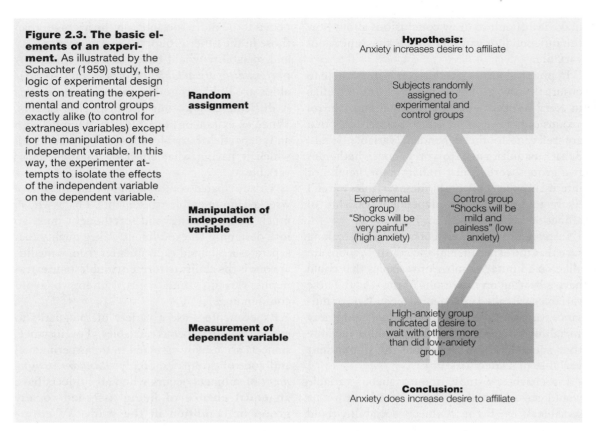

Figure 2.3. The basic elements of an experiment. As illustrated by the Schachter (1959) study, the logic of experimental design rests on treating the experimental and control groups exactly alike (to control for extraneous variables) except for the manipulation of the independent variable. In this way, the experimenter attempts to isolate the effects of the independent variable on the dependent variable.

Random assignment

Manipulation of independent variable

Measurement of dependent variable

Hypothesis:
Anxiety increases desire to affiliate

Subjects randomly assigned to experimental and control groups

Experimental group "Shocks will be very painful" (high anxiety)

Control group "Shocks will be mild and painless" (low anxiety)

High-anxiety group indicated a desire to wait with others more than did low-anxiety group

Conclusion:
Anxiety does increase desire to affiliate

reasonably confident that the groups will be similar in most ways.

To summarize the essentials of experimental design, Figure 2.3 provides an overview of the elements in an experiment, using Schachter's study as an example.

Variations in Designing Experiments

We have discussed the experiment in only its simplest format, with just one independent variable and one dependent variable. Actually, many variations are possible in conducting experiments. *Sometimes it is advantageous to use only one group of subjects who serve as their own control group.* The effects of the independent variable are evaluated by exposing this single group to two different conditions: an experimental condition and a control condition. For example, imagine that you wanted to study the effects of loud music on typing performance. You could have a group of subjects work on a typing task while loud music was played (experimental condition) and in the absence of music (control condition). This approach would ensure that the subjects in the experimental and control conditions would be alike on any extraneous variables involving their personal characteris-

tics, such as motivation or typing skill. After all, the same people would be studied in both conditions.

It is also possible to manipulate more than one independent variable or measure more than one dependent variable in a single experiment. For example, in another study of typing performance, you could vary both room temperature and the presence of distracting music as independent variables (see Figure 2.4), while measuring two aspects of typing performance (speed and accuracy) as dependent variables.

Advantages and Disadvantages of Experimental Research

The experiment is a powerful research method. Its principal advantage is that it permits conclusions about cause-and-effect relationships between variables. Researchers are able to draw these conclusions about causation because the precise control allows them to isolate the relationship between the independent variable and the dependent variable, while neutralizing the effects of extraneous variables. No other research method can duplicate this strength of the experiment. This advantage is why psychologists usually prefer to use the experimental method whenever possible.

For all its power, however, the experiment has limitations. One problem is that experiments are often artificial. Because experiments require great control over proceedings, researchers must often construct simple, contrived situations to test their hypotheses experimentally. For example, to investigate decision making in juries, psychologists have conducted many experiments in which subjects read a brief summary of a trial and then record their individual "verdicts" of innocence or guilt. This approach allows the experimenter to manipulate a variable, such as the race of the defendant, to see whether it affects the subjects' verdicts. However, critics have pointed out that having a subject read a short case summary and make an individual decision is terribly artificial in comparison to the complexities of real trials (Weiten & Diamond, 1979). In actual court cases, jurors may spend weeks listening to confusing testimony while making subtle judgments about the credibility of witnesses. They then retire for hours of debate to arrive at a verdict. Many researchers have failed to do justice to this complex process in their laboratory experiments. When experiments are highly artificial, doubts arise about the applicability of findings to everyday behavior outside the experimental laboratory.

Another disadvantage is that the experimental method can't be used to explore some research questions. Psychologists are frequently interested in the effects of factors that cannot be manipulated as independent variables because of ethical concerns or practical realities. For instance, you might be interested in the relation of a nutritionally poor diet during pregnancy to the likelihood of birth defects. This clearly is a significant issue. However, you obviously cannot take 100 pregnant women and assign 50 of them to an experimental condition in which they consume an inadequate diet. The potential risk to the health of the women and their unborn children would make this research strategy unethical.

In other cases, manipulations of variables are difficult or impossible. For example, you might want to know whether being brought up in an urban as opposed to a rural area affects people's values. An experiment would require you to assign similar families to live in urban and rural areas, which obviously is impossible to do. To explore this question, you would have to use descriptive/correlational research methods, which we turn to next.

Distracting music
Present   Absent

Room temperature
High
Normal

Figure 2.4. Manipulation of two independent variables in an experiment. As this example shows, when two independent variables are manipulated in a single experiment, the researcher has to compare four groups of subjects (or conditions) instead of the usual two. The main advantage of this procedure is that it allows an experimenter to see whether two variables interact. An interaction means that the effect of one variable depends on the effect of another. For instance, if we found that distracting music impaired typing performance only when room temperature was high, we would be detecting an interaction.

LOOKING FOR LINKS: DESCRIPTIVE/CORRELATIONAL RESEARCH

As we just saw, in some situations psychologists cannot exert experimental control over the variables they want to study. Thomas Holmes's research on the relationship between life change and illness provides another example of this problem. Obviously, Holmes could not manipulate the amount of life change experienced by his subjects. Their divorces, retirements, pregnancies, promotions, mortgages, and such were far beyond his control.

In such situations, investigators must rely on *descriptive/correlational research methods*. What distinguishes these methods is that the researcher cannot manipulate the variables under study. This lack of control means that these methods cannot be used to demonstrate a cause-and-effect relationship between variables. *Descriptive/correlational methods permit investigators only to see whether there is a link or association between the variables of interest.* Such an association is called a *correlation*, and the results of descriptive research are often summarized with a statistic called the *correlation coefficient*. In this section, we'll take a close look at the concept of correlation and then examine three specific approaches to descriptive research: naturalistic observation, case studies, and surveys.

Figure 2.5. Positive and negative correlation. Notice that the terms positive and negative refer to the direction of the relationship between two variables, not to its strength. Variables are positively correlated if they tend to increase and decrease together and are negatively correlated if one tends to increase when the other decreases.

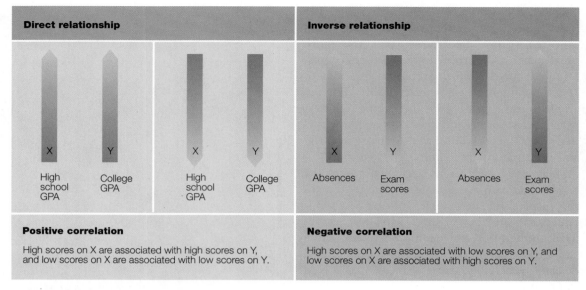

Direct relationship

X — High school GPA   Y — College GPA

X — High school GPA   Y — College GPA

Inverse relationship

X — Absences   Y — Exam scores

X — Absences   Y — Exam scores

Positive correlation

High scores on X are associated with high scores on Y, and low scores on X are associated with low scores on Y.

Negative correlation

High scores on X are associated with low scores on Y, and low scores on X are associated with high scores on Y.

The Concept of Correlation

In descriptive research, investigators often want to determine whether there is a correlation between two variables. **A *correlation* exists when two variables are related to each other.** A correlation may be either positive or negative, depending on the nature of the association between the variables measured. A *positive* correlation indicates a *direct* relationship between two variables. This means that high scores on variable *X* are associated with high scores on variable *Y* and that low scores on variable *X* are associated with low scores on variable *Y*. For example, there is a positive correlation between high school grade point average (GPA) and subsequent college GPA. That is, people who do well in high school tend to do well in college, and those who perform poorly in high school tend to perform poorly in college (see Figure 2.5).

In contrast, a *negative* correlation indicates an *inverse* relationship between two variables. This means that people who score high on variable *X* tend to score low on variable *Y*, whereas those who score low on *X* tend to score high on *Y*. For example, in most college courses, there is a negative correlation between how frequently students are absent and how well they perform on exams.

Students who have a high number of absences tend to get low exam scores, while students who have a low number of absences tend to earn higher exam scores (see Figure 2.5).

Strength of the Correlation

The strength of an association between two variables can be measured with a statistic called the correlation coefficient. **The *correlation coefficient* is a numerical index of the degree of relationship between two variables.** This coefficient can vary between 0 and +1.00 (if the correlation is positive) or between 0 and –1.00 (if the correlation is negative). A coefficient near zero indicates no relationship between the variables. That is, high or low scores on variable *X* show no consistent relationship to high or low scores on variable *Y*. A coefficient of +1.00 or –1.00 indicates a perfect, one-to-one correspondence between the two variables. Most correlations fall between these extremes.

The closer the correlation is to either –1.00 or +1.00, the stronger the relationship (see Figure 2.6). Thus, a correlation of .90 represents a stronger tendency for variables to be associated than does a correlation of .40. Likewise, a correlation of –.75 represents a stronger relationship

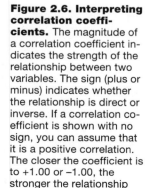

Figure 2.6. Interpreting correlation coefficients. The magnitude of a correlation coefficient indicates the strength of the relationship between two variables. The sign (plus or minus) indicates whether the relationship is direct or inverse. If a correlation coefficient is shown with no sign, you can assume that it is a positive correlation. The closer the coefficient is to +1.00 or –1.00, the stronger the relationship between the variables.

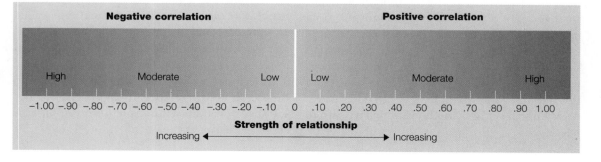

Negative correlation

High   Moderate   Low

Positive correlation

Low   Moderate   High

–1.00 –.90 –.80 –.70 –.60 –.50 –.40 –.30 –.20 –.10   0   .10 .20 .30 .40 .50 .60 .70 .80 .90 1.00

Strength of relationship

Increasing ◄————————————► Increasing

than does a correlation of –.45. Keep in mind that the *strength* of a correlation depends only on the size of the coefficient. The positive or negative sign simply shows whether the correlation is direct (positive) or inverse (negative). Therefore, a correlation of –.60 reflects a stronger relationship than a correlation of +.30.

Correlation and Prediction

You may recall that one of the key goals of scientific research is accurate *prediction*. There is a close link between the magnitude of a correlation and the power it gives scientists to make predictions. *As a correlation increases in strength (gets closer to either –1.00 or +1.00), the ability to predict one variable based on knowledge of the other variable increases.*

To illustrate, consider how college admissions tests (such as the SAT or ACT) are used to predict college performance. When students' admissions test scores and college GPA are correlated, researchers generally find moderate positive correlations in the .40s and .50s (Donlon, 1984). Because of this relationship, college admissions committees can predict with modest accuracy how well prospective students will do in college. Admittedly, the predictive power of these admissions tests is far from perfect. But it's substantial enough to justify the use of the tests as one factor in making admissions decisions. However, if this correlation were much higher, say .90, admissions tests could predict with superb accuracy how students would perform. In contrast, if this correlation were much lower, say .20, the tests' prediction of college performance would be so poor that considering the test scores in admissions decisions would be unreasonable.

Correlation and Causation

Although a high correlation allows us to predict one variable on the basis of another, it does not tell us whether a cause-effect relationship exists between the two variables. The problem is that variables can be highly correlated even though they are not causally related.

When we find that variables X and Y are correlated, we can safely conclude only that X and Y are related. We do not know *how* X and Y are related. We do not know whether X causes Y or Y causes X, or whether both are caused by a third variable. For example, survey studies have found a positive correlation between individuals' ratings of their marital satisfaction and their sexual satisfaction (Hunt, 1974; Tavris & Sadd, 1977). Although it's clear that a healthy marriage and good sex go hand in hand, it's hard to tell what's causing what. We don't know whether healthy marriages promote good sex or whether good sex promotes healthy marriages. Moreover, we can't rule out the possibility that both are caused by a third variable (Z). Perhaps sexual satisfaction and marital satisfaction are both influenced by partners' compatibility in values. The plausible causal relationships in this case are diagrammed in Figure 2.7, which illustrates the "third variable problem" in interpreting correlations. This is a common problem in descriptive research, and you'll see this type of diagram again when we discuss other correlations. Thus, it is important to remember that *correlation is not equivalent to causation.*

Naturalistic Observation

Are males more likely to take risks than females? Harvey Ginsburg and Shirley Miller (1982) wanted to know whether young boys and young girls differ in their willingness to take risks. Popular belief suggests that males are bigger risk takers than females are. However, there was a notable lack of empirical evidence before Ginsburg and Miller conducted their study. They probably could have devised an experiment to examine this question. However, they wanted to focus on risk taking in the real world rather than in the laboratory.

The setting for their study was the San Antonio Zoo, where they used *naturalistic observation* to study children's risk taking. **In *naturalistic observation* a researcher engages in careful, usually prolonged, observation of behavior without intervening directly with the sub-**

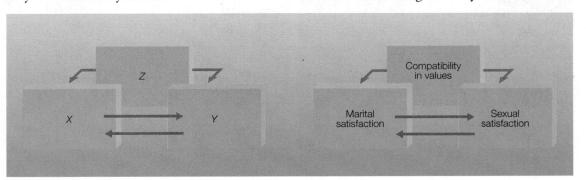

Figure 2.7. Three possible causal relations between correlated variables. If variables X and Y are correlated, does X cause Y, does Y cause X, or does some hidden third variable, Z, account for the changes in both X and Y? As the relationship between marital and sexual satisfaction illustrates, a correlation alone does not provide the answer. We will encounter this problem of interpreting the meaning of correlations at many points in this text.

jects. Ginsburg and Miller identified four specific risky behaviors that children might engage in at this zoo: going for a ride on an elephant, petting a burro, feeding animals, and climbing a steep embankment. Without making their presence readily apparent, they carefully recorded the number of boys and girls who engaged in each of these risky behaviors. Their observations revealed that a correlation did indeed exist between sex and risk taking, at least for these behaviors. They found that boys engaged in the risky behaviors more frequently than girls.

This type of research is called *naturalistic* because behavior is allowed to unfold naturally (without interference) in its natural environment—that is, the setting in which it would normally occur. The major strength of naturalistic observation is that it allows researchers to study behavior under conditions that are less artificial than in experiments. The major problem with this method is that researchers often have trouble making their observations unobtrusively so they don't affect their subjects' behavior.

Case Studies

Are death-row inmates the shrewd, coldly calculating individuals that many people believe them to be? A research team at New York University wanted to investigate the psychological characteristics of people given the death penalty (Lewis et al., 1986). Until this study, no one had done research either confirming or refuting the popular image of criminals sentenced to die.

The research team decided that their question called for a case study approach. **A *case study* is an in-depth investigation of an individual subject.** The researchers compiled case studies for 15 condemned individuals whose execution dates were close at hand. The findings were surprising. All 15 inmates had histories of severe head injuries. Twelve of them showed signs of brain damage, and most were well below average in intelligence. The investigators concluded that their data showed an unexpected correlation between neurological impairment and ending up on death row. Their findings suggest that our legal system doles out its harshest penalty to individuals who are anything but shrewd.

A variety of data collection techniques can be used in case studies. Typical techniques include interviewing the subject, direct observation of the subject, examination of records, and psychological testing. Clinical psychologists, who diagnose and treat psychological problems, routinely do case studies of their clients. When clinicians assemble a case study, they are *not* conducting empirical research. Case study *research* takes place

As the name implies, naturalistic observation allows behavior to unfold naturally, without interference by the researcher. These photographs were taken in 1988 by Harvey Ginsburg during naturalistic observation of boys and girls in a "risky behavior" situation.

only when investigators analyze a collection of case studies, looking for threads of consistency that permit general conclusions.

Case studies are particularly well suited for investigating some issues, such as the causes of psychological disorders. The main problem with case studies is that they are highly subjective. Information from several sources must be knit together in an impressionistic way. In this process, researchers may focus selectively on information that fits with their expectations, which usually reflect their theoretical slant. Thus, it is relatively easy for investigators to see what they expect to see in case study research.

Surveys

How common is it for college men to force women into sexual acts against their will? Karen Rapaport and Barry Burkhart (1984) set out to answer this question by conducting a survey. **In a *survey* researchers use questionnaires or interviews to gather information about specific aspects of subjects' behavior.**

In their study, Rapaport and Burkhart defined coercive sexual behavior as any sexual act with a woman that is engaged in "against her will." They administered a questionnaire to 201 college men. It inquired whether the subjects had ever engaged in any of 11 coercive sexual acts, such as placing a hand on a woman's breast or removing her underclothing, against her will. As you can see in Table 2.2, the survey revealed that a substantial proportion of the men had engaged in sexually coercive acts.

CONCEPT CHECK 2.3
Understanding Correlation

Check your understanding of correlation by interpreting the meaning of the correlation in item 1 and by guessing the direction (positive or negative) of the correlations in item 2. You'll find the answers in Appendix A.

1. Researchers have found a substantial positive correlation between youngsters' self-esteem and their academic achievement (measured by grades in school). Check any acceptable conclusions based on this correlation.
   _____ a. Low grades cause low self-esteem.
   _____ b. There is an association between self-esteem and academic achievement.
   _____ c. High self-esteem causes high academic achievement.
   _____ d. High ability causes both high self-esteem and high academic achievement.
   _____ e. Youngsters who score low in self-esteem tend to get low grades, and those who score high in self-esteem tend to get high grades.

2. Indicate whether you would expect the following correlations to be positive or negative.
   _____ a. The correlation between age and visual acuity (among adults).
   _____ b. The correlation between years of education and income.
   _____ c. The correlation between shyness and the number of friends one has.

Surveys are often used to obtain information on aspects of behavior that are difficult to observe directly (such as sexual behavior). Surveys also make it relatively easy to collect data on attitudes and opinions from large samples of subjects. The major problem with surveys is that they depend on self-report data. As we'll discuss later, intentional deception and wishful thinking can distort subjects' verbal reports about their behavior.

Table 2.2 College Men's Responses to Items on Coercive Sexuality Scale (%)

Coercive Act Engaged in "Against Her Will"	Never	Once or Twice	Several Times	Often
Held a woman's hand	57	34	7	1
Kissed a woman	47	41	10	2
Placed hand on a woman's knee	39	43	15	3
Placed hand on a woman's breast	39	37	18	5
Placed hand on a woman's thigh or crotch	42	40	16	2
Unfastened a woman's outer clothing	51	34	13	2
Removed or disarranged a woman's outer clothing	58	31	9	2
Removed or disarranged a woman's underclothing	68	27	3	2
Removed own underclothing	78	18	3	2
Touched a woman's genital area	63	30	6	1
Had intercourse with a woman	85	13	2	0

Note: Some rows do not total 100% because of rounding.
Source: Rapaport and Burkhart (1984)

Advantages and Disadvantages of Descriptive/Correlational Research

Descriptive/correlational research methods have advantages and disadvantages, which are compared to the strengths and weaknesses of experimental research in Figure 2.8. As a whole, the foremost advantage of these methods is that they give researchers a way to explore questions that they could not examine with experimental procedures. For example, after-the-fact analyses would be the only ethical way to investigate the possible link between poor maternal nutrition and birth defects in humans. In a similar vein, if researchers hope to learn how urban and rural upbringing relate to people's values, they have to depend on descriptive methods, since they can't control where subjects grow up. Thus, *descriptive research broadens the scope of phenomena that psychologists are able to study.*

Unfortunately, descriptive methods have one significant disadvantage: Investigators cannot control events to isolate cause and effect. *Consequently, descriptive/correlational research cannot demonstrate conclusively that correlated variables are causally related.* As an example, consider the study of children's risk taking that we discussed earlier. Although Ginsburg and Miller (1982) found an association

Figure 2.8. Comparison of major research methods. This chart pulls together a great deal of information on key research methods in psychology and gives a simple example of how each method might be applied in research on aggression. As you can see, the various research methods each have their strengths and weaknesses.

Overview of key research methods in psychology

Research method		Description	Example	Advantages	Disadvantages
Experiment		Manipulation of an independent variable under carefully controlled conditions to see whether any changes occur in a dependent variable	Youngsters are ramdomly assigned to watch a violent or nonviolent film, and their aggression is measured in a laboratory situation.	Precise control over variables; ability to draw conclusions about cause-and-effect relationships	Contrived situations often artificial; ethical concerns and practical realities preclude experiments on many important questions
Naturalistic observation		Careful, usually prolonged observation of behavior without direct intervention	Youngsters' spontaneous acts of aggression during recreational activities are observed unobtrusively and recorded.	Minimizes artificiality; can be good place to start when little is known about phenomena under study	Often difficult to remain unobtrusive; can't explain *why* certain patterns of behavior were observed
Case studies		In-depth investigation of a single subject using direct interview, direct observation, and other data collection techniques	Detailed case histories are worked up for youngsters referred to counseling because of excessive aggressive behavior.	Well-suited for study of certain phenomena; can provide compelling illustrations to support a theory	Subjectivity makes it easy to see what one expects to see based on one's theoretical slant; clinical samples often unrepresentative
Surveys		Use of questionnaires or interviews to gather information about specific aspects of subjects' behavior.	Youngsters are given questionnaire that describes hypothetical scenarios and are asked about the likelihood of aggressive behavior.	Can gather data on difficult-to-observe aspects of behavior; relatively easy to collect data from large sample	Self-report data often unreliable, due to intentional deception, social desirability bias, response sets, memory lapses, and wishful thinking

between sex and risk taking, their data do not permit us to conclude that a child's sex *causes* these differences. Too many factors were left uncontrolled in the study. For example, we do not know how similar the groups of boys and girls were. The groups could have differed in age distribution or other factors that might have led to the observed differences in risk taking.

LOOKING FOR FLAWS: EVALUATING RESEARCH

Scientific research is a more reliable source of information than casual observation or popular belief. However, it would be wrong to conclude that all published research is free of errors. Scientists are fallible human beings, and flawed studies do make their way into the body of scientific literature.

That is one of the reasons why scientists often try to replicate studies. *Replication* **is the repetition of a study to see whether the earlier results are duplicated.** The replication process helps science to identify and purge erroneous findings. Of course, the replication process sometimes leads to contradictory results. You'll see some examples in the upcoming chapters. Fortunately, one of the strengths of the empirical approach is that scientists work to reconcile or explain conflicting results. In fact, scientific advances often emerge out of efforts to explain contradictory findings.

Like all sources of information, scientific studies need to be examined with a critical eye. This section describes a number of common methodological problems that often spoil studies. Being aware of these pitfalls will make you more skilled in evaluating research.

Sampling Bias

A *sample* **is the collection of subjects selected for observation in an empirical study.** In contrast, **the** *population* **is the much larger collection of animals or people (from which the sample is drawn) that researchers want to generalize about** (see Figure 2.9). For example, when political pollsters attempt to predict elections, all of the voters in a jurisdiction represent the population, and the voters who are actually surveyed constitute the sample. If researchers were interested in the ability of six-year-old children to form concepts, those six-year-olds actually studied would be the sample, and all similar six-year-

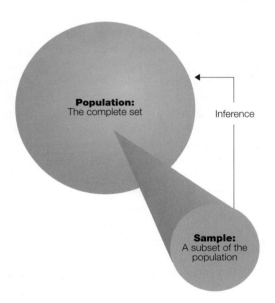

Figure 2.9. The relationship between the population and the sample. In research, we are usually interested in a broad population but can observe only a small subset, so we obtain a sample from the population. After making observations of our sample, we draw inferences about the population based on the sample. This inferential process works well as long as the sample is reasonably representative of the population.

old children (perhaps those in modern, Western cultures) would be the population.

The strategy of observing a limited sample in order to generalize about a much larger population rests on the assumption that the sample is reasonably *representative* of the population. A sample is representative if its composition is similar to the composition of the population. *Sampling bias* **exists when a sample is not representative of the population from which it was drawn.** When a sample is not representative, generalizations about the population may be inaccurate. For instance, if a political pollster were to survey only people in posh shopping areas frequented by the wealthy, the pollster's generalizations about the voting public as a whole would be off the mark.

Limits on available time and money often prevent researchers from obtaining as representative a sample as they would like. Consider the study of stress and illness that we discussed earlier. Wyler, Masuda, and Holmes (1971) surveyed hospital patients instead of a cross section of the local population. The latter approach would have been better, but it would have been much more time consuming and expensive. The makeup of the sample in the study may explain why the researchers found a somewhat stronger relationship between stress and illness than most subsequent studies. In general, when you have doubts about the results of a study, the first thing to examine is the composition of the sample.

Placebo Effects

In pharmacology, a *placebo* is a substance that resembles a drug but has no actual pharmacological effect. In studies that assess the effectiveness of medications, placebos are given to some subjects to control for the effects of a treacherous extraneous variable: subjects' expectations. Placebos are used because researchers know that subjects' expectations can influence their feelings, reactions, and behavior. Thus, *placebo effects* **occur when subjects' expectations lead them to experience some change even though they receive empty, fake, or ineffectual treatment.** In medicine, placebo effects are legendary. Many physicians tell of patients being "cured" by prescriptions of sugar pills. Similarly, psychologists have found that subjects' expectations can be powerful determinants of their perceptions and behavior when they are under the microscope in an empirical study.

In describing placebo effects, I cannot help but recall a friend from my college days who would gulp one drink and start behaving in a drunken fashion before the alcohol could possibly have taken effect. In fact, this sort of placebo effect has been observed in a number of laboratory experiments on the effects of alcohol (Wilson, 1982). In these studies, some subjects are led to believe that they are drinking alcoholic beverages when in reality the drinks only seem to contain alcohol. Many of the subjects act intoxicated, even though they haven't really consumed any alcohol.

Researchers should guard against placebo effects whenever subjects are likely to have expectations that a treatment will affect them in a certain way. The possible role of placebo effects can be assessed by including a fake version of the experimental treatment (a placebo condition) in a study.

Distortions in Self-Report Data

Research psychologists often work with *self-report data*, made up of subjects' verbal accounts of their behavior. This is the case whenever questionnaires, interviews, or personality inventories are used to measure variables. Self-report methods can be quite useful, taking advantage of the fact that people have a unique opportunity to observe themselves full-time. However, self-reports can be plagued by several kinds of distortion.

One of the most problematic of these distortions is **the *social desirability bias*, which is a tendency to give socially approved answers to questions about oneself.** Subjects who are influenced by this bias work overtime trying to create a favorable impression. For example, many survey respondents will report that they voted in an election or gave to a charity when in fact it is possible to determine that they did not.

Other problems can also produce distortions in self-report data (Schuman & Kalton, 1985). Subjects misunderstand questionnaire items surprisingly often. Memory errors can undermine the accuracy of verbal reports. In responding to certain kinds of scales, some people tend to agree with nearly all of the statements, while others tend to disagree with nearly everything. Obviously, distortions like these can produce inaccurate results. Although researchers have devised ways to neutralize these problems, we should be especially cautious in drawing conclusions from self-report data.

Experimenter Bias

As scientists, psychologists try to conduct their studies in an objective, unbiased way so that their own views will not influence the results. However, objectivity is a *goal* that scientists strive for, not an accomplished fact that can be taken for granted. In reality, most researchers have an emotional investment in the outcome of their research. Often they are testing hypotheses that they have developed themselves and that they would like to see supported by the data. It is understandable, then, that *experimenter bias* is a possible source of error in research.

Experimenter bias **occurs when a researcher's expectations or preferences about the outcome of a study influence the results ob-**

tained. Experimenter bias can slip through to influence studies in many subtle ways. One problem is that researchers, like others, sometimes *see what they want to see.* For instance, when experimenters make apparently honest mistakes in recording subjects' responses, the mistakes tend to be heavily slanted in favor of supporting the hypothesis (O'Leary, Kent, & Kanowitz, 1975).

Research by Robert Rosenthal (1976) suggests that experimenter bias may lead researchers to unintentionally influence the behavior of their subjects. In one study, Rosenthal and Fode (1963) recruited undergraduate psychology students to serve as the "experimenters." The students were told that they would be collecting data for a study of how subjects rated the success of people portrayed in photographs. In a pilot study, photos were selected that generated (on the average) neutral ratings on a scale extending from –10 (extreme failure) to +10 (extreme success). Rosenthal and Fode then manipulated the expectancies of their experimenters. Half of them were told that they would probably obtain average ratings of –5. The other half were led to expect average ratings of +5. The experimenters were forbidden from conversing with their subjects except for reading some standardized instructions. Even though the photographs were exactly the same for both groups, the experimenters who *expected* positive ratings *obtained* significantly higher ratings than those who expected negative ones.

How could the experimenters have swayed the subjects' ratings? According to Rosenthal, the experimenters may have unintentionally influenced their subjects by sending subtle nonverbal signals as the experiment progressed. Without realizing it, they may have smiled, nodded, or sent other positive cues when subjects made ratings that were in line with the experimenters' expectations. Thus, experimenter bias may influence both researchers' observations and their subjects' behavior.

The problems associated with experimenter bias can be neutralized by using a double-blind procedure. **The *double-blind procedure* is a research strategy in which neither subjects nor experimenters know which subjects are in the experimental or control groups.** It's not particularly unusual for subjects to be "blind" about their

"Quite unconsciously, a psychologist interacts in subtle ways with the people he is studying so that he may get the response he expects to get."
ROBERT ROSENTHAL

CONCEPT CHECK 2.5
Detecting Flaws in Research

Check your understanding of how to conduct sound research by looking for methodological flaws in the following studies. You'll find the answers in Appendix A.

Study 1. A researcher announces that he will be conducting an experiment to investigate the detrimental effects of sensory deprivation on perceptual-motor coordination. The first 40 students who sign up for the study are assigned to the experimental group, and the next 40 who sign up serve in the control group. The researcher supervises all aspects of the study's execution. Experimental subjects spend 2 hours in a sensory deprivation chamber, where sensory stimulation is minimal. Control subjects spend 2 hours in a waiting room that contains magazines and a TV. All subjects then perform ten 1-minute trials on a pursuit-rotor task that requires them to try to keep a stylus on a tiny rotating target. The dependent variable is their average score on the pursuit-rotor task.

Study 2. A researcher wants to know whether there is a relationship between age and racial prejudice. She designs a survey in which respondents are asked to rate their prejudice against six different ethnic groups. She distributes the survey to over 500 people of various ages who are approached at a shopping mall in a low-income, inner-city neighborhood.

Check the flaws that are apparent in each study.

Methodological flaw	Study 1	Study 2
Sampling bias	_____	_____
Placebo effects	_____	_____
Confounding of variables	_____	_____
Distortions in self-report data	_____	_____
Experimenter bias	_____	_____

treatment condition. However, the double-blind procedure keeps the experimenter in the dark as well. Of course, a member of the research team who isn't directly involved with subjects keeps track of who is in which group.

LOOKING AT ETHICS: DO THE ENDS JUSTIFY THE MEANS?

Think back to Stanley Schachter's (1959) study on anxiety and affiliation. Imagine how you would have felt if you had been one of the subjects in Schachter's high-anxiety group. You show up at a research laboratory, expecting to participate in a harmless experiment. The room you are sent to is full of unusual electronic equipment. An official-looking man in a lab coat announces that this equipment will be used to give you a series of painful electric shocks. His statement that the shocks will leave "no permanent tissue damage" is hardly reassuring. Surely, you think, there must be a mistake. All of a sudden, your venture into research has turned into a nightmare! Your stomach knots up in anxiety. The researcher explains that there will be a delay while he prepares his apparatus. He asks you to fill out a short questionnaire about whether you would prefer to wait alone or with others. Still reeling in dismay at the prospect of being shocked, you fill out the questionnaire. He takes it and then announces that you won't be shocked after all—it was all a hoax! Feelings of relief wash over you, but they're mixed with feelings of anger. You feel as though the experimenter has just made a fool out of you, and you're embarrassed and resentful.

Should researchers be allowed to play with your feelings in this way? Should they be permitted to deceive subjects in such a manner? Is this the cost that must be paid to advance scientific knowledge? As these questions indicate, the research enterprise sometimes presents scientists with difficult ethical dilemmas. *These dilemmas reflect concern about the possibility for inflicting harm on subjects.* In psychological research, the major ethical dilemmas center on the use of deception and the use of animals.

The Question of Deception

Elaborate deception, such as that seen in Schachter's study, has been fairly common in psychological research since the 1960s, especially in the area of social psychology (Christensen, 1988). Over the years, psychologists have faked fights, thefts, muggings, faintings, epileptic seizures, rapes, and automobile breakdowns to ex-

plore a host of issues. They have led subjects to believe that they were hurting others with electrical shocks, that they had homosexual tendencies, and that they were overhearing negative comments about themselves. Why have psychologists used so much deception in their research? Because of the methodological problems discussed in the last section. Subjects are often misled to avoid problems such as placebo effects and distortions in self-report data.

Critics argue against the use of deception on several grounds (Baumrind, 1985; Kelman, 1982). First, they assert that deception is only a nice word for lying, which they see as inherently immoral. Second, they argue that by deceiving unsuspecting subjects, psychologists may undermine many individuals' trust in others. Third, they point out that many deceptive studies produce distress for subjects who were not forewarned about that possibility. Specifically, subjects may experience great stress during a study or be made to feel foolish when the true nature of a study is explained.

Those who defend the use of deception in research maintain that many important issues could not be investigated if experimenters were not permitted to mislead subjects (Aronson, Brewer, & Carlsmith, 1985). They argue that most research deceptions involve "white lies" that are not likely to harm participants. A review of the relevant research by Larry Christensen (1988) suggests that deception studies are *not* harmful to subjects. Indeed, most subjects who participate in experiments involving deception report that they enjoyed the experience and that they didn't mind being misled. Moreover, a recent study found no support for the notion that deceptive research undermines subjects' trust in others (Sharpe, Adair, & Roese, 1992). Finally, researchers who defend deception argue that the benefits—advances in knowledge that often improve human welfare—are worth the costs.

The issue of deception creates a difficult dilemma for scientists, pitting honesty against the desire to advance knowledge. Today, most institutions that conduct research have committees that evaluate the ethics of research proposals before studies are allowed to proceed. These committees have often blocked studies requiring substantial deception. Many psychologists believe that this conservativism has obstructed important lines of research and slowed progress in the field. Although this may be true, it is not easy to write off the points made by the critics of deception.

"Who are the cruel and inhumane ones, the behavioral scientists whose research on animals led to the cures of the anorexic girl and the vomiting child, or those leaders of the radical animal activists who are making an exciting career of trying to stop all such research and are misinforming people by repeatedly asserting that it is without any value?"
NEAL MILLER

CHAPTER TWO

Warwick (1975) states the issue eloquently: "If it is all right to use deceit to advance knowledge, then why not for reasons of national security, for maintaining the Presidency, or to save one's own hide?" (p. 105). That's a tough question regarding a tough dilemma that will probably generate heated debate for a long time to come.

The Question of Animal Research

Psychology's other major ethics controversy concerns the use of animals in research. Psychologists use animals as research subjects for several reasons. Sometimes they simply want to know more about the behavior of a specific type of animal. In other instances, they want to identify general laws of behavior that apply to both humans and animals. Finally, in some cases psychologists use animals because they can expose them to treatments that clearly would be unacceptable with human subjects. For example, most of the research on the relationship between deficient maternal nutrition during pregnancy and the incidence of birth defects has been done with animals.

It's this third reason for using animals that has generated most of the controversy. Some people maintain that it is wrong to subject animals to harm or pain for research purposes. Essentially, they argue that animals are entitled to the same rights as humans (Regan, 1989). They accuse researchers of violating these rights by subjecting animals to unnecessary cruelty in many "trivial" studies (Hollands, 1989). They also argue that most animal studies are a waste of time because the results may not even apply to humans (Millstone, 1989; Ulrich, 1991). Some of the more militant animal rights activists have broken into laboratories, destroyed scientists' equipment and research records, and stolen experimental animals (Johnson, 1990).

In spite of the great furor, only 7%–8% of all psychological studies involve animals (mostly rodents and birds). Relatively few of these studies require subjecting the animals to painful or harmful manipulations (American Psychological Association, 1984). Psychologists who defend animal research point to the progress achieved through such work. Neal Miller (1985), a prominent psychologist who has done pioneering work in several areas, has compiled a list of major advances attributable to psychological research on animals. Among them are advances in the treatment of mental disorders, neuromuscular disorders, strokes, brain injuries, visual defects, headaches,

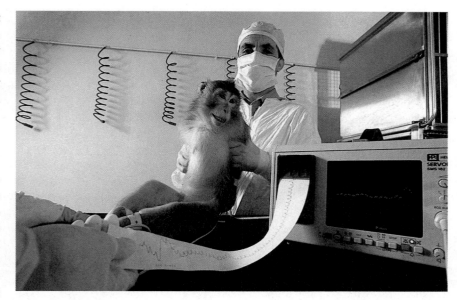

The use of animals in scientific research raises difficult ethical issues. The American Psychological Association's ethical guidelines call for humane treatment for experimental animals and clear justification for any procedure that may inflict harm or pain.

memory defects, high blood pressure, and problems with pain.

The manner in which animals can ethically be used for research is a highly charged controversy. Psychologists are becoming increasingly sensitive to this issue. Although animals continue to be used in research, psychologists are taking greater pains to justify their use in relation to the potential benefits of the research. They are also striving to ensure that laboratory animals receive humane care.

The ethics issues that we have discussed in this section have led the APA to develop a set of ethical standards for researchers (American Psychological Association, 1992). Although most psychological studies are fairly benign, these ethical principles are intended to ensure that both human and animal subjects are treated with dignity. Some of the key guidelines in these ethical principles are summarized in Figure 2.10 on the next page.

PUTTING IT IN PERSPECTIVE

Two of our seven unifying themes have emerged strongly in this chapter. First, the entire chapter is a testimonial to the idea that psychology is empirical. Second, the discussion of methodological flaws in research provides numerous examples of how people's experience of the world can be highly subjective. Let's examine each of these points in more detail.

As explained in Chapter 1, the empirical approach entails testing ideas, basing conclusions on systematic observation, and relying on a healthy brand of skepticism. All of those features of the

1 A subject's participation in research should be voluntary and based on informed consent. Subjects should never be coerced into participating in research. They should be informed in advance about any aspects of the study that might be expected to influence their willingness to cooperate. Furthermore, they should be permitted to withdraw from a study at any time if they so desire.

2 Subjects should not be exposed to harmful or dangerous research procedures. This guideline is intended to protect subjects from psychological as well as physical harm. Thus, even stressful procedures that might cause emotional discomfort are largely prohibited. However, procedures that carry a modest risk of moderate mental discomfort may be acceptable.

3 If an investigation requires some deception of subjects (about matters that do not involve risks), the researcher is required to explain and correct any misunderstandings as soon as possible. The deception must be disclosed to subjects in "debriefing" sessions as soon as it is practical to do so without compromising the goals of the study.

4 Subjects' rights to privacy should never be violated. Information about a subject that might be acquired during a study must be treated as highly confidential and should never be made available to others without the consent of the participant.

5 Harmful or painful procedures imposed upon animals must be thoroughly justified in terms of the knowledge to be gained from the study. Furthermore, laboratory animals are entitled to decent living conditions that are spelled out in detailed rules that relate to their housing, cleaning, feeding, and so forth.

6 Prior to conducting studies, approval should be obtained from host institutions and their research review committees. Research results should be reported fully and accurately, and raw data should be promptly shared with other professionals who seek to verify substantive claims. Retractions should be made if significant errors are found in a study subsequent to its publication.

Figure 2.10. Ethics in research. Key ethical principles in psychological research, as set forth by the American Psychological Association (1992), are summarized here. These principles are meant to ensure the welfare of both human and animal subjects.

empirical approach have been apparent in this chapter. As you have seen, psychologists test their ideas by formulating clear hypotheses that involve predictions about relations between variables. They then use a variety of research methods to collect data, so they can see whether their predictions are supported. The data collection methods are designed to make researchers' observations systematic and precise. The entire venture is saturated with skepticism. In planning and executing their research, scientists are constantly on the lookout for methodological flaws. They publish their findings so that other experts can subject their methods and conclusions to critical scrutiny. Collectively, these procedures represent the essence of the empirical approach.

The subjectivity of personal experience became apparent in the discussion of methodological problems, especially placebo effects and experimenter bias. When subjects report beneficial effects from a fake treatment (the placebo), it's because they

expected to see these effects. The studies showing that many subjects start feeling intoxicated just because they *think* that they have consumed alcohol are striking demonstrations of the enormous power of people's expectations. As pointed out in Chapter 1, psychologists and other scientists are not immune to the effects of subjective experience. Although they are trained to be objective, even scientists may see what they expect to see or what they want to see. This is one reason why the empirical approach emphasizes precise measurement and a skeptical attitude. The highly subjective nature of experience is exactly what the empirical approach attempts to neutralize.

The publication of empirical studies allows us to apply our skepticism to the research enterprise. However, you cannot critically analyze studies unless you know where and how to find them. In the upcoming Application, we will discuss where studies are published, how to find studies on specific topics, and how to read research reports.

Finding and Reading Journal Articles

Answer the following "yes" or "no."

1 I have read about scientific studies in newspapers and magazines and sometimes wondered, "How did they come to those conclusions?"

2 When I go to the library, I often have difficulty figuring out how to find information based on research.

3 I have tried to read scientific reports and found them to be too technical and difficult to understand.

If you responded "yes" to any of the above statements, you have struggled with the information explosion in the sciences. We live in a research-oriented society. The number of studies conducted in most sciences is growing at a dizzying pace. This expansion has been particularly spectacular in psychology (see Figure 2.11). Moreover, psychological research increasingly commands attention from the popular press because it is often relevant to people's personal concerns.

This Application is intended to help you cope with the information explosion in psychology. It assumes that there may come a time when you need to examine original psychological research. Perhaps it will be in your role as a student (working on a term paper, for instance), in another role (parent, teacher, nurse, administrator), or merely out of curiosity. In any case, this Application explains the nature of technical journals and discusses how to find and read articles in them. You can learn more about how to use library resources in psychology from an excellent little book titled *Library Use: A Handbook for Psychology* (Reed & Baxter, 1992).

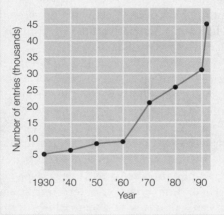

Figure 2.11. Increase in psychological literature. The number of entries included in *Psychological Abstracts,* a journal that indexes and summarizes the research literature in psychology, has increased dramatically over the years. The sharp increase since 1990 occurred in part because *Psychological Abstracts* began indexing books and book chapters in addition to journal articles.

The Nature of Technical Journals

As you will recall from earlier in the chapter, a *journal* is a periodical that publishes technical and scholarly material, usually in a narrowly defined area of inquiry. Scholars in most fields—whether economics, chemistry, education, or psychology—publish the bulk of their work in these journals. Journal articles represent the core of intellectual activity in any academic discipline. There are over 1100 journals that publish psychological research!

In general, journal articles are written for other professionals in the field. Hence, authors assume that their readers are other interested economists or chemists or psychologists. Because journal articles are written in the special language unique to a particular discipline, they are often difficult for nonprofessionals to understand. You will be learning a great deal of psychology's special language in this course, which will improve your ability to understand articles in psychology journals.

In psychology, most journal articles are reports that describe original empirical studies. These reports permit researchers to disseminate their findings to the scientific community. Another common type of article is the review article. *Review articles* summarize and reconcile the findings of a large number of studies on a specific issue. Some psychology journals also publish comments or critiques of previously published research, book reviews, theoretical treatises, and descriptions of methodological innovations.

Finding Journal Articles

Reports of psychological research are commonly mentioned in newspapers and popular magazines. These summaries can be helpful to readers, but they often embrace the most sensational conclusions that might be drawn from the research. They also tend to include many oversimplifications and factual errors. Hence, if a study mentioned in the press is of interest to you, you may want to track down the original article to ensure that you get accurate information.

Most discussions of research in the popular press do not mention where you can find the original technical article. However, there is a way to find out. A journal devoted exclusively to summarizing and indexing the research literature in psychology, called *Psychological Abstracts*, makes it possible to locate specific articles. It is also valuable for finding the research literature on general topics. For instance, you could locate

articles on topics such as intelligence testing or the effects of day care.

Psychological Abstracts contains brief summaries, or abstracts, of journal articles reporting psychological research. This monthly publication also contains various kinds of indexes to help you find articles relevant to your interests. Over 1100 journals are scanned regularly in order to select items for inclusion. The abstracts are concise—about 75 to 175 words. They briefly describe the hypotheses, methods, results, and conclusions of the studies. Each abstract should allow you to determine whether an article is relevant to your interest. If it is, you should be able to find the article in your library (or to order it) because a complete bibliographic reference is provided (see Figure 2.12).

Your search for a specific article or information on a broad topic can be greatly aided by judicious use of the subject and author indexes. These indexes list all the articles on a particular topic or by a particular author. The relevant articles are listed according to the index numbers they have been assigned. The subject and author indexes can be found in the back of each issue of *Psychological Abstracts*. Cumulative indexes are published every six months.

Although news accounts of research rarely mention where a study was published, they often mention the name of the researcher. If you have this information, the easiest way to find a specific article is to look up the author in the author index of *Psychological Abstracts*. For example, in June of 1987, a newspaper article summarized an interesting study about optimism as a personality trait. The article provided no information about which journal the study had been published in, but it did include quotes from Charles Carver, one of the researchers. To track down the original article, you would look up Carver's name in the cumulative author indexes of *Psychological Abstracts* for late 1986 and early 1987. The upper portion of Figure 2.12 shows what you would find. The author index reveals that Carver published one article during that period. The abstract for this article, found by its index number (13163), is shown at the bottom of Figure 2.12. As you can see, it shows that the original report was published in the December 1986 issue of the *Journal of Personality and Social Psychology*. Armed with this information, you could obtain the article easily.

You can conduct a search for articles on a particular topic by working through the subject index. It allows you to look up specific topics, such as achievement

Figure 2.12. Using the author index of *Psychological Abstracts*. The name of a researcher can be used via the author index (upper portion of figure) to locate abstracts of the researcher's journal articles (lower portion). Each abstract provides a summary of the article and complete bibliographical information.

Brown, Rupert 12923, 13087
Bronstein, Aaron J., 12392
Bruce, Katherine E., 12292
Bruce, Willa, 14250
Brug, A., 13764
Brull, Franz, 13524
Brulle, Andrew R., 13606
Brunswick, Ann F., 13849
Brusa, G., 13368, 13384
Brutus, Martin, 12695
Bryant, H. U., 12777
Bucci, Silvana, 13226
Buccio, M., 13639
Bucher, Richard E., 12237, 13127
Buchsbaum, Monte S., 13203
Buckalew, L.W., 14059
Buckelew, Susan P., 13178
Budeboska, Wanda, 13372

Carrier, Carol A., 14007
Carrigan, Philip, 12512
Carroll, Marilyn E., 12655
Carson, David K., 12975
Carson, Eleanor, 12818
Carstensen, Laura L., 13773
Carter, Daniel L., 13323
Carter, Michael V., 14323
Carter, R.M., 12405
Carterette, Edward C., 12819
Caruso, Keith A., 13659
Caruso, Lynn A., 13913
Carvell, Theresa, 12765
Carver, Charles S., 13163
Casalta, Henry, 13086
Casey, Jeff T., 12442
Cassel, Russell N., 13129
Cassiloth, Bernie R., 12304

Colbert, Patrick, 13251
Colbus, Debra, 13237
Cole, David A., 13774
Cole, Eric S., 13600
Cole, F. Russell, 12555
Coleman, Mick, 13479
Colletti, Gep, 13077
Colley, Ann, 12941
Collier, George, 12560
Collins, Allan C., 12778
Collins, D. A., 12550
Collins, Frank L., 13634
Collyer, Charles E., 12420
Colombo, G., 13639
Colombo, Michael, 12499
Compton, William C., 13348
Comstock, Clyde, 13798
Comstock, William, 13248

Record number

Authors

Date, volume, and pages of journal the article appeared in

Targeted author

Record number of abstract listing this person as author

First author's affiliation

13163. **Scheier, Michael F.; Weintraub, Jagdish K. & Carver, Charles S**. (Carnegie-Mellon U) **Coping with stress: Divergent strategies of optimists and pessimists**. *Journal of Personality & Social Psychology*, 1986(Dec), Vol 51(6), 1257–1264. —Previous research has shown that dispositional optimism is a prospective predictor of successful adaptation to stressful encounters. In this research we attempted to identify possible mechanisms underlying these effects by examining how optimists differ from pessimists in the kinds of coping strategies that they use. The results of two separate studies revealed modest but reliable positive correlations between optimism and problem-focused coping, seeking of social support, and emphasizing positive aspects of the stressful situation. Pessimism was associated with denial and distancing (Study 1), with focusing on stressful feelings, and with disengagement from the goal with which the stressor was interfering (Study 2). Study 1 also found a positive association between optimism and acceptance/resignation, but only when the event was construed as uncontrollable. Discussion centers on the implications of these findings for understanding the meaning of people's coping efforts in stressful circumstances. (42 ref)—*Journal abstract*.

Title of journal article

Summary of article

Name of journal

Figure 2.13. Using the subject index of *Psychological Abstracts*. In a search by subject rather than by author, the subject index is used to locate relevant abstracts by topic.

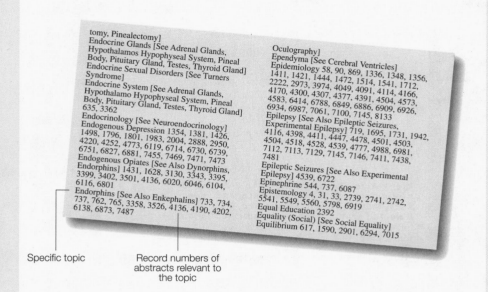

Figure 2.13. Using the subject index of *Psychological Abstracts*. In a search by subject rather than by author, the subject index is used to locate relevant abstracts by topic.

Specific topic

Record numbers of abstracts relevant to the topic

motivation, aggressive behavior, alcoholism, appetite disorders, or artistic ability. After each subject heading you will find a list of index numbers referring you to relevant abstracts. For instance, let's say that a professor's lecture sparks your interest in *endorphins*, morphinelike substances that are produced in the brain. If you wanted to do a term paper on endorphins, the place to start would be in the subject index of *Psychological Abstracts*, where you would find the term and a list of abstract numbers as seen in Figure 2.13. You could then examine the identified abstracts to decide which articles to obtain.

The widespread availability of computers is beginning to revolutionize the task of searching through mountains of technical literature in many disciplines, including psychology. The information contained in *Psychological Abstracts* from 1967 through the present is now stored in a computerized database called PsycINFO. Today, owners of personal computers can access this database through phone lines (for a modest fee, of course) and conduct literature searches almost instantaneously. This database is also available at some libraries that have the information stored on a CD-ROM

disc. This version of the database is called PsycLIT.

Computerized literature searches can be much more powerful, precise, and thorough than traditional, manual searches. Computers can sift through a half-million articles in a matter of seconds. Then, they can print out abstracts of *all* the articles on a subject, such as birth order. Obviously, there is no way you can match this efficiency stumbling around in the stacks at your library. Moreover, the computer allows you to pair up topics to swiftly narrow your search to exactly those issues that interest you. For example, Figure 2.14 shows a PsycINFO search that identified all the articles on birth order *and* intelligence. If you were preparing a term paper on whether birth order is related to intelligence, this precision would be invaluable.

Reading Journal Articles

Once you find the journal articles you want to examine, you need to know how to decipher them. You can process the information in such articles more efficiently if you understand how they are organized. Depending on your needs and purpose, you may want to simply

skim through some of the sections. Journal articles follow a fairly standard organization, which includes the following sections and features.

Abstract

Most journals print a concise summary at the beginning of each article. This abstract allows readers scanning the journal to quickly decide whether articles are relevant to their interests.

Introduction

The introduction presents an overview of the problem studied in the research. It mentions relevant theories and quickly reviews previous research that bears on the problem, usually citing shortcomings in previous research that necessitate the present study. This review of the current state of knowledge on the topic usually progresses to a specific and precise statement regarding the hypotheses under investigation.

Method

The next section provides a thorough description of the research methods used in the study. Information is provided on the subjects used, the procedures followed, and the data collection techniques employed. This description is made detailed enough to permit another researcher to attempt to replicate the study.

Results

The data obtained in the study are reported in the results section. This section often creates problems for novice readers because it includes complex statistical analyses, figures, tables, and graphs. This section does *not* include any inferences based on the data, as such conclusions are supposed to follow in the next section. Instead, it simply contains a concise summary of the raw data and the statistical analyses.

Discussion

In the discussion section you will find the conclusions drawn by the author(s). In contrast to the results section, which is a straightforward summary of empirical observations, the discussion section al-

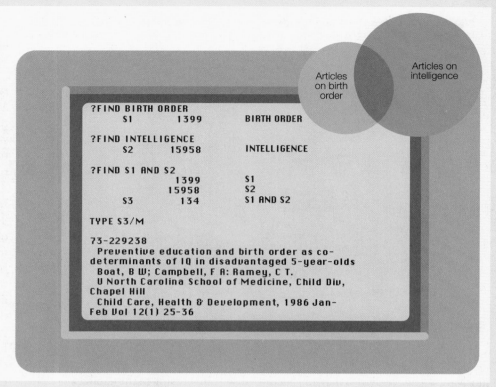

Figure 2.14. Using PsycINFO to locate journal articles. A computerized literature search can be a highly efficient way to locate relevant research. In this example, the first command ("?FIND BIRTH ORDER") asks the computer to find all the entries on birth order in the database. The computer labels the 1399 articles it finds Set 1 (S1). The second command searches for all the articles on intelligence; the 15,958 such articles make up Set 2 (S2). To identify those articles that deal with both birth order and intelligence, the third command searches S1 and S2 to find any articles that are listed in both sets (as depicted by the overlap in the circles). The resulting Set 3 (S3) includes 134 such articles. The fourth command directs the computer to print out the titles of all the articles in Set 3, from the most recent to the oldest. The computer can also print out the abstract of any article selected from this set.

lows for interpretation and evaluation of the data. Implications for theory and factual knowledge in the discipline are discussed. Conclusions are usually qualified carefully, and any limitations in the study may be acknowledged. This section may also include suggestions for future research on the issue.

References

At the end of each article is a list of bibliographic references for any studies cited. This list permits the reader to examine firsthand other relevant studies mentioned in the article. The references list is often a rich source of leads about other articles that are germane to the topic that you are looking into.

Chapter 2 Review

KEY IDEAS

Looking for Laws: The Scientific Approach to Behavior

♦ The scientific approach assumes that there are laws of behavior that can be discovered through empirical research. The goals of the science of psychology include (1) the measurement and description of behavior, (2) the understanding and prediction of behavior, and (3) the application of this knowledge to the task of controlling behavior.

♦ A scientific investigation follows a systematic pattern that includes five steps: (1) formulate a testable hypothesis, (2) select the research method and design the study, (3) collect the data, (4) analyze the data and draw conclusions, and (5) report the findings. The two major advantages of the scientific approach are its clarity in communication and its relative intolerance of error.

Looking for Causes: Experimental Research

♦ Experimental research involves the manipulation of an independent variable to ascertain its effect on a dependent variable. This research is usually done by comparing experimental and control groups, which must be alike in regard to important extraneous variables. Any differences between the groups in the dependent variable presumably are due to the manipulation of the independent variable.

♦ Experimental designs may vary. Sometimes an experimental group serves as its own control group. And in many experiments, there is more than one independent variable or more than one dependent variable.

♦ An experiment is a powerful research method that permits conclusions about cause-and-effect relationships between variables. However, the experimental method is often not usable for a specific problem, and many experiments tend to be artificial.

Looking for Links: Descriptive/ Correlational Research

♦ When psychologists are unable to manipulate the variables they want to study, they use descriptive/correlational research methods that seek to discover correlations between variables. Key descriptive methods include naturalistic observation, case studies, and surveys.

♦ Correlations may be either positive (reflecting a direct association) or negative (reflecting an inverse relationship). The closer a correlation is to either +1.00 or –1.00, the stronger the association is. Higher correlations yield greater predictability. However, a high correlation is no assurance of causation.

♦ Descriptive/correlational research methods allow psychologists to explore issues that might not be open to experimental investigation. They are also less artificial than experiments. However, these research methods cannot demonstrate cause-effect relationships.

Looking for Flaws: Evaluating Research

♦ Scientists often try to replicate research findings to double-check their validity. Although this process leads to some contradictory findings, science works toward reconciling and explaining inconsistent results.

♦ Sampling bias occurs when a sample is not representative of the population of interest. Placebo effects occur when subjects' expectations cause them to change in response to a fake treatment. Distortions in self-reports are a source of concern whenever questionnaires and personality inventories are used to collect data. Experimenter bias occurs when researchers' expectations and desires sway their observations.

Looking at Ethics: Do the Ends Justify the Means?

♦ Research sometimes raises complex ethical issues. In psychology, the key questions concern the use of deception with human subjects and the use of harmful or painful manipulations with animal subjects. The APA has formulated ethical principles to serve as guidelines for researchers.

Putting It in Perspective

♦ Two of the book's unifying themes are apparent in this chapter's discussion of the research enterprise in psychology: psychology is empirical, and people's experience of the world can be highly subjective.

Application: Finding and Reading Journal Articles

♦ Journals publish technical and scholarly material. Journal articles are usually written for other professionals in a narrow area of inquiry. Over 1100 journals publish psychological research.

♦ *Psychological Abstracts* contains brief summaries of journal articles. Articles on specific topics can be found by using the author and subject indexes or by conducting a computerized literature search.

♦ Journal articles are easier to understand if one is familiar with the standard format. Most articles include six elements: abstract, introduction, method, results, discussion, and references.

KEY TERMS

Case study	Journal
Confounding of variables	Naturalistic observation
Control group	Operational definition
Correlation	Placebo effects
Correlation coefficient	Population
	Random assignment
Data collection techniques	Replication
Dependent variable	Research methods
Double-blind procedure	Sample
	Sampling bias
Experiment	Social desirability bias
Experimental group	Statistics
Experimenter bias	Subjects
Extraneous variables	Survey
Hypothesis	Variables
Independent variable	

KEY PEOPLE

Neal Miller	Stanley Schachter
Robert Rosenthal	

3 The Biological Bases of Behavior

If you have ever visited an aquarium, you may have encountered one of nature's more captivating animals: the octopus. Although this jellylike mass of arms and head appears to be a relatively simple creature, it is capable of a number of interesting behaviors. The octopus has highly developed eyes that enable it to respond to stimuli in the darkness of the ocean. When threatened, it can release an inky cloud to befuddle enemies while it makes good its escape by a kind of jet propulsion. If that doesn't work, it can camouflage itself by changing color and texture to blend into its surroundings. Furthermore, the animal is surprisingly intelligent. In captivity, an octopus can learn, for example, to twist the lid off a jar with one of its tentacles to get at a treat that is inside.

Despite its talents, there are many things an octopus cannot do. An octopus cannot study psychology, plan a weekend, dream about its future, or discover the Pythagorean theorem. Yet the biological processes that underlie these uniquely human behaviors are much the same as the biological processes that enable an octopus to escape from a predator or forage for food. Indeed, some of science's most important insights about how the nervous system works came from studies of a relative of the octopus, the squid.

Organisms as diverse as humans and squid share many biological processes. However, their unique behavioral capacities depend on the differences in their physiological makeup. You and I have a larger repertoire of behaviors than the octopus primarily because we come equipped with a more complex brain and nervous system. The activity of the human brain is so complex that no computer has ever come close to duplicating it. Your nervous system contains as many cells busily integrating and relaying information as there are stars in our galaxy. Whether you are scratching your nose or composing an essay, the activity of those cells underlies what you do. It is little wonder, then, that many psychologists have dedicated themselves to exploring the biological bases of behavior.

How do mood-altering drugs work? Are the two halves of the brain specialized to perform different functions? What happens inside your body when you feel a strong emotion? Are some mental illnesses the result of chemical imbalances in the brain? To what extent is intelligence determined by biological inheritance? These questions only begin to suggest the countless ways in which biology is fundamental to the study of behavior.

In this chapter we will examine the principal biological structures and processes that make be-havior possible. In the first two sections of the chapter, we'll discuss the workings of the nervous system. We'll then take an extended look at the most important behavioral organ of all, the brain. After completing our review of behavioral physiology with a brief discussion of the endocrine system, we will consider a key issue raised by the importance of biology: the impact of heredity on behavior. Finally, the chapter's Application examines the furor about the specialized abilities of the right and left halves of the brain.

COMMUNICATION IN THE NERVOUS SYSTEM

Imagine that you are watching a scary movie. As the tension mounts, your palms sweat and your heart beats faster. You begin shoveling popcorn into your mouth, carelessly spilling some in your lap. If someone were to ask you what you are doing at this moment, you would probably say, "Nothing—just watching the movie." Yet some very complicated processes are occurring without your thinking about them. A stimulus (the light from the screen) is striking your eye. Almost instantaneously, your brain is interpreting the light stimulus, and signals are flashing to other parts of your body, leading to a flurry of activity. Your sweat glands are releasing perspiration, your heartbeat is quickening, and muscular movements are enabling your hand to find the popcorn and, more or less successfully, lift it to your mouth.

Even in this simple example, you can see that behavior depends on rapid information processing. Information travels almost instantaneously from your eye to your brain, from your brain to the muscles of your arm and hand, and from your palms back to your brain. In essence, your nervous system is a complex communication network in which signals are constantly being received, integrated, and transmitted. The nervous system handles *information*, just as the circulatory system handles blood. In this section, we take a close look at communication in the nervous system.

Nervous Tissue: The Basic Hardware

Your nervous system is living tissue. It is composed entirely of cells, just like the rest of your body. The cells in the nervous system fall into two major categories: *glia* and *neurons*.

Glia are cells found throughout the nervous system that provide structural support and insulation for neurons. Glia (literally "glue") hold

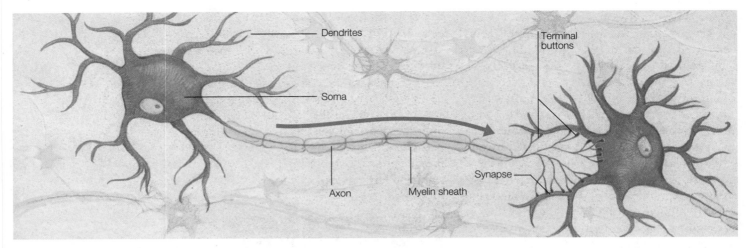

Dendrites

Soma

Terminal
buttons

Axon

Myelin sheath

Synapse

Figure 3.1. Structure of the neuron. Neurons are the communication links of the nervous system. This diagram highlights the key parts of a neuron, including specialized receptor areas (dendrites), the cell body (soma), the fiber along which impulses are transmitted (axon), and the junctions across which chemical messengers carry signals to other neurons (synapses). Neurons vary considerably in size and shape and are usually densely interconnected.

the nervous system together and help maintain the chemical environment of the neurons. Although glia provide many important services, neurons perform the crucial functions of the nervous system.

Neurons **are individual cells in the nervous system that receive, integrate, and transmit information.** They are the basic links that permit communication within the nervous system. *Most neurons communicate only with other neurons.* However, a privileged few receive signals from outside the nervous system (through sensory organs) or transmit signals from the nervous system to the muscles that allow your body to move about.

A highly simplified drawing of two "typical" neurons is shown in Figure 3.1. Actually, neurons come in a tremendous variety of types and shapes that no drawing can adequately represent. Trying to draw the "typical" neuron is like trying to draw the "typical" tree. In spite of this diversity, the drawing in Figure 3.1 highlights some common features of neurons.

The *soma,* **or cell body, contains the cell nucleus and much of the chemical machinery common to most cells** (*soma* is Greek for "body"). The rest of the neuron is devoted exclusively to handling information. We usually think of information as flowing from left to right, so the diagram in Figure 3.1 is set up for just such a flow. The neuron at the left has a number of branched, feelerlike structures called *dendritic trees* (*dendrite* is a Greek word for "tree"). Each individual branch is a *dendrite.* **Dendrites are the parts of a neuron that are specialized to receive information.** Most neurons receive information from many other cells—sometimes thousands of others—and so have extensive dendritic trees.

From the many dendrites, information flows into the cell body and then travels away from the soma along the *axon* (from the Greek for "axle"). **The** *axon* **is a long, thin fiber that transmits signals away from the soma to other neurons or to muscles or glands.** Axons may be quite long (sometimes several feet), and they may branch off to communicate with a number of other cells.

In humans, many axons are wrapped in a white, fatty substance called *myelin.* **The** *myelin sheath* **is insulating material, derived from glial cells, that encases some axons.** This insulation speeds up the transmission of signals that move along axons. Furthermore, if certain axons aren't properly insulated from each other, signals in the nervous system can get scrambled. The loss of muscle control seen with the disease *multiple sclerosis* appears to be due to a degeneration of myelin sheaths (McKhann, 1987).

The axon ends in a cluster of *terminal buttons,* **which are small knobs that secrete chemicals called neurotransmitters.** These chemicals serve as messengers that may activate neighboring neurons. The points at which neurons interconnect are called *synapses.* **A** *synapse* **is a junction where information is transmitted from one neuron to another** (*synapse* is from the Greek for "junction").

To summarize, information is received at the dendrites, passed through the soma and along the axon, and transmitted to the dendrites of other cells at meeting points called synapses. Unfortunately, this nice, simple picture has more exceptions than the U.S. Tax Code. For example, some neurons do not have an axon, while others have multiple axons. Also, although neurons typically synapse on the dendrites of other cells, they may also synapse on a soma or an axon. Despite these and other complexities, however, the fundamental function of neurons is clear: They do the work of the nervous system by receiving, integrating, and transmitting informational signals.

The Neural Impulse: Using Energy to Send Information

What happens when a neuron is stimulated? What is the nature of the signal—the *neural impulse*—that moves through the neuron? These were the questions that Alan Hodgkin and Andrew Huxley set out to answer in their experiments with axons removed from squid. Why did they choose to work with squid axons? Because the squid has a pair of "giant" axons that are about a hundred times larger than those in humans (which still makes them only about as thick as a human hair). These giant axons serve the squid well. The thick size speeds up the transmission of messages to the squid's muscles, enabling it to make its remarkable, jet-propelled escape from its enemies. The axons also serve physiologists well. Their large size permitted Hodgkin and Huxley to insert into them fine wires called *microelectrodes*. By using the microelectrodes to record the electrical activity in individual neurons, Hodgkin and Huxley unraveled the mystery of the neural impulse.

The Neuron at Rest: A Tiny Battery

Hodgkin and Huxley (1952) learned that the neural impulse is a complex electrochemical reaction. Both inside and outside the neuron are fluids containing electrically charged atoms and molecules called *ions*. Positively charged sodium and potassium ions and negatively charged chloride ions flow back and forth across the cell membrane, but they do not cross at the same rate. The difference in flow rates leads to a slightly higher concentration of negatively charged ions inside the cell. The net result is that the neuron membrane becomes *polarized*—negatively charged on the inside and positively charged on the outside.

The voltage difference that results from this polarization means that the neuron at rest is a tiny battery, a store of potential energy. **The *resting potential* of a neuron is its stable, negative charge when the cell is inactive.** As shown in Figure 3.2(a), this charge is about –70 millivolts, roughly 1/20 of the voltage of a flashlight battery.

The Action Potential

As long as the voltage of a neuron remains constant, the cell is quiet, and no messages are being sent. However, stimulation of sufficient intensity (signals from other neurons or from sensory stimuli) will disrupt this stability by momentarily altering the permeability of the cell membrane. When the neuron is stimulated, channels in its cell membrane open, briefly allowing positively charged sodium ions to rush in. For an instant, the neuron's charge is less negative, or even positive, creating an *action potential*. **An *action potential* is a brief change in a neuron's electrical charge.** The firing of an action potential is reflected in the voltage spike shown in Figure 3.2(b). Like a spark traveling along a trail of gunpowder, the voltage change races down the axon. The firing of the action potential in one segment of the axon triggers the firing of the action potential in the next segment, and so on down the line, just as a burning grain of gunpowder ignites neighboring grains.

Thus, a neural impulse is an electric current that flows along the axon as a result of an action potential. After the firing of an action potential, the channels in the cell membrane that opened to let in sodium close up. Until they are ready to reopen, the neuron cannot fire again. **The *absolute refractory period* is the minimum length of time after an action potential during which another action potential cannot begin.**

The All-or-None Law

The neural impulse is an all-or-none proposition, like firing a gun. You can't half-fire a gun. The same is true of the neuron's firing of action potentials. Either the neuron fires or it doesn't. A weaker stimulus does not produce a weaker neural impulse.

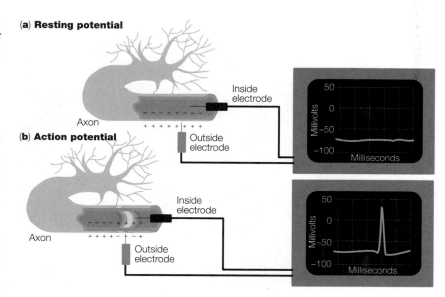

Figure 3.2. The neural impulse. The electrochemical properties of the neuron allow it to transmit signals. The electric charge of a neuron can be measured with a pair of electrodes connected to an oscilloscope, as Hodgkin and Huxley showed with a squid axon. Because of its exceptionally thick axons, the squid has frequently been used by scientists studying the neural impulse. (**a**) At rest, the neuron is like a tiny wet battery with a resting potential of about –70 millivolts. (**b**) When a neuron is stimulated, a brief jump in its electric potential occurs, resulting in a spike on the oscilloscope recording of the neuron's electrical activity. This change in voltage, called an action potential, travels along the axon like a spark traveling along a trail of gunpowder.

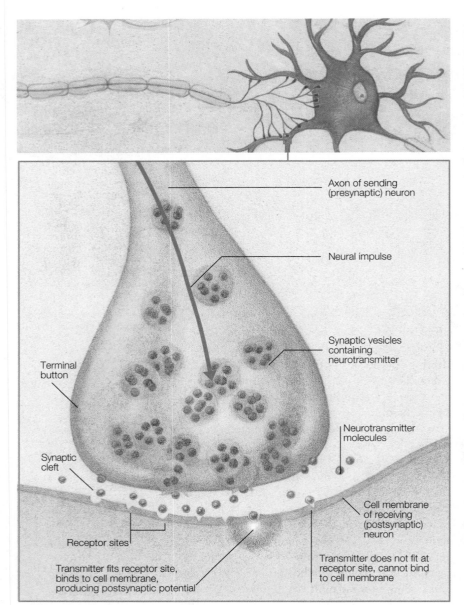

Figure 3.3. The synapse.
When a neural impulse reaches an axon's terminal buttons, it triggers the release of chemical messengers called neurotransmitters. The neurotransmitter molecules diffuse across the synaptic cleft and bind to receptor sites on the postsynaptic neuron. A specific neurotransmitter can bind only to receptor sites that its molecular structure will fit into, much like a key must fit a lock.

Labels in figure:
Axon of sending (presynaptic) neuron
Neural impulse
Synaptic vesicles containing neurotransmitter
Neurotransmitter molecules
Cell membrane of receiving (postsynaptic) neuron
Transmitter does not fit at receptor site, cannot bind to cell membrane
Transmitter fits receptor site, binds to cell membrane, producing postsynaptic potential
Receptor sites
Synaptic cleft
Terminal button

Even though the action potential is an all-or-nothing event, neurons *can* convey information about the strength of a stimulus. They do so by varying the *rate* at which they fire action potentials. In general, a stronger stimulus will cause a cell to fire a more rapid volley of neural impulses than a weaker stimulus will.

Different neurons transmit neural impulses at different speeds, depending on the thickness of their axons and other factors. Although neural impulses do not travel as fast as electricity along a wire, they *are* very fast. The entire, complicated process takes only a few thousandths of a second. In the time it has taken you to read this description of the neural impulse, billions of such impulses have been transmitted in your nervous system!

The Synapse: Where Neurons Meet

In the nervous system, the neural impulse functions as a signal. For that signal to have any meaning for the system as a whole, it must be transmitted from the neuron to other cells. As noted earlier, this transmission takes place at special junctions called *synapses*, which depend on *chemical* messengers.

Sending Signals: Chemicals as Couriers

A "typical" synapse is shown in Figure 3.3. The first thing that you should notice is that the two neurons don't actually touch. They are separated by the **synaptic cleft, a microscopic gap between the terminal button of one neuron and the cell membrane of another neuron.** Signals have to jump this gap to permit neurons to communicate. In this situation, the neuron that sends a signal across the gap is called the *presynaptic neuron*, and the neuron that receives the signal is called the *postsynaptic neuron.*

How do messages travel across the gaps between neurons? The arrival of an action potential at an axon's terminal buttons triggers the release of **neurotransmitters—chemicals that transmit information from one neuron to another.** Within the buttons, the chemicals are stored in small sacs, called *synaptic vesicles.* The neurotransmitters are released when a vesicle fuses with the membrane of the presynaptic cell and squeezes its contents into the synaptic cleft. After their release, neurotransmitters diffuse across the synaptic cleft to the membrane of the receiving cell. There they may bind with special molecules in the postsynaptic cell membrane at various *receptor sites.* These sites are specifically "tuned" to recognize and respond to some neurotransmitters but not to others.

Receiving Signals: Postsynaptic Potentials

When a neurotransmitter and a receptor molecule combine, reactions in the cell membrane cause a **postsynaptic potential (PSP), a voltage change at a receptor site on a postsynaptic cell membrane.** Postsynaptic potentials do *not* follow the all-or-none law as action potentials do. Instead, postsynaptic potentials are *graded.* That is, they increase or decrease the *probability* of a neural impulse in the receiving cell in proportion to their size (the amount of voltage change).

If the voltage in the postsynaptic neuron shifts in a positive direction, the cell comes closer to its threshold for firing a neural impulse. If the voltage shifts in a negative direction, the postsynaptic neuron moves farther away from its threshold for firing a neural impulse. The direction of the voltage shift (positive or negative) depends on which receptor sites are activated in the postsynaptic neuron (Kandel & Schwartz, 1991).

Because of these positive and negative shifts, there are two types of messages that can be sent from cell to cell: excitatory and inhibitory. Both types are essential to the functioning of the nervous system. If cells could only excite other cells, any excitation would grow and reverberate throughout the nervous system like a nuclear chain reaction. In fact, many kinds of seizures are due to insufficient inhibitory effects at synapses. Strychnine, perhaps the nastiest of poisons, works its deadly effects by disabling many inhibitory synapses. The resulting excitation causes uncontrollable convulsions that can be fatal.

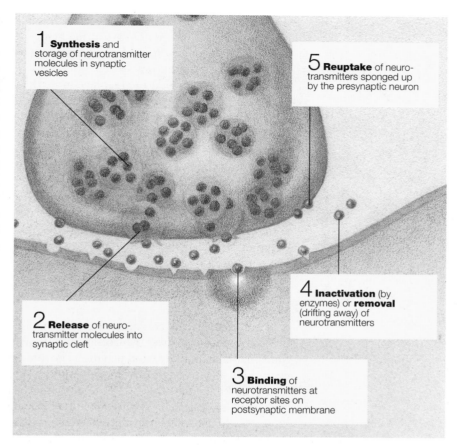

1 **Synthesis** and storage of neurotransmitter molecules in synaptic vesicles

5 **Reuptake** of neurotransmitters sponged up by the presynaptic neuron

2 **Release** of neurotransmitter molecules into synaptic cleft

3 **Binding** of neurotransmitters at receptor sites on postsynaptic membrane

4 **Inactivation** (by enzymes) or **removal** (drifting away) of neurotransmitters

The excitatory or inhibitory effects produced at a synapse last only a fraction of a second. Then neurotransmitters drift away from receptor sites or are inactivated by enzymes that metabolize (convert) them into inactive forms. Most are reabsorbed into the presynaptic neuron through *reuptake,* a process in which neurotransmitters are sponged up from the synaptic cleft by the presynaptic membrane. This process allows neurons to recycle their materials.

The various processes in synaptic transmission are diagrammed in Figure 3.4. As you can see, communication at synapses involves five steps: (1) the synthesis and storage of transmitters, (2) the release of transmitters into the synaptic cleft, (3) the binding of transmitters at receptor sites on the postsynaptic membrane, (4) the inactivation (by enzymes) or removal (drifting away) of transmitters from receptor sites, and (5) the reuptake of transmitters by the presynaptic neuron.

Integrating Signals: A Balancing Act

We have seen how neurons receive signals, transmit signals along axons, and send signals across synaptic clefts to other neurons. Keep in mind, however, that most neurons are interlinked in complex, dense networks. In fact, a neuron may

Figure 3.4. Overview of synaptic transmission. The main elements in synaptic transmission are summarized here, superimposed on a blowup of the synapse seen in Figure 3.3. The five key processes involved in communication at synapses are (1) synthesis, (2) release, (3) binding, (4) inactivation, and (5) reuptake of neurotransmitters. As you'll see in this chapter and the remainder of the book, the effects of many phenomena—such as stress, drug use, and some diseases—can be explained in terms of how they alter one or more of these processes (usually at synapses releasing a specific neurotransmitter).

have as many as 15,000 synapses receiving a symphony of signals from thousands of other neurons. The same neuron may pass its messages along to thousands of other neurons as well.

Thus, a neuron must do a great deal more than simply relay messages it receives. It must integrate signals arriving at many synapses before it "decides" whether to fire a neural impulse. If enough excitatory PSPs occur in a neuron, the electrical currents can add up, causing the cell's voltage to reach the threshold at which an action potential will be fired. However, if many inhibitory PSPs also occur, they will tend to cancel the effects of excitatory PSPs. The state of the neuron is a weighted balance between excitatory and inhibitory influences.

Neurotransmitters and Behavior

We have seen that the nervous system relies on chemical couriers to communicate information between neurons. These neurotransmitters are fundamental to our behavior, playing a key role in everything from our muscle movements to our moods and mental health.

You might guess that the nervous system would require only two neurotransmitters—one for excitatory signals and one for inhibitory signals. However, at least ten chemical substances clearly qualify as neurotransmitters (Kolb & Whishaw, 1990). In addition, scientists suspect that a number of other substances *may* function as transmit-

ters, and new candidates are still being discovered. In general, a specific type of neuron contains the chemical factory for manufacturing only one of the transmitters. However, some neurons also release related chemicals called *neuromodulators*, which we'll discuss later.

Specific neurotransmitters work at specific kinds of synapses. You may recall that transmitter substances deliver their messages by binding to receptor sites on the postsynaptic membrane. However, a transmitter cannot bind to just any site. The binding process operates much like a lock and key, as was shown in Figure 3.3. Just as a key has to fit a lock to work, a transmitter has to fit into a receptor site for binding to occur. Hence, specific transmitters can deliver signals only at certain locations, thus making the nervous system's control of our behavior more precise. Let's briefly review some of the most interesting findings about how neurotransmitters regulate behavior.

Acetylcholine

The discovery that cells communicate by releasing chemicals was first made in connection with the transmitter acetylcholine (ACh). ACh has been found throughout the nervous system. It is the only transmitter at synapses that communicate directly with voluntary muscles. Every move you make—typing, walking, talking, breathing—depends on ACh released to your muscles (Kandel & Schwartz, 1991).

Neurotransmitters underlie all aspects of behavior. For example, specific neurotransmitters are known to be involved in depression, in the stimulant effects of nicotine, and in the experience of pain.

ACh appears to contribute to attention, arousal, and memory processes. An inadequate supply of ACh in the brain has been implicated in the memory losses seen with *Alzheimer's disease*. This disease is endured by about 5 to 15% of people over the age of 65, as well as some younger people (Albert, 1992). People with Alzheimer's disease gradually lose their ability to remember anything. Eventually, they don't even recognize family members and can't find their way home. Examinations of the brains of people who have died from Alzheimer's disease reveal abnormally low levels of ACh (Goldman & Coté, 1991). Researchers believe that cells responsible for the synthesis of ACh degenerate in victims of Alzheimer's, leaving the brain with a depleted supply of this crucial neurotransmitter (Allen, Dawbarn, & Wilcock, 1988).

The activity of ACh (and other neurotransmitters) may be influenced by other chemicals in the brain. Although synaptic receptor sites are sensitive to specific neurotransmitters, sometimes they can be "fooled" by other chemical substances. For example, if you smoke tobacco, some of your ACh synapses will be stimulated by the nicotine that arrives in your brain. At these synapses, the nicotine acts like ACh itself. It binds to receptor sites for ACh, causing postsynaptic potentials (PSPs). In technical language, nicotine is an ACh agonist. **An *agonist* is a chemical that mimics the action of a neurotransmitter.** In other words, an agonist functions as a substitute, producing some of the effects of the regular transmitter.

Not all chemicals that fool synaptic receptors are agonists. Some chemicals bind to receptors but fail to produce a PSP (the key slides into the lock, but doesn't work). In effect, they temporarily *block* the action of the natural transmitter by occupying its receptor sites, rendering them unusable. Thus, they act as antagonists. **An *antagonist* is a chemical that opposes the action of a neurotransmitter.** For example, *curare* is an ACh antagonist. It blocks action at the same ACh synapses that are fooled by nicotine. As a result, muscles are unable to move. Some South American natives use a form of curare on arrows. If they wound an animal, the curare blocks the synapses from nerve to muscle, paralyzing the animal.

Biogenic Amines

The *biogenic amines* include three neurotransmitters: dopamine, norepinephrine, and serotonin. Neurons using these transmitters regulate many aspects of everyday behavior, including muscular movements, physiological arousal, sleep and wakefulness, feelings of pleasure and other mood fluctuations, and reactions to certain drugs, such as cocaine and amphetamines.

The importance of these neurotransmitters is illustrated by evidence linking abnormal levels of biogenic amines in the brain to the development of certain psychological disorders. For example, people who suffer from depression appear to have lowered levels of activation at norepinephrine (NE) synapses. Studies suggest that this reduced activation may be due to changes in the sensitivity of NE *receptors* rather than to decreases in the *release* of NE (Schildkraut, Green, & Mooney, 1989).

In a similar fashion, alterations in activity at dopamine (DA) synapses have been implicated in the development of *schizophrenia*. This severe mental illness is marked by irrational thought, hallucinations, poor contact with reality, and deterioration of routine adaptive behavior (see Chapter 14). Afflicting roughly 1% of the population, schizophrenia requires hospitalization more often than any other psychological disorder. Many investigators believe that schizophrenia is caused by overactivity at DA synapses. Why? Primarily because the therapeutic drugs that tame schizophrenic symptoms are known to be DA antagonists that reduce the neurotransmitter's activity. Solomon Snyder (1986) has shown that most of these drugs work by binding to DA receptor sites and blocking normal DA activity at these sites. Complexities in the biochemical explanations of depression and schizophrenia continue to be debated (Kandel, 1991), as you'll see in Chapter 14. Nonetheless, it's clear that disturbances in the activity of biogenic amine neurotransmitters contribute to some forms of mental illness.

GABA

Gamma-aminobutyric acid (GABA) is a widely distributed neurotransmitter that only produces *inhibitory* postsynaptic potentials. GABA appears to be responsible for much of the inhibition in the central nervous system. Studies suggest that GABA contributes to the regulation of anxiety in humans (Paul, Crawley, & Skolnick, 1986). Generally, the inhibitory effects of GABA keep a lid on neural excitement. However, lowered levels of GABA may permit heightened neural excitement that translates into feelings of anxiety. Consistent with this theory, researchers have found that antianxiety drugs, better known as tranquilizers, exert their effects by increasing inhibitory activity at GABA synapses (Julien, 1992). Ironically, millions of prescriptions were written for tranquiliz-

"Brain research of the past decade, especially the study of neurotransmitters, has proceeded at a furious pace, achieving progress equal in scope to all the accomplishments of the preceding fifty years—and the pace of discovery continues to accelerate. The final years of the twentieth century may witness unparalleled advances in our understanding of the brain and, even more exciting, in our ability to put this understanding to therapeutic use."
SOLOMON SNYDER

ers (such as Valium) before scientists discovered their mechanism of action in the late 1970s.

Endorphins

"When human beings engage in various activities, it seems that neurojuices are released that are associated with either pain or pleasure. And the endorphins are very pleasurable."
CANDACE PERT

In 1970, after a horseback-riding accident, Candace Pert, a graduate student in neuroscience, lay in a hospital bed receiving frequent shots of *morphine*, a painkilling drug derived from the opium plant. This experience left her with a driving curiosity about how morphine works. A few years later, she and Solomon Snyder rocked the scientific world by showing that *morphine exerts its effects by binding to specialized receptors in the brain* (Pert & Snyder, 1973).

This discovery raised a perplexing question: Why would the brain be equipped with receptors for morphine, a powerful, addictive opiate drug not normally found in the body? It occurred to Pert and others that the nervous system must have its own, endogenous (internally produced) morphinelike substances. Investigators dubbed these as-yet undiscovered substances "endorphins" (endogenous morphines). A search for the body's natural opiate ensued. In short order, a number of endogenous, opiatelike substances were identified (Hughes et al., 1975). Subsequent studies revealed that endorphins and their receptors are widely distributed in the human body. Our homemade opiates appear to contribute to our feelings of pain, pleasure, and hunger.

The term *endorphins* **refers to the entire family of internally produced chemicals that resemble opiates in structure and effects.** Given

that opiate drugs are highly addicting, you may be wondering why people don't become addicted to their own endorphins. Apparently, the reason is that endorphins are quickly inactivated by enzymes. Unlike opiate drugs, they don't remain at receptor sites long enough to cause the tissue changes that probably underlie addiction (Snyder, 1986).

Although they may serve as transmitters at some synapses, *endorphins seem to function primarily as neuromodulators* (Elliott & Barchas, 1986). **Neuromodulators are chemicals that increase or decrease (modulate) the activity of specific neurotransmitters.** Some endorphins, for instance, appear to reduce pain by preventing the release of *substance P*, a transmitter that delivers pain signals to the brain.

The discovery of endorphins has led to revolutionary new theories and findings on the neurochemical bases of pain and pleasure. In addition to their painkilling effects, opiate drugs such as morphine and heroin produce highly pleasurable feelings of euphoria. This euphoric effect explains why heroin is so widely abused. Researchers suspect that the body's natural endorphins may also be capable of producing feelings of pleasure. This capacity might explain why joggers sometimes experience a "runner's high." The pain caused by a long run may trigger the release of endorphins, which neutralize some of the pain and create a feeling of exhilaration (Colt, Wardlaw, & Frantz, 1981). Experts can't help but wonder whether endorphins might be the chemical basis for other pleasant emotions as well (Hopson, 1988).

In this section we have highlighted just a few of the more interesting connections between neurotransmitters and behavior. These highlights barely begin to convey the rich complexity of biochemical processes in the nervous system. Most aspects of behavior are probably regulated by several types of transmitters, and most transmitters appear to be involved in many aspects of behavior (Panksepp, 1986). Although scientists have learned a great deal about neurotransmitters and behavior, much still remains to be discovered.

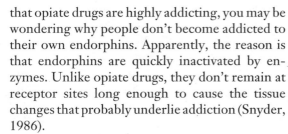

ORGANIZATION OF THE NERVOUS SYSTEM

Clearly, communication in the nervous system is fundamental to behavior. So far we have looked at

---

CONCEPT CHECK 3.2
Linking Brain Chemistry to Behavior

Check your understanding of relations between brain chemistry and behavior by indicating which neurotransmitters (or neuromodulators) have been linked to the phenomena listed below. Choose your answers from the following list: (a) acetylcholine, (b) norepinephrine, (c) dopamine, (d) GABA, (e) endorphins. Indicate your choice (by letter) in the spaces on the left. You'll find the answers in Appendix A.

_____ 1. An inhibitory transmitter linked to anxiety; tranquilizers increase the activity of this transmitter.

_____ 2. A biogenic amine that has been linked to depression.

_____ 3. Chemicals that resemble opiate drugs in structure and that are involved in feelings of pain and pleasure.

_____ 4. A neurotransmitter for which abnormal levels have been implicated in Parkinsonism and schizophrenia.

_____ 5. The only neurotransmitter between motor neurons and voluntary muscles; it also plays a role in memory.

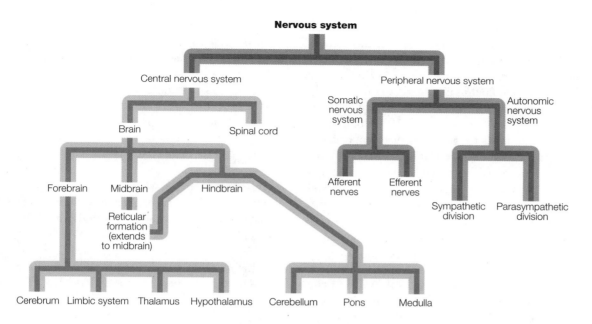

Nervous system

Central nervous system
— Brain
— Spinal cord

Brain:
— Forebrain
— Midbrain
— Hindbrain
— Reticular formation (extends to midbrain)

Forebrain: Cerebrum, Limbic system, Thalamus, Hypothalamus
Hindbrain: Cerebellum, Pons, Medulla

Peripheral nervous system
— Somatic nervous system
— Autonomic nervous system

Somatic nervous system: Afferent nerves, Efferent nerves
Autonomic nervous system: Sympathetic division, Parasympathetic division

Figure 3.5. Organization of the human nervous system. The central nervous system is composed mostly of the brain, which is traditionally divided into three regions: the hindbrain, the midbrain, and the forebrain. The reticular formation runs through both the midbrain and hindbrain on its way up and down the brainstem. These and other parts of the brain are discussed in detail later in the chapter. The peripheral nervous system is made up of the somatic nervous system, which controls voluntary muscles and sensory receptors, and the autonomic nervous system, which controls smooth muscles, blood vessels, and glands.

how individual cells communicate with one another. In this section, we examine the organization of the nervous system as a whole.

Experts believe that there are *100 to 180 billion* neurons in the human brain (Hubel, 1979; Kolb & Whishaw, 1990). Obviously, this is only an *estimate*. If you counted them nonstop at the rate of one per second, you'd be counting for about 6000 years! The multitudes of neurons in your nervous system have to work together to keep information flowing effectively. To do so, they are organized into teams. The various teams have specialized functions and duties that depend primarily on their location. To see how the nervous system is organized, we will perform a series of "cuts" that will divide it into parts. In many instances, the parts will be divided once again. Figure 3.5 presents an organizational chart that shows the relationships of all the parts of the nervous system.

The Peripheral Nervous System

The first and most important cut separates the *central nervous system* (the brain and spinal cord) from the *peripheral nervous system* (see Figure 3.6). **The *peripheral nervous system* is made up of all those nerves that lie outside the brain and spinal cord.** *Nerves* **are bundles of neuron fibers (axons) that are routed together in the peripheral nervous system.** This portion of the nervous system is just what it sounds like, the part that extends to the periphery (the outside) of the body. The peripheral nervous system can be subdivided into the *somatic nervous system* and the *autonomic nervous system*.

The Somatic Nervous System

The *somatic nervous system* is made up of nerves that connect to voluntary skeletal muscles and to sensory receptors. These nerves are the cables that carry information from receptors in the skin, muscles, and joints to the central nervous system and that carry commands from the CNS to the muscles. These functions require two kinds of nerve fibers. **Afferent nerve fibers are axons that carry information inward to the central nervous system from the periphery of the body. Efferent nerve fibers are axons that carry information outward from the central nervous system to the periphery of the body.** Each body nerve contains many axons of each type. Thus, somatic nerves are "two-way streets" with incoming (afferent) and outgoing (efferent) lanes. The somatic nervous system lets you feel the world and move around in it.

The Autonomic Nervous System

The *autonomic nervous system* is made up of nerves that connect to the heart, blood vessels, smooth muscles, and glands. As its name hints, the autonomic system is a separate (autonomous) system, although it is ultimately controlled by the central nervous system. The autonomic nervous system controls automatic, involuntary, visceral functions that people don't normally think about, such as heart rate, digestion, and perspiration.

The autonomic nervous system mediates much of the physiological arousal that occurs when people experience emotions. For example, imagine that you are walking home alone one night

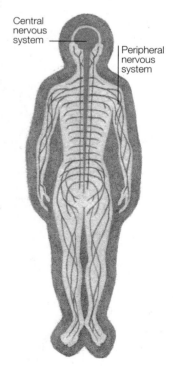

Figure 3.6. The central and peripheral nervous systems. The human nervous system is divided into the *central nervous system*, which consists of the brain and the spinal cord, and the *peripheral nervous system*, which consists of the remaining nerves that fan out throughout the body.

Central nervous system

Peripheral nervous system

when a seedy-looking character falls in behind you and begins to follow you. If you feel threatened, your heart rate and breathing will speed up. Your blood pressure may surge, you may get goose bumps, and your palms may begin to sweat. These difficult-to-control reactions are aspects of autonomic arousal. Walter Cannon (1932), one of the first psychologists to study this reaction, called it the *fight-or-flight response*. Cannon carefully monitored this response in animals. He concluded that organisms generally respond to threat by preparing physically for attacking (fight) or fleeing (flight) the enemy.

The autonomic nervous system can be subdivided into two branches: the sympathetic division and the parasympathetic division (see Figure 3.7). **The *sympathetic division* is the branch of the autonomic nervous system that mobilizes the body's resources for emergencies.** It creates the fight-or-flight response. Activation of the sympathetic division slows digestive processes and drains blood from the periphery, lessening bleeding in the case of an injury. Key sympathetic nerves send signals to the adrenal glands, triggering the release of hormones that ready the body for exer-

tion. In contrast, **the *parasympathetic division* is the branch of the autonomic nervous system that generally conserves bodily resources.** It activates processes that allow the body to save and store energy. For example, actions by parasympathetic nerves slow heart rate, reduce blood pressure, and promote digestion.

The Central Nervous System

The central nervous system is the portion of the nervous system that lies within the skull and spinal column. Thus, **the *central nervous system (CNS)* consists of the brain and the spinal cord.** The CNS is bathed in its own special nutritive "soup," called *cerebrospinal fluid* (CSF). This fluid nourishes the brain and provides a protective cushion for it. Although derived from the blood, the CSF is carefully filtered. To enter the CSF, substances in the blood have to cross **the *blood-brain barrier*, a semipermeable membranelike mechanism that stops some chemicals from passing between the bloodstream and the brain.** This barrier prevents some drugs from entering the CSF and affecting the brain.

The Spinal Cord

The *spinal cord* connects the brain to the rest of the body through the peripheral nervous system. Although the spinal cord looks like a cable from which the somatic nerves branch, it is part of the central nervous system. The spinal cord runs from the base of the brain to just below the level of the waist. It houses bundles of axons that carry the brain's commands to peripheral nerves and that relay sensations from the periphery of the body to the brain. Many forms of paralysis result from spinal cord damage, a fact that underscores the critical role it plays in transmitting signals from the brain to the neurons that move the body's muscles.

The Brain

The crowning glory of the central nervous system is, of course, the brain. Anatomically, the *brain* is the part of the central nervous system that fills the upper portion of the skull. Although it weighs only about three pounds and could be held in one hand, the brain contains billions of interacting cells that integrate information from inside and outside the body, coordinate the body's actions, and enable us to talk, think, remember, plan, create, and dream. Because of its central importance for behavior, the brain is the subject of the next two sections of the chapter.

Figure 3.7. The autonomic nervous system (ANS). The ANS is composed of the nerves that connect to the heart, blood vessels, smooth muscles, and glands. The ANS is divided into the *sympathetic division*, which mobilizes bodily resources in times of need, and the *parasympathetic division*, which conserves bodily resources. Some of the key functions controlled by each division of the ANS are summarized in the diagram.

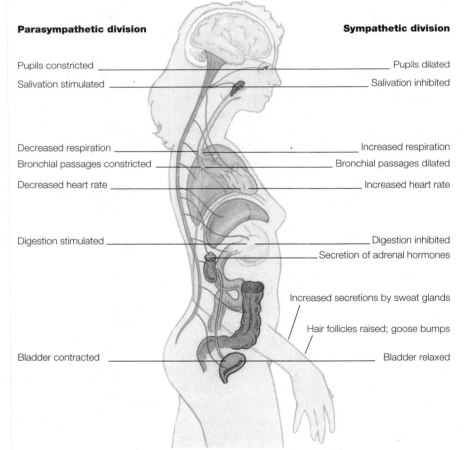

Parasympathetic division

Pupils constricted

Salivation stimulated

Decreased respiration

Bronchial passages constricted

Decreased heart rate

Digestion stimulated

Bladder contracted

Sympathetic division

Pupils dilated

Salivation inhibited

Increased respiration

Bronchial passages dilated

Increased heart rate

Digestion inhibited

Secretion of adrenal hormones

Increased secretions by sweat glands

Hair follicles raised; goose bumps

Bladder relaxed

THE BRAIN AND BEHAVIOR

Scientists who want to find out how parts of the brain are related to behavior are faced with a formidable task because mapping out brain *function* requires a working brain. These scientists use a variety of specialized techniques to investigate brain-behavior relations. For instance, researchers sometimes observe what happens when specific brain structures in animals are purposely destroyed through a process called *lesioning*. This is typically done by inserting an electrode into a brain structure and passing a high-frequency electric current through it to burn the tissue and disable the structure. Another valuable technique is *electrical stimulation of the brain (ESB)*, which involves sending a weak electric current into a brain structure to stimulate (activate) it. As in lesioning, the current is delivered through an implanted electrode, but the current is different. This sort of electrical stimulation does not ex-

actly duplicate normal electrical signals in the brain. However, it is usually a close enough approximation to activate the brain structures in which the electrodes are lodged. Obviously, these invasive procedures are largely limited to animal research, although ESB is occasionally used on humans in the context of brain surgery required for medical purposes.

Fortunately, in recent years, the invention of new brain-imaging devices has led to spectacular advances in scientists' ability to look inside the human brain. The *CT (computerized tomography) scan* is a computer-enhanced X ray of brain structure. Multiple X rays are shot from many angles, and the computer combines the readings to create a vivid image of a horizontal slice of the brain (see Figure 3.8). The more recently developed *MRI (magnetic resonance imaging) scan* uses magnetic fields, radio waves, and computerized enhancement to map out brain structure. MRI scans provide much better images of brain structure than

Figure 3.8. CT technology. CT scans are widely used in research to examine aspects of brain structure. They provide computer-enhanced X rays of horizontal slices of the brain.

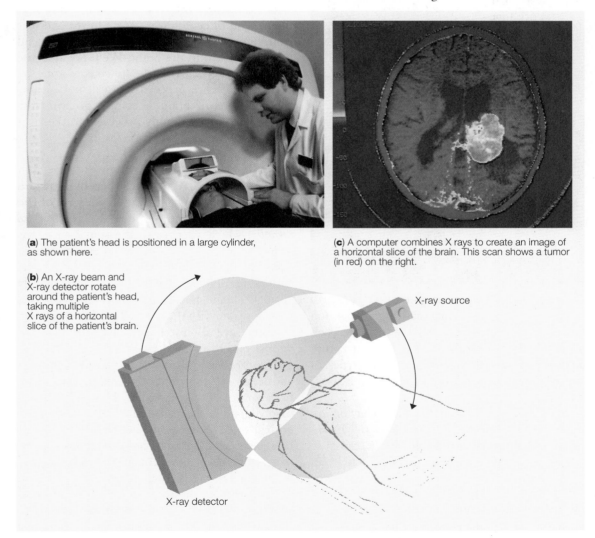

(**a**) The patient's head is positioned in a large cylinder, as shown here.

(**c**) A computer combines X rays to create an image of a horizontal slice of the brain. This scan shows a tumor (in red) on the right.

(**b**) An X-ray beam and X-ray detector rotate around the patient's head, taking multiple X rays of a horizontal slice of the patient's brain.

X-ray source

X-ray detector

Figure 3.9. MRI scans.
MRI scans can be used to produce remarkably high-resolution pictures of brain structure. A vertical view of the left side of a woman's brain is shown here.

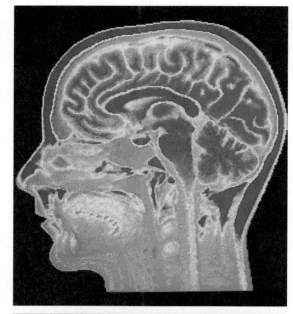

Figure 3.10. PET scans.
PET scans are used to map brain activity. They provide color-coded maps that show areas of high activity in the brain over time. The PET scan shown here pinpointed three areas of high activity (indicated by the color yellow) when a subject worked on a language task.

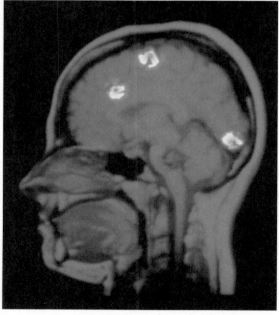

CT scans, producing three-dimensional pictures of the brain that have remarkably high resolution (see Figure 3.9). CT and MRI scans have been used to look for abnormalities in brain structure among people suffering from specific types of mental illness, such as schizophrenia (Andreasen, 1988).

In research on how brain and behavior are related, *PET (positron emission tomography) scans* may prove especially valuable. PET scans use radioactive markers to map chemical activity in the brain over time. Thus, a PET scan can provide a color-coded map indicating which areas of the brain become active and which neurotransmitters are used when subjects clench their fist, sing, or contemplate the mysteries of the universe (see Figure 3.10). In this way, neuroscientists are using PET scans to better pinpoint the brain areas that handle various types of mental activities (Volkow & Tancredi, 1991). Unfortunately, brain imaging techniques are very expensive (for instance, the initial cost of an MRI is $1–$3 million), so their availability for research purposes is limited.

Now that we have discussed a few approaches to brain research, let's look at what scientists have discovered about the functions of different parts of the brain. The brain can be divided into three major regions: the hindbrain, the midbrain, and the forebrain. The principal structures found in each of these regions are listed in the organizational chart of the nervous system in Figure 3.5. You can see where these regions are located in the brain by looking at Figure 3.11. They can be found easily in relation to the *brainstem*. The brainstem looks like its name—it appears to be a stem from which the rest of the brain "flowers," like a head of cauliflower. At its lower end it is contiguous with the spinal cord. At its higher end it lies deep within the brain. We'll begin at the brain's lower end, where the spinal cord joins the brainstem. As we proceed upward, notice how the functions of brain structures go from the regulation of basic bodily processes to the control of "higher" mental processes.

The Hindbrain

The *hindbrain* includes the cerebellum and two structures found in the lower part of the brainstem: the medulla and the pons. The *medulla*, which attaches to the spinal cord, has charge of largely unconscious but essential functions, such as breathing, maintaining muscle tone, and regulating circulation. The *pons* (literally "bridge") includes a bridge of fibers that connects the brainstem with the cerebellum. The pons also contains several clusters of cell bodies involved with sleep and arousal.

The *cerebellum* ("little brain") is a relatively large and deeply folded structure located adjacent to the back surface of the brainstem. The cerebellum is involved in the coordination of movement and is critical to the sense of equilibrium, or physical balance (Ghez, 1991). Although the actual commands for muscular movements come from higher brain centers, the cerebellum plays a key role in the execution of these commands. It is your cerebellum that allows you to hold your hand out to the side and then smoothly bring your finger to a

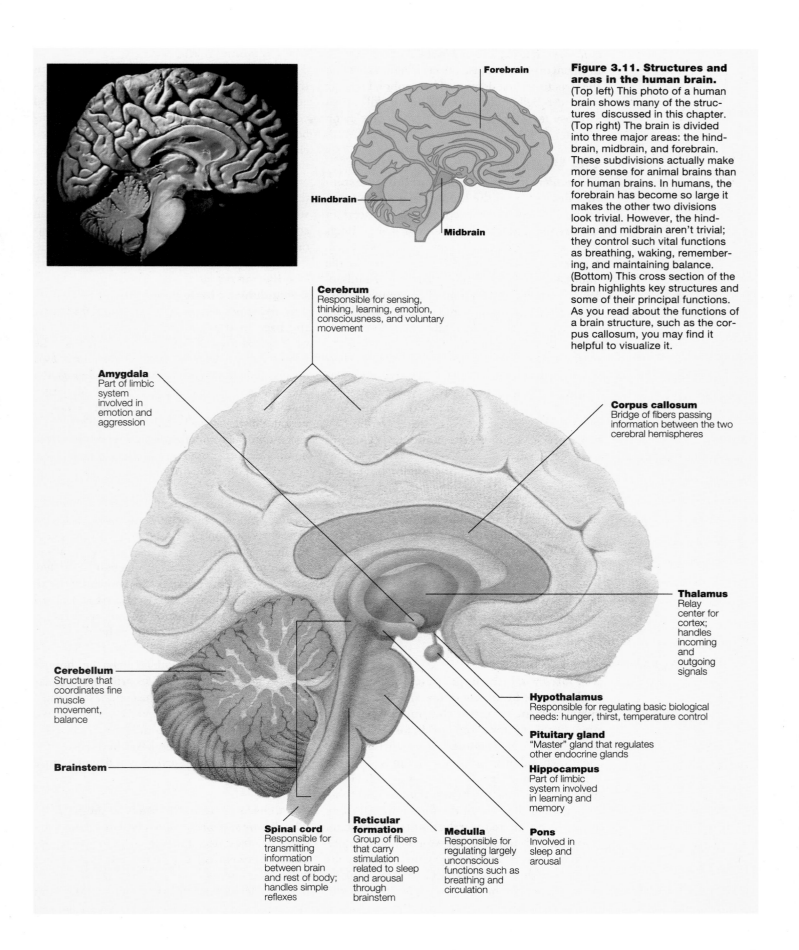

Forebrain

Hindbrain

Midbrain

Figure 3.11. Structures and areas in the human brain. (Top left) This photo of a human brain shows many of the structures discussed in this chapter. (Top right) The brain is divided into three major areas: the hindbrain, midbrain, and forebrain. These subdivisions actually make more sense for animal brains than for human brains. In humans, the forebrain has become so large it makes the other two divisions look trivial. However, the hindbrain and midbrain aren't trivial; they control such vital functions as breathing, waking, remembering, and maintaining balance. (Bottom) This cross section of the brain highlights key structures and some of their principal functions. As you read about the functions of a brain structure, such as the corpus callosum, you may find it helpful to visualize it.

Cerebrum
Responsible for sensing, thinking, learning, emotion, consciousness, and voluntary movement

Amygdala
Part of limbic system involved in emotion and aggression

Corpus callosum
Bridge of fibers passing information between the two cerebral hemispheres

Thalamus
Relay center for cortex; handles incoming and outgoing signals

Cerebellum
Structure that coordinates fine muscle movement, balance

Hypothalamus
Responsible for regulating basic biological needs: hunger, thirst, temperature control

Pituitary gland
"Master" gland that regulates other endocrine glands

Brainstem

Hippocampus
Part of limbic system involved in learning and memory

Spinal cord
Responsible for transmitting information between brain and rest of body; handles simple reflexes

Reticular formation
Group of fibers that carry stimulation related to sleep and arousal through brainstem

Medulla
Responsible for regulating largely unconscious functions such as breathing and circulation

Pons
Involved in sleep and arousal

stop on your nose. This is a useful roadside test for drunken driving because the cerebellum is one of the structures first depressed by alcohol. Damage to the cerebellum disrupts fine motor skills, such as those involved in writing, typing, or playing tennis.

The Midbrain

The *midbrain* is the segment of the brainstem that lies between the hindbrain and the forebrain. The midbrain is concerned with certain sensory processes, such as locating where things are in space. For instance, when a sound triggers a reflexive turning of the head, an area in the midbrain is at work (Middlebrooks & Knudsen, 1984). An important system of dopamine-releasing neurons that projects into various higher brain centers originates in the midbrain. Among other things, this dopamine system is involved in the performance of voluntary movements. *Parkinsonism*, a disease marked by tremors, muscular rigidity, and reduced control over voluntary movements, is apparently caused by a decline in dopamine synthesis that is due to degeneration of a structure located in the midbrain (Coté & Crutcher, 1991).

Running through both the hindbrain and the midbrain is the *reticular formation*. Lying at the central core of the brainstem, the reticular formation contributes to the modulation of muscle reflexes, breathing, and pain perception (Role & Kelly, 1991). It is best known, however, for its role in the regulation of sleep and wakefulness. Activity in the ascending fibers of the reticular formation is essential to maintaining an alert brain (Steriade et al., 1980). Indeed, damage to this area can cause a coma.

The Forebrain

The *forebrain* is the largest and most complex region of the brain, encompassing a variety of structures, including the thalamus, hypothalamus, limbic system, and cerebrum. This list is not exhaustive, and some of these structures have their own subdivisions, as you can see in the organizational chart of the nervous system (Figure 3.5). The thalamus, hypothalamus, and limbic system form the core of the forebrain. All three structures are located near the top of the brainstem. Above them is the *cerebrum*—the seat of complex thought. This relatively large structure may contain 70% of the neurons in the CNS. The wrinkled surface of the cerebrum is the *cerebral cortex*—the outer layer of the brain, the part that looks like a cauliflower.

The Thalamus: A Way Station

The *thalamus* is a structure in the forebrain through which all sensory information (except smell) must pass to get to the cerebral cortex. This way station is made up of a number of clusters of cell bodies, or somas. Each cluster is concerned with relaying sensory information to a particular part of the cortex. However, it would be a mistake to characterize the thalamus as nothing more than a passive relay station. The thalamus also appears to play an active role in integrating information from various senses.

The Hypothalamus:
A Regulator of Biological Needs

The *hypothalamus* is a structure found near the base of the forebrain that is involved in the regulation of basic biological needs. The hypothalamus lies beneath the thalamus (*hypo* means "under," making the hypothalamus the area under the thalamus). Although no larger than a kidney bean, the hypothalamus contains various clusters of cells that have many key functions. One such function is to control the autonomic nervous system.

The hypothalamus plays a major role in the regulation of basic biological drives related to survival, including the so-called "four F's": fighting, fleeing, feeding, and mating. For example, when researchers lesion the lateral areas (the sides) of the hypothalamus, animals lose interest in eating. The animals must be fed intravenously or they starve, even in the presence of abundant food. In contrast, when electrical stimulation (ESB) is used to *activate* the lateral hypothalamus, animals eat constantly and gain weight rapidly (Grossman et al., 1978; Keesey & Powley, 1975). Does this mean that the lateral hypothalamus is the "hunger center" in the brain? Not necessarily. The regulation of hunger turns out to be complex and multifaceted, as you'll see in Chapter 10. Nonetheless, the hypothalamus clearly contributes to the control of hunger and other basic biological processes, including thirst, sex drive, and temperature regulation.

The Limbic System: The Seat of Emotion

The *limbic system* is a loosely connected network of structures located roughly along the border between the cerebral cortex and deeper subcortical areas (hence the term *limbic*, which means "edge"). First described by Paul MacLean (1954), the limbic system is *not* a well-defined anatomical system with clear boundaries. Indeed,

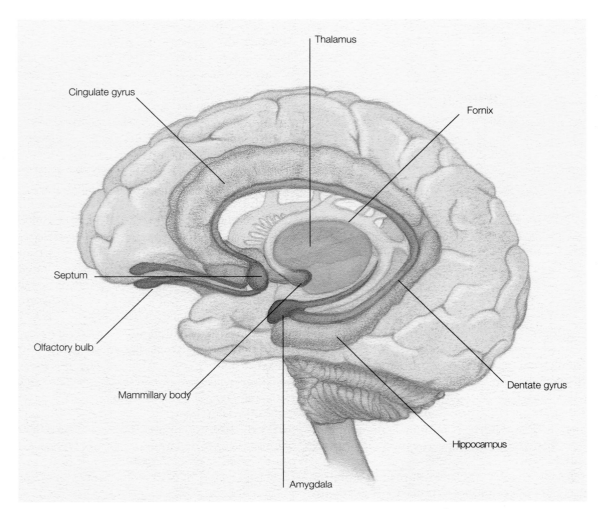

Figure 3.12. The limbic system. The limbic system is a network of interconnected structures that play a role in emotion, motivation, memory, and many other aspects of behavior. These structures fall mostly along the border between the cortex and deeper, subcortical areas.

Thalamus

Cingulate gyrus

Fornix

Septum

Olfactory bulb

Mammillary body

Dentate gyrus

Hippocampus

Amygdala

scientists disagree about which structures should be included in the limbic system. Broadly defined, the limbic system includes parts of the thalamus and hypothalamus, the *hippocampus*, the *amygdala*, the *septum*, and other structures that are shown in Figure 3.12.

The hippocampus makes an important contribution to the formation of memories (Berger, 1984), but the limbic system is best known for its role in the regulation of emotion. The limbic system appears to contain emotion-tinged "pleasure centers." This intriguing possibility first surfaced, quite by chance, in brain stimulation research with rats.

James Olds and Peter Milner (1954) accidentally discovered that a rat would press a lever repeatedly to send brief bursts of electrical stimulation to a specific spot in its brain where an electrode was implanted (see Figure 3.13). They thought that they had inserted the electrode in the rat's reticular formation. However, they learned later that the electrode had been bent during implantation and ended up elsewhere (probably in the hypothalamus). Much to their

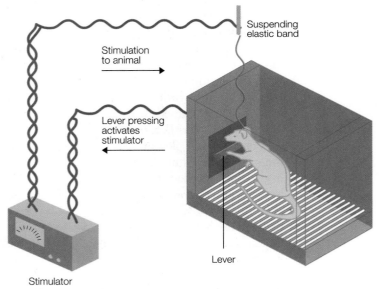

Suspending elastic band

Stimulation to animal

Lever pressing activates stimulator

Lever

Stimulator

Figure 3.13. Electrical stimulation of the brain (ESB) in the rat. Olds and Milner (1954) were using an apparatus like that depicted here when they discovered self-stimulation centers, or "pleasure centers," in the brain of a rat. In this setup, the rat's lever pressing earns brief electrical stimulation that is sent to a specific spot in the rat's brain where an electrode has been implanted.

Figure 3.14. The cerebral hemispheres and the corpus callosum. In this drawing the cerebral hemispheres have been "pulled apart" to reveal the corpus callosum. This band of fibers is the communication bridge between the right and left halves of the human brain.

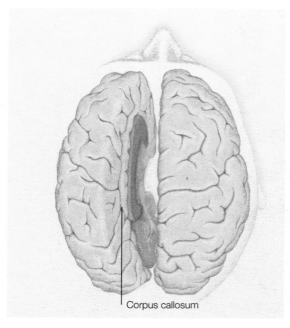

Corpus callosum

surprise, the rat kept coming back for more self-stimulation in this area. Subsequent studies showed that rats and monkeys would press a lever *thousands of times per hour* to stimulate certain brain sites. Although the experimenters obviously couldn't ask the animals about it, they *inferred* that the animals were experiencing some sort of pleasure.

Brain surgery cases have afforded neuroscientists a few opportunities to probe for similar pleasure centers in human subjects. Since they're often conscious during brain surgery, human subjects *can* be asked about their feelings, and electrically activated pleasure centers have indeed been found in humans (Delgado, 1969; Heath, 1964). However, the emotional reactions in humans have not been as strong as anticipated, given the ferocious way laboratory animals work to earn stimulation of pleasure centers (Valenstein, 1973).

Where are the pleasure centers located in the brain? Many self-stimulation sites have been found in the limbic system (Olds & Fobe, 1981). The heaviest concentration appears to be where the *medial forebrain bundle* (a bundle of axons) passes through the hypothalamus. The medial forebrain bundle is rich in dopamine-releasing neurons. The rewarding effects of ESB at self-stimulation sites may be largely mediated by the activation of these dopamine circuits (Wise & Rompre, 1989). The rewarding, pleasurable effects of opiate and stimulant drugs (cocaine and amphetamines) may also depend on excitation of this dopamine system (Wise & Bozarth, 1987).

The Cerebrum:
The Seat of Complex Thought

The *cerebrum* is the largest and most complex part of the human brain. It includes the brain areas that are responsible for our most complex mental activities, including learning, remembering, thinking, and consciousness itself. **The *cerebral cortex* is the convoluted outer layer of the cerebrum.** The cortex is folded and bent, so that its large surface area—about 1.5 square feet—can be packed into the limited volume of the skull (Hubel & Wiesel, 1979).

The cerebrum is divided into two halves called hemispheres. Hence, **the *cerebral hemispheres* are the right and left halves of the cerebrum** (see Figure 3.14). The hemispheres are separated in the center of the brain by a longitudinal fissure that runs from the front to the back. This fissure descends to a thick band of fibers called the *corpus callosum* (also shown in Figure 3.14). **The *corpus callosum* is the structure that connects the two cerebral hemispheres.** We'll discuss the functional specialization of the cerebral hemispheres in the next section of this chapter.

Each cerebral hemisphere is divided into four parts called *lobes*, more for our convenience than because there really are four distinct pieces. To some extent, each of these lobes is dedicated to specific purposes. The location of these lobes can be seen in Figure 3.15.

The *occipital lobe*, at the back of the head, includes the cortical area where most visual signals are sent and visual processing is begun. This area is called the *primary visual cortex*. We will discuss how it is organized in Chapter 4.

The *parietal lobe* is forward of the occipital lobe. It includes the area that registers the sense of touch, called the *primary somatosensory cortex*. Various sections of this area receive signals from different regions of the body. When ESB is delivered in these parietal lobe areas, people report physical sensations—as if someone actually touched them on the arm or cheek, for example. The parietal lobe is also involved in integrating visual input and in monitoring the body's position in space.

The *temporal lobe* (meaning "near the temples") lies below the parietal lobe. Near its top, the temporal lobe contains an area devoted to auditory processing, the *primary auditory cortex*. As we will see momentarily, damage to an area in the temporal lobe on the left side of the brain can impair the ability to comprehend speech and language.

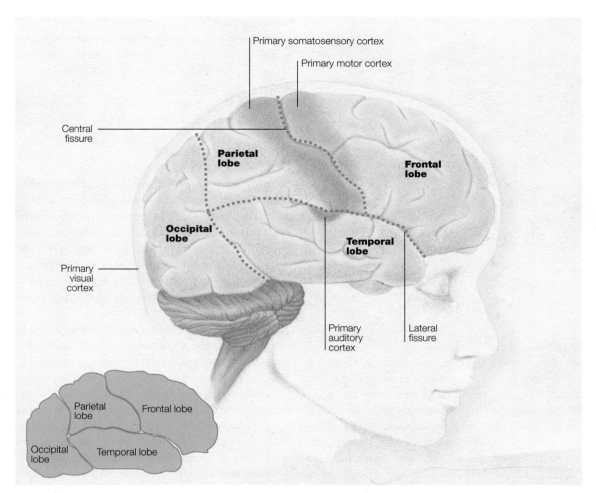

Figure 3.15. The cerebral cortex in humans. The cerebrum is divided into right and left halves, called cerebral hemispheres. This diagram provides a view of the right hemisphere. The cerebral cortex is the outer layer of the cerebrum. It can be thought of as a huge sheet of neural tissue crammed and folded into a small space. The cerebral cortex handles many "higher" intellectual functions. Each cerebral hemisphere can be divided into the four lobes shown in the diagram. Each lobe has areas that handle particular functions, such as visual processing or speech comprehension.

Continuing forward, we find the *frontal lobe*, the largest lobe in the human brain. It contains the principal areas that control the movement of muscles, the *primary motor cortex*. ESB applied in these areas can cause actual muscle contractions. The amount of motor cortex allocated to the control of a body part depends not on the part's size but on the diversity and precision of its movements. Thus, more of the cortex is given to parts we have fine control over, such as fingers, lips, and the tongue. Less of the cortex is devoted to larger parts that make crude movements, such as the thighs and shoulders.

RIGHT BRAIN/LEFT BRAIN: CEREBRAL SPECIALIZATION

As we noted a moment ago, the cerebrum—the seat of complex thought—is divided into two separate hemispheres (see Figure 3.14). Recent decades have seen an exciting flurry of research on the specialized abilities of the right and left cerebral hemispheres. Some theorists have gone so far as to suggest that we really have two brains in one!

Hints of this hemispheric specialization have been available for many years, from cases in which one side of a person's brain has been damaged. The left hemisphere was implicated in the control of language as early as 1861, by Paul Broca, a French surgeon. Broca was treating a patient who had been unable to speak for 30 years. After the patient died, Broca showed that the probable cause of his speech deficit was a localized lesion on the left side of the frontal lobe. Since then, many similar cases have shown that this area of the brain—known as *Broca's area*—plays an important role in the *production* of speech (see Figure 3.16 on the next page). Another major language center—*Wernicke's area*—was identified in the temporal lobe of the left hemisphere in 1874. Damage in Wernicke's area (see Figure 3.16) usually leads to problems with the *comprehension* of language.

Evidence that the left hemisphere usually processes language led scientists to characterize it as

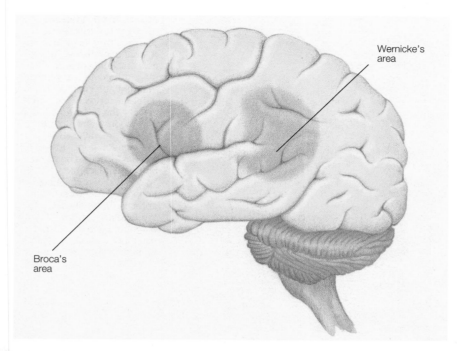

Wernicke's area

Broca's area

Figure 3.16. Language processing in the brain. This view of the left hemisphere highlights the location of two centers for language processing in the brain: *Broca's area*, which is involved in speech production, and *Wernicke's area*, which is involved in language comprehension.

Gazzaniga, and their colleagues who studied "split-brain" patients: individuals whose cerebral hemispheres had been surgically disconnected (Gazzaniga, 1970; Gazzaniga, Bogen, & Sperry, 1965; Levy, Trevarthen, & Sperry, 1972; Sperry, 1982). In 1981 Sperry received a Nobel prize in physiology/medicine for this work.

Bisecting the Brain: Split-Brain Research

In *split-brain surgery* **the bundle of fibers that connects the cerebral hemispheres (the corpus callosum) is cut to reduce the severity of epileptic seizures.** It is a radical procedure that is chosen only in exceptional cases that have not responded to other forms of treatment. But the surgery provides scientists with an unusual opportunity to study people who have had their brain literally split in two.

To appreciate the logic of split-brain research, you need to understand how sensory and motor information is routed to and from the two hemispheres. *Each hemisphere's primary connections are to the opposite side of the body.* Thus, the left hemisphere controls, and communicates with, the right hand, right arm, right leg, right eyebrow, and so on. In contrast, the right hemisphere controls, and communicates with, the left side of the body.

Vision and hearing are more complex. Both eyes deliver information to both hemispheres, but there still is a separation of input. Stimuli in the right half of the *visual field* are registered by receptors on the left side of each eye, which send signals to the left hemisphere. Stimuli in the left half of the

the "dominant" hemisphere. Because thoughts are usually coded in terms of language, the left hemisphere was given the lion's share of credit for handling the "higher" mental processes, such as reasoning, remembering, planning, and problem solving. Meanwhile, the right hemisphere came to be viewed as the "nondominant," or "dumb," hemisphere, lacking any special functions or abilities.

This characterization of the left and right hemispheres as major and minor partners in the brain's work began to change in the 1960s. It all started with landmark research by Roger Sperry, Michael

---

CONCEPT CHECK 3.3

Relating Disorders to the Nervous System

Imagine that you are working as a neuropsychologist at a clinic. You are involved in the diagnosis of the cases described below. You are asked to identify the probable cause(s) of the disorders in terms of nervous system malfunctions. Based on the information in this chapter, indicate the probable location of any brain damage or the probable disturbance of neurotransmitter activity. The answers can be found in the back of the book in Appendix A.

Case 1. Miriam is exhibiting language deficits. In particular, she does not seem to comprehend the meaning of words.

Case 2. Camille displays spastic motor coordination and is diagnosed as having Parkinsonism.

Case 3. Neal, a 72-year-old retired dockworker, has gradually seen his everyday memory deteriorate badly. Sometimes he can't even find his way home from the grocery store a few blocks away. He is diagnosed as having Alzheimer's disease.

Case 4. Wendy is highly irrational, has poor contact with reality, and reports hallucinations. She is given a diagnosis of schizophrenic disorder.

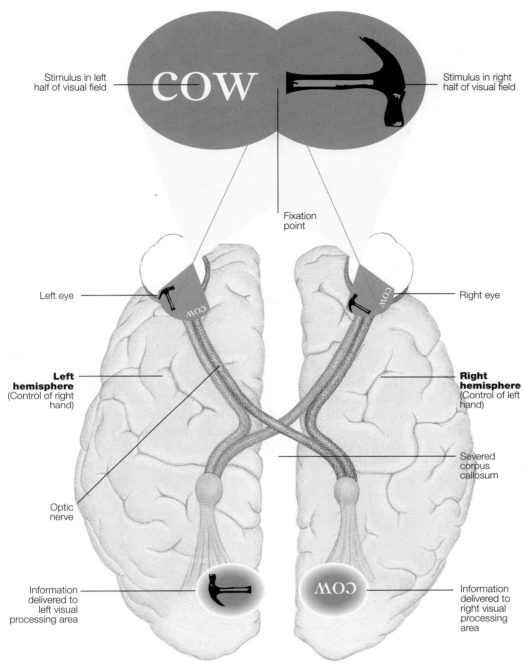

Stimulus in left half of visual field

Stimulus in right half of visual field

Fixation point

Left eye

Right eye

Left hemisphere (Control of right hand)

Right hemisphere (Control of left hand)

Severed corpus callosum

Optic nerve

Information delivered to left visual processing area

Information delivered to right visual processing area

Figure 3.17. Visual input in the split brain. If a subject stares at a fixation point, the point divides the subject's visual field into right and left halves. Input from the right visual field strikes the left side of each eye and is transmitted to the left hemisphere. Input from the left visual field strikes the right side of each eye and is transmitted to the right hemisphere. Normally, the hemispheres share the information from the two halves of the visual field, but in split-brain patients, the corpus callosum is severed, and the two hemispheres cannot communicate. Hence, the experimenter can present a visual stimulus to just one hemisphere at a time.

visual field are transmitted by both eyes to the right hemisphere (see Figure 3.17). Auditory inputs to each ear also go to both hemispheres. However, connections to the opposite hemisphere are stronger or more immediate. That is, sounds presented to the right ear are registered in the left hemisphere first, while sounds presented to the left ear are registered more quickly in the right hemisphere.

For the most part, people don't notice this asymmetric, "crisscrossed" organization because the two hemispheres are in close communica-

tion with each other. Information received by one hemisphere is readily shared with the other via the corpus callosum. However, when the two hemispheres are surgically disconnected, the functional specialization of the brain becomes apparent.

In their classic study of split-brain patients, Gazzaniga, Bogen, and Sperry (1965) presented visual stimuli such as pictures, symbols, and words in a single visual field (the left or the right), so that the stimuli would be sent to only one hemisphere. The stimuli were projected onto a screen in front

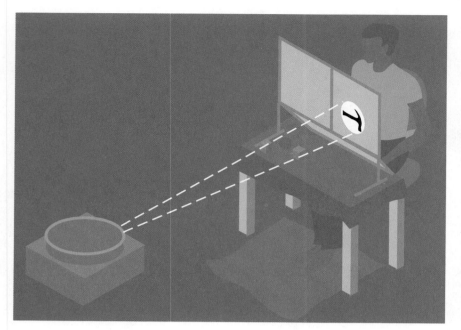

Figure 3.18. Experimental apparatus in split-brain research. On the left is a special slide projector that can present images very briefly, before the subject's eyes can move and thus change the visual field. Images are projected on one side of the screen to present stimuli to just one hemisphere. The portion of the apparatus beneath the screen is constructed to prevent subjects from seeing objects that they may be asked to handle with their right or left hand, another procedure that can be used to send information to just one hemisphere.

"Both the left and right hemispheres of the brain have been found to have their own speciliazed forms of intellect."
ROGER SPERRY

of the subjects, who stared at a fixation point (a spot) in the center of the screen (see Figure 3.18). The images were flashed to the right or the left of the fixation point for only a split second. Thus, the subjects did not have a chance to move their eyes, and the stimuli were only glimpsed in one visual field.

When pictures were flashed in the right visual field and thus sent to the left hemisphere, the split-brain subjects were able to name and describe the objects depicted (such as a cup or spoon). However, the subjects were *not* able to name and describe the same objects when they were flashed in the left visual field and sent to the right hemisphere. In a similar fashion, an object placed out of view in the right hand (communicating with the left hemisphere) could be named. However, the same object placed in the left hand (right hemisphere) could not be. These findings supported the notion that language is housed in the left hemisphere.

Although the split-brain subjects' right hemisphere was not able to speak up for itself, further tests revealed that it *was* processing the information presented. If subjects were given an opportunity to *point out a picture* of an object they had held in their left hand, they were able to do so. They were also able to point out pictures that had been flashed to the left visual field. Furthermore, the right hemisphere (left hand) turned out to be *superior* to the left hemisphere (right hand) in assembling little puzzles and copying drawings, even though the subjects were right-handed. These findings provided the first compelling demonstration that the right hemisphere has its own special

talents. Subsequent studies of additional split-brain patients showed the right hemisphere to be better than the left on a variety of visual-spatial tasks, including discriminating colors, arranging blocks, and recognizing faces.

Hemispheric Specialization in the Intact Brain

The problem with the split-brain operation, of course, is that it creates an abnormal situation. The vast majority of us remain "neurologically intact." Moreover, the surgery is done only with people who suffer from prolonged, severe cases of epilepsy. These people may have had somewhat atypical brain organization even before the operation. Thus, theorists couldn't help wondering whether it is safe to generalize broadly from the split-brain studies. For this reason, researchers developed methods that allowed them to study cerebral specialization in the intact brain.

One method involves looking at left-right imbalances in visual or auditory processing, called *perceptual asymmetries*. As we just discussed, it is possible to present visual stimuli to just one visual field at a time. In normal individuals, the input sent to one hemisphere is quickly shared with the other. However, subtle differences in the "abilities" of the two hemispheres can be detected by precisely measuring how long it takes subjects to recognize different types of stimuli.

For instance, when *verbal* stimuli are presented to the right visual field (and thus sent to the *left hemisphere* first), they are identified more quickly and more accurately than when they are presented to the left visual field (and sent to the right hemisphere first). The faster reactions in the left hemisphere presumably occur because it can recognize verbal stimuli on its own, while the right hemisphere has to take extra time to "consult" the left hemisphere. In contrast, the *right hemisphere* is faster than the left on *visual-spatial* tasks, such as locating a dot or recognizing a face (Bradshaw, 1989; Bryden, 1982).

Researchers have also used a variety of other approaches to explore hemispheric specialization in normal people. Ultimately, they have concluded that the two hemispheres handle different cognitive tasks (Springer & Deutsch, 1993). *The left hemisphere usually handles verbal processing, such as language, speech, reading, and writing. The right hemisphere usually handles nonverbal processing, such as that required by spatial, musical, and visual recognition tasks.* These findings have interesting implications for our understanding of mental processes. We will examine these provocative implications in

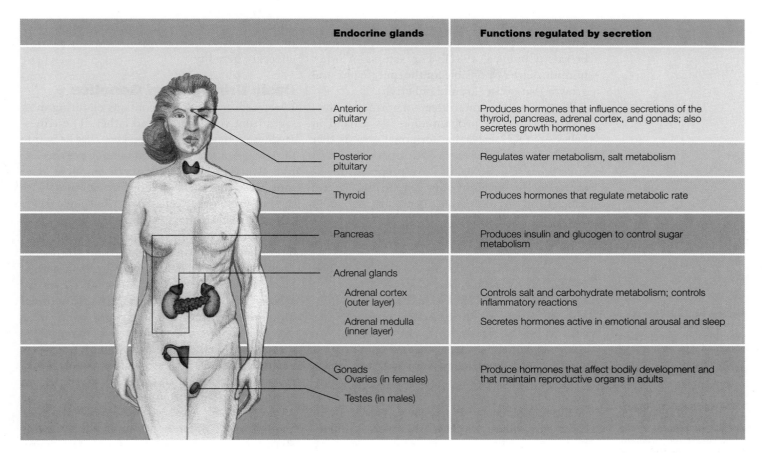

Endocrine glands	Functions regulated by secretion
Anterior pituitary	Produces hormones that influence secretions of the thyroid, pancreas, adrenal cortex, and gonads; also secretes growth hormones
Posterior pituitary	Regulates water metabolism, salt metabolism
Thyroid	Produces hormones that regulate metabolic rate
Pancreas	Produces insulin and glucogen to control sugar metabolism
Adrenal glands	
Adrenal cortex (outer layer)	Controls salt and carbohydrate metabolism; controls inflammatory reactions
Adrenal medulla (inner layer)	Secretes hormones active in emotional arousal and sleep
Gonads Ovaries (in females) Testes (in males)	Produce hormones that affect bodily development and that maintain reproductive organs in adults

Figure 3.19. The endocrine system. The endocrine glands secrete hormones into the bloodstream. These hormones regulate physical functions and may affect behavior.

the Application. For now, however, let's leave the brain and turn our attention to the endocrine system.

THE ENDOCRINE SYSTEM: ANOTHER WAY TO COMMUNICATE

The major way the brain communicates with the rest of the body is through the nervous system. However, the body has a second communication system that is also important to behavior. **The** *endocrine system* **consists of glands that secrete chemicals into the bloodstream that help control bodily functioning.** The messengers in this communication network are called hormones. *Hormones* **are the chemical substances released by the endocrine glands.** The endocrine system tends to be involved in the long-term regulation of basic bodily processes, as its action can't match the high speed of neural transmission. The major endocrine glands and their functions are shown in Figure 3.19.

Much of the endocrine system is controlled by the nervous system through the *hypothalamus*. This structure at the base of the forebrain has intimate connections with the pea-sized *pituitary gland*, to

which it is adjacent. **The** *pituitary gland* **releases a great variety of hormones that fan out around the body, stimulating actions in the other endocrine glands.** In this sense, the pituitary is the "master gland" of the endocrine system, although the hypothalamus is the real power behind the throne.

The intermeshing of the nervous system and the endocrine system can be seen in the fight-or-flight response described earlier. In times of stress, the hypothalamus sends signals along two pathways—through the autonomic nervous system and through the pituitary gland—to the adrenal glands (Sapolsky, 1992). In response, the adrenal glands secrete hormones that radiate throughout the body, preparing it to cope with an emergency (see Chapter 13).

Hormones also play important roles in modulating human physiological development. For example, among the more interesting hormones released by the pituitary are the *gonadotropins*, which affect the *gonads*, or sexual glands. Prior to birth, these hormones direct the formation of the external sexual organs in the developing fetus (Breedlove, 1992). Thus, your sexual identity as a male or female was shaped during prenatal development by the actions of hormones. At puberty, increased levels of sexual hormones are responsible for the emergence of secondary sexual characteristics, such as male facial hair and female breasts (Chumlea, 1982). The actions of other hormones are responsible for the spurt in physical growth that occurs around puberty.

These developmental effects of hormones illustrate how genetic programming has a hand in behavior. Obviously, the hormonal actions that launched your adolescent growth spurt and sparked your interest in sexuality were preprogrammed over a decade earlier by your genetic inheritance, which brings us to the role of heredity in shaping behavior.

HEREDITY AND BEHAVIOR: IS IT ALL IN THE GENES?

Most people realize that physical characteristics such as height, hair color, blood type, and eye color are largely shaped by heredity. But what about psychological characteristics, such as intelligence, moodiness, impulsiveness, and shyness? To what extent are people's behavioral qualities molded by their genes? As we saw in Chapter 1, questions about the relative importance of heredity versus environment are very old ones in psychology. The nature versus nurture debate will continue to surface in many of the upcoming chapters. To help you appreciate the complexities of this debate, we will outline some basic principles of genetics and describe the methods that investigators use to assess the effects of heredity.

Basic Principles of Genetics

Every cell in your body contains enduring messages from your mother and father. These messages are found on the *chromosomes* that lie within the nucleus of each cell. **Chromosomes are thread-like strands of DNA (deoxyribonucleic acid) molecules that carry genetic information.** With the exception of sex cells (sperm and eggs), every cell in humans contains 46 chromosomes. These chromosomes operate in 23 pairs, with one chromosome of each pair coming from each parent. Each chromosome, in turn, contains thousands of biochemical messengers called genes. **Genes are DNA segments that serve as the key functional units in hereditary transmission.**

If all offspring are formed by a union of the parents' sex cells, why aren't family members identical clones? The reason is that a single pair of parents can produce an extraordinary variety of combinations of chromosomes. Each parent's 23 chromosome pairs can be scrambled in over 8 million (2^{23}) different ways, yielding roughly 70 trillion possible configurations when sperm and egg unite. Thus, genetic transmission is a complicated process, and everything is a matter of probability. Except for identical twins, each person ends up with a unique genetic blueprint.

Although different combinations of genes explain why family members aren't all alike, the overlap among these combinations explains why family members do tend to resemble one another. Members of a family share more of the same genes than nonmembers. Ultimately, each person shares half of her or his genes with each parent. On the average, full siblings (except identical twins) also share half their genes. More distant relatives share smaller proportions of genes. Figure 3.20 shows the amount of genetic overlap for various kinship relations. The proportion of shared genes ranges from 100% for identical twins down to a mean of 6.25% for second cousins.

Like chromosomes, genes operate in pairs, with one gene of each pair coming from each parent. In the simplest scenario, a single pair of genes determines a trait. Eye color provides a nice example. However, most human characteristics appear to be **polygenic traits, or characteristics that are influenced by more than one pair of genes.** For example, three to five gene pairs are thought to interactively determine skin color.

Figure 3.20. Genetic overlap in relatives. Research on the genetic bases of behavior takes advantage of the different degrees of genetic overlap between various types of relatives. If heredity influences a trait, then relatives who share more genes should be more similar with regard to that trait than are more distant relatives, who share fewer genes. Comparisons involving various degrees of biological relationships will come up frequently in later chapters.

Relationship	Degree of relatedness	Genetic overlap
Identical twins		100%
Fraternal twins Brother or sister Parent or child	First degree	50%
Grandparent or grandchild Uncle, aunt, nephew, or niece Half-brother or half-sister	Second degree	25%
First cousin	Third degree	12.5%
Second cousin	Fourth degree	6.25%
Unrelated		0%

Complex physical abilities, such as motor coordination, may be influenced by tangled interactions among a great many pairs of genes. Most psychological characteristics that appear to be affected by heredity seem to involve very complex polygenic inheritance.

Detecting Hereditary Influence: Research Methods

How do scientists disentangle the effects of genetics and experience to determine how heredity affects human behavior? Researchers have designed special types of studies to assess the impact of heredity. The three most important methods are family studies, twin studies, and adoption studies.

Family Studies

In *family studies* researchers assess hereditary influence by examining blood relatives to see how much they resemble one another on a specific trait. If heredity affects the trait under scrutiny, researchers should find trait similarity among relatives. Furthermore, they should find more similarity among relatives who share more genes. For instance, siblings should exhibit more similarity than cousins.

Illustrative of this method are the numerous family studies conducted to assess the contribution of heredity to the development of schizophrenic disorders. These disorders strike approximately 1% of the population, yet 9% of the siblings of schizophrenic patients exhibit schizophrenia themselves (Gottesman, 1991). Thus, these first-degree relatives of schizophrenic patients show a risk for the disorder that is nine times higher than normal. This risk is greater than that observed for more distantly related, second-degree relatives, such as nieces and nephews (4%), which is greater than that found for third-degree relatives, such as second cousins (2%), and so on. This pattern of results is consistent with the hypothesis that genetic inheritance influences the development of schizophrenic disorders (Gottesman, 1993).

Family studies can indicate whether a trait runs in families. However, this correlation does not provide conclusive evidence that the trait is influenced by heredity. Why not? Because family members generally share not only genes but also similar environments. Furthermore, closer relatives are more likely to live together than more distant relatives. Thus, genetic similarity and environmental similarity *both* tend to be greater for closer relatives. Either of these confounded variables could be responsible when greater trait similarity is found in closer relatives. Family studies can offer useful insights about the possible impact of heredity, but they cannot provide definitive evidence.

Twin Studies

Twin studies can yield better evidence about the possible role of genetic factors. **In *twin studies* researchers assess hereditary influence by comparing the resemblance of identical twins and fraternal twins with respect to a trait.** *Identical (monozygotic) twins* emerge when a single fertilized egg splits for unknown reasons. Thus, they have exactly the same genetic blueprint; their genetic overlap is 100%. *Fraternal (dizygotic) twins* result when two separate eggs are fertilized simultaneously. Fraternal twins are no more alike in genetic makeup than any two siblings born to a pair of parents at different times. Their genetic overlap averages 50%.

Fraternal twins provide a useful comparison to identical twins because in both cases the twins usually grow up in the same home, at the same time, exposed to the same configuration of relatives, neighbors, peers, teachers, events, and so forth. Thus, both kinds of twins normally develop under equally similar environmental conditions. However, identical twins share more genetic kinship than fraternal twins. Consequently, if sets of identical twins tend to exhibit more similarity on a trait than sets of fraternal twins do, it is reasonable to infer that this greater similarity is probably due to heredity.

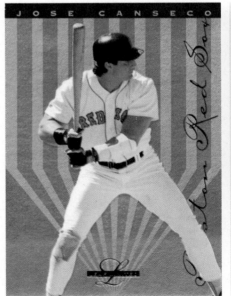

Ozzie Canseco

The Canseco twins appear to provide a dramatic illustration of how heredity and experience jointly influence many complex behavioral traits—in this case, baseball ability. Jose and Ozzie Canseco are identical twins, and the genetic inheritance that they share probably has much to do with the fact that both have demonstrated exceptional baseball ability by becoming professional baseball players. However, differences in their experiences probably explain why one brother (Jose) has become a superstar, whereas the other (Ozzie) has knocked around in the minor leagues for most of his career.

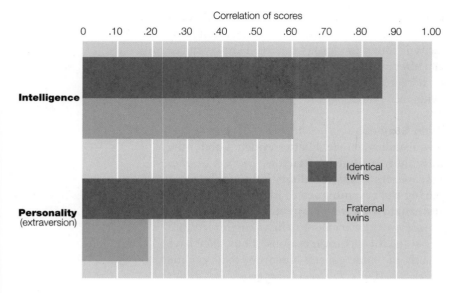

Correlation of scores

0   .10   .20   .30   .40   .50   .60   .70   .80   .90   1.00

Intelligence

Personality
(extraversion)

Identical twins

Fraternal twins

Figure 3.21. Twin studies of intelligence and personality. Identical twins tend to be more similar than fraternal twins (as reflected in higher correlations) with regard to general mental ability and specific personality traits, such as extraversion. These findings suggest that intelligence and personality are influenced by heredity. (Intelligence data from McGue et al., 1993; extraversion data based on Loehlin, 1992)

Twin studies have been conducted to assess the impact of heredity on many different traits. Some representative results are summarized in Figure 3.21. The higher correlations found for identical twins indicate that they tend to be more similar to each other than fraternal twins on measures of general intelligence (McGue et al., 1993) and measures of specific personality traits, such as extraversion (Loehlin, 1992). These results support the notion that these traits are influenced to some degree by genetic makeup.

Adoption Studies

Adoption studies **assess hereditary influence by examining the resemblance between adopted**

children and both their biological and their adoptive parents. If adopted children resemble their biological parents on a trait, even though they were not raised by them, genetic factors probably influence that trait. In contrast, if adopted children resemble their adoptive parents, even though they inherited no genes from them, environmental factors probably influence the trait.

In recent years, adoption studies have contributed to science's understanding of how genetics and the environment influence intelligence. The research shows significant similarity between adopted children and their biological parents, as indicated by an average correlation of .36 (Vandenberg & Vogler, 1985). Interestingly, adopted children resemble their adoptive parents nearly as much (average correlation of .31). These findings indicate that both heredity and environment have an influence on intelligence.

The Cutting Edge: Genetic Mapping

While behavioral geneticists have recently made great progress in documenting the influence of heredity on behavior, *molecular geneticists*, who study the biochemical bases of genetic inheritance, have made even more spectacular advances in their efforts to unravel the genetic code. *Genetic mapping* **is the process of determining the location and chemical sequence of specific genes on specific chromosomes.** New methods of manipulating DNA are now allowing scientists to create detailed physical maps of the genetic material on chromosomes in plants, animals, and humans. A huge, 15-year international project intended to map out the estimated 100,000 genes found on the 23 pairs of human chromosomes is well under way. Gene maps, by themselves, do not reveal which genes govern which traits. However, the compilation of a precise genetic atlas will produce a quantum leap in the ability of scientists to pinpoint links between specific genes and specific traits and disorders. For example, medical researchers have already identified the genes responsible for cystic fibrosis, Huntington's chorea, and muscular dystrophy (Wingerson, 1990). These discoveries promise to yield dramatic advances in the diagnosis and treatment of these diseases.

Will genetic mapping permit researchers to discover the genetic basis for intelligence, extraversion, musical ability, and other *behavioral* traits? Perhaps eventually, but progress is likely to be very gradual. Thus far, the major medical breakthroughs from genetic mapping have involved dichotomous traits (you either do or do not have

CONCEPT CHECK 3.4
Recognizing Hereditary Influence

Check your understanding of the methods scientists use to explore hereditary influences on specific behavioral traits by filling in the blanks in the descriptive statements below. The answers can be found in the back of the book in Appendix A.

1. The findings from family studies indicate that heredity may influence a trait if _____ show more trait similarity than _____.

2. The findings from twin studies suggest that heredity influences a trait if _____ show more trait similarity than _____.

3. The findings from adoption studies suggest that heredity influences a trait if children adopted at a young age share more trait similarity with their _____ than their _____.

4. The findings from family studies, twin studies, or adoption studies suggest that heredity does not influence a trait when _____ is not related to _____.

the trait, such as muscular dystrophy) governed by a single gene pair. However, most behavioral traits do not involve a dichotomy, as everyone has varying amounts of intelligence, musical ability, and so forth. Moreover, virtually all behavioral traits appear to be *polygenic* traits that are shaped by many genes rather than a single gene pair. Because of these complexities, scientists are not likely to find the gene that controls intelligence, extraversion, or musical talent (Plomin, 1993). Instead, the challenge will be to identify specific constellations of genes that each exert modest influence over particular aspects of behavior (McClearn et al., 1991).

The Interplay of Heredity and Environment

We began this section by asking, is it all in the genes? When it comes to behavioral traits, the answer clearly is no. According to Robert Plomin (1993), perhaps the leading behavioral genetics researcher in the last decade, what scientists find again and again is that heredity and experience jointly influence most aspects of behavior. Moreover, their effects are interactive—they play off each other.

For example, consider what researchers have learned about the development of schizophrenic disorders. Although the evidence indicates that genetic factors influence the development of schizophrenia, it does *not* appear that anyone directly inherits the disorder itself. Rather, what people appear to inherit is a certain degree of *vulnerability* to the disorder (Zubin, 1986). Whether this vulnerability is ever converted into an actual disorder depends on each person's experiences in life. As we will discuss in Chapter 14, certain types of experience seem to evoke the disorder in people who are more vulnerable to it.

PUTTING IT IN PERSPECTIVE

Three of our seven themes stood out in this chapter: (1) heredity and environment jointly influence behavior, (2) behavior is determined by multiple causes, and (3) psychology is empirical. Let's look at each of these points.

In Chapter 1, when it was first emphasized that heredity and environment jointly shape behavior, you may have been a little perplexed about how your genes could be responsible for your sarcastic wit or your interest in art. In fact, there are no genes for behavior per se. Experts do not expect to find genes for sarcasm or artistic interest, for example. Insofar as your hereditary endowment plays a role in your behavior, it does so *indirectly*, by molding the physiological machine that you work with. Thus, your genes influence your physiological makeup, which in turn influences your personality, temperament, intelligence, interests, and other traits. Bear in mind, however, that genetic factors do not operate in a vacuum. Genes exert their effects in an environmental context. The impact of genetic makeup depends on environment, and the impact of environment depends on genetic makeup.

It was evident throughout the chapter that behavior is determined by multiple causes, but this reality was particularly apparent in the discussions of schizophrenia. At different points in the chapter we saw that schizophrenia may be a function of (1) abnormalities in neurotransmitter activity (especially dopamine), (2) structural abnormalities in the brain identified with CT and MRI scans, and (3) genetic vulnerability to the illness. These findings do not contradict one another. Rather, they demonstrate that a complex array of biological factors are involved in the development of schizophrenia. In Chapter 14, we'll see that a host of environmental factors also play a role in the multifactorial causation of schizophrenia.

The empirical nature of psychology was apparent in the numerous discussions of the specialized research methods used to study the physiological bases of behavior. As you know, the empirical approach depends on precise observation. Throughout this chapter, you've seen how investigators have come up with innovative methods to observe and measure elusive phenomena such as neural impulses, brain function, cerebral specialization, and the impact of heredity on behavior. The point is that empirical methods are the lifeblood of the scientific enterprise. When researchers figure out how to better observe something, their findings usually facilitate major advances in our scientific knowledge. That is why the new brain-imaging techniques hold exciting promise for neuroscientists.

The importance of empiricism will also be apparent in the upcoming Application, which looks at popular ideas about the specialized abilities of the right and left halves of the brain as they relate to cognitive processes. You'll see that it is important to learn to distinguish between scientific findings and conjecture based on those findings.

"During the 1970s, I found I had to speak gingerly about genetic influence, gently suggesting that heredity might be important in behavior. Now, however, the transformation of the social and behavioral sciences from environmentalism to biological determinism is happening so fast that I find I more often have to say, 'Yes, genetic influences are substantial, but environmental influences are important, too.'"
ROBERT PLOMIN

Thinking Critically About the Concept of "Two Minds in One"

Answer the following "true" or "false."

___ 1 Each half of the brain has its own special mode of thinking.

___ 2 Some people are left-brained while others are right-brained.

___ 3 Our schools should devote more effort to teaching the overlooked right side of the brain.

Do we have two minds in one that think differently? Do some of us depend on one side of the brain more than the other? Is the right side of the brain neglected? These questions are too complex to resolve with a simple "true" or "false," but in this Application we'll take a closer look at the issues involved in these proposed extensions of the findings on cerebral specialization. You'll learn that some of

these ideas are plausible, but in many cases the hype has outstripped the evidence.

Cerebral Specialization and Cognitive Processes

Using a variety of methods, scientists have compiled mountains of data on the specialized abilities of the right and left hemispheres. These findings have led to extensive theorizing about how the right and left brains might be related to cognitive processes. Some of the more intriguing ideas include the following:

1. *The two hemispheres are specialized to process different types of cognitive tasks* (Corballis, 1991; Ornstein, 1977). Research findings have been widely interpreted as showing that the left hemisphere handles verbal tasks, including language, speech, writing, math, and logic, while

the right hemisphere handles nonverbal tasks, including spatial problems, music, art, fantasy, and creativity. These conclusions have attracted a great deal of public interest and media attention. For example, Figure 3.22 shows a *Newsweek* artist's depiction of how the brain supposedly divides its work.

2. *The two hemispheres have different modes of thinking* (Galin, 1974; Joseph, 1992). According to this notion, the documented differences between the hemispheres in dealing with verbal and nonverbal materials are due to more basic differences in *how* the hemispheres process information. This theory holds that the reason the left hemisphere handles verbal material well is that it is analytic, abstract, rational, logical, and linear. In contrast, the right hemisphere is thought to be better equipped to handle spatial and musical material because it is

Figure 3.22. Popular conceptions of hemispheric specialization. As this *Newsweek* diagram illustrates, depictions of hemispheric specialization in the popular press have often been oversimplified.

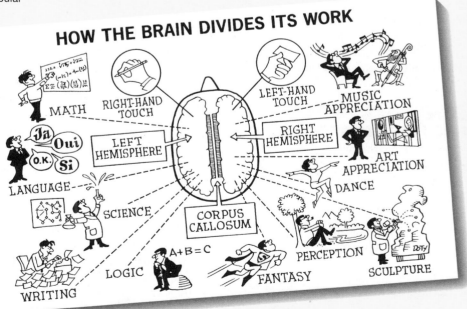

Figure 3.23. Proposed differences between the left and right hemispheres in cognitive style. It is popular to suggest that the two hemispheres exhibit different modes of thinking. This summary, adapted from Edwards (1989), shows that theorists have tried to relate many polarities in cognitive style to the right and left brains. However, as the text explains, there is little evidence to support these proposed dichotomies.

Left Hemisphere's Modes of Thinking	Right Hemisphere's Modes of Thinking
Verbal: Using words to name, describe, define	**Nonverbal:** Showing an awareness of things but minimal connection with words
Analytic: Figuring things out step by step and part by part	**Synthetic:** Putting things together to form wholes
Symbolic: Using a symbol to stand for something	**Analogic:** Seeing likenesses between things; understanding metaphoric relationships
Abstract: Taking out a small bit of information and using it to represent a whole thing	**Concrete:** Relating to things as they are at the present moment
Temporal: Keeping track of time; sequencing one thing after another, doing first things first, second things second, and so forth	**Nontemporal:** Being without a sense of time
Rational: Drawing conclusions based on reason and facts	**Nonrational:** Not requiring a basis of reason or facts; willing to suspend judgment
Digital: Using numbers as in counting	**Spatial:** Seeing where things are in relation to other things and how parts go together to form a whole
Logical: Drawing conclusions based on logic: one thing following another in logical order—for example, developing a mathematical theorem or a well-stated argument	**Intuitive:** Making leaps of insight, often based on incomplete patterns, hunches
Linear: Thinking in terms of linked ideas, one thought directly following another, often leading to a convergent conclusion	**Holistic:** Seeing whole things all at once; perceiving overall patterns and structures, which often leads to divergent conclusions

synthetic, concrete, nonrational, intuitive, and holistic. These proposed hemispheric differences in cognitive style are summarized in Figure 3.23.

3. *People vary in their reliance on one hemisphere as opposed to the other* (Bakan, 1971; Zenhausen, 1978). Allegedly, some people are "left-brained." Their greater dependence on their left hemisphere supposedly makes them analytic, rational, and logical. Other people are "right-brained." Their greater use of their right hemisphere supposedly makes them intuitive, holistic, and irrational. Being right-brained or left-brained is thought to explain many personal characteristics, such as whether an individual likes to read, is good with maps, or enjoys music. This notion of "brainedness" has even been used to explain occupational choice. Supposedly, right-brained people are more likely to become artists or musicians, while left-brained people are more likely to become writers or scientists.

4. *Schools should place more emphasis on teaching the right side of the brain* (Blakeslee, 1980; Prince, 1978). Some educational experts have argued that American schools overemphasize logical, analytical left-hemisphere thinking (required by English, math, and science) while shortchanging intuitive, holistic right-hemisphere thinking (required by art and music). These educators have concluded that modern schools turn out an excess of left-brained graduates. They advocate curriculum reform to strengthen the right side of the brain in their students.

Complexities and Qualifications

The ideas just outlined are the source of considerable debate among psychologists and neuroscientists. These ideas are intriguing and have clearly captured the imagination of the general public. However, the research on cerebral specialization is complex, and these ideas have to be qualified very carefully (Corballis, 1980; Efron, 1990; Kinsbourne, 1982). Let's examine each point.

1. There *is* ample evidence that the right and left hemispheres are specialized to handle different types of cognitive tasks, *but only to a degree*. Doreen Kimura (1973) compared the abilities of the right and left hemispheres to quickly recognize letters, words, faces, and melodies in a series of perceptual asymmetry studies, like those described earlier in the chapter. She found that the superiority of one hemisphere over the other on specific types of tasks was usually quite modest.

In a neurologically intact person, the hemispheres don't work alone. Most tasks probably engage *both* hemispheres, al-

Judith Jamison, a dancer and choreographer, and Marcia Clark, noted prosecutor, exemplify two types of thinking: creative/spatial and logical/analytical. Did the talents of each arise from a different hemisphere?

beit to different degrees (Hellige, 1990). For instance, imagine that you are asked the following question: "In what direction are you headed if you start north and make two right turns and a left turn?" In answering this question, you're confronted with a *spatial* task that should engage the right hemisphere. However, first you have to process the wording of the question, a *language* task that should engage the left hemisphere.

Furthermore, people differ in their patterns of cerebral specialization (Springer & Deutsch, 1993). Some people display little specialization—that is, their hemispheres seem to have equal abilities on various types of tasks. Others even reverse the usual specialization, so that verbal processing might be housed in the right hemisphere. These unusual patterns are especially common among left-handed people (Rasmussen & Milner, 1977). These variations are not well understood yet. However, they clearly indicate that the special abilities of the cerebral hemispheres are not set in concrete.

2. There is little direct evidence to support the notion that each hemisphere has its own mode of thinking, or *cognitive style* (Bradshaw, 1989). The key problem with this idea is that aspects of cognitive style have proven difficult to define and measure (Brownell & Gardner, 1981). For instance, there is great debate about the meaning of analytic versus synthetic thinking, or linear versus holistic thinking.

3. The evidence on the assertion that some people are left-brained while others are right-brained is inconclusive at best (Hellige, 1990). This notion has some plausibility—*if* it means only that some people consistently display more activation of one hemisphere than the other. However, the practical significance of any such "preferences" remains to be determined. At present, researchers do not have convincing data linking brainedness to musical ability, occupational choice, or the like.

4. The idea that schools should be reformed to better exercise the right side of the brain borders on nonsense. In neurologically intact people it is impossible to teach just one hemisphere at a time, and there is no evidence that it is beneficial to "exercise" a part of the brain (Levy, 1985). There are many sound arguments for reforming American schools to encourage more holistic, intuitive thinking, but these arguments have nothing to do with cerebral specialization.

In summary, the theories linking cerebral specialization to cognitive processes are highly speculative. There's nothing wrong with theory-based speculation. Unfortunately, the tentative, conjectural nature of these ideas about hemispheric specialization has gotten lost in the popular magazine descriptions of research on right and left brains (Coren, 1992). Commenting on this popularization, Hooper and Teresi (1986) note: "A widespread cult of the right brain ensued, and the duplex house that Sperry built grew into the K mart of brain science. Today our hairdresser lectures us about the Two Hemispheres of the Brain" (p. 223). Cerebral specialization is an important and intriguing area of research. However, it is unrealistic to expect that the hemispheric divisions in the brain will provide a biological explanation for every dichotomy or polarity in modes of thinking.

Chapter 3 Review

KEY IDEAS

Communication in the Nervous System

♦ Cells in the nervous system receive, integrate, and transmit information. Neurons are the basic communication links. They normally transmit a neural impulse (a change in electrical charge, called an action potential) along an axon to a synapse with another neuron. The action potential is an all-or-none event.

♦ Action potentials trigger the release of chemicals called neurotransmitters that diffuse across a synapse to communicate with other neurons. Transmitters bind with receptors in the postsynaptic cell membrane, causing excitatory or inhibitory postsynaptic potentials that vary in magnitude.

♦ There are a variety of neurotransmitters that bind at specific receptor sites according to a lock-and-key model. The first transmitter identified was ACh, which plays a key role in muscular movement. Disturbances in the activity of the biogenic amine transmitters have been related to the development of depression and schizophrenia. GABA appears to be involved in the regulation of anxiety. Endorphins contribute to the body's feelings of pain and pleasure.

Organization of the Nervous System

♦ The nervous system can be divided into two main subdivisions, the central nervous system and the peripheral nervous system. The central nervous system consists of the brain and spinal cord. The brain plays a crucial role in virtually all aspects of behavior.

♦ The peripheral nervous system consists of the nerves that lie outside the brain and spinal cord. It can be subdivided into the somatic nervous system, which connects to muscles and sensory receptors, and the autonomic nervous system, which connects to blood vessels, smooth muscles, and glands. The autonomic nervous system mediates the largely automatic arousal that accompanies emotion.

The Brain and Behavior

♦ Neuroscientists use a variety of invasive and noninvasive techniques to study the living brain. These methods include lesioning, electrical stimulation, CT scans, MRI scans, and PET scans. The brain has three major regions: the hindbrain, midbrain, and forebrain. Structures in the hindbrain and mid-brain handle essential functions such as breathing, circulation, coordination of movement, and the rhythm of sleep and arousal.

♦ The forebrain includes many structures that handle higher functions. The thalamus is primarily a relay station. The hypothalamus is involved in the regulation of basic biological drives such as hunger and sex. The limbic system is a network of loosely connected structures involved in emotion, motivation, and memory.

♦ The cerebrum is the brain area implicated in most complex mental activities. The cortex is the cerebrum's convoluted outer layer, which is subdivided into four areas. These areas and their primary known functions are the occipital lobe (vision), the parietal lobe (touch), the temporal lobe (hearing), and the frontal lobe (movement of the body).

Right Brain/Left Brain: Cerebral Specialization

♦ The cerebrum is divided into right and left hemispheres connected by the corpus callosum. Evidence that the left cerebral hemisphere usually processes language led scientists to view it as the dominant hemisphere. However, studies of split-brain patients and perceptual asymmetries revealed that the right and left halves of the brain each have unique talents, with the right hemisphere being specialized to handle visual-spatial functions.

The Endocrine System: Another Way to Communicate

♦ The endocrine system consists of the glands that secrete hormones, which are chemicals involved in the regulation of basic bodily processes. The control centers for the endocrine system are the hypothalamus and the pituitary gland.

Heredity and Behavior: Is It All in the Genes?

♦ The basic units of genetic transmission are genes housed on chromosomes. Most behavioral qualities appear to involve polygenic inheritance. Researchers assess hereditary influence through family studies, twin studies, adoption studies, and genetic mapping. These studies indicate that most behavioral traits are influenced by a complex interaction between heredity and environment.

Putting It in Perspective

♦ Three of the book's unifying themes stand out in this chapter. First, we saw how heredity interacts with experience to govern behavior. Second, the discussions of biological factors underlying schizophrenia highlighted the multifactorial causation of behavior. Third, we saw how innovations in research methods often lead to advances in knowledge, underscoring the empirical nature of psychology.

Application: Thinking Critically About the Concept of "Two Minds in One"

♦ Some theorists believe that each cerebral hemisphere has its own special abilities and cognitive style. Some also believe that people vary in their reliance on the right and left halves of the brain and that schools should work more to exercise the right half of the brain.

♦ The cerebral hemispheres are specialized for handling different cognitive tasks, but only to a degree, and people vary in their patterns of specialization. Evidence on whether people vary in braineddness and whether the two hemispheres vary in cognitive style is inconclusive. There is no evidence that exercising a hemisphere of the brain is useful. Popular ideas about the right and left brain have gone far beyond research findings.

KEY TERMS

Absolute refractory period	Hypothalamus
Action potential	Limbic system
Adoption studies	Midbrain
Afferent nerve fibers	Myelin sheath
Agonist	Nerves
Antagonist	Neuromodulators
Autonomic nervous system (ANS)	Neurons
Axon	Neurotransmitters
Blood-brain barrier	Parasympathetic division
Central nervous system (CNS)	Peripheral nervous system
Cerebral cortex	Pituitary gland
Cerebral hemispheres	Polygenic traits
Chromosomes	Postsynaptic potential (PSP)
Corpus callosum	Resting potential
Dendrites	Soma
Efferent nerve fibers	Somatic nervous system
Endocrine system	Split-brain surgery
Endorphins	Sympathetic division
Family studies	Synapse
Forebrain	Synaptic cleft
Genes	Terminal buttons
Genetic mapping	Thalamus
Hindbrain	Twin studies
Hormones	

KEY PEOPLE

Alan Hodgkin and Andrew Huxley	Robert Plomin
James Olds and Peter Milner	Roger Sperry and Michael Gazzaniga
Candace Pert and Solomon Snyder	

4 Sensation and Perception

Take a look at the adjacent photo. What do you see?

You probably answered, "a rose" or "a flower." But is that what you really see? No, this isn't a trick question. Let's examine the odd case of "Dr. P." It shows that there's more to seeing than meets the eye.

Dr. P was an intelligent and distinguished music professor who began to exhibit some worrisome behaviors that seemed to be related to his vision. Sometimes he failed to recognize familiar students by sight, though he knew them instantly by the sound of their voices. Sometimes he acted as if he saw faces in inanimate objects, cordially greeting fire hydrants and parking meters as if they were children. On one occasion, reaching for what he thought was his hat, he took hold of his wife's head and tried to put it on! Except for these kinds of visual mistakes, Dr. P was a normal, talented man.

Ultimately Dr. P was referred to Oliver Sacks, a neurologist, for an examination. During one visit, Sacks handed Dr. P a fresh red rose to see whether he would recognize it. Dr. P took the rose as if he were being given a model of a geometric solid rather than a flower. "About six inches in length," Dr. P observed, "a convoluted red form with a linear green attachment."

"Yes," Sacks persisted, "and what do you think it is, Dr. P?"

"Not easy to say," the patient replied. "It lacks the simple symmetry of the Platonic solids . . ."

"Smell it," the neurologist suggested. Dr. P looked perplexed, as if being asked to smell symmetry, but he complied and brought the flower to his nose. Suddenly, his confusion cleared up. "Beautiful. An early rose. What a heavenly smell" (Sacks, 1987, pp. 13–14).

What accounted for Dr. P's strange inability to recognize faces and familiar objects by sight? There was nothing wrong with his eyes. He could readily spot a pin on the floor. If you're thinking that he *must* have had something wrong with his vision, look again at the photo of the rose. What you see *is* "a convoluted red form with a linear green attachment." It doesn't occur to you to describe it that way only because, without thinking about it, you instantly perceive that combination of form and color as a flower. This is precisely what Dr. P was unable to do. He could see perfectly well, but he was losing the ability to assemble what he saw into a meaningful picture of the world. Technically, he suffered from a condition called *visual agnosia*, an inability to recognize objects through sight. As Sacks (1987) put it,

"Visually, he was lost in a world of lifeless abstractions" (p. 15).

As Dr. P's case illustrates, without effective processing of sensory input, our familiar world can become a chaos of bewildering sensations. To acknowledge the need to both take in and process sensory information, psychologists distinguish between sensation and perception. **Sensation is the stimulation of sense organs. Perception is the selection, organization, and interpretation of sensory input.** Sensation involves the absorption of energy, such as light or sound waves, by sensory organs, such as the eyes and ears. Perception involves organizing and translating sensory input into something meaningful (see Figure 4.1). For example, when you look at the photo of the rose, your eyes are *sensing* the light reflected from the page, including areas of low reflectance where ink has been deposited in an irregular shape. What you *perceive*, however, is a picture of a rose.

The distinction between sensation and perception stands out in Dr. P's case of visual agnosia. His eyes were doing their job of registering sensory input and transmitting signals to the brain. However, damage in his brain interfered with his ability to put these signals together into organized wholes. Thus, Dr. P's process of visual *sensation* was intact, but his process of visual *perception* was severely impaired.

Dr. P's case is unusual, of course. Normally, the processes of sensation and perception are difficult to separate because people automatically start organizing incoming sensory stimulation the

Figure 4.1. The distinction between sensation and perception. Sensation involves the stimulation of sensory organs, whereas perception involves the processing and interpretation of sensory input. As this illustration shows, the two processes merge at the point where sensory receptors convert physical energy into neural impulses.

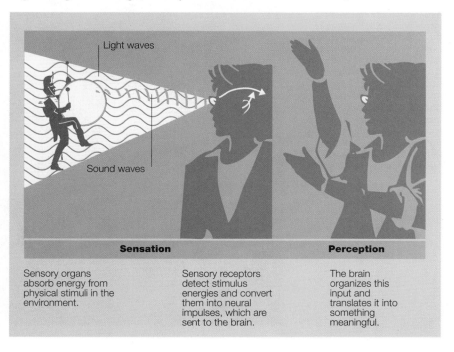

Light waves

Sound waves

Sensation

Perception

Sensory organs absorb energy from physical stimuli in the environment.

Sensory receptors detect stimulus energies and convert them into neural impulses, which are sent to the brain.

The brain organizes this input and translates it into something meaningful.

moment it arrives. The distinction between sensation and perception has been useful in organizing theory and research, but in actual operation the two processes merge.

We'll begin our discussion of sensation and perception with a long look at vision and then take a briefer look at the other senses. As we examine each of the sensory systems, we'll see repeatedly that people's experience of the world depends on both the physical stimuli they encounter (sensation) and their active processing of stimulus inputs (perception). The chapter's Application explores how principles of visual perception come into play in art and illusion.

OUR SENSE OF SIGHT: THE VISUAL SYSTEM

"Seeing is believing." Good ideas are "bright," and a good explanation is "illuminating." This section is an "overview." Do you see the point? As these common expressions show, humans are visual animals. People rely heavily on their sense of sight, and they virtually equate it with what is trustworthy (seeing is believing). Although it is taken for granted, you'll see (there it is again) that the human visual system is amazingly complex.

Furthermore, as in all sensory domains, what people "sense" and what they "perceive" may be quite different.

The Stimulus: Light

For people to see, there must be light. *Light* is a form of electromagnetic radiation that travels as a wave, moving, naturally enough, at the speed of light. As Figure 4.2(a) shows, light waves vary in *amplitude* (height) and in *wavelength* (the distance between peaks). Amplitude affects mainly the perception of brightness, while wavelength affects mainly the perception of color. The lights humans normally see are mixtures of different wavelengths. Hence, light can also vary in its *purity* (how varied the mix is). Purity influences perception of the saturation or richness of colors. Saturation is difficult to describe, but if you glance ahead to Figure 4.9, you'll find it clearly illustrated. Of course, most objects do not emit light, they reflect it (the sun, lamps, and fireflies being some exceptions).

What most people call light includes only the wavelengths that humans can see. But as Figure 4.2(c) shows, the visible spectrum is only a slim portion of the total range of wavelengths. Vision is a filter that permits people to sense only a fraction of the real world. Other animals have

Figure 4.2. Light, the physical stimulus for vision. (**a**) Light waves vary in amplitude and wavelength. (**b**) Within the spectrum of visible light, amplitude (corresponding to physical intensity) affects mainly the experience of brightness. Wavelength affects mainly the experience of color, and purity is the key determinant of saturation. (**c**) If white light (such as sunlight) passes through a prism, the prism separates the light into its component wavelengths, creating a rainbow of colors. However, visible light is only the narrow band of wavelengths to which human eyes happen to be sensitive.

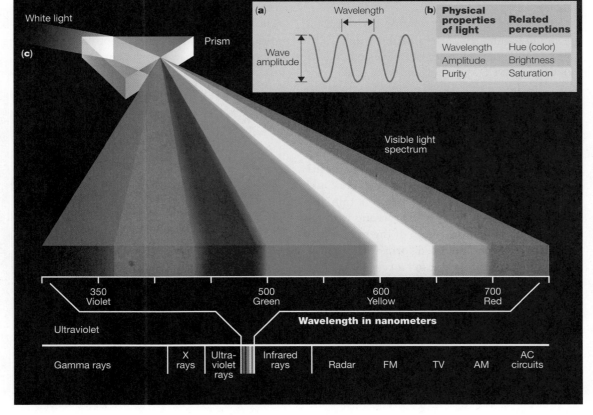

different capabilities and so live in a quite different visual world. For example, many insects can see shorter wavelengths than humans can see, in the *ultraviolet* spectrum, whereas many fish and reptiles can see longer wavelengths, in the *infrared* spectrum.

Although the sense of sight depends on light waves, for people to *see*, incoming visual input must be converted into neural impulses that are sent to the brain. Let's investigate how this transformation is accomplished.

The Eye: A Living Optical Instrument

The eyes serve two main purposes: they channel light to the neural tissue that receives it, called the *retina*, and they house that tissue. The structure of the eye is shown in Figure 4.3. Each eye is a living optical instrument that creates an image of the visual world on the light-sensitive retina lining its inside back surface.

Light enters the eye through a transparent "window" at the front, the *cornea*. The cornea and the

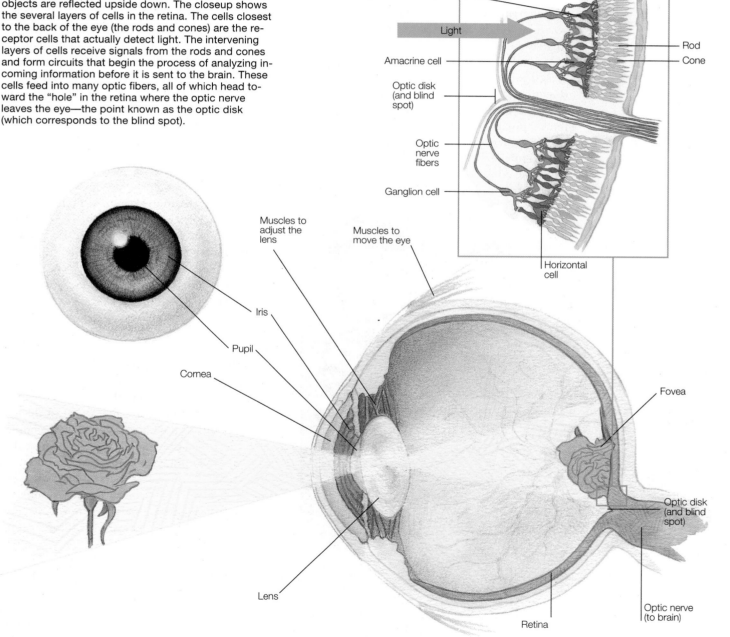

Figure 4.3. The human eye and retina. Light passes through the cornea, pupil, and lens and falls on the light-sensitive surface of the retina, where images of objects are reflected upside down. The closeup shows the several layers of cells in the retina. The cells closest to the back of the eye (the rods and cones) are the receptor cells that actually detect light. The intervening layers of cells receive signals from the rods and cones and form circuits that begin the process of analyzing incoming information before it is sent to the brain. These cells feed into many optic fibers, all of which head toward the "hole" in the retina where the optic nerve leaves the eye—the point known as the optic disk (which corresponds to the blind spot).

crystalline *lens*, located behind it, form an upside-down image of objects on the retina. It might seem disturbing that the image is upside down, but the arrangement works. It doesn't matter how the image sits on the retina, as long as the brain knows the rule for relating positions on the retina to the corresponding positions in the world. **The *lens* is the transparent eye structure that focuses the light rays falling on the retina.** The lens is made up of relatively soft tissue, capable of adjustments that facilitate a process called accommodation. *Accommodation* occurs when the curvature of the lens adjusts to alter visual focus. When you focus on a close object, the lens of your eye gets fatter (rounder) in order to give you a clear image. When you focus on distant objects, the lens flattens out to give you a better image of them.

A number of common visual deficiencies are caused by focusing problems or defects in the lens (Guyton, 1991). For example, **in *nearsightedness*, close objects are seen clearly but distant objects appear blurry** because the focus of light from distant objects falls a little short of the retina (see Figure 4.4). This focusing problem occurs when the cornea or lens bend light too much, or when the eyeball is too long. **In *farsightedness*,**

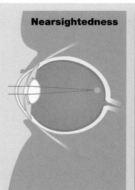
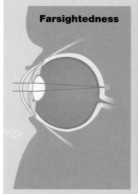

Figure 4.4. Nearsightedness and farsightedness. The photos on the right simulate how a scene might look to nearsighted and farsighted people. Nearsightedness occurs because light from distant objects focuses in front of the retina. Farsightedness is due to the opposite situation—light from close objects focuses behind the retina.

distant objects are seen clearly but close objects appear blurry because the focus of light from close objects falls behind the retina (see Figure 4.4). This focusing problem typically occurs when the eyeball is too short. A *cataract* is a lens that is clouded. This defect occurs mainly in older age groups, affecting three out of four people over the age of 65.

The eye also makes adjustments to alter the amount of light reaching the retina. The *iris* is the colored ring of muscle surrounding the *pupil*, or black center of the eye. **The *pupil* is the opening in the center of the iris that helps regulate the amount of light passing into the rear chamber of the eye.** When the pupil constricts, it lets less light into the eye, but it sharpens the image falling on the retina. When the pupil dilates (opens), it lets more light in, but the image is less sharp. In bright light, the pupils constrict to take advantage of the sharpened image. But in dim light, the pupils dilate. Image sharpness is sacrificed to allow more light to fall on the retina so that more remains visible.

The Retina: The Brain's Envoy in the Eye

The *retina* **is the neural tissue lining the inside back surface of the eye; it absorbs light, processes images, and sends visual information to the brain.** You may be surprised to learn that the retina *processes* images. But it's a piece of the central nervous system that happens to be located in the eyeball. Much as the spinal cord is a complicated extension of the brain, the retina is the brain's envoy in the eye. Although the retina is only a paper-thin sheet of neural tissue, it contains a complex network of specialized cells arranged in layers, as shown in Figure 4.3.

The axons that run from the retina to the brain converge at a single spot where they exit the eye. At that point, all the fibers dive through a hole in the retina called the *optic disk*. Since the optic disk is a *hole* in the retina, you cannot see the part of an image that falls on it. It is therefore known as the *blind spot*. You may not be aware that you have a blind spot in each eye, since each normally compensates for the blind spot of the other.

Visual Receptors: Rods and Cones

The retina contains millions of receptor cells that are sensitive to light. Surprisingly, these receptors are located in the innermost layer of the retina. Hence, light must pass through several layers of cells before it gets to the receptors that actually detect it. Surprisingly, only about 10% of the light arriving at the cornea reaches these receptors (Leibovic, 1990). The retina contains two types of receptors, *rods* and *cones*. Their names are based on their shapes, as rods are elongated and cones are stubbier. Rods outnumber cones by a huge margin, about 125 million to 6.4 million (Pugh, 1988).

Cones are specialized visual receptors that play a key role in daylight vision and color vision. The cones handle most of our daytime vision, because bright lights dazzle the rods. The special sensitivities of cones also allow them to play a major role in the perception of color. However, cones do not respond well to dim light, which is why you don't see color very well in low illumination. Nonetheless, cones provide better *visual acuity*—that is, sharpness and precise detail—than rods. Cones are concentrated most heavily in the center of the retina and quickly fall off in density toward its periphery. **The *fovea* is a tiny spot in the center of the retina that contains only cones; visual acuity is greatest at this spot.** When you want to see something sharply, you usually move your eyes to center the object in the fovea.

Rods are specialized visual receptors that play a key role in night vision and peripheral vision. Rods handle night vision because they are more sensitive than cones to dim light. They handle the lion's share of peripheral vision because they greatly outnumber cones in the periphery of the retina. The density of the rods is greatest just outside the fovea and gradually decreases toward the periphery of the retina. Because of the distribution of rods, when you want to see a faintly illuminated object in the dark, it's best to look slightly above or below the place it should be. Averting your gaze this way moves the image from the cone-filled fovea, which requires more light, to the rod-dominated area just outside the fovea, which requires less light. This trick of averted vision is well known to astronomers, who use it to study dim objects viewed through the eyepiece of a telescope.

Dark and Light Adaptation

You've probably noticed that when you enter a dark theater on a bright day, you stumble about almost blindly. But within minutes you can make your way about quite well in the dim light. This adjustment is called *dark adaptation*—**the process in which the eyes become more sensitive to light in low illumination.** Figure 4.5 maps out the course of this process. It shows how, as time passes, you require less and less light to see. Dark adaptation is virtually complete in about 30 min-

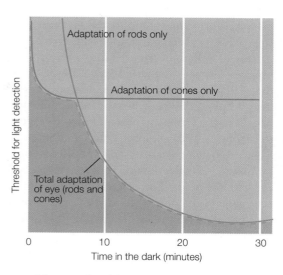

Figure 4.5. The process of dark adaptation. Visual sensitivity improves markedly during the first 5 to 10 minutes after entering a dark room, as the eye's bright-light receptors (the cones) rapidly adapt to low light levels. Further improvement comes from the rods, which are slower to adapt but are capable of far greater visual sensitivity in low levels of light.

utes, with considerable progress occurring in the first 10 minutes. The curve in Figure 4.5 that charts this progress consists of two segments because cones adapt more rapidly than rods (Walraven et al., 1990).

When you emerge from a dark theater on a sunny day, you need to squint to ward off the overwhelming brightness, and the reverse of dark adaptation occurs. *Light adaptation* is the process whereby the eyes become less sensitive to light in high illumination. As with dark adaptation, light adaptation improves your visual acuity under the prevailing circumstances.

CONCEPT CHECK 4.1
Understanding Sensory Processes in the Retina

Check your understanding of sensory receptors in the retina by completing the following exercise. Consult Appendix A for the answers.

The receptors for vision are rods and cones in the retina. These two types of receptors have many important differences, which are compared systematically in the chart below. Fill in the missing information to finish the chart.

Dimension	Rods	Cones
Physical shape	Elongated	
Number in the retina		6.4 million
Area of the retina in which they are dominant receptor	Periphery	
Critical to color vision		
Critical to peripheral vision		No
Sensitivity to dim light	Strong	
Speed of dark adaptation		Rapid

Information Processing in the Retina

In processing visual input, the retina transforms a pattern of light falling onto it into a very different representation of the visual scene. Light striking the retina's receptors (rods and cones) triggers neural signals that pass into the intricate network of cells in the retina. Signals move from receptors to bipolar cells to ganglion cells (see the inset in Figure 4.3), which in turn send impulses along the *optic nerve*—a collection of axons that connect the eye with the brain. These axons, which depart the eye through the optic disk, carry visual information, encoded as a stream of neural impulses, to the brain.

A great deal of complex information processing goes on in the retina itself before visual signals are sent to the brain. Ultimately, the information from over 130 million rods and cones converges to travel along "only" 1 million axons in the optic nerve (Slaughter, 1990). This means that the bipolar and ganglion cells in the intermediate layers of the retina integrate and compress signals from many receptors. The collection of rod and cone receptors that funnel signals to a particular visual cell in the retina (or ultimately in the brain) make up that cell's *receptive field*. Thus, **the receptive field of a visual cell is the retinal area that, when stimulated, affects the firing of that cell.**

Receptive fields in the retina come in a variety of shapes and sizes. Particularly common are circular fields with a center-surround arrangement (Tessier-Lavigne, 1991). In these receptive fields, light falling in the center has the opposite effect of light falling in the surrounding area (see Figure 4.6). For example, the rate of firing of a visual cell might be *increased* by light in the center of its receptive field and *decreased* by light in the *surrounding area*, as Figure 4.6 shows. Other visual cells may work in just the opposite way. Either

way, when receptive fields are stimulated, retinal cells send signals both toward the brain and *laterally* (sideways) toward nearby visual cells. These lateral signals, carried by the horizontal and amacrine cells (see the inset in Figure 4.3), allow visual cells in the retina to have interactive effects on each other.

Vision and the Brain

Light falls on the eye, but you see with your brain. Although the retina does an unusual amount of information processing for a sensory organ, visual input is meaningless until it is processed in the brain.

Visual Pathways to the Brain

How does visual information get to the brain? Axons leaving the back of each eye form the optic nerves, which travel to the *optic chiasm*. At the optic chiasm, the axons from the inside half of each eye cross over and then project to the opposite half of the brain (as we first discussed in Chapter 3—refer to Figure 3.17). This arrangement ensures that signals from both eyes go to both hemispheres of the brain. Thus, as Figure 4.7 shows, axons from the left half of each retina carry signals to the left side of the brain, and axons from the right half of each retina carry information to the right side of the brain.

After reaching the optic chiasm, the optic nerve fibers diverge along two pathways (Coren & Ward, 1989). The main pathway projects into the thalamus, where visual signals are processed and then distributed to areas in the occipital lobe that make up the *visual cortex*. The second visual pathway leaving the optic chiasm branches off to an area in the midbrain (the *superior colliculus*) before traveling through the thalamus and on to the occipital lobe. However, the second pathway

Figure 4.6. Receptive fields in the retina. Visual cells' receptive fields in the retina are often circular with a center-surround arrangement, so that light striking the center of the field produces the opposite result of light striking the surround. In the receptive field depicted here, light in the center produces increased firing in the visual cell, whereas light in the surround produces decreased firing; the arrangement in other receptive fields may be just the opposite.

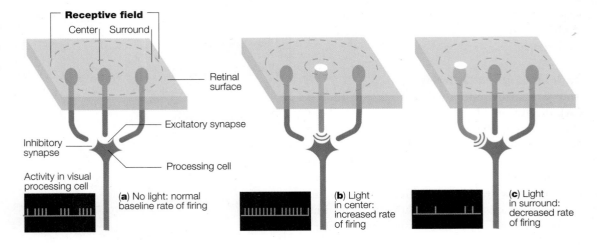

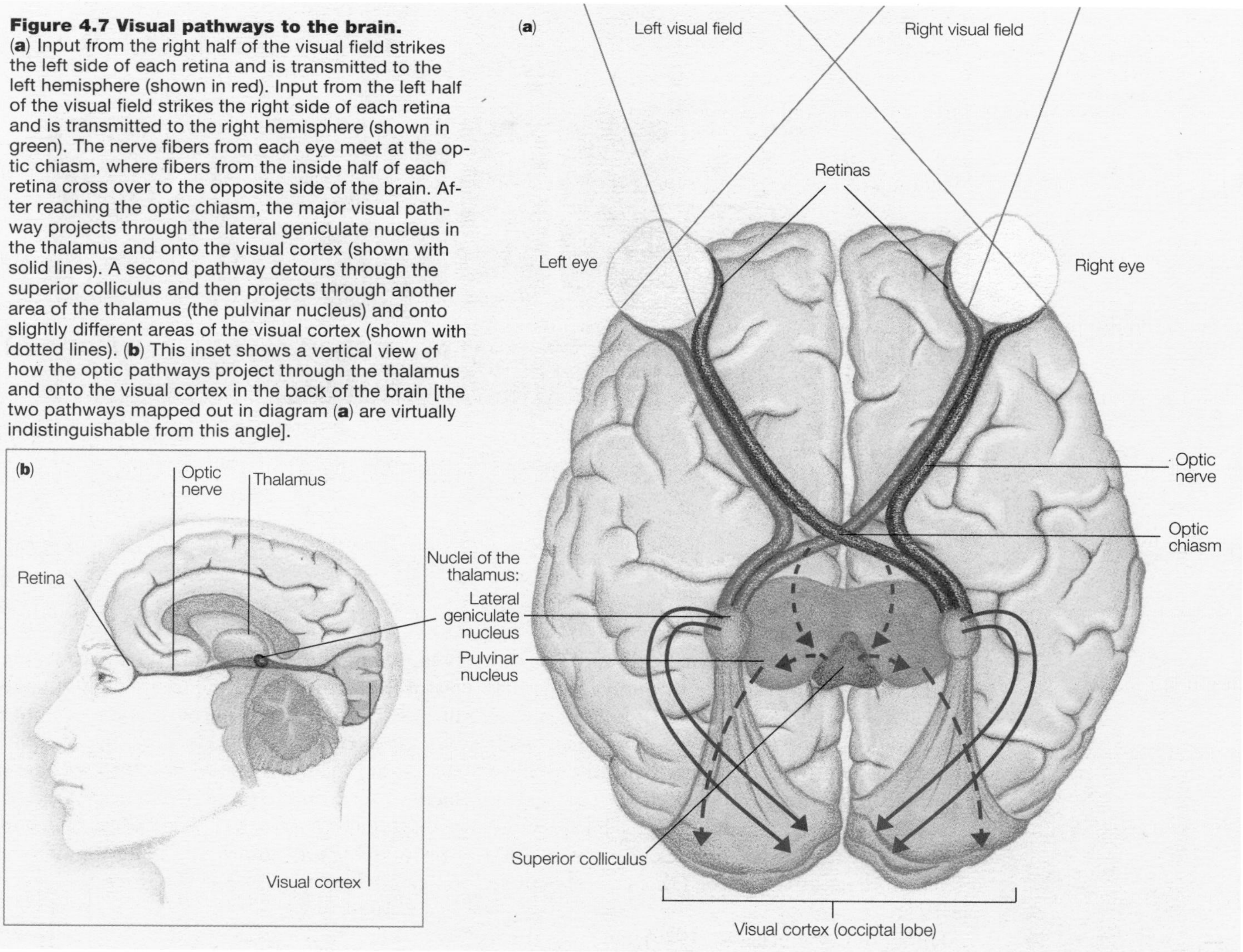

Figure 4.7 Visual pathways to the brain.
(a) Input from the right half of the visual field strikes the left side of each retina and is transmitted to the left hemisphere (shown in red). Input from the left half of the visual field strikes the right side of each retina and is transmitted to the right hemisphere (shown in green). The nerve fibers from each eye meet at the optic chiasm, where fibers from the inside half of each retina cross over to the opposite side of the brain. After reaching the optic chiasm, the major visual pathway projects through the lateral geniculate nucleus in the thalamus and onto the visual cortex (shown with solid lines). A second pathway detours through the superior colliculus and then projects through another area of the thalamus (the pulvinar nucleus) and onto slightly different areas of the visual cortex (shown with dotted lines). (b) This inset shows a vertical view of how the optic pathways project through the thalamus and onto the visual cortex in the back of the brain [the two pathways mapped out in diagram (a) are virtually indistinguishable from this angle].

projects into different areas of the thalamus and the occipital lobe than the main visual pathway does.

This segregation is necessary because the two visual pathways are specialized. They engage in *parallel processing*, simultaneously extracting different kinds of information from the same visual input. The main pathway appears to handle information relating to the perception of form, color, brightness, contrast, and depth (Livingstone & Hubel, 1988). The second pathway appears to handle the localization of objects in space and the coordination of visual input with other sensory input (Meredith & Stein, 1983; Sparks, 1988). Actually, the assertion that there are two parallel visual pathways is something of an understatement, since the main visual pathway apparently is subdivided into still more specialized pathways that operate in parallel (Lennie et al., 1990).

Information Processing in the Visual Cortex

Visual input ultimately arrives in the occipital lobe of the cortex. The cells in the visual areas of the cortex communicate with one another extensively in a rich processing network (Gilbert & Wiesel, 1985). How these cortical cells respond to light once posed a perplexing problem. Researchers investigating the question placed microelectrodes in the visual cortex of animals to record action potentials from individual cells. They would flash spots of light in the retinal receptive fields that the cells were thought to monitor, but there was rarely any response.

According to David Hubel and Torsten Wiesel (1962, 1963), they discovered the solution to this mystery quite by accident. One of the projector slides they used to present a spot to a cat had a crack in it. The spot elicited no response, but when they removed the slide, the crack moved

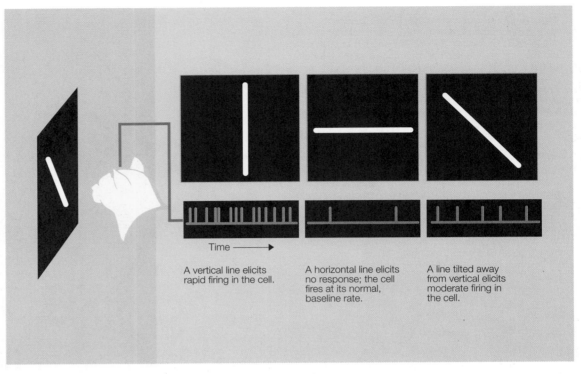

Figure 4.8. Hubel and Wiesel's procedure for studying the activity of neurons in the visual cortex. As the cat is shown various stimuli, a microelectrode records the firing of a neuron in the cat's visual cortex. The figure shows the electrical responses of a simple cell apparently "programmed" to respond to lines oriented vertically.

Time →

A vertical line elicits rapid firing in the cell.

A horizontal line elicits no response; the cell fires at its normal, baseline rate.

A line tilted away from vertical elicits moderate firing in the cell.

"One can now begin to grasp the significance of the great number of cells in the visual cortex. Each cell seems to have its own specific duties."
DAVID HUBEL

through the cell's receptive field, and the cell fired like crazy in response to the moving dark line. It turns out that cortical cells don't really respond much to little spots—they are much more sensitive to lines, edges, and other more complicated stimuli. Armed with new slides, Hubel and Wiesel embarked on years of painstaking study of the visual cortex (see Figure 4.8). Their work eventually earned them a Nobel prize in 1981.

Hubel and Wiesel (1962, 1979) identified three major types of visual cells in the cortex, which they called simple cells, complex cells, and hypercomplex cells. *Simple cells* are quite specific about which stimuli will make them fire. A simple cell responds best to a line of the correct width, oriented at the correct angle, and located in the correct position in its receptive field. *Complex cells* also care about width and orientation, but they respond to any position in their receptive fields. Some complex cells are most responsive if a line sweeps across their receptive field—but only if it's moving in the "right" direction. *Hypercomplex cells* are cells that are particularly fussy about the length of a stimulus line.

The key point of all this is that the cells in the visual cortex seem to be highly specialized. They have been characterized as *feature detectors,* **neurons that respond selectively to very specific features of more complex stimuli.** Ultimately, most visual stimuli could be represented by com-

binations of lines such as those registered by these feature detectors. Some theorists believe that feature detectors are registering the basic building blocks of visual perception and that the brain somehow assembles the blocks into a coherent picture of complex stimuli (Maguire, Weisstein, & Klymenko, 1990). Other theorists think that this model is too simple to explain the immense range of human visual capabilities (Sekuler & Blake, 1990).

Viewing the World in Color

So far, we've considered only how the visual system deals with light and dark. Let's journey now into the world of color. On the one hand, you can see perfectly well without seeing in color. Many animals get by with little or no color vision, and no one seemed to suffer back when all photographs, movies, and TV shows were in black and white. On the other hand, color adds not only spectacle but information to human perceptions of the world. Emotionally, color clearly is important to many people, as you well know if you've ever spent a great deal of time deciding on the color of sweater to wear or the color of car to buy.

The Stimulus for Color

As noted earlier, the lights people see are mixtures of different wavelengths. Perceived color is primarily a function of the dominant wavelength in these mixtures. In the visible spectrum, lights with the longest wavelengths appear red, whereas those with the shortest appear violet. Notice the word *appear*. Color is a psychological interpretation. It's not a physical property of light itself.

Although wavelength wields the greatest influence, perception of color depends on complex blends of all three properties of light. Wavelength is most closely related to hue, amplitude to brightness, and purity to saturation. These three dimensions of color are illustrated in the *color solid* shown in Figure 4.9.

As a color solid demonstrates systematically, people can perceive many different colors. Indeed, experts estimate that humans can discriminate between roughly a million colors (Boynton, 1990). Most of these diverse variations are the result of mixing a few basic colors. There are two kinds of color mixture: subtractive and additive (see Figure 4.10). **Subtractive color mixing works by removing some wavelengths of light, leaving less light than was originally there.** You probably became familiar with subtractive mixing as a child when you mixed yellow and blue paints to make green. Paints yield subtractive mixing because pigments *absorb* most wavelengths, selectively reflecting back specific wavelengths that give rise to particular colors. Subtractive color mixing can also be demonstrated by stacking color filters. If you look through a sandwich of yellow and blue cellophane filters, they will block out certain wavelengths. The middle wavelengths that are left will look green.

Additive color mixing works by superimposing lights, putting more light in the mixture than exists in any one light by itself. If you shine a beam from a blue spotlight and one from a yellow spotlight on the same white surface, you'll have an additive mixture. What color is it? Not green, but very nearly *white*. Additive and subtractive mixtures of the same colors, then, produce different results.

White light actually includes the entire visible spectrum, as you can demonstrate by allowing white light to pass through a prism (consult Figure 4.2 once again). Accordingly, when all wavelengths are mixed additively, they yield natural white light. Human processes of color perception parallel additive color mixing much more closely than subtractive mixing, as you'll see in the following discussion of theories of color vision.

Trichromatic Theory of Color Vision

The *trichromatic theory* of color vision (*tri* for "three," *chroma* for "color") was first stated by

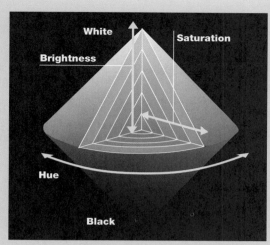

Figure 4.9. The color solid. The color solid shows how color varies along three perceptual dimensions: brightness (increasing from the bottom to the top of the solid), hue (changing around the solid's perimeter), and saturation (decreasing toward the center of the solid).

Figure 4.10. Color mixing. Additive color mixing is shown at the top, where red, green, and blue lights are combined, producing white at the intersection of all three colors. Subtractive color mixing is shown at the bottom, where red, yellow, and blue filters screen out various portions of the spectrum, producing black at the intersection of all three colors.

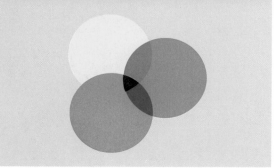

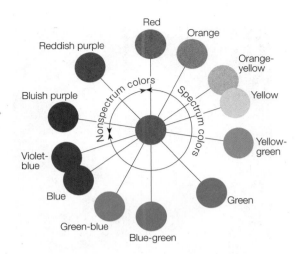

Figure 4.11. Complementary colors. Colors opposite each other on this color circle are complements, or "opposites." Additively, mixing complementary colors produces gray. Opponent process principles help explain this effect as well as the other peculiarities of complementary colors noted in the text.

Red
Orange
Reddish purple
Orange-yellow
Nonspectrum colors
Spectrum colors
Bluish purple
Yellow
Violet-blue
Yellow-green
Blue
Green
Green-blue
Blue-green

Thomas Young and modified later by Hermann von Helmholtz (1852). *The trichromatic theory holds that the human eye has three types of receptors with differing sensitivities to different light wavelengths.* Helmholtz believed that the eye contains specialized receptors specially sensitive to the wavelengths associated with red, green, and blue. According to this model, people can see all the colors of the rainbow because the eye does its own "color mixing" by varying the ratio of neural activity among these three types of receptors.

The impetus for the trichromatic theory was the demonstration that a light of any color can be matched by the additive mixture of three *primary colors.* (Any three colors that are appropriately spaced out in the visible spectrum can serve as primary colors, although red, green, and blue are usually used.) Does it sound implausible that three colors should be adequate for creating all other colors? If so, consider that this is exactly what happens on your color TV screen. Additive mix-

tures of red, green, and blue fool you into seeing all the colors of a natural scene.

Most of the known facts about color blindness also meshed well with trichromatic theory. *Color blindness encompasses a variety of deficiencies in the ability to distinguish among colors.* Color blindness occurs much more frequently in males than in females. Actually, the term color *blindness* is somewhat misleading, since complete blindness to differences in colors is quite rare. Most people who are color blind are *dichromats*; that is, they make do with only two color channels. There are three types of dichromats, and each type is insensitive to a different color (red, green, or blue, although the latter is rare) (Gouras, 1991). The three deficiencies seen among dichromats support the notion that there are three channels for color vision, as proposed by trichromatic theory.

Opponent Process Theory of Color Vision

Although trichromatic theory explained some facets of color vision well, it ran aground in other areas. Consider complementary afterimages, for instance. *Complementary colors* are pairs of colors that produce gray tones when mixed together. The various pairs of complementary colors can be arranged in a *color circle*, such as the one in Figure 4.11. If you stare at a strong color and then look at a white background, you'll see an *afterimage—a visual image that persists after a stimulus is removed.* The color of the afterimage will be the *complement* of the color you originally stared at. Trichromatic theory cannot account for the appearance of complementary afterimages.

Here's another peculiarity to consider. If you ask people to describe colors but restrict them to using three names, they run into difficulty. For example, using only red, green, and blue, they simply don't feel comfortable describing yellow as "reddish green." However, if you let them have just one more name, they usually choose yellow. Then they can describe any color quite well (Boynton & Gordon, 1965). If colors are reduced to three channels, why are four color names required to describe the full range of possible colors?

In an effort to answer questions such as these, Ewald Hering proposed the *opponent process theory* of color vision in 1878. *The opponent process theory holds that color perception depends on receptors that make antagonistic responses to three pairs of colors.* The three pairs of opponent colors posited by Hering were red versus green, yellow versus blue,

---

CONCEPT CHECK 4.2
Comparing Theories of Color Vision

Check your understanding of the differences between the trichromatic and opponent process theories of color vision by filling in the blanks below. The answers are in Appendix A.

	Trichromatic theory	*Opponent process theory*
Theory proposed by:	_____	_____
Can/can't account for complementary afterimages	_____	_____
Explains first/later stage of color processing	_____	_____
Does/doesn't account for need for four terms to describe colors	_____	_____

and black versus white. The antagonistic processes in this theory provide plausible explanations for complementary afterimages and the need for four names (red, green, blue, and yellow) to describe colors. Opponent process theory also explains some aspects of color blindness. For instance, it can explain why dichromats typically find it hard to distinguish either green from red or yellow from blue.

Reconciling Theories of Color Vision

Advocates of trichromatic theory and opponent process theory argued about the relative merits of their models for almost a century. Most researchers assumed that one theory must be wrong and the other must be right. In recent decades, however, it has become clear that it takes *both theories to explain color vision.* Eventually a physiological basis for both theories was found. Research that earned George Wald a Nobel prize demonstrated that *the eye has three types of cones,* with each type being most sensitive to a different band of wavelengths, as shown in Figure 4.12 (Bowmaker & Dartnall, 1980; Wald, 1964). The three types of cones represent the three different color receptors predicted by trichromatic theory.

Researchers also discovered a biological basis for opponent processes. They found cells in the retina, the thalamus, and the visual cortex *that respond in opposite ways to red versus green and blue versus yellow* (DeValois & Jacobs, 1984; Zrenner et al., 1990). For example, there are ganglion cells in the retina that are excited by green and inhibited by red. Other ganglion cells in the retina work in

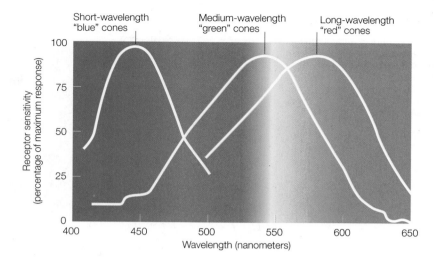

just the opposite way, as predicted by opponent process theory.

In summary, the perception of color appears to involve sequential stages of information processing (Hurvich, 1981). The receptors that do the first stage of processing (the cones) seem to follow the principles outlined in trichromatic theory. In later stages of processing, cells in the retina and the brain seem to follow the principles outlined in opponent process theory (see Figure 4.13). As you can see, vigorous theoretical debate about color vision produced a solution that went beyond the contributions of either theory alone.

Perceiving Forms, Patterns, and Objects

The drawing in Figure 4.14 is a poster for a circus act involving a trained seal. What do you see?

Figure 4.12. Three types of cones. Research has identified three types of cones that show varied sensitivity to different wavelengths of light. As the graph shows, these three types of cones correspond only roughly to the red, green, and blue receptors predicted by trichromatic theory, so it is more accurate to refer to them as cones sensitive to short, medium, and long wavelengths.

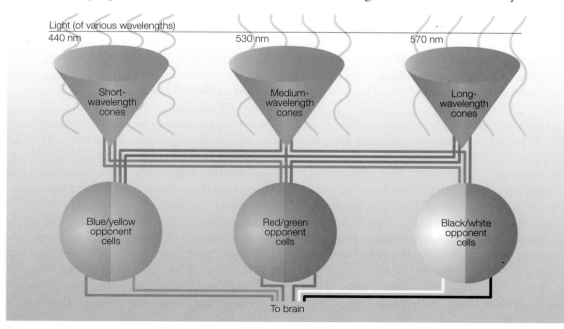

Figure 4.13. Explaining color perception. Contemporary theories of color vision include aspects of both the trichromatic and opponent process theories. As predicted by trichromatic theory, there are three types of receptors for color—cones sensitive to short, medium, and long wavelengths. However, these cones are organized into receptive fields that excite or inhibit the firing of higher-level visual cells in the retina, thalamus, and cortex. As predicted by opponent process theory, these cells respond in antagonistic ways to blue versus yellow, red versus green, and black versus white when lights of these colors stimulate their receptive fields.

Figure 4.14. A poster for a trained seal act. Or is it? The picture is an ambiguous figure, which can be interpreted as either of two scenes.

"The fundamental 'formula' of Gestalt theory might be expressed in this way: There are wholes, the behaviour of which is not determined by that of their individual elements."
MAX WERTHEIMER

No doubt you see a seal balancing a ball on its nose and a trainer holding a fish and a whip. But suppose you had been told that the drawing is actually a poster for a costume ball. Would you have perceived it differently?

If you focus on the idea of a costume ball (stay with it a minute if you still see the seal and trainer), you will probably see a costumed man and woman in Figure 4.14. She's handing him a hat, and he has a sword in his right hand. This tricky little sketch was made ambiguous quite intentionally. It's a *reversible figure*, **a drawing that is compatible with two different interpretations that can shift back and forth.**

The point of this demonstration is simply this: *The same visual input can result in radically different perceptions.* There is no one-to-one correspondence between sensory input and what you perceive. *This is a principal reason why people's experience of the world is subjective.* Perception involves much more than passively receiving signals from the outside world. It involves the *interpretation* of sensory input.

In this case, your interpretations result in two different "realities" because your *expectations* have been manipulated. Information given to you about the drawing has created a *perceptual set*—**a readiness to perceive a stimulus in a particular way.** A perceptual set creates a certain slant in how you interpret sensory input. An understanding of how people perceive forms, patterns, and objects requires knowledge of how people *organize and*

interpret visual input. Several influential approaches to this question emphasize *feature analysis*.

Feature Analysis: Assembling Forms

The information received by your eyes would do you little good if you couldn't recognize objects and forms, ranging from words on a page to mice in your cellar and friends in the distance. This was exactly the fate that befell Dr. P. As you recall, Dr. P could "see" perfectly well. Yet he couldn't make sense out of the world because he was unable to translate what he saw into the recognition of objects and faces. Even people without visual defects can find form perception to be challenging. For example, professors reading essay exams routinely complain about difficulty recognizing the letter forms that make up their students' handwriting.

According to some theories, perceptions of form and pattern entail *feature analysis* (Lindsay & Norman, 1977; Maguire et al., 1990). **Feature analysis is the process of detecting specific elements in visual input and assembling them into a more complex form.** In other words, you start with the components of a form, such as lines, edges, and corners, and build them into perceptions of squares, triangles, stop signs, bicycles, ice cream cones, and telephones. An application of this model of form perception is diagrammed in Figure 4.15. It shows how, in theory, people might recognize the letter T by registering and assembling the configuration of features that make up this letter. The plausibility of this model was bolstered greatly when Hubel and Wiesel showed that cells in the visual cortex operate as highly specialized feature detectors. It appears that at least some (but probably not all) aspects of form perception involve feature analysis.

Looking at the Whole Picture: Gestalt Principles

Sometimes a whole, as we perceive it, may have qualities that don't exist in any of the parts. This insight became the basic tenet of *Gestalt psychology*, an influential school of thought that emerged out of Germany during the first half of this century. (*Gestalt* is a German word for "form" or "shape.")

A simple example of this principle, which you have experienced innumerable times, is the *phi phenomenon*, first described by Max Wertheimer in 1912. **The *phi phenomenon* is the illusion of movement created by presenting visual stimuli in rapid succession.** You encounter examples of the phi phenomenon nearly every day. For ex-

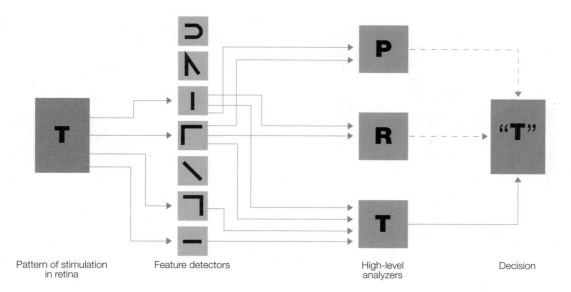

Pattern of stimulation in retina — Feature detectors — High-level analyzers — Decision

Figure 4.15. Feature analysis in form perception. One vigorously debated theory of form perception is that the brain has cells that respond to specific aspects or features of stimuli, such as lines and angles. Neurons functioning as higher-level analyzers then respond to input from these "feature detectors." The more input each analyzer receives, the more active it becomes. Finally, other neurons weigh signals from these analyzers and make a "decision" about the stimulus. In this way perception of a form is arrived at by assembling elements from the bottom up.

ample, movies and TV consist of separate still pictures projected rapidly one after the other. You *see* smooth motion, but in reality the "moving" objects merely take slightly different positions in successive frames. Viewed as a whole, a movie has a property (motion) that isn't evident in any of its parts (the individual frames).

The Gestalt psychologists formulated a series of principles that describe how the visual system organizes a scene into discrete forms. Let's examine some of these principles.

FIGURE AND GROUND Take a look at Figure 4.16. Do you see the figure as two silhouetted faces against a white background, or as a white vase against a black background? This reversible figure illustrates the Gestalt principle of *figure and ground.* Dividing visual displays into figure and ground is a fundamental way in which people organize visual perceptions. The *figure* is the thing being looked at, and the *ground* is the background against which it stands. The figure seems to have substance and appears to stand out in front of the ground. More often than not, your visual field may contain many figures sharing a background. The following Gestalt principles relate to how these elements are grouped into higher-order figures.

PROXIMITY Things that are near one another seem to belong together. The black dots in the upper left panel of Figure 4.17 (on the next page) could be grouped into vertical columns or horizontal rows. However, people tend to perceive rows because of the effect of proximity (the dots are closer together horizontally).

Figure 4.16. The principle of figure and ground. Whether you see two faces or a vase depends on which part of this drawing you see as figure and which as background. Although this reversible drawing allows you to switch back and forth between two ways of organizing your perception, you can't perceive the drawing both ways at once.

The illusion of movement in a highway construction sign is an instance of the phi phenomenon, which is also at work in motion pictures and television. The phenomenon illustrates the Gestalt principle that the whole can have properties that are not found in any of its parts.

Figure 4.17. Gestalt principles of perceptual organization. Gestalt principles help explain how people subjectively organize perception. **Proximity:** These dots might well be organized in columns (that is, top to bottom) rather than horizontal rows, but because of proximity (the dots are closer together horizontally), they tend to be perceived in rows. **Closure:** Even though the figures are incomplete, you fill in the missing contours and see a circle and a dog. **Similarity:** Because of similarity of color, you see dots organized into the number 2 instead of a random array. If you did not group similar elements, you wouldn't see the number 2 here. **Simplicity:** You tend to see (**a**) as made up of the elements shown in the simplest alternative, (**b**), instead of the more complex alternatives shown in (**c**) and (**d**), even though they could represent its structure equally well. **Continuity:** You tend to group these dots in a way that produces a smooth path rather than an abrupt shift in direction.

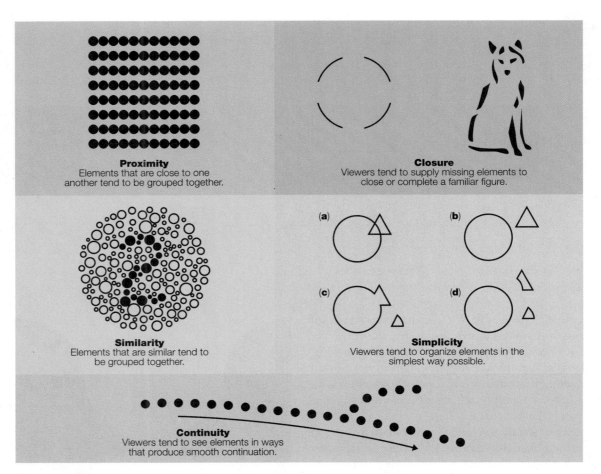

Proximity
Elements that are close to one another tend to be grouped together.

Closure
Viewers tend to supply missing elements to close or complete a familiar figure.

Similarity
Elements that are similar tend to be grouped together.

Simplicity
Viewers tend to organize elements in the simplest way possible.

Continuity
Viewers tend to see elements in ways that produce smooth continuation.

SIMILARITY People also tend to group stimuli that are similar. This principle is apparent in the middle left panel of Figure 4.17, where we group elements of similar darkness into the number two.

CONTINUITY The principle of continuity reflects people's tendency to follow in whatever direction they've been led. Thus, people tend to connect points that result in straight or gently curved lines that create "smooth" paths, as shown in the bottom panel of Figure 4.17.

SIMPLICITY The Gestaltists' most general principle was the law of *Pragnanz*, which translates from German as "good form." The idea is that people tend to group elements that combine to form a good figure. This principle is somewhat vague in that it's often difficult to spell out what makes a figure "good." Some theorists maintain that goodness is largely a matter of simplicity, asserting that people tend to organize forms in the simplest way possible (see the middle right panel of Figure 4.17).

CLOSURE People often group elements to create a sense of *closure*, or completeness. Thus, you may

"complete" figures that actually have gaps in them. This principle is demonstrated in the upper right panel of Figure 4.17.

Although Gestalt psychology is no longer an active theoretical orientation in modern psychology, its influence is still felt in the study of perception (Banks & Krajicek, 1991). The Gestalt psychologists raised many important questions that still occupy researchers, and they left a legacy of many useful insights about form perception that have stood the test of time.

Formulating Perceptual Hypotheses

The Gestalt principles provide some indications of how people organize visual input. However, scientists are still one step away from understanding how these organized perceptions result in a representation of the real world. Understanding the problem requires distinguishing between two kinds of stimuli: distal and proximal (Hochberg, 1988). ***Distal stimuli are stimuli that lie in the distance (that is, in the world outside the body).*** In vision, these are the objects that you're looking at. They are "distant" in that your eyes don't touch them.

What your eyes do "touch" are the images formed by patterns of light falling on your retinas. These images are *proximal stimuli*, **the stimulus energies that impinge directly on sensory receptors.** The distinction is important, because there are great differences between the objects you perceive and the stimulus energies that represent them.

In visual perception, the proximal stimuli are distorted, two-dimensional versions of their actual, three-dimensional counterparts. For example, consider the distal stimulus of a square such as the one in Figure 4.18. If the square is lying on a desk in front of you, it is actually projecting a trapezoid (the proximal stimulus) on your retinas, because the top of the square is farther from your eyes than the bottom. Obviously, the trapezoid is a distorted representation of the square. If what people have to work with is so distorted a picture, how do they get an accurate view of the world out there?

One explanation is that people bridge the gap between distal and proximal stimuli by constantly making and testing *hypotheses* about what's out there in the real world (Gregory, 1973). Thus, **a *perceptual hypothesis* is an inference about which distal stimuli could be responsible for the proximal stimuli sensed.** In effect, people make educated guesses about what form could be responsible for a pattern of sensory stimulation. The square in Figure 4.18 may project a trapezoidal image on your retinas, but your perceptual system "guesses" correctly that it's a square—and that's what you see.

Let's look at another ambiguous drawing to further demonstrate the process of making a perceptual hypothesis. Figure 4.19 is a famous reversible figure, first published as a cartoon in a humor magazine. Perhaps you see a drawing of a young woman looking back over her right shoulder. Alternatively, you might see an old woman with her chin down on her chest. The ambiguity exists because there isn't enough information to force your perceptual system to accept only one of these hypotheses.

If you can see only one of the women, you may be wondering where the other is. To guide you, Figure 4.20 shows unambiguous drawings of the young woman on the left and of the old woman on the right. Now you should be able to find either woman in Figure 4.19. You just needed some guidance as to how to make the other perceptual hypothesis. Incidentally, studies show that people who are led to *expect* the young woman or the old woman tend to see the one they expect (Leeper,

Retinal image

Figure 4.18. Distal and proximal stimuli.
Proximal stimuli are often distorted, shifting representations of distal stimuli in the real world. If you look directly down at a small, square piece of paper on a desk (**a**), the distal stimulus (the paper) and the proximal stimulus (the image projected on your retina) will both be square. But as you move the paper away on the desktop (**b**) and (**c**), the square distal stimulus projects an increasingly trapezoidal image on your retina, making the proximal stimulus more and more distorted. Nevertheless, you continue to perceive a square.

Figure 4.19. A famous reversible figure. What do you see?

Figure 4.20. Unambiguous drawings of the young and old woman in Figure 4.18.

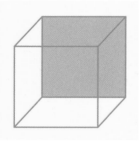

Figure 4.21. The Necker cube. The tinted surface can become either the front or the back of the cube.

THE CHT

Figure 4.22. Context effects. The context in which a stimulus is seen can affect your perceptual hypotheses.

1935). This is another example of how perceptual sets influence what people see.

Psychologists have used a variety of reversible figures to study how people formulate perceptual hypotheses. Another example can be seen in Figure 4.21, which shows the *Necker cube*. The shaded surface can appear as either the front or the rear of the transparent cube. If you look at the cube for a while, your perception will alternate between these possibilities. Later, in the Application on art and illusion, you'll see how M. C. Escher used the Necker cube to create a fascinating piece of art. The *context* in which something appears often guides our perceptual hypotheses. To illustrate, take a look at Figure 4.22. What do you see?

You probably saw the words "THE CAT." But look again; the middle characters in both words are identical. You identified an "H" in the first word and an "A" in the second because of the surrounding letters, which shaped your expectations.

Perceiving Depth or Distance

More often than not, forms and figures are objects in space. Spatial considerations add a third dimension to visual perception. ***Depth perception* involves interpretation of visual cues that indicate how near or far away objects are.** To make judgments of distance, people rely on quite a variety of clues, which can be classified into two types: binocular cues and monocular cues (Hochberg, 1988).

Binocular Cues

Because the eyes are set apart, each eye has a slightly different view of the world. ***Binocular cues* are clues about distance based on the differing views of the two eyes.** "Stereo" viewers (such as the Viewmaster toy you may have had as a child) make use of this principle by presenting slightly

different flat images of the same scene to each eye. The brain then supplies the "depth," and you perceive a three-dimensional scene.

The principal binocular depth cue is *retinal disparity*. Objects within 25 feet project images to slightly different locations on your right and left retinas. Closer objects project to locations a little farther apart. Thus, retinal disparity increases as objects come closer, providing information about distance. Another binocular cue is *convergence*, which involves sensing the eyes converging toward each other as they focus on closer objects.

If you cover one eye, the world does *not* collapse into a flat sheet. Thus, binocular cues are really just frosting on the cake—you don't need them to see depth. You can get by with only monocular cues, which we discuss next.

Monocular Cues

***Monocular cues* are clues about distance based on the image in either eye alone.** There are two kinds of monocular cues to depth. One kind is the result of active use of the eye in viewing the world. For example, as an object comes closer, you may sense the accommodation (the change in the curvature of the lens) that must occur for the eye to adjust its focus. Similarly, if you cover one eye and move your head from side to side, closer objects appear to move more than distant objects.

The other kind of monocular cue is *pictorial*—a cue that can be given in a flat picture. There are many pictorial cues to depth, which is why paintings and photographs can seem so realistic that you feel you can climb right into them. Six prominent pictorial depth cues are described and illustrated in Figure 4.23. *Linear perspective* is a depth cue reflecting the fact that lines converge in the distance. Because details are too small to see when they are far away, *texture gradients* can provide information about depth. If an object comes between you and another object, it must be closer to you, a cue called *interposition*. *Relative size* is a cue because closer objects appear larger. *Height in plane* reflects the fact that distant objects appear higher in a picture. Finally, the familiar effects of shadowing make *light and shadow* useful in judging distance.

There appear to be some cultural differences in the ability to take advantage of pictorial depth cues in two-dimensional drawings. These differences were first investigated by Hudson (1960, 1967), who presented pictures like that shown in Figure 4.24 (on page 102) to various cultural groups in South Africa. Hudson's approach was based on

Linear perspective Parallel lines that run away from the viewer seem to get closer together.

Texture gradient A texture is coarser for near areas and finer for more distant ones.

Interposition The shapes of near objects overlap or mask those of more distant ones.

Relative size If separate objects are expected to be of the same size, the larger ones are seen as closer.

Height in plane Near objects are low in the visual field; more distant ones are higher up.

Light and shadow Patterns of light and dark suggest shadows that can create an impression of three-dimensional forms.

Figure 4.23. Six monocular cues to depth. In most visual experiences, several monocular cues are present at once. The world rarely looks "flat," even through only one eye. Try looking at the light and shadow picture upside down. The change in shadowing reverses what you see.

Painters routinely attempt to create the perception of depth on a flat canvas by using pictorial depth cues. Figure 4.23 describes and illustrates six pictorial depth cues, most of which are apparent in van Gogh's colorful piece, titled *Hospital Corridor at Saint Remy* (1889). Check your understanding of depth perception by trying to spot the depth cues in the painting.

In the list below, check off the depth cues used by van Gogh. The answers can be found in Appendix A. You can learn more about how artists use the principles of visual perception in the Application at the end of this chapter.

_____ 1. Interposition

_____ 2. Height in plane

_____ 3. Texture gradient

_____ 4. Relative size

_____ 5. Light and shadow

_____ 6. Linear perspective

(Collection, The Museum of Modern Art, New York, Abby Aldrich Rockefeller Bequest)

Figure 4.24. Testing understanding of pictorial depth cues. In his cross-cultural research, Hudson (1960) asked subjects to indicate whether the hunter is trying to spear the antelope or the elephant. He found cultural disparities in subjects' ability to make effective use of the pictorial depth cues, which place the elephant in the distance and make it an unlikely target.

the assumption that subjects who indicate that the hunter is trying to spear the elephant instead of the antelope don't understand the depth cues (interposition, relative size, height in plane) in the picture, which place the elephant in the distance. Hudson found that subjects from a rural South African tribe (the Bantu), which had little exposure at that time to pictures and photos, frequently misinterpreted the depth cues in his pictures. Similar difficulties with depth cues in pictures have been documented for other cultural groups that have little experience with two-dimensional representations of three-dimensional space (Berry et al., 1992). Based on this evidence, Deregowski (1989) concludes that the application of pictorial depth cues to pictures is partly an acquired skill that depends on experience.

Although this conclusion seems reasonable, most theorists do not accept Deregowski's further assertion that perceptual processes vary to some degree across cultures. Among other things, critics of this idea point out that people from pictureless societies quickly learn how to interpret depth in pictures and that there is little evidence of cultural variability in the perception of depth in *real space* (as opposed to pictures). Hence, most other theorists seem to believe that the basic processes involved in depth perception are probably much the same across cultures (Halpern, 1989a; Hubbard, Baird, & Ajmal, 1989).

Perceptual Constancies in Vision

When a person approaches you from the distance, his or her image on your retinas gradually changes in size. Do you perceive that the person is growing right before your eyes? Of course not. Your perceptual system constantly makes allowances for this variation in visual input. The task of the perceptual system is to provide an accurate rendition of distal stimuli based on distorted, everchanging proximal stimuli. In doing so, it relies in part on perceptual constancies. A *perceptual constancy* **is a tendency to experience a stable perception in the face of continually changing sensory input.** Among other things, people tend to view objects as having a stable size, shape, brightness, hue (color), and location in space. Perceptual constancies such as these help impose some order on the surrounding world.

The Power of Misleading Cues: Optical Illusions

In general, perceptual constancies, depth cues, and principles of visual organization (such as the Gestalt laws) help people perceive the world accurately. Sometimes, however, perceptions are based on inappropriate assumptions, and *optical illusions* can result. **An *optical illusion* involves an apparently inexplicable discrepancy between the appearance of a visual stimulus and its physical reality.**

One famous optical illusion is the *Müller-Lyer* illusion, shown in Figure 4.25. The two vertical lines in this figure are equally long, but they certainly don't look that way. Why not? Several mechanisms probably play a role (Day, 1965; Gregory, 1978). In Figure 4.26, the figure on the left looks like the outside of a building, thrust toward the viewer, while the one on the right looks like an inside corner, thrust away. The vertical line in the left figure therefore seems closer. If two lines cast equally long retinal images but one seems closer, the closer one is assumed to be shorter. Thus, the Müller-Lyer illusion may be due largely to a combination of size constancy processes and misperception of depth.

The *Ponzo illusion*, which is shown in Figure 4.27, appears to result from the same factors (Coren & Girgus, 1978). The upper and lower horizontal

lines are the same length, but the upper one appears longer. This probably occurs because the converging lines convey linear perspective, a key depth cue suggesting that the upper line lies farther in the distance. The Ponzo illusion and the other geometric illusions shown in Figure 4.27 demonstrate that visual stimuli can be highly deceptive.

Impossible figures create another form of illusion. ***Impossible figures*** **are objects that can be represented in two-dimensional pictures but cannot exist in three-dimensional space.** These figures may look fine at first glance, but a closer look reveals that they are geometrically inconsistent or impossible. Three impossible figures are

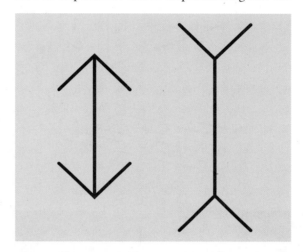

Figure 4.25. The Müller-Lyer illusion. Go ahead, measure them: The two vertical lines are of equal length.

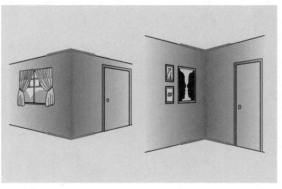

Figure 4.26. Explaining the Müller-Lyer illusion. Because of this illusion, the figure on the left seems to be closer, since it looks like an outside corner, thrust toward you. Given retinal images of the same length, you assume that the "closer" line is shorter.

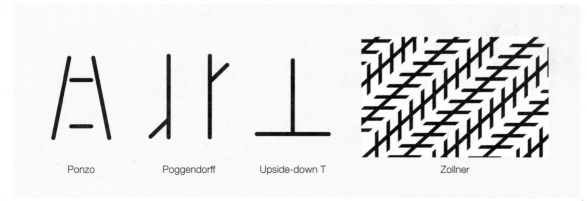

Ponzo   Poggendorff   Upside-down T   Zollner

Figure 4.27. Four geometric illusions. Ponzo: The horizontal lines are the same length. **Poggendorff**: The two diagonal segments lie on the same straight line. **Upside-down T**: The vertical and horizontal lines are the same length. **Zollner**: The long diagonals are all parallel (try covering up some of the short lines if you don't believe it).

Figure 4.28. Three impossible figures. The figures are impossible, yet they clearly exist—on the page. What makes them impossible is that they appear to be three-dimensional representations yet are drawn in a way that frustrates mental attempts to "assemble" their features into possible objects. It's difficult to see the drawings simply as lines lying in a plane—even though this perceptual hypothesis is the only one that resolves the contradiction.

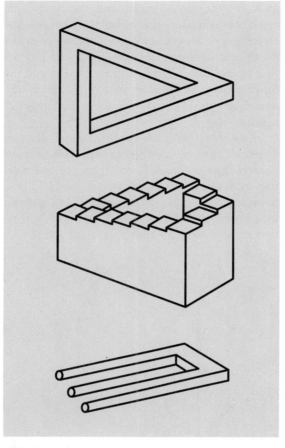

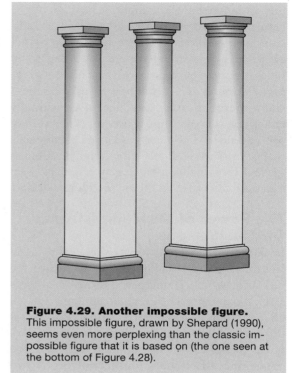

Figure 4.29. Another impossible figure. This impossible figure, drawn by Shepard (1990), seems even more perplexing than the classic impossible figure that it is based on (the one seen at the bottom of Figure 4.28).

shown in Figure 4.28 and a dramatic new impossible figure drawn by Roger Shepard (1990) can be seen in Figure 4.29. Notice that you perceive specific features of the figure as acceptable but are baffled as they are built into a whole. Your perceptual hypothesis about one portion of the figure turns out to be inconsistent with your hypothesis about another portion.

Illusions such as impossible figures involve a conspiracy of cues intended to deceive the viewer. Many visual illusions, however, occur quite naturally. A well-known example is the *moon illusion*. The full moon appears to be much smaller when overhead than when looming over the horizon. As with many of the other illusions we have discussed, the moon illusion appears to be due mainly to size constancy effects coupled with the misperception of distance (Coren & Aks, 1990; Kaufman & Rock, 1962). The moon illusion shows that optical illusions are part of everyday life. Indeed, many people are virtually addicted to an optical illusion—television (an illusion of movement created by a series of still images presented in quick succession).

Cross-cultural studies have uncovered some interesting differences among cultural groups in their propensity to see certain illusions. For example, Segall, Campbell, and Herskovits (1966) found that people from a variety of non-Western cultures are less susceptible to the

A puzzling perceptual illusion common in everyday life is the moon illusion: The moon looks larger when at the horizon than when overhead.

Unlike people in Western nations, the Zulus live in a culture where straight lines and right angles are scarce, if not entirely absent. Thus, they are not affected by such phenomena as the Müller-Lyer illusion nearly as much as people raised in environments that abound with rectangular structures.

Müller-Lyer illusion than Western samples. What could account for this difference? The most plausible explanation is that in the West, we live in a "carpentered world" dominated by straight lines, right angles, and rectangular rooms, buildings, and furniture. Thus, our experience prepares us to readily view the Müller-Lyer figures as inside and outside corners of buildings—inferences that help foster the illusion (Segall et al., 1990). In contrast, people in many non-Western cultures, such as the Zulu (see photo on page 104) who were tested by Segall and associates (1966), live in a less carpentered world, making them less likely to see the Müller-Lyer figures as building corners. In a similar vein, some investigators have found that cultural groups with little exposure to roads and railroad tracks are less susceptible to the Ponzo illusion than Western groups (Berry et al., 1992). Although there is some debate about the matter (Coren, 1989; Pollack, 1989), these cultural differences in illusion susceptibility suggest that our perceptual inferences can be shaped by experience (Segall et al., 1990).

What do optical illusions reveal about visual perception? They drive home the point that people go through life formulating perceptual hypotheses about what lies out there in the real world. The fact that these are only hypotheses becomes especially striking when the hypotheses are wrong, as they are with illusions. Optical illusions also show how context factors such as depth cues shape perceptual hypotheses. Finally, like ambiguous figures, illusions clearly demonstrate that human perceptions are not simple reflections of objective reality. Once again, we see that perception of the world is subjective.

These insights do not apply to visual perception only. We will encounter these lessons again as we examine other sensory systems, such as hearing, which we turn to next.

OUR SENSE OF HEARING: THE AUDITORY SYSTEM

Stop reading for a moment, close your eyes, and listen carefully. What do you hear?

Chances are, you'll discover that you're immersed in sounds: street noises, a high-pitched laugh from the next room, the hum of a fluorescent lamp, perhaps some background music you put on a while ago but forgot about. As this little demonstration shows, physical stimuli producing sound

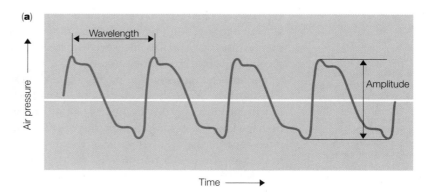

are present almost constantly, but you're not necessarily aware of these sounds.

Like vision, the auditory (hearing) system provides input about the world "out there," but not until incoming information is processed by the brain. A distal stimulus—a screech of tires, someone laughing, the hum of the refrigerator—produces a proximal stimulus in the form of sound waves reaching the ears. The perceptual system must somehow transform this stimulation into the psychological experience of hearing. We'll begin our discussion of hearing by looking at the stimulus for auditory experience: sound.

The Stimulus: Sound

Sound waves are vibrations of molecules, which means that they must travel through some physical medium, such as air. They move at a fraction of the speed of light. Sound waves are usually generated by vibrating objects, such as a guitar string, a loudspeaker cone, or your vocal cords. However, sound waves can also be generated by forcing air past a chamber (as in a pipe organ), or by suddenly releasing a burst of air (as when you clap).

Like light waves, sound waves are characterized by their *amplitude*, their *wavelength*, and their *purity* (see Figure 4.30). The physical properties of amplitude, wavelength, and purity affect mainly the perceived (psychological) qualities of loudness, pitch, and timbre, respectively. However, the physical properties of sound interact in complex ways to produce perceptions of these sound qualities.

Figure 4.30. Sound, the physical stimulus for hearing. (**a**) Like light, sound travels in waves—in this case, waves of air pressure. A smooth curve would represent a pure tone, such as that produced by a tuning fork. Most sounds, however, are complex. For example, the wave shown here is for middle C played on a piano. The sound wave for the same note played on a violin would have the same wavelength (or frequency) as this one, but the "wrinkles" in the wave would be different, corresponding to the differences in timbre between the two sounds. (**b**) The table shows the main relations between objective aspects of sound and subjective perceptions.

Human Hearing Capacities

Wavelengths of sound are described in terms of their *frequency*, which is measured in cycles per second, or *hertz (Hz)*. For the most part, higher frequencies are perceived as having higher pitch. That is, if you strike the key for high C on a piano, it will produce higher-frequency sound waves than the key for low C. Although the perception of pitch depends mainly on frequency, the amplitude of the sound waves also influences it.

Just as the visible spectrum is only a portion of the total spectrum of light, so, too, what people can hear is only a portion of the available range of sounds. Humans can hear sounds ranging in frequency from a low of 20 Hz up to a high of about 20,000 Hz. Sounds at either end of this range are harder to hear, and sensitivity to high-frequency tones declines as adults grow older. Other organisms have different capabilities. Low-frequency sounds under 10 Hz are audible to homing pigeons, for example. At the other extreme, bats and porpoises can hear frequencies well above 20,000 Hz.

In general, the greater the amplitude of sound waves, the louder the sound perceived. Whereas frequency is measured in hertz, amplitude is measured in *decibels (dB)*. The relationship between decibels (which measure a physical property of sound) and loudness (a psychological quality) is complex. A rough rule of thumb is that perceived loudness doubles about every 10 decibels (Stevens, 1955). To make this less abstract, Figure 4.31 shows approximate decibel levels for a wide range of common sounds. Very loud sounds can jeopardize the quality of your hearing. Even brief exposure to sounds over 120 decibels can be painful and may cause damage to your auditory system (Henry, 1984). As shown in Figure 4.31, the weakest sound a person can hear depends on its frequency. The human ear is most sensitive to sounds at frequencies between 1000 and 5000 Hz. Thus, loudness ultimately depends on an interaction between amplitude and frequency.

People are also sensitive to variations in the purity of sounds. The purest sound is one that has only a single frequency of vibration, such as that produced by a tuning fork. Most everyday sounds are complex mixtures of many frequencies. The

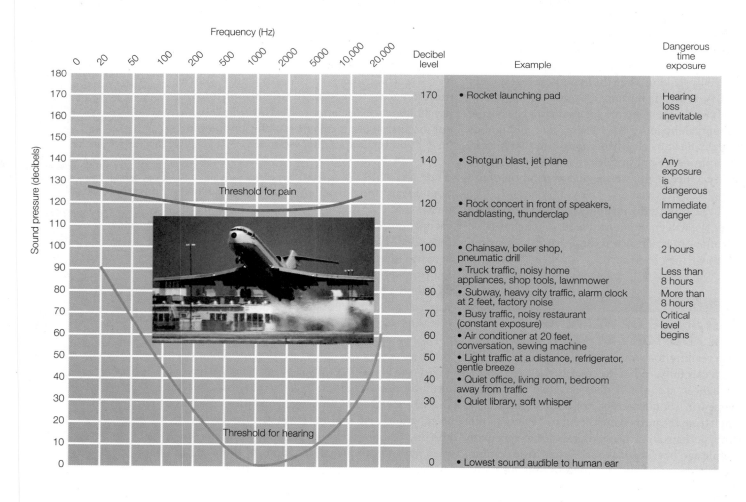

purity or complexity of a sound influences how *timbre* is perceived. To understand timbre, think of a note with precisely the same loudness and pitch played on a French horn and then on a violin. The difference you perceive in the sounds is a difference in timbre.

Sensory Processing in the Ear

Like your eyes, your ears channel energy to the neural tissue that receives it. Figure 4.32 shows that the human ear can be divided into three sections: the external ear, the middle ear, and the inner ear. Sound is conducted differently in each section. The external ear depends on the *vibration of air molecules*. The middle ear depends on the *vibration of movable bones*. And the inner ear depends on *waves in a fluid*, which are finally converted into a stream of neural signals sent to the brain (Kiang & Peake, 1988).

The *external ear* consists mainly of the *pinna*, a sound-collecting cone. When you cup your hand behind your ear to try to hear better, you are augmenting that cone. Many animals have large external ears that they can aim directly toward a sound source. However, humans can adjust their aim only crudely, by turning their heads. Sound waves collected by the pinna are funneled along the auditory canal toward the *eardrum*, a taut membrane that vibrates in response.

In the *middle ear*, the vibrations of the eardrum are transmitted inward by a mechanical chain made up of the three tiniest bones in your body (the hammer, anvil, and stirrup), known collectively as the *ossicles*. The ossicles form a three-stage lever system that converts relatively large movements with little force into smaller motions with greater force. The ossicles serve to amplify tiny changes in air pressure.

The *inner ear* consists largely of **the cochlea, a fluid-filled, coiled tunnel that contains the receptors for hearing.** The term *cochlea* comes from the Greek word for a spiral-shelled snail, which this chamber resembles (see Figure 4.32). Sound enters the cochlea through the *oval window*, which is vibrated by the ossicles. The ear's neural tissue, analogous to the retina in the eye, lies

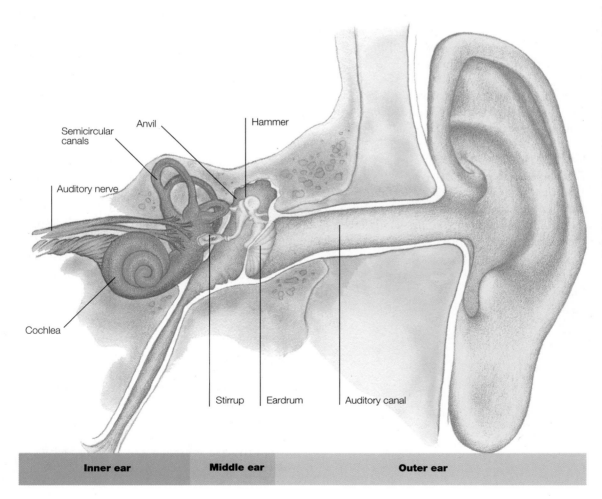

Figure 4.32. The human ear. Converting sound pressure to information processed by the nervous system involves a complex relay of stimuli: Waves of air pressure create vibrations in the eardrum, which in turn cause oscillations in the tiny bones in the inner ear (the hammer, anvil, and stirrup). As they are relayed from one bone to the next, the oscillations are magnified and then transformed into pressure waves moving through a liquid medium in the cochlea. These waves cause the basilar membrane to oscillate, stimulating the hair cells that are the actual auditory receptors (see Figure 4.33).

Semicircular canals

Anvil

Hammer

Auditory nerve

Cochlea

Stirrup   Eardrum

Auditory canal

Inner ear   Middle ear   Outer ear

Check your understanding of both vision and audition by comparing key aspects of sensation and perception in these senses. The dimensions of comparison are listed in the first column below. The second column lists the answers for the sense of vision. Fill in the answers for the sense of hearing in the third column. The answers can be found in Appendix A in the back of the book.

Dimension	Vision	Hearing
1. Stimulus	Light waves	
2. Elements of stimulus and related perceptions	Wavelength/hue Amplitude/brightness Purity/saturation	
3. Receptors	Rods and cones	
4. Location of receptors	Retina	
5. Main location of processing in brain	Occipital lobe, visual cortex	

Figure 4.33. The basilar membrane. The figure shows the cochlea unwound and cut open to reveal the basilar membrane, which is covered with thousands of hair cells (the auditory receptors). Pressure waves in the fluid filling the cochlea cause oscillations to travel in waves down the basilar membrane, stimulating the hair cells to fire. Although the entire membrane vibrates, as predicted by frequency theory, the point along the membrane where the wave peaks depends on the frequency of the sound stimulus, as suggested by place theory.

within the cochlea. This tissue sits on the basilar membrane that divides the cochlea into upper and lower chambers. **The *basilar membrane*, which runs the length of the spiraled cochlea, holds the auditory receptors, called hair cells.** Waves in the fluid of the inner ear stimulate the hair cells. Like the rods and cones in the eye, the hair cells convert this physical stimulation into neural impulses that are sent to the brain (Dallos, 1981). These signals are routed through the thalamus to the auditory cortex, which is located mostly in the temporal lobes of the brain.

Auditory Perception: Theories of Hearing

Theories of hearing need to account for how sound waves are physiologically translated into the perceptions of pitch, loudness, and timbre. To date, most of the theorizing about hearing has focused on the perception of pitch, which is reasonably well understood. Researchers' understanding of loudness and timbre perception is primitive by comparison. Hence, we'll limit our coverage to theories of pitch perception.

Place Theory

There have been two influential theories of pitch perception: *place theory* and *frequency theory*. You'll be able to follow the development of these theories more easily if you can imagine the spiraled cochlea unraveled, so that the basilar membrane becomes a long, thin sheet, lined with about 25,000 individual hair cells (see Figure 4.33). Long ago, Hermann von Helmholtz (1863) proposed that specific sound frequencies vibrate specific portions of the basilar membrane, producing distinct pitches, just as plucking specific strings on a harp produces sounds of varied pitch. *Thus, place theory holds that perception of pitch corresponds to the vibration of different portions, or places, along the basilar membrane.* Place theory assumes that hair cells at various locations respond independently and that different sets of hair cells are vibrated by different sound frequencies. The brain then detects the frequency of a tone according to which area along the basilar membrane is most active.

Frequency Theory

Other theorists in the 19th century proposed an alternative theory of pitch perception, called frequency theory (Rutherford, 1886). *Frequency theory holds that perception of pitch corresponds to the rate, or frequency, at which the entire basilar membrane vibrates.* This theory views the basilar membrane as more like a drumhead than a harp. According to frequency theory, the whole membrane vibrates in unison in response to sounds. However, a particular sound frequency, say 3000 Hz, causes the basilar membrane to vibrate at a corresponding rate of 3000 times per second. The brain detects the frequency of a tone by the rate at which the auditory nerve fibers fire.

Reconciling Place and Frequency Theories

The competition between these two theories is reminiscent of the dispute between the trichromatic and opponent process theories of color vision. Like that argument, the debate between place and frequency theories generated roughly a century of research. Although both theories proved to have some flaws, *both turned out to be valid in part.*

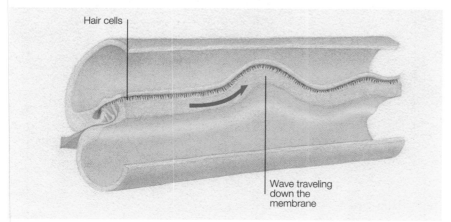

Hair cells

Wave traveling down the membrane

Helmholtz's place theory was basically on the mark except for one detail. The hair cells along the basilar membrane are not independent. They vibrate together, as suggested by frequency theory. The actual pattern of vibration, described in Nobel prize–winning research by Georg von Békésy (1947), is a traveling wave that moves along the basilar membrane. Place theory is correct, however, in that the wave peaks at a particular place, depending on the frequency of the sound wave.

Frequency theory was also found to be flawed when investigators learned that neurons are hard pressed to fire at a maximum rate of about 1000 impulses per second. How, then, can frequency theory account for the translation of 4000 Hz sound waves, which would require 4000 impulses per second? The answer, suggested by Wever and Bray (1937), is that groups of hair cells operate according to the volley principle. **The *volley principle* holds that groups of auditory nerve fibers fire neural impulses in rapid succession, creating volleys of impulses.** These volleys exceed the 1000-per-second limit. Studies suggest that auditory nerves can team up like this to generate volleys of up to 5000 impulses per second (Zwislocki, 1981).

Although the original theories had to be revised, the current thinking is that pitch perception depends on both place and frequency coding of vibrations along the basilar membrane (Goldstein, 1989). Sounds under 1000 Hz appear to be translated into pitch through frequency coding. For sounds between 1000 and 5000 Hz, pitch perception seems to depend on a combination of frequency and place coding. Sounds over 5000 Hz seem to be handled through place coding only. Again we find that theories that were pitted against each other for decades are complementary rather than contradictory.

OUR CHEMICAL SENSES: TASTE AND SMELL

Psychologists have devoted most of their attention to the visual and auditory systems. Although less is known about the chemical senses, taste and smell also play a critical role in people's experience of the world. Let's take a brief look at what psychologists have learned about **the *gustatory system*—the sensory system for taste**—and its close cousin, **the *olfactory system*—the sensory system for smell.**

Taste: The Gustatory System

True wine lovers go through an elaborate series of steps when they are served a good bottle of wine. Typically, they begin by drinking a little water to clean their palate. Then they sniff the cork from the wine bottle, swirl a small amount of the wine around in a glass, and sniff the odor emerging from the glass. Finally, they take a sip of the wine, rolling it around in their mouth for a short time before swallowing it. At last they are ready to confer their approval or disapproval. Is all this activity really a meaningful way to put the wine to a sensitive test? Or is it just a harmless ritual passed on through tradition? You'll find out in this section.

The physical stimuli for the sense of taste are chemical substances that are soluble (dissolvable in water). The gustatory receptors are clusters of taste cells found in the *taste buds* that line the trenches around tiny bumps on the tongue. When these cells absorb chemicals dissolved in saliva, they trigger neural impulses that are routed through the thalamus to the cortex. Interestingly, taste cells have a short life, spanning only about ten days, and they are constantly being replaced (Pfaffman, 1978). New cells are born at the edge of the taste bud and migrate inward to die at the center.

It's generally (but not universally) agreed that there are four *primary tastes:* sweet, sour, bitter, and salty (Bartoshuk, 1988). Sensitivity to these tastes is distributed somewhat unevenly across the tongue. However, Linda Bartoshuk (1993), a leading authority on taste research, emphasizes that these variations in sensitivity are quite small and very complicated (see Figure 4.34). Although most taste cells respond to more than one of the primary tastes, they typically respond best to one. Perceptions of taste quality appear to depend on complex patterns of neural activity initiated by taste receptors (Castelloci, 1986; Pfaffmann, 1974).

"Good and bad are so intimately associated with taste and smell that we have special words for the experiences (e.g., repugnant, foul). The immediacy of the pleasure makes it seem absolute and thus inborn. This turns out to be true for taste but not for smell."
LINDA BARTOSHUK

Figure 4.34. The "classic view" of the tongue and taste. For decades, it has been widely reported that the taste buds sensitive to the four primary tastes are distributed unevenly across the tongue, in the manner shown here. However, these classic tongue maps were based on a misinterpretation of early research data and they greatly oversimplify the spatial representation of taste sensitivity on the tongue (Bartoshuk, 1993). Sensitivity to the primary tastes does vary across the tongue, but these variations are small, and all four primary tastes can be detected wherever there are taste receptors.

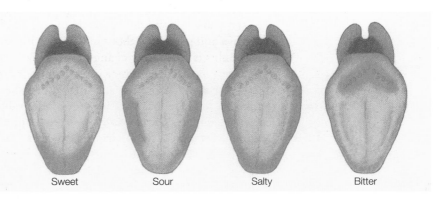

Sweet   Sour   Salty   Bitter

Figure 4.35. Culture and taste preferences. Taste preferences are largely learned, and they vary dramatically from one society to the next, as these examples demonstrate.

Blood. Several tribes in East Africa supplement their diet with fresh blood that is cometimes mixed with milk. They obtain the blood by puncturing a cow's jugular vein with a sharp arrow. The blood-milk drink provides a rich source of protein and iron.

Fish eyes. For some Eskimo children, raw fish eyes are like candy. Here you see a young girl using the Eskimo's all-purpose knife to gouge out the eye of an already-filleted Arctic fish.

Grubs. For most North Americans, the thought of eating a worm would be totally unthinkable. For the Asmat of New Guinea, however, a favorite delicacy is the plump, white, 2-inch larva or beetle grub.

Although some basic aspects of taste perception may be innate, taste preferences are largely learned and heavily influenced by social processes (Rozin, 1990). Most parents are aware of this reality and intentionally try—with varied success—to mold their children's taste preferences early in life (Casey & Rozin, 1989). This extensive social influence contributes greatly to the striking ethnic and cultural disparities found in taste preferences (Kittler & Sucher, 1989). Foods that are a source of disgust in Western cultures—such as worms, fish eyes, and blood—may be delicacies in other cultures (see Figure 4.35). Indeed, Rozin (1990) asserts that feces may be the only universal source of taste-related disgust in humans. To a large degree, variations in taste preferences depend on what one has been exposed to (Capaldi & VandenBos, 1991). Exposure to various foods varies along ethnic lines because different cultures have different traditions in food preparation, different agricultural resources, different climates to work with, and so forth.

When you eat, you are constantly mixing food and saliva and moving it about in your mouth, so the stimulus is constantly changing. However, if you place a flavored substance in a single spot on your tongue, the taste will fade until it vanishes (Krakauer & Dallenbach, 1937). This fading effect is an example of *sensory adaptation*—a gradual **decline in sensitivity to prolonged stimulation.** Sensory adaptation is not unique to taste. This phenomenon occurs in other senses as well. In the taste system, sensory adaptation can leave aftereffects (Bartoshuk, 1968). For example, adaptation to a sour solution makes water taste sweet, whereas adaptation to a sweet solution makes water taste bitter.

So far, we've been discussing taste, but what we are really interested in is the *perception of flavor.* You probably won't be surprised to learn that odor contributes greatly to flavor (Bartoshuk, 1991). The ability to identify flavors declines noticeably when odor cues are absent (Mozell et al., 1969). Although taste and smell are distinct sensory systems, they interact extensively. You might have noticed this interaction when you ate a favorite meal while enduring a severe head cold. The food probably tasted bland, because your stuffy nose impaired your sense of smell—and taste.

Now that we've explored the dynamics of taste, we can return to our question about the value of the wine-tasting ritual. This elaborate ritual is indeed an authentic way to put wine to a sensitive test. The aftereffects associated with sensory adaptation make it wise to clean one's palate before tasting the wine. Sniffing the cork, and the wine in the glass, is important because odor is a major determinant of flavor. Swirling the wine in the glass helps release the wine's odor inside the glass. Rolling the wine around in your mouth is especially critical because it distributes the wine over the full diversity of taste cells. It also forces the wine's odor up into the nasal passages. Thus, each action in this age-old ritual makes a meaningful contribution to the tasting.

Smell: The Olfactory System

In many ways, the sense of smell is much like the sense of taste. The physical stimuli are chemical substances—volatile ones that can evaporate and be carried in the air. These chemical stimuli are dissolved in fluid—specifically, the mucus in the nose. The receptors for smell are *olfactory cilia*, hairlike structures located in the upper portion of the nasal passages (Cagen & Rhein, 1980) (see Figure 4.36). They resemble taste cells in that they have a short life and are constantly being replaced. The olfactory receptors have axons that synapse directly with cells in the olfactory bulb at the base of the brain. This arrangement is unique. *Smell is the only sensory system that is not routed through the thalamus before it projects to the cortex.*

Odors cannot be classified as neatly as tastes, since efforts to identify primary odors have proven unsatisfactory. If primary odors exist, there must be a fairly large number of them. Most olfactory receptors respond to a wide range of odors (Sicard & Holley, 1984). Hence, the perception of various odors probably depends on patterns of activation across millions of receptors. As with taste, the sense of smell shows *sensory adaptation*. The perceived strength of an odor usually declines to less than half its original strength within about 4 minutes (Cain, 1988). For example, let's say you walk into your kitchen and find that the garbage has started to smell. If you stay in the kitchen without removing the garbage, the stench will soon start to fade.

Overall, humans have greater olfactory capacities than widely believed (Cain, 1979). Although there are some species whose sense of smell is superior (dogs, for instance), human olfaction compares favorably with that of many animals.

OUR OTHER SENSES

We have discussed the dynamics of sensation and perception in four sensory domains: vision, hearing, taste, and smell. Since it is widely known that humans have five senses, all that remains is touch. Right? Wrong! In addition to touch, people have still other sensory systems, including the kinesthetic system (which monitors positions of the body) and the vestibular system (sense of balance). Let's take a brief look at these three sensory systems.

Touch: Sensory Systems in the Skin

The physical stimuli for touch are mechanical, thermal, and chemical energy that impinge upon the skin. These stimuli can produce perceptions of tactile stimulation (the pressure of touch against the skin), warmth, cold, and pain. The human skin is saturated with at least six different types of sensory receptors (Gardner, 1975). To some degree, these different types of receptors are specialized for different functions, such as the registration of pressure, hot, cold, and so forth. However, these distinctions are not as clear as researchers had originally thought (Sinclair, 1981).

If you've been to a mosquito-infested picnic lately, you'll appreciate the need to quickly know where tactile stimulation is coming from. The sense of touch is set up to meet this need for tactile localization with admirable precision and efficiency. Cells in the nervous system that respond to touch are sensitive to specific patches of skin. These skin patches, which vary considerably in size, are the functional equivalents of *receptive fields* in vision. Like visual receptive fields, they often involve a center-surround arrange-

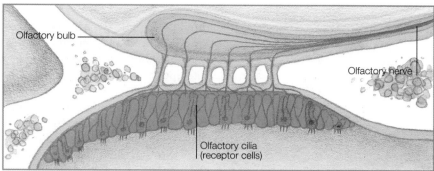
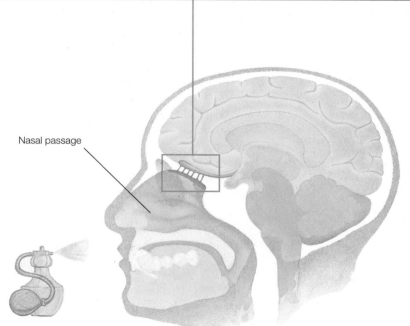

Figure 4.36. The olfactory system. Odor molecules travel through the nasal passages and stimulate olfactory cilia. An enlargement of these hairlike olfactory receptors is shown in the inset. The olfactory nerve transmits neural impulses through the olfactory bulb to the brain.

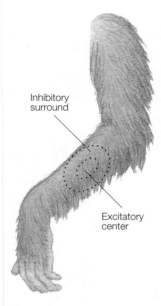

Figure 4.37. Receptive field for touch. A receptive field for touch is an area on the skin surface that, when stimulated, affects the firing of a cell that responds to pressure on the skin. Shown here is a center-surround receptive field for a cell in the thalamus of a monkey.

(labels on figure: Inhibitory surround; Excitatory center)

ment, as shown in Figure 4.37 (Kandel & Jessell, 1991). If a stimulus is applied continuously to a specific spot on the skin, the perception of pressure gradually fades. Thus, *sensory adaptation* occurs in the perception of touch, as it does in other sensory systems.

The nerve fibers that carry incoming information about tactile stimulation are routed through the spinal cord to the brainstem. The tactile pathway then projects through the thalamus and onto the *somatosensory cortex* in the brain's parietal lobe. The entire body is sensitive to touch. However, in humans the bulk of the somatosensory cortex is devoted to processing signals coming from the fingers, lips, and tongue. Some cells in the somatosensory cortex function like the *feature detectors* discovered in vision (Cholewiak & Collins, 1991). They respond to specific features of touch, such as a movement across the skin in a particular direction.

The receptors for pain are mostly free nerve endings in the skin. As unpleasant as pain is, the sensation of pain is crucial to survival. Pain is a marvelous warning system. It tells people when they should stop shoveling snow, or it lets them know that they have a pinched nerve that requires treatment.

Pain messages are transmitted to the brain via two pathways that pass through different areas in the thalamus (Willis, 1985). One is a *fast pathway* that registers localized pain and relays it to the cortex in a fraction of a second. This is the system that hits you with sharp pain when you first cut your finger. The second system uses a *slow pathway*, routed through the limbic system, that lags a second or two behind the fast system. This pathway (which also carries information about temperature) conveys the less localized, longer-lasting, aching or burning pain that comes after the initial injury (see Figure 4.38).

As with other perceptions, pain is not an automatic result of certain types of stimulation. The perception of pain can be influenced greatly by expectations, personality, mood, and other factors involving higher mental processes. The psychological element in pain perception becomes clear when something distracts your attention from pain and the hurting temporarily disappears. For example, imagine that you've just hit your thumb with a hammer and it's throbbing with pain. Suddenly, your child cries out that there's a fire in the laundry room. As you race to deal with this emergency, you forget all about the pain in your thumb.

Cultural variations in the experience of pain provide further evidence for the subjective quality of pain. Melzack and Wall (1982) have described a number of anecdotal examples of remarkable pain tolerance in non-Western cultures. More-

Figure 4.38 The two pathways for pain signals. Pain signals are sent from receptors to the brain along the two pathways depicted here. The fast pathway, shown in red, and the slow pathway, shown in black, depend on different types of nerve fibers and are routed through different parts of the thalamus. The gate control mechanism posited by Melzack and Wall (1965) apparently depends on descending signals originating in an area of the midbrain (the pathway shown in green).

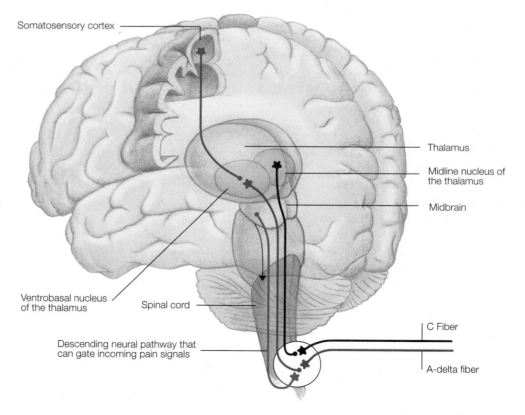

(labels on figure: Somatosensory cortex; Thalamus; Midline nucleus of the thalamus; Midbrain; Ventrobasal nucleus of the thalamus; Spinal cord; C Fiber; A-delta fiber; Descending neural pathway that can gate incoming pain signals)

over, systematic empirical comparisons have found ethnic and cultural differences in the experience of chronic pain (Bates, Edwards, & Anderson, 1993) and the pain associated with childbirth (Jordan, 1983). According to Melzack and Wall (1982), culture doesn't affect the process of pain perception so much as the willingness to tolerate certain types of pain, a conclusion echoed by Zatzick and Dimsdale (1990). In any case, cross-cultural research provides support for Beecher's (1956) widely cited conclusion that "the intensity of suffering is largely determined by what the pain means to the patient" (p. 1609).

As you can see, then, tissue damage that sends pain impulses on their way to the brain doesn't necessarily result in the experience of pain. Cognitive and emotional processes that unfold in higher brain centers can somehow block pain signals coming from peripheral receptors.

How are incoming pain signals blocked? In an influential effort to answer this question, Ronald Melzack and Patrick Wall (1965) devised the gate-control theory of pain. *Gate-control theory holds that incoming pain sensations must pass through a "gate" in the spinal cord that can be closed, thus blocking ascending pain signals.* The gate in this model is not an anatomical structure but a pattern of neural activity that inhibits incoming pain signals. Melzack and Wall suggested that this imaginary gate can be closed by signals from peripheral receptors or by signals from the brain. They theorized that the latter mechanism can help explain how factors such as attention and expectations can shut off pain signals. As a whole, research suggests that the concept of a gating mechanism for pain has merit (Rollman, 1991). However, relatively little support has been found for the neural circuitry originally hypothesized by Melzack and Wall. Other neural mechanisms, discovered after gate-control theory was proposed, appear to be responsible for blocking the perception of pain.

One of these discoveries was the identification of endorphins. As discussed in Chapter 3, *endorphins* are the body's own natural morphinelike painkillers, which are widely distributed in the central nervous system. The other discovery involved the identification of a descending neural pathway that mediates the suppression of pain (Basbaum & Fields, 1984). This pathway appears to originate in an area of the midbrain (see Figure 4.38). Neural activity in this pathway is probably initiated by endorphins. The circuits in this pathway synapse in the spinal cord, where they inhibit the activity of neurons that would normally transmit incoming pain impulses to the brain. The impact of cognitive and emotional factors on pain may be mediated by signals sent down this pathway from higher brain centers.

CONCEPT CHECK 4.5
Comparing Taste, Smell, and Touch

Check your understanding of taste, smell, and touch by comparing these sensory systems on the dimensions listed in the first column below. A few answers are supplied; see whether you can fill in the rest. The answers can be found in Appendix A.

Dimension	Taste	Smell	Touch
Stimulus	_____	Volatile chemicals in air	_____
Receptors	_____	_____	Many (at least 6) types
Location of receptors	_____	Upper areas of nasal passages	_____
Basic elements of perception	Sweet, sour, salty, bitter	_____	_____

The Kinesthetic System

The *kinesthetic system* **monitors the positions of the various parts of the body.** To some extent, you know where your limbs are because you commanded the muscles that put them there. Nonetheless, the kinesthetic system allows you to double-check these locations. Where are the receptors for your kinesthetic sense? Some reside in the joints, indicating how much they are bending. Others reside within the muscles, registering their tautness, or extension. Most kinesthetic stimulation is transmitted to the brain along the same pathway as tactile stimulation. However, the two types of information are kept separate (Vierck, 1978).

The Vestibular System

When you're jolting along in a bus, the world outside the bus window doesn't seem to jump about as your head bounces up and down. Yet a movie taken with a camera fastened to the bus would show a bouncing world. How are you and the camera different? Unlike the camera, you are equipped with a *vestibular system,* **which responds to gravity and keeps you informed of your body's location in space.** The vestibular system provides the sense of balance, or equilibrium, compensating for changes in the body's position (Parker, 1980).

The vestibular system shares space in the inner ear with the auditory system. The *semicircular canals* make up the largest part of the vestibular

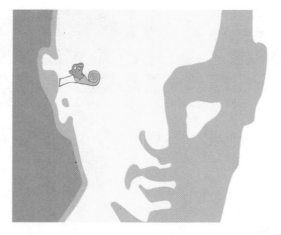

Figure 4.39. The vestibular system. The semicircular canals in the inner ear (which are shown disproportionately large here) are the sensory organ for balance and head movement. Fluid movements in these canals stimulate neural impulses that travel along the vestibular nerve to the brain.

system (see Figure 4.39). They look like three inner tubes joined at the base. Any rotational motion of the head is uniquely represented by a combination of fluid flows in the semicircular canals (Kelly, 1991). These shifts in fluid are detected by hair cells similar to those found along the basilar membrane in the cochlea. Your perceptual system integrates the vestibular input about your body's position with information from other senses. After all, you can see where you are and you know where you've instructed your muscles to take you.

This integration of sensory input raises a point that merits emphasis as we close our tour of the human sensory systems. Although we have discussed the various sensory domains separately, it's important to remember that all the senses send signals to the same brain, where the information is pooled. Sensory integration is the norm in perceptual experience. For example, when you sit beside a campfire, you *see* it blazing, you *hear* it crackling, you *smell* it burning, and you feel the *touch* of its warmth. If you cook something over it, you may even *taste* it. Thus, perception involves building a unified model of the world out of integrated input from all the senses.

PUTTING IT IN PERSPECTIVE

In this chapter, three of our unifying themes stood out in sharp relief: (1) psychology is theoretically diverse, (2) people's experience of the world is highly subjective, and (3) our behavior is shaped by our cultural heritage. Let's discuss the value of theoretical diversity first.

Contradictory theories about behavior can be disconcerting and frustrating for theorists, researchers, teachers, and students alike. Most of us show a natural human tendency to want to tie things up in a neat, sensible package. Yet this chapter provides two dramatic demonstrations of how theoretical diversity can lead to progress in the long run. For decades, the trichromatic and opponent process theories of color vision and the place and frequency theories of pitch perception were viewed as fundamentally incompatible. These competing theories generated and guided the research that now provides a fairly solid understanding of how people perceive color and pitch. As you know, in each case the evidence eventually revealed that the opposing theories were not really incompatible. Both were needed to fully explain the sensory processes that each sought to explain individually. If it hadn't been for these theoretical debates, current understanding of color vision and pitch perception might be far more primitive, as the understanding of timbre still is.

This chapter should also have enhanced your appreciation of why human experience of the world is highly subjective. As ambiguous figures and optical illusions clearly show, there is no one-to-one correspondence between sensory input and perceived experience of the world. Perception is an active process in which people organize and interpret the information received by the senses. These interpretations are shaped by a host of factors, including the environmental context and perceptual sets. Small wonder, then, that people often perceive the same event in very different ways. Thus, individuals' experience of the world is subjective because the process of perception is inherently subjective.

Finally, this chapter provided numerous examples of how cultural factors can shape behavior—in an area of research where one might expect to find little cultural influence. Most people are not surprised to learn that there are cultural differences in attitudes, values, social behavior, and development. But perception is widely viewed as a basic, universal process that should be invariant across cultures. In some respects it is, as the similarities among cultural groups in perception far outweigh the differences. Nonetheless, we saw cultural variations in depth perception, susceptibility to illusions, taste preferences, and pain tolerance. Thus, even a fundamental, heavily physiological process such as perception can be modified to some degree by one's cultural background.

The following Application will highlight the subjectivity of perception once again. It focuses on how painters have learned to use the principles of visual perception to achieve a variety of artistic goals.

Thinking About Art and Illusion

Answer the following multiple-choice question:
Artistic works such as paintings

___ **1** render an accurate picture of reality

___ **2** create an illusion of reality

___ **3** provide an interpretation of reality

___ **4** make us think about the nature of reality

___ **5** all of the above

The answer to this question is (5), "all of the above." Historically, artists have had many and varied purposes, including each of those listed in the question. To realize their goals, artists have had to use a number of principles of perception—sometimes quite deliberately, and sometimes not. Let's use the example of painting to explore the role of perceptual principles in art and illusion.

The goal of most early painters was to produce a believable picture of reality. This goal immediately created a problem familiar to most of us who have attempted to draw realistic pictures: the real world is three-dimensional, but a canvas or a sheet of paper is flat. Paradoxically, then, painters who set out to re-create reality had to do so by creating an *illusion* of three-dimensional reality.

Prior to the Renaissance, these efforts to create a convincing illusion of reality were awkward by modern standards. Why? Because artists did not understand how to use depth cues. This is apparent in Figure 4.40, a religious scene painted around 1300. The paint-

Figure 4.40. *The Kiss of Judas* by Jacopo Torriti (circa 1300). Notice how the absence of depth cues makes the painting seem flat and unrealistic.

Figure 4.41. A painting by the Italian Renaissance artists Gentile and Giovanni Bellini (circa 1480). In this painting a number of depth cues—including linear perspective, relative size, height in plane, and interposition—enhance the illusion of three-dimensional reality.

ing clearly lacks a sense of depth. The people seem paper-thin. They have no real position in space.

Many of the principles of geometric perspective that relate to depth perception were discovered during the Renaissance. Figure 4.41 dramatizes the resulting transition in art. This scene, painted by Italian Renaissance artists Gentile and Giovanni Bellini, seems much more realistic and lifelike than the painting in Figure 4.40 because it

employs a number of pictorial depth cues. Notice how the buildings on the sides converge to make use of linear perspective. Additionally, distant objects are smaller than nearby ones, an application of relative size. This painting also uses height in plane, as well as interposition. By taking advantage of pictorial depth cues, an artist can enhance a painting's illusion of reality.

In the centuries since the Renaissance, painters have adopted a number of view-

Figure 4.42. Georges Seurat's *Sunday Afternoon on the Island of La Grande Jatte* (without artist's border) (1884–1886). Seurat used thousands of tiny dots of color and the principles of color mixing (see detail at the right); the eye and brain combine the points into the colors the viewer actually sees. (The Art Institute of Chicago; Helen Birch Bartlett Memorial Collection, 1926.224)

points about the portrayal of reality. For instance, the French Impressionists of the 19th century did not want to re-create the photographic "reality" of a scene. They set out to interpret a viewer's fleeting perception or *impression* of reality. To accomplish this end, they worked with color in unprecedented ways.

Consider, for instance, the work of Georges Seurat, a French artist who used a technique called *pointillism*. Seurat carefully studied what scientists knew about the composition of color in the 1880s, then applied this knowledge in a calculated, laboratory-like manner. Indeed, critics in his era dubbed him the "little chemist." Seurat constructed his paintings out of tiny dots of pure, intense colors. He used additive color mixing, a departure from the norm in painting, which usually depends on subtractive mixing of pigments. A famous result of Seurat's "scientific" approach to painting was his renowned *Sunday Afternoon on the Island of La Grande Jatte* (see Figure 4.42). As the work of Seurat illustrates, modernist painters were moving away from attempts to re-create the world as it is literally seen.

If 19th-century painters liberated color, their successors at the turn of the 20th century liberated form. This was particularly true of the Cubists. Cub-

ism was begun in 1909 by Pablo Picasso, a Spanish artist who went on to experiment with other styles in his prolific career. The Cubists didn't try to *portray* reality so much as to *reassemble* it. They attempted to reduce everything to combinations of geometric forms (lines, circles, triangles, rectangles, and such) laid out in a flat space, lacking depth. In a sense, *they applied the theory of feature analysis to canvas*, as they built

their figures out of simple features.

The resulting paintings were decidedly unrealistic, but the painters would leave realistic fragments that provided clues about the subject. Picasso liked to challenge his viewers to decipher the subject of his paintings. Take a look at the painting in Figure 4.43 and see whether you can figure out what Picasso was portraying.

The work in Figure 4.43 is titled *Violin*

Figure 4.43. *Violin and Grapes* by Pablo Picasso (1912). This painting makes use of Gestalt principles of perceptual organization. (Collection, The Museum of Modern Art, New York, Mrs. David M. Levy Bequest)

Figure 4.44. Salvador Dali's *Slave Market with the Disappearing Bust of Voltaire* (1940). This painting playfully includes a reversible figure (two nuns form the bust of Voltaire, a philosopher known for his stringent criticisms of the Catholic church).

and Grapes. Note how Gestalt principles of perceptual organization are at work to create these forms. Proximity and similarity serve to bring the grapes together in the bottom right corner. Closure accounts for your being able to see the essence of the violin.

The Surrealists toyed with reality in a different way. Influenced by Sigmund Freud's writings on the unconscious, the Surrealists explored the world of dreams and fantasy. Specific elements in their paintings are often depicted realistically, but the strange juxtaposition of elements yields a disconcerting irrationality reminiscent of dreams. A prominent example of this style is Salvador Dali's *Slave Mar-*

ket with the Disappearing Bust of Voltaire, shown in Figure 4.44. Notice the reversible figure near the center of the painting. The "bust of Voltaire" is made up of human figures in the distance, standing in front of an arch. Dali often used reversible figures to enhance the ambiguity of his bizarre visions.

Perhaps no one has been more creative in manipulating perceptual ambiguity than M. C. Escher, a modern Dutch artist. Escher closely followed the work of the Gestalt psychologists, and he readily acknowledged his debt to psychology as a source of inspiration (Teuber, 1974). *Waterfall*, a 1961 lithograph by Escher, is an impossible figure

that appears to defy the law of gravity (see Figure 4.45). The puzzling problem here is that a level channel of water terminates in a waterfall that "falls" into the *same* channel two levels "below." This drawing is made up of two of the impossible triangles shown earlier, in Figure 4.28. In case you need help seeing them, the waterfall itself forms one side of each triangle.

The Necker cube, a reversible figure mentioned earlier (see Figure 4.21), was the inspiration for Escher's 1958 lithograph *Belvedere*, shown in Figure 4.46. You have to look carefully to realize that this is another impossible figure. Note that the top story runs at a right angle

Figure 4.45. Escher's lithograph *Waterfall* (1961). Escher's use of depth cues and impossible triangles deceives the brain into seeing water flow uphill.

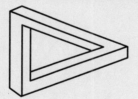

Figure 4.46. Escher's *Belvedere* (1958). This lithograph depicts an impossible figure inspired by the Necker cube. The cube appears in the architecture of the building, in the model held by the boy on the bench, and in the drawing lying at his feet.

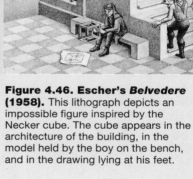

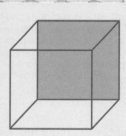

from the first story. Note also how the pillars are twisted around. The pillars that start on one side of the building end up supporting the second story on the other side! Escher's debt to the Necker cube is manifested in several places. Notice, for instance, the drawing of a Necker cube on the floor next to the seated boy (on the lower left). As you can see, Escher's chief goal was to stimulate viewers to think about the nature of reality and the process of visual perception itself.

Chapter 4 Review

KEY IDEAS

Our Sense of Sight: The Visual System

♦ Light varies in terms of wavelength, amplitude, and purity. Light enters the eye through the cornea and pupil and is focused on the retina by the lens. Rods and cones are the visual receptors found in the retina. Cones play a key role in daylight vision and color perception, while rods are critical to night vision and peripheral vision. Dark adaptation and light adaptation both involve changes in the retina's sensitivity to light, which allow the eye to adapt to changes in illumination.

♦ The retina transforms light into neural impulses that are sent to the brain via the optic nerve. Receptive fields are areas in the retina that affect the firing of visual cells. They vary in shape and size, but center-surround arrangements are common. Two visual pathways to the brain send signals through the thalamus to different areas of the visual cortex. The visual cortex contains cells that appear to function as feature detectors.

♦ Perceptions of color (hue) are primarily a function of light wavelength, while amplitude affects brightness and purity affects saturation. Perceptions of colors depend on processes that resemble additive color mixing. The trichromatic theory holds that people have three types of receptors that are sensitive to different wavelengths. The opponent process theory holds that color perception depends on receptors that make antagonistic responses to red versus green, blue versus yellow, and black versus white. The evidence now suggests that both theories are necessary to account for color vision.

♦ According to feature analysis theories, people detect specific elements in stimuli and build them into recognizable forms. Gestalt psychology emphasized that the whole may be greater than the sum of its parts (features), as illustrated by Gestalt principles of form perception, including figure-ground, proximity, similarity, continuity, closure, and simplicity. Other approaches to form perception emphasize that people develop perceptual hypotheses about the distal stimuli that could be responsible for the proximal stimuli that are sensed.

♦ Depth perception depends primarily on monocular cues such as linear perspective, texture gradient, interposition, relative size, height in plane, and light and shadow. Binocular cues such as retinal disparity and convergence can also contribute to depth perception. Cultures may vary in their use of pictorial depth cues.

♦ Perceptual constancies in vision help viewers deal with the ever-shifting nature of proximal stimuli. Optical illusions demonstrate that perceptual hypotheses can be inaccurate and that perceptions are not simple reflections of objective reality. Researchers have found some interesting cultural variations in the susceptibility to certain illusions.

Our Sense of Hearing: The Auditory System

♦ Sound varies in terms of wavelength (frequency), amplitude, and purity. These properties affect mainly perceptions of pitch, loudness, and timbre, respectively.

♦ Sound is transmitted through the external ear via air conduction to the middle ear. In the inner ear, fluid conduction vibrates hair cells along the basilar membrane in the cochlea. These hair cells are the receptors for hearing. Auditory signals are transmitted through the brainstem and thalamus to the primary auditory cortex in the temporal lobe.

♦ Place theory proposed that pitch perception depends on where vibrations occur along the basilar membrane. Frequency theory countered with the idea that pitch perception depends on the rate at which the basilar membrane vibrates. Modern evidence suggests that these theories are complementary rather than incompatible.

Our Chemical Senses: Taste and Smell

♦ The taste buds are sensitive to four basic tastes: sweet, sour, bitter, and salty. Sensitivity to these tastes is distributed unevenly across the tongue. Taste preferences are shaped by experience and culture. The perception of flavor is influenced greatly by the odor of food.

♦ Like taste, smell is a chemical sense. Chemical stimuli activate olfactory receptors lining the nasal passages. Most of these receptors respond to more than one odor.

Our Other Senses

♦ Sensory receptors in the skin respond to pressure, temperature, and pain. Pain signals are sent to the brain along two pathways that are characterized as fast and slow. The perception of pain is highly subjective. Gate-control theory holds that incoming pain signals can be blocked in the spinal cord. Endorphins and a descending neural pathway appear responsible for the suppression of pain.

♦ The kinesthetic system monitors the position of various body parts. The sense of balance depends primarily on activity in the vestibular system.

Putting It in Perspective

♦ This chapter underscored three of our unifying themes: the value of theoretical diversity, the subjective nature of experience, and the importance of one's cultural heritage.

Application: Thinking About Art and Illusion

♦ The principles of visual perception are often applied to artistic endeavors. Painters routinely use pictorial depth cues to make their scenes more lifelike. Color mixing, feature analysis, Gestalt principles, reversible figures, and impossible figures have also been used in influential paintings.

KEY TERMS

Additive color mixing	Nearsightedness
Afterimage	Olfactory system
Basilar membrane	Optical illusion
Binocular cues	Perception
Cochlea	Perceptual constancy
Color blindness	Perceptual hypothesis
Complementary colors	Perceptual set
Cones	Phi phenomenon
Dark adaptation	Proximal stimuli
Depth perception	Pupil
Distal stimuli	Receptive field of a visual cell
Farsightedness	Retina
Feature analysis	Reversible figure
Feature detectors	Rods
Fovea	Sensation
Gustatory system	Sensory adaptation
Impossible figures	Subtractive color mixing
Kinesthetic sense	
Lens	Vestibular system
Light adaptation	Volley principle
Monocular cues	

KEY PEOPLE

Linda Bartoshuk	Ronald Melzack and Patrick Wall
Hermann von Helmholtz	Max Wertheimer
David Hubel and Torsten Wiesel	

5 Variations in Consciousness

A young woman sat alone in a room. Attached to her skull were recording electrodes from an electroencephalograph (EEG)—a machine that monitors the electrical activity of the brain. Connected to the EEG was another device that increased the sound of a tone when the EEG registered a particular pattern of brain waves. As long as the brain-wave pattern persisted, the tone filled the room. When the woman's EEG pattern changed, the room fell silent. As the woman sat quietly, the tone gradually began to sound more frequently. What was happening here?

The young woman was a subject in one of a series of experiments conducted by Joe Kamiya. Kamiya set out to see whether people could learn to control the electrical activity in their brains by altering their mental states (Kamiya, 1969; Nowlis & Kamiya, 1970). The tone provided the subjects with *biofeedback*—information about internal bodily changes that would normally be imperceptible. In the experiment described here, the tone sounded whenever the young woman produced a specific pattern of brain waves called *alpha waves*. Kamiya found that when people are provided with EEG biofeedback, the vast majority *can* learn to alter their brain-wave activity to some extent.

In the course of this research, Kamiya also made some other interesting observations. Although subjects could increase alpha activity, they had difficulty explaining *how* they did it. When pressed, subjects would offer explanations, but the explanations tended to be tentative and vague. Their responses were equally hazy when Kamiya asked them to describe *what it felt like* when they were producing alpha-wave activity. They mostly agreed that the alpha state was quite pleasant, but beyond that they had great difficulty describing it. When questioned, one subject replied, "You keep asking me to describe this darned alpha state. I can't do it. It has a certain feel about it, sure, but really, it's best left undescribed" (Kamiya, 1969, p. 515).

The difficulty Kamiya's subjects experienced when asked to describe their mental state during alpha activity is hardly unique. Researchers find that people also have difficulty describing the states of consciousness associated with hypnosis, meditation, and drug use. Even everyday mental states can defy description. Can you provide a lucid description of exactly how you feel when you daydream? Ironically, the very thing people are most intimately acquainted with—their conscious experience—eludes their best efforts to describe it. The problem may be that consciousness is the ultimate in subjective experience. Your consciousness can be directly experienced by only one person—you.

Our review will begin with a few general points about the nature of consciousness. After that, much of the chapter will be a "bedtime story," as we take a long look at sleep and dreams. We'll continue our tour of variations in consciousness by examining hypnosis, meditation, and the effects of mind-altering drugs. Finally, the Application will address a number of practical questions about sleep and dreams.

ON THE NATURE OF CONSCIOUSNESS

What is consciousness? **Consciousness is the awareness of internal and external stimuli.** Your consciousness includes (1) your awareness of external events ("The professor just asked me a difficult question about medieval history"), (2) your awareness of your internal sensations ("My heart is racing and I'm beginning to sweat"), (3) your awareness of your *self* as the unique being having these experiences ("Why me?"), and (4) your awareness of your thoughts about these experiences ("I'm going to make a fool of myself!"). To put it more concisely, consciousness is personal awareness.

The contents of your consciousness are continually changing. Rarely does consciousness come to a standstill. It moves, it flows, it fluctuates, it wanders. Recognizing this reality, William James (1902) christened this continuous flow the *stream of consciousness*. If you could tape-record your thoughts, you would find an endless flow of ideas that zigzag all over the place. As you will soon learn, even when you sleep your consciousness moves through a series of transitions. To be constantly shifting and changing seems to be part of the essential nature of consciousness.

Variations in Levels of Awareness

While William James emphasized the stream of consciousness, Sigmund Freud (1900) wanted to examine what went on beneath the surface of this stream. As explained in Chapter 1, Freud argued that people's feelings and behavior are influenced by *unconscious* needs, wishes, and conflicts that lie below the surface of conscious awareness. According to Freud, the stream of consciousness has depth. Conscious and unconscious processes are different *levels of awareness*.

Freud was one of the first theorists to recognize that consciousness is not an all-or-none phenomenon. Instead, levels of awareness vary along a continuum between alert, focused awareness and the minimal awareness characteristic of sleep. Like other aspects of consciousness, this continuum is difficult to describe. However, a few examples will illustrate some of the levels included along this continuum.

Near the top of the continuum of awareness are the states of consciousness experienced during activities demanding high concentration, such as taking an exam, planning a move in chess, playing a video game, or learning to drive a car with a stick shift. These kinds of activities require alert awareness, absorb attention, and interfere with other ongoing activities.

At a lower level of awareness we find the states of consciousness that you experience when you're awake but on "automatic pilot." For example, once you learn to drive with a stick shift, working the shift will no longer require much attention. People can walk, talk, and chew gum at the same time because these are automatic processes that occur with little awareness, require minimal attention, and do not interfere much with other activities.

Further down the continuum of levels of awareness are the states of consciousness people experience when asleep or when they are put under anesthesia for surgery. Even in these situations, people continue to maintain some awareness. How do we know? Because some stimuli can still penetrate awareness. For example, people under surgical anesthesia occasionally hear comments made during their surgery, which they later repeat to their surprised surgeons (Bennett, 1993). Admittedly, relatively few surgical patients report recollections of events that occurred while they were anesthesized (Goldmann, 1990). However, studies employing subtle, sensitive measures of recall suggest that memory processes are more active during anesthesia than previously believed (Kihlstrom et al., 1990). Furthermore, in laboratory studies of sleep processes, subjects who are clearly asleep (based on monitoring of physiological indicators) have responded to faint tones by pressing a palm-mounted button (Ogilvie & Wilkinson, 1988).

Not only are people aware of some stimuli when they are largely unconscious, they can also discriminate among different stimuli. A good example is the new parent who can sleep through a loud thunderstorm or a buzzing alarm clock but who immediately hears the muffled sound of the baby crying down the hall. The parent's selective sensitivity to sounds means that some mental processing must be going on even during sleep. This minimal awareness marks the lower end of the continuum of levels of awareness.

Consciousness and Brain Activity

Variations in consciousness are intimately related to changes in electrical activity in the brain. Investigators have been exploring this relationship ever since Hans Berger (1929) invented the EEG. **The electroencephalograph (EEG) is a device that monitors the electrical activity of the brain over time by means of recording electrodes attached to the surface of the scalp.** The EEG records and amplifies electrical activity in the outer layer of the brain, the cortex.

Ultimately, the EEG summarizes the rhythm of cortical activity in the brain in terms of line tracings called *brain waves*. These brain-wave tracings vary in *amplitude* (height) and *frequency* (cycles per second, abbreviated *cps*). You can see what brain waves look like if you glance ahead to Figure 5.5. Human brain-wave activity is usually divided into four principal bands based on the frequency of the brain waves. These bands, named after letters in the Greek alphabet, are *beta* (13–24 cps), *alpha* (8–12 cps), *theta* (4–7 cps), and *delta* (under 4 cps).

Different patterns of EEG activity are associated with different states of consciousness, as is summarized in Table 5.1. For instance, when you are alertly engaged in problem solving, beta waves tend to dominate. When you are relaxed and resting, alpha waves increase. When you slip into deep, dreamless sleep, delta waves become more prevalent. Although these correlations are far from perfect, changes in brain activity are

Recording electrodes attached to the surface of the scalp permit the electroencephalograph (EEG) to record the brain's electrical activity over time. The EEG provides output in the form of tracings, called brain waves, that indicate the person's state of consciousness.

closely related to variations in consciousness (Guyton, 1991).

As is often the case with correlations, researchers are faced with a chicken-or-egg puzzle when it comes to the relationship between mental states and the brain's electrical activity. If you become drowsy while you are reading this passage, your brain-wave activity will probably change. But are these changes causing your drowsiness, or is your drowsiness causing the changes in brain-wave activity? Or are the drowsiness and the shifts in brain-wave activity both caused by a *third* factor—perhaps signals coming from a subcortical area in the brain? (See Figure 5.1.) Frankly, no one knows. All that is known for sure is that variations in consciousness are correlated with variations in brain activity.

Measures of brain-wave activity have provided investigators with a method for mapping out the mysterious state of consciousness called sleep. As we will see in the next section, this state turns out to be far more complex and varied than you might expect.

THE SLEEP AND WAKING CYCLE

Sleep is a variation in consciousness that is familiar to everyone. If you live to be 75, you'll probably spend somewhere between 18 and 25 years lost in sleep. Although it is a familiar state of consciousness, sleep is widely misunderstood. Generally, people consider sleep to be a single, uniform state of physical and mental inactivity, during which the brain is "turned off." In reality, sleepers pass through several states of consciousness and experience quite a bit of physical and mental activity.

The advances in our understanding of sleep have been the result of hard work by researchers who have spent countless nighttime hours watching other people sleep. This work is done in sleep laboratories, where volunteer subjects come to spend the night. Sleep labs have one or more "bedrooms" in which the subjects retire, usually after being hooked up to a variety of physiological recording devices. In addition to an EEG, these devices typically include **an *electromyograph* (EMG), which records muscular activity and tension; an *electrooculograph* (EOG), which records eye movements; and an *electrocardiograph* (EKG), which records the contractions of the heart**. Other instruments monitor breathing, pulse rate, and body temperature. The researchers observe the sleeping subject through a

Table 5.1 EEG Patterns Associated with States of Consciousness

EEG Pattern	Frequency (cps)	Typical States of Consciousness
Beta (β)	13–24	Normal waking thought, alert problem solving
Alpha (α)	8–12	Deep relaxation, blank mind, meditation
Theta (θ)	4–7	Light sleep
Delta (Δ)	0–3	Deep sleep

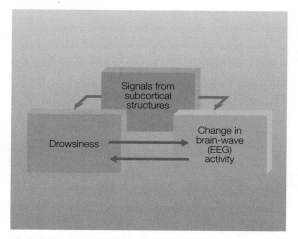

Figure 5.1. The correlation between mental states and electrical activity in the brain. Correlations alone do not establish causation. For example, there is a strong correlation between the occurrence of drowsiness and a particular pattern of brain-wave activity. But does drowsiness cause a change in brain waves, or do changes in brain waves cause drowsiness? Or does some third variable account for the changes in both?

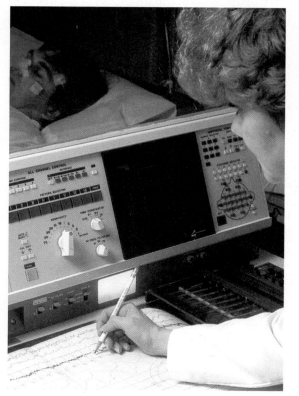

Researchers in a sleep laboratory can observe subjects while using elaborate equipment to record physiological changes during sleep. This kind of research has disclosed that sleep is a complex series of physical and mental states.

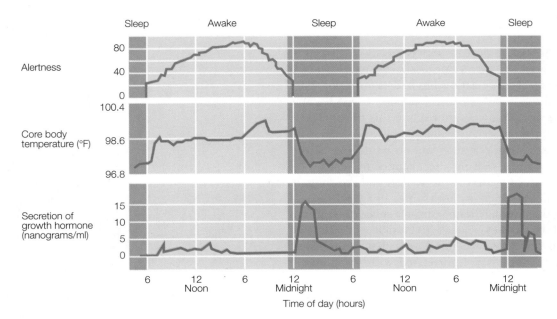

Figure 5.2. Examples of circadian rhythms. These graphs show how alertness, core body temperature, and the secretion of growth hormone typically fluctuate in a 24-hour rhythm. Note how alertness tends to diminish with declining body temperature.

Sleep as a Biological Rhythm

Rhythm pervades the world around us. The daily alternation of light and darkness, the annual pattern of the seasons, and the phases of the moon all reflect this rhythmic quality of repeating cycles. Humans and many other animals display biological rhythms that are tied to these planetary rhythms (Winfree, 1987). *Biological rhythms* **are periodic fluctuations in physiological functioning.** Birds beginning a winter migration and raccoons going into hibernation show the influence of a yearly cycle. In humans, females' 28-day menstrual cycle has been related to fluctuations in mood, although the data are complex and controversial (Reid, 1991). Males may experience similar but less obvious 28-day cycles that affect their hormonal secretions (Parlee, 1973, 1982). The existence of these rhythms means that organisms have internal "biological clocks" that somehow monitor the passage of time.

Circadian Rhythms

Circadian rhythms **are the 24-hour biological cycles found in humans and many other species.** In humans, circadian rhythms are particularly influential in the regulation of sleep (Moore, 1990). However, daily cycles also produce rhythmic variations in blood pressure, urine production, hormonal secretions, and other physical functions, some of which are highlighted in Figure 5.2 (Aschoff & Wever, 1981). For instance, body temperature varies rhythmically in a daily cycle, usually peaking in the afternoon and reaching its low point in the depths of the night.

A study by Charles Czeisler and his colleagues (1980) indicates that people generally fall asleep as their body temperature begins to drop and awaken as it begins to ascend once again. Researchers have concluded that circadian rhythms can leave individuals physiologically primed to fall asleep most easily at a particular time of day. This optimal time varies from one person to another, depending on their schedules, but it's interesting to learn that each individual may have an "ideal" time for going to bed.

To study biological clocks, researchers have monitored physiological processes while subjects are cut off from exposure to the cycle of day and night. For instance, some subjects have spent weeks in a cave or a closed-off room without windows or clocks. These studies reveal that circadian rhythms generally persist even when information about the light-dark cycle is eliminated. Interestingly, however, when people are isolated in this way, *they often drift toward a 25-hour cycle* (Welsh, 1993). That is, subjects tend to go to sleep and awaken a little later each day. This trend is charted for one experimental subject in Figure 5.3. Investigators aren't sure why this drift toward a 25-hour day occurs.

Although people's biological clocks continue to function when they're cut off from the daily cycle of light and darkness, their biological rhythms often become more erratic in these circumstances. This observation led many theorists to conclude that *exposure to daylight readjusts people's biological clocks*. The readjustments may be necessary to correct for the tendency to drift toward a 25-hour cycle.

Based on animal studies, researchers have a pretty good idea of how the day-night cycle resets human biological clocks. Exposure to sunlight apparently affects the activity of a small structure in the hypothalamus (Rietveld, 1985). This structure sends signals to the nearby *pineal gland*, whose secretion of the hormone melatonin appears to play a key role in adjusting biological clocks (Wever, 1989).

Ignoring Circadian Rhythms

What happens when you ignore your biological clock and go to sleep at an unusual time? Typically, the quality of your sleep suffers. Getting out of sync with your circadian rhythms also causes *jet lag*. When you fly across several time zones, your biological clock keeps time as usual, even though official clock time changes. You then go to sleep at the "wrong" time and are likely to experience difficulty falling asleep and poor quality sleep (Tepas, 1982). This inferior sleep, which can continue to occur for several days, can make you feel fatigued, sluggish, and irritable.

People differ in how quickly they can reset their biological clocks to compensate for jet lag, but a rough rule of thumb is that the readjustment process takes about a day for each time zone crossed (Colquhoun, 1984; Moline, 1993). In addition, the speed of readjustment depends on the direction traveled. Generally, it's easier to fly westward and lengthen your day than it is to fly eastward and shorten it (Moore-Ede, Sulzman, Fuller, 1982). Why does it takes longer to resynchronize after flying east (see Figure 5.4)? Perhaps because of our curious tendency to drift toward a 25-hour cycle. Flying westward allows you to follow this natural drift toward lengthening the daily cycle. Flying eastward goes against this drift, much like swimming against a river current.

Of course, you don't have to hop on a jet to get out of sync with your biological clock. Just going to bed a couple hours later than usual can affect how you sleep (Czeisler, Moore-Ede, & Coleman, 1980). Rotating work shifts that force many nurses, firefighters, and other workers to keep changing their sleep schedule play havoc with biological

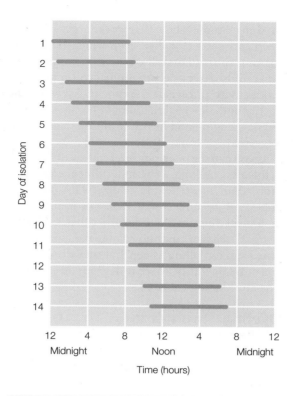

Figure 5.3. Changes in sleep periods of a subject isolated from the day-night cycle. The drift of the sleep periods to the right is characteristic of studies in which subjects are deprived of information about day and night. Subjects typically drift toward a 25-hour "day," retiring later and later with each day spent in isolation. When subjects are reexposed to light-cycle cues, they quickly return to a 24-hour rhythm.

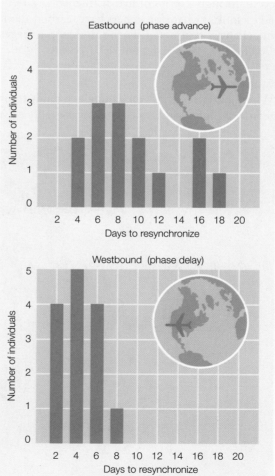

Figure 5.4. Circadian rhythms and jet lag. Air travelers generally adjust to local time more slowly after flying east (which shortens their day) than after flying west (which lengthens it). The explanation for this phenomenon may be the natural drift toward a longer daily cycle; it is easier to extend the biological cycle than to shorten it. (Data from Moore-Ede, Sulzman, & Fuller, 1982)

rhythms. Studies show that workers get less total sleep and poorer quality sleep when they go on rotating shifts (Torsvall et al., 1989). Shift rotation can also have a negative impact on employees' productivity and accident-proneness at work, the quality of their social relations at home, and their physical and mental health (Johnson et al., 1981; Regestein & Monk, 1991).

As you can see from our brief review of research in this area, biological rhythms influence behavior more than most people realize. However, it's important to understand that the influence of biological rhythms is subtle rather than overpowering. Circadian rhythms may make a particular time ideal for falling asleep, but they don't knock you out. Obviously, to some degree you can override your biological clock.

Cycling Through the Stages of Sleep

Not only does sleep occur in a context of daily rhythms, but subtler rhythms are evident within the experience of sleep itself. During sleep, people cycle through a series of five distinct stages. Let's take a look at what researchers have learned about the changes that occur during these sleep stages (Anch et al., 1988; Dement, 1978).

Stages 1–4

When you first fall asleep, your sleep tends to be relatively light and you can be awakened easily.

Stage 1 is a brief transitional stage that usually lasts only 5 to 10 minutes. Your breathing and heart rate slow as your muscle tension and body temperature decline. The alpha waves that probably dominated your EEG activity just before you fell asleep give way to lower-frequency EEG activity in which theta waves are prominent (see Figure 5.5).

As you descend through stages 2, 3, and 4 of the sleep cycle, your respiration rate, heart rate, muscle tension, and body temperature continue to decline. During stage 2, brief bursts of higher-frequency brain waves, called *sleep spindles*, appear against a background of mixed EEG activity (see Figure 5.5 once again). Gradually, your brain waves become higher in amplitude and slower in frequency, as you move into a deeper form of sleep, called slow-wave sleep. **Slow-wave sleep consists of sleep stages 3 and 4, during which low-frequency delta waves become prominent in EEG recordings.** Typically you reach slow-wave sleep in less than an hour and stay there for roughly a half-hour. Then the sleep cycle reverses itself and you gradually move upward through lighter stages of sleep. That's when things start to get interesting.

REM Sleep

When you reach what should be stage 1 once again, you usually go into the *fifth* stage of sleep, which is most widely known as *REM sleep*. REM is

Figure 5.5. EEG patterns in sleep and wakefulness. Characteristic brain waves vary depending on one's state of consciousness. Generally, as people move from an awake state through deeper stages of sleep, their brain waves decrease in frequency (cycles per second) and increase in amplitude (height). However, brain waves during REM sleep resemble "wide-awake" brain waves.

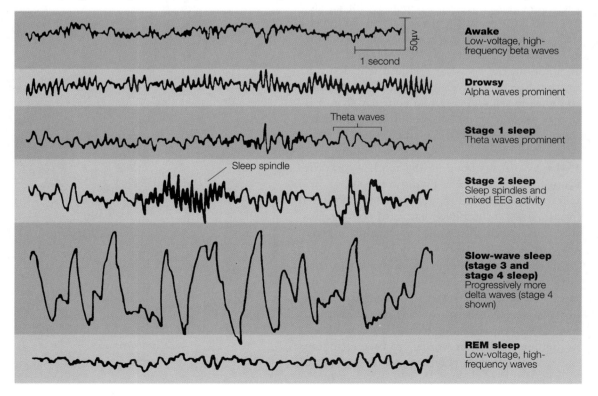

Awake
Low-voltage, high-frequency beta waves

Drowsy
Alpha waves prominent

Stage 1 sleep
Theta waves prominent

Stage 2 sleep
Sleep spindles and mixed EEG activity

Slow-wave sleep (stage 3 and stage 4 sleep)
Progressively more delta waves (stage 4 shown)

REM sleep
Low-voltage, high-frequency waves

an abbreviation for *rapid eye movements*, which are prominent during this stage of sleep. In a sleep lab, researchers use an electrooculograph to monitor these lateral movements that occur beneath the sleeping person's closed eyelids. However, they can be seen with the naked eye if you closely watch someone in the REM stage of sleep (little ripples move back and forth across his or her closed eyelids).

REM sleep was discovered accidentally in the 1950s in Nathaniel Kleitman's lab at the University of Chicago (Aserinsky & Kleitman, 1953; Dement & Kleitman, 1957). Kleitman and his colleagues found that the REM stage is a deep stage of sleep in the conventional sense that it is relatively hard to awaken a person from it. The REM stage is also marked by irregular breathing and pulse rate. Muscle tone is extremely relaxed—so much so that bodily movements are minimal and the sleeper is virtually paralyzed. Although REM is a deep stage of sleep, EEG activity is dominated by high-frequency beta waves that resemble those observed when people are alert and awake (see Figure 5.5 again). This pairing of deep sleep with "wide awake" brain waves is a paradox that continues to leave scientists perplexed.

This paradox is probably related to the association between REM sleep and dreaming. Soon after the discovery of REM sleep, researchers learned that *this is the stage of sleep during which most dreaming occurs.* How do we know that? When researchers systematically awaken subjects to ask them whether they have been dreaming, most dream reports come from awakenings during the REM stage. William Dement (1978), who coined the term REM sleep, compiled the results of eight early studies of this sort, involving nearly 1500 awakenings of subjects. REM awakenings produced dream recall 78% of the time. Awakenings from other stages were accompanied by dream recall only 14% of the time. Although some dreaming occurs in other stages, dreaming is most frequent, vivid, and memorable during REM sleep.

To summarize, **REM sleep** *is a deep stage of sleep marked by rapid eye movements, high-frequency brain waves, and dreaming.* It is such a special stage of sleep that the other four stages are often characterized simply as "non-REM sleep." **Non-REM (NREM) sleep** *consists of sleep stages 1 through 4, which are marked by an absence of rapid eye movements, relatively little dreaming, and varied EEG activity.*

"[The discovery of REM sleep] was the breakthrough—the discovery that changed the course of sleep research."
WILLIAM DEMENT

CONCEPT CHECK 5.1
Comparing REM and NREM Sleep

A table here could have provided you with a systematic comparison of REM sleep and NREM sleep, but that would have deprived you of the opportunity to check your understanding of these sleep phases by creating your own table. Try to fill in each of the blanks below with a word or phrase highlighting the differences between REM and NREM sleep with regard to the various characteristics specified. As usual, you can find the answers at the back of the book in Appendix A.

Characteristic	REM sleep	NREM sleep
Type of EEG activity		
Eye movements		
Dreaming		
Depth (difficulty in awakening)		
Percentage of total sleep (in adults)		
Increases or decreases (as percentage of sleep) during childhood		
Timing in sleep cycle (dominates early or late)		

Figure 5.6. An overview of the cycle of sleep. The green line charts how a typical person moves through the various stages of sleep during the course of a night. This diagram also shows how dreams and rapid eye movements coincide with REM sleep, whereas posture changes occur in between REM periods (because the body is nearly paralyzed during REM sleep). Notice how the person cycles into REM four times, as descents into NREM sleep get shallower and REM periods get longer. Thus, slow-wave sleep is prominent early in the night, while REM and stage 2 sleep dominate the second half of a night's sleep.

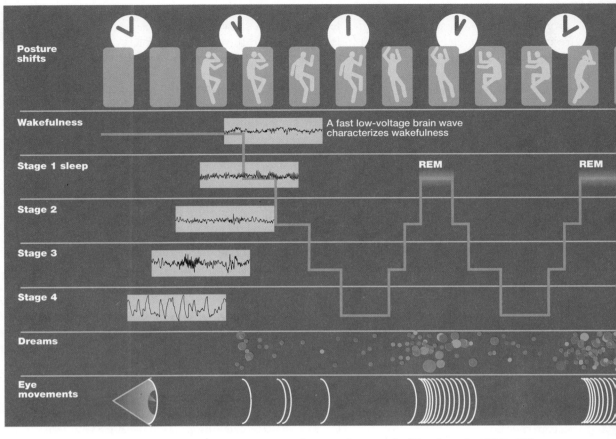

Repeating the Cycle

During the course of a night, people usually repeat the sleep cycle about four times. As the night wears on, the cycle changes gradually. The first REM period is relatively short, lasting only a few minutes. Subsequent REM periods get progressively longer, peaking around 40–60 minutes in length. Additionally, NREM intervals tend to get shorter, and descents into NREM stages usually become more shallow. These trends can be seen in Figure 5.6, which provides an overview of a typical night's sleep cycle.

These trends mean that most slow-wave sleep occurs early in the sleep cycle, gradually giving way to alternating periods of REM sleep and stage 2 sleep. Most dreaming occurs during the later part of a night's sleep. Summing across the entire sleep cycle, young adults typically spend about 60% of their sleep time in light sleep (stages 1 and 2), 20% in slow-wave sleep (stages 3 and 4), and 20% in REM sleep (Mendelson, 1987). Individuals have their unique variations from the typical pattern of sleep, but a person's sleep pattern tends to be moderately consistent from night to night. Heredity may influence some aspects of individuals' sleep patterns, such as what time they habitually go to bed, how long they sleep, and whether they nap frequently (Heath et al., 1990). Of course, personal sleep patterns can be disrupted by many things, including stress, depression, and drug use (Borbely, 1986).

Age, Culture, and Sleep

Now that we have described the basic architecture of sleep, let's take a look at a couple of factors that contribute to variations in patterns of sleeping: age and culture.

Age Trends

Age alters the sleep cycle. What we have described so far is the typical pattern for young to middle-aged adults. Children, however, display different patterns (Roffwarg, Muzio, & Dement, 1966; Williams, Karacan, & Hursch, 1974). Newborns will sleep six to eight times in a 24-hour period, often exceeding a total of 16 hours of sleep (see Figure 5.7). Fortunately for parents, during the first several months much of this sleep begins to get consolidated into one particularly long nighttime sleep period (Webb, 1992a). Interestingly, infants spend much more of their sleep time than adults do in the REM stage. In the first few months, REM accounts for about 50% of babies' sleep, as compared to 20% of adults' sleep. During

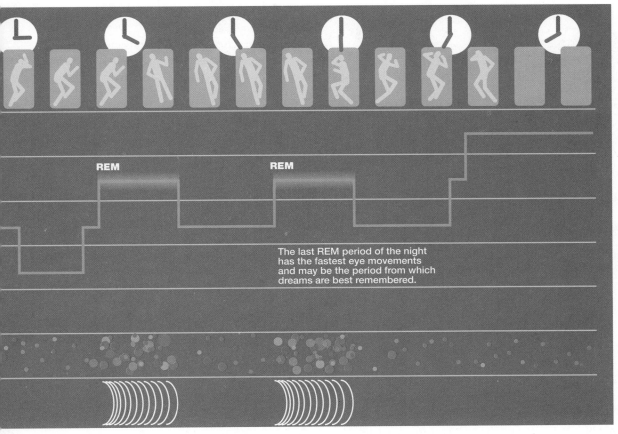

REM

REM

The last REM period of the night has the fastest eye movements and may be the period from which dreams are best remembered.

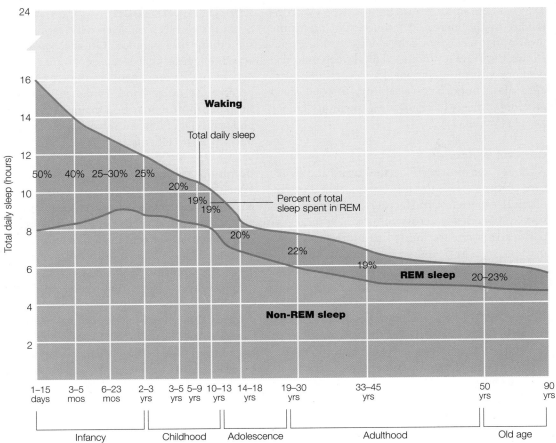

Figure 5.7. Changes in sleep patterns over the life span. Both the total amount of sleep per night and the portion of REM sleep change with age. Sleep patterns change most dramatically during infancy, with total sleep time and amount of REM sleep declining sharply in the first two years of life. After a noticeable drop in the average amount of sleep in adolescence, sleep patterns remain relatively stable, although total sleep and slow-wave sleep continue to decline gradually with age. (Adapted from Roffwarg, Muzio, & Dement, 1966; revised by authors since publication)

Although the siesta, or afternoon nap, has been a traditional part of Mexican culture, the practice is rapidly diminishing as industrialization and modernization alter traditional lifestyles.

the remainder of the first year, the REM portion of infants' sleep declines to roughly 30%. The REM portion of sleep continues to decrease gradually until it levels off at about 20% during adolescence (see Figure 5.7).

During adulthood, gradual, age-related changes in sleep continue. The proportion of slow-wave sleep declines and the percentage of time spent in stage 1 increases (Bliwise, 1989; Ehlers & Kupfer, 1989). These shifts toward lighter sleep *may* contribute to the increased frequency of nighttime awakenings seen among the elderly. As Figure 5.7 shows, the average amount of total sleep time also declines with advancing age. However, these averages mask important variability, as total sleep *increases* with age in a substantial portion of older people (Webb, 1992a).

Cultural Variations

Although age clearly affects the nature and structure of sleep itself, the psychological and physiological experience of sleep does not appear to vary systematically across cultures. Cultural disparities in sleep are limited to more peripheral matters, such as sleeping arrangements and napping customs. For example, there are cultural differences in *co-sleeping*, the practice of children and parents sleeping together (McKenna, 1993). In modern Western societies, co-sleeping is actively discouraged. As part of their effort to foster self-reliance, American parents teach their children to sleep alone. In contrast, co-sleeping is more widely accepted in Japanese culture, which emphasizes interdependence and group harmony. Around the world as a whole, co-sleeping is the norm rather than the exception. Strong pressure

against co-sleeping appears to be largely an urban, Western phenomenon.

Napping practices also vary along cultural lines. For example, the Temiars of Indonesia depend heavily on daytime naps because their nighttime routines (fishing, cooking, watching over the fire) limit their nocturnal sleep to about 4 to 6 hours per night (Stampi, 1989). In many societies, shops close and activities are curtailed in the afternoon to permit people to enjoy a 1- to 2-hour midday nap. These "siesta cultures" are found mostly in tropical regions of the world (Webb & Dinges, 1989). There, this practice is adaptive in that it allows people to avoid working during the hottest part of the day. The siesta is not a fixture in all tropical societies, however. It is infrequent among nomadic groups and those that depend on irregular food supplies. As a rule, the siesta tradition is not found in industrialized societies, where it conflicts with the emphasis on productivity and the philosophy that "time is money." Moreover, when industrialization comes to a siesta culture, it undermines the practice. For instance, modernization in Spain has led to a decline in midday napping there (Kribbs, 1993).

Doing Without: Sleep Deprivation

Scientific research on sleep deprivation presents something of a paradox. On the one hand, research suggests that sleep deprivation is not as detrimental as most people subjectively feel it to be. On the other hand, evidence suggests that sleep deprivation may be a major social problem, undermining efficiency at work and contributing to countless accidents.

Complete Deprivation

What happens when people go completely without sleep for a period of days? As you might expect, complete deprivation of sleep has been related to various negative effects, including weariness, poor concentration, reduced motivation, irritability, and lapses in attention (Johnson, 1982). However, these negative effects tend to be mild, and researchers have been impressed by how *well* sleep-deprived subjects can perform if they are motivated to do so (Anch et al., 1988). In 1965, a 17-year-old student named Randy Gardner, who wanted to set a world record, managed to stay awake for 264 consecutive hours. Gardner's accomplishment was astonishing enough by itself, but he did it *without experiencing any major ill effects* (Bonnet, 1993; Dement, 1978).

Partial Deprivation

Partial sleep deprivation occurs when people make do with substantially less sleep than normal over a period of time. Partial deprivation occurs far more often in everyday life than complete sleep deprivation. Indeed, many sleep experts believe that much of American society chronically suffers from partial sleep deprivation. It appears that more and more people are trying to squeeze additional waking hours out of their days as they attempt to juggle conflicting work, family, household, and school responsibilities, leading William Dement to comment that "Most Americans no longer know what it feels like to be fully alert" (Toufexis, 1990, p. 79).

How serious are the effects of partial sleep deprivation? Partial deprivation has an inconsistent impact on performance that depends on the amount of sleep lost and on the nature of the task at hand (Bonnet, 1991; Johnson, 1982). Negative effects are most likely when subjects are asked to work on long-lasting, difficult, or uninteresting tasks, but many studies find little or no deterioration in performance.

Overall, sleep deprivation is not as harmful as one might expect (Anch et al., 1988). *The most consistent result of sleep deprivation is simply an increase in sleepiness. However, this increased sleepiness may not be as benign as it sounds.* This drowsiness can impair individuals' capacity for attention, especially when working on monotonous, routine tasks. Evidence indicates that such lapses in attention contribute to a large share of transportation accidents and mishaps in the workplace (Lauber, 1993; Mitler, 1993). Obviously, if a person is driving a bus or working as an air traffic controller, a momentary lapse in attention could be very, very costly.

Fortunately, research indicates that sleep loss can be made up fairly quickly (Carskadon & Dement, 1981). Randy Gardner, for example, recovered from most of the effects of his 264 sleepless hours in just one 15-hour session of sleep (Spinweber, 1993). Most people compensate for sleep deprivation by getting a few hours of extra sleep for one to three nights.

Selective Deprivation

The unique quality of REM sleep led researchers to look into the effects of a special type of partial sleep deprivation—*selective deprivation.* In a number of laboratory studies, subjects were awakened over a period of nights whenever they began to go into the REM stage. These subjects usually got a decent amount of sleep in NREM stages, but they were selectively deprived of REM sleep.

What are the effects of REM deprivation? The evidence indicates that it has little impact on daytime functioning and task performance (Pearlman, 1982). However, REM deprivation *does* have some interesting effects on subjects' patterns of sleeping (Ellman et al., 1991). As the nights go by in REM-deprivation studies, it becomes necessary to awaken the subjects more and more often to deprive them of their REM sleep, because they spontaneously shift into REM more and more frequently. Whereas most subjects normally go into REM about four times a night, REM-deprived subjects start slipping into REM every time the researchers turn around. In one study, researchers had to awaken a subject 64 times by the third night of REM deprivation (Borbely, 1986). Furthermore, when a REM-deprivation experiment comes to an end and subjects are allowed to sleep without interruption, they experience a "rebound effect." That is, they spend extra time in REM periods for one to three nights to make up for their REM deprivation.

Similar results have been observed when subjects have been selectively deprived of slow-wave sleep (Klerman, 1993). After seven nights of stage 4 deprivation, subjects experience a rebound effect and spend extra time in stage 4 sleep. Also, as the nights go by, progressively more awakenings are required to prevent stage 4 sleep (Agnew, Webb, & Williams, 1964, 1967).

What do theorists make of these spontaneous pursuits of REM and slow-wave sleep? They conclude that people must have specific *needs* for

A large number of transportation mishaps result from dozing on the job. Although train accidents, for example, occur for a variety of reasons, one study of train engineers found that 59% admitted falling asleep while on duty.

REM and slow-wave sleep—and rather strong needs, at that. The realization that humans need these specific types of sleep has contributed to new theorizing about why people sleep, a perplexing question that we turn to next.

Why Do We Sleep?

Theories about why people sleep generally fall into two categories: restorative theories and circadian theories. *Restorative theories* propose that sleep promotes physiological processes that rejuvenate the body each night (Hartmann, 1973; Oswald, 1974). *Circadian theories* propose that sleep is an aspect of circadian rhythms regulated by neural mechanisms that are a product of evolution (Enright, 1980; Wever, 1979). The demonstration that people need both slow-wave and REM sleep has suggested to some theorists that the restorative and circadian explanations of sleep may *both* be correct.

For example, Alexander Borbely (1984) argues that *the need for slow-wave sleep reflects the restorative function of sleep* and that *the need for REM sleep reflects the circadian regulation of sleep.* Among other things, Borbely's theory is based on evidence that the time spent in slow-wave sleep depends mainly on how long one has been awake, whereas time spent in REM sleep depends mainly on a circadian rhythm (Borbely et al., 1989; Knowles et al., 1990). More research is needed to fully test Borbely's model, but it is an intriguing integration of restorative and circadian theories.

Problems in the Night: Insomnia

People are plagued by a variety of sleep problems, but insomnia is far and away the most common sleep disorder. **Insomnia refers to chronic problems in getting adequate sleep.** It occurs in three basic patterns: (1) difficulty in falling asleep initially, (2) difficulty in remaining asleep, and (3) persistent early-morning awakening. Insomnia may sound like a minor problem to those who haven't struggled with it, but it can be a very unpleasant malady. Insomniacs have to endure the agony of watching their precious sleep time tick away as they toss and turn in restless frustration.

Prevalence

Nearly everyone suffers occasional sleep difficulties because of stress, disruptions of biological rhythms, or other temporary circumstances. Fortunately, these problems clear up spontaneously for most people. However, about 15% of adults report severe or frequent insomnia, and another 15% complain of mild or occasional insomnia (Bootzin et al., 1993). The prevalence of insomnia increases noticeably during old age (Mellinger, Balter, & Uhlenhuth, 1985).

Causes

Insomnia has many causes (Bootzin et al., 1993; Kales & Kales, 1984). In some cases, excessive anxiety and tension prevent relaxation and keep people awake. Insomnia is frequently a side effect of emotional problems, such as depression, or of significant stress, such as pressures at work. Understandably, health problems such as back pain, ulcers, and asthma can lead to insomnia. The use of certain drugs, especially stimulants such as cocaine and amphetamines, may also lead to problems in sleeping.

Treatment

The most common approach to the treatment of insomnia is the prescription of sedative drugs (sleeping pills). Sedatives are fairly effective in helping people fall asleep more quickly, and they reduce nighttime awakenings and increase total sleep (Mendelson, 1990). Nonetheless, these drugs are probably used to combat insomnia *too* frequently. Sleep experts are virtually unanimous in maintaining that in the past physicians prescribed sleeping pills far too readily. As a result of this criticism, prescriptions for sleeping pills declined significantly during the 1970s and 1980s (Ray & Ksir, 1990).

Sedatives are a poor long-range solution for insomnia for a number of reasons (Mendelson, 1993). For example, there is the danger of overdose, and some people become dependent on sedatives in order to fall asleep. Sedatives also have carryover effects that can make people drowsy and sluggish the next day. Moreover, with continued use sedatives gradually become less effective, so people need to increase their dose to more dangerous levels, creating a vicious circle of escalating dependency (see Figure 5.8). Ironically, sedatives also interfere with the normal cycle of sleep. Although they promote sleep, they reduce the proportion of time spent in REM and slow-wave sleep (Borbely, 1986).

Sedatives do have a place in the treatment of insomnia, but they need to be used cautiously and conservatively. They should be used primarily for short-term treatment of sleep problems. Fortunately, the next generation of sleeping pills may reduce many of the problems that have long

"When we go to bed at night, we enter an altered state of consciousness that lasts for a number of hours. We cease to see, hear, and feel consciously what occurs around us. The world of sleep and the world of wakefulness are so different that each of us could be said to live in two worlds."
ALEXANDER BORBELY

been associated with sedatives. For example, preliminary evidence on a new sleep agent (trade name: Ambien) suggests that it leaves the normal sleep cycle intact while reducing the likelihood of next-day grogginess and other side effects (Scharf et al., 1991). In the chapter Application, we'll discuss some alternative strategies for grappling with insomnia.

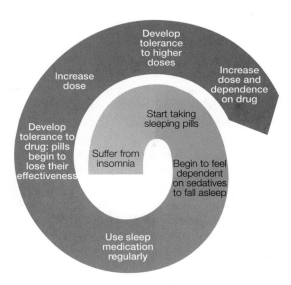

Figure 5.8. The vicious circle of dependence on sleeping pills. Because of the body's ability to develop tolerance to drugs, using sedatives routinely to "cure" insomnia can lead to a vicious circle of escalating dependency as larger and larger doses of the sedative are needed to produce the same effect.

THE WORLD OF DREAMS

One of the most fascinating aspects of sleep is the state of dreaming. **A *dream* is a mental experience during sleep that includes vivid visual images.** Dreams are not strongly constrained by logic or rationality. They often are disorganized and highly unrealistic, as their plots take unpredictable and even impossible turns.

People have always been intrigued by dreams, seeking to find hidden meanings in this seemingly magical world of consciousness. Only in recent years have dreams been subjected to empirical study. In the laboratory, researchers investigate dreaming by awakening subjects from sleep to ask them whether they were dreaming and what they were dreaming about. As you have already learned, this kind of research has shown that most dreaming occurs during REM sleep. Psychologists also learn about dreams by instructing research subjects or therapy patients to try to awaken during the night at home to record their dreams. These kinds of studies have cast some light on when people dream and what they dream about. What remains obscure is *why* people dream.

The Contents of Dreams

What do people dream about? Overall, dreams are not as exciting as advertised. Perhaps dreams are seen as exotic because people are more likely to remember their more bizarre nighttime dramas. After analyzing the contents of more than 10,000 dreams, Calvin Hall (1966) concluded that most dreams are relatively mundane. They tend to unfold in familiar settings with a cast of characters dominated by family, friends, and colleagues, with a sprinkling of strangers.

Researchers have found that certain themes are more common than others in dreams. Table 5.2 lists the most common dreams reported by college students in one study (Griffith, Miyago, & Tago, 1958). If you glance through this list, you will see that people dream quite a bit about sex, aggres-

sion, and misfortune. According to Hall, dreams tend to center on classic sources of internal conflict, such as the conflict between taking chances and playing it safe. Hall was struck by how little people dream about public affairs and current events. Typically, dreams are very self-centered; people dream mostly about themselves.

Table 5.2 Common Dreams of College Students and the Percentage Having Each Type of Dream

Type of Dream	Percentage of Students
Falling	83
Being attacked or pursued	77
Trying repeatedly to do something	71
School, teachers, studying	71
Sexual experiences	66
Arriving too late	64
Eating	62
Being frozen with fright	58
The death of a loved one	57
Being locked up	56
Finding money	56
Swimming	52
Snakes	49
Being inappropriately dressed	46
Being smothered	44
Being nude in public	43
Fire	41
Failing an examination	39
Seeing self as dead	33
Killing someone	26

Source: Griffith, Miyago, and Tago (1958)

Links Between the Dream World and the Real World

Though dreams seem to belong in a world of their own, what people dream about is affected by what is going on in their lives (Hall & Van de Castle, 1966). If you're struggling with financial problems, worried about an upcoming exam, or sexually attracted to a classmate, these themes may very well show up in your dreams. Freud noticed long ago that the contents of waking life tend to spill into dreams. He labeled this spillover the *day residue*. The connection between a person's real world and his or her dream world probably explains why there is some thematic continuity among successive dreams occurring in different REM periods on a given night (Cipolli et al., 1987).

On occasion, the contents of dreams can also be affected by external stimuli experienced while one is dreaming. For example, William Dement sprayed water on one hand of sleeping subjects while they were in the REM stage (Dement & Wolpert, 1958). Subjects who weren't awakened by the water were awakened by the experimenter a short time later and asked what they had been dreaming about. Dement found that 42% of the subjects had incorporated the water into their dreams. They said that they had dreamt that they were in rainfalls, floods, baths, swimming pools, and the like. Some people report that they occasionally experience the same thing at home when the sound of their alarm clock fails to awaken them. The alarm is incorporated into their dream as a loud engine or a siren, for instance. As with day residue, the incorporation of external stimuli into dreams shows that people's dream world is not entirely separate from their real world.

Culture and Dreams

Striking cross-cultural variations occur in beliefs about the nature of dreams and the importance attributed to them. In modern Western society, we typically make a distinction between the "real" world we experience while awake and the "imaginary" world we experience while dreaming. Some people realize that events in the real world can affect their dreams, but few believe that events in their dreams hold any significance for their waking life. Although a small minority of individuals take their dreams seriously, in Western cultures dreams are largely written off as insignificant, meaningless meanderings of the unconscious (Tart, 1988).

In many non-Western cultures, however, dreams are viewed as important sources of information about oneself, about the future, or about the spiritual world (Kracke, 1991). Although no culture confuses dreams with waking reality, many view events in dreams as another type of reality that may be just as important as, or perhaps even more important than, events experienced while awake. In some instances, people are even held responsible for their dream actions. Among the New Guinea Arapesh, for example, an erotic dream about someone may be viewed as the equivalent of an adulterous act. In many cultures, dreams are seen as a window into the spiritual world, permitting communication with ancestors or supernatural beings (Bourguignon, 1972). People in some cultures believe that dreams provide information about the future—good or bad omens about upcoming battles, hunts, births, and so forth (Tedlock, 1992).

The tendency to remember one's dreams varies across cultures. In modern Western societies where little significance is attributed to dreams, dream recall tends to be mediocre. Many people remember their dreams only infrequently. In contrast, dream recall tends to be much better in cultures that take dreams seriously. For example, among the Parintinin of Brazil, most people can remember several dreams per night, which they routinely share with others (Kracke, 1992).

In regard to dream content, both similarities and differences occur across cultures in the types of dreams that people report (Hunt, 1989). Some basic dream themes appear to be nearly universal

Dreaming is the focal point of traditional Aboriginal existence as it is in many other cultures.

(dreams of falling, being pursued, having sex). However, the contents of dreams vary some from one culture to another because people in different societies deal with different worlds while awake. For example, in a 1950 study of the Siriono, a hunting-and-gathering people of the Amazon who were almost always hungry and spent most of their time in a grim search for food, *half* of the reported dreams focused on hunting, gathering, and eating food (D'Andrade, 1961). Shared systems for interpreting the contents of dreams also vary from one society to another. Table 5.3 lists a number of common dream interpretations among the Toraja of Indonesia (Hollan, 1989). Although some of these interpretations (example: standing on moutaintop = becoming a leader) might be common in other societies, some clearly are peculiar to Toraja society (example: buffalo in the rice fields = rats will eat the rice harvest).

Theories of Dreaming

Many theories have been proposed regarding the purposes of dreaming. Sigmund Freud (1900), who analyzed clients' dreams in therapy, believed that the principal purpose of dreams is *wish fulfillment*. He thought that people fulfill ungratified needs from waking hours through wishful thinking in dreams. For example, someone who is sexually frustrated would tend to have highly erotic dreams, while an unsuccessful person would dream about great accomplishments.

Other theorists, such as Rosalind Cartwright, have proposed that dreams provide an opportunity to work through everyday problems (Cartwright, 1977; Cartwright & Lamberg, 1992). According to her cognitive, *problem-solving view*, there is considerable continuity between waking and sleeping thought. Proponents of this view believe that dreams allow people to engage in creative thinking about problems because dreams are not restrained by logic or realism.

J. Allan Hobson and Robert McCarley have argued that dreams are simply the by-product of bursts of activity emanating from subcortical areas in the brain (Hobson, 1988; Hobson & McCarley, 1977). Their *activation-synthesis model* proposes that dreams are side effects of the neural activation that produces "wide awake" brain waves during REM sleep. According to this model, neurons firing periodically in lower brain centers send random signals to the cortex (the seat of complex thought). The cortex supposedly constructs a dream to make sense out of these signals. In contrast to the theories of Freud and Cartwright, this theory obviously downplays

Table 5.3 Examples of Common Dream Interpretations Among the Toraja of Indonesia	
"Good" Dreams	*Interpretation*
Receive gold	Good rice harvest
Carry pig or buffalo meat	Good rice harvest
Act "crazy"	Receive wealth
Objects are thrown at dreamer	Rain will fall
Stand on mountaintop	Become a leader
Steal objects	Receive those objects/become wealthy
Swim in ocean or river	Receive wealth
Jump over or cross water	Become wise/clever
Gored by a buffalo	Buy a buffalo
"Bad" Dreams	*Interpretation*
Buffalo in the rice fields	Rats will eat rice harvest
Naked	Get sick
Enter a burial cave	Die
Carried off by an ancestor	Die
Objects are stolen/lost/carried away	Lose those objects
House burns or is destroyed	Lose wealth/become poor

Source: Adapted from Hollan (1989)

the role of emotional factors as determinants of dreams.

These theories, which are summarized in Figure 5.9, are only three of at least seven major theories about the functions of dreams. All seven

Figure 5.9. Three theories of dreaming. Dreams can be explained in a variety of ways. Freud stressed the wish-fulfilling function of dreams. Cartwright emphasizes the problem-solving function of dreams. Hobson and McCarley assert that dreams are merely a by-product of periodic neural activation.

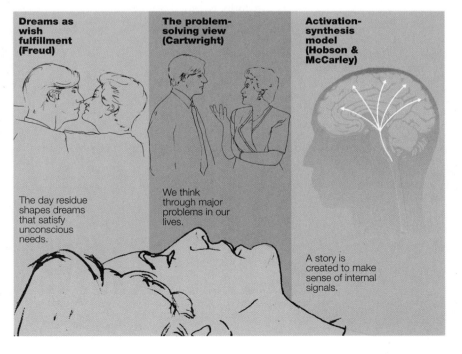

Dreams as wish fulfillment (Freud)
The day residue shapes dreams that satisfy unconscious needs.

The problem-solving view (Cartwright)
We think through major problems in our lives.

Activation-synthesis model (Hobson & McCarley)
A story is created to make sense of internal signals.

theories are based more on conjecture than research (Webb & Cartwright, 1978). In part, this is because the private, subjective nature of dreams makes it difficult to put the theories to an empirical test. Thus, the purpose of dreaming remains a mystery.

We'll encounter more unsolved mysteries in the next two sections of this chapter as we discuss hypnosis and meditation. Whereas sleep and dreams are familiar to everyone, most people have little familiarity with hypnosis and meditation, which both involve deliberate efforts to temporarily alter consciousness.

HYPNOSIS: ALTERED CONSCIOUSNESS OR ROLE PLAYING?

Hypnosis has a long and checkered history. It all began with a flamboyant 18th-century Austrian by the name of Franz Anton Mesmer. Working in Paris, Mesmer claimed to cure people of illnesses through an elaborate routine involving a "laying on of hands." Mesmer had some complicated theories about how he had harnessed "animal magnetism." However, we know today that he had simply stumbled onto the power of suggestion. Eventually he was dismissed as a charlatan and run out of town by the local authorities. Although officially discredited, Mesmer inspired followers—practitioners of "mesmerism"—who continued to ply their trade. To this day, our language preserves the memory of Franz Mesmer: When we are under the spell of an event or a story, we are "mesmerized."

Eventually, a Scottish physician, James Braid, became interested in the trancelike state that could be induced by the mesmerists. It was Braid who popularized the term *hypnotism* in 1843, borrowing it from the Greek word for sleep. Braid thought that hypnotism could be used to produce anesthesia for surgeries. However, just as hypnosis was catching on as a general anesthetic, more powerful and reliable chemical anesthetics were discovered, and interest in hypnotism dwindled.

Since then, hypnotism has led a curious dual existence. On the one hand, it has been the subject of numerous scientific studies. Furthermore, it has enjoyed considerable use as a clinical tool by physicians, dentists, and psychologists for over a century (Gibson & Heap, 1991). On the other hand, an assortment of entertainers and quacks have continued in the less respectable tradition of mesmerism, using hypnotism for parlor tricks and chicanery. It is little wonder, then, that most people don't know what to make of the whole subject. In this section, we'll work on clearing up some of the confusion surrounding hypnosis.

Hypnotic Induction and Susceptibility

Hypnosis is a systematic procedure that typically produces a heightened state of suggestibility. It may also lead to passive relaxation, narrowed attention, and enhanced fantasy.

If only in popular films, virtually everyone has seen a *hypnotic induction* enacted with a swinging pendulum. Actually, there are many techniques for inducing hypnosis (Meyer, 1992). Usually, the hypnotist will suggest to the subject that he or she is relaxing. Repetitively, softly, subjects are told that they are getting tired, drowsy, or sleepy. Often, the hypnotist vividly describes bodily sensations that should be occurring. Subjects are told that their arms are going limp, that their feet are getting warm, that their eyelids are getting heavy. Gradually, most subjects succumb and become hypnotized.

People differ in how well they respond to hypnotic induction. Ernest and Josephine Hilgard have done extensive research on this variability in *hypnotic susceptibility*. Not everyone can be hypnotized. About 10% of the population doesn't respond well at all, while at the other end of the continuum, about 10% of people are exceptionally good hypnotic subjects (Hilgard, 1965). Responsiveness to hypnosis can be estimated with the Stanford Hypnotic Susceptibility Scale (SHSS). The distribution of scores on the SHSS is graphed in Figure 5.10.

Figure 5.10. Variation in hypnotic susceptibility. This graph shows the distribution of scores of more than 500 subjects on the Stanford Hypnotic Susceptibility Scale. As you can see, responsiveness to hypnotism varies widely, and many people are not very susceptible to hypnotic induction. (Based on data from Hilgard, 1965)

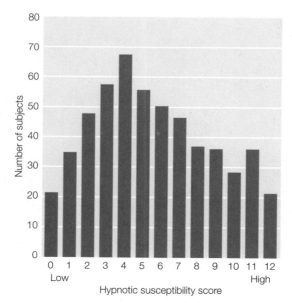

Hypnotic Phenomena

Many interesting effects can be produced through hypnosis. Some of the more prominent ones include:

1. *Anesthesia.* Under the influence of hypnosis, some subjects can withstand treatments that would normally cause considerable pain (Finer, 1980). As a result, some physicians and dentists have used hypnosis as a substitute for anesthetic drugs. Although drugs are more reliable, hypnosis is a surprisingly effective anesthetic for some people.

2. *Sensory distortions and hallucinations.* Hypnotized subjects may be led to experience auditory or visual hallucinations. They may hear sounds or see things that are not there, or fail to hear or see stimuli that are present (Spiegel et al., 1985). Subjects may also have their sensations distorted so that something sweet tastes sour or an unpleasant odor smells fragrant.

3. *Disinhibition.* Hypnosis can sometimes reduce inhibitions that would normally prevent subjects from acting in ways that they would see as immoral or unacceptable. In experiments, hypnotized subjects have been induced to throw what they believed to be nitric acid into the face of a research assistant. Similarly, stage hypnotists are sometimes successful in getting people to disrobe in public. This disinhibition effect may occur simply because hypnotized people feel that they cannot be held responsible for their actions while they are hypnotized.

4. *Posthypnotic suggestions and amnesia.* Suggestions made during hypnosis may influence a subject's later behavior (Kihlstrom, 1985). The most common posthypnotic suggestion is the creation of posthypnotic amnesia. That is, subjects are told that they will remember nothing that happened while they were hypnotized. Such subjects usually claim to remember nothing, as ordered.

Theories of Hypnosis

Although a number of theories have been developed to explain hypnosis, it is still not well understood. Most theories attribute hypnotic effects either to dramatic role playing or to a special, altered state of consciousness (a trance).

Hypnosis as Role Playing

Although hypnotized subjects may feel as though they are in an altered state, their patterns of EEG activity cannot be distinguished from their EEG patterns in normal waking states (Orne & Dinges, 1989). The failure to find any special physiological changes associated with hypnosis has led theorists such as Theodore Barber (1979) and Nicholas Spanos (1986) to conclude that hypnosis produces a normal state of consciousness in which suggestible people act out the role of a hypnotized subject and behave as they think hypnotized people are supposed to. According to this notion, it is subjects' role expectations that produce hypnotic effects, rather than a special trancelike state of consciousness.

Two other lines of evidence support the role-playing view. First, many of the seemingly amazing effects of hypnosis can be duplicated by nonhypnotized subjects (Meeker & Barber, 1971). For example, much has been made of the fact that hypnotized subjects can be used as "human planks" (see the photo below), but it turns out that nonhypnotized subjects can easily match this and other hypnotic feats (Barber, 1986). This finding suggests that no special state of consciousness is required to explain hypnotic feats.

The second line of evidence involves demonstrations that hypnotized subjects are often acting out a role. For example, Martin Orne (1951) regressed hypnotized subjects back to their sixth birthday and asked them to describe it. They responded with detailed descriptions that appeared to represent great feats of hypnosis-enhanced memory. However, instead of accepting this information at face value, Orne compared it with

"Thousands of books, movies and professional articles have woven the concept of 'hypnotic trance' into the common knowledge. And yet there is almost no scientific support for it."
THEODORE BARBER

Some feats performed under hypnosis can be performed equally well by nonhypnotized subjects. Here, the "Amazing Kreskin" demonstrates that proper positioning is the only requirement for the famous human plank feat.

information that he had obtained from the subjects' parents. It turned out that many of the subjects' memories were inaccurate and invented! Many other studies have also found that age-regressed subjects' recall of the distant past tends to be more fanciful than factual (Nash, 1987). Thus, the role-playing explanation of hypnosis suggests that situational factors lead suggestible subjects to act out a certain role in a highly cooperative manner.

Hypnosis as an Altered State of Consciousness

Despite the doubts raised by role-playing explanations, many prominent theorists still maintain that hypnotic effects are attributable to a special, altered state of consciousness (Beahrs, 1983; Fromm, 1979; Hilgard, 1986). **These theorists argue that it is doubtful that role playing can explain all hypnotic phenomena. For instance, they assert that even the most cooperative subjects are unlikely to endure surgery without a drug anesthetic just to please their physician** and live up to their expected role.

Of late, the most influential explanation of hypnosis as an altered state of awareness has been offered by Ernest Hilgard (1986). According to Hilgard, hypnosis creates a *dissociation* in consciousness. **Dissociation is a splitting off of mental processes into two separate, simultaneous streams of awareness.** In other words, Hilgard theorizes that hypnosis splits consciousness into two streams. One stream is in communication with the hypnotist and the external world, while the other is a difficult-to-detect "hidden observer." Hilgard believes that many hypnotic effects are a product of this divided consciousness. For instance, he suggests that a hypnotized subject might appear unresponsive to pain because the pain isn't registered in the portion of consciousness that communicates with other people.

One appealing aspect of Hilgard's theory is that *divided consciousness* is a common, normal experience. For example, people will often drive a car a great distance, responding to traffic signals and other cars, with no recollection of having consciously done so. In such cases, consciousness is clearly divided between driving and the person's thoughts about other matters. Interestingly, this common experience has long been known as *highway hypnosis*. In this condition, there even is an "amnesia" for the component of consciousness

"Many psychologists argue that the hypnotic trance is a mirage. It would be unfortunate if this skeptical view were to gain such popularity that the benefits of hypnosis are denied to the numbers of those who could be helped."
ERNEST HILGARD

that drove the car, similar to posthypnotic amnesia. In summary, Hilgard presents hypnosis as a plausible variation in consciousness that has continuity with everyday experience.

The debate about whether hypnosis involves an altered or a normal state of consciousness appears likely to continue for the foreseeable future. As you will see momentarily, a similar debate has dominated the scientific discussion of meditation.

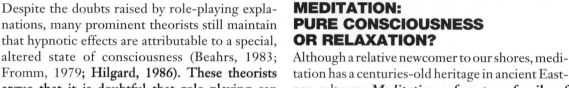

MEDITATION: PURE CONSCIOUSNESS OR RELAXATION?

Although a relative newcomer to our shores, meditation has a centuries-old heritage in ancient Eastern cultures. *Meditation* **refers to a family of mental exercises in which a conscious attempt is made to focus attention in a nonanalytical way.** There are many different approaches to meditation. In the United States, the most widely practiced approaches are those associated with yoga, Zen, and transcendental meditation (TM). All three of these approaches are rooted in Eastern religions (Hinduism, Buddhism, and Taoism). However, meditation can be divorced from religious beliefs. In fact, most Americans who practice meditation have only vague ideas regarding its religious significance. Of interest to psychology is the fact that meditation involves a deliberate effort to alter consciousness.

Most meditative techniques are deceptively simple. For example, in TM a person is supposed to sit in a comfortable position with eyes closed and silently focus attention on a *mantra*. A mantra is a specially assigned Sanskrit word that is personalized to each meditator. This exercise in mental self-discipline is to be practiced twice daily for about 20 minutes. The technique has been described as "diving from the active surface of the mind to its quiet depths" (Bloomfield & Kory, 1976, p. 49). Most proponents of TM believe that it involves an altered state of "pure consciousness." Many skeptics counter that meditation is simply an effective relaxation technique. Let's look at the evidence.

Short-Term Effects

What happens when an experienced meditator goes into the meditative state? An intriguing finding in many studies is that alpha waves and theta waves become more prominent in EEG recordings (Fenwick, 1987). Most studies also find that subjects' heart rate, respiration rate, oxygen consumption, and carbon dioxide elimination decline (see Figure 5.11). Many researchers have also observed increases in skin resistance and decreases in blood lactate—physiological indicators associated with relaxation (Davidson, 1976; Dillbeck & Orme-Johnson, 1987; Woolfolk, 1975). Taken together, these changes suggest that meditation leads to a potentially beneficial physiological state characterized by suppression of bodily arousal.

However, some researchers argue that many systematic relaxation training procedures can produce similar results (Shapiro, 1984). Hence, there is debate about whether the physiological changes associated with meditation are unique to it (Holmes, 1987).

Long-Term Effects

The evidence on the long-term effects of meditation is also controversial. Some studies have found that meditation can improve mood, lessen fatigue, and reduce anxiety and drug abuse (Carrington, 1987; Eppley, Abrams, & Shear, 1989; Gelderloos et al., 1991). Studies also suggest that meditation is associated with improved physical health (Orme-Johnson, 1987), superior mental health (Alexander, Rainforth, & Gelderloos, 1991), and even increased longevity among the elderly (Alexander et al., 1989). Some psychologists argue that at least some of these effects may be just as attainable through systematic relaxation or other mental focusing procedures (Shapiro, 1984; Smith, 1975). Critics also wonder whether placebo effects, sampling bias, and other methodological problems may contribute to some of the reported benefits of meditation (Shapiro, 1987).

In summary, it seems safe to conclude that meditation is a potentially worthwhile relaxation strategy. And it's possible that meditation involves more than mere relaxation, as TM advocates insist. At present, however, there is little evidence that meditation produces a unique state of "pure consciousness."

ALTERING CONSCIOUSNESS WITH DRUGS

Like hypnosis and meditation, drugs are commonly used in deliberate efforts to alter con-

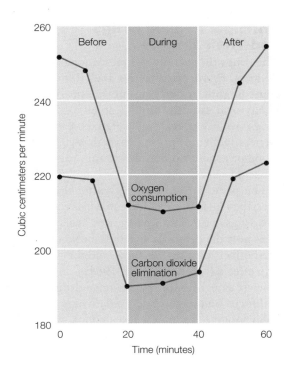

Figure 5.11. The suppression of physiological arousal during transcendental meditation. The physiological changes shown in the graph are evidence of physical relaxation during the meditative state. However, such changes can also be produced by systematic relaxation procedures. (Based on data from Wallace & Benson, 1972)

sciousness. In this section, we focus on the use of drugs for nonmedical purposes, commonly referred to as "drug abuse" or "recreational drug use." Drug abuse reaches into every corner of American society. Recreational drug use involves personal, moral, political, and legal issues that are not matters for science to resolve. However, the more knowledgeable you are about drugs, the more informed your decisions and opinions about them will be. Accordingly, this section describes the types of drugs that are most commonly used for recreational purposes and summarizes their effects on consciousness, behavior, and health.

CONCEPT CHECK 5.2
Relating EEG Activity to Variations in Consciousness

Early in the chapter we emphasized the intimate relationship between brain activity and variations in consciousness. Check your understanding of this relationship by indicating the kind of EEG activity (alpha, beta, theta, or delta) that would probably be dominant in each of the following situations. The answers are in Appendix A.

_____ 1. You are playing a video game.

_____ 2. You are deep in meditation.

_____ 3. You have just fallen asleep.

_____ 4. You are in the midst of a terrible nightmare.

_____ 5. You are a novice typist, practicing your typing.

Principal Abused Drugs and Their Effects

The drugs that people use recreationally are *psychoactive*. **Psychoactive drugs are chemical substances that modify mental, emotional, or behavioral functioning.** Not all psychoactive drugs produce effects that lead to recreational use. Generally, people prefer drugs that elevate their mood or produce other pleasurable alterations in consciousness.

The principal types of recreational drugs are described in Table 5.4. The table lists representative drugs in each of six categories. It also summarizes how the drugs are taken, their medical uses, their effects on consciousness, and their common side effects (based on Blum, 1984; Julien, 1992). The six categories of psychoactive drugs that we will focus on are narcotics, sedatives, stimulants, hallucinogens, cannabis, and alcohol.

Narcotics, or *opiates,* are drugs derived from opium that are capable of relieving pain. The main drugs in this category are heroin and morphine, although less potent opiates such as codeine, Demerol, and methadone are also abused. In sufficient dosages these drugs can produce an overwhelming sense of euphoria or well-being. This euphoric effect has a relaxing, "Who cares?" quality that makes the high an attractive escape from reality.

Sedatives **are sleep-inducing drugs that tend to decrease central nervous system activation and behavioral activity.** Over the years, the most widely abused sedatives have been the *barbiturates,* which are compounds derived from barbituric acid. People abusing sedatives, or "downers," generally consume larger doses than are prescribed for medical purposes. The desired effect is a euphoria similar to that produced by drink-

Table 5.4 Psychoactive Drugs: Methods of Ingestion, Medical Uses, and Effects

Drugs	Methods of Ingestion	Principal Medical Uses	Desired Effects	Short-Term Side Effects
Narcotics (opiates) Morphine Heroin	Injected, smoked, oral	Pain relief	Euphoria, relaxation, anxiety reduction, pain relief	Lethargy, drowsiness, nausea, impaired coordination, impaired mental functioning, constipation
Sedatives Barbiturates (e.g., Seconal) Nonbarbiturates (e.g., Quaalude)	Oral, injected	Sleeping pill, anticonvulsant	Euphoria, relaxation, anxiety reduction, reduced inhibitions	Lethargy, drowsiness, severely impaired coordination, impaired mental functioning, emotional swings, dejection
Stimulants Amphetamines Cocaine	Oral, sniffed, injected, freebased, smoked	Treatment of hyperactivity and narcolepsy, local anesthetic (cocaine only)	Elation, excitement, increased alertness, increased energy, reduced fatigue	Increased blood pressure and heart rate, increased talkativeness, restlessness, irritability, insomnia, reduced appetite, increased sweating and urination, anxiety, paranoia, increased aggressiveness, panic
Hallucinogens LSD Mescaline Psilocybin	Oral	None	Increased sensory awareness, euphoria, altered perceptions, hallucinations, insightful experiences	Dilated pupils, nausea, emotional swings, paranoia, jumbled thought processes, impaired judgment, anxiety, panic reaction
Cannabis Marijuana Hashish THC	Smoked, oral	Treatment of glaucoma; other uses under study	Mild euphoria, relaxation, altered perceptions, enhanced awareness	Bloodshot eyes, dry mouth, reduced short-term memory, sluggish motor coordination, sluggish mental functioning, anxiety
Alcohol	Drinking	None	Mild euphoria, relaxation, anxiety reduction, reduced inhibitions	Severely impaired coordination, impaired mental functioning, increased urination, emotional swings, depression, quarrelsomeness, hangover

Note: The principal omission from this table is PCP (phencyclidine hydrochloride), which does not fit neatly into any of the listed categories. PCP has sedative, stimulant, hallucinogenic, and anesthetic effects. Its short-term side effects can be very dangerous. Common side effects include agitation, paranoia, confusion, and severe mental disorientation that has been linked to accidents and suicides.

ing large amounts of alcohol. Feelings of tension or dejection are replaced by a relaxed, pleasant state of intoxication, accompanied by loosened inhibitions.

Stimulants **are drugs that tend to increase central nervous system activation and behavioral activity.** Stimulants range from mild, widely available drugs, such as caffeine and nicotine, to stronger, carefully regulated ones, such as cocaine. We will focus on cocaine and amphetamines. Cocaine is a natural substance that comes from the coca shrub. In contrast, amphetamines ("speed") are synthesized in a pharmaceutical laboratory. Cocaine and amphetamines have fairly similar effects, except that cocaine produces a briefer high. Stimulants produce a euphoria very different from that created by narcotics or sedatives. They produce a buoyant, elated, energetic, "I can conquer the world!" feeling accompanied by increased alertness. In recent years, cocaine and amphetamines have become available in much more potent (and dangerous) forms than before. "Freebasing" is a chemical treatment used to extract nearly pure cocaine from ordinary street cocaine. "Crack" is the most widely distributed by-product of this process, consisting of chips of pure cocaine that are usually smoked. Amphetamines are increasingly sold as a crystalline powder, called "crank," that may be snorted or injected intravenously. Drug dealers are also marketing a smokable form of methamphetamine called "ice."

Hallucinogens **are a diverse group of drugs that have powerful effects on mental and emotional functioning, marked most prominently by distortions in sensory and perceptual experience.** The principal hallucinogens are LSD, mescaline, and psilocybin. These drugs have similar effects, although they vary in potency. Hallucinogens produce euphoria, increased sensory awareness, and a distorted sense of time. In some users, they lead to profound, dreamlike, "mystical" feelings that are difficult to describe. The latter effect is why they have been used in religious ceremonies for centuries in some cultures. Unfortunately, at the other end of the emotional spectrum hallucinogens can also produce nightmarish feelings of anxiety and paranoia, commonly called a "bad trip."

Cannabis **is the hemp plant from which marijuana, hashish, and THC are derived.** Marijuana is a mixture of dried leaves, flowers, stems, and seeds taken from the plant. Hashish comes from the plant's resin. Smoking is the usual route of ingestion for both marijuana and hashish. THC, the active chemical ingredient in cannabis, can be synthesized for research purposes (for example, to give to animals, who can't very well smoke marijuana). When smoked, cannabis has an immediate impact that may last several hours. The desired effects of the drug are a mild, relaxed euphoria and enhanced sensory awareness.

Alcohol **encompasses a variety of beverages containing ethyl alcohol,** such as beers, wines, and distilled spirits. The concentration of ethyl alcohol varies from about 4% in most beers up to 40% in 80-proof liquor, and occasionally more in higher-proof liquors. When people drink heavily, the central effect is a relaxed euphoria that temporarily boosts self-esteem, as problems seem to melt away and inhibitions diminish. Alcohol is the most widely used recreational drug in our society. Because alcohol is legal, many people use it casually without even thinking of it as a drug. Yet experts estimate that the dollar costs (due to absenteeism at work, medical expenses, treatment costs, and so on) of alcohol abuse are nearly double the costs of all other types of drug abuse *combined* (Segal, 1988).

We'll limit our discussion to the six categories of drugs just described. However, it should be noted that there are other recreational drugs that do not fit into any of these categories, such as PCP or "designer drugs" like MDMA ("ecstasy").

Factors Influencing Drug Effects

The drug effects summarized in Table 5.4 are the *typical* ones. Drug effects can vary from person to person and even for the same person in different situations. The impact of any drug depends in part on the user's age, mood, motivation, personality, previous experience with the drug, body weight, and physiology. The dose and potency of a drug, the method of administration, and the setting in which a drug is taken also influence its effects (Leavitt, 1982). Our theme of *multifactorial causation* clearly applies to the effects of drugs.

So, too, does our theme emphasizing the *subjectivity of experience.* Expectations are potentially powerful factors that can influence the user's perceptions of a drug's effects. You may recall from our discussion of placebo effects in Chapter 2 that some people who are misled to *think* that they are drinking alcohol show signs of intoxication (Wilson, 1982). If people *expect* a drug to make them feel giddy, serene, or profound, their expectation may contribute to the feelings they experience.

Table 5.5 Psychoactive Drugs: Tolerance, Dependence, Potential for Fatal Overdose, and Health Risks

Drugs	Tolerance	Risk of Physical Dependence	Risk of Psychological Dependence	Fatal Overdose Potential	Health Risks
Narcotics (opiates)	Rapid	High	High	High	Infectious diseases, accidents
Sedatives	Rapid	High	High	High	Accidents
Stimulants	Rapid	Moderate	High	Moderate to high	Sleep problems, malnutrition, nasal damage, hypertension, stroke, liver disease
Hallucinogens	Gradual	None	Very low	Very low	Accidents
Cannabis	Gradual	None	Low to moderate	Very low	Accidents, lung cancer, respiratory disease, pulmonary disease
Alcohol	Gradual	Moderate	Moderate	Low to high	Accidents, liver disease, malnutrition, brain damage, neurological disorders, heart disease, stroke, hypertension, ulcers, cancer, birth defects

Figure 5.12. Amphetamines and neurotransmitters. Like other drugs, amphetamines alter neurotransmitter activity. Depicted here are two ways in which amphetamines appear to increase dopamine (DA) and norepinephrine (NE) activity.

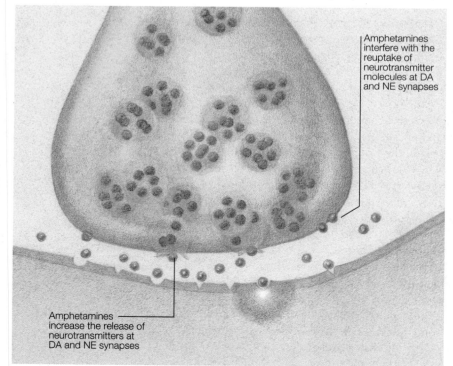

Amphetamines interfere with the reuptake of neurotransmitter molecules at DA and NE synapses

Amphetamines increase the release of neurotransmitters at DA and NE synapses

A drug's effects can also change as the person's body develops a *tolerance* to the chemical. **Tolerance refers to a progressive decrease in a person's responsiveness to a drug as a result of continued use.** Tolerance usually leads people to consume larger and larger doses of a drug to attain the effects they desire. Most drugs produce tolerance, but some do so more rapidly than others. For example, tolerance to alcohol usually builds slowly, while tolerance to heroin increases much more quickly. Table 5.5 indicates whether various categories of drugs tend to produce tolerance rapidly or gradually.

Mechanisms of Drug Action

Most drugs have effects that reverberate throughout the body. However, psychoactive drugs work primarily by altering neurotransmitter activity in the brain. As we discussed in Chapter 3, *neurotransmitters* are chemicals that transmit information between neurons at junctions called *synapses*.

The actions of amphetamines illustrate how drugs have selective, multiple effects on neurotransmitter activity. Amphetamines exert their effects on two of the biogenic amine neurotransmitters: norepinephrine (NE) and dopamine (DA). Indeed, the name amphet*amines* reflects the kinship between these drugs and the biogenic *amines*. Amphetamines appear to have two key effects at DA and NE synapses (Cooper, Bloom, & Roth, 1991; King & Ellinwood, 1992), which are summarized in Figure 5.12. First, they increase the release of DA and NE by presynaptic neurons. Second, they interfere with the reuptake of DA and NE from synaptic clefts. All three of these actions serve to increase the levels of dopamine and norepinephrine at the affected synapses. The key point is that amphetamines selectively influence NE and DA activity in a *variety* of ways. Cocaine shares some of these actions, which is why cocaine and amphetamines produce similar stimulant effects.

Sedatives and alcohol appear to exert many of their key effects at GABA synapses (Giannini & Miller, 1989; Tabakoff & Hoffman, 1992). The convergence of alcohol and sedatives on the same synapses probably explains why these drugs are *synergistic*. Drugs are said to be synergistic when their combined effect is greater than the sum of their individual effects. Synergistic effects explain why mixing alcohol and sedatives is so dangerous. The combination of these drugs has caused many fatal overdoses by depressing CNS activity excessively.

The discovery of special receptor sites in the brain for opiates (see Chapter 3) has led to new insights about the actions of narcotic drugs. These drugs apparently bind to opiate receptors, and their actions at these receptor sites indirectly elevate dopamine activity (Koob & Bloom, 1988). The impact of hallucinogens and marijuana on neurotransmitter activity remains obscure.

Drug Dependence

People can become either physically or psychologically dependent on a drug. Physical dependence is a common problem with narcotics, sedatives, and alcohol and is an occasional problem with stimulants. **Physical dependence exists when a person must continue to take a drug to avoid withdrawal illness.** The symptoms of withdrawal illness depend on the specific drug. Withdrawal from heroin, barbiturates, and alcohol can produce fever, chills, tremors, convulsions, vomiting, cramps, diarrhea, and severe aches and pains. Withdrawal from stimulants leads to a more subtle syndrome, marked by fatigue, apathy, irritability, depression, and disorientation.

Psychological dependence **exists when a person must continue to take a drug to satisfy intense mental and emotional craving for the drug.** Psychological dependence is more subtle than physical dependence, but the need it creates can be powerful. Cocaine, for instance, can produce an overwhelming psychological need for continued use. Psychological dependence is possible with all recreational drugs, although it seems rare for hallucinogens.

Both types of dependence are established gradually with repeated use of a drug. Drugs vary in their potential for creating either physical or psy-

chological dependence. Table 5.5 provides estimates of the risk of each kind of dependence for the six categories of recreational drugs covered in our discussion.

Some theorists have begun to raise doubts about the value of distinguishing between physical and psychological dependence (Koob & Bloom, 1988; Ray & Ksir, 1990). This distinction was originally based on two assumptions. First, it was assumed that there is a physiological basis (tissue changes) for physical dependence but not for psychological dependence. Second, it was assumed that a person who is physically dependent on a drug continues to use it to avoid aversive effects, while a person who is psychologically dependent on a drug continues to use it to experience pleasant effects. Both of these assumptions appear dubious today in light of new research. Increased knowledge of how drugs alter synaptic transmission suggests that physiological mechanisms underlie both types of dependence. Evidence also suggests that the motivation to avoid withdrawal may be less important in explaining physical dependence than was previously believed. Thus, the pursuit of pleasant effects may be the critical force underlying both types of dependence. Although the concepts of physical and psychological dependence remain widely used, these concepts are going through a period of transition.

CONCEPT CHECK 5.3
Recognizing the Unique Characteristics of Commonly Abused Drugs

From our discussion of the principal abused drugs, it is clear that considerable overlap exists among the categories of drugs in terms of their methods of ingestion, medical uses, desired effects, and short-term side effects. Each type of drug, however, has at least one or two characteristics that make it different from the other types. Check your understanding of the unique characteristics of each type of drug by indicating which of them has the characteristics listed below. Choose from the following: (a) narcotics, (b) sedatives, (c) stimulants, (d) hallucinogens, (e) cannabis, and (f) alcohol. You'll find the answers in Appendix A.

_____ 1. Increases alertness and energy, reduces fatigue.

_____ 2. No recognized medical use. May lead to insightful or "mystical" experiences.

_____ 3. Used as a "sleeping pill" because it reduces CNS activity.

_____ 4. Contributes to half of all traffic fatalities.

_____ 5. Derived from opium. Used medically for pain relief.

_____ 6. Most likely health risk is respiratory and pulmonary disease.

Drugs and Physical Health

Recreational drug use can affect physical health in a variety of ways. The three principal risks are overdose, tissue damage (direct effects), and health-impairing behavior that results from drug use (indirect effects).

Overdose

Any drug can be fatal if a person takes enough of it, but some drugs are much more dangerous than others. Table 5.5 shows estimates of the risk of accidentally consuming a *lethal* overdose of each listed drug. Drugs that are CNS depressants—sedatives, narcotics, and alcohol—carry the greatest risk of overdose. It's important to remember that these drugs are synergistic with each other, so many overdoses involve lethal *combinations* of CNS depressants. What happens when a person overdoses on these drugs? The respiratory system usually grinds to a halt, producing coma, brain damage, and death within a brief period.

Fatal overdoses with CNS stimulants usually involve a heart attack, stroke, or cortical seizure. Deaths due to overdoses of stimulant drugs used to be relatively infrequent (Kalant & Kalant, 1979). However, cocaine overdoses have increased sharply as more people have experimented with more potent forms of cocaine, such as crack (Gold, 1992).

Direct Effects

In some cases, drugs cause tissue damage directly. For example, snorting cocaine can damage nasal membranes. Cocaine can also alter cardiovascular functioning in ways that increase the risk of heart attack and stroke, and crack smoking is associated

Our society discourages some types of drug use more than others, but all drugs have side effects and carry risks.

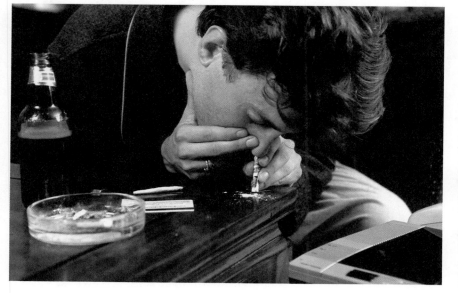

with a host of respiratory problems (Gold, 1992; Morris, 1991). Long-term, excessive alcohol consumption is associated with an elevated risk for a wide range of serious health problems, including liver damage, ulcers, hypertension, stroke, heart disease, neurological disorders, and some types of cancer (D. Goodwin, 1992).

The health risks associated with marijuana use have generated considerable debate in recent years. The preponderance of evidence suggests that heavy use of marijuana *probably* increases the chances for respiratory and pulmonary disease, including lung cancer (Gold, 1989). However, many other widely publicized dangers are either unfounded or greatly exaggerated by the popular press. Based on current evidence, there is little reason for concern about marijuana causing (1) brain damage, (2) increased chromosome breakage, (3) birth defects, (4) impaired immune response, or (5) impotence and sterility in men (Blum, 1984; Cohen, 1980; Grinspoon & Bakalar, 1992; Relman, 1982).

Health-Impairing Behavior

The negative effects of drugs on physical health are often indirect results of the drugs' impact on behavior (Blum, 1984). For instance, people using stimulants often do not eat or sleep properly. Sedatives increase the risk of accidental injuries because they severely impair motor coordination. People who abuse downers often trip down stairs, fall off stools, and suffer other mishaps. Many drugs impair driving ability, increasing the risk of automobile accidents. Alcohol, for instance, may contribute to roughly *half* of all automobile fatalities (Coleman, 1993). Intravenous drug users risk contracting infectious diseases that can be spread by unsterilized needles, including AIDS.

The major health risks (other than overdose) of various recreational drugs are listed in the sixth column of Table 5.5. As you can see, alcohol appears to have the most diverse negative effects on physical health. The irony, of course, is that alcohol is the only recreational drug listed that is legal.

PUTTING IT IN PERSPECTIVE

This chapter highlights four of our unifying themes. First, we can see how psychology evolves in a sociohistorical context. Psychology began as the science of consciousness in the 19th century, but consciousness proved difficult to study empirically. Research on consciousness dwindled after John B. Watson and others redefined psychology as the science of behavior. However, in the 1960s, people began to turn inward, showing a new interest in altering consciousness through drug use, meditation, hypnosis, and biofeedback. Psychologists responded to these social trends by beginning to study variations in consciousness in earnest. This renewed interest in consciousness shows how social forces can have an impact on psychology's evolution.

A second theme that predominates in this chapter is the idea that people's experience of the world is highly subjective. We encountered this theme at the start of the chapter when we discussed the difficulty that people have describing their states of consciousness. The subjective nature of consciousness was apparent elsewhere in the chapter, as well. For instance, we found that the alterations of consciousness produced by drugs depend significantly on personal expectations.

Third, we saw once again how culture molds some aspects of behavior. Although the basic physiological process of sleep appears largely invariant from one society to another, culture influences certain aspects of sleep habits and has a dramatic impact on whether people remember their dreams and how they interpret and feel about their dreams. If not for space constraints, we might also have discussed cross-cultural differences in patterns of recreational drug use, which vary considerably from one society to the next.

Finally, the chapter illustrates psychology's theoretical diversity. We discussed conflicting theories about dreams, hypnosis, meditation, and the functions of sleep. For the most part, we did not see these opposing theories converging toward reconciliation, as we did in the previous chapter. However, it's important to emphasize that rival theories do not always merge neatly into tidy models of behavior. While it's always nice to resolve a theoretical debate, the debate itself can advance knowledge by stimulating and guiding empirical research.

Indeed, our upcoming Application demonstrates that theoretical debates need not be resolved in order to advance knowledge. Many theoretical controversies and enduring mysteries remain in the study of sleep and dreams. Nonetheless, researchers have accumulated a great deal of practical information on these topics, which we'll discuss in the next few pages.

Addressing Practical Questions about Sleep and Dreams

Indicate whether the following statements are "true" or "false":

___ **1** Everyone needs 8 hours of sleep a night to maintain sound mental health.

___ **2** Naps rarely have a refreshing effect.

___ **3** Some people never dream.

___ **4** When people cannot recall their dreams, it's because they are trying to repress them.

These assertions were all drawn from the Sleep and Dreams Information Questionnaire (Palladino & Carducci, 1984), which measures practical knowledge about sleep and dreams. Are they true or false? You'll see in this Application.

People typically get very upset when they have difficulty falling asleep. Unfortunately, this emotional distress tends to make it even harder for people to get to sleep.

Common Questions About Sleep

How much sleep do people need? The average amount of daily sleep for young adults is 7.5 hours. However, people vary considerably in how long they sleep. Based on a synthesis of data from many studies, Webb (1992b) estimates that sleep time is distributed as shown in Figure 5.13. As the diagram shows, sleep needs vary from person to person. Asking how much sleep the average person needs isn't a very useful question, much like asking what shoe size the average person needs. If everyone were given average-size shoes to wear, most people would be very uncomfortable.

Can people learn to get by with less sleep? Some can. There are well-documented cases of people who have learned to live with less than 3 hours of sleep per night for years without any ill effects (Jones & Oswald, 1968). Thus, the first statement

in our series of true-false items is false. If you want to spend less time sleeping, try reducing your sleep time gradually and see how you feel. In one study of subjects

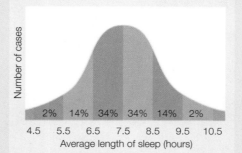

Figure 5.13. Variation in sleep needs. Based on data from a variety of sources, Webb (1992b) estimates that average sleep length among young adults is distributed normally, as shown here. Although most young adults sleep an average of 6.5 to 8.5 hours per night, some people need less and some people need more sleep. (Adapted from Webb, 1992b)

Number of cases

2% 14% 34% 34% 14% 2%

4.5   5.5   6.5   7.5   8.5   9.5   10.5

Average length of sleep (hours)

who gradually reduced their sleep time, all were still sleeping an hour or two less when questioned a year after the study was finished (Friedmann et al., 1977). However, bear in mind the point made earlier in the main body of the chapter—although the effects of sleep deprivation seem pretty benign, lapses of attention due to sleepiness can be quite dangerous if they occur in the wrong place at the wrong time.

Can short naps be refreshing? Some naps are beneficial and some are not. The effectiveness of napping varies from person to person. Also, the benefits of any specific nap depend on the time of day and the amount of sleep one has had recently (Gillberg, 1984). In general, naps are *not* a very efficient way to sleep because you're often just getting into the deeper stages of sleep when your nap time is up. Napping can also disrupt nighttime sleep (Dinges, 1989). Nonetheless, most naps enhance subsequent alertness and reduce sleepiness (Dinges & Broughton, 1989). Many highly productive people, including Thomas Edison, Winston Churchill, and John F. Kennedy, have made effective use of naps. In conclusion, naps can be refreshing for many people, so the second statement opening this Application is false.

Is there such a thing as sleep learning? Yes, but it won't get you through college. Studies show that cognitive responding to external stimuli can occur during the lighter stages (1 and 2) of sleep (Ogilvie, Wilkinson, & Allison, 1989). This and other lines of evidence suggest that sleep learning is a legitimate possibility (Eich, 1990). However, studies indicate that people have minimal ability to assimilate information of any complexity into long-term memory while asleep (Badia, 1990; Bonnet, 1982). It would be nice if people could learn Spanish by listening to an audiotape while they slept. But the evidence indicates that trying to do so is pointless.

What can be done to avoid sleep problems? There are many ways to improve your chances of getting satisfactory sleep (see Figure 5.14). Most of them involve developing sensible daytime habits that won't interfere with sleep (Catalano, 1990; Coleman, 1986; Hales, 1987). For example, if you've been having trouble sleeping at night, it's wise to avoid daytime naps, so you're *tired* when bedtime arrives. Some people find that daytime exercise helps them fall asleep more readily at bedtime.

It's wise to minimize consumption of stimulants such as caffeine or nicotine. Because coffee and cigarettes aren't prescription drugs, people don't appreciate how much the stimulants they contain can heighten physical arousal. Many foods (such as chocolate) and beverages (such as cola drinks) contain more caffeine than people realize. Also, bear in mind that ill-advised eating habits can interfere with sleep. Try to avoid going to bed hungry, uncomfortably stuffed, or soon after eating foods that disagree with you. It's also a good idea to try to establish a reasonably regular bedtime. This habit will allow you to take advantage of your circadian rhythm, so you'll be trying to fall asleep when your body is primed to cooperate.

What can be done about insomnia? First, don't panic if you run into a little trouble sleeping. An overreaction to sleep problems can begin a vicious circle of escalating problems, like that depicted in Figure 5.15. If you jump to the conclusion that you are becoming an insomniac, you may approach sleep with anxiety that will aggravate the problem. The harder you work at falling asleep, the less success you're likely to have. As noted earlier, temporary sleep problems are common and generally clear up on their own.

One sleep expert, Dianne Hales (1987), lists 101 suggestions for combating insomnia in her book *How to Sleep Like a Baby*. Many involve "boring yourself to sleep" by playing alphabet games, reciting poems, or listening to your clock. Another recommended strategy is to engage in some not-so-engaging activity. For instance, you might try reading your dullest textbook. It could turn out to be a superb sedative.

It's often a good idea to simply launch yourself into a pleasant daydream. This normal presleep process can take your mind off your difficulties. Whatever you think about, try to avoid ruminating about the current stresses and problems in your life. Research has shown that the tendency to ruminate is one of the key fac-

Figure 5.14. Suggestions for better sleep. Dianne Hales, in *How to Sleep Like a Baby*, offers the following advice for avoiding or minimizing sleep problems.

1 Keep regular hours.

2 Remember that quality of sleep matters more than quantity.

3 Exercise every day—but not in the evening.

4 Don't smoke.

5 Don't have coffee late in the day.

6 Don't drink alcohol after dinner.

7 Don't nap during the day.

8 Unwind in the evening.

9 Don't go to bed starved or stuffed.

10 Develop a bedtime sleep ritual.

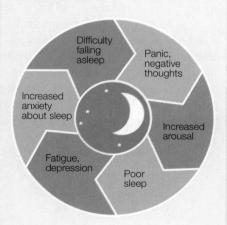

Figure 5.15. The vicious circle of anxiety and sleep difficulty. Anxiety about sleep difficulties leads to poorer sleep, which increases anxiety further, which in turn leads to even greater difficulties in sleeping.

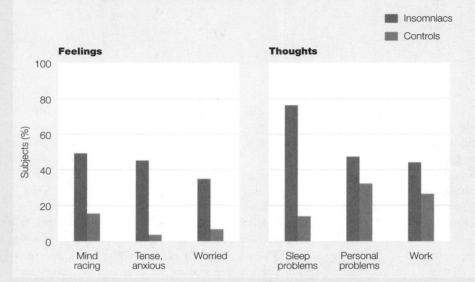

Figure 5.16. Thoughts and emotions associated with insomnia. This graph depicts the percentage of insomniacs and control subjects reporting various presleep feelings and thoughts. Insomniacs' tendency to ruminate about their problems contributes to their sleep difficulties. (Based on data from Kales et al., 1984)

tors contributing to insomnia (Kales et al., 1984), as the data in Figure 5.16 show. Anything that relaxes you—whether it's music, meditation, prayer, a warm bath, or a systematic relaxation procedure—can aid you in falling asleep.

Common Questions About Dreams

Does everyone dream? Yes. Some people just don't *remember* any of their dreams. However, when these people are brought into a sleep lab and awakened from REM sleep, they report having been dreaming—much to their surprise (Hall & Nordby, 1972). Thus, statement 3 at the start of this Application is false.

Why don't some people remember their dreams? The evaporation of dreams appears to be quite normal. Given the lowered level of awareness during sleep, it's understandable that memory of dreams is mediocre. Dream recall is best when people are awakened during or soon after a dream (Goodenough, 1991). Most of the time, people who *do* recall dreams upon waking are remembering either their *last* dream from their final REM

period or a dream that awakened them earlier in the night. Hobson's (1989) educated guess is that people probably forget 95%–99% of their dreams. This forgetting is natural and is not due to repression (statement 4 is also false). People who never remember their dreams probably have a sleep pattern that puts too much time between their last REM/dream period and awakening, so even their last dream is forgotten.

Can people improve their recall of dreams? Yes. Most people don't have any significant reason to work at recalling their dreams, so they just let them float away. However, many people have found that they can remember more dreams if they merely place that goal uppermost in their minds as they go to sleep (Goodenough, 1991). Dream recall is also aided by making a point of trying to remember dreams upon first awakening, before opening one's eyes or getting out of bed.

Do dreams require interpretation? Yes, but interpretation may not be as difficult as generally assumed. People have long believed that dreams are symbolic and that it is necessary to interpret the sym-

bols to understand the meaning of dreams. Freud, for instance, made a distinction between the *manifest content* and the *latent content* of a dream. **The *manifest content* consists of the plot of a dream at a surface level. The *latent content* refers to the hidden or disguised meaning of the events in the plot.** Thus, a Freudian therapist might equate such dream events as walking into a tunnel, mounting a horse, or riding a roller coaster with sexual intercourse. Freudian theorists assert that dream interpretation is a complicated task requiring considerable knowledge of symbolism.

However, many dream theorists argue that symbolism in dreams is less deceptive and mysterious than Freud thought (Faraday, 1974; Foulkes, 1985; Hall, 1979). Calvin Hall makes the point that dreams require some interpretation simply because they are more visual than verbal. That is, pictures need to be translated into ideas. According to Hall, dream symbolism is highly personal and the dreamer may be the person best equipped to decipher a dream. Unfortunately, you'll never know whether you're "correct," because there is no definitive way to judge the validity of different dream interpretations.

Could a shocking dream be fatal? According to folklore, if you fall from a height in a dream, you'd better wake up on the plunge downward, because if you hit the bottom the shock to your system will be so great that you will actually die in your sleep. Think about this one for a moment. *If* it were a genuine problem, who would have reported it? You can be sure that no one has ever testified to experiencing a fatal dream. This myth presumably exists because many people do awaken during the downward plunge, thinking they've averted a close call. A study by Barrett (1988–1989) suggests that dreams of one's own death are relatively infrequent. However, people do have such dreams—and live to tell about them.

Chapter 5 Review

KEY IDEAS

On the Nature of Consciousness
♦ Consciousness is the continually changing stream of mental activity. Consciousness varies along a continuum of levels of awareness. There is some minimal awareness even during sleep. Variations in consciousness are related to brain activity, as measured by the EEG.

The Sleep and Waking Cycle
♦ Sleep is influenced by our biological rhythms, especially 24-hour circadian rhythms. Biological clocks are internally regulated mechanisms that run even when people are cut off from the light-darkness cycle. Ignoring your biological clock by going to sleep at an unusual time may have a negative effect on your sleep. Being out of sync with circadian rhythms is one reason for jet lag and for the unpleasant nature of rotating shift work.

♦ When you fall asleep, you evolve through a series of stages in cycles of approximately 90 minutes. During the REM stage you experience rapid eye movements, a brain wave that is characteristic of waking thought, and the bulk of your dreaming. The sleep cycle tends to be repeated about four times in a night, as REM sleep gradually becomes more predominant and NREM sleep dwindles.

♦ The REM portion of sleep declines during childhood, leveling off at around 20% during adolescence. During adulthood, slow-wave sleep declines. Culture appears to have little impact on the architecture of sleep, but it does influence sleeping arrangements and napping patterns.

♦ The impact of sleep loss on performance is highly variable, with the typical effects being less damaging than expected. The only consistent effect of sleep deprivation is sleepiness. However, increased sleepiness can contribute to work accidents and other mishaps. Research on sleep deprivation suggests that people need REM sleep and slow-wave sleep.

♦ Some theorists believe that slow-wave sleep is regulated by a restorative process, and REM sleep by a circadian process. Insomnia involves three distinct patterns of sleep difficulty. Insomnia has a variety of causes. Sleeping pills generally are a poor solution for insomnia.

The World of Dreams
♦ Research on dream content indicates that dreams are not as exotic as widely believed. The content of one's dreams may be affected by events in one's life, as well as by external stimuli that are experienced during the dream.

♦ There are dramatic variations across cultures in beliefs about the nature of dreams and their importance, dream recall, dream content, and dream interpretation. Theories of dreaming remain largely untested, and scientists do not really know why people dream.

Hypnosis: Altered Consciousness or Role Playing?
♦ People vary in their susceptibility to hypnosis. Among other things, hypnosis can produce anesthesia, sensory distortions, disinhibition, and posthypnotic amnesia. Theories of hypnosis view it either as an altered state of consciousness or as a normal state in which subjects assume a hypnotic role.

Meditation: Pure Consciousness or Relaxation?
♦ Claims for the benefits of meditation have created some excitement in recent decades, and evidence does suggest that meditation can be beneficial. However, some experts suggest that these benefits are not unique to meditation and are a product of any effective relaxation procedure.

Altering Consciousness with Drugs
♦ Most recreational drug use involves an effort to alter consciousness with psychoactive drugs. The principal categories of abused drugs are narcotics, sedatives, stimulants, hallucinogens, cannabis, and alcohol. Although it's possible to describe the typical effects of various drugs, the actual effect on any individual depends on a host of factors, including subjective expectations and tolerance to the drug.

♦ Psychoactive drugs exert their main effects in the brain, where they alter neurotransmitter activity at synaptic sites in a variety of ways. Drugs vary in their potential for psychological and physical dependence. Likewise, the dangers to physical health vary depending on the drug. Recreational drug use can prove harmful to health by producing an overdose, by causing tissue damage, or by increasing health-impairing behavior.

Putting It in Perspective
♦ Four of our unifying themes were highlighted in this chapter. First, we saw how psychology's study of consciousness reflects concurrent social trends, showing that psychology evolves in a sociohistorical context. Second, we saw how states of consciousness are highly subjective. Third, we saw how culture molds some aspects of sleep and dreaming. Fourth, we saw extensive theoretical diversity that continues to generate vigorous debate about many issues in this area.

Application: Addressing Practical Questions About Sleep and Dreams
♦ Sleep needs vary and some people can learn to get by with less sleep. The value of short naps depends on many factors, including one's biological rhythm. Learning can occur during sleep, but it has little practical value. People can do many things to avoid or reduce sleep problems. Mostly, it's a matter of developing good daytime habits that do not interfere with sleep. People troubled by transient insomnia should avoid panic, pursue effective relaxation, and try distracting themselves so they don't work too hard at falling asleep.

♦ Everyone dreams, but some people cannot remember their dreams, probably because of the nature of their sleep cycle. Dream recall can be improved, and there's no evidence that dreams can be fatal. Most theorists believe that dreams require some interpretation, but this may not be as complicated as once assumed.

KEY TERMS

Alcohol	Latent content
Biological rhythms	Manifest content
Cannabis	Meditation
Circadian rhythms	Meditation
Consciousness	Narcotics
Dissociation	Non-REM (NREM) sleep
Dream	Opiates
Electrocardiograph (EKG)	Physical dependence
Electroencephalograph (EEG)	Psychoactive drugs
Electromyograph (EMG)	Psychological dependence
Electrooculograph (EOG)	REM sleep
Hallucinogens	Sedatives
Hypnosis	Slow-wave sleep
Insomnia	Stimulants
	Tolerance

KEY PEOPLE

William Dement	Ernest Hilgard
Sigmund Freud	J. Alan Hobson
Calvin Hall	

6 Learning Through Conditioning

- You're sitting in the waiting room of your dentist's office. You cringe when you hear the whirring of a dental drill coming from the next room.

- A 4-year-old boy pinches his hand in one of his toys and curses loudly. His mother looks up in dismay and says to his father, "Where did he pick up that kind of language?"

- A seal waddles across the stage, bows ceremoniously, and "doffs his cap" by flipping it into the air and catching it in his mouth. The spectators at the aquatic show clap appreciatively as the trainer tosses the seal a fish as a reward.

- The crowd hushes as an Olympic diver prepares to execute her dive. In a burst of motion she propels herself into the air and glides smoothly through a dazzling corkscrew somersault.

What do all of these scenarios have in common? At first glance, very little. They are a diverse collection of events, some trivial, some impressive. However, they do share one common thread: *they all involve learning*. This may surprise you. When most people think of learning, they envision students reading textbooks or novices working to acquire a specific skill, such as riding a bicycle or skiing. Although these activities do involve learning, they represent only the tip of the iceberg in psychologists' eyes.

Learning refers to a relatively durable change in behavior or knowledge that is due to experience. This broad definition means that learning is one of the most fundamental concepts in all of psychology. Learning includes the acquisition of knowledge and skills, but it also shapes personal habits such as nailbiting, personality traits such as shyness, emotional responses such as a fear of storms, and personal preferences, such as a taste for tacos or a distaste for formal clothes. Most of your behavior is the result of learning. If it were possible to strip away your learned responses, little behavior would be left. You would not be able to read this book, find your way home, or cook yourself a hamburger. You would be about as complex and exciting as a turnip.

Although you and I depend on learning, it is *not* an exclusively human process. Most organisms are capable of learning. Even the lowly flatworm can acquire a learned response. As this chapter unfolds, you may be surprised to see that much of the research on learning has been conducted using lower animals as subjects. Why?

Mainly because researchers can exert much better experimental control over animal subjects than human subjects. As we saw in Chapter 1, that was one of the reasons why the noted behaviorist John B. Watson advocated the study of animal behavior. For the most part, Watson's plan has worked out well. Decades of research have shown that many principles of learning discovered in animal research apply quite well to humans.

In this chapter, we will focus most of our attention on a specific kind of learning: conditioning. *Conditioning* involves learning associations between events that occur in an organism's environment. In investigating conditioning, psychologists study learning at a very fundamental level. This strategy has paid off with fruitful insights that have laid the foundation for the study of more complex forms of learning, including learning by means of observation. In our chapter Application, you'll see how you can harness the principles of conditioning to improve your self-control.

CLASSICAL CONDITIONING

Do you go weak in the knees at the thought of standing on the roof of a tall building? Does your heart race when you imagine encountering a harmless garter snake? If so, you can understand, at least to some degree, what it's like to have a phobia. *Phobias* are irrational fears of specific objects or situations. Mild phobias are commonplace (Costello, 1982). Over the years, students in my classes have described their phobic responses to a diverse array of stimuli, including bridges, elevators, tunnels, heights, dogs, cats, bugs, snakes, professors, doctors, strangers, thunderstorms, and germs. If you have a phobia, you may have wondered how you managed to acquire such a foolish fear. Chances are, it was through classical conditioning.

Classical conditioning is a type of learning in which a stimulus acquires the capacity to evoke a response that was originally evoked by another stimulus. The process was first described in 1903 by Ivan Pavlov, and it is sometimes called *Pavlovian conditioning* in tribute to him.

Pavlov's Demonstration: "Psychic Reflexes"

Pavlov was a prominent Russian physiologist who did Nobel prize–winning research on digestion. Something of a "classic" himself, he was an ab-

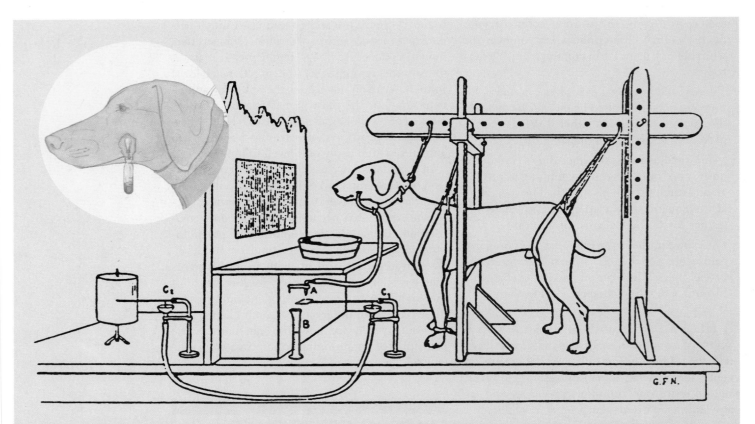

Figure 6.1. Classical conditioning apparatus. An experimental arrangement similar to the one depicted here (taken from Yerkes & Morgulis, 1909) has typically been used in demonstrations of classical conditioning, although Pavlov's original setup (see inset) was quite a bit simpler. The dog is restrained in a harness. A tone is used as the conditioned stimulus (CS), and the presentation of meat powder is used as the unconditioned stimulus (UCS). The tube inserted into the dog's salivary gland allows precise measurement of its salivation response. The pen and rotating drum of paper on the left are used to maintain a continuous record of salivary flow. (Inset) The less elaborate setup that Pavlov originally used to collect saliva on each trial is shown here (Goodwin, 1991).

sent-minded but brilliant professor obsessed with his research. Legend has it that Pavlov once reprimanded an assistant who arrived late for an experiment because of trying to avoid street fighting in the midst of the Russian Revolution. The assistant defended his tardiness, saying, "But Professor, there's a revolution going on with shooting in the streets!" Pavlov supposedly replied, "What the hell difference does a revolution make when you've work to do in the laboratory? Next time there's a revolution, get up earlier!" Apparently, dodging bullets wasn't an adequate excuse for delaying the march of scientific progress (Fancher, 1979; Gantt, 1975).

Pavlov was studying the role of saliva in the digestive processes of dogs when he stumbled onto what he called "psychic reflexes" (Pavlov, 1906). Like many great discoveries, Pavlov's was partly accidental, although he had the insight to recognize its significance. His subjects were dogs restrained in harnesses in an experimental chamber (see Figure 6.1). Their saliva was collected by

"Next time there's a revolution, get up earlier!"
IVAN PAVLOV

means of a surgically implanted tube in the salivary gland. Pavlov would present meat powder to a dog and then collect the resulting saliva. As his research progressed, he noticed that dogs accustomed to the procedure would start salivating *before* the meat powder was presented. For instance, they would salivate in response to a clicking sound made by the device that was used to present the meat powder.

Intrigued by this unexpected finding, Pavlov decided to investigate further. To clarify what was happening, he paired the presentation of the meat powder with various stimuli that would stand out in the laboratory situation. For instance, he used a simple, auditory stimulus—the presentation of a tone. After the tone and the meat powder had been presented together a number of times, the tone was presented alone. What happened? The dogs responded by salivating to the sound of the tone alone.

What was so significant about a dog salivating when a tone was sounded? The key is that the tone had started out as a *neutral* stimulus. That is, it did not originally produce the response of salivation. However, Pavlov managed to change that by pairing the tone with a stimulus (meat powder) that *did* produce the salivation response. Through this process, the tone acquired the capacity to trigger the response of salivation. What Pavlov had demonstrated was how stimulus-response bonds—the basic building blocks of learning—are formed by events in an organism's environment.

Terminology and Procedures

There is a special vocabulary associated with classical conditioning. It often looks intimidating to the uninitiated, but it's really not all that mysterious. The bond Pavlov noted between the meat powder and salivation was a natural, unlearned association. It did not have to be created through conditioning. It is therefore called an *unconditioned* association. In unconditioned bonds, **the *unconditioned stimulus (UCS)* is a stimulus that evokes an unconditioned response without previous conditioning. The *unconditioned response (UCR)* is an unlearned reaction to an unconditioned stimulus that occurs without previous conditioning.**

In contrast, the link between the tone and salivation was established through conditioning. It is therefore called a *conditioned* association. In conditioned bonds, **the *conditioned stimulus (CS)* is a previously neutral stimulus that has, through conditioning, acquired the capacity to evoke a conditioned response. The *conditioned response (CR)* is a learned reaction to a conditioned stimulus that occurs because of previous conditioning.**

To avoid possible confusion, it is worth noting that the unconditioned response and conditioned response are virtually the same behavior, although there may be subtle differences between them. In Pavlov's initial demonstration, the UCR and CR were both salivation. When evoked by the UCS (meat powder), salivation was an unconditioned response. When evoked by the CS (the tone), salivation was a conditioned response. The procedures involved in classical conditioning are outlined in Figure 6.2.

Pavlov's "psychic reflex" came to be called the *conditioned reflex.* Classically conditioned responses have traditionally been characterized as reflexes and said to be *elicited* (drawn forth) because most of them are relatively automatic or involuntary.

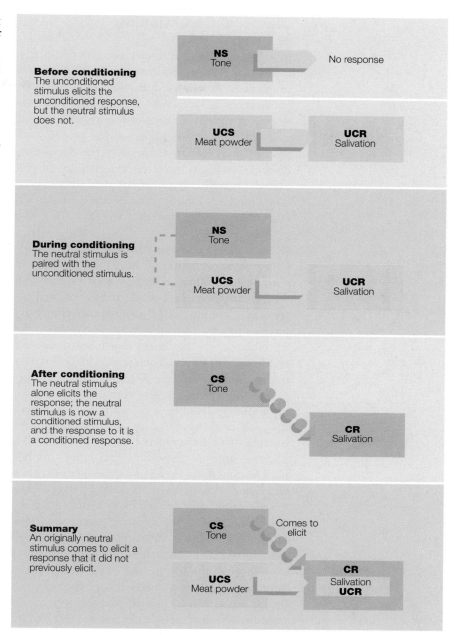

Figure 6.2. The sequence of events in classical conditioning. As we encounter examples of classical conditioning throughout the book, we will see many diagrams like the one in the fourth panel, which summarizes the process.

However, research in recent decades has demonstrated that classical conditioning is involved in a wider range of human and animal behavior than previously appreciated, including some types of nonreflexive responding (Turkkan, 1989). Finally, **a *trial* in classical conditioning consists of any presentation of a stimulus or pair of stimuli.** Psychologists are interested in how many trials are required to establish a particular conditioned bond. The number needed to form an association varies considerably. Although classical conditioning generally proceeds gradually, it *can* occur quite rapidly, sometimes in just one pairing of the CS and UCS.

Classical Conditioning in Everyday Life

In laboratory experiments on classical conditioning, researchers have generally worked with extremely simple responses. Besides salivation, frequently studied favorites include eyelid closure, knee jerks, the flexing of various limbs, and fear responses. The study of such simple responses has proven both practical and productive. However, these responses do not even begin to convey the rich diversity of everyday behavior that is regulated by classical conditioning. Let's look at some examples of classical conditioning drawn from everyday life.

Conditioned Fear and Anxiety

Classical conditioning often plays a key role in shaping emotional responses such as fear and anxiety. Phobias are a good example of such responses. Case studies of patients suffering from phobias suggest that many irrational fears can be traced back to experiences that involve classical conditioning (Merckelbach et al., 1989). It is easy to imagine how such conditioning can occur outside of the laboratory. For example, a student of mine was troubled by a bridge phobia so severe that she couldn't drive on interstate highways because of all the viaducts that had to be crossed. She was able to pinpoint as the source of her phobia something that had happened during her childhood. Whenever her family drove to visit her grandmother, they had to cross a little-used, rickety, dilapidated bridge out in the countryside. Her father, in a misguided attempt at humor, made a major production out of these crossings. He would stop short of the bridge and carry on about the enormous danger. Obviously, he thought the bridge was safe or he wouldn't have driven across it. However, the naive young girl was terrified by her father's scare tactics. Hence, the bridge became a conditioned stimulus eliciting great fear (see Figure 6.3). Unfortunately, the fear spilled over to *all* bridges. Forty years later she was still carrying the burden of this phobia. A number of processes besides conditioning can contribute to the development of phobias (Marks, 1987). None-theless, it's clear that classical conditioning is responsible for a great many irrational fears.

Everyday anxiety responses that are less severe than phobias may also be products of classical conditioning. For instance, if you cringe when you hear the sound of a dentist's drill, this response is due to classical conditioning. In this case, the pain you have experienced from dental drilling is the UCS. This pain has been paired with the sound of the drill, which became a CS eliciting your cringe.

Other Conditioned Emotional Responses

Classical conditioning is not limited to producing unpleasant emotions such as fear and anxiety. Many pleasant emotional responses are also acquired through classical conditioning. Consider the following example, described by a 53-year-old woman who wrote a letter to newspaper columnist Bob Greene about the news that a company was bringing back a discontinued product—Beemans gum. She wrote:

That was the year (1949) I met Charlie. I guess first love is always the same.... Charlie and I went out a lot. He chewed Beemans gum and he smoked.... We would go to all the passion pits—the drive-in movies and the places to park. We did a lot of necking, but we always stopped at a certain point. Charlie wanted to get married when we got out of high school ... [but] Charlie and I drifted apart. We both ended up getting married to different people.

And the funny thing is ... for years the combined smell of cigarette smoke and Beemans gum made my knees weak. Those two smells were Charlie to me. When I would smell the Beemans and the cigarette smoke, I could feel the butterflies dancing all over my stomach.

The writer clearly had a unique and long-lasting emotional response to the smell of Beemans gum and cigarettes. The credit for this *pleasant* response goes to classical conditioning (see Figure 6.4).

Advertising campaigns often try to take advantage of classical conditioning (see Figure 6.5). Advertisers routinely pair their products with UCSs that elicit pleasant emotions (Gorn, 1982; Smith & Engel, 1968). The most common strategy is to present a product in association with an attractive person or enjoyable surroundings. Advertisers hope that these pairings will make their products conditioned stimuli that evoke good feelings. For example, Kodak used a child playing with puppies in one of its TV commercials to help associate warm feelings with its film products.

Figure 6.3. Classical conditioning of a fear response. Many emotional responses that would otherwise be puzzling can be explained by classical conditioning. In the case of one woman's bridge phobia, the fear originally elicited by her father's scare tactics has become a conditioned response to the stimulus of bridges.

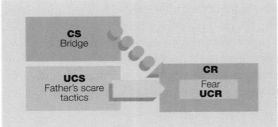

Conditioning and Physiological Responses

Classical conditioning affects not only overt behaviors but physiological processes as well. Consider, for example, your body's immune functioning. When an infectious agent invades your body, your immune system attempts to repel the invasion by producing specialized proteins called *antibodies*. The critical importance of the immune response becomes evident when the immune system is disabled, as occurs with the fatal disease AIDS (acquired immune deficiency syndrome).

Recent advances have revealed that the functioning of the immune system can be influenced by psychological factors, including conditioning. Robert Ader and Nicholas Cohen (1981, 1984, 1993) have shown that classical conditioning procedures can lead to *immunosuppression*—a decrease in the production of antibodies. In a typical study, animals are injected with a drug (the UCS) that *chemically* causes immunosuppression while they are simultaneously given an unusual-tasting liquid to drink (the CS). Days later, after the chemical immunosuppression has ended, some of the animals are reexposed to the CS by giving them the unusual-tasting solution. Measurements of antibody production indicate that animals exposed to the CS show a reduced immune response.

Immune resistance is only one example of the subtle physiological processes that can be influenced by classical conditioning. Studies suggest that classical conditioning can also modulate *drug tolerance* (Siegel, 1983, 1989), *allergic reactions* (MacQueen et al., 1989), and the *release of endorphins* (Fanselow, 1991), the brain's opiatelike painkillers (see Chapters 3 and 4). Thanks in part to findings on the conditioning of physiological processes, experts are reappraising traditional theories of health, pain, and disease to include a larger role for psychological factors.

Basic Processes in Classical Conditioning

Classical conditioning is often portrayed as a mechanical process that inevitably leads to a certain result. This view reflects the reality that most conditioned responses are reflexive and difficult to control. Pavlov's dogs would have been hard pressed to withhold their salivation. Similarly, most people with phobias have great difficulty suppressing their fear. However, this vision of classical conditioning as an "irresistible force" is misleading because it fails to consider the many factors involved in classical conditioning. In this section, we'll look at basic processes in classical

conditioning to expand on the rich complexity of this form of learning.

Acquisition: Forming New Responses

We have already discussed *acquisition* without attaching a formal name to the process. *Acquisition is the formation of a new conditioned response*

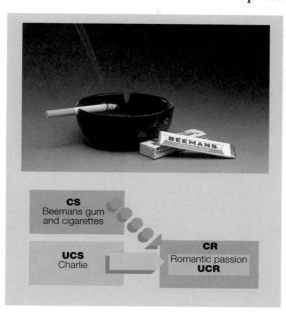

Figure 6.4. Classical conditioning and romance. Pleasant emotional responses can be acquired through classical conditioning, as illustrated by one woman's unusual conditioned response to the aroma of Beemans gum and cigarette smoke.

Figure 6.5. Classical conditioning in advertising. Many advertisers attempt to make their products conditioned stimuli that elicit pleasant emotional responses.

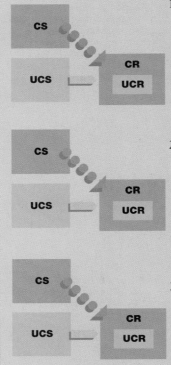
tendency. Pavlov theorized that the acquisition of a conditioned response depends on stimulus *contiguity*, which literally means "touching." **Stimulus contiguity is a temporal (time) association between two events.** Thus, Pavlov thought that the key to classical conditioning is the *pairing* of stimuli in time. Do the two stimuli have to occur simultaneously to produce conditioning? No, but some CS-UCS timing arrangements work better than others. Conditioning is most likely to occur when the CS begins about a half-second before the UCS and stops at the same time as the UCS (Heth & Rescorla, 1973; Kamin, 1965).

Stimulus contiguity is important, but learning theorists now realize that contiguity alone doesn't automatically produce conditioning. People are bombarded daily by countless stimuli that could be perceived as being paired, yet only some of these pairings produce classical conditioning.

Consider the woman who developed a conditioned emotional reaction to the smell of Beemans gum and cigarettes. Certainly, there were other stimuli that shared contiguity with her boyfriend, Charlie. He smoked, so ashtrays were probably present, but she doesn't get weak in the knees at the sight of an ashtray.

If conditioning does not occur to all the stimuli present in a situation, what determines its occurrence? Evidence suggests that *stimuli that are novel, unusual, or especially intense have more potential to become CSs than routine stimuli*, probably because they are more likely to stand out among other stimuli (Hearst, 1988).

Extinction: Weakening Conditioned Responses

Fortunately, a newly formed stimulus-response bond does not necessarily last indefinitely. If it did, learning would be inflexible, and organisms would have difficulty adapting to new situations. Instead, the right circumstances produce **extinction, the gradual weakening and disappearance of a conditioned response tendency.**

What leads to extinction in classical conditioning? The consistent presentation of the conditioned stimulus *alone*, without the unconditioned stimulus. For example, when Pavlov consistently presented *only* the bell to a previously conditioned dog, the bell gradually lost its capacity to elicit the response of salivation. Such a sequence of events is depicted in the left portion of Figure 6.6, which graphs the amount of salivation by a dog over a series of conditioning trials. Note how the salivation response declines during extinction.

For an example of extinction from outside the laboratory, let's assume that you cringe at the sound of a dentist's drill, which has been paired with pain in the past. You take a job as a dental assistant and you start hearing the drill (the CS) day in and day out without experiencing any pain (the UCS). Your cringing response will gradually diminish and extinguish altogether.

How long does it take to extinguish a conditioned response? That depends on many factors, but particularly the strength of the conditioned bond when extinction begins. Some conditioned responses extinguish quickly, while others are difficult to weaken.

Spontaneous Recovery: Resurrecting Responses

Some conditioned responses display the ultimate in tenacity by "reappearing from the dead" after

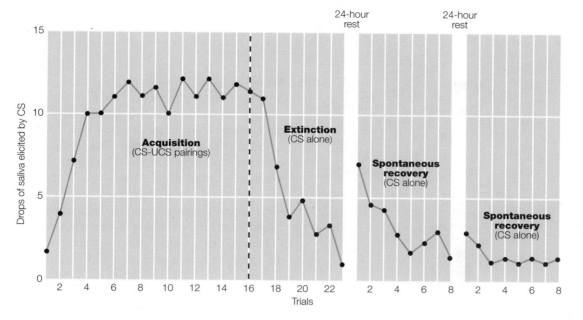

Figure 6.6. Acquisition, extinction, and spontaneous recovery. During acquisition, the strength of the dog's conditioned response (measured by the amount of salivation) increases rapidly and then levels off near its maximum. During extinction, the CR declines erratically until it's extinguished. After a "rest" period in which the dog is not exposed to the CS, a spontaneous recovery occurs, and the CS once again elicits a (weakened) CR. Repeated presentations of the CS alone reextinguish the CR, but after another "rest" interval, a weaker spontaneous recovery occurs.

being extinguished. Learning theorists use the term *spontaneous recovery* to describe such a resurrection from the graveyard of conditioned associations. **Spontaneous recovery is the reappearance of an extinguished response after a period of nonexposure to the conditioned stimulus.**

Pavlov (1927) observed this phenomenon in some of his pioneering studies. He fully extinguished a dog's CR of salivation to a tone and then returned the dog to its home cage for a "rest interval" (a period of nonexposure to the CS). On a subsequent day, when the dog was brought back to the experimental chamber for retesting, the tone was sounded and the salivation response reappeared. Although it had returned, the rejuvenated response was weak. There was less salivation than when the response was at its peak strength. If Pavlov consistently presented the CS by itself again, the response reextinguished quickly. However, in some of the dogs the response made still another spontaneous recovery (typically even weaker than the first) after they had spent another period in their cages (consult Figure 6.6 once again).

The theoretical meaning of spontaneous recovery is complex and hotly debated. However, its practical meaning is quite simple. Even if you manage to rid yourself of a conditioned response (such as cringing when you hear a dental drill), it may make a surprise reappearance later. This result is particularly likely if you go for a while without being exposed to the CS that elicited the response. For example, suppose you quit your job as a dental assistant and are not exposed to the sound of a dentist's drill for a year or so. There's a good chance that if you stop by a dentist's office to pick up a friend, you'll cringe once again at the sound of the drill.

Stimulus Generalization and the Case of Little Albert

After conditioning has occurred, organisms often show a tendency to respond not only to the exact CS used but also to other, similar stimuli. For example, Pavlov's dogs might have salivated in response to a different bell, or you might cringe at the sound of a jeweler's as well as a dentist's drill. These are examples of stimulus generalization. **Stimulus generalization occurs when an organism that has learned a response to a specific stimulus responds in the same way to new stimuli that are similar to the original stimulus.**

Generalization is adaptive given that organisms rarely encounter the exact same stimulus more than once (Thomas, 1992). Stimulus generalization is also commonplace. We have already discussed a real-life example: the woman who acquired a bridge phobia during her childhood because her father scared her whenever they went over a particular old bridge. The original CS for her fear was that specific bridge, but her fear was ultimately *generalized* to all bridges.

John B. Watson, the founder of behaviorism (see Chapter 1), conducted an influential early study of generalization. Watson and a colleague, Rosalie Rayner, examined the generalization of conditioned fear in an 11-month-old boy, known in the annals of psychology as "Little Albert." Like

Figure 6.7. The conditioning of Little Albert. The diagram shows how Little Albert's fear response to a white rat was established. Albert's fear response to other white, furry objects illustrates generalization. In the photo, made from a 1919 film, Rosalie Rayner and John Watson are shown with little Albert before he was conditioned to fear the rat.

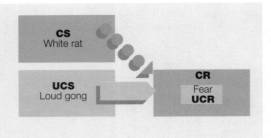

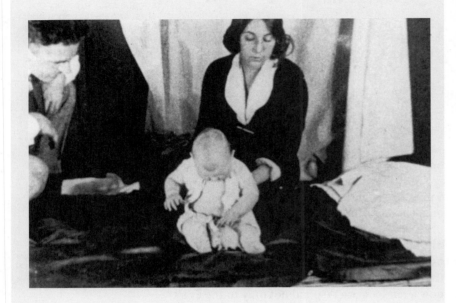

tioned fear did *not* generalize to wooden blocks that bore no resemblance to the original CS of the rat.

Stimulus Discrimination

Stimulus discrimination is just the opposite of stimulus generalization. **Stimulus discrimination occurs when an organism that has learned a response to a specific stimulus does *not* respond in the same way to new stimuli that are similar to the original stimulus.** Like generalization, discrimination is adaptive in that an animal's survival may hinge on its being able to distinguish friend from foe, or edible from poisonous food (Thomas, 1992). Organisms can gradually learn to discriminate between the original CS and similar stimuli if they have adequate experience with both. For instance, let's say your pet dog runs around, excitedly wagging its tail, whenever it hears your car pull up in the driveway. Initially it will probably respond to *all* cars that pull into the driveway (stimulus generalization). However, if there is anything distinctive about the sound of your car, your dog may gradually respond with excitement only to your car and not to other cars (stimulus discrimination).

The development of stimulus discrimination usually requires that the original CS (your car) continues to be paired with the UCS (your arrival), while similar stimuli (the other cars) are not paired with the UCS. As with generalization, a basic law governs discrimination: *The less similar new stimuli are to the original CS, the greater the likelihood (and ease) of discrimination.* Conversely, if a new stimulus is quite similar to the original CS, discrimination will be relatively difficult to learn.

Higher-Order Conditioning

Imagine that you were to conduct the following experiment. First, you condition a dog to salivate in response to the sound of a tone by pairing the tone with meat powder. Once the tone is firmly established as a CS, you pair the tone with a new stimulus, let's say a red light, for 15 trials. You then present the red light alone, without the tone. Will the dog salivate in response to the red light?

The answer is "yes." Even though the red light has never been paired with the meat powder, it will acquire the capacity to elicit salivation by virtue of being paired with the tone (see Figure 6.8). This is a demonstration of **higher-order conditioning, in which a conditioned stimulus functions as if it were an unconditioned stimulus.** Higher-order conditioning shows that classical conditioning does

many babies, Albert was initially unafraid of a live white rat. Then Watson and Rayner (1920) paired the presentation of the rat with a loud, startling sound (made by striking a steel bar with a hammer). Albert *did* show fear in response to the loud noise. After seven pairings of the rat and the gong, the rat was established as a CS eliciting a fear response (see Figure 6.7).

Five days later, Watson and Rayner exposed the youngster to other stimuli that resembled the rat in being white and furry. They found that Albert's fear response generalized to a variety of stimuli, including a rabbit, a dog, a fur coat, a Santa Claus mask, and Watson's hair.

Like conditioning itself, stimulus generalization does not occur in just any set of circumstances (Balsam, 1988). Generalization depends on the similarity between the new stimulus and the original CS. The basic law governing generalization is this: *The more similar new stimuli are to the original CS, the greater the likelihood of generalization.* Conversely, generalization becomes less likely as the similarity between the new and the original stimulus decreases. For example, Little Albert's condi-

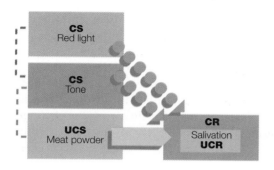
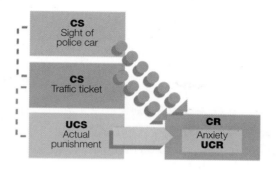

Figure 6.8. Higher-order conditioning. In higher-order conditioning, a neutral stimulus comes to elicit a conditioned response by being paired with an already established CS, as seen in the two examples diagrammed here.

not depend on the presence of a genuine, natural UCS. An already established CS will do just fine. In higher-order conditioning, new conditioned responses are built on the foundation of already established conditioned responses.

Many human conditioned responses are the product of higher-order conditioning (Rescorla, 1980). For instance, if your heart leaps into your throat when you spot a police car while driving—even if you're driving at the speed limit—this reflexive anxiety response is due to higher-order conditioning. The stimulus of a police car shouldn't elicit anxiety unless it has previously been paired with an anxiety-arousing event, such as getting a traffic ticket. However, a traffic ticket is not an unconditioned stimulus for anxiety. People aren't born fearing traffic tickets. A traffic ticket is a conditioned stimulus that elicits anxiety in certain people because of their previous learning (see Figure 6.8). Thus, conditioning can occur when

CONCEPT CHECK 6.2
Recognizing Basic Processes in Classical Conditioning

Check your understanding of basic processes in classical conditioning by reading each of the following vignettes and identifying the process at work. Choose from the following: (a) acquisition, (b) extinction, (c) spontaneous recovery, (d) stimulus generalization, (e) stimulus discrimination, (f) higher-order conditioning.

_____ 1. Lucy has flunked algebra twice. Now whenever she sees any kind of math book, she begins to get that same old sick feeling in the pit of her stomach.

_____ 2. Little Suzy is experiencing her first thunderstorm. A bolt of lightning flashes across the sky, but this doesn't bother her; she thinks it's pretty. A second later, however, she just about jumps out of her skin when a tremendous crash of thunder shakes the room.

_____ 3. Otto has gotten A's on all of his quizzes in history, so he likes Professor Olden quite a bit. But he's not too crazy about Professor Datum, because Otto's received nothing but C's and D's in his research methods class.

_____ 4. Glenda tried sushi for the first time when she visited her cousin in San Francisco, and she loved it. Back home in Kansas City she eagerly searched until she found a restaurant that served sushi, but the fish wasn't fresh, so she didn't like it much. On a visit to St. Louis she tried again, but she was disappointed once more. Glenda no longer gets excited by the prospect of eating sushi, unless it's San Francisco sushi, which still makes her mouth water.

_____ 5. On his first day at work at the Joy Ice Cream Shop, Arnold helped himself and overdid it. He got sick and swore he'd never eat ice cream again. True to his word, he stayed off the stuff for the rest of the summer, though he continued working at the shop. For a while it was hard, because the sight and smell of the ice cream made him feel nauseous, but eventually those feelings faded. The following summer Arnold decided to visit his old employer, but as soon as he walked in the door, he felt so sick he had to turn around and leave immediately.

_____ 6. Little Timmy used to get so excited whenever Grandpa would come to visit, because Grandpa always brought Timmy some neat new toy. As Grandpa got older, however, he became forgetful. He no longer brings toys when he visits. Now Grandpa's visits don't excite Timmy as much.

"Operant conditioning shapes behavior as a sculptor shapes a lump of clay."
B. F. SKINNER

neutral stimuli are paired with previously established CSs. The phenomenon of higher-order conditioning greatly extends the reach of classical conditioning.

OPERANT CONDITIONING

Even Pavlov recognized that classical conditioning is not the only form of conditioning. Classical conditioning best explains reflexive responding that is largely controlled by stimuli that *precede* the response. However, humans and other animals make a great many responses that don't fit this description. Consider the response that you are engaging in right now: studying. It is definitely not a reflex (life might be easier if it were). The stimuli that govern it (exams and grades) do not precede it. Instead, your studying is mainly influenced by stimulus events that *follow* the response—specifically, its *consequences*.

In the 1930s, this kind of learning was christened *operant conditioning* by B. F. Skinner (1938, 1953, 1969). The term was derived from his belief that in this type of responding, an organism "operates" on the environment instead of simply reacting to stimuli. Learning occurs because responses come to be influenced by the consequences that follow them. Thus, *operant conditioning* **is a form of learning in which voluntary responses come to be controlled by their consequences.** Learning theorists originally distinguished between classical and operant conditioning on the grounds that the former regulated reflexive, involuntary responses, whereas the lat-

ter governed voluntary responses. This distinction holds up much of the time, but it is not absolute. Research in recent decades has shown that classical conditioning sometimes contributes to the regulation of voluntary behavior, that operant conditioning can influence involuntary, visceral responses, and that the two types of conditioning jointly and interactively govern some aspects of behavior (Domjan, 1993; Turkkan, 1989).

Skinner's Demonstration: It's All a Matter of Consequences

Like Pavlov, Skinner conducted some deceptively simple research that became enormously influential (Lattal, 1992). The fundamental principle of operant conditioning is uncommonly elementary. *Skinner demonstrated that organisms tend to repeat those responses that are followed by favorable consequences.* This fundamental principle is embodied in Skinner's concept of reinforcement. *Reinforcement* **occurs when an event following a response increases an organism's tendency to make that response.** In other words, a response is strengthened because it leads to rewarding consequences (see Figure 6.9).

The principle of reinforcement may be simple, but it is immensely powerful. Skinner and his followers have shown that much of our everyday behavior is regulated by reinforcement. For example, you study hard because good grades are likely to follow as a result. You go to work because this behavior leads to your receiving paychecks. Perhaps you work extra hard because promotions and raises tend to follow such behavior. You tell

Figure 6.9. Reinforcement in operant conditioning. According to Skinner, reinforcement occurs when a response is followed by rewarding consequences and the organism's tendency to make the response increases. The two examples diagrammed here illustrate the basic premise of operant conditioning—that voluntary behavior is controlled by its consequences. These examples involve positive reinforcement (for a comparison of positive and negative reinforcement, see Figure 6.14).

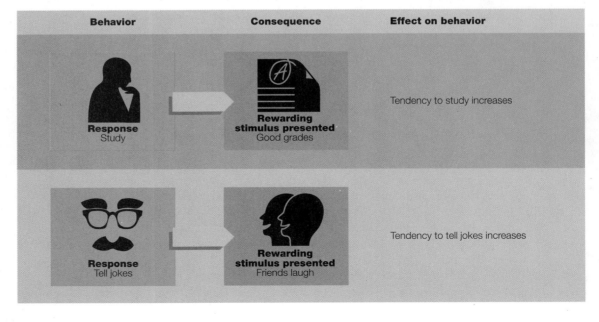

jokes, and your friends laugh—so you tell some more. The principle of reinforcement clearly governs complex aspects of human behavior. Paradoxically, though, this principle emerged out of Skinner's research on the behavior of rats and pigeons in exceptionally simple situations. Let's look at that research.

Terminology and Procedures

Like Pavlov, Skinner created a prototype experimental procedure that has been repeated (with variations) thousands of times. In this procedure, an animal, typically a rat or a pigeon, is placed in an *operant chamber* that has come to be better known as a "Skinner box." **A *Skinner box* is a small enclosure in which an animal can make a specific response that is systematically recorded while the consequences of the response are controlled.** In the boxes designed for rats, the main response made available is pressing a small lever mounted on one side wall (see Figure 6.10). In the boxes made for pigeons, the designated response is pecking a small disk mounted on a side wall.

Operant responses such as lever pressing and disk pecking are said to be *emitted* rather than *elicited*. **To *emit* means to send forth.** This word was chosen because operant conditioning governs mainly *voluntary* responses. In contrast, classical conditioning governs mainly *involuntary*, reflexive responses.

The Skinner box permits the experimenter to control the reinforcement contingencies that are in effect for the animal. ***Reinforcement contingencies* are the circumstances or rules that determine whether responses lead to the presentation of reinforcers.** Typically, the experimenter manipulates whether positive consequences occur when the animal makes the designated response. The main positive consequence is usually delivery of a small bit of food into a food cup mounted in the chamber. Because the animals are deprived of food for a while prior to the experimental session, their hunger virtually ensures that the food serves as a reinforcer.

The key dependent variable in most research on operant conditioning is the subjects' *response rate* over time. An animal's rate of lever pressing or disk pecking in the Skinner box is monitored continuously by a device known as a cumulative recorder (see Figure 6.10). **The *cumulative recorder* creates a graphic record of responding and reinforcement in a Skinner box as a function of time.** The recorder works by means of a

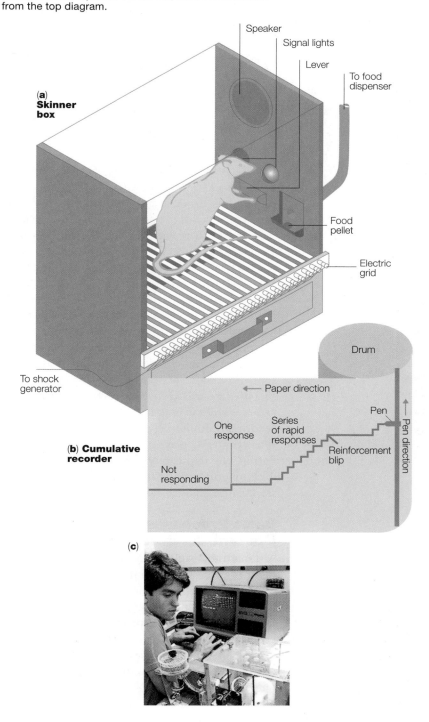

Figure 6.10. Skinner box and cumulative recorder. (**a**) This diagram highlights some of the key features of a Skinner box. In this apparatus designed for rats, the response under study is lever pressing. Food pellets, which may serve as reinforcers, are delivered into the food cup on the right. The speaker and light permit manipulations of visual and auditory stimuli, and the electric grid gives the experimenter control over aversive consequences (shock) in the box. (**b**) A cumulative recorder connected to the box keeps a continuous record of responses and reinforcements. Each lever press moves the pen up a step, and each reinforcement is marked with a slash. (**c**) This photo shows the real thing—a rat being conditioned in a Skinner box. Note the food dispenser on the left, which was omitted from the top diagram.

Figure 6.11. A graphic portrayal of operant responding. The results of operant conditioning are often summarized in a graph of cumulative responses over time. The insets magnify small segments of the curve to show how an increasing response rate yields a progressively steeper slope (bottom); a high, steady response rate yields a steep, stable slope (middle); and a decreasing response rate yields a progressively flatter slope (top).

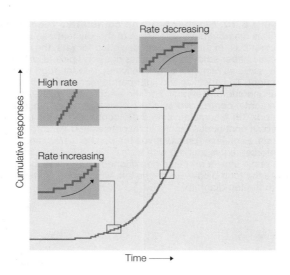

roll of paper that moves at a steady rate underneath a movable pen. When there is no responding, the pen stays still and draws a straight horizontal line, reflecting the passage of time. Whenever the designated response occurs, however, the pen moves upward a notch. The pen's movements produce a graphic summary of the animal's responding over time. The pen also makes slash marks to record the delivery of each reinforcer.

The results of operant-conditioning studies are usually portrayed in graphs. In these graphs, the horizontal axis is used to mark the passage of time, while the vertical axis is used to plot the accumulation of responses, as shown in Figure 6.11. In interpreting these graphs, the key consideration is the *slope* of the line that represents the record of responding. *A rapid response rate produces a steep slope, whereas a slow response rate produces a shallow slope.* Because the response record is cumulative, the line never goes down. It can only go up as more responses are made or flatten out if the response rate slows to zero. The magnifications in Figure 6.11 show how slope and response rate are related.

Basic Processes in Operant Conditioning

Although the principle of reinforcement is strikingly simple, many other processes are involved in operant conditioning that make this form of learning just as complex as classical conditioning. In fact, some of the same processes are involved in both types of conditioning. In this section, we'll discuss how the processes of acquisition, extinction, generalization, and discrimination occur in operant conditioning.

Acquisition and Shaping

As in classical conditioning, *acquisition* in operant conditioning is the formation of a new response tendency. However, the procedures used to establish a tendency to emit a voluntary operant response are different from those used to create a reflexive conditioned response. Operant responses are typically established through a gradual process called *shaping*: the reinforcement of closer and closer approximations of a desired response.

Shaping is necessary when an organism does not, on its own, emit the desired response. For example, when a rat is first placed in a Skinner box, it may not press the lever at all. In this case an experimenter begins shaping by releasing food pellets whenever the rat moves toward the lever. As this response becomes more frequent, the experimenter starts requiring a closer approximation of the desired response, possibly releasing food only when the rat actually touches the lever. As reinforcement increases the rat's tendency to touch the lever, the rat will spontaneously press the lever on occasion, finally providing the experimenter with an opportunity to reinforce the designated response. These reinforcements will gradually increase the rate of lever pressing.

Shaping molds many aspects of both human and animal behavior. For instance, it is the key to training animals to perform impressive tricks. When you go to a zoo, circus, or marine park and see bears riding bicycles, monkeys playing the piano, and whales leaping through hoops, you are witnessing the results of shaping. To demonstrate the power of shaping techniques, Skinner once trained some pigeons so that they appeared to play Ping-Pong! They would run about on opposite ends of a Ping-Pong table and peck the ball back and forth. Keller and Marian Breland, a couple of psychologists influenced by Skinner, went into the business of training animals for advertising and entertainment purposes. One of their better known feats was shaping "Priscilla, the Fastidious Pig," to turn on a radio, eat at a kitchen table, put dirty clothes in a hamper, run a vacuum, and then "go shopping" with a shopping cart (see photo). Of course, Priscilla picked the sponsor's product off the shelf in her shopping expedition (Breland & Breland, 1961).

Extinction

In operant conditioning, *extinction* refers to the gradual weakening and disappearance of a response tendency because the response is no longer followed by a reinforcer. Extinction begins in operant conditioning whenever previously available reinforcement is stopped. In laboratory studies with rats, this usually means that the experimenter stops delivering food when the rat presses the lever. When the extinction process is begun, a brief surge often occurs in the rat's responding, followed by a gradual decline in response rate until it approaches zero.

The same effects are generally seen in the extinction of human behavior. Let's say that a child routinely cries at bedtime and that this response is reinforced by attention from mom and dad. If the parents decided to cut off further reinforcement by ignoring the crying, they would be attempting to extinguish this undesirable response. Typically, the child would increase the crying behavior for a few evenings, and then the crying would taper off fairly quickly (Williams, 1959).

A key issue in operant conditioning is how much *resistance to extinction* an organism will display when reinforcement is halted. **Resistance to extinction occurs when an organism continues to make a response after delivery of the reinforcer for it has been terminated.** The greater the resistance to extinction, the longer the responding will continue. Thus, if a researcher stops giving reinforcement for lever pressing and the response tapers off very slowly, the response shows high resistance to extinction. However, if the response tapers off quickly, it shows relatively little resistance to extinction.

Resistance to extinction may sound like a matter of purely theoretical interest, but actually it's quite practical. People often want to strengthen a response in such a way that it will be relatively resistant to extinction. For instance, most parents want to see their child's studying response survive even if the child hits a rocky stretch when studying doesn't lead to reinforcement (good grades). In a similar fashion, a casino wants to see patrons continue to gamble, even if they encounter a lengthy losing streak.

Stimulus Control: Generalization and Discrimination

Operant responding is ultimately controlled by its consequences, as organisms learn response-outcome (R-O) associations (Colwill, 1993). However, stimuli that *precede* a response can also influence operant behavior. When a response is consistently followed by a reinforcer in the presence of a particular stimulus, that stimulus comes to serve as a "signal" indicating that the response is likely to lead to a reinforcer. Once an organism learns the signal, it tends to respond accordingly (Honig & Alsop, 1992). For example, a pigeon's disk

Shaping—an operant technique in which an organism is rewarded for closer and closer approximations of the desired response—is used in teaching both animals and humans. It is the main means of training animals to perform tricks.

This pigeon is learning that pecking the disk pays off only if the disk is lit. The light that signals the availability of the food reinforcer is a discriminative stimulus.

pecking may be reinforced only when a small light behind the disk is lit (see the above photo). When the light is out, pecking does not lead to the reward. Pigeons quickly learn to peck the disk only when it is lit. The light that signals the availability of reinforcement is called a discriminative stimulus. **Discriminative stimuli are cues that influence operant behavior by indicating the probable consequences (reinforcement or nonreinforcement) of a response.**

Discriminative stimuli play a key role in the regulation of operant behavior. For example, birds learn that hunting for worms is likely to be reinforced after a rain. Children learn to ask for sweets when their parents are in a good mood. Drivers learn to slow down when the highway is wet. Human social behavior is also regulated extensively by discriminative stimuli. Consider the behavior of asking someone out for a date. Many people emit this response only very cautiously, after receiving many signals, such as eye contact, smiles, and encouraging conversational exchanges (the discriminative stimuli), that a favorable answer (reinforcement) is fairly likely.

Reactions to a discriminative stimulus are governed by the processes of *stimulus generalization* and *stimulus discrimination*, just like reactions to a CS in classical conditioning. For instance, envision a cat that comes running into the kitchen whenever it hears the sound of a can opener because that sound has become a discriminative stimulus signaling a good chance of its getting fed. If the cat also responded to the sound of a new kitchen appliance (say a blender), this response would represent *generalization*—responding to a new stimulus as if it were the original. *Discrimination* would occur if the cat learned to respond only to the can opener and not to the blender.

As you have learned in this section, the processes of acquisition, extinction, generalization, and discrimination in operant conditioning parallel these same processes in classical conditioning. Table 6.1 compares these processes in the two kinds of conditioning.

Reinforcement: Consequences That Strengthen Responses

Although it is convenient to equate reinforcement with reward and the experience of pleasure, strict behaviorists object to this practice. Why? Because the experience of pleasure is an unobservable

Table 6.1 Comparison of Basic Processes in Classical and Operant Conditioning

Process and Definition	Description in Classical Conditioning	Description in Operant Conditioning
Acquisition: The formation of a conditioned response tendency	CS and UCS are paired, gradually resulting in CR.	Responding gradually increases because of reinforcement, possibly through shaping.
Extinction: The gradual weakening and disappearance of a conditioned response tendency	CS is presented alone until it no longer elicits CR.	Responding gradually slows and stops after reinforcement is terminated.
Stimulus generalization: An organism's responding to stimuli other than the original stimulus used in conditioning	CR is elicited by new stimulus that resembles original CS.	Responding increases in the presence of new stimulus that resembles original discriminative stimulus.
Stimulus discrimination: An organism's lack of response to stimuli that are similar to the original stimulus used in conditioning	CR is not elicited by new stimulus that resembles original CS.	Responding does not increase in the presence of new stimulus that resembles original discriminative stimulus.

event that takes place within an organism. As explained in Chapter 1, most behaviorists believe that scientific assertions must be limited to what can be observed.

In keeping with this orientation, Skinner said that reinforcement occurs whenever an outcome strengthens a response, as measured by an increase in the rate of responding. This definition avoids the issue of what the organism is feeling and focuses on observable events. The central process in reinforcement is the *strengthening of a response tendency*. To know whether an event is reinforcing, researchers must make it contingent upon a response and observe whether the rate of this response increases after the supposed reinforcer has been presented.

Thus, reinforcement is defined *after the fact*, in terms of its *effect* on behavior. Something that is clearly reinforcing for an organism at one time may not function as a reinforcer later (Catania, 1992). Food will reinforce lever pressing by a rat only if the rat is hungry. Similarly, something that serves as a reinforcer for one person may not function as a reinforcer for another person. For example, parental approval is a potent reinforcer for most children, but not all.

Delayed Reinforcement

In operant conditioning, a favorable outcome is much more likely to strengthen a response if the outcome follows the response *immediately*. If a delay occurs between a response and the positive outcome, the response may not be strengthened. Furthermore, studies show that the longer the delay between the designated response and the delivery of the reinforcer, the more slowly conditioning proceeds (Church, 1989; Mazur, 1993).

Conditioned Reinforcement

Operant theorists make a distinction between unlearned, or primary, reinforcers as opposed to conditioned, or secondary, reinforcers. **Primary reinforcers are events that are inherently reinforcing because they satisfy biological needs.** A given species has a limited number of primary reinforcers because they are closely tied to physiological needs. In humans, primary reinforcers include food, water, warmth, sex, and perhaps affection expressed through hugging and close bodily contact.

Secondary, or conditioned, reinforcers are events that acquire reinforcing qualities by being associated with primary reinforcers. The events that function as secondary reinforcers vary among members of a species because they depend on learning. Examples of common secondary reinforcers in humans include money, good grades, attention, flattery, praise, and applause. Most of the material things that people work hard to earn are secondary reinforcers. For example, people learn to find stylish clothes, sports cars, fine jewelry, elegant china, and state-of-the-art stereos reinforcing.

Schedules of Reinforcement

Organisms make innumerable responses that do *not* lead to favorable consequences. It would be nice if people were reinforced every time they took an exam, watched a movie, hit a golf shot, asked for a date, or made a sales call. However, in the real world most responses are reinforced only some of the time. How does this reality affect the potency of reinforcers? To find out, operant psychologists have devoted an enormous amount of attention to how *schedules of reinforcement* influence operant behavior (Ferster & Skinner, 1957; Skinner, 1938, 1953).

A *schedule of reinforcement* is a specific pattern of presentation of reinforcers over time. The simplest pattern is continuous reinforcement. ***Continuous reinforcement* occurs when every instance of a designated response is reinforced.** In the laboratory, experimenters often use continuous reinforcement to shape and establish a new response before moving on to more realistic schedules involving intermittent, or partial reinforcement. ***Intermittent reinforcement* occurs when a designated response is reinforced only some of the time.**

Which do you suppose leads to longer-lasting effects—being reinforced every time you emit a response, or being reinforced only some of the time? Studies show that, given an equal number of reinforcements, *intermittent* reinforcement makes a response more resistant to extinction than continuous reinforcement does (Robbins, 1971). In other words, organisms continue responding longer after removal of reinforcers when a response has been reinforced only *some* of the time.

In fact, intermittent schedules of reinforcement that provide only sporadic delivery of reinforcers can yield great resistance to extinction. This explains why behaviors that are reinforced only occasionally can be very durable. Consider a child who persists in throwing temper tantrums on a regular basis. The parents may be proud of the fact that they give in to these temper tantrums

Figure 6.12. Reinforcement schedules in everyday life. Complex human behaviors are regulated by schedules of reinforcement. Piecework in factories is reinforced on a fixed-ratio schedule. Playing roulette is based on variable-ratio reinforcement. Watching the clock at work is rewarded on a fixed-interval basis (the arrival of quitting time is the reinforcer). Surfers waiting for a big wave are rewarded on a variable-interval basis.

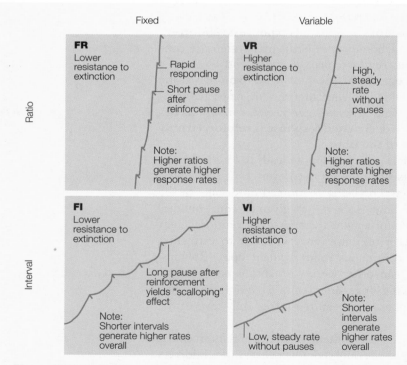

Figure 6.13. Schedules of reinforcement and patterns of response. Each type of reinforcement schedule tends to generate a characteristic pattern of responding. In general, ratio schedules tend to produce more rapid responding than interval schedules (note the steep slopes of the FR and VR curves). In comparison to fixed schedules, variable schedules tend to yield steadier responding (note the smoother lines for the VR and VI schedules on the right) and greater resistance to extinction.

(thus reinforcing them) only about one in seven times. They believe that they are working toward eliminating the tantrums, and they may be mystified when the tantrums persist. Parents in this situation usually fail to realize that they are providing steady intermittent reinforcement for the tantrums. This schedule of reinforcement will make the temper tantrums relatively difficult to eliminate.

Reinforcement schedules come in many varieties, but four particular types of intermittent schedules have attracted the most interest. These schedules are described here along with examples drawn from the laboratory and everyday life (see Figure 6.12 for additional examples).

Ratio schedules require the organism to make the designated response a certain number of times to gain each reinforcer. **In a *fixed-ratio (FR) schedule*, the reinforcer is given after a fixed number of nonreinforced responses.** *Examples:* (1) A rat is reinforced for every tenth lever press. (2) A salesperson receives a bonus for every fourth set of encyclopedias sold. **In a *variable-ratio (VR) schedule*, the reinforcer is given after a variable number of nonreinforced responses.** The number of nonreinforced responses varies around a predetermined average. *Examples:* (1) A rat is reinforced for every tenth lever press on the average. The exact number of responses required for reinforcement varies from one time to the next. (2) A slot machine in a casino pays off once every six tries on the average. The number of nonwinning responses between payoffs varies greatly from one time to the next.

Interval schedules require a time period to pass between the presentation of reinforcers. **In a *fixed-interval (FI) schedule*, the reinforcer is given for the first response that occurs after a fixed time interval has elapsed.** *Examples:* (1) A rat is reinforced for the first lever press after a 2-minute interval has elapsed and then must wait 2 minutes before receiving the next reinforcement. (2) Students can earn grades (let's assume the grades are reinforcing) by taking exams every three weeks. **In a *variable-interval (VI) schedule*, the reinforcer is given for the first response after a variable time interval has elapsed.** The interval length varies around a predetermined average. *Examples:* (1) A rat is reinforced for the first lever press after a 1-minute interval has elapsed, but the following intervals are 3 minutes, 2 minutes, 4 minutes, and so on—with an average length of 2 minutes. (2) A person repeatedly dials a busy phone number (getting through is the reinforcer).

More than 40 years of research has yielded an enormous volume of data on how these schedules of reinforcement are related to patterns of responding (Williams, 1988; Zeiler, 1977). Some of the more prominent findings are summarized in Figure 6.13, which depicts typical response patterns generated by each schedule. For example, with fixed-interval schedules, a pause in responding usually occurs after each reinforcer is delivered, and then responding gradually increases to a rapid rate at the end of the interval. This pattern of behavior yields a "scalloped" response curve. In general, ratio schedules tend to produce more rapid responding than interval schedules. Why? Because faster responding leads to quicker reinforcement when a ratio schedule is in effect. Variable schedules tend to generate steadier response rates and greater resistance to extinction than their fixed counterparts.

Most of the research on reinforcement schedules was conducted on rats and pigeons in Skinner boxes. However, psychologists have found that humans react to schedules of reinforcement in much the same way as lower animals (De Villiers, 1977; Perone, Galizio, & Baron, 1988). For example, when animals are placed on ratio schedules, shifting to a higher ratio (that is, requiring more responses per reinforcement) tends to generate faster responding. Managers who run factories that pay on a piecework basis (a fixed-ratio schedule) have seen the same reaction in humans.

There are many other parallels between ani-mals' and humans' reactions to schedules of reinforcement. For instance, in rats and pigeons variable-ratio schedules yield steady responding and great resistance to extinction. Similar effects are routinely observed among people who gamble. Most gambling is reinforced according to variable-ratio schedules, which tend to produce rapid, steady responding and great resistance to extinction—exactly what casino operators want.

Positive Reinforcement Versus Negative Reinforcement

According to Skinner, reinforcement can take two forms, which he called *positive reinforcement* and *negative reinforcement*. **Positive reinforcement occurs when a response is strengthened because it is followed by the presentation of a rewarding stimulus.** Thus far, for purposes of simplicity, our examples of reinforcement have involved positive reinforcement. Good grades, tasty meals, paychecks, scholarships, promotions, nice clothes, nifty cars, attention, and flattery are all positive reinforcers.

In contrast, **negative reinforcement occurs when a response is strengthened because it is followed by the removal of an aversive (unpleasant) stimulus.** Don't let the word *negative* confuse you. Negative reinforcement *is* reinforcement. Like all reinforcement it involves a favorable outcome that *strengthens* a response tendency. However, this strengthening takes place because a response leads to the *removal of an aversive stimulus* rather than the arrival of a pleasant stimulus (see Figure 6.14 on the next page).

In laboratory studies, negative reinforcement is

CONCEPT CHECK 6.3
Recognizing Schedules of Reinforcement

Check your understanding of schedules of reinforcement in operant conditioning by indicating the type of schedule that would be in effect in each of the examples below. In the spaces on the left, fill in CR for continuous reinforcement, FR for fixed-ratio, VR for variable-ratio, FI for fixed-interval, and VI for variable-interval. The answers can be found in Appendix A in the back of the book.

_____ 1. Sarah is paid on a commission basis for selling computer systems. She gets a bonus for every third sale.

_____ 2. Artie's parents let him earn some pocket money by doing yard work *approximately* once a week.

_____ 3. Martha is fly-fishing. Think of each time that she casts her line as the response that may be rewarded.

_____ 4. Mort, who is in the fourth grade, gets a gold star from his teacher for every book he reads.

_____ 5. Skip, a professional baseball player, signs an agreement that his salary increases will be renegotiated every third year.

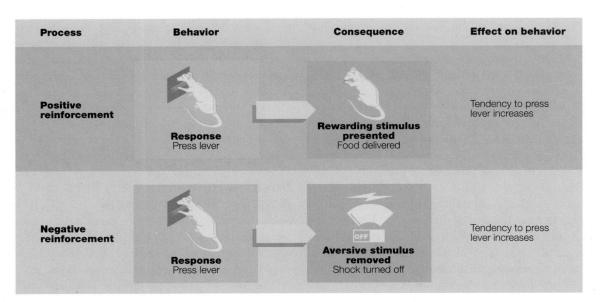

Figure 6.14. Positive reinforcement versus negative reinforcement. In positive reinforcement, a response leads to the presentation of a rewarding stimulus. In negative reinforcement, a response leads to the removal of an aversive stimulus. Both types of reinforcement involve favorable consequences and both have the same effect on behavior: the organism's tendency to emit the reinforced response is strengthened.

Process	Behavior	Consequence	Effect on behavior
Positive reinforcement	Response Press lever	Rewarding stimulus presented Food delivered	Tendency to press lever increases
Negative reinforcement	Response Press lever	Aversive stimulus removed Shock turned off	Tendency to press lever increases

Figure 6.15. Escape and avoidance learning. (**a**) Escape and avoidance learning are often studied with a shuttle box like that shown here. Warning signals, shock, and the animal's ability to flee from one compartment to another can be controlled by the experimenter. (**b**) Avoidance behavior involves both classical and operant conditioning. Avoidance *begins* because classical conditioning creates a conditioned fear that is elicited by the warning signal (panel 1). Avoidance *continues* because it is maintained by operant conditioning (panel 2). Specifically, the avoidance response is strengthened through negative reinforcement, since it leads to removal of the conditioned fear.

(a)

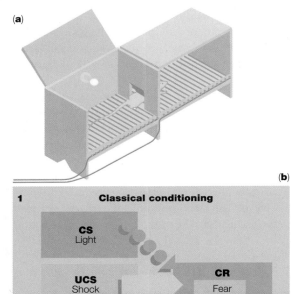

(b)

1   **Classical conditioning**

CS
Light

UCS
Shock

CR
Fear
UCR

2   **Operant conditioning**
(negative reinforcement)

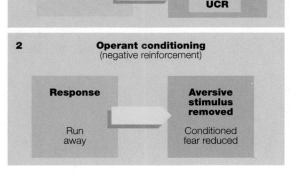

Response

Run away

Aversive stimulus removed

Conditioned fear reduced

usually accomplished as follows. While a rat is in a Skinner box, a moderate electric shock is delivered to the animal through the floor of the box. When the rat presses the lever, the shock is turned off for a period of time. Thus, lever pressing leads to removal of an aversive stimulus (shock). Al-

though this sequence of events is different from those for positive reinforcement, it reliably strengthens the rat's lever-pressing response.

Everyday human behavior is regulated extensively by negative reinforcement. Consider a handful of examples. You rush home in the winter to get out of the cold. You clean house to get rid of a disgusting mess. You give in to your child's begging to halt the whining. You give in to a roommate or spouse to bring an unpleasant argument to an end.

Negative reinforcement plays a key role in both escape learning and avoidance learning. **In *escape learning*, an organism acquires a response that decreases or ends some aversive stimulation.** Psychologists often study escape learning in the laboratory with dogs or rats that are conditioned in a *shuttle box*. The shuttle box has two compartments connected by a doorway, which can be opened and closed by the experimenter, as depicted in Figure 6.15. In a typical study, an animal is placed in one compartment and the shock in the floor of that chamber is turned on, with the doorway open. The animal learns to escape the shock by running to the other compartment. This escape response leads to the removal of an aversive stimulus (shock), so it is strengthened through negative reinforcement. If you were to leave a party where you were getting picked on by peers, you would be engaging in an escape response.

Escape learning often leads to avoidance learning. **In *avoidance learning* an organism acquires a response that prevents some aversive stimulation from occurring.** In shuttle box studies of avoidance learning, the experimenter simply gives the animal a signal that shock is forthcoming. The typical signal is a light that goes on a few seconds prior to the shock. At first the dog or rat runs only when shocked (escape learning). Gradually, however, the animal learns to run to the safe compartment as soon as the light comes on, demonstrating avoidance learning. Similarly, if you were to quit going to parties because of your concern about being picked on by peers, this would represent avoidance learning.

Avoidance learning presents an interesting example of how classical conditioning and operant conditioning can work together to regulate behavior (Levis, 1989; Mowrer, 1947). In avoidance learning, the warning light that goes on before the shock becomes a CS (through classical conditioning) eliciting reflexive, conditioned fear in the animal. However, the response of fleeing to the other side of the box is operant behavior. This response is strengthened through negative reinforcement *because it reduces the animal's conditioned fear*—see Figure 6.15(b).

The principles of avoidance learning shed some light on why phobias are so resistant to extinction (Levis, 1989). For example, suppose you have a phobia of elevators. Chances are you acquired your phobia through classical conditioning. At some point in your past, elevators became paired with a frightening event. Now whenever you need to use an elevator, you experience conditioned fear. If your phobia is severe, you probably take the stairs instead. Taking the stairs is an avoidance response that should lead to consistent negative reinforcement by relieving your conditioned fear. Thus, it's hard to get rid of phobias for two reasons. First, responses that allow you to avoid a phobic stimulus earn negative reinforcement each time they are made—so avoidance behavior is strengthened and continues. Second, these avoidance responses prevent any opportunity to extinguish the phobic conditioned response because you're never exposed to the conditioned stimulus (in this case, riding in an elevator).

Punishment: Consequences That Weaken Responses

Reinforcement is defined in terms of its consequences. It *strengthens* an organism's tendency to make a certain response. Are there also consequences that *weaken* an organism's tendency to make a particular response? Yes. In Skinner's model of operant behavior, such consequences are called *punishment*.

Punishment occurs when an event following a response weakens the tendency to make that response. In a Skinner box, the administration of punishment is very simple. When a rat presses the lever or a pigeon pecks the disk, it receives a brief shock. This procedure usually leads to a rapid decline in the animal's response rate. Punishment typically involves presentation of an aversive stimulus (for instance, spanking a child). However, punishment may also involve the removal of a rewarding stimulus (for instance, taking away a child's TV-watching privileges).

The concept of punishment in operant conditioning is confusing to many students on two counts. First, they often confuse it with negative reinforcement, which is entirely different. Negative reinforcement involves the *removal* of an aversive stimulus, thereby *strengthening* a response. Punishment, on the other hand, involves the *presentation* of an aversive stimulus, thereby *weakening* a response. Thus, punishment and negative reinforcement are opposite procedures that yield opposite effects on behavior (see Figure 6.16).

The second source of confusion involves the tendency to equate punishment with *disciplinary procedures* used by parents, teachers, and other authority figures. In the operant model, punishment occurs any time undesirable consequences weaken a response tendency. Defined in this way, the concept of punishment goes far beyond things like parents spanking children and teach-

---

CONCEPT CHECK 6.4
Recognizing Outcomes in Operant Conditioning

Check your understanding of the various types of consequences that can occur in operant conditioning by indicating whether the examples below involve positive reinforcement (PR), negative reinforcement (NR), punishment (P), or extinction (E). The answers can be found in Appendix A.

_____ 1. Lyle gets a speeding ticket.

_____ 2. Diane's supervisor compliments her on her hard work.

_____ 3. Leon goes to the health club for a rare workout and pushes himself so hard that his entire body aches and he throws up.

_____ 4. Audrey lets her dog out so she won't have to listen to its whimpering.

_____ 5. Richard shoots up heroin to ward off tremors and chills associated with heroin withdrawal.

_____ 6. Edna constantly complains about minor aches and pains to obtain sympathy from colleagues at work. Three co-workers who share an office with her decide to ignore her complaints instead of responding with sympathy.

Figure 6.16. Comparison of negative reinforcement and punishment. Although punishment can occur when a response leads to the removal of a rewarding stimulus, it more typically involves the presentation of an aversive stimulus. Students often confuse punishment with negative reinforcement because they associate both with aversive stimuli. However, as this diagram shows, punishment and negative reinforcement represent opposite consequences that have opposite effects on behavior.

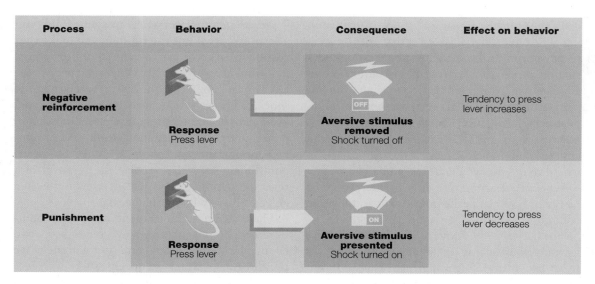

Process	Behavior	Consequence	Effect on behavior
Negative reinforcement	Response Press lever	Aversive stimulus removed Shock turned off	Tendency to press lever increases
Punishment	Response Press lever	Aversive stimulus presented Shock turned on	Tendency to press lever decreases

ers handing out detentions. For example, if you wear a new outfit and your schoolmates make fun of it, your behavior will have been punished and your tendency to emit this response (wear the same clothing) will probably decline. Similarly, if you go to a restaurant and have a horrible meal, your response will have been punished, and your tendency to go to that restaurant will probably decline.

Although punishment in operant conditioning encompasses far more than disciplinary acts, it *is* used frequently for disciplinary purposes. In light of this reality, research on punishment takes on special significance. Let's look at the implications of operant research for the use of punishment as a disciplinary measure.

Side Effects of Punishment

A key problem with punishment is that even when it is effective in weakening a response, it can have unintended side effects (Newsom, Favell, & Rincover, 1983; Van Houten, 1983). One of these side effects is the *general suppression of behavioral activity*. In other words, punishment can suppress many responses besides the punished one. In the laboratory, punished rats may simply freeze up. Similarly, some children who are frequently and severely punished become withdrawn, inhibited, and less active than other children. It is also common for punishment to trigger *strong emotional responses*, including fear, anxiety, anger, and resentment. Strong emotions can temporarily disrupt normal functioning and generate hostility toward the source of the punishment, such as a parent.

Finally, studies show that *physical* punishment often leads to an increase in *aggressive behavior*.

Children who are subjected to a lot of physical punishment tend to become more aggressive than the average youngster (Parke & Slaby, 1983). You'll see why shortly, when we discuss observational learning.

The truckload of side effects associated with punishment make it less than ideal as a disciplinary procedure. Research on operant conditioning suggests that disciplinary goals can often be accomplished more effectively by *reinforcing desirable behavior* than by *punishing undesirable behavior*.

Making Punishment More Effective

Although punishment is probably overused in disciplinary efforts, it does have a role to play. Fortunately, the undesirable side effects of punishment can be minimized if punishment is handled skillfully. The following guidelines summarize evidence on how to make punishment effective while reducing its side effects (Axelrod & Apsche, 1983; Parke, 1977; Walters & Grusec, 1977).

1. *Apply punishment swiftly*. A delay in delivering punishment—like a delay in delivering reinforcement—undermines its impact. When a mother says, "Wait until your father gets home . . ." she is making a fundamental mistake in the use of punishment. This problem with delayed punishment also explains the ineffectiveness of punishing a pet hours after it has misbehaved, when the owner finally returns home. For instance, it won't do any good to hit your dog with a newspaper while shoving its face in the feces it previously left on your carpet. This common punishment doesn't teach your dog to stop defecating on your carpet—it teaches the dog to keep its face out of its feces.

2. *Use punishment just severe enough to be effective.* The intensity of punishment is a two-edged sword. Severe punishments usually are more effective in weakening unwanted responses. However, they also increase the likelihood of undesirable side effects. Thus, it's best to use the least severe punishment that seems likely to have some impact.

3. *Make punishment consistent.* If you want to eliminate a response, you should punish the response every time it occurs. When parents are inconsistent about punishing a particular behavior, they create more confusion than learning.

4. *Explain the punishment.* When children are punished, the reason for their punishment should be explained as fully as possible, given the constraints of their age. The more that children understand why they were punished, the more effective the punishment tends to be.

5. *Minimize dependence on physical punishment.* Modest physical punishment may be necessary when children are too young to understand a verbal reprimand or the withdrawal of privileges. A light slap on the hand or bottom should suffice. Otherwise, physical punishment should be avoided, because it tends to increase aggressive behavior in children. Also, physical punishment often isn't as effective as most parents assume. Even a vigorous spanking isn't felt by a child an hour later. In contrast, withdrawing valued privileges can give children hours to contemplate the wisdom of changing their ways.

NEW DIRECTIONS IN THE STUDY OF CONDITIONING

As you learned in Chapter 1, science is constantly evolving and changing in response to new research and new thinking. Such change certainly has occurred in the study of conditioning (Domjan, 1993). In this section, we will examine two major changes in thinking about conditioning. First, we'll consider the recent recognition that an organism's biological heritage can limit or channel conditioning. Second, we'll discuss the increased appreciation of the role of cognitive processes in conditioning.

Recognizing Biological Constraints on Conditioning

Learning theorists have traditionally assumed that the fundamental laws of conditioning have great generality—that they apply to a wide range of

---

CONCEPT CHECK 6.5
Distinguishing Between Classical Conditioning and Operant Conditioning

Check your understanding of the usual differences between classical conditioning and operant conditioning by indicating the type of conditioning process involved in each of the following examples. In the space on the left, place a C if the example involves classical conditioning, an O if it involves operant conditioning, or a B if it involves both. The answers can be found in Appendix A.

_____ 1. Whenever Marcia takes her dog out for a walk, she wears the same old blue windbreaker. Eventually, she notices that her dog becomes excited whenever she puts on this windbreaker.

_____ 2. The Creatures are a successful rock band with three hit albums to their credit. They begin their U.S. tour featuring many new, unreleased songs, all of which draw silence from their concert fans. The same fans cheer wildly when the Creatures play any of their old hits. Gradually, the band reduces the number of new songs it plays and starts playing more of the old standbys.

_____ 3. When Cindy and Mel first fell in love, they listened constantly to the Creatures' hit song "Transatlantic Obsession." Although several years have passed, whenever they hear this song they experience a warm, romantic feeling.

_____ 4. For nearly 20 years Ralph has worked as a machinist in the same factory. His new foreman is never satisfied with his work and criticizes him constantly. After a few weeks of heavy criticism, he experiences anxiety whenever he arrives at work. He starts calling in sick more and more frequently to evade this anxiety.

---

species. Although no one ever suggested that hamsters could learn physics, until the 1960s most psychologists assumed that associations could be conditioned between any stimulus an organism could register and any response it could make. However, findings in recent decades have demonstrated that there are limits to the generality of conditioning principles—limits imposed by an organism's biological heritage.

One biological constraint on learning is instinctive drift. *Instinctive drift* occurs when an animal's innate response tendencies interfere with conditioning processes. Instinctive drift was first described by the Brelands, the operant psychologists who went into the business of training animals for commercial purposes (Breland & Breland, 1966). They have described many amusing examples of their "failures" to control behavior through conditioning. For instance, they once were training some raccoons to deposit coins in a piggy bank. They were successful in shaping the raccoons to pick up a coin and put it into a small box, using food as the reinforcer. However, when they gave the raccoons a couple of coins, an unexpected problem arose: the raccoons wouldn't give the coins up! In spite of the reinforcers available for depositing the coins, they would sit and rub the coins together like so many little misers.

What had happened to disrupt the conditioning program? Apparently, associating the coins with food had brought out the raccoons' innate food-washing behavior. Raccoons often rub things together to clean them. The Brelands report that they have run into this sort of instinct-related interference on many occasions with a wide variety of species.

Research on *conditioned taste aversion* also demonstrates that an organism's biological heritage can channel conditioning in certain directions. A number of years ago a prominent psychologist, Martin Seligman, dined out with his wife and enjoyed a steak with sauce béarnaise. About 6 hours afterward, he developed a wicked case of stomach flu and endured severe nausea. Subsequently, when he ordered sauce béarnaise, he was chagrined to discover that its aroma alone nearly made him throw up.

Seligman's experience was not unique. Many people develop aversions to food that has been followed by nausea from illness, alcohol intoxication, or food poisoning. However, Seligman was puzzled by his problem (Seligman & Hager, 1972). On the one hand, it appeared to be the straightforward result of classical conditioning. A neutral stimulus (the sauce) had been paired with an unconditioned stimulus (the flu), which caused an unconditioned response (the nausea). Hence, the sauce béarnaise became a conditioned stimulus eliciting nausea (see Figure 6.17).

On the other hand, Seligman recognized that his aversion to béarnaise sauce violated certain basic principles of conditioning. First, the lengthy delay of six hours between the CS (the sauce) and the UCS (the flu) should have prevented conditioning from occurring. In laboratory studies, a delay of more than *30 seconds* between the CS and UCS makes it very difficult to establish a conditioned response, yet this conditioning occurred in just one pairing. Second, why was it that *only* the béarnaise sauce became a CS eliciting nausea?

Why not other stimuli that were present in the restaurant? Shouldn't plates, knives, tablecloths, or his wife, for example, also trigger Seligman's nausea?

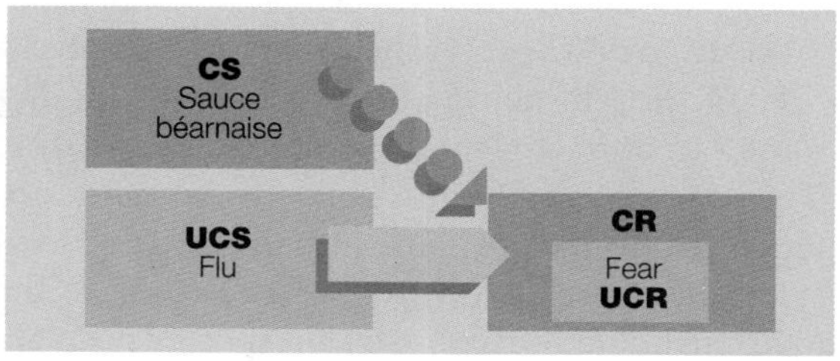

The riddle of Seligman's aversion to sauce béarnaise was solved by John Garcia (1989) and his colleagues. They conducted a series of studies on conditioned taste aversion (Garcia & Koelling, 1966; Garcia, Clarke, & Hankins, 1973; Garcia & Rusiniak, 1980). In these studies, they manipulated the kinds of stimuli preceding the onset of nausea and other noxious experiences in rats, using radiation to artificially induce the nausea. They found that when taste cues were followed by nausea, rats quickly acquired conditioned taste aversions. However, when taste cues were followed by other types of noxious stimuli (such as shock), rats did *not* develop conditioned taste aversions. Furthermore, visual and auditory stimuli followed by nausea also failed to produce conditioned aversions.

In short, Garcia and his co-workers found that taste aversions were conditioned *only* through the pairing of taste stimuli and stimuli inducing nausea. When taste stimuli or nausea-inducing stimuli were paired with other types of stimuli—rather than each other—minimal conditioning occurred. In contrast, the taste-nausea connection was made so readily that conditioned taste aversions could develop in spite of remarkably long CS-UCS delays. These findings contradicted the long-held belief that associations could be created between virtually any stimulus and any response. Garcia found that it was almost impossible to create certain associations, whereas taste-nausea associations (and odor-nausea associations) were almost impossible to prevent.

What is the theoretical significance of this unique readiness to make connections between taste and nausea? Garcia argues that it is a by-product of the evolutionary history of mammals. Animals that consume poisonous foods and survive must learn not to repeat their mistakes. Natural selection will favor organisms that quickly learn what *not* to eat. Thus, evolution may have biologically programmed some organisms to learn certain types of associations more easily than others.

Conditioned taste aversion has practical as well as theoretical significance. After learning how easy it is to condition food aversions, Garcia decided to apply this discovery to a practical problem: the control of predators' attacks on livestock. He gave coyotes, which normally prey on sheep, the opportunity to eat tainted sheep carcasses that

Figure 6.17. Conditioned taste aversion. Taste aversions can be established through classical conditioning. However, as the text explains, taste aversions can be acquired in ways that violate basic principles of classical conditioning.

made them ill. As a result, the coyotes experienced nausea at the sight of sheep—and failed to attack them. In a subsequent study at a real sheep ranch, Garcia and his colleagues demonstrated that this technique could be used to reduce coyotes' attacks on livestock (Gustavson et al., 1976).

Recognizing Cognitive Processes in Conditioning

Pavlov, Skinner, and their followers traditionally viewed conditioning as a mechanical process in which stimulus-response associations are stamped in by experience. Learning theorists asserted that if a flatworm can be conditioned, then conditioning can't depend on higher mental processes. Although this viewpoint did not go entirely unchallenged (for example, Tolman, 1922, 1932), mainstream theories of conditioning did not allocate a major role to cognitive processes. In recent decades, however, research findings have led theorists to shift toward more cognitive explanations of conditioning.

The cognitive element in classical conditioning is especially prominent in research conducted by Robert Rescorla (1978, 1980; Rescorla & Wagner, 1972). Rescorla asserts that environmental stimuli serve as signals and that some stimuli are better, or more dependable, signals than others. Hence, he has manipulated *signal relations* in classical conditioning—that is, CS-UCS relations that influence whether a CS is a good signal. A "good" signal is one that allows accurate prediction of the UCS.

In essence, Rescorla manipulates the *predictive value* of a conditioned stimulus. How does he do so? He varies the proportion of trials in which the CS and UCS are paired. Consider the following example. A tone and shock are paired 20 times for one group of rats. Otherwise, these rats are never shocked. For these rats the CS (tone) and UCS (shock) are paired in 100% of the experimental trials. Another group of rats also receives 20 pairings of the tone and shock. However, this group is also exposed to the shock on 20 other trials when the tone does *not* precede it. For this group, the CS and UCS are paired in only 50% of the trials. Thus, the two groups of rats have had an equal number of CS-UCS pairings, but the CS is a better signal or predictor of shock for the 100% CS-UCS group than for the 50% CS-UCS group.

What did Rescorla find when he tested the two groups of rats for conditioned fear? He found that the CS elicits a much stronger response in the 100% CS-UCS group than in the 50% CS-UCS group. Given that the two groups have received an equal number of CS-UCS pairings, this difference must be due to the greater predictive power of the CS for the 100% group. Numerous studies of signal relations have shown that the predictive value of a CS is an influential factor governing classical conditioning (Rescorla, 1978). These studies of signal relations suggest that classical conditioning may involve information processing rather than reflexive responding.

Let's turn to operant behavior for one more example of cognitive processes in conditioning. Imagine that on the night before an important exam you study very hard while repeatedly playing a Bruce Springsteen album. The next morning you earn an A on your exam. Does this result strengthen your tendency to play Springsteen albums before exams? Probably not. Chances are, you will recognize the logical relation between the response of studying hard and the reinforcement of a good grade, and only the response of studying will be strengthened (Killeen, 1981).

Thus, reinforcement is *not* automatic when favorable consequences follow a response. People actively reason out the relations between responses and the outcomes that follow. When a response is followed by a desirable outcome, the response is more likely to be strengthened if the person thinks that the response *caused* the outcome. You might guess that only humans would engage in this causal reasoning. However, evidence suggests that under the right circumstances even pigeons can learn to recognize causal relations between responses and outcomes (Killeen, 1981).

In sum, modern, reformulated models of conditioning view it as a matter of detecting the

Coyotes given tainted sheep develop a conditioned response of nausea at the sight of sheep. Sheep ranchers have reduced coyotes' attacks on their livestock by spreading tainted sheep carcasses around their ranches.

Observational learning is seen in animals as well as humans. For instance, the English titmouse has learned how to open cardboard caps on milk bottles to swipe milk and cream from its human neighbors. This clever learned behavior has been passed down from one generation of titmouse to the next through observational learning.

OBSERVATIONAL LEARNING

Can classical and operant conditioning account for all of our learning? Absolutely not. Consider how people learn a fairly basic skill such as driving a car. They do not hop naively into an automobile and start emitting random responses until one leads to favorable consequences. On the contrary, most people learning to drive know exactly where to place the key and how to get started. How are these responses acquired? Through *observation*. Most new drivers have years of experience observing others drive and they put those observations to work. Learning through observation accounts for a great deal of learning in both animals and humans.

Observational learning occurs when an organism's responding is influenced by the observation of others, who are called models. This process has been investigated extensively by Albert Bandura (1977, 1986). Bandura does not see observational learning as entirely separate from classical and operant conditioning. Instead, he asserts that it greatly extends the reach of these conditioning processes. Whereas previous conditioning theorists emphasized the organism's direct experience, Bandura has demonstrated that both classical and operant conditioning can take place vicariously through observational learning.

Essentially, observational learning involves being conditioned indirectly by virtue of observing another's conditioning (see Figure 6.18). To illustrate, suppose you observe a friend behaving assertively with a car salesperson. You see your friend's assertive behavior reinforced by the exceptionally good buy she gets on the car. Your own tendency to behave assertively with salespeople might well be strengthened as a result. Notice that the reinforcement is experienced by your friend, not you. The good buy should strengthen your friend's tendency to bargain assertively, but your tendency to do so may also be strengthened indirectly.

Bandura has identified four key processes that are crucial in observational learning. The first two—attention and retention—highlight the importance of cognition in this type of learning.

- *Attention.* To learn through observation, you must pay attention to another person's behavior and its consequences.

- *Retention.* You may not have occasion to use an observed response for weeks, months, or even years. Hence, you must store a mental represen-

contingencies among environmental events. According to these theories, organisms actively try to figure out what leads to what (the contingencies) in the world around them. Stimuli are viewed as signals that help organisms minimize their aversive experiences and maximize their pleasant experiences.

The new, cognitively oriented theories of conditioning are quite a departure from older theories that depicted conditioning as a mindless, mechanical process. We can also see this new emphasis on cognitive processes in our next subject, observational learning.

Figure 6.18. Observational learning. In observational learning, an observer attends to and stores a mental representation of a model's behavior (*example:* assertive bargaining) and its consequences (*example:* a good buy on a car). If the observer sees the modeled response lead to a favorable outcome, the observer's tendency to emit the modeled response will be strengthened.

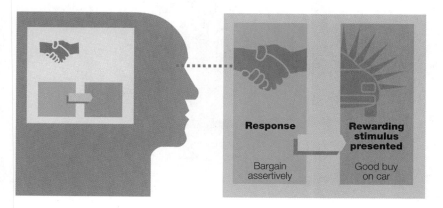

Response

Bargain assertively

Rewarding stimulus presented

Good buy on car

tation of what you have witnessed in your memory.

- *Reproduction*. Enacting a modeled response depends on your ability to reproduce the response by converting your stored mental images into overt behavior. This may not be easy for some responses. For example, most people cannot execute a breathtaking windmill dunk after watching Michael Jordan do it in a basketball game.

- *Motivation*. Finally, you are unlikely to reproduce an observed response unless you are motivated to do so. Your motivation depends on whether you encounter a situation in which you believe that the response is likely to pay off for you.

Bandura's theory of observational learning has shed light on many important aspects of behavior. For example, it explains why physical punishment tends to increase aggressive behavior in children, even when it is intended to do just the opposite. Parents who depend on physical punishment often punish a child for hitting other children—by spanking the child. The parents may sincerely intend to reduce the child's aggressive behavior, but they are unwittingly serving as *models* of such behavior. Although they may tell the child that "hitting people won't accomplish anything," they are in the midst of hitting the child in order to accomplish something. Because parents usually accomplish their immediate goal of stopping the child's hitting, the child witnesses the reinforcement of aggressive behavior. In this situation, actions speak louder than words—because of observational learning.

Clearly, observational learning plays an important role in regulating behavior. It represents a third major type of learning that builds on the first two types—classical conditioning and operant conditioning. These three basic types of learning are summarized and compared in a pictorial table on pages 176–177.

PUTTING IT IN PERSPECTIVE

Two of our unifying themes stand out in this chapter: (1) nature and nurture interactively govern behavior, and (2) psychology evolves in a sociohistorical context. Let's examine each of these points in more detail.

In regard to nature versus nurture, research on learning clearly demonstrates the enormous power

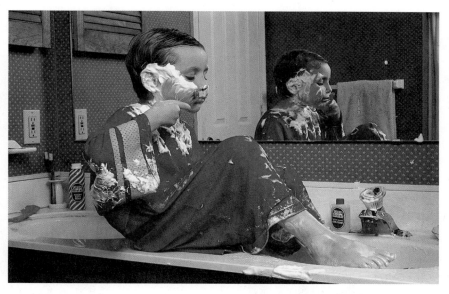

Performance of a task is often learned by observing how a model performs the task.

of the environment in shaping behavior. Pavlov's model of classical conditioning shows how experiences can account for everyday fears and other emotional responses. Skinner's model of operant conditioning shows how reinforcement and punishment can mold everything from a child's bedtime whimpering to an adult's restaurant preferences. Indeed, many learning theorists once believed that *all* aspects of behavior could be explained in terms of environmental determinants. In recent decades, however, evidence on instinctive drift and conditioned taste aversion has shown that there are biological constraints on conditioning. Thus, even in explanations of learning—an area once dominated by nurture theories—we see again that heredity and environment jointly influence behavior.

The history of research on conditioning also shows how progress in psychology can seep into every corner of society. For example, Skinner's ideas on the power of reinforcement and the ineffectiveness of punishment have influenced patterns of discipline in our society. Today's parents and educators appear to depend less on punitive measures than previous generations. Research on operant conditioning has also affected management styles in the business world, leading to an increased emphasis on positive reinforcement. The fact that the principles of conditioning are routinely applied in homes, businesses, schools, and factories clearly shows that psychology is not an ivory tower endeavor.

In the upcoming Application, you will see how you can apply the principles of conditioning to improve your self-control, as we discuss the technology of behavior modification.

"Most human behavior is learned by observation through modeling."
ALBERT BANDURA

THREE TYPES OF LEARNING

Type of learning	Procedure	Diagram	Result
Classical conditioning Ivan Pavlov	A neutral stimulus (for example, a bell) is paired with an unconditioned stimulus (such as food) that elicits an unconditioned response (salivation).	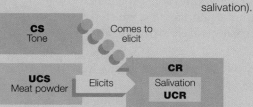	The neutral stimulus becomes a conditioned stimulus that elicits the conditioned response (for example, a bell triggers salivation).
Operant conditioning B. F. Skinner	In a stimulus situation, a response is followed by favorable consequences (reinforcement) or unfavorable consequences (punishment).	**Response** Press lever → Followed by → **Rewarding or aversive stimulus presented or removed** Food delivery or shock	If reinforced, the response is strengthened (emitted more frequently); if punished, the response is weakened (emitted less frequently).
Observational learning Albert Bandura	An observer attends to a model's behavior (for example, aggressive bargaining) and its consequences (for example, a good buy on a car).		The observer stores a mental representation of the modeled response; the observer's tendency to emit the response may be strengthened or weakened, depending on the consequences observed.

Diagram for Classical conditioning: **CS** Tone — Comes to elicit → **CR** Salivation **UCR**; **UCS** Meat powder — Elicits →

Diagram for Observational learning: **Response** Bargain assertively — **Rewarding stimulus presented** Good buy on car

Typical kinds of responses	Examples in animals	Examples in humans
Mostly (but not always) involuntary reflexes and visceral responses	Coyotes given tainted sheep develop a conditioned response of nausea elicited by the sight of sheep. 	Little Albert learns to fear a white rat and other white, furry objects through classical conditioning 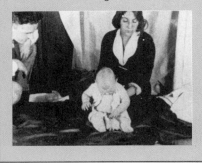
Mostly (but not always) voluntary, spontaneous responses	Circus bears and other trained animals perform remarkable feats because they have been reinforced for gradually learning closer and closer approximations of responses they do not normally emit. 	Casino patrons tend to exhibit high, steady rates of gambling, as most games of chance involve complex variable-ratio schedules of reinforcement. 
Mostly voluntary responses, often consisting of novel and complex sequences	An English titmouse learns to break into humans' milk bottles by observing the thievery of other titmice. 	A young boy tries to perform a response that he has acquired through observational learning. 

Achieving Self-Control Through Behavior Modification

Answer the following "yes" or "no":

1 Do you have a hard time passing up food, even when you're not hungry?

2 Do you wish you studied more often?

3 Would you like to cut down on your smoking or drinking?

4 Do you experience difficulty in getting yourself to exercise regularly?

If you answered "yes" to any of these questions, you have struggled with the challenge of self-control. This Application discusses how you can use the techniques of behavior modification to improve your self-control.

Behavior modification **is a systematic approach to changing behavior through the application of the principles of conditioning.** Advocates of behavior modification assume that behavior is mainly a product of learning, conditioning, and environmental control. They further assume that *what is learned can be unlearned*. Thus, they set out to "recondition" people to produce more desirable patterns of behavior.

The technology of behavior modification has been applied with great success in schools, businesses, hospitals, factories, child-care facilities, prisons, and mental health centers (Goodall, 1972; Kazdin, 1982; Rachman, 1992). Moreover, behavior modification techniques have proven particularly valuable in efforts to improve self-control. Our discussion will borrow liberally from an excellent book on self-modification by David Watson and Roland Tharp (1993). We will discuss five steps in the process

of self-modification, which are outlined in Figure 6.19.

Specifying Your Target Behavior

The first step in a self-modification program is to specify the target behavior(s) that you want to change. Behavior modification can only be applied to a clearly defined, overt response, yet many people have difficulty pinpointing the behavior they hope to alter. They tend to describe their problems in terms of unobservable personality *traits* rather than overt *behaviors*. For example, asked what behavior he would like to change, a man might say, "I'm too irritable." That may be true, but it is of little help in designing a self-modification program. To use a behavioral approach, vague statements about traits need to be translated into precise descriptions of specific target behaviors.

To identify target responses, you need to ponder past behavior or closely observe future behavior and list specific *examples* of responses that lead to the trait description. For instance, the man who regards himself as "too irritable" might identify two overly frequent responses, such as arguing with his wife and snapping at his children. These are specific behaviors for which he could design a self-modification program.

Gathering Baseline Data

The second step in behavior modification is to gather baseline data. You need to systematically observe your target behavior for a period of time (usually a week or two) before you work out the details of your program. In gathering your baseline data, you need to monitor three things.

First, you need to determine the initial response level of your target behavior. After all, you can't tell whether your

program is working effectively unless you have a baseline for comparison. In most cases, you would simply keep track of how often the target response occurs in a certain time interval. Thus, you might count the daily frequency of snapping at your children, smoking cigarettes, or biting your fingernails. *It is crucial to gather accurate data.* You should keep perma-

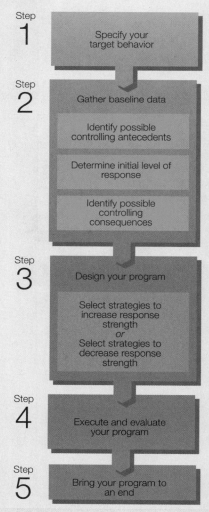

Figure 6.19. Steps in a self-modification program. This flowchart provides an overview of the steps necessary to execute a self-modification program.

Step 1
Specify your target behavior

Step 2
Gather baseline data
Identify possible controlling antecedents
Determine initial level of response
Identify possible controlling consequences

Step 3
Design your program
Select strategies to increase response strength
or
Select strategies to decrease response strength

Step 4
Execute and evaluate your program

Step 5
Bring your program to an end

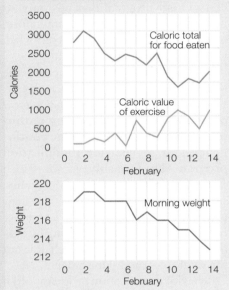

Figure 6.20. Example of record keeping in a self-modification program for losing weight. Graphic records are ideal for tracking progress in behavior modification efforts.

nent written records, and it is usually best to portray these records graphically (see Figure 6.20).

Second, you need to monitor the antecedents of your target behavior. *Antecedents are events that typically precede the target response.* Often these events play a major role in evoking your target behavior. For example, if your target is overeating, you might discover that the bulk of your overeating occurs late in the evening while you watch TV. If you can pinpoint this kind of antecedent-response connection, you may be able to design your program to circumvent or break the link.

Third, you need to monitor the typical consequences of your target behavior. Try to identify the reinforcers that are maintaining an undesirable target behavior or the unfavorable outcomes that are suppressing a desirable target behavior. In trying to identify reinforcers, remember that avoidance behavior is usually maintained by negative reinforcement. That is, the payoff for avoidance is usually the removal of something aversive,

such as anxiety or a threat to self-esteem. You should also take into account the fact that a response may not be reinforced every time, as most behavior is maintained by intermittent reinforcement.

Designing Your Program

Once you have selected a target behavior and gathered adequate baseline data, it is time to plan your intervention program. Generally speaking, your program will be designed either to increase or to decrease the frequency of a target response.

Increasing Response Strength

Efforts to increase the frequency of a target response depend largely on the use of positive reinforcement. In other words, you reward yourself for behaving properly. Although the basic strategy is quite simple, doing it skillfully involves a number of considerations.

SELECTING A REINFORCER To use positive reinforcement, you need to find a reward that will be effective for you. Reinforcement is subjective. What is reinforcing for one person may not be reinforcing for another. Figure 6.21 lists questions you can ask yourself to help you determine your personal reinforcers.

You don't have to come up with spectacular new reinforcers that you've never experienced before. *You can use reinforcers that you are already getting.* However, you have to restructure the contingencies so that you get them only if you behave appropriately. For example, if you normally buy two compact discs per week, you might make these purchases contingent on studying a certain number of hours during the week.

ARRANGING THE CONTINGENCIES Once you have chosen your reinforcer, you have to set up reinforcement contingencies. These contingencies will describe the exact behavioral goals that must be met and the reinforcement that may then

Figure 6.21. Selecting a reinforcer. The questions listed here may help you identify your personal reinforcers. (From Watson & Tharp, 1989)

What Are Your Reinforcers?

1. What will be the rewards of achieving your goal?
2. What kind of praise do you like to receive, from yourself and others?
3. What kinds of things do you like to have?
4. What are your major interests?
5. What are your hobbies?
6. What people do you like to be with?
7. What do you like to do with those people?
8. What do you do for fun?
9. What do you do to relax?
10. What do you do to get away from it all?
11. What makes you feel good?
12. What would be a nice present to receive?
13. What kinds of things are important to you?
14. What would you buy if you had an extra $20? $50? $100?
15. On what do you spend your money each week?
16. What behaviors do you perform every day? (Don't overlook the obvious or commonplace.)
17. Are there any behaviors you usually perform instead of the target behavior?
18. What would you hate to lose?
19. Of the things you do every day, which would you hate to give up?
20. What are your favorite daydreams and fantasies?
21. What are the most relaxing scenes you can imagine?

be awarded. For example, in a program to increase exercise, you might make spending $40 on clothes (the reinforcer) contingent on having jogged 15 miles during the week (the target behavior).

Try to set behavioral goals that are both challenging and realistic. You want your goals to be challenging so that they lead to improvement in your behavior. However, setting unrealistically high goals—a common mistake in self-modification—often leads to unnecessary discouragement.

You also need to be concerned about doling out too much reinforcement. If reinforcement is too easy to get, you may become *satiated*, and the reinforcer may lose its motivational power. For example, if you were to reward yourself with virtually all the compact discs you wanted, this reinforcer would lose its incentive value.

One way to avoid the satiation problem is to put yourself on a token economy. **A *token economy* is a system for doling out symbolic reinforcers that are exchanged later for a variety of genuine reinforcers.** Thus, you might develop a point system for exercise behavior, accumulating points that can be spent on compact discs, movies, restaurant meals, and so forth (see Figure 6.22).

Decreasing Response Strength

Let's turn now to the challenge of reducing the frequency of an undesirable response. You can go about this task in a number of ways. Your principal options include reinforcement, control of antecedents, and punishment.

REINFORCEMENT Reinforcers can be used in an indirect way to decrease the frequency of a response. This may sound paradoxical, since you have learned that reinforcement strengthens a response. The trick lies in how you define the target behavior. For example, in the case of overeating you might define your target behavior as eating more than 1600 calories a day (an excess response that you want to decrease) or eating less than 1600 calories a day (a deficit response that you want to increase). You can choose the latter definition and reinforce yourself whenever you eat less than 1600 calories in a day. Thus, you can reinforce yourself for *not* emitting a response, or for emitting it less, and thereby decrease a response through reinforcement.

CONTROL OF ANTECEDENTS A worthwhile strategy for decreasing the occurrence of an undesirable response may be to identify its antecedents and avoid exposure to them. This strategy is especially useful when you are trying to decrease the frequency of a consummatory response, such as smoking or eating. In the case of overeating, for instance, the easiest way to resist temptation is to avoid having to face it. Thus, you might

Figure 6.22. Example of a token economy to reinforce exercise. This token economy was set up to strengthen three types of exercise behavior. The person can exchange tokens for four different types of reinforcers.

Response Earning Tokens		
Response	Amount	Number of Tokens
Jogging	1/2 mile	4
Jogging	1 mile	8
Jogging	2 miles	16
Tennis	1 hour	4
Tennis	2 hours	8

Redemption Value of Tokens	
Reinforcer	Tokens Required
Purchase one compact disc of your choice	30
Go to movie	50
Go to nice restaurant	100
Take special weekend trip	500

stay away from enticing restaurants, minimize time spent in your kitchen, shop for groceries just after eating (when willpower is higher), and avoid purchasing favorite foods.

PUNISHMENT The strategy of decreasing unwanted behavior by punishing yourself for that behavior is an obvious option that people tend to overuse. The biggest problem with punishment in a self-modification effort is that it is difficult to follow through and punish yourself. Nonetheless, there may be situations in which your manipulations of reinforcers need to be bolstered by the threat of punishment.

If you're going to use punishment, keep two guidelines in mind. First, do not use punishment alone. Use it in conjunction with positive reinforcement. If you set up a program in which you can earn only negative consequences, you probably won't stick to it. Second, use a relatively mild punishment so that you will actually be able to administer it to yourself.

Executing and Evaluating Your Program

Once you have designed your program, the next step is to put it to work by enforcing the contingencies that you have carefully planned. During this period, you need to continue to accurately record the frequency of your target behavior so you can evaluate your progress. The success of your program depends on your not "cheating." The most common form of cheating is to reward yourself when you have not actually earned it.

You can do two things to increase the likelihood that you will comply with your program. One is to make up **a *behavioral contract*—a written agreement outlining a promise to adhere to the contingencies of a behavior modification program.** The formality of signing such a contract in front of friends or family seems to make many people take their program more seriously. You can further reduce the likelihood of cheating by having someone other than yourself dole out the reinforcers and punishments.

Behavior modification programs often require some fine-tuning. So don't be surprised if you need to make a few adjustments. Several flaws are especially common in designing self-modification programs. Among those that you should look out for are (1) depending on a weak reinforcer, (2) permitting lengthy delays between appropriate behavior and delivery of reinforcers, and (3) trying to do too much too quickly by setting unrealistic goals. Often, a small revision or two can turn a failing program around and make it a success.

Ending Your Program

Generally, when you design your program you should spell out the conditions under which you will bring it to an end. This involves setting terminal goals such as reaching a certain weight, studying with a certain regularity, or going without cigarettes for a certain length of time. Often, it is a good idea to phase out your program by planning a gradual reduction in the frequency or potency of your reinforcement for appropriate behavior.

Chapter 6 Review

KEY IDEAS

Classical Conditioning

♦ Classical conditioning explains how a neutral stimulus can acquire the capacity to elicit a response originally evoked by another stimulus. This kind of conditioning was originally described by Ivan Pavlov, who conditioned dogs to salivate when a tone was presented. Many kinds of everyday responses are regulated through classical conditioning, including phobias, anxiety responses, pleasant emotional responses, and physiological responses.

♦ Stimulus contiguity plays a key role in the acquisition of new conditioned responses. A conditioned response may be weakened and extinguished entirely when the CS is no longer paired with the UCS. In some cases, spontaneous recovery occurs, and an extinguished response reappears after a period of nonexposure to the CS.

♦ Conditioning may generalize to additional stimuli that are similar to the original CS. The opposite of generalization is discrimination, which involves not responding to stimuli that resemble the original CS. Higher-order conditioning occurs when a CS functions as if it were a UCS, to establish new conditioning.

Operant Conditioning

♦ Operant conditioning, which was pioneered by B. F. Skinner, involves largely voluntary responses that are governed by their consequences. The key dependent variable in operant conditioning is the rate of response over time. New operant responses can be shaped by gradually reinforcing closer and closer approximations of the desired response.

♦ In operant conditioning, when reinforcement is terminated, the response rate usually declines and extinction may occur. There are variations in how long an organism continues to make a response that is no longer reinforced. Operant responses are regulated by discriminative stimuli that are cues for the likelihood of obtaining reinforcers.

♦ The central process in reinforcement is the strengthening of a response. Something that is reinforcing for an organism at one time may not be reinforcing later. Delayed reinforcement slows the process of conditioning. Primary reinforcers are unlearned. In contrast, secondary reinforcers acquire their reinforcing quality through conditioning.

♦ Schedules of reinforcement influence patterns of operant responding. Intermittent schedules produce greater resistance to extinction than similar continuous schedules. Ratio schedules tend to yield higher rates of response than interval schedules. Shorter intervals and higher ratios are associated with faster responding.

♦ Responses can be strengthened either through the presentation of positive reinforcers or through the removal of negative reinforcers. Negative reinforcement regulates escape and avoidance learning.

♦ Punishment involves unfavorable consequences that lead to a decline in response strength. Some of the problems associated with the application of punishment are an increase in aggressive behavior and suppression of behavioral activities. Punishment is more effective when it is swift, severe, consistent, and explained.

New Directions in the Study of Conditioning

♦ Recent decades have brought profound changes in our understanding of conditioning. The findings on instinctive drift and conditioned taste aversion have led to the recognition that there are biological constraints on conditioning. Studies have also demonstrated that cognitive processes play a larger role in conditioning than originally believed. Modern theories hold that conditioning is a matter of detecting the contingencies that govern events.

Observational Learning

♦ In observational learning, an organism is conditioned by watching a model's conditioning. Both classical and operant conditioning can occur through observational learning, which depends on the processes of attention, retention, reproduction, and motivation. Modeling appears to explain why physical punishment increases youngsters' aggressiveness.

Putting It in Perspective

♦ Two of our key themes were especially apparent in our coverage of learning and conditioning. One theme involves the interaction of heredity and the environment in governing behavior. The other involves the way progress in psychology affects society at large.

Application: Achieving Self-Control Through Behavior Modification

♦ Behavior modification techniques can be used to increase one's self-control. The first step in self-modification is to specify the overt target behavior to be increased or decreased. The second step involves gathering baseline data about the initial rate of the target response and identifying any typical antecedents and consequences associated with the behavior.

♦ The third step is to design a program. If you are trying to increase the strength of a response, you'll depend on positive reinforcement. A number of strategies can be used to decrease the strength of a response, including reinforcement, control of antecedents, and punishment. The fourth step involves executing and evaluating your program. Self-modification programs often require some fine-tuning. The final step is to determine how and when you will phase out your program.

KEY TERMS

Acquisition	Operant conditioning
Antecedents	Pavlovian conditioning
Avoidance learning	Positive reinforcement
Behavioral contract	
Behavior modification	Primary reinforcers
Classical conditioning	Punishment
Conditioned reinforcers	Reinforcement
Conditioned response (CR)	Reinforcement contingencies
Conditioned stimulus (CS)	Resistance to extinction
Continuous reinforcement	Schedule of reinforcement
Cumulative recorder	Secondary reinforcers
Discriminative stimuli	Shaping
Elicit	Skinner box
Emit	Spontaneous recovery
Escape learning	Stimulus contiguity
Extinction	Stimulus discrimination
Fixed-interval (FI) schedule	Stimulus generalization
Fixed-ratio (FR) schedule	Token economy
Higher-order conditioning	Trial
Intermittent reinforcement	Unconditioned response (UCR)
Learning	Unconditioned stimulus (UCS)
Negative reinforcement	Variable-interval (VI) schedule
Observational learning	Variable-ratio (VR) schedule

KEY PEOPLE

Albert Bandura	B. F. Skinner
Ivan Pavlov	John B. Watson
Robert Rescorla	

7 Human Memory

If you live in the United States, you've undoubtedly handled thousands upon thousands of American pennies. Surely, then, you remember what a penny looks like—or do you? Take a look at Figure 7.1. Which drawing corresponds to a real penny?

Did you have a hard time selecting the real one? If so, you're not alone. Nickerson and Adams (1979) found that most people can't recognize the real penny in this collection of drawings. And their surprising finding was not a fluke. Undergraduates in England showed even worse memory for British coins (G. Jones, 1990). How can that be? Why do most of us have so poor a memory for an object we see every day?

Let's try another exercise. A definition of a word follows. It's not a particularly common word, but there's a good chance that you're familiar with it. Try to think of the word.

Definition: Favoritism shown or patronage granted by persons in high office to relatives or close friends.

If you can't think of the word, perhaps you can remember what letter of the alphabet it begins with, or what it sounds like. If so, you're experiencing the *tip-of-the-tongue phenomenon*, in which forgotten information feels like it's just out of reach. In this case, the word you may be reaching for is *nepotism*.

You've probably endured the tip-of-the-tongue phenomenon while taking exams. You blank out on a term that you're sure you know. You may feel as if you're on the verge of remembering the term, but you can't quite come up with it. Later, perhaps while you're driving home, the term suddenly comes to you. "Of course," you may say to yourself, "how could I forget that?" That's an interesting question. Clearly, the term was stored in your memory.

As these examples suggest, memory involves more than taking in information and storing it in some mental compartment. In fact, psychologists probing the workings of memory have had to grapple with three enduring questions: (1) How does information get *into* memory? (2) How is information *maintained* in memory? (3) How is information *pulled back out* of memory? These three questions correspond to the three key processes involved in memory (see Figure 7.2): *encoding* (getting information in), *storage* (maintaining it), and *retrieval* (getting it out).

Encoding involves forming a memory code. For example, when you form a memory code for a word, you might emphasize how it looks, how it

sounds, or what it means. Encoding usually requires attention, which is why you may not be able to recall exactly what a penny looks like—most people don't pay much attention to the appearance of a penny. As you'll see throughout this chapter, memory is largely an active process. For the most part, you're unlikely to remember something unless you make a conscious effort to do so. **Storage involves maintaining encoded information in memory over time.** Psychologists have focused much of their memory research on trying to identify just what factors help or hinder memory storage. But, as the tip-of-the-tongue phenomenon shows, information storage isn't enough to guarantee that you'll remember something. You need to be able to get information out

Figure 7.1. A simple memory test. Nickerson and Adams (1979) presented these 15 versions of an object most people have seen hundreds or thousands of times and asked, "Which one is correct?"

Figure 7.2. Three key processes in memory. Memory depends on three sequential processes: encoding, storage, and retrieval. Some theorists draw an analogy between these processes and elements of information processing by computers.

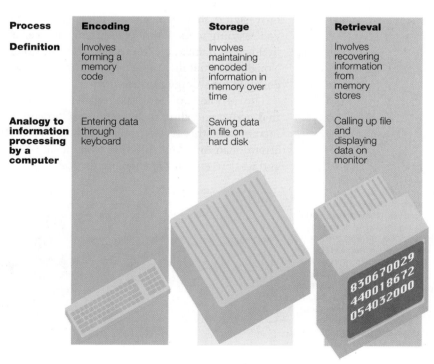

Process	Encoding	Storage	Retrieval
Definition	Involves forming a memory code	Involves maintaining encoded information in memory over time	Involves recovering information from memory stores
Analogy to information processing by a computer	Entering data through keyboard	Saving data in file on hard disk	Calling up file and displaying data on monitor

of storage. *Retrieval* **involves recovering information from memory stores.** Research issues concerned with retrieval include the study of how people search memory and why some retrieval strategies are more effective than others.

Most of this chapter is devoted to an examination of memory encoding, storage, and retrieval. As you'll see, these basic processes help explain the ultimate puzzle in the study of memory: why people forget. Just as memory involves more than storage, forgetting involves more than "losing" something from the memory store. Forgetting may be due to deficiencies in any of the three key processes in memory—encoding, storage, or retrieval. After our discussion of forgetting, we will take a brief look at the physiological bases of memory. Finally, we will discuss the theoretical controversy about whether there are separate memory systems for different types of information. The chapter's Application provides some practical advice on how to improve your memory.

ENCODING: GETTING INFORMATION INTO MEMORY

Have you ever been embarrassed because you couldn't remember someone's name? Perhaps there have been times when you realized only 30 seconds after meeting someone that you had already "forgotten" his or her name. More often than not, this familiar kind of forgetting is due to a failure to form a memory code for the name. When you're introduced to people, you're often busy sizing them up and thinking about what you're going to say. With your attention diverted in this way, names go in one ear and out the other. You don't remember them because they are never encoded for storage into memory.

The problem of forgetting names illustrates that active encoding is an important process in memory. In this section, we discuss the role of attention in encoding, different types of encoding, and ways to enrich the encoding process.

The Role of Attention

Generally, you need to pay attention to information if you want to remember it. For example, if you sit through a class lecture but pay little attention to it, you're unlikely to remember much of what the professor had to say.

Attention **involves focusing awareness on a narrowed range of stimuli or events.** Psychologists routinely refer to "selective attention," but the words are really redundant. Attention is selection of input. If you pause to devote a little attention to the matter, you'll realize that selective attention is critical to everyday functioning. If your attention were distributed equally among all stimulus inputs, life would be utter chaos. If you weren't able to filter out most of the potential stimulation around you, you wouldn't be able to read a book, converse with a friend, or even carry on a coherent train of thought.

Attention is usually likened to a *filter* that screens out most potential stimuli while allowing a select few to pass through into conscious awareness. However, a great deal of debate has been devoted to *where* the filter is located in the information-processing system. The key issue in this debate is whether stimuli are screened out early, during sensory input, or late, after the brain has processed the meaning or significance of the input. Hence, models of attention are often characterized as *early-selection* or *late-selection* theories (see Figure 7.3).

Which view is supported by the weight of evidence—early selection or late selection? There is ample evidence for *both* as well as for intermediate selection (Cowan, 1988; Johnston & Dark, 1986). These findings have led some theorists to conclude that the location of the attention filter may be flexible rather than fixed (Johnston & Heinz, 1978; Shiffrin, 1988).

Levels of Processing

Attention is critical to the encoding of memories, but not all attention is created equal. You can attend to things in different ways, focusing on

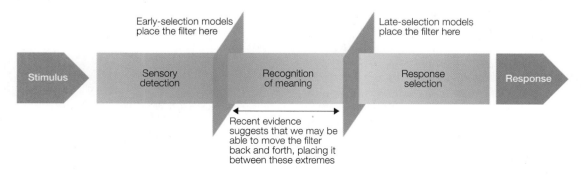

Figure 7.3. Models of selective attention. Early-selection models propose that input is filtered before meaning is processed. Late-selection models hold that filtering occurs after the processing of meaning. There is evidence to support early, late, and intermediate selection, suggesting that the location of the attentional filter may not be fixed.

different aspects of the stimulus input. According to some theorists, these qualitative differences in *how* people attend to information are the main factors influencing how much they remember. For example, Fergus Craik and Robert Lockhart (1972) argue that different rates of forgetting occur because some methods of encoding create more durable memory codes than others.

Craik and Lockhart propose that incoming information can be processed at different levels. For instance, they maintain that in dealing with verbal information, people engage in three progressively deeper levels of processing: structural, phonemic, and semantic encoding (see Figure 7.4). *Structural encoding* is relatively shallow processing that emphasizes the physical structure of the stimulus. For example, if words are flashed on a screen, structural encoding registers such things as how they were printed (capital, lowercase, and so on) or the length of the words (how many letters). Further analysis may result in *phonemic encoding*, which emphasizes what a word sounds like. Phonemic encoding involves naming or saying (perhaps silently) the words. Finally, *semantic encoding* emphasizes the meaning of verbal input. Semantic encoding involves thinking about the objects and actions the words represent. **Levels-of-processing theory** **proposes that deeper levels of processing result in longer-lasting memory codes.**

In one experimental test of levels-of-processing theory, Craik and Tulving (1975) compared the durability of structural, phonemic, and semantic encoding. They directed subjects' attention to particular aspects of briefly presented stimulus words by asking them questions about various characteristics of the words (examples are in Figure 7.4). The questions were designed to engage the subjects in different levels of processing. The key hypothesis was that retention of the stimulus words would increase as subjects moved from structural to phonemic to semantic encoding. After responding to 60 words, the subjects received an unexpected test of their memory for the words. As predicted, the subjects' recall was low after structural encoding, notably better after phonemic encoding, and highest after semantic encoding.

The hypothesis that deeper processing leads to enhanced memory has been replicated in many studies (Koriat & Melkman, 1987; Lockhart & Craik, 1990). Nonetheless, the levels-of-processing model is not without its weaknesses. Critics ask, what exactly is a "level" of processing? And how do we determine whether one level is deeper than another? Craik and Lockhart had hoped that

the *time required for processing* would prove to be a good indicator of depth. However, they found that it's possible to design a task in which structural encoding takes longer than deeper, semantic encoding. Thus, processing time has not proven to be a reliable index of processing depth, and the levels in levels-of-processing theory remain vaguely defined.

Enriching Encoding

Structural, phonemic, and semantic encoding do not exhaust your options when it comes to forming memory codes. There are other dimensions to encoding, dimensions that can enrich the encoding process and thereby improve memory.

Elaboration

Semantic encoding can often be enhanced through a process called elaboration. **Elaboration is linking a stimulus to other information at the time of encoding.** For example, let's say you read that phobias are often caused by classical conditioning, and you apply this idea to your own fear of spiders. In doing so, you are engaging in elaboration. The additional associations created by elaboration usually help people remember information. Differences in elaboration can help explain why different approaches to semantic processing result in varied amounts of retention (Craik & Tulving, 1975).

Visual Imagery

Imagery—the creation of visual images to represent the words to be remembered—can also be used to enrich encoding. Of course, some words are easier to create images for than others. If you were asked to remember the word *juggler*, you could readily form an image of someone juggling balls. However, if you were asked to remember the word *truth*, you would probably have more difficulty forming a suitable image. The difference is that *juggler* refers to a concrete object whereas *truth* refers to an abstract concept. Allan

Figure 7.4. Levels-of-processing theory. According to Craik and Lockhart (1972), structural, phonemic, and semantic encoding—which can be elicited by questions such as those shown on the right—involve progressively deeper levels of processing, which should result in more durable memories.

Level of processing	Type of encoding	Example of questions used to elicit appropriate encoding
Shallow processing	Structural encoding: emphasizes the physical structure of the stimulus	Is the word written in capital letters?
Intermediate processing	Phonemic encoding: emphasizes what a word sounds like	Does the word rhyme with weight?
Deep processing	Semantic encoding: emphasizes the meaning of verbal input	Would the word fit in the sentence: "He met a _____ on the street"?

Depth of processing

Figure 7.5. The effect of visual imagery on retention. Subjects given pairs of words to remember showed better recall for high-imagery pairings, demonstrating that visual imagery enriches encoding. (Data from Paivio, Smythe, & Yuille, 1968)

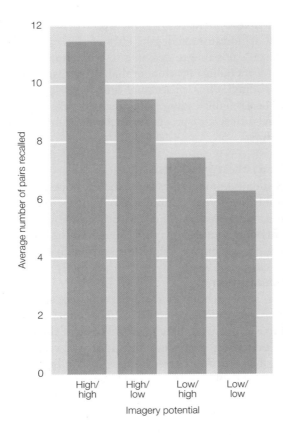

Paivio (1969) points out that it is easier to form images of concrete objects than of abstract concepts. He believes that this ease of image formation affects memory.

The beneficial effect of imagery on memory was demonstrated in a study by Paivio, Smythe, and Yuille (1968). They asked subjects to learn a list of 16 pairs of words. They manipulated whether the words were concrete, high-imagery words or abstract, low-imagery words. In terms of imagery potential, the list contained four types of pairings: high-high (*juggler-dress*), high-low (*letter-effort*), low-high (*duty-hotel*), and low-low (*quality-necessity*). Figure 7.5 shows the recall for each type of pairing. The impact of imagery is quite evident. The best recall was of high-high pairings, and the worst recall was of low-low pairings.

According to Paivio (1986), imagery facilitates memory because it provides a second kind of memory code, and two codes are better than one. His **dual-coding theory** holds that memory is **enhanced by forming both semantic and visual codes, since either can lead to recall.** The value of visual imagery demonstrates once again that encoding plays a critical role in memory. But encoding is only one of the three key processes in memory. We turn next to the process of storage, which for many people is virtually synonymous with memory.

STORAGE: MAINTAINING INFORMATION IN MEMORY

In their efforts to understand memory storage, theorists have historically related it to the technologies of their age (Roediger, 1980). One of the earliest models used to explain memory storage was the wax tablet. Both Aristotle and Plato compared memory to a block of wax that differed in size and hardness for various individuals. Remembering, according to this analogy, was like stamping an impression into the wax. As long as the image remained in the wax, the memory would remain intact.

Current theories of memory reflect the technological advances of the 20th century. Many modern theories draw an analogy between information storage by computers and information storage in human memory. These *information-processing theories* emphasize how information flows through a series of separate memory stores.

CONCEPT CHECK 7.1

Recognizing Factors in Memory Encoding

Check your understanding of various factors at work in memory encoding by identifying each of the vignettes below as an example of one of the following: (a) semantic encoding, (b) elaboration, (c) visual imagery, (d) attention. You'll find the answers in Appendix A.

_____ 1. As Craig reads the next chapter in his psychology textbook for the first time, he stops whenever he comes across a word he doesn't understand and looks it up in a dictionary. In addition, at the end of each paragraph he stops and quizzes himself to determine whether he understands what he's just read.

_____ 2. On the bus riding home from work, Pat relaxes by reading books about baseball. He's really interested in learning the intricacies of baseball strategy. It's a more challenging subject than he thought, so he really has to concentrate on shutting out the noise and other distractions that go along with riding a bus during rush hour.

_____ 3. Lulu has discovered that many of the foreign-sounding vocabulary terms in her anatomy and physiology course are similar to common English words and that if she forms mental pictures of the things these English words remind her of, she's often better able to remember the meanings of the vocabulary terms.

_____ 4. While Dr. Riley is lecturing on theories of motivation, Harold is thinking of examples in his own life of each of the concepts she's introducing.

The most prominent information-processing model of memory holds that there are three memory stores: a *sensory store*, a *short-term store*, and a *long-term store*. Many psychologists have contributed to this theory, but Richard Atkinson and Richard Shiffrin (1968, 1971) were especially influential. We will use their model, which is diagrammed in Figure 7.6, as a general guide in our discussion of memory storage. According to this model, incoming information must pass through two temporary storage buffers (the sensory and short-term stores) before it can be transferred into long-term storage.

Sensory Memory

The *sensory memory* preserves information in its original sensory form for a brief time, usually only a fraction of a second. Sensory memory allows the sensation of a visual pattern, sound, or touch to linger for a brief moment after the sensory stimulation is over. In the case of vision, people really perceive an *afterimage* rather than the actual stimulus. You can demonstrate the existence of afterimages for yourself by rapidly moving a lighted sparkler in circles in the dark. If you move the sparkler fast enough, you should see a complete circle even though the light source is only a single point (see the adjacent photo). The sensory memory preserves the sensory image long enough for you to perceive a continuous circle rather than separate points of light.

The brief preservation of sensations in sensory memory gives you additional time to try to recognize stimuli. However, you'd better take advantage of sensory storage immediately, because it doesn't last long. In a classic experiment, George Sperling (1960) demonstrated that the memory trace in the visual sensory store decays in about one-quarter of a second. Memory traces may last a little longer (perhaps up to 2 seconds) in other senses, but sensory storage is still fleeting, to say the least. However, the sensory store has a fairly large capacity. It can register up to 25 stimuli and perhaps more.

Short-Term Memory

Short-term memory (STM) is a limited-capacity store that can maintain unrehearsed information for about 20 to 30 seconds. In contrast, information stored in long-term memory may last weeks, months, or years. Actually, you can maintain information in your short-term store for longer than 30 seconds. How? Primarily, by engaging in *rehearsal*—**the process of repetitively verbalizing or thinking about information.** You surely have used the rehearsal process on many occasions. For instance, when you obtain a phone number from the information operator, you probably recite it over and over until you can dial the

Because the image of the sparkler persists briefly in sensory memory, when the sparkler is moved fast enough, the blending of afterimages causes people to see a continuous circle instead of a succession of individual points.

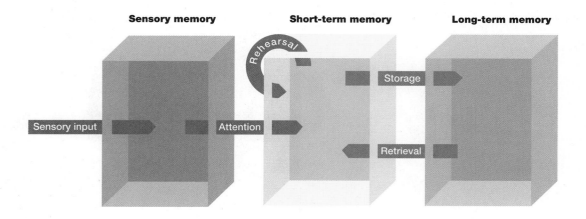

Figure 7.6. The Atkinson and Shiffrin (1971) model of memory storage. Atkinson and Shiffrin proposed that memory is made up of three information stores. *Sensory memory* can hold a large amount of information just long enough for a small portion of it to be selected for longer storage. *Short-term memory* has a limited capacity, and unless aided by rehearsal, its storage duration is brief. *Long-term memory* can store an apparently unlimited amount of information for indeterminate periods.

Sensory memory — Short-term memory — Long-term memory

Rehearsal

Sensory input — Attention — Storage — Retrieval

number. Rehearsal keeps recycling the information through your short-term memory. In theory, this recycling could go on indefinitely, but in reality something eventually distracts you and breaks the rehearsal loop.

People's dependence on recitation to maintain information in short-term memory is apparent from the kinds of mistakes they tend to make when their efforts break down. For example, suppose that you were asked to remember a list of random letters such as

Q P L H S X

presented briefly on a screen. Mistakes on this task usually involve *acoustic confusions*, in which the incorrect answers *sound* like the correct answers (Conrad, 1964; Sperling, 1967). For instance, you might mistakenly convert P to E because they sound alike. Notice, you are far less likely to convert P to R because they *look* alike. Even when information is presented visually, people tend to make acoustic mistakes, because they largely depend on phonemic encoding in short-term memory.

Durability of Storage

Without rehearsal, information in short-term memory quickly decays with the passage of time. This rapid decay was demonstrated in a study by Peterson and Peterson (1959). They measured how long undergraduates could remember three consonants if they couldn't rehearse them. To prevent rehearsal, the Petersons required the students to count backward by threes from the time the consonants were presented until they saw a light that signaled the recall test (see Figure 7.7). The recall test occurred 3, 6, 9, 12, 15, or 18 seconds after the subjects began counting. The Petersons found that subjects' recall accuracy declined rapidly between 3 and 18 seconds. Their results indicated that when people cannot rehearse unfamiliar material, the material is quickly lost from STM. Without rehearsal, the maximum duration of STM storage is only about 20–30 seconds.

Capacity of Storage

Short-term memory is also limited in the number of items it can hold. The small capacity of STM was pointed out by George Miller (1956) in a famous paper called "The Magical Number Seven, Plus or Minus Two: Some Limits on Our Capacity for Processing Information." Miller noticed that people could recall only about seven items in tasks that required them to remember unfamiliar material. The common thread in these tasks, Miller argued, was that they required the use of STM.

When short-term memory is filled to capacity, the insertion of new information often *displaces* some of the information currently in STM. For example, if you're memorizing a ten-item list of

"The Magical Number Seven, Plus or Minus Two."
GEORGE MILLER

Figure 7.7. Peterson and Peterson's (1959) study of short-term memory. After a warning light was flashed, the subjects were given three consonants to remember. The researchers prevented rehearsals by giving the subjects a three-digit number at the same time and telling them to count backward by three from that number until given the signal to recall the letters. By varying the amount of time between stimulus presentation and recall, Peterson and Peterson were able to measure the rate of decay in short-term memory.

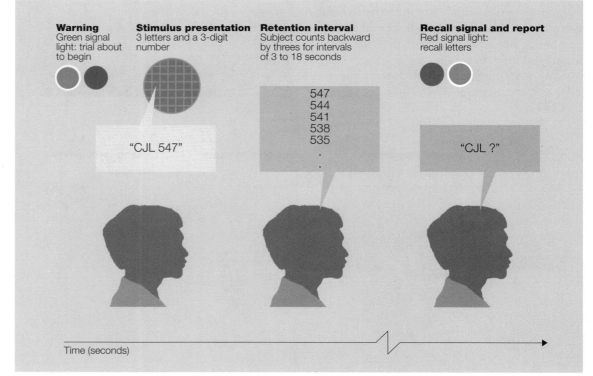

CHAPTER SEVEN

basic chemical elements, the eighth, ninth, and tenth items in the list will begin to "bump out" earlier items. Similarly, if you're reciting the phone number of a pizza parlor you're about to call when someone asks, "How much is this pizza going to cost?" your retrieval of the cost information into STM may knock part of the phone number out of STM. The limited capacity of STM constrains people's ability to perform tasks in which they need to mentally juggle various pieces of information (Baddeley & Hitch, 1974).

You can increase the capacity of your short-term memory by combining stimuli into larger, possibly higher-order, units called *chunks* (Simon, 1974). **A *chunk* is a group of familiar stimuli stored as a single unit.** You can demonstrate the effect of chunking by asking someone to recall a sequence of 12 letters grouped in the following way:

FB - ITW - AC - IAIB - M

As you read the letters aloud, pause at the hyphens. Your subject will probably attempt to remember each letter separately because there are no obvious groups or chunks. But a string of 12 letters is too long for STM, so errors are likely. Now present the same string of letters to another person, but place the pauses in the following locations:

FBI - TWA - CIA - IBM

The letters now form four familiar chunks that should occupy only four slots in short-term memory, resulting in successful recall (Bower & Springston, 1970).

To successfully chunk the letters I B M, a subject must first recognize these letters as a familiar unit. This familiarity has to be stored somewhere in long-term memory. Hence, in this case information was transferred from long-term into short-term memory. This is not unusual. People routinely draw information out of their long-term memory banks to evaluate and understand information that they are working with in short-term memory.

Short-Term Memory as "Working Memory"

Twenty years of research eventually uncovered a number of problems with the original model of short-term memory (Cowan, 1988; Hilgard & Bower, 1981). Among other things, studies showed that short-term memory is *not* limited to phonemic encoding and that decay and displacement are

not the only processes responsible for the loss of information from STM. These and other findings suggest that short-term memory involves more than a simple rehearsal buffer, as originally envisioned. To make sense of such findings, Alan Baddeley (1976, 1989) has proposed a more complex model of short-term memory that characterizes it as "working memory."

According to Baddeley, working memory consists of three components. The first is the *rehearsal loop* that represented all of STM in the original model. This component is at work when you use recitation to temporarily hold on to a phone number. The second component in working memory is a *visuospatial sketchpad* that permits people to temporarily hold and manipulate visual images. This component is at work when you try to mentally rearrange the furniture in your bedroom. The third component is an *executive control system*. It handles the limited amount of information that people can juggle at one time, as they engage in reasoning and decision making. This component is at work when you mentally weigh all the pros and cons before deciding whether to buy a particular car.

The two key characteristics that originally defined short-term memory—small capacity and short storage duration—are still present in the concept of working memory. However, Baddeley's model accounts for evidence that STM handles a greater variety of functions and depends on more complicated processes than previously thought.

Long-Term Memory

Long-term memory (LTM) is an unlimited capacity store that can hold information over lengthy periods of time. Unlike sensory and short-term memory, which decay rapidly, LTM can store information indefinitely. Long-term memories are durable. Some information may remain in LTM across an entire lifetime.

Durability: Is Storage Permanent?

One point of view is that all information stored in long-term memory is stored there *permanently*. According to this view, forgetting occurs only because people sometimes cannot *retrieve* needed information from LTM. To draw an analogy, imagine that memories are stored in LTM like marbles in a barrel. According to this view, none of the marbles ever leak out. When you forget, you just aren't able to dig out the right marble, but it's there—somewhere. An alternative point of view assumes that some memories stored in LTM do vanish forever. According to this view, the barrel

People throughout the United States were watching on television when the *Challenger* space shuttle exploded in the skies over Florida in 1986. For these observers, their experience of the *Challenger* tragedy is likely to be a *flashbulb memory*—one that will persist in vivid detail.

Figure 7.8. The serial-position effect. After hearing a list of items to remember, people reliably recall more of the items from the beginning (primacy effect) and the end (recency effect) of the list than from the middle, producing the characteristic U-shaped curve shown here.

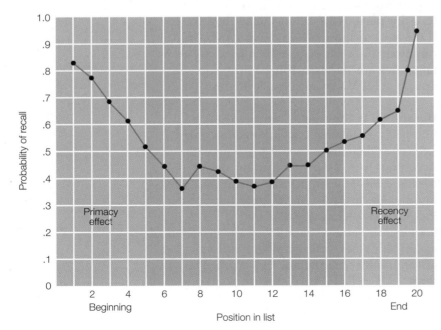

is leaky and some of the marbles roll out, never to return.

The existence of *flashbulb memories* provides some support for the notion that LTM storage may be permanent. ***Flashbulb memories*, which are unusually vivid and detailed recollections of momentous events**, provide striking examples of seemingly permanent storage (Brown & Kulik, 1977). Many American adults, for instance, can remember exactly where they were, what they were doing, and how they felt when they learned that President John F. Kennedy had been shot. You may have a similar recollection related to the explosion of the *Challenger* spacecraft (see the above photo).

Evidence consistent with the notion of permanent memory storage also comes from reports of

exceptional recall through hypnosis. Hypnotized subjects who have been regressed back to early childhood have described in remarkable detail events that they thought they had forgotten (Spiegel & Spiegel, 1985). These hypnosis-aided recoveries of lost memories suggest that normal forgetfulness is just a matter of poor retrieval.

Do these lines of evidence demonstrate that LTM storage is permanent? No, there are problems with both lines of evidence just discussed. Although flashbulb memories are remarkably durable, studies suggest that they are neither as accurate nor as special as once believed (Neisser & Harsch, 1992). Like other memories, they become less detailed and complete with time (Christianson, 1989; McCloskey, Wible, & Cohen, 1988). Similarly, when hypnosis-aided recollections have been double-checked, they have often turned out to be inaccurate (Orne & Dinges, 1989). That is, hypnotized subjects often make things up and distort recollections to be consistent with their current beliefs. Thus, although psychologists can't absolutely rule out the possibility, there is no convincing evidence that all memories are stored away permanently (Loftus & Loftus, 1980).

Transferring Information into Long-Term Memory

How is information transferred from short-term memory into long-term memory? According to Atkinson and Shiffrin (1971), information that is being maintained in short-term memory through *rehearsal* is gradually absorbed into long-term memory. Rundus (1971) investigated this hypothesis by asking undergraduates to recall a list of 20 words immediately after they had rehearsed the words aloud. The words were presented slowly, one at a time, so subjects had time to rehearse some of the list before hearing a new word. Rundus kept track of how often each word was rehearsed.

Figure 7.8 shows the probability of recall for each word as a function of its position on Rundus's list. The resulting U-shaped curve, called the *serial-position effect*, is often observed when subjects are tested on their memory of lists. **The *serial-position effect* occurs when subjects show better recall for items at the beginning and end of a list than for items in the middle.** This effect includes two components—a primacy effect and a recency effect— that are often seen in memory research. A ***primacy effect*** occurs when items near the beginning of a list are recalled better than other items. A ***recency effect*** occurs when

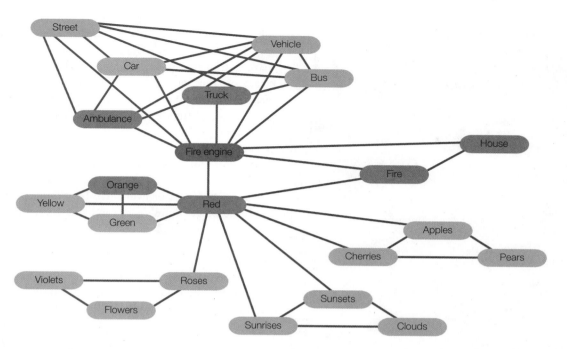

Figure 7.9. A semantic network. Much of the organization of long-term memory depends on networks of associations among concepts. In this highly simplified depiction of a fragment of a semantic network, the shorter the line linking any two concepts, the stronger the association between them. The coloration of the concept boxes represents activation of the concepts. This is how the network might look just after a person hears the words *fire engine.* (Adapted from Collins & Loftus, 1975)

items near the end of a list are recalled better than other items.

The mechanisms underlying the serial-position effect are the subject of considerable debate (Greene, 1992). The most widely cited explanation asserts that the seemingly incompatible primacy and recency effects occur together because the short-term and long-term memory stores operate separately. The primacy effect reflects LTM storage. The words at the beginning of the list get rehearsed more often than the others. Hence, they're more likely to be transferred into LTM than later words. In contrast, the recency effect reflects STM storage. Since the words at the end of the list are the ones most recently presented, they're still available in STM if subjects' recall is tested promptly.

Organization in Long-Term Memory

Consider what your plight would be if your college or local library did not organize its holdings. Imagine searching among hundreds of thousands of randomly shelved books for a specific book on 17th-century Canadian history. Your term paper would probably be long overdue before you found the needed book.

Organization is just as important for long-term memory. Although LTM storage does not appear to be permanent, long-term memory undeniably houses a vast amount of information. Without at least some organization, that huge amount of information would be virtually useless. Unfortunately, long-term memory stores do not appear to be organized as systematically as a well-run library. Research suggests that LTM is characterized by a hodgepodge of overlapping organizational frameworks.

SEMANTIC NETWORKS Much of people's knowledge seems to be organized into semantic networks (Collins & Loftus, 1975). **A *semantic network* consists of nodes representing concepts, joined together by pathways that link related concepts.** Figure 7.9 shows a small semantic network. The ovals are the nodes, and the words inside the ovals are the interlinked concepts. The lines connecting the nodes are the pathways. A more detailed figure would label the pathways to show how the concepts are related to one another. However, in this instance the relations should be fairly clear. For example, *fire engine* is linked to *red* because of its color, to *vehicle* because it's a vehicle, and to *house* because fires often occur in houses. The length of each pathway represents the degree of association between two concepts. Shorter pathways imply stronger associations.

Semantic networks have proven useful in explaining why thinking about one word (such as *butter*) can make a closely related word (such as *bread*) easier to remember (Meyer & Schvaneveldt, 1976). According to Collins and Loftus (1975), when people think about a word, their thoughts naturally go to related words. These theorists call this process *spreading activation* within a semantic network. They assume that activation spreads out along the pathways of the semantic network surrounding the word. They also theorize that the strength of this activation decreases as it travels

Professor Smith's office is shown in this photo. Follow the instructions in the text to learn how Brewer and Treyens (1981) used it in a study of memory.

who had briefly visited the office shown in the photo. Most subjects recalled the desks and chairs, but few recalled the wine bottle or the picnic basket. Indeed, the tendency to recall things that are consistent with a schema can lead to memory errors. For instance, nine subjects in the Brewer and Treyens study falsely recalled that the office contained books. Perhaps you made the same mistake.

Information stored in memory is often organized around schemas (Thorndyke, 1984). Thus, recall of an object or event will be influenced by both the actual details observed and the person's schemas for these objects and events.

In summary, memory storage is a complex matter, involving several memory stores and a host of organizational devices. To help you make sense of all this information, Figure 7.10 provides an overview of memory storage. It summarizes how we have elaborated on, and sometimes amended, the model of three memory stores introduced at the beginning of this section. It closes out our discussion of memory storage, as we now turn to the process of retrieval.

outward, much as ripples decrease in size as they radiate outward from a rock tossed into a pond. Consider again the semantic network shown in Figure 7.9. If subjects see the word *red*, words that are closely linked to it (such as *orange*) should be easier to recall than words that have longer links (such as *sunrises*).

SCHEMAS Imagine that you've just visited Professor Smith's office, which is shown in the above photo. Take a brief look at the photo and then cover it up. Now pretend that you want to describe Professor Smith's office to a friend. Write down what you saw in the office (the picture).

After you finish, compare your description with the picture. Chances are, your description will include elements—filing cabinets, for instance—that were *not* in the office. This common phenomenon demonstrates how *schemas* can influence memory.

A *schema* **is an organized cluster of knowledge about a particular object or sequence of events.** For example, college students have schemas for what professors' offices are like. People are more likely to remember things that are consistent with their schemas than things that are not. This principle was quite apparent when Brewer and Treyens (1981) tested the recall of 30 subjects

RETRIEVAL: GETTING INFORMATION OUT OF MEMORY

Entering information into long-term memory is a worthy goal, but an insufficient one if you can't get the information back out again when you need it. Fortunately, recall often occurs without much effort. But occasionally a planned search of LTM is necessary. For instance, imagine that you were asked to recall the names of all 50 states in the United States. You would probably conduct your memory search systematically, recalling states in alphabetical order or by geographical location. Although this example is rather simple, retrieval is a complex process, as you'll see in this section.

Using Cues to Aid Retrieval

At the beginning of this chapter we discussed the *tip-of-the-tongue phenomenon*—**the temporary inability to remember something you know, accompanied by a feeling that it's just out of reach.** The tip-of-the-tongue phenomenon is a common experience that occurs to the average person about once a week (A. Brown, 1991). It clearly represents a failure in retrieval. Fortunately, memories can often be jogged with *retrieval cues*—stimuli that help gain access to memo-

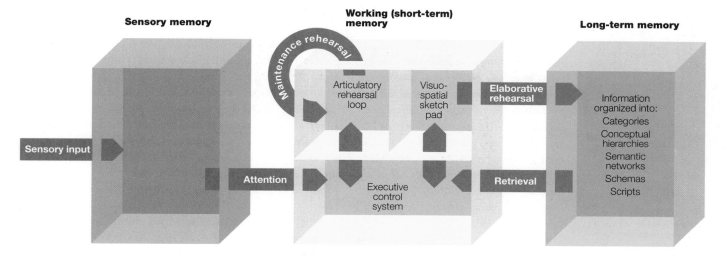

Sensory memory

Working (short-term) memory

Maintenance rehearsal

Sensory input

Articulatory rehearsal loop

Visuo-spatial sketch pad

Elaborative rehearsal

Long-term memory

Attention

Executive control system

Retrieval

Information organized into:
Categories
Conceptual hierarchies
Semantic networks
Schemas
Scripts

ries. This was apparent when Roger Brown and David McNeill (1966) studied the tip-of-the-tongue phenomenon. They gave subjects definitions of obscure words and asked them to think of the words. Our example at the beginning of the chapter (the definition for *nepotism*) was taken from their study. Brown and McNeill found that subjects groping for obscure words were correct in guessing the first letter of the missing word 57% of the time. This figure far exceeds chance and shows that partial recollections are often headed in the right direction. Thus, when partial recollections give you clues about the sound or first letter of a word on the tip of your tongue, it pays to follow up on these clues (Read & Bruce, 1982).

Reinstating the Context of an Event

Let's test your memory: What did you have for breakfast two days ago? If you can't immediately answer, you might begin by imagining yourself sitting at the breakfast table. Trying to recall an event by putting yourself back in the context in which it occurred involves working with *context cues* to aid retrieval.

Context cues often facilitate the retrieval of information (Smith, 1988). Most people have experienced the effects of context cues on many occasions. For instance, when people return after a number of years to a place where they used to live, they typically are flooded with long-forgotten memories. Or consider how often you have gone from one room to another to get something (scissors, perhaps), only to discover that you can't remember what you were after. However, when you return to the first room (the original context), you suddenly recall what it was ("Of course, the scissors!"). These examples illustrate the po-

tentially powerful effects of context cues on memory.

Reconstructing Memories

When you retrieve information from long-term memory, you're not able to pull up a "mental videotape" that provides an exact replay of the past. To some extent, your memories are sketchy *reconstructions* of the past. The reconstructive nature of retrieval is emphasized in schema theories of memory (Brewer & Nakamura, 1984). These theories propose that part of what people recall about an event is the details of that particular event and part is a reconstruction of the event based on their schemas. (Remember your visit to Professor Smith's office?) According to this view, general, schematic knowledge becomes more influential in determining recall as the details of an event blur with the passage of time.

Sulin and Dooling (1974) demonstrated how memory becomes progressively more reconstruc-

Figure 7.10. An updated overview of memory storage. This diagram builds on the Atkinson and Shiffrin model (see Figure 7.6) to summarize our coverage of memory storage. The model shown here depicts short-term memory as a multicomponent working memory, differentiates between maintenance and elaborative rehearsal, and lists some of the organizational frameworks used in long-term memory. Also consult Concept Check 7.2 to compare the encoding, storage capacity, and storage duration of the three memory stores.

CONCEPT CHECK 7.2
Comparing the Memory Stores

Check your understanding of the three memory stores by filling in the blanks in the table below. The answers can be found in Appendix A.

Feature	Sensory memory	Short-term memory	Long-term memory
Encoding format	Copy of input	_____	_____
Storage capacity	Large	_____	_____
Storage duration	_____	Up to 30 seconds	_____

"One reason most of us, as jurors, place so much faith in eyewitness testimony is that we are unaware of how many factors influence its accuracy."
ELIZABETH LOFTUS

Figure 7.11. The effect of leading questions on eyewitness recall. Subjects who were asked leading questions in which cars were described as *hitting* or *smashing* each other were prone to recall the same accident differently one week later, demonstrating the reconstructive nature of memory.

tive. In their study, subjects read the following biographical passage:

Adolf Hitler strove to undermine the existing government to satisfy his political ambitions. Many of the people of his country supported his efforts. Current political problems made it relatively easy for Hitler to take over. Certain groups remained loyal to the old government and caused Hitler trouble. He confronted these groups directly and so silenced them. He became a ruthless, uncontrollable dictator. The ultimate effect of his rule was the downfall of his country. (Sulin & Dooling, 1974, p. 256)

Subjects were given a true-false memory test on information in the story either 5 minutes or 1 week after reading the passage. If people reconstructed the passage, they should have falsely "recalled" information that fit with their preexisting knowledge of Hitler. Subjects who were tested 5 minutes after reading the passage made relatively few mistakes of this type. However, subjects who were tested a week later made more reconstructive errors. They were much more likely to falsely recall information such as "He was obsessed with the desire to conquer the world," which reflected their general knowledge of Hitler rather than the content of the passage.

Research by Elizabeth Loftus (1979, 1992) and others on the *misinformation effect* has shown that reconstructive distortions show up frequently in eyewitness testimony. For example, in one study Loftus and Palmer (1974) showed subjects a vid-

eotape of an automobile accident. Subjects were then "grilled" as if they were providing eyewitness testimony, and biasing information was introduced. Some subjects were asked, "How fast were the cars going when they *hit* each other?" Other subjects were asked, "How fast were the cars going when they *smashed into* each other?" A week later, subjects' recall of the accident was tested and they were asked whether they remembered seeing any broken glass in the accident (there was none). Subjects who had earlier been asked about the cars *smashing into* each other were more likely to "recall" broken glass. Why would they add this detail to their reconstructions of the accident? Probably because broken glass is consistent with their schemas for cars *smashing* together (see Figure 7.11). Although postevent misinformation does not inevitably introduce errors into recollections of events, the misinformation effect has been replicated in numerous studies by Loftus and other researchers (Lindsay, 1993).

However, there is considerable debate about the mechanisms underlying the effect (Ceci & Bruck, 1993). Loftus (1979) has argued for an "overwriting" explanation in which the new misinformation destroys and replaces the original memory of the event (much like saving a new version of a file on a computer). An alternative explanation is that the new misinformation interferes with the retrieval of the original memory (Bekerian & Bowers, 1983). Other theorists argue that subjects can access both the original memory and the altered memory, but they have difficulty distinguishing which one was the original (Lindsay & Johnson, 1989). This explanation attributes the misinformation effect to difficulties in *source monitoring—the process of making attributions about the origins of memories.* According to Marcia Johnson and her colleagues (Johnson, Hashtroudi, & Lindsay, 1993; Lindsay & Johnson, 1991), memories are not tagged with labels that specify their sources. Hence, when people pull up specific memory records, they have to make decisions *at the time of retrieval* about where the memories came from. **A *source-monitoring error* occurs when a memory derived from one source is misattributed to another source.** For example, you might "remember" something that your roomate said as having been said by your psychology professor, or you may recall something you heard on *Oprah* as having been in your psychology textbook.

Evidence on the reconstructive nature of memory clearly shows that people's recollections are not exact replicas of their experiences. How-

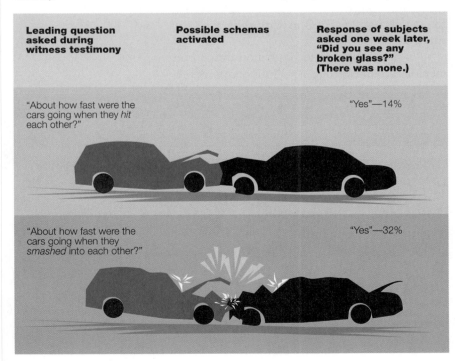

Leading question asked during witness testimony	Possible schemas activated	Response of subjects asked one week later, "Did you see any broken glass?" (There was none.)
"About how fast were the cars going when they *hit* each other?"		"Yes"—14%
"About how fast were the cars going when they *smashed* into each other?"		"Yes"—32%

ever, memory distortions are not due solely to loose reconstruction during retrieval. Some of these distortions are introduced during encoding or storage. This interdependence of encoding, storage, and retrieval will be particularly apparent in our discussion of forgetting.

FORGETTING: WHEN MEMORY LAPSES

Why do people forget information—even information they would like very much to remember? Many theorists believe that there isn't one simple answer to this perplexing question. They point to the complex, multifaceted nature of memory and assert that forgetting can be caused by deficiencies in encoding, storage, retrieval, or some combination of these processes.

How Quickly We Forget: Ebbinghaus's Forgetting Curve

The first person to conduct scientific studies of forgetting was Hermann Ebbinghaus. He published a series of insightful memory studies way back in 1885. Ebbinghaus studied only one subject—himself. To give himself lots of new material to memorize, he invented *nonsense syllables—* **consonant-vowel-consonant arrangements that do not correspond to words** (such as BAF, XOF, VIR, and MEQ). He wanted to work with meaningless materials that would be uncontaminated by his previous learning.

Ebbinghaus was a remarkably dedicated researcher. For instance, in one study he went through over 14,000 practice repetitions, as he tirelessly memorized 420 lists of nonsense syllables (Slamecka, 1985). He tested his memory of these lists after various time intervals had elapsed. Figure 7.12 shows what he found. This diagram, called **a** *forgetting curve,* **graphs retention and forgetting over time.** Ebbinghaus's forgetting curve shows a precipitous drop in retention during the first few hours after the nonsense syllables were memorized. He forgot more than 60% of the syllables in less than 9 hours! Thus, he concluded that most forgetting occurs very rapidly after learning something.

That's a depressing conclusion. What is the point of memorizing information if you're going to forget it all right away? Fortunately, subsequent research showed that Ebbinghaus's forgetting curve was unusually steep (Postman, 1985). Forgetting usually isn't as swift or as extensive as Ebbinghaus thought. One problem was that he

was working with such meaningless material. When subjects memorize more meaningful material, such as prose or poetry, forgetting curves aren't nearly as steep. Studies of how well people recall their high school classmates suggest that forgetting curves for autobiographical information are even shallower (Bahrick, Bahrick, & Wittlinger, 1975). Also, different methods of measuring forgetting yield varied estimates of how quickly people forget. This variation underscores the importance of the methods used to measure forgetting, the matter we turn to next.

Measures of Forgetting

To study forgetting empirically, psychologists need to be able to measure it precisely. Measures of forgetting inevitably measure retention as well. *Retention* **refers to the proportion of material retained (remembered).** In studies of forgetting, the results may be reported in terms of the amount forgotten or the amount retained. In these studies, the *retention interval* is the length of time between the presentation of materials to be remembered and the measurement of forgetting. Psychologists use three methods to measure forgetting: recall, recognition, and relearning (Lockhart, 1992).

Who is the current U.S. secretary of state? What movie won the Academy Award for best picture last year? These questions involve recall measures of forgetting. **A** *recall* **measure of retention requires subjects to reproduce information on their own without any cues.** If you were to take a recall test on a list of 25 words you had memorized, you would simply be told to write down on a blank sheet of paper as many of the words as you could remember.

In contrast, in a recognition test you might be shown a list of 100 words and asked to choose the 25 words that you had memorized. **A** *recognition* **measure of retention requires subjects to se-**

Figure 7.12. Ebbinghaus's forgetting curve for nonsense syllables. From his experiments on himself, Ebbinghaus concluded that forgetting is extremely rapid immediately after the original learning and then levels off. However, subsequent research has suggested that this forgetting curve is unusually steep. (Data from Ebbinghaus, 1885)

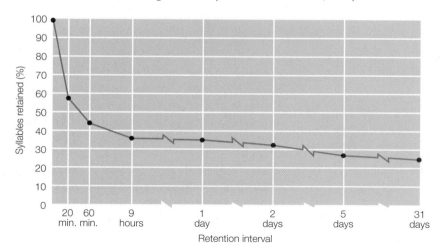

lect previously learned information from an array of options. Subjects not only have cues to work with, they have the answers right in front of them. In educational testing, essay questions and fill-in-the-blanks questions are recall measures of retention. Multiple-choice, true-false, and matching questions are recognition measures.

If you're like most students, you probably prefer multiple-choice tests over essay tests. This preference is understandable, because evidence shows that recognition measures (such as multiple-choice tests) tend to yield higher scores than recall measures (such as essay tests) of memory for the same information (Nelson, 1978). There are two ways of looking at this difference. One view is that recognition tests are especially *sensitive* measures of retention. The other view is that recognition tests are excessively *easy* measures of retention.

Actually, there is no guarantee that a recognition test will be easier than a recall test. This tends to be the case, but the difficulty of a recognition test can vary greatly, depending on the number, similarity, and plausibility of the options provided as possible answers. To illustrate, see whether you know the answer to the following multiple-choice question:

> *The capital of Washington is:*
> *a. Seattle*
> *b. Spokane*
> *c. Tacoma*
> *d. Olympia*

Most students who aren't from Washington find this a fairly difficult question. The answer is Olympia. Now take a look at the next question:

> *The capital of Washington is:*
> *a. London*
> *b. New York*
> *c. Tokyo*
> *d. Olympia*

Virtually anyone can answer this question because the incorrect options are readily dismissed. Although this illustration is a bit extreme, it shows that two recognition measures of the same information can be dramatically different in difficulty.

The third method of measuring forgetting is relearning. **A *relearning* measure of retention requires a subject to memorize information a second time to determine how much time or effort is saved by having learned it before.** To use this method, a researcher measures how much time (or how many practice trials) a subject needs to memorize something. At a later date, the subject is asked to relearn the information. The researcher measures how much more quickly the material is memorized the second time. Subjects' *savings scores* provide an estimate of their retention. For example, if it takes you 20 minutes to memorize a list the first time and only 5 minutes to memorize it a week later, you've saved 15 minutes. Your savings score of 75% ($^{15}/_{20} = ^3/_4 = 75\%$) suggests that you have retained 75% and forgotten the remaining 25% of the information. Relearning measures can detect retention that is overlooked by recognition tests (Nelson, 1978).

Why We Forget

Measuring forgetting is only the first step in the long journey toward explaining why forgetting occurs. In this section, we explore the possible causes of forgetting, looking at factors that may affect encoding, storage, and retrieval processes.

Ineffective Encoding

A great deal of forgetting may only *appear* to be forgetting. The information in question may never have been inserted into memory in the first place. Since you can't really forget something you never learned, this phenomenon is sometimes called *pseudoforgetting*. We opened the chapter with an example of pseudoforgetting. People usually assume that they know what a penny looks like, but most have actually failed to encode this information. Pseudoforgetting is usually due to *lack of attention*.

Even when memory codes *are* formed for new information, subsequent forgetting may be due to *ineffective* encoding. The research on levels of processing shows that some approaches to encoding lead to more forgetting than others (Craik & Tulving, 1975). For example, if you're distracted while you read your textbooks, you may be doing little more than saying the words to yourself. This is *phonemic encoding*, which is inferior to *semantic encoding* for retention of verbal material. When you can't remember the information that you've read, your forgetting may be due to ineffective encoding.

Decay

Instead of focusing on encoding, decay theory attributes forgetting to the impermanence of memory *storage*. **Decay theory** proposes that for-

getting occurs because memory traces fade with time. The implicit assumption is that decay occurs in the physiological mechanisms responsible for memories. According to decay theory, the mere passage of time produces forgetting. This notion meshes nicely with commonsense views of forgetting.

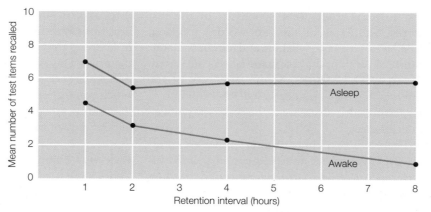

As we saw earlier, decay does contribute to the loss of information from the sensory and short-term memory stores. However, the critical task for theories of forgetting is to explain the loss of information from long-term memory. Researchers have *not* been able to demonstrate that decay causes LTM forgetting.

If decay theory is correct, the principal cause of forgetting should be the passage of time. In studies of long-term memory, however, researchers have found that time passage is not as influential as what happens during the time interval. This was first shown in a clever experiment by Jenkins and Dallenbach (1924). Their subjects memorized a list of nonsense syllables and were tested for recall after 1, 2, 4, or 8 hours. The catch was that half the subjects slept during the retention interval and the other half went about their normal waking activities. According to decay theory, since the same amount of time had elapsed for both groups, they should have exhibited an equal amount of forgetting. However, as you can see in Figure 7.13, the subjects who remained awake forgot more than those who slept.

Why did the subjects who remained awake forget more? Their greater forgetting was blamed on interference from the competing information that they had to process while awake. Many subsequent studies have shown that forgetting depends not on the amount of time that has passed since learning but on the amount, complexity, and type of information that subjects have had to assimilate during the retention interval. The negative impact of competing information on retention is called *interference*.

Interference

Interference theory **proposes that people forget information because of competition from other material.** Although demonstrations of decay in long-term memory have remained elusive, hun-

dreds of studies have shown that interference influences forgetting (Postman, 1971). In the experiment on interference that we mentioned earlier, Jenkins and Dallenbach (1924) manipulated the amount of interference by having their subjects sleep or remain awake during the retention interval.

In many other studies, researchers have controlled interference by varying the *similarity* between the original material given to subjects (the test material) and the material studied in the intervening period. Interference is assumed to be greatest when intervening material is most similar to the test material. Decreasing the similarity should reduce interference and cause less forgetting. This is exactly what McGeoch and McDonald (1931) found in an influential study (see Figure 7.14). They had subjects memorize test material that consisted of a list of two-syllable adjectives. They varied the similarity of intervening learning by having subjects then memorize one of five lists. In order of decreasing similarity to the

Figure 7.13. Interference and retention. By sending some of their subjects off to bed after learning a list of nonsense syllables while allowing others to engage in their normal waking activities, Jenkins and Dallenbach (1924) demonstrated that much of forgetting is attributable to interference. The subjects who slept forgot the least.

Figure 7.14. Effects of interference. According to interference theory, more interference from competing information should produce more forgetting. McGeoch and McDonald (1931) controlled the amount of interference with a learning task by varying the similarity of an intervening task. The results were consistent with interference theory. The amount of interference is greatest at the left of the graph, as is the amount of forgetting. As interference decreases (moving to the right on the graph), retention improves.

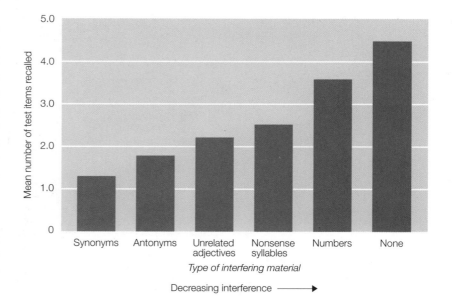

test material, they were synonyms of the test words, antonyms of the test words, unrelated adjectives, nonsense syllables, and numbers. Later, subjects' recall of the test material was measured. As Figure 7.14 shows, as the similarity of the intervening material decreased, the amount of forgetting also decreased—because of reduced interference.

There are two kinds of interference (see Figure 7.15): *retroactive* interference and *proactive* interference. **Retroactive interference occurs when new information impairs the retention of previously learned information.** Retroactive interference occurs between the original learning and the retest on that learning, during the retention interval. For example, the interference manipulated by McGeoch and McDonald (1931) was retroactive interference. In contrast, *proactive interference* **occurs when previously learned**

information **interferes with the retention of new information.** Proactive interference is rooted in learning that comes *before* exposure to the test material. The evidence indicates that both types of interference can have powerful effects on how much you forget. They may exert their effects by disrupting *retrieval* (Tulving & Psotka, 1971), which we turn to next.

Retrieval Failure

People often remember things that they were unable to recall at an earlier time. This may be obvious only during struggles with the tip-of-the-tongue phenomenon, but it happens frequently. In fact, a great deal of forgetting may be due to breakdowns in the process of retrieval.

Why does an effort to retrieve something fail on one occasion and succeed on another? That's a tough question. One theory is that retrieval failures may be more likely when there is a mismatch between retrieval cues and the encoding of the information you're searching for. According to Tulving and Thomson (1973), a good retrieval cue is consistent with the original encoding of the information to be recalled. If the sound of a word—its phonemic quality—was emphasized during encoding, an effective retrieval cue should emphasize the sound of the word. If the meaning of the word was emphasized during encoding, semantic cues should be best. A general statement of the principle at work here was formulated by Tulving and Thomson (1973). **The *encoding specificity principle* states that the value of a retrieval cue depends on how well it corresponds to the memory code.** This principle provides one explanation for the inconsistent success of retrieval efforts.

Motivated Forgetting

Many years ago, Sigmund Freud (1901) came up with an entirely different explanation for retrieval failures. As we noted in Chapter 1, Freud asserted that people often keep embarrassing, unpleasant, or painful memories buried in their unconscious. For example, a person who was deeply wounded by perceived slights at a childhood birthday party might suppress all recollection of that party. In his therapeutic work with patients, Freud recovered many such buried memories. He theorized that the memories were there all along, but their retrieval was blocked by unconscious avoidance tendencies.

The tendency to forget things one doesn't want to think about is called *motivated forgetting*, or to

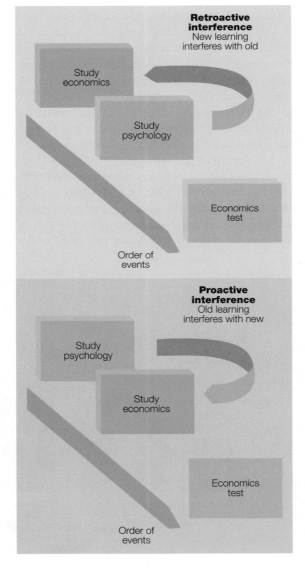

Figure 7.15. Retroactive and proactive interference. Retroactive interference occurs when learning produces a "backward" effect, reducing recall of previously learned material. Proactive interference occurs when learning produces a "forward" effect, reducing recall of subsequently learned material.

use Freud's terminology, *repression*. In Freudian theory, **repression** **refers to keeping distressing thoughts and feelings buried in the unconscious** (see Chapter 12). Psychologists have not been able to unambiguously demonstrate the operation of repression in controlled laboratory experiments (Holmes, 1990). Nonetheless, a number of experiments *suggest* that people don't remember anxiety-laden material as readily as emotionally neutral material, just as Freud proposed (Guenther, 1988). Thus, when you forget unpleasant things such as a dental appointment, a promise to help a friend move, or a term paper deadline, motivated forgetting may be at work.

The Repressed Memories Controversy

Although the concept of repression has been around for a century, interest in this phenomenon has surged in recent years, thanks to a spate of prominent reports involving the return of long-lost memories of sexual abuse and other traumas during childhood. The media have been flooded with reports of people—including some celebrities—who have remembered long-buried incidents of sexual abuse. For example, in 1991 TV star Roseanne Barr Arnold suddenly recalled years of abuse by her parents, and a former Miss America remembered being sexually assaulted by her father (Wielawski, 1991). In another 1991 case, a woman won a $1.4 million settlement from a church-run school in Washington, where she claimed she had been repeatedly raped by her teacher two decades previously (Toufexis, 1991). A similar case in Akron, Ohio, resulted in a $5 million settlement for a woman who accused her uncle of having sexually abused her many years earlier.

Thus, the 1990s have brought a rash of lawsuits in which adult plaintiffs have sued their parents, teachers, and neighbors for alleged child abuse decades earlier, based on previously repressed memories of these travesties. For the most part, these parents, teachers, and neighbors have denied the allegations. Many of them have seemed genuinely befuddled by the accusations, which have torn some previously happy families apart. In an effort to make sense of the charges, some accused parents have argued that their children's recollections are false memories created inadvertently by well-intentioned therapists through the power of suggestion.

What do psychologists have to say about the authenticity of repressed memories? They seem

In a well-publicized example of false repressed memories, Cardinal Bernadin, the Archbishop of Chicago, was accused by Steve Cook (with microphone below) of having molested him decades earlier when Bernadin was a priest in Cincinnati. A few months later Cook recanted his accusations of molestation.

to be sharply divided on the issue. Many psychologists, especially clinicians involved in the treatment of psychological disorders, accept repressed memories at face value (Briere & Conte, 1993; Dawes, 1992). They assert that it is common for patients to bury traumatic incidents in their unconscious. Citing new evidence that sexual abuse in childhood is far more widespread than most people realize, they argue that most repressed memories of abuse are probably genuine. They attribute the recent upsurge in reports of repressed memories to therapists' and clients' increased sensitivity to an issue that people used to be reluctant to discuss.

In contrast, many other psychologists have expressed skepticism about the recent flood of repressed memories (Loftus, 1993). These psychologists do not argue that people are lying about their repressed memories. Rather, they maintain that some suggestible people wrestling with emotional problems have been convinced by persuasive therapists that their emotional problems must be the result of abuse that occurred years before. Critics blame a small minority of therapists who presumably have good intentions but who operate under the dubious assumption that virtually all psychological problems are attributable to childhood sexual abuse. Using hypnosis, dream interpretation, and leading questions, they supposedly prod and probe patients until they inadvertently create the memories of abuse that they are searching for. Psychologists who doubt the authenticity of repressed memories support their analysis by pointing to published case histories that clearly involved suggestive questioning and to cases in which patients have recanted repressed memories of sexual abuse after realizing that these memories were implanted by their therapists (see Figure 7.16). Those who question the accuracy of repressed memories also point to research on the misinformation effect, source monitoring, and other studies that demonstrate the relative ease of creating "memories" of events that never happened.

The debate about repressed memories of sexual abuse has grown increasingly bitter and emotionally charged. Those who are skeptical about repressed memories argue that thousands of innocent families are being ripped apart by unquestioned acceptance of recovered memories of sexual abuse. The other camp raises an equally disturbing concern that the recent skepticism about repressed memories will turn the clock back to a time when women and children were reluctant to report abuse because they were often ignored, ridiculed, or made to feel guilty. Unfortunately, the repressed memories controversy isn't likely to be settled soon, given that there is no way to definitively evaluate the authenticity of most recovered recollections of child abuse.

IN SEARCH OF THE MEMORY TRACE: THE PHYSIOLOGY OF MEMORY

For decades, neuroscientists have ventured forth in search of the physiological basis for memory. On several occasions scientists have been excited by new leads, only to be led down blind alleys. For example, in the 1960s James McConnell rocked the world of science when he reported that he had chemically transferred a specific memory from one flatworm to another. McConnell (1962) created a conditioned reflex (contraction in response to light) in flatworms and then transferred RNA (a

Figure 7.16. False memory syndrome. Revelations of repressed memories of sexual abuse are viewed with skepticism in some quarters. One reason is that some people who have recovered previously repressed recollections of child abuse have subsequently realized that their "memories" were the product of suggestion. A number of case histories, such as the one summarized here (from Jaroff, 1993), have demonstrated that therapists who relentlessly search for memories of child abuse in their patients sometimes instill the memories they are seeking.

A CASE HISTORY OF FALSE MEMORY SYNDROME

Suffering from a prolonged bout of depression and desperate for help, Melody Gavigan, 39, a computer specialist from Long Beach, California, checked herself into a local psychiatric hospital. As Gavigan recalls the experience, her problems were just beginning. During five weeks of treatment there, a family and marriage counselor repeatedly suggested that her depression stemmed from incest during her childhood. While at first Gavigan had no recollection of any abuse, the therapist kept prodding. "I was so distressed and needed help so desperately, I latched on to what he was offering me," she says. "I accepted his answers."

When asked for details, she wrote page after page of what she believed were emerging repressed memories. She told about running into the yard after being raped in the bathroom. She incorporated into another lurid rape scene an actual girlhood incident, in which she had dislocated a shoulder. She went on to recall being molested by her father when she was only a year old—as her diapers were being changed—and sodomized by him at five. Following what she says was the therapist's advice, Gavigan confronted her father with her accusations, severed her relationship with him, moved away, and formed an incest survivors' group.

But she remained uneasy. Signing up for a college psychology course, she examined her newfound memories more carefully and concluded that they were false. Now Gavigan has begged her father's forgiveness and filed a lawsuit against the psychiatric hospital for the pain that she and her family suffered.

basic molecular constituent of all living cells) from trained worms to untrained worms. The untrained worms showed evidence of "remembering" the conditioned reflex. McConnell boldly speculated that in the future, chemists might be able to formulate pills containing the information for Physics 201 or History 101! Unfortunately, the RNA transfer studies proved difficult to replicate (Gaito, 1976). Today, 30 years after McConnell's "breakthrough," we are still a long way from breaking the chemical code for memory.

Investigators continue to explore a variety of leads about the physiological bases for memory. In light of past failures, these lines of research should probably be viewed with guarded optimism. Nonetheless, in this section we'll look at some of the more promising leads, emphasizing research on the anatomy of memory.

Cases of amnesia (extensive memory loss) due to head injury are a useful source of clues about the anatomical bases of memory. There are two basic types of amnesia: retrograde and anterograde. **In *retrograde amnesia* a person loses memories for events that occurred prior to the injury.** For example, a 25-year-old gymnast who sustains a head trauma might find 3 years, 7 years, or perhaps her entire lifetime erased. In ***anterograde amnesia* a person loses memories for events that occur after the injury.** For instance, after her accident, the injured gymnast might suffer impaired ability to remember people she meets, where she has parked her car, and so on.

Because victims' current memory functioning is impaired, cases of anterograde amnesia have been especially rich sources of information about the brain and memory. One well-known case, that of a man referred to as H. M., has been followed since 1953 (Corkin, 1984; Scoville & Milner, 1957). H. M. had surgery to relieve debilitating epileptic seizures. Unfortunately, the surgery inadvertently wiped out most of his ability to form long-term memories. H. M.'s short-term memory is fine, but he has no recollection of anything that has happened since 1953 (other than about the most recent 30 seconds of his life). He doesn't recognize the doctors treating him, he can't remember routes to and from places, and he doesn't know his age. He can't remember what he did yesterday, let alone what he has done for the last 35 to 40 years. He doesn't even recognize a current photo of himself, as aging has changed his appearance considerably.

H. M.'s memory losses have been attributed to the removal of his *hippocampus*, a structure in the *limbic system* (see Figure 7.17). Damage to the hippocampus has also been found in other cases of anterograde amnesia (Shimamura, 1992). However, it appears that amnesia can also be caused by damage to other areas of the limbic system, specifically the *amygdala* and certain nuclei in the *thalamus* (Markowitsch & Pritzel, 1985; Mishkin, Malamut, & Backevalier, 1984).

Do these findings mean that memories are housed in the limbic system? Probably not. Instead, the hippocampus and amygdala appear to play a key role in the *consolidation* of memories (McGaugh, 1989). **Consolidation is a hypothetical process involving the gradual conversion of information into durable memory codes stored in long-term memory.** The current thinking is that memories are consolidated in subcortical structures in the limbic system but that they are stored in various areas of the cortex. Which areas? Memories are probably stored in the same cortical areas that were originally involved in processing the sensory input that led to the memories (Mishkin & Appenzeller, 1987; Squire, 1987). For instance, memories of visual information may be stored in the visual cortex.

Various other lines of research have related memory functioning to (1) alterations in neurotransmitter secretions at specific synaptic sites (Alkon, 1989), (2) the formation of localized neural circuits that correspond to specific memories (Thompson, 1989), (3) synthesis of acetylcholine, the neurotransmitter that is depleted by Alzheimer's disease (Albert & Moss, 1992), (4) hor-

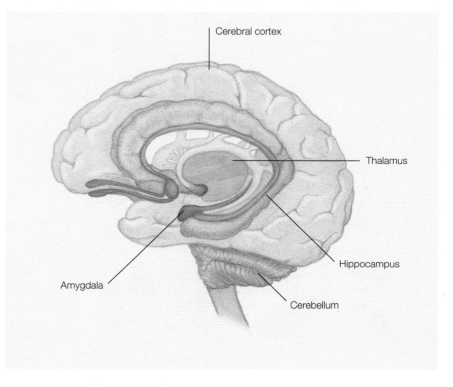

Figure 7.17. The anatomy of memory. All of the brain structures identified here have been implicated in efforts to discover the anatomical structures involved in memory. Although researchers have made some exciting discoveries, the physiological bases of memory are extremely complex and are not yet well understood.

Cerebral cortex

Thalamus

Hippocampus

Cerebellum

Amygdala

monal fluctuations (McGaugh, 1992), (5) protein synthesis in the brain (Rose, 1992), and (6) the stimulation of neural growth (increased branching of dendritic trees) in the brain (Greenough, 1985).

In summary, a host of biochemical processes, neural circuits, and anatomical structures have been implicated as playing a role in memory. Does all this sound confusing? It should, because it is. The bottom line is that neuroscientists are still assembling the pieces of the puzzle that will explain the physiological basis of memory. Although they have identified many of the puzzle pieces, they're not sure how the pieces fit together. Their difficulty is probably due to the complex, multifaceted nature of memory. Looking for the physiological basis for memory is only slightly less daunting than looking for the physiological basis for thought itself.

ARE THERE MULTIPLE MEMORY SYSTEMS?

Some theorists believe that evidence on the physiology of memory is confusing because investigators are unwittingly probing into several distinct memory systems that have different physiological bases. A number of research findings inspired this view, foremost among them the discovery of *implicit memory*. Let's look at this perplexing phenomenon.

Implicit Versus Explicit Memory

As we noted earlier, patients with anterograde amnesia often appear to have virtually no ability to form long-term memories. If they're shown a list of words and subsequently given a test of retention, their performance is miserable. However, different findings emerge when "sneaky" techniques are used to measure their memory indirectly. For instance, they might be asked to work on a word recognition task in which they are shown fragments of words (example: _ss_ss__ for assassin) and are asked to complete the fragments with the first appropriate word that comes to mind. The series of word fragments includes ones that correspond to words on a list they saw earlier. In this situation, the amnesiac subjects respond with words that were on the list just as frequently as normal subjects who also saw the initial list. Thus, the amnesiacs *do* remember words from the list. However, when asked, they don't even remember having been shown the first list!

The demonstration of long-term retention in amnesiacs who previously appeared to have no long-term memory shocked experts when it was first reported by Warrington and Weiskrantz (1970). However, this surprising finding has been replicated in many subsequent studies. This phenomenon has come to be known as implicit memory. **Implicit memory is apparent when retention is exhibited on a task that does not require intentional remembering.** Implicit memory is contrasted with *explicit memory*, **which involves intentional recollection of previous experiences.**

Is implicit memory peculiar to people suffering from amnesia? No. When normal subjects are exposed to material and their retention of it is

CONCEPT CHECK 7.4
Recognizing Pioneers in Memory Research

Below are quotations from some of the pioneers in memory research whose work is discussed in Chapter 7. Check your understanding of the contributions of these researchers by matching the quotations with the names of those who made them. Choose from the following: (a) Richard Atkinson and Richard Shiffrin, (b) Fergus Craik and Robert Lockhart, (c) Hermann Ebbinghaus, and (d) Elizabeth Loftus. You'll find the answers in Appendix A at the back of the book.

_____ 1. "In considering information flow in the system, we start with its initial input into the sensory register. . . . The next step is a subject-controlled scan of the information in the register; as a result of this scan . . . information is introduced into the short-term store. We assume that transfer to the long-term store takes place throughout the period that information resides in the short-term store."

_____ 2. "One hour after the end of the learning, the forgetting had already progressed so far that one-half the amount of the original work had to be expended before the series could be reproduced again. . . . After 24 hours about one-third was always remembered . . . and after a whole month fully one-fifth of the first work persisted in effect."

_____ 3. "Perception involves the rapid analysis of stimuli at a number of levels or stages. Preliminary stages are concerned with the analysis of such physical or sensory features as lines, angles, brightness, pitch, and loudness, while later stages are more concerned with . . . the extraction of meaning. This conception of a series or hierarchy of processing stages is often referred to as 'depth of processing.'"

_____ 4. "This result raises obvious issues about the whole process of questioning witnesses. . . . [T]he questions asked may deposit information in memory that radically alters subsequent testimony. The theoretical account . . . involves the postulation of two types of information in memory: information acquired during the acquisition stage and information acquired during the retention stage. These two types of information may become inextricably integrated, and the person may therefore be unable to distinguish them at the retrieval stage."

measured indirectly, they, too, show implicit memory (Schachter, 1987). To draw a parallel with everyday life, implicit memory is simply incidental, unintentional remembering (Mandler, 1989). People frequently remember things that they didn't deliberately store in memory. For example, you might recall the color of a jacket that your professor wore yesterday. Likewise, people remember things without deliberate retrieval efforts. For instance, you might be telling someone about a restaurant, which somehow reminds you of an unrelated story about a mutual friend.

Research has uncovered many interesting differences between implicit and explicit memory (Roediger, 1990; Tulving & Schachter, 1990). Explicit memory is conscious, is accessed directly, and can be best assessed with recall or recognition measures of retention. Implicit memory is unconscious, must be accessed indirectly, and can be best assessed with variations on relearning (savings) measures of retention. Implicit memory is largely unaffected by amnesia, age, the administration of certain drugs (such as alcohol), the length of the retention interval, and manipulations of interference. In contrast, explicit memory is affected very much by all these factors.

Some theorists think these differences are found because implicit and explicit memory rely on *different cognitive processes* in encoding and retrieval (Graf & Mandler, 1984; Roediger, Weldon, & Challis, 1989). However, many other theorists argue that the differences exist because implicit and explicit memory are handled by *independent memory systems* (Schachter, 1992; Squire, 1986). These independent systems are referred to as declarative and procedural memory.

Declarative Versus Procedural Memory

Many theorists have suggested that people have separate memory systems for different kinds of information (see Figure 7.18). The most basic division of memory into distinct systems contrasts declarative memory with procedural memory (Winograd, 1975). **The *declarative memory system* handles factual information.** It contains recollections of words, definitions, names, dates, faces, events, concepts, and ideas. **The *procedural memory system* houses memory for actions, skills, and operations.** It contains memories of how to execute such actions as riding a bike, typing, and tying one's shoes. To illustrate the distinction, if you know the rules of tennis (the number of games in a set, scoring, and such), this

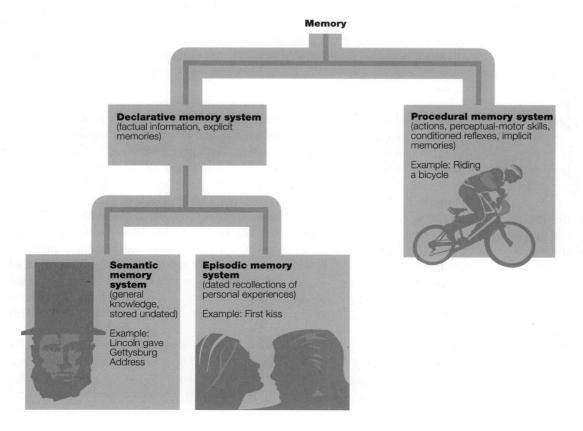

Figure 7.18. Theories of independent memory systems. There is some evidence that different types of information are stored in separate memory systems, which may have distinct physiological bases. The diagram shown here, which blends the ideas of several theorists, is an adaptation of Larry Squire's (1987) scheme. Endel Tulving (1985, 1987), another highly influential theorist in this area, makes similar distinctions but would diagram the relations among systems differently. Tulving's theory proposes a "nested" organization, in which episodic memory is part of semantic memory, which is part of declarative memory. Note also that implicit and explicit memory are *not* memory systems. They are observed behavioral phenomena that appear to be handled by different hypothetical memory systems (the procedural and declarative memory systems), which cannot be observed directly.

Perceptual-motor skills, such as those used in playing tennis, are stored in procedural memory.

"Memory systems constitute the major subdivisions of the overall organization of the memory complex. . . . An operating component of a system consists of a neural substrate and its behavioral or cognitive correlates."
ENDEL TULVING

factual information is stored in declarative memory. If you remember how to hit a serve and swing through a backhand, these perceptual-motor skills are stored in procedural memory.

Some theorists believe that an association exists between implicit memory and the procedural memory system (Squire & Cohen, 1984). Why? Because memory for skills is largely unconscious. People execute perceptual-motor tasks such as playing the piano or typing with little conscious awareness of what they're doing. In fact, performance on such tasks often deteriorates if people think too much about what they're doing. Another parallel with implicit memory is that the memory for skills (such as typing and bike riding) doesn't decline much over long retention intervals. Thus, the procedural memory system may handle implicit remembering, while the declarative memory system handles explicit remembering.

The notion that declarative and procedural memories are separate is supported by certain patterns of memory loss seen in amnesiacs. In many cases, declarative memory is severely impaired while procedural memory is left largely intact (Squire, 1987). For example, H. M., the victim of amnesia discussed earlier, can learn and remember new motor skills, even though he can't remember what he currently looks like. The sparing of procedural memory in amnesia could ex-

plain why implicit remembering is largely unaffected.

Procedural memory is considered a relatively primitive type of memory. It can be observed even in lower animals. Among the "operations" thought to be stored in procedural memory are automatic glandular and muscular reflexes governed by classical conditioning. Declarative memory involves more complex mental processes that are seen only in higher organisms.

There is considerable debate about whether procedural and declarative memory are independent systems with separate neural bases. At present, the evidence is complex and often contradictory (Hintzman, 1990).

Semantic Versus Episodic Memory

Endel Tulving (1986, 1993) has further subdivided declarative memory into semantic and episodic memory (see Figure 7.18). Both contain factual information, but episodic memory contains *personal facts* and semantic memory contains *general facts*. **The *episodic memory system* is made up of chronological, or temporally dated, recollections of personal experiences.** Episodic memory is a record of things you've done, seen, and heard. It includes information about *when* you did these things, saw them, or heard them. It contains recollections about being in a ninth-grade play, visiting the Grand Canyon, attending a Depeche Mode concert, or going to a movie last weekend.

The *semantic memory system* contains general knowledge that is not tied to the time when the information was learned. Semantic memory contains information such as Christmas is December 25th, dogs have four legs, and Phoenix is located in Arizona. You probably don't remember when you learned these facts. Information like this is usually stored undated. The distinction between episodic and semantic memory can be better appreciated by drawing an analogy to books: Episodic memory is like an autobiography, while semantic memory is like an encyclopedia.

The memory deficits seen in some cases of amnesia suggest that episodic and semantic memory are separate systems. For instance, some amnesiacs forget most personal facts, while their recall of general facts is largely unaffected (Wood, Ebert, & Kinsbourne, 1982). However, debate continues about whether episodic and semantic memory represent physiologically separate systems (Humphreys, Bain, & Pike, 1989; Neely,

1989). Hence, this issue promises to be a fertile source of future research.

PUTTING IT IN PERSPECTIVE

One of our integrative themes—the idea that people's experience of the world is subjective—stood head and shoulders above the rest in this chapter. Let's briefly review how the study of memory has illuminated this idea.

First, our discussion of attention as inherently selective should have shed light on why people's experience of the world is subjective. To a great degree, what you see in the world around you depends on where you focus your attention. This is one of the main reasons why two people can be exposed to the "same" events and walk away with entirely different perceptions.

Second, the reconstructive nature of memory should further explain people's tendency to view the world with a subjective slant. When you observe an event, you don't store an exact copy of the event in your memory. Instead, you store a rough, "bare bones" approximation of the event that may be reshaped as time goes by. With the passage of time, people tend to put more and more of a personal, subjective imprint on memories.

Finally, people sometimes forget those things that they don't want to remember. This propensity for motivated forgetting introduces yet another source of personal bias into people's views of the past. In short, a host of natural processes in memory conspire to make each individual's experience of the world highly subjective.

Another of our unifying themes also surfaced in this chapter. The multifaceted nature of memory demonstrates once again that behavior is governed by multiple causes. For instance, your memory of a specific event may be influenced by the following factors:

- The amount of attention you devote to the event
- The level at which you process the incoming information
- Whether you enrich your encoding with some form of elaboration
- Whether you have an opportunity to transfer the information into long-term memory
- How you organize the information
- How you search through your memory store
- The extent to which you use schemas to reconstruct the event
- The amount of interference you experience

Given the multifaceted nature of memory, it should come as no surprise that there are many ways to improve memory. We discuss a variety of strategies in our Application section.

Improving Everyday Memory

Answer the following "true" or "false":

___ 1 Memory strategies were recently invented by psychologists.

___ 2 Overlearning of information leads to poor retention.

___ 3 Outlining what you read is not likely to affect retention.

___ 4 Massing practice in one long study session is better than distributing practice across several shorter sessions.

***Mnemonic devices* are strategies for enhancing memory.** They have a long and honorable history, so the first statement is false. In fact, one of the mnemonic devices covered in this Application—the method of loci—was described in Greece as early as 86–82 B.C. (Yates, 1966). Actually, mnemonic devices were even more crucial in ancient times than they are today. In ancient Greece and Rome, for instance, paper and pencils were not readily available for people to write down things they needed to remember, so they had to depend heavily on mnemonic devices.

In this Application, we consider how the principles of memory can be used to enhance memory, with an emphasis on effective studying for school. In the process, you'll learn that all of the true-false statements above are false.

Engage in Adequate Rehearsal

Practice makes perfect, or so you've heard. In reality, practice is not likely to guarantee perfection, but it usually leads to improved retention. Studies show that retention improves with increased rehearsal (Greene, 1992). This improvement occurs because rehearsal can help transfer information into long-term memory.

Continued rehearsal may also improve your *understanding* of assigned material. This payoff was apparent in a study that examined the effects of repetition (Bromage & Mayer, 1986). Undergraduate subjects listened to an audiotaped lecture on photography, from one to three times. Information in the lecture was classified into three levels of importance. As Figure 7.19 shows, increased repetition led to increased recall for information at all three levels of importance. However, repetition had its greatest impact on the retention of the *most important* information, yielding enhanced understanding of the lecture. Thus, as you go over information again and again, your increased familiarity with the material may permit you to focus selectively on the most important points.

It even pays to overlearn material (Driskell, Willis, & Copper, 1992). ***Overlearning* refers to continued rehearsal of material after you first appear to have mastered it.** In one study, after subjects had mastered a list of nouns (they recited the list without error), Krueger (1929) required them to continue rehearsing for 50% or 100% more trials. Measuring retention at intervals up to 28 days, Krueger found that greater overlearning was related to better recall of the list. The practical implication of this finding is simple: you should not quit rehearsing material just because you appear to have mastered it.

Schedule Distributed Practice

Let's assume that you need to study 9 hours for an exam. Should you "cram" all your studying into one 9-hour period

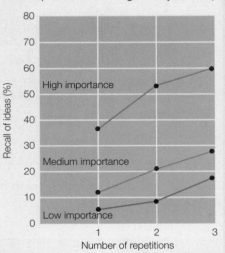

Figure 7.19. Effects of repetition on understanding. In this study, repetition most aided the recall of high-importance ideas. (Data from Bromage & Mayer, 1986)

(massed practice)? Or is it better to distribute your study among, say, three 3-hour periods on successive days (distributed practice)? The evidence indicates that retention tends to be greater after distributed practice than after massed practice (Glenberg, 1992). This advantage is especially apparent if the intervals between practice periods are fairly long, such as 24 hours (Zechmeister & Nyberg, 1982). For instance, Underwood (1970) studied children (ages 9 to 14) who practiced a list of words four times, either in one long session or in four separate sessions. He found that distributed practice led to better recall than a similar amount of massed practice (see Figure 7.20). The superiority of distributed practice suggests that cramming is an ill-advised approach to studying for exams.

Minimize Interference

Because interference is a major cause of forgetting, you'll probably want to think

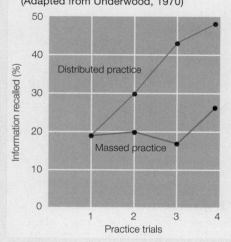

Figure 7.20. Effects of massed versus distributed practice on retention. Children in this study showed better recall of information when practice sessions were distributed over time. (Adapted from Underwood, 1970)

about how you can minimize it. This issue is especially important for students, because memorizing information for one course can interfere with the retention of information for another course. It may help to allocate study for specific courses to separate days. Thorndyke and Hayes-Roth (1979) found that similar material produced less interference when it was learned on different days. Thus, the day before an exam in a course, you should study for that course only—if possible. If demands in other courses make that plan impossible, you should study the test material last.

Of course, studying for other classes is not the only source of interference in a student's life. Other normal waking activities also produce interference. Therefore, it's a good idea to conduct one last, thorough review of material as close to exam time as possible (Anderson, 1980). This strategy will help you avoid memory loss due to interference from intervening activities.

Engage in Deep Processing

Research on levels of processing suggests that how *often* you go over material is less critical than the *depth* of processing that you engage in (Craik & Tulving, 1975). Thus, if you expect to remember what you read, you have to wrestle fully with its meaning. Many students could probably benefit if they spent less time on rote repetition and devoted more effort to actually paying attention to and analyzing the meaning of their reading assignments. In particular, it is useful to make material *personally* meaningful. When you read your textbooks, try to relate information to your own life and experience. For example, when you read about classical conditioning, try to think of responses that you display that are attributable to classical conditioning.

Enrich Encoding with Verbal Mnemonics

Although it's often helpful to make information personally meaningful, it's not always easy to do so. For instance, when you study chemistry you may have a hard time relating to polymers at a personal level. Thus, many mnemonic devices—such as acrostics, acronyms, and narrative methods—are designed to make abstract material more meaningful.

Acrostics and Acronyms

Acrostics are phrases (or poems) in which the first letter of each word (or line) functions as a cue to help you recall information to be remembered. For instance, you may remember the order of musical notes with the saying "Every good boy does fine" (or "deserves favor"). A slight variation on acrostics is the *acronym*—a word formed out of the

first letters of a series of words. Students memorizing the order of colors in the light spectrum often store the name "Roy G. Biv" to remember red, orange, yellow, green, blue, indigo, and violet. Notice that this acronym takes advantage of the principle of chunking.

Narrative Methods

Another useful way to remember a list of words is to create a story that includes the words in the appropriate order. The narrative both increases the meaningfulness of the words and links them in a specific order. Examples of this technique can be seen in Figure 7.21. Bower and Clark

Figure 7.21. Narrative methods of remembering. In this study, 12 lists of words were presented. Subjects in the "narrative group" were asked to recall the words by constructing a story out of them (like the stories shown below). Subjects in the control group were not given any special instructions. (From Bower & Clark, 1969)

Word lists	Stories
Bird Costume Mailbox Head River Nurse Theater Wax Eyelid Furnace	A man dressed in a *Bird Costume* and wearing a *Mailbox* on his *Head* was seen leaping into the *River*. A *Nurse* ran out of a nearby *Theater* and applied *Wax* to his *Eyelids*, but her efforts were in vain. He died and was tossed into the *Furnace*.
Rustler Penthouse Mountain Sloth Tavern Fuzz Gland Antler Pencil Vitamin	A *Rustler* lived in a *Penthouse* on top of a *Mountain*. His specialty was the three-toed *Sloth*. He would take his captive animals to a *Tavern* where he would remove *Fuzz* from their *Glands*. Unfortunately, all this exposure to sloth fuzz caused him to grow *Antlers*. So he gave up his profession and went to work in a *Pencil* factory. As a precaution he also took a lot of *Vitamin* E.

Figure 7.22. Effects of narrative methods of remembering.

Recoding the material in story form dramatically improved recall, as the graph clearly shows. (Data from Bower & Clark, 1969)

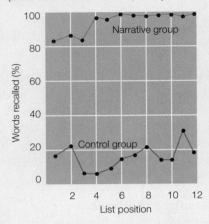

(1969) found that this procedure greatly enhanced subjects' recall of lists of unrelated words (see Figure 7.22).

Rhymes

Another verbal mnemonic that people often rely on is rhyming. You've probably repeated, "I before E except after C . . ." thousands of times. Perhaps you also remember the number of days in each month with the old standby, "Thirty days hath September . . ." Rhyming something to remember it is an old and useful trick.

Enrich Encoding with Visual Imagery

Memory can be enhanced by the use of visual imagery. As you may recall, Allan Paivio (1986) believes that visual images create a second memory code and that two codes are better than one for enhancing recall. Many popular mnemonic devices depend on visual imagery, including the link method and the method of loci.

Link Method

The *link method* involves forming a mental image of items to be remembered in a way that links them together. For instance, suppose that you need to remember some items to pick up at the drugstore: a news magazine, shaving cream, film, and pens. To remember

Figure 7.23. The method of loci.

In this example from Bower (1970), a person about to go shopping pairs items to remember with familiar places (*loci*) arranged in a natural sequence: (1) hot dogs/driveway; (2) cat food/garage interior; (3) tomatoes/front door; (4) bananas/coat closet shelf; (5) whiskey/kitchen sink. The shopper then uses imagery to associate the items on the shopping list with the loci, as shown in the drawing: (1) giant *hot dog* rolls down a *driveway;* (2) a cat noisily devours *cat food* in the *garage;* (3) ripe *tomatoes* are splattered on the *front door;* (4) bunches of *bananas* are hung from the *closet shelf;* (5) the contents of a bottle of *whiskey* gurgle down the *kitchen sink.* As the last panel shows, the shopper recalls the items by mentally touring the loci associated with them.

these items, you might visualize a public figure on the magazine cover shaving with a pen while being photographed. The more bizarre you make your image, the more helpful it is likely to be (McDaniel & Einstein, 1986).

Method of Loci

The *method of loci* involves taking an imaginary walk along a familiar path where images of items to be remembered are associated with certain locations. The first step is to commit to memory a series of loci, or places along a path. Usually these loci are specific locations in your home or neighborhood. Then envision each thing you want to remember in one of these locations. Try to form distinctive, vivid images. When you need to remember the items, imagine yourself walking along the path. The various loci on your path should serve as cues for the retrieval of the images that you formed (see Figure 7.23). The method of loci assures that items are remembered in their correct order because the order is determined by the sequence of locations along the pathway.

Organize Information

Retention tends to be greater when information is well organized. The value of organization has been apparent in studies of people who exhibit remarkable memory capability. For example, Ericsson and Polson (1988) have studied a waiter, known as J. C., who can remember up to 20 complicated dinner orders without taking notes. They found that J. C. organized information by dinner element (salad dressings, vegetables, and so on), whereas other people memorized dinner requests in the order in which the requests were presented. J. C. also used acronyms to remember orders within a dinner element. For instance, he used the word *boot* to remember salad dressing orders for blue cheese, oil and vinegar, oil and vinegar, and thousand island.

Gordon Bower (1970) has shown that hierarchical organization is particularly helpful when it is applicable. Thus, it may be a good idea to *outline* reading assignments for school, since outlining forces you to organize material hierarchically. Outlining is also valuable because it forces you to wrestle with the meaning of information in a text.

Chapter 7 Review

KEY IDEAS

Encoding: Getting Information into Memory

♦ The multifaceted process of memory begins with encoding. Attention, which facilitates encoding, is inherently selective and has been compared to a filter.

♦ According to levels-of-processing theory, deeper processing results in better recall of information. Structural, phonemic, and semantic encoding represent progressively deeper and more effective levels of processing.

♦ Elaboration enriches encoding by linking a stimulus to other information. Visual imagery may work in much the same way, creating two memory codes rather than just one.

Storage: Maintaining Information in Memory

♦ Information-processing theories of memory assert that people have three kinds of memory stores: a sensory memory, a short-term memory, and a long-term memory. The sensory store preserves information in its original form, sometimes for only a fraction of a second.

♦ Short-term memory has a limited capacity (capable of holding about seven chunks of information) and can maintain unrehearsed information for about 20 to 30 seconds. Short-term memory is working memory, and it appears to involve more than a simple rehearsal loop.

♦ Long-term memory is an unlimited capacity store that may hold information indefinitely. Phenomena such as flashbulb memories and reports of exceptional recall through hypnosis suggest that LTM storage may be permanent, but the evidence is not convincing. Information is transferred from STM to LTM primarily through rehearsal.

♦ Information in LTM can be organized in a variety of ways. Semantic networks consist of concepts joined together by pathways. A schema is an organized cluster of knowledge about a particular object or sequence of events.

Retrieval: Getting Information out of Memory

♦ Recall is often guided by partial information. Reinstating the context of an event can facilitate recall. Memories are not exact replicas of past experiences. Memory is partially reconstructive.

♦ Information learned after an event can alter our memory of it. Source monitoring is the process of making attributions about the origins of memories. Source-monitoring errors may explain why people sometimes "recall" something that was only suggested to them.

Forgetting: When Memory Lapses

♦ Ebbinghaus's early studies of nonsense syllables suggested that we forget very rapidly. Subsequent research showed that Ebbinghaus's forgetting curve was exceptionally steep. Forgetting can be measured by asking people to either recall, recognize, or relearn information.

♦ Some forgetting, including pseudo-forgetting, is due to ineffective encoding of information. Decay theory proposes that forgetting occurs spontaneously with the passage of time. It has proven difficult to show that decay occurs in long-term memory.

♦ Interference theory proposes that people forget information because of competition from other material. Evidence that either prior (proactive interference) or subsequent (retroactive interference) material can cause forgetting supports interference theory.

♦ Forgetting may also be a matter of retrieval failure. According to the encoding specificity principle, the effectiveness of a retrieval cue depends on how well it corresponds to the original encoding method. Retrieval may be prevented by repression. Recent years have seen a surge of reports of repressed memories of sexual abuse in childhood. There is a hotly debated controversy about the authenticity of these recovered memories.

In Search of the Memory Trace: The Physiology of Memory

♦ Research on amnesia has implicated the hippocampus, amygdala, and thalamus as brain structures involved in the consolidation of memories. Research on the physiological basis of memory has also provided many other interesting leads, but the picture remains confusing.

Are There Multiple Memory Systems?

♦ Differences between implicit and explicit memory suggest that people may have several separate memory systems. Declarative memory is memory for facts, while procedural memory is memory for actions and skills. Declarative memory can be subdivided into episodic memory, for personal facts, and semantic memory, for general facts.

Putting It in Perspective

♦ Our discussion of attention and memory enhances our understanding of why our experience of the world is highly subjective.

Work in this area also shows that behavior is governed by multiple factors.

Application: Improving Everyday Memory

♦ Rehearsal, even when it involves overlearning, facilitates retention. Distributed practice tends to be more efficient than massed practice. It is wise to plan study sessions so as to minimize interference. Deep processing during rehearsal enhances recall.

♦ Meaningfulness can be enhanced through the use of verbal mnemonics such as acrostics, acronyms, and narrative methods. The link method and the method of loci are mnemonic devices that depend on the value of visual imagery. Evidence also suggests that organization enhances retention, so outlining texts may be valuable.

KEY TERMS

Anterograde amnesia	Proactive interference
Attention	Procedural memory system
Chunk	Recall
Consolidation	Recency effect
Decay theory	Recognition
Declarative memory system	Rehearsal
Dual-coding theory	Relearning
Elaboration	Repression
Encoding	Retention
Encoding specificity principle	Retrieval
Episodic memory system	Retroactive interference
Explicit memory	Retrograde amnesia
Flashbulb memories	Schema
Forgetting curve	Semantic memory system
Implicit memory	Semantic network
Interference theory	Sensory memory
Levels-of-processing theory	Serial-position effect
Link method	Short-term memory (STM)
Long-term memory (LTM)	Source monitoring
Method of loci	Source-monitoring error
Mnemonic devices	Storage
Nonsense syllables	Tip-of-the-tongue phenomenon
Overlearning	
Primacy effect	

KEY PEOPLE

Richard Atkinson and Richard Shiffrin	Hermann Ebbinghaus
Fergus Craik and Robert Lockhart	Elizabeth Loftus
	George Miller
	Endel Tulving

8 Language and Thought

"Mr. Watson—Mr. Sherlock Holmes," said Stamford, introducing us.

"How are you?" he said, cordially, gripping my hand with a strength for which I should hardly have given him credit. "You have been in Afghanistan, I perceive."

"How on earth did you know that?" I asked, in astonishment. (From A Study in Scarlet *by Arthur Conan Doyle)*

I f you've ever read any Sherlock Holmes stories, you know that the great detective continually astonished his stalwart companion, Dr. Watson, with his extraordinary deductions. Obviously, Holmes could not arrive at his conclusions without a chain of reasoning. Yet to him even an elaborate reasoning process was a simple, everyday act. Consider his feat of knowing at once, upon first meeting Watson, that the doctor had been in Afghanistan. When asked, Holmes explained his reasoning as follows:

"I knew you came from Afghanistan. From long habit the train of thought ran so swiftly through my mind that I arrived at the conclusion without being conscious of the intermediate steps. There were such steps, however. The train of reasoning ran: 'Here is a gentleman of a medical type, but with the air of a military man. Clearly an army doctor, then. He has just come from the tropics, for his face is dark, and that is not the natural tint of his skin, for his wrists are fair. He has undergone hardship and sickness, as his haggard face says clearly. His left arm has been injured. He holds it in a stiff and unnatural manner. Where in the tropics could an English army doctor have seen much hardship and got his arm wounded? Clearly in Afghanistan.' The whole train of thought did not occupy a second."

Admittedly, Sherlock Holmes's deductive feats are fictional. But even to read about them appreciatively—let alone imagine them, as Sir Arthur Conan Doyle did—is a remarkably complex mental act. Our everyday thought processes seem ordinary to us only because we take them for granted, just as Holmes saw nothing extraordinary in what to him was a simple deduction.

In reality, everyone is a Sherlock Holmes, continually performing magical feats of thought. Even elementary perception—for instance, watching a football game or a ballet—involves elaborate cognitive processes. People must sort through distorted, constantly shifting perceptual inputs and deduce what they see out there in the real world. Imagine, then, the complexity of thought required to read a book, fix an automobile, or balance a

checkbook. Of course, all this is not to say that human thought processes are flawless or unequaled. You probably own a $10 calculator that can run circles around you when it comes to computing square roots. As we'll see, some of the most interesting research in this chapter focuses on ways in which people's thinking can be limited, simplistic, or outright illogical.

THE COGNITIVE REVOLUTION IN PSYCHOLOGY

As we have noted before, **cognition refers to the mental processes involved in acquiring knowledge.** In other words, cognition involves thinking. When psychology first emerged as an independent science in the 19th century, it focused on the mind. Mental processes were explored through *introspection*—analysis of one's own conscious experience (see Chapter 1). Unfortunately, early psychologists' study of mental processes ran aground, as the method of introspection yielded unreliable results. Psychology's empirical approach depends on observation, and private mental events proved difficult to observe. Furthermore, during the first half of the 20th century, the study of cognition was actively discouraged by the theoretical dominance of behaviorism. Herbert Simon, a pioneer of cognitive psychology, recalls that "you couldn't use a word like *mind* in a psychology journal—you'd get your mouth washed out with soap" (Holden, 1986).

Although it wasn't fully recognized until much later, the 1950s brought a "cognitive revolution" in psychology (Baars, 1986). Renegade theorists, such as Herbert Simon, began to argue that behaviorists' exclusive focus on overt responses was doomed to yield an incomplete understanding of human functioning. More important, creative new approaches to research on cognitive processes led to exciting progress. For example, in his book on the cognitive revolution, Howard Gardner (1985) notes that three major advances were reported at a watershed 1956 conference—in just one day! First, Herbert Simon and Allen Newell described the first computer program to successfully simulate human problem solving. Second, Noam Chomsky outlined a new model that changed the way psychologists studied language. Third, George Miller delivered the legendary paper that we discussed in Chapter 7, arguing that the capacity of short-term memory is seven (plus or minus two) items.

Today, cognitive psychology is a robust, grow-

"You couldn't use a word like *mind* in a psychology journal—you'd get your mouth washed out with soap."
HERBERT SIMON

ing area of research. Besides memory (which we covered in Chapter 7), cognitive psychologists investigate the complexities of language, problem solving, decision making, and reasoning. We'll look at all these topics in this chapter, beginning with language.

LANGUAGE: TURNING THOUGHTS INTO WORDS

Language obviously plays a fundamental role in human behavior. Indeed, if you were to ask people, "What characteristic most distinguishes humans from other living creatures?" a great many would reply, "Language." In this section, we'll discuss the nature, structure, and development of language.

What Is Language?

A *language* consists of symbols that convey meaning, plus rules for combining those symbols, that can be used to generate an infinite variety of messages. Language systems include a number of critical properties (Ratner & Gleason, 1993).

First, language is *symbolic*. People use spoken sounds and written words to represent objects, actions, events, and ideas. The word *lamp*, for instance, refers to a class of objects that have certain properties. The symbolic nature of lan-

guage greatly expands what people can communicate about. Symbols allow one to refer to objects that may be in another place and to events that happened at another time (for example, a lamp broken at work yesterday). Language symbols are flexible in that a variety of somewhat different objects may be called by the same name (consider the diversity of lamps, for example).

Second, language is *semantic*, or meaningful. The symbols used in a language are arbitrary in that no built-in relationship exists between the look or sound of words and the objects they stand for. Take, for instance, the writing object that you may have in your hand right now. It's represented by the word *pen* in English, *stylo* in French, and *pluma* in Spanish. Although these words are arbitrary (others could have been chosen), they have *shared meanings* for people who speak English, French, and Spanish.

Third, language is *generative*. A limited number of symbols can be combined in an infinite variety of ways to *generate* an endless array of novel messages. Everyone has some "stock sayings," but every day you create sentences that you have never spoken before. You also comprehend many sentences that you have never encountered before (like this one).

Fourth, language is *structured*. Although people can generate an infinite variety of sentences, these sentences must be structured in a limited number of ways. There are rules that govern the arrange-

---

CONCEPT CHECK 8.1
Understanding the Critical Properties of Language

Some of the most interesting research on language has involved efforts to teach apes to use language. Below are several vignettes drawn from this research. Check your understanding of the four critical properties of language by deciding which property is highlighted by each of the vignettes. Place the letter corresponding to the appropriate property in the space next to the vignette: (a) language is symbolic; (b) language is semantic; (c) language is generative; (d) language is structured. You'll find the answers in Appendix A.

_____ 1. In order to communicate his wishes clearly, Kanzi the chimpanzee used word order correctly. For instance, if he wanted to be chased, he constructed the sentence "Person chase Kanzi" (on a specially designed symbol board), but if he wanted to do the chasing, he changed the word order to "Kanzi chase Person."

_____ 2. Washoe was the first chimpanzee to successfully learn the hand gestures used in American Sign Language to stand for words.

_____ 3. Many of the sentences Kanzi constructed by combining symbols were spontaneous—that is, they were not prompted by his trainers—and many of them appeared to be original and novel.

_____ 4. Many researchers agree that the apes involved in language research have successfully demonstrated the ability to convey meaningful messages. Examples are "Me Nim eat more apple" and "Gimme flower."

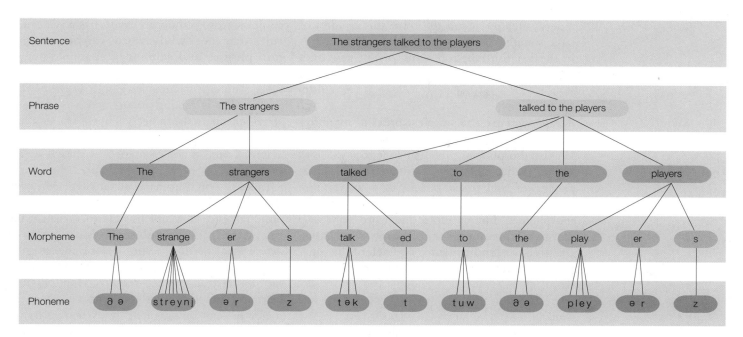

Sentence	The strangers talked to the players
Phrase	The strangers / talked to the players
Word	The / strangers / talked / to / the / players
Morpheme	The / strange / er / s / talk / ed / to / the / play / er / s
Phoneme	ə e / streynj / ə r / z / t ə k / t / t u w / ə e / p l e y / ə r / z

ment of words into phrases and sentences. Some arrangements are acceptable and some are not. For example, you might say, "The swimmer jumped into the pool," but you would never recombine the same words to say, "Pool the into the jumped swimmer." The structure of language allows people to be inventive with words and still understand each other. Let's take a closer look at the structural properties of language.

The Structure of Language

Human languages have a hierarchical structure (Ratner & Gleason, 1993). As Figure 8.1 shows, basic sounds are combined into units with meaning, which are combined into words. Words are combined into phrases, which are combined into sentences.

Phonemes

At the base of the language hierarchy are *phonemes,* **the basic units of sound in a spoken language.** Considering that an unabridged English dictionary contains more than 450,000 words, you might imagine that there must be a huge number of phonemes. In fact, linguists estimate that humans are capable of producing only about 100 such basic sounds. Moreover, no one language uses all of these phonemes. Different languages use different groups of about 20 to 80 phonemes.

For all its rich vocabulary, the English language is composed of about 40 to 45 phonemes, corresponding roughly to the 26 letters of the alphabet plus several variations. Some represen-

tative English phonemes are listed in Table 8.1. A letter in the alphabet is represented by more than one phoneme if it has more than one pronunciation. For example, the letter *a* is pronounced differently in the words *father*, *had*, *call*, and *take*. Each of these pronunciations is represented by a different phoneme. In addition, some phonemes are represented by combinations of

Table 8.1 Examples of Some English Language Phonemes

Symbol	Examples
p	**p**at, a**pp**le
b	**b**at, am**b**le
d	**d**ip. love**d**
g	**g**uard, o**g**re
f	**f**at, **ph**ilosophy
s	**s**ap, pa**ss**, peace
z	**z**ip, pad**s**, **x**ylophone
y	**y**ou, ba**y**, fe**u**d
w	**w**itch, q**u**een
l	**l**eaf, pa**l**ace
ē	b**ee**t, b**ea**t, bel**ie**ve
e	**a**te, b**ai**t, **ei**ght
i	b**i**t, **i**njury
u	b**oo**t, tw**o**, thr**ou**gh
U	p**u**t, f**oo**t, c**ou**ld
oy	b**oy**, d**oi**ly
ay	b**i**te, s**igh**t, **i**sland
š	**sh**oe, mu**sh**, deduc**ti**on

Source: Adapted from Moates and Schumacher (1980)

Figure 8.1. An analysis of a simple English sentence. As this example shows, verbal language has a hierarchical structure. At the base of the hierarchy are the *phonemes,* which are units of vocal sound that do not, in themselves, have meaning. The smallest units of meaning in a language are *morphemes,* which include not only root words but such meaning-carrying units as the past tense suffix *ed* and the plural *s.* Complex rules of syntax govern how the words constructed from morphemes may be combined into phrases, and phrases into meaningful statements, or sentences.

letters, such as *ch* and *th*. From this handful of basic sounds, speakers can generate all the words in the English language—and invent new ones besides.

Morphemes

Morphemes **are the smallest units of meaning in a language**. There are approximately 50,000 English morphemes, which include root words as well as prefixes and suffixes. Many words, such as *fire*, *guard*, and *friend*, consist of a single morpheme. Many others represent combinations of morphemes. For example, the word *unfriendly* consists of three morphemes: the root word *friend*, the prefix *un*, and the suffix *ly*. Each of the morphemes contributes to the meaning of the entire word.

Syntax

Of course, most utterances consist of more than a single word. As we've already noted, people don't combine words randomly. *Syntax* **is a system of rules that specify how words can be arranged into phrases and sentences**. A simple rule of syntax is that declarative sentences (sentences that make a statement) must have both a *subject* (what the speaker is talking about) and a *predicate* (a statement about the subject). Thus, "The sound of cars is annoying" is a sentence. However, "The sound of cars" is not a sentence, because it lacks a predicate.

Rules of syntax underlie all language use, even though you may not be aware of them. Thus, although they may not be able to verbalize the rule, virtually all English speakers know that an *article* (such as *the*) comes before the word it modifies. For example, you would never say *swimmer the* instead of *the swimmer*. How children learn the complicated rules of syntax is one of the major puzzles investigated by psychologists interested in language. Like other aspects of language development, children's acquisition of syntax seems to progress at an amazingly rapid pace. Let's look at how this remarkable development unfolds.

Milestones in Language Development

Learning to use language requires learning a number of skills that become important at different points in a child's development (Siegler, 1986). We'll examine this developmental sequence by looking first at how children learn to pronounce words, then at their use of single words, and then at their ability to combine words to form sentences (see Table 8.2).

Moving Toward Producing Words

During the first six months of life, a baby's vocalizations are dominated by crying, cooing, and laughter, which have limited value as a means of communication. Soon, infants are *babbling*, producing a wide variety of sounds that correspond to phonemes and, eventually, many consonant-vowel combinations. Babbling becomes more complex and increasingly resembles the language spoken by parents and others in the child's environment (Boysson-Bardies et al., 1989). These trends probably reflect ongoing neural development and the maturation of the infant's vocal apparatus (Sachs, 1985). Babbling lasts until around 18 months, continuing even after children utter their first words.

At around 10 to 13 months of age, most children begin to utter sounds that correspond to words.

Table 8.2 Overview of Typical Language Development

Age	General Characteristics
Months 1–5	Reflexive communication: Vocalizes randomly, coos, laughs, cries, engages in vocal play, discriminates language from nonlanguage sounds
6–18	Babbling: Verbalizes in response to speech of others; responses increasingly approximate human speech patterns
10–13	First words: Uses words typically to refer to objects rather than actions
12–18	One-word sentence stage: Vocabulary grows slowly; uses nouns primarily
18–24	Vocabulary spurt: Fast-mapping facilitates rapid acquisition of new words
Years 2	Two-word sentence stage: Uses telegraphic speech; uses more pronouns and verbs
2.5	Three-word sentence stage: Modifies speech to take listener into account
3	Uses complete simple active sentence structure; uses sentences to tell stories that are understood by others; uses plurals
3.5	Expanded grammatical forms: Expresses concepts with words; uses four-word sentences
4	Uses imaginary speech; uses five-word sentences
5	Well-developed and complex syntax: Uses more complex syntax. Uses more complex forms to tell stories
6	Displays metalinguistic awareness

Note: Children often show individual differences in the exact ages at which they display the various developmental achievements outlined here.

Most infants' first words are similar in phonetic form and meaning—even in different languages (Gleason & Ratner, 1993). The initial words resemble the syllables that infants most often babble spontaneously. For example, words such as *dada*, *mama*, and *papa* are names for parents in many languages because they consist of sounds that are easy to produce.

Using Words

After children utter their first words, their vocabulary grows slowly for the next few months (Barrett, 1989). Toddlers typically can say between 3 and 50 words by 18 months. However, their *receptive vocabulary* is larger than their *productive vocabulary*. That is, they can comprehend more words spoken by others than they can actually produce to express themselves (Pease & Gleason, 1985). Thus, toddlers can *understand* 50 words months before they can *say* 50 words. Toddlers' early words tend to refer to *objects* more often than *actions* (Gentner, 1982).

Youngsters' vocabularies soon begin to grow at a dizzying pace, as a vocabulary spurt often begins at around 18 months (Goldfield & Reznick, 1990). By the age of 6, the average child has a vocabulary of approximately 10,000 words (Clark, 1983). To build such a large vocabulary, a child must learn about 5 to 8 new words every day! *Fast mapping* appears to be the key to this rapid growth of vocabulary (Dollaghan, 1985; Taylor & Gelman, 1989). **Fast mapping is the process by which children map a word onto an underlying concept after only one exposure to the word.** Thus, children often add words like *ball*, *dog*, and *cookie* to their vocabularies after their first encounter with objects that illustrate these concepts.

Of course, these efforts to learn new words are not flawless. Toddlers often make errors, such as overextensions (G. Miller, 1991). **An *overextension* occurs when a child incorrectly uses a word to describe a wider set of objects or actions than it is meant to.** For example, a child might use the word *ball* for anything round—oranges, apples, even the moon. Overextensions usually appear in children's speech between ages one and two and a half. Specific overextensions typically last up to several months (Clark, 1983). These mistakes show that toddlers are actively trying to learn the rules of language—albeit with mixed success. Overextensions sometimes lead parents and others to provide corrective information, so overextensions may help children to learn new words and concepts.

While toddlers increase their ability to communicate as they learn new words, they remain unable to express themselves in sentences. They appear to compensate for this limitation by using a single word to represent the meaning of several words. **Holophrases are single-word utterances that appear to function like sentences.** Some theorists doubt the idea that these one-word utterances represent primitive sentences (Dore, 1985). However, children do appear to be intentionally selective in choosing words that convey their needs (Barrett, 1982). For example, a child who wants a banana will say *banana* rather than *want* because *banana* is the more informative term (Greenfield & Smith, 1976). After all, there are many things a child could want, but relatively few reasons why a child would be interested in a banana.

Combining Words

Children typically begin to combine words into sentences near the end of their second year. Early sentences are characterized as "telegraphic" because they resemble telegrams (Reich, 1986). **Telegraphic speech consists mainly of content words; articles, prepositions, and other less critical words are omitted.** Thus, a child might say, "Give doll" rather than "Please give me the doll."

Researchers sometimes track language development by keeping tabs on subjects' **mean length of utterance (MLU)—the average length of youngsters' spoken statements (measured in morphemes).** After children begin to combine words, their vocal expressions gradually become longer, as Figure 8.2 shows (Riley, 1987).

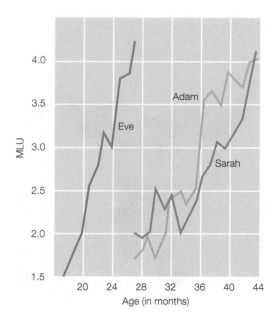

Figure 8.2. Age and mean length of utterance. These graphs depict the age-related increase in mean length of utterance (MLU) for three children studied by Brown (1973). As you can see, MLU increases rapidly among 2- and 3-year-old children.

By the end of their third year, most children can express complex ideas such as the plural or the past tense. However, their efforts to learn the rules of language continue to generate revealing mistakes. ***Overregularizations* occur when grammatical rules are incorrectly generalized to irregular cases where they do not apply.** For example, children will say things like "The girl goed home" or "I hitted the ball." Cross-cultural research suggests that these overregularizations occur in all languages (Slobin, 1985). Children don't learn the fine points of grammar and usage in a single leap but gradually acquire them in small steps.

Refining Language Skills

Youngsters make their largest strides in language development in their first 4 to 5 years. However, they continue to refine their language skills during their school-age years. They generate longer and more complicated sentences as they receive formal training in written language.

As their language skills develop, school-age children begin to appreciate ambiguities in language. They can, for instance, recognize two possible meanings in sentences such as "Visiting relatives can be bothersome." This interest in ambiguities indicates that they're developing *metalinguistic awareness*—**the ability to reflect on the use of language.** As metalinguistic awareness grows, children begin to "play" with language, coming up with puns and jokes. They also learn to recognize hidden meanings often found in everyday discourse, such as sarcastic comments (Capelli, Nakagawa, & Madden, 1990).

In the final analysis, what's most striking about children's language development is how swiftly it occurs. Bright college students often struggle to learn a foreign language, yet even toddlers with below-average intelligence acquire a decent mastery of their native tongue in a mere 30 months or so. How do they do it? Theorists have proposed several explanations of language acquisition. We examine these theories next.

Theories of Language Acquisition

Since the 1950s, a great debate has raged about the key processes involved in language acquisition. As with arguments in other areas of psychology that we have seen previously, this one centers on the *nature versus nurture* issue. The debate was stimulated by the influential behaviorist B. F. Skinner (1957), who argued that environmental factors govern language development. His provocative analysis brought a rejoinder from Noam Chomsky (1959), who emphasized biological determinism. Let's examine their views and subsequent theories that stake out a middle ground.

Behaviorist Theories

The behaviorist approach to language was first outlined by Skinner (1957) in his book *Verbal Behavior*. He argued that children learn language the same way they learn everything else: through imitation, reinforcement, and other established principles of conditioning. According to Skinner, vocalizations that are not reinforced gradually decline in frequency. The remaining vocalizations are shaped with reinforcers until they are correct. Behaviorists assert that by controlling reinforcement, parents encourage their children to learn the correct meaning and pronunciation of words (Staats & Staats, 1963). For example, as children grow older, parents may insist on closer and closer approximations of the word *water* before supplying the requested drink.

Behavioral theorists also use the principles of imitation and reinforcement to explain how children learn syntax. According to the behaviorists' view, children learn how to construct sentences by imitating the sentences of adults and older children. If children's imitative statements are understood, parents are able to answer their questions or respond to their requests, thus reinforcing their verbal behavior. Learning theory asserts that parents shape children's syntax by translating under-

Humans seem uniquely well-suited for learning language. Although researchers have made some remarkable advances in teaching apes language, the language development of a typical human toddler quickly surpasses that of even the most successfully trained chimps. The most amazing aspect of children's language development is how rapidly it proceeds. By the age of 30 months, most children have acquired a decent mastery of their native tongue.

standable but ungrammatical statements into correct grammatical form.

Nativist Theories

Skinner's explanation of language acquisition soon inspired a critique and rival explanation from Noam Chomsky (1959, 1965). Chomsky pointed out that there are an infinite number of sentences in a language. It's therefore unreasonable to expect that children learn language by imitation. For example, in English, we add *ed* to the end of a verb to construct past tense. Children routinely overregularize this rule, producing incorrect verbs such as *goed*, *eated*, and *thinked*. Mistakes such as these are inconsistent with Skinner's emphasis on imitation, because most adult speakers don't use ungrammatical words like *goed*. Children can't imitate things they don't hear. According to Chomsky, children learn *the rules of language*, not specific verbal responses, as Skinner proposed. Chomsky asserts that youngsters' misapplication of rules explains many of their early errors in language.

Critics have also challenged the behaviorist position that children learn to construct correct sentences through reinforcement. An influential study by Brown and Hanlon (1970) indicated that parents typically respond to meaning and factual accuracy in their youngsters' speech rather than to grammar. Thus, a mother curling her daughter's hair probably won't correct the ungrammatical statement "Her curl my hair," because it is factually accurate. In other words, parents may not engage in much of the language shaping that is critical to the behavioral explanation of language development (Maratsos, 1983; Pinker, 1990).

An alternative theory favored by Chomsky and others is that humans have an inborn or "native" propensity to develop language (Chomsky, 1975, 1986; Crain, 1991; McNeill, 1970). In this sense, *native* is a variation on the word *nature* as it's used in the nature versus nurture debate. *Nativist theory* proposes that humans are equipped with a *language acquisition device (LAD)—an innate mechanism or process that facilitates the learning of language.* According to this view, humans learn language for the same reason that birds learn to fly—because they're biologically equipped for it. The exact nature of the LAD has not been spelled out in nativist theories. It presumably consists of brain structures and neural wiring that leave humans well prepared to discriminate among phonemes, to fast-map morphemes, to acquire rules of syntax, and so on.

Why does Chomsky believe that children have an innate capacity for learning language? One reason is that children seem to acquire language quickly and effortlessly. How could they develop so complex a skill in such a short time unless they have a built-in capacity for it? Another reason is that language development tends to unfold at roughly the same pace for most children, even though children obviously are reared in diverse home environments. This finding suggests that language development is determined by biological maturation more than personal experience. The nativists also cite evidence that the early course of language development is similar across very different cultures (Slobin, 1985). They interpret this to mean that children all over the world are guided by the same innate capabilities.

Interactionist Theories

Like Skinner, Chomsky has his critics. His nativist theory has been attacked on a number of grounds. Some critics assert that Chomsky's "language acquisition device" isn't much of an explanation. They ask: What exactly is a language acquisition device? How does the LAD work? What are the neural mechanisms involved? They argue that the LAD concept is terribly vague.

Other critics question whether the rapidity of early language development is as exceptional as nativists assume. They assert that it isn't fair to compare the rapid progress of toddlers, who are immersed in their native language, against the struggles of students, who may devote only 10–15 hours per week to their foreign language course. It is more appropriate to compare youngsters and adults who are learning the same second language after having moved to a new country. Although

"Even at low levels of intelligence, at pathological levels, we find a command of language that is totally unattainable by an ape."
NOAM CHOMSKY

The Eskimo language has numerous words for *snow*. Does that mean that Eskimo people think differently from English speakers, who have a more limited snow vocabulary?

the human organism is biologically well equipped for learning language. They also agree that much of this learning involves the acquisition of rules. However, they stress that these realities do *not* mean that language development is automatic or that environment is irrelevant. Like the behaviorists, they believe that social exchanges with parents and others play a critical role in molding language skills. Thus, interactionist theories maintain that an innate predisposition and a supportive environment both contribute to language development.

Culture, Language, and Thought

Another long-running controversy in the study of language concerns the relations between culture, language, and thought. Obviously, people from different cultures generally speak different languages. But does your training in English lead you to think about certain things differently than someone who was raised to speak Chinese or French? In other words, does a cultural group's language determine their thought? Or does thought determine language?

Benjamin Lee Whorf (1956) has been the most prominent advocate of **linguistic relativity, the hypothesis that one's language determines the nature of one's thought.** Whorf speculated that different languages lead people to view the world differently. His classic example compared English and Eskimo views of snow. He asserted that the English language has just one word for snow, whereas the Eskimo language has many words that distinguish among falling snow, wet snow, and so on. Because of this language gap, Whorf argued that Eskimos perceive snow differently than English-speaking people do. However, Whorf's conclusion about these perceptual differences was based on casual observation rather than systematic cross-cultural comparisons of perceptual processes. Moreover, critics subsequently noted that advocates of the linguistic relativity hypothesis had carelessly overestimated the number of Eskimo words for snow, while conveniently ignoring the variety of English words that refer to snow, such as slush and blizzard (Martin, 1986; Pullum, 1991).

Nonetheless, Whorf's hypothesis has been the subject of spirited debate. In one of the betterdesigned experimental tests of this hypothesis, Eleanor Rosch (1973) compared the color perceptions of English-speaking people with those of the Dani, an agricultural people who live in New Guinea. The Dani were chosen because their

some studies find that children have an advantage in this situation (Johnson & Newport, 1989), many others suggest that adults can learn a second language about as readily as young children (Snow, 1993). Nativist theories have also been undermined by recent evidence that parents *do* provide their children with subtle corrective feedback about grammar (Bohannon, MacWhinney, & Snow, 1990; Bohannon & Stanowicz, 1988).

The problems apparent in Skinner's and Chomsky's explanations of language development have led some psychologists to outline *interactionist theories* of language acquisition. These theories assert that biology and experience *both* make important contributions to the development of language.

Interactionist theories come in two basic varieties. *Cognitive theories* assert that language development is simply an important aspect of more general cognitive development (Meltzoff & Gopnik, 1989; Piaget, 1983). Hence, language acquisition is tied to children's progress in thinking—which depends on both maturation and experience. According to this view, when children begin to add *ed* to verbs to express past tense, it's because they understand the *idea* of the past. *Social communication theories* emphasize the functional value of interpersonal communication and the social context in which language evolves (Bohannon & Warren-Leubecker, 1989; Farrar, 1990). According to this view, language development is modulated to some extent by interaction with mature language users and the feedback they provide.

Like the nativists, interactionists believe that

language includes relatively few *basic color terms* (widely used words for widely agreed upon colors). In fact, the Dani have terms for only two basic colors (bright and dark). In contrast, the English language includes eleven basic color terms. Previous research had shown that English speakers learn arbitrary, nonsense names for these eleven basic colors more easily than for nonbasic colors. If language determines thought, this advantage in learning new names for the eleven basic colors should *not* be seen among the Dani, since they don't think in terms of these colors. However, the Dani also found it easier to learn nonsense names for the eleven basic colors. Thus, Rosch concluded that the Dani think about color much as English speakers do, even though their language treats color differently. Rosch's findings clearly contradict Whorf's hypothesis.

Is there any evidence that is consistent with the linguistic relativity hypothesis? Yes. Bloom's (1981) research on *counterfactual thinking* suggests that language may shape thought. *Counterfactual assertions* are propositions that begin with a premise that is implied to be false. For example, the statement "If I knew French, I could read the works of Voltaire" implies that the speaker does *not* know French. The English language easily accommodates such "If only" hypotheticals, but the Chinese language is ill-equipped to handle them. Thus, a Chinese speaker would express the same idea in a factual rather than hypothetical manner ("I don't know French, so I can't read the works of Voltaire"). Bloom investigated the repercussions of this linguistic disparity by comparing Chinese and American college students' ability to understand counterfactual assertions. He found that the Chinese students made many more errors in interpreting counterfactual statements. Hence, he concluded that the Chinese and English languages foster somewhat different types of thinking.

So, what is the status of the linguistic relativity hypothesis? The preponderance of evidence provides little support for the original, strong version of the hypothesis—that a given language makes certain ways of thinking obligatory or impossible (Berry et al., 1992; Eysenck, 1984). However, a weaker version of the linguistic relativity hypothesis—that a given language makes certain ways of thinking easier or more difficult—may be tenable in light of the evidence on counterfactual thinking (and other research).

In everyday life, many people clearly recognize that language may slant thought along certain lines. This possibility is the basis for concern about sexist language. Women who object to being called "girls," "chicks," and "babes" believe that these terms influence the way people think about women. Concerns about words such as "mankind," "manpower," "policeman," "chairman," and "foreman" are also based on the belief that these words constrain the way people think about women's roles in modern society. In a similar vein, car dealers who sell "preowned cars," airlines that outline precautions for "water landings," and politicians who refer to tax increases as "revenue enhancement initiatives" are manipulating language to influence thought. We'll see additional examples of how language can sway thinking in our later discussion of decision making, but first we turn to the subject of problem solving.

PROBLEM SOLVING: IN SEARCH OF SOLUTIONS

Look at the two problems below. Can you solve them?

In the Thompson family there are five brothers, and each brother has one sister. If you count Mrs. Thompson, how many females are there in the Thompson family?

Fifteen percent of the people in Topeka have unlisted telephone numbers. You select 200 names at random from the Topeka phone book. How many of these people can be expected to have unlisted phone numbers?

These problems, borrowed from Sternberg (1986, p. 214), are exceptionally simple, but many people fail to solve them. The answer to the first problem is two. The only females in the family are Mrs. Thompson and her one daughter, who is a sister to each of her brothers. The answer to the second problem is none. You won't find any people with unlisted phone numbers in the phone book.

Why do many people fail to solve these simple problems? You'll learn why in a moment, when we discuss barriers to effective problem solving. But first, let's examine a scheme for classifying problems into a few basic types.

Types of Problems

Problem solving **refers to active efforts to discover what must be done to achieve a goal that is not readily attainable.** Obviously, if a goal is readily attainable, there isn't a problem. But in problem-solving situations, one must go

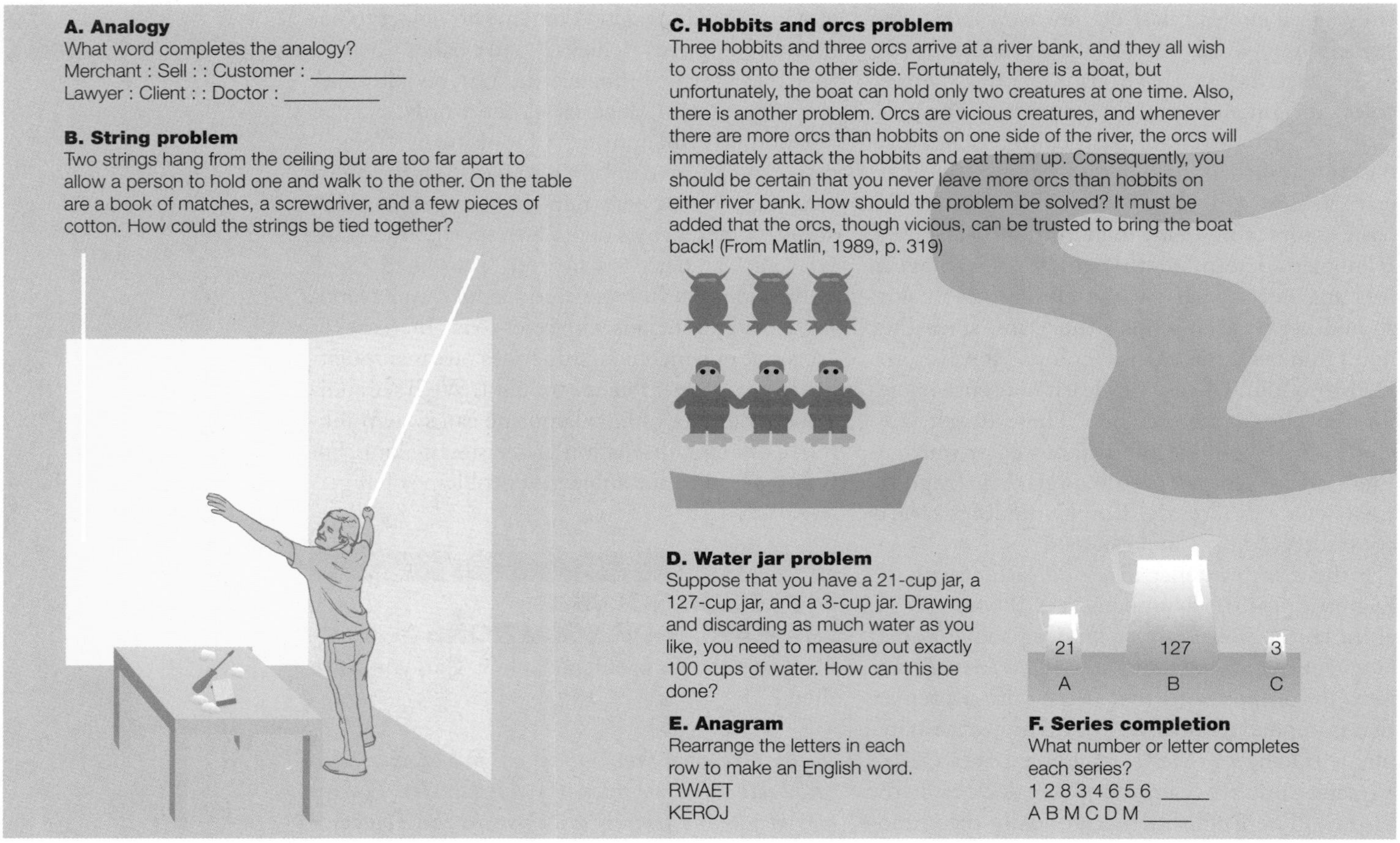

A. Analogy
What word completes the analogy?
Merchant : Sell : : Customer : _____
Lawyer : Client : : Doctor : _____

B. String problem
Two strings hang from the ceiling but are too far apart to allow a person to hold one and walk to the other. On the table are a book of matches, a screwdriver, and a few pieces of cotton. How could the strings be tied together?

C. Hobbits and orcs problem
Three hobbits and three orcs arrive at a river bank, and they all wish to cross onto the other side. Fortunately, there is a boat, but unfortunately, the boat can hold only two creatures at one time. Also, there is another problem. Orcs are vicious creatures, and whenever there are more orcs than hobbits on one side of the river, the orcs will immediately attack the hobbits and eat them up. Consequently, you should be certain that you never leave more orcs than hobbits on either river bank. How should the problem be solved? It must be added that the orcs, though vicious, can be trusted to bring the boat back! (From Matlin, 1989, p. 319)

D. Water jar problem
Suppose that you have a 21-cup jar, a 127-cup jar, and a 3-cup jar. Drawing and discarding as much water as you like, you need to measure out exactly 100 cups of water. How can this be done?

21   127   3
 A   B   C

E. Anagram
Rearrange the letters in each row to make an English word.
RWAET
KEROJ

F. Series completion
What number or letter completes each series?
1 2 8 3 4 6 5 6 _____
A B M C D M_____

Figure 8.3. Six standard problems used in studies of problem solving. Try solving the problems and identifying which class each belongs to before reading further. The problems can be classified as follows. The *analogy problems* and *series completion problems* are problems of inducing structure. The solutions for the analogy problems are *Buy* and *Patient*. The solutions for the series completion problems are *4* and *E*. The *string problem* and the *anagram problems* are problems of arrangement. To solve the string problem, attach the screwdriver to one string and set it swinging as a pendulum. Hold the other string and catch the swinging screwdriver. Then you need only untie the screwdriver and tie the strings together. The solutions for the anagram problems are *WATER* and *JOKER*. The *hobbits and orcs problem* and the *water jar problem* are problems of transformation. The solutions for these problems are outlined in Figures 8.4 and 8.5.

beyond the information given to overcome obstacles and reach a goal. Jim Greeno (1978) has proposed that problems can be categorized into three basic classes:

1. *Problems of inducing structure.* The subject must discover the relations among the parts of the problem. The *series completion problems* and the *analogy problems* in Figure 8.3 are examples of problems of inducing structure.

2. *Problems of arrangement.* The subject must arrange the parts in a way that satisfies some criterion. The parts can usually be arranged in many ways, but only one or a few of the arrangements form a solution. The *string problem* and the *anagrams* in Figure 8.3 fit in this category. Arrangement problems are often solved with a burst of insight. **Insight is the sudden discovery of the correct solution following incorrect attempts based primarily on trial and error.**

3. *Problems of transformation.* The subject must carry out a sequence of transformations in order to reach a specific goal. The *hobbits and orcs problem* and the *water jar problem* in Figure 8.3 are examples of transformation problems. Transformation problems can be challenging. Even though

you know exactly what the goal is, it's often not obvious how the goal can be achieved.

Greeno's list is not an exhaustive scheme for classifying problems, but it provides a useful system for understanding some of the variety seen in everyday problems.

Barriers to Effective Problem Solving

On the basis of their studies of problem solving, psychologists have identified a number of barriers that frequently impede subjects' efforts to arrive at solutions. Common obstacles to effective problem solving include a focus on irrelevant information, functional fixedness, mental set, and imposition of unnecessary constraints.

Irrelevant Information

We began our discussion of problem solving with two simple problems that people routinely fail to solve. The catch is that these problems contain *irrelevant information* that leads people astray. In the first problem, the number of brothers is irrelevant in determining the number of females in the Thompson family. In the second problem, subjects tend to focus on the figures of 15% and 200 names. But this numerical information is irrelevant, since all the names came out of the phone book.

Sternberg (1986) points out that people often incorrectly assume that all the numerical information in a problem is necessary to solve it. They therefore try to figure out how to use quantitative information before they even consider whether it's relevant. Effective problem solving requires that you attempt to figure out what information is relevant and what is irrelevant before proceeding.

Functional Fixedness

Another common barrier to successful problem solving is *functional fixedness*—the tendency to perceive an item only in terms of its most common use. Functional fixedness has been seen in the difficulties that people have with the string problem (Maier, 1931). Solving this problem requires finding a novel use for one of the objects: the screwdriver. Subjects tend to think of the screwdriver in terms of its usual functions—turning screws and perhaps prying things open. They have a hard time viewing the screwdriver as a weight. Their rigid way of thinking about the screwdriver illustrates functional fixedness.

Mental Set

Rigid thinking is also at work when a mental set interferes with effective problem solving. A *mental set* exists when people persist in using problem-solving strategies that have worked in the past. The effects of mental set were seen in a classic study by Abraham Luchins (1942). Luchins asked subjects to work a series of water jar problems, like the one introduced earlier. Six such problems are outlined in Figure 8.6, which shows the capacities of the three jars and the amounts of water to be measured out. Try solving these problems.

Were you able to develop a formula for solving these problems? The first four all require the same strategy, which was described in Figure 8.5. You have to fill jar B, draw off the amount that jar A holds once, and draw off the amount that jar C holds twice. Thus, the formula for your solution is B − A − 2C. Although there is an obvious and much simpler solution (A − C) for the fifth problem (see Figure 8.10 on page 224), Luchins found that most subjects stuck with the more cumbersome strategy that they had used in problems 1–4. Moreover, most subjects couldn't solve the sixth prob-

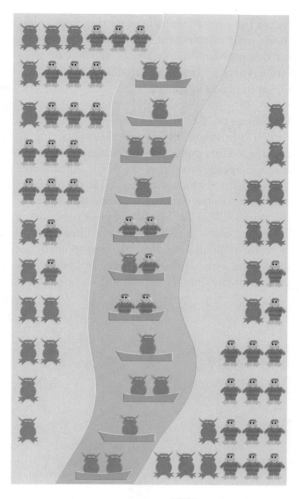

Figure 8.4. Solution to the hobbits and orcs problem. This problem is difficult because it is necessary to temporarily work "away" from the goal.

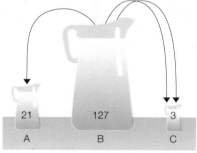

Figure 8.5. The method for solving the water jar problem. The formula is B − A − 2C.

	Capacity of empty jars			
Problem	A	B	C	Desired amount of water
1	14	163	25	99
2	18	43	10	5
3	9	42	6	21
4	20	59	4	31
5	23	49	3	20
6	28	76	3	25

Figure 8.6. Additional water jar problems. Using jars A, B, and C, with the capacities indicated in each row, figure out how to measure out the desired amount of water specified on the far right. (Based on Luchins, 1942)

lem in the allotted time, because they kept trying to use their proven strategy, which does *not* work for this problem. The subjects' reliance on their "tried and true" strategy is an illustration of mental set in problem solving.

Unnecessary Constraints

Effective problem solving requires specifying all the constraints governing a problem *without assuming any constraints that don't exist.* An example of a problem in which people place an unnecessary constraint on the solution is shown in Figure 8.7 (Adams, 1980). Without lifting your pencil from the paper, try to draw four straight lines that will cross through all nine dots. Most people will not draw lines outside the imaginary boundary that surrounds the dots. Notice that this constraint is not part of the problem statement. It's imposed only by the problem solver. Correct solutions, two of which are shown in Figure 8.11 on page 224, extend outside the imaginary boundary. People often make assumptions that impose unnecessary constraints on problem-solving efforts.

Approaches to Problem Solving

People use a variety of strategies in attempting to solve problems. In this section, we'll examine some general strategies.

Trial and Error

Trial and error is a common, albeit primitive, approach to solving problems. **Trial and error involves trying possible solutions sequentially and discarding those that are in error until one works.** Trial and error can be effective when there are relatively few possible solutions to be tried out. However, this method becomes impractical when the number of possible maneuvers is large. Consider, for instance, the problem shown in Figure 8.8. The challenge is to move just two matches to create a pattern containing four equal squares. Sure, you could use a trial-and-error approach in moving pairs of matches about. But you'd better allocate plenty of time to this effort, as there are over 60,000 possible rearrangements to check out (see Figure 8.12 on page 224 for the solution).

Because trial and error is inefficient, people often use shortcuts called *heuristics* in problem solving. **A *heuristic* is a guiding principle or "rule of thumb" used in solving problems or making decisions.** Heuristics are often useful, but they don't guarantee success. Helpful heuristics in problem solving include forming subgoals, working backward, searching for analogies, and changing the representation of the problem.

Forming Subgoals

It is often useful to tackle problems by formulating *subgoals*, intermediate steps toward a solution. When you reach a subgoal, you've solved part of the problem. Some problems have fairly obvious subgoals, and research has shown that people take advantage of them. For instance, in analogy problems, the first subgoal usually is to figure out the possible relations between the first two parts of the analogy.

The wisdom of formulating subgoals can be seen in the *tower of Hanoi problem*, depicted in Figure 8.9. The terminal goal for this problem is to move all three rings on peg A to peg C, while abiding by two restrictions: only the top ring on a

Figure 8.7. The nine-dot problem. Without lifting your pencil from the paper, draw no more than four lines that will cross through all nine dots.

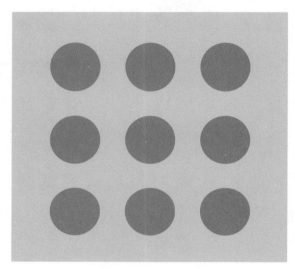

Figure 8.8. The matchstick problem. Move two matches to form four equal squares.

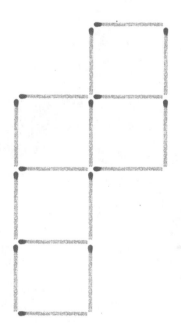

peg can be moved and a ring must never be placed above a smaller ring. See whether you can solve the problem before continuing.

Dividing this problem into subgoals facilitates a solution (Kotovsky, Hayes, & Simon, 1985). If you think in terms of subgoals, your first task is to get ring 3 to the bottom of peg C. Breaking this task into sub-subgoals, subjects can figure out that they should move ring 1 to peg C, ring 2 to peg B, and ring 1 from peg C to peg B. These maneuvers allow you to place ring 3 at the bottom of peg C, thus meeting your first subgoal. Your next subgoal—getting ring 2 over to peg C—can be accomplished in just two steps: move ring 1 to peg A and ring 2 to peg C. It should then be obvious how to achieve your final subgoal—getting ring 1 over to peg C.

Working Backward

Try to work the *lily pond problem* described below:

The water lilies on the surface of a small pond double in area every 24 hours. From the time the first water lily appears until the pond is completely covered takes 60 days. On what day is half of the pond covered with lilies?

If you're working on a problem that has a well-specified end point, you may find the solution more readily if you begin at the end and work backward. This strategy is the key to solving the lily pond problem. If the entire pond is covered on the 60th day, and the area covered doubles every day, how much is covered on the 59th day? One-half of the pond will be covered, and that happens to be the exact point you were trying to reach. The lily pond problem is remarkably simple when you work backward. In contrast, if you move forward from the starting point, you wrestle with questions about the area of the pond and the size of the lilies, and you find the problem riddled with ambiguities.

Working backward is a good strategy when you can see that you have many options available at the beginning of a problem but will have relatively few options available near the end. It's also worth considering when you stop making progress by working forward.

Searching for Analogies

Searching for analogies is another of the major heuristics for solving problems. If you can spot an analogy between problems, you may be able to use the solution to a previous problem to solve a current one. Of course, using this strategy de-

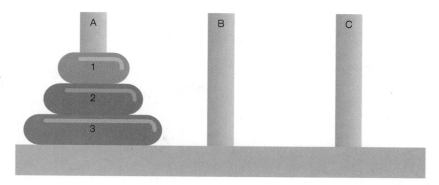

Figure 8.9. The tower of Hanoi problem. Your mission is to move the rings from peg A to peg C. You can move only the top ring on a peg and can't place a larger ring above a smaller one. The solution is explained in the text.

pends on recognizing the similarity between two problems, which may itself be a challenging problem. People often are unable to recognize that two problems are similar, but once informed of the similarity, they do reasonably well in making use of the analogous solution (Gick & Holyoak, 1980; Reed, Ernst, & Banerji, 1974). Try applying this strategy to the following two problems:

A teacher had 23 pupils in his class. All but 7 of them went on a museum trip and thus were away for the day. How many students remained in class that day?

Susan gets in her car in Boston and drives toward New York City, averaging 50 miles per hour. Twenty minutes later, Ellen gets in her car in New York City and starts driving toward Boston, averaging 60 miles per hour. Both women take the same route, which extends a total of 220 miles between the two cities. Which car is nearer to Boston when they meet?

These problems, taken from Sternberg (1986, pp. 213 and 215), resemble the ones that opened our discussion of problem solving. Each has an obvious solution that's hidden in irrelevant quantitative information. If you recognized this similarity, you probably solved the problems easily. If not, take another look now that you know what the analogy is. Neither problem requires any calculation whatsoever. The answer to the first problem is 7. As for the second problem, when the two cars meet they're in the same place. Obviously, they have to be the same distance from Boston.

Changing the Representation of the Problem

Whether you solve a problem often hinges on how you envision it—your *representation of the problem*. Many problems can be represented in a variety of ways, such as verbally, mathematically, or spatially. You might represent a problem with a list, a table, an equation, a graph, a matrix of facts or

Figure 8.10. Solutions to the additional water jar problems. The solution for problems 1–4 is the same (B – A – 2C) as the solution shown in Figure 8.5. This method will work for problem 5, but there also is a simpler solution (A – C), which is the only solution for problem 6. Many subjects exhibit a mental set on these problems, as they fail to notice the simpler solution for problem 5.

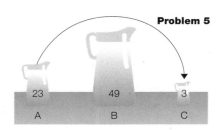

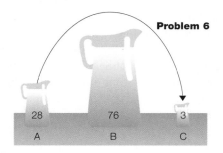

Figure 8.11. Two solutions to the nine-dot problem. The key to solving the problem is to recognize that nothing in the problem statement forbids going outside the imaginary boundary surrounding the dots.

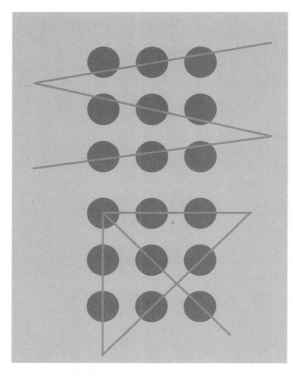

Figure 8.12. Solution to the matchstick problem. The key to solving this problem is to "open up" the figure, something many subjects are reluctant to do because they impose unnecessary constraints on the problem.

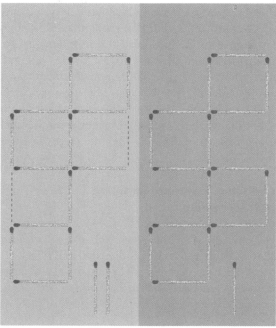

numbers, a hierarchical tree diagram, or a sequential flowchart (Halpern, 1989b). When you fail to make progress with your initial representation of a problem, changing your representation is often a good strategy. As an illustration, see whether you can solve the *Buddhist monk problem:*

At sunrise, a Buddhist monk sets out to climb a tall mountain. He follows a narrow path that winds around the mountain and up to a temple. He stops frequently to rest and climbs at varying speeds, arriving around sunset. After staying a few days, he begins his return journey. As before, he starts at sunrise, rests often, walks at varying speeds, and arrives around sunset. Prove that there must be a spot along the path that the monk will pass on both trips at precisely the same time of day.

Why should there be such a spot? The monk's walking speed varies. Shouldn't it all be a matter of coincidence if he reaches a spot at the same time each day? Moreover, if there is such a spot, how would you prove it? Subjects who represent this problem in terms of verbal, mathematical, or spatial information struggle. Subjects who work with a graphic representation fare much better. The best way to represent the problem is to envision the monk (or two different monks) ascending and descending the mountain at the same time. The two monks must meet at some point. If you construct a graph (see Figure 8.13) you can vary the speed of the monks' descent in endless ways, but you can see that there's always a place where they meet.

Culture, Cognitive Style, and Problem Solving

Do the varied experiences of people from different cultures lead to cross-cultural variations in problem solving? Yes, researchers have found cultural differences in the cognitive style that people exhibit in solving problems.

Back in the 1940s, Herman Witkin was intrigued by the observation that some airplane pilots would fly into a cloud bank upright but exit it upside down without realizing that they had turned over. Witkin's efforts to explain this aviation problem led to the discovery of an interesting dimension of cognitive style (Witkin, 1950; Witkin et al., 1962). **Field dependence-independence refers to individuals' tendency to rely primarily on external versus internal frames of reference when orienting themselves in space.** People who are *field dependent* rely on external frames of reference and tend to accept the physical environment as a given instead of trying to analyze or restructure it. People who are *field independent* rely on internal frames of reference and tend to analyze and try to restructure the physical environment rather than accepting it as is. In solving problems, field-dependent people tend to focus on the total context of a problem instead of zeroing in on specific aspects or breaking it into component parts. In contrast, field-independent people are more likely to focus on specific features of a problem and to reorganize the component parts. A person's field dependence-independence can be measured with the Embedded Figures Test, which requires subjects to identify simple designs from within more complex ones (see Figure 8.14).

Research has shown that field dependence-independence is related to diverse aspects of cognitive, emotional, and social functioning (Witkin & Goodenough, 1981). Each style has its strengths and weaknesses, but in many types of problem solving, field independence seems more advantageous. For example, studies have shown that field-independent subjects outperform field-dependent subjects on a variety of classic laboratory problems, including the string problem, matchstick problem, candle problem, and water jar problem (Witkin et al., 1962).

An extensive body of research suggests that some cultures encourage a field-dependent cognitive style, whereas others foster a field-independent style (Berry, 1990; Witkin & Berry, 1975). The educational practices in modern Western societies seem to nourish field independence. A field-independent style is also more likely to be predominant in nomadic societies that depend on hunting and gathering for subsistence and in societies with lenient child-rearing practices that encourage personal autonomy. In contrast, a field-dependent style is found more in sedentary agricultural societies and in societies that stress strict child-rearing practices and conformity. According to John Berry (1976), the predominant cognitive style in a society depends in large part on

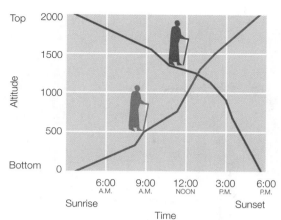

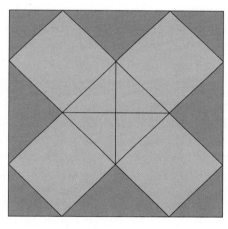

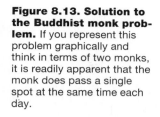

Figure 8.13. Solution to the Buddhist monk problem. If you represent this problem graphically and think in terms of two monks, it is readily apparent that the monk does pass a single spot at the same time each day.

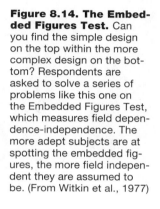

Figure 8.14. The Embedded Figures Test. Can you find the simple design on the top within the more complex design on the bottom? Respondents are asked to solve a series of problems like this one on the Embedded Figures Test, which measures field dependence-independence. The more adept subjects are at spotting the embedded figures, the more field independent they are assumed to be. (From Witkin et al., 1977)

the culture's ecological demands—that is, the types of skills that are necessary to survive or flourish in the culture. For example, in cultures that depend on hunting and gathering for subsistence, the need to extract information from the surrounding field to locate game and food makes a field-independent style more adaptive. Consistent with this analysis, the Eskimo hunters of the Arctic wastelands and the Aboriginal hunters of the desert wastelands in Australia, who both need to extract information from particularly difficult environments, are among the most field-independent peoples of the world (Goodenough, 1986).

Problems are not the only kind of cognitive challenge that people grapple with on a regular basis. Life also seems to constantly demand deci-

Cultural factors appear to influence whether people become field-dependent or field-independent. For example, because of their demanding environment, the Aboriginal hunters of the desert wastelands of Australia are among the most field-independent people in the world.

require more thought. Big decisions—such as selecting a car, a home, or a job—tend to be difficult. The alternatives usually have a number of facets that need to be weighed. For instance, in choosing among several cars, you may want to compare their costs, roominess, fuel economy, handling, acceleration, stylishness, reliability, safety features, and warranties.

Decision making involves evaluating alternatives and making choices among them. Most people try to be systematic and rational in their decision making. However, the work that earned Herbert Simon the 1978 Nobel prize in economics showed that people don't always live up to these goals. Before Simon's work, most traditional theories in economics assumed that people made rational choices to maximize their economic gains. Simon (1957) noted that people have a limited ability to process and evaluate information on numerous facets of possible alternatives. He demonstrated that people tend to use simple strategies in decision making that focus on only a few facets of the available options. According to Simon's theory of *bounded rationality*, people use sensible decision strategies, given their cognitive limitations, but these limitations often result in "irrational" decisions that are less than optimal. In this section, we examine research on decision making to better understand how this happens.

sions. As you might expect, cognitive psychologists have shown great interest in the process of decision making, which is our next subject.

DECISION MAKING: CHOICES AND CHANCES

Decisions, decisions. Life is full of them. You decided to read this book today. Earlier today you decided when to get up, whether to eat breakfast, and if so, what to eat. Usually you make routine decisions like these with little effort. But on occasion you need to make important decisions that

Making Choices: Selecting an Alternative

Many decisions involve choices about *preferences*, which can be made using a variety of strategies (Hogarth, 1987). For instance, imagine that Boris has found two reasonably attractive apartments and is trying to decide between them. How should he go about selecting between his alternatives? Let's look at some strategies Boris might use in trying to make his decision.

If Boris wanted to use an *additive strategy*, he would list the attributes that influence his decision. Then he would rate the desirability of each apartment on each attribute. For example, let's say that Boris wants to consider four attributes: rent, noise level, distance to campus, and cleanliness. He might make ratings from −3 to +3, like those shown in Table 8.3, add up the ratings for each alternative, and select the one with the largest total. Given the ratings in Table 8.3, Boris should select apartment B.

To make an additive strategy more useful, you can *weight* attributes differently, based on their

Table 8.3 Application of the Additive Model to Choosing an Apartment

	Apartment	
Attribute	A	B
Rent	+1	+2
Noise level	−2	+3
Distance to campus	+3	−1
Cleanliness	+2	+2
Total	**+4**	**+6**

Check your understanding of problem solving by answering some questions about the following problem. Begin by trying to solve the problem.

The candle problem. Using the objects shown—candles, a box of matches, string, and some tacks—figure out how you could mount a candle on a wall so that it could be used as a light.

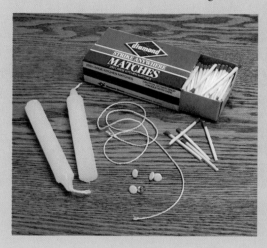

Work on the problem for a while before you turn to page 228 to see the solution. After you've seen the solution, respond to the following questions. The answers are in Appendix A.

1. If it didn't occur to you that the matchbox could be converted from a container to a platform, this illustrates _____ _____.

2. While working on the problem, if you thought to yourself, "How can I create a platform attached to the wall?" you used the heuristic of _____ _____.

3. If it occurred to you suddenly that the matchbox could be used as a platform, this realization would be an example of _____.

4. If you had a hunch that there might be some similarity between this problem and the string problem in Figure 8.3 (the similarity is the novel use of an object), your hunch would illustrate the heuristic of _____ _____ _____.

5. In terms of Greeno's three types of problems, the candle problem is a(n) _____ problem.

importance (Goldstein, 1990). For example, if Boris considers distance to campus to be twice as important as the other considerations, he could multiply his ratings of this attribute by 2. The distance rating would then be +6 for apartment A and –2 for apartment B, and apartment A would become the preferred choice.

People also make choices by gradually eliminating less attractive alternatives (Slovic, 1990; Tversky, 1972). This strategy is called *elimination by aspects* because it assumes that alternatives are eliminated by evaluating them on each attribute or aspect in turn. Whenever any alternative fails to satisfy some minimum criterion for an attribute, it is eliminated from further consideration.

To illustrate, suppose Juanita is looking for a new car. She may begin by eliminating all cars that cost over $10,000. Then she may eliminate cars that don't average at least 20 miles per gallon of gas. By continuing to reject choices that don't satisfy some minimum criterion on selected attributes, she can gradually eliminate alternatives until only a single car remains.

The final choice in elimination by aspects depends on the order in which attributes are evaluated. For example, if cost was the last attribute Juanita evaluated, she could have previously eliminated all cars that cost under $10,000! If she has only $10,000 to spend, her decision-making strategy would not have brought her very far. Thus, when using elimination by aspects, it's best to evaluate attributes in the order of their importance.

Both the additive and the elimination-by-aspects strategies have advantages, but which strategy do people actually tend to use? Research by John Payne (1976) suggests that when decisions involve relatively few options that need to be evaluated on only a few attributes, people tend to use additive strategies. However, as more options and factors are added to a decision task, people tend to shift to elimination by aspects. Thus, subjects adapt their approach to the demands of the task. When their choices become very complex, they shift toward simpler decision strategies.

Risky decision making occurs in any situation where the outcome is uncertain. Gamblers deal with a high degree of uncertainty, and chess players make dozens of risky decisions in any game. President Clinton risked his relationship with voters by getting involved in the Mid-East peace process.

The solution to the candle problem in Concept Check 8.3.

Taking Chances: Risky Decision Making

Suppose you have the chance to play a dice game in which you might win some money. You must decide whether it would be to your advantage to play. You're going to roll a fair die. If the number 6 appears, you win $5. If one of the other five numbers appears, you win nothing. It costs you $1 every time you play. Should you participate?

This problem calls for a type of decision making that is somewhat different from making choices about preferences. In selecting alternatives that reflect preferences, people generally weigh known outcomes (apartment A will require a long commute to campus, car B will get 30 miles per gallon, and so forth). In contrast, *risky decision making* **involves making choices under conditions of uncertainty.** Uncertainty exists when people don't know what will happen. At best, they know, or can estimate, the probability that a particular event will occur.

Factors Weighed in Risky Decisions

One way to decide whether to play the dice game would be to figure out the *expected value* of participation in the game. To do so, you would need to calculate the average amount of money you could expect to win or lose each time you play. The value of a win is $4 ($5 minus the $1 entry fee). The value of a loss is –$1. To calculate expected value, you also need to know the probability of a win or loss. Since a die has six faces, the probability of a win is 1 out of 6, and the probability of a loss is 5 out of 6. Thus, on five out of every six trials, you lose $1. On one out of six, you win $4. The game is beginning to sound unattractive, isn't it? We can figure out the precise expected value as follows:

$$\text{Expected value} = (1/6 \times 4) + (5/6 \times -1)$$
$$= 4/6 + (-5/6)$$
$$= -1/6$$

The expected value of this game is $-\frac{1}{6}$ of a dollar, which means that you lose an average of about 17 cents per turn. Now that you know the expected value, surely you won't agree to play. Or will you?

If we want to understand why people make the decisions they do, the concept of expected value is not enough. People frequently behave in ways that are inconsistent with expected value (Slovic, Lichtenstein, & Fischoff, 1988). Any time the expected value is negative, a gambler should expect to lose money. Yet a great many people gamble at racetracks and casinos and buy lottery tickets. Although they realize that the odds are against them, they continue to gamble. Even people who don't gamble buy homeowner's insurance, which has a negative expected value. After all, when you buy insurance, your expectation (and hope!) is that you will lose money on the deal.

To explain decisions that violate expected value, some theories replace the objective value of an outcome with its *subjective utility* (Fischoff, 1988). Subjective utility represents what an outcome is personally worth to an individual. For example, buying a few lottery tickets may allow you to dream about becoming wealthy. Buying insurance may give you a sense of security. Subjective utilities like these vary from one person to another. If we know an individual's subjective utilities, we can better understand that person's risky decision making.

Another way to improve our understanding of risky decision making is to consider individuals' estimates of the *subjective probability* of events (Shafer & Tversky, 1988). If people don't know actual probabilities, they must rely on their personal estimates of probabilities. Subjective probabilities introduce another bit of illogic into our decision making.

Heuristics in Judging Probabilities

- What are your chances of passing your next psychology test if you study only 3 hours?
- How likely is a major downturn in the stock market during the upcoming year?
- What are the odds of your getting into graduate school in the field of your choice?

These questions ask you to make probability estimates. Amos Tversky and Daniel Kahneman (1982) have conducted extensive research on the *heuristics*, or mental shortcuts, that people use in grap-

pling with probabilities. Sometimes these heuristics yield reasonable estimates, but often they do not.

Availability is one such heuristic. **The *availability heuristic* involves basing the estimated probability of an event on the ease with which relevant instances come to mind.** For example, you may estimate the divorce rate by recalling the number of divorces among your friends' parents. Recalling specific instances of an event is a reasonable strategy to use in estimating the event's probability. However, if instances occur frequently but you have difficulty retrieving them from memory, your estimate will be biased. For instance, it's easier to think of words that begin with a certain letter than words that contain that letter at some other position. Hence, people should tend to respond that there are more words starting with the letter K than words having a K in the third position. To test this hypothesis, Tversky and Kahneman (1973) selected five consonants (K, L, N, R, V) that occur more frequently in the third position of a word than in the first. Subjects were asked whether each of the letters appears more often in the first or third position. Most of the subjects erroneously believed that all five letters were much more frequent in the first than in the third position, confirming the hypothesis.

Representativeness is another guide in estimating probabilities identified by Kahneman and Tversky (1982). **The *representativeness heuristic* involves basing the estimated probability of an event on how similar it is to the typical prototype of that event.** To illustrate, imagine that you flip a coin six times and keep track of how often the result is heads (H) or tails (T). Which of the following sequences is more likely?

1. T T T T T T
2. H T T H T H

People generally believe that the second sequence is more likely. After all, coin tossing is a random affair, and the second sequence looks much more representative of a random process than the first. In reality, the probability of each exact *sequence* is precisely the same ($\frac{1}{2} \times \frac{1}{2} \times \frac{1}{2} \times \frac{1}{2} \times \frac{1}{2} \times \frac{1}{2} = \frac{1}{64}$). We'll see more examples of how the representativeness heuristic works in our upcoming Application on pitfalls in decision making.

The Framing of Questions

Another consideration in making decisions involving risks is the *framing of questions* (Tversky &

"People treat their own cases as if they were unique, rather than part of a huge lottery. You hear this silly argument that 'The odds don't apply to me.' Why should God, or whoever runs this lottery, give you special treatment?"
AMOS TVERSKY

"The human mind suppresses uncertainty. We're not only convinced that we know more about our politics, our businesses, and our spouses than we really do, but also that what we don't know must be unimportant."
DANIEL KAHNEMAN

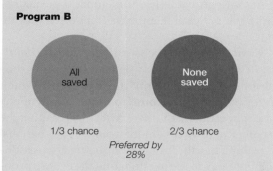

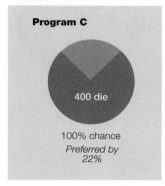

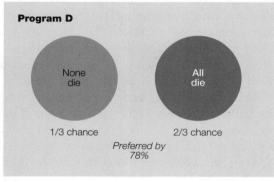

Figure 8.15. The framing of questions. This chart shows that Programs A and C involve an identical probability situation, as do Programs B and D. When choices are framed in terms of possible gains, people prefer the safer plan. However, when choices are framed in terms of losses, people are more willing to take a gamble.

Kahneman, 1988, 1991). **Framing refers to how issues are posed or how choices are structured.** People often allow a decision to be shaped by the language or context in which it's presented, rather than explore it from different perspectives. Consider the following scenario, adapted from Kahneman and Tversky (1984, p. 343):

Imagine that the U.S. is preparing for the outbreak of a dangerous disease, which is expected to kill 600 people. Two alternative programs to combat the disease have been proposed. Assume that the exact scientific estimates of the consequences of the programs are as follows.
- *If Program A is adopted, 200 people will be saved.*
- *If Program B is adopted, there is a one-third probability that all 600 people will be saved and a two-thirds probability that no people will be saved.*

Kahneman and Tversky found that 72% of their subjects chose the "sure thing" (Program A) over the "risky gamble" (Program B). However, they obtained different results when the alternatives were reframed as follows:

- *If Program C is adopted, 400 people will die.*
- *If Program D is adopted, there is a one-third probability that nobody will die and a two-thirds probability that all 600 people will die.*

Although framed differently, Programs A and B

represent exactly the same probability situation as Programs C and D (see Figure 8.15). In spite of this equivalence, 78% of the subjects chose Program D. Thus, subjects chose the sure thing when the decision was framed in terms of lives saved, but they went with the risky gamble when the decision was framed in terms of lives lost. On the basis of many additional experiments, Kahneman and Tversky concluded that these results reflected an interesting general trend: *When seeking to obtain gains, people tend to avoid risky options. However, when seeking to cut their losses, people are much more likely to take risks.*

Although there are some limiting conditions that reduce the likelihood of framing effects (Miller & Fagley, 1991), these effects have been found in many studies, which have examined everything from gambling behavior (Elliott & Archibald, 1989), to product preferences (Neale & Northcraft, 1986), to decisions about genetic risks (Huys, Evers-Kiebooms, & d'Ydewalle, 1990). Clearly, framing is a factor in many of the choices people face in everyday life. For instance, some oil companies charge gas station patrons an extra nickel or so per gallon when they pay with a credit card. This fee clearly is a credit surcharge that results in a small financial loss. However, the oil companies never explicitly label it as a surcharge. Instead, they assert that they offer a discount for cash. Thus, they frame the decision as a choice between the normal price or an opportunity for a gain. They understand that it's easier for customers to foresake a gain than to absorb a loss.

In summary, the evidence on decision making suggests that people try to follow systematic and logical strategies, but they often aren't as rational as they could be—even when they think they are.

PUTTING IT IN PERSPECTIVE

Four of our unifying themes have been especially prominent in this chapter. The first is the continuing question about the relative influence of heredity and environment. The controversy about how children acquire language skills replays the nature versus nurture debate. The behaviorist theory, that children learn language through imitation and reinforcement, emphasizes the importance of the environment. The nativist theory, that children come equipped with an innate language acquisition device, argues for the importance of biology. The debate is far from settled, but the

Check your understanding of heuristics in decision making by trying to identify the heuristics used in the following example. Each numbered element in the anecdote below illustrates a problem-solving heuristic. Write the relevant heuristic in the space on the left. You can find the answers in Appendix A.

_____ 1. Marsha can't decide on a college major. She evaluates all the majors available at her college on the attributes of how much she would enjoy them (likability), how challenging they are (difficulty), and how good the job opportunities are in the field (employability). She drops from consideration any major that she regards as "poor" on any of these three attributes.

_____ 2. When she considers history as a major, she thinks to herself, "Gee, I know four history graduates who are still looking for work," and concludes that the probability of getting a job using a history degree is very low.

_____ 3. She finds that every major gets a "poor" rating on at least one attribute, so she eliminates everything. Because this is unacceptable, she decides she has to switch to another strategy. Marsha finally focuses her consideration on five majors that received just one "poor" rating. She uses a 4-point scale to rate each of these majors on each of the three attributes she values. She totals the ratings and selects the major with the largest sum as her leading candidate.

accumulating evidence suggests that language development depends on both nature and nurture, as more recent interactionist theories of language acquisition have proposed.

The second pertinent theme is the empirical nature of psychology. For many decades, psychologists paid little attention to cognitive processes, because most of them assumed that thinking is too private to be studied scientifically. During the 1950s and 1960s, however, psychologists began to devise creative new ways to measure mental processes. These innovations fueled the cognitive revolution that put the *psyche* (the mind) back in psychology. Thus, once again, we see how empirical methods are the lifeblood of the scientific enterprise.

Third, the study of cognitive processes shows how there are both similarities and differences across cultures in behavior. On the one hand, we saw that language development unfolds in much the same way in widely disparate cultures and that thought processes are largely invariant in spite of sharp differences in cultures' linguistic heritage. On the other hand, we learned that there are cultural variations in cognitive style that reflect the ecological demands of one's environment. And, although the evidence does not support the strong version of the linguistic relativity hypothesis, we saw that a culture's language may make certain ways of thinking easier or more difficult. Thus, cognitive processes are moderated—albeit to a limited degree—by cultural factors.

The fourth theme is the subjective nature of human experience. We have seen that decision making is a highly subjective process. Indeed, reframed in new language, choices that are objectively identical can subjectively seem very different. The subjectivity of decision processes will continue to be prominent in the upcoming Application, which discusses common pitfalls in decision making.

Understanding Pitfalls in Reasoning About Decisions

Consider the following scenario:

Beth is in a casino watching people play roulette. The 38 slots in the roulette wheel include 18 black numbers, 18 red numbers, and 2 green numbers. Hence, on any one spin, the probability of red or black is slightly less than 50-50 (.474 to be exact). Although Beth hasn't been betting, she has been following the pattern of results in the game very carefully. The ball has landed in red seven times in a row. Beth concludes that black is long overdue and she jumps into the game, betting heavily on black.

Has Beth made a good bet? Do you agree with Beth's reasoning? Or do you think that Beth misunderstands the laws of probability? You'll find out momentarily, as we discuss how people reason their way to decisions—and how their reasoning can go awry.

The pioneering work of Amos Tversky and Daniel Kahneman (1982) has led to an explosion of research on risky decision making. In their efforts to identify the heuristics that people use in decision making, investigators have stumbled onto quite a few misconceptions, oversights, and illusions. As a whole, many decisions are not as rational or as systematic as people believe they are. Fortunately, there is evidence that increased awareness of shortcomings in reasoning about decisions can lead to improved decision making (Agnoli & Krantz, 1989; Keren, 1990). With this goal in mind, let's look at some common pitfalls in reasoning about decisions.

The Gambler's Fallacy

As you may have guessed by now, Beth's reasoning in our opening scenario is flawed. A great many people tend to

believe that Beth has made a good bet (Tversky & Kahneman, 1982). However, they're wrong. Beth's behavior illustrates **the *gambler's fallacy*—the belief that the odds of a chance event increase if the event hasn't occurred recently.** People believe that the laws of probability should yield fair results and that a random process must be self-correcting. These aren't bad assumptions in the long run. However, they don't apply to individual, independent events.

The roulette wheel does not remember its recent results and make adjustments for them. Each spin of the wheel is an independent event. The probability of black on each spin remains at .474, even if red comes up 100 times in a row! The gambler's fallacy reflects the pervasive influence of the *representativeness heuristic*. In betting on black, Beth is predicting that future results will be more representative of a random process. This logic can be used to estimate the probability of black across a *string of spins*. But it doesn't apply to a *specific spin* of the roulette wheel.

Ignoring Base Rates and the Laws of Probability

Steve is very shy and withdrawn, invariably helpful, but with little interest in people or in the world of reality. A meek and tidy soul, he has a need for order and structure and a passion for detail. Do you think Steve is a salesperson or a librarian? (Adapted from Tversky & Kahneman, 1974, p. 1124)

Using the *representativeness heuristic*, subjects tend to guess that Steve is a librarian, because he resembles their prototype of a librarian (Tversky & Kahneman, 1982). In reality, this is not a very wise guess, because it *ignores the base*

rates of librarians and salespeople in the population. Virtually everyone knows that salespeople outnumber librarians by a wide margin (roughly 75 to 1 in the United States). This fact makes it much more likely that Steve is in sales. But in estimating probabilities, people often ignore information on base rates.

Obviously, people do not always neglect base rate information (Bar-Hillel, 1990). However, people are particularly bad about applying base rates to themselves. For instance, Weinstein (1984) found that people underestimated the risks of their own health-impairing habits while viewing others' risks much more accurately. Similarly, people starting new companies ignore the high failure rate for new businesses, and burglars underestimate the likelihood that they will end up in jail. Thus, in risky decision making, people often think that they can beat the odds. As Amos Tversky puts it, "People treat their own cases as if they were unique, rather than part of a huge lottery. You hear this silly argument that 'The odds don't apply to me.' Why should God, or whoever runs this lottery, give you special treatment?" (McKean, 1985, p. 27).

The Law of Small Numbers

Envision a small urn filled with a mixture of red and green beads. You know that two-thirds of the beads are one color and one-third are the other color. However, you don't know whether red or green predominates. A blindfolded person reaches into the urn and comes up with 3 red beads and 1 green bead. These beads are put back in the urn and a second person scoops up 14 red beads and 10 green beads. Both samplings suggest that red beads outnumber green beads in the urn. But which sample provides better evidence? (Adapted from McKean, 1985, p. 25)

Many subjects report that the first sampling is more convincing, because of the greater preponderance of red over green. What are the actual odds that each sampling accurately reflects the dominant color in the urn? The odds for the first sampling are 4 to 1. These aren't bad odds, but the odds that the second sampling is accurate are much higher—16 to 1. Why? Because the second sample is substantially larger than the first. The likelihood of misleading results is much greater in a small sample than a large one. For example, in flipping a fair coin, the odds of getting all heads in a sample of 5 coin flips dwarfs the odds of getting all heads in a sample of 100 coin flips.

Most people appreciate the value of a large sample as an abstract principle, but they don't fully understand that results based on small samples are more variable and more likely to be a fluke (Well, Pollatsek, & Boyce, 1990). Hence, they frequently assume that results based on small samples are representative of the population. Tversky and Kahneman (1971) call this the *belief in the law of small numbers*. This misplaced faith in small numbers explains why people are often willing to draw general conclusions based on a few individual cases.

Overestimating the Improbable

Various causes of death are paired up below. In each pairing, which is the more likely cause of death?

> *Asthma or tornadoes?*
> *Syphilis or botulism (food poisoning)?*
> *Tuberculosis or floods?*
> *Suicide or murder?*

Table 8.4 shows the actual mortality rates for each of the causes of death just

Table 8.4 Actual Mortality Rates for Selected Causes of Death

Cause of Death	Rate	Cause of Death	Rate
Asthma	920	Tornadoes	44
Syphilis	200	Botulism	1
Tuberculosis	1,800	Floods	100
Suicide	12,000	Homicide	9,200

Note: Mortality rates are per 1 billion people and are based on U.S. statistics.
Source: Halpern (1989b)

listed. As you can see, the first choice in each pair is the more common cause of death. If you guessed wrong for several pairings, don't feel bad. Like many other people, you may be a victim of the tendency to *overestimate the improbable*. People tend to greatly overestimate the likelihood of dramatic, vivid—but infrequent—events that receive heavy media coverage. Thus, the number of fatalities due to tornadoes, floods, food poisonings, and murders is usually overestimated (Slovic, Fischoff, & Lichtenstein, 1982). Fatalities due to asthma and other common diseases, which receive less media coverage, tend to be underestimated. This tendency to exaggerate the improbable reflects the operation of the *availability heuristic*. Instances of floods, tornadoes, and such are readily available in memory because people are exposed to a great deal of publicity about such events.

Confirmation Bias and Belief Perseverance

Imagine a young physician examining a sick patient. The patient is complaining of a high fever and a sore throat. The physician must decide on a diagnosis from among myriad possible diseases. The physician thinks that it may be the flu. She asks the patient if he feels "achy all over." The answer is "yes." The physician asks if the symptoms began a few days ago. Again, the response is "yes." The physician concludes that the patient has the flu. (Adapted from Halpern, 1984, pp. 215–216)

Do you see any flaws in the physician's reasoning? Has she probed into the causes of the patient's malady effectively? No, she has asked about symptoms that would be consistent with her preliminary diagnosis, but she has not inquired about symptoms that could rule it out. Her questioning of the patient illustrates *confirmation bias*—the tendency to seek information that supports one's decisions and beliefs while ignoring disconfirming information. This bias is common in medical diagnosis and other forms of decision making (Green, 1990; Klayman & Ha, 1987). There's nothing wrong with searching for supportive evidence. However, people should also seek disconfirming evidence—which they often neglect to do.

Confirmation bias contributes to another, related problem called *belief perseverance*—the tendency to hang onto beliefs in the face of contradictory evidence (Gorman, 1989). It is difficult to dislodge an idea after having embraced it. To investigate this phenomenon, researchers have given subjects evidence to establish a belief (example: high risk takers make better firefighters) and later exposed the subjects to information discrediting the idea. These studies have shown that the disconfirming evidence tends to fall on deaf ears (Ross & Anderson, 1982). Thus, once people arrive at a decision, they are prone to accept supportive evidence at face value while subjecting contradictory evidence to tough, skeptical scrutiny.

The Overconfidence Effect

Make high and low estimates of the total U.S. Defense Department budget in 1986. Choose estimates far enough apart to be 98% confident that the actual figure lies between them. In other words, you should feel that there is only a 2% chance that the correct figure is lower than your low estimate or higher than your high estimate. Write your estimates in the spaces provided, before reading further.

       *High estimate:*_____
       *Low estimate:*_____

When working on problems like this one, people reason their way to their best estimate and then create a confidence interval around it. For instance, let's say that you arrived at $200 billion as your best estimate of the defense budget. You would then expand a range around that estimate—say $150 billion to $250 billion—that you're sure will contain the correct figure. The answer in this case is $286 billion. If the answer falls outside your estimated range, you are not unusual. In making this type of estimate, people consistently tend to make their confidence intervals too narrow (Lichtenstein, Fischoff, & Phillips, 1982). For example, subjects' 98% confidence intervals should include the correct answer 98% of the time, but they actually do so only about 60% of the time.

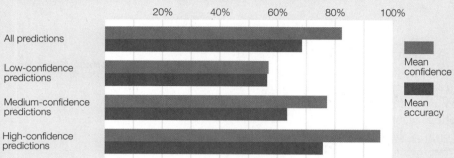

Figure 8.16. Results of the Vallone et al. (1990) study. The subjects in this study (sample 1) made 3776 predictions about personal matters. Their mean confidence level for all these predictions was 82.3%, but their mean accuracy was only 68.2%. When the predictions were divided into low-, medium-, and high-confidence predictions, an interesting pattern emerged. As subjects' confidence level went up, the gap between their confidence and their accuracy increased. This finding suggests that the more confident you are about a personal prediction, the more likely it is that you are overconfident.

The crux of the problem is that people tend to put too much faith in their estimates, beliefs, and decisions, a principle called the *overconfidence effect*. (Gigerenzer, Hoffrage, & Kleinbölting, 1991). This effect is seen even when people make probability predictions about themselves. For instance, in one study (Vallone et al., 1990), college students were asked to make predictions about personal matters for the upcoming fall quarter and the entire academic year. Their predictions concerned such things as whether they would drop any courses, whether they would vote in an upcoming election, or whether they would break up with their boyfriend or girlfriend. The subjects were also asked to rate their confidence in each of their predictions, from 50% confidence to 100% confidence (the predictions were either/or propositions, making 50% a chance level of accuracy and the lowest possible level of confidence). The accuracy of the subjects' predictions was as-sessed at the end of the year. The analyses of thousands of predictions revealed that the students were more confident than accurate. Moreover, the more confident subjects were about their predictions, the more likely it was that they were *over*confident (see Figure 8.16).

The overconfidence effect is also seen among experts in many walks of life (Fischoff, 1988). Studies have shown that physicians, weather forecasters, military leaders, gamblers, investors, and scientists tend to be overconfident about their predictions. As Daniel Kahneman puts it, "The human mind suppresses uncertainty. We're not only convinced that we know more about our politics, our businesses, and our spouses than we really do, but also that what we don't know must be unimportant" (McKean, 1985, p. 27). Thus, in making major decisions, it usually pays to gather as much information as possible and to move forward cautiously.

Chapter 8 Review

KEY IDEAS

The Cognitive Revolution in Psychology

♦ During the first half of the 20th century, the study of cognition was largely suppressed by the theoretical dominance of behaviorism. However, the 1950s brought a cognitive revolution in psychology, as Simon, Chomsky, Miller, and many others reported major advances in the study of mental processes.

Language: Turning Thoughts into Words

♦ Languages are symbolic, semantic, generative, and structured. Human languages are structured hierarchically. At the bottom of the hierarchy are the basic sound units, called phonemes. At the next level are morphemes, the smallest units of meaning. Words are morphemes or are formed of morphemes. At higher levels, words are combined into phrases and sentences according to the rules of syntax.

♦ Language in humans begins with infants' attempts to produce sounds. The initial sounds are similar across languages, but beginning when the child is about 6 months of age, the sounds begin to resemble the surrounding language. Children utter their first words at around 10 to 13 months and can usually say between 3 and 50 words by 18 months.

♦ These early words are often overextended to refer to objects that look similar to the correctly named object. Single words, called holophrases, are also used to express the meaning of several words. Children begin to combine words by the end of their second year. Their early sentences are telegraphic, in that they omit many nonessential words. Over the next several years, children gradually learn the complexities of syntax.

♦ According to Skinner, children acquire a language through imitation and reinforcement. Chomsky argued that people have an innate capacity to learn language rules. Today, theorists are moving toward interactionist perspectives, which emphasize the role of both biology and experience.

♦ The theory of linguistic relativity asserts that language determines thought, thus suggesting that people from different cultures may think about the world somewhat differently. To date, the balance of evidence suggests that thought determines language more than vice versa and that cognitive processes are largely invariant across cultures. However, a weak version of the linguistic relativity hypothesis, which simply proposes that one's language makes certain ways of thinking easier or more difficult, may be tenable.

Problem Solving: In Search of Solutions

♦ In studying problem solving, psychologists have differentiated among several types of problems. Transformation problems require that the problem solver carry out a sequence of transformations (moves) in order to reach a specific goal. Arrangement problems require the problem solver to arrange the parts in a way that satisfies a general goal. In problems that require inducing structure, the problem solver must discover the relations among the parts of a problem.

♦ Common barriers to problem solving include functional fixedness, mental set, getting bogged down in irrelevant information, and placing unnecessary constraints on one's solutions. A variety of strategies, or heuristics, are used for solving problems. When people form subgoals, they try breaking the problem into several parts. Sometimes it is useful to start at the goal state and work backward toward the initial state. Another general strategy involves searching for analogies between new problems and old problems.

♦ Because of varied ecological demands, some cultures encourage a field-dependent cognitive style, whereas others foster more field independence. People who are field independent tend to analyze and restructure problems more than those who are field dependent. These tendencies appear to give field-independent subjects the advantage on some types of problems.

Decision Making: Choices and Chances

♦ The additive model is used when people make decisions by rating the attributes of each alternative and selecting the alternative that has the highest sum of ratings. When elimination by aspects is used, people gradually eliminate alternatives if their attributes fail to satisfy some minimum criterion. To some extent, people adapt their decision-making strategy to the situation, moving toward simpler strategies when choices become very complex.

♦ Models of how people make risky decisions focus on the expected value or subjective utility of various outcomes and the objective or subjective probability that these outcomes will occur. People use the representativeness and availability heuristics in estimating probabilities. Decisions can be influenced by how they are framed.

Putting It in Perspective

♦ Four of our unifying themes surfaced in the chapter. Our discussion of language acquisition revealed once again that most aspects of behavior are shaped by both nature and nurture. The recent progress in the study of cognitive processes showed how science depends on empirical methods. Research on decision making illustrated the importance of subjective perceptions. We also saw that cognitive processes are moderated—to a limited degree—by cultural factors.

Application: Understanding Pitfalls in Reasoning About Decisions

♦ The heuristics that people use in decision making lead to various flaws in reasoning. For instance, the use of the representativeness heuristic contributes to the gambler's fallacy, to ignoring of the base rate, and to faith in small numbers. The availability heuristic underlies the tendency to overestimate the improbable.

♦ People tend to cling to their beliefs in spite of contradictory evidence, in part because they exhibit confirmation bias. People generally fail to appreciate these shortcomings, which lead to the overconfidence effect.

KEY TERMS

Availability heuristic	Linguistic relativity
Belief perseverance	Mean length of utterance (MLU)
Cognition	
Confirmation bias	Mental set
Decision making	Metalinguistic awareness
Fast mapping	
Field dependence-independence	Morphemes
	Overextension
Framing	Overregularizations
Functional fixedness	Phonemes
Gambler's fallacy	Problem solving
Heuristic	Representativeness heuristic
Holophrases	
Insight	Risky decision making
Language	Syntax
Language acquisition device (LAD)	Telegraphic speech
	Trial and error

KEY PEOPLE

Noam Chomsky	B. F. Skinner
Daniel Kahneman	Amos Tversky
Herbert Simon	

9 Intelligence and Psychological Testing

Have you ever thought about the role that psychological testing has played in your life? In all likelihood, your years in grade school and high school were punctuated with a variety of intelligence tests, achievement tests, creativity tests, aptitude tests, and occupational interest tests. In the lower grades, you were probably given standardized achievement tests once or twice a year. For instance, you may have taken the Iowa Tests of Basic Skills, which measured your progress in reading, language, vocabulary, mathematics, and study skills. Perhaps you still have vivid memories of the serious atmosphere in the classroom, the very formal instructions ("Do not break the seal on this test until your examiner tells you to do so"), and the heavy pressure to work fast (I can still see Sister Dominic marching back and forth with her intense gaze riveted on her stopwatch). Where you're sitting at this very moment may have been influenced by your performance on standardized tests. That is, the college you chose to attend may have hinged on your SAT or ACT scores.

The vast enterprise of modern testing evolved from psychologists' pioneering efforts to measure *general intelligence*. The first useful intelligence tests, which were created soon after the turn of the century, left a great many "descendants." Today, there are over 2600 published psychological tests that measure a diverse array of mental abilities and other behavioral traits (Katz & Slomka, 1990).

Clearly, American society has embraced psychological testing. Each year in the United States alone, people take *hundreds of millions* of intelligence and achievement tests (Anderson, 1982). Scholarships, degrees, jobs, and self-concepts are on the line as Americans attempt to hurdle a seemingly endless succession of tests. It's apparent that your life is affected by how you perform on psychological tests. Hence, it pays to be aware of their strengths and limitations. In this chapter we'll explore many questions about testing, including the following:

- How did psychological testing become so prevalent in modern society?

- How do psychologists judge the validity of their tests?

- What exactly do intelligence tests measure?

- Is intelligence inherited? If so, to what extent?

We'll begin by introducing some basic concepts in psychological testing. Then we'll explore the history of intelligence tests, because they provided the model for subsequent psychological tests. Next we'll address practical questions about how intelligence tests work. After examining the nature versus nurture debate as it relates to intelligence, we'll explore some new directions in the study of intelligence. In the Application, we'll discuss efforts to measure and understand another type of mental ability: creativity.

KEY CONCEPTS IN PSYCHOLOGICAL TESTING

A *psychological test* is a standardized measure of a sample of a person's behavior. Psychological tests are measurement instruments. They're used to measure the *individual differences* that exist among people in abilities, aptitudes, interests, and aspects of personality.

Your responses to a psychological test represent a *sample* of your behavior. The word *sample* should alert you to one of the key limitations of psychological tests: A particular behavior sample may not be representative of your characteristic behavior. Everyone has bad days. A stomachache, a fight with a friend, a problem with your car—all might affect your responses to a particular test on a particular day. Because of the limitations of the sampling process, test scores should always be interpreted *cautiously*. Many psychological tests are precise measurement devices. However, because of the ever-present sampling problem, test results should *not* be viewed as the final word on one's personality and abilities.

Principal Types of Tests

Psychological tests are used extensively in research, but most of them were developed to serve a practical purpose outside of the laboratory. Most tests can be placed in one of two broad categories: mental ability tests and personality tests.

Mental Ability Tests

Psychological testing originated with efforts to measure general mental ability. Today, tests of mental abilities remain the most common kind of psychological test. This broad class of tests includes three principal subcategories: intelligence tests, aptitude tests, and achievement tests.

Intelligence tests measure general mental ability. They're intended to assess intellectual potential rather than previous learning or accumulated knowledge. *Aptitude tests* are also designed to measure potential more than knowledge, but they break mental ability into separate components. Thus, *aptitude tests* **assess talent for specific kinds of learning.** In other words, aptitude tests measure particular types of mental ability, such as numerical ability, clerical speed and accuracy, mechanical reasoning, and spatial reasoning. Like aptitude tests, *achievement tests* have a specific focus, but they're supposed to measure previous learning instead of potential. Thus, *achievement tests* **gauge a person's mastery and knowledge of various subjects** (such as reading, English, or history).

Personality Tests

If you had to describe yourself in a few words, what words would you use? Are you introverted? Independent? Ambitious? Conventional? Assertive? Words such as these refer to personality traits. These traits can be assessed systematically with over 500 personality tests. *Personality tests* **measure various aspects of personality, including motives, interests, values, and attitudes.** Many psychologists prefer to call these tests personality *scales* because, unlike tests of mental abilities, the questions do not have right and wrong answers. We'll look at the different types of personality scales in our upcoming chapter on personality (Chapter 12).

Standardization and Norms

Both personality scales and tests of mental abilities are *standardized* measures of behavior. *Standardization* **refers to the uniform procedures used in administrating and scoring a test.** All subjects get the same instructions, the same questions, and the same time limits, so that their scores can be compared meaningfully. This means, for instance, that a person taking the Differential Aptitude Tests (DAT) in 1972 in San Diego, another taking the DAT in 1981 in Atlanta, and another taking it in 1990 in Peoria all confront exactly the same test-taking task.

The standardization of a test's scoring system includes the development of test norms. *Test norms* **provide information about where a score on a psychological test ranks in relation to other scores on that test.** Why are test norms needed? Because in psychological testing, everything is relative. Psychological tests tell you how you score *relative to other people*. They tell you, for instance, that you are average in creativity or slightly above average in clerical ability. These interpretations are derived from the test norms

that help you understand what your test score means.

Usually, test norms allow you to convert your "raw score" on a test into a *percentile*. **A** *percentile score* **indicates the percentage of people who score at or below the score one has obtained.** For example, imagine that you take a 40-item assertiveness scale and obtain a raw score of 26. In other words, you indicate a preference for the assertive option on 26 of the questions. Your score of 26 has little meaning until you consult the test norms and find out that it places you at the 82nd percentile. This normative information would indicate that you appear to be as assertive as or more assertive than 82% of the sample of people who provided the basis for the test norms.

The sample of people that the norms are based on is called a test's *standardization group*. Ideally, test norms are based on a large sample of people who were carefully selected to be representative of the broader population. In reality, the representativeness of standardization groups varies considerably from one test to another.

Reliability

Any kind of measuring device, whether it's a tire gauge, a stopwatch, or a psychological test, should be reasonably consistent. That is, repeated measurements should yield reasonably similar results. Psychologists call this quality *reliability*. To better appreciate the importance of reliability, think about how you would react if a tire pressure gauge were to give you several different readings for the same tire. You would probably conclude that the gauge is broken and toss it into the trash. Consistency in measurement obviously is essential to accuracy in measurement.

Reliability **refers to the measurement consistency of a test (or of other kinds of measurement techniques).** A reliable test is one that yields similar results on repetition of the test (see Figure 9.1). Like most other types of measuring devices, psychological tests are not perfectly reliable. That is, they usually don't yield exactly the same scores when repeated. A certain amount of inconsistency is unavoidable, because human behavior is variable. For example, if you take the Beck Depression Inventory twice, you're not likely to respond to all 21 items in the same way both times.

Although a test's reliability can be estimated in several ways, the most widely used approach is to check test-retest reliability. *Test-retest* **reliability is estimated by comparing subjects' scores on**

two administrations of a test. If we wanted to check the test-retest reliability of a newly developed test of assertiveness, we would ask a group of subjects to take the test on two occasions, probably a few weeks apart. The underlying assumption is that assertiveness is a fairly stable aspect of personality that won't change in a matter of a few weeks. Thus, changes in subjects' scores across the two administrations of the test would presumably reflect inconsistency in measurement.

Reliability estimates require the computation of correlation coefficients, which we introduced in Chapter 2. Correlation plays a critical role in research on testing, so let's reexamine the concept briefly (see Figure 9.2). *A correlation coefficient is a numerical index of the degree of relationship between two variables.* A *positive* correlation indicates a direct relationship between two variables. Thus, high scores on variable X are associated with high scores on variable Y, and low scores on X tend to go with low scores on Y. A negative correlation indicates an inverse relationship between two variables. Hence, high scores on X are associated with low scores on Y, and high scores on Y go with low scores on X. The actual coefficient of correlation can vary between 0 and ±1.00. The closer a correlation comes to either +1.00 or −1.00 (that is, the farther it is from 0), the stronger the association between the two variables.

In estimating test-retest reliability, the two variables that must be correlated are the two sets of scores from the two administrations of the test. If people get fairly similar scores on the two administrations of our hypothetical assertiveness test, this consistency yields a substantial positive correlation. The magnitude of the correlation gives us a precise indication of the test's consistency. The closer the correlation comes to +1.00, the more reliable the test is.

There are no absolute guidelines about acceptable levels of reliability. What's acceptable depends to some extent on the nature and purpose of the test. The reliability estimates for most psychological tests are above .70. Many exceed .90. The

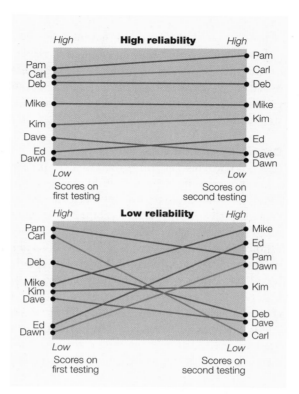

Figure 9.1. Test-retest reliability. Subjects' scores on the first administration of an assertiveness test are represented on the left, and their scores on a second administration of the same test a few weeks later are shown on the right. If subjects obtain similar scores on both administrations, as in the top graph, the test measures assertiveness consistently and has high reliability. If they get very different scores on the second administration, as in the bottom graph, the test has low reliability.

higher the reliability coefficient, the more consistent the test is. As reliability goes down, concern about measurement error increases.

Validity

Even if a test is quite reliable, we still need to be concerned about its validity. *Validity* **refers to the ability of a test to measure what it was designed to measure.** If we develop a new test of assertiveness, we have to provide some evidence that it really measures assertiveness. Validity can be estimated in several ways, depending on the nature of the test (Golden, Sawicki, & Franzen, 1990).

Content Validity

Achievement tests and educational tests such as classroom exams should have adequate content validity. *Content validity* **refers to the degree to which the content of a test is representative of**

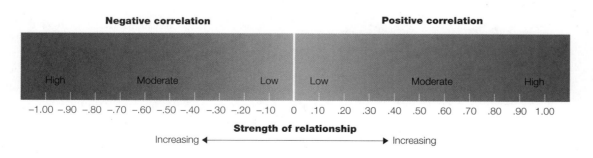

Figure 9.2. Correlation and reliability. As you may recall from Chapter 2, a positive correlation means that two variables are directly related; a negative correlation means that the variables are inversely related. The closer the correlation coefficient gets to either −1.00 or +1.00, the stronger the relationship. At a minimum, reliability estimates for psychological tests must be moderately high positive correlations.

the domain it's supposed to cover. Imagine a poorly prepared physics exam that includes questions on material that was not covered in class or in assigned reading. The professor has compromised the content validity of the exam. Content validity is evaluated with logic more than with statistics.

Criterion-Related Validity

Psychological tests are often used to make predictions about specific aspects of individuals' behavior. They are used to predict performance in college, job capability, and suitability for training programs, as just a few examples. Criterion-related validity is a central concern in such cases. ***Criterion-related validity*** **is estimated by correlating subjects' scores on a test with their scores on an independent criterion (another measure) of the trait assessed by the test** (see Figure 9.3).

For example, let's say you developed a test to measure aptitude for becoming an airplane pilot. You could check its validity by correlating subjects' scores on your aptitude test with subsequent ratings of their performance in their pilot training program. The performance ratings would be the independent criterion of pilot aptitude. If your test has reasonable validity, people who score high on the test should tend to earn high performance ratings during training, and low scorers should tend to get low ratings. In other words, there ought to be a reasonably strong positive correlation between the test and the criterion measure. Such a correlation would help validate your test's predictive ability.

Construct Validity

Many psychological tests attempt to measure abstract personal qualities, such as creativity, intelligence, or independence. There are no obvious criterion measures for these abstract qualities, which are called *hypothetical constructs*. In measuring abstract qualities, psychologists are concerned about ***construct validity***—**the extent to which there is evidence that a test measures a particular hypothetical construct.**

The process of demonstrating construct validity can be complicated. It usually requires a series of studies that examine the correlations between the test and various measures *related* to the trait in question. For example, the construct validity of intelligence tests has been investigated by correlating intelligence test scores with grades in school. No one would argue that grades in school are a pure criterion of intelligence. However, they are undoubtedly related to intelligence. Hence, it can be reasoned that if an intelligence test really measures intelligence, there should be a positive correlation between scores on the test and school grades. If this is found to be the case, the results provide support for the test's construct validity.

A thorough demonstration of construct validity requires looking at the relations between a test and as many related measures as can be found. Ultimately, it's the overall pattern of correlations that provides convincing (or unconvincing) evidence of a test's construct validity.

The complexities involved in demonstrating construct validity will be apparent in our upcoming discussion of intelligence testing. The ongoing debate about the construct validity of intelligence tests is one of the oldest debates in psychology. Let's look first at the origins of intelligence tests. This historical review will help you appreciate the current controversies about intelligence testing.

THE EVOLUTION OF INTELLIGENCE TESTING

Psychological tests play a prominent role in our society, but this wasn't always so. The first psychological tests were invented only a little over a hundred years ago. Since then, the reliance on psychological tests has grown gradually. In this

Figure 9.3. Criterion-related validity. To evaluate the criterion-related validity of a pilot aptitude test, a psychologist would correlate subjects' test scores with a criterion measure of their aptitude, such as ratings of their performance in a pilot training program. Test validity is high if scores on the two measures are highly correlated. If little or no relationship exists between the two sets of scores, validity is low, which means that the aptitude test does not measure what it is supposed to measure.

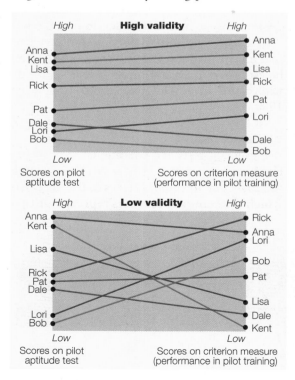

CHAPTER NINE

section, we discuss the pioneers who launched psychological testing with their efforts to measure general intelligence.

Galton's Studies of Hereditary Genius

It all began with the work of a British scholar, Sir Francis Galton, in the later part of the 19th century. Galton studied family trees and found that success and eminence appeared consistently in some families over generations. For the most part, these families were much like Galton's: well-bred, upper-class families with access to superior schooling and social connections that pave the way to success. Yet Galton discounted the advantages of such an upbringing. In his book *Hereditary Genius*, Galton (1869) concluded that success runs in families because great intelligence is passed from generation to generation through genetic inheritance.

To better demonstrate that intelligence is governed by heredity, Galton needed an objective measure of intelligence. His approach to this problem was guided by the theoretical views of his day. Thus, he assumed that the contents of the mind are built out of elementary *sensations*, and he hypothesized that exceptionally bright people should exhibit exceptional sensory acuity. Working from this premise, he tried to assess innate mental ability by measuring simple sensory processes. Among other things, he measured sensitivity to high-pitched sounds, color perception, and reaction time (the speed of one's response to a stimulus). His efforts met with little success. Research eventually showed that the sensory processes that he measured were largely unrelated to other criteria of mental ability that he was trying to predict (such as success in school or professional life). Although Galton's mental tests were a failure, his work created an interest in the measurement of mental ability, setting the stage for a subsequent breakthrough by Alfred Binet, a prominent French psychologist.

Binet's Breakthrough

In 1904 a commission on education in France asked Alfred Binet to devise a test to identify mentally subnormal children. The commission was motivated by admirable goals. It wanted to single out youngsters in need of special training. It also wanted to avoid complete reliance on teachers' evaluations, which might often be subjective and biased.

In response to this need, Binet and a colleague,

CONCEPT CHECK 9.1
Recognizing Basic Concepts in Testing

Check your understanding of basic concepts in psychological testing by answering the questions below. Select your responses from the following concepts:

Test norms
Test-retest reliability
Content validity
Criterion-related validity
Construct validity

The answers are in Appendix A.

1. At the request of the HiTechnoLand computer store chain, Professor Charlz develops a test to measure aptitude for selling computers. Two hundred applicants for sales jobs at HiTechnoLand stores are asked to take the test on two occasions, a few weeks apart. A correlation of +.82 is found between applicants' scores on the two administrations of the test. Thus, the test appears to possess reasonable _____.

2. All 200 of these applicants are hired and put to work selling computers. After six months Professor Charlz correlates the new workers' aptitude test scores with the dollar value of the computers that each sold during the first 6 months on the job. This correlation turns out to be –21. This finding suggests that the test may lack _____.

3. Back at the university, Professor Charlz is teaching a course in theories of personality. He decides to use the same midterm exam that he gave last year, even though the exam includes questions about theorists that he did not cover or assign reading on this year. There are reasons to doubt the _____ of Professor Charlz's midterm exam.

Theodore Simon, published the first useful test of general mental ability in 1905. They had the insight to load it with items that required abstract reasoning skills, rather than the sensory skills Galton had measured. Their scale was a success because it was inexpensive, easy to administer, objective, and capable of predicting children's performance in school fairly well (Siegler, 1992). Thanks to these qualities, its use spread across Europe and America.

The Binet-Simon scale expressed a child's score in terms of "mental level" or "mental age." A child's ***mental age indicated that he or she displayed the mental ability typical of a child of that chronological (actual) age.*** Thus, a child with a mental age of 6 performed like the average 6-year-old on the test. Binet realized that his scale was a somewhat crude initial effort at measuring mental ability. He revised it in 1908 and again in 1911. Unfortunately, his revising came to an abrupt end with his death in 1911. However, other psychologists continued to build on Binet's work.

"The intelligence of anyone is susceptible of development. With practice, enthusiasm, and especially with method one can succeed in increasing one's attention, memory, judgment, and in becoming literally more intelligent than one was before."
ALFRED BINET

Terman and the Stanford-Binet

In America, Lewis Terman and his colleagues at Stanford University soon went to work on a major expansion and revision of Binet's test. Their work led to the 1916 publication of the Stanford-Binet Intelligence Scale (Terman, 1916). Although this revision was quite loyal to Binet's original conceptions, it incorporated a new scoring scheme based on the "intelligence quotient" suggested by William Stern (1914). **An *intelligence quotient (IQ)* is a child's mental age divided by chronological age, multiplied by 100.** As you can see below, IQ scores originally involved actual quotients:

$$IQ = \frac{\text{Mental age}}{\text{Chronological age}} \times 100$$

The ratio of mental age to chronological age made it possible to compare children of different ages. In Binet's system, such comparisons were awkward. The IQ ratio placed all children (regardless of age) on the same scale, which was centered at 100 if their mental age corresponded to their chronological age (see Table 9.1 for examples of IQ calculations).

The Stanford-Binet quickly became the world's foremost intelligence test and the standard of comparison for virtually all intelligence tests that followed (Zimmerman & Woo-Sam, 1984). Although many new IQ tests geared to specific populations, age groups, and purposes have been developed, the apparent variety is somewhat misleading. Most of the tests remain loyal to the conception of intelligence originally formulated by Binet and Terman. Since its publication in 1916, the Stanford-Binet has been updated periodically (in 1937, 1960, and 1986), and it remains one of the world's most widely used psychological tests.

"It is the method of tests that has brought psychology down from the clouds and made it useful to men; that has transformed the 'science of trivialities' into the 'science of human engineering.'"
LEWIS TERMAN

"The subtests [of the WAIS] are different measures of intelligence, not measures of different kinds of intelligence."
DAVID WECHSLER

Wechsler's Innovations

As chief psychologist at New York's massive Bellevue Hospital, David Wechsler was charged with overseeing the psychological assessment of thousands of adult patients. He found the Stanford-Binet somewhat unsatisfactory for this purpose. Thus, Wechsler set out to improve on the measurement of intelligence *in adults*. In 1939 he published the first high-quality IQ test designed specifically for adults, which came to be known as the Wechsler Adult Intelligence Scale (WAIS) (Wechsler, 1955, 1981). Ironically, Wechsler (1949, 1967, 1991) eventually devised downward extensions of his scale for children.

The Wechsler scales were characterized by at least two major innovations (Frank, 1983). First, Wechsler made his scales less dependent on subjects' verbal ability than the Stanford-Binet. He included many items that required nonverbal reasoning. To highlight the distinction between verbal and nonverbal ability, he formalized the computation of separate scores for verbal IQ, performance (nonverbal) IQ, and full-scale (total) IQ. Sample Wechsler items are presented in Figure 9.4.

Second, Wechsler discarded the intelligence quotient in favor of a new scoring scheme based on the *normal distribution*. This scoring system has since been adopted by most other IQ tests, including the Stanford-Binet. Although the term *intelligence quotient* lingers on in our vocabulary, scores on intelligence tests are no longer based on an actual quotient. We'll take a close look at the modern scoring system for IQ tests a little later.

Intelligence Testing Today

Today, psychologists and educators have many IQ tests available for their use. Basically, these tests fall into two categories: *individual tests* and *group tests*. Individual IQ tests are administered only by psychologists who have special training for this purpose. A psychologist works face to face with a single examinee at a time. The Stanford-Binet and the Wechsler scales are both individual IQ tests.

The problem with individual IQ tests is that they're expensive and time-consuming to administer. Therefore, researchers have developed a number of IQ tests that can be administered to large groups of people at once. Because they're much more cost-effective, group tests such as the Otis-Lennon School Ability Test and the Lorge-Thorndike Intelligence Test enjoy wide usage at

Table 9.1 Calculating the Intelligence Quotient

Measure	Child 1	Child 2	Child 3	Child 4
Mental age (MA)	6 years	6 years	9 years	12 years
Chronological age (CA)	6 years	9 years	12 years	9 years
$IQ = \frac{MA}{CA} \times 100$	$\frac{6}{6} \times 100 = 100$	$\frac{6}{9} \times 100 = 67$	$\frac{9}{12} \times 100 = 75$	$\frac{12}{9} \times 100 = 133$

Wechsler Adult Intelligence Scale (WAIS)

Test	Description	Example
Verbal scale		
Information	Taps general range of information	On what continent is France?
Comprehension	Tests understanding of social conventions and ability to evaluate past experience	Why are children required to go to school?
Arithmetic	Tests arithmetic reasoning through verbal problems	How many hours will it take to drive 150 miles at 50 miles per hour?
Similarities	Asks in what way certain objects or concepts are similar; measures abstract thinking	How are a calculator and a typewriter alike?
Digit span	Tests attention and rote memory by orally presenting series of digits to be repeated forward or backward	Repeat the following numbers backward: 2 4 3 5 1 8 6
Vocabulary	Tests ability to define increasingly difficult words	What does *audacity* mean?
Performance scale		
Digit symbol	Tests speed of learning through timed coding tasks in which numbers must be associated with marks of various shapes	Shown: 1 2 3 4 Fill in: 1 4 3 2 
Picture completion	Tests visual alertness and visual memory through presentation of an incompletely drawn figure; the missing part must be discovered and named	Tell me what is missing: 
Block design	Tests ability to perceive and analyze patterns by presenting designs that must be copied with blocks	Assemble blocks to match this design: 
Picture arrangement	Tests understanding of social situations through a series of comic-strip-type pictures that must be arranged in the right sequence to tell a story	Put the pictures in the right order: 
Object assembly	Tests ability to deal with part/whole relationships by presenting puzzle pieces that must be assembled to form a complete object	Assemble the pieces into a complete object: 

Figure 9.4. Subtests on the Wechsler Adult Intelligence Scale (WAIS). The WAIS is subdivided into a series of tests that yield separate verbal and performance (nonverbal) IQ scores. Sample test items that closely resemble those on the WAIS are shown on the right.

all educational levels (Vane & Motta, 1990). Indeed, if you've taken an IQ test, chances are that it was a group test.

Most IQ testing is conducted by school districts, which are largely free to formulate their own unique testing programs. There is little federal or state policy regarding ideal patterns of testing. Some districts administer group IQ tests to all students at regular intervals. Others only administer individual IQ tests on an occasional basis, as needed. Schools use IQ tests to screen for mental retardation, to group students according to their academic ability ("tracking"), to identify gifted children, and to evaluate educational programs (Boehm, 1985).

BASIC QUESTIONS ABOUT INTELLIGENCE TESTING

Misconceptions abound when it comes to intelligence tests. In this section we'll use a question-

Recognizing the Ideas of Pioneers in Intelligence Testing

Check your understanding of some of the key ideas of pioneers in intelligence testing by identifying the authors of each of the following quotations. Choose from among (a) Francis Galton, (b) Alfred Binet, (c) Lewis Terman, and (d) David Wechsler.

_____ 1. "I propose to show in this book that man's natural abilities are derived from inheritance, under exactly the same limitations as are the form and physical features of the whole organic world."

_____ 2. "The grouping of the subtests into Verbal (1–6) and Performance (7–11), while intending to emphasize a dichotomy as regards possible types of ability called for by the individual tests, does not imply that these are the only abilities involved in the tests. Nor does it presume that there are different kinds of intelligence, e.g., verbal, manipulative, etc. It merely implies that these are different ways in which intelligence may manifest itself."

_____ 3. "We here present the first rough sketch of a work which was directly inspired by the desire to serve the interesting cause of the education of subnormals. . . . [T]he Minister of Public Instruction named a commission which was charged with the study of measures to be taken for insuring the benefits of instruction to defective children. . . . They decided that no child suspected of retardation should be eliminated from the ordinary school and admitted into a special class, without first being subjected to a pedagogical and medical examination from which it could be certified that because of the state of his intelligence, he was unable to profit, in an average measure, from the instruction given in the ordinary school."

_____ 4. "The mental age of a subject is meaningless if considered apart from chronological age. It is only the ratio of retardation or acceleration to chronological age (that is, the IQ) which has significance."

and-answer format to explain the basic principles underlying intelligence testing.

What Kinds of Questions Are on Intelligence Tests?

The nature of the questions found on IQ tests varies somewhat from test to test. These variations depend on whether the test is intended for children or adults (or both) and whether the test is designed for individuals or groups. Overall, the questions are fairly diverse in format. The Wechsler scales, with their numerous subtests, provide a representative example of the kinds of items that appear on most IQ tests. As you can see in Figure 9.4, the items in the Wechsler subtests require subjects to furnish information, recognize vocabulary, and demonstrate basic memory. Generally speaking, examinees are required to manipulate words, numbers, and images through abstract reasoning.

What Do Modern IQ Scores Mean?

As we discussed, scores on intelligence tests once represented a ratio of mental age to chronological age. However, this system has given way to one based on the normal distribution and the standard deviation, a statistical index of variability in a data distribution, which is explained in Appendix B. **The *normal distribution* is a symmetrical, bell-shaped curve that represents the pattern in which many characteristics are dispersed in the population.** When a trait is normally distributed, most cases fall near the center of the distribution (an average score) and the number of cases gradually declines as one moves away from the center in either direction. The normal distribution provides a precise way to measure how people stack up in comparison to each other. The scores under the normal curve are dispersed in a fixed pattern, with the standard deviation serving as the unit of measurement, as shown in Figure 9.5. About 68% of the scores in the distribution fall within plus or minus one standard deviation of the mean, whereas 95% of the scores fall within plus or minus two standard deviations of the mean. Given this fixed pattern, if you know the mean and standard deviation of a normally distributed trait, you can tell where any score falls in the distribution for the trait.

The normal distribution was first discovered by 18th-century astronomers. They found that their measurement errors were distributed in a predictable way that resembled a bell-shaped curve. Since then, research has shown that many human traits, ranging from height to running speed to spatial ability, also follow a normal distribution. Psychologists eventually recognized that intelligence scores also fall into a normal distribution. This insight permitted David Wechsler to devise a more sophisticated scoring system for his tests that has been adopted by virtually all subsequent IQ tests. In this system, raw scores are translated into ***deviation IQ scores*** **that locate subjects precisely within the normal distribution.**

For most IQ tests, the mean of the distribution is set at 100 and the standard deviation (SD) is set at 15. These choices were made to provide continuity with the original IQ ratio (mental age to chronological age) that was centered at 100. In this system, which is depicted in Figure 9.5, a score of 115 means that a person scored exactly one SD (15 points) above the mean. A score of 85 means that a person scored one SD below the mean. A score of 100 means that a person showed average

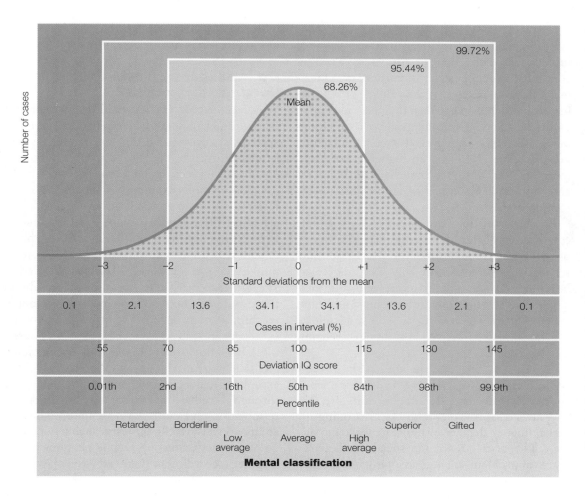

Figure 9.5. The normal distribution. Many characteristics are distributed in a pattern represented by this bell-shaped curve. The horizontal axis shows how far above or below the mean a score is (measured in plus or minus standard deviations). The vertical axis is used to graph the number of cases obtaining each score. In a normal distribution, the cases are distributed in a fixed pattern. For instance, 68.26% of the cases fall between +1 and −1 standard deviation. Modern IQ scores indicate where a person's measured intelligence falls in the normal distribution. On most IQ tests, the mean is set at an IQ of 100 and the standard deviation at 15. Thus, an IQ of 130 means that a person scored 2 standard deviations above the mean. Any deviation IQ score can be converted into a percentile score, which indicates the percentage of cases obtaining a lower score. The mental classifications at the bottom of the figure are descriptive labels that roughly correspond to ranges of IQ scores.

performance. *The key point is that modern IQ scores indicate exactly where you fall in the normal distribution of intelligence.* Thus, a score of 120 does not indicate that you answered 120 questions correctly. Nor does it mean that you have 120 "units" of intelligence. A deviation IQ score places you at a specific point in the normal distribution of intelligence (based on the norms for your age group). Deviation IQ scores can be converted into percentile scores, as shown in Figure 9.5.

Do Intelligence Tests Have Adequate Reliability?

Do IQ tests produce consistent results when people are retested? Yes. Most IQ tests report commendable reliability estimates. The correlations often range into the .90s. In comparison to most other types of psychological tests, IQ tests are exceptionally reliable. However, like other tests, they *sample* behavior, and a specific testing may yield an unrepresentative score.

Variations in examinees' motivation to take an IQ test or in their anxiety about the test can sometimes produce misleading scores (Zimmer-

man & Woo-Sam, 1984). The most common problem is that low motivation or high anxiety may drag a person's score down on a particular occasion. For instance, a fourth-grader who is made to feel that the test is terribly important may get jittery and be unable to concentrate. The same child might score much higher on a subsequent testing by another examiner who creates a more comfortable atmosphere. Although the reliability of IQ tests is excellent, caution is always in order in interpreting test scores. IQ scores should be viewed as estimates that are accurate within plus or minus 5 points about two-thirds of the time.

Do Intelligence Tests Have Adequate Validity?

Do intelligence tests measure what they're supposed to measure? Yes, but this answer has to be qualified very carefully. IQ tests are valid measures of the kind of intelligence that's necessary to do well in academic work. But if the purpose is to assess intelligence in a broader sense, the validity of IQ tests is questionable.

As you may recall, intelligence tests were originally designed with a relatively limited purpose in mind: to predict school performance. This has continued to be the principal purpose of IQ testing. Efforts to document the validity of IQ tests have usually concentrated on their relationship to grades in school. Typically, positive correlations in the .50s are found between IQ scores and school grades (Kline, 1991). Even higher correlations (between .60 and .80) are found between IQ scores and the number of years of school that people complete (Ceci, 1991).

These correlations are about as high as one could expect, given that many factors besides a person's intelligence are likely to affect grades and school progress. For example, school grades may be influenced by a student's motivation, diligence, or personality, not to mention teachers' subjective biases. Thus, IQ tests are reasonably valid indexes of school-related intellectual ability, or academic intelligence.

However, over the years people have mistakenly come to believe that IQ tests measure mental ability in a truly general sense. In reality, IQ tests have always focused on the abstract reasoning and verbal fluency that are essential to academic success. The tests do not tap social competence, practical problem solving, creativity, mechanical ingenuity, or artistic talent.

When Robert Sternberg and his colleagues (1981) asked people to list examples of intelligent behavior, they found that the examples fell into three categories: (1) *verbal intelligence*, (2) *practical intelligence*, and (3) *social intelligence* (see Figure 9.6). Thus, people generally recognize three basic types of intelligence. For the most part, IQ tests assess only the first of these three types. Although IQ tests are billed as measures of *general* mental ability, they actually focus somewhat narrowly on a specific type of intelligence: academic/verbal intelligence. Hence, IQ tests are not valid indicators of intelligence in a truly general sense.

Do Intelligence Tests Predict Vocational Success?

Vocational success is a vague, value-laden concept that's difficult to quantify. Nonetheless, researchers have tackled this question by examining correlations between IQ scores and specific indicators of vocational success, such as the prestige of subjects' occupations or ratings of subjects' job performance. On the positive side of the ledger, it's clear that IQ is related to occupational attainment. People who score high on IQ tests are more likely than those who score low to end up in high-status jobs (Austin & Hanisch, 1990; Ree & Earles, 1992). Because IQ tests measure school ability fairly well and school performance is important in reaching certain occupations, this link between IQ scores and job status makes sense. Of course, the correlations between IQ and occupational attainment are moderate, and there are plenty of exceptions to the general trend. Some people plow through the educational system with bulldog determination and hard work, in spite of limited ability as measured by IQ tests. Such people may go on to prestigious jobs, while people who are brighter (according to their test results), but less motivated, settle for lower-status jobs.

On the negative side of the ledger, IQ scores are mediocre predictors of performance within a particular occupation (Ghiselli, 1966, 1973; Sternberg & Wagner, 1993). For example, in summarizing data for 446 occupations, Jensen (1993a) reported a median correlation of .27 between general intelligence and job performance. Thus, knowing the IQ scores of 100 freshly graduated engineers will not be much help in predicting which graduates will go on to become the best engineers.

Doubts about the ability of IQ tests to predict job performance have led to controversy over the use of IQ tests in employee selection. Over the years, many companies have used intelligence tests in deciding whom to hire or promote. However, there's lively debate about whether IQ tests are sufficiently valid indicators of job potential in most occupational areas (Barrett & Depinet, 1991; Hunter & Hunter, 1984; McClelland, 1973, 1993). Moreover, the use of intelligence testing in making employment decisions has been challenged on legal grounds. Because of these challenges, the practice has declined dramatically (Gatewood & Perloff, 1990).

Figure 9.6. Layperson's conceptions of intelligence. Robert Sternberg and his colleagues (1981) asked subjects to list examples of behaviors characteristic of intelligence. The examples tended to sort into three groups that represent the three types of intelligence recognized by the average person: verbal intelligence, practical intelligence, and social intelligence.

Verbal intelligence	Practical intelligence	Social intelligence
Speaks clearly and articulately	Sees all aspects of a problem	Accepts others for what they are
Is verbally fluent	Sizes up situations well	Has social conscience
Is knowledgeable about a particular field	Makes good decisions	Thinks before speaking and doing
Reads with high comprehension	Poses problems in an optimal way	Is sensitive to other people's needs and desires

Are IQ Tests Widely Used in Other Cultures?

In other Western cultures with European roots the answer is yes. In most non-Western cultures, the answer is only very little. IQ testing has a long history and continues to be a major enterprise in many Western countries, such as Britain, France, Norway, Canada, and Australia (Irvine & Berry, 1988). However, efforts to export IQ tests to non-Western societies have met with mixed results. The tests have been well received in some non-Western cultures, such as Japan, where the Binet-Simon scales were introduced as early as 1908 (Iwawaki & Vernon, 1988), but they have been met with indifference or resistance in other cultures, such as China and India (Chan & Vernon, 1988; Sinha, 1983).

The bottom line is that Western IQ tests do not translate well into the language and cognitive frameworks of many non-Western cultures. Using an intelligence test with a cultural group other than the one for which it was originally designed can be problematic. The entire process of test administration, with its emphasis on rapid information processing, decisive responding, and the notion that ability can be quantified, is foreign to some cultures. Moreover, different cultures have different conceptions of what intelligence is and value different mental skills (Segall et al., 1990). In a landmark treatise on culture and cognition, Cole and his colleagues (1971) concluded that "people

will be good at doing things that are important to them, and that they have occasion to do often" (p. xi). *In other words, the ingredients of intelligence are culture-specific.* Even when a non-Western culture is largely in agreement with Western views about the ingredients of intelligent behavior, it can be difficult to construct equivalent tests that measure these ingredients with equal reliability and validity in both cultural contexts.

HEREDITY AND ENVIRONMENT AS DETERMINANTS OF INTELLIGENCE

Most early pioneers of intelligence testing, such as Sir Francis Galton, Lewis Terman, and Henry Goddard, maintained that intelligence is inherited (Cravens, 1992). Small wonder, then, that this view lingers on in our society. Gradually, however, it has become clear that both heredity and environment influence intelligence (Locurto, 1991; Plomin, 1990; Scarr, 1989). Does this mean that the nature versus nurture debate has been settled with respect to intelligence? Absolutely not. Theorists and researchers continue to argue vigorously about which is more important, in part because the issue has such far-reaching sociopolitical implications.

Theorists who believe that intelligence is largely inherited downplay the value of special

These accomplished individuals exemplify the three basic types of intelligence recognized by most people (based on research by Sternberg et al., 1981). Johnny Cochran's oratorical skills as a trial lawyer demonstrate *verbal intelligence*. Oprah Winfrey's ability to empathize and put people at ease demonstrates *social intelligence*. Martha Stewart's knowledge of home management and entertaining demonstrates *practical intelligence*.

educational programs for underprivileged groups (Jensen, 1980). They assert that a child's intelligence cannot be increased noticeably, because a child's genetic destiny cannot be altered. Theorists who believe that intelligence is shaped by experience are highly critical of this view. Lewontin, Rose, and Kamin (1984) assert that "the IQ test in practice has been used both in the United States and England to shunt vast numbers of working-class and minority children into inferior and dead-end educational tracks" (p. 87). Such critics maintain that even more funds should be allocated for remedial education programs, improved schooling in lower-class neighborhoods, and college financial aid for the underprivileged. Because the debate over the role of heredity in intelligence has direct relevance to important social issues and political decisions, we'll take a detailed look at this complex controversy.

Evidence for Hereditary Influence

Galton's observation that intelligence runs in families was quite accurate. However, *family studies* can determine only whether genetic influence on a trait is *plausible*, not whether it is certain. Family members share not just genes, but similar environments. If high intelligence (or low intelligence) appears in a family over several generations, this consistency could reflect the influence of either shared genes or shared environment. Because of this problem, researchers must turn to *twin studies* and *adoption studies* to obtain more definitive evidence on whether heredity affects intelligence.

Twin Studies

The best evidence regarding the role of genetic factors in intelligence comes from studies that compare identical and fraternal twins. The rationale for twin studies is that both identical and fraternal twins normally develop under similar environmental conditions. However, identical twins share more genetic kinship than fraternal twins. Hence, if pairs of identical twins are more similar in intelligence than pairs of fraternal twins, it's presumably because of their greater genetic similarity. (See Chapter 3 for a more detailed explanation of the logic underlying twin studies.)

Figure 9.7. Studies of IQ similarity. The graph shows the mean correlations of IQ scores for people of various types of relationships, as obtained in studies of IQ similarity. Higher correlations indicate greater similarity. The results show that greater genetic similarity is associated with greater similarity in IQ, suggesting that intelligence is partly inherited (compare, for example, the correlations for identical and fraternal twins). However, the results also show that living together is associated with greater IQ similarity, suggesting that intelligence is partly governed by environment (compare, for example, the scores of siblings reared together and reared apart). (Data from Bouchard & McGue, 1981; McGue et al., 1993)

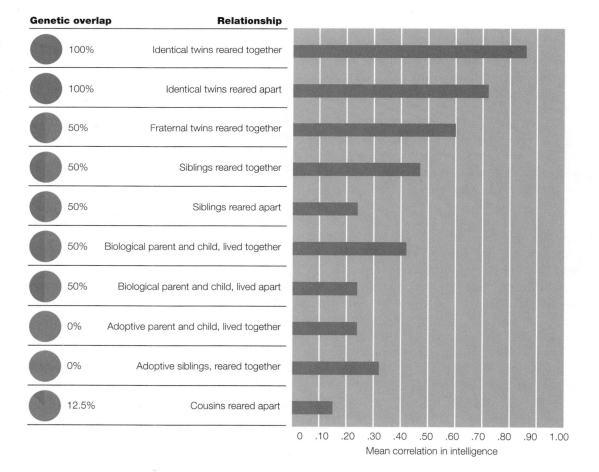

What are the findings of twin studies regarding intelligence? McGue and colleagues (1993) reviewed the results of over 100 studies of intellectual similarity for various kinds of kinship relations and child-rearing arrangements. The key findings from their review are highlighted in Figure 9.7. This figure plots the average correlation observed for various types of relationships. As you can see, the average correlation reported for identical twins (.86) is very high, indicating that identical twins tend to be quite similar in intelligence. The average correlation for fraternal twins (.60) is significantly lower. This correlation indicates that fraternal twins also tend to be similar in intelligence, but noticeably less so than identical twins. These results support the notion that IQ is inherited to a considerable degree.

Of course, critics have tried to poke holes in this line of reasoning. They argue that identical twins are more alike in IQ because parents and others treat them more similarly than they treat fraternal twins. This environmental explanation of the findings has some merit. After all, identical twins are always the same sex, and gender influences how a child is raised. However, a clever study of twins who were mislabeled as identical or fraternal suggests that this environmental hypothesis cannot account for identical twins' greater IQ similarity (Scarr & Carter-Saltzman, 1979). In this study, IQ tests were given to 400 pairs of same-sex twins. The sample included identical twins who had mistakenly been thought to be fraternals, and fraternal twins who had mistakenly been thought to be identicals. The sample also included twins of both types who had been correctly labeled. If identical twins are more similar in intelligence because they are treated more alike, then fraternal twins reared as identicals should also be highly similar in intelligence. Furthermore, identical twins mistakenly raised as fraternals should be less similar in intelligence than identical twins raised as identicals. Neither of these hypotheses was borne out by the results. Intellectual similarity depended not on whether the twins were raised as identical or fraternal but on whether they really *were* identical or fraternal.

Evidence favorable to the genetic hypothesis also comes from a handful of studies that have focused on identical twins reared apart because of family breakups or adoption (Bouchard et al., 1990). Although reared in different environments, these twins still display greater similarity in IQ (average correlation: .72) than fraternal twins reared together (average correlation: .60). More-

over, the gap in IQ similarity between identical twins reared apart and fraternal twins reared together appears to widen in middle and late adulthood (Pedersen et al., 1992). This finding suggests, paradoxically, that the influence of heredity increases with age.

Adoption Studies

Research comparing adopted children to their biological parents also provides evidence about the effects of heredity (and of environment, as we shall see). If adopted children resemble their biological parents in intelligence even though they were not reared by these parents, this finding supports the genetic hypothesis. The relevant studies indicate that there is indeed more than chance similarity between adopted children and their biological parents (Turkheimer, 1991; refer again to Figure 9.7).

Heritability Estimates

Various experts have sifted through mountains of correlational evidence to estimate the *heritability* of intelligence. **A *heritability ratio* is an estimate of the proportion of trait variability in a population that is determined by variations in genetic inheritance.** Given the strong views that experts bring to the IQ debate, it should come as no surprise that heritability estimates for intelligence vary (see Figure 9.8).

At the high end, a few theorists, such as Arthur Jensen (1980), maintain that the heritability of IQ is about 80%. That is, they believe that only about 20% of the variation in intelligence is attributable to environmental factors. Many researchers in this area assert that the 80% figure is higher than the data really support. Most studies suggest that the

Figure 9.8. The concept of heritability. A heritability ratio is an estimate of the portion of variation in a trait determined by heredity—with the remainder presumably determined by environment—as these pie charts illustrate. Typical heritability estimates for intelligence range between a high of 70% and a low of 50%, although some estimates (such as Jensen's) have fallen outside this range. Bear in mind that heritability ratios are *estimates* and have certain limitations that are discussed in the text.

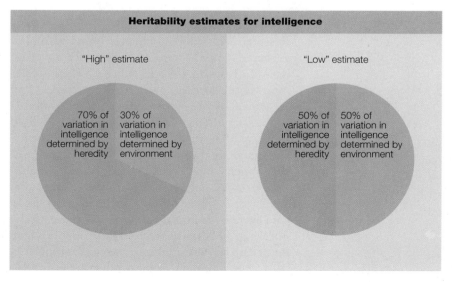

Heritability estimates for intelligence

"High" estimate

70% of variation in intelligence determined by heredity

30% of variation in intelligence determined by environment

"Low" estimate

50% of variation in intelligence determined by heredity

50% of variation in intelligence determined by environment

heritability of IQ is between 50% and 70% (Bouchard et al., 1990; Loehlin, 1989). The consensus estimate of experts hovers around 60% (Snyderman & Rothman, 1987).

Even the estimates at the low end suggest that heredity has a substantial impact on intelligence. However, it's important to understand that heritability estimates have certain limitations (Erdle, 1990; Rutter, Silberg, & Simonoff, 1993). First, a heritability estimate is a *group statistic* based on studies of trait variability within a specific group. A heritability estimate cannot be applied meaningfully to *individuals*. In other words, even if the heritability of intelligence truly is 70%, this does not mean that each individual's intelligence is 70% inherited. Second, the heritability of a specific trait may vary from one group to another depending on a variety of factors. For instance, in a group with a given gene pool, heritability will increase if there's a shift toward rearing group members in more similar circumstances. Why? Because the extent of environmental differences will be reduced. To date, heritability estimates for intelligence have been based largely on research with white, middle-class subjects. Hence, they should be applied only to such groups.

Evidence for Environmental Influence

Heredity unquestionably influences intelligence, but a great deal of evidence indicates that upbringing also affects mental ability. We'll examine three lines of research—concerning adoption, environmental deprivation or enrichment, and home environment—that show how life experiences shape intelligence.

Adoption Studies

Research with adopted children provides useful evidence about the impact of experience as well as heredity (Locurto, 1990; Plomin & DeFries, 1980). Many of the correlations in Figure 9.7 reflect the influence of the environment. For example, adopted children show some resemblance to their foster parents in IQ. This similarity is usually attributed to the fact that their foster parents shape their environment. Adoption studies also indicate that siblings reared together are more similar in IQ than siblings reared apart. This is true even for identical twins. Moreover, entirely unrelated children who are raised in the same home also show a significant resemblance in IQ. All of these findings indicate that environment influences intelligence.

Environmental Deprivation and Enrichment

If environment affects intelligence, then children who are raised in substandard circumstances should experience a gradual decline in IQ as they grow older (since other children will be progressing more rapidly). This *cumulative deprivation hypothesis* was tested decades ago. Researchers studied children consigned to understaffed orphanages and children raised in the poverty and isolation of the back hills of Appalachia (Sherman & Key, 1932; Stoddard, 1943). Generally, investigators *did* find that environmental deprivation led to the predicted erosion in IQ scores.

Conversely, children who are removed from a deprived environment and placed in circumstances more conducive to learning should benefit from their environmental enrichment. Their IQ scores should gradually increase. This hypothesis has been tested by studying children who have been moved from understaffed orphanages or disadvantaged homes into high-quality, middle-class adoptive homes (Scarr & Weinberg, 1977, 1983; Schiff & Lewontin, 1986). Although there are limits on the improvements seen, the IQs of these children tend to increase noticeably (typically 10–12 points). These findings also show that environment influences IQ.

Home-Environment Studies

In the last 20 years, researchers have examined the influence of environment on intelligence in another way. This new approach involves going into intact homes (mother and father living together with their children) to make an elaborate, systematic assessment of the quality of the intellectual environment there. If environment shapes intelligence, these assessments of home environments should correlate with youngsters' IQ scores. They do. Several large-scale studies have yielded an average correlation of .30 between children's IQ scores and assessments of the quality of the intellectual environment in their homes (Gottfried, 1984).

What kind of home environment nurtures the development of intelligence? Many factors appear to be involved (Bradley, 1989; Bradley & Caldwell, 1980; Hanson, 1975). It helps if parents run an orderly household *and* encourage exploration, experimentation, and independence. In the ideal home, parents are warm, affectionate, and highly involved with their children. They provide a diverse array of age-appropriate toys, as well as more formal learning materials (such as books). The parents speak articulately and are interested in intellectual pursuits (and therefore serve as role

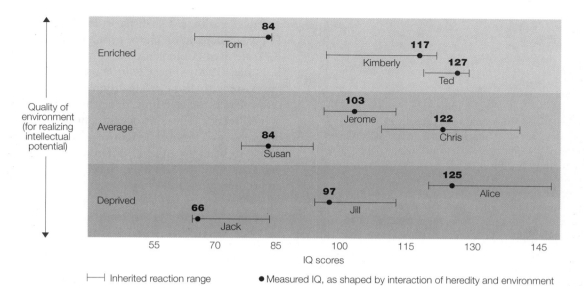

Figure 9.9. Reaction range. The concept of reaction range posits that heredity sets limits on one's intellectual potential (represented by the horizontal bars), while the quality of one's environment influences where one scores within this range (represented by the dots on the bars). People raised in enriched environments should score near the top of their reaction range, whereas people raised in poor-quality environments should score near the bottom of their range. Genetic limits on IQ can be inferred only indirectly, so theorists aren't sure whether reaction ranges are narrow (like Ted's) or wide (like Chris's). The concept of reaction range can explain how two people with similar genetic potential can be quite different in intelligence (compare Tom and Jack) and how two people reared in environments of similar quality can score quite differently (compare Alice and Jack).

models for these behaviors). When children reach school age, parents encourage them to work hard in school and reward them when they make progress. Throughout childhood, the parents emphasize achievement motivation and provide tangible assistance with schoolwork.

The Interaction of Heredity and Environment

Clearly, heredity and environment both influence intelligence to a significant degree. Indeed, many theorists now assert that the question of which is more important ought to take a backseat to the question of *how they interact* to govern IQ.

The current thinking is that heredity may set certain limits on intelligence and that environmental factors determine where individuals fall within these limits (Scarr & Carter-Saltzman, 1982; Weinberg, 1989). According to this idea, genetic makeup places an upper limit on a person's IQ that can't be exceeded even when environment is ideal. Heredity is also thought to place a lower limit on an individual's IQ, although extreme circumstances (for example, being locked in an attic until age 20) could drag a person's IQ beneath this boundary. Theorists use the term *reaction range* **to refer to these genetically determined limits on IQ (or other traits).** Sandra Scarr, a prominent theorist who emphasizes the reaction-range concept, explains it as follows:

Each person has a range of potential in development. For example, a person with "medium-tall" genes for height who grows up in a poor environment may be shorter than average. In a good nutritional environment, the person would grow up taller than average. But no matter how well-fed, someone with "short" *genes will never be taller than average. It works the same way with shyness, intelligence, and almost any other aspect of personality and behavior. (Quoted in Hall, 1987, p. 18)*

According to the reaction-range model, children reared in high-quality environments that promote the development of intelligence should score near the top of their potential IQ range. Children reared under less ideal circumstances should score lower in their reaction range. The reaction range for most people is *estimated* to be around 20–25 points on the IQ scale (Weinberg, 1989). Thus, most people are probably born with a reaction range in the vicinity of 90 to 110. Their actual score within this range will then depend on the quality of their intellectual environment. Of course, other people are assumed to be born with ranges such as 70–90, 80–105, 110–130, 120–145, and so forth (see Figure 9.9).

The concept of a reaction range can explain why high-IQ children sometimes come from poor environments. It can also explain why low-IQ children sometimes come from very good environments. Moreover, it can explain these apparent paradoxes without discounting the role that environment undeniably plays. But how can the genetic boundaries on a person's intelligence be measured? That's the problem with the reaction-range concept. There is no readily apparent way to measure the range, which makes it difficult to test the reaction-range model empirically. The impossibility of measuring individuals' genetically determined intellectual potential also makes it difficult to resolve the debate about the causes of ethnic differences in IQ scores. We'll try to sort through this complex issue in the next section.

"My research has been aimed at asking in what kind of environments genetic differences shine through and when do they remain hidden."
SANDRA SCARR

Cultural Differences in IQ Scores

The age-old nature versus nurture debate lies at the core of the current controversy about ethnic differences in average IQ. Although the full range of IQ scores is seen in all ethnic groups, the average IQ for many of the larger minority groups in the United States (such as blacks, Native Americans, and Hispanics) is somewhat lower than the

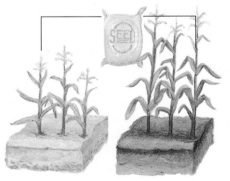

Between-group differences (cause: the soils in which the plants were grown)

Figure 9.10. Genetics and between-group differences on a trait. Kamin's analogy (see text) shows how between-group differences on a trait (the height of corn plants) could be due to environment, even if the trait is largely inherited. The same reasoning presumably applies to the trait of human intelligence.

Barren field Within-group differences (cause: genetic variations in the seeds)

Fertile field Within-group differences (cause: genetic variations in the seeds)

average for whites. The disparity ranges from 3 to 15 points, depending on the group tested and the IQ scale used (Coleman et al., 1966; Perlman & Kaufman, 1990). There is little argument about the existence of these group differences, variously referred to as racial, ethnic, or cultural differences in intelligence. The controversy concerns *why* the differences are found. A vigorous debate continues as to whether cultural differences in intelligence are due to the influence of heredity or of environment.

Jensen's Heritability Explanation

In 1969 Arthur Jensen sparked a heated war of words by arguing that cultural differences in IQ are largely due to heredity. The cornerstone for Jensen's argument was his analysis suggesting that the heritability of intelligence is about 80%. Essentially, he asserted that (1) intelligence is largely genetic in origin, and (2) therefore, genetic factors are "strongly implicated" as the cause of ethnic differences in intelligence. Jensen's article triggered a flurry of rebuttals and research that shed additional light on the determinants of intelligence.

Jensen's critics asserted that his heritability estimate was too high, and they pointed to weaknesses in his reasoning (Kagan, 1969; Lewontin, 1976; Mackenzie, 1984). For example, a heritability estimate applies only to the specific group on which the estimate is based. Jensen's data were drawn from studies dominated almost entirely by white subjects. Hence, there is doubt about the validity of applying this estimate to other cultural groups.

Moreover, even if one accepts Jensen's assumption that the heritability of IQ is about 80%, it does not follow logically that differences in group averages must be due largely to heredity. Leon Kamin has presented a compelling analogy that highlights the logical fallacy in Jensen's reasoning (see Figure 9.10):

We fill a white sack and a black sack with a mixture of different genetic varieties of corn seed. We make certain that the proportions of each variety of seed are identical in each sack. We then plant the seed from the white sack in fertile Field A, while that from the black sack is planted in barren Field B. We will observe that within Field A, as within Field B, there is considerable variation in the height of individual corn plants. This variation will be due largely to genetic factors (seed differences). We will also observe, however, that the average height of plants in Field A is greater than that in Field B. That difference will be entirely due to environmental factors (the soil). The same is true of IQs: differences in the average IQ of various human populations could be entirely due to environmental differences, even if within each population all variation were due to genetic differences! (Eysenck & Kamin, 1981, p. 97)

Kamin's analogy shows that even if the heritability of intelligence is high, group differences in average IQ *could* still be caused entirely (or in part) by environmental factors.

Further evidence on how group differences in a heritable trait could be environmental in origin comes from recent observations of dramatic generational changes in the average height of Japanese males. Angoff (1988) notes that between 1946 and 1982, the average height of young adult males in Japan increased by 3.3 inches. Obviously, the gene pool of a population as large as Japan's could not have changed overnight (in evolutionary terms, one or two generations is more like a fraction a second). Instead, this increased stature has been attributed to environmental factors (mostly nutritional changes). Thus, although height is a highly heritable trait (surely more so than intelligence), we see that group differences (between generations) in average height can be environmental in origin.

Cultural Disadvantage as an Explanation

Many social scientists argue that minority students' IQ scores are depressed because these children tend to grow up in deprived environments that create a cultural disadvantage—both in school and on IQ tests. There is no question that, on the average, whites and minorities tend to be raised in very different circumstances. Most minority groups have endured a long history of economic discrimination and are greatly overrepresented in the lower social classes. A lower-class upbringing tends to carry a number of disadvantages that work against the development of a youngster's full intellectual potential (Blau, 1981). In comparison to the middle and upper classes, lower-class children tend to be exposed to fewer books, to have fewer learning supplies, to have less privacy for concentrated study, and to get less parental assistance in learning. Typically, they also have poorer role models for language development, experience less pressure to work hard on intellectual pursuits, and attend poorer-quality schools (Wolf, 1965).

In light of these disadvantages, it's not surprising that children from higher classes tend to get higher IQ scores (Bouchard & Segal, 1985; White, 1982). The average IQ in the lowest social classes runs about 20–30 points lower than the average IQ in the highest social classes (Locurto, 1991). This is true even if race is factored out of the picture by studying whites exclusively. Given the overrepresentation of minorities in the lower classes, many researchers argue that ethnic differences in intelligence are really social class differences in disguise.

Cultural Bias on IQ Tests as an Explanation

Some critics of IQ tests have argued that cultural differences in IQ scores are partly due to a cultural bias built into IQ tests. They argue that because IQ tests are constructed by white, middle-class psychologists, they naturally draw on experience and knowledge typical of white, middle-class lifestyles and employ language and vocabulary that reflect the white, middle-class origins of their developers (Helms, 1992).

According to Jane Mercer (1975), when IQ tests are given to minorities, they measure *both mental ability and assimilation into the mainstream culture*. She assessed the degree to which Mexican American and black children came from homes that were assimilated into the dominant Anglo-American culture. She found that the IQ scores of these ethnic children were correlated with the "Anglicization" of their home backgrounds.

Other lines of research also suggest that IQ tests are slanted in favor of white middle-class students, at the expense of lower-class ethnic minorities (Bernal, 1984; Cole, 1981; Hilliard, 1984; Williams et al., 1980). Hence, most testing experts assert that minority students' IQ scores should be interpreted with extra caution (Puente, 1990). However, the balance of evidence suggests that the cultural slant on IQ tests is modest. Cultural bias produces only weak and inconsistent effects on the IQ scores of minority examinees (R. Kaplan, 1985; Oakland & Parmelee, 1985). Thus, cultural bias on IQ tests appears to be less of a problem than the cultural disadvantage associated with a lower-class upbringing.

Taken together, the various rebuttals of Jensen's views provide serious challenges to his theory. Genetic explanations for ethnic differences in IQ appear weak at best—and suspiciously racist at worst. In fairness to Jensen, his writings focus squarely on empirical data and theoretical issues. He studiously avoids racist rhetoric. But Block and Dworkin (1976) note that others have cited his conclusions while advocating social programs with racist overtones.

Unfortunately, since the earliest days of IQ

"Despite more than half a century of repeated efforts by psychologists to improve the intelligence of children, particularly those in the lower quarter of the IQ distribution relative to those in the upper half of the distribution, strong evidence is still lacking as to whether or not it can be done."
ARTHUR JENSEN

testing, some people have used IQ tests to further elitist goals. The current controversy about ethnic differences in IQ is just another replay of a record that has been heard before. For instance, beginning in 1913, Henry Goddard tested a great many immigrants to the United States at Ellis Island in New York. Goddard reported that 79% of the Italian immigrants, 80% of the Hungarian immigrants, and 83% of the Jewish immigrants tested out as *feeble-minded*. As you can see, claims about ethnic deficits in intelligence are nothing new. Only the victims have changed.

There is, however, one new twist to the debate about cultural differences in intelligence. A handful of recent studies have suggested that some ethnic minority groups—those of Asian American descent—score slightly *above average* on IQ tests (Lynn, 1987, 1991; Vernon, 1982). Admittedly, the comparative data on Asian Americans' IQ performance are still sparse, and a great deal of additional research is needed. But the IQ data are consistent with the much more extensive data available on Asian Americans' school performance. These data clearly show that most Asian American groups tend to earn higher grade point averages and to have higher graduation rates than those of other ethnic groups, including whites (Sue & Okazaki, 1990).

The outstanding intellectual and educational attainments of Asian Americans constitute a perplexing phenomenon in search of an explanation. The tentative explanations proposed thus far focus primarily on how Asian cultural values may encourage and nurture educational achievement. Investigators theorize that in comparison to most other groups, Asian families place greater emphasis on the value of education, put their children under more pressure to succeed in school, instill more respect for elders such as teachers, and exert more control over their children's study habits. Sue and Okazaki (1990) also speculate that Asian Americans have come to view education as their most realistic route to upward mobility, as racial discrimination has limited their opportunities for advancement through noneducational routes (such as entertainment, politics, and sports). Evidence on most of these hypotheses is lacking, but one recent study of black, white, Hispanic, and Asian American students did find that Asian American students (1) are more likely to report that their parents have high standards for school performance, (2) are more prone to attribute academic success to hard work, (3) spend about twice as much time on homework as other students, and (4) are more likely to

belong to a peer group that emphasizes academic success (Steinberg, Dornbusch, & Brown, 1992). A great deal of additional study is needed to pin down the reasons for Asian Americans' academic prowess. One investigator (Lynn, 1987, 1991) has proposed a highly speculative genetic theory, but most researchers are confident that cultural factors are responsible for Asian Americans' educational success.

The debate about cultural differences in intelligence illustrates how IQ tests have often become entangled in thorny social conflicts. This is unfortunate, because it brings politics to the testing enterprise. Intelligence testing has many legitimate and valuable uses. However, the controversy associated with intelligence tests has undermined their value, leading to some of the new trends that we discuss in the next section.

NEW DIRECTIONS IN THE ASSESSMENT AND STUDY OF INTELLIGENCE

Intelligence testing has been through a period of turmoil, and changes are on the horizon. In fact, many changes have occurred already. Let's discuss some of the major new trends and projections for the future.

Reducing Reliance on IQ Tests

In 1982 a task force assembled by the National Academy of Sciences recommended a reduced emphasis on standardized tests in the United States. Today, such a reduction is clearly under way. Many school districts are shifting from IQ tests to achievement and aptitude tests. The problem is not so much that IQ tests are flawed—experts generally agree that they are reasonably sound measurement instruments (Snyderman & Rothman, 1987). However, these experts also agree that intelligence tests are terribly misunderstood by the general public. IQ scores are typically viewed as "magical" numbers that capture the essence of individuals' ability (Weinberg, 1989). Far too many people believe that IQ tests measure an innate, fixed mental capacity that is truly general in scope and of the utmost significance for success in life. Some authorities (Reschly, 1981; Turnbull, 1979) have argued that the concept of IQ is so bound up in myth that it has outlived its usefulness. They suggest that the term "IQ" should be done away with and that intelligence scales

"To understand intelligent behavior, we need to move beyond the fairly restrictive tasks that have been used both in experimental laboratories and in psychometric tests of intelligence."
ROBERT STERNBERG

should be relabeled as tests of scholastic ability or academic aptitude. Some slow movement in this direction is apparent.

Exploring Biological Indexes of Intelligence

Recent years have also seen an increased interest in biological indexes of intelligence. Arthur Jensen (1987, 1993b), Hans Eysenck (1988, 1989), and other researchers are attempting to find raw physiological indicators of general intelligence. Their search for a "culture-free" measure of intelligence has led them to focus on sensory processes, much as Sir Francis Galton did over a hundred years ago. Armed with much more sophisticated equipment, they hope to succeed where Galton failed.

Jensen's (1982, 1987) studies of mental speed are representative of this line of inquiry. In his studies, Jensen measures *reaction time* (RT), using a panel of paired buttons and lights. On each trial, the subject rests a hand on a "home button." When one of the lights is activated, the subject is supposed to push the button for that light as quickly as possible. The time between the onset of the stimulus light and the release of the home button is the subject's reaction time. RT is typically averaged over a number of trials involving varied numbers of lights. Modest correlations (.20s to .30s) have been found between faster RTs and higher scores on conventional IQ tests.

Jensen's findings suggest an association between raw mental speed and intelligence, as Galton originally suggested. This correlation is theoretically interesting and, in retrospect, not all that surprising. Many conventional IQ tests have imposed demanding time limits on examinees, working under the assumption that "fast is smart."

However, the correlation between RT and IQ appears to be too weak to give RT any practical value as an index of intelligence. Critics also argue that RT is not a pure measure of neural processing (Lohman, 1989). They assert that RTs are affected by subjects' prior practice, their motivation, and their strategy for dealing with the trade-off between speed and accuracy (Carroll, 1987; Longstreth, 1984). Furthermore, research on cognitive processes in intelligent behavior suggests that speed is *not* the critical factor in intelligence (Sternberg, 1985). We turn to some of this cognitive research next.

Investigating Cognitive Processes in Intelligent Behavior

As noted in Chapters 1 and 8, psychologists are increasingly taking a cognitive perspective in their

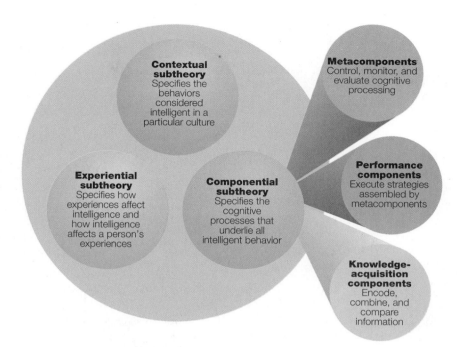

efforts to study many topics. For over a century, the investigation of intelligence has been approached primarily from a *testing perspective*. This perspective emphasizes measuring the *amount* of intelligence people have and figuring out why some have more than others. In contrast, the *cognitive perspective* focuses on how people *use* their intelligence. The interest is in process rather than amount. In particular, cognitive psychologists focus on the information-processing strategies that underlie intelligence. This new perspective is generating intriguing insights that are changing the way psychologists think about intelligence.

The application of the cognitive perspective to intelligence has been spearheaded by Robert Sternberg (1984, 1988b, 1991). His *triarchic theory of human intelligence* consists of three parts: the contextual, experiential, and componential subtheories, which are outlined in Figure 9.11. In his *contextual subtheory*, Sternberg argues that intelligence is a culturally defined concept. He asserts that different manifestations of intelligent behavior are valued in different contexts. For example, the verbal skills emphasized in North American culture may take a backseat to hunting skills in another culture.

In his *experiential subtheory*, Sternberg explores the relationships between experience and intelligence. He emphasizes two factors as the hallmarks of intelligent behavior. The first is the ability to deal effectively with novelty—new tasks, demands, and situations. The second factor is the ability to learn how to handle familiar tasks automatically and effortlessly.

Figure 9.11. Sternberg's triarchic theory of intelligence. Sternberg's model of intelligence consists of three parts: the contextual subtheory, the experiential subtheory, and the componential subtheory. Much of Sternberg's research has been devoted to the componential subtheory, as he has attempted to identify the cognitive processes that contribute to intelligence. He believes that these processes fall into three groups: metacomponents, performance components, and knowledge-acquisition components.

Table 9.2 Gardner's Seven Intelligences

Intelligence	End-States	Core Components
Logical-mathematical	Scientist Mathematician	Sensitivity to, and capacity to discern, logical or numerical patterns; ability to handle long chains of reasoning
Linguistic	Poet Journalist	Sensitivity to the sounds, rhythms, and meanings of words; sensitivity to the different functions of language
Musical	Composer Violinist	Abilities to produce and appreciate rhythm, pitch, and timbre; appreciation of the forms of musical expressiveness
Spatial	Navigator Sculptor	Capacities to perceive the visual-spatial world accurately and to perform transformations on one's initial perceptions
Bodily-kinesthetic	Dancer Athlete	Abilities to control one's body movements and to handle objects skillfully
Interpersonal	Therapist Salesperson	Capacities to discern and respond appropriately to the moods, temperaments, motivations, and desires of other people
Intrapersonal	Person with detailed, accurate self-knowledge	Access to one's own feelings and the ability to discriminate among them and draw upon them to guide behavior; knowledge of one's own strengths, weaknesses, desires, and intelligences

Source: Gardner and Hatch (1989)

Sternberg's *componential subtheory* proposes that intelligent thought depends on three sets of mental processes: metacomponents, performance components, and knowledge-acquisition components. He calls *metacomponents* "executive" processes because they give directions to the other two kinds of components. They are high-level processes used in planning how to attack a problem. Meta-components include processes such as defining the nature of a problem, selecting the steps needed to solve a problem, allocating resources (attention) to problems, and monitoring solutions to problems. According to Sternberg, "meta-components decide what to do, *performance components* actually do it." For purposes of illustration, consider an analogy problem: LAWYER is to CLIENT as DOCTOR is to _____. Some of the processes involved in solving this problem include *encoding* the concepts in the problem, *inferring* the relationship between lawyer and client, and *applying* the inferred relation to a new domain, arriving at the answer of PATIENT.

Performance components vary depending on the nature of the problem. Sternberg assumes, however, that there are certain performance components on which everyone depends heavily. Much of his research is intended to identify these crucial performance components.

Knowledge-acquisition components are the processes involved in learning and storing information. The strategies that you may use to help memorize things exemplify the processes that fall in this category. A mnemonic device such as using a rhyme to remember something (example: "Thirty days hath September . . .") represents a knowledge-acquisition component.

Investigations of cognitive processes in intelligent behavior have interesting implications for intelligence testing. Cognitive research has shown that more-intelligent subjects spend more time figuring out how to best represent problems and planning how to solve them than less-intelligent subjects do. Thus, Sternberg (1985) concludes that metacomponents are crucial to intelligent behavior. Furthermore, because planning takes time, Sternberg argues that traditional IQ tests place too much emphasis on speed.

Expanding the Concept of Intelligence

In recent years, many theorists have concluded that traditional IQ tests are too narrow in focus (Ceci & Liker, 1986; Frederiksen, 1986). These theorists argue that to assess intelligence in a truly general sense, tests should sample from a broader range of tasks. This view has been articulated particularly well by Howard Gardner (Gardner, 1983; Gardner & Hatch, 1989).

According to Gardner, IQ tests have generally emphasized verbal and mathematical skills, to the exclusion of other important skills. He suggests the existence of a number of relatively autonomous *human intelligences*, which are listed in Table 9.2 (Gardner & Hatch, 1989). To build his list of separate intelligences, Gardner reviewed the evidence on cognitive capacities in normal individuals, people suffering from brain damage, and special populations, such as prodigies and idiot savants. He concluded that humans exhibit seven intelligences: logical-mathematical, linguistic, musical, spatial, bodily-kinesthetic, interpersonal, and intrapersonal. These intelligences obviously include a variety of talents that are not assessed by conventional IQ tests.

Gardner is currently investigating whether these intelligences are largely independent, as his theory asserts. He has devised scales to measure each form of intelligence to examine interrelations among them. Subjects who score more than one standard deviation above the mean on a scale are said to have a "strength" in that area. Subjects who score more than one standard deviation below the mean on a scale are said to have a "weakness" in that area. If subjects were to show strength in most areas or weakness in most areas, this result would undermine Gardner's argument that there are a number of basic mental abilites that are largely independent of one another. For the most part, however, Gardner has found that people tend to display a mixture of strong, intermediate, and weak abilities. A great deal of additional research is needed to evaluate Gardner's ambitious and refreshing theory of intelligence. However, demands for broader assessments of intelligence appear likely to continue for the foreseeable future.

PUTTING IT IN PERSPECTIVE

As you probably noticed, three of our integrative themes dominated this chapter. Our discussions repeatedly illustrated that cultural factors shape behavior, that heredity and environment jointly influence behavior, and that psychology evolves in a sociohistorical context.

Pervasive psychological testing is largely a Western phenomenon. Most non-Western cultures depend far less than we do on standardized tests. Indeed, the entire enterprise of testing is downright foreign to many cultures. The concept of general intelligence also has a special, Western flavor to it. Many non-Western cultures have very different ideas about the nature of intelligence. Within Western societies, the observed ethnic differences in average intelligence also illustrate the importance of cultural factors, as these disparities appear to be due in large part to cultural disadvantage and cultural bias on IQ tests. Thus, we see once again that if we hope to achieve a sound understanding of behavior, we need to appreciate the cultural contexts in which behavior unfolds.

Human intelligence is shaped by a complex interaction of hereditary and environmental factors. We've drawn a similar conclusion before in other chapters where we examined other topics. However, this chapter should have enhanced your appreciation of this idea by illustrating in detail how scientists arrive at this conclusion. Thus, you saw how psychologists have conducted family studies, twin studies, adoption studies, environmental

enrichment studies, environmental deprivation studies, and home environment studies in their efforts to document the joint influence of genetics and experience.

Finally, we saw more evidence that psychology evolves in a sociohistorical context. Prevailing social attitudes have always exerted some influence on testing practices and the interpretation of test results. In the first half of the 20th century, a strong current of racial and class prejudice was apparent in the United States and Britain. This prejudice supported the idea that IQ tests measured innate ability and that "undesirable" groups scored poorly because of their genetic inferiority. Although these beliefs did not go unchallenged within psychology, their widespread acceptance in the field reflected the social values of the time. Today, the continuing, ferocious debate about the roots of cultural differences in intelligence shows that issues in psychology often have far-reaching social and political implications.

It's ironic that IQ tests have sometimes been associated with social prejudice. When used properly, intelligence tests provide relatively objective measures of mental ability that are probably less prone to bias than the subjective judgments of teachers or employers. Today, psychological tests serve many diverse purposes. In the upcoming Application, we focus on creativity tests and on the nature of creative thinking and creative people.

CONCEPT CHECK 9.4
Recognizing Theories of Intelligence

Check your understanding of various theories on the nature of intelligence by matching the names of their originators with the brief descriptions of the theories' main themes that appear below. Choose from the following theorists: (a) Sir Francis Galton, (b) Howard Gardner, (c) Arthur Jensen, (d) Sandra Scarr, and (e) Robert Sternberg. The answers are in Appendix A.

_____ 1. This theorist posited seven human intelligences: logical-mathematical, linguistic, musical, spatial, bodily-kinesthetic, interpersonal, and intrapersonal.

_____ 2. On the basis of a study of eminence and success in families, this theorist concluded that intelligence is inherited.

_____ 3. This theorist stated that the heritability of intelligence is about 80% and that IQ differences between ethnic groups are mainly due to genetics.

_____ 4. This theorist stated that heredity sets certain limits on intelligence and that environmental factors determine where one falls within those limits.

_____ 5. This person's theory of intelligence is divided into three parts: the contextual, experiential, and componential subtheories.

Measuring and Understanding Creativity

Answer the following "true" or "false":

___ **1** Creative ideas often come out of nowhere.

___ **2** Creativity usually occurs in a burst of insight.

___ **3** Creativity depends on inspiration far more than on perspiration.

___ **4** Creativity and intelligence are unrelated.

Intelligence is not the only type of mental ability that psychologists have studied. They have devised tests to explore a variety of mental abilities. Among these, creativity is certainly one of the most interesting. People tend to view creativity as an essential trait for artists, musicians, and writers, but it is important in *many* walks of life. In this Application, we'll discuss psychologists' efforts to measure and understand creativity. As we progress, you'll learn that all the statements above are false.

The Nature of Creativity

What makes thought creative? *Creativity* **involves the generation of ideas that are original, novel, and useful.** Creative thinking is fresh, innovative, and inventive. But novelty by itself is not enough. In addition to being unusual, creative thinking must be adaptive. It must be appropriate to the situation and problem.

Does Creativity Occur in a Burst of Insight?

It is widely believed that creativity usually involves sudden flashes of insight and great leaps of imagination. Robert Weisberg (1986) calls this belief the "Aha!

myth." Undeniably, creative bursts of insight do occur (Feldman, 1988). However, the evidence suggests that major creative achievements generally are logical extensions of existing ideas, involving long, hard work and many small, faltering steps forward (Weisberg, 1988). Creative ideas do not come out of nowhere. They come from a deep well of experience and training in a specific area, whether it's music, painting, business, or science. As Snow (1986) puts it, "Creativity is not a light bulb in the mind, as most cartoons depict it. It is an accomplishment born of intensive study, long reflection, persistence, and interest" (p. 1033).

Does Creativity Depend on Divergent Thinking?

According to many theorists, the key to creativity lies in *divergent thinking*—thinking "that goes off in different directions," as J. P. Guilford (1959) put it. In his model of mental abilities Guilford distinguished between convergent thinking and divergent thinking. **In *convergent thinking* one tries to narrow down a list of alternatives to converge on a single correct answer.** For example, when you take a multiple-choice exam, you try to eliminate incorrect options until you hit on the correct response. Most training in school encourages convergent thinking. **In *divergent thinking* one tries to expand the range of alternatives by generating many possible solutions.** Imagine that you work for an advertising agency. To come up with as many slogans as possible for a client's product, you must use divergent thinking. Some of your slogans may be clear losers, and eventually you will have to engage in convergent thinking to pick the best, but coming up with the range of

new possibilities depends on divergent thinking.

Thirty years of research on divergent thinking has yielded mixed results. As a whole, the evidence suggests that divergent thinking contributes to creativity, but it clearly does not represent the *essence* of creativity, as originally proposed (Barron & Harrington, 1981; Brown, 1989). In retrospect, it was probably unrealistic to expect creativity to depend on a single cognitive skill. According to Sternberg (1988a), the cognitive processes that underlie creativity are multifaceted.

Measuring Creativity

Although its nature may be elusive, creativity clearly is important in today's world. Creative masterpieces in the arts and literature enrich human existence. Creative insights in the sciences illuminate people's understanding of the world. Creative inventions fuel our technological progress. Thus, it is understandable that psychologists have been interested in measuring creativity with psychological tests.

How Do Psychological Tests Assess Creativity?

A diverse array of psychological tests have been devised to measure individuals' creativity (Cooper, 1991). Usually, the items on creativity tests give respondents a specific starting point and then require them to generate as many possibilities as they can in a short period of time. Typical items on a creativity test might include the following: (1) List as many uses as you can for a newspaper. (2) Think of as many fluids that burn as you can. (3) Imagine that people no longer need sleep and think of as many consequences as you can. (See Figure 9.12 for

Figure 9.12. Examples of problems used to measure creativity. Tests of creativity contain problems like these, which require divergent thinking. Respondents attempt to generate a large number of solutions in a short amount of time.

1. Many words begin with an L and end with an N. List as many words as possible, in a 1-minute period, that have the form L____N. (They can have any number of letters in between the L and the N.)

2. Suppose that people reached their final height at the age of 2, and so normal adult height was less than 3 feet. In a 1-minute period, list as many consequences as possible that would result from this change.

3. Here are four shapes. Combine them to make each of the following objects: a face, a lamp, a piece of playground equipment, a tree. Each shape may be used once, many times, or not at all in forming each object, and it may be expanded or shrunk to any size.

How Well Do Tests Predict Creative Productivity?

In general, studies indicate that creativity tests are mediocre predictors of creative achievement in the real world (Hocevar & Bachelor, 1989). Why? One reason is that these tests measure creativity in the abstract, as a *general trait*. However, the accumulation of evidence suggests that *creativity is specific to particular domains* (Amabile, 1983, 1990; Brown, 1989). Despite some rare exceptions, creative people usually excel in a single field, in which they typically have considerable training and expertise. An innovative physicist might have no potential to be a creative poet or an inventive advertising executive. Measuring this person's creativity outside of physics may be meaningless. Thus, creativity tests may have limited value because they measure creativity out of context.

Even if better tests of creativity were devised, predicting creative achievement would probably still prove difficult. Why?

Because creative achievement depends on many factors besides creativity. Creative productivity over the course of an individual's career will depend on his or her motivation, personality, and intelligence, as well as on situational factors, including training, mentoring, and good fortune (Amabile, 1983).

Research by Benjamin Bloom (1985) and his colleagues on the development of talent highlights the importance of training and hard work. Investigators put together richly detailed case histories for 120 exceptionally successful people from six fields, including concert pianists and sculptors. In all fields, they found that great success depended on high-quality training. The accomplished pianists and sculptors had moved through a succession of outstanding teachers and mentors during their formative years. The study also found that creative success was attributable to dogged determination in the face of adversity and endless hours of hard work.

additional examples.) Subjects' scores on these tests depend on the *number* of alternatives they generate and on the *originality* and *usefulness* of the alternatives.

One of the more widely used creativity tests is the Remote Associates Test (RAT) developed by Sarnoff and Martha Mednick (1967). This test is based on the assumption that creative people see unusual relationships and make nonobvious connections between ideas. Items on the test require subjects to figure out the obscure links (the remote associations) among three words by coming up with a fourth word that is related to the three stimulus words. Examples of items similar to those found on the RAT are shown in Figure 9.13.

Instructions: For each set of three words, try to think of a fourth word that is related to all three words. For example, the words ROUGH, RESISTANCE, and BEER suggest the word DRAFT because of the phrases ROUGH DRAFT, DRAFT RESISTANCE, and DRAFT BEER.

1. CHARMING	STUDENT	VALIANT
2. FOOD	CATCHER	HOT
3. HEARTED	FEET	BITTER
4. DARK	SHOT	SUN
5. CANADIAN	GOLF	SANDWICH
6. TUG	GRAVY	SHOW
7. ATTORNEY	SELF	SPENDING
8. MAGIC	PITCH	POWER
9. ARM	COAL	PEACH
10. TYPE	GHOST	STORY

Figure 9.13 Remote associates as an index of creativity. One of the more widely used creativity tests is the Remote Associates Test (RAT) developed by Sarnoff and Martha Mednick (1967). The items shown here (from Matlin, 1989) are similar to those on the RAT. See whether you can identify the remote associations between the three stimulus words by coming up with a fourth word that is related to all three. The answers can be found in Figure 9.14.

Creativity takes many forms. Laurie Anderson expresses her creativity as a performance artist. Chef Wolfgang Puck has displayed creativity in the preparation of gastronomic delights. Marc Andreesen, the developer of Netscape Navigation, a widely heralded web browser, has demonstrated his creativity in the field of computers.

Correlates of Creativity

What are creative people like? Are they brighter, or more open minded, or less well adjusted than average? A great deal of research has been conducted on the correlates of creativity.

Is There a Creative Personality?

Creative people exhibit the full range of personality traits, but investigators *have* found modest correlations between certain personality characteristics and creativity (Barron & Harrington, 1981; Ochse, 1990). At the core of this set of personality characteristics are the related traits of independence, autonomy, self-confidence, and nonconformity. Creative people tend to think for themselves and are less easily influenced by the opinions of others than the average person is. Creative people also tend to be more tolerant of complexity, contradiction, and

ambiguity than others. They don't feel compelled to simplify everything, and they're not as troubled by uncertainty as many people are. Sternberg and Lubart (1992) also assert that creative people are willing to grow and change, willing to take risks, and willing to work at overcoming obstacles.

Are Creativity and Intelligence Related?

Are creative people exceptionally smart? Conceptually, creativity and intelligence represent different types of mental ability. Thus, it's not surprising that creativity and intelligence are only weakly related (Horn, 1976; Wallach & Kogan, 1965). They're not entirely unrelated, however (Haensly & Reynolds, 1989), as creativity in most fields requires a minimum level of intelligence. Hence, most highly creative people are probably above average in intelligence (Ochse, 1990).

Is There a Connection Between Creativity and Mental Illness?

There may be a connection between truly exceptional creativity and mental illness. The list of creative geniuses who suffered from psychological disorders is endless (Prentky, 1989). Kafka, Heming-

way, Rembrandt, Van Gogh, Chopin, Tchaikovsky, Descartes, and Newton are but a few examples. Of course, a statistical association cannot be demonstrated by citing a handful of examples. In this case, however, some statistical data are available. And these data *do* suggest a correlation between creative genius and maladjustment—in particular, mood disorders such as depression. When Jamison (1988) studied 47 British writers and artists who had achieved certain major honors, she found that 38% of her sample had been treated for mood disorders. Similarly, Andreasen (1987) found that 24 of 30 writers (80%) who had been invited as visiting faculty to the prestigious Iowa Writers Workshop had suffered a mood disorder at some point in their lives. These figures are far above the base rate (roughly 8%) for mood disorders in the general population.

Thus, preliminary data tentatively suggest that there may be a correlation between major creative achievement and vulnerability to mood disorders. According to Prentky (1989), creativity and maladjustment probably are *not* causally related. Instead, he speculates that certain cognitive styles may both foster creativity and predispose people to psychological disorders.

Figure 9.14. Answers to the remote associates items.

1. PRINCE	6. BOAT
2. DOG	7. DEFENSE
3. COLD	8. BLACK
4. GLASSES	9. PIT
5. CLUB	10. WRITER

Chapter 9 Review

KEY IDEAS

Key Concepts in Psychological Testing

♦ Psychological tests are standardized measures of behavior—usually mental abilities or aspects of personality. Test scores are interpreted by consulting test norms to find out what represents a high or low score. As measuring devices, psychological tests should produce consistent results, a quality called reliability.

♦ Validity refers to the degree to which there is evidence that a test measures what it was designed to measure. Content validity is crucial on classroom tests. Criterion-related validity is critical when tests are used to predict performance. Construct validity is critical when a test is designed to measure a hypothetical construct.

The Evolution of Intelligence Testing

♦ The first crude efforts to devise intelligence tests were made by Sir Francis Galton, who wanted to show that intelligence is inherited. Modern intelligence testing began with the work of Alfred Binet, who devised a scale to measure a child's mental age.

♦ Lewis Terman revised the original Binet scale to produce the Stanford-Binet in 1916. It introduced the intelligence quotient and became the standard of comparison for subsequent intelligence tests. David Wechsler devised an improved measure of intelligence for adults and a series of IQ tests that reduced the emphasis on verbal ability and used a new scoring system based on the normal distribution. Today, there are many individual and group intelligence tests.

Basic Questions About Intelligence Testing

♦ Intelligence tests contain a diverse mixture of questions. In the modern scoring system, deviation IQ scores indicate where people fall in the normal distribution of intelligence for their age group. IQ tests are exceptionally reliable. They are reasonably valid measures of academic intelligence, but they do not tap social or practical intelligence.

♦ IQ scores are correlated with occupational attainment. Nonetheless, they do not predict performance within an occupation very well. There is little evidence for their validity in selecting employees. Intelligence testing is largely a Western enterprise and IQ tests are not widely used in most non-Western cultures.

Heredity and Environment as Determinants of Intelligence

♦ Twin studies show that identical twins are more similar in IQ than fraternal twins, suggesting that intelligence is inherited, at least in part. Estimates of the heritability of intelligence range from 50% to 70%, but heritability ratios have certain limitations.

♦ Many lines of evidence indicate that environment is also an important determinant of intelligence. The concept of reaction range posits that heredity places limits on one's intellectual potential and the environment determines where one falls within these limits.

♦ Genetic explanations for cultural differences in IQ have been challenged on a variety of grounds. Even if the heritability of IQ is great, group differences in intelligence may not be due to heredity. Moreover, ethnicity varies with social class, so cultural disadvantage may account for low IQ scores among minority students. Test bias may make a small contribution to ethnic differences in IQ. Asian American students' comparative success in the educational arena appears to be due to cultural factors.

New Directions in the Assessment and Study of Intelligence

♦ In the future, schools and society may place less emphasis on intelligence tests because of widespread misconceptions about them. Although biological indexes of intelligence are being explored, far more research is using a cognitive perspective that advocates an expanded concept of intelligence.

Putting It in Perspective

♦ Three of our integrative themes stood out in the chapter. Our discussions of intelligence showed how heredity and environment interact to shape behavior, how psychology evolves in a sociohistorical context, and how one has to consider cultural contexts to fully understand behavior.

Application: Measuring and Understanding Creativity

♦ Creativity involves the generation of original, novel, and useful ideas. Creativity does not usually involve sudden insight and it consists of more than divergent thinking.

♦ Creativity tests are mediocre predictors of creative productivity in the real world. Creativity is only weakly related to intelligence and personality. Recent evidence suggests that creative geniuses may exhibit heightened vulnerability to mood disorders.

KEY TERMS

Achievement tests	Intelligence tests
Aptitude tests	Mental age
Construct validity	Normal distribution
Content validity	Percentile score
Convergent thinking	Personality tests
Correlation coefficient	Psychological test
Creativity	Reaction range
Criterion-related validity	Reliability
Deviation IQ score	Standardization
Divergent thinking	Test norms
Heritability ratio	Test-retest reliability
Intelligence quotient (IQ)	Validity

KEY PEOPLE

Alfred Binet	Robert Sternberg
Sir Francis Galton	Lewis Terman
Arthur Jensen	David Wechsler
Sandra Scarr	

10 Motivation and Emotion

In September 1983, for the first time in 132 years the United States lost the America's Cup, the foremost trophy in the sport of sailing. An Australian team with a superior new boat design won the Cup. The U.S. team was devastated by its unexpected defeat. Dennis Conner, the team's skipper, wept openly in despair after the last race.

Within months, however, Conner had begun a relentless campaign to recapture the America's Cup in the next race in 1987. Working 365 days a year, he investigated hundreds of new boat designs, supervised the building of four boats, assembled and trained a crackerjack crew, and sailed in hundreds of races to prepare. Describing his frantic pace, Conner's wife said, "He never relaxes, and we never go on vacations. Hell to Dennis would be a day on the beach." Conner's crew would certainly agree with his wife. Working 12 to 15 hours a day, six or seven days a week, they were pushed through a grueling training regimen for 17 months. Training thousands of miles from their homes, most of them saw their wives or girlfriends only once during this time.

In 1987 the long hours of hard work and sacrifice paid off. Conner and his crew trounced their opponents and recaptured the America's Cup. The jubilation of victory is readily apparent in Conner's face in the top photo on the right. So did Conner finally relax after the vindication of his 1987 victory? No, he continued his frenetic work pace in the ensuing years in the hopes of successfully defending the America's Cup. In 1992 and 1995, however, he once again experienced the bitter taste of defeat.

The saga of Dennis Conner and his crew is packed with motivational riddles. What motivates these men to dedicate their lives to the pursuit of a yachting trophy? Money? No, the well-educated crew members get little pay for their months of brutal training. Fame? For Conner perhaps, but the other crew members know that their names won't become household words. A deep-rooted love of sailing? Maybe for some of them, but Conner noted, "I don't like to sail. I like to compete." That was the key theme for most of the crew. More than anything else, they seemed to be propelled by the excitement of competition and the thrill of victory. As Conner put it, "The bottom line is, people like to win."

Conner's story is also filled with strong emotions. When he won the Cup in 1987, he experienced enormous joy and happiness. When he lost the America's Cup in 1983 and again in subsequent years, he experienced dejection and disappointment. His tale illustrates the intimate relation between motivation and emotion—the topics we'll examine in this chapter.

We'll begin by discussing theoretical perspectives on motivation. Then we'll take a close look at a handful of selected motives that have been studied extensively, including hunger, sex, and achievement. To close, we'll analyze the elements of emotion and examine theories that attempt to explain emotional experience. In the Application we'll expand on practical issues related to hunger and eating, as we discuss the roots of obesity.

MOTIVATIONAL THEORIES AND CONCEPTS

Why did many of Dennis Conner's crew members give up good jobs to join his quest for the America's Cup? Why did the renowned artist Vincent van Gogh cut off his own ear? Why did Greta Garbo suddenly retire from making movies at the peak of her highly acclaimed movie career? Why did you decide to attend college? Why did you start reading this chapter today? In asking these questions, we're looking for the motives underlying the actions. *Motives* are the needs, wants, interests, and desires that propel people in certain directions. In short, **motivation involves goal-directed behavior.**

There are a number of theoretical approaches to motivation. These theories differ most basically in whether they emphasize the innate, biological basis of motivation or the learned, social basis of motivation. Let's look at some motivational theories and the concepts they employ.

Sociobiology's View

Sociobiology **is the study of the genetic and evolutionary basis of social behavior in all organisms, including humans.** Sociobiology came of age in 1975 with the publication of Edward Wilson's *Sociobiology: A New Synthesis*. Wilson's theory is descended from earlier instinct theories in that it proposes that some human motives are genetically programmed.

Sociobiologists argue that natural selection favors social behaviors that maximize reproductive success—that is, passing on genes to the next generation (Hamilton, 1970; Wilson, 1980). Thus, they explain social motives such as competition, dominance, aggression, and sexual activity in terms of their evolutionary value. If humans are in-

Dennis Conner was jubilant when he and his crew won the America's Cup yacht race in 1987 (top), but his emotions were quite different when his crew lost the cup in 1995 (bottom).

Many animal species, including wolves, form complex social structures, comparable to human families or tribes. Many biologists and psychologists believe that social and emotional behavior patterns are products of evolution in the same way that anatomical and physiological characteristics are.

tensely competitive, sociobiologists say, it's because competitiveness gives a survival advantage, so that proportionately more competitive genes are passed on to the next generation.

You may wonder: If behavior is as selfish as sociobiologists make it sound, how do they explain self-sacrifice? Why does a blackbird risk death to signal the approach of a hawk to others in the flock? Why does a soldier throw himself on a hand grenade to protect a comrade? Sociobiologists offer an interesting explanation for this apparent paradox (Krebs, 1987). They point out that an organism may contribute to passing on its genes by sacrificing itself to save others that share the same genes. Altruistic (self-sacrificing) behavior that evolves as members of a species protect their own offspring, for example, can be extended to other, more distantly related members of the species. Thus, the principle of genetic selfishness may operate to produce behavior that seems remarkably unselfish.

Sociobiology's basic thesis—that evolution has influenced human motivation—seems reasonable. Many psychologists believe that sociobiological analyses have enriched psychology's repertoire of explanatory concepts and broadened its understanding of the factors that motivate social behavior in many species (Crawford, 1987). However, efforts to apply sociobiological concepts to human motivation have generated a highly charged debate (Ruse, 1987). Some critics argue that Wilson's theory overemphasizes the influence of biology on social behavior. Other critics assert that sociobiological theory can be used to maintain that the status quo in society is the inevitable

outcome of evolutionary forces (Lewontin, Rose, & Kamin, 1984). For example, if males have dominant status over females, sociobiological theory suggests that natural selection must have favored this arrangement.

You can probably see why some people are concerned about the political implications of this line of thought. Wilson has tried to address these concerns by asserting that sociobiology should try to avoid "the naturalistic fallacy of ethics, which uncritically concludes that what is, should be." However, Wilson's disclaimers have not satisfied many of his critics, and sociobiology theory remains controversial.

Drive Theories

Many theories view motivational forces in terms of *drives*. The drive concept appears in a diverse array of theories that otherwise have little in common, such as psychoanalytic (Freud, 1915) and behaviorist formulations (Hull, 1943). This approach to understanding motivation was explored most fully by Clark Hull in the 1940s and 1950s.

Hull's concept of drive was derived from Walter Cannon's (1932) observation that organisms seek to maintain **homeostasis, a state of physiological equilibrium or stability.** The body maintains homeostasis in various ways. For example, human body temperature normally fluctuates around 98.6° Fahrenheit (see Figure 10.1). If your body temperature rises or drops noticeably, automatic responses occur: If your temperature goes up, you perspire; if your temperature goes down, you shiver. These reactions are designed to move your temperature back toward 98.6°. Thus, your body reacts to many disturbances in physiological stability by trying to restore equilibrium.

Drive theories apply the concept of homeostasis to behavior. **A *drive* is an internal state of tension that motivates an organism to engage in activities that should reduce this tension.** These unpleasant states of tension are viewed as disruptions of the preferred equilibrium. According to drive theories, when individuals experience a drive, they're motivated to pursue actions that will lead to *drive reduction*. The hunger motive provides a simple example of drive theory in action. If you go without food for a while, you begin to experience some discomfort. This internal tension (the drive) motivates you to obtain food. Eating reduces the drive and restores physiological equilibrium. Most drive theories assume that people begin life with a small set of unlearned, biological drives and that they gradually develop a larger, more diverse set of acquired drives through learning and socialization.

Drive theories have been very influential, and the drive concept continues to be widely used in modern psychology. *However, drive theories cannot explain all motivation.* Homeostasis appears irrelevant to some human motives, such as a "thirst for knowledge." Also, motivation may exist without drive arousal. This point is easy to illustrate. Think of all the times that you've eaten when you weren't the least bit hungry. You're driving or walking home from class, amply filled by a solid lunch, when an ice cream parlor beckons seductively. You stop in and have a couple of scoops of your favorite flavor. Not only are you motivated to eat in the absence of internal tension, you may actually *cause* yourself some internal tension—from overeating. Because drive theories assume that people always try to reduce internal tension, they can't explain this behavior very well. Incentive theories, which represent a different approach to motivation, can account for this behavior more readily.

Incentive Theories

Incentive theories propose that external stimuli regulate motivational states (Bolles, 1975; McClelland, 1975; Skinner, 1953). **An *incentive* is an external goal that has the capacity to motivate behavior.** Ice cream, a juicy steak, a monetary prize, approval from friends, an A on an exam, and a promotion at work are all incentives. Some of these incentives may reduce drives, but others may not.

Drive and incentive models of motivation are often contrasted as *push versus pull* theories. Drive theories emphasize how *internal* states of tension *push* people in certain directions. Incentive theories emphasize how *external* stimuli *pull* people in certain directions. According to drive theories, the source of motivation lies *within* the organism. According to incentive theories, the source of motivation lies *outside* the organism, in the environment. This means that incentive models don't operate according to the principle of homeostasis, which hinges on internal changes in the organism. Thus, in comparison to drive theories, incentive theories emphasize environmental factors and downplay the biological bases of human motivation.

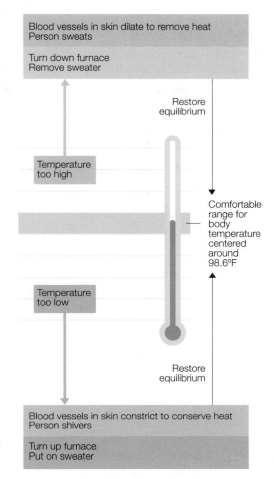

Blood vessels in skin dilate to remove heat
Person sweats

Turn down furnace
Remove sweater

Restore equilibrium

Temperature too high

Comfortable range for body temperature centered around 98.6°F

Temperature too low

Restore equilibrium

Blood vessels in skin constrict to conserve heat
Person shivers

Turn up furnace
Put on sweater

Figure 10.1. Temperature regulation as an example of homeostasis. The regulation of body temperature provides a simple example of how organisms often seek to maintain homeostasis, or a state of physiological equilibrium. When your temperature moves out of an acceptable range, automatic bodily reactions (such as sweating or shivering) respond to restore equilibrium. Of course, these automatic reactions may not be sufficient by themselves, so you may have to take other actions (such as turning a heater up or down) to bring your body temperature back into its comfort zone.

As you're painfully aware, people can't always obtain the goals they desire, such as good grades or choice promotions. *Expectancy-value models* of motivation are incentive theories that take this reality into account (Atkinson & Birch, 1978). According to expectancy-value models, one's motivation to pursue a particular course of action will depend on two factors: (1) *expectancy* about one's chances of attaining the incentive and (2) the *value* of the desired incentive.

Thus, your motivation to pursue a promotion at work will depend on your estimate of the likelihood that you can snare the promotion (expectancy) and on how appealing the promotion is to you (value). In a similar fashion, your motivation to buy lottery tickets will depend on the size of the prize and your belief about your chances of winning. State-run lotteries clearly recognize this reality. To lure people into playing these lotteries, officials make incentive value high by offering games with huge financial prizes (but with very low odds of winning). They also elevate the expectancy of winning by offering games in which there are many daily winners (of small prizes).

The Range and Diversity of Human Motives

Motivational theorists of all persuasions agree that humans display an enormous diversity of motives. Most theories distinguish between *biological motives* that originate in bodily needs, such as hunger, and *social motives* that originate in social experiences, such as the need for achievement.

People have a limited number of biological needs. According to K. B. Madsen (1968, 1973), most theories enumerate 10 to 15 such needs, some of which are listed on the left side of Figure 10.2. As you can see, most biological motives reflect needs that are essential to survival, such as the needs for food, water, and maintenance of normal body temperature.

People all share the same biological needs, but their social needs vary depending on their experiences. For example, some people acquire a need for orderliness, and some don't. Although people have a limited number of biological needs, they can acquire an unlimited number of social needs through learning and socialization. Some examples of social motives—from an influential list compiled by Henry Murray (1938)—are shown on the right side of Figure 10.2. Murray theorized that most people have needs for achievement, autonomy, affiliation, dominance, exhibition, and order, among other things. Of course, the strength of these needs varies from person to person, depending on personal history.

The distinction between biological needs and social needs is *not* clear-cut. A specific motive may be viewed as a biological motive by one theorist and as a social motive by another. These differences of opinion exist because human motives vary in the *degree* to which they depend on biology. Even a heavily biological motive such as hunger is shaped to some extent by social factors. Sexual motivation clearly has both biological and social origins. Furthermore, sociobiologists and other theorists maintain that many social needs, such as dominance, affiliation, and curiosity, have biological foundations that are not fully appreciated.

Although the distinction between biological and social needs is not absolute, this dichotomy allows us to impose some organization on the diverse motives seen in human behavior. We turn next to a theory that provides a more elaborate scheme for organizing human motives.

Arranging Needs in a Hierarchy: Maslow's Theory

Abraham Maslow (1962, 1970), a prominent humanistic theorist, proposed a sweeping overview of human motivation. His theory strikes a unique balance between biological and social needs and integrates many of the motivational concepts that we've discussed.

Maslow's theory assumes that people have many needs that compete for expression. At this very moment, your need for sleep may be pitted against your need for achievement, as you work to earn a good grade in your psychology class. Of course, not all needs are created equal. Maslow proposed that human motives are organized hierarchically. Maslow's *hierarchy of needs* is a systematic arrangement of needs according to priority, which assumes that basic needs must be met before less basic needs are aroused.

This hierarchical arrangement is usually portrayed as a pyramid (see Figure 10.3). The needs at

Figure 10.2. The diversity of human motives. People are motivated by a wide range of needs, which can be divided into two broad classes: biological motives and social motives. The list on the left (adapted from Madsen, 1973) shows some important biological needs in humans. The list on the right (adapted from Murray, 1938) provides examples of prominent social needs in humans.

Examples of Biological Needs in Humans	Examples of Social Needs in Humans
Hunger motive	Achievement motive (need to excel)
Thirst motive	Affiliation motive (need for social bonds)
Sex motive	Autonomy motive (need for independence)
Temperature motive (need for appropriate body temperature)	Nurturance motive (need to nourish and protect others)
Excretory motive (need to eliminate bodily wastes)	Dominance motive (need to influence or control others)
Sleep and rest motive	Exhibition motive (need to make an impression on others)
Activity motive (need for optimal level of stimulation and arousal)	Order motive (need for orderliness, tidiness, organization)
Aggression motive	Play motive (need for fun, relaxation, amusement)

CHAPTER TEN

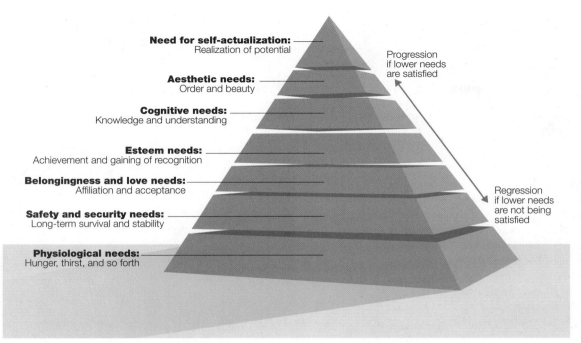

Need for self-actualization:
Realization of potential

Aesthetic needs:
Order and beauty

Cognitive needs:
Knowledge and understanding

Esteem needs:
Achievement and gaining of recognition

Belongingness and love needs:
Affiliation and acceptance

Safety and security needs:
Long-term survival and stability

Physiological needs:
Hunger, thirst, and so forth

Progression if lower needs are satisfied

Regression if lower needs are not being satisfied

Figure 10.3. Maslow's hierarchy of needs. According to Maslow, human needs are arranged in a hierarchy, and people must satisfy their basic needs before they can satisfy higher needs. In the diagram, higher levels in the pyramid represent progressively less basic needs. Individuals progress upward in the hierarchy when lower needs are satisfied reasonably well, but they may regress back to lower levels if basic needs are no longer satisfied.

the bottom of the pyramid are the most basic. They are fundamental physiological needs that are essential to survival, such as the needs for food, water, a stable body temperature, and so on. They must be satisfied fairly well before the individual can become concerned about needs at higher levels in the hierarchy. When a person manages to satisfy a level of needs reasonably well (complete satisfaction is not necessary), *this satisfaction activates needs at the next level.*

The second tier in Maslow's pyramid is made up of safety and security needs. These needs reflect concern about *long-term* survival. People seek to live in an orderly, stable, safe world. They want to be protected from assault, mayhem in the streets, environmental poisons, economic chaos, and so forth. Safety and security needs motivate adults to seek a stable job, to buy insurance, and to put money in their savings accounts.

When safety and security needs are met adequately, needs for love and belongingness become more prominent. These needs lead people to seek affection—from family, from friends, and in intimate relationships. When these needs are gratified, esteem needs are activated. People then become more concerned about their achievements and the recognition, respect, and status that they earn. Maslow's key point is that lower needs must be satisfied reasonably well before higher needs are aroused.

Consistent with his humanistic perspective, Maslow theorized that people have growth needs that emerge out of the human striving for *personal growth*—that is, evolution toward a higher state of

being (see Chapter 1). The growth needs—such as the needs for knowledge, understanding, and aesthetic beauty—are found in the uppermost reaches of Maslow's hierarchy. Foremost among them is the *need for self-actualization*, **which is the need to fulfill one's potential.** It is the highest need in Maslow's motivational hierarchy. Maslow summarized this concept with a very simple statement: "What a man *can* be, he *must* be." According to Maslow, people will be frustrated if they are unable to fully use their talents or pursue their true interests. For example, if you have musical talent but must work as an accountant, or if you have scholarly interests but must work as a sales clerk, your need for self-actualization will be thwarted.

Maslow believed that human nature dictates the order of the various levels of needs. His hierarchy systematically organizes needs according to their biological and social foundations. As one moves upward in the hierarchy, each level of needs becomes less biological and more social in origin. Thus, according to Maslow, the degree to which a person's behavior is dominated by biological needs depends on which level of needs is activated. This level varies depending on the individual and the circumstances.

Maslow's theory has been highly influential. However, aspects of the theory are difficult to test empirically. In particular, growth needs such as self-actualization have proven difficult to measure and study. Thus, portions of Maslow's theory rest on a thin foundation of research (Geller, 1982). Nonetheless, Maslow contributed to the understanding of motivation by suggesting a hi-

"What a man can be, he must be."
ABRAHAM MASLOW

Check your understanding of the motivational concepts that we've discussed by analyzing the examples of motivated behavior described here. In the first column of blank spaces, indicate which theoretical approach seems to provide the best explanation for the behavior. In the second column, indicate which level of needs in Maslow's hierarchy has been activated. The answers are in Appendix A.

Scenario	*Level of needs*	*Relevant theory*
1. You're alone in a strange city, and you feel lonely. You yearn for someone to talk to. You go for a walk along the waterfront, hoping to meet someone.	_____	_____
2. You're working 2 hours overtime every night. You don't like staying late, but your company really needs to get the work done and you can't pass up the substantial bonus (triple pay) they're offering.	_____	_____
3. You become fascinated by modern architecture, so you check a bunch of books out of the library because you want to understand the thinking behind postmodernism.	_____	_____
4. You're among the nation's poor, and you can't put adequate food on the table for your family. You give your children all of the food available for dinner, telling them you don't feel hungry, when you're really starving.	_____	_____

erarchical principle that takes both the biological and social foundations of human motives into consideration.

Maslow's theory has its strengths and its weaknesses—just as all the other motivational theories do. No one theory has come to dominate the investigation of motivation in contemporary psychology. Perhaps it's unrealistic to expect a single theory to explain the great variety of motives that inspire goal-directed behavior. In any case, in the remainder of this chapter you'll see the influence of all the motivational theories that we've discussed.

Our next task is to take a closer look at selected motives. Given the range and diversity of human motives, we can only examine a handful in depth. To a large degree, our choices reflect the motives psychologists have studied the most: hunger, sex, and achievement. As we explore these motives we'll be moving upward through Maslow's hierarchy. Thus, you'll see the influence of physiological factors gradually declining, giving way to social and environmental factors.

THE MOTIVATION OF HUNGER AND EATING

Why do people eat? Because they're hungry. What makes them hungry? A lack of food. Any grade-

school child can explain these basic facts. So hunger is a simple motivational system, right? Wrong! Hunger is deceptive. It only looks simple. Actually, it's a terribly puzzling and complex motivational system. Despite extensive studies of hunger, psychologists and other scientists are still struggling to understand the factors that regulate eating behavior.

Biological Factors in the Regulation of Hunger

You have probably had embarrassing occasions when your stomach growled loudly at an inopportune moment. Someone may have commented, "You must be starving!" Most people equate a rumbling stomach with hunger, and, in fact, the first scientific theories of hunger were based on this simple equation. In an elaborate 1912 study, Walter Cannon and A. L. Washburn verified what most people have noticed based on casual observation: A strong association exists between stomach contractions and the experience of hunger.

Based on this correlation, Cannon theorized that stomach contractions *cause* hunger. However, as we've seen before, correlation is no assurance of causation, and his theory was eventually discredited. Stomach contractions often accompany hunger, but they don't cause it. How do we know? Because later research showed that people continue to experience hunger even after their stomach has been removed out of medical necessity (Wangensteen & Carlson, 1931). If hunger can occur without a stomach, then stomach contractions can't be the cause of hunger. This realization led to more elaborate theories of hunger that focus on (1) the role of the brain, (2) blood sugar level, and (3) hormones.

Brain Regulation

Research with laboratory animals eventually suggested that the experience of hunger is controlled in the brain—specifically, in the hypothalamus. As we have noted before, the *hypothalamus* is a tiny structure involved in the regulation of a variety of biological needs related to survival (see Figure 10.4). Researchers have typically investigated the role of the hypothalamus in behavior by subjecting animals to *electrical stimulation of the brain (ESB)*. They implant an electrode in the hypothalamus and then pass different currents through the electrode to either destroy (lesion) or activate the area of the brain at the base of the electrode (see Chapter 3).

A great many animal studies have shown that the activation and destruction of two areas in the hypothalamus are associated with changes in eating. Investigators have found that when they activate the *lateral hypothalamus* (LH) through ESB, animals promptly begin to eat, even if they're already full. The animals stop eating when the electrical stimulation of the LH is halted. In contrast, when researchers destroy the LH, animals typically ignore available food and frequently starve (Anand & Brobeck, 1951; Teitelbaum & Epstein, 1962). The opposite pattern is seen when researchers stimulate or lesion the *ventromedial nucleus of the hypothalamus* (VMH) (Brobeck, Tepperman, & Long, 1943; Wyrwicka & Dobrzecka, 1960). Activation of the VMH curtails eating behavior, whereas destroying the VMH leads to extensive overeating and obesity. Indeed, it is not unusual for animals with VMH lesions to balloon up to three times their original weight.

The typical results of these studies of hypothalamic manipulations and eating are summarized in Figure 10.5. Given these results, investigators originally concluded that activation of the lateral hypothalamus *starts* the experience of hunger and that activation of the ventromedial hypothalamus *stops* the experience of hunger. They weren't entirely sure what normally leads to the activation of these areas in the absence of artificial electrical stimulation, but they concluded that the LH and VMH are the brain's on-off switches or start-stop centers that control hunger (Stellar, 1954).

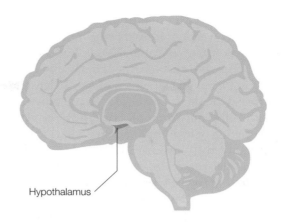

Figure 10.4. The hypothalamus. This small structure at the base of the forebrain plays a role in regulating a variety of human biological needs, including hunger. (Consult Figure 3.11 for a more detailed view.)

Hypothalamus

Doubts about this dual-centers model of hunger soon surfaced, however. Researchers noticed that hypothalamic stimulation and lesioning lead to some peculiarities in the eating behavior of experimental animals. For example, rats with VMH lesions usually engage in massive overeating. However, they're *lazy*, and if they're forced to work for their food (by pressing a lever), they end up eating less than normal (Graff & Stellar, 1962). They also are *picky* and reject food that doesn't taste good (Ferguson & Keesey, 1975). Critics argued that if the animals were really hungry, they wouldn't be so lazy or picky.

Researchers shed some light on these riddles when they found that the effects of LH and VMH manipulations *are not unique to hunger*. For instance, LH stimulation, which triggers eating when food is present, will elicit drinking if water alone is present. Furthermore, if neither food nor water is available, LH stimulation elicits running. Thus, Elliot Valenstein (1973) reasoned that LH stimulation does not produce hunger but rather *generalized arousal*. He argued that this arousal led to eating in many studies simply because the animals were confined to cages with food present—what else could they do? In a similar fashion, Valenstein

Figure 10.5. The hypothalamus and eating behavior. Researchers found that destroying or activating the lateral hypothalamus (LH) or ventromedial hypothalamus (VMH) in rats and other animals caused opposite effects on eating. These results suggested that the LH and VMH are the brain's on-off centers for hunger, but the text discusses doubts raised by subsequent studies.

Section of hypothalamus	Destroyed (by lesioning)	Activated (by electrical stimulation)
Lateral area	Animal stops eating	Animal overeats
Ventromedial nucleus	Animal overeats	Animal stops eating

argued that VMH activation blocks eating by inhibiting general arousal. Finally, he asserted that hypothalamic manipulations lead to peculiarities in eating because the animals aren't experiencing genuine hunger. Although Valenstein's theory is the subject of debate, several other lines of evidence support the idea that the activation or destruction of hypothalamic areas influences eating indirectly (Grossman, 1979).

The dual-centers model has been further complicated by recent research on how neurotransmitters and endorphins (see Chapter 3) contribute to the brain's regulation of hunger and eating. Armed with new methods for tracking chemical activity in the brain, investigators have found that increased levels of norepinephrine and endorphins are associated with increased eating in laboratory animals and that serotonin activity is associated with the inhibition of hunger (Hoebel, 1988; Le Magnen, 1990). Moreover, they have found that some of these neurochemical changes related to eating unfold in a third area of the hypothalamus (the paraventricular nucleus) that may be yet another center involved in the regulation of hunger.

These findings have muddied the waters quite a bit. Most theorists still believe that the LH and VMH are involved in the control of hunger. However, the exact nature of their role is unclear. The once popular notion that they are on-off centers for hunger has been discarded as too simplistic (Logue, 1991). They appear to be just two elements in a large, complex homeostatic system that regulates hunger. Let's look at some other physiological mechanisms that play a role in this system.

Blood Glucose Regulation

Much of the food taken into the body is converted into *glucose*, which circulates in the blood. **Glucose is a simple sugar that is an important source of energy.** Manipulations that decrease blood glucose level can increase hunger. Manipulations that increase glucose level can make people feel satiated (full). Based on these findings, Jean Mayer (1955, 1968) proposed that hunger is regulated by the rise and fall of blood glucose levels.

Glucostatic theory proposed that fluctuations in blood glucose level are monitored in the brain by *glucostats*—**neurons sensitive to glucose in the surrounding fluid.** Glucostats located in the hypothalamus were thought to control the experience of hunger. In its simplest form, glucostatic theory quickly ran into a major complication. People who are diabetic typically have high levels

of glucose in their blood (which should make them feel full), but they still feel hungry much of the time. Mayer accounted for this fact by reasoning that it's not the *level of glucose* in the blood that is monitored by glucostats but rather *cells' uptake of glucose* from the blood. Thus, diabetics' frequent hunger makes sense because their disease involves a deficiency in extracting glucose from the blood.

Associations between blood glucose utilization and hunger have been found (Thompson & Campbell, 1977). It appears likely that hunger is regulated, at least in part, through glucostatic mechanisms. However, the *location* of the glucostats remains open to debate. Although neurons sensitive to glucose have been found in the hypothalamus (Oomura, 1976), glucose fluctuations in the brain seem too slow and too small to account for swings in hunger.

The current evidence suggests that the glucostatic regulation of hunger is accomplished primarily through the liver (Niijima, 1982; Novin et al., 1983). Such an arrangement would make sense, in that the liver is the first stop for nutrients after they are absorbed from the intestine. It appears that glucostats in the liver send signals to the hypothalamus by way of the vagus nerve that connects the liver with the brain. The liver may also monitor other physiological changes that affect hunger.

Hormonal Regulation

Insulin **is a hormone secreted by the pancreas.** It must be present for cells to extract glucose from the blood. Indeed, an inadequate supply of insulin is what causes diabetes. Many diabetics are unable to use the glucose in their blood unless they are given insulin injections. In nondiabetic individuals, insulin injections stimulate hunger. Normal secretion of insulin by the pancreas is also associated with increased hunger (Rodin et al., 1985).

These findings indicate that insulin fluctuations contribute to the experience of hunger. Indeed, research suggests that insulin may not be the only hormone involved in hunger regulation. For instance, a hormone called cholecystokinin (CCK) is apparently secreted when food enters the digestive system. Investigators suspect that CCK plays a role in the experience of satiety that brings eating to a halt (McHugh & Moran, 1985; Smith & Gibbs, 1992).

Environmental Factors in the Regulation of Hunger

Hunger clearly is a biological need, but eating is not regulated by biological factors alone. Studies show that social and environmental factors govern eating to a considerable extent. Three key environmental factors are (1) learned preferences and habits, (2) food-related cues, and (3) stress.

Learned Preferences and Habits

Are you fond of eating calves' brains? How about eels or snakes? Could I interest you in a grasshopper or some dog meat? Probably not, but these are delicacies in some regions of the world. Arctic Eskimos like to eat maggots! You probably prefer chicken, apples, eggs, lettuce, potato chips, pizza, cornflakes, or ice cream. These preferences are acquired through learning. People from different cultures display very different patterns of food consumption (Kittler & Sucher, 1989). If you doubt this, just visit a grocery store in an ethnic neighborhood (not your own, of course).

Humans do have some innate taste preferences of a general sort (for sweet over sour, for instance). But learning wields a great deal of influence over *what* people prefer to eat (Birch, 1987). Taste preferences are partly a function of learned associations formed through classical conditioning. For example, youngsters can be conditioned to prefer flavors paired with high caloric intake or pleasant social interactions (Logue, 1991). Of course, as we learned in Chapter 6, taste aversions can also be acquired through conditioning when foods are followed by nausea (Bernstein & Meachum, 1990).

Eating habits are also shaped by obervational learning (see Chapter 6). To a large degree, food preferences are a matter of exposure (Rozin, 1990). People generally prefer familiar foods. But geographical, cultural, religious, and ethnic factors limit people's exposure to various foods. Repeated exposures to a new food usually lead to increased liking. Individuals' reactions to foods are also shaped by the reactions of others around them, such as parents, siblings, and peers. For instance, if you're trying squid for the first time, you're more likely to have a favorable reaction if a companion savors a bite with delight, as opposed to spitting it out in disgust.

Learned habits and social considerations also influence *how much* people eat. For instance, most people tend to consume more food when they are with others than when alone (de Castro & Brewer, 1992). The influence of habit is apparent when artificial sugar is substituted for real sugar in subjects' diets *without their knowledge*. Because of this substitution, they get far fewer calories, which should lead to increased eating to compensate for the caloric loss.

But most people don't increase their food intake for at least six days (Bellisle, 1979). They continue to eat in their usual way—out of habit.

Food-Related Cues

You have no doubt had your hunger aroused by television commercials for delicious-looking food or by seductive odors coming from the kitchen. These experiences illustrate how food-related environmental cues can trigger hunger (Birch et al., 1989). Stanley Schachter (1971) conducted numerous studies on how external cues influence hunger. In one study, Schachter and Gross (1968) manipulated the apparent time by altering the clock in a room so that it ran fast or slow. The subjects had been asked to remove their watches, so they were misled about the time of day. When offered crackers, obese subjects ate nearly twice as many when they thought (erroneously) that it was late rather than early in the afternoon. Nonobese subjects, on the other hand, ate fewer crackers when they thought it was late—because they didn't

Food preferences are shaped to a considerable degree by learning and socialization. The foods shown here are not likely to be appetizing to you because of your cultural background. (Top) Snakes are among the small crawling things that Chinese people consume for medicinal purposes. (Bottom) A Vietnamese man preparing to cook a dog.

want to spoil their appetite for dinner. Thus, the control of time cues affected eating in both groups, but with opposite results.

In other studies Schachter manipulated external cues such as how tasty and appealing food appeared, how obvious its availability was, and how much effort was required to eat. All of these external cues were found to influence eating behavior to some extent (Schachter & Rodin, 1974). Thus, it's clear that hunger and eating are governed in part by a variety of food-related cues.

Stress, Arousal, and Eating

When I have an exceptionally stressful day, I often head for the refrigerator, a grocery store, or a restaurant—usually in pursuit of something chocolate. In other words, I sometimes deal with life's hassles by stuffing myself with my favorite foods. My response is not particularly unusual. Studies have shown that stress leads to increased eating in a substantial portion of people (Grunberg & Straub, 1992; Slochower, Kaplan, & Mann, 1981). Actually, it may be stress-induced *arousal* rather than stress itself that stimulates eating. Stressful events often lead to physiological arousal (see Chapter 13), and several lines of evidence suggest a link between heightened arousal and overeating (Striegel-Moore & Rodin, 1986). Thus, stress is another environmental factor that can influence hunger, although it's not clear whether these effects are direct or indirect.

As you can see then, hunger is a basic motive, but it's not a simple one. Neither is sex, the motivational system that we'll consider next.

SEXUAL MOTIVATION: THE MYSTERY OF SEXUAL ORIENTATION

How does sex resemble food? Sometimes it seems that people are obsessed with both. People joke and gossip about sex constantly. Magazines, novels, movies, and television shows are saturated with sexual activity and innuendo. The advertising industry uses sex to sell everything from mouthwash to designer jeans to automobiles. This intense interest in sex reflects the importance of sexual motivation.

Researchers interested in sexual motivation have learned a great deal about a variety of issues. For example, Masters and Johnson (1966, 1970) have provided a detailed description of the physiology of the human sexual response. And a host of investigators have contributed to our understanding of how sexual desire is influenced by a complicated network of biological and social factors. Although much of this research is fascinating, we will limit our discussion in this section to the single question that has most intrigued sex researchers (and the public) in recent years: What are the determinants of sexual orientation?

The factors that modulate sexual desire are reasonably well understood, but the determinants of *sexual orientation* are much more obscure. *Sexual orientation* **refers to a person's preference for emotional and sexual relationships with individuals of the same sex, the other sex, or either sex.** *Heterosexuals* **seek emotional-sexual relationships with members of the other sex,** *bisexuals* **with members of either sex, and** *homo-*

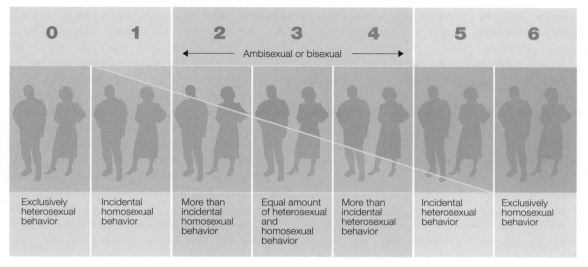

Figure 10.6. Homosexuality and heterosexuality as endpoints on a continuum. Sex researchers view heterosexuality and homosexuality as falling on a continuum rather than make an all-or-none distinction. Kinsey and his associates (1948, 1953) created this seven-point scale (from 0 to 6) to describe people's sexual orientation. They used the term *ambisexual* to describe those who fall in the middle of the scale, but such people are commonly called *bisexual* today.

sexuals **with members of the same sex.** In recent years, the terms *gay* and *straight* have become widely used to refer to homosexuals and heterosexuals, respectively. Although *gay* can refer to homosexuals of either sex, most homosexual women prefer to call themselves *lesbians*.

People tend to view heterosexuality and homosexuality as an all-or-none distinction. However, in a large-scale survey of sexual behavior, Alfred Kinsey and his colleagues (1948, 1953) discovered that many people who define themselves as heterosexuals have had homosexual experiences—and vice versa. Thus, Kinsey and others have concluded that it is more accurate to view heterosexuality and homosexuality as end points on a continuum. Indeed, Kinsey devised a seven-point scale, shown in Figure 10.6, that can be used to characterize individuals' sexual orientation.

How are people distributed on this scale? No one knows for sure. Prejudicial attitudes about homosexuality make it hard to get candid information from people. Estimates of the incidence of homosexuality vary widely—from 4% to 17% (Gonsiorek & Weinrich, 1991). A frequently cited estimate of the number of people who are homosexual is 10%. If homosexuals and bisexuals are lumped together, recent studies *suggest* that this figure is reasonably accurate for males but perhaps an overestimate for females (Ellis & Ames, 1987; Janus & Janus, 1993).

Over the years, many theories have been floated to explain the origins of homosexuality, but when tested empirically, these theories have garnered remarkably little support. For example, psychoanalytic and behavioral theorists, who usually agree on very little, both proposed environmental explanations for the development of homosexuality. The Freudian theorists argued that a male is likely to become gay when raised by a weak, detached, ineffectual father who is a poor heterosexual role model and an overprotective, close-binding mother, with whom the boy identifies. Behavioral theorists argued that homosexuality is a learned preference acquired when same-sex stimuli have been paired with sexual arousal, perhaps through chance seductions by adult homosexuals. Extensive research on homosexuals' upbringing and childhood experiences have failed to support either of these theories (Bell, Weinberg, & Hammersmith, 1981).

However, efforts to research homosexuals' personal histories have yielded a couple of interesting insights. Gay men and women consistently report that they can trace their homosexual leanings back to their early childhood, even before they understood what sex was really about (Garnets & Kimmel, 1991). Most also report that

In spite of fascinating, ground-breaking research in recent years, the determinants of sexual orientation remain obscure. Like so many other issues in psychology, the debate about the roots of homosexuality centers around the relative importance of nature versus nurture.

because of negative parental and societal attitudes about homosexuality, they initially struggled to deny their sexual orientation. Hence, they felt that their homosexuality was not a matter of choice and not something that they could readily change.

These findings obviously suggest that the roots of homosexuality are more biological than environmental. But initial efforts to find a biological basis for homosexuality met with little success. Most theorists originally assumed that hormonal differences between heterosexuals and homosexuals must underlie a person's sexual orientation (Doerr et al., 1976, Dorner, 1988). However, studies comparing circulating hormone levels in gays and straights found only small, inconsistent differences that could not be linked to sexual orientation in any convincing way (Garnets & Kimmel, 1991; Ricketts, 1984).

Thus, like environmental theorists, biological theorists were stymied in their efforts to explain the roots of homosexuality. However, several recent studies have provided some impressive support for the idea that homosexuality is largely biological in origin. One example is a study by Bailey and Pillard (1991), whose subjects were gay men who had either a twin brother or an adopted brother. They found that 52% of the subjects' identical twins were gay, that 22% of their fraternal twins were gay, and that 11% of their adoptive brothers were gay. A companion study (Bailey et al., 1993) of lesbians has yielded a similar pattern of results (see Figure 10.7). Given that identical twins share more genetic overlap than fraternal twins, who share more genes than unrelated adop-

tive siblings, these results suggest that there is a genetic predisposition to homosexuality (see Chapter 3 for an explanation of the logic underlying twin and adoption studies). A similar conclusion emerged from another recent study that used genetic mapping techniques. In this study, Hamer and associates (1993) linked male homosexuality to genetic material on the X chromosome.

In another line of research, LeVay (1991) has reported anatomical differences between gay and straight men in a region of the brain thought to influence sexual behavior. He focused on a tiny cluster of neurons in the anterior hypothalamus that is known to be larger in men than women. Because the structure is too small to be measured effectively in the living brain, it is studied posthumously. LeVay compared the autopsied brains of 19 homosexual and 16 heterosexual men and found that the targeted structure tended to be about half as large in the gay men. LeVay acknowledges that his findings should be interpreted with caution, as many of his subjects (including all the gay men) had died of AIDS, which clearly can wreak havoc in the brain. But like other recent findings, his data point to a biological basis for sexual orientation.

Despite the recent breakthroughs, much remains to be learned about the determinants of sexual orientation. The fact that identical twins of gay subjects turn out to be gay only about half the time suggests that the genetic predisposition to homosexuality is not overpowering. Environmental influences of some kind probably contribute to the development of homosexuality, but the nature of these environmental factors remains a mystery.

Once again, though, we can see that the nature versus nurture debate can have far-reaching social and political implications. Homosexuals have long been victims of extensive—and in many instances *legal*—discrimination. Gays cannot legally formalize their unions in marriage, they are not allowed to openly join the U.S. military, and they are barred from some jobs (for example, many school districts will not hire gay teachers). However, if research were to show that being gay is a matter of biological destiny, much like being black or female or short, many of the arguments against equal rights for gays would disintegrate. Why ban gays from teaching, for instance, if their sexual preference cannot "rub off" on their students? Although I would argue that discrimination against gays should be brought to an end either way, many individuals' opinions about gay rights may be

Figure 10.7. Genetics and sexual orientation. A *concordance rate* indicates the percentage of twin pairs or other pairs of relatives that exhibit the same characteristic. If relatives who share more genetic relatedness show higher concordance rates than relatives who share less genetic overlap, this evidence suggests a genetic predisposition to the characteristic. Recent studies of both gay men and lesbian women have found higher concordance rates among identical twins than fraternal twins, who, in turn, exhibit more concordance than adoptive siblings. These findings are consistent with the hypothesis that genetic factors influence sexual orientation. (Data from Bailey & Pillard, 1991; Bailey et al., 1993)

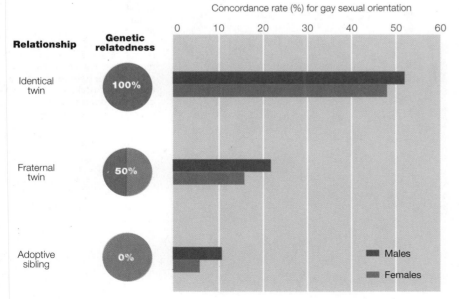

swayed by the outcome of the nature-nurture debate on the roots of homosexuality.

ACHIEVEMENT: IN SEARCH OF EXCELLENCE

At the beginning of this chapter, we discussed Dennis Conner's lengthy, laborious, and tenacious pursuit of the America's Cup. He and his crew made great sacrifices and worked countless hours to try to achieve their goal. What motivates people to push themselves so hard? In all likelihood, it's a strong need for achievement. **The *achievement motive* is the need to master difficult challenges, to outperform others, and to meet high standards of excellence.** Above all else, the need for achievement involves the desire to excel—especially in competition with others. In Maslow's hierarchy of needs, achievement is found at the fourth level, among the esteem needs. Although some people have tried to link achievement to biological factors such as hormonal fluctuations (Baker, 1980), the need for achievement is generally viewed as a product of social training.

David McClelland and his colleagues (McClelland, 1985; McClelland et al., 1953) have been studying the achievement motive for about 40 years. McClelland believes that achievement motivation is of the utmost importance. He sees the need for achievement as the spark that ignites economic growth, scientific progress, inspirational leadership, and masterpieces in the creative arts. It's difficult to argue with his assertion about the immense importance of achievement motivation. Consider how much poorer our culture would be if people such as Charles Darwin, Thomas Edison, Ernest Hemingway, Pablo Picasso, Marie Curie, Abraham Lincoln, Susan B. Anthony, Winston Churchill, and Martin Luther King hadn't had a fire burning in their hearts.

Individual Differences in the Need for Achievement

The need for achievement is a fairly stable aspect of personality. Hence, research in this area has focused mostly on individual differences in achievement motivation. In this research, investigators usually measure subjects' need for achievement with some variant of the Thematic Apperception Test (TAT), which was originally developed by Christina Morgan and Henry Murray in 1935. The TAT is a *projective test*, a test that requires subjects to respond to vague, ambiguous stimuli in ways that may reveal personal motives and traits (see Chapter 12). The stimulus materials for the TAT are pictures of people in ambiguous scenes open to interpretation. Examples include a man working at a desk and a woman seated in a chair staring off into space. Subjects are asked to write or tell stories about what's happening in the scenes and what the characters are feeling. The themes of these stories are then scored to measure the strength of various needs. Figure 10.8 shows examples of stories dominated by affiliation and achievement themes.

The research on individual differences in achievement motivation has yielded interesting findings on the characteristics of people who score high in the need for achievement. They tend to work harder and more persistently on tasks than people low in the need for achievement (Brown, 1974). They also are more likely than others to delay gratification in order to pursue long-term goals (Mischel, 1961). In terms of careers, they typically go into competitive occupations that provide them with an opportunity to excel (McClelland, 1987). Apparently, their persistence

"People with a high need for achievement are not gamblers; they are challenged to win by personal effort, not by luck."
DAVID McCLELLAND

Affiliation arousal
George is an engineer who is working late. He is *worried that his wife will be annoyed* with him for neglecting her. She has been *objecting* that he cares more about his work than his wife and family. He seems *unable to satisfy* both his boss and his wife, but he *loves her* very much and will do his best to *finish up* fast and get home to her.

Achievement arousal
George is an engineer who *wants to win* a competition in which the man with *the most practicable drawing* will be awarded the contract to build a bridge. He is taking a moment to think *how happy he will be* if he wins. He has been *baffled* by how to make *such a long span strong*, but he remembers *to specify a new steel alloy* of great strength, submits his entry, but does not win, and *is very unhappy*.

Figure 10.8. Measuring motives with the Thematic Apperception Test (TAT). Subjects taking the TAT tell or write stories about what is happening in a scene, such as this one showing a man at work. The two stories shown here illustrate strong affiliation motivation and strong achievement motivation. The italicized parts of the stories are thematic ideas that would be identified by a TAT scorer.

and hard work often pay off. High achievement motivation correlates positively with measures of career success and with upward social mobility among lower-class men (Crockett, 1962; McClelland & Boyatzis, 1982).

Do people high in achievement need always tackle the biggest challenges available? Not necessarily. A curious finding has emerged in laboratory studies in which subjects have been asked to choose how difficult of a task they want to work on. Subjects high in the need for achievement tend to select tasks of intermediate difficulty (McClelland & Koestner, 1992). For instance, in one study, where subjects playing a ring-tossing game were allowed to stand as close to or far away from the target peg as they wanted, high achievers tended to prefer a moderate degree of challenge (Atkinson & Litwin, 1960). Research on the situational determinants of achievement behavior has suggested a reason why.

Situational Determinants of Achievement Behavior

Your achievement drive is not the only determinant of how hard you work. Situational factors can also influence achievement strivings. John Atkinson (1974, 1981, 1992) has elaborated extensively on McClelland's original theory of achievement motivation and has identified some important situational determinants of achievement behavior. Atkinson theorizes that the tendency to pursue achievement in a particular situation depends on the following factors:

- The strength of one's *motivation* to *achieve success*. This is viewed as a stable aspect of personality.

- One's estimate of the *probability of success* for the task at hand. This varies from task to task.

- The *incentive value of success*. This depends on the tangible and intangible rewards for success on the specific task.

The last two variables are situational determinants of achievement behavior. That is, they vary from one situation to another. According to Atkinson, the pursuit of achievement increases as the probability and incentive value of success go up.

Let's apply Atkinson's model to a simple example. According to his theory, your tendency to pursue a good grade in calculus should depend on your general motivation to achieve success, your estimate of the probability of getting a good grade in the class, and the value you place on getting a good grade in calculus. Thus, given a certain motivation to achieve success, you will pursue a good grade in calculus less vigorously if your professor gives impossible exams (thus lowering your expectancy of success) or if a good grade in calculus is not required for your major (lowering the incentive value of success).

The joint influence of these situational factors may explain why high achievers prefer tasks of intermediate difficulty. Atkinson notes that the probability of success and the incentive value of success on tasks are interdependent to some degree. As tasks get easier, success becomes less satisfying. As tasks get harder, success becomes more satisfying, but its likelihood obviously declines. When the probability and incentive value of success are weighed together, moderately challenging tasks seem to offer the best overall value in terms of maximizing one's sense of accomplishment.

Factoring in the Fear of Failure

According to Atkinson, a person's fear of failure must also be considered to understand achievement behavior (Atkinson & Birch, 1978). He maintains that people vary in their *motivation to avoid failure*. This motive is considered a stable aspect of personality. Together with situational factors such as the probability of failure and the negative value placed on failure, it influences achievement strivings. Figure 10.9 diagrams the factors in

Figure 10.9. Determinants of achievement behavior. According to John Atkinson, a person's pursuit of achievement in a particular situation depends on several factors. Some of these factors, such as need for achievement or fear of failure, are relatively stable motives that are part of the person's personality. Many other factors, such as the likelihood and value of success or failure, vary from one situation to another, depending on the circumstances.

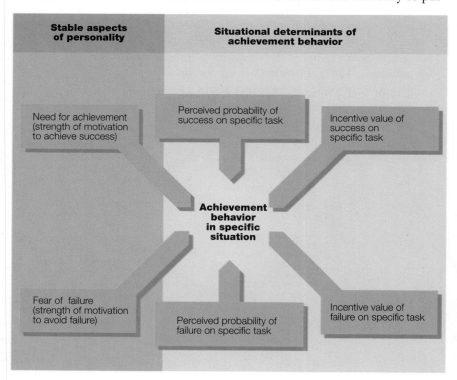

Atkinson's model that are thought to govern achievement behavior.

As with the motive to achieve success, the motive to avoid failure can stimulate achievement. For example, you might work very hard and very persistently in calculus primarily because you couldn't tolerate the shame associated with failure. In other words, you might work more to avoid a bad grade than to earn a good grade.

Fear is one of the most fundamental emotions. Thus, the relationship between achievement behavior and *fear* of failure illustrates how motivation and emotion are often intertwined. On the one hand, *emotion can cause motivation*. For example, *anger* about your work schedule may motivate you to look for a new job. *Jealousy* of an ex-girlfriend may motivate you to ask out her roommate. On the other hand, *motivation can cause emotion*. For example, your motivation to win a photography contest may lead to great *anxiety* during the judging and either great *joy* if you win or great *gloom* if you don't. Although motivation and emotion are closely related, they're *not* the same thing. We'll analyze the nature of emotion in the next section.

THE ELEMENTS OF EMOTIONAL EXPERIENCE

The most profound and important experiences in life are saturated with emotion. Think of the *joy* that people feel at weddings, the *grief* they feel at funerals, the *ecstasy* they feel when they fall in love. Emotions also color everyday experiences. For instance, you might experience *anger* when a professor treats you rudely, *dismay* when you learn that your car needs expensive repairs, and *happiness* when you see that you aced your economics exam. In some respects, emotions lie at the core of mental health. The two most common complaints that lead people to seek psychotherapy are *depression* and *anxiety*. Clearly, emotions play a pervasive role in people's lives. Reflecting this reality, modern psychologists have increased their research on emotion in recent decades (Davidson & Cacioppo, 1992).

Exactly what is an emotion? Everyone has plenty of personal experience with emotion, but it's an elusive concept to define. Emotion includes cognitive, physiological, and behavioral components, which are summarized in the following definition: *Emotion* involves (1) a sub-jective conscious experience (the cognitive component) accompanied by (2) bodily arousal (the physiological component) and (3) characteristic overt expressions (the behavioral component). That's a pretty complex definition. Let's take a closer look at each of these three components of emotion.

The Cognitive Component: Subjective Feelings

Over 550 words in the English language refer to emotions (Averill, 1980). Nonetheless, people often have difficulty describing their emotions to others (Zajonc, 1980). Emotion is a highly personal, subjective experience. In studying the cognitive component of emotions, psychologists generally rely on subjects' verbal reports of what they're experiencing. Their reports indicate that emotions are potentially intense internal feelings that sometimes seem to have a life of their own. Although some degree of control is possible, people can't click their emotions on and off like a bedroom light.

Our cognitive appraisals of events in our lives are key determinants of the emotions that we experience (Lazarus, 1991). A specific event, such as giving a speech, may be highly threatening and thus anxiety arousing for one person but a "ho-

---

CONCEPT CHECK 10.3
Understanding the Determinants of Achievement Behavior

According to John Atkinson, one's pursuit of achievement in a particular situation depends on several factors. Check your understanding of these factors by identifying each of the following vignettes as an example of one of the following six determinants of achievement behavior: (a) need for achievement; (b) perceived probability of success; (c) incentive value of success; (d) fear of failure; (e) perceived probability of failure; (f) incentive value of failure. The answers can be found in Appendix A.

_____ 1. Donna has just received a B in biology. Her reaction is typical of the way she responds to many situations involving achievement: "I didn't get an A, it's true, but at least I didn't flunk; that's what I was really worried about."

_____ 2. Belinda is nervously awaiting the start of the finals of the 200-meter dash in the last meet of her high school career. "I've gotta win this race! This is the most important race of my life!"

_____ 3. Corey grins as he considers the easy time he's going to have this semester. "I won't need to study much for this course. This teacher never flunks anyone."

_____ 4. Diana's gotten the highest grade on every test throughout the semester, yet she's still up all night studying for the final. "I know I've got an A in the bag, but I want to be the best student Dr. McClelland's ever had!"

hum," routine matter for another. The conscious experience of emotion includes an eval*uative* aspect. People characterize their emotions as pleasant or unpleasant (Schlosberg, 1954). Of course, individuals often experience "mixed emotions" that include both pleasant and unpleasant qualities (Polivy, 1981). For example, an executive just given a promotion with challenging new responsibilities may experience both happiness and anxiety. A young man who has just lost his virginity may experience a mixture of apprehension, guilt, and delight.

The Physiological Component: Autonomic Arousal

Imagine your reaction as your car spins out of control on an icy highway. Your fear is accompanied by a variety of physiological changes. Your heart rate and breathing accelerate. Your blood pressure surges, and your pupils dilate. The hairs on your skin stand erect, giving you "goose bumps," and you start to perspire. Although the physical reactions may not always be as obvious as in this scenario, *emotions are accompanied by physiological arousal.* Surely, you've experienced a "knot in your stomach" or a "lump in your throat"—thanks to anxiety.

The physiological arousal associated with emotion occurs mainly through the actions of the *autonomic nervous system,* which regulates the activity of glands, smooth muscles, and blood vessels (see Figure 10.10). As you may recall from Chapter 3, the autonomic nervous system is responsible for the *fight-or-flight response,* which is heavily laden with emotion. One prominent part of emo-tional arousal is **the *galvanic skin response (GSR)*, an increase in the electrical conductivity of the skin that occurs when sweat glands increase their activity.** GSR is a convenient and sensitive index of autonomic arousal that has been used as a measure of emotion in many laboratory studies.

The connection between emotion and autonomic arousal provides the basis for **the *polygraph*, or *lie detector*, a device that records autonomic fluctuations while a subject is questioned.** A polygraph can't actually detect lies. It's really an emotion detector. It monitors key indicators of autonomic arousal, typically heart rate, blood pressure, respiration rate, and GSR (see Figure 10.11). The assumption is that when subjects lie, they experience emotion (presumably anxiety) that produces noticeable changes in these physiological indicators. The polygraph examiner asks a subject a number of nonthreatening questions to establish the subject's baseline on these autonomic indicators. Then the examiner asks the critical questions (for example, "Where were you on the night of the burglary?") and observes whether the subject's autonomic arousal changes.

The polygraph is a potentially useful tool that can help police check out leads and alibis. However, its capacity to assess truthfulness is *far* from perfect (Lykken, 1981). Part of the problem is that people who are telling the truth may experience emotional arousal when they respond to incriminating questions. Thus, polygraph tests often lead to accusations against people who are actually innocent. Another problem is that some people can lie without experiencing anxiety or autonomic arousal.

Figure 10.10. Emotion and autonomic arousal. The autonomic nervous system (ANS) is composed of the nerves that connect to the heart, blood vessels, smooth muscles, and glands (consult Figure 3.7 for a more detailed view). The ANS is divided into the *sympathetic system,* which mobilizes bodily resources in response to stress, and the *parasympathetic system,* which conserves bodily resources. Emotions are frequently accompanied by sympathetic ANS activation, which leads to goose bumps, sweaty palms, and the other physical responses listed on the left side of the diagram.

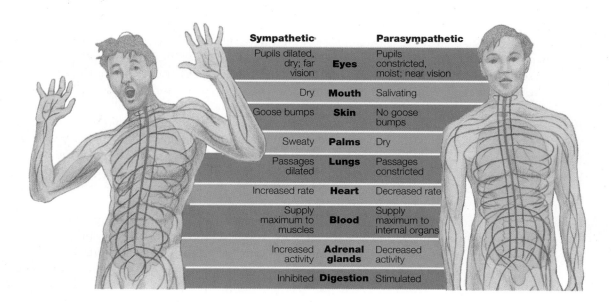

Sympathetic		Parasympathetic
Pupils dilated, dry; far vision	**Eyes**	Pupils constricted, moist; near vision
Dry	**Mouth**	Salivating
Goose bumps	**Skin**	No goose bumps
Sweaty	**Palms**	Dry
Passages dilated	**Lungs**	Passages constricted
Increased rate	**Heart**	Decreased rate
Supply maximum to muscles	**Blood**	Supply maximum to internal organs
Increased activity	**Adrenal glands**	Decreased activity
Inhibited	**Digestion**	Stimulated

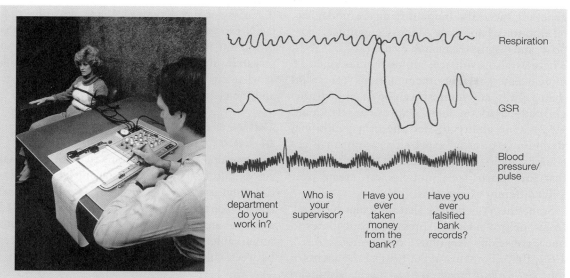

Respiration

GSR

Blood
pressure/
pulse

What
department
do you
work in?

Who is
your
supervisor?

Have you
ever
taken
money
from the
bank?

Have you
ever
falsified
bank
records?

Figure 10.11. Emotion and the polygraph. A lie detector measures the autonomic arousal that most people experience when they tell a lie. After using nonthreatening questions to establish a baseline, a polygraph examiner looks for signs of arousal (such as the sharp change in GSR shown here) on incriminating questions.

A study by Benjamin Kleinmuntz and Julian Szucko (1984) suggests that polygraph exams are inaccurate about one-fourth to one-third of the time. They arranged for lie detector tests for theft suspects, including 50 suspects who ultimately confessed their guilt and 50 suspects who were ultimately proven innocent by others' confessions. Their results indicated that the lie detector tests would have led to guilty verdicts for about one-third of the suspects who were proven innocent. Furthermore, about one-fourth of the suspects who later confessed would have been judged innocent based on their lie detector results. As a general rule, polygraph examiners do a better job of identifying guilty suspects than ruling out innocent ones (Honts & Perry, 1992).

Because of their high error rates, polygraph results cannot be submitted as evidence in most types of courtrooms. In spite of the courts' conservativism, many companies required prospective and current employees to take lie detector tests to weed out thieves. In 1988, however, the U.S. Congress passed a law curtailing this practice. The passage of this law was stimulated in part by research results such as those seen in the Kleinmuntz and Szucko study.

The Behavioral Component: Nonverbal Expressiveness

At the behavioral level, people reveal their emotions through characteristic overt expressions such as smiles, frowns, furrowed brows, clenched fists, and slumped shoulders. In other words, *emotions are expressed in "body language," or nonverbal behavior.*

Facial expressions reveal a variety of basic emotions. In an extensive research project, Paul Ekman and Wallace Friesen have asked subjects to identify what emotion a person was experiencing on the basis of facial cues in photographs (see Figure 10.12). They have found that subjects are

Figure 10.12. Recognizing emotions from facial expressions. Ekman and Friesen (1975, 1984) have used these photographs to study people's ability to distinguish emotions based on facial expressions. Their data indicate that people generally can identify the six fundamental emotions portrayed in these photos: happiness, anger, sadness, surprise, disgust, and fear.

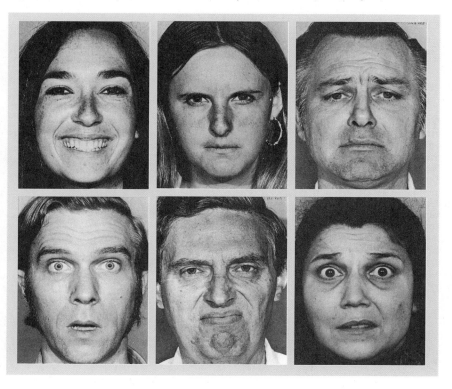

generally successful in identifying six fundamental emotions: happiness, sadness, anger, fear, surprise, and disgust (Ekman & Friesen, 1975, 1984). There is also evidence, although it is open to more debate, that four other emotions (contempt, shame, guilt, and interest) can be reliably distinguished based on facial expressions (Ekman, 1992). Our ability to decipher the emotional significance of facial expressions is no small accomplishment in that Ekman (1980) estimates that the human facial muscles can create over 7000 different expressions.

Some theorists believe that muscular feedback from one's own facial expressions contributes to one's conscious experience of emotions (Izard, 1971, 1990; Tomkins, 1980, 1991). Proponents of the *facial-feedback hypothesis* assert that facial muscles send signals to the brain and that these signals help the brain recognize the emotion that one is experiencing. According to this view, smiles, frowns, and furrowed brows help create the subjective experience of various emotions. Consistent with this idea, studies show that if subjects are instructed to contract their facial muscles to mimic facial expressions associated with certain emotions, they tend to report that they actually experience these emotions (Laird, 1984; Levenson, 1992). For example, a subject induced to frown would begin to feel angry. As a whole, the evidence supports the idea that facial feedback exerts some influence over the experience of emotions (Adelmann & Zajonc, 1989).

The facial expressions that go with different emotions may be largely innate (Eibl-Ebesfeldt, 1975). People who have been blind since birth smile and frown much like everyone else, even though they've never seen a smile or frown (Charlesworth & Kreutzer, 1973). The idea that facial expressions of emotion might be biologically built in has led to extensive cross-cultural research on the dynamics of emotion. Let's look at what investigators have learned about culture and the elements of emotional experience.

Culture and the Elements of Emotion

Are emotions innate reactions that are universal across cultures? Or are they socially learned reactions that are culturally variable? The voluminous research on this lingering question has not yielded a simple answer. Investigators have found both remarkable similarities and dramatic differences between cultures in the experience of emotion.

Cross-Cultural Similarities in Emotional Experience

After demonstrating that Western subjects could discern specific emotions from facial expressions, Ekman and Friesen (1975) took their facial-cue photographs on the road to other societies to see whether nonverbal expressions of emotion transcend cultural boundaries. Testing subjects in Argentina, Spain, Japan, and other countries, they found considerable cross-cultural agreement in the identification of happiness, sadness, anger, fear, surprise, and disgust based on facial expressions (see Figure 10.13). Still, Ekman and Friesen wondered whether this agreement might be the result of learning rather than biology, given that people in different cultures often share considerable exposure to Western mass media (magazines, newspapers, television, and so forth), which provide many visual depictions of people's emotional reactions. To rule out this possibility they took

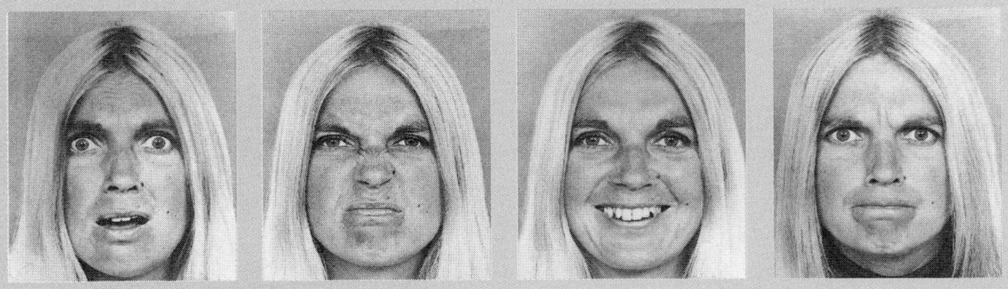

Figure 10.13. Cross-cultural comparisons of people's ability to recognize emotions from facial expressions.
Ekman and Friesen (1975) found that people in highly disparate cultures showed fair agreement on the emotions portrayed in these photos. This consensus across cultures suggests that facial expressions of emotions may have a biological basis.

Country	Fear	Disgust	Happiness	Anger
		Agreement in judging photos (%)		
United States	85	92	97	67
Brazil	67	97	95	90
Chile	68	92	95	94
Argentina	54	92	98	90
Japan	66	90	100	90
New Guinea	54	44	82	50

their photos to a remote area in New Guinea and showed them to a group of natives (the Fore) who had had virtually no contact with Western culture. Even the people from this preliterate culture did a fair job of identifying the emotions portrayed in the pictures (see the data in the bottom row of Figure 10.13). Subsequent comparisons of many other societies have also shown considerable cross-cultural congruence in the judgment of facial expressions (Ekman, 1992, 1993; Izard, 1991). Thus, there is compelling evidence that people in widely disparate cultures express their emotions and interpret those expressions in much the same way. As Russell (1991) puts it, "There is a core of emotional communication that has to do with being human rather than being a member of a particular culture" (p. 437).

As one might expect, the physiological arousal that accompanies emotion also appears to be largely invariant across cultures. When people from different cultures are asked to describe the physiological reactions associated with their emotions, they tend to describe the same physical sensations, such as tensed muscles, a lump in the throat, perspiration, and feeling warm (Wallbott & Scherer, 1988). Thus, researchers have found a great deal of cross-cultural continuity and uniformity in the physiological and behavioral (expressive) elements of emotional experience.

Cross-Cultural Differences in Emotional Experience

The cross-cultural similarities in emotional experience are impressive, but researchers have also found many cultural disparities in how people think about and express their emotions. Foremost among these disparities are the fascinating variations in how cultures categorize emotions. Some basic categories of emotion that are universally understood in Western cultures appear to go unrecognized—or at least unnamed—in some non-Western cultures. James Russell (1991) has compiled numerous examples of English words for emotions that have no equivalent in other languages. For example, Tahitians have no word that corresponds to *sadness*. Many non-Western groups, including the Yoruba of Nigeria, the Kaluli of New Guinea, and the Chinese, lack a word for *depression*. The concept of *anxiety* seems to go unrecognized among Eskimos and the Yoruba. The Quichua of Ecuador lack a word for *remorse*, and the Ifaluk of Micronesia have no word for *fear*.

Russell (1991) also notes that the English language lacks words for certain emotions that are viewed as basic emotions in other cultures. For example, we do not have an equivalent of the German word *Schadenfreude*, which refers to pleasure derived from another's displeasure. The English language also lacks an equivalent for the Japanese concept of *itoshii* (longing for an absent loved one) and the Bengali concept of *obhiman* (sorrow caused by the insensitivity of a loved one). Thus, although there is considerable cross-cultural overlap in the categorization of emotions (most basic emotions are recognized in most languages), there also are some striking cultural variations in how people think about emotions (Russell, 1991).

A similar conclusion can be drawn about nonverbal expressions of emotion. Although the natural facial expressions associated with basic emotions appear to be pancultural, people can and do learn to control and modify these expressions. Sometimes we consider it inappropriate to express certain feelings, so we try to hide them. At one time or another, we have all attempted to stifle a smile, frown, or furrowed brow to disguise our pleasure, anger, or anxiety. ***Display rules* are cultural norms that regulate the appropriate expression of emotions.** Display rules prescribe when, how, and to whom people can show various emotions.

These norms vary from one culture to another (Ekman, 1992). The Ifaluk, for instance, severely restrict expressions of happiness because they believe that this emotion often leads people to neglect their duties (Lutz, 1987). Japanese culture emphasizes the suppression of negative emotions in public. More so than in other cultures, the Japanese are socialized to mask emotions such as anger, sadness, and disgust with stoic facial expressions or polite smiling (Ekman, 1972). Thus, nonverbal expressions of emotions vary somewhat across cultures because of culture-specific display rules.

THEORIES OF EMOTION

How do psychologists explain the experience of emotion? A variety of theories and conflicting models exist. Some have been vigorously debated for over a century. As we describe these theories, you'll recognize a familiar bone of contention. Like theories of motivation, theories of emotion differ in their emphasis on the innate biological basis of emotion versus the social, environmental basis.

James-Lange Theory

As we noted in Chapter 1, William James was a prominent early theorist who urged psychologists to explore the functions of consciousness. James (1884) developed a theory of emotion over 100 years ago that remains influential today. At about the same time, he and Carl Lange (1885) independently proposed that the *conscious experience of emotion results from one's perception of autonomic arousal*. Their theory stood common sense on its head. Everyday logic suggests that when you stumble onto a rattlesnake in the woods, the conscious experience of fear leads to visceral arousal (the fight-or-flight response). The James-Lange theory of emotion asserts the opposite: that the perception of visceral arousal leads to the conscious experience of fear (see Figure 10.14). In other words, while you might assume that your pulse is racing because you're fearful, James and Lange argue that you're fearful because your pulse is racing.

The James-Lange theory emphasizes the physiological determinants of emotion. According to this view, *different patterns of autonomic activation lead to the experience of different emotions*. Hence, people supposedly distinguish emotions such as fear, joy, and anger on the basis of the exact configuration of physical reactions they experience.

Cannon-Bard Theory

Walter Cannon (1927) found the James-Lange theory unconvincing. Cannon, who developed the concepts of homeostasis and the fight-or-flight response, pointed out that physiological arousal may occur without the experience of emotion (if one exercises vigorously, for instance). He also argued that visceral changes are too slow to precede the conscious experience of emotion. Finally, he argued that people experiencing very different emotions, such as fear, joy, and anger, exhibit almost identical patterns of autonomic arousal.

Thus, Cannon espoused a different explanation of emotion. Later, Philip Bard (1934) elaborated on it. The resulting Cannon-Bard theory argues that emotion occurs when the *thalamus* sends signals *simultaneously* to the cortex (creating the conscious experience of emotion) and to the autonomic nervous system (creating visceral arousal). The Cannon-Bard model is compared to the James-Lange model in Figure 10.14. Cannon and Bard were off the mark a bit in pinpointing the thalamus as the neural center for emotion. As we

Figure 10.14. Theories of emotion. Three influential theories of emotion are contrasted here with one another and with the common-sense view. The James-Lange theory was the first to suggest that feelings of arousal cause emotion, rather than vice versa. Schachter built on this idea by adding a second factor—interpretation (appraisal and labeling) of arousal.

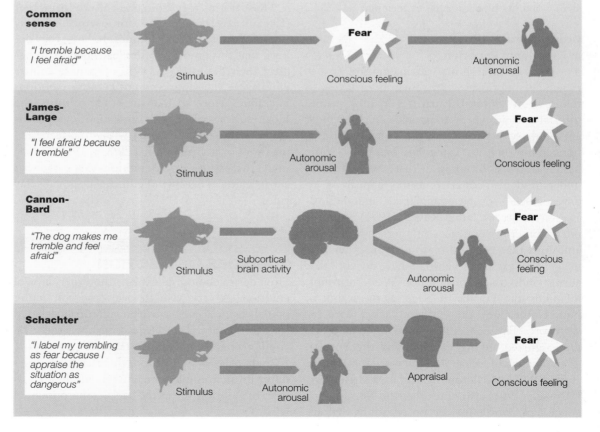

discussed in Chapter 3, the limbic system, the hypothalamus, and other neural structures have been implicated as the seats of emotion. However, many modern theorists agree with the Cannon-Bard view that emotions originate in subcortical brain structures (Buck, 1984; Izard, 1984; Tomkins, 1980).

Ultimately, the key issue in the debate between the James-Lange and Cannon-Bard views turned out to be whether different emotions are associated with different patterns of autonomic arousal. The research findings mostly supported the Cannon-Bard point of view for several decades. Investigators found that different emotions are *not* reliably associated with different patterns of autonomic activation (Strongman, 1978). However, more recent studies have detected some subtle differences in the patterns of visceral arousal that accompany basic emotions such as happiness, sadness, anger, and fear (Ekman, Levenson, & Friesen, 1983; Levenson, 1992).

The debate continues, because many psychologists doubt whether people can actually *distinguish* between these slightly different patterns of physiological activation (Zillmann, 1983). Humans are not particularly adept at recognizing their autonomic fluctuations. Thus, there must be some other explanation for how people differentiate various emotions.

Schachter's Two-Factor Theory

Stanley Schachter believes that people look at situational cues to differentiate between alternative emotions. According to Schachter (1964; Schachter & Singer, 1962, 1979), the experience of emotion depends on two factors: (1) autonomic arousal and (2) cognitive interpretation of that arousal. Schachter proposes that when you experience visceral arousal, you search your environment for an explanation (see Figure 10.14). If you're stuck in a traffic jam, you'll probably label your arousal as anger. If you're taking an important exam, you'll probably label it as anxiety. If you're celebrating your birthday, you'll probably label it as happiness.

Schachter agrees with the James-Lange view that emotion is inferred from arousal. However, he also agrees with the Cannon-Bard position that different emotions yield indistinguishable patterns of arousal. He reconciles these views by arguing that people look to external rather than internal cues to differentiate and label their specific emotions. In essence, Schachter suggests that people think along the following lines: "If I'm aroused and you're obnoxious, I must be angry."

The two-factor theory of emotion has been tested in numerous studies that have produced mixed results. Some aspects of the model have been supported and some have not (Reisenzein, 1983). A naturalistic study of interpersonal attraction by Dutton and Aron (1974) provides a particularly clever example of research that supported the two-factor theory. They arranged for young men crossing a footbridge in a park to encounter a young woman who asked them to stop briefly to fill out a questionnaire. The woman offered to explain the research at some future time and gave the men her phone number. Autonomic arousal was manipulated by enacting this scenario on two very different bridges. One was a long suspension bridge that swayed precariously 230 feet above a river (see the adjacent photo). The other bridge was a solid, safe structure a mere 10 feet above a small stream. The experimenters reasoned that the men crossing the shaky, frightening bridge would be experiencing emotional arousal and that some of them might attribute that arousal to the woman rather than to the bridge. If so, they might mislabel their emotion as lust rather than fear and infer that they were attracted to the woman. The dependent variable was how many of the men later called the woman to pursue a date. As predicted, more of the men who met the woman on the precarious bridge called her for a date than did those who met her on the safe bridge.

The Dutton and Aron study supports the hypothesis that people often infer emotion from their physiological arousal and label that emotion in accordance with their cognitive explanation for it. The fact that the explanation may be inaccurate

"Cognitive factors play a major role in determining how a subject interprets his bodily feelings."
STANLEY SCHACHTER

In their naturalistic study of the two-factor theory of emotion, Dutton and Aron (1974) manipulated emotional arousal by arranging for males to encounter a female confederate on this precarious-looking bridge.

Silvan Tomkins	Carroll Izard	Robert Plutchik
Fear	Fear	Fear
Anger	Anger	Anger
Enjoyment	Joy	Joy
Disgust	Disgust	Disgust
Interest	Interest	Anticipation
Surprise	Surprise	Surprise
Contempt	Contempt	
Shame	Shame	
	Sadness	Sadness
Distress		
	Guilt	
		Acceptance

Figure 10.15. Primary emotions. Evolutionary theories of emotion attempt to identify primary emotions. Three leading theorists—Silvan Tomkins, Carroll Izard, and Robert Plutchik—have compiled different lists of primary emotions, but this chart shows great overlap among the basic emotions identified by these theorists. (Based on Mandler, 1984)

sheds light on why people frequently seem confused about their own emotions.

Evolutionary Theories of Emotion

In recent years, some theorists interested in emotion have returned to ideas espoused by Charles Darwin over a century ago. Darwin (1872) believed that emotions developed because of their adaptive value. Fear, for instance, would help an organism avoid danger and thus would aid in survival. Hence, Darwin viewed human emotions as a product of evolution. This premise serves as the foundation for several modern prominent theories of emotion developed independently by S. S. Tomkins (1980, 1991), Carroll Izard (1984, 1991), and Robert Plutchik (1984).

These *evolutionary theories* consider emotions to be largely innate reactions to certain stimuli. As such, emotions should be immediately recognizable under most conditions without much thought.

Figure 10.16. Mixing primary emotions. Eight primary emotions (shown inside the circle) are identified in Robert Plutchik's model of emotion. Plutchik's theory assumes that additional emotions (such as those shown on the outside of the circle) are created by blending primary emotions. For example, awe is viewed as a blend of fear and surprise. Many more combinations are possible than are shown here.

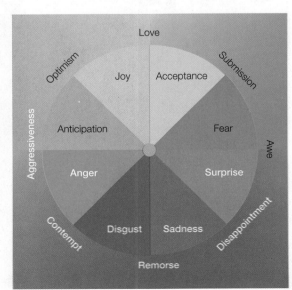

After all, primitive animals that are incapable of complex thought seem to have little difficulty in recognizing their emotions. Evolutionary theorists believe that emotion evolved before thought. They assert that thought plays a relatively small role in emotion, although they admit that learning and cognition may have some influence on human emotions. Evolutionary theories generally assume that emotions originate in subcortical brain structures (such as the hypothalamus and most of the limbic system) that evolved before the higher brain areas (in the cortex) associated with complex thought.

Evolutionary theories also assume that evolution has equipped humans with a small number of innate emotions with proven adaptive value. Hence, the principal question that evolutionary theories of emotion wrestle with is, *What are the fundamental emotions?* Evolutionary theorists attempt to identify these primary emotions by searching for universals—emotions that are expressed and recognized in the same way in widely disparate cultures. Figure 10.15 summarizes the conclusions of the leading theorists in this area. As you can see, Tomkins, Izard, and Plutchik have not come up with identical lists, but there is considerable agreement. All three conclude that people exhibit eight to ten primary emotions. Moreover, six of these emotions appear on all three lists: fear, anger, joy, disgust, interest, and surprise.

Of course, people experience more than just eight to ten emotions. How do evolutionary theories account for this variety? They propose that the many emotions that people experience are produced by (1) blends of primary emotions and (2) variations in intensity. For example, Robert Plutchik (1980) has devised an elegant model of how primary emotions such as fear and surprise may blend into secondary emotions such as awe (see Figure 10.16). Plutchik's model also posits that various emotions, such as apprehension, fear, and terror, involve one primary emotion experienced at different levels of intensity.

PUTTING IT IN PERSPECTIVE

Five of our organizing themes were particularly prominent in this chapter: the influence of cultural contexts, the dense connections between psychology and society at large, psychology's theoretical diversity, the interplay of heredity and environment, and the multiple causes of behavior.

Our discussion of motivation and emotion demonstrated once again that there are both similarities and differences across cultures in behavior. The neural, biochemical, genetic, and hormonal processes underlying hunger and eating, for instance, are universal. But cultural factors influence what people prefer to eat. In a similar vein, researchers have found a great deal of cross-cultural congruence in the physiological and expressive elements of emotional experience, but they have also found cultural variations in how people think about and express their emotions. Thus, as we have seen in previous chapters, psychological processes are characterized by both cultural variance and invariance.

Our discussion of the controversies surrounding sociobiology and the determinants of sexual orientation show once again that psychology is not an ivory tower enterprise. It evolves in a sociohistorical context that helps shape the debates in the field, and these debates often have far-reaching social and political ramifications for society at large.

We began the chapter with a discussion of various theoretical perspectives on motivation and ended with a review of various theories of emotion. Obviously, this area of inquiry is marked by great theoretical diversity, and there has been little movement toward reconciling the contradictory theories. Why are there so many conflicting theories? In this case, theoretical diversity appears to exist because motivation and emotion are such broad areas of study.

The age-old nature versus nurture question was at the center of many of the theoretical debates in the chapter. We repeatedly saw that biological and social factors jointly govern behavior. For example, we learned that eating behavior and the experience of emotion depend on complicated interactions between biological and environmental determinants.

Indeed, complicated interactions permeated the entire chapter, demonstrating that if we want to fully understand behavior, we have to take multiple causes into account. For instance, we saw that achievement behavior is a function of the motive to achieve success, the probability of success, the value of success, the motive to avoid failure, the probability of failure, and the negative impact of failure. We'll see more of these complicated interactions among variables in our Application, which discusses research on the causes of weight problems and obesity.

Understanding the Roots of Weight Problems

Answer the following "true" or "false."

___ 1 Approximately 7% of Americans are overweight.

___ 2 Obese people simply eat much more than normal weight people.

___ 3 People who lose weight through dieting usually gain the weight back.

___ 4 Studies suggest that there is a genetic vulnerability to obesity.

We saw in the main body of the chapter that hunger is regulated by a complex interaction of biological and psychological factors. You'll see the same kinds of complexities emerge in this Application, as we explore the roots of weight problems and obesity. Along the way, you'll learn that the first two statements above are false and the second two are true.

Although American culture seems obsessed with slimness, more and more people are struggling with the problem of obesity. Depending on where one draws the line between obesity and normality, anywhere from 12% to 40% of American adults are overweight (Gray, 1989). If obesity merely frustrated people's vanity, there would be little cause for concern. Unfortunately, obesity is a significant health problem that elevates one's mortality risk (see Figure 10.17). Overweight people are more vulnerable than others to cardiovascular diseases, diabetes, hypertension, respiratory problems, digestive diseases, stroke, arthritis, and back problems (Bray, 1986; Kissebah, Freedman, & Peiris, 1989). Why do some people de-

velop troublesome weight problems? A number of theories have been advanced to answer this question. We'll begin by examining Stanley Schachter's analysis, which focuses on the critical role of external cues for eating.

Sensitivity to External Cues

Stanley Schachter (1971) advanced the hypothesis that obese people are extrasensitive to external cues that affect hunger and are relatively insensitive to internal physiological signals. According to this notion, fat people pay little attention to messages from their bodies but respond readily to environmental cues such as the availability of food, the attractiveness of food, and the time of day. Schachter argued that obese people eat excessively because they can't ignore food-related cues that trigger eating. Such people may walk into a shopping mall intending to eat nothing, just to shop in

a few stores. But they end up eating because their hunger is aroused by the sight and aroma of others' cinnamon rolls, hot dogs, and tacos.

Although Schachter's theory has received some support, studies have also led to some modifications in the theory. Judith Rodin's (1978, 1981) research has blurred Schachter's key distinction between the internal and external determinants of hunger. She has demonstrated that the sight, smell, and sound of a grilling steak (external determinants) can elicit insulin secretions (internal determinants) that lead to increased hunger. She has also found that food-related stimuli produce the greatest insulin responses in people who tend to respond to food-related cues by eating. Rodin's findings raise the possibility that people who are responsive to external food cues may really be responding to internal signals (insulin secretion). Their problem

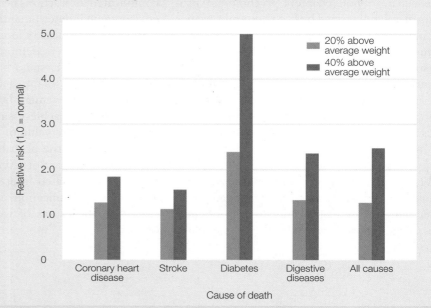

Figure 10.17. Obesity and mortality. This graph shows the increased mortality risks for men who are either 20% or 40% above average weight for their age and height. Clearly, obesity is a significant health risk. (Data from VanItallie, 1979)

may be that they secrete insulin too readily in response to food-related cues.

After reviewing the accumulated evidence, Rodin (1981) has argued that the link between sensitivity to external cues and obesity is weaker than Schachter believed. Many obese people are not exceptionally responsive to food-related stimuli. Indeed, obese people do not overeat as much as is widely assumed (Rodin, Schank, & Striegel-Moore, 1989). Moreover, many people who are highly responsive to food cues and eat a great deal still remain slender. Thus, Rodin asserts that obesity must depend on factors besides sensitivity to external food cues. She theorizes that responsiveness to external cues contributes to obesity, but only in conjunction with genetic and other factors, such as those we are about to discuss.

Genetic Predispositions

You may know some people who can eat constantly without gaining weight. You may also know less fortunate people who get chubby despite a controlled intake. Differences in physiological makeup must be the cause of this paradox. Research suggests that these differences may have a genetic basis.

In one influential adoption study, adults raised by foster parents were compared to their biological and foster parents in regard to weight (Stunkard et al., 1986). The investigators found that the adoptees resembled their biological parents in weight, but not their adoptive parents. In a subsequent twin study, Stunkard and associates (1990) found that identical twins reared apart were far more similar in weight than fraternal twins reared together. On the basis of their correlational data, these researchers estimate that genetic factors account for roughly 70% of the variation among people in weight (see Chapter 9 for a discussion of the logic underlying twin studies and heritability estimates). Thus, weight

Are obese people simply those who are more responsive to external food cues? The answer is not a simple one, as the text discusses.

seems to be influenced by genetic makeup. This finding suggests that some people may inherit a vulnerability to obesity.

What, exactly, is inherited by people who are prone to obesity? One obvious hypothesis is that some people inherit a sluggish metabolism. **The *basal metabolic rate* is the body's rate of energy output at rest after a 12-hour fast.** Although metabolic rate can be increased by exercise, basal metabolic processes generally account for about two-thirds of a person's energy output. People vary in their basal metabolic rate. This means that some burn off calories faster than others. Calories that are burned off won't be stored as fat.

Thus, it's plausible to speculate that hereditary factors lead obese people to have relatively low metabolic rates. However, investigators who have compared the average metabolic rates of obese and lean subjects have *not* found slower metabolism in the obese group (Garrow, 1986). Thus, the physiological bases for inherited differences in the tendency to gain weight remain obscure. Some theo-

rists believe that obese people are genetically programmed to develop an excessive number of fat cells (Grinker, 1982). This hypothesis remains unproven, but it brings us to set-point theory, which concerns how the body might regulate fat deposits.

The Concept of Set Point

People who lose weight on a diet have a rather strong (and depressing) tendency to gain back the weight they lose. The reverse is also true: People who have to work to put weight on often have trouble keeping it on. These observations suggest that each person's body may have **a *set point*, a natural point of stability in body weight**. Theorists who subscribe to this view believe that obesity is usually the result of an elevated set point (Keesey & Powley, 1975, 1986; Nisbett, 1972).

According to set-point theory, the body monitors levels of fat stores to keep them fairly stable. When fat stores slip below a crucial set point, the body supposedly begins to compensate for this change. This compensation process apparently

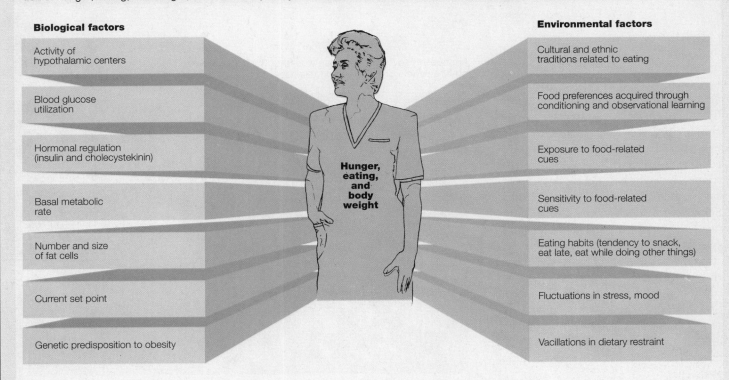

Figure 10.18. The factors influencing hunger, eating, and body weight. Multifactorial causation is readily apparent in the regulation of hunger, eating, and weight, which are shaped by a complex array of interacting biological and environmental factors.

Biological factors

Activity of hypothalamic centers

Blood glucose utilization

Hormonal regulation (insulin and cholecystekinin)

Basal metabolic rate

Number and size of fat cells

Current set point

Genetic predisposition to obesity

Hunger, eating, and body weight

Environmental factors

Cultural and ethnic traditions related to eating

Food preferences acquired through conditioning and observational learning

Exposure to food-related cues

Sensitivity to food-related cues

Eating habits (tendency to snack, eat late, eat while doing other things)

Fluctuations in stress, mood

Vacillations in dietary restraint

leads to increased hunger and decreased metabolism. The location and nature of the cells that monitor fat stores are unknown. Some proponents of this theory believe that the hypothalamus is involved (Keesey, 1986). In fact, they maintain that the stimulation and destruction of hypothalamic centers in animals affect eating by altering the animals' set point.

What determines a person's set point? Advocates of set-point theory note that when people gain or lose weight, these shifts do *not* lead to an increase or decrease in the *number* of fat cells. Instead, fat cells increase or decrease in average *size* (Hirsch et al., 1989). Although the number of fat cells in the body can be increased at any age (through persistent

overeating), the count typically stabilizes in early childhood (Knittle et al., 1981). This curious stability suggests that the number of fat cells has something to do with one's set point.

Can a person's set point be changed? The evidence on this issue is not very encouraging. Studies suggest that long-term excessive eating can gradually increase one's set point, but decreasing it seems to be very difficult (Keesey, 1986). This finding does *not* mean that all obese people are doomed to remain obese forever. However, it does suggest that most overweight people must be prepared to make *permanent* changes in their eating and exercise habits if they expect to keep their weight down (Keesey, 1988).

Many people, even if they aren't obese, also struggle to maintain a weight that they consider ideal. Their hunger and weight are governed by the same complex array of factors that influence hunger and weight in the obese. These factors, which are summarized in Figure 10.18, include activity in hypothalamic centers, blood glucose fluctuations, insulin secretion, metabolic rate, fat cell distribution, body weight set point, acquired food preferences, learned eating habits, exposure and sensitivity to food cues, and stress. As you can see then, eating behavior provides us with another excellent example of how behavior is governed by a multiplicity of factors.

Chapter 10 Review

KEY IDEAS

Motivational Theories and Concepts

♦ Motivation involves goal-oriented behavior. Some motivational theories emphasize the biological roots of motives; others emphasize the social roots. Sociobiologists maintain that there is an evolutionary basis for many human motives.

♦ Drive theories apply a homeostatic model to motivation. They assume that organisms seek to reduce unpleasant states of tension called drives. In contrast, incentive theories emphasize how external goals energize behavior. Madsen's list of biological needs and Murray's list of social needs illustrate that a diverse array of motives govern human behavior.

♦ Maslow's hierarchy of needs assumes that basic needs must be satisfied reasonably well before higher needs are activated. His model integrates biological and social needs. According to Maslow, people's growth needs include the need to realize their full potential, a motive called the need for self-actualization.

The Motivation of Hunger and Eating

♦ Eating is regulated by a complex interaction of biological and environmental factors. In the brain the lateral and ventromedial areas of the hypothalamus appear to be involved in the control of hunger, but their exact role is unclear.

♦ Fluctuations in blood glucose also seem to play a role, but the exact location of the glucostats and their mode of functioning are yet to be determined. Hormonal regulation of hunger depends primarily on insulin secretions.

♦ Learned habits also exert a great deal of influence over both what people eat and how much they eat. For example, culture influences food preferences. Food-related cues in the environment and stress can also influence eating.

Sexual Motivation: The Mystery of Sexual Orientation

♦ The determinants of sexual orientation are not well understood. Research has not provided convincing support for either environmental theories or hormonal theories of sexual orientation. Recent studies suggest that there may be a genetic predisposition to homosexuality, but much remains to be learned.

Achievement: In Search of Excellence

♦ Achievement involves the need to excel, especially in competition with others. The need for achievement is usually measured with the TAT. People who are relatively high in the need for achievement work harder and more persistently than others. They delay gratification well and pursue competitive careers.

♦ The pursuit of achievement tends to increase when the probability of success and the incentive value of success are high. However, the pursuit of achievement can also be influenced by fear of failure.

The Elements of Emotional Experience

♦ Emotion is made up of cognitive, physiological, and behavioral components. The cognitive component involves subjective feelings that have an evaluative aspect. The physiological component is dominated by autonomic arousal. This is the basis for the lie detector, which is really an emotion detector. At the behavioral level, emotions are expressed through body language, with facial expressions being particularly prominent.

♦ Ekman and Friesen have found considerable cross-cultural agreement in the identification of emotions based on facial expressions. Cross-cultural similarities have also been found in the physiological components of emotion. However, there are some striking cultural variations in how people categorize and display their emotions.

Theories of Emotion

♦ The James-Lange theory asserts that emotion results from one's perception of autonomic arousal. The Cannon-Bard theory counters with the proposal that emotions originate in subcortical areas of the brain.

♦ According to Schachter's two-factor theory, people infer emotion from arousal and then label it in accordance with their cognitive explanation for the arousal. Evolutionary theories of emotion maintain that emotions are innate reactions that require little cognitive interpretation.

Putting It in Perspective

♦ Our look at motivation and emotion showed once again that psychology is characterized by theoretical diversity, that biology and environment shape behavior interactively, that behavior is governed by multiple causes, that psychological processes are characterized by both cultural variance and invariance, and that psychology evolves in a sociohistorical context.

Application: Understanding the Roots of Weight Problems

♦ Schachter hypothesizes that obesity develops mainly in people who are overly sensitive to external cues that trigger eating. However, Rodin concludes that oversensitivity to external cues is only one factor among many determinants of obesity.

♦ Evidence indicates that there is a genetic predisposition to obesity. Weight problems can also be caused by an elevated set point for body weight. According to set-point theory, our bodies monitor fat stores to keep them fairly stable.

KEY TERMS

Achievement motive	Homeostasis
Basal metabolic rate	Homosexuals
Bisexuals	Incentive
Display rules	Insulin
Drive	Lie detector
Emotion	Motivation
Galvanic skin response (GSR)	Need for self-actualization
Glucose	Polygraph
Glucostats	Set point
Heterosexuals	Sexual orientation
Hierarchy of needs	Sociobiology

KEY PEOPLE

Walter Cannon	Henry Murray
William James	Judith Rodin
Abraham Maslow	Stanley Schachter
David McClelland	

11 Human Development Across the Life Span

Archie Leach grew up in a lower-middle-class British home saturated with frustration and unhappiness. Archie's mother was obsessed with money and felt that her husband never earned enough. When Archie wanted anything, she constantly harped on the fact that money didn't "grow on trees." As a youngster, Archie was a frail, sad-eyed boy. He was often sullen and wrapped up in himself. His parents were miserable with each other, and his mother suffered from depression. When Archie was 10, his father had his mother committed to a mental hospital. Archie was bewildered by his mother's disappearance. His father gave him only a vague explanation, saying that she had gone away for a "rest." Archie, who didn't learn the truth for more than 20 years, thought that his mother had abandoned him. Understandably, he was deeply hurt and felt betrayed.

As a young man, Archie tried to break into theater in New York. However, at the age of 25, "Archie Leach possessed a low opinion of himself as an actor" (Harris, 1987, p. 42). He was a shy, moody young man who was especially awkward with the opposite sex. One acquaintance remarked, "He was literally tongue-tied around women."

In spite of these humble beginnings, Archie Leach eventually enjoyed great success in the world of entertainment. Blessed with classic good looks, he began to cultivate the image of an elegant man-about-town. "He looked graceless at first, but he knew that to succeed he had to become someone else, and he was not to be put off" (Wansell, 1983, p. 50).

Archie moved to Los Angeles and started working in films. He made remarkable progress in his effort to transform himself into a sophisticated ladies' man. He earned leading roles in better and better films and went on to star in 72 movies spanning four decades, using the stage name Cary Grant. He became a matinee idol, involved in romances with some of the world's most beautiful and desirable women. As one of his biographers put it, by the end of his career Cary Grant had come to personify such adjectives as "dapper, debonair, charming, jaunty, ageless, dashing, blithe, witty, [and] stylish" (Harris, 1987, p. 4).

Archie Leach's transformation into Cary Grant was a stunning triumph, but many remnants of Archie's past were apparent beneath the surface of Cary Grant's public persona. Having felt betrayed by his mother when she mysteriously disappeared, he had lifelong difficulties trusting women. This lack of trust and the moody self-absorption that he

had shown as a child contributed greatly to his four failed marriages. Although he could be glib and charming, he continued to feel strained in social encounters, and he spent much of his time in seclusion. In spite of his acclaimed brilliance as a movie star, he remained terribly insecure. He was never able to shake his mother's obsessive concern about money. Indeed, his miserliness was legendary. He amassed a fortune estimated to be worth $40 million, but he "saved the string from parcels and the tinsel from the Christmas tree, cut the buttons off the shirts he was about to discard in order to save them for future use, [and] marked the wine bottle to make sure that none was drunk while he was not there" (Wansell, 1983, p. 233).

What does Cary Grant have to do with developmental psychology? His story provides an interesting illustration of the two themes that permeate the study of human development: *transition* and *continuity*. In investigating human development, psychologists try to shed light on how people arrive at their various destinations in life. They focus on how people evolve through transitions over time. In looking at these transitions, developmental psychologists inevitably find continuity with the past. This continuity may be the most fascinating element in the story of Cary Grant's personal development. The metamorphosis of shy, awkward little Archie Leach into urbane, debonair Cary Grant was a more radical transformation than most people go through. Nonetheless, the threads of continuity connecting Archie's childhood to the development of Cary Grant's adult personality were quite obvious.

Development **is the sequence of age-related changes that occur as a person progresses from conception to death.** It is a reasonably orderly, cumulative process that includes both the biological and the behavioral changes that take place as people grow older. An infant's newfound ability to grasp objects, a child's gradual mastery of grammar, an adolescent's spurt in physical

Archie Leach's evolution into Cary Grant is a developmental story marked by both continuity and transition.

growth, a young adult's increasing commitment to a vocation, and an elderly person's struggle with reduced hearing sensitivity all represent development. These transitions are predictable changes that are related to age.

Traditionally, psychologists have been most interested in development during childhood. Our coverage reflects this emphasis. However, as Cary Grant's story illustrates, development is a lifelong process. We'll divide the life span into four broad periods: (1) the prenatal period, (2) childhood, (3) adolescence, and (4) adulthood. We'll examine aspects of development that are especially dynamic during each period. Let's begin by looking at events that occur before birth, during prenatal development.

PROGRESS BEFORE BIRTH: PRENATAL DEVELOPMENT

Development begins with conception. Conception occurs when fertilization creates **a *zygote*, a one-celled organism formed by the union of a sperm and an egg.** All of the other cells in your body developed from this single cell. Each of your cells contains enduring messages from your parents carried on the *chromosomes* that lie within its nucleus. Each chromosome houses many *genes*, the functional units in hereditary transmission. Genes carry the details of your hereditary blueprints, which are revealed gradually throughout life (see Chapter 3 for more information on genetic transmission).

The *prenatal period* extends from conception to birth, usually encompassing nine months of pregnancy. A great deal of important development occurs before birth. In fact, development during the prenatal period is remarkably rapid. If you were an average-sized newborn and your physical growth had continued during the first year of your life at a prenatal pace, by your first birthday you would have weighed 200 pounds! Fortunately, you didn't grow at that rate—and no human does—because in the final weeks before birth the frenzied pace of prenatal development tapers off dramatically.

In this section, we'll examine the usual course of prenatal development and discuss how environmental events can leave their mark on development even before birth exposes the newborn to the outside world.

Prenatal development is remarkably rapid. (Top left) This 30-day-old embryo is just six millimeters in length. (Bottom left) At 14 weeks, the fetus is approximately two inches long. Note the well-developed fingers. The fetus can already move its legs, feet, hands, and head and displays a variety of basic reflexes. (Right) After four months of prenatal development, facial features are beginning to emerge.

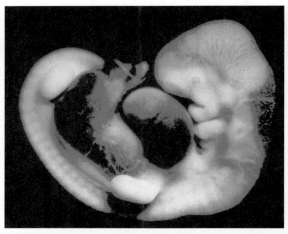

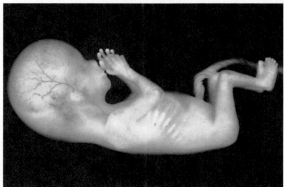

The Course of Prenatal Development

The prenatal period is divided into three phases: (1) the germinal stage (the first two weeks), (2) the embryonic stage (two weeks to two months), and (3) the fetal stage (two months to birth). Some key developments in these phases are outlined here.

Germinal Stage

The *germinal stage* is the first phase of prenatal development, encompassing the first two weeks after conception. This brief stage begins when a zygote is created through fertilization. Within 36 hours, rapid cell division begins, and the zygote becomes a microscopic mass of multiplying cells. This mass of cells slowly migrates along the mother's fallopian tube to the uterine cavity. On about the seventh day, the cell mass begins to implant itself in the uterine wall. This process takes about a week and is far from automatic. Many zygotes are rejected at this point. Research suggests that as many as one in five pregnancies end with the woman never being aware that conception has occurred (Wilcox et al., 1988).

During the implantation process, the placenta begins to form. The *placenta* is a structure that allows oxygen and nutrients to pass into the fetus from the mother's bloodstream and bodily wastes to pass out to the mother. This critical exchange takes place across thin membranes that block the passage of blood cells, keeping the fetal and maternal bloodstreams separate.

Embryonic Stage

The *embryonic stage* is the second stage of prenatal development, lasting from two weeks until the end of the second month. During this stage, most of the vital organs and bodily systems begin to form in the developing organism, which is now called an *embryo*. Structures such as the heart, spine, and brain emerge gradually as cell division becomes more specialized. Although the embryo is typically only about an inch long at the end of this stage, it's already beginning to look human. Arms, legs, hands, feet, fingers, toes, eyes, and ears are already discernible.

The embryonic stage is a period of great vulnerability because virtually all the basic physiological structures are being formed. If anything interferes with normal development during the embryonic phase, the effects can be devastating. Most miscarriages occur during this period (Simpson, 1991). Most major structural birth defects are also due to problems that occur during the embryonic stage (Mortensen, Sever, & Oakley, 1991).

Fetal Stage

The *fetal stage* is the third stage of prenatal development, lasting from two months through birth. The first two months of the fetal stage bring rapid bodily growth, as muscles and bones begin to form (Moore & Persaud, 1993). The developing organism, now called a *fetus*, becomes capable of physical movements as skeletal structures harden. Organs formed in the embryonic stage continue to grow and gradually begin to function. Sex organs start to develop during the third month.

During the final three months of the prenatal period, brain cells multiply at a brisk pace. A layer of fat is deposited under the skin to provide insulation, and the respiratory and digestive systems mature. All of these changes ready the fetus for life outside the cozy, supportive environment of its mother's womb. Sometime between 22 weeks and 26 weeks the fetus reaches the *age of viability—the age at which a baby can survive in the event of a premature birth.* The probability of survival is still pretty slim at 22 or 23 weeks, but it climbs steadily over the next month to an 85% survival rate at 26 to 28 weeks (Main & Main, 1991).

CONCEPT CHECK 11.1
Understanding the Stages of Prenatal Development

Check your understanding of the stages of prenatal development by filling in the blanks in the chart below. The first column contains descriptions of a main event from each of the three stages. In the second column, write the name of the stage, in the third column, write the term used to refer to the developing organism during that stage; and in the fourth column, write the time span (in terms of weeks or months) covered by the stage. The answers are in Appendix A at the back of the book.

Event	Stage	Term for organism	Time span
1. Uterine implantation	_____	_____	_____
2. Muscle and bone begin to form	_____	_____	_____
3. Vital organs and body systems begin to form	_____	_____	_____

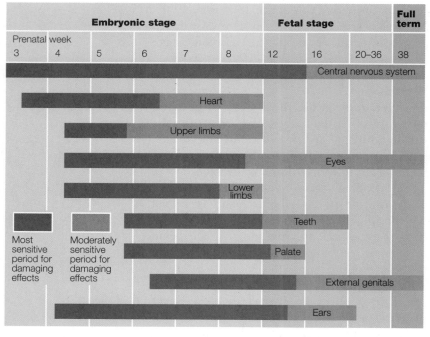

	Embryonic stage					Fetal stage			Full term

Prenatal week
3 4 5 6 7 8 12 16 20–36 38

Central nervous system

Heart

Upper limbs

Eyes

Lower limbs

Teeth

Palate

External genitals

Ears

Most sensitive period for damaging effects

Moderately sensitive period for damaging effects

Figure 11.1. Periods of vulnerability in prenatal development. Generally, structures are most susceptible to damage when they are undergoing rapid development. The darker regions of the bars indicate the most sensitive periods for various organs and structures, while the lighter regions indicate periods of continued, but lessened, vulnerability.

Premature births and infant deaths are much more common in the United States than most people realize. Shown here is the author's son, born prematurely in September 1992, receiving postnatal treatment in a hospital intensive care unit. Although prematurity is associated with a variety of developmental problems, T. J., like a great many premature infants, has matured into a robust, healthy child (see page 216 for a picture of him at age 15 months).

Environmental Factors and Prenatal Development

Although the fetus develops in the protective buffer of the womb, events in the external environment can affect it indirectly through the mother because the developing organism and its mother are linked via the placenta. Figure 11.1 shows the periods of prenatal development during which various structures are most vulnerable to damage.

Maternal nutrition is very important, as the developing fetus needs a variety of essential nutrients. Severe maternal malnutrition increases the risk of birth complications and neurological deficits for the newborn (Rosenblith, 1992). The impact of moderate malnutrition is more difficult

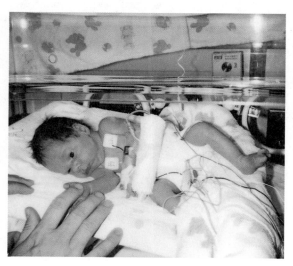

to gauge. However, some studies have found a correlation between moderate maternal dietary deficits during the prenatal period and subsequent poor motor skills, apathy, and irritability during infancy (Chandra, 1991; Zeskind & Ramey, 1981).

Another major source of concern is the mother's consumption of drugs. Unfortunately, most drugs consumed by a pregnant woman can slip through the membranes of the placenta. Virtually all "recreational" drugs can be harmful, with sedatives, narcotics, and cocaine being particularly dangerous (Finnegan & Kandall, 1992; Lester et al., 1991). Problems can even be caused by drugs prescribed for legitimate medical reasons and by some over-the-counter drugs (Niebyl, 1991). Tobacco use during pregnancy is also problematic, as pregnant women who smoke have an increased risk for miscarriage, stillbirth, and other birth complications (Niswander, 1982; Wen et al., 1990). Maternal smoking may also increase a child's risk for sudden infant death syndrome (Haglund & Cnattinguis, 1990).

Alcohol consumption during pregnancy may also carry unnecessary risks. It has long been clear that *heavy* drinking by a mother can be hazardous to a fetus. ***Fetal alcohol syndrome* is a collection of congenital (inborn) problems associated with excessive alcohol use during pregnancy.** Typical problems include microcephaly (a small head), heart defects, irritability, hyperactivity, and retarded mental and motor development (Julien, 1992). Previously, the available evidence suggested that it was safe for women to drink in moderation during pregnancy. However, more recent studies indicate that even normal social drinking *may* be harmful to the fetus. For example, slight deficits in IQ, reaction time, motor skills, and attention span have been found in children born to women who consumed about three drinks a day during pregnancy (Barr et al., 1990; Streissguth et al., 1984, 1989).

The placenta is able to screen out quite a number of infectious agents, but not all. Thus, many maternal illnesses can interfere with prenatal development. Diseases such as rubella (German measles), syphilis, cholera, smallpox, mumps, and even severe cases of the flu can be hazardous to the fetus (Isada & Grossman, 1991). Genital herpes and AIDS are two severe diseases that pregnant women can transmit to their offspring. Both are typically transmitted during the birth process itself (Hanshaw, Dudgeon, & Marshall, 1985; Mott, Fazekas, & James, 1985).

The Importance of Prenatal Health Care

Many of the prenatal dangers that we have discussed are preventable if pregnant women receive adequate care and guidance from health professionals. Good quality medical care that begins early in pregnancy is associated with reduced prematurity and higher survival rates for infants (Malloy, Kao, & Lee, 1992). Because of poverty and a lack of health insurance, however, many pregnant women in the United States receive little or no prenatal medical care. This problem is particularly acute among racial minorities, especially African Americans (Edelman, 1987). Other factors surely contribute, but the lack of readily available health care for low-income groups is thought to be the main cause of the surprisingly high infant mortality in the United States. **Infant mortality, which is the death rate in the first year of life per 1000 births**, varies considerably from one country to another. In spite of its relative affluence and its leadership in medical technology, the United States ranks an embarrassing 21st in the world in the prevention of infant mortality (see Figure 11.2). Moreover, infant mortality among American blacks (18.0 per 1000 births) is more than double that of whites (7.6 per 1000). Black infants born in Washington, D.C., for example, have lower survival rates than infants born in Nigeria, Jamaica, or Costa Rica (Cowley, 1991). Experts on child development from psychology, medicine, and many other fields have argued that the U.S. government sorely needs to increase its funding of prenatal health care for low-income groups (Gibbs, 1990). Given the high cost of intensive care for prematurely born infants, this investment would almost surely save money in the long run (see Figure 11.3). Unfortunately, in recent years, federal spending on children's programs has *declined* rather than increased.

Science has a long way to go before it uncovers all the factors that shape development before birth. For example, the effects of fluctuations in maternal emotions are not well understood. Nonetheless, it's clear that critical developments unfold quickly during the prenatal period. In the next section, you'll learn that

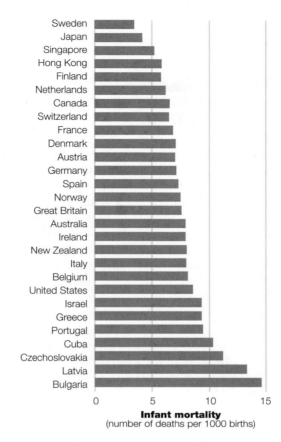

Infant mortality
(number of deaths per 1000 births)

Figure 11.2. Cross-cultural comparisons of infant mortality. Infant mortality is the death rate per 1000 births during the first year of life. Although the United States takes pride in its modern, sophisticated medical system, it ranks only 21st in the prevention of infant mortality. One of the main factors underlying this poor showing appears to be low-income mothers' limited access to medical care during pregnancy.

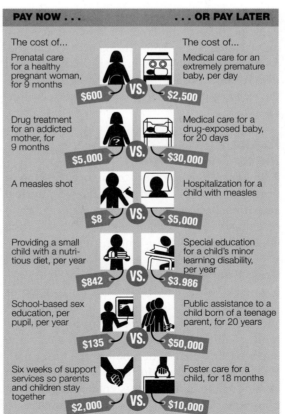

Figure 11.3. The high cost of not investing in preventive care for children. This *Time* magazine graphic shows why it would be financially prudent to spend more public funds on preventive health care measures for young children. As you can see, the cost of providing medical care to pregnant women who cannot afford it is a pittance in comparison to the cost that government agencies often absorb later when a child is born prematurely. Infants born six to eight weeks early often spend a month or more in an intensive care unit, at a cost of $75,000 to $100,000.

development continues at a fast pace during the early years of childhood.

THE WONDROUS YEARS OF CHILDHOOD

There's a certain magic associated with childhood. Young children have an extraordinary ability to captivate adults' attention, especially their parents'. Legions of parents apologize repeatedly to friends and strangers alike as they talk on and on about the cute things their kids do. Most wondrous of all are the rapid and momentous developmental changes of the childhood years. Helpless infants become curious toddlers almost overnight. Before parents can catch their breath, these toddlers are schoolchildren engaged in spirited play with young friends. Then, suddenly, they're insecure adolescents, worrying about dates, part-time jobs, cars, and college. The whirlwind transitions of childhood often seem miraculous.

Of course, the transformations that occur in childhood only *seem* magical. In reality, they reflect an orderly, predictable, gradual progression. In this section you'll see what psychologists have learned about this progression. We'll examine various aspects of development that are especially dynamic during childhood. Language development, which is very rapid during early childhood, is omitted from this section because we covered it in the chapter on language and thought (see Chapter 8). Let's begin by looking at motor development.

Exploring the World: Motor Development

Motor development refers to the progression of muscular coordination required for physical activities. Basic motor skills include grasping and reaching for objects, manipulating objects, sitting up, crawling, walking, running, and so forth.

Basic Principles

A number of principles are apparent in motor development. One is the *cephalocaudal trend—* the head-to-foot direction of motor development. Children tend to gain control over the upper part of their bodies before the lower part. You've seen this trend in action if you've seen an infant learn to crawl. Infants gradually shift from using their arms for propelling themselves to using their legs. The *proximodistal trend* is the center-outward direction of motor develop-

ment. Children gain control over their torso before their extremities. Thus, infants initially reach for things by twisting their entire body, but gradually they learn to extend just their arms.

Early motor development depends in part on physical growth, which is very rapid during infancy and is apparently more uneven than previously appreciated. In a study of infants' growth from birth to 21 months, Lampl, Veldhuis, and Johnson (1992) found that lengthy periods of no growth were punctuated by sudden bursts of growth. Infants routinely went two to four weeks, and sometimes even 60 days, with no growth and then grew as much as a half-inch in just one day. These remarkable growth spurts tend to be accompanied by restlessness and irritability.

Understanding Developmental Norms

Parents often pay close attention to early motor development, comparing their child's progress with developmental norms. *Developmental norms* indicate the average (median) age at which individuals display various behaviors and abilities. Developmental norms are useful benchmarks as long as parents don't expect their children to progress exactly at the pace specified in the norms. Some parents get unnecessarily alarmed when their children fall behind developmental norms. What these parents overlook is that developmental norms are group *averages*. Variations from the average are entirely normal. This normal variation stands out in Figure 11.4, which indicates the age at which 25%, 50%, and 90% of youngsters can demonstrate various motor skills. As Figure 11.4 shows, a substantial portion of children often don't achieve a particular milestone until long after the average time cited in norms.

Cultural Variations and Their Significance

Early progress in motor skills has largely been attributed to the process of maturation. *Maturation* is development that reflects the gradual unfolding of one's genetic blueprint. It is a product of genetically programmed physical changes that come with age—as opposed to experience and learning. Although infants' acquisition of motor skills is *primarily* a function of maturation, cross-cultural research on early motor development shows that it can be influenced to some degree by environmental factors.

Relatively rapid motor development has been observed in some cultures that provide special practice in basic motor skills. For example, soon after birth the Kipsigis people of Kenya begin

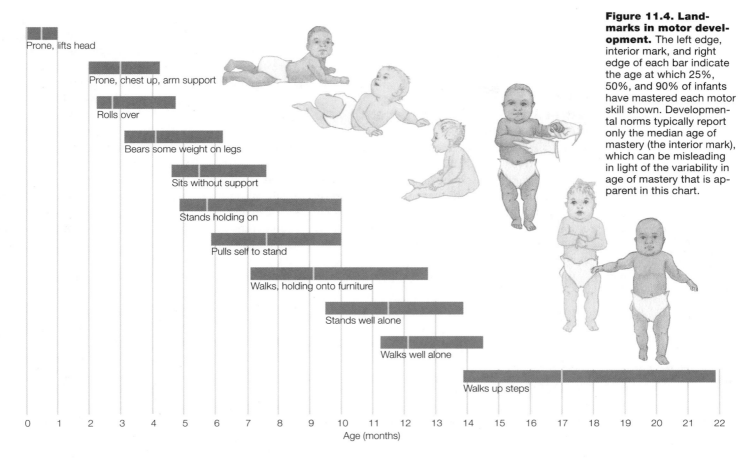

Prone, lifts head

Prone, chest up, arm support

Rolls over

Bears some weight on legs

Sits without support

Stands holding on

Pulls self to stand

Walks, holding onto furniture

Stands well alone

Walks well alone

Walks up steps

0 1 2 3 4 5 6 7 8 9 10 11 12 13 14 15 16 17 18 19 20 21 22
Age (months)

Figure 11.4. Landmarks in motor development. The left edge, interior mark, and right edge of each bar indicate the age at which 25%, 50%, and 90% of infants have mastered each motor skill shown. Developmental norms typically report only the median age of mastery (the interior mark), which can be misleading in light of the variability in age of mastery that is apparent in this chart.

active efforts to train their infants to sit up, stand, and walk. Thanks to this training, Kipsigis children achieve these developmental milestones (but not others) about a month earlier than babies in the United States (Super, 1976). West Indian children in Jamaica also exhibit advanced motor development that has been linked to a special regimen of motor exercises practiced in early infancy (Hopkins & Westra, 1988, 1990). In contrast, relatively slow motor development has been found in some cultures that discourage motor exploration. For example, among the Ache, a nomadic people living in the rain forests of Paraguay, safety concerns dictate that children under age 3 rarely venture more than 3 feet from their mothers, who carry them virtually everywhere. As a result of these constraints, Ache children are delayed in acquiring a variety of motor skills and typically begin walking about a year later than other children (Kaplan & Dove, 1987).

Cultural variations in the emergence of basic motor skills demonstrate that environmental factors can accelerate or slow early motor development. Nonetheless, the similarities across cultures in the sequence and timing of early motor development outweigh the differences, and the fact

remains that *early* motor development depends first and foremost on maturation. *Later* motor development is another matter, however. As children in any culture grow older, they acquire more specialized motor skills, some of which may be unique to their culture. Maturation becomes less influential and experience becomes more criti-

Tribes around the world use a variety of methods to foster rapid development of motor abilities in their children. The !Kung San of Kalahari, Botswana, teach their young to dance quite early, using poles to develop the kinesthetic sense of balance.

cal. Obviously, maturation by itself will never lead to the development of ballet or football skills, for example, without exposure to appropriate training.

Easy and Difficult Babies: Differences in Temperament

Infants show considerable variability in temperament. *Temperament* **refers to characteristic mood, activity level, and emotional reactivity.** From the very beginning, some babies seem animated and cheerful while others seem sluggish and ornery. Infants show consistent differences in emotional tone, tempo of activity, and sensitivity to environmental stimuli very early in life (Stifter & Fox, 1990).

Alexander Thomas and Stella Chess have conducted a major *longitudinal* study of the development of temperament (Thomas & Chess, 1977, 1989; Thomas, Chess, & Birch, 1970). **In a *longitudinal study* investigators observe one group of subjects repeatedly over a period of time.** This approach to the study of development is often contrasted with the cross-sectional approach (the logic of both approaches is diagrammed in Figure 11.5). **In a *cross-sectional study* investigators compare groups of subjects of differ-**ing age at a single point in time. For example, in a cross-sectional study an investigator tracing the growth of children's vocabulary might compare 50 six-year-olds, 50 eight-year-olds, and 50 ten-year-olds. In contrast, an investigator using the longitudinal method would assemble one group of 50 six-year-olds and measure their vocabulary at age six, again at age eight, and once more at age ten.

Each method has its advantages. Cross-sectional studies can be completed more quickly, easily, and cheaply than longitudinal studies, which often extend over many years. But longitudinal studies tend to be more sensitive to developmental changes (Nunnally, 1982).

To some extent, the choice between the longitudinal approach and the cross-sectional approach depends on what the investigators want to learn about development. Thomas and Chess wanted to learn about the long-term stability of children's temperaments. Given this goal, they needed to follow the same children in a longitudinal study to assess their temperamental stability over time. They began their study in 1956 with a group of 141 middle-class children. In 1961 they added a second group of 95 children of working-class parents. They have tracked the development of most of these subjects into adolescence and adulthood.

Thomas and Chess found that "temperamental individuality is well established by the time the infant is two to three months old" (Thomas & Chess, 1977, p. 153). They identified three basic styles of temperament that were apparent in most of the children. About 40% of the youngsters were *easy children* who tended to be happy, regular in sleep and eating, adaptable, and not readily upset. Another 15% were *slow-to-warm-up children* who tended to be less cheery, less regular in their sleep and eating, and slower in adapting to change. These children were wary of new experiences, and their emotional reactivity was moderate. *Difficult children* constituted 10% of the group. They tended to be glum, erratic in sleep and eating, resistant to change, and relatively irritable. The remaining 35% of the children showed mixtures of these three temperaments.

A child's temperament at three months was a fair predictor of the child's temperament at age ten. Infants categorized as "difficult" developed more emotional problems requiring counseling than other children. Although basic changes in temperament were seen in some children, Thomas and Chess concluded that temperament was

Figure 11.5. Longitudinal versus cross-sectional research. In a longitudinal study of development between ages 6 and 10, the same children would be observed at 6, again at 8, and again at 10. In a cross-sectional study of the same age span, a group of 6-year-olds, a group of 8-year-olds, and a group of 10-year-olds would be compared simultaneously. Note that data collection could be completed immediately in the cross-sectional study, whereas the longitudinal study would require four years to complete.

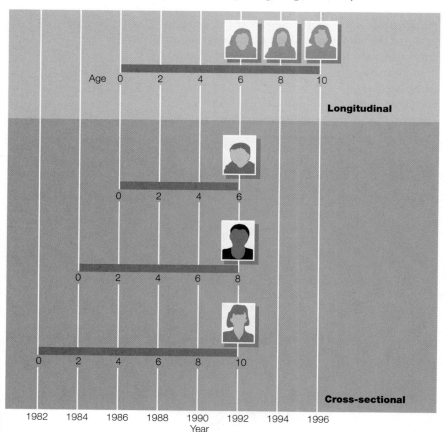

generally stable over time. Their conclusion has been echoed by other investigators who assert that temperament has a strong biological basis (Kagan & Snidman, 1991; Robinson et al., 1992).

Early Emotional Development: Attachment

Do mothers and infants forge lasting emotional bonds in the first few hours after birth? Do early emotional bonds affect later development? These are just some of the questions investigated by psychologists interested in attachment. **Attachment refers to the close, emotional bonds of affection that develop between infants and their caregivers.** Researchers have shown a keen interest in how infant-mother attachments are formed early in life. Children eventually form attachments to many people, including their fathers, siblings, grandparents, and others. However, a child's first important attachment usually occurs with his or her mother because she is typically the principal caregiver in the early months of life (Lamb, 1987).

Patterns of Attachment

Contrary to popular belief, infants' attachment to their mothers is *not* instantaneous. Initially, babies show little in the way of a special preference for their mothers. They can be handed over to strangers such as babysitters with relatively little difficulty. This typically changes at around 6 to 8 months of age, when infants begin to show a preference for their mother's company and often protest when

separated from her (Lamb, Ketterlinus, & Fracasso, 1992). This is the first manifestation of *separation anxiety*—**emotional distress seen in many infants when they are separated from people with whom they have formed an attachment.** Separation anxiety, which may occur with other familiar caregivers as well as the mother, typically peaks at around 14 to 18 months and then begins to decline.

Research by Mary Ainsworth and her colleagues (1978) suggests that attachment emerges out of a complex interplay between infant and mother (see Figure 11.6). Studies reveal that mothers who are sensitive and responsive to their children's needs tend to evoke stronger attachments than mothers who are relatively insensitive or inconsistent in their responding (Cox et al., 1992; Isabella & Belsky, 1991). However, infants are not passive bystanders as this process unfolds. They are active participants who influence the process with their crying, smiling, fussing, and babbling. Difficult infants who spit up most of their food, make bathing a major battle, refuse to go to sleep, and rarely smile may sometimes slow the process of attachment in the mother by undermining her responsiveness (Mangelsdorf et al., 1990).

Infant-mother attachments vary in quality. Ainsworth and her colleagues (1978) found that these attachments fall into three categories, which are shown in Figure 11.6. Fortunately, most infants develop a *secure attachment*. However, some become very anxious when separated from their mother, a pattern called *anxious-ambivalent attach-*

"Where familial security is lacking, the individual is handicapped by the lack of what might be called a secure base from which to work."
MARY SALTER AINSWORTH

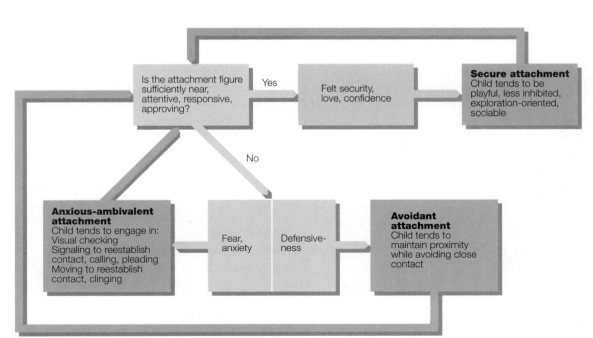

Figure 11.6. Overview of the attachment process. The unfolding of attachment depends on the interaction between a mother (or other caregiver) and an infant. Research by Mary Ainsworth and others suggests that attachment relations fall into three categories—secure, avoidant, and anxious-ambivalent—which depend on how sensitive and responsive caregivers are to their children's needs. The feedback loops shown in the diagram reflect the fact that babies are not passive bystanders in the attachment drama; their reactions to caregivers can affect the caregivers' behavior. (Adapted from Shaver & Hazan, 1994)

ment. Children in the third category seek little contact with their mothers, a condition labeled *avoidant attachment.* The type of attachment that emerges between an infant and mother may depend to a large degree on the infant's temperament (Vaughn et al., 1992). Evidence suggests that the quality of the attachment relationship can have important consequences for children's subsequent social development.

Bonding at Birth, Day Care, and Attachment

Does a strong attachment relationship depend on infant-mother "bonding" during the first few hours after birth? Some theorists think so. For instance, Klaus and Kennell (1982) have suggested that extensive skin-to-skin contact between a newborn and its mother immediately after birth can promote more effective attachment later. This practice is intuitively appealing and can be a highly pleasurable "magic moment" for both infants and mothers. However, the data on its effects are unimpressive. Even short-term benefits have proven difficult to demonstrate. And there is no convincing evidence that this practice leads to healthier attachment relationships in the long run (Bretherton, 1992; Myers, 1987; Rosenblith, 1992).

As for day care, its impact on attachment is the subject of heated debate. The crucial question is whether daily infant-mother separations might disrupt the attachment process. The issue is an important one, given that 53% of mothers with an infant under the age of 1 work outside the home. Research by Jay Belsky (1988, 1990, 1992) suggests that babies who receive nonmaternal care for more than 20 hours per week have an increased risk of developing insecure attachments to their mothers. Belsky's findings have raised many eyebrows, but they need to be put in perspective. The effects of day care appear to depend on the quality of the care provided. Negative effects seem minimal and may even be outweighed by positive effects when children are cared for in spacious, well-equipped, adequately staffed facilities that provide lots of individual attention and carefully planned activities (Howes, Phillips, & Whitebook, 1992; Scarr et al., 1993).

Unfortunately, the United States has not invested as heavily in the provision of high-quality day care as many other industrialized nations. For example, publicly funded, strictly regulated, high-caliber day care is widely available in most Western European nations (Kamerman, 1993). In contrast, in the United States there is no federal regulation of day care and little funding to subsidize low-income parents who cannot afford quality care. Many states do not require caregivers to have any special training and do not license or even inspect child-care facilities (Wingert & Kantrowitz, 1990). Day-care centers are often understaffed, and their employees are notoriously underpaid, which results in high turnover (Zigler & Gilman, 1993). Obviously, children from low-income homes are especially likely to be placed in less expensive, poor-quality day-care arrangements. Thus, research on the possible negative effects of day care highlights the urgent need to improve American children's access to high-quality care.

Culture and Attachment

Separation anxiety emerges in children at about 6–8 months and peaks at about 14–18 months in cultures around the world (Grossman & Grossman, 1990). This finding suggests that attachment is a universal feature of human development. However, studies have found some interesting cultural variations in the proportion of infants who fall into the three attachment categories described by Ainsworth. Working with white, middle-class subjects in the United States, Ainsworth and colleagues (1978) found that 67% of infants displayed a secure attachment, 21% an anxious-ambivalent attachment, and 12% an avoidant attachment. As Table 11.1 shows, studies in Germany and Japan have yielded very different figures. Avoidant attachments were far more common in the German sample but were nonexistent in the Japanese sample, which yielded more anxious-ambivalent attachments than the U.S. sample.

Researchers have attributed these disparities in attachment patterns to cultural variations in child-rearing practices. More so than American parents, German parents intentionally try to encourage independence rather than clinging dependence at an early age, thus producing more avoidant attachments (Grossman et al., 1985). In contrast, Japanese parents do not attempt to fos-

Table 11.1 Patterns of Attachment (%) from Three Cultural Samples

Country (study)	Avoidant	Secure	Anxious-Ambivalent
USA (Ainsworth et al., 1978)	21	67	12
Germany (Grossman et al., 1981)	52	35	13
Japan (Takahashi, 1986)	0	68	32

Source: Adapted from Cole (1992)

ter a similar kind of early independence, and infants are rarely away from their mothers during the first year, so avoidant attachments are rare (Takahashi, 1990). Clearly, cultural differences in child-rearing attitudes and practices can influence patterns of attachment.

Becoming Unique: Personality Development

How do individuals develop their unique constellations of personality traits over time? Many theories have addressed this question. The first major theory of personality development was put together by Sigmund Freud back around the turn of the century. As we'll discuss in Chapter 12, he claimed that the basic foundation of an individual's personality is firmly laid down by age 5. Half a century later, Erik Erikson (1963) proposed a sweeping revision of Freud's theory that has proven very influential. Like Freud, Erikson concluded that events in early childhood leave a permanent stamp on adult personality. However, unlike Freud, Erikson theorized that personality continues to evolve over the entire life span.

Building on Freud's earlier work, Erikson devised a stage theory of personality development. As you'll see in reading this chapter, many theories describe development in terms of stages. **A *stage* is a developmental period during which characteristic patterns of behavior are exhibited and certain capacities become established.** Stage theories assume that (1) individuals must progress through specified stages in a particular order because each stage builds on the previous stage and (2) progress through these stages is strongly related to age.

Erikson's Stage Theory

Erikson partitioned the life span into eight stages, each of which brings a *psychosocial crisis* involving transitions in important social relationships. According to Erikson, personality is shaped by how individuals deal with these psychosocial crises. Each crisis is a potential turning point that can yield different outcomes. Erikson described the stages in terms of these alternative outcomes, which represent personality traits that people display over the remainder of their lives. All eight stages in Erikson's theory are charted in Table 11.2. We describe the first four childhood stages here and discuss the remaining stages in the upcoming sections on adolescence and adulthood.

TRUST VERSUS MISTRUST Erikson's first stage encompasses the first year of life, when an infant has to depend completely on adults to take care of its basic needs for such necessities as food, a warm blanket, and changed diapers. If an infant's basic biological needs are adequately met by its caregivers and sound attachments are formed, the child should develop an optimistic, trusting attitude toward the world. However, if the infant's basic needs are taken care of poorly, a more distrusting, insecure personality may result.

AUTONOMY VERSUS SHAME AND DOUBT Erikson's second stage unfolds during the second and third years of life, when parents begin toilet training and other efforts to regulate the child. The child must begin to take some personal responsibility for feeding, dressing, and bathing. If all goes well, he or she acquires a sense of self-sufficiency. But if parents are never satisfied with the child's efforts

"Human personality in principle develops according to steps predetermined in the growing person's readiness to be driven toward, to be aware of, and to interact with a widening social radius."
ERIK ERIKSON

Table 11.2 Erikson's Stages of Psychosocial Development

Stage	Psychosocial Crisis	Significant Social Relationships	Favorable Outcome
1. First year of life	Trust versus mistrust	Mother or mother substitute	Trust and optimism
2. Second and third years	Autonomy versus doubt	Parents	A sense of self-control and adequacy
3. Fourth through sixth years	Initiative versus guilt	Basic family	Purpose and direction; ability to initiate one's own activities
4. Age six through puberty	Industry versus inferiority	Neighborhood; school	Competence in intellectual, social, and physical skills
5. Adolescence	Identity versus confusion	Peer groups and outgroups; models of leadership	An integrated image of oneself as a unique person
6. Early adulthood	Intimacy versus isolation	Partners in friendship and sex; competition, cooperation	An ability to form close and lasting relationships, to make career commitments
7. Middle adulthood	Generativity versus self-absorption	Divided labor and shared household	Concern for family, society, and future generations
8. The aging years	Integrity versus despair	"My kind"	A sense of fulfillment and satisfaction with one's life; willingness to face death

Source: Adapted from Erikson (1963)

According to Erik Erikson, school-age children face the challenge of learning how to function in social situations outside of their family, especially with peers and at school. If they succeed, they will develop a sense of competence; if they fail, they may feel inferior.

and there are constant parent-child conflicts, the child may develop a sense of personal shame and self-doubt.

INITIATIVE VERSUS GUILT In Erikson's third stage, roughly from ages 3 to 6, the challenge facing children is to function socially within their families. If children think only of their own needs and desires, family members may begin to instill feelings of guilt, and self-esteem may suffer. But if children learn to get along well with siblings and parents, a sense of self-confidence should begin to grow.

INDUSTRY VERSUS INFERIORITY In the fourth stage (age 6 through puberty), the challenge of learning to function socially is extended beyond the family to the broader social realm of the neighborhood and school. Children who are able to function effectively in this less nurturant social sphere where productivity is highly valued should develop a sense of competence.

Evaluating Erikson's Theory

The strength of Erikson's theory is that it accounts for both continuity and transition in personality development. It accounts for transition by showing how new challenges in social relations stimulate personality development throughout life. It accounts for continuity by drawing connections between early childhood experiences and aspects of adult personality.

On the negative side, Erikson's theory is vague and hence has not stimulated as much empirical research as a good theory should (Miller, 1989). Also, it's an "idealized" description of "typical"

developmental patterns. Thus, it's not well suited for explaining the enormous personality differences that exist among people. Inadequate explanation of individual differences is a common problem with stage theories of development. This shortcoming surfaces again in the next section, where we'll examine Jean Piaget's stage theory of cognitive development.

The Growth of Thought: Cognitive Development

Cognitive development **refers to transitions in youngsters' patterns of thinking, including reasoning, remembering, and problem solving.** The investigation of cognitive development has been dominated in recent decades by the theory of Jean Piaget (1929, 1952, 1983). Although other approaches to cognitive development have yielded important insights, we'll focus our discussion on Piaget's theory and the research it has generated.

Overview of Piaget's Stage Theory

Jean Piaget was a Swiss scholar whose own cognitive development was exceptionally rapid. In his early 20s, after he had earned a doctorate in natural science and published a novel, Piaget's interest turned to psychology. He met Theodore Simon, who had collaborated with Alfred Binet in devising the first useful intelligence tests. Working in Simon's Paris laboratory, Piaget administered intelligence tests to many children to develop better test norms. In doing this testing, Piaget was intrigued by the reasoning underlying the children's *wrong* answers. He decided that measuring children's intelligence was less interesting than studying how children *use* their intelligence. In 1921 he moved to Geneva, where he spent the remainder of his life studying cognitive development. Many of his ideas were based on insights gleaned from careful observations of his own three children during their infancy.

Noting that children actively explore the world around them, Piaget asserted that interaction with the environment and maturation gradually alter the way children think. Like Erikson's theory, Piaget's model is a *stage theory* of development. Piaget proposed that children's thought processes go through a series of four major stages: (1) the *sensorimotor period* (birth to age 2), (2) the *preoperational period* (ages 2 to 7), (3) the *concrete operational period* (ages 7 to 11), and (4) the *formal operational period* (age eleven onward). Table 11.3 provides an overview of each of these periods. Piaget regarded

Table 11.3 Piaget's Stages of Cognitive Development

Approximate Age Range	Stage	Major Characteristics
Birth to 2 years	Sensorimotor period	Coordination of sensory input and motor responses Development of object permanence Little or no capacity for symbolic representation
2 to 7 years	Preoperational period	Development of symbolic thought Irreversible, egocentric thinking
7 to 11 years	Concrete operational period	Mental operations applied to concrete objects and events Development of conservation, mastery of concept of reversibiltiy
11 through adulthood	Formal operational period	Mental operations applied to abstractions Development of logical and systematic thinking

his age norms as approximations and acknowledged that transitional ages may vary from one child to another.

Sensorimotor Period

One of Piaget's foremost contributions was to greatly enhance our understanding of mental development in the earliest months of life. The first stage in his theory is the *sensorimotor period*, which lasts from birth to about age 2. Piaget called this stage *sensorimotor* because infants are developing the ability to coordinate their sensory input with their motor actions.

The major development during the sensorimotor stage is the gradual appearance of symbolic thought. At the beginning of this stage, a child's behavior is dominated by innate reflexes. But by the end of the stage, the child can use mental symbols to represent objects (for example, a mental image of a favorite toy). The key to this transition is the acquisition of the concept of object permanence.

Object permanence develops when a child recognizes that objects continue to exist even when they are no longer visible. Although you surely take the permanence of objects for granted, infants aren't aware of this permanence at first. If you show a 4-month-old child an eye-catching toy and then cover the toy with a pillow, the child will not attempt to search for the toy. Piaget inferred from this observation that the child does not understand that the toy continues to exist under the pillow. The notion of object permanence does not dawn on children overnight. The first signs of this insight usually appear between 4 and 8 months of age, when children will often pursue an object that is *partially* covered in their presence. Progress

is gradual, and children typically don't master the concept of object permanence until they're about 18 months old.

The significance of object permanence is immense. Once children realize that disappearing objects continue to exist, they begin to use mental images to represent the absent objects. This is the primitive beginning of symbolic thought, which will gradually expand the boundaries of their thinking.

Preoperational Period

During the *preoperational period*, which extends roughly from age 2 to age 7, children gradually improve in their use of mental images. Although progress in symbolic thought continues, Piaget

When this young boy's view of a toy is blocked, he doesn't attempt to search for the toy, because he doesn't yet understand that the toy continues to exist behind the barrier. According to Piaget, the eventual acquisition of the concept of object permanence is the foremost development during the sensorimotor period.

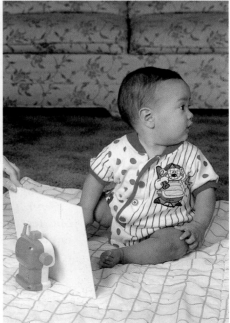

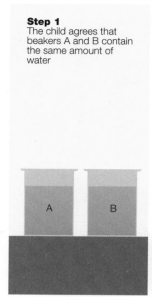

Step 1
The child agrees that beakers A and B contain the same amount of water

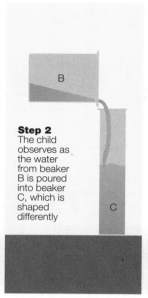

Step 2
The child observes as the water from beaker B is poured into beaker C, which is shaped differently

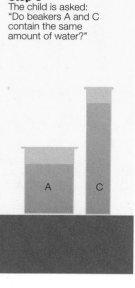

Step 3
The child is asked: "Do beakers A and C contain the same amount of water?"

Figure 11.7. Piaget's conservation task. After watching the transformation shown, a preoperational child will usually answer that the taller beaker contains more water. In contrast, the child in the concrete operations period tends to respond correctly, recognizing that the amount of water in beaker C remains the same as the amount in beaker A.

emphasized the *shortcomings* in preoperational thought.

Consider a simple problem that Piaget presented to youngsters. He would take two identical beakers and fill each with the same amount of water. After a child had agreed that the two beakers contained the same amount of water, he would pour the water from one of the beakers into a much taller and thinner beaker (see Figure 11.7). He would then ask the child whether the two differently shaped beakers still contained the same amount of water. Confronted with a problem like this, children in the preoperational period generally said "no." They typically focused on the higher water line in the taller beaker and insisted that there was more water in the slender beaker. They had not yet mastered the principle of conservation. *Conservation* is **Piaget's term for the awareness that physical quantities remain constant in spite of changes in their shape or appearance.**

Why are preoperational children unable to solve conservation problems? According to Piaget, their inability to understand conservation is due to some basic flaws in preoperational thinking. These flaws include centration, irreversibility, and egocentrism.

Centration **is the tendency to focus on just one feature of a problem, neglecting other important aspects.** When working on the conservation problem with water, preoperational children tend to concentrate on the height of the water while ignoring the width. They have difficulty focusing on several aspects of a problem at once.

Irreversibility **is the inability to envision re-**versing an action. Preoperational children can't mentally "undo" something. For instance, in grappling with the conservation of water, they don't think about what would happen if the water were poured back from the tall beaker into the original beaker.

Egocentrism **in thinking is characterized by a limited ability to share another person's viewpoint.** Indeed, Piaget felt that preoperational children fail to appreciate that there are points of view other than their own. For instance, if you ask a preoperational girl whether her sister has a sister, she'll probably say no if they are the only two girls in the family. She's unable to view sisterhood from her sister's perspective (this also shows irreversibility).

A notable feature of egocentrism is *animism*—**the belief that all things are living,** just like oneself. Thus, youngsters attribute lifelike, human qualities to inanimate objects, asking questions such as, "When does the ocean stop to rest?" or "Why does the wind get so mad?"

As you can see, Piaget emphasized the weaknesses apparent in preoperational thought. Indeed, that is why he called this stage *pre*operational. The ability to perform *operations*—internal transformations, manipulations, and reorganizations of mental structures—emerges in the next stage.

Concrete Operational Period

The development of mental operations marks the beginning of the *concrete operational period*, which usually lasts from about age 7 to age 11. Piaget called this stage *concrete* operations because children can perform operations only on images of tangible objects and actual events.

Among the operations that children master during this stage are reversibility and decentration. *Reversibility* permits a child to mentally undo an action. *Decentration* allows the child to focus on more than one feature of a problem simultaneously. The newfound ability to coordinate several aspects of a problem helps the child appreciate that there are several ways to look at things. This ability in turn leads to a decline in egocentrism.

As children master concrete operations, they develop a variety of new problem-solving capacities. Let's examine another problem studied by Piaget. Give a preoperational child seven carnations and three daisies. Tell the child the names for the two types of flowers and ask the child to sort them into carnations and daisies. That should be no problem. Now ask the child whether there are more carnations or more daisies. Most chil-

Typical tasks used to measure conservation	Typical age of mastery
Conservation of number Two equivalent rows of objects are shown to the child, who agrees that they have the same number of objects	6–7
One row is lengthened, and the child is asked whether one row has more objects	
Conservation of mass The child acknowledges that two clay balls have equal amounts of clay	7–8
The experimenter changes the shape of one of the balls and asks the child whether they still contain equal amounts of clay	
Conservation of length The child agrees that two sticks aligned with each other are the same length	7–8
After moving one stick to the left or right, the experimenter asks the child whether the sticks are of equal length	
Conservation of area Two identical sheets of cardboard have wooden blocks placed on them in identical positions; the child confirms that the same amount of space is left on each piece of cardboard	8–9
The experimenter scatters the blocks on one piece of cardboard and again asks the child whether the two pieces have the same amount of unoccupied space	

Figure 11.8. The gradual mastery of conservation. Children master Piaget's conservation problem during the concrete operations period, but their mastery is gradual. As outlined here, children usually master the conservation of number at age 6 or 7, but they may not understand the conservation of area until age 8 or 9.

dren will correctly respond that there are more carnations. Now ask the child whether there are more carnations or more flowers. At this point, most preoperational children will stumble and respond incorrectly that there are more carnations than flowers. Generally, preoperational children can't handle *hierarchical classification* problems that require them to focus simultaneously on two levels of classification. However, the child who has advanced to the concrete operational stage is not as limited by centration and can work successfully with hierarchical classification problems.

Children in the concrete operational period are also able to grasp the principle of conservation as it applies to liquid, mass, number, volume, area, and length (see Figure 11.8). Children master some conservation problems (conservation of number, for instance) earlier than others (such as volume). This difference in mastery may be due in part to differences in the complexity of the concepts involved. However, this piecemeal progress also illustrates the *gradual* nature of cognitive development. Children in the concrete operational period also begin to appreciate the logic of relations. Unlike preoperational children, they can understand that if Sue is younger than Sara and Sara is younger than Sandy, then Sue is younger than Sandy.

Formal Operational Period

The final stage in Piaget's theory is the *formal operational period*, which typically begins around 11 years of age. In this stage, children begin to apply their operations to *abstract* concepts in addition to concrete objects. Indeed, during this stage, youngsters come to *enjoy* the heady contemplation of abstract concepts. Many adolescents spend hours mulling over hypothetical possibilities related to abstractions such as justice, love, and free will.

According to Piaget, youngsters graduate to relatively adult modes of thinking in the formal operations stage. He did *not* mean to suggest that no further cognitive development occurs once children reach this stage. However, he believed that after children achieve formal operations, further developments in thinking are changes in *degree* rather than fundamental changes in the *nature* of thinking.

"It is virtually impossible to draw a clear line between innate and acquired behavior patterns."
JEAN PIAGET

Adolescents in the formal operational period become more *systematic* in their problem-solving efforts. Children in earlier developmental stages tend to attack problems quickly, with a trial-and-error approach. In contrast, children who have achieved formal operations are more likely to think things through. They envision possible courses of action and try to use logic to reason out the likely consequences of each possible solution before they act. Thus, thought processes in the formal operational period can be characterized as abstract, systematic, logical, and reflective.

Evaluating Piaget's Theory

Jean Piaget made a landmark contribution to psychology's understanding of children in general and their cognitive development in particular (Beilin, 1992). Above all else, he sought answers to new questions. As he acknowledged in a 1970 interview, "It's just that no adult ever had the idea of asking children about conservation. It was so obvious that if you change the shape of an object, the quantity will be conserved. Why ask a child? The novelty lay in asking the question" (Hall, 1987, p. 56). Piaget's daring ideas sparked an explosion of research that continues through today. This research has supported a great many of Piaget's central propositions (Siegler, 1991). In such a far-reaching theory, however, there are bound to be some weak spots. Let's briefly examine some criticisms of Piaget's theory:

1. In some areas, Piaget may have underestimated young children's cognitive development. Some researchers have found evidence that children begin to develop object permanence earlier than Piaget thought (Baillargeon & DeVos, 1991). Others have marshaled evidence that preoperational children exhibit less egocentrism and animism than Piaget believed (Newcombe & Huttenlocher, 1992).

2. Piaget's model suffers from problems that plague most stage theories. Like Erikson, Piaget had little to say about individual differences in development (Siegler, 1994). Also, people often simultaneously display patterns of thinking that are characteristic of several different stages. This "mixing" of stages calls into question the value of organizing development in terms of stages (Flavell, 1992; Miller, 1989).

3. Piaget believed that his theory described universal processes that should lead children everywhere to progress through uniform stages of thinking at roughly the same ages. Subsequent research has shown that the *sequence* of stages is largely invariant, but the *timetable* that children follow in passing through these stages varies considerably across cultures (Dasen, 1994; Rogoff, 1990). Thus, Piaget underestimated the influence of cultural factors on cognitive development.

As with any theory, Piaget's is not flawless. However, without Piaget's theory to guide research, many crucial questions about children's development might not have been confronted until decades later (if at all). For instance, Piaget's work stimulated fruitful new approaches to moral development, the topic we consider next.

The Development of Moral Reasoning

In Europe, a woman was near death from cancer. One drug might save her, a form of radium that a druggist in the same town had recently discovered. The druggist was charging $2,000, ten times what the drug cost him to make. The sick woman's husband, Heinz, went to everyone he knew to borrow the money, but he could only get together about half of what it cost. He told the druggist that his wife was dying and asked him to sell it cheaper or let him pay later. But the druggist said, "No." The husband got desperate and broke into the man's store to steal the drug for his wife. Should the husband have done that? Why? (Kohlberg, 1969, p. 379)

What's your answer to Heinz's dilemma? Would you have answered the same way 3 years ago? In the fifth grade? Can you guess what you might have said at age 6?

By presenting similar dilemmas to subjects and studying their responses, Lawrence Kohlberg (1976, 1984; Colby & Kohlberg, 1987) developed a model of *moral development*. What is morality? That's a complicated question that philosophers have debated for centuries. For our purposes, it will suffice to say that *morality* involves the ability to discern right from wrong and to behave accordingly.

Kohlberg's Stage Theory

Kohlberg's model is the most influential of a number of competing theories that attempt to explain how youngsters develop a sense of right and wrong. His work was derived from much earlier work by Piaget (1932). Piaget theorized that moral development is determined by cognitive development. By this he meant that the way individuals think out moral issues depends on their level of cognitive development. This assumption provided the springboard for Kohlberg's research.

Kohlberg's theory focuses on moral *reasoning* rather than overt *behavior*. This point is best illustrated by describing Kohlberg's method of investigation. He presented his subjects with thorny moral questions such as Heinz's dilemma, then asked the subjects what the actor in the dilemma should do, and more important, why. It was the *why* that interested Kohlberg. He examined the nature and progression of subjects' moral reasoning.

The result of this work is the stage theory of moral reasoning outlined in Table 11.4. Kohlberg found that individuals progress through a series of three levels of moral development, each of which can be broken into two sublevels, yielding a total of six stages. Each stage represents a different approach to thinking about right and wrong. Examples of how people reason out Heinz's dilemma in each of Kohlberg's six stages are shown in Table 11.4.

Younger children at the *preconventional level* think in terms of external authority. Acts are wrong because they are punished, or right because they lead to positive consequences. Older children who have reached the *conventional level* of moral reasoning see rules as necessary for maintaining social order. They therefore accept these rules as their own. They "internalize" these rules not to avoid punishment but to be virtuous and win approval from others. Moral thinking at this stage is relatively inflexible. Rules are viewed as absolute guidelines that should be enforced rigidly.

During adolescence, some youngsters move on

"Children are almost as likely to reject moral reasoning beneath their level as to fail to assimilate reasoning too far above their level."
LAWRENCE KOHLBERG

Table 11.4 Kohlberg's Levels of Moral Development

Kohlberg's Levels and Stages	Description	Example of Characteristic Reasoning Regarding Heinz's Dilemma
Level I. Preconventional morality		
Stage 1. Punishment orientation	Compliance with rules to avoid punishment	"If he steals the drug, he might go to jail." (Punishment is the primary consideration.)
Stage 2. Naive reward orientation	Compliance with rules to get rewards, sharing in order to get returns	"He can steal the drug and save his wife, and he'll be with her when he gets out of jail." (Act is motivated by its hedonistic consequences for the actor.)
Level II. Conventional morality		
Stage 3. Good-boy/good-girl orientation	Conformity to rules that are defined by others' approval/disapproval	"People will understand if you steal the drug to save your wife, but they'll think you're cruel and a coward if you don't." (Reactions of others and the effects of the act on social relationships become important.)
Stage 4. Authority orientation	Rigid conformity to society's rules, law-and-order mentality, avoiding censure for rule breaking	"It is the husband's duty to save his wife even if he feels guilty afterward for stealing the drug." (Institutions, law, duty, honor, and guilt motivate behavior.)
Level III. Postconventional morality		
Stage 5. Social contract orientation	More flexible understanding that people obey rules because they are necessary for social order, but the rules could be changed if there were better alternatives	"The husband has a right to the drug even if he can't pay now. If the druggist won't charge it, the government should look after it." (Democratic laws guarantee individual rights; contracts are mutually beneficial.)
Stage 6. Morality of individual principles and conscience	Behavior conforms to internal principles (justice, equality) to avoid self-condemnation, and sometimes may violate society's rules	"Although it is legally wrong to steal, the husband would be morally wrong not to steal to save his wife. A life is more precious than financial gain." (Conscience is individual. Laws are socially useful but not sacrosanct.)

Source: Adapted from Kohlberg (1969)

to the *postconventional level*, which involves working out a personal code of ethics. Acceptance of rules is less rigid, and moral thinking shows some flexibility. Subjects at the postconventional level allow for the possibility that someone might not comply with some of society's rules if they conflict

with personal ethics. For example, subjects at this level might applaud a newspaper reporter who goes to jail rather than reveal a source of information who was promised anonymity.

Evaluating Kohlberg's Theory

How has Kohlberg's theory fared in research? The central ideas have received reasonable support. Progress in moral reasoning is indeed closely tied to cognitive development (Walker, 1988). Studies also show that youngsters generally do progress through Kohlberg's stages of moral reasoning in the order that he proposed (Walker, 1989). Furthermore, relations between age and level of moral reasoning are in the predicted directions (Rest, 1986). Representative age trends are shown in Figure 11.9. As children get older, stage 1 and stage 2 reasoning declines, while stage 3 and stage 4 reasoning increases. However, there is great variation in the age at which people reach specific stages. Furthermore, only a small percentage of people ever reach stage 6.

Like all influential theorists, Kohlberg has his critics. They have raised the following issues:

1. It's not unusual to find that a person shows signs of several adjacent levels of moral reasoning at a particular point in development (Walker & Taylor, 1991). As we noted in the critique of Piaget, this mixing of stages is a problem for virtually all stage theories.

2. Evidence is mounting that Kohlberg's dilemmas may not be valid indicators of moral development in some cultures. Some critics believe that the value judgments built into Kohlberg's theory reflect a liberal, individualistic ideology characteristic of modern Western nations that is much more culture-specific than Kohlberg appreciated (Shweder, Mahapatra, & Miller, 1990).

3. According to Carol Gilligan (1982), Kohlberg equates morality with justice, a view that reflects males' typical socialization. She maintains that females are socialized to equate morality with caring for others and self-sacrifice. Hence, she has hypothesized that Kohlberg's approach may underestimate the moral development of female subjects. This assertion has *not* been supported by subsequent research, which has failed to find significant gender differences in age-related progress through Kohlberg's stages (Thoma, 1986; Walker, 1991). However, there is some evidence that females are more likely than males to interpret moral dilemmas in terms

Figure 11.9. Age and moral reasoning. The percentages of different types of moral judgments made by subjects at various ages are graphed here (based on Kohlberg, 1963, 1969). As predicted, preconventional reasoning declines as children mature, conventional reasoning increases during middle childhood, and postconventional reasoning begins to emerge during adolescence; but at each age, children display a mixture of various levels of moral reasoning.

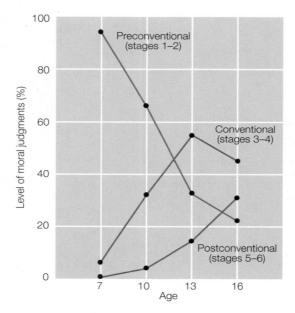

of caring rather than justice (Donenberg & Hoffman, 1988; Gilligan, Hamner, & Lyons, 1990). Thus, Kohlberg's theory may capture the essence of moral development in males better than in females.

Social Development: Trends in Altruism and Aggression

Psychologists have studied many aspects of social development. In sampling from this domain, we'll look at two kinds of social behavior that have been the focus of much research: altruism and aggression. *Altruism* **is selfless concern for the welfare of others that leads to helping behavior.** *Aggression* **is any behavior that is intended to hurt someone, either physically or verbally** (through insults, for instance). These two very different kinds of interpersonal behavior tend to show opposite developmental trends.

Altruism begins to emerge in children as they approach age 2 and tends to increase as they grow older, at least through the grade-school years (Zahn-Waxler & Smith, 1992). Interestingly, a modest positive correlation exists between a child's altruism and his or her level of moral reasoning. Children who exhibit more sophisticated moral reasoning tend to be more helpful and concerned about others than children who display lower levels of moral reasoning (Eisenberg et al., 1991).

In contrast, aggression generally declines with age, although this generalization has to be qualified carefully, because aggression changes in form as children grow older. Younger children display more *instrumental aggression*, which is intended to achieve some goal such as retrieving a toy. Older children display more *hostile aggression*, which is intended solely to hurt another (McCabe & Lipscomb, 1988). With increasing age, aggression also tends to become less physical and more verbal.

In spite of these age trends, huge differences occur in altruism and aggression among children of the same age. Some children are much more altruistic or more aggressive than others. Among grade-school children, for instance, a small minority (10%–15%) of highly aggressive children account for the vast majority of aggressive acts (Perry, Kusel, & Perry, 1988). Furthermore, there is ample evidence of gender differences in aggression. From age 2 onward, boys tend to be noticeably more aggressive than girls (Hyde, 1986; Legault & Strayer, 1990).

THE TRANSITION OF ADOLESCENCE

Adolescence is a bridge between childhood and adulthood. During this time, individuals continue to make significant progress in cognitive, moral, and social development. However, the most dynamic areas of development are physical changes and related transitions in emotional and personality development.

Puberty and the Growth Spurt

Recall for a moment your junior high school days. Didn't it seem that your body grew so fast about this time that your clothes just couldn't "keep up"? This phase of rapid growth in height and weight is called the *adolescent growth spurt*. Brought on by hormonal changes, it typically starts about 11 years of age in girls and about age 13 in boys (Malina, 1990). (Technically, this spurt should be called the *pre*adolescent growth spurt because it actually occurs *prior* to puberty, which is generally recognized as the beginning of adolescence.)

The term *pubescence* **is used to describe the two-year span preceding puberty during which the changes leading to physical and sexual maturity take place.** In addition to growing taller and heavier during pubescence, children begin to develop the physical features that characterize adults of their respective sexes. These features are termed *secondary sex characteristics*—**physical features that distinguish one sex from the other but that are not essential for reproduction.** For example, males go through a voice change, develop facial hair, and experience greater skeletal and muscle growth in the upper torso, leading to broader shoulders (see Figure 11.10 on the next page). Females experience breast growth and a widening of the pelvic bones plus increased fat deposits in this area, resulting in wider hips (Litt & Vaughan, 1992).

Note, however, that the capacity to reproduce is not attained in pubescence. This comes later. *Puberty* **is the stage during which sexual functions reach maturity, which marks the beginning of adolescence.** It is during puberty that the *primary sex characteristics*—**the structures necessary for reproduction**—develop fully. In the male, these include the testes, penis, and related internal structures. Primary sex characteristics in the female include the ovaries, vagina, uterus, and other internal structures.

In females, the onset of puberty is typically signaled by *menarche*—**the first occurrence of**

Figure 11.10. Physical development at puberty. Hormonal changes during puberty lead not only to a growth spurt but also to the development of secondary sexual characteristics. The pituitary gland sends signals to the adrenal glands and gonads (ovaries and testes), which secrete hormones responsible for various physical changes that differentiate males and females.

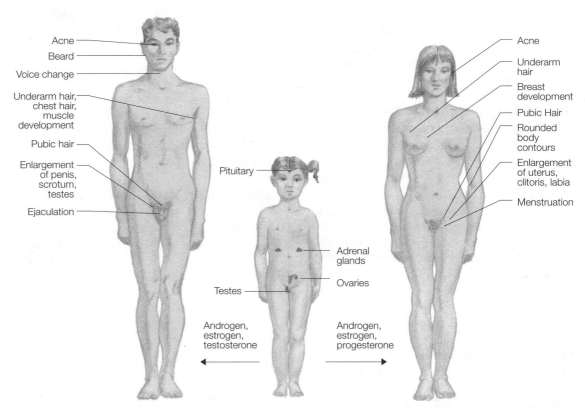

Acne
Beard
Voice change
Underarm hair, chest hair, muscle development
Pubic hair
Enlargement of penis, scrotum, testes
Ejaculation

Pituitary

Adrenal glands

Testes

Ovaries

Androgen, estrogen, testosterone

Androgen, estrogen, progesterone

Acne
Underarm hair
Breast development
Pubic Hair
Rounded body contours
Enlargement of uterus, clitoris, labia
Menstruation

menstruation. American girls typically reach menarche at about age 12½, with further sexual maturation continuing until approximately age 16. Most American boys begin to produce sperm by age 14, with complete sexual maturation occurring around age 18 (Brooks-Gunn & Reiter, 1990; Tanner, 1978). Interestingly, there have been *generational* changes in the timing of puberty. Today's adolescents begin puberty at a younger age, and complete it more rapidly, than did their counterparts in earlier generations. This trend apparently reflects improvements in nutrition and medical care (Brooks-Gunn, 1991; Bullough, 1981).

Time of Turmoil? Adolescent Suicide

Back around the turn of the century, G. Stanley Hall (1904), one of psychology's great pioneers, proposed that the adolescent years are characterized by convulsive instability and disturbing inner turmoil. Hall attributed this turmoil to adolescents' erratic physical changes and resultant confusion about self-image. Over the decades, a host of theorists have agreed with Hall's characterization of adolescence as a stormy period.

Statistics on *adolescent suicide* would seem to support the idea that adolescence is a time marked by turmoil, but the figures can be interpreted in various ways. On the one hand, suicide rates among

adolescents have risen alarmingly in recent decades. This is apparent in Figure 11.11(a), which shows a 154% increase in suicide among young people ages 15 to 24 between 1960 and 1990, while the overall suicide rate rose only slightly. On the other hand, even with this steep increase, suicide rates for adolescents are low in comparison to the rates for older age groups. Figure 11.11(b) plots suicide rates as a function of age. The figure reveals that the incidence of suicide in the 15–24 age group is lower than that for any older age group.

Actually, the suicide crisis among teenagers involves *attempted* suicide more than *completed* suicide. It's estimated that when all age groups are lumped together, suicide attempts outnumber actual suicidal deaths by a ratio of about 8 to 1 (Cross & Hirschfeld, 1986). However, this ratio of attempted to completed suicides is much higher for adolescents than for any other age group. Studies suggest that the ratio among adolescents may be anywhere from 50:1 to 200:1 (Garland & Zigler, 1993). According to David Curran (1987), suicide attempts by adolescents tend to be a "communicative gesture designed to elicit caring" (p. 12). Put another way, they are desperate cries for attention, help, and support.

Returning to our original question, does the weight of evidence support the idea that adolescence is usually a period of turmoil and turbu-

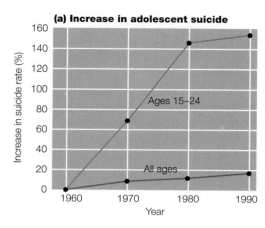

(a) Increase in adolescent suicide

Ages 15–24

All ages

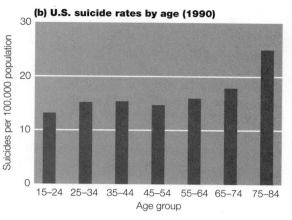

(b) U.S. suicide rates by age (1990)

Figure 11.11. Adolescent suicide. (a) The suicide rate for adolescents and young adults (15–24 years old) has increased in recent decades far more than the suicide rate for the population as a whole. (b) Nonetheless, suicide rates remain lower for this youthful age group than for older age groups. [Data from *Statistical Abstract of the United States,* 1990, and *Monthly Vital Statistics Report,* January 7, 1993]

lence? Overall, the consensus of the experts appears to be that it is not (Petersen, 1988). The increase in adolescent suicide is a disturbing social tragedy that requires attention from parents, schools, and the helping professions (see the Chapter 14 Application for a discussion of suicide prevention). But even with the recent increases in suicidal behavior, only a small minority of adolescents attempt suicide (Meehan et al., 1992).

What about the remainder of the adolescent population? Research suggests that most teenagers navigate through adolescence without any more turmoil than one is likely to encounter in other periods of life (Hauser & Bowlds, 1990; Offer et al., 1988). Although turbulence and turmoil are not *universal* features of adolescence, challenging adaptations *do* have to be made during this period. In particular, most adolescents struggle to some extent in their effort to achieve a sound sense of identity.

The Search for Identity

Erik Erikson was especially interested in personality development during adolescence, which is the fifth of the eight major life stages he described. The psychosocial crisis during this stage pits *identity* against *confusion* as potential outcomes. According to Erikson (1968), the main challenge of adolescence is the struggle to form a clear sense of identity. This struggle involves working out a stable concept of oneself as a unique individual and embracing an ideology or system of values that provides a sense of direction. In Erikson's view, adolescents grapple with questions such as "Who am I, and where am I going in life?"

Erikson recognized that the process of identity formation begins before adolescence and often extends beyond it, as his own life illustrates (Coles, 1970; Roazen, 1976). Erikson's mother, who was

Jewish, was abandoned by his Danish father before Erik's birth in 1902 in Germany. Within a few years, his mother married a Jewish doctor and the two of them raised Erik in the Jewish faith as Erik Homburger. Erik was viewed as a Jew by his schoolmates, but he was viewed as a gentile at his temple because of his decidedly Scandinavian appearance. Thus, Erikson struggled with identity confusion early in life.

During adolescence Erikson began to resist family pressures to study medicine. Instead, he wandered about Europe until he was 25, trying to "find himself" as an artist. His interest in psychoanalysis was sparked by an introduction to Sigmund Freud's youngest daughter, Anna, a pioneer of child psychoanalysis. After his psychoanalytic training, he moved to the United States. When he became a naturalized citizen in 1939, he changed his surname from Homburger to Erikson. Clearly, Erikson was struggling with the question of "Who am I?" well into adulthood. Small wonder, then, that he focused a great deal of attention on identity formation.

Although the struggle for a sense of identity neither begins nor ends in adolescence, it does tend to be especially intense during this period. Adolescents' increased concern about identity is probably due to the conjunction of several significant transitions (Lloyd, 1985). First, rapid physical changes stimulate thought about self-image during adolescence. Second, changes in cognitive processes (in Piaget's terminology, the arrival of formal operations) promote personal introspection. Third, decisions about vocational direction require self-contemplation.

Adolescents deal with identity formation in a variety of ways. According to James Marcia (1966, 1980), the presence or absence of *crisis* and *commitment* can combine in various ways to produce four different *identity statuses* (see Figure 11.12 on the next page). These are not stages

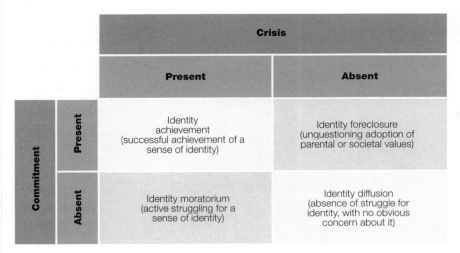

		Crisis	
		Present	**Absent**
Commitment	**Present**	Identity achievement (successful achievement of a sense of identity)	Identity foreclosure (unquestioning adoption of parental or societal values)
	Absent	Identity moratorium (active struggling for a sense of identity)	Identity diffusion (absence of struggle for identity, with no obvious concern about it)

Figure 11.12. Marcia's four identity statuses. According to Marcia (1980), the occurrence of an identity crisis and the development of personal commitments can combine into four possible identity statuses, as shown in this diagram.

that people pass through, but orientations that may occur at a particular time. An individual may get locked into one of these patterns or go through several at various times. Marcia's four identity statuses are as follows:

• *Foreclosure* is a premature commitment to visions, values, and roles prescribed by one's parents. This path allows a person to circumvent much of the "struggle" for an identity. However, it may backfire and cause problems later.

• A *moratorium* involves delaying commitment for a while to experiment with alternative ideologies and careers. Such experimentation can be valuable. Unfortunately, some people remain indefinitely in what should be a temporary phase.

• *Identity diffusion* is a state of rudderless apathy. Some people simply refuse to confront the challenge of charting a life course and committing to an ideology. Although this stance allows them to evade the struggle, the lack of direction can become problematic.

• *Identity achievement* involves arriving at a sense of self and direction after some consideration of alternative possibilities. Commitments have the strength of some conviction, although they're not absolutely irrevocable.

Erikson, Marcia, and many other theorists believe that adequate identity formation is a cornerstone of sound psychological health. Identity confusion can interfere with important developmental transitions that should happen during the adult years, as you'll see in the next section, which explores developmental trends during adulthood.

THE EXPANSE OF ADULTHOOD

As people progress through adulthood, they periodically ask themselves, "How am I doing for my age?" In pondering this question, they are likely to be influenced by their social clocks. **A *social clock* is a person's notion of a developmental schedule that specifies what he or she should have accomplished by certain points in life.** For example, if you feel that you should be married by the time you're 30, that belief creates a marker on your social clock. Social clocks are personalized to some degree but are very much a product of one's culture. Social clocks may influence the stressfulness of various life changes. Important transitions that come too early or too late according to one's social clock produce more stress than transitions that occur "on time" (Chiriboga, 1987). In particular, it appears that lagging behind one's personal schedule in regard to certain achievements produces frustration and reduced self-esteem (Helson, Mitchell, & Moane, 1984). Thus, many people pay great heed to their social clocks as they proceed through adulthood. With this thought in mind, let's look at some of the major developmental transitions in adult life.

Personality Development

In recent years, research on adult personality development has been dominated by one key question: How stable is personality over the life span? We'll look at this issue, the question of the midlife crisis, and Erikson's view of adulthood in our discussion of personality development in the adult years.

The Question of Stability

At midlife, Jerry Rubin went from being an outraged, radical political activist to being a subdued, conventional Wall Street businessman. His transformation illustrates that major personality changes sometimes occur during adulthood. But how common are such changes? Is a grouchy 20-year-old going to be a grouchy 40-year-old and a grouchy 65-year-old? Or can the grouchy young adult become a mellow senior citizen?

After tracking subjects through adulthood, many researchers have been impressed by the amount of change observed. Roger Gould (1975) studied two samples of men and women and concluded that the evolution of personality continues through the fifth decade of life. In a study following women from their college years through their 40s, Helson and Moane (1987) found that "personality does change from youth to middle age in consistent and often predictable ways."

In contrast, many other researchers have been struck by the persistence and durability they have found in personality. The general conclusion that emerged from several longitudinal studies based on large samples and objective assessments of personality was that personality tends to be quite stable over periods of 20 to 40 years (Block, 1981; Costa & McCrae, 1994). These studies found that personality in early adulthood was an excellent predictor of personality right through to late adulthood.

In sum, researchers assessing the stability of personality in adulthood have reached very different conclusions (Kogan, 1990). How can these contradictory conclusions be reconciled? This appears to be one of those debates in which researchers are eyeing the same findings—but from different perspectives. Hence, some conclude that the glass is half full, whereas others conclude that it's half empty. In his discussion of this controversy, Lawrence Pervin (1994) concludes that personality is characterized by *both* stability and change. It appears that some personality traits (such as emotional stability, extraversion, and assertiveness) tend to remain stable, while others (such as masculinity and femininity) tend to change systematically as people grow older (Conley, 1985; Helson & Stewart, 1994).

The Question of the Midlife Crisis

There has also been a spirited debate about whether most people go through a *midlife crisis*. The two most influential studies of adult development in the 1970s both concluded that a midlife crisis is a normal transition experienced by a majority of people. Daniel Levinson and his colleagues (1978) found that most of their subjects (all men) went through a midlife crisis around the ages of 40 to 45. This transition was marked by reappraisal of one's life and emotional turmoil. Roger Gould (1978) found that people tended to go through a midlife crisis between the ages of 35 and 45. Gould's subjects reported feeling pressed by time. They heard their social clocks ticking loudly as they struggled to achieve their life goals.

Since the landmark studies of Levinson and Gould, many other researchers have questioned whether the midlife crisis is a normal developmental transition. A host of studies have failed to detect an increase in emotional turbulence at midlife (Eisler & Ragsdale, 1992; Roberts & New-

Major transitions in adulthood are common, as illustrated by the life of one-time radical Jerry Rubin.

ton, 1987). How can we explain this discrepancy? Levinson and Gould both depended primarily on interview and case study methods to gather their data. As we noted in Chapter 2, when knitting together impressionistic case studies, it is easy for investigators to see what they expect to see. Given that the midlife crisis has long been part of developmental folklore, Levinson and Gould may have been prone to interpret their case study data in this light (McCrae & Costa, 1984). In any case, investigators relying on more objective measures of emotional stability have found signs of midlife crises in a distinct minority of subjects (McCrae & Costa, 1990). Thus, it's clear that the fabled midlife crisis is not universal, and it may not even be typical.

Erikson's View of Adulthood

Insofar as personality changes during the adult years, Erik Erikson's (1963) theory offers some clues about the kinds of changes people can expect. In his eight-stage model of development over the life span, Erikson divided adulthood into three stages (see again Table 11.2):

INTIMACY VERSUS ISOLATION In early adulthood, the key concern is whether one can develop the capacity to share intimacy with others. Successful resolution of the challenges in this stage should promote empathy and openness, rather than shrewdness and manipulativeness.

GENERATIVITY VERSUS SELF-ABSORPTION In middle adulthood, the key challenge is to acquire a genuine concern for the welfare of future generations, which results in providing unselfish guidance to younger people. Self-absorption is characterized by self-indulgent concerns with meeting one's own needs and desires.

INTEGRITY VERSUS DESPAIR During the retirement years, the challenge is to avoid the tendency to dwell on the mistakes of the past and on one's imminent death. People need to find meaning and satisfaction in their lives, rather than wallow in bitterness and resentment.

Transitions in Family Life

Many of the important transitions in adulthood involve changes in family responsibilities and relationships. Everyone emerges from a family, and most people go on to form their own families. However, the transitional period during which young adults are "between families" until they form a new family is being prolonged by more and more people. The percentage of young adults who are postponing marriage until their late twenties or early thirties has risen dramatically (Sporakowski, 1988). This trend is probably the result of a number of factors. Chief among them are the availability of new career options for women, increased educational requirements in the world of work, and increased emphasis on personal autonomy. Remaining single is a much more acceptable option today than it was a few decades ago. The classic stereotype of single people, which depicted them as lonely, frustrated, and unchosen, is gradually evaporating (Stein, 1989). Nonetheless, over 90% of adults eventually marry.

Adjusting to Marriage

The newly married couple usually settle into their roles as husband and wife gradually. Difficulties with this transition are more likely when spouses come into a marriage with different expectations about marital roles (Kitson & Sussman, 1982). Unfortunately, substantial differences in role expectations seem particularly likely in this era of transition in gender roles. For instance, males differ from females in their view of what equality

in marriage means. When the subjects in one survey (Machung, 1989) were asked to define an egalitarian marriage, half the men could not. The other half defined it in purely psychological terms, saying a marriage is "equal" if it is based on mutual understanding and trust. The women were considerably more concrete and task oriented. They defined marital equality in terms of an equal sharing of chores and responsibilities. However, the evidence indicates that such equality is extremely rare. As Figure 11.13 shows, wives are still doing the bulk of the housework in America, even when they are employed outside the home (Berardo, Shehan, & Leslie, 1987; Blair & Johnson, 1992). Obviously, women's and men's marital role expectations often are at odds.

In general, however, the first few years of married life tend to be characterized by great happiness—the proverbial "marital bliss." As Figure 11.14 shows, spouses' satisfaction with their relationship tends to be relatively high early in marriage, before the arrival of the first child (Glenn, 1990). This prechildren phase used to be rather short for most newly married couples. Traditionally, couples just *assumed* that they would proceed to have children. However, in recent years more couples have found themselves struggling to decide *whether* to have children. Often, this decision occurs after numerous postponements, when the couple finally acknowledges that "the right time" is never going to arrive (Crane, 1985). People who choose to not have children cite factors such as the financial burdens of having children, the loss of educational or career opportunities, reduced leisure time, and worry about the responsibilities associated with child rearing (Bram, 1985; Seccombe, 1991).

Adjusting to Parenthood

Although an increasing number of people are choosing to not have children, the vast majority

Figure 11.13. Who does the housework? Berardo, Shehan, and Leslie (1987) studied the proportion of housework done by husbands, wives, and other family members. As these pie charts show, wives continue to do a highly disproportionate share of the housework, even if they are employed.

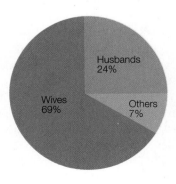

Wife employed

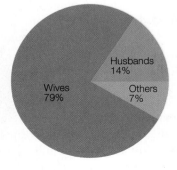

Wife not employed

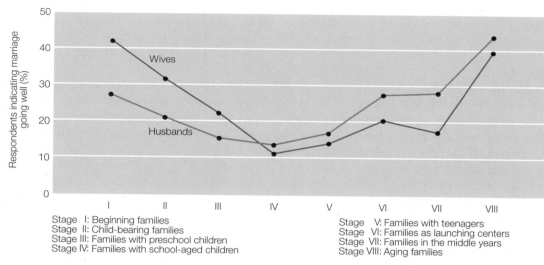

Figure 11.14. Marital satisfaction across the family life cycle. This graph depicts the percentage of husbands and wives who said their marriage was going well "all the time" at various stages of the family life cycle. Rollins and Feldman (1970) broke the family life cycle into eight stages. The U-shaped relationship shown here has been found in other studies as well.

Stage I: Beginning families
Stage II: Child-bearing families
Stage III: Families with preschool children
Stage IV: Families with school-aged children

Stage V: Families with teenagers
Stage VI: Families as launching centers
Stage VII: Families in the middle years
Stage VIII: Aging families

of married couples continue to plan on becoming parents (Roosa, 1988). Despite the challenges involved in rearing children, most parents report no regret about their choice and rate parenthood as a very positive experience (Demo, 1992). Nonetheless, the arrival of the first child represents a *major* transition. The disruption of old routines can create a full-fledged crisis. The new mother, already physically exhausted by the birth process, is particularly prone to postpartum stress (Harriman, 1986). Wives are especially vulnerable when they have to shoulder the major burden of infant care (Kalmuss, Davidson, & Cushman, 1992).

Crisis during the transition to first parenthood is far from universal, however (Ruble et al., 1988). Couples who have high levels of intimacy, closeness, and commitment tend to experience a smoother transition to parenthood (Lewis, Owen, & Cox, 1988). Another key to making this transition less stressful may be to have *realistic expectations* about parental responsibilities. Belsky (1985) found that stress was greatest in new parents who had overestimated the benefits and underestimated the costs of their new role.

As children grow up, parental influence over them tends to decline, and the early years of parenting—that once seemed so difficult—are often recalled with fondness. When youngsters reach adolescence and seek to establish their own identities, gradual realignments occur in parent-child relationships. Parent-adolescent relations generally are not as bitter or contentious as widely assumed, but conflicts over values are common, and power struggles frequently ensue (Silverberg, Tennenbaum, & Jacob, 1992). When conflict does occur, mothers often are more adversely affected by it than fathers (Steinberg & Silverberg, 1987).

This may be because women's self-esteem tends to be more closely tied to the quality of their family relationships. Ironically, although recent studies have shown that adolescence is not as turbulent or difficult for youngsters as once believed, their parents *are* stressed out. Parents overwhelmingly rate adolescence as the most difficult stage of child rearing (Gecas & Seff, 1990).

Adjusting to the Empty Nest

When parents have launched all their children into the adult world, they find themselves faced with an "empty nest." This was formerly thought to be a difficult period of transition for many parents, especially mothers familiar only with the maternal role. Today, however, more women have experience with other roles outside the home, and most look forward to their "liberation" from child-rearing responsibilities (Reinke et al., 1985).

The postparental period often provides couples with new freedom to devote attention to each other. Many couples take advantage of this opportunity by traveling or developing new leisure interests. Thus, as offspring strike out on their own, couples' marital satisfaction tends to start climbing to higher levels once again (Brubaker, 1990). It tends to remain fairly high until one of the spouses (usually the husband) dies.

Aging and Physical Changes

People obviously experience many physical changes as they progress through adulthood. In both sexes, hair tends to thin out and become gray, and many males confront receding hairlines and baldness. To the dismay of many, the proportion of body fat tends to increase with age. Overall, weight tends to increase in most adults through the mid-50s, when a gradual decline may begin. These changes have little functional significance, but in our youth-oriented society, they often lead people to view themselves as less attractive.

The number of active neurons in the brain declines during adulthood. The rate of neuronal loss is hard to measure and appears to vary in different parts of the brain (Duara, London, & Rapoport, 1985). There is no clear evidence that this gradual loss of brain cells has any functional significance (LaRue & Jarvik, 1982). It doesn't appear to contribute to *senile dementia,* **an abnormal deterioration in mental faculties seen in the elderly.** Senile dementia occurs in about 15% of people over age 65 (Elias, Elias, & Elias, 1990).

In the sensory domain, the key developmental changes occur in vision and hearing. The proportion of people with 20/20 visual acuity declines with age. Farsightedness, difficulty adapting to darkness, and poor recovery from glare are common among older people (Fozard, 1990; Kline & Schieber, 1985). Hearing sensitivity begins declining gradually in early adulthood. Noticeable hearing losses requiring corrective treatment are apparent in about three-quarters of people over the age of 75 (Olsho, Harkins, & Lenhardt, 1985). These sensory losses could be problematic, but in modern society they can usually be compensated for with glasses and hearing aids.

Age-related changes also occur in hormonal functioning during adulthood. Among women, these changes lead to *menopause.* This ending of menstrual periods, accompanied by a loss of fertility, typically occurs in the early 50s. Not long ago, menopause was thought to be almost universally accompanied by severe emotional strain. However, it is now clear that women's reactions to menopause vary greatly, depending on their expectations (Matthews, 1992). Most women experience little psychological distress (McKinlay, McKinlay, & Brambilla, 1987). Although people sometimes talk about "male menopause," men don't really go through an equivalent experience. Middle-aged males experience hormonal changes, but they're very gradual.

Aging and Cognitive Changes

The current evidence suggests that general intelligence is fairly stable throughout most of adulthood. However, a small decline often begins after age 60 (Hertzog & Schaie, 1988; Schaie, 1990). Also, people's IQ scores tend to drop sharply within the last several years before death (Berg, 1987). This phenomenon is referred to as "terminal drop." It probably reflects the effects of declining health in those who are approaching their death.

Numerous studies report decreases in older adults' memory capabilities (Baltes & Kliegl, 1992; Hultsch & Dixon, 1990). However, most of these studies have asked subjects to memorize simple lists of words or paired associations. Older subjects often find these artificial laboratory tasks meaningless and uninteresting. Investigators have only recently begun to study age-related changes in memory for more realistic content. There *do* seem to be some modest decreases in memory for prose, television shows, conversations, past activities, and personal plans (Kausler, 1985), but the memory losses associated with aging are moderate in size and are *not* universal.

In the cognitive domain, aging seems to take its toll on *speed* first. Many studies indicate that speed in learning, solving problems, and processing information tends to decline with age (Drachman, 1986). These changes probably reflect reductions in the effectiveness of working memory, which appear to be largely mediated by decreases in raw processing speed (Salthouse & Babcock, 1991). Although additional data are needed, some evidence suggests that the erosion of processing speed may be a gradual, lengthy trend commencing in middle adulthood. The general nature of this trend (across differing tasks) suggests that it may be due to age-related changes in neurological functioning (Cerella, 1990; Myerson et al., 1990). Alternatively, it could reflect increased cautiousness among older adults (Reese & Rodeheaver, 1985). Although mental speed declines with age, problem-solving ability remains largely unimpaired if older people are given adequate time to compensate for their reduced speed.

It should be emphasized that many people remain capable of great intellectual accomplishments well into their later years (Simonton, 1990). This reality was verified in a study of scholarly, scientific, and artistic productivity that examined lifelong patterns of work among 738 men who lived at least through the age of 79 (Dennis, 1966). Figure 11.15 plots the percentage of professional works completed by these men in their 20s, 30s, 40s, 50s, 60s, and 70s. As you can see, the 40s decade was the most productive in most professions. However, productivity was remarkably stable through the 60s and even the 70s in many areas.

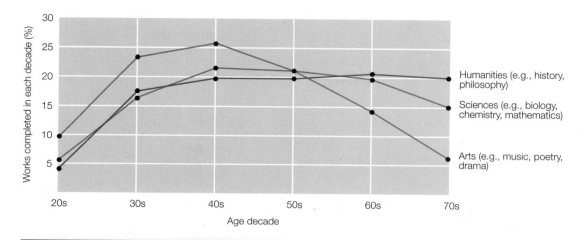

Figure 11.15. Professional productivity over the life span. Dennis (1966) compiled the percentage of professional works completed in each decade of life by 738 men who lived to be at least 79 years old. Productivity peaked in the 40s decade, but professional output remained strong through the 60s decade and, for the humanities and sciences, even into the 70s decade.

PUTTING IT IN PERSPECTIVE

Five of our seven integrative themes surfaced to some degree in our coverage of human development. We saw theoretical diversity in our discussions of cognitive development and personality development. We saw that psychology evolves in a sociohistorical context, investigating complex, real-world issues—such as the controversies over the effects of prenatal health care and day care—that emerge as our society changes. We encountered multifactorial causation of behavior in the development of temperament and attachment, among other things. We saw cultural invariance and cultural diversity in our examination of attachment, motor development, cognitive development, and moral development.

But above all else, we saw how heredity and environment jointly mold behavior. We've encountered the dual influence of heredity and environment before, but this theme is rich in complexity, and each chapter draws out different aspects and implications. Our discussion of development amplified the point that genetics and experience work *interactively* to shape behavior. What does it mean to say that heredity and environment interact? In the language of science, an interaction means that the effects of one variable depend on the effects of another. In other words, heredity and environment do not operate independently. Children with "difficult" temperaments will elicit different reactions from different parents, depending on the parents' personalities and expectations. Likewise, a particular pair of parents will affect different children in different ways, depending on the inborn characteristics of the children. An interplay, or feedback loop, exists between biological and environmental factors.

All aspects of development are shaped jointly by heredity and experience. We often estimate their relative weight or influence, as if we could cleanly divide behavior into genetic and environmental components. Although we can't really carve up behavior that neatly, such comparisons can be of great theoretical interest, as you'll see in our upcoming Application, which discusses the nature and origins of gender differences in behavior.

AN OVERVIEW OF HUMAN DEVELOPMENT

Stage of development	Infancy (birth–2)	

Physical and sensorimotor development

Rapid brain growth; 75% of adult brain weight is attained by age 2.

Ability to localize sounds is apparent at birth; ability to recognize parent's voice within first week.

Rapid improvement occurs in visual acuity; depth perception is clearly present by 6 months, perhaps earlier.

Landmarks in motor development: infants sit without support around 6 months, walk around 12–14 months, run freely around 2 years.

Major stage theories	Piaget	Sensorimotor	
	Kohlberg	Premoral	
	Erikson	Trust vs. distrust	Autonomy vs. shame
	Freud (see Chapter 12)	Oral	Anal

Cognitive development

Object permanence gradually develops; by age 2, infants understand that absent objects continue to exist.

Infant shows orienting response (pupils dilate, head turns) and attention to new stimulus, habituation (reduced orienting response) to repeated stimulus.

Babbling increasingly resembles spoken language.

First word is used around age 1; holophrases (one-word "sentences") are used around 18 months; frequent overextensions (words applied too broadly) occur.

Social and personality development

Temperamental individuality is established by 2–3 months; infants tend to be easy, difficult, or slow to warm up.

Attachment to caregiver(s) is usually evident around 6–8 months; secure attachment facilitates exploration.

"Stranger anxiety" often appears around 6–7 months; separation anxiety peaks around 14–18 months.

Information compiled by Barbara Hansen Lemme, College of DuPage

Early childhood (2–6)	Middle childhood (6–12)

Early childhood
(2–6)

Connections among neurons continue to increase in density.

Visual acuity reaches 20/20.

Bladder and bowel control is established.

Hand preference is usually solidified by 3–4 years; coordination improves; children learn to dress themselves.

Middle childhood
(6–12)

In girls, growth spurt begins around age 10½, bringing dramatic increases in height and weight.

Level of pituitary activity and sex hormones increases.

In girls, puberty begins around age 12; menstruation starts.

Girls' secondary sexual characteristics (such as breast development and widening hips) begin to emerge.

Preoperational	Concrete operational
Preconventional	Conventional
Initiative vs. guilt	Industry vs. inferiority
Phallic	Latency

Development of symbolic thought (use of symbols to represent objects and activities begins); thought is marked by egocentrism (limited ability to view world from another's perspective).

Thought is marked by centration (inability to focus on more than one aspect of a problem at a time) and irreversibility (inability to mentally undo an action).

Telegraphic speech (omitting nonessential words) appears at 2–3 years; syntax is well developed by age 5; vocabulary increases dramatically.

Short-term memory capacity increases from two items at age 2 to five items around age 6–7; attention span improves.

Conservation (understanding that physical qualities can remain constant in spite of transformations in shape) is gradually mastered.

Child develops decentration (ability to focus on more than one feature of a problem at a time) and reversibility (ability to mentally undo an action).

Metalinguistic awareness (ability to reflect on use of language) leads to play with language, use of puns, riddles, metaphors.

Long-term memory improves with increasing use of encoding strategies of rehearsal and organization.

Child realizes that gender does not change and begins to learn gender roles and form gender identity; social behavior is influenced by observational learning, resulting in imitation.

Child progresses from parallel (side-by-side, noninteractive) play to cooperative play.

Social world is extended beyond family; first friendships are formed.

Child experiences great increase in social skills, improved understanding of others' feelings; social world is dominated by same-sex peer relationships.

Role-taking skills emerge; fantasy is basis for thoughts about vocations and jobs.

Altruism tends to increase, aggression tends to decrease; aggression tends to become verbal rather than physical, hostile more than instrumental.

Adolescence
(12–20)

In boys, growth spurt begins around age 12½, bringing dramatic increases in height and weight.

Level of pituitary activity and hormones increases.

In boys, puberty begins around age 14; boys become capable of ejaculation.

Boys' secondary sexual characteristics (such as voice change and growth of facial hair) begin to emerge.

Young adulthood
(20–40)

Reaction time and muscular strength peak in early to mid-20s.

External signs of aging begin to show in 30s; skin loses elasticity; hair is thinner, more likely to be gray.

Maximum functioning of all body systems, including senses, attained; slow decline begins in 20s.

Lowered metabolic rate contributes to increased body fat relative to muscle; gain in weight is common.

Formal operations

Postconventional (if attained)

Identity vs. confusion | Intimacy vs. isolation

Genital

Deductive reasoning improves; problem solving becomes more systematic, with alternative possibilities considered before solution is selected.

Thought becomes more abstract and reflective; individual develops ability to mentally manipulate abstract concepts as well as concrete objects.

Individual engages in idealistic contemplation of hypotheticals, "what could be."

Long-term memory continues to improve as elaboration is added to encoding strategies.

Intellectual abilities and speed of information processing are relatively stable.

Greater emphasis is on application, rather than acquisition, of knowledge.

There is some evidence of a trend toward dialectical thought (ideas stimulate opposing ideas), leading to more contemplation of contradictions, pros and cons.

Person experiences increased interactions with opposite-sex peers; dating begins.

Attention is devoted to identify formation, questions such as "Who am I?" and "What do I want out of life?"

Realistic considerations about abilities and training requirements become more influential in thoughts about vocations and jobs.

Energies are focused on intimate relationships, learning to live with marriage partner, starting a family, managing a home.

Trial period is given for occupational choices, followed by stabilization of vocational commitment; emphasis is on self-reliance, becoming one's own person.

For many, close relationship develops with mentor (older person who serves as role model, advisor, and teacher).

Middle adulthood
(40–65)

Changes occur in vision: increased farsightedness and difficulty recovering from glare; slower dark adaptation.

Number of active brain cells declines, but significance of this neural loss is unclear.

In women, menopause occurs around age 50; in both sexes, sexual activity declines, although capacity for arousal changes only slightly.

Sensitivity to high-frequency sounds decreases especially in males after age 55.

Late adulthood
(65 and older)

Height decreases slightly because of changes in vertebral column; decline in weight also common.

Sensitivity of vision, hearing, and taste noticeably decreases.

Chronic diseases, especially heart disease, cancer, and stroke, increase.

Rate of aging is highly individualized.

Generativity vs. self-absorption

Integrity vs. despair

There is some evidence for a trend toward improved judgment or "wisdom" based on accumulation of life experiences.

Effectiveness of retrieval from long-term memory begins slow decline, usually not noticeable until after age 55.

Individual experiences gradual decline in speed of learning, problem solving, and information processing.

In spite of decreased speed in cognitive processes, intellectual productivity and problem-solving skills usually remain stable.

Individual experiences continued gradual decline in cognitive speed and effectiveness of long-term memory.

Intellectual productivity depends on factors such as health and lifestyle; many people in 60s and 70s remain quite productive.

Decision making tends to become more cautious.

Terminal drop: a marked decrease in intellectual performance occurs in the 2–3 years preceding death.

Midlife transition around age 40 leads to reflection, increased awareness of mortality and passage of time; may or may not be personal crisis.

"Sandwich generation" is caught between needs of aging parents and children reaching adulthood.

Career development peaks; there is some tendency to shift energy from career concerns to family concerns.

Physical changes associated with aging require adjustments that affect life satisfaction.

Marital satisfaction often increases, but eventually death of spouse presents coping challenge.

Living arrangements are a significant determinant of satisfaction, as 60–90% of time is spent at home.

Understanding Gender Differences

Answer the following "true" or "false."

___ **1** Females are more socially oriented than males.

___ **2** Males outperform females on spatial tasks.

___ **3** Females are more irrational than males.

___ **4** Males are less sensitive to nonverbal cues than females.

___ **5** Females are more emotional than males.

Are there genuine behavioral differences between the sexes similar to those mentioned above? If so, why do these differences exist? How do they develop? These are the complex and controversial questions that we'll explore in this Application.

Before proceeding further, we need to clarify how some key terms are used, as terminology in this area of research has been evolving and remains a source of confusion (Deaux, 1993; Unger & Crawford, 1993). *Sex* **refers to the biologically based categories of female and male.** In contrast, *gender* **refers to culturally constructed distinctions between femininity and masculinity.** Individuals are *born* female or male. However, they *become* feminine or masculine through complex developmental processes that take years to unfold.

The statements at the beginning of this Application reflect popular gender stereotypes in our society. *Gender stereotypes* **are widely held beliefs about females' and males' abilities, person-** ality traits, and social behavior. Table 11.5 lists some characteristics that are part of the masculine and feminine stereotypes in North American society. The table shows something you may have already noticed on your own. The male stereotype is much more flattering, suggesting that men have virtually cornered the market on competence and rationality. After all, everyone knows that females are more dependent, emotional, irrational, submissive, and talkative than males. Right? Or is that not the case? Let's look at the research.

Table 11.5 Elements of Traditional Gender Stereotypes	
Masculine	Feminine
Active	Aware of others' feelings
Adventurous	Considerate
Aggressive	Creative
Ambitious	Cries easily
Competitive	Devotes self to others
Dominant	Emotional
Independent	Enjoys art and music
Leadership qualities	Excitable in a crisis
Likes math and science	Expresses tender feelings
Makes decisions easily	Feelings hurt
Mechanical aptitude	Gentle
Not easily influenced	Home oriented
Outspoken	Kind
Persistent	Likes children
Self-confident	Neat
Skilled in business	Needs approval
Stands up under pressure	Tactful
Takes a stand	Understanding

Source: Adapted from Ruble (1983)

How Do the Sexes Differ in Behavior?

Gender differences **are actual disparities between the sexes in typical behavior or average ability.** Mountains of research, literally thousands of studies, exist on gender differences. It's difficult to sort through this huge body of research, but fortunately, many review articles on gender differences have been published in recent years. As noted in Chapter 2, *review articles* summarize and reconcile the findings of a large number of studies on a specific issue.

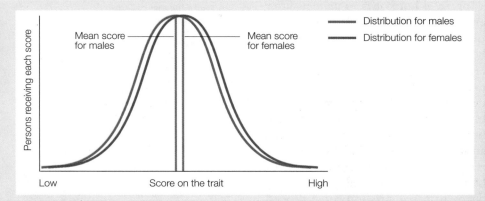

Figure 11.16. The nature of gender differences. Gender differences are group differences that indicate little about individuals because of the great overlap between the groups. For a given trait, one sex may score higher on the average, but far more variation occurs within each sex than between the sexes.

What does this research show? Are the stereotypes of males and females accurate? For the most part, no. The research indicates that genuine behavioral differences *do* exist between the sexes, but they are far fewer in number than stereotypes suggest. As you'll see, only two of the differences mentioned in our opening true-false questions (the even-numbered items) have been supported by the research.

Cognitive Abilities

In the cognitive domain, it appears that there are three genuine—albeit very small—gender differences. First, on the average, females tend to exhibit slightly better *verbal skills* than males (Halpern, 1992). However, recent studies suggest that the gender gap in verbal ability has been shrinking since the 1970s and is now so small it is of negligible importance (Hyde & Linn, 1988). Second, starting during high school, males show a slight advantage on tests of *mathematical ability*. When all students are compared, males' advantage is quite small and appears to be declining (Feingold, 1988a; Hyde, Fennema, & Lamon, 1990). However, at the high end of the ability distribution, the gender gap is larger, as far more males than females are found to be mathematically precocious (Benbow, 1988). Third, starting in the grade-school years, males tend to score higher than

females on various measures of *visual-spatial ability* (Halpern, 1992). Once again, these gender differences are rather small and some of them appear to be shrinking (Linn & Hyde, 1989).

Social Behavior

In regard to social behavior, research findings support the existence of three more gender differences. First, studies indicate that males tend to be more *aggressive* than females, both verbally and physically (Eagly, 1987; Hyde, 1986). This disparity shows up early in childhood. Its continuation into adulthood is supported by the fact that men account for a grossly disproportionate number of the violent crimes in our society (Kenrick, 1987). Second, there are gender differences in *nonverbal communication*. The evidence indicates that females are more sensitive than males to subtle nonverbal cues (Hall, 1990). Females also smile and gaze at others more than males do (Hall & Halberstadt, 1986). Third, two separate reviews conclude that gender differences occur in *influenceability* (Becker, 1986; Eagly & Carli, 1981). That is, females appear to be slightly more susceptible to persuasion and conforming to group pressure than males are.

Some Qualifications

Although there are some genuine gender differences in behavior, bear in mind that

these are *group* differences that indicate nothing about individuals. Essentially, research results compare the "average man" with the "average woman." However, you are—and every individual is—unique. The average female and male are ultimately figments of our imagination. Furthermore, the genuine group differences noted are relatively small. Figure 11.16 shows how scores on a trait, perhaps verbal ability, might be distributed for men and women. Although the group averages are detectably different, you can see the great variability within each group (sex) and the huge overlap between the two group distributions.

Thus, the behavioral differences between males and females are fewer and smaller than popular stereotypes suggest. Many supposed gender differences have turned out to be more mythical than real (Tavris, 1992). Nonetheless, there are some genuine gender differences that require explanation, which is the matter we'll attend to next.

Biological Origins of Gender Differences

What accounts for the development of the gender differences that do exist? To what degree are they the product of learning or of biology? This question is yet another manifestation of the nature versus nurture issue. Investigations of the biological origins of gender differences have centered on hormones and brain organization.

Hormones

To investigate the possible contribution of prenatal hormones to gender differences, John Money and his colleagues tracked the development of a small number of females who were exposed to high levels of androgens (the principal class of male hormones) during their prenatal development. The girls were born to mothers who either had a hormonal malfunction during pregnancy or were given an androgenlike drug to prevent miscarriage. These *androgenized females* were born with masculinized genitals. The degree of masculinization varied, depending on the extent of prenatal hormonal imbalance. In some cases, the masculinization was so subtle that it went unnoticed for months and even years. Once noticed, most cases were treated with a combination of hormone (cortisone) therapy and surgical correction of the genitals.

Money and his colleagues wondered whether the prenatal dose of male hormones had affected the behavioral tendencies of these androgenized females. When they researched this question, they found that the androgenized females showed "tomboyish" interests in vigorous outdoor activities and had preferences for male playmates and "male" toys (Money & Erhardt, 1972).

The findings on androgenized females suggested to many theorists that prenatal hormones shape gender differences in humans. But there are a few problems with this evidence (Huston, 1983). First, it's always dangerous to draw conclusions about the general population based on a handful of people who have an abnormal condition. Second, most of the androgenized girls received drug treatments (cortisone) for their condition. These treatments could have influenced their activity levels. Third, the girls were born with masculine-looking genitals that often were not surgically corrected until age 2 or 3. Hence, their families may not have reared them quite the same way

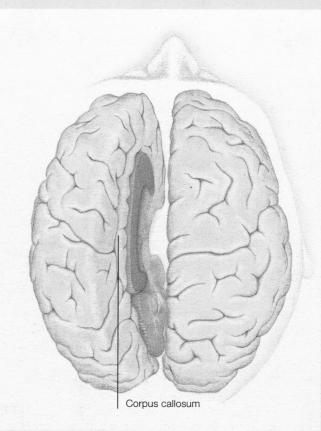

Figure 11.17. The cerebral hemispheres and the corpus callosum. As explained in Chapter 3, the cerebral cortex is divided into left and right halves, called the cerebral hemispheres, which are specialized (to some extent) to handle different cognitive functions. In this drawing the cerebral hemispheres have been "pulled apart" to reveal the corpus callosum. This band of fibers is the communication bridge between the right and left halves of the human brain. Some theorists have related gender differences in cognitive abilities to sexual disparities in hemispheric specialization and the size of the corpus callosum.

Corpus callosum

they would have reared "normal" girls. In light of these considerations, research on androgenized females cannot conclusively demonstrate that prenatal hormones mold gender differences in behavior.

Brain Organization

Interpretive problems have also cropped up in efforts to link gender differences to specialization of the cerebral hemispheres in the brain (see Figure 11.17). As you may recall from Chapter 3, in most people the left hemisphere is more actively involved in verbal processing, whereas the right hemisphere is more active in visual-spatial processing (Sperry, 1982; Springer & Deutsch, 1993). After these findings surfaced, theorists began to wonder whether this division of labor in the brain might be related to gender differences in verbal and spatial skills. Consequently, they began looking for sex-related disparities in brain organization.

Some thought-provoking findings *have* been reported. For instance, some stud-

ies have found that *males tend to exhibit more cerebral specialization than females* (Bryden, 1988; Hines, 1990). In other words, there's a trend for males to depend more heavily than females do on the left hemisphere in verbal processing and more heavily on the right in spatial processing. Differences between males and females have also been found in the size of the corpus callosum, the band of fibers that connects the two hemispheres of the brain (Hines, 1990). Some studies suggest that *females tend to have a larger corpus callosum*, which might allow for better interhemispheric transfer of information, which, in turn, might underlie the more bilateral organization of females' brains (see Figure 11.17). Thus, some theorists have concluded that differences between the sexes in brain organization are responsible for gender differences in verbal and spatial ability (Geschwind & Galaburda, 1987; Kimura, 1987).

This idea is intriguing, but psychologists have a long way to go before they can explain gender differences in terms of right brain/left brain specialization. Studies have not been consistent in finding that males have more specialized brain organization than females (Halpern, 1992; Kinsbourne, 1980), and the finding of a larger corpus callosum in females has proven difficult to replicate (Bleier, 1988). Moreover, even if men *do* show stronger cerebral specialization than women, no one is really sure just how that would account for the observed gender differences in cognitive abilities. It seems peculiar that strong specialization would produce an advantage for males on one kind of task (spatial) and a disadvantage on another kind of task (verbal). Thus, the theory linking cerebral specialization to gender differences in mental abilities remains highly speculative.

In summary, researchers have made relatively little progress in their efforts to document the biological roots of gender differences in behavior. The idea that "anatomy is destiny" has proven difficult to demonstrate. Theorists remain convinced that biological factors contribute to gender differences. However, the overall evidence, or rather the lack of it, suggests that biology must play a relatively minor role, creating predispositions that are largely shaped by experience. In contrast, efforts to link gender differences to disparities in the way males and females are reared have proven more fruitful.

Environmental Origins of Gender Differences

Socialization is the acquisition of the norms and behaviors expected of people in a particular society. It includes all the efforts made by a society to ensure that its members learn to behave in a manner that's considered appropriate. The socialization process has traditionally included efforts to train children about gender roles. *Gender roles* are expectations about what is appropriate behavior for each sex. Investigators have identified three key processes involved in the socialization of gender roles:

operant conditioning, observational learning, and self-socialization. First we'll examine these processes. Then we'll look at the principal sources of gender-role socialization: families, schools, and the media.

Operant Conditioning

In part, gender roles are shaped by the power of reward and punishment—the key processes in *operant conditioning*. Parents, teachers, peers, and others often reinforce (usually with tacit approval) "gender-appropriate" behavior and respond negatively to "gender-inappropriate" behavior (Fagot, Leinbach, & O'Boyle, 1992). If you're a man, you might recall getting hurt as a young boy and being told that "men don't cry." If you succeeded in inhibiting your crying, you may have earned an approving smile or even something tangible like an ice cream cone. The reinforcement probably strengthened your tendency to "act like a man" and suppress emotional displays. If you're a woman, chances are your crying wasn't discouraged as gender-inappropriate.

Observational Learning

Observational learning by children can lead to the imitation of adults' sex-

appropriate behavior. Children imitate both males and females, but most children tend to imitate same-sex role models more than opposite-sex role models (Bussey & Bandura, 1984; Perry & Bussey, 1979). Thus, imitation often leads young girls to play with dolls, dollhouses, and toy stoves. Young boys are more likely to tinker with toy trucks, miniature gas stations, or tool kits.

Self-Socialization

Children themselves are active agents in their own gender-role socialization. Several *cognitive theories* of gender-role development emphasize self-socialization (Bem, 1985; Kohlberg, 1966; Martin & Halverson, 1987). Self-socialization entails three steps. First, children learn to classify themselves as male or female and to recognize their sex as a permanent quality (around ages 5 to 7). Second, this self-categorization motivates them to value those characteristics and behaviors associated with their sex. Third, they strive to bring their behavior in line with what is considered gender-appropriate in their culture. In other words, children get involved in their own socialization, working diligently to discover the rules that are supposed to govern their behavior.

As more women enter traditionally male professions, what was once a novelty—female firefighters, construction workers, corporate officers—is now much more commonplace. The debate is over how such changes in roles are affecting man-woman relationships.

Sources of Gender-Role Socialization

There are three main sources of influence in gender-role socialization: families, schools, and the media. Of course, we are now in an era of transition in gender roles, so the generalizations that follow may say more about how you were socialized than about how children will be socialized in the future. We'll discuss this transition after describing the traditional picture.

FAMILIES A great deal of gender-role socialization takes place in the home. Fathers engage in more "rough-housing" play with their sons than with their daughters, even in infancy. As children grow, boys and girls are encouraged to play with different types of toys (Etaugh & Liss, 1992). Generally, boys have less leeway to play with "feminine" toys than girls do with "masculine" toys. When children are old enough to help with household chores, the assignments tend to depend on sex (McHale et al., 1990). For example, girls wash dishes and boys mow the lawn.

SCHOOLS Schools also contribute to the socialization of gender roles. Books that children use in learning to read influence their ideas about what is suitable behavior for males and females (Schau & Scott, 1984). Traditionally, males have been more likely to be portrayed as clever, heroic, and adventurous in these books, while females have been more likely to be shown doing domestic chores. As youngsters progress through the school system, they are often channeled in career directions considered appropriate for their sex (Read, 1991). For example, males have been more likely to be encouraged to study mathematics and to work toward becoming engineers or doctors. Females have often been encouraged to take classes in home economics and to work toward becoming nurses or homemakers.

MEDIA Television is another source of gender-role socialization. Television shows have traditionally depicted men and women in highly stereotypic ways (Signorielli, 1989). Women are often portrayed as submissive, passive, and emotional. Men are more likely to be portrayed as independent, assertive, and competent. Even commercials contribute to the socialization of gender roles (Bretl & Cantor, 1988). Women are routinely shown worrying about trivial matters such as a ring around their husband's shirt collar or the shine of their dishes. Music videos frequently portray women as sex objects, and these portrayals appear to influence viewers' attitudes about sexual conduct (Hansen & Hansen, 1988).

Gender Roles in Transition

Gender roles are in a period of transition in our society. Many women and men are rebelling against traditional role expectations based on sex. Many parents are trying to raise their children with fewer preconceived notions about how males and females "ought" to behave. Some social critics view this as a healthy trend because they believe that traditional roles have been too narrow and restrictive for both sexes (Bem, 1985; Goldberg, 1983). Such theorists argue that conventional sex roles lock people into rigid straitjackets that prevent them from realizing their full potential. Other social critics (Davidson, 1988; Gilder, 1986), believe that changes in gender roles may harm intimate relationships between men and women and hurt the quality of family life. Thus, vigorous debate continues about the effects of evolving gender roles.

Chapter 11 Review

KEY IDEAS

Progress Before Birth: Prenatal Development

♦ Prenatal development proceeds through the germinal, embryonic, and fetal stages as the zygote is differentiated into a human organism. During this period, development may be affected by maternal drug use, maternal malnutrition, and some maternal illnesses. Many problems can be avoided if expectant mothers have access to good health care.

The Wondrous Years of Childhood

♦ Motor development follows cephalocaudal (head-to-foot) and proximodistal (center-outward) trends and depends in part on physical growth, which appears to be more uneven than previously appreciated. Developmental norms for motor skills and other types of development are only group averages, and parents should not be alarmed if their children's progress does not match these norms exactly. Early motor development depends more on maturation than learning. However, cultural variations in the pacing of motor development show that both clearly play a role.

♦ Cross-sectional and longitudinal studies are both well suited to developmental research. Temperamental differences among children are apparent during the first few months of life. Thomas and Chess found that most infants could be classified as easy, slow-to-warm-up, or difficult children. These differences in temperament are fairly stable over time.

♦ Infants' attachments to their mothers develop gradually. Separation anxiety usually appears around six to eight months of age. Research shows that attachment emerges out of an interplay between infant and mother. Infant-mother attachments fall into three categories: secure, anxious-ambivalent, and avoidant. Bonding during the first few hours after birth does not appear to be crucial to secure attachment. The effects of day care on attachment are a source of concern, but the evidence is hotly debated. Cultural variations in child rearing can affect the patterns of attachment seen in a society.

♦ Erik Erikson's theory of personality development proposes that individuals evolve through eight stages over the life span. In each stage the person wrestles with changes (crises) in social relationships. Successful progress through the four childhood stages should yield a trustful, autonomous person with a sense of initiative and industry.

♦ According to Piaget's theory of cognitive development, the key advance during the sensorimotor period is the child's gradual recognition of the permanence of objects. The preoperational period is marked by certain deficiencies in thinking—notably, centration, irreversibility, and egocentrism. During the concrete operations period, children develop the ability to perform operations on mental representations, making them capable of conservation and hierarchical classification. Formal operations ushers in more abstract, systematic, and logical thought. Although critics have identified some problems with Piaget's theory, his work has greatly improved psychology's understanding of cognitive development.

♦ According to Kohlberg, moral reasoning progresses through three levels that are related to age and determined by cognitive development. Age-related progress in moral reasoning has been found in research, although there is a great deal of overlap between adjacent stages. Altruism and aggression, two important aspects of social behavior, tend to increase and decrease, respectively, with age.

The Transition of Adolescence

♦ The growth spurt at puberty is a prominent event involving the development of reproductive maturity and secondary sexual characteristics. Adolescence appears no more tumultuous than other periods of life, in spite of the recent surge in attempted suicide by adolescents.

♦ According to Erikson, the key challenge of adolescence is to make some progress toward a sense of identity. Marcia identified four patterns of identity formation: foreclosure, moratorium, identity diffusion, and identity achievement.

The Expanse of Adulthood

♦ During adulthood, personality is marked by both stability and change. Doubts have surfaced about whether a midlife crisis is a normal developmental transition. Many landmarks in adult development involve transitions in family relationships, including adjusting to marriage, parenthood, and the empty nest.

♦ During adulthood, age-related physical transitions include changes in appearance, neuron losses, sensory losses (especially in vision and hearing), and hormonal changes. Menopause is not as problematic as widely suggested. In the cognitive domain, mental speed declines first, followed in late adulthood by decreases in memory and problem-solving ability.

Putting It in Perspective

♦ Five of our seven integrative themes stood out in this chapter, including the value of theoretical diversity, the influence of cultural factors, the importance of sociohistorical contexts, and the inevitability of multifactorial causation. But above all else, our discussion of development showed how heredity and environment interactively shape behavior.

Application: Understanding Gender Differences

♦ Gender differences in behavior are fewer in number and smaller in magnitude than gender stereotypes suggest. Research reviews suggest that there are genuine gender differences in verbal ability, mathematical ability, spatial ability, aggression, nonverbal communication, and influenceability.

♦ There is research linking gender differences in humans to hormones and brain organization, but the research is marred by interpretive problems. Efforts to link gender differences to socialization processes have been more successful. Operant conditioning, observational learning, and self-socialization contribute to the development of gender differences. Families, schools, and the media are among the main sources of gender-role socialization.

KEY TERMS

Age of viability	Infant mortality
Aggression	Irreversibility
Altruism	Longitudinal study
Animism	Maturation
Attachment	Menarche
Centration	Motor development
Cephalocaudal trend	Object permanence
Cognitive development	Placenta
Conservation	Prenatal period
Cross-sectional study	Primary sex characteristics
Development	Proximodistal trend
Developmental norms	Puberty
Egocentrism	Pubescence
Embryonic stage	Secondary sex characteristics
Fetal alcohol syndrome	Senile dementia
Fetal stage	Separation anxiety
Gender	Sex
Gender differences	Social clock
Gender roles	Socialization
Gender stereotypes	Stage
Germinal stage	Temperament
	Zygote

KEY PEOPLE

Mary Ainsworth	Jean Piaget
Erik Erikson	Alexander Thomas and Stella Chess
Lawrence Kohlberg	

12 Personality: Theory, Research, and Assessment

have a close friend who has to be one of the world's great optimists. A few years ago, he was riding an all-terrain vehicle in a California desert and flipped it into the air. The vehicle landed on him, shattering one of his legs. Two days later, he called me long-distance (from the hospital) to tell me about the accident. Still in great pain from extensive surgery, and facing more operations, not to mention a year or two on crutches, he was joking about it. He was in his usual—make that unalterable—cheerful, lighthearted mood. Most of us, of course, would have been rather dejected and gloomy under such circumstances.

My friend's optimism is a key facet of his *personality*. In this chapter, we'll explore the mystery of personality. What exactly is personality? How does personality develop over time? For instance, how does someone like my friend get to be so upbeat and optimistic? Is personality largely biological in origin, or is experience critical? What makes for a healthy personality?

Traditionally, the study of personality has been dominated by "grand theories," broad in scope, attempting to explain a great many facets of behavior. Our discussion will reflect this emphasis, as we'll devote most of our time to the sweeping theories of Freud, Jung, Skinner, Rogers, and several others. In the chapter Application, we'll discuss how psychological tests are used to measure various aspects of personality.

THE NATURE OF PERSONALITY

Personality is a complex hypothetical construct that has been defined in a variety of ways. Let's take a closer look at the concepts of personality and personality traits.

Defining Personality: Consistency and Distinctiveness

What does it mean to say that my friend has an optimistic personality? This assertion indicates that he has a fairly *consistent tendency* to behave in a cheerful, hopeful, enthusiastic way, looking at the bright side of things, across a wide variety of situations. Although no one is entirely consistent in behavior, this quality of *consistency across situations* lies at the core of the concept of personality.

Distinctiveness is also central to the concept of personality. Personality is used to explain why people do not act the same in similar situations.

If you were stuck in an elevator with three people, each might react differently. One might crack jokes to relieve tension. Another might make ominous predictions that "we'll never get out of here." The third person might calmly think about how to escape. These varied reactions to the same situation occur because each person has a different personality. Each person has traits that are seen in other people, but each individual has his or her own distinctive *set* of personality traits.

In summary, the concept of personality is used to explain (1) the stability in a person's behavior over time and across situations (consistency) and (2) the behavioral differences among people reacting to the same situation (distinctiveness). We can combine these ideas into the following definition: **Personality refers to an individual's unique constellation of consistent behavioral traits.** Let's explore the concept of *traits* in more detail.

Personality Traits: Dispositions and Dimensions

Everyone makes remarks like "Jan is very *conscientious*." Or you might assert that "Bill is too *timid* to succeed in that job." These descriptive statements refer to personality traits. **A *personality trait* is a durable disposition to behave in a particular way in a variety of situations.** Adjectives such as *honest, dependable, moody, impulsive, suspicious, anxious, excitable, domineering*, and *friendly* describe dispositions that represent personality traits. People use an enormous number of these trait terms to describe one another's personality. One prominent personality theorist, Gordon Allport (1937, 1961), went through an unabridged dictionary and identified over 4500 personality traits!

Most approaches to personality assume that some traits are more basic than others. According to this notion, a small number of fundamental traits determine other, more superficial traits. For example, a person's tendency to be impulsive, restless, irritable, boisterous, and impatient might all be derived from a more basic tendency to be excitable.

A number of psychologists have taken on the challenge of identifying the basic traits that form the core of personality. For example, Raymond Cattell (1950, 1966, 1990) has used complex statistical procedures to reduce Allport's list of traits to just 16 basic dimensions of personality. Cattell believes that psychologists can thoroughly describe an individual's personality by measuring these 16 traits. In the chapter Application, we'll discuss a personality test he designed to assess these traits.

Robert McCrae and Paul Costa (1985, 1987) have arrived at an even simpler, *five-factor model of personality*. McCrae and Costa maintain that most aspects of personality are derived from just five critical traits: neuroticism, extraversion, openness to experience, agreeableness, and conscientiousness. These dimensions of personality are described in Table 12.1. Like Cattell, McCrae and Costa maintain that personality can be described adequately by measuring the basic traits that they've identified. Their bold claim has been supported in many studies by other researchers (Digman, 1990; Goldberg, 1993; John, 1990). However, many theorists still maintain that more than five traits are necessary to account for most of the variation seen in human personality (Briggs, 1989; Wiggins, 1992).

The debate about how many dimensions are necessary to describe personality is likely to continue for many years to come. As you'll see throughout the chapter, the study of personality is an area in psychology that has a long history of "dueling theories." We'll divide these diverse personality theories into four broad groups that share certain assumptions, emphases, and interests: (1) psychodynamic perspectives, (2) behavioral perspectives, (3) humanistic perspectives, and (4) biological perspectives. We'll begin our discussion of personality theories by examining the life and work of Sigmund Freud.

"No one who, like me, conjures up the most evil of those half-tamed demons that inhabit the human beast, and seeks to wrestle with them, can expect to come through the struggle unscathed."
SIGMUND FREUD

Table 12.1 McCrae and Costa's Five-Factor Model of Personality

Factor	Description
Neuroticism	Anxious, insecure, guilt-prone, self-conscious
Extraversion	Talkative, sociable, fun-loving, affectionate
Openness to experience	Daring, nonconforming, showing unusually broad interests, imaginative
Agreeableness	Sympathetic, warm, trusting, cooperative
Conscientiousness	Ethical, dependable, productive, purposeful

Source: McCrae and Costa (1987)

PSYCHODYNAMIC PERSPECTIVES

Psychodynamic theories include all the diverse theories descended from the work of Sigmund Freud that focus on unconscious mental forces. Freud inspired many brilliant scholars who followed in his intellectual footsteps. Some of these followers simply refined and updated Freud's theory. Others veered off in new directions and established independent, albeit related, schools of thought. Today, the psychodynamic umbrella covers a large collection of loosely related theories that we can only sample from in this text. In this section, we'll examine the ideas of Sigmund Freud in some detail. Then we'll take a briefer look at the psychodynamic theories of Carl Jung and Alfred Adler.

Freud's Psychoanalytic Theory

Born in 1856, Sigmund Freud grew up in a middle-class Jewish home in Vienna, Austria. He showed an early interest in intellectual pursuits and became an intense, hardworking young man, driven to achieve fame. Freud lived in the Victorian era, which was marked by sexual repression. His life was also affected by World War I, which devastated Europe, and by the growing anti-Semitism of the times. We'll see that the sexual repression and aggressive hostilities that Freud witnessed left their mark on his view of human nature.

Freud was a physician specializing in neurology when he began his medical practice in Vienna toward the end of the 19th century. Like other neurologists in his era, he often treated people troubled by nervous problems such as irrational fears, obsessions, and anxieties. Eventually he devoted himself to the treatment of mental disorders using an innovative procedure he had developed, called psychoanalysis, that required lengthy verbal interactions with patients during which Freud probed deeply into their lives.

Freud's (1901, 1924, 1940) *psychoanalytic theory* grew out of his decades of interactions with his clients in psychoanalysis. Psychoanalytic theory attempts to explain personality, motivation, and psychological disorders by focusing on the influence of early childhood experiences, on unconscious motives and conflicts, and on the methods people use to cope with their sexual and aggressive urges.

Most of Freud's contemporaries were uncomfortable with his theory for at least three reasons. First, in arguing that people's behavior is governed by unconscious factors of which they are unaware, Freud made the disconcerting suggestion that individuals are not masters of their own minds. Second, in claiming that our adult personalities are shaped by childhood experiences and other factors beyond our control, he suggested that people are not masters of their own destinies. Third, by emphasizing the great importance of how people cope with their sexual urges, he offended those who held the conservative, Victorian values of his time.

Thus, Freud endured a great deal of criticism, condemnation, and outright ridicule, even after his work began to attract favorable attention. Consider the following recollection from one of Freud's friends: "In those days when one mentioned Freud's name everyone would begin to laugh, as if someone had told a joke. Freud was the queer fellow who wrote a book about dreams. . . . He was the man who saw sex in everything. It was considered bad taste to bring up Freud's name in the presence of ladies. They would blush when his name was mentioned" (Donn, 1988, p. 57). Let's examine the ideas that generated so much controversy.

Structure of Personality

Freud divided personality structure into three components: the id, the ego, and the superego. He saw a person's behavior as the outcome of interactions among these three components.

The *id* is the primitive, instinctive component of personality that operates according to the pleasure principle. Freud referred to the id as the reservoir of psychic energy. By this he meant that the id houses the raw biological urges (to eat, sleep, defecate, copulate, and so on) that energize human behavior. The id operates according to **the *pleasure principle*, which demands immediate gratification of its urges.** The id engages in *primary-process thinking*, which is primitive, illogical, irrational, and fantasy oriented.

The *ego* is the decision-making component of personality that operates according to the reality principle. The ego mediates between the id, with its forceful desires for immediate satisfaction, and the external social world, with its expectations and norms regarding suitable behavior. The ego considers social realities—society's norms, etiquette, rules, and customs—in deciding how to behave. The ego is guided by **the *reality principle*, which seeks to delay gratification of the id's urges until appropriate outlets and situations can be found.** In short, to stay out of trouble, the ego often works to tame the unbridled desires of the id.

In the long run, the ego wants to maximize gratification, just as the id does. However, the ego engages in *secondary-process thinking*, which is relatively rational, realistic, and oriented toward problem solving. Thus, the ego strives to avoid negative consequences from society and its representatives (for example, punishment by parents or teachers) by behaving "properly." It also attempts to achieve long-range goals that sometimes require putting off gratification.

While the ego concerns itself with practical realities, **the *superego* is the moral component of personality that incorporates social standards about what represents right and wrong.** Throughout their lives, but especially during childhood, people receive training about what constitutes good and bad behavior. Many social norms regarding morality are eventually internalized. The superego emerges out of the ego at around 3 to 5 years of age. In some people, the superego can become irrationally demanding in its striving for moral perfection. Such people are plagued by excessive feelings of guilt.

According to Freud, the id, ego, and superego are distributed differently across three levels of awareness, which we'll describe next.

Freud's psychoanalytic theory was based on decades of clinical work. He treated a great many patients in the consulting room pictured here. The room contains numerous artifacts from other cultures—and the original psychoanalytic couch.

Levels of Awareness

Perhaps Freud's most enduring insight was his recognition of how unconscious forces can influence behavior. He inferred the existence of the unconscious from a variety of observations that he made with his patients. For example, he noticed that "slips of the tongue" often revealed a person's true feelings. He also realized that his patients' dreams often expressed hidden desires. Most important, through psychoanalysis he often helped patients discover feelings and conflicts they had previously been unaware of.

Freud contrasted the unconscious with the conscious and preconscious, creating three levels of awareness. **The *conscious* consists of whatever one is aware of at a particular point in time.** For example, at this moment your conscious may include the train of thought in this text and a dim awareness in the back of your mind that your eyes are getting tired and you're beginning to get hungry. **The *preconscious* contains material just beneath the surface of awareness that can** easily be retrieved. Examples might include your middle name, what you had for supper last night, or an argument you had with a friend yesterday. **The *unconscious* contains thoughts, memories, and desires that are well below the surface of conscious awareness but that nonetheless exert great influence on behavior.** Examples of material that might be found in your unconscious include a forgotten trauma from childhood, hidden feelings of hostility toward a parent, and repressed sexual desires.

Freud's conception of the mind is often compared to an iceberg that has most of its mass hidden beneath the water's surface (see Figure 12.1). He believed that the unconscious (the mass below the surface) is much larger than the conscious or preconscious. As you can see in Figure 12.1, he proposed that the ego and superego operate at all three levels of awareness. In contrast, the id is entirely unconscious, expressing its urges at a conscious level through the ego. Of course, the id's desires for immediate satisfaction

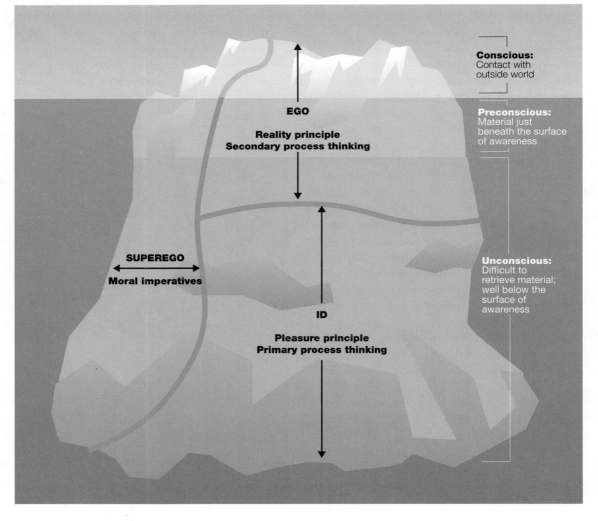

Figure 12.1. Freud's model of personality structure. Freud theorized that people have three levels of awareness: the conscious, the preconscious, and the unconscious. The enormous size of the unconscious is often dramatized by comparing it to the portion of an iceberg that lies beneath the water's surface. Freud also divided personality structure into three components—id, ego, and superego—that operate according to different principles and exhibit different modes of thinking. In Freud's model, the id is entirely unconscious, but the ego and superego operate at all three levels of awareness.

EGO
Reality principle
Secondary process thinking

SUPEREGO
Moral imperatives

ID
Pleasure principle
Primary process thinking

Conscious: Contact with outside world

Preconscious: Material just beneath the surface of awareness

Unconscious: Difficult to retrieve material; well below the surface of awareness

often trigger internal conflicts with the ego and superego. These conflicts play a key role in Freud's theory.

Conflict and the Tyranny of Sex and Aggression

Freud assumed that behavior is the outcome of an ongoing series of internal conflicts. He saw internal battles between the id, ego, and superego as routine. Why? Because the id wants to gratify its urges immediately, but the norms of civilized society frequently dictate otherwise. For example, your id might feel an urge to clobber a co-worker who constantly irritates you. However, society frowns on such behavior, so your ego would try to hold this urge in check. Hence, you would find yourself in conflict. You may be experiencing conflict at this very moment. In Freudian terms, your id may be secretly urging you to abandon reading this chapter so that you can fix a snack and watch some television. Your ego may be weighing this appealing option against your society-induced need to excel in school.

Freud believed that people's lives are dominated by conflict. He asserted that individuals careen from one conflict to another. The following scenario provides a concrete illustration of how the three components of personality interact to create constant conflicts:

Imagine lurching across your bed to shut off your alarm clock as it rings obnoxiously. It's 7 A.M. and time to get up for your history class. However, your id (operating according to the pleasure principle) urges you to return to the immediate gratification of additional sleep. Your ego (operating according to the reality principle) points out that you really must go to class since you haven't been able to decipher the textbook on your own. Your id (in its typical unrealistic fashion) smugly assures you that you will get the A grade that you need and suggests lying back to dream about how impressed your roommates will be. Just as you're relaxing, your superego jumps into the fray. It tries to make you feel guilty about all the money your parents paid in tuition for the class that you're about to skip. You haven't even gotten out of bed yet, but there's already a pitched battle in your psyche.

Let's say your ego wins the battle. You pull yourself out of bed and head for class. On the way, you pass a donut shop and your id clamors for cinnamon rolls. Your ego reminds you that you're getting overweight and that you're supposed to be on a diet. Your id wins this time. After you've attended your history lecture, your ego reminds you that you need to do some library

research for a paper in philosophy. However, your id insists on returning to your apartment to watch some sitcom reruns. As you reenter your apartment, you're overwhelmed by how messy it is. It's your roommates' mess, and your id suggests that you tell them off. As you're about to lash out, however, your ego convinces you that diplomacy will be more effective. Three sitcoms later you find that you're in a debate with yourself about whether to go to the gym to work out or to the student union to watch MTV. It's only midafternoon—and already you've been through a series of internal conflicts.

Freud believed that conflicts centering on sexual and aggressive impulses are especially likely to have far-reaching consequences. Why did he emphasize sex and aggression? Two reasons were prominent in his thinking. First, he thought that sex and aggression are subject to more complex and ambiguous social controls than other basic motives. The norms governing sexual and aggressive behavior are subtle, and people often get inconsistent messages about what's appropriate. Thus, Freud believed that these two drives are the source of much confusion. Second, he noted that the sexual and aggressive drives are thwarted more regularly than other basic, biological urges. Think about it: If you get hungry or thirsty, you can simply head for a nearby vending machine or a drinking fountain. But if a department store clerk infuriates you, you aren't likely to reach across the counter and slug him or her. Likewise, when you see an attractive person who inspires lustful urges, you don't normally walk up and propose a tryst in a nearby broom closet. There's nothing comparable to vending machines or drinking fountains for the satisfaction of sexual and aggressive urges. Freud ascribed great importance to these needs because social norms dictate that they're routinely frustrated.

Anxiety and Defense Mechanisms

Most internal conflicts are trivial and are quickly resolved one way or the other. Occasionally, however, a conflict will linger for days, months, or even years, creating internal tension. More often than not, such prolonged and troublesome conflicts involve sexual and aggressive impulses that society wants to tame. These conflicts are often played out entirely in the unconscious. Although you may not be aware of these unconscious battles, they can produce *anxiety* that slips to the surface of conscious awareness. The anxiety can be attributed to your ego worrying about (1) the id getting out of control and doing something terrible that leads to severe negative consequences or (2) the superego getting out of control and making you feel guilty about a real or imagined transgression.

The arousal of anxiety is a crucial event in Freud's theory of personality functioning. Anxiety is distressing, so people try to rid themselves of this unpleasant emotion any way they can. This effort to ward off anxiety often involves the use of defense mechanisms. *Defense mechanisms* **are largely unconscious reactions that protect a person from unpleasant emotions such as anxiety and guilt.** Typically, they're mental maneuvers that work through self-deception. Consider *rationalization*, **which is creating false but plausible excuses to justify unacceptable behavior.** For example, after cheating someone in a business transaction, you might reduce your guilt by rationalizing that "everyone does it."

According to Freud, the most basic and widely used defense mechanism is repression. *Repression* **is keeping distressing thoughts and feelings buried in the unconscious.** People tend to repress desires that make them feel guilty, conflicts that make them anxious, and memories that are painful. Repression has been called "motivated forgetting." If you forget a dental appointment or the name of someone you don't like, repression may be at work.

Self-deception can also be seen in projection and displacement. *Projection* **is attributing one's own thoughts, feelings, or motives to another.** Usually, the thoughts one projects onto others are those that would make one feel guilty. For example, if lusting for a co-worker makes you feel guilty, you might attribute any latent sexual tension between the two of you to the *other person's* desire to seduce you. *Displacement* **is diverting emotional feelings (usually anger) from their original source to a substitute target.** If your boss gives you a hard time at work and you come home and slam the door, kick the dog, and scream at your spouse, you're displacing your anger onto irrelevant targets. Unfortunately, social constraints often force people to hold back their anger, and they end up lashing out at the people they love the most.

Other prominent defense mechanisms include reaction formation, regression, and identification. *Reaction formation* **is behaving in a way that's exactly the opposite of one's true feelings.** Guilt about sexual desires often leads to reaction formation. Freud theorized that many males who ridicule homosexuals are defending against their own latent homosexual impulses. The telltale sign of reaction formation is the exaggerated quality of the opposite behavior. *Regression* **is a reversion to immature patterns of behavior.** When anxious about their self-worth, some adults respond with childish boasting and bragging (as opposed to subtle efforts to impress others). For example, a fired executive having difficulty finding a new job might start making ridiculous statements about his incomparable talents and achievements. Such bragging is regressive when it's marked by massive

Table 12.2 Defense Mechanisms, with Examples

Defense Mechanism	Definition	Example
Repression	Keeping distressing thoughts and feelings buried in the unconscious	A traumatized soldier has no recollection of the details of a close brush with death.
Projection	Attributing one's own thoughts, feelings, or motives to another	A woman who dislikes her boss thinks she likes her boss but feels that the boss doesn't like her.
Displacement	Diverting emotional feelings (usually anger) from their original source to a substitute target	After parental scolding, a young girl takes her anger out on her little brother.
Reaction formation	Behaving in a way that is exactly the opposite of one's true feelings	A parent who unconsciously resents a child spoils the child with outlandish gifts.
Regression	A reversion to immature patterns of behavior	An adult has a temper tantrum when he doesn't get his way.
Rationalization	Creating false but plausible excuses to justify unacceptable behavior	A student watches TV instead of studying, saying that "additional study wouldn't do any good anyway."
Identification	Bolstering self-esteem by forming an imaginary or real alliance with some person or group	An insecure young man joins a fraternity to boost his self-esteem.

Note: See Table 13.2 for additional examples of defense mechanisms.

exaggerations that virtually anyone can see through. *Identification* **is bolstering self-esteem by forming an imaginary or real alliance with some person or group.** Youngsters often shore up precarious feelings of self-worth by identifying with rock stars, movie stars, or famous athletes. Adults may join exclusive country clubs or civic organizations as a means of boosting their self-esteem via identification.

Additional examples of the defense mechanisms we've described can be found in Table 12.2. If you see defensive maneuvers that you've used, you shouldn't be surprised. According to Freud, everyone uses defense mechanisms to some extent. They become problematic only when people depend on them excessively. The seeds for psychological disorders are sown only when defenses lead to wholesale distortion of reality.

Various theorists have added to Freud's original list of defenses (Vaillant, 1992). We'll examine some of these additional defense mechanisms in the next chapter, when we discuss the role of defenses in coping with stress. For now, however, let's turn our attention to Freud's ideas about the development of personality.

Development: Psychosexual Stages

Freud made the rather startling assertion that the basic foundation of an individual's personality has been laid down by the tender age of 5. To shed light on these crucial early years, Freud formulated a stage theory of development. He emphasized how young children deal with their immature but powerful sexual urges (he used the term *sexual* in a general way to refer to many urges for physical pleasure). According to Freud, these sexual urges shift in focus as children progress from one stage

CONCEPT CHECK 12.1
Identifying Defense Mechanisms

Check your understanding of defense mechanisms by identifying specific defenses in the story below. Each example of a defense mechanism is underlined, with a number beneath it. Write in the defense at work in each case in the numbered spaces after the story. The answers are in Appendix A.

My boyfriend recently broke up with me after we had dated seriously for several years. At first, I cried a great deal and <u>locked myself in my room, where I pouted endlessly.</u> I was sure that my former boyfriend felt as miserable as I did. <u>I told several friends that he was probably lonely and depressed.</u> Later, I decided that I hated him. <u>I was happy about the breakup and talked about how much I was going to enjoy my newfound freedom.</u> I went to parties and socialized a great deal and just forgot about him. It's funny—<u>at one point I couldn't even remember his phone number!</u> Then I started pining for him again. But eventually I began to look at the situation more objectively. I realized that he had many faults and that <u>we were bound to break up sooner or later, so I was better off without him.</u>

1. _____   4. _____

2. _____   5. _____

3. _____

of development to another. Indeed, the names for the stages (oral, anal, genital, and so on) are based on where children are focusing their erotic energy during that period. Thus, *psychosexual stages* **are developmental periods with a characteristic sexual focus that leave their mark on adult personality.**

Freud theorized that each psychosexual stage has its own, unique developmental challenges or tasks (see Table 12.3). The way these challenges

Table 12.3 Freud's Stages of Psychosexual Development

Stage	Approximate Ages	Erotic Focus	Key Tasks and Experiences
Oral	0–1	Mouth (sucking, biting)	Weaning (from breast or bottle)
Anal	2–3	Anus (expelling or retaining feces)	Toilet training
Phallic	4–5	Genitals (masturbating)	Identifying with adult role models; coping with Oedipal crisis
Latency	6–12	None (sexually repressed)	Expanding social contacts
Genital	Puberty onward	Genitals (being sexually intimate)	Establishing intimate relationships; contributing to society through working

are handled supposedly shapes personality. The notion of *fixation* plays an important role in this process. **Fixation involves a failure to move forward from one stage to another as expected.** Essentially, the child's development stalls for a while. Fixation can be caused by *excessive gratification* of needs at a particular stage or by *excessive frustration* of those needs. Either way, fixations left over from childhood affect adult personality. Generally, fixation leads to an over-emphasis on the psychosexual needs prominent during the fixated stage. Freud described a series of five psychosexual stages. Let's examine some of the highlights in this sequence.

ORAL STAGE The oral stage encompasses the first year of life. During this period, the main source of erotic stimulation is the mouth (in biting, sucking, chewing, and so on). In Freud's view, the handling of the child's feeding experiences is crucial to subsequent development. He attributed considerable importance to the manner in which the child is weaned from the breast or the bottle. According to Freud, fixation at the oral stage could form the basis for obsessive eating or smoking later in life (among many other things).

ANAL STAGE In their second year, children get their erotic pleasure from their bowel movements, through either the expulsion or retention of feces. The crucial event at this time is toilet training, which represents society's first systematic effort to regulate the child's biological urges. Severely punitive toilet training leads to a variety of possible outcomes. For example, excessive punishment might produce a latent feeling of hostility toward the "trainer," usually the mother. This hostility might generalize to women as a class. Another possibility is that heavy reliance on punitive measures could lead to an association between genital concerns and the anxiety that the punishment arouses. This genital anxiety derived from severe toilet training could evolve into anxiety about sexual activities later in life.

PHALLIC STAGE In the third through fifth years, the genitals become the focus for the child's erotic energy, largely through self-stimulation. During this pivotal stage, the *Oedipal complex* emerges. That is, little boys develop an erotically tinged preference for their mother. They also feel hostility toward their father, whom they view as a competitor for mom's affection. Similarly, little girls develop a special attachment to their father.

Around the same time, they learn that little boys have very different genitals, and supposedly they develop *penis envy*. According to Freud, young girls feel hostile toward their mother because they blame her for their anatomical "deficiency."

To summarize, in the **Oedipal complex children manifest erotically tinged desires for their opposite-sex parent, accompanied by feelings of hostility toward their same-sex parent.** The name for this syndrome was taken from the Greek myth in which Oedipus, not knowing the identity of his real parents, inadvertently killed his father and married his mother.

According to Freud, the way parents and children deal with the sexual and aggressive conflicts inherent in the Oedipal complex is of paramount importance. The child has to resolve the Oedipal dilemma by purging the sexual longings for the opposite-sex parent and by crushing the hostility felt toward the same-sex parent. In Freud's view, healthy psychosexual development hinges on the resolution of the Oedipal conflict. Why? Because continued hostility toward the same-sex parent may prevent the child from identifying adequately with that parent. Freudian theory predicts that without such identification, many aspects of the child's development won't progress as they should.

LATENCY AND GENITAL STAGES From around age five through puberty, the child's sexuality is largely suppressed—it becomes *latent*. Important events during this *latency stage* center on expanding social contacts beyond the immediate family. With the advent of puberty, the child progresses into the *genital stage*. Sexual urges reappear and focus on the genitals once again. At this point, sexual energy is normally channeled toward peers of the other sex, rather than toward oneself as in the phallic stage.

In arguing that the early years shape personality, Freud did not mean that personality development comes to an abrupt halt in middle childhood. However, he did believe that the foundation for adult personality has been solidly entrenched by this time. He maintained that future developments are rooted in early, formative experiences and that significant conflicts in later years are replays of crises from childhood.

In fact, Freud believed that unconscious sexual conflicts rooted in childhood experiences cause most personality disturbances. His steadfast belief in the psychosexual origins of psychological disorders eventually led to bitter theoretical disputes with two of his most brilliant colleagues: Carl Jung and Alfred Adler. Jung and Adler both argued that Freud overemphasized sexuality. Freud summarily rejected their ideas, and the other two theorists felt compelled to go their own way, developing their own psychodynamic theories of personality.

Jung's Analytical Psychology

Carl Jung was born to middle-class Swiss parents in 1875. The son of a Protestant pastor, he was a deeply introverted, lonely child, but an excellent student. Jung had earned his medical degree and was an established young psychiatrist in Zurich when he began to write to Freud in 1906. When the two men had their first meeting, they were so taken by each other's insights, they talked nonstop for 13 hours! They exchanged 359 letters before their friendship and theoretical alliance were torn apart in 1913.

Jung called his new approach *analytical psychology* to differentiate it from Freud's psychoanalytic theory. Unlike Freud, Jung encouraged his followers to develop their own theoretical views.

Perhaps because of his conflict with Freud, he deplored the way schools of thought often become dogmatic, discouraging creative, new ideas. Although many theorists came to characterize themselves as "Jungians," Jung himself often remarked, "I am not a Jungian" and said, "I do not want anybody to be a Jungian. I want people above all to be themselves" (van der Post, 1975).

Like Freud, Jung (1921, 1933) emphasized the unconscious determinants of personality. However, he proposed that the unconscious consists of two layers. The first layer, called the *personal unconscious*, is essentially the same as Freud's version of the unconscious. The personal unconscious houses material that is not within one's conscious awareness because it has been repressed or forgotten. In addition, Jung theorized the existence of a deeper layer he called the collective unconscious. **The *collective unconscious* is a storehouse of latent memory traces inherited from people's ancestral past.** According to Jung, each person shares the collective unconscious with the entire human race (see Figure 12.2). It con-

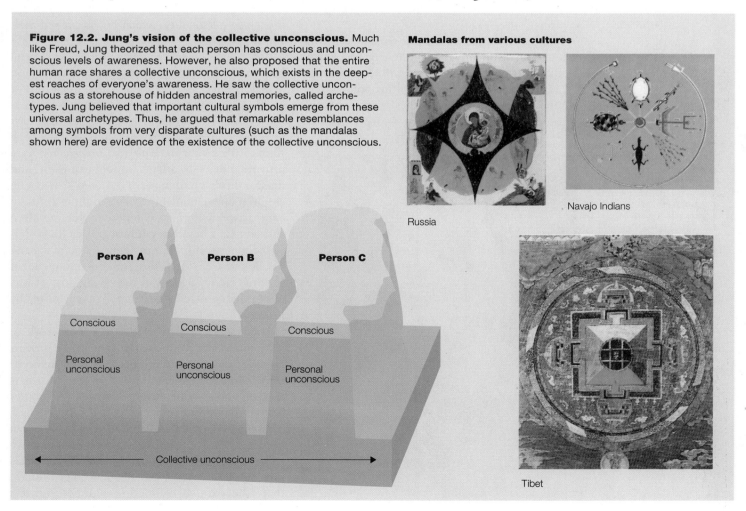

Figure 12.2. Jung's vision of the collective unconscious. Much like Freud, Jung theorized that each person has conscious and unconscious levels of awareness. However, he also proposed that the entire human race shares a collective unconscious, which exists in the deepest reaches of everyone's awareness. He saw the collective unconscious as a storehouse of hidden ancestral memories, called archetypes. Jung believed that important cultural symbols emerge from these universal archetypes. Thus, he argued that remarkable resemblances among symbols from very disparate cultures (such as the mandalas shown here) are evidence of the existence of the collective unconscious.

Mandalas from various cultures

Russia

Navajo Indians

Tibet

Person A

Person B

Person C

Conscious

Conscious

Conscious

Personal unconscious

Personal unconscious

Personal unconscious

Collective unconscious

tains the "whole spiritual heritage of mankind's evolution, born anew in the brain structure of every individual" (Jung, quoted in Campbell, 1971, p. 45).

Jung called these ancestral memories *archetypes*. They are not memories of actual, personal experiences. Instead, ***archetypes* are emotionally charged images and thought forms that have universal meaning.** These archetypal images and ideas show up frequently in dreams and are often manifested in a culture's use of symbols in art, literature, and religion. According to Jung, symbols from very different cultures often show striking similarities because they emerge from archetypes that are shared by the entire human race. For instance, Jung found numerous cultures in which the *mandala*, or "magic circle," has served as a symbol of the unified wholeness of the self (see Figure 12.2). Jung felt that an understanding of archetypal symbols helped him make sense of his patients' dreams. This was of great concern to him, as he thought that dreams contain important messages from the unconscious. Like Freud, he depended extensively on dream analysis in his treatment of patients.

Jung's unusual ideas about the collective unconscious had little impact on the mainstream of thinking in psychology. Their influence was felt more in other fields, such as anthropology, philosophy, art, and religious studies. However, many of Jung's other ideas *have* been incorporated into the mainstream of psychology. For instance, Jung was the first to describe the introverted (inner-directed) and extraverted (outer-directed) personality types. **Introverts tend to be preoccupied with the internal world of their own thoughts, feelings, and experiences.** Like Jung himself, they generally are contemplative and aloof. In contrast, **extraverts tend to be interested in the external world of people and things.** They're more likely to be outgoing, talkative, and friendly, instead of reclusive.

Adler's Individual Psychology

Like Freud, Alfred Adler grew up in Vienna in a middle-class Jewish home. He was a sickly child who struggled to overcome rickets and an almost fatal case of pneumonia. At home, he was overshadowed by an exceptionally bright and successful older brother. Nonetheless, he went on to earn his medical degree, and he practiced ophthalmology and general medicine before his interest turned to psychiatry. He was a charter member of Freud's inner circle—the Vienna Psychoanalytic Society. However, he soon began to develop his own approach to personality, which he christened *individual psychology*.

Like Jung, Adler (1917, 1927) argued that Freud had gone overboard in centering his theory on sexual conflicts. According to Adler, the foremost source of human motivation is a striving for superiority. In his view, this striving does not necessarily translate into the pursuit of dominance or high status. Adler saw ***striving for superiority* as a universal drive to adapt, improve oneself, and master life's challenges.** He noted that young children understandably feel weak and helpless in comparison with more competent older children and adults. These early inferiority feelings supposedly motivate them to acquire new skills and develop new talents. Thus, Adler maintained that striving for superiority is the prime goal of life, rather than physical gratification (as suggested by Freud).

Adler asserted that everyone has to work to overcome some feelings of inferiority—a process he called compensation. ***Compensation* involves efforts to overcome imagined or real inferiorities by developing one's abilities.** Adler believed that compensation is entirely normal. However, in some people inferiority feelings can become excessive, resulting in what is widely known today as an *inferiority complex*—exaggerated feelings of weakness and inadequacy. Adler thought that either parental pampering or parental neglect

"The goal of the human soul is conquest, perfection, security, superiority."
ALFRED ADLER

Adler's theory has been used to analyze the tragic life of the legendary sex symbol Marilyn Monroe (Ansbacher, 1970). During her childhood, Monroe suffered from parental neglect that left her with acute feelings of inferiority. These inferiority feelings led her to overcompensate by flaunting her beauty, marrying celebrities (Joe DiMaggio and Arthur Miller), keeping film crews waiting for hours, and seeking the adoration of her fans.

could cause an inferiority complex. Thus, he agreed with Freud on the importance of early childhood experiences, although he focused on different aspects of parent-child relations.

Adler explained personality disturbances by noting that excessive inferiority feelings can pervert the normal process of striving for superiority. He asserted that some people engage in *overcompensation* to conceal, even from themselves, their feelings of inferiority. Instead of working to master life's challenges, people with an inferiority complex work to achieve status, gain power over others, and acquire the trappings of success (fancy clothes, impressive cars, or whatever looks important to them). They tend to flaunt their success in an effort to cover up their underlying inferiority complex.

Adler's theory stressed the social context of personality development. For instance, it was Adler who first focused attention on the possible importance of *birth order* as a factor governing personality. He noted that only children, firstborns, second children, and subsequent children enter different home environments that are likely to affect their personality. Thus, he hypothesized that children without siblings are often spoiled by excessive attention from parents, that firstborns often are problem children because they become upset when they're "dethroned" by a second child, and that second-born children tend to be competitive because they have to struggle to catch up with an older sibling. Adler's hypotheses stimulated hundreds of studies on the effects of birth order. This research has proven very interesting, although birth order effects have turned out to be weaker and less consistent than Adler expected (Ernst & Angst, 1983; Falbo & Polit, 1986).

Evaluating Psychodynamic Perspectives

The psychodynamic approach has provided a number of far-reaching, truly "grand" theories of personality. These theories yielded some bold new insights when they were first presented. Although one might argue about exact details of interpretation, psychodynamic theory and research have demonstrated (1) that unconscious forces can influence behavior, (2) that internal conflict often plays a key role in generating psychological distress, and (3) that early childhood experiences can influence adult personality (Kihlstrom, 1990; Westen, 1990). Many widely used concepts in psychology emerged out of psychodynamic theo-

ries, including the unconscious, defense mechanisms, introversion-extraversion, and the inferiority complex.

In addition to being praised, psychodynamic formulations have also been criticized on several grounds (Eysenck, 1990; Fine, 1990; Fisher & Greenberg, 1985). Among other things, critics argue (1) that psychodynamic theories have often been too vague to permit a clear scientific test, (2) that empirical studies have provided only modest support for central psychodynamic hypotheses, and (3) that the psychodynamic approach has generally provided a rather male-centered point of view resulting in a sexist bias against women.

It's easy to ridicule Freud for concepts such as penis envy, and it's easy to point to Freudian ideas that have turned out to be wrong. However, you have to remember that Freud, Jung, and Adler began to fashion their theories about a century ago. It's not entirely fair to compare these theories to other models that are only a decade or two old. That's like asking the Wright brothers to race the Concorde. Freud and his colleagues deserve great credit for breaking new ground with their speculations about psychodynamics. Standing at a distance a century later, we have to be impressed by the extraordinary impact that psychodynamic theory has had on modern intellectual thought. In psychology as a whole, no other school has been so influential, with the exception of behaviorism, which we turn to next.

CONCEPT CHECK 12.2
Comparing Psychodynamic Theorists

As followers of Freud, Jung and Adler shared some ideas with their mentor. However, both eventually broke with Freud and established their own theoretical systems because of disagreements on some issues. Below are terms for eight concepts about which Freud, Jung, and Adler agreed or disagreed. Check your understanding of the theorists and their ideas by placing check marks in the appropriate spaces to indicate which theorists emphasized which concepts. Then check your answers in Appendix A.

	Freud	*Jung*	*Adler*
1. archetypes	____	____	____
2. physical gratification	____	____	____
3. striving for superiority	____	____	____
4. collective unconscious	____	____	____
5. early childhood experiences	____	____	____
6. dream analysis	____	____	____
7. birth order	____	____	____
8. unconscious determinants	____	____	____

"The practice of looking inside the organism for an explanation of behavior has tended to obscure the variables which are immediately available for a scientific analysis. These variables lie outside the organism, in its immediate environment and in its environmental history. . . . The objection to inner states is not that they do not exist, but that they are not relevant."

B. F. SKINNER

BEHAVIORAL PERSPECTIVES

Behaviorism **is a theoretical orientation based on the premise that scientific psychology should study only observable behavior.** As we saw in Chapter 1, behaviorism has been a major school of thought in psychology since 1913, when John B. Watson began campaigning for the behavioral point of view. Research in the behavioral tradition has focused largely on learning. For many decades behaviorists devoted relatively little attention to the study of personality. However, their interest in personality began to pick up after John Dollard and Neal Miller (1950) attempted to translate selected Freudian ideas into behavioral terminology. Dollard and Miller showed that behavioral concepts could provide enlightening insights about the complicated subject of personality.

In this section, we'll examine three behavioral views of personality, as we discuss the ideas of B. F. Skinner, Albert Bandura, and Walter Mischel. For the most part, you'll see that behaviorists explain personality the same way they explain everything else—in terms of learning.

Skinner's Ideas Applied to Personality

As we noted in Chapters 1 and 6, modern behaviorism's most prominent theorist has been B. F. Skinner, an American psychologist who lived from 1904 to 1990. After earning his doctorate in 1931, Skinner spent most of his career at Harvard University. There he achieved renown for his research on learning in lower organisms, mostly rats and pigeons. Skinner's (1953, 1957) principles of *operant conditioning* were never meant to be a theory of personality. However, his ideas have affected thinking in all areas of psychology and have been applied to the explanation of personality. Here we'll examine Skinner's views as they relate to personality structure and development.

Personality Structure: A View from the Outside

Skinner made no provision for internal personality structures similar to Freud's id, ego, and superego because such structures can't be observed. Following in the tradition of Watson, Skinner showed little interest in what goes on "inside" people. He argued that it's useless to speculate about private, unobservable cognitive processes. Instead, he focused on how the external environment molds overt behavior. Indeed, he argued for a strong brand of *determinism*, asserting that behavior is fully determined by environmental stimuli. He claimed that free will is but an illusion, saying, "There is no place in the scientific position for a self as a true originator or initiator of action" (Skinner, 1974, p. 225).

How can Skinner's theory explain the consistency that can be seen in individuals' behavior? According to his view, people show some consistent patterns of behavior because they have some stable *response tendencies* that they have acquired through experience. These response tendencies may change in the future, as a result of new experience, but they're enduring enough to create a certain degree of consistency in a person's behavior.

Implicitly, then, Skinner viewed an individual's personality as a *collection of response tendencies that are tied to various stimulus situations*. A specific situation may be associated with a number of response tendencies that vary in strength, depending on past conditioning (see Figure 12.3). As an example, consider the rather general stimulus situation of a large party where you know relatively few people. Your response tendencies in this situation, in order of strength, might be (1) to circulate, speaking to others only if they approach you first, (2) to stick close to the few guests you already know while making no effort to meet anyone new, (3) to politely withdraw by getting wrapped up in your host's book or record collection (or whatever else is available), or (4) to leave as soon as you can.

Figure 12.3. A behavioral view of personality. Staunch behaviorists devote little attention to the structure of personality because it is unobservable, but they implicitly view personality as an individual's collection of response tendencies. A possible hierarchy of response tendencies for a specific stimulus situation is shown here.

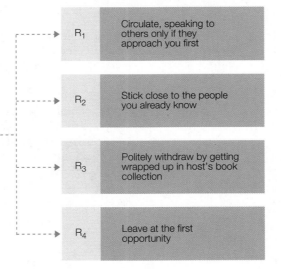

Personality Development as a Product of Conditioning

Skinner's theory accounts for personality development by explaining how various response tendencies are acquired through learning. He believed that most human responses are shaped by the type of conditioning that he described: operant conditioning. As we discussed in Chapter 6, Skinner maintained that environmental consequences—reinforcement, punishment, and extinction—determine people's patterns of responding. On the one hand, when responses are followed by favorable consequences (reinforcement), they are strengthened. For example, if your joking at a party pays off with favorable attention, your tendency to joke at parties will increase (see Figure 12.4). On the other hand, when responses lead to negative consequences (punishment), they are weakened. Thus, if your impulsive decisions always backfire, your tendency to be impulsive will decline.

Because response tendencies are constantly being strengthened or weakened by new experiences, Skinner's theory views personality development as a continuous, lifelong journey. Unlike Freud and many other theorists, Skinner saw no reason to break the developmental process into stages. Nor did he attribute special importance to early childhood experiences.

Bandura's Social Learning Theory

Albert Bandura is a modern theorist who has helped to reshape the theoretical landscape of behaviorism. He has spent his entire academic career at Stanford University, where he has conducted influential research on behavior therapy and the determinants of aggression.

Bandura is one of several behaviorists who have added a cognitive flavor to behaviorism since the 1960s. Bandura (1977), Walter Mischel (1973), and Julian Rotter (1982) take issue with Skinner's "pure" behaviorism. They point out that humans obviously are conscious, thinking, feeling beings. Moreover, these theorists argue that in neglecting cognitive processes, Skinner ignored the most distinctive and important feature of human behavior. Bandura and like-minded theorists call their modified brand of behaviorism *social learning theory*.

Bandura (1982, 1986) agrees with the fundamental thrust of behaviorism in that he believes that personality is largely shaped through learning. However, he contends that conditioning is

Stimulus context

Party

Telling jokes → Followed by → Attention, compliments

Response   **Reinforcer**

Figure 12.4. Personality development and operant conditioning. According to Skinner, people's characteristic response tendencies are shaped by reinforcers and other consequences that follow behavior. Thus, if your joking at a party leads to attention and compliments, your tendency to be witty and humorous will be strengthened.

not a mechanical process in which people are passive participants. Instead, he maintains that people actively seek out and process information about their environment to maximize favorable outcomes. In focusing on information processing, he brings unobservable cognitive events into the picture.

Observational Learning

Bandura's foremost theoretical contribution has been his description of observational learning, which we introduced in Chapter 6. *Observational learning occurs when an organism's responding is influenced by the observation of others.* According to Bandura, both classical and operant conditioning can occur vicariously when one person observes another's conditioning. For example, watching your sister get burned by a bounced check upon selling her old stereo could strengthen your tendency to be suspicious of others. Although your sister would be the one actually experiencing the negative consequences, they might also influence you—through observational learning. Bandura maintains that people's characteristic patterns of behavior are shaped by the *models* that they're exposed to. In observational learning, **a *model* is a person whose behavior is observed by another.** At one time or another, everyone serves as a model for others. Bandura's key point is that many response tendencies are the product of imitation.

"Most human behavior is learned by observation through modeling."
ALBERT BANDURA

As social learning theory has been refined, it has become apparent that some models are more influential than others (Bandura, 1986). Both children and adults tend to imitate people they like or respect more than people they don't. People are also especially prone to imitate the behavior of those whom they consider attractive or powerful (such as rock stars or athletes). In addition, imitation is more likely when people see similarity between models and themselves. Thus, children tend to imitate same-sex role models somewhat more than opposite-sex models. Finally, people are more likely to copy a model if they observe that the model's behavior leads to positive outcomes.

According to social learning theory, models have a great impact on personality development. Children learn to be assertive, conscientious, self-sufficient, dependable, easygoing, and so forth by observing others behaving in these ways. Parents, teachers, relatives, siblings, and peers serve as models for young children. Bandura and his colleagues have done extensive research showing how models influence the development of aggressiveness, sex roles, and moral standards in children (Bandura, 1973; Bussey & Bandura, 1984; Mischel & Mischel, 1976). Their research on modeling and aggression has been particularly influential.

In a classic study, Bandura, Ross, and Ross (1963) showed how the observation of filmed models can influence the learning of aggressive behavior in children. They manipulated whether or not nursery-school children saw an aggressive model on film and whether the aggressive model experienced positive or negative consequences. Soon after the manipulations, the children were taken to a toy room, where their play was observed through a one-way mirror. Children who saw the aggressive model rewarded engaged in more aggression toward toys than did children in the other conditions. This landmark study was one of the earliest experimental demonstrations of a cause-and-effect relationship between exposure to media aggression and aggressive behavior.

Self-Efficacy

Bandura discusses how a variety of personal factors (aspects of personality) govern behavior. In recent years, the factor he has emphasized the most is self-efficacy (Bandura, 1990, 1993). *Self-efficacy* **refers to one's belief about one's ability to perform behaviors that should lead to expected outcomes.** When self-efficacy is high, individuals feel confident that they can execute the

responses necessary to earn reinforcers. When self-efficacy is low, individuals worry that the necessary responses may be beyond their abilities. Perceptions of self-efficacy are subjective and specific to certain kinds of tasks. For instance, you might feel extremely confident about your ability to handle difficult social situations but doubtful about your ability to handle academic challenges. Perceptions of self-efficacy can influence which challenges people tackle and how well they perform. Studies have found, for example, that feelings of greater self-efficacy are associated with greater success in giving up smoking (Garcia, Schmitz, & Doerfler, 1990), higher levels of academic performance (Multon, Brown, & Lent, 1991), enhanced performance in athletic competition (Bandura, 1990), and consideration of a broader range of occupations in making career choices (Bores-Rangel et al., 1990).

Mischel and the Person-Situation Controversy

Walter Mischel was born in Vienna, not far from Freud's home. His family immigrated to the United States in 1939, when he was 9. After earning his doctorate in psychology, he spent many years on the faculty at Stanford, as a colleague of Bandura's. He has since moved to Columbia University.

Like Bandura, Mischel (1973, 1984) is an advocate of social learning theory. Mischel's chief contribution to personality theory has been to focus attention on the extent to which situational factors govern behavior. This contribution has embroiled him in a fundamental controversy about the consistency of human behavior across varying situations.

According to social learning theory, people make responses that they think will lead to reinforcement in the situation at hand. They try to gauge the reinforcement contingencies and adjust their behavior to the circumstances. Thus, if you believe that hard work in your job will pay off by leading to raises and promotions, you'll probably be diligent and industrious. But if you think that hard work in your job is unlikely to be rewarded, you may behave in a lazy and irresponsible manner.

Social learning theory predicts that people will often behave differently in different situations. Mischel (1968, 1973) reviewed decades of research and concluded that, indeed, people exhibit far less consistency across situations than had been widely assumed. For example, studies show that a person who is honest in one situation may be dishonest in another. Someone who wouldn't

"It seems remarkable how each of us generally manages to reconcile his seemingly diverse behavior into one self-consistent whole."
WALTER MISCHEL

dream of being dishonest in a business deal might engage in wholesale cheating in filling out tax returns. Similarly, some people are quite shy in one situation and outgoing in another. In light of these realities, Mischel maintains that behavior is characterized more by *situational specificity* than by consistency.

Mischel's position strikes at the heart of the concept of personality itself. As we discussed at the beginning of the chapter, the concept of personality is used to explain consistency in people's behavior over time and situations. If there isn't much consistency, then there isn't much need for the concept of personality. Thus, Mischel's provocative ideas have sparked a robust debate about the relative importance of the *person* as opposed to the *situation* in determining behavior.

This debate has led to a growing recognition that both the person and the situation are important determinants of behavior. The concept of personality doesn't require anything approaching *complete* consistency in behavior. There clearly is enough cross-situational consistency in humans' behavior to warrant interest in person variables, or personality. In fact, Mischel has never advocated that the personality concept should be discarded. Mischel (1990) merely asserts that more attention should be paid to the situational determinants of behavior and how they interact with personality variables. His arguments and the ensuing debate have led many psychologists to do just that (Kenrick & Funder, 1988).

Evaluating Behavioral Perspectives

Behavioral theories are firmly rooted in extensive empirical research. Skinner's ideas have shed light on how environmental consequences and conditioning mold people's characteristic behavior. Bandura's social learning theory has expanded the horizons of behaviorism and increased its relevance to the study of personality. Mischel deserves credit for increasing psychology's awareness of how situational factors shape behavior.

Of course, each theoretical approach has its shortcomings, and the behavioral approach is no exception. Critics argue (1) that behaviorists have depended too much on animal research and have indiscriminately generalized from animal behavior to human behavior, (2) that they have made little effort to integrate biological factors into their theories, and (3) that in carving personality into stimulus-response bonds, behaviorists have provided a fragmented view of personality (Liebert & Spiegler, 1990; Maddi, 1989). Humanistic theo-

rists, whom we shall cover next, have been particularly vocal in criticizing this piecemeal analysis of personality.

HUMANISTIC PERSPECTIVES

Humanistic theory emerged in the 1950s as something of a backlash against the behavioral and psychodynamic theories that we have just discussed. The principal charge hurled at these two models was that they are dehumanizing. Freudian theory was criticized for its belief that behavior is dominated by primitive, animalistic drives. Behaviorism was criticized for its preoccupation with animal research and for its mechanistic, fragmented view of personality. Critics argued that both schools of thought are too deterministic and that both fail to recognize the unique qualities of human behavior.

Many of these critics blended into a loose alliance that came to be known as humanism, because of its exclusive focus on human behavior. **Humanism is a theoretical orientation that emphasizes the unique qualities of humans, especially their freedom and their potential for personal growth.** In contrast to most psychodynamic and behavioral theorists, humanistic theorists, such as Carl Rogers and Abraham Maslow, take an optimistic view of human nature. They assume (1) that people can rise above their primitive animal heritage and control their biological urges and (2) that people are largely conscious and rational beings who are not dominated by unconscious, irrational needs and conflicts. Humanistic theorists also maintain that a person's subjective view of the world is more important than objective reality. According to this notion, if you think that you're homely or bright or sociable, then this belief will influence your behavior more than the realities of how homely, bright, or sociable you actually are.

Rogers's Person-Centered Theory

Carl Rogers (1951, 1961, 1980) was one of the fathers of the human potential movement. This movement emphasizes self-realization through sensitivity training, encounter groups, and other exercises intended to foster personal growth. Like Freud, Rogers based his personality theory on his extensive therapeutic interactions with many clients. Because of its emphasis on a person's subjective point of view, Rogers called his approach a *person-centered theory*.

"I have little sympathy with the rather prevalent concept that man is basically irrational, and that his impulses, if not controlled, will lead to destruction of others and self. Man's behavior is exquisitely rational, moving with subtle and ordered complexity toward the goals his organism is endeavoring to achieve."
CARL ROGERS

The Self

Rogers viewed personality structure in terms of just one construct. He called this construct the *self*, although it's more widely known today as the *self-concept*. **A *self-concept* is a collection of beliefs about one's own nature, unique qualities, and typical behavior.** Your self-concept is your own mental picture of yourself. It's a collection of self-perceptions. For example, a self-concept might include beliefs such as "I'm easygoing" or "I'm sly and crafty" or "I'm pretty" or "I'm hardworking." According to Rogers, individuals are aware of their self-concept. It's not buried in their unconscious.

Rogers stressed the subjective nature of the self-concept. Your self-concept may not be entirely consistent with your experiences. Most people tend to distort their experiences to some extent to promote a relatively favorable self-concept. For example, you may believe that you're quite bright, but your grade transcript might suggest otherwise. Rogers called the gap between self-concept and reality incongruence. ***Incongruence* is the degree of disparity between one's self-concept and one's actual experience.** In contrast, if a person's self-concept is reasonably accurate, it's said to be *congruent* with reality (see Figure 12.5). Everyone experiences *some* incongruence. The crucial issue is how much. As we'll see, Rogers maintained that too much incongruence undermines one's psychological well-being.

Development of the Self

In terms of personality development, Rogers was concerned with how childhood experiences promote congruence or incongruence between one's self-concept and one's experience. According to Rogers, people have a strong need for affection, love, and acceptance from others. Early in life, parents provide most of this affection. Rogers

maintained that some parents make their affection very *conditional*. That is, it depends on the child's behaving well and living up to expectations. When parental love seems conditional, children often block out of their self-concept those experiences that make them feel unworthy of love. They do so because they're worried about parental acceptance, which appears precarious. At the other end of the spectrum, some parents make their affection *unconditional*. Their children have less need to block out unworthy experiences because they've been assured that they're worthy of affection, no matter what they do.

Hence, Rogers believed that unconditional love from parents fosters congruence and that conditional love fosters incongruence. He further theorized that if individuals grow up believing that affection from others is highly conditional, they will go on to distort more and more of their experiences in order to feel worthy of acceptance from a wider and wider array of people.

A person's self-concept evolves throughout childhood and adolescence. As individuals' self-concept gradually stabilizes, they begin to feel comfortable with it and are usually loyal to it. This loyalty produces two effects. First, the self-concept becomes a "self-fulfilling prophecy" in that the person tends to behave in ways that are consistent with it. If you see yourself as an even-tempered, reflective person, you'll consciously work at behaving in these ways. If you happen to behave impulsively, you'll probably feel some discomfort because you're acting "out of character." Second, people become resistant to information that contradicts their self-concept. Contradictory information threatens their comfortable equilibrium. If your experiences begin to suggest that you're not as even-tempered as you thought, you'll probably try to find ways to dismiss this evidence.

Anxiety and Defense

According to Rogers, experiences that threaten people's personal views of themselves are the principal cause of troublesome anxiety. The more inaccurate your self-concept is, the more likely you are to have experiences that clash with your self-perceptions. Thus, people with highly incongruent self-concepts are especially likely to be plagued by recurrent anxiety.

To ward off this anxiety, individuals often behave defensively in an effort to reinterpret their experience so that it appears consistent with their self-concept. Thus, they ignore, deny, and twist reality to protect and perpetuate their self-concept. Consider a young lady who, like most people,

Figure 12.5. Rogers's view of personality structure. In Rogers's model, the self-concept is the only important structural construct. However, Rogers acknowledged that one's self-concept may not be consistent with the realities of one's actual experience—a condition called incongruence.

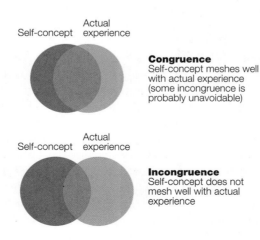

Self-concept   Actual experience

Congruence
Self-concept meshes well with actual experience (some incongruence is probably unavoidable)

Self-concept   Actual experience

Incongruence
Self-concept does not mesh well with actual experience

considers herself a "nice person." Let's suppose that in reality she is rather conceited and selfish. She gets feedback from both boyfriends and girlfriends that she is a "self-centered, snotty brat." How might she react in order to protect her self-concept? She might ignore or block out those occasions when she behaves selfishly. She might attribute her girlfriends' negative comments to their jealousy of her good looks. Perhaps she would blame her boyfriends' negative remarks on their disappointment because she won't get more serious with them. Meanwhile, she might start doing some kind of charity work to show everyone (including herself) that she really is a nice person. As you can see, people will sometimes go to great lengths to defend their self-concept.

Maslow's Theory of Self-Actualization

Abraham Maslow, who grew up in Brooklyn, described his childhood as "unhappy, lonely, [and] isolated." To follow through on his interest in psychology, he had to resist parental pressures to go into law. Maslow spent much of his career at Brandeis University, where he created an influential theory of motivation and provided crucial leadership for the fledgling humanistic movement.

Like Rogers, Maslow (1968, 1970) argued that psychology should take an optimistic view of human nature instead of dwelling on the causes of disorders. "To oversimplify the matter somewhat," he said, "it's as if Freud supplied to us the sick half of psychology and we must now fill it out with the healthy half" (1968, p. 5). Maslow's key contribution to personality theory was his description of the *self-actualizing person* as an example of the healthy personality.

As you may recall from Chapter 10, Maslow theorized that humans are driven by a ***need for self-actualization,*** **which is the need to fulfill one's potential.** Thus, Maslow agreed with Rogers that people have an innate drive toward fulfillment and personal growth. Moreover, he believed that this fulfillment is crucial to psychological health, saying, "A musician must make music, an artist must paint, a poet must write, if he is to be ultimately at peace with himself. What a man can be, he *must* be" (1970, p. 46).

Working from this premise, Maslow set out to discover the nature of the healthy personality. He tried to identify people of exceptional mental health, so that he could investigate their characteristics. In one case, he used psychological tests and interviews to sort out the healthiest

1% of a sizable population of college students. He also studied admired historical figures (such as Thomas Jefferson and William James) and personal acquaintances characterized by superior adjustment. Over a period of years, he accumulated his case histories and gradually sketched, in broad strokes, a picture of ideal psychological health.

According to Maslow, ***self-actualizing persons*** **are people with exceptionally healthy personalities, marked by continued personal growth.** Maslow identified various traits characteristic of self-actualizing people. Many of these traits are listed in Figure 12.6. In brief, Maslow found that self-actualizers are accurately tuned in to reality and that they're at peace with themselves. He found that they're open and spontaneous and that they retain a fresh appreciation of the world around them. Socially, they're sensitive to others' needs and enjoy rewarding interpersonal relations. However, they're not dependent on others for approval or uncomfortable with solitude. They thrive on their work, and they enjoy their sense of humor. Maslow also noted that they have "peak experiences" (profound emotional highs) more often than others do. Finally, he found that they strike a nice balance between many polarities in personality. For instance, they can be both childlike and mature, both rational and intuitive, both conforming and rebellious.

Evaluating Humanistic Perspectives

The humanists added a refreshing new perspective to the study of personality. Their argument that a person's subjective views may be more important than objective reality has proven compelling. As we noted earlier, even behavioral theo-

"It is as if Freud supplied to us the sick half of psychology and we must now fill it out with the healthy half."
ABRAHAM MASLOW

Figure 12.6. Maslow's view of the healthy personality. Humanistic theorists emphasize psychological health instead of maladjustment. Maslow's description of characteristics of self-actualizing people evokes a picture of the healthy personality.

Characteristics of self-actualizing people

- Clear, efficient perception of reality and comfortable relations with it

- Spontaneity, simplicity, and naturalness

- Problem centering (having something outside themselves they "must" do as a mission)

- Detachment and need for privacy

- Autonomy, independence of culture and environment

- Continued freshness of appreciation

- Mystical and peak experiences

- Feelings of kinship and identification with the human race

- Strong friendships, but limited in number

- Democratic character structure

- Ethical discrimination between good and evil

- Philosophical, unhostile sense of humor

- Balance between polarities in personality

rists have begun to take into account subjective personal factors such as beliefs and expectancies. The humanistic approach also deserves credit for making the self-concept an important construct in psychology. Today, theorists of many persuasions use the self-concept in their analyses of personality. Finally, the humanists have often been applauded for focusing attention on the issue of what constitutes a healthy personality.

Of course, there's a negative side to the balance sheet as well (Burger, 1993). Critics argue (1) that many aspects of humanistic theory are difficult to put to a scientific test, (2) that humanists have been unrealistically optimistic in their assumptions about human nature and their descriptions of the healthy personality, and (3) that more experimental research is needed to catch up with the theorizing in the humanistic camp. The latter complaint is precisely the opposite of what we'll encounter in the next section, on biological perspectives, where more theorizing is needed to catch up with the research.

BIOLOGICAL PERSPECTIVES

Like many identical twins reared apart, Jim Lewis and Jim Springer found they had been leading eerily similar lives. Separated four weeks after birth in 1940, the Jim twins grew up 45 miles apart in Ohio and were reunited in 1979. Eventually, they discovered that both drove the same model blue Chevrolet, chain-smoked Salems, chewed their fingernails and owned dogs named Toy. Each had spent a good deal of time vacationing at the same three-block strip of beach in Florida. More important, when tested for such personality traits as flexibility, self-control, and sociability, the twins responded almost exactly alike. (Leo, 1987, p. 63)

So began a *Time* magazine summary of a major twin study conducted at the University of Minnesota Center for Twin and Adoption Research. Since 1979 the investigators at this center have been studying the personality resemblance of identical twins reared apart. Not all the twin pairs have been as similar as Jim Lewis and Jim Springer, but many of the parallels have been uncanny (Lykken et al., 1992). Identical twins Oskar Stohr and Jack Yufe were separated soon after birth. Oskar was sent to a Nazi-run school in Czechoslovakia while Jack was raised in a Jewish home on a Caribbean island. When they were reunited for the first time during middle age, they showed up wearing similar mustaches, haircuts, shirts, and wire-rimmed glasses! A pair of previously separated female twins both arrived at the Minneapolis airport wearing seven rings on their fingers. One had a son named Richard Andrew and the other had a son named Andrew Richard!

Could personality be largely inherited? These anecdotal reports of striking resemblances between identical twins reared apart certainly raise this possibility. In this section we'll discuss Hans Eysenck's theory, which emphasizes the influence of heredity, and look at recent behavioral genetics research on the heritability of personality.

Eysenck's Theory

Hans Eysenck was born in Germany but fled to London during the era of Nazi rule. He went on to become one of Britain's most prominent psychologists. Eysenck (1967, 1982, 1990a) views personality structure as a hierarchy of traits, in which many superficial traits are derived from a smaller number of more basic traits, which are

derived from a handful of fundamental higher-order traits, as shown in Figure 12.7. His studies suggest that all aspects of personality emerge from just three higher-order traits: extraversion, neuroticism, and psychoticism. *Extraversion* involves being sociable, assertive, active, and lively. *Neuroticism* involves being anxious, tense, moody, and low in self-esteem. *Psychoticism* involves being egocentric, impulsive, cold, and antisocial.

According to Eysenck, "Personality is determined to a large extent by a person's genes" (1967, p. 20). How is heredity linked to personality in Eysenck's model? In part, through conditioning concepts borrowed from behavioral theory. Eysenck theorizes that some people can be conditioned more readily than others because of differences in their physiological functioning. These variations in "conditionability" are assumed to influence the personality traits that people acquire through conditioning processes.

Eysenck has shown a special interest in explaining variations in *extraversion-introversion*, the trait dimension first described years earlier by Carl Jung. He has proposed that introverts tend to have high levels of physiological arousal, which make them more easily conditioned than extraverts. According to Eysenck, people who condition easily acquire more conditioned inhibitions than others. These inhibitions make them more bashful, tentative, and uneasy in social situations. This social discomfort leads them to turn inward. Hence, they become introverted.

Is personality largely inherited? The story of these identical twins would certainly suggest so. Although they were reared apart from four weeks after their birth, Jim Lewis (left) and Jim Springer (right) exhibit remarkable correspondence in personality. Some of the similarities in their lives—such as the benches built around trees in their yards—seem uncanny.

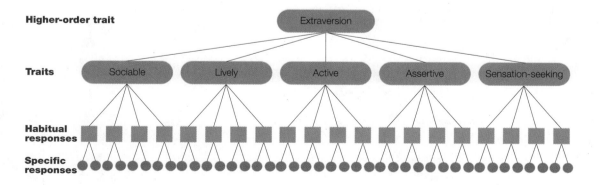

Higher-order trait

Extraversion

Traits

Sociable Lively Active Assertive Sensation-seeking

Habitual responses

Specific responses

Figure 12.7. Eysenck's model of personality structure. Eysenck described personality structure as a hierarchy of traits. In this scheme, a few higher-order traits, such as extraversion, determine a host of lower-order traits, which determine a person's habitual responses.

"Personality is determined to a large extent by a person's genes."
HANS EYSENCK

Behavioral Genetics and Personality

Recent research in behavioral genetics has provided impressive support for the idea that personality is largely inherited (Plomin, Chipuer, & Loehlin, 1990). For instance, in one study, 573 pairs of twins responded to five personality scales that measured altruism, empathy, nurturance, aggressiveness, and assertiveness (Rushton et al., 1986). On all five traits, identical twins were found to be much more similar to each other than were fraternal twins. Based on these data, Rushton and his co-workers concluded that genetic factors exert considerable influence over personality. Similar conclusions have been drawn by many researchers who have investigated the heritability of the "Big Five" personality traits (neuroticism, extraversion, openness to experience, agreeableness, conscientiousness) described at the beginning of the chapter (Loehlin, 1992).

Some skeptics wonder whether identical twins might exhibit more trait similarity than fraternal twins because they're treated more alike. In other words, they wonder whether environmental factors (rather than heredity) could be responsible for identical twins' greater personality resemblance. This nagging question can be answered only by studying identical twins reared apart, which is why the twin study at the University of Minnesota is so important.

The Minnesota study (Tellegen et al., 1988) was the first to administer the same personality test to identical and fraternal twins reared apart, as well as together. Most of the twins reared apart were separated quite early in life (median age of 2.5 months) and remained separated for a long time (median period of almost 34 years).

Figure 12.8 shows the correlations for all four types of twin sets with regard to the three basic dimensions of personality measured in the study: (1) *positive emotionality* (extraverted, achievement oriented, having a sense of well-being), (2) *negative emotionality* (anxious, angry, alienated), and (3) *constraint* (inhibited, cautious, deferential, conventional). These correlations reveal that identical twins reared together are more similar on all three traits than fraternal twins reared together. More telling, though, are the results for the identical twins reared apart. On all three traits, identical twins reared apart are still more similar to each other than are fraternal twins reared together.

Figure 12.8 also shows the proportion of variation in each trait allocated to heredity, family environment, and unique experience, as determined by statistical modeling procedures. The

Figure 12.8. Personality resemblance in the Tellegen et al. (1988) study. On all three basic personality traits examined in this study, identical twins were more similar than fraternal twins—even if the identical twins were reared apart. These correlational data yielded relatively high estimates of heritability. Evidence of environmental influence on personality was also apparent in the data, but the investigators were surprised to find that the impact of family environment appeared negligible on two out of three personality traits.

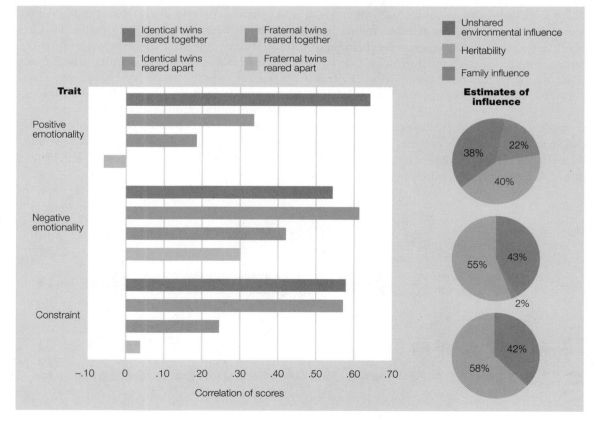

genetic components, which are heritability estimates, range from 40% to 58%. A noticeable effect for family environment was found only for the positive emotionality trait. The investigators maintain that their results support the hypothesis that genetic blueprints shape the contours of personality.

Research on the heritability of personality has inadvertently turned up an interesting finding that was apparent in the Minnesota twin study. A number of studies have found that shared family environment has surprisingly little impact on personality (Plomin & Daniels, 1987; Hoffman, 1991). For many years, social scientists assumed that the environment shared by children growing up together led to some personality resemblance among them, but these studies have seriously undermined this widespread belief. These findings have led Robert Plomin (1990) to ask, "Why are children in the same family so different from one another?" Researchers have only just begun to explore this question. Plomin speculates that children in the same family experience home environments that are not nearly as homogeneous as previously assumed. He notes that children in the same home may be treated quite differently, because gender and birth order can influence parents' approaches to child rearing. Temperamental differences between children may also evoke differences in parenting. Focusing on how environmental factors vary *within* families represents a promising new way to explore the determinants of personality.

Evaluating Biological Perspectives

Researchers have compiled convincing evidence that biological factors help shape personality, and findings on the meager effects of shared family environment have launched intriguing new approaches to the investigation of personality development. Nonetheless, we must take note of some weaknesses in biological approaches to personality. Critics assert (1) that heritability ratios should be regarded as ballpark estimates that will vary depending on sampling procedures (McGuire & Haviland, 1985), and (2) that there's no comprehensive biological theory of personality, so additional theoretical work is needed to catch up with recent empirical findings.

CULTURE AND PERSONALITY

Are there connections between culture and personality? The investigation of this question dates back to the 1940s and 1950s, when researchers set out to describe various cultures' *modal personality* (Kardiner & Linton, 1945) or *national character* (Kluckhohn & Murray, 1948). These investigations, which were largely guided by Freud's psychoanalytic theory, met with relatively little success (Bruner, 1974). Studies of the links between culture and personality dwindled after the disappointments of the 1940s and 1950s. However, in recent years, psychology's new interest in cultural factors has led to a renaissance of culture-

CONCEPT CHECK 12.4
Understanding the Implications of Major Theories: Who Said This?

Check your understanding of the implications of the personality theories we've discussed by indicating which theorist is likely to have made the statements below. The answers are in Appendix A.

Choose from the following theorists:

Alfred Adler

Albert Bandura

Hans Eysenck

Sigmund Freud

Abraham Maslow

Walter Mischel

Quotes

1. "If you deliberately plan to be less than you are capable of being, then I warn you that you'll be deeply unhappy for the rest of your life." _____

2. "I feel that the major, most fundamental dimensions of personality are likely to be those on which [there is] strong genetic determination of individual differences." _____

3. "People are in general not candid over sexual matters . . . they wear a heavy overcoat woven of a tissue of lies, as though the weather were bad in the world of sexuality." _____

Culture can shape personality. Children in Asiatic cultures, for example, grow up with a value system that allows them to view themselves as interconnected parts of large social units. Hence, they tend to avoid positioning themselves so that they stand out from others.

personality research. Like cross-cultural research in other areas of psychology, this research has found evidence of both continuity and variability across cultures.

For the most part, continuity has been apparent in cross-cultural comparisons of the *trait structure* of personality. When English language personality scales have been translated and administered in other cultures, the predicted dimensions of personality have emerged from the statistical analyses. For example, in cross-cultural studies of the Eysenck Personality Questionnaire, the same four factors originally identified in Great Britain have consistently been found in other cultures (Eysenck & Eysenck, 1983). Similarly, when scales that tap the "Big Five" personality traits have been administered and subjected to statistical analysis in other cultures, the usual five traits have typically emerged (Paunonen et al., 1992; Stumpf, 1993). Far more data are needed before theorists are ready to conclude that the basic structure of personality is pancultural, but the cross-cultural similarities observed thus far are impressive.

In contrast, when researchers have compared cultural groups on specific aspects of personality, some intriguing disparities have surfaced. Perhaps the most interesting work has been that of Hazel Markus and Shinobu Kitayama (1991) comparing American and Asian conceptions of the self. According to Markus and Kitayama, American parents teach their children to be self-reliant, to feel good about themselves, and to view themselves as special individuals. Children are encouraged to excel in competitive endeavors and to strive to stand out from the crowd. They are told that "the squeaky wheel gets the grease" and that "you have to stand up for yourself." Thus, Markus and

Kitayama argue that *American culture fosters an independent view of the self*. American youngsters learn to define themselves in terms of their personal attributes, abilities, accomplishments, and possessions. Their unique strengths and achievements become the basis for their sense of self-worth. Hence, they are prone to exaggerate their uniqueness and to overestimate their abilities.

Most of us take this individualistic mentality for granted. Indeed, Markus and Kitayama maintain that "most of what psychologists currently know about human nature is based on one particular view—the so-called Western view of the individual as an independent, self-contained, autonomous entity" (1991, p. 224). However, they marshal convincing evidence that this view is *not* universal. They argue that in Asian cultures such as Japan and China, socialization practices foster a more *interdependent view of the self*, which emphasizes the fundamental connectedness of people to each other (see Figure 12.9). In these cultures, parents teach their children that they can rely on family and friends, that they should be modest about their personal accomplishments so they don't diminish others' achievements, and that they should view themselves as part of a larger social matrix. Children are encouraged to fit in with others and to avoid standing out from the crowd. A popular adage in Japan reminds children that "the nail that stands out gets pounded down." Hence, Markus and Kitayama assert that Asian youngsters typically learn to define themselves in terms of the groups they belong to. Their harmonious relations with others and their pride in group achievements become the basis for their sense of self-worth. Because their self-esteem does not hinge so much on personal strengths, they have little need to exaggerate their uniqueness or their abilities. Consistent with this analysis, Markus and Kitayama report that Asian subjects tend to view themselves as more similar to their peers than American subjects do and that they consistently downplay their personal achievements more than Americans do.

Markus and Kitayama speculate that the interdependent view of self may also be the norm in many African and Latin American cultures, but more comparative data are needed to evaluate this possibility. In any case, the cultural variations in conceptions of self that they have uncovered are fascinating and will surely be the subject of much future research. Their findings demonstrate once again that we cannot assume that Western models of psychological processes will apply equally well in other cultures.

Independent self-system

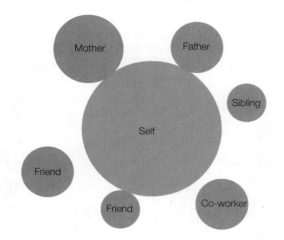

Interdependent self-system

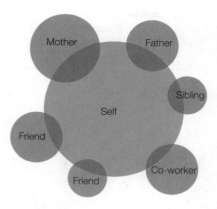

Figure 12.9. Culture and conceptions of self. According to Markus and Kitayama (1991), Western cultures foster an independent view of the self as a unique individual who is separate from others, as diagrammed on the left. In contrast, Asian cultures encourage an interdependent view of the self as part of an interconnected social matrix, as diagrammed on the right. The interdependent view leads people to define themselves in terms of their social relationships (for instance, as someone's daughter, employee, colleague, or neighbor).

PUTTING IT IN PERSPECTIVE

The preceding discussion of culture and personality obviously highlighted the text's theme that our behavior is influenced by our cultural heritage. This chapter has also been ideally suited for embellishing on two other unifying themes: psychology's theoretical diversity and the idea that psychology evolves in a sociohistorical context.

No other area of psychology is characterized by as much theoretical diversity as the study of personality, where there are literally dozens of insightful theories. Some of this diversity exists because different theories attempt to explain different facets of behavior. Of course, much of this diversity reflects genuine disagreements on basic questions about personality. These disagreements will be apparent on the next two pages, where you'll find an illustrated comparative overview of the ideas of Freud, Skinner, Rogers, and Eysenck, as representatives of the psychodynamic, behavioral, humanistic, and biological approaches to personality.

The study of personality also highlights the sociohistorical context in which psychology evolves. Personality theories have left many marks on modern culture—we can mention only a handful as illustrations. The theories of Freud, Adler, and Skinner have had an enormous impact on child-rearing practices. The ideas of Freud and Jung have found their way into literature (influencing the portrayal of fictional characters) and the visual arts. For example, Freud's theory helped inspire surrealism's interest in the world of dreams. Social learning theory has become embroiled in the public policy debate about whether media violence should be controlled, because of

its effects on viewers' aggressive behavior. Maslow's hierarchy of needs and Skinner's affirmation of the value of positive reinforcement have given rise to new approaches to management in the world of business and industry.

Sociohistorical forces also leave their imprint on psychology. This chapter provided many examples of how personal experiences, prevailing attitudes, and historical events have contributed to the evolution of ideas in psychology. For example, Freud's pessimistic view of human nature and his emphasis on the dark forces of aggression were shaped to some extent by his exposure to the hostilities of World War I and prevailing anti-Semitic sentiments. Freud's emphasis on sexuality surely was influenced by the Victorian climate of sexual repression that existed in his youth. Adler's views also reflected the social context in which he grew up. His interest in inferiority feelings and compensation appears to have sprung from his own sickly childhood and the difficulties he had to overcome. His interest in birth order probably stemmed, in part, from the way in which he was overshadowed by his older brother. Likewise, it's reasonable to speculate that Jung's childhood loneliness and introversion may have sparked his interest in the introversion-extraversion dimension of personality.

Progress in the study of personality has also been influenced by developments in other areas of psychology. For instance, the enterprise of psychological testing originally emerged out of efforts to measure general intelligence. Eventually, however, the principles of psychological testing were applied to the challenge of measuring personality. In the upcoming Application we discuss the logic and limitations of personality tests.

"Most of what psychologists currently know about human nature is based on one particular view—the so-called Western view of the individual as an independent, self-contained, autonomous entity."
HAZEL MARKUS and SHINOBU KITAYAMA

FOUR VIEWS OF PERSONALITY

Theorist and orientation	Source of data and observations	Key motivational forces
A psychodynamic view Sigmund Freud 	Case studies from clinical practice of psychoanalysis 	Sex and aggression; need to reduce tension resulting from internal conflicts
A behavioral view B. F. Skinner 	Laboratory experiments, primarily with animals 	Pursuit of primary (unlearned) and secondary (learned) reinforcers; priorities depend on personal history
A humanistic view Carl Rogers 	Case studies from clinical practice of client-centered therapy 	Actualizing tendency (motive to develop capacities, and experience personal growth) and self-actualizing tendency (motive to maintain self-concept and behave in ways that are consistent with self-concept)
A biological view Hans Eysenck 	Twin, family, and adoption studies of heritability; factor analysis studies of personality structure 	No specific motivational forces singled out.

Model of personality structure	View of personality development	Roots of disorders

Three interacting components (id, ego, superego) operating at three levels of consciousness

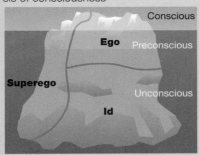

Emphasis on fixation or progress through psychosexual stages; experiences in early childhood (such as toilet training) can leave lasting mark on adult personality

Unconscious fixations and unresolved conflicts from childhood, usually centering on sex and aggression

Collections of response tendencies tied to specific stimulus situations

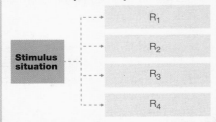

Personality evolves gradually over the life span (not in stages); responses (such as extraverted joking) followed by reinforcement (such as appreciative laughter) become more frequent

Maladaptive behavior due to faulty learning; the "symptom" *is* the problem, not a sign of underlying disease

Self-concept, which may or may not mesh well with actual experience

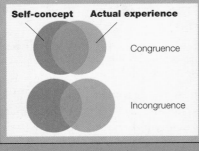

Children who receive unconditional love have less need to be defensive; they develop more accurate, congruent self-concept; conditional love fosters incongruence

Incongruence between self and actual experience (inaccurate self-concept); overdependence on others for approval and sense of worth

Hierarchy of traits, with specific traits derived from more fundamental, general traits

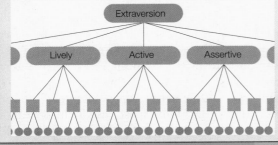

Emphasis on unfolding of genetic blueprint with maturation; inherited predispositions interact with learning experiences

Genetic vulnerability activated in part by environmental factors

Understanding Personality Assessment

Answer the following "true" or "false."

__ **1** Responses to personality tests are subject to unconscious distortion.

__ **2** The results of personality tests are often misunderstood.

__ **3** Personality test scores should be interpreted with caution.

__ **4** Personality tests serve many important functions.

If you answered "true" to all four questions, you earned a perfect score. Yes, personality tests are subject to distortion. Admittedly, test results are often misunderstood, and they should be interpreted cautiously. In spite of these problems, however, psychological tests can be quite useful.

Everyone engages in efforts to size up his or her own personality as well as that of others. When you think to yourself that "Mary Ann is shrewd and poised," or when you remark to a friend that "Howard is timid and submissive," you're making personality assessments. In a sense, then, personality assessment is an ongoing part of daily life. Given the popular interest in personality assessment, it's not surprising that psychologists have devised formal measures of personality.

The Uses of Personality Scales

When and why are psychological tests used to measure personality? They have a variety of purposes. Benjamin Kleinmuntz (1985) lists four principal uses of personality tests:

1. Personality tests are used extensively by mental health professionals in the *clinical diagnosis* of psychological dis-

orders. Although diagnoses are not made on the basis of test results alone, personality scales can be helpful in arriving at diagnostic decisions.

2. Personality measurement may be done for the purpose of *counseling* individuals about a variety of normal, everyday problems. Counselors often use personality scales to help people chart career plans and make vocational decisions.

3. Formal personality assessment often plays a key role in *personnel selection* in business, industry, government, and the military services. This use of personality testing has become controversial in recent years. Nonetheless, many organizations continue to use personality scales to assess applicants' suitability for various jobs.

4. Personality scales are frequently used in *psychological research*. Empirical studies on a great variety of issues require precise measurement of some aspect of personality. For instance, let's say you want to investigate whether introversion is related to a certain style of child rearing. Your task is simplified greatly if you have a personality test that measures introversion.

Personality tests can be divided into two broad categories: *self-report inventories* and *projective tests*. In this Application, we'll discuss some representative tests from both categories and discuss their strengths and weaknesses.

Self-Report Inventories

Self-report inventories are personality tests that ask individuals to answer a series of questions about their characteristic behavior. The logic underlying this approach is very simple: Who knows you better? Who has known you longer? Who has more access to your

private feelings? We'll look at three examples of self-report scales, the MMPI, the 16PF, and the NEO Personality Inventory.

The MMPI

The most widely used self-report inventory is the Minnesota Multiphasic Personality Inventory (MMPI). This test was developed in the 1940s (Hathaway & McKinley, 1943) but has recently undergone a major revision and modernization. The authors of MMPI-2 set out to maintain the original character of the scale while replacing obsolete items, eliminating sexist language, and updating the test norms (Graham, 1990).

The MMPI was originally designed to aid clinicians in the diagnosis of psychological disorders. Consequently, it measures mostly aspects of personality that, when manifested to an extreme degree, are thought to be symptoms of disorders. Examples include traits such as paranoia, depression, and hysteria.

The MMPI is a rather lengthy test. The revised version consists of 567 statements to which the subject answers "true," "false," or "cannot say." The MMPI yields scores on the 14 subscales described in Table 12.4. Four of the subscales are *validity scales* that provide indications about whether a subject has been careless or deceptive in taking the test. The remaining 10 are *clinical scales* that measure various aspects of personality.

Are the MMPI clinical scales valid? That is, do they measure what they were designed to measure? The validity of the MMPI has been investigated in hundreds of studies (Butcher & Keller, 1984). Originally, it was assumed that the 10 clinical subscales would provide direct indexes of specific types of disorders. In other words, a high score on the de-

Table 12.4 Personality Characteristics Associated with High MMPI Scores

Scale	Characteristics Associated with Higher Scores
Validity scales	
Cannot say (?)	May indicate evasiveness.
Lie scale (L)	Indicates a tendency to present oneself in an overly favorable or highly virtuous light.
Infrequency scale (F)	Items on this scale are endorsed very infrequently by most people. Suggests carelessness, confusion, or "faking illness."
Subtle defensiveness (K)	Measures defensiveness of a subtle nature.
Clinical scales	
Hypochondriasis (Hs)	Indicates person is preoccupied with self, complaining, hostile, and presenting numerous physical problems that tend to be chronic.
Depression (D)	Indicates person is moody, shy, despondent, pessimistic, and distressed; one of the most frequently elevated scales in clinical patients.
Hysteria (Hy)	Indicates person tends to rely on neurotic defenses such as denial and repression to deal with stress and tends to be dependent, naive, outgoing, infantile, and narcissistic.
Psychopathic deviation (Pd)	May indicate rebelliousness, impulsiveness, hedonism, antisocial behavior, difficulty in marital or family relationships, and trouble with the law or authority in general.
Masculinity/femininity (MF)	Indicates departure from traditional gender roles. High-scoring men are described as sensitive, aesthetic, passive, or feminine. They may show conflicts over sexual identity and low heterosexual drive. Because the direction of scoring is reversed, high-scoring women are seen as masculine, rough, aggressive, self-confident, unemotional, and insensitive.
Paranoia (Pa)	Often indicates person is suspicious, aloof, shrewd, guarded, worrisome, and overly sensitive and likely to project or externalize blame.
Psychasthenia (Pt)	Indicates person is tense, anxious, ruminative, preoccupied, obsessional, phobic, rigid, and frequently self-condemning and feeling inferior and inadequate.
Schizophrenia (Sc)	Often indicates person is withdrawn, shy, unusual, or strange and has peculiar thoughts or ideas, poor reality contact, and perhaps delusions and hallucinations.
Hypomania (Ma)	Indicates person is social, outgoing, impulsive, overly energetic, optimistic, and in some cases amoral, flighty, grandiose, and impulsive.
Social introversion (Sie)	Indicates person is introverted, shy, withdrawn, socially reserved, submissive, overcontrolled, lethargic, conventional, tense, inflexible, and guilt-prone.

Source: Adapted from Keller, Butcher, and Slutske (1990)

pression scale would be indicative of depression, a high score on the paranoia scale would be indicative of a paranoid disorder, and so forth. However, research revealed that the relations between MMPI scores and various types of pathology are much more complex than originally anticipated. People with most types of disorders show elevated scores on *several* MMPI subscales. This means that certain score *profiles* are indicative of specific disorders (see Figure 12.10 on the next page). Thus, the interpretation of the MMPI is quite complicated. Nonetheless, the MMPI can be a very helpful diagnostic tool for the clinician. The fact that the inventory has been translated into more than 115 languages is a testimonial to its usefulness (Butcher, 1990).

The 16PF and NEO Personality Inventory

Raymond Cattell (1957, 1965) set out to identify and measure the *basic dimensions* of the *normal* personality. He started with a previously compiled list of 4504 personality traits. This massive list was reduced to 171 traits by weeding out terms that were virtually synonymous. Cattell then used a statistical procedure called factor analysis to identify clusters of closely related traits and the factors underlying them. Eventually, he reduced the list of 171 traits to 16 *source traits*. The Sixteen Personality Factor (16PF) Questionnaire is a 187-item scale that assesses these 16 basic dimensions of personality (Cattell, Eber, & Tatsuoka, 1970), which are listed in Figure 12.11 (next page).

As we noted in the main body of the chapter, some theorists believe that only five trait dimensions are required to pro-

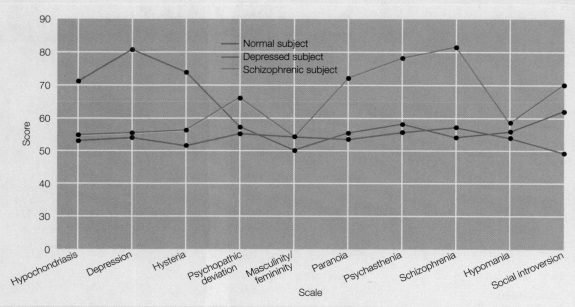

Figure 12.10. MMPI profiles. Scores on the 10 clinical scales of the MMPI are often plotted as shown here to create a profile for a client. The normal range for scores on each subscale is 50 to 65. People with disorders frequently exhibit elevated scores on several clinical scales rather than just one.

Normal subject
Depressed subject
Schizophrenic subject

Score

Hypochondriasis Depression Hysteria Psychopathic deviation Masculinity/ femininity Paranoia Psychasthenia Schizophrenia Hypomania Social introversion

Scale

vide a full description of personality. This view has led to the creation of a relatively new test—the NEO Personality Inventory. Developed by Paul Costa and Robert McCrae (1985, 1992), the NEO Inventory is designed to measure the Big Five traits: neuroticism, extraversion, openness to experience, agreeableness, and conscientiousness. In spite of its short life span, the NEO is already widely used

in research and clinical work. Some testing experts, such as Joseph Mattarazzo (1992), believe that the NEO represents the wave of the future in personality assessment.

Strengths and Weaknesses of Self-Report Inventories

To appreciate the strengths of self-report inventories, consider how else you might

inquire about an individual's personality. For instance, if you want to know how assertive someone is, why not just ask the person? Why administer an elaborate 50-item personality inventory that measures assertiveness? The advantage of the personality inventory is that it can provide a more objective and more precise estimate of the person's assertiveness.

Of course, self-report inventories are

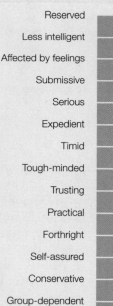

Figure 12.11. The Sixteen Personality Factor Questionnaire (16PF). Unlike the MMPI, Cattell's 16PF is designed to assess normal aspects of personality. The pairs of traits listed across from each other in the figure define the 16 factors measured by this self-report inventory. The profile shown is the average profile seen among a group of airline pilots who took the test.

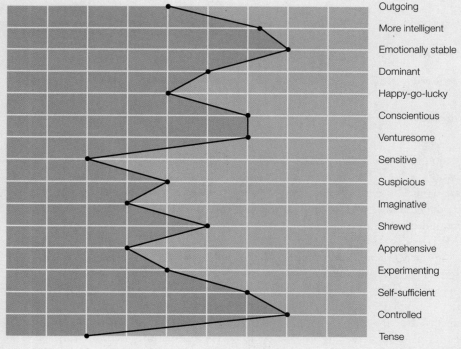

Reserved — Outgoing
Less intelligent — More intelligent
Affected by feelings — Emotionally stable
Submissive — Dominant
Serious — Happy-go-lucky
Expedient — Conscientious
Timid — Venturesome
Tough-minded — Sensitive
Trusting — Suspicious
Practical — Imaginative
Forthright — Shrewd
Self-assured — Apprehensive
Conservative — Experimenting
Group-dependent — Self-sufficient
Uncontrolled — Controlled
Relaxed — Tense

only as accurate as the information that respondents provide. They are susceptible to several sources of error (Furnham, 1986; Paulhus, 1991; Shedler, Mayman, & Manis, 1993), including the following:

1. *Deliberate deception.* Some self-report inventories include many questions whose purpose is easy to figure out. This problem makes it possible for some respondents to intentionally fake particular personality traits.

2. *Social desirability bias.* Without realizing it, some people consistently respond to questions in ways that make them look good. The social desirability bias isn't a matter of deception so much as wishful thinking.

3. *Response sets.* A response set is a systematic tendency to respond to test items in a particular way that is unrelated to the content of the items. For instance, some people, called "yea-sayers," tend to agree with virtually every statement on a test. Other people, called "nay-sayers," tend to disagree with nearly every statement.

Test developers have devised a number of strategies to reduce the impact of deliberate deception, social desirability bias, and response sets (Jackson, 1973). For instance, it's possible to insert a "lie scale" into a test to assess the likelihood that a respondent is engaging in deception. The best way to reduce the impact of social desirability bias is to identify items that are sensitive to this bias and drop them from the test. Problems with response sets can be reduced by systematically varying the way in which test items are worded.

Projective Tests

Projective tests, which all take a rather indirect approach to the assessment of personality, are used extensively in clinical work. **Projective tests ask subjects to respond to vague, ambiguous stimuli in ways that may reveal the subjects' needs, feelings, and personality traits.** The Rorschach test, for instance, con-

Figure 12.12. The Thematic Apperception Test (TAT). In taking the TAT, respondents are asked to tell stories about scenes such as this one. The themes apparent in each story can be scored to provide insight about the respondent's personality.

sists of a series of ten inkblots. Respondents are asked to describe what they see in the blots (see the photo below). In the Thematic Apperception Test (TAT), a series of pictures of simple scenes is presented to subjects who are asked to tell stories about what is happening in the scenes and what the characters are feeling. For instance, one TAT card shows a

young boy contemplating a violin resting on a table in front of him (see Figure 12.12 for another example).

The Projective Hypothesis

The "projective hypothesis" is that ambiguous materials can serve as a blank screen onto which people project their characteristic concerns, conflicts, and

Subjects are shown a series of ten inkblots from the Rorschach test and are asked to describe the forms that they see in these ambiguous stimuli. Evidence on the reliability and validity of the Rorschach is controversial.

desires (Frank, 1939). Thus, a competitive person who is shown the TAT card of the boy at the table with the violin might concoct a story about how the boy is contemplating an upcoming musical competition at which he hopes to excel. The same card shown to a person high in impulsiveness might elicit a story about how the boy is planning to sneak out the door to go dirt-bike riding with friends.

The scoring and interpretation of projective tests is very complicated. Rorschach responses may be analyzed in terms of content, originality, the feature of the inkblot that determined the response, and the amount of the inkblot used, among other criteria. In fact, five different systems exist for scoring the Rorschach (Edberg, 1990). TAT stories are examined in terms of heroes, needs, themes, and outcomes.

Strengths and Weaknesses of Projective Tests

Proponents of projective tests assert that the tests have two unique strengths. First, they are not transparent to subjects. That is, the subject doesn't know how the test provides information to the tester. Hence, it's difficult for people to engage in intentional deception. Second, the indirect approach used in these tests may make them especially sensitive to unconscious, latent features of personality.

Critics maintain that there is inadequate evidence for the reliability (consistency) and validity of projective measures. In spite of these problems, projective tests continue to be widely used by clinicians (Piotrowski, Sherry, & Keller, 1985). Although the subjectivity of the tests is a very real problem, their continued popularity suggests that they are effective in eliciting information that is valuable to many clinicians.

Despite the fact that the problems associated with self-report inventories and projective tests can't be eliminated entirely, these measurement strategies have proven useful in personality assessment. In light of the potential for distortion, however, the results of personality tests should be interpreted with caution. Of course, as we saw in Chapter 9, prudence is *always* in order when interpreting psychological test results of any kind.

Chapter 12 Review

KEY IDEAS

The Nature of Personality
◆ The concept of personality explains the consistency in people's behavior over time and situations while also explaining their distinctiveness. Personality traits are dispositions to behave in certain ways. There is considerable debate as to how many trait dimensions are necessary to fully describe personality.

Psychodynamic Perspectives
◆ Freud's psychoanalytic theory emphasizes the importance of the unconscious. Freud described personality structure in terms of three components—the id, ego, and superego—which are routinely involved in an ongoing series of internal conflicts.

◆ Freud theorized that conflicts centering on sex and aggression are especially likely to lead to significant anxiety. According to Freud, anxiety and other unpleasant emotions such as guilt are often warded off with defense mechanisms, which work primarily through self-deception.

◆ Freud believed that the first five years of life are extremely influential in shaping adult personality. He described a series of five psychosexual stages of development. Certain experiences during these stages can have lasting effects on adult personality. Resolution of the Oedipal complex is thought to be particularly critical to healthy development.

◆ Jung's most innovative and controversial concept was the collective unconscious. His analytical psychology also provided the first description of introversion and extraversion. Adler's individual psychology emphasizes how people strive for superiority to compensate for their feelings of inferiority.

◆ Overall, psychodynamic theories have produced many ground-breaking insights about the unconscious, the role of internal conflict, and the importance of early childhood experiences. However, psychodynamic theories have been criticized for their poor testability, their inadequate base of empirical evidence, and their male-centered views.

Behavioral Perspectives
◆ Behavioral theories explain how personality is shaped through learning. Skinner saw personality as a collection of response tendencies tied to specific stimulus situations. He assumed that personality development is a lifelong process in which response tendencies are shaped and reshaped by learning.

◆ Social learning theory focuses on how cognitive factors such as expectancies and self-efficacy regulate learned behavior. Bandura's concept of observational learning accounts for the acquisition of responses from models. Mischel's work has increased psychologists' awareness of the situational determinants of behavior.

◆ Behavioral approaches to personality are based on rigorous research. They have provided ample insights into how environmental factors and learning mold personalities. The behaviorists have been criticized for their overdependence on animal research, their neglect of biological factors, and their fragmented analysis of personality.

Humanistic Perspectives
◆ Humanistic theories take an optimistic view of people's conscious, rational ability to chart their own courses of action. Rogers focused on the self-concept as the critical aspect of personality. He maintained that anxiety is attributable to incongruence between one's self-concept and reality.

◆ Maslow theorized that psychological health depends on meeting one's need for self-actualization, which is the need to fulfill one's human potential. His work led to the description of self-actualizing persons as idealized examples of psychological health.

◆ Humanistic theories deserve credit for highlighting the importance of subjective views of oneself and for confronting the question of what makes for a healthy personality. Humanistic theories lack a firm base of research, are difficult to put to an empirical test, and may be overly optimistic about human nature.

Biological Perspectives
◆ Biological theories stress the genetic origins of personality. Eysenck suggests that heredity influences individual differences in physiological functioning that affect how easily people acquire conditioned responses. The Minnesota study on the personality resemblance of twins reared apart provides impressive evidence that genetic factors shape personality.

◆ The biological approach has been criticized because of methodological problems with heritability ratios and because it offers no systematic model of how physiology governs personality.

Culture and Personality
◆ Although far more research is needed, some studies suggest that the basic trait structure of personality may be much the same across cultures. However, notable differences have been found when researchers have compared cultural groups on specific personality traits, such as their conceptions of self.

Putting It in Perspective
◆ The study of personality illustrates how psychology is characterized by great theoretical diversity. There has been relatively little movement toward reconciling contradictory theories of personality. The study of personality also demonstrates how ideas in psychology are shaped by sociohistorical forces and how cultural factors influence psychological processes.

Application: Understanding Personality Assessment
◆ Personality assessment is useful in clinical diagnosis, counseling, personnel selection, and research. Self-report inventories, such as the MMPI, 16PF, and NEO Personality Inventory, ask subjects to describe themselves. Self-report inventories are vulnerable to certain sources of error, including deception, the social desirability bias, and response sets.

◆ Projective tests, such as the Rorschach and TAT, assume that subjects' responses to ambiguous stimuli reveal something about their personality. Projective tests may discourage deception by subjects and facilitate the exploration of unconscious dimensions of personality. While the projective hypothesis seems plausible, projective tests' reliability and validity are disturbingly low.

KEY TERMS

Archetypes	Personality trait
Behaviorism	Pleasure principle
Collective unconscious	Preconscious
Compensation	Projection
Conscious	Projective tests
Defense mechanisms	Psychodynamic theories
Displacement	Psychosexual stages
Ego	Rationalization
Extraverts	Reaction formation
Fixation	Reality principle
Humanism	Regression
Id	Repression
Identification	Self-actualizing persons
Incongruence	Self-concept
Introverts	Self-efficacy
Model	Self-report inventories
Need for self-actualization	Striving for superiority
Observational learning	Superego
Oedipal complex	Unconscious
Personality	

KEY PEOPLE

Alfred Adler	Abraham Maslow
Albert Bandura	Walter Mischel
Hans Eysenck	Carl Rogers
Sigmund Freud	B. F. Skinner
Carl Jung	

13 Stress, Coping, and Health

You're in your car headed home from school with a classmate. Traffic is barely moving. A radio report indicates that the traffic jam is only going to get worse. You groan audibly as you fiddle impatiently with the radio dial. Another motorist nearly takes your fender off trying to cut into your lane. Your pulse quickens as you shout insults at the unknown driver, who can't even hear you. You think about the term paper that you have to work on tonight. Your stomach knots up as you recall all the crumpled drafts you tossed into the wastebasket last night. If you don't finish that paper soon, you won't be able to find any time to study for your math test, not to mention your biology quiz. Suddenly, you remember that you promised the person you're dating that the two of you would get together tonight. There's no way. Another fight looms on the horizon. Your classmate asks how you feel about the tuition increase that the college announced yesterday. You've been trying not to think about it. You're already in debt up to your ears. Your parents are bugging you about changing schools, but you don't want to leave your friends. Your heartbeat quickens as you contemplate the debate you're sure to have with your parents. You feel wired with tension as you realize that the stress in your life never seems to let up.

Many circumstances can create stress. It comes in all sorts of packages: big and small, pretty and ugly, simple and complex. All too often, the package comes as a surprise. In this chapter we'll try to sort out these packages. We'll discuss the nature of stress, how people cope with stress, and the potential effects of stress.

Our examination of the relationship between stress and physical illness will lead us into a broader discussion of the psychology of health. The way people in health professions think about physical illness has changed considerably in the past 10 to 20 years. The traditional view of physical illness as a purely biological phenomenon has given way to a biopsychosocial model of illness (Smilkstein, 1990). **The *biopsychosocial model* holds that physical illness is caused by a complex interaction of biological, psychological, and sociocultural factors.** This model does not suggest that biological factors are unimportant. It simply asserts that these factors operate in a psychosocial context that is also influential.

What has led to this shift in thinking? In part, it's a result of changing patterns of illness. Prior to the 20th century, the principal threats to health were *contagious diseases* caused by infectious agents—diseases such as smallpox, typhoid fever, diphtheria, yellow fever, malaria, cholera, tuberculosis, and polio. Today, none of these diseases is among the leading killers in the United States (Shank, 1983). They were tamed by improvements in nutrition, public hygiene, sanitation, and medical treatment (Grob, 1983). Unfortunately, the void left by contagious diseases has been filled all too quickly by *chronic diseases* that develop gradually, such as heart disease, cancer, and stroke (see Figure 13.1). Psychosocial factors, such as stress and lifestyle, play a large role in the development of these chronic diseases.

The growing recognition that psychological factors influence physical health has led to the

Figure 13.1. Changing patterns of illness. Trends in the death rates for various diseases during the 20th century reveal that contagious diseases (shown in green) have declined as a threat to health. However, the death rates for stress-related chronic diseases (shown in red) have remained quite high. The pie chart (*inset*) shows the results of these trends: three chronic diseases (heart disease, cancer, and stroke) account for 64% of all deaths.

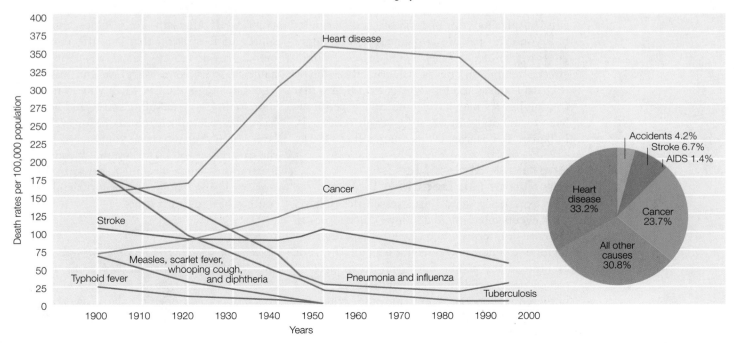

emergence of a new specialty in psychology. *Health psychology* **is concerned with how psychosocial factors relate to the promotion and maintenance of health and with the causation, prevention, and treatment of illness.** In the second half of this chapter, we'll explore this new domain of psychology. In our chapter Application, we'll focus on strategies for improving stress management. However, you can't manage stress very effectively if you can't recognize it, so let's take an in-depth look at the nature of stress.

THE NATURE OF STRESS

The term *stress* has been used in different ways by different theorists. We'll define s*tress* **as any circumstances that threaten or are perceived to threaten one's well-being and that thereby tax one's coping abilities.** The threat may be to immediate physical safety, long-range security, self-esteem, reputation, peace of mind, or many other things that one values. This is a complex concept, so let's explore it a little further.

Stress as an Everyday Event

The word *stress* tends to spark images of overwhelming, traumatic crises. People may think of hijackings, hurricanes, military combat, and nuclear accidents. Undeniably, major disasters of this sort are extremely stressful events (Rubonis & Bickman, 1991; Weisaeth, 1993). However, these unusual events are only a small part of what stress is. Many everyday events such as waiting in line, having car trouble, shopping for Christmas presents, misplacing your checkbook, and staring at bills you can't pay are also stressful. You might guess that minor stresses would produce minor effects, but that isn't necessarily true. Research by Richard Lazarus and his colleagues indicates that routine hassles may have significant harmful effects on mental and physical health (Delongis, Folkman, & Lazarus, 1988; Kanner et al., 1981).

Appraisal: Stress Lies in the Eye of the Beholder

The experience of feeling stressed depends on what events one notices and how one chooses to appraise or interpret them. Events that are stressful for one person may be routine for another. For example, many people find flying in an airplane somewhat stressful, but frequent fliers may not be bothered at all. Some people enjoy the excitement of going out on a date with someone new; others find the uncertainty terrifying.

Often, people aren't very objective in their appraisals of potentially stressful events. A study of hospitalized patients awaiting surgery showed only a slight correlation between the objective seriousness of a person's upcoming surgery and the amount of fear experienced by the patient (Janis, 1958). Thus, stress lies in the eye (actually, the mind) of the beholder. People's appraisals of stressful events are highly subjective (Lazarus & Folkman, 1984).

Major Types of Stress

An enormous variety of events can be stressful for one person or another. Although they're not entirely independent, the four principal types of stress are (1) frustration, (2) conflict, (3) change, and (4) pressure. As you read about each of these, you'll surely recognize four very familiar adversaries.

Frustration

I had a wonderful relationship with a married man for three months. One day when we planned to spend the entire day together, he called and said he wouldn't be meeting me. Someone had mentioned me to his wife, and he said that to keep his marriage together he would have to stop seeing me. I cried all morning. The grief was like losing someone through death. I still hurt, and I wonder if I'll ever get over him.

This scenario illustrates frustration. As psychologists use the term, *frustration* **occurs in any situation in which the pursuit of some goal is thwarted.** In essence, you experience frustration when you want something and you can't have it. Everyone has to deal with frustration virtually every day. Traffic jams, for instance, are a routine source of frustration that can affect mood and blood pressure (Schaeffer et al., 1988). Fortunately, most frustrations are brief and insignificant. You may be quite upset when you go to a repair shop to pick up your ailing stereo and find that it hasn't been fixed as promised. However, a week later you'll probably have your stereo back, and the frustration will be forgotten. Of course, some frustrations—such as failing to get a promotion at work or losing a boyfriend or girlfriend—can be sources of significant stress.

Conflict

Should I or shouldn't I? I became engaged at Christmas. My fiance surprised me with a ring. I knew if I refused the ring he would be terribly hurt and our relationship would suffer. However, I don't really know whether or not I want to marry him. On the other hand, I don't want to lose him either.

"We developed the Hassle Scale because we think scales that measure major events miss the point. They don't tell us anything about what goes on day in and day out, hour after hour, in a person's life. The constant, minor irritants may be much more important than the large, landmark changes."
RICHARD LAZARUS

Like frustration, conflict is an unavoidable feature of everyday life. The perplexing question "Should I or shouldn't I?" comes up countless times in one's life. *Conflict* **occurs when two or more incompatible motivations or behavioral impulses compete for expression.** As we discussed in Chapter 12, Sigmund Freud proposed nearly a century ago that internal conflicts generate considerable psychological distress. This link between conflict and distress was measured with new precision in a study by Robert Emmons and Laura King (1988). They used a questionnaire to assess the overall amount of internal conflict experienced by 88 subjects. They found that higher levels of conflict were associated with higher levels of anxiety, depression, and physical symptoms.

Conflicts come in three types, which were originally described by Kurt Lewin (1935) and investigated extensively by Neal Miller (1944, 1959). These three basic types of conflict—approach-approach, avoidance-avoidance, and approach-avoidance—are diagrammed in Figure 13.2.

In an *approach-approach conflict* **a choice must be made between two attractive goals.** The problem, of course, is that you can choose just one of the two goals. For example: You have a free afternoon—should you play tennis or racquetball? You're out for a meal—do you want the pizza or the spaghetti? You can't afford both—should you buy the blue sweater or the gray jacket? Among the three kinds of conflict, the approach-

approach type tends to be the least stressful. Nonetheless, approach-approach conflicts over important issues may sometimes be troublesome. If you're torn between two appealing college majors or two attractive boyfriends, for example, you may find the decision-making process quite stressful.

In an *avoidance-avoidance conflict* **a choice must be made between two unattractive goals.** Forced to choose between two repellent alternatives, you are, as they say, "caught between a rock and a hard place." For example, should you continue to collect unemployment checks, or should you take that degrading job at the car wash? Or suppose you have painful backaches. Should you submit to surgery that you dread, or should you continue to live with the pain? Obviously, avoidance-avoidance conflicts are most unpleasant and highly stressful.

In an *approach-avoidance conflict* **a choice must be made about whether to pursue a single goal that has both attractive and unattractive aspects.** For instance, imagine that you're offered a career promotion that will mean a large increase in pay, but you'll have to move to a city that you hate. Approach-avoidance conflicts are common and can be quite stressful. Any time you have to take a risk to pursue some desirable outcome, you're likely to find yourself in an approach-avoidance conflict. Should you risk rejection by approaching that attractive person in class? Should you risk your savings by investing in

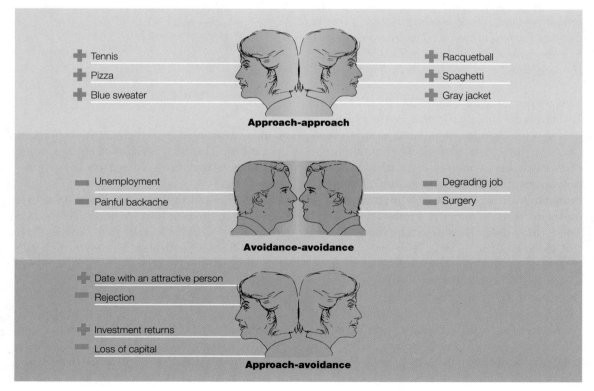

Tennis
Pizza
Blue sweater
Approach-approach
Racquetball
Spaghetti
Gray jacket

Unemployment
Painful backache
Avoidance-avoidance
Degrading job
Surgery

Date with an attractive person
Rejection
Investment returns
Loss of capital
Approach-avoidance

Figure 13.2. Types of conflict. Psychologists have identified three basic types of conflict. In approach-approach and avoidance-avoidance conflicts, a person is torn between two goals. In an approach-avoidance conflict, there is only one goal under consideration, but it has both positive and negative aspects.

CONCEPT CHECK 13.1
Identifying Types of Conflict

Check your understanding of the three basic types of conflict by identifying the type experienced in each of the following examples. The answers are in Appendix A.

Examples

_____ 1. John can't decide whether to take a demeaning job in a car wash or to go on welfare.

_____ 2. Mary wants to apply to a highly selective law school, but she hates to risk the possibility of rejection.

_____ 3. Ellen has been shopping for a new car and is torn between a nifty little sports car and a classy sedan, both of which she really likes.

Types of conflict

a. approach-approach

b. avoidance-avoidance

c. approach-avoidance

Table 13.1 Social Readjustment Rating Scale

Life Event	Mean Value
Death of spouse	100
Divorce	73
Marital separation	65
Jail term	63
Death of close family member	63
Personal injury or illness	53
Marriage	50
Fired at work	47
Marital reconciliation	45
Retirement	45
Change in health of family member	44
Pregnancy	40
Sex difficulties	39
Gain of a new family member	39
Business readjustment	39
Change in financial state	38
Death of a close friend	37
Change to a different line of work	36
Change in number of arguments with spouse	35
Mortgage or loan for major purchase (home, etc.)	31
Foreclosure of mortgage or loan	30
Change in responsibilities at work	29
Son or daughter leaving home	29
Trouble with in-laws	29
Outstanding personal achievement	28
Wife begins or stops work	26
Begin or end school	26
Change in living conditions	25
Revision of personal habits	24
Trouble with boss	23
Change in work hours or conditions	20
Change in residence	20
Change in school	20
Change in recreation	19
Change in church activities	19
Change in social activities	18
Mortgage or loan for lesser purchase (car, TV, etc.)	17
Change in sleeping habits	16
Change in number of family get-togethers	15
Change in eating habits	15
Vacation	13
Christmas	12
Minor violations of the law	11

a new business that could fail? Approach-avoidance conflicts often produce *vacillation* (Miller, 1944). That is, you go back and forth, beset by indecision. You decide to go ahead, then you decide not to, and then you decide to go ahead again.

Change

After my divorce, I lived alone for four years. Six months ago I married a wonderful woman who has two children from her previous marriage. My biggest stress is suddenly having to adapt to living with three people instead of by myself. I was pretty set in my ways. I had certain routines. Now everything is chaos. I love my wife and I'm fond of the kids. They're not really doing anything wrong. But my house and my life just aren't the same, and I'm having trouble dealing with it all.

As we discussed in Chapter 2, Thomas Holmes, Richard Rahe, and their colleagues pioneered the idea that life changes—including positive events, such as getting married or getting a promotion—represent a key type of stress. **Life changes are any noticeable alterations in one's living circumstances that require readjustment.** Based on their theory, Holmes and Rahe (1967) developed the Social Readjustment Rating Scale (SRRS) to measure life change as a form of stress. The scale assigns numerical values to 43 major life events. These values are supposed to reflect the magnitude of the readjustment required by each change (see Table 13.1). In using the scale, respondents are asked to indicate how often they experienced any of these 43 events during a certain time period (typically, the past year). The numbers associated with each event checked are then added. This total is an index of the amount of change-related stress the person has recently experienced.

The SRRS and similar scales based on it have been used in thousands of studies by researchers all over the world. Overall, these studies have shown that people with higher scores on the SRRS tend to be more vulnerable to many kinds of physical illness and to many types of psychological problems as well (Creed, 1993; Derogatis & Coons, 1993: Gruen, 1993). These results have attracted a great deal of attention, and the SRRS has been reprinted in many popular newspapers and magazines. The attendant publicity has led to the widespread conclusion that life change is inherently stressful.

However, experts have criticized this research, citing problems with the methods used (Rabkin, 1993; Raphael, Cloitre, & Dohrenwend, 1991) and problems in interpreting the findings (Brett et al., 1990; Watson & Pennebaker, 1989). At this point, it's a key interpretive issue that concerns us. Many critics have argued that the SRRS does not measure *change* exclusively. The main problem is that the list of life changes on the SRRS is dominated by events that are clearly negative or undesirable (death of a spouse, being fired from a job, and so on). These negative events probably generate great frustration. Although there are some positive events on the scale, it could be that frustration (generated by negative events), rather than change, creates most of the stress assessed by the scale.

To investigate this possibility, researchers began to take into account the desirability and undesirability of subjects' life changes. Subjects were asked to indicate the desirability of the events that they checked off on the SRRS and similar scales. The findings in these studies clearly indicated that life change is not the crucial dimension measured by the SRRS. Although positive events *can* be stressful for some people (Brown & McGill, 1989), negative life events cause most of the stress tapped by the SRRS (Perkins, 1982; J. Smith, 1993).

In conclusion, the SRRS assesses a wide range of different kinds of stressful experiences, not just life change. At present, there's little reason to believe that change is *inherently or inevitably* stressful. Undoubtedly, some life changes may be quite challenging, but others may be quite benign.

Pressure

My father questioned me at dinner about some things I didn't want to talk about. I know he doesn't want to hear my answers, at least not the truth. My father told me when I was little that I was his favorite because I was "pretty near perfect." I've spent my life trying to keep up that image, even though it's obviously not true. Recently, he has begun to realize this, and it's made our relationship very strained and painful.

At one time or another, most people have remarked that they're "under pressure." What does this mean? **Pressure involves expectations or demands that one behave in a certain way.** You are under pressure to *perform* when you're expected to execute tasks and responsibilities quickly, efficiently, and successfully. For example, sales-people are usually under pressure to move merchandise. Professors at research institutions are often under pressure to publish in prestigious journals. Stand-up comedians are under intense pressure to make people laugh. Pressures to *conform* to others' expectations are also common in our lives. Businessmen are expected to wear suits and ties. Suburban homeowners are expected to keep their lawns well manicured. Teenagers are expected to adhere to their parents' values and rules.

Although widely discussed by the general public, the concept of pressure has received scant attention from researchers. Specific aspects of pressure, such as work overload, have been examined in a few studies of work-related stress (Holt, 1993), but until recently no attempt had been made to investigate pressure as a general form of stress. However, in the 1980s researchers began to explore the effects of pressure.

For instance, an effort was made to devise a scale to measure pressure as a form of life stress. The result was a 48-item self-report measure called the Pressure Inventory. It assesses self-imposed pressure, pressure from work and school, and pressure from family relations, peer relations, and intimate relations. In the first two studies with this scale, a strong relationship has been found between pressure and a variety of psychological symptoms and problems (Weiten, 1988; Weiten & Dixon, 1984). In fact, pressure has turned out to be more strongly

---

CONCEPT CHECK 13.2
Recognizing Sources of Stress

Check your understanding of the major sources of stress by indicating which type or types of stress are at work in each of the examples below. Bear in mind that the four basic types of stress are not mutually exclusive. There's some potential for overlap, so that a specific experience might include both change and pressure, for instance. The answers are in Appendix A.

Examples

_____ 1. Marie is late for an appointment but is stuck in line at the bank.

_____ 2. Maureen decides that she won't be satisfied unless she gets straight A's this year.

_____ 3. Melvin has just graduated from business school and has taken an exciting new job.

_____ 4. Morris has just been fired from his job and needs to find another.

Types of stress

a. frustration

b. conflict

c. change

d. pressure

related to measures of mental health than the SRRS and other established measures of stress are. This research suggests that pressure may be an important form of stress that merits more attention from stress theorists.

RESPONDING TO STRESS

The human response to stress is complex and multidimensional. Stress affects the individual at several levels. Consider again the chapter's opening scenario, in which you're driving home in heavy traffic and thinking about overdue papers, tuition increases, and parental pressures. Let's look at some of the reactions that were mentioned. When you groan audibly in reaction to the traffic report, you're experiencing an *emotional response* to stress, in this case annoyance and anger. When your pulse quickens and your stomach knots up, you're exhibiting *physiological responses* to stress. When you shout insults at another driver, your verbal aggression is a *behavioral response* to the stress at hand. Thus, we can analyze a person's reactions to stress at three levels: (1) emotional responses, (2) physiological responses, and (3) behavioral responses. Figure 13.3 is a diagram of these three levels of response. It provides an overview of the stress process.

Emotional Responses

When people are under stress, they often react emotionally. More often than not, stress elicits unpleasant emotions rather than pleasurable ones (Lazarus, 1993). The link between stress and emotion was apparent in a study of 96 women who filled out daily diaries about the stresses and moods that they experienced over a period of 28 days (Caspi, Bolger, & Eckenrode, 1987). The investigators found that daily fluctuations in stress correlated with daily fluctuations in mood. As stress increased, mood tended to become more negative. As the researchers put it, "Some days everything seems to go wrong, and by day's end, minor difficulties find their outlet in rotten moods" (p. 184).

Emotions Commonly Elicited

There are no simple one-to-one connections between certain types of stressful events and particular emotions, but researchers *have* begun to uncover some strong links between specific *cognitive reactions to stress (appraisals)* and specific emotions (Smith & Lazarus, 1993). For example, self-blame tends to lead to guilt, helplessness to sadness, and so forth. Although many emotions can be evoked by stressful events, some are certainly more likely than others. Common emotional responses to stress include the following (Lazarus, 1993; Woolfolk & Richardson, 1978):

1. *Annoyance, anger, and rage.* Stress frequently produces feelings of anger ranging from mild annoyance to uncontrollable rage. Frustration is particularly likely to generate anger.

2. *Apprehension, anxiety, and fear.* Stress probably evokes anxiety and fear more frequently than any other emotions. As we saw in Chapter 12, Freudian theory has long recognized the link between conflict and anxiety. However, anxiety can also be elicited by the pressure to perform, the threat of impending frustration, or the uncertainty associated with change.

3. *Dejection, sadness, and grief.* Sometimes stress—especially frustration—simply brings you down. Routine setbacks, such as traffic tickets and poor grades, often produce feelings of dejection. More profound setbacks, such as deaths and divorces, typically leave one grief-stricken.

Figure 13.3. Overview of the stress process. A potentially stressful event, such as a major exam, elicits a subjective appraisal of how threatening the event is. If the event is viewed with alarm, the stress may trigger emotional, physiological, and behavioral reactions, as people's response to stress is multidimensional.

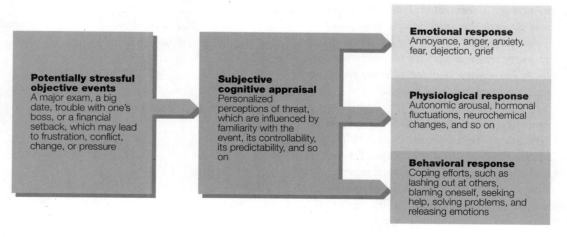

CHAPTER THIRTEEN

Effects of Emotional Arousal

Emotional reponses are a natural and normal part of life. Even unpleasant emotions serve important purposes. Like physical pain, painful emotions can serve as warnings that one needs to take action. However, it's important to note that strong emotional arousal may sometimes interfere with efforts to cope with stress. For example, there's evidence that high emotional arousal can interfere with attention and memory retrieval and can impair judgment and decision making (Janis, 1993; Mandler, 1993).

Although emotional arousal may hurt coping efforts, this isn't *necessarily* the case. The *inverted-U hypothesis* predicts that task performance should improve with increased emotional arousal—up to a point, after which further increases in arousal become disruptive and performance deteriorates (Anderson, 1990; Mandler, 1993). This idea is referred to as the inverted-U hypothesis because when performance is plotted as a function of arousal, the resulting graphs approximate an up-side-down U (see Figure 13.4). In these graphs, the level of arousal at which performance peaks is characterized as the *optimal level of arousal* for a task.

This optimal level of arousal appears to depend in part on the complexity of the task at hand. The conventional wisdom is that *as a task becomes more complex, the optimal level of arousal (for peak performance) tends to decrease*. This relationship is depicted in Figure 13.4. As you can see, a fairly high level of arousal should be optimal on simple tasks (such as driving 8 hours to help a friend in a crisis). However, performance should peak at a lower level of arousal on complex tasks (such as making a major decision in which you have to weigh many factors).

The research evidence on the inverted-U hypothesis is inconsistent and subject to varied interpretations (Neiss, 1988, 1990). Nonetheless, the inverted-U hypothesis provides a plausible model of how emotional arousal could have either beneficial or disruptive effects on coping, depending on the nature of the stressful demands.

Physiological Responses

As we just discussed, stress frequently elicits strong emotional responses. Now we'll look at the important physiological changes that often accompany these responses.

The General Adaptation Syndrome

Concern about the physical effects of stress was first voiced by Hans Selye (1936, 1956, 1982), a Canadian scientist who launched stress research decades ago. Selye was born in Vienna but spent his entire professional career at McGill University in Montreal. Beginning in the 1930s, Selye exposed laboratory animals to a diverse array of both physical and psychological stressors (heat, cold, pain, mild shock, restraint, and so on). The patterns of physiological arousal seen in the animals were largely the same, regardless of the type of stress. Thus, Selye concluded that stress reactions are *nonspecific*. In other words, he maintained that the reactions do not vary according to the specific type of stress encountered. Initially, Selye wasn't sure what to call this nonspecific response to a variety of noxious agents. In the 1940s he decided to call it *stress*, and the word has been part of our vocabulary ever since.

Selye (1956, 1974) explained stress reactions in terms of the general adaptation syndrome. **The *general adaptation syndrome* is a model of the body's stress response, consisting of**

"There are two main types of human beings: 'racehorses,' who thrive on stress and are only happy with a vigorous, fast-paced lifestyle; and 'turtles,' who in order to be happy require peace, quiet, and a generally tranquil environment."
HANS SELYE

Figure 13.4. Arousal and performance. According to the inverted-U hypothesis, graphs of the relationship between emotional arousal and task performance tend to resemble an inverted U, as increased arousal is associated with improved performance up to a point, after which higher arousal leads to poorer performance. The optimal level of arousal for a task depends on the complexity of the task. On complex tasks, a relatively low level of arousal tends to be optimal. On simple tasks, however, performance may peak at a much higher level of arousal.

Level of task complexity

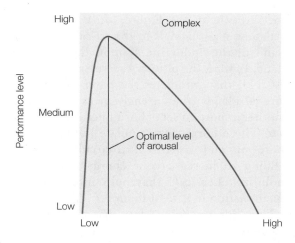

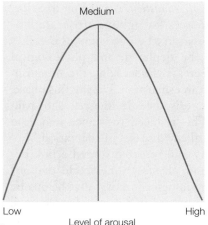

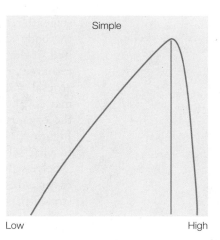

Level of arousal

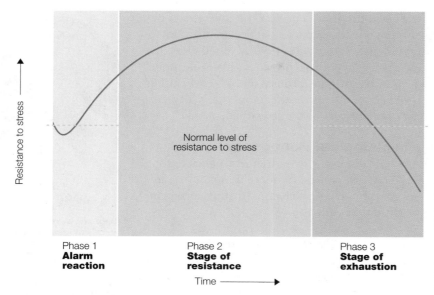

Resistance to stress →

Normal level of
resistance to stress

Phase 1
**Alarm
reaction**

Phase 2
**Stage of
resistance**

Phase 3
**Stage of
exhaustion**

Time ——→

Figure 13.5. The general adaptation syndrome. Selye breaks the physiological response to stress into three phases. During the first phase, the body mobilizes its resources for resistance after a brief initial shock. In the second phase, resistance levels off and eventually begins to decline. If the third phase of the general adaptation syndrome is reached, resistance is depleted, leading to health problems and exhaustion.

three stages: alarm, resistance, and exhaustion. In the first stage, an *alarm reaction* occurs when an organism first recognizes the existence of a threat: physiological arousal occurs as the body musters its resources to combat the challenge. Selye's alarm reaction is essentially the fight-or-flight response described in Chapters 3 and 10.

However, Selye took his investigation of stress a few steps further by exposing laboratory animals to *prolonged* stress, similar to the chronic stress often endured by humans. As stress continues, the organism may progress to the second phase of the general adaptation syndrome, the *stage of resistance*. During this phase, physiological changes stabilize as coping efforts get under way. Typically, physiological arousal continues to be higher than normal, although it may level off somewhat as the organism becomes accustomed to the threat.

If the stress continues over a substantial period of time, the organism may enter the third stage, the *stage of exhaustion*. According to Selye, the body's resources for fighting stress are limited. If the stress can't be overcome, the body's resources may be depleted, and physiological arousal will decrease. Eventually, the organism may collapse from exhaustion. During this phase, the organism's resistance declines, as shown in Figure 13.5. This reduced resistance may lead to what Selye called "diseases of adaptation."

Selye's theory and research forged a link between stress and physical illness. He demonstrated that physiological arousal that begins by being adaptive can lead to diseases if prolonged. His belief that stress reactions are nonspecific

remains controversial (Mason, 1975). Nonetheless, his model provided guidance for a generation of researchers who worked out the details of how stress reverberates throughout the body. Let's look at some of those details.

Brain-Body Pathways

Even in cases of moderate stress, you may notice that your heart has started beating faster, you've begun to breathe harder, and you're perspiring more than usual. How does all this (and much more) happen? It appears that there are two major pathways along which the brain sends signals to the endocrine system (Asterita, 1985; Koranyi, 1989). As we noted in Chapter 3, the *endocrine system* consists of glands located at various sites in the body that secrete chemicals called hormones. The hypothalamus is the part of the brain that appears to initiate action along these two pathways.

The first pathway (see Figure 13.6) is routed through the autonomic nervous system. Your hypothalamus activates the sympathetic division of the ANS. A key part of this activation involves stimulating the central part of the adrenal glands (the adrenal medulla) to release large amounts of *catecholamines* into the bloodstream. These hormones radiate throughout your body, producing the physiological changes seen in the fight-or-flight response. The net result of catecholamine elevation is that your body is mobilized for action. Heart rate and blood flow increase, and more blood is pumped to your brain and muscles. Respiration and oxygen consumption speed up, which facilitates alertness. Digestive processes are inhibited to conserve your energy. The pupils of your eyes dilate, increasing visual sensitivity.

The second pathway involves more direct communication between the brain and the endocrine system (see Figure 13.6). The hypothalamus sends signals to the so-called master gland of the endocrine system, the pituitary gland. In turn, the pituitary secretes a hormone (ACTH) that stimulates the outer part of the adrenal glands (the adrenal cortex) to release another important set of hormones—*corticosteroids*. These hormones stimulate the release of more fats and proteins into circulation, thus helping to increase your energy. They also mobilize chemicals that help inhibit tissue inflammation in case of injury.

Thus, it's becoming clear that physiological responses to stress extend into all parts of the

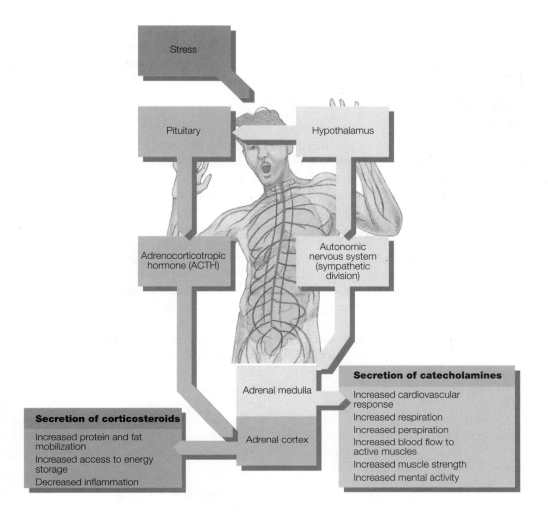

Stress

Pituitary

Hypothalamus

Adrenocorticotropic hormone (ACTH)

Autonomic nervous system (sympathetic division)

Adrenal medulla

Adrenal cortex

Secretion of corticosteroids

Increased protein and fat mobilization

Increased access to energy storage

Decreased inflammation

Secretion of catecholamines

Increased cardiovascular response

Increased respiration

Increased perspiration

Increased blood flow to active muscles

Increased muscle strength

Increased mental activity

Figure 13.6. Brain-body pathways in stress. In times of stress, the brain sends signals along two pathways. The pathway through the autonomic nervous system controls the release of catecholamine hormones that help mobilize the body for action. The pathway through the pituitary gland and the endocrine system controls the release of corticosteroid hormones that increase energy and ward off tissue inflammation.

body. As you'll see, these physiological reactions can affect both mental and physical health.

Behavioral Responses

Although people respond to stress at several levels, it's clear that behavior is the crucial dimension of their reactions. Most behavioral responses to stress involve coping. *Coping* **refers to active efforts to master, reduce, or tolerate the demands created by stress.** Notice that this definition is neutral as to whether coping efforts are healthful or maladaptive. The popular use of the term often implies that coping is inherently healthful. When people say that someone "coped with her problems," the implication is that she handled them effectively.

In reality, however, coping responses may be adaptive or maladaptive (Moos & Schaefer, 1993). For example, if you were flunking a history course at midterm, you might cope with this stress by (1) increasing your study efforts, (2) seeking help from a tutor, (3) blaming your professor, or (4) giving up on the class without really trying. Clearly, the first two of these coping responses would be more adaptive than the last two.

People cope with stress in many ways, but most individuals exhibit certain styles of coping that are fairly consistent across situations (Endler & Parker, 1990; Haan, 1993). Given the immense variety in coping strategies, we can only highlight some of the more common patterns. In this section we'll focus most of our attention on styles of coping that tend to be less than ideal. We'll discuss more-healthful coping strategies in the chapter Application on stress management.

Striking Out at Others

People often respond to stressful events by striking out at others with aggressive behavior. *Aggression* **is any behavior that is intended to hurt someone, either physically or verbally.** Many years ago, a team of psychologists (Dollard et al., 1939) proposed the *frustration-aggression hypothesis*, which held that aggression is always caused by frustration. Decades of research have supported this idea of a causal link between frus-

Lashing out at others is a typical, but not very healthful, response to stress.

tration and aggression (Berkowitz, 1989). However, this research has also shown that there isn't an inevitable, one-to-one correspondence between frustration and aggression.

In discussing qualifications to the frustration-aggression hypothesis, Leonard Berkowitz (1969, 1989) has concluded that (1) frustration does not *necessarily* lead to aggression, (2) many situational factors influence whether frustration will lead to aggression, (3) the likelihood of aggression increases with the amount of negative emotions aroused, and (4) frustration may produce responses other than aggression (for example, apathy). Although these are important qualifications, it's clear that frustration often leads to aggression.

Giving Up

When confronted with stress, people sometimes simply give up and withdraw from the battle. This response of apathy and inaction tends to be associated with the emotional reactions of sadness and dejection. Martin Seligman (1974, 1983) has developed a model of this giving-up syndrome that appears to shed light on its causes.

In Seligman's research, animals were subjected to electric shocks they couldn't escape. The animals were then given an opportunity to learn a response that would allow them to escape the shock. However, many of the animals became so apathetic and listless that they didn't even try to learn the escape response. When researchers made similar manipulations with *human* subjects using inescapable noise (rather than shock), they observed parallel results (Hiroto & Seligman, 1975). Seligman called this syndrome learned helplessness. **Learned helplessness is passive behavior produced by exposure to unavoidable aversive events.**

Seligman originally considered learned helplessness to be a product of conditioning. However, research with human subjects has led Seligman and his colleagues to revise their theory. The current model proposes that a person's *cognitive interpretation* of aversive events determines whether he or she develops learned helplessness (Abramson, Seligman, & Teasdale, 1978; Seligman, 1990). Specifically, helplessness seems to occur when

people believe that events are beyond their control. This belief is particularly likely to emerge when they attribute setbacks to personal inadequacies instead of situational factors (see the discussion of attributional style and depression in Chapter 14).

Indulging Oneself

Stress sometimes leads to self-indulgence. When troubled by stress, many people engage in excessive consummatory behavior—unwise patterns of eating, drinking, smoking, using drugs, spending money, and so forth. As I mentioned in Chapter 10, when I have an exceptionally stressful day, I often head for the refrigerator, the grocery store, or a restaurant in pursuit of something chocolate. I have a friend who copes with stress by making a beeline for the nearest shopping mall to indulge in a spending spree.

It appears that my friend and I are not unusual in our excessive consummatory behavior. It makes sense that when things are going poorly in one area of their lives, people may try to compensate by pursuing substitute forms of satisfaction. When this happens, consummatory responses probably rank high among the substitutes. They're relatively easy to execute, and they tend to be pleasur-

---

CONCEPT CHECK 13.3
Tracing Brain-Body Pathways in Stress

Check your understanding of the two major pathways along which the brain sends signals to the endocrine system in the event of stress by separating the eight terms below into two sets of four and arranging each set in the appropriate sequence. You'll find the answers in Appendix A.

ACTH	corticosteriods
adrenal cortex	hypothalamus
adrenal medulla	pituitary
catecholamines	sympathetic division of the ANS

Pathway 1 *Pathway 2*

_____ _____

_____ _____

_____ _____

_____ _____

able. Thus, it's not surprising that studies have linked stress to increases in eating (Grunberg & Straub, 1992), smoking (Cohen & Lichtenstein, 1990), and the consumption of alcohol and drugs (Peyser, 1993).

Defensive Coping

Defensive coping is a common response to stress. We noted in the previous chapter that Sigmund Freud originally developed the concept of the defense mechanism. Though rooted in the psychoanalytic tradition, this concept has gained widespread acceptance from psychologists of most persuasions. Building on Freud's initial insights, modern psychologists have broadened the scope of the concept and added to Freud's list of defense mechanisms.

***Defense mechanisms* are largely unconscious reactions that protect a person from unpleasant emotions such as anxiety and guilt.** Many specific defense mechanisms have been identified. For example, Laughlin (1979) lists 49 different defenses. We described 7 common defense mechanisms in our discussion of Freud's theory in the previous chapter. Table 13.2 introduces another 5 defenses that people use with some regularity: denial, fantasy, intellectualization, undoing, and overcompensation. Although widely discussed in the popular press, defense mechanisms are often misunderstood. To clear up some of the misconceptions, we'll use a question/answer format to elaborate on the nature of defense mechanisms.

What exactly do defense mechanisms defend against? Above all else, defense mechanisms shield the individual from the emotional discomfort that's so often elicited by stress. Their main purpose is to ward off or reduce the intensity of unwelcome emotions such as anxiety, anger, guilt, and dejection.

How do they work? They work through *self-deception*. Defense mechanisms accomplish their goals by distorting reality so that it doesn't appear so threatening. For example, suppose you're not doing well in school and you're in danger of flunking out. You might use *denial* to block awareness of the possibility that you could flunk, temporarily fending off feelings of anxiety.

Are they conscious or unconscious? Both. Freud originally assumed that defenses operate entirely at an unconscious level. However, the concept of the defense mechanism has been broadened by other theorists to include maneuvers that people may be aware of. Thus, defense mechanisms may operate at varying levels of awareness, although they're largely unconscious.

Are they normal? Definitely. Everyone uses defense mechanisms on a fairly regular basis. They're entirely normal patterns of coping. The notion that only neurotic people use defense mechanisms is inaccurate.

Are they healthy? This is a much more complicated question. More often than not, the answer is "no." Generally, defensive coping is less than optimal for several reasons. First, defensive coping is an avoidance strategy, and avoidance rarely provides a genuine solution to problems. Holahan and Moos (1985, 1990) found that people who exhibit high resistance to stress use avoidance strategies less than people who are frequently troubled by stress. Second, a repressive coping style has been related to poor health, in part because repression often leads people to delay facing up to their problems (Weinberger, 1990).

Table 13.2 Common Defense Mechanisms

Mechanism	Description	Example
Denial of reality	Protecting oneself from unpleasant reality by refusing to perceive or face it	A smoker concludes that the evidence linking cigarette use to health problems is scientifically worthless.
Fantasy	Gratifying frustrated desires by imaginary achievements	A socially inept and inhibited young man imagines himself chosen by a group of women to provide them with sexual satisfaction.
Intellectualization (isolation)	Cutting off emotion from hurtful situations or separating incompatible attitudes so that they appear unrelated	A prisoner on death row awaiting execution resists appeal on his behalf and coldly insists that the letter of the law be followed.
Undoing	Atoning for or trying to magically dispel unacceptable desires or acts	A teenager who feels guilty about masturbation ritually touches door knobs a prescribed number of times following each occurrence of the act.
Overcompensation	Covering up felt weaknesses by emphasizing some desirable characteristic, or making up for frustration in one area by overgratification in another	A dangerously overweight woman goes on eating binges when she feels neglected by her husband.

Note: See Table 12.2 for another list of defense mechanisms.

For example, if you were to block out obvious warning signs of cancer or diabetes and fail to obtain needed medical care, your defensive behavior could be fatal. Third, defenses such as denial and fantasy represent wishful thinking, which appears to have little adaptive value (Bolger, 1990).

Although defensive behavior tends to be relatively unhealthful, Vaillant (1994) emphasizes that some defenses are healthier than others and that defense mechanisms can sometimes be adaptive. For example, *overcompensation* for athletic failures could lead you to work extra hard in the classroom. Creative use of *fantasy* is sometimes the key to dealing effectively with a temporary period of frustration, such as a stint in the military service or a period of recovery in the hospital. Shelley Taylor (1989) has reviewed several lines of evidence indicating that *illusions may sometimes be adaptive for mental health and physical well-being*. For example, she notes that in comparison to depressed subjects, normal subjects overestimate the degree to which they control chance events, have overly favorable self-images, and display unrealistic optimism about the future.

Thus, it is hard to make sweeping generalizations about the adaptive value of self-deception. Some of the personal illusions that people create through defensive coping may help them deal with life's difficulties. Roy Baumeister (1989) theorizes that it's all a matter of degree and that there is an "optimal margin of illusion." According to Baumeister, extreme distortions of reality are maladaptive, but small illusions are often beneficial.

Constructive Coping

Our discussion thus far has focused on coping strategies that usually are less than ideal. Of course, people also exhibit many healthful strategies for dealing with stress. We'll use the term **constructive coping to refer to relatively healthful efforts that people make to deal with stressful events.** No strategy of coping can *guarantee* a successful outcome. Even the healthiest coping responses may turn out to be ineffective in some circumstances. Thus, the concept of constructive coping is simply meant to connote a healthful, positive approach, without promising success.

What makes certain coping strategies constructive? Frankly, it's a gray area in which psychologists' opinions vary to some extent. Nonetheless, a consensus about the nature of constructive coping has emerged from the sizable literature on stress management. Key themes in this literature include the following:

1. Constructive coping involves confronting problems directly. It is task relevant and action oriented. It entails a conscious effort to rationally evaluate your options so that you can try to solve your problems.

2. Constructive coping is based on reasonably realistic appraisals of your stress and coping resources. A little self-deception may sometimes be adaptive, but excessive self-deception and highly unrealistic negative thinking are not.

3. Constructive coping involves learning to recognize, and in some cases inhibit, potentially disruptive emotional reactions to stress.

4. Constructive coping includes making efforts to ensure that your body is not especially vulnerable to the possibly damaging effects of stress.

The principles just described provide a rather general and abstract picture of constructive coping. We'll look at patterns of constructive coping in more detail in the Application, which discusses various stress management strategies that people can use.

Thus far, we've probed the nature of stress and described how people typically respond to stress. We turn next to the possible outcomes of struggles with stress. Research on the effects of stress has focused mainly on negative health outcomes, so our coverage is slanted in that direction. However, it's important to emphasize that stress is not inherently bad. You would probably suffocate from boredom if you lived a stress-free existence. Stress makes life challenging and interesting. Moreover, it can have beneficial effects. Stress can force people to develop new skills, learn new insights, and acquire new personal strengths (Holahan & Moos, 1990). Along the way, though, stress can be harrowing, sometimes leading to psychological disorders and physical illness.

THE EFFECTS OF STRESS ON PHYSICAL HEALTH

People struggle with many stresses every day. Most stresses come and go without leaving any enduring imprint. However, when stress is severe or when many stressful demands pile up, one's mental or physical health may be affected. In Chapter 14 you'll learn that chronic stress contributes to many types of psychological disorders, including depression, schizophrenia, and anxiety disorders. In this section, we'll discuss the link between stress and physical illness.

"Rather than perceiving themselves, the world, and the future accurately, most people regard themselves, their circumstances, and the future as considerably more positive than is objectively likely. . . . These illusions are not merely characteristic of human thought; they appear actually to be adaptive, promoting rather than undermining good mental health."
SHELLEY TAYLOR

Prior to the 1970s, it was thought that stress contributed to the development of only a few physical diseases, such as high blood pressure, ulcers, and asthma, which were called *psychosomatic diseases*. However, in the 1970s, research began to uncover new links between stress and a great variety of diseases previously believed to be purely physiological in origin (Elliott, 1989). Let's look at some of this research.

Type A Behavior and Heart Disease

Heart disease accounts for nearly 40% of the deaths in the United States every year. *Coronary* heart disease involves a reduction in blood flow in the coronary arteries, which supply the heart with blood. This type of heart disease accounts for about 90% of heart-related deaths.

In the 1960s and 1970s a pair of cardiologists, Meyer Friedman and Ray Rosenman (1974), were investigating the causes of coronary heart disease. Originally, Friedman and Rosenman were interested in the usual factors thought to produce a high risk of heart attack: smoking, obesity, physical inactivity, and so forth. Although they found that these factors were relevant, they eventually recognized that a piece of the puzzle was missing. Many people who smoked constantly, got little exercise, and were severely overweight avoided the ravages of heart disease. At the same time, other people who seemed to be in much better shape in regard to these risk factors experienced the misfortune of a heart attack.

Gradually, Friedman and Rosenman unraveled the riddle. What was their explanation for these perplexing findings? Stress! Specifically, they found a connection between coronary risk and a syndrome they called *Type A behavior*, which involves self-imposed stress and intense reactions to stress.

Elements of Type A Behavior

Friedman and Rosenman divided people into two basic types—Type A and Type B—who exhibit differing characteristics (Rosenman, 1993). **The *Type A personality* includes three elements: (1) a strong competitive orientation, (2) impatience and time urgency, and (3) anger and hostility.** Type A's are ambitious, hard-driving perfectionists who are exceedingly time-conscious. They routinely try to do several things at once. Thus, a Type A person may watch TV, talk on the phone, work on a report, and eat dinner all at the same time. Type A's are so impatient that they frequently finish others' sentences for them! They

---

Measuring Type A behavior

You can use the checklist below to estimate the likelihood of your being a Type A personality. However, the checklist should be regarded as providing only a rough estimate, because Friedman and Rosenman (1974) emphasize that how you answer certain questions in their interview is often more significant than the answers themselves. Nonetheless, if you answer "yes" to a majority of the items below, you may want to consider reading their book, Type A Behavior and Your Heart.

_____ **1.** Do you find it difficult to restrain yourself from hurrying others' speech (finishing their sentences for them)?

_____ **2.** Do you often try to do more than one thing at a time (such as eat and read simultaneously)?

_____ **3.** Do you often feel guilty if you use extra time to relax?

_____ **4.** Do you tend to get involved in a great number of projects at once?

_____ **5.** Do you find yourself racing through yellow lights when you drive?

_____ **6.** Do you need to win in order to derive enjoyment from games and sports?

_____ **7.** Do you generally move, walk, and eat rapidly?

_____ **8.** Do you agree to take on too many responsibilities?

_____ **9.** Do you detest waiting in lines?

_____ **10.** Do you have an intense desire to better your position in life and impress others?

Figure 13.7. The Type A personality. The ten questions shown here highlight some of the behavioral traits associated with the Type A personality.

---

fidget frantically over the briefest delays. Often they are highly competitive, achievement-oriented workaholics who drive themselves with many deadlines. They speak rapidly and emphatically. They are cynical about life and hostile toward others. They are easily irritated and are quick to anger. In contrast, **the *Type B personality* is marked by relatively relaxed, patient, easygoing, amicable behavior.** Type B's are less hurried, less competitive, and less easily angered than Type A's. The strength of one's Type A tendencies can be measured with either structured interviews or questionnaires. Figure 13.7 lists some questions that are representative of those used in measurements of Type A behavior.

Which aspects of Type A behavior are most strongly related to increased coronary risk? Are competitiveness, time urgency, and hostility equally important? These are questions of current interest in research on the Type A syndrome. Based on recent studies, many researchers believe that hostility may be more important for coronary risk than other elements of the Type A personality (Houston et al., 1992; T. Smith, 1992; Williams & Barefoot, 1988). In particular, investigators have

People who are classified as being a Type A personality tend to be workaholics. They try to do several things at the same time, and they put themselves under constant time pressure. The extra stress that such people experience may be associated with a higher risk of heart attack.

been impressed by the apparent relationship between *cynical hostility* and coronary disease, hypertension, and early mortality. People high in cynical hostility are moody, suspicious, resentful, and distrusting. They are quick to anger and to criticize others. When they get upset, they tend to show relatively strong physiological reactions. In comparison to others, they exhibit elevated heart rate and blood pressure reactivity (Smith & Brown, 1991) and elevated secretions of stress hormones (Pope & Smith, 1991). More research is needed and the evidence is far from conclusive (Rosenman, 1991), but cynical hostility may prove to be the most toxic element of the Type A syndrome.

Evaluating the Risk

How strong is the link between Type A personality and coronary risk? Based on preliminary data, Friedman and his associates originally estimated that Type A's are *six* times more prone to heart attack than Type B's. At the other extreme, some studies have failed to find an association between Type A behavior and coronary risk (Ragland & Brand, 1988; Shekelle et al., 1985). What can we make of these inconsistent findings? Miller and his associates (1991) have demonstrated convincingly that most of the studies that have not found a link between Type A behavior and coronary disease have been characterized by one or more of several methodological limitations (chief among them being poor sample selection). Nonetheless, the mixed findings suggest that the relationship

between Type A behavior and coronary risk is more modest than originally believed. Taken as a whole, the data suggest that the increased coronary risk for Type A's is perhaps double that for Type B's (Lyness, 1993; Weaver & Rodnick, 1986). The modest nature of this relationship probably means that Type A behavior increases coronary risk for only a portion of the population.

Stress and Other Diseases

The development of questionnaires to measure life stress has allowed researchers to look for correlations between stress and a variety of diseases. These researchers have uncovered many connections between stress and illness. For example, Thomason and colleagues (1992) found an association between life stress and the course of rheumatoid arthritis. Working with a sample of female students, Williams and Deffenbacher (1983) found that life stress was correlated with the number of vaginal (yeast) infections the women reported in the previous year. Other studies have connected stress to the development of genital herpes (VanderPlate, Aral, & Magder, 1988) and periodontal disease (Green et al., 1986). Researchers have also found an association between high stress and flareups of inflammatory bowel disease (Garrett et al., 1991).

These are just a handful of representative examples of studies relating stress to physical diseases. Table 13.3 provides a longer list of health problems that have been linked to stress. Many of these stress-illness connections are based on very tentative or inconsistent findings, but the sheer length and diversity of the list is remarkable. Why should stress increase our risk for so many kinds of illness? A partial answer may lie in our immunal functioning.

Stress and Immunal Functioning

The link between stress and illness raises the possibility that stress may undermine immunal functioning. **The *immune response* is the body's defensive reaction to invasion by bacteria, viral agents, or other foreign substances.** The immune response works to protect people from many forms of disease. Immunal reactions are multifaceted, but they depend heavily on actions initiated by specialized white blood cells called *lymphocytes*.

A wealth of studies indicates that experimentally induced stress can impair immunal functioning *in animals* (Ader & Cohen, 1984, 1993). Stressors such as crowding, shock, and restraint reduce various aspects of lymphocyte reactivity in laboratory animals.

Some studies have also related stress to suppressed immunal activity *in humans*. In one study, medical students provided researchers with blood samples so that their immune response could be assessed (Kiecolt-Glaser et al., 1984). They provided a baseline sample a month before final exams and contributed a high-stress sample on the first day of their finals. The subjects also responded to the SRRS to measure recent stress. Reduced levels of immune activity were found during the extremely stressful finals week. Reduced immunal activity was also correlated with higher scores on the SRRS. In another study, investigators exposed quarantined volunteers to respiratory viruses that cause the common cold and found that those under high stress were more likely to be infected by the viruses (Cohen, Tyrell, & Smith, 1993). Thus, scientists are beginning to assemble some impressive evidence that stress can temporarily suppress immunal functioning. This immunosuppression may be the key to many of the links between stress and illness.

Sizing Up the Link Between Stress and Illness

A wealth of evidence shows that stress is related to physical health, and converging lines of evidence suggest that stress contributes to the *causation* of illness. But we have to put this intriguing

Table 13.3 Health Problems That May Be Linked to Stress	
Health Problem	Representative Evidence
Common cold	Stone et al. (1992)
Ulcers	Ellard et al. (1990)
Asthma	Plutchik et al. (1978)
Headaches	Featherstone & Beitman (1984)
Menstrual discomfort	Siegel, Johnson, & Sarason (1979)
Vaginal infections	Williams & Deffenbacher (1983)
Genital herpes	VanderPlate, Aral, & Magder (1988)
Skin disorders	Fava et al. (1989)
Rheumatoid arthritis	Thomason et al. (1992)
Chronic back pain	Craufurd, Creed, & Jayson (1990)
Female reproductive problems	Fries, Nillius, & Petersson (1974)
Diabetes	Gonder-Frederick et al. (1990)
Complications of pregnancy	Pagel et al. (1990)
Hernias	Rahe & Holmes (1965)
Glaucoma	Cohen & Hajioff (1972)
Hyperthyroidism	Weiner (1978)
Hemophilia	Buxton et al. (1981)
Tuberculosis	Wolf & Goodell (1968)
Leukemia	Greene & Swisher (1969)
Stroke	Harmsen et al. (1990)
Appendicitis	Creed (1989)
Multiple sclerosis	Grant et al. (1989)
Periodontal disease	Green et al. (1986)
Hypertension	Egan et al. (1983)
Cancer	Cooper (1984)
Coronary heart disease	Rosengren, Tibblin, & Wilhelmsen (1991)
Inflammatory bowel disease	Garrett et al. (1991)

finding in perspective. Virtually all of the relevant research is correlational, so it can't demonstrate *conclusively* that stress causes illness (see Figure 13.8 on the next page). Subjects' elevated levels of stress and illness could both be due to a third variable, perhaps some aspect of personality. For instance, some evidence suggests that neuroticism may make people overly prone to interpret events as stressful and overly prone to interpret unpleasant sensations as symptoms of illness, thus inflating the correlation between stress and illness (Brett et al., 1990; Watson & Pennebaker, 1989).

In spite of methodological problems favoring inflated correlations, the research in this area consistently indicates that the *strength* of the relationship between stress and health is modest. The correlations typically fall in the .20s and .30s.

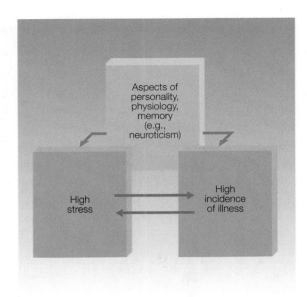

Figure 13.8. The stress-illness correlation. One or more aspects of personality, physiology, or memory could play the role of a postulated third variable in the relationship between high stress and high incidence of illness. For example, neuroticism may lead some subjects to view more events as stressful and to remember more illness, thus inflating the apparent correlation between stress and illness.

Clearly, stress is not an irresistible force that produces inevitable effects on health. Actually, this should come as no surprise, as stress is but one factor operating in a complex network of biopsychosocial determinants of health. Other key factors include one's genetic endowment, exposure to infectious agents and environmental toxins, nutrition, exercise, alcohol and drug use, smoking, use of medical care, and cooperation with medical advice. Furthermore, some people handle stress better than others, which is the matter we turn to next.

Factors Moderating the Impact of Stress

Some people seem to be able to withstand the ravages of stress better than others. Why? Because a number of *moderator variables* can lessen the impact of stress on physical and mental health. We'll look at two key moderator variables—social support and optimism—to shed light on individual differences in how well people tolerate stress.

Social Factors: Social Support

Friends may be good for your health! This startling conclusion emerges from studies on social support as a moderator of stress. **Social support refers to various types of aid and succor provided by members of one's social networks.** In one study, Jemmott and Magloire (1988) examined the effect of social support on immunal functioning in a group of students going through the stress of final exams. They found that students who reported stronger social support had higher levels of an antibody that plays a key role in warding off respiratory infections. Positive cor-

relations between high social support and greater immunal functioning were also seen in another study, which focused on spouses of cancer patients (Baron et al., 1990).

Many other studies have also found evidence that social support is favorably related to physical health (Cohen, 1988; Vogt et al., 1992). Social support seems to be good medicine for the mind as well as the body, as most studies find an association between social support and mental health (Leavy, 1983). The mechanisms underlying the connection between social support and wellness are the subject of considerable debate (Hobfoll & Vaux, 1993). It appears that social support serves as a protective buffer for us during times of high stress, reducing the negative impact of stressful events. Furthermore, social support has its own positive effects on health, which may be apparent even when we aren't under great stress (Cohen & Syme, 1985).

Optimism

Defining **optimism as a general tendency to expect good outcomes,** Michael Scheier and Charles Carver (1985) found a correlation between optimism and relatively good physical health in a sample of college students. In another study that focused on surgical patients, optimism was found to be associated with a faster recovery and a quicker return to normal activities after coronary artery bypass surgery (Scheier et al., 1989). Research suggests that optimists cope with stress in more adaptive ways than pessimists (Aspinwall & Taylor, 1992; Scheier & Carver, 1992). Optimists are more likely to engage in action-oriented, problem-focused coping. They are more willing than pessimists to seek social support, and they are more likely to emphasize the positive in their appraisals of stressful events. In comparison, pessimists are more likely to deal with stress by giving up or engaging in denial.

In a related line of research, Christopher Peterson and Martin Seligman have studied how people explain bad events (personal setbacks, mishaps, disappointments, and such). They identified a *pessimistic explanatory style* in which some people tend to blame setbacks on their personal shortcomings. In a retrospective study of men who graduated from Harvard back in the 1940s, they found an association between this pessimistic explanatory style and relatively poor health (Peterson, Seligman, & Vaillant, 1988). In their attempt to explain this association, they speculate that pessimism leads to passive coping efforts and poor

CHAPTER THIRTEEN

health care practices. A subsequent study also found an association between pessimism and suppressed immune function (Kamen-Siegel et al., 1991).

Individual differences among people in social support and optimism explain why stress doesn't have the same impact on everyone. Differences in lifestyle may play an even larger role in determining health. We'll examine some critical aspects of lifestyle in the next section.

HEALTH-IMPAIRING LIFESTYLES

Some people seem determined to dig an early grave for themselves. They do precisely those things that are bad for their health. For example, some people drink heavily even though they know that they're damaging their liver. Others eat all the wrong foods even though they know that they're increasing their risk of a second heart attack. Behavior that's downright *self-destructive* is surprisingly common. In this section we'll discuss how health is affected by smoking, poor nutrition, and lack of exercise, and we'll look at lifestyle factors in AIDS. (The health risks of alcohol and drug use are discussed in Chapter 5.) We'll also discuss *why* people develop health-impairing lifestyles.

Smoking

The smoking of tobacco is widespread in our culture. Current consumption in the United States is around 2800 cigarettes a year per adult (Fiore, 1992). Smokers face a much greater risk of premature death than nonsmokers (U.S. Department of Health and Human Services, 1989, 1990). For example, a 30-year-old male who smokes two packs a day has an estimated life expectancy that is *8 years shorter* than a comparable nonsmoker. The increased health risks from smoking are positively correlated with the number of cigarettes smoked and their tar and nicotine content. Jarvik and Schneider (1992) put the health costs of smoking in perspective by noting that smoking accounts for roughly 60 times as many deaths per year as cocaine and heroin use combined.

Why are mortality rates higher for smokers? Smoking increases the likelihood of developing a surprisingly large range of diseases. Lung cancer and heart disease are the two types of illness that kill the largest number of smokers (Fielding, 1985).

Knowing that their personal habits adversely affect their well-being, many people nonetheless persist in doing things that are self-descructive.

However, smokers also have an elevated risk for oral, bladder, and kidney cancer, as well as cancer of the larynx, esophagus, and pancreas (Newcomb & Carbone, 1992); arteriosclerosis, hypertension, stroke, and other cardiovascular diseases (McBride, 1992); and bronchitis, emphysema, and other pulmonary diseases (Sherman, 1992).

Studies show that if people can give up smoking, their health risks decline reasonably quickly (Samet, 1992). Five years after people stop smoking, their health risk is already noticeably lower than that of people who have continued to smoke. The health risks of people who give up tobacco continue to decline until they reach a normal level after about 15 years.

Unfortunately, it's very difficult to give up cigarettes. People who enroll in formal smoking cessation programs aren't any more successful than people who try to quit on their own (Cohen et al., 1989). Long-term success rates are in the vicinity of only 25%. In fact, as Figure 13.9 shows, relapse rates for quitting smoking often are as bad as those

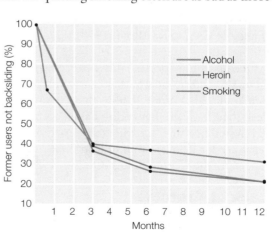

Figure 13.9. Relapse in efforts to quit smoking. It is quite difficult to give up smoking. As the graph shows, the relapse rates for returning to smoking within a year are similar to those for returning to alcohol and heroin use. (From Hunt & Matarazzo, 1982)

seen in efforts to give up heroin or alcohol (Hunt & Matarazzo, 1982). Nonetheless, the fact that there are nearly 40 million ex-smokers in the United States indicates that it is possible to quit smoking successfully. Interestingly, many people fail several times before they eventually succeed. Evidence suggests that the readiness to give up smoking builds gradually as people cycle through periods of abstinence and relapse (Biener & Abrams, 1991; Prochaska, 1994).

Poor Nutritional Habits

Evidence is accumulating that patterns of nutrition influence susceptibility to a variety of diseases and health problems. Possible connections between eating patterns and diseases include the following:

1. Many factors influence the development of obesity, but chronic overeating often plays a prominent role. Overweight people have an increased risk of heart disease, hypertension, stroke, respiratory ailments, arthritis, diabetes, and back problems (Bray, 1990).

2. Heavy consumption of foods that elevate serum cholesterol level (eggs, cheeses, butter, shellfish, sausage, and the like) appears to increase the risk of heart disease (Muldoon, Manuck, & Matthews, 1990).

3. High salt intake has long been thought to be a contributing factor to the development of high blood pressure (Kaplan, 1986), although there's still some debate about its role.

4. Diets high in fats and low in fiber have been implicated as possible contributors to some forms of cancer, especially cancers of the colon, prostate, and breast (S. Levy, 1985).

5. Vulnerability to osteoporosis, an abnormal loss of bone mass observed most commonly in postmenopausal women, appears to be elevated by a life-long pattern of inadequate calcium intake (Fahey & Gallagher-Allred, 1990).

Of course, nutritional habits interact with other factors to determine whether one develops a particular disease. Nonetheless, the examples just described indicate that eating habits are relevant to physical health. Unfortunately, nutritional patterns are far from ideal in industrialized nations, especially the United States (Quillin, 1987).

Lack of Exercise

There is considerable evidence linking lack of exercise to poor health. Research indicates that

regular exercise is associated with increased longevity (Paffenbarger, Hyde, & Wing, 1990). Why would exercise help people live longer? Because physical fitness promotes a diverse array of specific benefits. For one thing, an appropriate exercise program can enhance cardiovascular fitness and thereby reduce susceptibility to deadly cardiovascular problems. Fitness is associated with reduced risk for both coronary disease and hypertension (Froelicher, 1990; Hagberg, 1990). Second, regular physical activity can contribute to the avoidance of obesity (Bray, 1990). Hence, fitness may indirectly reduce one's risk for a variety of obesity-related health problems, such as diabetes and respiratory illnesses. Third, recent studies suggest that physical fitness is also associated with a decreased risk for colon cancer in men and for breast and reproductive cancer in women (Blair et al., 1992; Calabrese, 1990). The apparent link between exercise and reduced cancer risk has been a pleasant surprise for scientists, who are now scrambling to figure out the physiological mechanisms underlying this association.

Admittedly, exercise programs may carry their own hazards. For example, jogging can elevate one's risk of muscular and skeletal injuries (it's especially hard on the knees) and can elicit heat stroke and even a heart attack (Siscovick, 1990). However, the potential hazards of exercise can be minimized by developing a workout regimen gradually and following it regularly. Most exercise-related problems occur when people work out sporadically and try to do too much in one session (Siscovick et al., 1984).

Behavior and AIDS

At present, some of the most problematic links between behavior and health may be those related to AIDS. *AIDS* stands for *acquired immune deficiency syndrome*, **a disorder in which the immune system is gradually weakened and eventually disabled by the human immunodeficiency virus (HIV).** Being infected with the HIV virus is *not* equivalent to having AIDS. AIDS is the final stage of the HIV infection process, typically manifested about ten years after the original infection, during which a person is left virtually defenseless against a host of opportunistic infectious agents. AIDS inflicts its harm indirectly by opening the door to other diseases. The symptoms of AIDS vary widely depending on the specific constellation of diseases that one develops. Ultimately, AIDS is a fatal disorder and there is no cure on the horizon. Unfortunately, the prevalence of this deadly disease continues to increase at an alarming rate. Although the average length of survival for AIDS patients has increased slightly, the typical patient dies 18 to 24 months after the AIDS syndrome is manifested (Libman, 1992).

The HIV virus is transmitted through person-to-person contact involving the exchange of bodily fluids, primarily semen and blood. The two principal modes of transmission in the United States have been sexual contact and the sharing of needles by intravenous (IV) drug users. In the United States, sexual transmission has occurred primarily among gay and bisexual men, but in the world as a whole, infection through heterosexual relations is more common, with male-to-female transmission particularly prevalent (Ickovics & Rodin, 1992). The HIV virus can be found in the tears and saliva of infected individuals, but the concentrations are low and there is no evidence that the infection can be spread through casual contact (Friedland et al, 1986). Even most forms of noncasual contact, including kissing, hugging, and sharing food with infected individuals, appear safe.

Misconceptions about AIDS are widespread. Ironically, the people who hold these misconceptions fall into two polarized camps. On the one hand, a great many people have unrealistic fears that AIDS can be readily transmitted through casual contact with infected individuals. These people worry unnecessarily about contracting AIDS from a handshake, a sneeze, or an eating utensil. They tend to be paranoid about interacting with homosexuals, thus fueling discrimination against gays in regard to housing, employment and so forth. Some people also believe that it is dangerous to donate blood, when, in fact, blood donors are at no risk whatsoever.

On the other hand, many young heterosexuals who are sexually active with a variety of partners, foolishly downplay their risk for HIV, naively assuming that they are safe as long as they avoid IV drug use and sexual relations with gay or bisexual men (Friedman & Goodman, 1992). They greatly underestimate the probability that their sexual partners may have previously used IV drugs or had unprotected sex with an infected individual. Also, because AIDS is usually accompanied by discernible symptoms, many young people believe that prospective sexual partners who carry the HIV virus will exhibit telltale signs of illness. However, as we have already noted, having AIDS and being infected with HIV are not the same thing, and HIV carriers often remain healthy and symptom-

free for years after they are infected. In sum, many myths about AIDS persist, in spite of extensive efforts to educate the public about this complex and controversial disease. Figure 13.10 contains a short quiz to test your knowledge of the facts about AIDS.

The behavioral changes that minimize the risk of developing AIDS are fairly straightforward, although making the changes is often much easier said than done. In all groups, the more sexual partners one has, the higher the risk that one will be exposed to the HIV virus. Thus, people can reduce their risk by having sexual contacts with fewer partners and by using condoms to control the exchange of semen. It is also important to curtail certain sexual practices (in particular, anal sex) that increase the probability of semen/blood mixing. Intravenous drug users could greatly reduce their risk by abandoning their drug use, but this is unlikely, since most are physically dependent on the drugs. Alternatively, they need to improve the sterilization of their needles and avoid sharing syringes with other users.

How Do Health-Impairing Lifestyles Develop?

It may seem puzzling that people behave in self-destructive ways. How does this happen? Several factors are involved. First, many health-impairing habits creep up on people slowly. For instance, alcohol use may grow imperceptibly over years, or exercise habits may decline ever so gradually.

A quiz on AIDS

Answer the following "true" or "false."

T F **1.** AIDS is caused by a virus.

T F **2.** AIDS is caused by inheriting a bad gene or genes.

T F **3.** AIDS is caused by a kind of bacterium.

T F **4.** A person can "carry" and pass on whatever causes AIDS without necessarily having AIDS or looking sick.

T F **5.** Whatever causes AIDS can be passed on through semen.

T F **6.** Whatever causes AIDS can be passed on through blood or blood products.

T F **7.** You can catch AIDS like you catch a cold because whatever causes AIDS can be carried in the air.

T F **8.** You can catch AIDS by being in the same room with someone who has AIDS.

T F **9.** You can catch AIDS by shaking hands with someone who has AIDS.

T F **10.** Having a monogamous relationship decreases the risk of getting AIDS.

T F **11.** Using condoms reduces the risk of getting AIDS.

T F **12.** A vaccine for AIDS will be available within a year.

Answers: 1.T 2.F 3.F 4.T 5.T 6.T 7.F 8.F 9.F 10.T 11.T 12.F

Figure 13.10. A quiz on knowledge of AIDS. Because misconceptions about AIDS abound, it may be wise to take this brief quiz to test your knowledge of AIDS. (Adapted from Temoshok, Sweet, & Zich, 1987)

Second, many health-impairing habits involve activities that are quite pleasant at the time. Actions such as eating favorite foods, smoking cigarettes, or getting "high" are potent reinforcing events. Third, the risks associated with most health-impairing habits are chronic diseases such as cancer that usually lie 10, 20, or 30 years down the road. It's relatively easy to ignore risks that lie in the distant future.

Finally, people have a curious tendency to underestimate the risks that accompany their own health-impairing behaviors while viewing the risks associated with others' self-destructive behaviors much more accurately (van der Velde, van der Pligt, & Hooykaas, 1994; Weinstein, 1989). Many people are well aware of the dangers associated with certain habits, but when it's time to apply this information to themselves, they often discount it. They figure, for instance, that smoking will lead to cancer or a heart attack in *someone else*.

So far, we've seen that physical health may be affected by stress and by aspects of lifestyle. Next, we'll look at the importance of how people react to physical symptoms, health problems, and health care efforts.

"A person will not carry out a health behavior if significant barriers stand in the way, or if the steps interfere with favorite or necessary activities."
ROBIN DiMATTEO

REACTIONS TO ILLNESS

Some people respond to physical symptoms and illnesses by ignoring warning signs of developing diseases, while others actively seek to conquer their diseases. Let's examine the decision to seek medical treatment, the sick role, and adherence to medical advice.

The Decision to Seek Treatment

Have you ever experienced nausea, diarrhea, stiffness, headaches, cramps, chest pains, or sinus problems? Of course you have; we all experience some of these problems periodically. However, whether we view these sensations as *symptoms* is a matter of individual interpretation. When two persons experience the same unpleasant sensations, one may shrug them off as a nuisance while the other may rush to a physician. Studies suggest that people who are relatively high in anxiety and low in self-esteem tend to report more symptoms of illness than others (Pennebaker, 1982). Those who are extremely attentive to bodily sensations and health concerns also report more symptoms than the average person (Barsky, 1988).

Variations in the perceived seriousness and disruptiveness of symptoms help explain the differences among people in their readiness to seek medical treatment (Cameron, Leventhal, & Leventhal, 1993). The biggest problem in regard to treatment seeking is the tendency of many people to delay the pursuit of needed professional consultation. Delays can be critical because early diagnosis and quick intervention may facilitate more effective treatment of many health problems. Unfortunately, procrastination is the norm even when people are faced with a medical emergency, such as a heart attack. Why do people dawdle in the midst of a crisis? Robin DiMatteo (1991), a leading expert on patient behavior, mentions a number of reasons, noting that people delay because they often (a) misinterpret and downplay the significance of their symptoms, (b) fret about looking silly if the problem turns out to be nothing, (c) worry about "bothering" their physician, (d) are reluctant to disrupt their plans (to go out to dinner, see a movie, and so forth), and (e) waste time on trivial matters (such as taking a shower, gathering personal items, or packing clothes) before going to a hospital emergency room.

The Sick Role

Although many people tend to delay medical consultations, some people are positively eager to seek care. These people have learned that there are potential benefits to adopting the "sick role" (Lubkin, 1990; Parsons, 1979). For instance, fewer demands are placed on sick people, who often can selectively decide which demands to ignore. Sick people may also find themselves to be the center of attention from friends and relatives. This increase in attention from others can be highly rewarding, especially to those who have received little attention previously. Moreover, much of this attention is favorable, in that the sick person is showered with affection, concern, and sympathy.

Thus, some people grow to *like* the sick role, although they may not be aware of this feeling. Such people readily seek professional care, but they also tend to behave in subtle ways that prolong their illness (Kinsman, Dirks, & Jones, 1982). For example, they may only pretend to go along with the medical advice they receive, a common problem that we'll discuss next.

Adherence to Medical Advice

Many patients fail to adhere to the instructions they receive from physicians and other health care

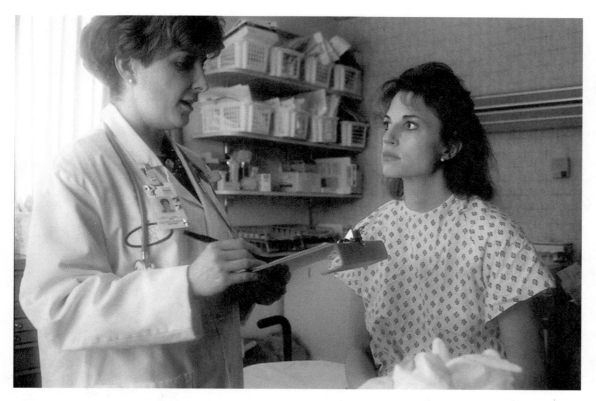

Many patients do not comply with the directions they receive from their physicians. Research suggests that improvements in doctor-patient communication can increase medical compliance.

professionals. Such nonadherence is not limited to people who have come to like the sick role, and it's a major problem in our medical care system. The evidence suggests that noncompliance with medical advice may occur 30% to 60% of the time (Kaplan & Simon, 1990).

This point is not intended to suggest that you should passively accept all professional advice from medical personnel. However, when you have doubts about a prescribed treatment, you should speak up and ask questions. Passive resistance can backfire. For instance, if a physician sees no improvement in a patient who falsely insists that he has been taking his medicine, the physician may abandon an accurate diagnosis in favor of an inaccurate one. The inaccurate diagnosis could lead to inappropriate treatments that might be harmful to the patient.

Why don't people comply with the advice that they've sought out from highly regarded health care professionals? Physicians tend to attribute noncompliance to patients' personality traits, but research indicates that other factors are more important. Three considerations are especially prominent (DiMatteo & Friedman, 1982; Evans & Haynes, 1990):

1. Frequently, noncompliance is due to a failure by the patient to understand the instructions as given. Highly trained professionals often forget that what seems obvious and simple to them may be obscure and complicated to many of their patients.

2. Another key factor is how aversive or difficult the instructions are. If the prescribed regimen is unpleasant, compliance will tend to decrease. And the more that following instructions interferes with routine behavior, the less probable it is that the patient will cooperate successfully.

3. If a patient has a negative attitude toward a physician, the probability of noncompliance will increase. When patients are unhappy with their interactions with the doctor, they're more likely to ignore the medical advice provided, no matter how important it may be.

In response to the noncompliance problem, some health psychologists are exploring ways to increase patients' adherence to medical advice. They've found that the communication process between the practitioner and the patient is of critical importance. Courtesy, encouragement, reassurance, taking time to answer questions, and decreased reliance on medical jargon can improve compliance (DiNicola & DiMatteo, 1984; Hall, Roter, & Katz, 1988). Thus, there's a new emphasis in medicine on enhancing health care professionals' communication skills.

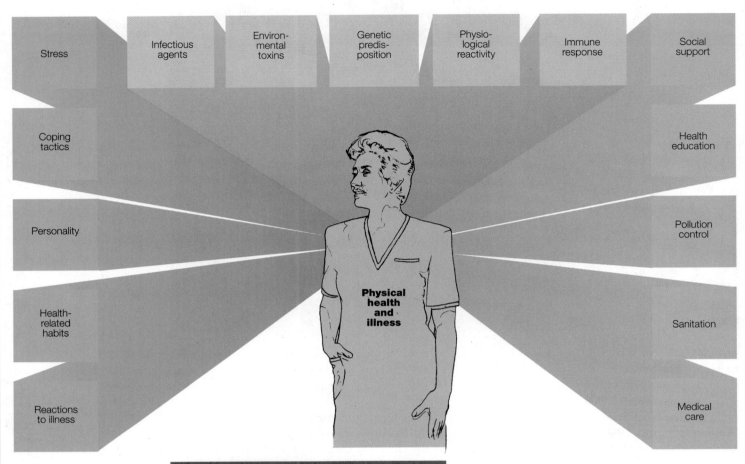

Psychological (behavioral) factors

Biological factors

Social (system) factors

Stress

Infectious agents

Environmental toxins

Genetic predisposition

Physiological reactivity

Immune response

Social support

Coping tactics

Health education

Personality

Pollution control

Health-related habits

Sanitation

Reactions to illness

Medical care

Physical health and illness

**Figure 13.11.
Biopsychosocial factors
in health.** Physical health
can be influenced by a remarkably diverse set of variables, including biological,
psychological, and social
factors. The host of factors
that affect health provide an
excellent example of multifactorial causation.

PUTTING IT IN PERSPECTIVE

Which of our themes were prominent in this
chapter? As you probably noticed, our discussion
of stress and health illustrated multifactorial causation and the subjectivity of experience.

Our discussion of the psychology of health provided a particularly complex illustration of multifactorial causation. As we noted in Chapter 1,
people are likely to think simplistically, in terms of
single causes. In recent years, the highly publicized research linking stress to health has led many
people to point automatically to stress as an explanation for illness. In reality, stress has only a
modest impact on physical health. Stress can increase the risk for illness, but health is governed by
a dense network of factors. Important factors
include inherited vulnerabilities, exposure to infectious agents, health-impairing habits, reactions
to symptoms, treatment-seeking behavior, compliance with medical advice, optimism, and social

support. In other words, stress is but one actor on
a crowded stage. This should be apparent in Figure 13.11, which shows the multitude of
biopsychosocial factors that jointly influence physical health. It illustrates multifactorial causation in
all its complexity.

The subjectivity of experience was demonstrated by the frequently repeated point that
stress lies in the eye of the beholder. The same
promotion at work may be stressful for one
person and invigorating for another. One
person's pressure is another's challenge. When
it comes to stress, objective reality is not nearly
as important as subjective perceptions. More
than anything else, the impact of stressful events
seems to depend on how people view them. The
critical importance of individual stress appraisals will continue to be apparent in our Application on stress management. Many stress-management strategies depend on altering one's
appraisals of events.

Improving Coping and Stress Management

Answer the following "true" or "false."

___ **1** The key to managing stress is to avoid or circumvent it.

___ **2** It's best to suppress emotional reactions to stress.

___ **3** Laughing at one's problems is immature.

___ **4** Exercise has little or no impact on stress resistance.

Courses and books on stress management have multiplied at a furious pace in the last decade. They summarize experts' advice on how to cope with stress more effectively. How do these experts feel about the four statements above? As you'll

see in this Application, most would agree that all four are false.

The key to managing stress does *not* lie in avoiding it. Stress is an inevitable element in the fabric of modern life. As Hans Selye (1973) noted, "contrary to public opinion, we must not—and indeed can't—avoid stress" (p. 693). Thus, most stress-management programs train people to use more effective coping strategies. In this Application, we'll examine a variety of constructive coping tactics, beginning with Albert Ellis's ideas about changing one's appraisals of stressful events.

Reappraisal: Ellis's Rational Thinking

Albert Ellis (1977, 1985) is a prominent theorist who believes that people can

short-circuit their emotional reactions to stress by altering their appraisals of stressful events. Ellis's insights about stress appraisal are the foundation for a widely used system of therapy that he devised. *Rational-emotive therapy* **is an approach that focuses on altering clients' patterns of irrational thinking to reduce maladaptive emotions and behavior.**

Ellis maintains that *you feel the way you think*. He argues that problematic emotional reactions are caused by negative self-talk, which he calls catastrophic thinking. *Catastrophic thinking* **involves unrealistically pessimistic appraisals of stress that exaggerate the magnitude of one's problems.** Ellis uses a simple A-B-C sequence to explain his ideas (see Figure 13.12):

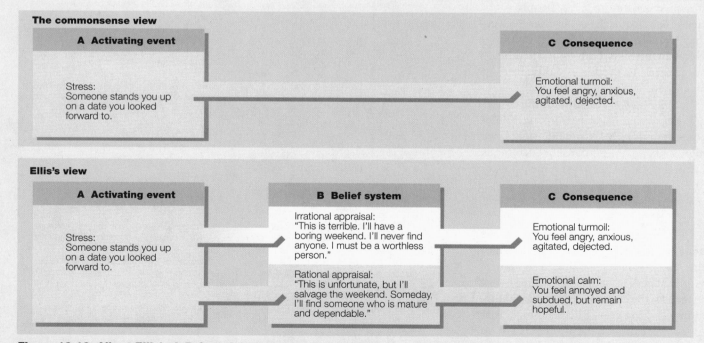

Figure 13.12. Albert Ellis's A-B-C model of emotional reactions. Although most people are prone to attribute their negative emotional reactions directly to events, Ellis argues that people *feel* the way they *think*.

"People largely disturb themselves by thinking in a self-defeating, illogical, and unrealistic manner."
ALBERT ELLIS

A: *Activating event.* The A in Ellis's system stands for the activating event that produces the stress. The activating event may be any potentially stressful transaction. Examples might include an automobile accident, the cancellation of a date, a delay while waiting in line at the bank, or a failure to get a promotion you were expecting.

B: *Belief system.* B stands for your belief about the event, or your appraisal of the stress. According to Ellis, people often view minor setbacks as disasters. Thus, they engage in catastrophic thinking: "How awful this is. I can't stand it! Things never turn out fair for me. I'll never get promoted."

C: *Consequence.* C stands for the consequences of your negative thinking. When your appraisals of stressful events are highly negative, the consequence tends to be emotional distress. Thus, people feel angry, outraged, anxious, panic stricken, disgusted, or dejected.

Ellis asserts that most people don't understand the importance of phase B in this three-stage sequence. We unwittingly believe that the activating event (A) causes the consequent emotional turmoil (C). However, Ellis maintains that A does *not* cause C. It only appears to do so. Instead, Ellis asserts, B causes C. One's emotional distress is actually caused by one's catastrophic thinking in appraising stressful events.

According to Ellis, it's commonplace for people to turn inconvenience into disaster and to make mountains out of molehills. For instance, imagine that someone stands you up on a date that you were looking forward to eagerly. You might think as follows: "Oh, this is terrible. I'm going to have another rotten, boring weekend. People always mistreat me. I'll never find anyone to fall in love with. I must be a crummy, worthless person." Ellis would argue that such thoughts are highly irrational. He would point out that it doesn't follow logically that, just because you were stood up, (1) you must have a lousy weekend, (2) you will never fall in love, and (3) you are a worthless person.

Ellis theorizes that unrealistic appraisals of stress are derived from irrational assumptions that people hold. He maintains that if you scrutinize your catastrophic thinking, you'll find that your reasoning is based on a logically indefensible premise, such as "I must have approval from everyone" or "I must perform well in all endeavors." These faulty assumptions, which people often hold unconsciously, generate catastrophic thinking and emotional turmoil. Irrational assumptions that are especially common are described in Figure 13.13.

How can you reduce your unrealistic appraisals of stress? To accomplish this, Ellis asserts that you must learn (1) how to detect catastrophic thinking and

Figure 13.13. Irrational assumptions that can cause and sustain emotional disturbance. According to Ellis, assumptions such as these are often held unconsciously, and one may have to work at detecting them before one can change to a more positive way of thinking. (Adapted by Basil Najjar from Ellis, 1977)

	Irrational assumption	Rational alternative
1	I must be loved or approved by everyone for everything I do.	It's best to concentrate on my own self-respect, on winning approval for practical purposes, and on loving rather than being loved.
2	I must be thoroughly competent, adequate, and achieving in order to be worthwhile.	I'm an imperfect creature who has limitations and fallibilities like anyone else—and that's okay.
3	It's horrible when things aren't going the way I'd like them to be.	I can try to change or control the things that disturb me—or temporarily accept conditions I can't change.
4	There isn't much I can do about my sorrows and disturbances, because unhappiness comes from what happens to you.	I *feel* how I *think*. Unhappiness comes mostly from how I look at things.
5	If something is dangerous or fearsome, I'm right to be terribly upset about it and to dwell on the possibility of its occurring.	I can frankly face what I fear and either render it nondangerous or accept the inevitable.
6	It's easier to avoid facing difficulties and responsibilities than to face them.	The "easy way out" is invariably the much harder alternative in the long run.
7	I'm dependent on others and need someone stronger than I am to rely on.	It's better to take the risk of relying on myself and thinking and acting independently.
8	There's always a precise and perfect solution to human problems, and it's catastrophic not to find it.	The world is full of probability and chance, and I can enjoy life even though there isn't always an ideal solution to a problem.
9	The world—especially other people—should be fair, and justice (or mercy) must triumph.	I can work toward seeking fair behavior, realizing that there are few absolutes in life.
10	I must not question the beliefs held by society or respected authorities.	It's better to evaluate beliefs for myself—on their own merits, not on who happens to hold them.

(2) how to dispute the irrational assumptions that cause it.

Humor as a Stress Reducer

A few years ago, the Chicago suburbs experienced their worst flooding in about a century. Thousands of people saw their homes wrecked when two rivers spilled over their banks. As the waters receded, the flood victims returning to their homes were subjected to the inevitable TV interviews. A remarkable number of victims, surrounded by the ruins of their homes, *joked* about their misfortune. When the going gets tough, it may pay to laugh about it. In a study of coping styles, McCrae (1984) found that 40% of his subjects used humor to deal with stress.

In analyzing the stress-reducing effects of humor, Dixon (1980) noted that finding a humorous aspect in a stressful situation redefines the situation in a less threatening way. Dixon also pointed out that laughter and mirth can serve to discharge pent-up emotions. These dual functions of humor may make joking about life's difficulties a particularly useful coping strategy (Martin & Lefcourt, 1983; Nezu, Nezu, & Blissett, 1988).

Releasing Pent-Up Emotions

Try as you might to redefine situations as less stressful, you no doubt still go through times when you feel wired with stress-induced tension. When this happens, there's merit in the commonsense notion that you should try to release the emotions welling up inside. Why? Because the physiological arousal that accompanies emotions can become problematic. One study of high school students found that those who tended to hold their anger in exhibited higher blood pressure (Spielberger et al., 1985).

Verbalization or "talking it out" can be valuable in dealing with stress (Clark, 1993). James Pennebaker and his colleagues (1988) have shown that talking or writing about traumatic events can have beneficial effects. For example, in one study of college students, half of the subjects were asked to write three essays about their difficulties in adjusting to college. The other half wrote three essays about superficial topics. The subjects who wrote about their personal problems and traumas enjoyed better health in the following months than the other subjects (Pennebaker, Colder, & Sharp, 1990). Thus, if you can find a good listener, you may be able to discharge problematic emotions by letting your secret fears, misgivings, and suspicions spill out in a candid conversation.

Learning to Relax

Relaxation is a valuable stress-management technique that can soothe emotional turmoil and suppress problematic physiological arousal (Lehrer & Woolfolk, 1984). One study even suggests that relaxation training may improve the effectiveness of the immune response (Kiecolt-Glaser et al., 1985).

The value of relaxation became apparent to Herbert Benson (1975; Benson & Klipper, 1988) as a result of his research on meditation. Benson, a Harvard Medical School cardiologist, believes that relaxation is the key to the beneficial effects of meditation. According to Benson, the elaborate religious rituals and beliefs associated with meditation are irrelevant to its effects. After "demystifying" meditation, Benson set out to devise a simple, nonreligious procedure that could provide similar benefits. He calls his procedure the *relaxation response*. From his study of a variety of relaxation techniques, Benson concluded that four factors promote effective relaxation: (1) a quiet, distraction-free environment, (2) a mental device to focus on (such as a sound or word recited repetitively), (3) a passive attitude, and (4) a comfortable position that isn't conducive to sleep. Benson's simple relaxation procedure is described in Figure 13.14. For full benefit, it should be practiced daily.

Minimizing Physiological Vulnerability

Your body is intimately involved in your response to stress, and the wear and tear

1 Sit quietly in a comfortable position.

2 Close your eyes.

3 Deeply relax all your muscles, beginning at your feet and progressing up to your face. Keep them relaxed.

4 Breathe through your nose. Become aware of your breathing. As you breathe out, say the word "one" silently to yourself. For example, breathe in . . . out, "one"; in . . . out, "one"; and so forth. Breathe easily and naturally.

5 Continue for 10 to 20 minutes. You may open your eyes to check the time, but do not use an alarm. When you finish, sit quietly for several minutes, at first with your eyes closed and later with your eyes opened. Do not stand up for a few minutes.

Figure 13.14. Benson's relaxation procedure. To benefit from the procedure, you should practice it daily. (From Benson, 1975, pp. 114–115)

6 Do not worry about whether you are successful in achieving a deep level of relaxation. Maintain a passive attitude and permit relaxation to occur at its own pace. When distracting thoughts occur, try to ignore them by not dwelling on them, and return to repeating "one." With practice, the response should come with little effort. Practice the technique once or twice daily but not within two hours after any meal, since digestive processes seem to interfere with the elicitation of the relaxation response.

Figure 13.15. Physical fitness and mortality. Blair et al. (1989) studied death rates among men and women who exhibited low, medium, or high fitness. As you can see, fitness was associated with lower mortality rates in both sexes.

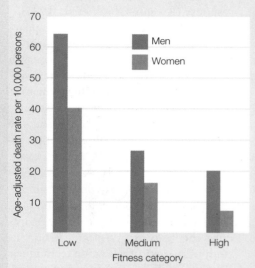

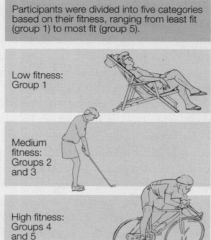

Participants were divided into five categories based on their fitness, ranging from least fit (group 1) to most fit (group 5).

Low fitness: Group 1

Medium fitness: Groups 2 and 3

High fitness: Groups 4 and 5

of stress can be injurious to your health. To combat this potential problem, it helps to keep your body in relatively sound shape. The potential benefits of regular exercise are substantial. Regular exercise is associated with increased longevity (Paffenbarger, Hyde, & Wing, 1986). Moreover, research has shown that you don't have to be a dedicated athlete to benefit from exercise (Blair et al., 1989). Even a moderate amount of exercise reduces your risk of disease (see Figure 13.15). Successful participation in an exercise program can also lead to improvements in your mood, self-concept, and work efficiency (Folkins & Sime, 1981; King, Taylor, & Haskell, 1993).

Embarking on an exercise program is difficult for many people. Exercise is time-consuming, and if you're out of shape, your initial attempts may be painful and discouraging. To avoid these problems, it's wise to do the following: (1) select an activity that you find enjoyable, (2) increase your participation gradually, (3) exercise regularly without overdoing it, and (4) reinforce yourself for your efforts (Greenberg, 1990). If you choose a competitive sport (such as basketball or tennis), try to avoid falling into the competition trap. If you become obsessed with winning, you'll put yourself under pressure and *add* to the stress in your life.

Chapter **13** Review

KEY IDEAS

The Nature of Stress
♦ Stress involves circumstances and experiences that are perceived as threatening. Stress is a common, everyday event, and even seemingly minor stressors or hassles can be problematic. To a large degree, stress lies in the eye of the beholder. Whether one feels threatened by events depends on how one appraises them.

♦ Major types of stress include frustration, conflict, change, and pressure. Frustration occurs when an obstacle prevents one from attaining some goal. There are three principal types of conflict: approach-approach, avoidance-avoidance, and approach-avoidance. The third type is especially stressful. Vacillation is a common response to conflict.

♦ A large number of studies with the SRRS suggest that change is stressful. Although this may be true, it is now clear that the SRRS is a measure of general stress rather than just change-related stress. Two kinds of pressure (to perform and conform) also appear to be stressful .

Responding to Stress
♦ Emotional reactions to stress typically include anger, fear, and sadness. Emotional arousal may interfere with coping. According to the inverted-U hypothesis, task performance improves with increased arousal up to a point and then declines. The optimal level of arousal on a task depends on the complexity of the task.

♦ Selye's general adaptation syndrome describes three stages in physiological reactions to stress: alarm, resistance, and exhaustion. Diseases of adaptation may appear during the stage of exhaustion. There are two major pathways along which the brain sends signals to the endocrine system in response to stress. Actions along these paths release two sets of hormones, catecholamines and corticosteroids, into the bloodstream.

♦ The behavioral response to stress takes the form of coping. Some coping responses are less than optimal. One of these is striking out at others with acts of aggression. Giving up and indulging oneself are other coping patterns that tend to be of limited value. Defensive coping is particularly common. Defense mechanisms protect against emotional distress through self-deception. Defensive illusions may sometimes be adaptive. Relatively healthy coping tactics are called constructive coping.

The Effects of Stress on Physical Health
♦ Stress appears to play a role in many types of illnesses, not just psychosomatic diseases. Type A behavior has been implicated as a contributing cause of coronary heart disease. Cynical hostility may be the most toxic element of the Type A syndrome. Researchers have found associations between stress and the onset of a great variety of specific diseases, although the evidence on many is highly tentative. Stress may play a role in a host of diseases because it can temporarily suppress the effectiveness of the immune system.

♦ While there's little doubt that stress can contribute to the development of physical illness, the link between stress and illness is modest in strength. Stress is only one factor in a complex network of biopsychosocial variables that shape health. There are individual differences in how much stress people can tolerate without experiencing ill effects. Social support and optimism are key moderators of the relationship between stress and illness.

Health-Impairing Lifestyles
♦ People frequently display health-impairing lifestyles. Smokers have much higher mortality rates than nonsmokers because they are more vulnerable to a host of diseases. Poor nutritional habits have been linked to obesity, heart disease, hypertension, and cancer. Lack of exercise elevates one's risk for cardiovascular diseases and perhaps for certain types of cancer.

♦ Aspects of behavior also influence one's risk of AIDS, which is transmitted through person-to-person contact involving the exchange of bodily fluids, primarily semen and blood. Misconceptions about AIDS are common, and the people who hold these misconceptions tend to fall into polarized camps, either overestimating or underestimating the risk of infection. Health-impairing habits tend to develop gradually and often involve pleasant activities. The risks may be easy to ignore because they lie in the distant future and because people tend to underestimate risks that apply to them personally.

Reactions to Illness
♦ Ignoring physical symptoms may result in the delay of needed medical treatment. At the other extreme, a minority of people learn to like the sick role because it earns them attention and allows them to avoid stress. Nonadherence to medical advice is a major problem. The likelihood of noncompliance is greater when instructions are difficult to understand, when recommendations are difficult to follow, and when patients are unhappy with their doctor.

Putting It in Perspective
♦ Two of our integrative themes were prominent in this chapter. First, we saw that behavior and health are influenced by multiple causes. Second, we saw that experience is highly subjective, as stress lies in the eye of the beholder.

Application: Improving Coping and Stress Management
♦ People use a variety of coping strategies, and some are healthier than others. Ellis emphasizes the importance of reappraising stressful events to detect and dispute catastrophic thinking. Humor may be useful in efforts to redefine stressful situations.

♦ In some cases, it may pay to release pent-up emotions by expressing them. Talking it out may help. Relaxation techniques, such as Benson's relaxation response, can reduce the wear and tear of stress. Physical vulnerability may also be reduced through regular exercise.

KEY TERMS

Acquired immune deficiency syndrome (AIDS)	Frustration
Aggression	General adaptation syndrome
Approach-approach conflict	Health psychology
Approach-avoidance conflict	Immune response
Avoidance-avoidance conflict	Learned helplessness
Biopsychosocial model	Life changes
Catastrophic thinking	Optimism
Conflict	Pressure
Constructive coping	Rational-emotive therapy
Coping	Social support
Defense mechanisms	Stress
	Type A personality
	Type B personality

KEY PEOPLE

Robin DiMatteo

Albert Ellis

Meyer Friedman and Ray Rosenman

Thomas Holmes and Richard Rahe

Richard Lazarus

Hans Selye

Shelley Taylor

14 Psychological Disorders

"The government of the United States was overthrown more than a year ago! I'm the president of the United States of America and Bob Dylan is vice president!" So said Ed, the author of a prominent book on journalism, who was speaking to a college journalism class, as a guest lecturer. Ed also informed the class that he had killed both John and Robert Kennedy, as well as Charles de Gaulle, the former president of France. He went on to tell the class that all rock music songs were written about him, that he was the greatest karate expert in the universe, and that he had been fighting "space wars" for 2000 years. The students in the class were mystified by Ed's bizarre, disjointed "lecture," but they assumed that he was putting on a show that would eventually lead to a sensible conclusion. However, their perplexed but expectant calm was shattered when Ed pulled a hatchet from the props he had brought with him and hurled the hatchet at the class! Fortunately, he didn't hit anyone, as the hatchet sailed over the students' heads. At that point, the professor for the class realized that Ed's irrational behavior was not a pretense. The professor evacuated the class quickly while Ed continued to rant and rave about his presidential administration, space wars, vampires, his romances with female rock stars, and his personal harem of 38 "chicks." (Adapted from Pearce, 1974)

Clearly, Ed's behavior was abnormal. Even *he* recognized that when he agreed later to be admitted to a mental hospital, signing himself in as the "President of the United States of America." What causes such abnormal behavior? Does Ed have a mental illness, or does he just behave strangely? What is the basis for judging behavior as normal versus abnormal? How common are psychological disorders? Can they be cured? These are just a few of the questions that we will address in this chapter as we discuss psychological disorders and their complex causes.

ABNORMAL BEHAVIOR: MYTHS, REALITIES, AND CONTROVERSIES

Misconceptions about abnormal behavior are common. Hence, we need to clear up some preliminary issues before we describe the various types of disorders. In this section, we will discuss (1) the medical model of abnormal behavior, (2) the criteria of abnormal behavior, and (3) the classification of psychological disorders.

The Medical Model Applied to Abnormal Behavior

In Ed's case, there's no question that his behavior was abnormal. But does it make sense to view his unusual and irrational behavior as an illness? This is a controversial question. **The *medical model* proposes that it is useful to think of abnormal behavior as a disease.** This point of view is the basis for many of the terms used to refer to abnormal behavior, including mental *illness*, psychological *disorder*, and psycho*pathology* (*pathology* refers to manifestations of disease). The medical model gradually became the dominant way of thinking about abnormal behavior during the 18th and 19th centuries, and its influence remains strong today.

The medical model clearly represented progress over earlier models of abnormal behavior. Prior to the 18th century, most conceptions of abnormal behavior were based on superstition. People who behaved strangely were thought to be possessed by demons, to be witches in league with the devil, or to be victims of God's punishment. Their disorders were "treated" with chants, rituals, exorcisms, and such. If the people's behavior was seen as threatening, they were candidates for chains, dungeons, torture, and death (see Figure 14.1).

Figure 14.1. Historical conceptions of mental illness. In the Middle Ages people who behaved strangely were sometimes thought to be in league with the devil. The drawing on the left depicts some of the cruel methods used to extract confessions from suspected witches and warlocks. Some psychological disorders were also thought to be caused by demonic possession. The painting on the right is a detail from Di Benvenuto's *St. Catherine Exorcising Possessed Woman*. (Denver Art Museum Collection)

The rise of the medical model brought great improvements in the treatment of those who exhibited abnormal behavior. As victims of an illness, they were viewed with more sympathy and less hatred and fear. Although living conditions in early asylums were often deplorable, gradual progress was made toward more humane care of the mentally ill. It took time, but ineffectual approaches to treatment eventually gave way to scientific investigation of the causes and cures of psychological disorders.

Problems with the Medical Model

In recent decades, critics have suggested that the medical model may have outlived its usefulness. A particularly vocal critic has been Thomas Szasz (1974, 1990). Szasz asserts that "strictly speaking, disease or illness can affect only the body; hence there can be no mental illness. . . . Minds can be 'sick' only in the sense that jokes are 'sick' or economies are 'sick'" (1974, p. 267). He further argues that abnormal behavior usually involves a deviation from social norms rather than an illness. He contends that such deviations are "problems in living" rather than medical problems. According to Szasz, the medical model's disease analogy converts moral and social questions about what is acceptable behavior into medical questions. Under the guise of "healing the sick," this conversion allegedly allows modern society to lock up deviant people and to enforce its norms of conformity.

Some critics are also troubled because medical diagnoses of abnormal behavior pin potentially derogatory labels on people (Becker, 1973; Rothblum, Solomon, & Albee, 1986). Being labeled as psychotic, schizophrenic, or mentally ill carries a social stigma that can be difficult to shake. Even after a full recovery, someone who has been labeled mentally ill may have difficulty finding a place to live, getting a job, or making friends. Deep-seated prejudice against people who have been labeled mentally ill is commonplace. The stigma of mental illness is not impossible to shed (Gove, 1975), but it undoubtedly creates additional difficulties for people who already have their share of problems.

Critics of the medical model also maintain that diagnostic labels such as *alcoholic* or *neurotic* can create unfortunate self-fulfilling prophecies (Scheff, 1975, 1984). Some people who are labeled *alcoholic*, for instance, seem to accept this designation as part of their identity. They proceed to live out the "alcoholic role" created for them, instead of working to alter their behavior and conquer their problems.

"Minds can be 'sick' only in the sense that jokes are 'sick' or economies are 'sick.'"
THOMAS SZASZ

Putting the Medical Model in Perspective

So, what position should we take on the medical model? In this chapter, we will assume an intermediate position, neither accepting nor discarding the model entirely. There certainly are significant problems with the medical model, and the issues raised by its critics deserve serious attention. However, in its defense, the medical model *has* stimulated scientific research on abnormal behavior. Moreover, some of the problems blamed on the disease analogy are not unique to this conception of abnormality. People who displayed strange, irrational behavior were labeled, stigmatized, and locked up in institutions long before the medical model came along.

Hence, we'll take the position that the disease analogy can be useful, as long as we remember that it is *only* an analogy. Medical concepts such as *diagnosis*, *etiology*, and *prognosis* have proven useful in the treatment and study of abnormality. **Diagnosis involves distinguishing one illness from another. Etiology refers to the apparent causation and developmental history of an illness. A prognosis is a forecast about the probable course of an illness.** These medically based concepts have widely shared meanings that permit clinicians, researchers, and the public to communicate more effectively in their discussions of abnormal behavior.

So, flawed though it may be, we will use the disease analogy and will use terms such as *abnormal behavior*, *mental illness*, and *psychological disorders* interchangeably. Remember, however, that the medical model *is* only an analogy. With this thought in mind, let's discuss the criteria used in judgments of mental health and mental illness.

Criteria of Abnormal Behavior

If your next-door neighbor scrubs his front porch twice every day and spends virtually all his time cleaning and recleaning his house, is he normal? If your sister-in-law goes to one physician after another seeking treatment for ailments that appear imaginary, is she psychologically healthy? How are we to judge what's normal and what's abnormal? More important, who's to do the judging?

These are complex questions. In a sense, *all* people make judgments about normality in that they all express opinions about others' (and perhaps their own) mental health. Of course, formal diagnoses of psychological disorders are made by mental health professionals. In making these judgments, clinicians and laypeople generally apply the same criteria, albeit with highly varied levels of knowledge. Let's examine the three criteria that are most frequently used in judgments of abnormality. Although two or three criteria may apply in a particular case, people are often viewed as disordered when only one criterion is met.

1. *Deviance.* As Szasz has pointed out, people often are said to have a disorder because their behavior deviates from what their society considers acceptable. What constitutes normality varies somewhat from one culture to another, but all cultures have such norms. When people ignore these standards and expectations, they may be labeled mentally ill. Consider transvestites, for instance. **Transvestism is a sexual disorder in which a man achieves sexual arousal by dressing in women's clothing.** This behavior is regarded as disordered because a man who wears a dress, brassiere, and nylons is deviating from our culture's norms. The example of transvestism illustrates the arbitrary nature of cultural standards regarding normality, as in our society it is normal for women to dress in men's clothing, but not vice versa. Thus, the same overt behavior (cross-sex dressing) is acceptable for women and deviant for men.

2. *Maladaptive behavior.* In many cases, people are judged to have a psychological disorder because their everyday adaptive behavior is impaired. This is the key criterion in the diagnosis of substance use (drug) disorders. In and of itself, recreational drug use is not terribly unusual or deviant. However, when the use of cocaine, for instance, begins to interfere with a person's social or occupational functioning, a substance use disorder exists. In such cases, it is the maladaptive quality of the behavior that makes it disordered.

3. *Personal distress.* Frequently, the diagnosis of a psychological disorder is based on an individual's report of great personal distress. This is usually the criterion met by people who are troubled by depression or anxiety disorders. Depressed people, for instance, may or may not exhibit deviant or maladaptive behavior. Such people are usually labeled as having a disorder when they describe their subjective pain and suffering to friends, relatives, and mental health professionals.

The Cultural Bounds of Normality

As we have already noted, judgments of normality and abnormality are influenced by cultural norms and values. Behavior that is considered deviant or maladaptive in one society may be quite acceptable in another. For example, in modern Western culture people who "hear voices" are assumed to be irrational and are routinely placed in mental

hospitals. However, in some cultures hearing voices is commonplace and hardly merits a raised eyebrow.

Cultural norms regarding acceptable behavior may change over time. For example, consider how views of homosexuality have changed in our society. Homosexuality used to be listed as a sexual disorder in the American Psychiatric Association's diagnostic system. However, in 1973 a committee appointed by the association voted to delete homosexuality from the official list of psychological disorders. This action occurred for several reasons. First, attitudes toward homosexuality in our society had become more accepting. Second, gay rights activists campaigned vigorously for the change. Third, research showed that gays and heterosexuals do not differ overall on measures of psychological health (Rothblum, Solomon, & Albee, 1986). As you might guess, this change stimulated a great deal of debate.

Behavior that is deviant in one culture or context may be quite normal in another. In what contexts might each of these men be considered "normal"? "abnormal"?

Vigorous campaigning by gay rights activists was one of several factors that led the American Psychiatric Association to delete homosexuality from its list of psychological disorders. Judgments regarding normality and abnormality reflect social trends and political forces, as well as scientific knowledge.

The key point is that diagnoses of psychological disorders involve *value judgments* about what represents normal or abnormal behavior. The criteria of mental illness are not nearly as value-free as the criteria of physical illness. In evaluating physical diseases, people can usually agree that a weak heart or a bad kidney is pathological, regardless of their personal values. However, judgments about mental illness reflect prevailing cultural values, social trends, and political forces, as well as scientific knowledge (Kirk & Kutchins, 1992).

Normality and Abnormality as a Continuum

Antonyms such as normal versus abnormal and mental health versus mental illness imply that people can be divided neatly into two distinct groups: those who are normal and those who are not. In reality, normality and abnormality exist on a continuum (see Figure 14.2).

Although it is widely believed that people with psychological disorders behave in bizarre ways that are very different from normal people, this is true only in a small minority of cases, usually involving relatively severe disorders. At first glance, people with psychological disorders usually are indistinguishable from those without disorders.

A study by David Rosenhan (1973) showed that even mental health professionals may have difficulty distinguishing normality from abnormality. To study diagnostic accuracy, Rosenhan arranged for a number of normal people to seek admission to mental hospitals. These "pseudopatients" arrived at the hospitals complaining of one false symptom: hearing voices. Except for this single symptom, they acted as they normally would and gave accurate information when interviewed about their personal history. All the pseudopatients were admitted, and the average length of their hospitalization was 19 days! Why is it so hard to distinguish normality from abnormality? The pseudopatients' observations about life on the psychiatric wards offer a clue. They noted that the real patients acted normal most of the time and acted in a deviant manner only infrequently. As

CONCEPT CHECK 14.1

Applying the Criteria of Abnormal Behavior

Check your understanding of the criteria of abnormal behavior by identifying the criteria met by each of the examples below and checking them off in the table provided. Remember, a specific behavior may meet more than one criterion. The answers are in Appendix A.

Behavioral examples

1. Alan's performance at work has suffered because he has been drinking alcohol to excess. Several co-workers have suggested that he seek help for his problem, but he thinks that they're getting alarmed over nothing. "I just enjoy a good time once in a while," he says.

2. Monica has gone away to college and feels lonely, sad, and dejected. Her grades are fine, and she gets along okay with the other students in the dormitory, but inside she's choked with gloom, hopelessness, and despair.

3. Walter believes that he's Napoleon reborn. He believes that he is destined to lead the U.S. military forces into a great battle to recover California from aliens.

4. Phyllis panics with anxiety whenever she leaves her home. Her problem escalated gradually until she was absent from work so often that she was fired. She hasn't been out of her house in nine months and is deeply troubled by her problem.

Criteria met by each example

	Maladaptive behavior	Deviance	Personal distress
1. Allan	_____	_____	_____
2. Monica	_____	_____	_____
3. Walter	_____	_____	_____
4. Phyllis	_____	_____	_____

you might imagine, Rosenhan's study evoked quite a controversy about our diagnostic system for mental illness. Let's take a look at how this diagnostic system has evolved.

Psychodiagnosis: The Classification of Disorders

Obviously, we cannot lump all psychological disorders together without giving up all hope of understanding them better. A sound taxonomy of mental disorders can facilitate empirical research and enhance communication among scientists and clinicians (Adams & Cassidy, 1993). Hence, a great deal of effort has been invested in devising an elaborate system for classifying psychological disorders.

Guidelines for psychodiagnosis were vague and informal prior to 1952 when the American Psychiatric Association unveiled its *Diagnostic and Statistical Manual of Mental Disorders* (Grob, 1991). Known as DSM-I, this classification scheme described about 100 disorders. Revisions intended to improve the system were incorporated into the second edition (DSM-II) published in 1968, but the diagnostic guidelines were still pretty sketchy, and there was widespread dissatisfaction with the lack of consistency in psychiatric diagnosis (Wilson, 1993). All too often, several clinicians evaluating the same patient would arrive at several different diagnoses. Thus, the revisions of the next two editions, DSM-III (1980) and DSM-III-R (1987), sought, first and foremost, to improve the consistency of psychodiagnosis. To achieve this

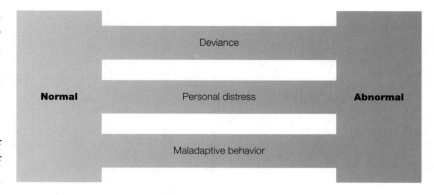

end, diagnostic guidelines were made more explicit, concrete, and detailed (see Figure 14.3). These revisions *did* lead to substantial increases in diagnostic consistency for many disorders, although there is still considerable room for improvement (Garfield, 1993). The current edition, DSM-IV, was introduced in 1994. More than ever before, the architects of the most recent DSM worked to base their revision on empirical research, as opposed to the consensus of experts (Widiger et al., 1991). Each revision of the DSM system has expanded the list of disorders covered.

The Multiaxial System

The publication of DSM-III in 1980 introduced a new multiaxial system of classification, which asks for judgments about individuals on five separate dimensions, or "axes." Figure 14.4 (on the next page) provides an overview of the entire system and the five axes. The diagnoses of disorders are made on Axes I and II. Clinicians record any major

Figure 14.2. Normality and abnormality as a continuum. No sharp boundary exists between normal and abnormal behavior. Behavior is normal or abnormal in degree, depending on the extent to which one's behavior is deviant, personally distressing, or maladaptive.

Diagnostic criteria for generalized anxiety disorder

A. Excessive anxiety and worry (apprehensive expectation), occurring more days than not for at least six months, about a number of events or activities (such as work or school performance).

B. The person finds it difficult to control the worry.

C. The anxiety and worry are associated with at least three of the following six symptoms (with at least some symptoms present for more days than not for the past six months):
  (1) restlessness or feeling keyed up or on edge
  (2) being easily fatigued
  (3) difficulty concentrating or mind going blank
  (4) irritability
  (5) muscle tension
  (6) sleep disturbance (difficulty falling or staying asleep, or restless unsatisfying sleep)

D. The focus of the anxiety and worry is not confined to features of an Axis I disorder, e.g., the anxiety or worry is not about having a panic attack (as in panic disorder), being embarrassed in public (as in social phobia), being contaminated (as in obsessive-compulsive disorder), being away from home or close relatives (as in separation anxiety disorder), gaining weight (as in anorexia nervosa), or having a serious illness (as in hypochondriasis), and is not part of posttraumatic stress disorder.

E. The anxiety, worry, or physical symptoms cause clinically significant distress or impairment in social, occupational, or other important areas of functioning.

F. Not due to the direct effects of a substance (e.g., drugs of abuse, medication) or a general medical condition (e.g., hyperthyroidism), and does not occur exclusively during a mood disorder, psychotic disorder, or a pervasive developmental disorder.

Figure 14.3. Example of the diagnostic criteria in the DSM diagnostic system. This list of the conditions to be met for a diagnosis of generalized anxiety disorder shows the degree of detail in modern diagnostic criteria. (Adapted with permission from the *Diagnostic and Statistical Manual of Mental Disorders*, 4th ed. [1994]. Copyright 1994 American Psychiatric Association.)

Figure 14.4. Overview of the DSM diagnostic system. Published by the American Psychiatric Association, the *Diagnostic and Statistical Manual of Mental Disorders* is the formal classification system used in the diagnosis of psychological disorders. It is a *multiaxial* system, which means that information is recorded on the five axes described here. (Adapted with permission from the *Diagnostic and Statistical Manual of Mental Disorders*, 4th ed. [1994]. Copyright 1994 American Psychiatric Association.)

Axis I
Clinical Syndromes

1. *Disorders usually first diagnosed in infancy, childhood, or adolescence*
This category includes disorders that arise before adolescence, such as attention deficit disorders, autism, mental retardation, enuresis, and stuttering.

2. *Organic mental disorders*
These disorders are temporary or permanent dysfunctions of brain tissue caused by diseases or chemicals. Examples are delirium, dementia, and amnesia.

3. *Substance-related disorders*
This category refers to the *maladaptive* use of drugs and alcohol. Mere consumption and recreational use of such substances are not disorders. This category requires an abnormal pattern of use, as with alcohol abuse and cocaine dependence.

4. *Schizophrenia and other psychotic disorders*
The schizophrenias are characterized by psychotic symptoms (for example, grossly disorganized behavior, delusions, and hallucinations) and by over six months of behavioral deterioration. This category also includes delusional disorder and schizoaffective disorder.

5. *Mood disorders*
The cardinal feature is emotional disturbance. Patients may, or may not, have psychotic symptoms. These disorders include major depression, bipolar disorder, dysthymic disorder, and cyclothymic disorder.

6. *Anxiety disorders*
These disorders are characterized by physiological signs of anxiety (for example, palpitations) and subjective feelings of tension, apprehension, or fear. Anxiety may be acute and focused (panic disorder) or continual and diffuse (generalized anxiety disorder).

7. *Somatoform disorders*
These disorders are dominated by somatic symptoms that resemble physical illnesses. These symptoms cannot be accounted for by organic damage. There *must* also be strong evidence that these symptoms are produced by psychological factors or conflicts. This category includes somatization and conversion disorders and hypochondriasis.

8. *Dissociative disorders*
These disorders all feature a sudden, temporary alteration or dysfunction of memory, consciousness, identity, and behavior, as in dissociative amnesia and multiple personality.

9. *Sexual and gender-identity disorders*
There are three basic types of disorders in this category: gender identity disorders (discomfort with identity as male or female), paraphilias (preference for unusual acts to achieve sexual arousal), and sexual dysfunctions (impairments in sexual functioning).

Axis II
Personality Disorders

These disorders are patterns of personality traits that are longstanding, maladaptive, and inflexible and involve impaired functioning or subjective distress. Examples include borderline, schizoid, and antisocial personality disorders.

Axis III
General Medical Conditions

Physical disorders or conditions are recorded on this axis. Examples include diabetes, arthritis, and hemophilia.

Axis IV
Psychosocial and Environmental Problems

Axis IV is for reporting psychosocial and environmental problems that may affect the diagnosis, treatment, and prognosis of mental disorders (Axis I and II). A psychosocial or environmental problem may be a negative life event, an environmental difficulty or deficiency, a familial or other interpersonal stress, an inadequacy of social support or personal resources, or another problem that describes the context in which a person's difficulties have developed.

Axis V
Global Assessment of Functioning (GAF) Scale

Code	Symptoms
100	Superior functioning in a wide range of activities
90	Absent or minimal symptoms, good functioning in all areas
80	Symptoms transient and expectable reactions to psychosocial stressors
70	Some mild symptoms or some difficulty in social, occupational, or school functioning, but generally functioning pretty well
60	Moderate symptoms or difficulty in social, occupational, or school functioning
50	Serious symptoms or impairment in social, occupational, or school functioning
40	Some impairment in reality testing or communication or major impairment in family relations, judgment, thinking, or mood
30	Behavior considerably influenced by delusions or hallucinations, serious impairment in communication or judgment, or inability to function in almost all areas
20	Some danger of hurting self or others, occasional failure to maintain minimal personal hygiene, or gross impairment in communication
10	Persistent danger of severely hurting self or others
1	

disorders that are apparent on Axis I (Clinical Syndromes). They use Axis II (Personality Disorders) to list milder, long-running personality disturbances, which often coexist with Axis I syndromes. People may receive diagnoses on both axes.

The remaining axes are used to record supplemental information. A patient's physical disorders are listed on Axis III (General Medical Conditions). On Axis IV (Psychosocial and Environmental Problems), the clinician makes notations regarding the types of stress experienced by the individual in the past year. On Axis V (Global Assessment of Functioning), estimates are made of the individual's current level of adaptive functioning (in social and occupational behavior, viewed as a whole), and of the individual's highest level of functioning in the past year.

Controversies Surrounding the DSM

Since the publication of the third edition in 1980, the DSM system has become the dominant classification scheme for mental disorders around the world (Maser, Kaelber, & Weise, 1991). Nonetheless, the DSM system has garnered its share of criticism. First, some critics argue that the heavy focus on improving the consistency of psychodiagnosis has drawn attention away from an equally basic issue—the *validity* of the diagnostic categories (Carson, 1991). Precise, detailed descriptions of disorders are of little value unless the descriptions mesh well with the constellations of problems that people actually experience. For example, as we will discuss shortly, some theorists have questioned whether *hypochondria* is a discrete, independent disorder or merely a general symptom of psychological distress associated with a variety of disorders (Iezzi & Adams, 1993). More research is needed on these kinds of validity issues.

Second, recent editions of the DSM sparked controversy by adding everyday problems that are not traditionally thought of as mental illnesses. For example, the DSM system includes a *developmental coordination disorder* (basically, extreme clumsiness in children), a *nicotine dependence disorder* (distress derived from quitting smoking), and a *pathological gambling disorder* (difficulty controlling one's gambling). Critics argue that this approach "medicalizes" everyday problems and casts the shadow of pathology on normal behavior (Kirk & Kutchins, 1992). In part, everyday problems were added to the diagnostic system so that more people could bill their insurance companies for professional treatment of the conditions (Garfield, 1986). Many health insurance policies permit reimbursement only for the treatment of disorders on the official (DSM) list. There's merit in making it easier for more people to seek needed professional help. Nonetheless, the pros and cons of including everyday problems in DSM are complicated.

We are now ready to start examining the specific types of psychological disorders. Obviously, we cannot cover all 200 or so disorders listed in DSM-IV. However, we will introduce most of the major categories of disorders to give you an overview of the many forms abnormal behavior takes. In discussing each set of disorders, we will begin with brief descriptions of the specific syndromes or subtypes that fall in the category. Then we'll focus on the *etiology* of the disorders in that category. Although many paths can lead to specific disorders, some are more common than others. We'll highlight some of the common paths to enhance your understanding of the roots of abnormal behavior.

ANXIETY DISORDERS

Everyone experiences anxiety from time to time. It is a natural and common reaction to many of life's difficulties. For some people, however, anxiety becomes a chronic problem. These people experience high levels of anxiety with disturbing regularity. *Anxiety disorders* **are a class of disorders marked by feelings of excessive apprehension and anxiety.** There are four principal types of anxiety disorders: generalized anxiety disorders, phobic disorders, panic disorders, and obsessive-compulsive disorders. Studies suggest that anxiety disorders are quite common, occurring in roughly 17% of the population (Robins & Regier, 1991).

Generalized Anxiety Disorder

The *generalized anxiety disorder* **is marked by a chronic, high level of anxiety that is not tied to any specific threat.** This anxiety is sometimes called "free-floating anxiety" because it is nonspecific. People with this disorder worry constantly about yesterday's mistakes and tomorrow's problems. In particular, they worry about minor matters related to family, finances, work, and personal illness (Sanderson & Barlow, 1990). They often dread decisions and brood over them endlessly. Their anxiety is frequently accompanied by physical symptoms, such as trembling, muscle tension, diarrhea, dizziness, faintness, sweating, and heart palpitations.

Phobic Disorder

In a phobic disorder, an individual's troublesome anxiety has a specific focus. **A *phobic disorder* is marked by a persistent and irrational fear of an object or situation that presents no realistic danger.** The following case provides an example of a phobic disorder:

Hilda is 32 years of age and has a rather unusual fear. She is terrified of snow. She cannot go outside in the snow. She cannot even stand to see snow or hear about it on the weather report. Her phobia severely constricts her day-to-day behavior. Probing in therapy revealed that her phobia was caused by a traumatic experience at age 11. Playing at a ski lodge, she was buried briefly by a small avalanche of snow. She had no recollection of this experience until it was recovered in therapy. (Adapted from Laughlin, 1967, p. 227)

As Hilda's unusual snow phobia illustrates, people can develop phobic responses to virtually anything. Nonetheless, certain types of phobias are relatively common, as the data in Figure 14.5 show. Particularly common are acrophobia (fear of heights), claustrophobia (fear of small, enclosed

places), brontophobia (fear of storms), hydrophobia (fear of water), and various animal and insect phobias (Eaton, Dryman, & Weissman, 1991). Many people troubled by phobias realize that their fears are irrational but still are unable to calm themselves when confronted by a phobic object.

Panic Disorder and Agoraphobia

A *panic disorder* is characterized by recurrent attacks of overwhelming anxiety that usually occur suddenly and unexpectedly. These paralyzing attacks are accompanied by physical symptoms of anxiety. After a number of anxiety attacks, victims often become apprehensive, wondering when their next panic will occur. Their concern about exhibiting panic in public may escalate to the point where they are afraid to leave home. This creates a condition called agoraphobia, which is a common complication of panic disorders.

Agoraphobia **is a fear of going out to public places** (its literal meaning is "fear of the market-place or open places"). Because of this fear, some people become prisoners confined to their homes. As its name suggests, agoraphobia has traditionally been viewed as a phobic disorder. However, recent studies suggest that agoraphobia shares more kinship with panic disorders than phobic disorders (Turner et al., 1986). Nonetheless, agoraphobia can occur independently of panic disorder, and some theorists question the wisdom of lumping panic and agoraphobia together in the DSM classification system (Noyes, 1988). The vast majority of people who suffer from panic disorder or agoraphobia are female (Rapee & Barlow, 1993).

Obsessive-Compulsive Disorder

Obsessions are *thoughts* that repeatedly intrude on one's consciousness in a distressing way. Compulsions are *actions* that one feels forced to carry out. Thus, an *obsessive-compulsive disorder* **(OCD) is marked by persistent, uncontrollable intrusions of unwanted thoughts (obsessions) and urges to engage in senseless rituals (compulsions).** To illustrate, let's examine the bizarre behavior of a man once reputed to be the wealthiest person in the world.

The famous industrialist Howard Hughes was obsessed with the possibility of being contaminated by germs. This led him to devise extraordinary rituals to minimize the possibility of such contamination. He would

Figure 14.5. Common phobias. The most frequently reported phobias in a large-scale survey of mental health (Eaton, Dryman, & Weissman, 1991) are listed here. The percentages reflect the portion of respondents who reported each type of phobia. Although the data show that phobias are quite common, people are said to have full-fledged phobic disorders only when their phobias seriously interfere with their activities. Overall, about 40% of the subjects who reported each fear qualified as having a phobic disorder.

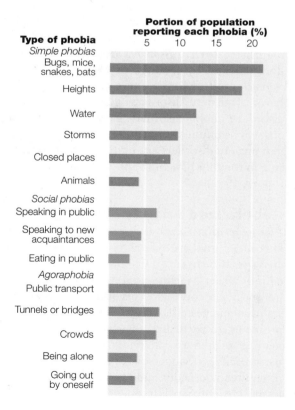

Portion of population reporting each phobia (%)

Type of phobia

Simple phobias
Bugs, mice, snakes, bats
Heights
Water
Storms
Closed places
Animals

Social phobias
Speaking in public
Speaking to new acquaintances
Eating in public

Agoraphobia
Public transport
Tunnels or bridges
Crowds
Being alone
Going out by oneself

spend hours methodically cleaning a single telephone. He once wrote a three-page memo instructing assistants on exactly how to open cans of fruit for him. The following is just a small portion of the instructions that Hughes provided for a driver who delivered films to his bungalow. "Get out of the car on the traffic side. Do not at any time be on the side of the car between the car and the curb. . . . Carry only one can of film at a time. Step over the gutter opposite the place where the sidewalk dead-ends into the curb from a point as far out into the center of the road as possible. Do not ever walk on the grass at all, also do not step into the gutter at all. Walk to the bungalow keeping as near to the center of the sidewalk as possible." (Adapted from Barlett & Steele, 1979, pp. 227–237)

The typical age of onset for OCD is early adulthood (Sturgis, 1993). Obsessions often center on inflicting harm on others, personal failures, suicide, or sexual acts. People troubled by obsessions may feel that they have lost control of their mind. Compulsions usually involve stereotyped rituals that temporarily relieve anxiety. Common examples include constant handwashing, repetitive cleaning of things that are already clean, and endless rechecking of locks, faucets, and such. Unusual rituals intended to bring good luck are also a common form of compulsive behavior. Although many of us can be compulsive at times, full-fledged obsessive-compulsive disorders occur in roughly 2%–4% of the population (Karno & Golding, 1991). The frequency of OCD seems to be increasing, but this trend may simply reflect changes in clinicians' diagnostic tendencies (Stoll, Tohen, & Baldessarini, 1992). Most victims of OCD exhibit both obsessions and compulsions, but some experience only one or the other (Marks, 1987).

Etiology of Anxiety Disorders

Like most psychological disorders, anxiety disorders develop out of complicated interactions among a variety of factors. Classical conditioning, observational learning, and cognitive factors appear especially important, but biological factors may also contribute to anxiety disorders.

Biological Factors

Recent studies suggest that there may be a weak genetic predisposition to anxiety disorders (Crowe, 1988; Kendler et al., 1992). These findings are consistent with the idea that inherited differences in temperament might make some people more vulnerable than others to anxiety disorders

As a young man (shown in the photo), Howard Hughes was a handsome, dashing daredevil pilot and movie producer who appeared to be reasonably well adjusted. However, as the years went by, his behavior gradually became more and more maladaptive, as obsessions and compulsions came to dominate his life. In his later years (shown in the drawing), he spent most of his time in darkened rooms, naked, unkempt, and dirty, following bizarre rituals to alleviate his anxieties. (The drawing was done by an NBC artist and was based on descriptions from men who had seen Hughes.)

(Rosenbaum et al., 1992). Some theorists maintain that *anxiety sensitivity* is the key to this vulnerability (Fowles, 1993; Reiss, 1991). According to this notion, some people are very sensitive to the internal physiological symptoms of anxiety and are prone to overreact with fear when they experience these symptoms. Anxiety sensitivity may fuel an inflationary spiral in which anxiety breeds more anxiety, which eventually spins out of control in the form of an anxiety disorder.

Recent evidence suggests that a link may exist between anxiety disorders and neurochemical activity in the brain. As you learned in Chapter 3, *neurotransmitters* are chemicals that carry signals from one neuron to another. Therapeutic drugs (such as Valium) that reduce excessive anxiety appear to alter neurotransmitter activity at GABA synapses. This finding and other lines of evidence suggest that disturbances in the neural circuits using GABA may play a role in some types of anxiety disorders (Paul, Crawley, & Skolnick, 1986). Abnormalities in other neural circuits using serotonin have recently been implicated in obsessive-compulsive disorders (Hollander et al., 1990; Rapoport, 1989). Thus, scientists are beginning to unravel the neurochemical bases for anxiety disorders.

Conditioning and Learning

Many anxiety responses may be *acquired through classical conditioning* and *maintained through operant conditioning* (see Chapter 6). According to Mowrer (1947), an originally neutral stimulus (the snow in Hilda's case, for instance) may be paired with a frightening event (the avalanche) so that it becomes a conditioned stimulus eliciting anxiety (see Figure 14.6). Once a fear is acquired through classical conditioning, the person may start avoiding the anxiety-producing stimulus. The avoidance response is negatively reinforced because it is followed by a reduction in anxiety. This process involves operant conditioning (see Figure 14.6). Thus, separate conditioning processes may create and then sustain specific anxiety responses (Levis, 1989).

The tendency to develop phobias of certain types of objects and situations may be explained by Martin Seligman's (1971) concept of *preparedness*. Like many theorists, Seligman believes that classical conditioning creates most phobic responses. *However, he suggests that people are biologically prepared by their evolutionary history to acquire some fears much more easily than others.* His theory would explain why people develop phobias of ancient sources of threat (such as snakes and spiders) much more readily than modern sources of threat (such as electrical outlets or hot irons). Some laboratory studies of conditioned fears have yielded evidence consistent with Seligman's theory. For example, Cook and Mineka (1989) found that monkeys acquired conditioned fears of stimuli that they should be prepared to fear, such as snakes, with relative ease in comparison to other stimuli, such

as flowers. As a whole, however, research has provided only modest support for the role of preparedness in the acquisition of phobias (McNally, 1987; Öhman & Soares, 1993).

There are a number of problems with conditioning models of phobias (Rachman, 1990). For instance, many people with phobias cannot recall or identify a traumatic conditioning experience that led to their phobia. Conversely, many people endure extremely traumatic experiences that should create a phobia but do not. To provide better explanations for these complexities, conditioning models of anxiety disorders are currently being revised to include a larger role for cognitive factors (much like conditioning theories in general, as we noted in Chapter 6).

One of these revisions is an increased emphasis on how observational learning can lead to the development of conditioned fears. *Observational learning* occurs when a new response is acquired through watching the behavior of another (consult Chapters 6 and 12). Case studies suggest that anxiety responses are often acquired indirectly (Rachman, 1990). In particular, parents frequently pass on their anxieties to their children. Thus, if a father hides in a closet every time there's a thunderstorm, his children may acquire their father's fear of storms.

Cognitive Factors

Cognitive theorists maintain that certain styles of thinking make some people particularly vulnerable to anxiety disorders. According to these theorists, some people are more likely to suffer from anxiety problems than others because they tend to (a) misinterpret harmless situations as threatening, (b) focus excessive attention on perceived threats, and (c) selectively recall information that seems threatening (Beck, 1988; McNally, 1990). In one intriguing test of the cognitive view, anxious and nonanxious subjects were asked to read 32 sentences that could be interpreted in either a threatening or a nonthreatening manner (Eysenck et al., 1991). For instance, one such sentence was "The doctor examined little Emma's growth," which could mean that the doctor checked her height or the growth of a tumor. As Figure 14.7 shows, the anxious subjects interpreted the sentences in a threatening way more often than the nonanxious subjects did. Thus, consistent with our theme that human experience is highly subjective, the cognitive view holds that some people are prone to anxiety disorders because they see threat in every corner of their lives.

Figure 14.6. Conditioning as an explanation for phobias. (a) Many phobias appear to be acquired through classical conditioning, as a neutral stimulus becomes paired with an anxiety-arousing stimulus. **(b)** Once acquired, a phobia may be maintained through operant conditioning: avoidance of the phobic stimulus reduces anxiety, resulting in negative reinforcement.

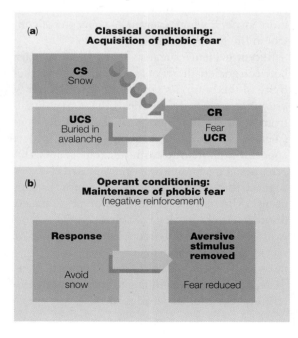

(a) **Classical conditioning: Acquisition of phobic fear**

CS
Snow

UCS
Buried in avalanche

CR
Fear
UCR

(b) **Operant conditioning: Maintenance of phobic fear**
(negative reinforcement)

Response

Avoid snow

Aversive stimulus removed

Fear reduced

Stress

Finally, recent studies have supported the long-held suspicion that anxiety disorders are stress related. For instance, Blazer, Hughes, and George (1987) found an association between stress and the development of generalized anxiety disorders. Men who experienced high stress were 8.5 times more likely to develop these disorders than men under low stress. In another study, Faravelli and Pallanti (1989) found that patients with panic disorder had experienced a dramatic increase in stress in the month prior to the onset of their disorder. Thus, there is reason to believe that high stress often helps to precipitate the onset of anxiety disorders.

SOMATOFORM DISORDERS

Chances are, you have met people who always seem to be complaining about aches, pains, and physical maladies of doubtful authenticity. You may have thought to yourself, "It's all in his head," and concluded that the person exhibited a "psychosomatic" condition. However, the term *psychosomatic* is widely misused. ***Psychosomatic diseases are genuine physical ailments caused in part by psychological factors, especially emotional distress.*** These diseases, which include maladies such as ulcers, asthma, and high blood pressure, have a genuine organic basis and are not imagined ailments. They are recorded on the DSM axis for physical problems (Axis III). When physical illness appears to be *entirely* psychological in origin, we are dealing with somatoform disorders, which are recorded on Axis I. ***Somatoform disorders are***

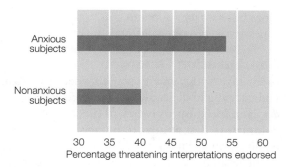

Figure 14.7. Cognitive factors in anxiety disorders. Eysenck and his colleagues (1991) compared how subjects with anxiety problems and nonanxious subjects tended to interpret sentences that could be viewed as threatening or nonthreatening. Consistent with cognitive models of anxiety disorders, anxious subjects were more likely to interpret the sentences in a threatening light.

physical ailments with no authentic organic basis that are due to psychological factors. Although their symptoms are more imaginary than real, victims of somatoform disorders are *not* simply faking illness. Deliberate feigning of illness for personal gain is another matter altogether, called *malingering.*

People with somatoform disorders typically seek treatment from physicians practicing neurology, internal medicine, or family medicine, instead of from psychologists or psychiatrists. Making accurate diagnoses of somatoform disorders can be difficult, because the causes of physical ailments are sometimes hard to identify. In some cases, somatoform disorders are misdiagnosed when a genuine organic cause for a person's physical symptoms goes undetected in spite of extensive medical examinations and tests (Rubin, Zorumski, & Guze, 1986).

We will discuss three specific types of somatoform disorders: somatization disorders, conversion disorders, and hypochondriasis (see Table 14.1). Diagnostic difficulties make it hard to obtain sound data on the prevalence of somatoform disorders. Hypochondriasis seems to be fairly com-

Table 14.1 Comparisons of Three Somatoform Disorders with Psychosomatic Diseases

Condition	Physical Complaints	Organic Basis	Psychological Basis	Typical Symptom Pattern	Typical Examples
Psychosomatic diseases	Yes	Yes	Yes*	Varied stress-related diseases	Ulcers, high blood pressure
Somatization disorders	Yes	No	Yes	History of minor symptoms in many organ systems	Vague complaints of back pain, chest pain, dizziness
Conversion disorders	Yes	No	Yes	Major loss of function in a single organ system	Hysterical paralysis, glove anesthesia
Hypochondriasis	Yes	No	Yes	Preoccupation with health concerns	Unwarranted fear of infection

*The psychological component in diseases that are usually psychosomatic may be minimal in some cases.

mon, but somatization and conversion disorders appear to be relatively infrequent (Barsky, 1989).

Somatization Disorder

Individuals with somatization disorders are often said to "cling to ill health." A *somatization disorder* is marked by a history of diverse physical complaints that appear to be psychological in origin. Somatization disorders occur mostly in women. Victims report an endless succession of minor physical ailments. They usually have a long and complicated history of medical treatment from many doctors. The distinguishing feature of this disorder is the diversity of victims' physical complaints. Over the years, they report a mixed bag of cardiovascular, gastrointestinal, pulmonary, neurological, and genitourinary symptoms. The unlikely nature of such a smorgasbord of symptoms occurring together often alerts a physician to the possible psychological basis for the patient's problems.

Conversion Disorder

Conversion disorder is characterized by a significant loss of physical function (with no apparent organic basis), usually in a single organ system. Common symptoms include partial or complete loss of vision, partial or complete loss of hearing, partial paralysis, severe laryngitis or mutism, and loss of feeling or

function in limbs, such as that seen in the following case:

Mildred was a rancher's daughter who lost the use of both of her legs during adolescence. Mildred was at home alone one afternoon when a male relative attempted to assault her. She screamed for help, and her legs gave way as she slipped to the floor. She was found on the floor a few minutes later when her mother returned home. She could not get up, so she was carried to her bed. Her legs buckled when she made subsequent attempts to walk on her own. Due to her illness, she was waited on hand and foot by her family and friends. Neighbors brought her homemade things to eat or to wear. She became the center of attention in the household. (Adapted from Cameron, 1963, pp. 312–313)

People with conversion disorders are usually troubled by more severe ailments than people with somatization disorders. In some cases of conversion disorder, there are telltale clues about the psychological origins of the illness because the patient's symptoms are not consistent with medical knowledge about their apparent disease. For instance, the loss of feeling in one hand that is seen in "glove anesthesia" is inconsistent with the known facts of neurological organization (see Figure 14.8).

Hypochondriasis

Hypochondriacs constantly monitor their physical condition, looking for signs of illness. Any tiny alteration from their physical norm leads them to conclude that they have contracted a disease. *Hypochondriasis* (more widely known as hypochondria) is characterized by excessive preoccupation with one's health and incessant worry about developing physical illnesses.

When hypochondriacs are assured by their physician that they do not have any real illness, they often are skeptical and disbelieving. They frequently assume that the physician must be incompetent, and they go shopping for another doctor. Hypochondriacs don't subjectively suffer from physical distress as much as they *overinterpret* every conceivable sign of illness. Hypochondria often appears alongside other psychological disorders, especially anxiety disorders and depression (Simon & VonKorff, 1991). For example, Howard Hughes's obsessive-compulsive disorder was coupled with profound hypochondria. Indeed, hypochondria coexists with other disorders so often, some theorists have raised doubts about whether it should be viewed as a separate diagnostic category (Iezzi & Adams, 1993).

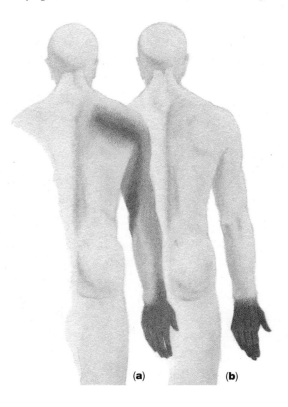

Figure 14.8. Glove anesthesia. In conversion disorders, the physical complaints are sometimes inconsistent with the known facts of physiology. For instance, given the patterns of nerve distribution in the arm shown in (**a**), it is impossible that a loss of feeling in the hand exclusively, as shown in (**b**), has a physical cause, indicating that the patient's problem is psychological in origin.

(a)　　　(b)

Etiology of Somatoform Disorders

Inherited aspects of physiological functioning may predispose people to somatoform disorders (Weiner, 1992). However, available evidence suggests that these disorders are largely a function of personality and learning. Let's look at personality factors first.

Personality Factors

People with certain types of personality traits seem to be particularly prone to develop somatoform disorders. The prime candidates are people with *histrionic* personality characteristics (Nemiah, 1985; Slavney, 1990). The histrionic personality tends to be self-centered, suggestible, excitable, highly emotional, and overly dramatic. Such people thrive on the attention that they get when they become ill.

Cognitive Factors

In recent years, theorists have devoted increased attention to how cognitive peculiarities might contribute to somatoform disorders. For example, Barsky, Wyshak, and Klerman (1990) assert that some people focus excessive attention on their internal physiological processes and amplify normal bodily sensations into symptoms of distress, which lead them to pursue unnecessary medical treatment. Recent evidence also suggests that people with somatoform disorders tend to have a faulty standard of good health, equating health with a complete absence of symptoms and discomfort, which is unrealistic (Barsky et al., 1993).

The Sick Role

As we discussed in Chapter 13, some people grow fond of the role associated with being sick (Lubkin, 1990; Pilowsky, 1978). Their complaints of physical symptoms may be reinforced by indirect benefits derived from their illness. What are the benefits commonly associated with physical illness? One payoff is that becoming ill is a superb way to avoid having to confront life's challenges. Many people with somatoform disorders are avoiding facing up to marital problems, career frustrations, family responsibilities, and the like. After all, when you're sick, others cannot place great demands on you.

Attention from others is another payoff that may reinforce complaints of physical illness. When people become ill, they command the attention of family, friends, co-workers, neighbors, and doctors. The sympathy that illness often brings may strengthen the person's tendency to feel ill. This clearly occurred in Mildred's case of conversion disorder. Her illness paid handsome dividends in terms of attention, consolation, and kindhearted assistance from others.

DISSOCIATIVE DISORDERS

Dissociative disorders are among the more unusual syndromes that we will discuss. *Dissociative disorders* **are a class of disorders in which people lose contact with portions of their consciousness or memory, resulting in disruptions in their sense of identity.** We'll describe three dissociative syndromes—dissociative amnesia, dissociative fugue, and multiple-personality disorder—all of them relatively uncommon.

Dissociative Amnesia and Fugue

Dissociative amnesia and fugue are overlapping disorders characterized by serious memory deficits. *Dissociative amnesia* **is a sudden loss of memory for important personal information that is too extensive to be due to normal forgetting.**

CONCEPT CHECK 14.2
Distinguishing Anxiety and Somatoform Disorders

Check your understanding of the nature of anxiety and somatoform disorders by making very preliminary diagnoses for the cases described below. Read each case summary and write your tentative diagnosis in the space provided. The answers are in Appendix A.

1. Morris religiously follows an exact schedule every day. His showering and grooming ritual takes 2 hours. He follows the same path in walking to his classes every day, and he always sits in the same seat in each class. He can't study until his apartment is arranged perfectly. Although he tries not to, he thinks constantly about flunking out of school. Both his grades and his social life are suffering from his rigid routines.

   Preliminary diagnosis: _____

2. Jane has been unemployed for the last eight years because of poor health. She has suffered through a bizarre series of illnesses of mysterious origin. Troubles with devastating headaches were followed by months of chronic back pain. Then she developed respiratory problems, frequently gasping for breath. Her current problem is stomach pain. Physicians have been unable to find any physical basis for her maladies.

   Preliminary diagnosis: _____

3. Nathan owns a small restaurant that's in deep financial trouble. He dreads facing the possibility that his restaurant will fail. One day, he suddenly loses all feeling in his right arm and the ability to control the arm. He's hospitalized for his condition, but physicians can't find any organic cause for his arm trouble.

   Preliminary diagnosis: _____

Memory losses may occur for a single traumatic event (such as an automobile accident or home fire) or for an extended period of time surrounding the event. **In *dissociative fugue*, people lose their memory for their entire lives along with their sense of personal identity.** These people forget their name, their family, where they live, and where they work! In spite of this wholesale forgetting, they remember matters unrelated to their identity, such as how to drive a car and how to do math.

Multiple-Personality Disorder

Multiple-personality disorder **involves the co-existence in one person of two or more largely complete, and usually very different, personalities.** The formal name for this disorder was changed to *dissociative identity disorder* in the recent revision of the DSM system, but it remains more widely known by its traditional name. In multiple-personality disorders, the divergences in behavior go far beyond those that people normally display in adapting to different roles in life. People with multiple personalities feel that they have more than one identity. Each personality has his or her own name, memories, traits, and physical mannerisms. Although rare, this "Dr. Jekyll and Mr. Hyde" syndrome is frequently portrayed in novels, movies, and television shows. In popular media portrayals, the syndrome is often mistakenly called *schizophrenia*. As you will see later, schizophrenic disorders are entirely different.

In a multiple-personality disorder, the original personality is often unaware of the alternate personalities. In contrast, the alternate personalities are usually aware of the original one and have varying amounts of awareness of each other. The alternate personalities commonly display traits that are quite foreign to the original personality. For instance, a shy, inhibited person might develop a flamboyant, extraverted alternate personality. Transitions between personalities often occur suddenly.

During the 1980s, there was a dramatic increase in the diagnosis of multiple-personality disorders (Ross et al., 1991). Some theorists believe that these disorders used to be underdiagnosed—that is, they often went undetected (Saxe et al., 1993). Other skeptics argue that a handful of clinicians have begun overdiagnosing the condition (Thigpen & Cleckley, 1984). The debate about the reason for the sudden upsurge in multiple-personality diagnoses is far from settled. It probably won't be resolved without a great deal of additional research.

Etiology of Dissociative Disorders

Psychogenic amnesia and fugue are usually attributed to excessive stress. However, relatively little is known about why this extreme reaction to stress occurs in a tiny minority of people but not in the vast majority who are subjected to similar stress.

The causes of multiple-personality disorders are equally obscure. Some skeptical theorists believe that people with multiple personalities are engaging in intentional role playing to use mental illness as a face-saving excuse for their personal failings (Spanos, Weekes, & Bertrand, 1985). Indeed, there is evidence that multiple-personality disorders are faked with some regularity, perhaps because of all the media attention garnered by the disorder. However, various lines of evidence suggest to most theorists that at least some cases are authentic (Kihlstrom, Tataryn, & Hoyt, 1993). Many of these cases seem to be rooted in severe emotional trauma that occurred during childhood. A substantial majority of people with multiple-personality disorder have a history of disturbed home life, beatings and rejection from parents, and sexual abuse (Ross et al., 1990). In the final analysis, however, very little is known about the causes of multiple-personality disorders.

MOOD DISORDERS

What did Abraham Lincoln, Marilyn Monroe, Ernest Hemingway, Winston Churchill, Janis Joplin, and Leo Tolstoy have in common? Yes, they all achieved great prominence, albeit in different ways at different times. But, more pertinent to our interest, they all suffered from severe mood disorders. Although mood disorders can be terribly debilitating, people with mood disorders may still achieve greatness, because such disorders tend to be *episodic*. In other words, mood disturbances often come and go, interspersed among periods of normality.

Mood disorders **are a class of disorders marked by emotional disturbances of varied kinds that may spill over to disrupt physical, perceptual, social, and thought processes.** There are two basic types of mood disorders: unipolar and bipolar (see Figure 14.9). People with *unipolar disorders* experience emotional extremes at just one end of the mood continuum, as they are troubled only by *depression*. People with *bipolar disorders* experience emotional extremes at both ends of the mood continuum, going through periods of both *depression and mania* (excitement and elation). The mood swings in bipolar disorders can be patterned in many ways.

Depressive Disorder

Everyone gets depressed once in a while. Thus, the line between normal and abnormal depression can be difficult to draw (Grove & Andreasen, 1992). Ultimately, a subjective judgment is required. Crucial considerations in this judgment include the duration of the depression and its disruptive effects. When a depression significantly impairs everyday adaptive behavior for more than a few weeks, there is reason for concern.

In *depressive disorders* **people show persistent feelings of sadness and despair and a loss of interest in previous sources of pleasure.** Negative emotions form the heart of the depressive syndrome, but many other symptoms may also appear. The most common symptoms of depressive disorders are summarized and compared with the symptoms of mania in Table 14.2. Depressed people often give up activities that they used to find enjoyable. For example, a depressed person might quit going bowling or might give up a favorite hobby like photography. Reduced appetite and insomnia are common. People with depression often lack energy. They tend to move sluggishly and talk slowly. Anxiety, irritability, and brooding are commonly observed. Self-esteem tends to sink as the depressed person begins to feel worthless. Depression plunges people into feelings of hopelessness, dejection, and boundless guilt. The severity of abnormal depression varies considerably. The onset of unipolar disorder can occur at any point in the life span and is *not* strongly related to age (Lewinsohn et al., 1986).

How common are depressive disorders? Very common. Recent studies suggest that about 7% of the population endure a unipolar depressive disorder at some time (Weissman et al., 1991). However, this figure may underestimate the amount of depression likely to be seen in future years, as there is evidence that the prevalence of depression is higher in more recent age cohorts (Lewinsohn et al., 1993). Researchers are scrambling to collect data that might shed light on this unanticipated trend. Researchers are also hard at work trying to figure out why the prevalence of depression is about twice as high in women as it is in men (Nolen-Hoeksema, 1990).

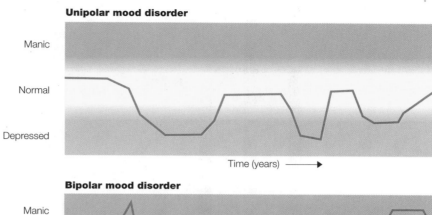

Unipolar mood disorder

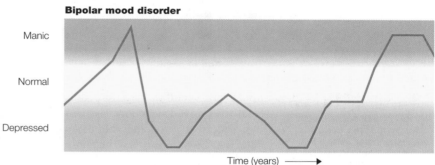

Bipolar mood disorder

Bipolar Mood Disorder

Bipolar mood disorders **(formerly known as manic-depressive disorders) are marked by the experience of both depressed and manic periods.** The symptoms seen in manic periods generally are the opposite of those seen in depression (see Table 14.2 for a comparison). In a manic episode, a person's mood becomes elevated to the point of euphoria. Self-esteem skyrockets as the person bubbles over with optimism, energy, and extravagant plans. He or she becomes hyperactive and may go for days without sleep. The individual talks rapidly and shifts topics wildly, as his or her mind races at breakneck speed. Judgment is often impaired. Some people in manic periods gamble

Figure 14.9. Episodic patterns in mood disorders. Time-limited episodes of emotional disturbance come and go unpredictably in mood disorders. People with unipolar disorders suffer from bouts of depression only, whereas people with bipolar disorders experience both manic and depressive episodes. The time between episodes of disturbance varies greatly with the individual and the type of disorder.

Table 14.2 Comparison of Common Symptoms in Manic and Depressive Episodes

Characteristics	Manic Episode	Depressive Episode
Emotional	Elated, euphoric, very sociable, impatient at any hindrance	Gloomy, hopeless, socially withdrawn, irritable
Cognitive	Characterized by racing thoughts, flight of ideas, desire for action, and impulsive behavior; talkative, self-confident; experiencing delusions of grandeur	Characterized by slowness of thought processes, obsessive worrying, inability to make decisions, negative self-image, self-blame, and delusions of guilt and disease
Motor	Hyperactive, tireless, requiring less sleep than usual, showing increased sex drive and fluctuating appetite	Less active, tired, experiencing difficulty in sleeping, showing decreased sex drive and decreased appetite

Source: Sarason and Sarason (1987)

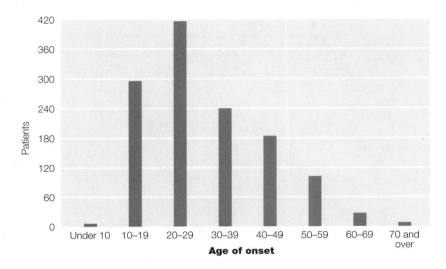

Figure 14.10. Age of on-set for bipolar mood dis-order. The onset of bipolar disorder typically occurs in adolescence or early adult-hood. The data graphed here, which were combined from ten studies, show the distribution of age of onset for 1304 bipolar patients. As you can see, bipolar disor-der emerges most frequently during the 20s decade. (Data from Goodwin & Jamison, 1990)

impulsively, spend money frantically, or become sexually reckless. Like depressive disorders, bipo-lar disorders vary considerably in severity.

You may be thinking that the euphoria in manic episodes sounds appealing. If so, you are not entirely wrong. In their milder forms, manic states can seem attractive. The increases in energy, self-esteem, and optimism can be deceptively seduc-tive. Because of the increase in energy, many bipolar patients report temporary surges of pro-ductivity and creativity (Goodwin & Jamison, 1990).

Although manic episodes may have some posi-tive aspects, bipolar mood disorders ultimately prove to be troublesome for most victims. Manic periods often have a paradoxical negative under-current of uneasiness and irritability (Rehm & Tyndall, 1993). Moreover, mild manic episodes usually escalate to higher levels that become scary and disturbing. Impaired judgment leads many victims to do things that they greatly regret later, as you'll see in the following case history:

Robert, a dentist, awoke one morning with the idea that he was the most gifted dental surgeon in his tri-state area. He decided that he should try to provide services to as many people as possible, so that more people could benefit from his talents. Thus, he decided to remodel his two-chair dental office, installing 20 booths so that he could simultaneously attend to 20 patients. That same day he drew up plans for this arrangement, telephoned a number of remodelers, and invited bids for the work. Later that day, impatient to get rolling on his remod-eling, he rolled up his sleeves, got himself a sledgeham-mer, and began to knock down the walls in his office. Annoyed when that didn't go so well, he smashed his dental tools, washbasins and X-ray equipment. Later, Robert's wife became concerned about his behavior and

summoned two of her adult daughters for assistance. The daughters responded quickly, arriving at the fam-ily home with their husbands. In the ensuing discussion, Robert—after bragging about his sexual prowess—made advances toward his daughters. He had to be subdued by their husbands. (Adapted from Kleinmuntz, 1980, p. 309)

Although not rare, bipolar disorders are much less common than unipolar disorders. Bipolar disorders affect a little under 1% of the population (Weissman et al., 1991). Unlike depressive disor-ders, bipolar disorders are seen equally often in males and females (Perris, 1992). As Figure 14.10 shows, the onset of bipolar disorders is age related, with the peak of vulnerability occurring between the ages of 20 and 29 (Goodwin & Jamison, 1990).

Etiology of Mood Disorders

Quite a bit is known about the etiology of mood disorders, although the puzzle hasn't been as-sembled completely. There appear to be a number of routes into these disorders, involving intricate interactions between psychological and biological factors.

Genetic Vulnerability

The evidence strongly suggests that genetic fac-tors influence the likelihood of developing major depression or a bipolar mood disorder. In studies that assess the impact of heredity on psychological disorders, investigators look at *concordance rates*. **A concordance rate indicates the percentage of twin pairs or other pairs of relatives that ex-hibit the same disorder.** If relatives who share more genetic similarity show higher concordance rates than relatives who share less genetic overlap, this finding supports the genetic hypothesis. Twin studies, which compare identical and fraternal twins (see Chapter 3), suggest that genetic factors *are* involved in mood disorders (Gershon, Berrettini, & Goldin, 1989). Concordance rates average around 67% for identical twins but only 15% for fraternal twins, who share less genetic similarity. Thus, it appears that heredity can cre-ate a *vulnerability* to mood disorders.

Neurochemical Factors

Heredity may influence susceptibility to mood disorders by creating a predisposition toward cer-tain types of neurochemical abnormalities in the brain. Correlations have been found between mood disorders and the activity of three neurotransmit-ters in the brain: norepinephrine, serotonin, and

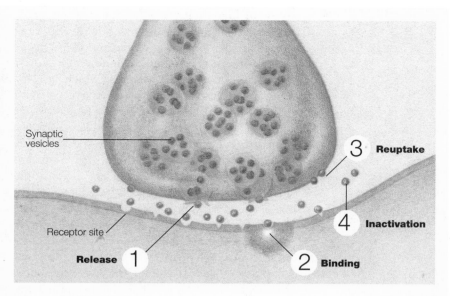

Figure 14.11. Hypotheses about the neuro-chemical bases for depression. Until recently, neurochemical models of depression centered on the hypothesis that depression is associated with lowered levels of activation at norepinephrine (NE) synapses. Originally, it was assumed that the reduction in NE activity was due to decreased release of NE (1), but studies eventually suggested that alterations in the sensitivity of NE receptors (2) also played a role. The hypothesis linking low NE levels to depression is supported by evidence that two major classes of antidepressant drugs increase NE levels. Tricyclic antidepressants appear to inhibit reuptake (3), leaving more NE in the synapse, while MAO inhibitors seem to slow the inactivation of NE (4). Although all these findings remain relevant to the understanding of the neurochemical bases of depression, recent studies suggest that complex imbalances in *several* neurotransmitter systems may contribute to depression and that abnormalities in serotonin circuits may be particularly critical.

acetylcholine—although evidence on acetylcholine is modest (Delgado et al., 1992). Originally, abnormalities at norepinephrine (NE) synapses were believed to be most critical (see Figure 14.11). Depression was thought to be due to decreased secretion of NE and mania to increased release of NE. Further research eventually demonstrated that alterations in the *release* of norepinephrine were not as important as changes in the sensitivity of the synaptic *receptors* that NE binds to (Schildkraut, Green, & Mooney, 1985). Although researchers still think that disturbances in neural circuits using norepinephrine contribute to mood disorders, the preponderance of recent evidence suggests that aberrations in serotonin circuits may be more important (Delgado et al., 1992).

Cognitive Factors

A variety of theories emphasize how cognitive factors contribute to depressive disorders (Abramson, Metalsky, & Alloy, 1988; Beck, 1976; Ellis, 1962; Seligman, 1983). In recent years, theories that focus on people's patterns of *attribution* have generated a great deal of research on the cognitive roots of depression. **Attributions are inferences that people draw about the causes of events, others' behavior, and their own behavior.** People routinely make attributions because they want to *understand* their personal fates and the events that take place around them. For example, if your boss criticizes your work, you will probably ask yourself why. Was your work really that sloppy? Was your boss just in a grouchy mood? Was the criticism a manipulative effort to

motivate you to work harder? Each of these potential explanations is an attribution.

Attributions can be analyzed along a number of dimensions. Three important dimensions are illustrated in Figure 14.12. The most prominent dimension is the degree to which people attribute events to *internal, personal factors versus external, situational factors*. For instance, if you performed poorly on a standardized mathematics test, you might attribute your poor showing to your lack of intelligence (an internal attribution) or to the horrible heat and humidity in the exam room (an external attribution).

Another key dimension is the degree to which people attribute events to factors that are *stable or unstable over time*. Thus, you might blame your poor test performance on exhaustion (an internal but unstable factor that could change next time) or

Figure 14.12. Attributional style and depression. Possible attributions for poor performance on a standardized math exam are shown here. Note how the explanations in each cell vary in terms of whether causes are seen as internal or external, stable or unstable, and specific or global. People who consistently explain their failures with internal, stable, and global attributions are particularly vulnerable to depression (the deeper the color in the cell, the more depressing the attribution tends to be).

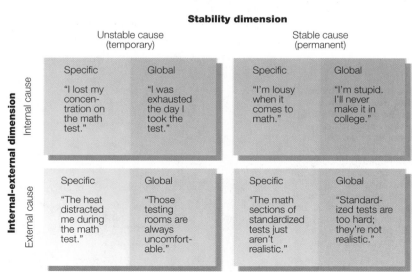

Stability dimension

	Unstable cause (temporary)		Stable cause (permanent)	
	Specific	Global	Specific	Global
Internal cause	"I lost my concentration on the math test."	"I was exhausted the day I took the test."	"I'm lousy when it comes to math."	"I'm stupid. I'll never make it in college."
External cause	"The heat distracted me during the math test."	"Those testing rooms are always uncomfortable."	"The math sections of standardized tests just aren't realistic."	"Standardized tests are too hard; they're not realistic."

(Internal-external dimension)

on your low intelligence (an internal but stable factor). Some theories also focus on the degree to which attributions have *global versus specific implications*. Thus, you might attribute your low test score to your lack of intelligence (which has general, global implications) or to your poor math ability (the implications are specific to math). Figure 14.12 provides additional examples of attributions that might be made for poor test performance.

Theories that link attribution to depression are interested in the *attributional style* that people display, especially when they are trying to explain failures, setbacks, and other negative events. Studies show that *people who consistently tend to make internal, stable, and global attributions are more prone to depression* than people who exhibit the opposite attributional styles (Robins, 1988; Sweeney, Anderson, & Bailey, 1986). Why? Because in making internal, stable, and global attributions, people blame their setbacks on personal inadequacies (internal), which they see as unchangeable (stable), and draw far-reaching (global) conclusions about their lack of worth as a human being. In other words, they draw depressing conclusions about themselves.

Thus, cognitive models of depression maintain that it is negative thinking that makes many people feel helpless, hopeless, and dejected. The principal problem with cognitive theories is their difficulty in separating cause from effect (Barnett & Gotlib, 1988). Does negative thinking cause depression? Or does depression cause negative thinking? Could both be caused by a third variable, such as neurochemical changes (see Figure 14.13)? Evidence can be mustered to support all three of these possibilities, suggesting that negative thinking, depression, and neurochemical alterations may feed off one another as depression deepens.

In accord with this line of thinking, Susan Nolen-Hoeksema (1990, 1991) has found that depressed people who ruminate about their depression re-main depressed longer than those who try to distract themselves. People who respond to depression with rumination repetitively focus their attention on their depressing feelings, thinking constantly about how sad, lethargic, and unmotivated they are. According to Nolen-Hoeksema, excessive rumination tends to extend and amplify individuals' episodes of depression. She believes that women are more likely to ruminate than men and that this disparity may be the primary reason why depression is more prevalent in women.

Interpersonal Roots

Behavioral approaches to understanding depression emphasize how inadequate social skills put people on the road to depressive disorders (Lewinsohn et al., 1985). According to this notion, depression-prone people lack the social finesse needed to acquire many important kinds of reinforcers, such as good friends, top jobs, and desirable spouses. This paucity of reinforcers could understandably lead to negative emotions and depression. Consistent with this theory, researchers have found correlations between poor social skills and depression (Dykman et al., 1991).

Another interpersonal factor is that depressed people tend to be depressing! Individuals suffering from depression often are irritable and pessimistic. They complain a lot and they aren't very enjoyable companions. Thus, depression, like other emotions, can be contagious. This creates a tendency for people to reject and avoid depressed individuals. Therefore, depressed people have fewer sources of social support than nondepressed people do (Billings, Cronkite, & Moos, 1983). In turn, this lack of support and social rejection may aggravate and deepen a person's depression (Segrin & Dillard, 1992).

Precipitating Stress

Mood disorders sometimes appear mysteriously in people who are leading benign, nonstressful lives. For this reason, experts used to believe that mood disorders are not influenced much by stress. However, recent advances in the measurement of personal stress have altered this picture. The evidence available today suggests the existence of a moderately strong link between stress and the onset of mood disorders (Paykel & Cooper, 1992).

SCHIZOPHRENIC DISORDERS

Literally, *schizophrenia* means "split mind." However, when Eugen Bleuler coined the term in

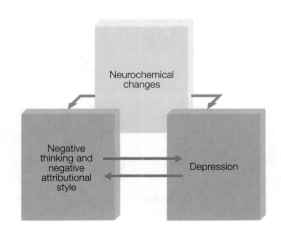

Figure 14.13. Interpreting the correlation between negative thinking and depression. Cognitive theories of depression assert that consistent patterns of negative thinking cause depression. Although these theories are highly plausible, depression could cause negative thoughts, or both could be caused by a third factor, such as neurochemical changes in the brain.

CHAPTER FOURTEEN

1911 he was referring to the fragmentation of thought processes seen in the disorder—not to a "split personality." Unfortunately, writers in the popular media often assume that the split-mind notion, and thus schizophrenia, refers to the rare syndrome in which a person manifests two or more personalities. As you have already learned, this syndrome is actually called *multiple-personality disorder*. Schizophrenia is a much more common, and altogether different, type of disorder.

***Schizophrenic disorders* are a class of disorders marked by disturbances in thought that spill over to affect perceptual, social, and emotional processes.** How common is schizophrenia? Prevalence estimates suggest that about 1%–1.5% of the population may suffer from schizophrenic disorders (Keith, Regier, & Rae, 1991). That may not sound like much, but it means that in the United States alone there may be 4 million people troubled by schizophrenic disturbances.

General Symptoms

There are a number of distinct schizophrenic syndromes, but they share some general characteristics that we will examine before looking at the subtypes. Many of these characteristics are apparent in the following case history, adapted from Sheehan (1982). Sylvia was first diagnosed as schizophrenic at age 15. She has been in and out of many different types of psychiatric facilities since then. She has never been able to hold a job for any length of time. During severe flare-ups of her disorder, her personal hygiene deteriorates. She rarely washes, wears clothes that neither fit nor match, smears makeup on heavily but randomly, and slops food all over herself. Sylvia occasionally hears voices talking to her. Sylvia tends to be argumentative, aggressive, and emotionally volatile. Over the years, she has been involved in innumerable fights with fellow patients, psychiatric staff members, and strangers. Her thoughts can be highly irrational, as is apparent from the following quote.

"Mick Jagger wants to marry me. If I have Mick Jagger, I don't have to covet Geraldo Rivera. Mick Jagger is St. Nicholas and the Maharishi is Santa Claus. I want to form a gospel rock group called the Thorn Oil, but Geraldo wants me to be the music critic on Eyewitness News, so what can I do? Got to listen to my boyfriend. Teddy Kennedy cured me of my ugliness. I'm pregnant with the son of God. I'm going to marry David Berkowitz and get it over with. Creedmoor is

The apathy, withdrawal, and severe deterioration in everyday adaptive behavior often seen in schizophrenic disorders leave many patients institutionalized for lengthy periods of time. Modern drug therapies have greatly reduced the amount of time that schizophrenic patients spend in mental hospitals, but these drug treatments can create their own problems (see Chapter 15).

the headquarters of the American Nazi Party. They're eating the patients here. Archie Bunker wants me to play his niece on his TV show. I work for Epic Records. I'm Joan of Arc. I'm Florence Nightingale. The door between the ward and the porch is the dividing line between New York and California. Divorce isn't a piece of paper, it's a feeling. Forget about Zip Codes. I need shock treatments. The body is run by electricity. My wiring is all faulty. A fly is a teenage wasp. I'm marrying an accountant. I'm in the Pentecostal Church, but I'm considering switching my loyalty to the Charismatic Church." (Adapted from Sheehan, 1982; quotation from pp. 104–105)

Sylvia's case clearly shows that schizophrenic thinking can be bizarre and that schizophrenia can be a severe and debilitating disorder. Although no single symptom is inevitably present, the following symptoms are commonly seen in schizophrenia (Grebb & Cancro, 1989).

Irrational Thought

Disturbed, irrational thought processes are the central feature of schizophrenic disorders. Various kinds of delusions are common. ***Delusions* are false beliefs that are maintained even though they clearly are out of touch with reality.** For example, one patient's delusion that he is a tiger (with a deformed body) has persisted for 15 years (Kulick, Pope, & Keck, 1990). More typically, affected persons believe that their private thoughts are being broadcast to other people. They may also believe that thoughts are being injected into their mind against their will. In *delusions of grandeur*, people maintain that they are famous or important.

Sylvia expressed an endless array of grandiose delusions, such as thinking that Mick Jagger wanted to marry her, that she had dictated the hobbit stories to J. R. R. Tolkien, and that she was going to win the Nobel prize for medicine.

In addition to delusions, the schizophrenic person's train of thought deteriorates. Thinking becomes chaotic rather than logical and linear. There is a "loosening of associations," as the person shifts topics in disjointed ways. The quotation from Sylvia illustrates this symptom dramatically. The entire quote involves a wild flight of ideas, but at one point (beginning with the sentence "Creedmoor is the headquarters . . .") she rattles off ten consecutive sentences that have no apparent connection to each other.

Deterioration of Adaptive Behavior

Schizophrenia usually involves a noticeable deterioration in the quality of the person's routine functioning in work, social relations, and personal care. Friends will often make remarks such as "Hal just isn't himself anymore." This deterioration is readily apparent in Sylvia's inability to get along with others or to function in the work world. It's also apparent in her neglect of personal hygiene.

Distorted Perception

A variety of perceptual distortions may occur with schizophrenia, the most common being auditory hallucinations. *Hallucinations* **are sensory perceptions that occur in the absence of a real, external stimulus or are gross distortions of perceptual input.** Schizophrenics frequently report that they hear voices of nonexistent or absent people talking to them. Sylvia, for instance, said she heard messages from Paul McCartney. These voices often provide an insulting, running commentary on the person's behavior ("You're an idiot for shaking his hand"). They may be argumentative ("You don't need a bath"), and they may issue commands ("Prepare your home for visitors from outer space").

Disturbed Emotion

Normal emotional tone can be disrupted in schizophrenia in a variety of ways. Some victims show a flattening of emotions. In other words, they show little emotional responsiveness. Others show inappropriate emotional responses that don't jell with the situation or with what they are saying. People with schizophrenia may also become emotionally volatile. This pattern was displayed by Sylvia, who often overreacted emotionally in erratic, unpredictable ways.

Subtypes

Four subtypes of schizophrenic disorders are recognized, including a category for people who don't fit neatly into any of the first three categories.

Paranoid Type

As its name implies, *paranoid schizophrenia* **is dominated by delusions of persecution, along with delusions of grandeur.** In this common form of schizophrenia, people come to believe that they have many enemies who want to harass and oppress them. They may become suspicious of friends and relatives or they may attribute the persecution to mysterious, unknown persons. They are convinced that they are being watched and manipulated in malicious ways. To make sense of this persecution, they often develop delusions of grandeur. They believe that they must be enormously important people, frequently seeing themselves as great inventors or as great religious or political leaders. For example, in the case described at the beginning of the chapter, Ed's belief that he was president of the United States was a delusion of grandeur.

Catatonic Type

Catatonic schizophrenia **is marked by striking motor disturbances, ranging from muscular rigidity to random motor activity.** Some patients go into an extreme form of withdrawal known as a catatonic stupor. They may remain virtually motionless and seem oblivious to the environment around them for long periods of time. Others go into a state of catatonic excitement. They become hyperactive and incoherent. Some alternate between these dramatic extremes. The catatonic subtype is not particularly common, and its prevalence seems to be declining.

Disorganized Type

In *disorganized schizophrenia*, **a particularly severe deterioration of adaptive behavior is seen.** Prominent symptoms include emotional indifference, frequent incoherence, and virtually complete social withdrawal. Aimless babbling and giggling are common. Delusions often center on bodily functions ("My brain is melting out my ears").

Undifferentiated Type

People who are clearly schizophrenic but who cannot be placed into any of the three previous categories are said to have *undifferentiated schizophrenia*, **which is marked by idiosyncratic mixtures of schizophrenic symptoms.** The undifferentiated subtype is fairly common.

Positive Versus Negative Symptoms

Some theorists are beginning to doubt the value of dividing schizophrenic disorders into the four subtypes just described (Nicholson & Neufeld, 1993). Critics note that the catatonic subtype is disappearing and that undifferentiated cases aren't so much a subtype as a hodgepodge of "leftovers." Critics also point out that there aren't meaningful differences between the classic schizophrenic subtypes in etiology, prognosis, or response to treatment. The absence of such differences casts doubt on the value of the current classification scheme.

Because of problems such as those just mentioned, Nancy Andreasen (1990) and others (Carpenter, 1992; McGlashan & Fenton, 1992) have proposed an alternative approach to subtyping. This new scheme divides schizophrenic disorders into just two categories based on the predominance of negative versus positive symptoms. *Negative symptoms* involve behavioral deficits, such as flattened emotions, social withdrawal, apathy, impaired attention, and poverty of speech. *Positive symptoms* involve behavioral excesses or peculiarities, such as hallucinations, delusions, bizarre behavior, and wild flights of ideas. Andreasen believes that researchers will find consistent differences between these two subtypes in etiology, prognosis, and response to treatment. Only time (and research) will tell whether this proposed subdivision will prove useful.

Etiology of Schizophrenia

You can probably identify, at least to some extent, with people who suffer from mood disorders, somatoform disorders, and anxiety disorders. You can probably imagine events that could unfold that might leave you struggling with depression, grappling with anxiety, or worrying about your physical health. But what could possibly have led Ed to believe that he had been fighting space wars and vampires? What could account for Sylvia's thinking that she was Joan of Arc or that she had dictated the hobbit novels to Tolkien? As mystifying as these delusions may seem, you'll see that the etiology of schizophrenic disorders is not all that different from the etiology of other psychological disorders. We'll begin our discussion by examining the matter of genetic vulnerability.

Genetic Vulnerability

Evidence is plentiful that hereditary factors play a role in the development of schizophrenic disorders (Cloninger, 1989). For instance, in twin studies, concordance rates average around 48% for identical twins, in comparison to about 17% for fraternal twins (Gottesman, 1991). Studies also indicate that a child born to two schizophrenic parents has about a 46% probability of developing a schizophrenic disorder (as compared to the probability in the general population of about 1%–1.5%). These and other findings that demonstrate the genetic roots of schizophrenia are summarized in Figure 14.14. Overall, the picture is similar to that seen for mood disorders. Several converging lines of evidence indicate that people inherit a genetically transmitted *vulnerability* to schizophrenia (Fowles, 1992).

Neurochemical Factors

Like mood disorders, schizophrenic disorders appear to be accompanied by changes in the activity of one or more neurotransmitters in the brain (Hollandsworth, 1990). *Dopamine* has been implicated as the critical neurotransmitter because most of the drugs that are useful in the treatment of schizophrenia are known to dampen dopamine activity in the brain (Snyder, 1986). However, the evidence linking schizophrenia to neurotransmitter disturbances is riddled with interpretive problems (Carson & Sanislow, 1993). Nonetheless, investigators continue to search for the neurochemical bases of schizophrenia.

Structural Abnormalities in the Brain

Various studies have suggested that schizophrenic individuals have difficulty in focusing their attention (Dawson et al., 1993). Some theorists believe that many bizarre aspects of schizophrenic behavior may be due mainly to an inability to filter out unimportant stimuli (Judd et al., 1992). This lack of selectivity supposedly leaves victims of the

"Schizophrenia disfigures the emotional and cognitive faculties of its victims, and sometimes nearly destroys them."
NANCY ANDREASEN

Figure 14.14. Genetic vulnerability to schizophrenic disorders. Relatives of schizophrenic patients have an elevated risk for schizophrenia. This risk is greater among closer relatives. Although environment also plays a role in the etiology of schizophrenia, the concordance rates shown here suggest that there must be a genetic vulnerability to the disorder. These concordance estimates are based on pooled data from 40 studies conducted between 1920 and 1987. (Data from Gottesman, 1991)

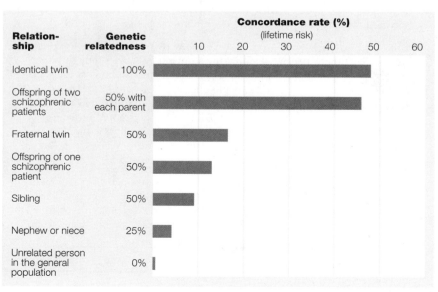

disorder flooded with overwhelming, confusing sensory input.

These problems with attention suggest that schizophrenic disorders may be caused by neurological defects (Perry & Braff, 1994). Until recently, this theory was based more on speculation than on actual research. However, new advances in brain imaging technology are beginning to yield some intriguing data. The findings suggest that there is an association between enlarged brain ventricles (the hollow, fluid-filled cavities in the brain) and chronic schizophrenic disturbance (Raz, 1993; Suddath et al., 1990). The significance of enlarged ventricles in the brain is hotly debated, however. Enlarged ventricles are not unique to schizophrenia—they are a sign of many kinds of brain pathology. Thus, it is difficult to sort out whether this brain abnormality is a cause or an effect of schizophrenia.

Communication Deviance

Various theorists assert that vulnerability to schizophrenia is increased by exposure to defective interpersonal communication during childhood. Studies have found a relationship between schizophrenia and *communication deviance* (Goldstein, 1984; Singer, Wynne, & Toohey, 1978). Communication deviance on the part of parents and family members includes unintelligible speech, stories with no endings, heavy use of unusual words, extensive contradictions, and poor attention to children's communication efforts. The evidence suggests that schizophrenia is more likely to develop when youngsters grow up in homes characterized by such vague, muddled, fragmented communication. Researchers speculate that communication deviance gradually undermines a child's sense of reality and encourages youngsters to withdraw into their own private world, setting the stage for schizophrenic thinking later in life.

Expressed Emotion

Studies of expressed emotion have primarily focused on how this element of family dynamics influences the *course* of schizophrenic illness, after the onset of the disorder (Leff & Vaughn, 1985). *Expressed emotion* is the degree to which a relative of a schizophrenic patient displays highly critical or emotionally overinvolved attitudes toward the patient. Audiotaped interviews of relatives' communication are carefully evaluated for critical comments, resentment toward the patient, and excessive emotional involvement (overprotective, overconcerned attitudes).

Studies show that a family's expressed emotion is a good predictor of the course of a schizophrenic patient's illness (Leff & Vaughn, 1981; Parker & Hadzi-Pavlovic, 1990). After release from a hospital, schizophrenic patients who return to a family high in expressed emotion show relapse rates three or four times that of patients who return to a family low in expressed emotion. Part of the problem for patients returning to homes high in expressed emotion is that their families probably are sources of stress rather than of social support. And like virtually all mental disorders, schizophrenia is influenced to some extent by life stress.

Precipitating Stress

Most theories of schizophrenia assume that stress plays a key role in triggering schizophrenic disorders (Fowles, 1992; Zubin, 1986). According to this notion, various biological and psychological factors influence individuals' *vulnerability* to schizophrenia. High stress may then serve to precipitate a schizophrenic disorder in someone who is vulnerable. A recent study indicates that high stress

---

CONCEPT CHECK 14.3
Distinguishing Schizophrenic and Mood Disorders

Check your understanding of the nature of schizophrenic and mood disorders by making very preliminary diagnoses for the cases described below. Read each case summary and write your tentative diagnosis in the space provided. The answers are in Appendix A.

1. Max hasn't slept in four days. He's determined to write the "great American novel" before his class reunion, which is a few months away. He expounds eloquently on his novel to anyone who will listen, talking at such a rapid pace that no one can get a word in edgewise. He feels like he's wired with energy and is supremely confident about the novel, even though he's only written 10 to 20 pages. Last week, he charged $8000 worth of new computer software, which is supposed to help him write his book.

   Preliminary diagnosis: _____

2. Maurice maintains that he invented the atomic bomb, even though he was born after its invention. He says he invented it to punish homosexuals, Nazis, and short people. It's short people that he's really afraid of. He's sure that all the short people on TV are talking about him. He thinks that short people are conspiring to make him look like a Republican. Maurice frequently gets in arguments with people and is emotionally volatile. His grooming is poor, but he says it's okay because he's the Secretary of State.

   Preliminary diagnosis: _____

3. Margaret has hardly gotten out of bed for weeks, although she's troubled by insomnia. She doesn't feel like eating and has absolutely no energy. She feels dejected, discouraged, spiritless, and apathetic. Friends stop by to try to cheer her up, but she tells them not to waste their time on "pond scum."

   Preliminary diagnosis: _____

can also trigger relapses in schizophrenic patients who have made progress toward recovery (Ventura et al., 1989).

PSYCHOLOGICAL DISORDERS AND THE LAW

Societies use the law to enforce their norms of conformity. Given this function, the law has something to say about many issues related to abnormal behavior. In this section we briefly examine the legal issues of insanity and involuntary commitment.

Insanity is *not* a diagnosis; it's purely a legal concept. ***Insanity* is a legal status indicating that a person cannot be held responsible for his or her actions because of mental illness.** Why is this an issue in the courtroom? Because criminal acts must be intentional. The law reasons that people who are "out of their mind" may not be able to appreciate the significance of what they're doing. The insanity defense is used in criminal trials by defendants who admit that they committed the crime but claim that they lacked intent.

No simple relationship exists between specific diagnoses of mental disorders and court findings of insanity. Most people with diagnosed psychological disorders would *not* qualify as insane. The people most likely to qualify are those troubled by severe, psychotic disturbances. The courts apply several rules in making judgments about a defendant's sanity, depending on the jurisdiction. According to the most widely used rule, called the M'naghten rule, *insanity exists when a mental disorder makes a person unable to distinguish right from wrong.* As you can imagine, evaluating insanity as defined in the M'naghten rule can be difficult for judges and jurors, not to mention the psychologists and psychiatrists who are called into court as expert witnesses. Although highly publicized and controversial, the insanity defense is actually used less frequently and less successfully than widely believed (Phillips, Wolf, & Coons, 1988).

The issue of insanity surfaces only in *criminal* proceedings. Far more people are affected by *civil* proceedings relating to involuntary commitment. In ***involuntary commitment* people are hospitalized in psychiatric facilities against their will.** What are the grounds for such a dramatic action? They vary some from state to state. Generally, people are subject to involuntary commitment when mental health professionals and legal authorities believe that a mental disorder makes

After his attempt to assassinate President Ronald Reagan, John Hinckley, Jr., was found not guilty by reason of insanity. The Hinckley verdict aroused controversy about the concept of insanity, which is a legal status and not a psychodiagnostic category.

them (1) dangerous to themselves (usually suicidal), (2) dangerous to others (potentially violent), or (3) in need of treatment (applied in cases of severe disorientation). In emergency situations psychologists and psychiatrists can authorize *temporary* commitment, usually for 24 to 72 hours. Orders for long-term involuntary commitment are usually set up for renewable six-month periods and can be issued by a court only after a formal

---

CONCEPT CHECK 14.4
Identifying Etiological Factors in Psychological Disorders

The abundance of theories concerning the etiology of psychological disorders exemplifies our theme that behavior is determined by multiple causes. Check your understanding of the etiological factors that appear to play a role in the three categories of disorders shown below by placing check marks in the appropriate spaces in the chart. The column on the left lists the categories of etiological factors. The top row lists three categories of disorders. You'll find the answers in Appendix A.

	Anxiety disorders	Mood disorders	Schizophrenic disorders
Brain structure abnormalities			
Cognitive factors			
Communication deviance			
Conditioning			
Genetic predisposition			
Interpersonal factors			
Neurochemical factors			
Observational learning			
Stress			

hearing. Mental health professionals provide extensive input in these hearings, but the courts make the final decisions.

CULTURE AND PATHOLOGY

The legal rules governing insanity and involuntary commitment obviously are culture-specific. And we noted earlier that judgments of normality and abnormality are influenced by cultural norms and values. In light of these realities, would it be reasonable to infer that psychological disorders are culturally variable phenomena? Many social scientists have concluded that the answer to this question is yes. Embracing a *relativistic view* of psychological disorders, they have argued that the criteria of mental illness vary greatly across cultures and that there are no universal standards of normality and abnormality (Lewis-Fernandez & Kleinman, 1994; Marsella, 1979). According to the relativists, the DSM diagnostic system reflects an ethnocentric, Western, white, urban, middle- and upper-class cultural orientation that has limited relevance in other cultural contexts.

Not everyone agrees with this conclusion, however. Many social scientists subscribe to a *pancultural view* of psychological disorders, arguing that the criteria of mental illness are much the same around the world and that basic standards of normality and abnormality are universal across cultures (Frances et al., 1991; Murphy, 1976). Theorists who accept the pancultural view of psychopathology typically maintain that Western diagnostic concepts have validity and utility in other cultural contexts.

The debate about culture and pathology basically boils down to this question: Are the psychological disorders seen in Western societies found throughout the world? Let's briefly examine the evidence on this issue.

Most investigators agree that the principal categories of serious psychological disturbance—schizophrenia, depression, and bipolar illness—are identifiable in all cultures (Butcher, Narikiyo, & Vitousek, 1993). Most behaviors that are regarded as clearly abnormal in Western culture are also viewed as abnormal in other cultures. People who are delusional, hallucinatory, disoriented, or incoherent are thought to be disturbed in all societies, although there are cultural disparities in exactly what is considered delusional or hallucinatory.

Cultural variations are more apparent in the recognition of less severe forms of psychological disturbance (Tseng et al., 1986). Additional research is needed, but relatively mild types of pathology that do not disrupt behavior in obvious ways appear to go unrecognized in many societies. Thus, syndromes such as generalized anxiety disorder, hypochondria, and somatization disorder, which are firmly established as important diagnostic categories in the DSM, are viewed in some cultures as "run-of-the-mill" difficulties and peculiarities rather than as full-fledged disorders.

Finally, researchers have discovered a small number of *culture-bound disorders* that further illustrate the diversity of abnormal behavior around the world (Simons & Hughes, 1993). **Culture-bound disorders are abnormal syndromes found only in a few cultural groups.** For example, *koro*, an obsessive fear that one's penis will withdraw into one's abdomen, is seen only among Chinese males in Malaya and several other regions of southern Asia. *Windigo*, which involves an intense craving for human flesh and fear that one will turn into a cannibal, is seen only among Algonquin Indian cultures. *Anorexia nervosa*, which involves an intense fear of becoming fat, a loss of appetite, and refusal to eat adequately, is seen only in affluent Western cultures.

So, what can we conclude about the validity of the relativistic versus pancultural views of psychological disorders? Both views appear to have some merit. As we have seen in other areas of research, psychopathology is characterized by both cultural variance and invariance.

PUTTING IT IN PERSPECTIVE

Our examination of abnormal behavior and its roots has highlighted four of our organizing themes: multifactorial causation, the interplay of heredity and environment, the sociohistorical context in which psychology evolves, and the influence of culture on psychological phenomena.

We can safely assert that every disorder described in this chapter has multiple causes. The development of mental disorders involves an interplay among a variety of psychological, biological, and social factors. Let's reconsider the etiology of schizophrenia to illustrate. The schematic diagram in Figure 14.15 provides an overview of how various factors are believed to contribute to the development of schizophrenic disorders. As you can see, a host of variables (some of which we didn't discuss) have been implicated. The model depicted in the diagram shows not only that many

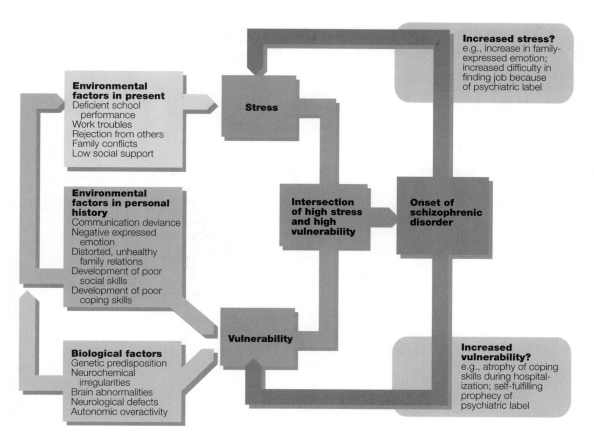

Figure 14.15. The stress-vulnerability model of schizophrenia. Multifactorial causation is readily apparent in current theories about the etiology of schizophrenic disorders. A variety of biological factors and personal history factors influence one's vulnerability to the disorder, which interacts with the amount of stress one experiences. Schizophrenic disorders appear to result from an intersection of high stress and high vulnerability.

variables are involved in the evolution of this disorder but also that these variables interact in complex ways.

We also saw that most psychological disorders depend on an interaction of genetics and experience. This interaction shows up most clearly in the *stress-vulnerability models* for mood disorders and schizophrenic disorders. *Vulnerability* to these disorders seems to depend primarily on heredity, although experience contributes. Stress is largely a function of environment, although physiological factors may influence people's stress reactions. According to stress-vulnerability theories, disorders emerge when high vulnerability intersects with high stress, as shown in Figure 14.15. A high biological vulnerability may not be converted into a disorder if a person's stress is low. Similarly, high stress may not lead to a disorder if vulnerability is low. Thus, the impact of heredity depends on the environment, and the effect of environment depends on heredity.

This chapter also demonstrated that psychology evolves in a sociohistorical context. We saw that the formal definitions of normality and abnormality codified in the DSM system are not shaped exclusively by scientific research. For instance, because of changing social values and lob-

bying by a special-interest group, homosexuality is no longer classified as pathological, while some relatively minor problems in living are officially regarded as pathological to accommodate our insurance system. These points are not raised to belittle the enormous contributions that science has made to our understanding of mental disorders. Modern conceptions of normality and abnormality are largely shaped by empirical research, but social trends, economic necessities, and political realities also play a role.

Finally, our discussion of psychological disorders showed once again that psychological phenomena are shaped to some degree by cultural parameters. Although some standards of normality and abnormality transcend cultural boundaries, cultural norms influence some aspects of psychopathology.

Indeed, a certain cultural orientation is implicit in our upcoming Application on suicide. Our culture views suicide as a cowardly, abnormal act to be prevented whenever possible. In contrast, there are other cultures in which suicide is considered to be an acceptable and even courageous act under certain circumstances. We'll take the traditional view in our culture and focus on suicide prevention.

Understanding and Preventing Suicide

Answer the following "true" or "false."

___ **1** People who talk about suicide don't actually commit suicide.

___ **2** Suicides usually take place with little or no warning.

___ **3** People who attempt suicide are fully intent on dying.

___ **4** People who are suicidal remain so forever.

These four statements are all false. They are myths about suicide that we will dispose of momentarily. First, however, let's discuss the magnitude of this tragic problem.

Prevalence of Suicide

There are about 250,000 suicide attempts in the United States each year. Roughly one in eight of these attempts is "successful." This makes suicide the eighth leading cause of death in the United States. Worse yet, official statistics may underestimate the scope of the problem. Many suicides are disguised as accidents, either by the suicidal person or by survivors who try to cover up afterward. Thus, experts estimate that there may be ten times more suicides than officially reported (Hirschfeld & Davidson, 1988).

Who Commits Suicide?

Anyone can commit suicide. No segment of society is immune. Nonetheless, some groups are at higher risk than others (Buda & Tsuang, 1990; Cross & Hirschfeld, 1986). For instance, the prevalence of suicide varies according to *marital status* (see Figure 14.16). Married people commit suicide less frequently than divorced, bereaved, or single people. *Sex* and *age* have complex relations to suicide rates. On the one hand, women

attempt suicide more often than men. On the other hand, men are more likely to actually kill themselves in an attempt, so they *complete* more suicides than women. In regard to age, suicide attempts peak between ages 24 and 44, but completed suicides are most frequent after age 55. However, age trends are different for men and women, as you can see in Figure 14.17, which graphs suicide rates by sex and age group.

Unfortunately, suicide rates have tripled among adolescents and young adults in the last several decades (Brent & Kolko, 1990). *College students* are at higher risk than their noncollege peers. Academic pressures and setbacks do *not* appear to be the principal cause of this elevated suicide rate among collegians. Interpersonal problems and loneliness seem to be more important.

Suicide is *not* limited to people with severe mental illness. However, elevated suicide rates are found for most catego-

ries of psychological disorders (Black & Winokur, 1990), and retrospective evaluations of suicide victims indicate that the vast majority experienced some type of mental illness around the time of their suicide (Henriksson et al., 1993). As you might predict, suicide rates are highest for people with mood disorders, especially depression (see Figure 14.18).

Myths About Suicide

We opened this application with four false statements about suicide. Let's examine these myths as they have been discussed by various suicide experts (Fremouw, Perczel, & Ellis, 1990; Shneidman, 1985).

Myth 1: People who talk about suicide don't actually commit suicide. Undoubtedly, there are many people who threaten suicide without ever going through with it. Nonetheless, there is no group at

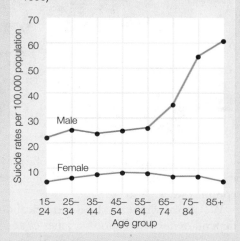

Figure 14.17. Suicide rates in the United States, by age and sex. At all ages, more men than women commit suicide. The age patterns for the two sexes are also noticeably different: whereas the rate of male suicides peaks in the retirement years, the rate of female suicides peaks in middle adulthood. (Data from *Statistical Abstract of the United States*, 1990)

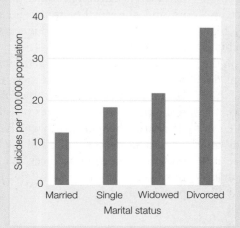

Figure 14.16. Marital status and suicide rates. As these data show, marital status is correlated with the likelihood of suicide. The suicide rate for singles is about 50% higher than for married individuals, and the rate for divorced people is about three times higher. (Adapted from McIntosh, 1991)

Preventing Suicide

There is no simple and dependable way to prevent someone from going ahead with a threatened suicide. One expert on suicide (Wekstein, 1979) makes the point that "perhaps nobody really knows *exactly* what to do when dealing with an imminent suicide" (p. 129). However, we will review some general advice that may be useful if you ever have to help someone through a suicidal crisis (Fremouw et al., 1990; Rosenthal, 1988; Shneidman, Farberow, & Litman, 1970).

1. *Take suicidal talk seriously.* When people talk about suicide in vague generalities, it's easy to dismiss it as "idle talk" and let it go. However, people who talk about suicide are a high-risk group, and their veiled threats should not be ignored. According to Rosenthal (1988), the first step in suicide prevention is to directly ask such people if they're contemplating suicide.

2. *Provide empathy and social support.* It's important to show the suicidal person that you care. People often contemplate suicide because they see the world around them as indifferent and uncaring. Hence, you must demonstrate to the suicidal person that you are genuinely concerned. Even if you are thrust into a situation where you barely know the suicidal person, you need to provide empathy. Suicide threats are often a last-ditch cry for help. It is therefore imperative that you offer to help.

3. *Identify and clarify the crucial problem.* The suicidal person is often terribly confused and feels lost in a sea of frustration and problems. It is a good idea to try to help sort through this confusion. Encourage the person to try to identify the crucial problem. Once it is isolated, it may not seem quite so overwhelming.

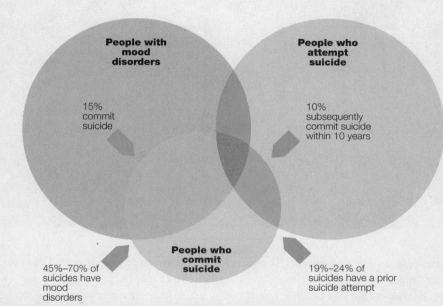

Figure 14.18. The relationship between suicide and mood disorders. Two groups with elevated risk of suicide are people with mood disorders and people who have made previous suicide attempts. Between them, these groups account for a high percentage of suicides. (Adapted from Avery & Winokur, 1978)

higher risk for suicide than those who openly discuss the possibility. Many people who kill themselves have a history of earlier threats that they did not carry out.

Myth 2: Suicide usually takes place with little or no warning. It is estimated that eight out of ten suicide attempts are preceded by some kind of warning. These warnings may range from clear threats to vague statements. For example, at dinner with friends the night before he committed suicide, one prominent attorney cut up his American Express card, saying, "I'm not going to need this anymore." The probability of an actual suicide attempt is greatest when a threat is clear, when it includes a detailed plan, and when the plan involves a relatively deadly method.

Myth 3: People who attempt suicide are fully intent on dying. It appears that only about 3%–5% of those who attempt suicide definitely want to die. About 30% of the people who make an attempt seem ambivalent. They arrange things so that their fate is largely a matter of chance. The remaining two-thirds of suicide attempts are made by people who appear to have no interest in dying! They only want to send out a dramatic distress signal. Thus, they arrange their suicide so that a rescue is quite likely. These variations in intent probably explain why only about one-eighth of suicide attempts end in death.

Myth 4: People who are suicidal remain so forever. Many people who become suicidal do so for a limited period of time. If they manage to ride through their crisis period, thoughts of suicide may disappear entirely. Apparently, time heals many wounds—if it is given the opportunity.

There is no sure way to talk someone out of attempting suicide, but it's important to provide empathy and social support, clarify the person's problem, and capitalize on any doubts.

You could also point out that the person's confusion is clouding his or her ability to rationally judge the seriousness of the problem.

4. *Suggest alternative courses of action.* People thinking about suicide often see it as the only solution to their problems. This is obviously an irrational view. Try to chip away at this premise by offering other possible solutions for the problem that has been identified as crucial. Suicidal people often are too distraught and disoriented to do this on their own.

5. *Capitalize on any doubts.* For most people, life is not easy to give up. They are racked by doubts about the wisdom of their decision. Many people will voice their unique reasons for doubting whether they should take the suicidal path. Zero in on these doubts. They may be your best arguments for life over death. For instance, if a person expresses concern about how her or his suicide will affect family members, capitalize on this source of doubt.

6. *Encourage professional consultation.* It is important to try to get a suicidal person to seek assistance from some sort of mental health professional. Just because you talk a person out of attempting a threatened suicide does not mean that the crisis is over. The contemplation of suicide indicates that a person is experiencing great distress. Given this reality, professional intervention is crucial.

Chapter 14 Review

KEY IDEAS

Abnormal Behavior: Myths, Realities, and Controversies

♦ The medical model assumes that it is useful to view abnormal behavior as a disease. This view has been criticized on the grounds that it turns ethical questions about deviance into medical questions and stigmatizes those labeled mentally ill. Although there are serious problems with the medical model, the concept is useful if one remembers that it is only an analogy.

♦ Three criteria are used in deciding whether people suffer from psychological disorders: deviance, personal distress, and maladaptive behavior. Often, it is difficult to clearly draw a line between normality and abnormality. Generally, people with psychological disorders do not exhibit bizarre behavior.

♦ DSM-IV is the official psychodiagnostic classification system in the United States. This system asks for information about patients on five axes or dimensions. Controversies about DSM illustrate that judgments about psychological disorders are not value-free and that they are influenced by social trends and political realities.

Anxiety Disorders

♦ The anxiety disorders include generalized anxiety disorder, phobic disorder, panic disorder, and obsessive-compulsive disorder. These disorders may have a genetic component and may be more likely in people who are especially sensitive to physiological symptoms of anxiety. High stress and abnormalities in neurotransmitter activity may also play a role.

♦ Many anxiety responses, especially phobias, may be caused by classical conditioning and maintained by operant conditioning. Parents who model anxiety may promote these disorders. Cognitive theorists maintain that certain styles of thinking—especially a tendency to overinterpret harmless situations as threatening—make some people vulnerable to anxiety disorders.

Somatoform Disorders

♦ Somatoform disorders include somatization disorder, conversion disorder, and hypochondriasis. These disorders often emerge in people with highly suggestible, histrionic personalities. Somatoform disorders may be a learned avoidance strategy reinforced by attention and sympathy.

Dissociative Disorders

♦ Dissociative disorders include dissociative amnesia and fugue and multiple personality (dissociative identity disorder). These disorders are uncommon and their causes are not well understood. Multiple-personality disorders may be rooted in emotional trauma that occurred during childhood.

Mood Disorders

♦ The principal mood disorders are unipolar depression and bipolar mood disorder. Mood disorders are episodic. Unipolar depressions are more common than bipolar disorders, and they appear to be increasing in prevalence.

♦ Evidence indicates that people vary in their genetic vulnerability to the severe mood disorders. These disorders are accompanied by changes in neurochemical activity in the brain. Cognitive models posit that negative thinking contributes to depression. An attributional style emphasizing internal, stable, and global attributions has been implicated. Depression is often rooted in interpersonal inadequacies and setbacks and sometimes is stress related.

Schizophrenic Disorders

♦ Schizophrenic disorders are characterized by deterioration of adaptive behavior, irrational thought, distorted perception, and disturbed mood. Schizophrenic disorders are classified as paranoid, catatonic, disorganized, or undifferentiated. A new classification scheme based on the predominance of positive versus negative symptoms is under study.

♦ Research has linked schizophrenia to a genetic vulnerability, changes in neurotransmitter activity, and structural abnormalities in the brain. Precipitating stress and unhealthy family dynamics, including communication deviance and a negative emotional climate (high expressed emotion), may also contribute to the development of schizophrenia.

Psychological Disorders and the Law

♦ Insanity is a legal concept applied to people who cannot be held responsible for their actions because of mental illness. When people appear to be dangerous to themselves or others, courts may rule that they are subject to involuntary commitment in a hospital.

Culture and Pathology

♦ The principal categories of psychological disturbance are identifiable in all cultures. But milder disorders may go unrecognized in some societies, and culture-bound disorders further illustrate the diversity of abnormal behavior around the world.

Putting It in Perspective

♦ This chapter highlighted four of our unifying themes, showing that psychological disorders are governed by multiple causes, that heredity and environment jointly influence mental disorders, that psychology evolves in a sociohistorical context, and that pathology is characterized by both cultural variance and invariance.

Application: Understanding and Preventing Suicide

♦ Suicide attempts result in death about one-eighth of the time, and suicide is the eighth leading cause of death in the United States. People with psychological disorders, especially mood disorders, show elevated suicide rates. Suicidal people usually provide warnings, often are not intent on dying, and may not remain suicidal if they survive their crisis. Efforts at suicide prevention emphasize empathy, clarification of the person's problems, and professional assistance.

KEY TERMS

Agoraphobia	Hypochondriasis
Anxiety disorders	Insanity
Attributions	Involuntary commitment
Bipolar mood disorders	Medical model
Catatonic schizophrenia	Mood disorders
Concordance rate	Multiple-personality disorder
Conversion disorder	Obsessive-compulsive disorder (OCD)
Culture-bound disorders	Panic disorder
Delusions	Paranoid schizophrenia
Depressive disorders	Phobic disorder
Diagnosis	Prognosis
Disorganized schizophrenia	Psychosomatic diseases
Dissociative amnesia	Schizophrenic disorders
Dissociative disorders	Somatization disorder
Dissociative fugue	Somatoform disorders
Dissociative identity disorder	Transvestism
Etiology	Undifferentiated schizophrenia
Generalized anxiety disorder	
Hallucinations	

KEY PEOPLE

Nancy Andreasen	Martin Seligman
David Rosenhan	Thomas Szasz

15 Psychotherapy

What do you picture when you hear the term *psychotherapy*? If you're like most people, you probably envision a troubled patient lying on a couch in a book-lined office, with the therapist asking penetrating questions and providing sage advice. Typically, people believe that psychotherapy is only for those who are "sick" and that therapists have special powers that allow them to "see through" their clients. It is also widely believed that successful therapy requires years of deep probing into a client's innermost secrets. Many people further assume that therapists routinely tell their patients how to lead their lives. Like most stereotypes, this picture of psychotherapy is a mixture of fact and fiction, as you'll see in the upcoming pages.

In this chapter, we'll take a down-to-earth look at the complex process of psychotherapy. We'll start by discussing some general questions about the provision of therapy, including:

- Who seeks therapy?
- What kinds of professionals provide therapy?
- What are the differences between psychiatrists and psychologists?
- How many different types of therapy are there?

After we've considered these general issues, we'll examine some of the more widely used approaches to psychotherapy, analyzing their goals, techniques, and effectiveness. In the Application at the end of the chapter, we focus on practical issues involved in finding and choosing a therapist, in case you ever have to advise someone about seeking psychotherapy.

THE ELEMENTS OF PSYCHOTHERAPY: TREATMENTS, CLIENTS, AND THERAPISTS

Sigmund Freud is widely credited with launching modern psychotherapy. Ironically, the landmark case that inspired Freud was actually treated by one of his colleagues, Josef Breuer. Around 1880, Breuer began to treat a young woman named Anna O (a pseudonym). Anna exhibited a variety of physical maladies, including headaches, coughing, and a loss of feeling and movement in her right arm. Much to his surprise, Breuer discovered that Anna's physical symptoms cleared up when he encouraged her to talk about emotionally charged experiences from her past.

When Breuer and Freud discussed the case, they speculated that talking things through had enabled Anna to drain off bottled up emotions that had caused her symptoms. Breuer found the intense emotional exchange in this treatment not to his liking, so he didn't follow through on his discovery. However, Freud applied Breuer's insight to other patients, and his successes led him to develop a systematic treatment procedure, which he called *psychoanalysis*. Anna O called her treatment "the talking cure." However, as you'll see, psychotherapy isn't always curative, and many modern therapies place little emphasis on talking.

Freud's breakthrough ushered in a century of progress for psychotherapy. Psychoanalysis spawned many offspring as Freud's followers developed their own systems of treatment. Since then, approaches to psychotherapy have steadily grown more numerous, more diverse, and more effective. Today, people can choose from a bewildering array of therapies.

Treatments: How Many Types Are There?

In their efforts to help people, psychotherapists use many treatment methods. One expert (Kazdin, 1994) estimates that there may be over 400 different approaches to psychotherapy! Fortunately, we can impose some order on this chaos. As varied as therapists' procedures are, approaches to treatment can be classified into three major categories:

1. *Insight therapies*. Insight therapy is "talk therapy" in the tradition of Freud's psychoanalysis. In insight therapies, clients engage in complex, often lengthy verbal interactions with their thera-

The case of Anna O., whose real name was Bertha Pappenheim, provided the inspiration for Sigmund Freud's invention of psychoanalysis.

In psychotherapy, a person with psychological problems enlists the help of a professional (the therapist) in dealing with those problems.

pists. The goal in these discussions is to pursue increased insight regarding the nature of the client's difficulties and to sort through possible solutions.

2. *Behavior therapies.* Behavior therapies are based on the principles of learning, which were introduced in Chapter 6. Instead of emphasizing personal insights, behavior therapists make direct efforts to alter problematic responses (phobias, for instance) and maladaptive habits (drug use, for instance). Most of their procedures involve classical conditioning, operant conditioning, or observational learning.

3. *Biomedical therapies.* Biomedical approaches to therapy involve interventions into a person's biological functioning. The most widely used procedures are drug therapy and electroconvulsive (shock) therapy. As the name bio*medical* therapies suggests, these treaments have traditionally been provided only by physicians with a medical degree (usually psychiatrists). This situation may change, however, as psychologists have begun to campaign for limited prescription privileges, and the federal government has funded a pilot study to assess the feasability of this proposal (VandenBos, Cummings, & DeLeon, 1992).

Later in this chapter we will examine approaches to therapy that fall into each of these three categories. Although we'll find very different methods in each category, the three major treatment classes are not entirely incompatible. For example, a client might be seen in insight therapy while also receiving medication.

Clients: Who Seeks Therapy?

People bring to therapy the full range of human problems: anxiety, depression, unsatisfactory in-

terpersonal relations, troublesome habits, poor self-control, low self-esteem, marital conflicts, self-doubt, a sense of emptiness, and feelings of personal stagnation. Therapy is sought by people who feel troubled, but the nature and severity of that trouble varies greatly from one person to another. The two most common presenting problems are excessive anxiety and depression (Lichtenstein, 1980).

A client in treatment does *not* necessarily have an identifiable psychological disorder. Some people seek professional help for everyday problems (career decisions, for instance) or vague feelings of discontent. Thus, therapy includes efforts to foster clients' personal growth, as well as professional interventions for mental disorders.

Therapists: Who Provides Professional Treatment?

Friends and relatives may provide you with excellent advice about your personal problems, but their assistance does not qualify as therapy. Psychotherapy refers to *professional* treatment by someone with special training. However, a common source of confusion about psychotherapy is the variety of "helping professions" involved (Murstein & Fontaine, 1993). Psychology and psychiatry are the principal professions involved in the provision of psychotherapy, but treatment is also provided by other types of therapists (see Table 15.1). Let's look at these mental health professions.

Psychologists

Two types of psychologists may provide therapy, although the distinction between them is more theoretical than real. *Clinical psychologists* and *counseling psychologists* specialize in the diag-

Table 15.1 The Principal Mental Health Professions: Different Types of Therapists

Title	Degree*	Years Beyond Bachelor's Degree	Typical Roles and Activities
Clinical or counseling psychologist	Ph.D. Psy.D. Ed.D.	5–7	Diagnosis, psychological testing, insight and behavior therapy
Psychiatrist	M.D.	8	Diagnosis; insight, behavior, and biomedical therapy
Social worker	M.S.W.	2	Insight and behavior therapy, family therapy, helping patients return to the community
Psychiatric nurse	B.S., B.A., M.A.	0–2	Inpatient care, insight and behavior therapy
Counselor	M.A.	2	Insight and behavior therapy, working primarily with everyday adjustment problems and marital and career issues

*Ph.D. = Doctor of Philosophy; Psy.D. = Doctor of Psychology; Ed.D. = Doctor of Education; M.D. = Doctor of Medicine; M.S.W. = Master of Social Work; B.S. = Bachelor of Science; B.A. = Bachelor of Arts; M.A. = Master of Arts.

nosis and treatment of psychological disorders and everyday behavioral problems. In theory, clinical psychologists' training emphasizes the treatment of full-fledged disorders. In contrast, counseling psychologists' training is supposed to be slanted toward the treatment of everyday adjustment problems in normal people. In practice, however, there is great overlap between clinical and counseling psychologists in training, skills, and the clientele that they serve.

Both types of psychologists must earn a doctoral degree (Ph.D., Psy.D., or Ed.D.). A doctorate in psychology requires about five to seven years of training beyond a bachelor's degree. The process of gaining admission to a Ph.D. program in clinical psychology is highly competitive (about as difficult as getting into medical school). Psychologists receive most of their training on university campuses, although they serve a one- to two-year internship in a clinical setting, such as a hospital. In providing therapy, psychologists use either insight or behavioral approaches. Clinical and counseling psychologists do psychological testing as well as psychotherapy, and many also conduct research.

Psychiatrists

Psychiatrists are physicians who specialize in the diagnosis and treatment of psychological disorders. Many psychiatrists also treat everyday behavioral problems. However, in comparison to psychologists, psychiatrists devote more time to relatively severe disorders (schizophrenia, mood disorders) and less time to everyday marital, family, job, and school problems.

Psychiatrists have an M.D. degree. Their graduate training requires four years of coursework in medical school and a four-year apprenticeship in a residency at a hospital. Their psychotherapy training occurs during their residency. In their provision of therapy, psychiatrists tend to emphasize biomedical treatments and psychoanalytic approaches to insight therapy.

Other Mental Health Professionals

Several other mental health professions provide psychotherapy services. *Psychiatric social workers* and *psychiatric nurses* often work as part of a treatment team with a psychologist or psychiatrist. Although social workers have traditionally worked in hospitals and social service agencies, many also provide a wide range of therapeutic services as independent practitioners. Many kinds of *counselors* also provide therapeutic services. Counselors are usually found working in schools, colleges, and assorted human service agencies. They often specialize in particular types of problems, such as vocational counseling, marital counseling, rehabilitation counseling, and drug counseling.

Although there are clear differences among the helping professions in education and training, their roles in the treatment process overlap considerably. In this chapter, we will refer to psychologists or psychiatrists as needed, but otherwise we'll use the terms *clinician*, *therapist*, and *mental health professional* to refer to psychotherapists of all kinds, regardless of their professional degree.

Now that we have discussed the basic elements in psychotherapy, we can examine specific approaches to treatment in terms of their goals, procedures, and effectiveness. We'll begin with a few, representative insight therapies.

INSIGHT THERAPIES

There are many schools of thought about how to do insight therapy. Therapists with various theoretical orientations use different methods to pursue different kinds of insights. However, what these varied approaches have in common is that **insight therapies involve verbal interactions intended to enhance clients' self-knowledge and thus promote healthful changes in personality and behavior.**

There probably are around 200 different insight therapies, but the leading eight or ten approaches appear to account for the lion's share of treatment.

Although people often think of therapists as being psychiatrists or psychologists, they may also be social workers, nurses, or counselors.

In this section, we'll delve into psychoanalysis, client-centered therapy, and cognitive therapy. We'll also discuss how insight therapy can be done with groups as well as individuals.

Psychoanalysis

After the case of Anna O, Sigmund Freud worked as a psychotherapist for almost 50 years in Vienna. Through a painstaking process of trial and error, he developed innovative techniques for the treatment of psychological disorders and distress. His system of *psychoanalysis* came to dominate psychiatry for many decades. Although the dominance of psychoanalysis has eroded in recent years (Reiser, 1989), a diverse collection of psychoanalytic approaches to therapy continue to evolve and to remain influential today (Eagle & Wolitzky, 1992).

Psychoanalysis **is an insight therapy that emphasizes the recovery of unconscious conflicts, motives, and defenses through techniques such as free association and transference.** To appreciate the logic of psychoanalysis, we have to look at Freud's thinking about the roots of mental disorders. Freud mostly treated anxiety-dominated disturbances, such as phobic, panic, obsessive-compulsive, and conversion disorders, that were then called *neuroses.*

Freud believed that neurotic problems are caused by unconscious conflicts left over from early childhood. As explained in Chapter 12, he thought that these inner conflicts involved battles among the id, ego, and superego, usually over sexual and aggressive impulses. He theorized that people depend on defense mechanisms to avoid confronting these conflicts, which remain hidden in the depths of the unconscious. However, he noted that defensive maneuvers often lead to self-defeating behavior. Furthermore, he asserted that defenses tend to be only partially successful in alleviating anxiety, guilt, and other distressing emotions. With this model in mind, let's take a look at the therapeutic procedures used in psychoanalysis.

Probing the Unconscious

Given Freud's assumptions, we can see that the logic of psychoanalysis is quite simple. The analyst attempts to probe the murky depths of the unconscious to discover the unresolved conflicts causing the client's neurotic behavior. In this effort to explore the unconscious, the therapist relies on two techniques: free association and dream analysis.

In *free association* **clients spontaneously express their thoughts and feelings exactly as** **they occur, with as little censorship as possible.** Clients lie on a couch so they will be better able to let their mind drift freely. In free associating, clients expound on anything that comes to mind, regardless of how trivial, silly, or embarrassing it might be. Gradually, most clients begin to let everything pour out without conscious censorship. The analyst studies these free associations for clues about what is going on in the unconscious.

In *dream analysis* **the therapist interprets the symbolic meaning of the client's dreams.** For Freud, dreams were the "royal road to the unconscious," the most direct means of access to patients' innermost conflicts, wishes, and impulses. Clients are encouraged and trained to remember their dreams, which they describe in therapy. The therapist then analyzes the symbolism in these dreams to interpret their meaning.

To better illustrate these matters, let's look at an actual case treated through psychoanalysis (adapted from Greenson, 1967, pp. 40–41). Mr. N was troubled by an unsatisfactory marriage. He claimed to love his wife, but he preferred sexual relations with prostitutes. Mr. N reported that his parents also endured lifelong marital difficulties. His childhood conflicts about their relationship appeared to be related to his problems. Both dream analysis and free association can be seen in the following description of a session in Mr. N's treatment:

Mr. N reported a fragment of a dream. All that he could remember is that he was waiting for a red traffic light to change when he felt that someone had bumped into him from behind. . . . The associations led to Mr. N's love of cars, especially sports cars. He loved the sensation, in particular, of whizzing by those fat, old expensive cars. . . . His father always hinted that he had been a great athlete, but he never substantiated it. . . . Mr. N doubted whether his father could really perform. His father would flirt with a waitress in a cafe or make sexual remarks about women passing by, but he seemed to be showing off. If he were really sexual, he wouldn't resort to that.

As is characteristic of free association, Mr. N's train of thought meandered about with little direction. Nonetheless, clues about his unconscious conflicts are apparent. What did Mr. N's therapist extract from this session? The therapist saw sexual overtones in the dream fragment, where Mr. N was bumped from behind. The therapist also inferred that Mr. N had a competitive orientation toward his father, based on the free association about whizzing by fat, old expensive cars. As you

"The news that reaches your consciousness is incomplete and often not to be relied on."
SIGMUND FREUD

can see, analysts must *interpret* their clients' dreams and free associations. This is a critical process throughout psychoanalysis.

Interpretation

Interpretation **refers to the therapist's attempts to explain the inner significance of the client's thoughts, feelings, memories, and behaviors.** Contrary to popular belief, analysts do not interpret everything, and they generally don't try to dazzle clients with startling revelations. Instead, analysts move forward inch by inch, offering interpretations that should be just out of the client's own reach. Mr. N's therapist eventually offered the following interpretations to his client:

I said to Mr. N near the end of the hour that I felt he was struggling with his feelings about his father's sexual life. He seemed to be saying that his father was sexually not a very potent man. . . . He also recalls that he once found a packet of condoms under his father's pillow when he was an adolescent and he thought, "My father must be going to prostitutes." I then intervened and pointed out that the condoms under his father's pillow seemed to indicate more obviously that his father used the condoms with his mother, who slept in the same bed. However, Mr. N wanted to believe his wish-fulfilling fantasy: mother doesn't want sex with father and father is not very potent. The patient was silent and the hour ended.

As you may have already guessed, the therapist concluded that Mr. N's difficulties were rooted in an Oedipal complex (see Chapter 12). He had unresolved sexual feelings toward his mother and hostile feelings about his father. These unconscious conflicts, rooted in Mr. N's childhood, were distorting his intimate relations as an adult.

Resistance

How would you expect Mr. N to respond to the therapist's suggestion that he was in competition with his father for the sexual attention of his mother? Obviously, most clients would have great difficulty accepting such an interpretation. Freud fully expected clients to display some resistance to therapeutic efforts. *Resistance* **refers to largely unconscious defensive maneuvers intended to hinder the progress of therapy.** Why would clients try to resist the helping process? Because they don't want to face up to the painful, disturbing conflicts that they have buried in their unconscious. Although they have sought help, they are reluctant to confront their real problems.

Resistance can take many forms. Clients may show up late for their sessions, may merely pretend to engage in free association, or may express hostility toward their therapist. For instance, Mr. N's therapist noted that after the session just described, "The next day he [Mr. N] began by telling me that he was furious with me . . ." Analysts use a variety of strategies to deal with their clients' resistance. Often, a key consideration is the handling of transference, which we consider next.

Transference

Transference **occurs when clients start relating to their therapists in ways that mimic critical relationships in their lives.** Thus, a client might start relating to a therapist as if the therapist were an overprotective mother, a rejecting brother, or a passive spouse. In a sense, the client *transfers* conflicting feelings about important people onto the therapist. For instance, in his treatment, Mr. N transferred some of the competitive hostility he felt toward his father onto his analyst.

Psychoanalysts often encourage transference so that clients can reenact relations with crucial people in the context of therapy. These reenactments can help bring repressed feelings and conflicts to the surface, allowing the client to work through them. The therapist's handling of transference is complicated and difficult, because transference may arouse confusing, highly charged emotions in the client.

Undergoing psychoanalysis is not easy. It can be a slow, painful process of self-examination that routinely requires three to five years of hard work. Ultimately, if resistance and transference can be handled effectively, the therapist's interpretations should lead the client to profound insights. For instance, Mr. N eventually admitted, "The old boy is probably right, it does tickle me to imagine that my mother preferred me and I could beat out my father. Later, I wondered whether this had something to do with my own screwed-up sex life with my wife." According to Freud, once clients recognize the unconscious sources of conflicts, they can resolve these conflicts and discard their neurotic defenses.

Modern Psychodynamic Treatment

Though still available, classical psychoanalysis as done by Freud is not widely practiced anymore. Freud's psychoanalytic method was geared to a particular kind of clientele that he was seeing in Vienna many years ago. As his followers fanned out across Europe and America, many found it necessary to adapt psychoanalysis to different cultures, changing times, and new kinds of patients. Thus, many variations on Freud's original approach to psychoanalysis have developed over the years. These descendants of psychoanalysis are collectively known as *psychodynamic approaches* to therapy.

Some of these adaptations, such as those by Carl Jung (1917) and Alfred Adler (1927), were sweeping revisions based on fundamental differences in theory. Other variations, such as those devised by Melanie Klein (1948) and Heinz Kohut (1971), involved more subtle changes in theory. Still other revisions (Alexander, 1954; Stekel, 1950) simply involved efforts to modernize and streamline psychoanalytic techniques. Hence, today we have a rich diversity of psychodynamic approaches to therapy.

Client-Centered Therapy

You may have heard of people going into therapy to "find themselves," or to "get in touch with their real feelings." These now-popular phrases emerged out of the human potential movement, which was stimulated in part by Carl Rogers's work (Rogers, 1951, 1986). Using a humanistic perspective, Rogers devised client-centered therapy (also known as person-centered therapy) in the 1940s and 1950s.

Client-centered therapy is an insight therapy that emphasizes providing a supportive emotional climate for clients, who play a major role in determining the pace and direction of their therapy. Rogers's theory about the principal causes of neurotic anxieties is quite different from the Freudian explanation. As discussed in Chapter 12, Rogers maintains that most personal distress is due to inconsistency, or "incongruence," between a person's self-concept and reality. According to his theory, incongruence makes people prone to feel threatened by realistic feedback about themselves from others. For example, if you inaccurately viewed yourself as a hard-working, dependable person, you would feel threatened by contradictory feedback from friends or co-workers. According to Rogers, anxiety about such feedback often leads to reliance on defense mechanisms, to distortions of reality, and to stifled personal growth. Excessive incongruence is thought to be rooted in clients' overdependence on others for approval and acceptance.

Given Rogers's theory, client-centered therapists stalk insights that are quite different from the repressed conflicts that psychoanalysts go after.

Client-centered therapists help clients realize that they do not have to worry constantly about pleasing others and winning acceptance. They encourage clients to respect their own feelings and values. They help people restructure their self-concept to correspond better to reality. Ultimately, they try to foster self-acceptance and personal growth.

Therapeutic Climate

According to Rogers, the *process* of therapy is not as important as the emotional *climate* in which the therapy takes place. He believes that it is critical for the therapist to provide a warm, supportive, accepting climate. This creates a safe environment in which clients can confront their shortcomings without feeling threatened. The lack of threat should reduce clients' defensive tendencies and thus help them open up. To create this atmosphere of emotional support, client-centered therapists must provide three conditions:

1. *Genuineness*. The therapist must be genuine with the client, communicating honestly and spontaneously. The therapist should not be phony or defensive.

2. *Unconditional positive regard*. The therapist must also show complete, nonjudgmental acceptance of the client as a person. The therapist should provide warmth and caring for the client, with no strings attached. This does not mean that the therapist must approve of everything that the client says or does. A therapist can disapprove of a particular behavior while continuing to value the client as a human being.

3. *Empathy*. Finally, the therapist must provide accurate empathy for the client. This means that the therapist must understand the client's world from the client's point of view. Furthermore, the therapist must be articulate enough to communicate this understanding to the client.

Therapeutic Process

In client-centered therapy, the client and therapist work together as equals. The therapist provides relatively little guidance and keeps interpretation and advice to a minimum. So, just what does the client-centered therapist do, besides creating a supportive climate? Primarily, the therapist provides feedback to help clients sort out their feelings. The therapist's key task is *clarification*. Client-centered therapists try to function like a human mirror, reflecting statements back to their clients, but with enhanced clarity. They help clients be-

come more aware of their true feelings by highlighting themes that may be obscure in the clients' rambling discourse.

By working with clients to clarify their feelings, client-centered therapists hope to gradually build toward more far-reaching insights. In particular, they try to help clients better understand their interpersonal relationships and become more comfortable with their genuine selves. Obviously, these are ambitious goals. Client-centered therapy resembles psychoanalysis in that both seek to achieve a major reconstruction of a client's personality. We'll see more limited and specific goals in cognitive therapy, which we consider next.

Cognitive Therapy

In Chapter 13, we saw that people's cognitive interpretations of events make all the difference in the world in how well they handle stress. In Chapter 14, we learned that cognitive factors play a key role in the development of depressive disorders. Citing the importance of findings such as these, Aaron Beck devised a treatment that focuses on clients' cognitive processes (Beck, 1987; Beck & Rush, 1989). *Cognitive therapy* **is an insight therapy that emphasizes recognizing and changing negative thoughts and maladaptive beliefs.**

In recent years cognitive therapy has been applied fruitfully to a wide range of disorders (Beck, 1991; Hollon & Beck , 1994), but it was originally devised as a treatment for depression. According to cognitive therapists, depression is caused by "errors" in thinking (see Table 15.2). They assert that depression-prone people tend to (1) blame their setbacks on personal inadequacies without considering circumstantial explanations, (2) focus selectively on negative events while ignoring positive events, (3) make unduly pessimistic projections about the future, and (4) draw negative conclusions about their worth as a person based on insignificant events. For instance, imagine that you got a low grade on a minor quiz in a class. If you made the kinds of errors in thinking just described, you might blame the grade on your woeful stupidity, dismiss comments from a classmate that it was an unfair test, gloomily predict that you will surely flunk the course, and conclude that you are not genuine college material.

Goals and Techniques

The goal of cognitive therapy is to change the way clients think. To begin, clients are taught to detect their automatic negative thoughts. These are self-defeating statements that people are prone to make when analyzing problems. Examples might include "I'm just not smart enough," "No one really likes me," or "It's all my fault." Clients are then trained to subject these automatic thoughts to reality testing. The therapist helps them to see how unrealistically negative the thoughts are.

The therapist's goal is not to promote unwarranted optimism but rather to help the client use more reasonable standards of evaluation. For example, a cognitive therapist might point out that a client's failure to get a desired promotion at work may be attributable to many factors and that this setback doesn't mean that the client is incompetent. Gradually, the therapist digs deeper, looking for the unrealistic assumptions that underlie clients' constant negative thinking. These, too, have to be changed.

Unlike client-centered therapists, cognitive therapists are actively involved in determining the pace and direction of treatment. They usually talk extensively in the therapy sessions. They may argue openly with clients as they try to persuade them to alter their patterns of thinking.

"Most people are barely aware of the automatic thoughts which precede unpleasant feelings or automatic inhibitions."
AARON BECK

Kinship with Behavior Therapy

Cognitive therapy borrows heavily from behavioral approaches to treatment, which we will discuss shortly. Specifically, cognitive therapists often use "homework assignments" that focus on changing clients' overt behaviors. Clients may be instructed to engage in overt responses on their own, outside of the clinician's office. For example, one shy, insecure young man in cognitive therapy was told to go to a singles bar and engage three

Table 15.2 Cognitive Errors That Promote Depression, According to Beck's Cognitive Theory

Cognitive Error	Description
Overgeneralizing	If it is true in one case, it applies to any case that is even slightly similar.
Selective abstraction	The only events that matter are failures, deprivation, and so on. I should measure myself by errors, weaknesses, etc.
Excessive responsibility (assuming personal causality)	I am responsible for all bad things, failures, and so on.
Assuming temporal causality (predicting without sufficient evidence)	If it has been true in the past, then it is always going to be true.
Self-references	I am the center of everyone's attention, especially when it comes to bad performances or personal attributes.
"Catastrophizing"	Always think of the worst. It is most likely to happen to you.
Dichotomous thinking	Everything is either one extreme or another (black or white; good or bad).

Source: Beck (1976)

different women in conversations for up to 5 minutes each (Rush, 1984). He was instructed to record his thoughts before and after each of the conversations. This assignment elicited various maladaptive patterns of thought that gave the young man and his therapist plenty to talk about in subsequent sessions. As this example illustrates, cognitive therapy is a creative blend of "talk therapy" and behavior therapy, although it is primarily an insight therapy.

Cognitive therapy was originally designed as a treatment for individuals. However, it has recently been adapted for use with groups (Covi & Primakoff, 1988). Most insight therapies can be conducted on either an individual or group basis (Kaplan & Sadock, 1993), so let's take a look at the dynamics of group therapy.

Group Therapy

Although it dates back to the early part of the 20th century, group therapy came of age during World War II and its aftermath in the 1950s (Rosenbaum, Lakin, & Roback, 1992). During this period, the expanding demand for therapeutic services forced clinicians to use group techniques (Scheidlinger, 1993). *Group therapy* **is the simultaneous treatment of several clients in a group.** Although group therapy can be conducted in a variety of ways, we can provide a general overview of the process as it usually unfolds (see Fuchs, 1984; Vinogradov & Yalom, 1988).

A therapy group typically consists of 4 to 15 people, with 8 participants regarded as an ideal number. The therapist usually screens the participants, excluding persons who seem likely to be disruptive. Some theorists maintain that judicious selection of participants is crucial to effective group treatment (Salvendy, 1993). There is some

debate about whether or not it is best to have a homogeneous group, made up of people who are similar in age, sex, and psychological problem. Practical necessities usually dictate that groups are at least somewhat diversified.

In group therapy, participants essentially function as therapists for one another. Group members describe their problems, trade viewpoints, share experiences, and discuss coping strategies. Most important, they provide acceptance and emotional support for each other. In this supportive atmosphere, group members work at peeling away the social masks that cover their insecurities. Once their problems are exposed, members work at correcting them. As members come to value one another's opinions, they work hard to display healthy changes to win the group's approval.

The therapist plays a subtle role in group therapy, often staying in the background and focusing mainly on promoting group cohesiveness. The therapist models supportive behaviors for the participants and tries to promote a healthy climate. He or she always retains a special status, but the therapist and clients are on much more equal footing in group therapy than in individual therapy. The leader in group therapy typically expresses emotions, shares feelings, and copes with challenges from group members.

Group therapies obviously save time and money, which can be critical in understaffed mental hospitals and other institutional settings. Therapists in private practice usually charge less for group than individual therapy, making therapy affordable for more people. However, group therapy is *not* just a less costly substitute for individual therapy. Group therapy has unique strengths of its own, and certain kinds of problems are especially well suited to group treatment (Piper, 1993; Yalom, 1985).

Whether insight therapies are conducted on a group or an individual basis, clients usually invest considerable time, effort, and money. Are these therapies worth the investment? Let's examine the evidence on their effectiveness.

Evaluating Insight Therapies

Evaluating the effectiveness of any approach to psychotherapy is a complex matter (Garfield, 1992). For one thing, psychological disorders sometimes clear up on their own, a phenomenon called *spontaneous remission*. Hence, if a client experiences a recovery after treatment, one cannot automatically assume that the recovery was attributable to

Insight therapies can be conducted with groups as well as individuals. Group treatments have proven particularly helpful when members share similar problems, such as alcoholism, overeating, or having been sexually abused as a child.

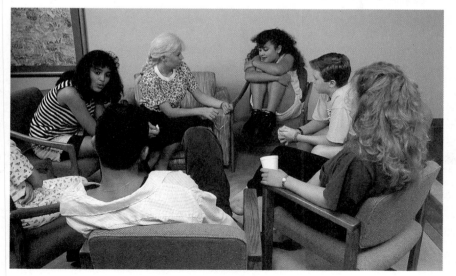

the treatment. Evaluations of insight therapies are especially complicated. If you were to undergo insight therapy, how would you judge its effectiveness? By how you felt? By looking at your behavior? By asking your therapist? By consulting your friends and family? What would you be looking for? Various schools of thought pursue entirely different goals. Thus, judgments of therapeutic outcome in insight therapy tend to be subjective, with little consensus about the best way to assess therapeutic progress (Lambert & Hill, 1994). Moreover, people enter therapy with diverse problems of varied severity, so the efficacy of treatment can only be evaluated meaningfully for specific clinical problems (Goldfried, Greenberg, & Marmar, 1990).

In spite of these difficulties, hundreds of therapy outcome studies have been conducted. These studies have used a diverse array of methods to assess therapeutic outcomes, including scores on psychological tests and ratings by family members, as well as therapists' and clients' ratings. As a whole, these studies consistently indicate that insight therapy is superior to no treatment or placebo treatment and that the effects of therapy are reasonably durable (Lambert & Bergin, 1994; Lipsey & Wilson, 1993). In one widely cited, comprehensive review of research, Smith, Glass, and Miller (1980) examined 475 studies and estimated that the average therapy client ended up better off than 80% of comparable, untreated controls. Admittedly, this outcome research does not indicate that insight therapy leads to miraculous results. The superiority of therapy over no treatment is usually characterized as modest. In light of the price of therapy, there is room for debate about its cost-effectiveness.

BEHAVIOR THERAPIES

Behavior therapy is different from insight therapy in that behavior therapists make no attempt to help clients achieve grand insights about themselves. Why not? Because behavior therapists believe that such insights aren't necessary to produce constructive change. For example, consider a client troubled by compulsive gambling. The behavior therapist doesn't care whether this behavior is rooted in unconscious conflicts or parental rejection. What the client needs is to get rid of the maladaptive behavior. Consequently, the therapist simply designs a program to eliminate the compulsive gambling.

The crux of the difference between insight

CONCEPT CHECK 15.1

Understanding Therapists' Conceptions of Disorders

Check your understanding of the three approaches to insight therapy covered in the text by matching each approach with the appropriate explanation of the typical origins of clients' psychological disorders. The answers are in Appendix A.

Theorized causes of disorders

_____ 1. Problems rooted in pervasive negative thoughts about self and errors in thinking

_____ 2. Problems rooted in unconscious conflicts left over from childhood

_____ 3. Problems rooted in inaccurate self-concept and excessive concern about pleasing others

Therapy

a. Psychoanalysis

b. Client-centered therapy

c. Cognitive therapy

---

therapy and behavior therapy is this: Insight therapists treat pathological symptoms as signs of an underlying problem, whereas behavior therapists think that the symptoms are the problem. Thus, *behavior therapies* **involve the application of the principles of learning to direct efforts to change clients' maladaptive behaviors.**

Behaviorism has been an influential school of thought in psychology since the 1920s. Nevertheless, behaviorists devoted little attention to clinical issues until the 1950s, when behavior therapy emerged out of three independent lines of research fostered by B. F. Skinner and his colleagues (Skinner, Solomon, & Lindsley, 1953) in the United States, Hans Eysenck (1959) and his colleagues in Britain, and Joseph Wolpe (1958) and his colleagues in South Africa (Glass & Arnkoff, 1992). Since then, there has been an explosion of interest in behavioral approaches to psychotherapy.

General Principles

Behavior therapies are based on certain assumptions (Agras & Berkowitz, 1988). *First, it is assumed that behavior is a product of learning.* No matter how self-defeating or pathological a client's behavior might be, the behaviorist believes that it is the result of past conditioning. *Second, it is assumed that what has been learned can be unlearned.* The same learning principles that explain how the maladaptive behavior was acquired can be used to get rid of it. Thus, behavior therapists attempt to change clients' behavior by applying the principles of classical conditioning, operant conditioning, and observational learning.

Behavior therapies are close cousins of the self-modification procedures described in the Chapter 6 Application. Both use the same principles of learning to alter behavior directly. In discussing *self-modification*, we examined some relatively simple procedures that people can apply to themselves to improve everyday self-control. In our discussion of *behavior therapy*, we will examine more complex procedures used by mental health professionals in the treatment of more severe problems.

Like self-modification, behavior therapy requires that clients' vague complaints ("My life is filled with frustration") be translated into concrete behavioral goals ("I need to learn assertive responses for dealing with colleagues"). Once the troublesome behaviors have been targeted, the therapist can design a program to alter these behaviors. The nature of the therapeutic program will depend on the types of problems identified. Specific procedures are designed for specific types of problems, as you'll see in our discussion of systematic desensitization.

Systematic Desensitization

Devised by Joseph Wolpe (1958), systematic desensitization revolutionized psychotherapy by giving therapists their first useful alternative to traditional "talk therapy" (Fishman & Franks, 1992). **Systematic desensitization is a behavior therapy used to reduce clients' anxiety responses through counterconditioning.** The treatment assumes that most anxiety responses are acquired through classical conditioning (as we discussed in Chapter 14). According to this model, a harmless stimulus (for instance, a bridge) may be paired with a fear-arousing event (lightning striking it), so that it becomes a conditioned stimulus eliciting anxiety. The goal of systematic desensitization is to weaken the association between the conditioned stimulus (the bridge) and the conditioned response of anxiety. Systematic desensitization involves three steps.

First, the therapist helps the client build an anxiety hierarchy. The hierarchy is a list of anxiety-arousing stimuli related to the specific source of anxiety, such as flying, academic tests, or snakes. The client ranks the stimuli from the least anxiety arousing to the most anxiety arousing. This ordered list of stimuli is the *anxiety hierarchy*. An example of an anxiety hierarchy for one woman's fear of heights is shown in Figure 15.1.

The second step involves training the client in deep muscle relaxation. This second phase may begin during early sessions while the therapist and client are still constructing the anxiety hierarchy. Various therapists use different relaxation training procedures. Whatever procedures are used, the client must learn to engage in deep, thorough relaxation on command from the therapist.

In the third step, the client tries to work through the hierarchy, learning to remain relaxed while imagining each stimulus. Starting with the least anxiety-arousing stimulus, the client imagines the situation as vividly as possible while relaxing. If the client experiences strong anxiety, he or she drops the imaginary scene and concentrates on relaxation. The client keeps repeating this process until he or she can imagine a scene with little or no anxiety. Once a particular scene is conquered, the client moves on to the next stimulus situation in the anxiety hierarchy. Gradually, over a number of therapy sessions, the client progresses through the hierarchy, unlearning troublesome anxiety responses.

As clients conquer *imagined* phobic stimuli, they may be encouraged to confront the *real* stimuli. Although desensitization to imagined stimuli can be effective by itself, many behavior therapists advocate following it up with direct exposures to the real anxiety-arousing stimuli (Emmelkamp & Scholing, 1990). The desensitization process should reduce anxiety enough so that clients will be able to confront situations they used to avoid. Usually, these real-life confrontations prove harmless, and the person's anxiety response declines further.

According to Wolpe (1958, 1990), the principle

"Neurotic anxiety is nothing but a conditioned response."
JOSEPH WOLPE

Figure 15.1. Example of an anxiety hierarchy. Systematic desensitization requires the construction of an anxiety hierarchy like the one shown here, which was developed for a woman who had a fear of heights but wanted to go hiking in the mountains.

An anxiety hierarchy for systematic desensitization	
Degree of fear	
5	I'm standing on the balcony of the top floor of an apartment tower.
10	I'm standing on a stepladder in the kitchen to change a light bulb.
15	I'm walking on a ridge. The edge is hidden by shrubs and treetops.
20	I'm sitting on the slope of a mountain, looking out over the horizon.
25	I'm crossing a bridge 6 feet above a creek. The bridge consists of an 18-inch-wide board with a handrail on one side.
30	I'm riding a ski lift 8 feet above the ground.
35	I'm crossing a shallow, wide creek on an 18-inch-wide board, 3 feet above water level.
40	I'm climbing a ladder outside the house to reach a second-story window.
45	I'm pulling myself up a 30-degree wet, slippery slope on a steel cable.
50	I'm scrambling up a rock, 8 feet high.
55	I'm walking 10 feet on a resilient, 18-inch-wide board, which spans an 8-foot-deep gulch.
60	I'm walking on a wide plateau, 2 feet from the edge of a cliff.
65	I'm skiing an intermediate hill. The snow is packed.
70	I'm walking over a railway trestle.
75	I'm walking on the side of an embankment. The path slopes to the outside.
80	I'm riding a chair lift 15 feet above the ground.
85	I'm walking up a long, steep slope.
90	I'm walking up (or down) a 15-degree slope on a 3-foot-wide trail. On one side of the trail the terrain drops down sharply; on the other side is a steep upward slope.
95	I'm walking on a 3-foot-wide ridge. The slopes on both sides are long and more than 25 degrees steep.
100	I'm walking on a 3-foot-wide ridge. The trail slopes on one side. The drop on either side of the trail is more than 25 degrees.

at work in systematic desensitization is simple: Anxiety and relaxation are incompatible responses; the trick is to recondition people so that the conditioned stimulus elicits relaxation instead of anxiety. Although it seems deceptively simple, systematic desensitization can be effective in eliminating specific anxieties (Spiegler & Guevremont, 1993).

Aversion Therapy

Aversion therapy is far and away the most controversial of the behavior therapies. It's not something that you would sign up for unless you were pretty desperate. Psychologists usually suggest it only as a treatment of last resort, after other interventions have failed. What's so terrible about aversion therapy? The client has to endure decidedly unpleasant stimuli, such as shock or drug-induced nausea.

Aversion therapy **is a behavior therapy in which an aversive stimulus is paired with a stimulus that elicits an undesirable response.** For example, alcoholics have had an *emetic drug* (one that causes nausea and vomiting) paired with their favorite drinks during therapy sessions (Cannon, Baker, & Wehl, 1981). By pairing the drug with alcohol, the therapist hopes to create a conditioned aversion to alcohol (see Figure 15.2).

Aversion therapy takes advantage of the automatic nature of responses produced through classical conditioning. Admittedly, alcoholics treated with aversion therapy know that they won't be given an emetic outside of their therapy sessions. However, their reflex response to the stimulus of alcohol may be changed so they respond to it with nausea and distaste. Obviously, this response should make it much easier to resist the urge to drink.

Troublesome behaviors eliminated successfully with aversion therapy have included drug abuse, sexual deviance, gambling, shoplifting, stuttering, cigarette smoking, and overeating (Sandler, 1975; Wolpe, 1990). Typically, aversion therapy is only one element in a larger treatment program. Of course, this procedure should be used only with willing clients when other options have failed (Rimm & Cunningham, 1985).

Social Skills Training

Many psychological problems grow out of interpersonal difficulties. Behavior therapists point out that people are not born with social finesse—they acquire social skills through learning. Unfortunately, some people have not learned how to be friendly, how to make conversation, how

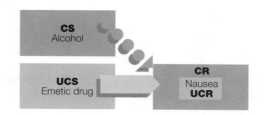

Figure 15.2. Aversion therapy. Aversion therapy uses classical conditioning to create an aversion to a stimulus that has elicited problematic behavior. For example, in the treatment of drinking problems, alcohol may be paired with a nausea-inducing drug to create an aversion to drinking.

to express anger appropriately, and so forth. Social ineptitude can contribute to anxiety, feelings of inferiority, and various kinds of disorders. In light of these findings, therapists are increasingly using social skills training in efforts to improve clients' social abilities (Liberman, Mueser, & DeRisi, 1989). This approach has yielded promising results in the treatment of depression, shyness, social anxiety, and even schizophrenia (Becker, 1990; Wixted, Bellack, & Hersen, 1990).

Social skills training **is a behavior therapy designed to improve interpersonal skills that emphasizes modeling, behavioral rehearsal, and shaping.** This type of behavior therapy can be conducted with individual clients or in groups. *Modeling* is used by encouraging clients to watch socially skilled friends and colleagues, so that they can acquire appropriate responses (eye contact, active listening, and so on) through observation. In *behavioral rehearsal*, the client tries to practice social techniques in structured role-playing exercises. The therapist provides corrective feedback and uses approval to reinforce progress. Eventually, of course, clients try their newly acquired skills in real-world interactions. Usually, they are given specific homework assignments. *Shaping* is used in that clients are gradually asked to handle more complicated and delicate social situations. For example, a nonassertive client may begin by

CONCEPT CHECK 15.2
Understanding the Types of Behavior Therapy

Check your understanding of the different varieties of behavior therapy discussed in your text by matching each therapy with the appropriate description. Choose from the following: (a) systematic desensitization, (b) social skills training, and (c) aversion therapy. The answers are in Appendix A.

_____ 1. Anxiety is reduced by conditioning the client to respond positively to stimuli that previously aroused anxiety.

_____ 2. Unwanted behaviors are eliminated by conditioning the client to have an unpleasant response to stimuli that previously triggered the behavior.

_____ 3. Behavioral techniques are used to teach clients new behaviors aimed at enhancing the quality of their interactions with others.

working on making requests of friends. Only much later will he be asked to tackle standing up to his boss at work.

Evaluating Behavior Therapies

How does the effectiveness of behavior therapy compare to that of insight therapy? In direct comparisons, the differences are usually small. However, these modest differences tend to favor behavioral approaches for certain types of disorders (Lambert & Bergin, 1992). Of course, behavior therapies are not well suited to the treatment of some types of problems (vague feelings of discontent, for instance). Furthermore, it's misleading to make global statements about the effectiveness of behavior therapies, because they include many procedures designed for different purposes. For example, the value of systematic desensitization for phobias has no bearing on the value of aversion therapy for sexual deviance.

For our purposes, it is sufficient to note that there is favorable evidence on the efficacy of most of the widely used behavioral interventions. Behavior therapies can make important contributions to the treatment of phobias, obsessive-compulsive disorders, sexual dysfunction, schizophrenia, drug-related problems, eating disorders, psychosomatic disorders, hyperactivity, autism, and mental retardation (Emmelkamp, 1994; Liberman & Bedell, 1989).

Many of these problems would not be amenable to treatment with the biomedical therapies, which we consider next. To some extent, the three major approaches to treatment have different strengths.

CONCEPT CHECK 15.3
Understanding Therapists' Goals

Check your understanding of therapists' goals by matching various therapies with the appropriate description. The answers are in Appendix A.

Principal therapeutic goals

_____ 1. Elimination of maladaptive behaviors or symptoms

_____ 2. Acceptance of genuine self, personal growth

_____ 3. Recovery of unconscious conflicts, character reconstruction

_____ 4. Detection and reduction of negative thinking

Therapy
a. Psychoanalysis
b. Client-centered therapy
c. Cognitive therapy
d. Behavior therapy

Let's see where the strengths of the biomedical therapies lie.

BIOMEDICAL THERAPIES

Biomedical therapies **are physiological interventions intended to reduce symptoms associated with psychological disorders.** These therapies assume that psychological disorders are caused, at least in part, by biological malfunctions. As we discussed in the previous chapter, this assumption clearly has merit for many disorders, especially the more severe ones. We will discuss two biomedical approaches to psychotherapy: drug therapy and electroconvulsive (shock) therapy.

Treatment with Drugs

Psychopharmacotherapy **is the treatment of mental disorders with medication,** which we will refer to more simply as *drug therapy*. Therapeutic drugs fall into three major groups (with one notable "leftover" that doesn't fit neatly into any of the basic categories): antianxiety drugs, antipsychotic drugs, and antidepressant drugs. The leftover is lithium, which is used in the treatment of bipolar mood disorders.

Antianxiety Drugs

You probably know someone who pops pills to relieve anxiety. *Antianxiety drugs*, **which relieve tension, apprehension, and nervousness,** are the drugs used in this common coping strategy. The most popular of these drugs are Valium and Xanax. These are trade names for the generic drugs diazepam and alprazolam, respectively.

In everyday language, Valium, Xanax, and similar drugs are called *tranquilizers*. These drugs are routinely prescribed for people with anxiety disorders. They are also given to millions of people who simply suffer from chronic nervous tension. In the mid 1970s, U.S. pharmacists were filling nearly *100 million* prescriptions each year for Valium and similar antianxiety drugs. Many critics characterized this level of use as excessive (Lickey & Gordon, 1991). Antianxiety drugs exert their effects almost immediately. They can be fairly effective in alleviating feelings of anxiety (Lader, 1984). However, their effects are measured in hours, so their impact is relatively short lived.

All the drugs used to treat psychological disorders have potentially troublesome side effects that show up in some patients, but not others. The antianxiety drugs are no exception. The most common side effects of Valium and Xanax are listed in Table 15.3. Some of these side effects—such as drowsiness, nausea, and confusion—present serious problems for certain patients. Another drawback is that antianxiety drugs can be abused, and some people become dependent on them (Salzman, 1989). Concerns about the abuse of tranquilizers led to a moderate decline in their use in the 1980s. Currently, researchers are studying the effects of a new antianxiety drug called Buspar (buspirone) that has less potential for abuse (Gorman & Davis, 1989). Unlike Valium, Buspar is slow acting, exerting its effects in seven to ten days, but with fewer sedative side effects (Norman & Burrows, 1990).

Antipsychotic Drugs

Antipsychotic drugs are used primarily in the treatment of schizophrenia. They are also given to people with severe mood disorders who become delusional. The trade names (and generic names) of some prominent drugs in this category are Thorazine (chlorpromazine), Mellaril (thioridazine), and Haldol (haloperidol). *Antipsychotic drugs* **are used to gradually reduce psychotic symptoms, including hyperactivity, mental confusion, hallucinations, and delusions.**

Studies suggest that about 90% of psychotic patients respond favorably (albeit in varied degrees) to antipsychotic medication (Davis, Barter, & Kane, 1989). When antipsychotic drugs are effective, they work their magic gradually, as shown in Figure 15.3. Patients usually begin to respond within two days to a week. Further improvement may occur for several months. Many schizophrenic patients are placed on antipsychotics indefinitely because these drugs can reduce the likelihood of a relapse into an active schizophrenic episode.

Antipsychotic drugs undeniably make a major contribution to the treatment of severe mental disorders, but they are not without problems. They have many unpleasant side effects (Lader & Herrington, 1990). Drowsiness, constipation, and cottonmouth are common. Tremors, muscular rigidity, and impaired coordination may also occur. After being released from a hospital, many patients who have been placed on antipsychotics discontinue their drug regimen because of the side effects. Unfortunately, relapse into another schizophrenic episode often occurs within three to nine months after a patient stops taking antipsychotic medication (Davis, 1985).

In addition to minor side effects, antipsychotics may cause a more severe and lasting problem

Table 15.3 Side Effects of Xanax and Valium

Side Effects	Patients Experiencing Side Effects (%)	
	Xanax	Valium
Drowsiness	36.0	49.4
Lightheadedness	18.6	24.0
Dry mouth	14.9	13.0
Depression	11.9	17.0
Nausea, vomiting	9.3	10.0
Constipation	9.3	11.3
Insomnia	9.0	6.7
Confusion	9.3	14.1
Diarrhea	8.5	10.5
Tachycardia, palpitations	8.1	7.2
Nasal congestion	8.1	7.2
Blurred vision	7.0	9.1

Source: Evans (1981)

called *tardive dyskinesia*. ***Tardive dyskinesia* is a neurological disorder marked by involuntary writhing and ticlike movements of the mouth, tongue, face, hands, or feet.** Tardive dyskinesia can be reversed if it is detected early and the patient is taken off antipsychotic medication. Once this debilitating syndrome is established, however, there is no cure. There has been a heated debate about how often this serious side effect occurs as a result of antipsychotic drug therapy (Brown & Funk, 1986). Recent evidence suggests that it occurs in a little less than 20% of patients who take antipsychotics over a prolonged period (Khot & Wyatt, 1991). As the prevalence of this problem has come to be recognized, many experts have urged psychiatrists to be more conservative about prescribing antipsychotic drugs on a long-term basis, but reliance on antipsychotics has

Figure 15.3. The time course of antipsychotic drug effects. Antipsychotic drugs reduce psychotic symptoms gradually, over a span of weeks, as graphed here. In contrast, patients given placebo pills show little improvement. (Data from Cole, Goldberg, & Davis, 1966; Davis, 1985)

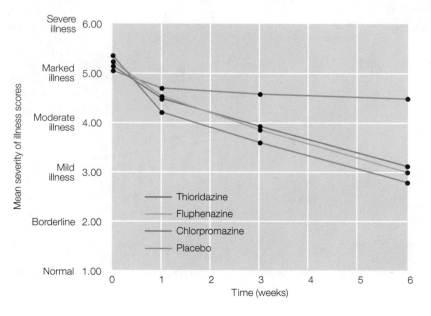

remained stable because of the lack of effective alternatives (Cohen & McCubbin, 1990).

A new antipsychotic drug called Clozaril (clozapine) was introduced in 1990. Unlike older antipsychotics, which exert their effects at dopamine synapses (see Chapters 3 and 14), Clozaril apparently alters neurotransmitter activity at serotonin synapses (Kahn et al., 1993). Although it's not risk-free, it seems to produce fewer side effects than traditional antipsychotics. Unfortunately, at present the cost of Clozaril therapy is prohibitively expensive, running about $5000 per year for each patient (Jann, Jenike, & Lieberman, 1994).

Antidepressant Drugs

As their name suggests, **antidepressant drugs gradually elevate mood and help bring people out of a depression.** Until recently, there were two principal classes of antidepressants: *tricyclics* (such as Elavil) and *MAO inhibitors* (such as Nardil). These two sets of drugs affect neurochemical activity in different ways and tend to work with different patients. The tricyclics are effective for a larger portion (60%–80%) of depressed patients (Davis & Glassman, 1989). They also have less-problematic side effects than the MAO inhibitors (Davidson, 1992). Like antipsychotic drugs, antidepressants exert their effects gradually over a period of weeks, rather than immediately.

Psychiatrists are currently enthusiastic about a new class of antidepressants, called *selective serotonin reuptake inhibitors*, which slow the reuptake process at serotonin synapses. The drugs in this class, which include Prozac (fluoxetine), Paxil

Prozac, an extremely popular antidepressant agent, has received a lot of publicity as a psychotherapeutic wonder drug. However, like all drugs for psychological disorders, Prozac has risks that must be carefully weighed againts its benefits.

(paroxetine), and Zoloft (sertraline), seem to yield rapid therapeutic gains in the treatment of depression (Jann et al., 1994). Prozac also appears to have value in the treatment of obsessive-compulsive disorders (Jenike, Baer, & Greist, 1990). However, Prozac is not a "miracle drug," as suggested by some popular magazines. A small minority of patients on Prozac have developed serious, unexpected side effects, such as intense suicidal preoccupations (Teicher, Glod, & Cole, 1990). Like all drugs for psychological disorders, Prozac has risks that must be carefully weighed against its benefits.

Lithium

Lithium **is a chemical used to control mood swings in patients with bipolar mood disorders.** It has excellent value in preventing *future* episodes of both mania and depression in patients with bipolar illness (Jefferson & Greist, 1989). Lithium can also be used in efforts to bring patients with bipolar illness out of *current* manic or depressed episodes. However, antipsychotics and antidepressants are more frequently used for these purposes. On the negative side of the ledger, lithium has some dangerous side effects if its use isn't managed skillfully (Abou-Saleh, 1992). Lithium levels in the patient's blood must be monitored carefully, because high concentrations can be toxic (and even fatal). Kidney and thyroid gland complications are the major problems associated with lithium therapy (Post, 1989).

Evaluating Drug Therapies

Drug therapies can produce clear therapeutic gains for many kinds of patients. What's especially impressive is that they can be effective with severe disorders that otherwise defy therapeutic endeavors. Nonetheless, drug therapies are controversial for two reasons.

First, some critics argue that drug therapies often produce superficial curative effects (Lickey & Gordon, 1991). For example, Valium does not really solve problems with anxiety. It merely provides temporary relief from an unpleasant symptom. Moreover, this temporary relief may lull patients into complacency about their problem and prevent them from working toward a more lasting solution. Thus, drug therapies may be more of a band-aid than a cure for psychological disorders.

Second, critics charge that many drugs are overprescribed and that many patients are overmedicated (Breggin, 1991; Leavitt, 1982). Drug interventions can be all too appealing as apparent "solutions" to psychiatrists and other hospital personnel. Writing out a prescription is much less challenging than conducting insight therapy or designing a behavior therapy program. Thus, many physicians habitually hand out prescriptions without giving adequate consideration to more complicated interventions. This problem is compounded by the fact that drugs calm patients, making it easier for hospital staff to run their wards. Thus, critics argue that there's a tendency in some institutions to overmedicate patients to minimize disruptive behavior.

Electroconvulsive Therapy (ECT)

In the 1930s, a Hungarian psychiatrist named Ladislas von Meduna speculated that epilepsy and schizophrenia could not coexist in the same body. On the basis of this observation, which turned out to be inaccurate, von Meduna theorized that it might be useful to induce epileptic-like seizures in schizophrenic patients. Initially, a drug was used to trigger these seizures. However, by 1938 a pair of Italian psychiatrists (Cerletti & Bini, 1938) demonstrated that it was safer to elicit the seizures with electric shock. Thus, modern electroconvulsive therapy was born.

Electroconvulsive therapy (ECT) **is a biomedical treatment in which electric shock is used to produce a cortical seizure accompanied by convulsions.** In ECT, electrodes are attached to the skull over the temporal lobes of the brain (see the adjacent photo). A light anesthesia is induced, and the patient is given a variety of drugs to minimize the likelihood of complications, such as spinal fractures. An electric current is then applied for about a second. The current triggers a brief (5–20 seconds) convulsive seizure, during which the patient usually loses consciousness. The patient normally awakes in an hour or two. People typically receive between 6 and 20 treatments as inpatients at a hospital (Fink, 1992).

The clinical use of ECT peaked in the 1940s and 1950s, before effective drug therapies were widely available. ECT has long been controversial, and its use did decline in the 1960s and 1970s. Nonetheless, there has been a recent resurgence in the use of ECT, and it is not a *rare* form of therapy. Estimates suggest that about 100,000 people receive ECT treatments yearly in the United States, mainly for depression (Rymer, 1989).

Effectiveness of ECT

The effectiveness of ECT is hotly debated. Ardent proponents maintain that it is a remarkably effective treatment (Abrams, 1992; Fink, 1992; Swartz, 1993). However, equally ardent opponents argue that it is no more effective than a placebo (Breggin, 1991; Friedberg, 1976). Reported improvement rates for ECT treatment range from negligible to very high (Small, Small, & Milstein, 1986). The findings on relapse rates after treatment are also inconsistent (Frank, 1990; Weiner, 1984).

In light of these problems, conclusions about the value of ECT must be tentative. Although ECT was once considered appropriate for a wide range of disorders, even most proponents now recommend it only for mood disorders (especially depression). Overall, there does seem to be enough favorable evidence to justify *conservative* use of ECT in treating severe mood disorders (Rudorfer & Goodwin, 1993; Weiner & Coffey, 1988). However, the possible benefits of ECT need to be weighed against the possible risks, which some critics believe are substantial.

Risks Associated with ECT

Even ECT proponents acknowledge that memory losses, impaired attention, and other cognitive deficits are common short-term side effects of electroconvulsive therapy. However, proponents assert that these deficits are mild and usually last less than six months (Calev et al., 1993). In contrast, ECT critics maintain that these cognitive losses are significant and often permanent (Breggin, 1991; Frank, 1990).

So, what can be concluded about ECT and cognitive deficits? The truth probably lies some-

This patient is being prepared for electroconvulsive therapy (ECT). In ECT an electric shock is used to elicit a brief cortical seizure. The shock is delivered through electrodes attached to the patient's skull.

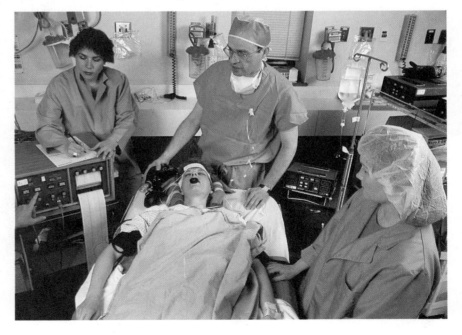

where in between the positions staked out by the proponents and opponents of ECT. In an unusually dispassionate review of the ECT controversy, Small and associates (1986) asserted that "there is little doubt that ECT produces both short- and long-term intellectual impairment." However, they concluded that this impairment isn't inevitable and that it isn't permanent in the vast majority of cases.

It appears that the use of ECT will remain controversial for some time to come. Perhaps more objective empirical research will eventually resolve some of the debates swirling around ECT.

BLENDING APPROACHES TO PSYCHOTHERAPY

In this chapter we have reviewed many approaches to therapy. However, there is no law that a client must be treated with just one approach. Often, a clinician will use several techniques in working with a client. For example, a depressed person might receive cognitive therapy (an insight therapy), social skills training (a behavior therapy), and antidepressant medication (a biomedical therapy). Multiple approaches are particularly likely when a treatment *team* provides therapy. Studies suggest that there is merit in combining approaches to treatment (Frank, 1991; Klerman et al., 1994).

The value of multiple approaches may explain why a significant trend seems to have crept into the field of psychotherapy: a movement away from strong loyalty to individual schools of thought and a corresponding move toward integrating various approaches to therapy (Arkowitz, 1992; Norcross

& Goldfried, 1992). Most clinicians used to depend exclusively on one system of therapy while rejecting the utility of all others. This era of fragmentation may be drawing to a close. In recent surveys of psychologists' theoretical orientations, researchers have been surprised to find that the greatest proportion of respondents described themselves as *eclectic* in approach (Garfield & Bergin, 1994) (see Figure 15.4). Eclecticism in the practice of therapy involves drawing ideas from two or more systems of therapy, instead of committing to just one system.

Increasing eclecticism is only one of several recent trends in the field of psychotherapy. Many other changes have also occurred in the delivery of mental health services. We'll examine some of these changes in the next two sections, which discuss efforts to respond to increasing cultural diversity in America and shifting patterns of institutional care for mental disorders.

CULTURE AND THERAPY

Modern psychotherapy emerged during the second half of the 19th century in Europe and America, spawned in part by a cultural milieu that viewed the self as an independent, reflective, rational being, capable of self-improvement (Cushman, 1992). Psychological disorders were assumed to have natural causes like physical diseases and to be amenable to medical treatments derived from scientific research. But the individualized, medicalized institution of modern psychotherapy reflects Western cultural values that are far from universal (Dana, 1993). In many nonindustrialized societies, psychological disorders are attributed to supernatural forces (possession, withcraft, angry gods, and so forth), and victims seek help from priests, shamans, and folk healers, rather than doctors (Wittkower & Warnes, 1984). Thus, efforts to export Western psychotherapies to non-Western cultures have met with mixed success. Indeed, the highly culture-bound origins of modern therapies have raised questions about their applicability to ethnic minorities *within* Western culture.

Research on how cultural factors influence the process and outcome of psychotherapy has burgeoned in recent years, motivated in part by the need to improve mental health services for ethnic minority groups in American society. The data are ambiguous for a couple of ethnic groups, but studies suggest that American minority groups

Figure 15.4. The leading approaches to therapy among psychologists. The pooled data from a survey of 415 clinical and counseling psychologists (Smith, 1982) and another survey of 479 clinical psychologists (Norcross & Prochaska, 1982) indicate that the most widely used approaches to therapy are (in order) eclectic, psychodynamic, behavioral, cognitive, and client-centered.

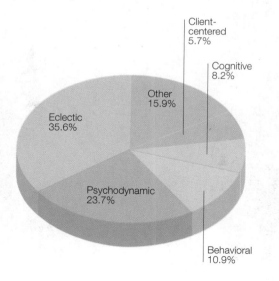

Client-centered 5.7%

Cognitive 8.2%

Other 15.9%

Eclectic 35.6%

Psychodynamic 23.7%

Behavioral 10.9%

generally underutilize therapeutic services (Mays & Albee, 1992). Why? A variety of barriers appear to contribute to this problem, including the following (Cheung, 1991; Mays & Albee, 1992; Sue, Zane, & Young, 1994):

1. *Cultural barriers.* In times of psychological distress, some cultural groups are reluctant to turn to formal, professional sources of assistance. Given their socialization, they prefer to rely on informal assistance from family members, the clergy, respected elders, herbalists, acupuncturists, and so forth, who share their cultural heritage. Many members of minority groups have a history of frustrating interactions with American bureaucracies and are distrustful of large, intimidating, foreign institutions, such as hospitals and community mental health centers.

2. *Language barriers.* Effective communication is crucial to the provision of psychotherapy. But most hospitals and mental health agencies are not adequately staffed with therapists who speak the languages used by minority groups in their service areas. The resulting communication problems make it awkward and difficult for many minority group members to explain their problems and obtain the type of help they need.

3. *Access barriers.* Many minority groups suffer from elevated rates of joblessness and poverty. In our society, people who are unemployed or employed in economically marginal jobs typically do not have health insurance. Their lack of health insurance severely restricts their options in pursuing treatment for psychological problems.

4. *Institutional barriers.* When all is said and done, Stanley Sue and Nolan Zane (1987) argue that the "single most important explanation for the problems in service delivery involves the inability of therapists to provide culturally responsive forms of treatment" (p. 37). The vast majority of therapists have been trained almost exclusively in the treatment of white middle-class Americans and are not familiar with the cultural backgrounds and unique characteristics of various ethnic groups. This culture gap often leads to misunderstandings and ill-advised treatment strategies (Hughes, 1993). Unfortunately, there is a grievous shortage of ethnic therapists to meet the needs of various ethnic groups (Mays & Albee, 1992).

What can be done to improve mental health services for American minority groups? Researchers in this area have offered a variety of

---

CONCEPT CHECK 15.4

Understanding Biomedical Therapies

Check your understanding of how psychiatrists use biomedical therapies by matching each treatment with its chief use. The answers are in Appendix A.

Treatment

_____ 1. Antianxiety drugs

_____ 2. Antipsychotic drugs

_____ 3. Antidepressant drugs

_____ 4. Lithium

_____ 5. Electroconvulsive therapy (ECT)

Chief purpose

a. To reduce psychotic symptoms

b. To bring a major depression to an end

c. To suppress tension, nervousness, and apprehension

d. To prevent future episodes of mania or depression in people with bipolar mood disorders

---

suggestions (Homma-True et al., 1993; Pedersen, 1994; Sue & Zane, 1987; Yamamoto et al., 1993). Discussions of possible solutions usually begin with the need to recruit and train more ethnic minority therapists. Studies show that ethnic minorities are more likely to go to mental health facilities that are staffed by a higher proportion of people who share their ethnic background (Sue et al., 1994). Furthermore, clients' satisfaction with therapy tends to be greater when they are treated by therapists from their own culture. Therapists can also be given special training to work more effectively with people from different cultural backgrounds. For example, Wade and Bernstein (1991) found that

Cultural barriers have emerged in the psychotherapy process. A number of minority groups in the United States shy away from using professional services in this field. Those who try it also tend to quickly terminate treatment more often than white Americans.

a cultural sensitivity training program for white therapists working with an African American clientele resulted in improved client satisfaction. Finally, most authorities urge further investigation of how traditional approaches to therapy can be modified and tailored to be more compatible with specific cultural groups' attitudes, values, norms, and traditions.

![gray bar]

INSTITUTIONAL TREATMENT IN TRANSITION

Traditionally, much of the treatment of mental illness has been carried out in institutional settings, primarily in mental hospitals. **A *mental hospital* is a medical institution specializing in providing inpatient care for psychological disorders.** In the United States, a national network of state-funded mental hospitals started to emerge in the 1840s through the efforts of Dorothea Dix and other reformers (see Figure 15.5). Prior to these reforms, the mentally ill who were poor were housed in jails and poorhouses or were left to wander the countryside. Today, mental hospitals continue to play an important role in the delivery of mental health services. However, since World War II, institutional care for mental illness has under-

gone a series of major transitions—and the dust hasn't settled yet. Let's look at how institutional care has evolved in recent decades.

Disenchantment with Mental Hospitals

By the 1950s, it had become apparent that public mental hospitals were not fulfilling their goals very well (Mechanic, 1980). Experts began to realize that hospitalization often *contributed* to the development of pathology instead of curing it.

What were the causes of these unexpected negative effects? Part of the problem was that the facilities were usually underfunded (Bloom, 1984). The lack of adequate funding meant that the facilities were overcrowded and understaffed. Hospital personnel were undertrained and overworked, making them hard-pressed to deliver minimal custodial care. Despite gallant efforts at treatment, the demoralizing conditions made most public mental hospitals decidedly nontherapeutic (Scull, 1990).

These problems were aggravated by the fact that state mental hospitals served large geographic regions but were rarely placed near major population centers. Hence, most patients were uprooted from their community. Institutionalized 50, 100, or 300 miles from their homes, they lost contact with their families, friends, and employers. This

Figure 15.5. Dorothea Dix and the advent of mental hospitals in America. During the 19th century, Dorothea Dix campaigned tirelessly to obtain funds for building mental hospitals. Many of these hospitals, such as the New York State Lunatic Asylum shown here, were extremely large facilities. Although public mental hospitals improved the care of the mentally ill, they had a variety of shortcomings, which eventually prompted the deinstitutionalization movement.

isolation deprived the patients of needed social support and made their potential return to the community more difficult. Thus, critics concluded that there were fundamental flaws in our system of mental hospitals.

Disenchantment with the public mental hospital system inspired the *community mental health movement* that emerged in the 1960s (Scull, 1990). The community mental health movement emphasizes (1) local, community-based care, (2) reduced dependence on hospitalization, and (3) the prevention of psychological disorders. The community mental health movement jumped into prominence in 1963 when John F. Kennedy became the first American president ever to address the nation on the subject of mental health. Kennedy enthusiastically endorsed the community mental health philosophy. He outlined an ambitious plan to build a national network of community mental health centers that would operate according to this philosophy. Thus, in the 1960s much of the responsibility for the treatment of psychological disorders was turned over to community mental health centers, which supplement mental hospitals with decentralized and more accessible services.

Deinstitutionalization

Mental hospitals continue to care for many people troubled by chronic mental illness, but their role in patient care has diminished. Since the 1960s, a policy of deinstitutionalization has been followed by the American mental health care establishment. *Deinstitutionalization* **refers to transferring the treatment of mental illness from inpatient institutions to community-based facilities that emphasize outpatient care.** This shift in responsibility was made possible by two developments: (1) the emergence of effective drug therapies for severe disorders and (2) the deployment of community mental health centers to coordinate local care (Wyatt, 1985).

The exodus of patients from mental hospitals has been dramatic. In 1955 about *one-half* of the hospital beds in the United States were occupied by psychiatric patients. Today that figure has declined to about one-fourth (Kiesler, 1993). The average inpatient population in state and county mental hospitals has dropped from a peak of nearly 550,000 in the mid-1950s to around 90,000 today, as shown in Figure 15.6. These trends do *not* mean that hospitalization for mental illness has become a thing of the past. A great many people are still hospitalized, but there's been a shift toward plac-

ing them in local general hospitals for brief periods instead of distant psychiatric hospitals for long periods (Kiesler, 1992). In keeping with the philosophy of deinstitutionalization, these local facilities try to get patients stabilized and back into the community as swiftly as possible.

How has deinstitutionalization worked out? It gets mixed reviews. On the positive side, many people have benefited by avoiding disruptive and unnecessary hospitalization. Ample evidence suggests that alternatives to hospitalization can be both more effective and less costly than inpatient care (Kiesler, 1982, 1992). Moreover, many authorities maintain that treatment *inside* mental hospitals has improved because of deinstitutionalization. This improvement would have been virtually impossible if the patient population hadn't been brought down to a more manageable size.

Unfortunately, some unanticipated problems have arisen (A. Johnson, 1990; Scull, 1990). Many patients suffering from chronic psychological disorders had nowhere to go when they were released. They had no families, friends, or homes to return to. Many had no work skills and were poorly prepared to live on their own. These people were supposed to be absorbed by "halfway houses," sheltered workshops, and other types of intermediate care facilities. Unfortunately, many communities were never able to fund and build the planned facilities. Meanwhile, the increased burden on community mental health centers left them strapped to provide needed services.

To some extent, patients were released into communities that weren't prepared to handle them. Thus, deinstitutionalization left two major problems in its wake: a "revolving door" population of people who flow in and out of psychiatric facilities, and a sizable population of homeless mentally ill people.

Mental Illness, the Revolving Door, and Homelessness

Although the proportion of hospital days attributable to mental illness has dwindled, admission

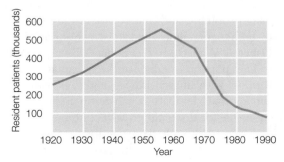

Figure 15.6. Declining inpatient population at state and county mental hospitals. The inpatient population in public mental hospitals has declined dramatically since the late 1950s, as a result of deinstitutionalization and the use of drug therapy. (Data from the National Institute of Mental Health)

Figure 15.7. Percentage
of psychiatric inpatient
admissions that are re-
admissions. The extent of
the revolving door problem
is apparent from these figures on the percentage of
inpatient admissions that are
readmissions at various
types of facilities. (Data from
the National Institute of
Mental Health)

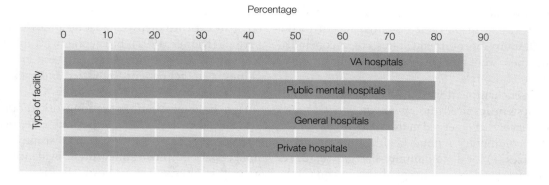

rates for psychiatric hospitalization have actually climbed. What has happened? Deinstitutionalization and drug therapy have created a revolving door through which many mentally ill people pass again and again (Geller, 1992).

Most of the people caught in the mental health system's revolving door suffer from chronic, severe disorders (usually schizophrenia) that frequently require hospitalization. However, they respond well to drug therapies in the hospital. Once they're stabilized through drug therapy, they no longer qualify for expensive hospital treatment according to the new standards created by deinstitutionalization. Thus, they're sent back out the door, into communities that often aren't prepared to provide adequate outpatient care. Because they lack appropriate care and support, their condition deteriorates and they soon require readmission to a hospital, where the cycle begins once again. Studies reveal that 50% of the patients released from public mental hospitals are readmitted within one year (Kiesling, 1983). Over two-thirds of all psychiatric inpatient admissions involve rehospitalizing a former patient, as Figure 15.7 shows.

Deinstitutionalization has also been blamed for the growing population of homeless people. Studies *have* consistently found elevated rates of mental illness among the homeless. Taken as a whole, the evidence suggests that roughly one-third of the homeless suffer from severe mental illness (schizophrenic and mood disorders), that another one-third or so are struggling with alcohol and drug problems, and that 10%–20% are troubled by both mental illness and substance abuse (Drake, Osher, & Wallach, 1991; Fischer & Breakey, 1991).

The popular media routinely equate homelessness with mental illness, and it is widely assumed that deinstitutionalization is largely responsible for the rapid growth of homelessness in America. Although deinstitutionalization probably has contributed to the growth of homeless-

ness, many experts in this area maintain that it is misleading to blame the problem of homelessness chiefly on deinstitutionalization (Kanter, 1989; Kiesler, 1991). They note, for instance, that although mental illness is common among the homeless, studies suggest that only about 5%–7% of the homeless population require psychiatric hospitalization (Dennis et al., 1991).

Those who criticize the tendency to equate homelessness with mental illness worry that this equation diverts attention from the real causes of the homelessness crisis (Kiesler, 1991). They marshall evidence to show that the sharp increase in the homeless population is due to a variety economic, social, and political trends, including increased unemployment and poverty, decreased support for welfare and subsidized housing programs, the loss of much low-income housing to urban renewal, and so forth (Cohen & Thompson, 1992; McCarty et al., 1991; Rossi, 1990). They maintain that homelessness is primarily an economic problem and that it requires economic solutions.

In light of the revolving door problem and homelessness among the mentally ill, what can we conclude about deinstitutionalization? It appears to be a worthwhile idea that has been poorly executed. Overall, the policy has probably been a benefit to countless people with milder disorders but a cruel trick on many others with severe, chronic disorders. Ultimately, it's clear that our society is not providing adequate care for a sizable segment of the mentally ill population (Shadish, Lurigio, & Lewis, 1989). That's not a new development. Inadequate care for mental illness has always been the norm. Societies always struggle with the problem of what to do with the mentally ill and how to pay for their care (English & McCarrick, 1989).

What's the solution? Virtually no one advocates returning to the era of custodial warehouses. Many do advocate increasing the quality and availability

Table 15.4 Comparison of Major Approaches to Psychotherapy

Type of Psychotherapy	Primary Founders	Origin of Disorder	Therapeutic Goals	Therapeutic Techniques
Psychoanalysis	Freud	Unconscious conflicts resulting from fixations in earlier development	Insights regarding unconscious conflicts and motives; personality reconstruction	Free association, dream analysis, interpretation, catharsis, transference
Client-centered therapy	Rogers	Incongruence between self-concept and actual experience; dependence on acceptance from others	Congruence between self-concept and experience; acceptance of genuine self; self-determination; personal growth	Genuineness, empathy, unconditional positive regard, clarification, reflecting back to client
Cognitive therapy	Beck Ellis	Irrational assumptions and negative, self-defeating thinking about events related to self	Detection of negative thinking; substitution of more realistic thinking	Thought stopping, recording automatic thoughts, refuting negative thinking, reattribution, homework assignments
Behavior therapy	Wolpe Bandura	Maladaptive patterns of behavior acquired through learning	Elimination of symptomatic, maladaptive behaviors; acquisition of more adaptive responses	Classical and operant conditioning, reinforcement, punishment, extinction, shaping, aversive conditioning, systematic desensitization, social skills training, biofeedback
Biomedical therapies		Physiological malfunction, primarily abnormal neurotransmitter activity	Elimination of symptoms; prevention of relapse	Antipsychotic, antianxiety, and antidepressant drugs; lithium; electroconvulsive therapy (ECT)

of intermediate care facilities and programs (Drake et al., 1991; McCarty et al., 1991). Only time will tell whether American society will be willing to make the financial commitment to follow through on this recommendation.

PUTTING IT IN PERSPECTIVE

In our discussion of psychotherapy, one of our unifying themes—the value of theoretical diversity—was particularly prominent, and one other theme—the importance of culture—surfaced briefly. Let's discuss the latter theme first. The approaches to psychotherapy described in this chapter are products of modern, white, middle-class, Western culture. Some of these therapies have proven useful in some other cultures, but many have turned out to be irrelevant or counterproductive when used with different cultural groups, including ethnic minorities in Western society. Thus, we have seen once again that cultural factors influence psychological processes and that Western psychology cannot assume that its theories and practices have universal applicability.

As for theoretical diversity, its value can be illustrated with a rhetorical question: Can you imagine what the state of modern psychotherapy would be if everyone in psychology and psychiatry had simply accepted Freud's theories about the nature and treatment of psychological disorders? If not for theoretical diversity, psychotherapy might still be in the dark ages. Psychoanalysis can

be a useful method of therapy, but it would be a tragic state of affairs if it were the *only* treatment available to people experiencing psychological distress. Multitudes of people have benefited from alternative approaches to treatment, such as client-centered therapy, cognitive therapy, behavior therapies, and biomedical therapies. These alternatives emerged out of tension between psychoanalytic theory and the four other major theoretical perspectives identified in Chapter 1: the humanistic perspective (which generated client-centered therapy), the behavioral perspective (behavior therapies), the physiological perspective (biomedical therapies), and the cognitive perspective (cognitive therapy).

We've seen throughout this text that human existence is complex and highly varied. People have diverse problems, rooted in varied origins, that call for the pursuit of different therapeutic goals. Thus, it's fortunate that people can choose from a diverse array of approaches to psychotherapy. Table 15.4 summarizes and compares the approaches that we've discussed in this chapter. The table shows that the major types of psychotherapy overlap relatively little. Each type has its own vision of the nature of human discontent and the ideal remedy.

Of course, diversity can be confusing. The range and variety of available treatments in modern psychotherapy leaves many people puzzled about their options. Thus, in our Application we'll sort through the practical issues involved in selecting a therapist.

Looking for a Therapist

Answer the following "true" or "false."

1 Psychotherapy is an art as well as a science.

2 Psychotherapy can be harmful or damaging to a client.

3 Psychotherapy does not have to be expensive.

4 It is a good idea to shop around when choosing a therapist.

5 The type of professional degree that a therapist holds is relatively unimportant.

All of these statements are true. Do any of them surprise you? If so, you're in good company. Many people know relatively little about the practicalities of selecting a therapist.

The task of finding an appropriate therapist is no less complex than shopping for any other major service. Should you see a psychologist or a psychiatrist? Should you opt for individual therapy or group therapy? Should you see a client-centered therapist or a behavior therapist? The unfortunate part of this complexity is that people seeking psychotherapy often feel overwhelmed by personal problems. The last thing they need is to be confronted by yet another complex problem.

Nonetheless, the importance of finding a good therapist cannot be overestimated. Therapy can sometimes have harmful rather than helpful effects. We have already discussed how drug therapies and ECT can sometimes be damaging, but problems are not limited to these interventions. Talking about your problems with a therapist may sound pretty harmless, but studies indicate that insight therapies can also backfire (Lambert & Bergin, 1994; McGlashan et al., 1990). Although a great many talented therapists are available, psychotherapy, like any other profession, has incompetent practitioners as well. Therefore, you should shop for a skilled therapist, just as you would for a good attorney or a good mechanic.

In this Application, we'll go over some information that should be helpful if you ever have to look for a therapist for yourself or for a friend or family member (based on Amada, 1985; Bruckner-Gordon, Gangi, & Wallman, 1988; Ehrenberg & Ehrenberg, 1986; Pittman, 1994).

Where Do You Find Therapeutic Services?

Psychotherapy can be found in a variety of settings. Contrary to general belief, most therapists are not in private practice. Many work in institutional settings such as community mental health centers, hospitals, and human service agencies. The principal sources of therapeutic services are described in Table 15.5. The exact configuration of therapeutic services available will vary from one community to another. To find out what your community has to offer, it is a good idea to consult your friends, your local phone book, or your local community mental health center.

Is the Therapist's Profession Important?

Psychotherapists may be trained in psychology, psychiatry, social work, counseling, psychiatric nursing, or marriage and family therapy. Researchers have *not*

Table 15.5 Principal Sources of Therapeutic Services

Source	Comments
Private practitioners	Self-employed therapists are listed in the Yellow Pages under their professional category, such as psychologists or psychiatrists. Private practitioners tend to be relatively expensive, but they also tend to be highly experienced therapists.
Community mental health centers	Community mental health centers have salaried psychologists, psychiatrists, and social workers on staff. The centers provide a variety of services and often have staff available on weekends and at night to deal with emergencies.
Hospitals	Several kinds of hospitals provide therapeutic services. There are both public and private mental hospitals that specialize in the care of people with psychological disorders. Many general hospitals have a psychiatric ward, and those that do not usually have psychiatrists and psychologists on staff and on call. Although hospitals tend to concentrate on inpatient treatment, many provide outpatient therapy as well.
Human service agencies	Various social service agencies employ therapists to provide short-term counseling. Depending on your community, you may find agencies that deal with family problems, juvenile problems, drug problems, and so forth.
Schools and workplaces	Most high schools and colleges have counseling centers where students can get help with personal problems. Similarly, some large businesses offer in-house counseling to their employees.

DIRECTORY

FIRST FLOOR FRONT →

John Steinhelber, Ph.D.
Betsy V. Hand, R.N., M.S.
John E. Johnson D.D.S., Inc.
John F. Herschleb, D.D.S., Inc.

Vitkoff Chiropractic
Jeffrey Felix, M.A., M.F.C.C.
Scott Thompson, D.D.S.

← FIRST FLOOR REAR

David G. Levine, M.D.
Edwyne Nazarian, M.D.

• Robin Gayle, Ph.D., M.F.C.C.

SECOND FLOOR

Otto Vanoni, Ph.D.
Julia Gombos, M.F.C.C.
Maggie Tuteur, M.F.C.C.
Anthony Piccione, Ph.D.
Donald Nadler, Ph.D.
Carol Freeburg, M.A., M.F.C.C.
Lawrence B. Katz, Ph.D.
Beth Becker, Ph.D.
Life After Breakfast
Warren R. Westerhoff, D.D.S.
Jeanette R. Margolin M.D., Inc.
Alva J. Ackley M.S.
Louis M. Flohr, M.D.

Max Boveri, M.S.
Jane Cunningham, M.F.C.C.
Psychological Health Center
Robert W. Lutz, Ph.D.
Ann Rivo, Ph.D.
Perry Grey, Ph.D.
Tony Sabatasso, Ph.D.
Charles R. Billings, Ph.D.
Barbara Rose Billings, D.C.H.
Penny Wright, M.S., M.F.C.
Patricia Grasso, Ph.D.
De Lima, Associates
Madeline Sheron, C.H.T.

Finding the right therapist is no easy task. You need to take into account the therapist's training and orientation, fees charged, and personality. An initial visit will give you a good idea of what the therapist is like, but you'll have to pay for the session.

found any reliable associations between therapists' professional background and therapeutic efficacy (Beutler, Machado, & Neufeldt, 1994), probably because many talented therapists can be found in all of these professions. Thus, the kind of degree that a therapist holds doesn't need to be a crucial consideration in your selection process. At the present time, it *is* true that only a psychiatrist can prescribe drugs for disorders that merit drug therapy. However, critics argue that many psychiatrists are too quick to use drugs to solve problems (Breggin, 1991). In any case, other types of therapists can refer you to a psychiatrist if they think that drug therapy would be helpful. If you have a health insurance policy that covers psychotherapy, you may want to check to see whether it carries any restrictions about the therapist's profession.

Is the Therapist's Sex Important?

This depends on your attitude. If *you* feel that the therapist's sex is important, then for you it is. The therapeutic relationship must be characterized by trust and rapport. Feeling uncomfortable with a therapist of one sex or the other could inhibit the therapeutic process. Hence, you should feel free to look for a male or female therapist if you prefer to do so. This point is probably most relevant to female clients whose troubles may be related to the extensive sexism in our society (A. Kaplan, 1985). It is entirely reasonable for women to seek a therapist with a feminist perspective if that would make them feel more comfortable.

Speaking of sex, you should be aware that sexual exploitation is an occasional problem in the context of therapy. Studies indicate that a small minority of therapists take advantage of their clients sexually (Pope, Keith-Spiegel, & Tabachnick, 1986). These incidents almost always involve a male therapist making advances to a female client. The available evidence indicates that these sexual liaisons are usually harmful to clients (Williams, 1992). There are absolutely no situations in which therapist-client sexual relations are an ethical therapeutic practice. If a therapist makes sexual advances, a client should terminate treatment.

Is Therapy Always Expensive?

Psychotherapy does not have to be prohibitively expensive. Private practitioners tend to be the most expensive, charging between $25 and $100 per (50-minute) hour. These fees may seem high, but they are in line with those of similar professionals, such as dentists and attorneys. Community mental health centers and social service agencies are usually supported by tax dollars. Hence, they can charge lower fees than most therapists in private practice. Many of these organizations use a sliding scale, so that clients are charged according to how much they can afford to pay. Thus, most communities have inexpensive opportunities for psychotherapy. Moreover, many health insurance plans provide at least partial reimbursement for the cost of psychotherapy.

Is the Therapist's Theoretical Approach Important?

Logically, you might expect that the diverse approaches to therapy vary in effectiveness. For the most part, this is *not* what researchers find, however. After reviewing the evidence, Jerome Frank (1961) and Lester Luborsky and his colleagues (1975) both quote the dodo bird who has just judged a race in *Alice in Wonderland*: "*Everybody* has won, and *all* must have prizes." Improvement rates for various theoretical orientations usually come out pretty close in most studies (Lambert & Bergin, 1994). In their landmark review of outcome studies, Smith and Glass (1977) estimated the effectiveness of many major approaches to therapy. As Figure 15.8 shows, the estimates cluster together closely.

These findings do not mean that all *therapists* are created equal. Some therapists unquestionably are more effective than others. However, these variations in effectiveness appear to depend on therapists' personal skills rather than on their theoretical orientation (Beutler et al., 1994). Good, bad, and mediocre therapists are found within each school of thought.

The key point is that effective therapy requires skill and creativity. Arnold Lazarus (1987), who devised multimodal therapy, emphasizes that therapists "straddle the fence between science and art" (p. 167). Therapy is scientific in that interventions are based on extensive theory and empirical research (Forsyth & Strong, 1986). Ultimately, though, each client is a unique human being, and the therapist has to creatively fashion a

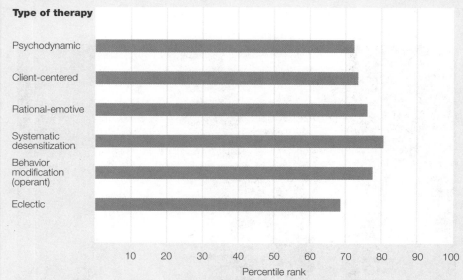

Figure 15.8. Estimates of the effectiveness of various approaches to psychotherapy. Smith and Glass (1977) reviewed nearly 400 studies in which clients who were treated with a specific type of therapy were compared with a control group made up of individuals with similar problems who went untreated. The bars indicate the percentile rank (on outcome measures) attained by the average client treated with each type of therapy when compared to control subjects. The higher the percentile, the more effective the therapy was. As you can see, the different approaches were fairly similar in their apparent effectiveness.

treatment program that will help that individual.

What Should You Look for in a Prospective Therapist?

Some clients are timid about asking prospective therapists questions about their training, approach, fees, and so forth. However, these are reasonable questions, and the vast majority of therapists will be most accommodating in providing answers. What should you look for in a therapist? First, you should look for personal warmth and sincere concern. Try to judge whether you will be able to talk to this person in a candid, nondefensive way. Second, look for empathy and understanding. Is the person capable of appreciating your point of view? Third, look for self-confidence. Self-assured therapists will communicate a sense of competence without trying to intimidate you with jargon or boasting needlessly about what they can do for you. When all

is said and done, you should *like* your therapist. Otherwise, it will be difficult to establish the needed rapport.

What Is Therapy Like?

It is important to have realistic expectations about therapy, or you may be unnecessarily disappointed. Some people expect miracles. They expect to turn their life around quickly with little effort. Others expect their therapist to run their lives for them. These are unrealistic expectations.

Therapy usually is a slow process. Your problems are not likely to melt away quickly. Moreover, therapy is hard work, and your therapist is only a facilitator. Ultimately, *you* have to confront the challenge of changing your behavior, your feelings, or your personality. This process may not be pleasant. You may have to face up to some painful truths about yourself. As Ehrenberg and Ehrenberg (1986) point out, "Psychotherapy takes time, effort, and courage."

Chapter 15 Review

KEY IDEAS

The Elements of Psychotherapy: Treatments, Clients, and Therapists

♦ Approaches to psychotherapy are diverse, but they can be grouped into three categories: insight therapies, behavior therapies, and biomedical therapies. Clients bring a wide variety of problems to therapy and do not necessarily have a disorder. Therapists come from various professional backgrounds. Each profession shows different preferences for various approaches to treatment.

Insight Therapies

♦ Insight therapies involve verbal interactions intended to enhance self-knowledge. Freudian approaches to therapy assume that neuroses originate from unresolved conflicts lurking in the unconscious. Therefore, in psychoanalysis free association and dream analysis are used to explore the unconscious.

♦ When an analyst's probing hits sensitive areas, resistance can be expected. The transference relationship may be used to overcome this resistance so the client can handle interpretations that lead to insight. Classical psychoanalysis is not widely practiced anymore, but Freud's legacy lives on in a rich diversity of modern psychodynamic therapies.

♦ Rogers's client-centered therapy assumes that neurotic anxieties are derived from incongruence between a person's self-concept and reality. Accordingly, the client-centered therapist tries to provide a supportive climate in which clients can restructure their self-concept. The process emphasizes clarification of the client's feelings and self-acceptance.

♦ Beck's cognitive therapy concentrates on changing the way clients think about events in their lives. Cognitive therapists reeducate clients to detect and challenge automatic negative thoughts that cause depression and anxiety. Cognitive therapists also use behavioral techniques in efforts to alter clients' overt behaviors.

♦ Most theoretical approaches to insight therapy have been adapted for use with groups. Group therapists usually play a subtle role, staying in the background and working to promote group cohesiveness. Participants essentially act as therapists for one another.

♦ Evaluating the effectiveness of any approach to therapy is complex and difficult. Nonetheless, the weight of the evidence suggests that insight therapies can be effective.

Behavior Therapies

♦ Behavior therapies use the principles of learning in direct efforts to change specific aspects of behavior. Wolpe's systematic desensitization, a treatment for phobias, involves the construction of an anxiety hierarchy, relaxation training, and step-by-step movement through the hierarchy, pairing relaxation with each phobic stimulus.

♦ In aversion therapy, a stimulus associated with an unwanted response is paired with an unpleasant stimulus in an effort to eliminate the maladaptive response. Social skills training can improve clients' interpersonal skills through shaping, modeling, and behavioral rehearsal. There is ample evidence that behavior therapies are effective.

Biomedical Therapies

♦ Biomedical therapies are physiological interventions for psychological problems. A variety of disorders are treated with drugs. The principal types of therapeutic drugs are antianxiety drugs, antipsychotic drugs, antidepressant drugs, and lithium. Drug therapies can be quite effective, but they have their drawbacks, such as problematic side effects.

♦ Electroconvulsive therapy (ECT) is used to trigger a cortical seizure that is believed to have therapeutic value for mood disorders, especially depression. There is contradictory evidence and heated debate about the effectiveness of ECT and about possible risks associated with its use.

Blending Approaches to Psychotherapy

♦ Combinations of insight, behavioral, and biomedical therapies are often used fruitfully in the treatment of psychological disorders. Many modern therapists are eclectic, using specific ideas, techniques, and strategies gleaned from two or more theoretical approaches.

Culture and Therapy

♦ The highly culture-bound origins of Western therapies have raised doubts about their applicability to other cultures and even to ethnic groups in Western society. Because of cultural, language, and access barriers, therapeutic services are underutilized by ethnic minorities in America. However, the crux of the problem is the failure of institutions to provide culturally sensitive and responsive forms of treatment for ethnic minorities.

♦ More culturally responsive approaches to treatment will require more minority therapists, special training for therapists, and additional investigation of how traditional therapies can be tailored to be more compatible with specific ethnic groups' cultural heritage.

Institutional Treatment in Transition

♦ Institutional treatment of mental illness has changed a great deal in the last 40 years. Disenchantment with the negative effects of mental hospitals led to the advent of more localized community mental health centers and a policy of deinstitutionalization. Long-term hospitalization for mental disorders is largely a thing of the past.

♦ Unfortunately, deinstitutionalization has left some unanticipated problems in its wake. Adequate outpatient facilities and care have not been provided for the mentally ill, resulting in the revolving door problem. Although deinstitutionalization may have made a small contribution to the growth of homelessness in America, homelessness appears to be primarily an economic problem.

Putting It in Perspective

♦ Our discussion of psychotherapy highlighted the value of theoretical diversity. Conflicting theoretical orientations have generated varied approaches to treatment. Variety in treatment options allows clients to look for interventions suited to their unique needs. Our coverage of therapy also showed once again that cultural factors shape psychological processes.

Application: Looking for a Therapist

♦ Therapeutic services are available in many settings, and such services do not have to be expensive. Excellent therapists and mediocre therapists can be found in all of the mental health professions, using the full range of therapeutic approaches. Thus, therapists' personal skills are more important than their professional degree or their theoretical orientation.

♦ In selecting a therapist, warmth, empathy, confidence, and likability are desirable traits, and it is reasonable to insist on a therapist of one sex or the other. Therapy requires time, hard work, and the courage to confront your problems.

KEY TERMS

Antianxiety drugs	Free association
Antidepressant drugs	Group therapy
Antipsychotic drugs	Insight therapies
Aversion therapy	Interpretation
Behavior therapies	Lithium
Biomedical therapies	Mental hospital
Client-centered therapy	Psychiatrists
	Psychoanalysis
Clinical psychologists	Psychopharmaco-therapy
Cognitive therapy	Resistance
Counseling psychologists	Social skills training
Deinstitutionalization	Systematic desensitization
Dream analysis	Tardive dyskinesia
Electroconvulsive therapy (ECT)	Transference

KEY PEOPLE

Aaron Beck	Carl Rogers
Sigmund Freud	Joseph Wolpe

16 Social Behavior

When Muffy, "the quintessential yuppie," met Jake, "the ultimate working-class stiff," her friends got very nervous.

Muffy is a 28-year-old stockbroker and a self-described "snob" with a group of about ten close women friends. Snobs all. They're graduates of fancy business schools. All consultants, investment bankers, and CPAs. All "cute, bright, fun to be with, and really intelligent," according to Muffy. They're all committed to their high-powered careers, but they all expect to marry someday, too.

Unfortunately, most of them don't date much. In fact, they spend a good deal of time "lamenting the dearth of "good men."" You know who the "good men" are. Those are the ones who are "committed to their work, open to the idea of marriage and family, and possessed of a good sense of humor."

Well, lucky Muffy actually met one of those "good men." Jake is a salesman. He comes from a working-class neighborhood. His clothes come from Sears.

He wasn't like the usual men Muffy dated. He treats Muffy the way she's always dreamed of being treated. He listens; he cares; he remembers. "He makes me feel safe and more cherished than any man I've ever known," she says.

So she decided to bring him to a little party of about 30 of her closest friends. . . .

Perhaps it was only Jake's nerves that caused him to commit some truly unforgivable faux pas that night. His sins were legion. Where do we start? First of all, he asked for a beer when everyone else was drinking white wine. He wore a worn turtleneck while everyone else had just removed the Polo tags from their clothing. He smoked. . . .

"The next day at least half of the people who had been at the party called to give me their impressions. They all said that they felt they just had to let me know that they thought Jake 'lacked polish' or 'seemed loud' or 'might not be a suitable match,'" Muffy says.

Now, you may think that Muffy's friends are simply very sensitive, demanding people. A group of princes and princesses who can detect a pea under the fluffiest stack of mattresses. But you'd be wrong. Actually, they've been quite accepting of some of the other men that Muffy has brought to their little parties. Or should we call them inquisitions? Winston, for example, was a great favorite.

"He got drunk, ignored me, and asked for other women's phone numbers right in front of me. But he was six-foot-four, the classic preppie, with blond hair, horn-rimmed glasses, and Ralph Lauren clothes."

And most important of all, he didn't ask for a Pabst Blue Ribbon. So now Muffy is confused. "Jake is the first guy I've been out with in a long time that I've

really liked. I was excited about him and my friends knew that. I was surprised by their reaction. I'll admit there's some validity to all their comments, but it's hard to express how violent it was. It made me think about what these women really want in a man. Whatever they say, what they really want is someone they can take to a business dinner. They want someone who comes with a tux. Like a Ken doll."

Muffy may have come to a crossroads in her young life. It's clear that there's no way she can bring Jake among her friends for a while.

"I don't want their reaction to muddy my feelings until I get them sorted out," she says.

It just may be time for Muffy to choose between her man and her friends.

The preceding account is a real story, taken from a book about contemporary intimate relationships titled *Tales from the Front* (Kavesh & Lavin, 1988, pp. 118–121). Muffy is on the horns of a difficult dilemma. Romantic relationships are very important to most people, but so are friendships, and Muffy may have to choose between the two. Muffy's story illustrates the significance of social relations in people's lives. It also foreshadows each of the topics that we'll cover in this chapter, as we look at behavior in its social context.

Social psychology is the branch of psychology concerned with the way individuals' thoughts, feelings, and behaviors are influenced by others. Our coverage of social psychology will focus on six broad topics, and an Application on prejudice will integrate ideas introduced in the main body of the chapter. Let's return to Muffy's story to get a glimpse of the various facets of social behavior that we'll examine in the coming pages:

- *Person perception.* The crux of Muffy's problem is that Jake didn't make a very good impression on her friends. To what extent do people's expectations color their impressions of others? Can a bad first impression be overcome?

- *Attribution processes.* Muffy is struggling to understand her friends' rejection of Jake. When she implies that Jake's rejection is due to their snotty elitism, she's engaging in attribution, making an inference about the causes of her friends' behavior. How do people use attributions to explain social behavior?

- *Interpersonal attraction.* Jake and Muffy are different in many important ways—is it true that opposites attract? Why does Jake's lack of similarity to Muffy's friends lead to such disdain?

- *Attitudes.* Muffy's girlfriends have negative attitudes about working-class men. How are attitudes formed? What leads to attitude change? How do attitudes affect people's behavior?

- *Conformity and obedience.* Muffy's friends discourage her from dating Jake, putting her under pressure to conform to their values. What factors influence conformity? Can people be coaxed into doing things that contradict their values?

- *Behavior in groups.* Muffy belongs to a tight-knit group of friends who think along similar lines. Is people's behavior in groups similar to their behavior when alone? Why do people in groups often think alike?

Social psychologists study how people are affected by the actual, imagined, or implied presence of others. Their interest is not limited to individuals' *interactions* with others, as people can engage in social behavior even when they're alone. For instance, if you were driving by yourself on a deserted highway and tossed your trash out your car window, your littering would be a social action. It would defy social norms, reflect your socialization and attitudes, and have repercussions (albeit, small) for other people in your society. Thus, social psychologists often study *individual* behavior in a social context. This interest in understanding individual behavior should be readily apparent in our first section, on person perception.

PERSON PERCEPTION: FORMING IMPRESSIONS OF OTHERS

Can you remember the first meeting of your introductory psychology class? What kind of impression did your professor make on you that day? Did your instructor appear to be confident? Easygoing? Pompous? Open-minded? Cynical? Friendly? Were your first impressions supported or undermined by subsequent observations? When you interact with people, you're constantly engaged in ***person perception***, **the process of forming impressions of others.** In this section we consider some of the factors that influence, and often distort, our perceptions of others.

Effects of Physical Appearance

"You shouldn't judge a book by its cover." "Beauty is only skin deep." People know better than to let physical attractiveness determine their perceptions of others' personal qualities. Or do they? Studies have shown that judgments of others' personality are often swayed by their appearance, especially their physical attractiveness. People tend to ascribe desirable personality characteristics to those who are good looking, seeing them as more sociable, friendly, poised, warm, and well adjusted than those who are unattractive (Dion, 1986; Eagly et al., 1991).

Physical attractiveness influences perceptions of competence less than perceptions of personality, but people nonetheless tend to view good-looking individuals as more intelligent and succesful than their less attractive counterparts (Eagly et al., 1991). For example, in a study of male employees in two large accounting firms, Ross and Ferris (1981) found that physical attractiveness was positively related to evaluations of the employees' performance and their salary increases. In general, people seem to assume that "what is beautiful is good." However, good looks have little impact on perceptions of honesty and integrity and may occasionally backfire in that beautiful people are assumed to be vain (Feingold, 1992).

In general, people have a bias toward viewing good-looking men and women as bright, competent, and talented. However, people sometimes downplay the talent of successful women who happen to be attractive, attributing their success to their good looks instead of to their competence.

Cognitive Schemas

Even though every individual is unique, people tend to categorize one another. For instance, in our opening story, Muffy is characterized as "the quintessential yuppie." In another story in *Tales from the Front*, a man describes his date as a "BUP"—a "boring, uptight prude." Such labels reflect the use of cognitive schemas in person perception.

As we discussed in our chapter on memory (Chapter 7), *schemas* are cognitive structures that guide our information processing. People have schemas for everything from inanimate objects (bicycles, apartments) to human activities (eating lunch, going to a gas station). Individuals use schemas to organize the world around them— including their social world. **Social schemas are organized clusters of ideas about categories of social events and people.** We have social schemas for events such as dates, picnics, committee meetings, and family reunions, as well as for certain categories of people, such as "dumb jocks," "social climbers," "frat rats," and "wimps" (see Figure 16.1).

When a schema is activated, it's likely to influence one's perceptions of a person (Fiske & Taylor, 1991). For example, in our opening story, Muffy's friends apparently categorized Jake as a "working-class stiff." The activation of this schema probably increased their tendency to notice behaviors that fit their schema for working-class stiffs, such as beer drinking and smoking, while overlooking his kindness and other good points.

Stereotypes

Some of the schemas that individuals apply to people, such as "BUP," are unique products of their personal experiences, while other schemas, such as "yuppie," may be part of their shared cultural background. *Stereotypes* are special types of schemas that fall into the latter category (Anderson & Klatzky, 1987). **Stereotypes are widely held beliefs that people have certain characteristics because of their membership in a particular group.**

The most common stereotypes in our society are those based on sex and on membership in ethnic or occupational groups. Preconceived notions that Jews are mercenary, blacks have rhythm, Germans are methodical, and Italians are passionate are examples of common *ethnic stereotypes*. People who subscribe to traditional *gender stereotypes* tend to assume that women are emotional, submissive, illogical, and passive, while men are

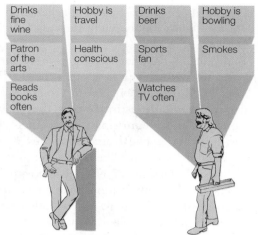

Figure 16.1. Examples of social schemas. Everyone has social schemas for various "types" of people, such as sophisticated professionals or working-class stiffs. Social schemas are clusters of beliefs that guide information processing.

Sophisticated professional — Working-class stiff

unemotional, dominant, logical, and aggressive. *Occupational stereotypes* suggest that lawyers are manipulative, accountants are conforming, artists are moody, and so forth.

Stereotyping is a normal cognitive process that saves on the time and effort required to get a handle on people individually (Macrae, Milne, & Bodenhausen, 1994). Stereotypes save energy by simplifying our social world. However, this conservation of energy often comes at some cost in terms of accuracy. Stereotypes frequently are broad overgeneralizations that ignore the diversity within social groups and foster inaccurate perceptions of people (Stephan, 1989). Obviously, all Jews, males, and lawyers do not behave alike. Most people who subscribe to stereotypes realize that not all members of a group are identical. For instance, they may admit that some Jews aren't mercenary, some men aren't competitive, and some lawyers aren't manipulative. However, they may still tend to assume that Jews, males, and lawyers are *more likely* than others to have these characteristics. These expectations may lead them to misperceive individuals with whom they interact. As we've noted in previous chapters, perception is subjective, and people often see what they expect to see.

Selectivity in Person Perception

Stereotypes and other schemas create biases in person perception that frequently lead to confirmation of people's expectations about others. If there's any ambiguity in someone's behavior, people are likely to interpret what they see in a way that's consistent with their expectations (E. Jones, 1990). Thus, after dealing with a pushy female customer, a salesman who holds traditional gender stereotypes might characterize the woman as "emotional." In contrast, he might characterize a pushy male who exhibits exactly the same behavior as "aggressive."

People not only see what they expect to see, they also tend to overestimate how often they see it (Johnson & Mullen, 1994)). *Illusory correlation* **occurs when people estimate that they have encountered more confirmations of an association between social traits than they have actually seen.** Statements like "I've never met an honest lawyer" illustrate this effect. Memory processes make major contributions to confirmatory biases in person perception. Often, individuals selectively recall facts that fit with the schemas they apply to people. Evidence for such a tendency was found in a study by Cohen (1981). In this experiment, subjects watched a videotape of a woman, described as either a waitress or a librarian, who engaged in a variety of activities, including listening to classical music, drinking beer, and watching TV. When asked to recall what the woman did during the filmed sequence, subjects tended to remember activities consistent with their stereotypes of waitresses and librarians. For instance, subjects who thought the woman was a waitress tended to recall her drinking beer. Subjects who thought she was a librarian tended to recall her listening to classical music.

Our discussion of social schemas, stereotypes, and memory distortion in person perception shows that cognitive processes influence impressions of others. This insight will be reinforced in the next section, where we discuss attribution processes.

"Often the momentary situation which, at least in part, determines the behavior of a person is disregarded and the behavior is taken as a manifestation of personal characteristics."
FRITZ HEIDER

ATTRIBUTION PROCESSES: EXPLAINING BEHAVIOR

It's Friday evening and you're sitting around at home feeling bored. You call a few friends to see whether they'd like to go out. They all say that they'd love to go, but they have other commitments and they can't. Their commitments sound vague, and you feel that their reasons for not going out with you are rather flimsy. How do you explain these rejections? Do your friends really have commitments? Are they worn out by school and work? Are they just lazy and apathetic about going out? When they said that they'd love to go, were they being sincere? These questions illustrate a process that people engage in routinely: the explanation of behavior. *Attributions* play a key role in these explanatory efforts, and they have significant effects on social relations.

Attributions: What? Why? When?

Although we discussed how patterns of attribution can contribute to depression in Chapter 14, let's review what attributions are, elaborate on why people make them, and discuss when people are likely to engage in attributional thinking.

What are attributions? **Attributions are inferences that people draw about the causes of events, others' behavior, and their own behavior.** If you conclude that a friend turned down your invitation because she's overworked, you've made an attribution about the cause of her behavior (and, implicitly, rejected other possible explanations). If you conclude that you're stuck at home with nothing to do because you failed to plan ahead, you've made an attribution about the cause of an event (being stuck at home). If you conclude that you failed to plan ahead because you're a procrastinator, you've made an attribution about the cause of your own behavior.

Why do people make attributions? Individuals make attributions because they have a strong need to understand their experiences. They want to make sense out of their own behavior, others' actions, and the events in their lives.

When do people make attributions? People don't attempt to explain everything that happens around them. You're not likely to mull over why a friend said "Hi" this morning, or why a colleague took the elevator to get to the 20th floor of the building you work in. However, if your friend *did not* say "Hi," or if your colleague *walked* up 20 flights of stairs instead of taking the elevator, you might wonder why. A variety of factors influence whether people are stimulated to engage in attributional thinking (Hilton, Fein, & Miller, 1993; E. Jones, 1990). Generally, people are more likely to make attributions (1) when unusual events grab their attention, (2) when events have personal consequences for them, and (3) when others behave in unexpected ways.

Having looked at the what, why, and when of attribution, we'll devote the remainder of our discussion in this section to *how* people explain the causes of behavior. Specifically, we'll examine theoretical models that identify the key dimensions of attributions and look at various sources of bias in attributional thinking.

Internal Versus External Attributions

Fritz Heider (1958) was the first to describe how people make attributions. He asserted that people tend to locate the cause of behavior either *within a person*, attributing it to personal factors, or *outside a person*, attributing it to environmental factors.

Elaborating on Heider's insight, various theorists have agreed that explanations of behavior and events can be categorized as internal or external attributions (Jones & Davis, 1965; Kelley, 1967; Weiner, 1974). **Internal attributions ascribe the causes of behavior to personal dispositions, traits, abilities, and feelings. External attributions ascribe the causes of behavior to situational demands and environmental constraints.** For example, if a friend's business fails, you might attribute it to your friend's lack of business acumen (an internal, personal factor) or to negative trends in the nation's economic climate (an external, situational explanation). Parents who find out that their teenage son has just banged up the car may blame it on his carelessness (a personal disposition) or on slippery road conditions (a situational factor).

Internal and external attributions can have a tremendous impact on everyday interpersonal interactions. Blaming a friend's business failure on poor business acumen as opposed to a poor economy will have a great impact on how you view your friend—not to mention on whether you'll lend him or her money in the future. Likewise, if parents attribute their son's automobile accident to slippery road conditions, they're likely to deal with the event very differently than if they attribute it to his carelessness.

Attributions for Success and Failure

Some psychologists have sought to discover additional dimensions of attributional thinking besides the internal-external dimension. After studying the attributions that people make in explaining success and failure, Bernard Weiner and his colleagues concluded that people often focus on the *stability* of the causes underlying behavior (Weiner, 1974; Weiner et al., 1972). According to Weiner, the stable-unstable dimension in attribution cuts across the internal-external dimension, creating four types of attributions for success and failure, as shown in Figure 16.2.

Let's apply Weiner's model to a concrete event. Imagine that you're contemplating why you failed to get a job that you wanted. You might attribute your setback to internal factors that are stable (lack of ability) or unstable (inadequate effort to put together an eye-catching résumé). Or you might attribute your setback to

external factors that are stable (too much outstanding competition) or unstable (bad luck). If you got the job, the explanations that you might offer for your success would fall into the same four categories: internal-stable (your excellent ability), internal-unstable (your hard work to assemble a superb résumé), external-stable (lack of topflight competition), and external-unstable (good luck). Clearly, attributions are complicated, and they have important implications for how people see themselves and others. However, attributions are not entirely logical and objective. We turn next to the matter of biases in attribution processes.

Bias in Attribution

Attributions are only inferences. Your attributions may not be the correct explanations for events. Paradoxical as it may seem, people often arrive at inaccurate explanations even when they contemplate the causes of *their own behavior*. Attributions ultimately represent *guesswork* about the

An internal attribution would ascribe this business failure to the owner's personal traits (poor planning, bad decisions, etc.). An external attribution would ascribe the failure to situational factors (a recession, changing demographics, etc.).

Figure 16.2. Attributions for success and failure. Weiner's model assumes that people's explanations for success and failure emphasize internal versus external causes and stable versus unstable causes. Examples of causal factors that fit into each of the four cells in Weiner's model are shown in the diagram.

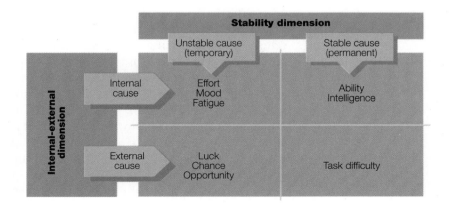

Check your understanding of attribution processes by analyzing possible explanations for an athletic team's success. Imagine that the women's track team at your school has just won a regional championship that qualifies it for the national tournament. Around the campus, you hear people attribute the team's success to a variety of factors. Examine the attributions shown below and place each of them in one of the cells of Weiner's model of attribution (just record the letter inside the cell). The answers are in Appendix A.

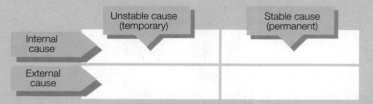

a. "They won only because the best two athletes on Central State's team were out with injuries—talk about good fortune!"
b. "They won because they have some of the best talent in the country."
c. "Anybody could win this region; the competition is far below average in comparison to the rest of the country."
d. "They won because they put in a great deal of last-minute effort and practice, and they were incredibly fired up for the regional tourney after last year's near miss."

causes of events, and these guesses tend to be slanted in certain directions. Let's look at the principal biases seen in attribution.

Actor-Observer Bias

Your view of your own behavior can be quite different from the view of someone else observing you. When an actor and an observer draw inferences about the causes of the actor's behavior, they often make different attributions. **The *fundamental attribution error* refers to observers' bias in favor of internal attributions in explaining others' behavior** (Ross, 1977). Of course, in many instances, an internal attribution may not be an "error" (Harvey, Town, & Yarkin, 1981). However, observers have a curious tendency to overestimate the likelihood that an actor's behavior reflects personal qualities rather than situational factors. Why? One reason is that attributing others' behavior to their dispositions is a relatively simple, effortless process that borders on automatic (Trope & Liberman, 1993). In contrast, explaining people's behavior in terms of situational factors is a more complex process that requires more thought and effort (Gilbert, Pelham, & Krull, 1988).

To illustrate the gap that often exists between actors' and observers' attributions, imagine that you're visiting your bank and you fly into a rage over a mistake made on your account. Observers who witness your rage are likely to make an internal attribution and infer that you are surly, temperamental, and quarrelsome. They may be right, but if asked, you'd probably attribute your rage to the frustrating situation. Perhaps you're normally a calm, easygoing person, but today you've been in line for 20 minutes, you just straightened out a similar error by the same bank last week, and you're being treated rudely by the teller. Observers often are unaware of situational considerations such as these, so they tend to make internal attributions for another's behavior (White & Younger, 1988).

In contrast, the circumstances that have influenced an actor's behavior tend to be more salient to the actor. Hence, actors are more likely than observers to locate the cause of their behavior in the situation. In general, then, *actors favor external attributions for their behavior, while observers are more likely to explain the same behavior with internal attributions* (Jones & Nisbett, 1971; Watson, 1982).

Defensive Attribution

In attempting to explain the calamities and setbacks that befall other people, an observer's tendency to make internal attributions becomes even stronger than normal. Let's say that a friend gets mugged and severely beaten. You may attribute the mugging to your friend's carelessness or stupidity ("He should have known better than to be in that neighborhood at that time") rather than to bad luck. Why? Because if you attribute your friend's misfortune to bad luck, you have to face the ugly reality that it could just as easily happen to you. To avoid disturbing thoughts such as these, people often attribute mishaps to victims' negligence (Thornton, 1984, 1992).

Defensive attribution **is a tendency to blame victims for their misfortune, so that one feels less likely to be victimized in a similar way.** Unfortunately, blaming victims for their setbacks causes them to be seen in a negative light, and undesirable traits are unfairly attributed to them. Thus, it is assumed that burglary victims must be careless, people who get fired must be incompetent, poor people must be lazy, rape victims must be seductive ("She probably asked for it"), and so on. As you can see, defensive attribution often leads to unwarranted derogation of victims of misfortune.

Self-Serving Bias

The self-serving bias in attribution comes into play when people attempt to explain success and failure. This bias may either strengthen or weaken one's normal attributional tendencies, depending on whether one is trying to explain positive or negative outcomes (Bradley, 1978; Brown & Rogers, 1991). **The *self-serving bias* is the tendency to attribute one's successes to personal factors and one's failures to situational factors.** Interestingly, this bias grows stronger as time passes after an event, so that people tend to take progressively more credit for their successes and less responsibility for their failures (Burger, 1986).

In explaining *failure*, the usual actor-observer biases are apparent. Actors tend to make external attributions, blaming their failures on unfavorable situational factors, while observers attribute the same failures to the actors' personal shortcomings. Thus, if you fail an exam, you may place the blame on the poorly constructed test items, lousy teaching, distractions in the hallway, or a bad week at work (all external attributions). However, an observer is more likely to attribute your failure to your lack of ability or lack of study (both internal attributions).

In explaining *success*, the usual actor-observer differences are reversed to some degree. Thus, if you get a high exam score, you'll probably make an internal attribution and point to your ability or your hard work (Forsyth & McMillan, 1981). In contrast, an observer may be more likely to infer that the test was easy or that you were lucky (external attributions). In other words, actors like to take credit for their success, while observers lean toward situational explanations for others' triumphs.

Culture and Attributional Tendencies

Do the patterns of attribution observed in subjects from Western societies transcend culture? More research is needed, but the preliminary evidence suggests not. Some interesting cultural disparities have emerged in research on attribution processes.

According to Harry Triandis (1989, 1994), cultural differences in *individualism* versus *collectivism* influence attributional tendencies as well as other aspects of social behavior. ***Individualism*** **involves putting personal goals ahead of group goals and defining one's identity in terms of personal attributes rather than group mem-**

CONCEPT CHECK 16.2
Recognizing Bias in Social Cognition

Check your understanding of bias in social cognition by identifying various types of errors that are common in person perception and attribution. Imagine that you're a nonvoting student member of a college committee at Southwest State University that is hiring a new political science professor. As you listen to the committee's discussion, you hear examples of (a) the illusory correlation effect, (b) stereotyping, (c) the fundamental attribution error, and (d) defensive attribution. Indicate which of these is at work in the excerpts from committee members' deliberations below. The answers are in Appendix A.

_____ 1. "I absolutely won't consider the fellow who arrived 30 minutes late for his interview. Anybody who can't make a job interview on time is either irresponsible or hopelessly disorganized. I don't care what he says about the airline messing up his reservations."

_____ 2. "You know, I was very, very impressed with the young female applicant, and I would love to hire her, but every time we add a young woman to the faculty in liberal arts, she gets pregnant within the first year." The committee chairperson, who has heard this line from this professor before replies, "You always say that, so I finally did a systematic check of what's happened in the past. Of the last 14 women hired in liberal arts, only 1 has become pregnant within a year."

_____ 3. "The first one I want to rule out is the guy who's been practicing law for the last ten years. Although he has an excellent background in political science, I just don't trust lawyers. They're all ambitious, power hungry, manipulative cutthroats. He'll be a divisive force in the department."

_____ 4. "I say we forget about the two candidates who lost their faculty slots in the massive financial crisis at Western Polytechnic last year. I know it sounds cruel, but they brought it on themselves with their fiscal irresponsiblity over at Western. Thank goodness we'll never let anything like that happen around here. As far as I'm concerned, if these guys couldn't see that crisis coming, they must be pretty dense."

---

berships. In contrast, ***collectivism*** **involves putting group goals ahead of personal goals and defining one's identity in terms of the groups one belongs to** (such as one's family, tribe, work group, social class, caste, and so on). In comparison to individualistic cultures, collectivist cultures place a higher priority on shared values and resources, cooperation, mutual interdependence, and concern for how one's actions will affect other group members. Child-rearing patterns in collectivist cultures emphasize the importance of obedience, reliability, and proper behavior, whereas individualistic cultures emphasize the development of independence, self-esteem, and self-reliance.

A variety of factors influence whether societies cherish individualism as opposed to collectivism. Among other things, increases in a culture's affluence, education, urbanization, and

The winning Olympic diving champions from mainland China, a collectivist society, probably possess a far different attributional bias about their success than that held by their Western colleagues, who are influenced by a culture centered on individualism.

error than those from individualistic societies. In Western culture, people are viewed as autonomous individuals who are responsible for their actions. Endorsing beliefs such as "You can do anything you put your mind to" or "You have no one to blame but yourself," Westerners typically explain behavior in terms of people's personality traits and unique abilities. In contrast, collectivists, who value interdependence and obedience, are more likely to assume that one's behavior reflects adherence to group norms. Consistent with this analysis, researchers have found that American subjects explain others' behavior in terms of internal attributions more than Hindu subjects (Miller, 1984) or Japanese subjects do (Weisz, Rothbaum, & Blackburn, 1984).

Although the *self-serving bias* has been documented in a variety of cultures (Fletcher & Ward, 1988), it may be particularly prevalent in individualistic, Western societies, where an emphasis on competition and high self-esteem motivates people to try to impress others, as well as themselves. In contrast, Japanese subjects exhibit a *self-effacing bias* in explaining success (Kashima & Triandis, 1986; Markus & Kitayama, 1991). They tend to attribute their successes to help they receive from others or to the ease of the task, while downplaying the importance of their ability. They attribute their failures mainly to inadequate effort. Studies have also failed to find the usual self-serving bias in Chinese and Nepalese subjects (Smith & Bond, 1994). A great deal of additional research is needed before any broad conclusions can be drawn, but collectivism may put a different spin on attributional bias.

Attributions are an important aspect of social behavior. For example, in recent years researchers have learned that certain patterns of attribution

social mobility tend to foster more individualism (Triandis, 1994). Many contemporary societies are in transition, but generally speaking, North American and Western European cultures tend to be individualistic, whereas Asian, African, and Latin American cultures tend to be higher in collectivism (Hofstede, 1980, 1983) (see Figure 16.3).

How does individualism versus collectivism relate to patterns of attribution? The evidence suggests that collectivist cultures may promote different attributional biases than individualistic cultures. For example, people from collectivist societies may be less prone to the *fundamental attribution*

Figure 16.3. Individualism versus collectivism around the world.
Hofstede (1980, 1983) used survey data from over 100,000 employees of a large, multinational corporation to estimate the emphasis on individualism versus collectivism in 50 nations and 3 "regions," for which he combined data for adjacent countries. Data were not available for much of what used to be the Communist bloc or for much of Africa, but his large, diverse international sample remains unequaled to date. As you can see, Hofstede's estimates suggest that most North American and Western European nations tend to be relatively individualistic, whereas more collectivism is found in Asian, African, and Latin American countries.

Hofstede's (1983) rankings of national cultures' individualism

1. United States	19. Israel	37. Hong Kong
2. Australia	20. Spain	38. Chile
3. Great Britain	21. India	40. Singapore
4. Canada	22. Argentina	40. Thailand
4. Netherlands	22. Japan	40. West Africa region
6. New Zealand	24. Iran	42. El Salvador
7. Italy	25. Jamaica	43. Taiwan
8. Belgium	26. Arab region	44. South Korea
9. Denmark	26. Brazil	45. Peru
10. France	28. Turkey	46. Costa Rica
11. Sweden	29. Uraguay	47. Indonesia
12. Ireland	30. Greece	47. Pakistan
13. Norway	31. Philippines	49. Colombia
14. Switzerland	32. Mexico	50. Venezuela
15. West Germany	34. East Africa region	51. Panama
16. South Africa	34. Portugal	52. Ecuador
17. Finland	34. Yugoslavia	53. Guatemala
18. Austria	36. Malaysia	

can play a key role in either the growth or the deterioration of intimate relationships (Fincham & Bradbury, 1993). In the next section, we'll look at a variety of other factors that influence the development of close relationships.

INTERPERSONAL ATTRACTION: LIKING AND LOVING

"I just don't know what she sees in him. She could do so much better for herself. I suppose he's a nice guy, but they're just not right for each other." Can't you imagine Muffy's friends making these comments in discussing her relationship with Jake? You've probably heard similar remarks on many occasions. These comments illustrate people's interest in analyzing the dynamics of attraction. *Interpersonal attraction* refers to positive feelings toward another. Social psychologists use this term broadly to encompass a variety of experiences, including liking, friendship, admiration, lust, and love. In this section, we'll analyze key factors that influence attraction and examine some theoretical perspectives on the mystery of love.

Key Factors in Attraction

Many factors influence who is attracted to whom. Here we'll discuss factors that promote the development of liking, friendship, and love. Although these are different types of attraction, the interpersonal dynamics at work in each are surprisingly similar. Each is influenced by proximity, physical attractiveness, similarity, and reciprocity.

Proximity Effects

It would be difficult for you to develop a friendship with someone you never met. It happens occasionally (among pen pals, for instance), but attraction usually depends on people being in the same place at the same time, making proximity a major factor in attraction. *Proximity* refers to geographic, residential, and other forms of spatial closeness (classroom seating, office arrangements, and so forth). Generally, people become acquainted with, and attracted to, people who live, work, shop, and play nearby. The importance of spatial factors in living arrangements was apparent in a study of friendship patterns among married graduate students living in university housing projects (Festinger, Schachter, & Back, 1950). The closer people's doors were, the more likely they were to become friends.

Proximity effects may seem self-evident, but it's sobering to realize that your friendships and love interests are shaped by arbitrary desk arrangements in offices, dormitory floor assignments, and traffic patterns in apartment complexes. In spite of the increasing geographic mobility in modern society, people still tend to marry someone who grew up nearby (Ineichen, 1979).

Physical Attractiveness

Although people often say that "beauty is only skin deep," the empirical evidence suggests that most people don't really believe that homily. The importance of physical attractiveness was demonstrated in a study of first-year college students whose dates for a dance were supposedly selected by a computer (Walster et al., 1966). Actually, the couples had been paired randomly, but the computer cover story provided a good rationale for asking students to rate their desire to go out with their dates again. These ratings were then correlated with the dates' physical attractiveness (assessed by impartial judges) and a host of personality, interest, and background variables.

For both sexes, a partner's good looks was the *only* variable that predicted subjects' desire to go out with their date again. Subsequent studies

According to the matching hypothesis, males and females who are similar in physical attractiveness are likely to be drawn together. This type of matching may also influence the formation of friendships.

have replicated the singular prominence of physical attractiveness in the initial stage of dating and have shown that it continues to influence the course of commitment as dating relationships evolve (Patzer, 1985). In the realm of romance, being physically attractive appears to be more important for females than males (Feingold, 1990).

Although people prefer physically attractive partners in romantic relationships, they may consider their own level of attractiveness in pursuing dates. **The *matching hypothesis* proposes that males and females of approximately equal physical attractiveness are likely to select each other as partners.** The matching hypothesis is supported by evidence that married couples tend to be very similar in level of physical attractiveness (Feingold, 1988b). However, there's some debate about whether people match up by their own choice (Aron, 1988; Kalick & Hamilton, 1986). Some theorists believe that people mostly pursue high attractiveness in partners and that their matching is the result of social forces beyond their control, such as rejection by more attractive others.

Similarity Effects

Is it true that "birds of a feather flock together," or do "opposites attract"? Research provides far more support for the former than the latter. Married and dating couples tend to be similar in age, race, religion, social class, education, intelligence, physical attractiveness, and attitudes (Brehm, 1992; Hendrick & Hendrick, 1992). Similarity is also seen among friends. For instance, adolescent best friends are similar in educational goals and performance, political and religious activities, and illicit drug use (Kandel, 1978).

The most obvious explanation for these correlations is that similarity causes attraction. Laboratory experiments on *attitude similarity*, conducted by Donn Byrne and his colleagues, suggest that similarity does cause liking (Byrne, 1971; Byrne, Clore, & Smeaton, 1986). In these studies, subjects who have previously provided information on their own attitudes are led to believe that they'll be meeting a stranger. They're given information about the stranger's views that has been manipulated to show various degrees of similarity to their own views. As attitude similarity increases, subjects' ratings of the likability of the stranger increase. This evidence supports the notion that similarity promotes attraction.

Reciprocity Effects

In his book *How to Win Friends and Influence People*, Dale Carnegie (1936) suggested that people can gain others' liking by showering them with praise and flattery. However, we've all heard that "flattery will get you nowhere." Which advice is right? The evidence suggests that flattery will get you somewhere, with some people, some of the time.

In interpersonal attraction, ***reciprocity* involves liking those who show that they like you.** In general, it appears that liking breeds liking and loving promotes loving (Byrne & Murnen, 1988). However, this principle must be qualified carefully. People realize that others sometimes try to butter them up. ***Ingratiation* is a conscious effort to cultivate others' liking by complimenting them, agreeing with them, and doing them favors.** If affection appears to be part of an ingratiation strategy, it's not likely to be reciprocated (Schlenker, 1980).

Studies of proximity, physical attractiveness, similarity, and reciprocity shed some light on the formation and evolution of friendships and romantic relationships but tell us very little about the mystery of love. We discuss some theoretical perspectives on love next.

Perspectives on the Mystery of Love

People have always been interested in love and romance, but the scientific study of love has a short history that, for all practical purposes, dates back only to the 1970s. Love has proven to be an elusive subject of study. It's difficult to define, difficult to measure, and frequently difficult to understand. Nonetheless, psychologists have begun to make some progress in their study of love. Let's look at their theories and research.

Passionate and Companionate Love

Perhaps no one has conducted more research on love than Elaine Hatfield (formerly Walster) and Ellen Berscheid (Berscheid, 1988; Berscheid & Walster, 1978; Hatfield, 1988; Hatfield & Rapson, 1993; Walster & Berscheid, 1974). They propose that romantic relationships are characterized by two kinds of love: passionate love and companionate love. ***Passionate love* involves a complete absorption in another that includes tender sexual feelings and the agony and ecstasy of intense emotion.** *Companionate love* **is warm, trusting, tolerant affection for another whose life is deeply intertwined with one's own.** Pas-

"Passionate love is like any other form of excitement. By its very nature, excitement involves a continuous interplay between elation and despair, thrills and terror."
ELAINE HATFIELD

"The emotion of romantic love seems to be distressingly fragile. As a 16th-century sage poignantly observed, 'the history of a love affair is the drama of its fight against time.'"
ELLEN BERSCHEID

Figure 16.4

Parents' caregiving style	Infant attachment	Adult attachment style
Warm/responsive She/he was generally warm and responsive; she/he was good at knowing when to be supportive and when to let me operate on my own; our relationship was almost always comfortable, and I have no major reservations or complaints about it.	**Secure attachment** An infant-caregiver bond in which the child welcomes contact with a close companion and uses this person as a secure base from which to explore the environment.	**Secure** I find it relatively easy to get close to others and am comfortable depending on them and having them depend on me. I don't often worry about being abandoned or about someone getting too close to me.
Cold/rejecting She/he was fairly cold and distant, or rejecting, not very responsive; I wasn't her/his highest priority, her/his concerns were often elsewhere; it's possible that she/he would just as soon not have had me.	**Avoidant attachment** An insecure infant-caregiver bond, characterized by little separation protest and a tendency of the child to avoid or ignore the caregiver.	**Avoidant** I am somewhat uncomfortable being close to others; I find it difficult to trust them, difficult to allow myself to depend on them. I am nervous when anyone gets too close, and often love partners want me to be more intimate than I feel comfortable being.
Ambivalent/inconsistent She/he was noticeably inconsistent in her/his reactions to me, sometimes warm and sometimes not; she/he had her/his own agenda, which sometimes got in the way of her/his receptiveness and responsiveness to my needs; she/he definitely loved me but didn't always show it in the best way.	**Anxious/ambivalent attachment** An insecure infant-caregiver bond, characterized by strong separation protest and a tendency of the child to resist contact initiated by the caregiver, particularly after a separation.	**Anxious/ambivalent** I find that others are reluctant to get as close as I would like. I often worry that my partner doesn't really love me or won't want to stay with me. I want to merge completely with another person, and this desire sometimes scares people away.

Figure 16.4. Infant attachment and romantic relationships. According to Hazan and Shaver (1987), people's romantic relationships in adulthood are similar in form to their attachment patterns in infancy, which are determined in part by parental caregiving styles. The theorized relations between parental styles, attachment patterns, and intimate relations are outlined here. Hazan and Shaver's (1987) study sparked a flurry of follow-up research, which has largely supported the basic premises of their groundbreaking theory, although the linkages between infant experiences and close relationships in adulthood appear to be somewhat more complex than those portrayed here (Shaver & Hazan, 1993). (Data for parental caregiving styles and adult attachment styles based on Hazan and Shaver, 1986, 1987; infant attachment patterns adapted from Shaffer, 1985)

sionate and companionate love *may* coexist, but they don't necessarily go hand in hand.

Although they're rigorous researchers who have made major contributions to the scientific study of love, Berscheid and Hatfield have also been willing to offer down-to-earth, practical insights about the nature of love. For instance, they've identified some common myths about love that can foster disappointment in romantic relationships (Berscheid & Walster, 1978).

Myth 1: When you fall in love, you'll know it. People often spend a great deal of time agonizing over whether they're really in love or only experiencing infatuation. When people consult others about their doubts, they're commonly told, "If it were true love, you'd know it." This assertion, which amounts to replying, "You must not be in love," just isn't true. In reality, confusion about a romantic relationship is not the least bit unusual, and it does *not* mean that you aren't really in love.

Myth 2: Love is a purely positive experience. Our society's idealized views of love often suggest that it should be a purely enjoyable experience. In reality, pain, anger, and ambivalent feelings are common in love relationships, and it's unrealistic to expect love to be entirely pleasant. People often are more critical and less tolerant of lovers than they are of friends. The intense nature of passionate love means that love is capable of taking you to emotional peaks in *either* direction.

Myth 3: True love lasts forever. Love may last forever, but you certainly can't count on it. Some people perpetuate this myth in an interesting way. If their love relationship disintegrates, they conclude that it was never genuine love, only infatuation or comfortable compatibility. According to Hatfield and Berscheid, passionate love typically peaks early in a relationship and then declines rapidly. Companionate love is more likely to continue to grow over the long haul, but there are no guarantees.

Love as Attachment

Cindy Hazan and Phillip Shaver (1987) have looked not at the types of love but at similarities between adult love and attachment relationships in infancy. We noted in Chapter 11 that infant-caretaker bonding, or *attachment*, emerges in the first year of life. Early attachments vary in quality, and infants tend to fall into three groups (Ainsworth et al., 1978). Most infants develop a *secure attachment*. However, some are very anxious when separated from their caretaker, a syndrome called *anxious-ambivalent attachment*. A third group of infants, characterized by *avoidant attachment*, never bond very well with their caretaker (see Figure 16.4).

According to Hazan and Shaver, romantic love is an attachment process, and people's intimate relationships in adulthood follow the same form as their attachments in infancy. According to their theory, a person who had an anxious-ambivalent attachment in infancy will tend to have romantic relations marked by anxiety and ambivalence in adulthood. In other words, people relive their early bonding with their parents in their adult relationships.

Hazan and Shaver's (1987) initial survey study provided some support for their theory. They found that adults' love relationships could be sorted into groups that paralleled the three patterns of attachment seen in infants. *Secure adults* found it relatively easy to get close to others and described their love relations as trusting. *Anxious-ambivalent adults* reported a preoccupation with love accompanied by expectations of rejection and described their love relations as volatile and marked by jealousy. *Avoidant adults* found it difficult to get close to others and described their love relations as lacking intimacy.

Hazan and Shaver found that the percentage of adults falling into each category was roughly the same as the percentage of infants in each comparable category. Also, subjects' recollections of their childhood relations with their parents were consistent with the idea that people relive their infant attachment experiences in adulthood. Subsequent studies by other researchers have supported the idea that attachment styles influence people's choices of lovers, as well as the nature and quality of their romantic relationships (Collins & Read, 1990; Feeney & Noller, 1990; Simpson, 1990).

Culture and Attraction

Relatively little cross-cultural research has been conducted on the dynamics of interpersonal attraction. The limited evidence suggests that there are both similarities and differences between cultures in romantic relationships. For the most part, similarities have been seen when research has focused on what people look for in prospective mates. David Buss (1989, 1994) has collected data on mate preferences in 37 divergent cultures and found that people all over the world value mutual attraction, kindness, intelligence, emotional stability, dependability, and good health. Moreover, he has found gender differences in mating priorities that seem to be nearly universal. Men around the globe are more interested than women in seeking youthfulness and physical attractiveness in their mates. Women, on the other hand, place a greater premium on prospective mates' ambition, industriousness, social status, financial potential, and material resources.

Cultures vary, however, in their emphasis on love—especially passionate love—as a prerequisite for marriage. Love as the basis for marriage is an 18th-century invention of Western culture (Stone, 1977). As Hatfield and Rapson (1993) note, "Marriage-for-love represents an ultimate expression of individualism" (p. 2). In contrast, marriages arranged by families and other go-betweens remain common in cultures high in collectivism, including India (Gupta, 1992), Japan (Iwao, 1993), and China (Xiaghe & Whyte, 1990). This practice is declining in some societies as a result of Westernization, but in collectivist societies people contemplating marriage still tend to think in terms of "What will my parents and other people say?" rather than "What does my heart say?" (Triandis, 1994). Studies show that attitudes about love in collectivist societies reflect these cultural priorities. For example, in comparison to Western subjects, Japanese subjects report that they value romantic love less (Simmons, von Kolke, & Shimizu, 1986) and rate their relationships as being lower in love commitment (Ting-Toomey, 1991). When compared to European subjects, samples from India and South Africa also indicated that they valued romantic love less (Furnham, 1984).

As you can see, research on love is in its infancy. Psychologists have more theory than data and very little consensus on the directions in which future research should proceed. In contrast, they have mountains of data and a great deal of practical knowledge about another important element of social behavior—attitudes.

ATTITUDES: MAKING SOCIAL JUDGMENTS

In our chapter-opening story, Muffy's friends exhibited decidedly negative attitudes about working-class men. Their example reveals a basic feature of attitudes: they're evaluative. They involve making social judgments. Social psychology's interest in attitudes has a much longer history than its interest in attraction. Indeed, in its early days social psychology was defined as the study of attitudes. In this section we'll discuss the nature of attitudes, efforts to change attitudes through persuasion, and theories about the process of attitude change.

What are attitudes? William McGuire (1985) provides a succinct definition in *The Handbook of*

Social Psychology: *Attitudes* locate objects of thought on dimensions of judgment. "Objects of thought" may include social issues (capital punishment or gun control, for example), groups (liberals, farmers), institutions (the Catholic church, the Supreme Court), consumer products (yogurt, computers), and people (the president, your next-door neighbor). "Dimensions of judgment" refers to the various ways in which people might make favorable or unfavorable evaluations of the objects of their thoughts. Although attitudes are social judgments, they're not exclusively cognitive. Attitudes are complex mixtures of cognitive, emotional, and behavioral components.

Components of Attitudes

Social psychologists have traditionally viewed attitudes as being made up of three components (Rajecki, 1990). We can see concrete examples of the three components of an attitude if we look at what one of my former teachers meant years ago when he told me that I had an "attitude problem." The *cognitive component* of an attitude is made up of the *beliefs* that people hold about the object of an attitude. I believed that my teacher was boring, incompetent, and uninterested in his students—you can imagine why he characterized my attitude as a "problem." The *affective component* of an attitude consists of the *emotional feelings* stimulated by an attitude object. At the time, my feelings for my teacher ranged from active dislike to contempt, with some occasional sympathy mixed in. The *behavioral component* of an attitude consists of *predispositions* to act in certain ways toward an attitude object. In the case of my attitude problem, my behavioral tendencies included ignoring lectures, talking in class, and not turning in assignments. (See Figure 16.5 for another example of an attitude divided into its components.) Of course, people exhibit positive as well as negative attitudes. For instance, I had many teachers whom I viewed as bright, dedicated individuals (cognitive component), who elicited feelings of liking and admiration (affective component), and who inspired rapt attention and hard work (behavioral component).

Trying to Change Attitudes: Factors in Persuasion

Every day you're bombarded by efforts to alter your attitudes. In light of this reality, let's examine some of the factors that determine whether persuasion works.

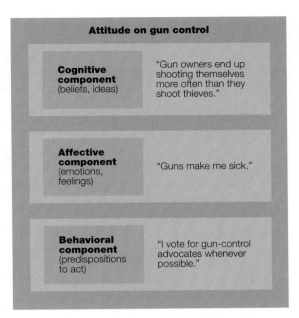

Figure 16.5. The components of attitudes. Attitudes can be broken into cognitive, affective, and behavioral components, as illustrated here for a hypothetical person's attitude about gun control.

The process of persuasion includes four basic elements: source, receiver, message, and channel (see Figure 16.6). **The *source* is the person who sends a communication, and the *receiver* is the person to whom the message is sent.** Thus, if you watch a presidential news conference on TV, the president is the source, and you and millions of other viewers are the receivers. **The *message* is the information transmitted by the source, and the *channel* is the medium through which the message is sent.** Although the research on communication channels is interesting, we'll confine our discussion to source, message, and receiver variables.

Source Factors

Persuasion tends to be more successful when the source has high *credibility* (O'Keefe, 1990). What gives a person credibility? Either expertise or trustworthiness. People try to convey their *expertise* by mentioning their degrees, their training, and their experience or by showing an impressive grasp of the issue at hand (Hass, 1981). Expertise

Figure 16.6. Overview of the persuasion process. The process of persuasion essentially boils down to *who* (the source) communicates *what* (the message) *by what means* (the channel) *to whom* (the receiver). Thus, there are four sets of variables that influence the process of persuasion: source, message, channel, and receiver factors. The diagram lists some of the more important factors in each category (including some that are not discussed in the text due to space limitations). (Adapted from Lippa, 1994)

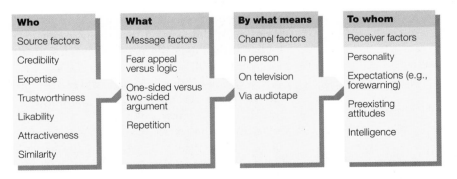

Who	What	By what means	To whom
Source factors	Message factors	Channel factors	Receiver factors
Credibility	Fear appeal versus logic	In person	Personality
Expertise	One-sided versus two-sided argument	On television	Expectations (e.g., forewarning)
Trustworthiness	Repetition	Via audiotape	Preexisting attitudes
Likability			Intelligence
Attractiveness			
Similarity			

is a plus, but *trustworthiness* is even more important (McGinnies & Ward, 1980). Trustworthiness is undermined when a source appears to have something to gain. In contrast, trustworthiness is enhanced when people appear to argue against their own best interests (Hunt, Smith, & Kernan, 1985). *Likability* also increases the effectiveness of a persuasive source (Roskos-Ewoldsen & Fazio, 1992).

The importance of source variables can be seen in advertising. Many companies spend a fortune to obtain an ideal spokesperson, such as Bill Cosby, who combines trustworthiness, expertise (a doctorate in education), and likability. Companies quickly abandon spokespersons when their likability declines. For example, Pepsi immediately canceled an advertising campaign centered on the rock star Madonna when one of her videos offended many people's religious values. Thus, source variables can be extremely important factors in persuasion.

Message Factors

If you were going to give a speech to a local community group advocating a reduction in state taxes on corporations, you'd probably wrestle with a number of questions about how to structure your message. Should you look at both sides of the issue, or should you just present your side? Should you deliver a low-key, logical speech? Or should you try to strike fear into the hearts of your listeners? These questions are concerned with message factors in persuasion.

In general, two-sided arguments seem to be more effective than one-sided presentations (O'Keefe, 1990). Just mentioning that there are two sides to an issue can increase your credibility with an audience (Jones & Brehm, 1970). One-sided messages are best only when your audience is uneducated about the issue or when they're already favorably disposed to your point of view (Lumsdaine & Janis, 1953).

Persuasive messages frequently attempt to arouse fear. Opponents of nuclear power scare us with visions of meltdowns. Antismoking campaigns emphasize the threat of cancer, and deodorant ads highlight the risk of embarrassment. *Do appeals to fear work?* Yes—if they are successful in arousing fear. Research reveals that many messages intended to induce fear fail to do so. However, studies involving a wide range of issues (nuclear policy, auto safety, dental hygiene, and so on) have shown that messages that are effective in arousing fear tend to increase persuasion (Perloff, 1993).

According to Rogers (1983), fear appeals are most likely to work when your listeners view the dire consequences that you describe as exceedingly unpleasant, fairly probable if they don't take your advice, and avoidable if they do.

Receiver Factors

What about the receiver of the persuasive message? Are some people easier to persuade than others? Undoubtedly, but the personality traits that account for these differences interact with other considerations in complicated ways. Transient factors such as the forewarning a receiver gets about a persuasive effort and the receiver's initial position on an issue seem to be more influential than the receiver's personality.

An old saying suggests that "to be forewarned is to be forearmed." The value of *forewarning* applies to targets of persuasive efforts (Petty & Cacioppo, 1979; Pfau et al., 1990). When you shop for a new TV, you *expect* salespeople to work at persuading you, and to some extent this forewarning reduces the impact of their arguments.

The effect of a persuasive effort also depends on the discrepancy between a *receiver's initial position* on an issue and the position advocated by the source. Persuasion tends to work best when a moderate discrepancy exists between the two positions. Why? According to *social judgment theory*, people are usually willing to consider alternative views on an issue if the views aren't too different from their own (Sherif & Hovland, 1961; Upshaw, 1969). **A *latitude of acceptance* is a range of potentially acceptable positions on an issue, centered on one's initial attitude position.** Persuasive messages that fall outside a receiver's latitude of acceptance usually fall on deaf ears. When a message falls within a receiver's latitude of acceptance, successful persuasion is much more likely (Rajecki, 1990). Moreover, within the latitude of acceptance, a larger discrepancy between the receiver's initial position and the position advocated should produce greater attitude change than a smaller discrepancy does (see Figure 16.7).

Our review of source, message, and receiver variables has shown that attempting to change attitudes through persuasion involves a complex interplay of factors—and we haven't even looked beneath the surface yet. How do people acquire attitudes in the first place? What dynamic processes within people produce attitude change? We turn to these theoretical issues next.

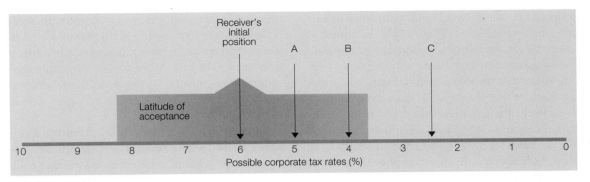

Theories of Attitude Formation and Change

Many theories have been proposed to explain the mechanisms at work in attitude change, whether or not it occurs in response to persuasion. We'll look at three theoretical perspectives: learning theory, dissonance theory, and the elaboration likelihood model.

Learning Theory

We've seen repeatedly that *learning theory* can help explain a wide range of phenomena, from conditioned fears to the acquisition of sex roles to the development of personality traits. Now we can add attitude formation and change to our list.

The affective, or emotional, component in an attitude can be created through *classical conditioning*, just as other emotional responses can (Staats & Staats, 1958; Stalling, 1970). As we discussed in Chapter 6, advertisers routinely try to take advantage of classical conditioning by pairing their products with stimuli that elicit pleasant emotional responses, such as extremely attractive models, highly likable spokespersons, and cherished events (the Olympics, for instance). This conditioning process is diagrammed in Figure 16.8.

Operant conditioning may come into play when you openly express an attitude, such as "I believe that husbands should do more housework." Some people may endorse your view, while others may jump down your throat. Agreement from other people generally functions as a reinforcer, strengthening your tendency to express a specific attitude (Insko, 1965). Disagreement often functions as a form of punishment, which may gradually weaken your commitment to your viewpoint.

Another person's attitudes may rub off on you through *observational learning* (Oskamp, 1991). If you hear your uncle say, "Republicans are nothing but puppets of big business," and your mother heartily agrees, your exposure to your uncle's attitude and your mother's reinforcement of your

uncle may influence your attitude toward the Republican party. Studies show that parents and their children tend to have similar political attitudes (Sears, 1975). Observational learning presumably accounts for much of this similarity. The opinions of teachers, coaches, co-workers, talk-show hosts, rock stars, and so forth are also likely to sway people's attitudes through observational learning.

Dissonance Theory

Leon Festinger's *dissonance theory* assumes that inconsistency among attitudes propels people in the direction of attitude change. Dissonance theory burst into prominence in 1959 when Festinger and J. Merrill Carlsmith published a famous study of counterattitudinal behavior. Let's look at their findings and at how dissonance theory explains them.

Festinger and Carlsmith (1959) had male college students come to a laboratory, where they

Figure 16.8. Classical conditioning of attitudes in advertising. Advertisers routinely pair their products with likable celebrities, such as Bill Cosby, in the hope that their products will come to elicit pleasant emotional responses.

worked on excruciatingly dull tasks, such as turning pegs repeatedly. When a subject's hour was over, the experimenter confided that some participants' motivation was being manipulated by telling them that the task was interesting and enjoyable before they started it. Then, after a moment's hesitation, the experimenter asked if the subject could help him out of a jam. His usual helper was delayed and he needed someone to testify to the next "subject" (really an accomplice) that the experimental task was interesting. He offered to pay the subject if he would tell the person in the adjoining waiting room that the task was enjoyable and involving.

This entire scenario was enacted to coax subjects into doing something that was inconsistent with their true feelings—that is, to engage in *counterattitudinal behavior*. Some subjects received a token payment of $1 for their effort, while others received a more substantial payment of $20 (an amount equivalent to about $60 today, in light of inflation). Later, a second experimenter inquired about the subjects' true feelings regarding the dull experimental task. Figure 16.9 summarizes the design of the Festinger and Carlsmith study.

Who do you think rated the task more favorably—the subjects who were paid $1 or those who were paid $20? Both common sense and learning

theory would predict that the subjects who received the greater reward ($20) should come to like the task more. In reality, however, the subjects who were paid $1 exhibited more favorable attitude change—just as Festinger and Carlsmith had predicted. Why? Dissonance theory provides an explanation.

According to Festinger (1957), ***cognitive dissonance* exists when related cognitions are inconsistent—that is, when they contradict each other.** Festinger's model assumes that dissonance is possible only when cognitions are relevant to each other, as unrelated cognitions ("I am hardworking" and "Fire engines are red") can't contradict each other. However, when cognitions are related, they may be consonant ("I am hardworking" and "I'm staying overtime to get an important job done") or dissonant ("I am hardworking" and "I'm playing hooky from work"). When aroused, cognitive dissonance is supposed to create an unpleasant state of tension that motivates people to reduce their dissonance—usually by altering their cognitions.

In the study by Festinger and Carlsmith (1959), the subjects' contradictory cognitions were "The task is boring" and "I told someone the task was enjoyable." The subjects who were paid $20 for lying had an obvious reason for behaving inconsistently with their true attitudes, so these subjects experienced little dissonance. In contrast, the subjects paid $1 had no readily apparent justification for their lie and experienced high dissonance. To reduce it, they tended to persuade themselves that the task was more enjoyable than they had originally thought. Thus, dissonance theory sheds light on why people sometimes come to believe their own lies.

Cognitive dissonance is also at work when people turn attitudinal somersaults to justify efforts that haven't panned out, a syndrome called *effort justification*. Aronson and Mills (1959) studied effort justification by putting college women through a "severe initiation" before they could qualify to participate in what promised to be an interesting discussion of sexuality. In the initiation, the women had to read obscene passages out loud to a male experimenter. After all that, the highly touted discussion of sexuality turned out to be a boring, taped lecture on reproduction in lower animals. Subjects in the severe initiation condition experienced highly dissonant cognitions ("I went through a lot to get here" and "This discussion is terrible"). How did they reduce their dissonance? Apparently by changing their attitude about the discus-

Figure 16.9. Design of the Festinger and Carlsmith (1959) study. The sequence of events in this landmark study of counterattitudinal behavior and attitude change is outlined here. The diagram omits a third condition (no dissonance), in which subjects were not induced to lie. The results in the non-dissonance condition were similar to those found in the low-dissonance condition.

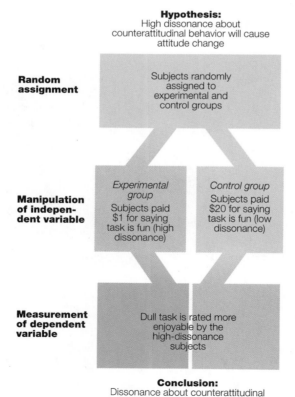

Hypothesis:
High dissonance about counterattitudinal behavior will cause attitude change

Random assignment
Subjects randomly assigned to experimental and control groups

Manipulation of independent variable

Experimental group
Subjects paid $1 for saying task is fun (high dissonance)

Control group
Subjects paid $20 for saying task is fun (low dissonance)

Measurement of dependent variable
Dull task is rated more enjoyable by the high-dissonance subjects

Conclusion:
Dissonance about counterattitudinal behavior does cause attitude change

sion, since they rated it more favorably than sub-jects in two control conditions.

Effort justification may be at work in many facets of everyday life. For example, people who wait in line for hours to get into an exclusive restaurant often praise the restaurant afterward even if they have been served a poorly prepared meal. Rock fans who pay $100 for scalped concert tickets will tend to rate the concert favorably, even if the artists show up in a stupor and play like a garage band.

Dissonance theory has been tested in hundreds of studies with mixed, but largely favorable, re-sults. The dynamics of dissonance appear to un-derlie many attitude changes (Aronson, 1980), and research has supported Festinger's claim that dissonance involves genuine physiological ten-sion and arousal (Croyle & Cooper, 1983). How-ever, it's difficult to predict when dissonance will occur because people may or may not recognize the inconsistencies among their cognitions (Aronson, 1980; Cooper & Fazio, 1984).

Elaboration Likelihood Model

A more recent theory of attitude change proposed by Richard Petty and John Cacioppo (1986) as-serts that there are two basic "routes" to persua-sion. The *central route* is taken when people care-fully ponder the content and logic of persuasive messages. The *peripheral route* is taken when per-suasion depends on nonmessage factors, such as the attractiveness and credibility of the source, or on conditioned emotional responses. For example, a politician who campaigns by delivering carefully researched speeches that thoughtfully analyze com-plex issues is following the central route to persua-sion. In contrast, a politician who depends on marching bands, flag waving, celebrity endorse-ments, and emotional slogans is following the peripheral route.

Both routes can lead to persuasion. However, according to the *elaboration likelihood model*, the durability of attitude change depends on the ex-tent to which people elaborate on (think about) the contents of persuasive communications. Stud-ies suggest that the central route to persuasion leads to more enduring attitude change than the peripheral route (Chaiken, 1987; Tesser & Shaffer, 1990). Research also suggests that attitudes changed through central processes predict behav-ior better than attitudes changed through periph-eral processes (Petty, Cacioppo, & Schumann, 1983).

The elaboration likelihood model adds another

CONCEPT CHECK 16.3
Understanding Attitudes and Persuasion

Check your understanding of the components of attitudes and the elements of persuasion by analyzing hypothetical political strategies. Imagine you're work-ing on a political campaign and you're invited to join the candidate's inner circle in strategy sessions, as staff members prepare the candidate for upcoming campaign stops. During the meetings, you hear various strategies discussed. For each strategy below, indicate which component of voters' attitudes (cogni-tive, affective, or behavioral) is being targeted for change, and indicate which element in persuasion (source, message, or receiver factors) is being manipu-lated. The answers are in Appendix A.

1. "You need to convince this crowd that your program for regulating nursing homes is sound. Whatever you do, don't acknowledge the two weaknesses in the program that we've been playing down. I don't care if you're asked point blank. Just slide by the question and keep harping on the program's advantages."
2. "You haven't been smiling enough lately, especially when the TV cameras are rolling. Remember, you can have the best ideas in the world, but if you don't seem likable, you're not gonna get elected. By the way, I think I've lined up some photo opportunities that should help us create an image of sincerity and compassion."
3. "This crowd is already behind you. You don't have to alter their opinions on any issue. Get right to work convincing them to contribute to the campaign. I want them lining up to give money."

complication to the complex relations between attitudes and behavior. We'll see more complica-tions in the next section, which is concerned with related aspects of social influence—conformity and obedience.

CONFORMITY AND OBEDIENCE: YIELDING TO OTHERS

A few years ago, the area I live in experienced a severe flood that required the mobilization of the National Guard and various emergency services. At the height of the crisis, a young man arrived at the scene of the flood, announced that he was from an obscure state agency that no one had ever heard of, and proceeded to take control of the emer-gency. City work crews, the fire department, local police, municipal officials, and the National Guard followed his orders with dispatch for several days, evacuating entire neighborhoods—until an official thought to check and found out that the man was just someone who had walked in off the street. The imposter, who had had small armies at his beck and call for several days, had no training in emergency services, just a history of unemployment and psychological problems.

After news of the hoax spread, people criticized red-faced local officials for their compliance with the imposter's orders. However, many of the critics probably would have cooperated in much the same way if they had been in the officials' shoes. For most people, willingness to obey someone in authority is the rule, not the exception. In this section, we'll analyze the dynamics of social influence at work in conformity and obedience.

Conformity

If you keep a well-manicured lawn and extoll the talents of the popular rock star Bruce Springsteen, are you exhibiting conformity? According to social psychologists, it depends on whether your behavior is the result of group pressure. **Conformity occurs when people yield to real or imagined social pressure.** For example, if you maintain a well-groomed lawn only to avoid complaints from your neighbors, you're yielding to social pressure. If you like Springsteen because you genuinely enjoy his records, that's *not* conformity. However, if you like Springsteen because it's "hip" and your friends would question your taste if you didn't, then you're conforming.

In the 1950s, Solomon Asch (1951, 1955, 1956) devised a clever procedure that minimized ambiguity about whether subjects were conforming, allowing him to investigate the variables that govern conformity. Let's re-create one of Asch's (1955) classic experiments. The subjects are male undergraduates recruited for a study of visual perception. A group of seven subjects are shown a large card with a vertical line on it and then are asked to indicate which of three lines on a second card

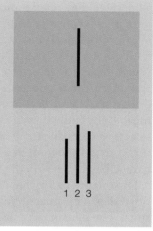

Figure 16.10. Stimuli used in Asch's conformity studies. Subjects were asked to match a standard line (top) with one of three other lines displayed on another card (bottom). The task was easy—until experimental accomplices started responding with obviously incorrect answers, creating a situation in which Asch evaluated subjects' conformity.

matches the original "standard line" in length (see Figure 16.10). All seven subjects are given a turn at the task, and they announce their choice to the group. The subject in the sixth chair doesn't know it, but everyone else in the group is an accomplice of the experimenter, and they're about to make him wonder whether he has taken leave of his senses.

The accomplices give accurate responses on the first two trials. On the third trial, line number 2 clearly is the correct response, but the first five "subjects" all say that line number 3 matches the standard line. The genuine subject is bewildered and can't believe his ears. Over the course of the next 15 trials, the accomplices all give the same incorrect response on 11 of them. How does the real subject respond? The line judgments are easy and unambiguous. So, if the subject consistently agrees with the accomplices, he isn't making honest mistakes—he's conforming.

Averaging across all 50 subjects, Asch (1955) found that the young men conformed on 37% of the trials. The subjects varied considerably in their tendency to conform, however. Of the 50 subjects, 13 never caved in to the group, while 14 conformed on more than half the trials.

In subsequent studies, *group size* and *group unanimity* turned out to be key determinants of conformity (Asch, 1956). To examine the impact of group size, Asch repeated his procedure with groups that included from 1 to 15 accomplices. Little conformity was seen when a subject was pitted against just one person, but conformity increased rapidly as group size went from 2 to 4, peaked at a group size of 7, and then leveled off (see Figure 16.11). Thus, Asch concluded that as groups grow larger, conformity increases—up to a point.

However, group size made little difference if

Figure 16.11. Conformity and group size. This graph shows the percentage of trials on which subjects conformed as a function of group size in Asch's research. Asch found that conformity became more frequent as group size increased up to about seven, and then conformity leveled off. (Data from Asch, 1955)

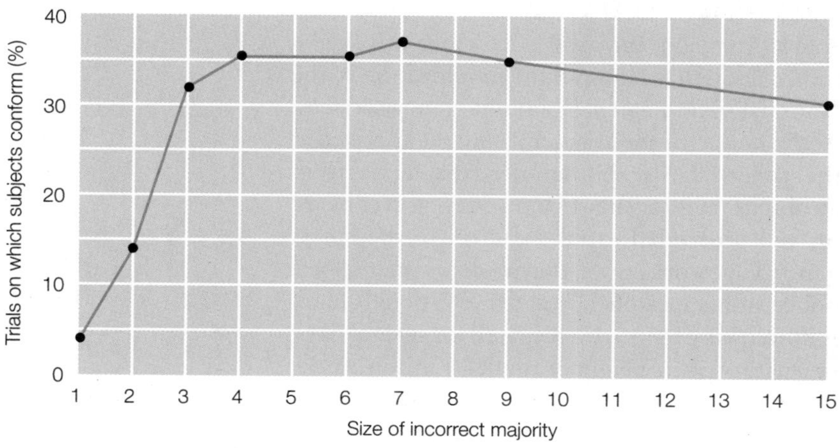

Size of incorrect majority (x-axis: 1–15)
Trials on which subjects conform (%) (y-axis: 0–40)

just one accomplice "broke" with the others, wrecking their unanimous agreement. The presence of another dissenter lowered conformity to about one-quarter of its peak, even when the dissenter made *inaccurate* judgments that happened to conflict with the majority view. Apparently, the subjects just needed to hear someone else question the accuracy of the group's perplexing responses. The importance of unanimity in fostering conformity has been replicated in subsequent research (Nemeth & Chiles, 1988).

Obedience

Obedience **is a form of compliance that occurs when people follow direct commands, usually from someone in a position of authority.** To a surprising extent, when an authority figure says, "Jump!" many people simply ask, "How high?"

Milgram's Studies

Stanley Milgram wanted to study this tendency to obey authority figures. Like many other people after World War II, he was troubled by how readily the citizens of Germany followed the orders of dictator Adolf Hitler, even when the orders required morally repugnant actions, such as the slaughter of millions of Jews. Milgram, who had worked with Solomon Asch, set out to design a standard laboratory procedure for the study of obedience, much like Asch's procedure for studying conformity. The clever experiment that Milgram devised became one of the most fa-mous and controversial studies in the annals of psychology.

Milgram's (1963) subjects were a diverse collection of 40 men from the local community. They were told that they would be participating in a study concerned with the effects of punishment on learning. When they arrived at the lab, they drew slips of paper from a hat to get their assignments. The drawing was rigged so that the subject always became the "teacher" and an experimental accomplice (a likable 47-year-old accountant) became the "learner."

The learner was strapped into an electrified chair through which a shock could be delivered whenever he made a mistake on the task (see Figure 16.12). The subject was then taken to an adjoining room that housed the shock generator that he would control in his role as the teacher. Although the apparatus looked and sounded realistic, it was a fake and the learner was never shocked.

As the "learning experiment" proceeded, the accomplice made many mistakes that necessitated shocks. The teacher was instructed to increase the shock level after each wrong answer. At 300 volts, the learner began to pound on the wall between the two rooms in protest and soon stopped responding to the teacher's questions. From this point forward, subjects frequently turned to the experimenter for guidance. Whenever they did so, the experimenter firmly indicated that the teacher should continue to give stronger and stronger shocks to the now-silent learner. The dependent

"The essence of obedience is that a person comes to view himself as the instrument for carrying out another person's wishes, and he therefore no longer regards himself as responsible for his actions."
STANLEY MILGRAM

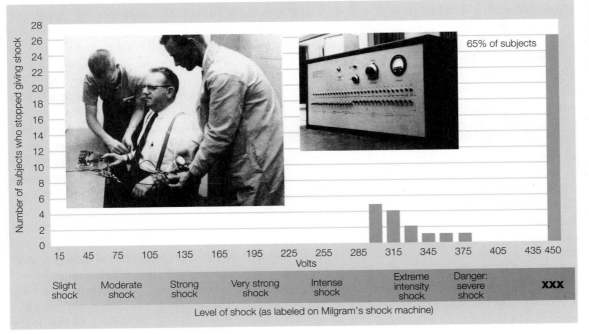

Figure 16.12. Milgram's experiment on obedience. The photo on the left shows the "learner" being connected to the shock generator during one of Milgram's experimental sessions. The photo on the right shows the fake shock generator used in the study. The surprising results of the Milgram (1963) study are summarized in the bar graph. Although subjects frequently protested, the vast majority (65%) delivered the entire series of shocks to the learner. (Photos copyright 1965 by Stanley Milgram. From the film *Obedience*, distributed by The Pennsylvania State University.)

variable was the maximum shock the subject was willing to administer before refusing to go on.

As Figure 16.12 shows, 26 of the 40 subjects (65%) administered all 30 levels of shock. Although they tended to obey the experimenter, many subjects voiced and displayed considerable distress about harming the learner. The horrified subjects groaned, bit their lips, stuttered, trembled, and broke into a sweat, but continued administering the shocks. Based on these results, Milgram concluded that obedience to authority was even more common than he or others anticipated.

In interpreting his results, Milgram argued that strong pressure from an authority figure can make decent people do terribly indecent things to others. Applying this insight to Nazi war crimes and other travesties, Milgram asserted that some sinister actions may not be due to actors' evil character so much as to situational pressures that can lead normal people to engage in acts of treachery and violence. Thus, he arrived at the disturbing conclusion that given the right circumstances, any of us might obey orders to inflict harm on innocent strangers.

After his initial demonstration, Milgram (1974) tried about 20 variations on his experimental procedure, looking for factors that influenced subjects' obedience. As a whole, Milgram was surprised at how stable subjects' obedience remained as he changed various aspects of his experiment.

The Ensuing Controversy

Milgram's study evoked a controversy that continues through today. Some critics argued that Milgram's results wouldn't generalize to the real world (Baumrind, 1964; Orne & Holland, 1968). They maintained that subjects who agree to participate in a scientific study *expect to obey* orders from an experimenter. Milgram (1964, 1968) replied by pointing out that so do soldiers and bureaucrats in the real world who are accused of villainous acts performed in obedience to authority. "I reject Baumrind's argument that the observed obedience doesn't count because it occurred where it is appropriate," said Milgram (1964). "That is precisely why it *does* count." Overall, the weight of evidence supports the generalizability of Milgram's results. They were consistently replicated for many years, in diverse settings, with a variety of subjects and procedural variations (Miller, 1986).

Critics also questioned the ethics of Milgram's procedure (Baumrind, 1964; Kelman, 1967). They noted that without prior consent, subjects were exposed to extensive deception that could undermine their trust in people and severe stress that could leave emotional scars. Milgram's defenders argued that the brief distress experienced by his subjects was a small price to pay for the insights that emerged from his obedience studies. Looking back, however, many psychologists seem to share the critics' concerns about the ethical implications of Milgram's work. His procedure is questionable by contemporary standards of research ethics, and no replications of his obedience study have been conducted in the United States since the mid-1970s (Blass, 1991)—a bizarre epitaph for what may be psychology's best-known experiment.

Cultural Variations in Conformity and Obedience

Are conformity and obedience unique to American culture? By no means. The Asch and Milgram experiments have been repeated in many different societies, where they have yielded results roughly similar to those seen in the United States. Thus, the phenomena of conformity and obedience seem to transcend culture.

The replications of Milgram's obedience study have largely been limited to industrialized nations similar to the United States. Comparisons of the results of these studies must be made with caution because the composition of the samples and the experimental procedures have varied somewhat. But many of the studies have reported even higher obedience rates than those seen in Milgram's American samples. For example, obedience rates over 80% have been reported for samples from Italy, Germany, Austria, Spain, and Holland (Smith & Bond, 1994). Thus, the surprisingly high level of obedience observed by Milgram does not appear to be peculiar to the United States.

The Asch experiment has been repeated in a more diverse range of societies than the Milgram experiment. As is often the case, cross-national comparisons are fraught with peril because of disparities in the makeup of the samples. But researchers have tentatively concluded that there are modest cultural variations in the propensity to conform. Like many other cultural differences in social behavior, these variations appear to be related to the degree of *individualism versus collectivism* seen in a society. Various theorists have argued that collectivistic cultures, which emphasize respect for group norms, cooperation, and harmony, probably encourage more conformity than individualistic cultures, with their emphasis on independence and assertiveness (Matsumoto, 1994; Schwartz, 1990). Consistent with this analysis, replications of the Asch experiment have tended to find somewhat higher levels of conformity in collectivistic cultures than in individualistic cultures (Smith & Bond, 1994).

Our discussion of conformity and obedience foreshadows our last major topic in this chapter, behavior in groups. Social pressure, for instance, is often at work in group interactions, and being part of a group can have a dramatic impact on an individual's behavior (as it did in the Asch studies). Our review of behavior in groups will begin with a look at the nature of groups.

BEHAVIOR IN GROUPS: JOINING WITH OTHERS

Social psychologists study groups as well as individuals, but exactly what is a group? Are all the divorced fathers living in Baltimore a group? Are three strangers moving skyward in an elevator a group? What if the elevator gets stuck? How about four students from your psychology class who study together regularly? A jury deciding a trial? The Boston Celtics? Some of these collections of people are groups and others aren't. Let's examine the concept of a group to find out which of these collections qualify.

In social psychologists' eyes, **a *group* consists of two or more individuals who interact and are interdependent.** The divorced fathers in Baltimore aren't likely to qualify on either count. Strangers sharing an elevator might interact briefly, but they're not interdependent. However, if the elevator got stuck and they had to deal with an emergency together, they could suddenly become a group. Your psychology classmates who study together are a group, as they interact and depend on each other to achieve shared goals. So do the members of a jury and a sports team such as the Celtics.

Groups vary in many ways. Obviously, a study group, the Celtics, and a jury are very different in terms of size, purpose, formality, longevity, similarity of members, and diversity of activities. Can anything meaningful be said about groups if they're so diverse? Yes. In spite of their immense variability, groups share certain features that affect their functioning. Among other things, most groups have *roles* that allocate special responsibilities to some members, *norms* about suit-

able behavior, a *communication structure* that reflects who talks to whom, and a *power structure* that determines which members wield the most influence (Forsyth, 1990). For example, a study group and the Celtics may appear to have little in common, but both might have a "harmonizer" whose role is to smooth over conflicts among members, a norm that "everyone pulls his own weight," and an unequal distribution of power among members.

Behavior Alone and in Groups: The Case of the Bystander Effect

Imagine that you have a precarious medical condition and that you must go through life worrying about whether someone will leap forward to provide help if the need ever arises. Wouldn't you feel more secure around larger groups? After all, there's "safety in numbers." Logically, as group size increases, the probability of having a good Samaritan on the scene increases. Or does it? We've seen before that human behavior isn't necessarily logical. When it comes to helping behavior, many studies have uncovered an apparent paradox called the **bystander effect: people are less likely to provide needed help when they are in groups than when they are alone.**

Evidence that your probability of getting help *declines* as group size increases was first described by John Darley and Bibb Latané (1968), who were conducting research on the determinants of helping behavior. In the Darley and Latané study, students in individual cubicles connected by an intercom participated in discussion groups of three sizes. Early in the discussion, a student who was an experimental accomplice hesitantly mentioned that he was prone to seizures. Later in the discussion, the same accomplice feigned a severe seizure and cried out for help. Although a majority of subjects sought assistance for the student, Figure 16.13 (on the next page) shows that the tendency to seek help *declined* with increasing group size.

Similar trends have been seen in many other experiments, in which over 6000 subjects have had opportunities to respond to apparent emergencies including fires, asthma attacks, faintings, crashes, and flat tires, as well as less pressing needs to answer a door or to pick up objects dropped by a stranger. Pooling the results of this research, Latané and Nida (1981) estimated that subjects who were alone provided help 75% of the time, whereas subjects in the presence of others provided help only 53% of the time.

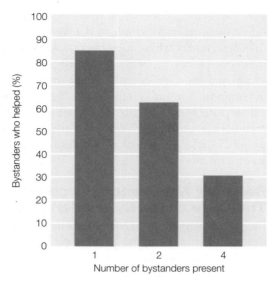

that they were all dawdling. And then again, perhaps not. Individuals' productivity often *does* decline in larger groups (Latané, Williams, & Harkins, 1979).

Two factors appear to contribute to reduced individual productivity in larger groups. One factor is *reduced efficiency* resulting from the *loss of coordination* among workers' efforts (Kravitz & Martin, 1986). As you put more people on a yearbook staff, for instance, you'll probably create more and more duplication of effort and increase how often group members end up working at cross purposes.

The second factor contributing to low productivity in groups involves *effort* rather than efficiency. **Social loafing is a reduction in effort by individuals when they work in groups as compared to when they work by themselves.** To investigate social loafing, Latané et al. (1979) measured the sound output produced by subjects who were asked to cheer or clap as loud as they could. So they couldn't see or hear other group members, subjects were told that the study concerned the importance of sensory feedback and were asked to don blindfolds and put on headphones through which loud noise was played. This maneuver permitted a simple deception: subjects were *led to believe* that they were working alone or in a group of two or six, when in fact *individual* output was actually measured.

When subjects *thought* that they were working in larger groups, their individual output declined. Since lack of coordination could not affect individual output, the subjects' decreased sound production had to be due to reduced effort. Latané and his colleagues also had the same subjects clap and shout in genuine groups of two and six and found an additional decrease in production that was attributed to loss of coordination. Figure 16.14 shows how social loafing and loss of coordination combined to reduce productivity as group size increased.

What accounts for the bystander effect? A number of factors may be at work. For instance, the *diffusion of responsibility* that occurs in a group is important. If you're by yourself when you encounter someone in need of help, the responsibility to provide help rests squarely on your shoulders. However, if other people are present, the responsibility is divided among you, and you may all say to yourselves "Someone else will help." A reduced sense of responsibility may contribute to other aspects of behavior in groups, as we'll see in the next section.

Group Productivity and Social Loafing

Have you ever driven through a road construction project—at a snail's pace, of course—and become irritated because so many workers seem to be just standing around? Maybe the irony of the posted sign "Your tax dollars at work" made you imagine

According to Latané (1981), the bystander effect and social loafing share a common cause: diffusion of responsibility in groups. As group size increases, the responsibility for getting a job done is divided among more people, and many group members ease up because their individual contribution is less recognizable. Thus, social loafing occurs in situations where individuals can "hide in the crowd." Consistent with this line of thinking, research shows that social loafing is more likely: (a) in larger groups, (b) on tasks where individual output is hard to evaluate, and (c) in situations where group members expect their co-workers to

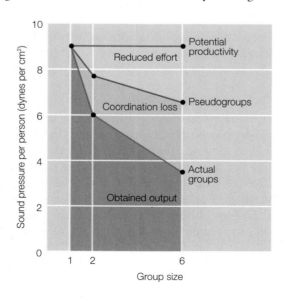

perform well and "carry them" (Karau & Williams, 1993).

Decision Making in Groups

Productivity is not the only issue that commonly concerns groups. When people join together in groups, they often have to make decisions about what the group will do and how it will use its resources. Whether it's your study group deciding what type of pizza to order, a jury deciding on a verdict, or Congress deciding whether to pass a bill, groups make decisions. Social psychologists have discovered some interesting tendencies in group decision making. We'll take a brief look at *group polarization* and *groupthink*.

Group Polarization

Who leans toward more cautious decisions: individuals or groups? Common sense suggests that groups will work out compromises that cancel out members' extreme views. Hence, the collective wisdom of the group should yield relatively conservative choices. Is common sense correct? To investigate this question, Stoner (1961) asked individual subjects to give their recommendations on tough decisions and then asked the same subjects to engage in group discussion to arrive at joint recommendations. When Stoner compared individuals' average recommendation against their group decision generated through discussion, he found that groups arrived at *riskier* decisions than individuals did. Stoner's finding was replicated in other studies (Pruitt, 1971), and the phenomenon acquired the name *risky shift*.

However, investigators eventually determined that groups can shift either way, toward risk or caution, depending on which way the group is leaning to begin with (Myers & Lamm, 1976). A shift toward a more extreme position, an effect called *polarization*, is often the result of group discussion. Thus, ***group polarization* occurs when group discussion strengthens a group's dominant point of view and produces a shift toward a more extreme decision in that direction** (see Figure 16.15). Group polarization does *not* involve widening the gap between factions in a group, as its name might suggest. In fact, group polarization can contribute to consensus in a group, as we'll see in our discussion of groupthink.

Groupthink

In contrast to group polarization, which is a normal process in group dynamics, groupthink is more like a "disease" that can infect decision making in groups. ***Groupthink* occurs when**

members of a cohesive group emphasize concurrence at the expense of critical thinking in arriving at a decision. As you might imagine, groupthink doesn't produce very effective decision making. Indeed, groupthink often leads to major blunders that may look incomprehensible after the fact. Irving Janis (1972) first described groupthink in his effort to explain how President John F. Kennedy and his advisers could have miscalculated so badly in deciding to invade Cuba at the Bay of Pigs in 1961. The attempted invasion failed miserably and, in retrospect, seemed re-

Figure 16.15. Group polarization. Two examples of group polarization are diagrammed here. In the first example (top), a group starts out mildly opposed to an idea, but after discussion there is stronger sentiment against the idea. In the second example (bottom), a group starts out with a favorable disposition toward an idea, and this disposition is strengthened by group discussion.

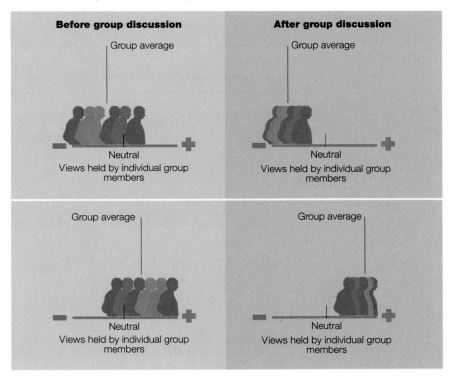

Before group discussion — Group average — Neutral — Views held by individual group members

After group discussion — Group average — Neutral — Views held by individual group members

Group average — Neutral — Views held by individual group members

Group average — Neutral — Views held by individual group members

Many types of groups have to arrive at collective decisions. The social dynamics of group decisions are complicated, and a variety of factors can undermine effective decision making.

Figure 16.16. A model of groupthink. The antecedent conditions and symptoms of groupthink are outlined here, along with the resultant effects on a group's decision making.

markably ill-conceived. Applying his many years of research on group dynamics to the Bay of Pigs fiasco, Janis developed a model of groupthink, which is summarized in Figure 16.16.

When groups get caught up in groupthink, members suspend their critical judgment and the group starts censoring dissent as the pressure to conform increases. Soon, everyone begins to think alike. Moreover, "mind guards" try to shield the group from information that contradicts the

Antecedent conditions

1. High cohesiveness
2. Insulation of the group
3. Lack of methodical procedures for search and appraisal
4. Directive leadership
5. High stress with low degree of hope for finding better solution than the one favored by the leader or other influential persons

Concurrence-seeking tendency

Symptoms of groupthink

1. Illusion of invulnerability
2. Collective rationalization
3. Belief in inherent morality of the group
4. Stereotypes of outgroups
5. Direct pressure on dissenters
6. Self-censorship
7. Illusion of unanimity
8. Self-appointed mind guards

Symptoms of defective decision making

1. Incomplete survey of alternatives
2. Incomplete survey of objectives
3. Failure to examine risks of preferred choice
4. Poor information search
5. Selective bias in processing information at hand
6. Failure to reappraise alternatives
7. Failure to work out contingency plans

group's view. If the group's view is challenged from outside, victims of groupthink tend to think in simplistic terms, dividing the world into the *ingroup*—**the group they belong to and identify with—and the *outgroup*—people who are not part of the ingroup.** When groups shift into this "us versus them" thinking, members begin to overestimate the ingroup's unanimity, and they begin to view the outgroup as the enemy. Groupthink also promotes incomplete gathering of information. The group's search for information is biased in favor of facts and opinions that support their decision.

What causes groupthink? The key precondition is high group cohesiveness. *Group cohesiveness* **refers to the strength of the liking relationships linking group members to each other and to the group itself.** Members of cohesive groups are close-knit, are committed, have "team spirit," and are very loyal to the group. Cohesiveness itself isn't bad. It can help groups achieve great things. But Janis maintains that the danger of groupthink is greater when groups are highly cohesive. Groupthink is also more likely when a group works in relative isolation, when its power structure is dominated by a strong, directive leader, and when it is under stress to make a major decision (see Figure 16.16). Under these conditions, group discussions can lead to group polarization, strengthening the group's dominant view.

After his description of groupthink, Janis and others reviewed other presidential blunders and found clear signs of groupthink underlying Franklin D. Roosevelt's lack of preparation for Japan's attack on Pearl Harbor, President Lyndon Johnson's continued escalation of the Vietnam war, and President Richard Nixon's cover-up of the Watergate break-in. Of course, groupthink is not limited to the highest levels of government. It may be even more prevalent in less public groups that make decisions every day in board rooms, committee rooms, courtrooms, and back rooms all over the world.

Only a handful of experiments have been conducted to test Janis's theory, because the antecedent conditions thought to foster groupthink—such as high decision stress, strong group cohesiveness, and dominating leadership—are difficult to create effectively in laboratory settings (Aldag & Fuller, 1993). Although one recent experimental study by Turner and her associates (1992) found support for certain aspects of Janis's theory, the evidence on groupthink consists almost entirely of retrospective case studies of major decision-making fiascos. In analyzing these cases Janis and other investigators may have tended to see what they expected to see (Tetlock et al., 1992). Thus, Janis's model of groupthink should probably be characterized as an innovative, sophisticated, intuitively appealing theory that needs to be subjected to much more empirical study.

PUTTING IT IN PERSPECTIVE

Our discussion of social psychology has provided a final embellishment on three of our seven unifying themes. One of these is the value of psychology's commitment to empiricism—that is, its reliance on systematic observation through research to arrive at conclusions. The second theme that stands out is the importance of cultural factors in shaping behavior, and the third is the extent to which people's experience of the world is highly subjective. Let's consider the virtues of empiricism first.

It's easy to question the need to do scientific research on social behavior, because studies in social psychology often seem to verify common sense. While most people wouldn't presume to devise their own theory of color vision or question the significance of REM sleep, everyone has beliefs about the nature of love, how to persuade others, and the limits of obedience. Thus, when studies demonstrate that credibility enhances persuasion, or that good looks facilitate attraction, it's tempting to conclude that social psychologists go to great lengths to document the obvious, and some critics say, "Why bother?"

You saw why in this chapter. Research in social psychology has repeatedly shown that the predictions of logic and common sense are often wrong. Consider just a few examples. Even psychiatric experts failed to predict the remarkable obedience to authority uncovered in Milgram's research. The bystander effect in helping behavior violates cold-blooded mathematical logic. Dissonance research has shown that after a severe initiation, the bigger the letdown, the more favorable people's feelings are. These principles defy common sense.

Thus, research on social behavior provides dramatic illustrations of why psychologists put their faith in empiricism. The moral of social psychology's story is this: Although scientific research often supports ideas based on common sense and logic, we can't count on this result. If psychologists want to achieve sound understanding of the principles governing behavior, they have to put their ideas to an empirical test.

Our coverage of social psychology also demonstrated once again that behavior is characterized by both cultural variance and invariance. Although basic social phenomena such as stereotyping, attraction, obedience, and conformity probably occur all over the world, cross-cultural studies of social behavior show that research findings based on American samples may not generalize precisely to other cultures.

Research in social psychology is also uniquely well suited for making the point that people's view of the world is highly personal and subjective. In this chapter we saw how physical appearance can color perception of a person's ability or personality, how social schemas can lead people to see what they expect to see in their interactions with others, how pressure to conform can make people begin to doubt their senses, and how groupthink can lead group members down a perilous path of shared illusions.

The subjectivity of social perception will surface once again in our chapter Application. It focuses on a practical problem that social psychologists have shown great interest in—prejudice.

Understanding Prejudice

Answer the following "true" or false."

___ **1** Prejudice and discrimination amount to the same thing.

___ **2** Stereotypes are always negative or unflattering.

___ **3** Ethnic and racial groups are the only widespread targets of prejudice in modern society.

___ **4** People see members of their own ingroup as being more alike than the members of outgroups.

Prejudice is a major social problem. It harms victims' self-concepts, suppresses human potential, creates tension and strife between groups, and even instigates wars. The first step toward reducing prejudice is to understand its roots. Hence, in this Application we'll strive to achieve a better understanding of why prejudice is so common. Along the way, you'll learn the answers to the true-false questions above.

Prejudice and discrimination are closely related concepts, and the terms have become nearly interchangeable in popular use. Social scientists, however, prefer to define their terms precisely, so let's clarify which is which. *Prejudice* **is a negative attitude held toward members of a group.** Like other attitudes, prejudice includes three components (see Figure 16.17): beliefs ("Indians are mostly alcoholics"), emotions ("I despise Jews"), and behavioral dispositions ("I wouldn't hire a Mexican"). Racial prejudice receives the lion's share of publicity, but prejudice is *not* limited to ethnic groups. Women, homosexuals, the aged, the handicapped, and the mentally ill are also targets of widespread prejudice. Thus, many people hold prejudicial attitudes toward one group or another, and many have been victims of prejudice.

Prejudice may lead to *discrimination,* **which involves behaving differently, usually unfairly, toward the members of a group.** Prejudice and discrimination tend to go hand in hand, but as we discussed earlier, attitudes and behavior do not necessarily correspond (see Figure 16.18). In our discussion, we'll concentrate primarily on the attitude of prejudice. Let's begin by looking at processes in person perception that promote prejudice.

Stereotyping and Selectivity in Person Perception

Perhaps no factor plays a larger role in prejudice than *stereotypes.* However, stereotypes are not inevitably negative. Although it's a massive overgeneralization, it's hardly insulting to assert that Americans are ambitious or that the Japanese are industrious. Unfortunately, many people *do* subscribe to derogatory stereotypes of various ethnic groups. Although studies suggest that negative racial stereotypes have diminished over the last 50 years, they're not a thing of the past (Dovidio & Gaertner, 1991; Smith, 1991; Trimble, 1988). According to a variety of investigators, modern racism has merely become more subtle (Ponterotto & Pedersen, 1993).

Stereotypes persist, in part, because the *selectivity* of person perception makes it likely that people will see what they expect to see when they actually come into contact with groups that they view with prejudice (Stephan, 1989). For example, Duncan (1976) had white subjects watch and evaluate interaction on a TV monitor that was supposedly live (actually it was a videotape), and varied the race of a person who gets into an argument and gives another person a slight shove. The shove was coded as

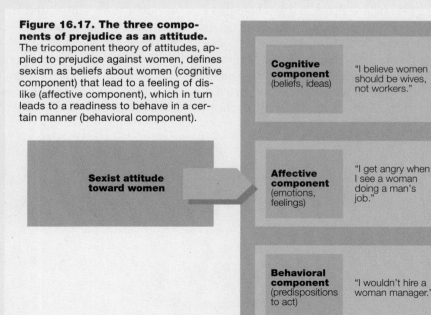

Figure 16.17. The three components of prejudice as an attitude. The tricomponent theory of attitudes, applied to prejudice against women, defines sexism as beliefs about women (cognitive component) that lead to a feeling of dislike (affective component), which in turn leads to a readiness to behave in a certain manner (behavioral component).

Sexist attitude toward women

Cognitive component (beliefs, ideas)
"I believe women should be wives, not workers."

Affective component (emotions, feelings)
"I get angry when I see a woman doing a man's job."

Behavioral component (predispositions to act)
"I wouldn't hire a woman manager."

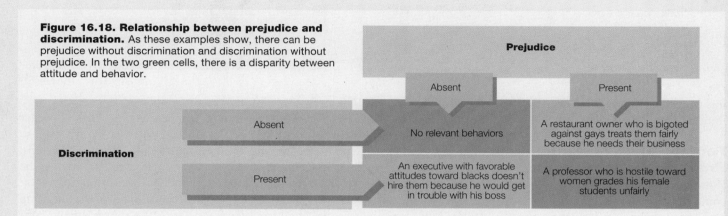

Figure 16.18. Relationship between prejudice and discrimination. As these examples show, there can be prejudice without discrimination and discrimination without prejudice. In the two green cells, there is a disparity between attitude and behavior.

		Prejudice	
		Absent	Present
Discrimination	Absent	No relevant behaviors	A restaurant owner who is bigoted against gays treats them fairly because he needs their business
	Present	An executive with favorable attitudes toward blacks doesn't hire them because he would get in trouble with his boss	A professor who is hostile toward women grades his female students unfairly

"violent behavior" by 73% of the subjects when the actor was black but by only 13% of the subjects when the actor was white. As we've noted before, people's perceptions are highly subjective. Because of stereotypes, even "violence" may lie in the eye of the beholder.

Memory biases are also tilted in favor of confirming people's prejudices. For example, if a man believes that "women are not cut out for leadership roles," he may dwell with delight on his female supervisor's mistakes and quickly forget about her achievements. Thus, the *illusory correlation effect* can contribute to the maintenance of prejudicial stereotypes (Hamilton & Sherman, 1989). Obviously, actual interaction can do only so much to counteract stereotypes, since gender stereotypes remain common even though men and women interact extensively.

Biases in Attribution

Attribution processes can also help perpetuate stereotypes and prejudice. Research taking its cue from Weiner's (1980) model of attribution has shown that people often make *biased attributions for success and failure*. For example, men and women don't get equal credit for their successes (Deaux, 1984). Observers often discount a woman's success by attrib-

uting it to good luck, sheer effort, or the ease of the task (except on traditional feminine tasks). In comparison, a man's success is more likely to be attributed to his outstanding ability. Figure 16.19 (on the next page) shows how sex bias tends to affect attributions for success and failure. These biased patterns of attribution help sustain the stereotype that men are more competent than women. Similar patterns of bias have been seen in attributional explanations of ethnic minorities' successes and failures (Jackson, Sullivan, & Hodge, 1993; Kluegel, 1990).

Recall that the *fundamental attribution error* is a bias toward explaining events by pointing to the personal characteristics of the actors as causes (internal attributions). Research suggests that people are particularly likely to make this error when evaluating targets of prejudice (Hewstone, 1990; Pettigrew, 1979). Thus, when people take note of ethnic neighborhoods dominated by crime and poverty, the personal qualities of the residents are blamed for these problems, while other explanations emphasizing situational factors (job discrimination, poor police service, and so on) are downplayed or ignored.

Defensive attribution, which involves unjustly blaming victims of misfortune

for their adversity, can also contribute to prejudice. A prominent example in recent years has been the assertion by some people that homosexuals brought the AIDS crisis on themselves and so deserve their fate (Anderson, 1992). By blaming AIDS on gays' alleged character flaws, heterosexuals may be unknowingly seek-

Members of many types of groups are victims of prejudice. Besides racial minorities, others than have been stereotyped and discriminated against include gays, women, the disabled, the homeless, and those who are overweight or obese.

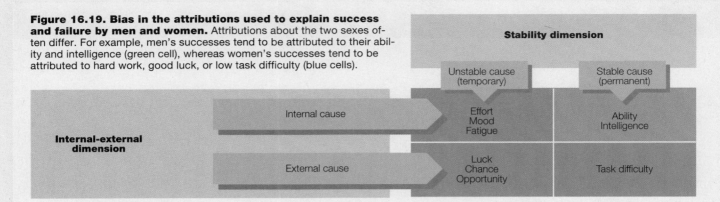

Figure 16.19. Bias in the attributions used to explain success and failure by men and women. Attributions about the two sexes often differ. For example, men's successes tend to be attributed to their ability and intelligence (green cell), whereas women's successes tend to be attributed to hard work, good luck, or low task difficulty (blue cells).

Internal-external dimension		Stability dimension	
		Unstable cause (temporary)	Stable cause (permanent)
Internal cause		Effort Mood Fatigue	Ability Intelligence
External cause		Luck Chance Opportunity	Task difficulty

ing to reassure themselves that they're immune to a similar fate.

Forming and Preserving Prejudicial Attitudes

If prejudice is an attitude, where does it come from? Many prejudices appear to be handed down as a legacy from parents (Ponterotto & Pedersen, 1993). Prejudicial attitudes can be found in children as young as ages 4 to 7 (Aboud, 1987). This transmission of prejudice across generations presumably depends to some extent on *observational learning*. For example, if a young boy hears his father ridicule homosexuals, his exposure to his father's attitude is likely to affect his attitude about gays. If the young boy then goes to school and makes disparaging remarks about gays that are reinforced by approval from

peers, his prejudice will be strengthened through *operant conditioning*. Consistent with this analysis, one recent study found that college students' opinions on racial issues were swayed by overhearing others voice racist or antiracist sentiments (Blanchard, Lilly, & Vaughn, 1991). Thus, social norms that condone expressions of prejudice help sustain prejudicial attitudes.

Dividing the World into Ingroups and Outgroups

As noted in our discussion of groupthink, people sometimes divide the social world into "us versus them," or *ingroups versus outgroups*. As you might anticipate, people tend to evaluate outgroup members less favorably than ingroup members (Meindl & Lerner, 1984; Wilder, 1981). The more strongly one identifies with an ingroup,

the more prejudiced one tends to be toward competing outgroups (Crocker & Luhtanen, 1990). People also tend to think simplistically about outgroups. They tend to see diversity among the members of their ingroup but to overestimate the homogeneity of the outgroup (Judd & Park, 1988). At a simple, concrete level, the essense of this process is captured by the statement "They all look alike." Indeed, studies have found that blacks and whites do have more difficulty distinguishing the faces of outgroup members (Anthony, Copper, & Mullen, 1992). The illusion of homogeneity in the outgroup makes it easier to sustain stereotypic beliefs about its members (Judd, Ryan, & Park, 1991). This point disposes of our last unanswered question from the list that opened the Application. Just in case you missed one of the answers, they all were false.

Our discussion has shown that a plethora of processes conspire to create and maintain personal prejudices. Most of the factors at work reflect normal, routine processes in social behavior. Thus, it is understandable that most people probably harbor some prejudicial attitudes. Our analysis of the causes of prejudice may have permitted you to identify prejudices of your own or their sources. Perhaps it's wishful thinking on my part, but an enhanced awareness of your personal prejudices may help you to become a little more tolerant of the endless diversity seen in human behavior. If so, that alone would mean that my efforts in writing this book have been amply rewarded.

People who say that gay men have brought AIDS upon themselves may be using defensive attribution, trying to be reassured that they are immune to the disease.

Chapter 16 Review

KEY IDEAS

Person Perception: Forming Impressions of Others
◆ Perceptions of others can be distorted by a variety of factors, including physical appearance. People attribute desirable characteristics, such as intelligence, competence, and warmth, to those who are good-looking.

◆ People use social schemas to categorize others into types. Stereotypes are widely held schemas that lead people to expect that others will have certain characteristics because of their membership in a specific group. Gender, ethnic, and occupational stereotypes are common. Stereotypes may lead people to see what they expect to see and to overestimate how often they see it.

Attribution Processes: Explaining Behavior
◆ Attributions are inferences about the causes of events and behavior. Internal attributions ascribe behavior to personal dispositions and traits, whereas external attributions locate the cause of behavior in the environment. Weiner's model proposes that attributions for success and failure should be analyzed in terms of the stability of causes, as well as along the internal-external dimension.

◆ Observers favor internal attributions to explain another's behavior (the fundamental attribution error), while actors favor external attributions to explain their own behavior. In defensive attribution, people unfairly blame victims for their misfortune (with internal attributions) to reduce their own feelings of vulnerability. The self-serving bias is the tendency to attribute one's good outcomes to personal factors and one's bad outcomes to situational factors.

◆ Cultures vary in their emphasis on individualism as opposed to collectivism, and these differences appear to influence attributional tendencies. The fundamental attribution error and the self-serving bias in attribution may be by-products of Western cultures' individualism.

Interpersonal Attraction: Liking and Loving
◆ People tend to like and love others who live in close proximity, who are similar, who reciprocate expressions of affection, and who are physically attractive. The matching hypothesis asserts that people who are similar in physical attractiveness are more likely to be drawn together than those who are not. Byrne's research suggests that attitude similarity causes attraction.

◆ Berscheid and Hatfield have identified some popular myths about love and made a distinction between passionate love and companionate love. Hazan and Shaver's theory suggests that love relationships in adulthood mimic attachment patterns in infancy.

◆ The characteristics that people seek in prospective mates and gender differences in mating preferences appear to transcend culture. However, cultures vary considerably in their emphasis on passionate love as a prerequisite for marriage.

Attitudes: Making Social Judgments
◆ Attitudes are made up of cognitive, affective, and behavioral components. A source of persuasion who is credible, expert, trustworthy, and likable tends to be relatively effective in stimulating attitude change. Although there are some situational limitations, two-sided arguments and fear arousal are effective elements in persuasive messages. Persuasion is undermined when a receiver is forewarned or when a receiver's initial position is highly discrepant from the position advocated.

◆ Attitudes may be shaped through classical conditioning, operant conditioning, and observational learning. Dissonance theory asserts that inconsistent attitudes cause tension and that people alter their attitudes to reduce dissonance. The elaboration likelihood model holds that the central route to persuasion tends to yield longer-lasting attitude change than the peripheral route.

Conformity and Obedience: Yielding to Others
◆ Asch found that conformity in groups becomes more likely as group size increases, up to a size of seven. If a small group isn't unanimous, conformity declines rapidly. In Milgram's landmark study of obedience to authority, adult men drawn from the community showed a remarkable tendency, in spite of their misgivings, to follow orders to shock an innocent stranger. Milgram concluded that situational pressures can make decent people do indecent things.

◆ The generalizability of Milgram's findings has stood the test of time, but his work also helped to stimulate stricter ethical standards for research. The Asch and Milgram experiments have been replicated in many cultures. These replications have uncovered modest cultural variations in the propensity to conform or to obey an authority figure.

Behavior in Groups: Joining with Others
◆ People who help someone in need when alone are less likely to provide help when a group is present. The bystander effect occurs primarily because a group creates diffusion of responsibility.

◆ Productivity often declines in larger groups because of loss of coordination and social loafing. Group polarization occurs when the group shifts toward a more extreme decision in the direction it was already leaning. In groupthink, a cohesive group suspends critical judgment in a misguided effort to promote agreement in decision making.

Putting It in Perspective
◆ Social psychology illustrates the value of empiricism because research in this area often proves that common sense is wrong. Additionally, several lines of research on social perception demonstrate that people's experience of the world is highly subjective.

Application: Understanding Prejudice
◆ Prejudice is a negative attitude toward a group. Prejudice is supported by selectivity in person perception and stereotyping. Attributional biases also contribute, including the tendency to assume that others' behavior reflects their dispositions, the tendency to attribute others' failures to personal factors, and the tendency to derogate victims.

◆ Negative attitudes about groups are often acquired through observational learning and supported by operant conditioning. The tendency to see outgroups as homogenous may also serve to strengthen prejudice.

KEY TERMS

Attitudes	Internal attribution
Attributions	Interpersonal attraction
Bystander effect	Latitude of acceptance
Channel	
Cognitive dissonance	Matching hypothesis
Collectivism	Message
Companionate love	Obedience
Conformity	Outgroup
Defensive attribution	Passionate love
Discrimination	Person perception
External attribution	Prejudice
Fundamental attribution error	Proximity
Group	Receiver
Group cohesiveness	Reciprocity
Group polarization	Self-serving bias
Groupthink	Social loafing
Illusory correlation	Social psychology
Individualism	Social schemas
Ingratiation	Source
Ingroup	Stereotypes

KEY PEOPLE

Solomon Asch	Fritz Heider
Ellen Berscheid	Irving Janis
Leon Festinger	Stanley Milgram
Elaine Hatfield	

Appendix

Answers to Concept Checks

Chapter 1
Concept Check 1.1

1. c. John B. Watson (1930, p. 103) dismissing the importance of genetic inheritance while arguing that traits are shaped entirely by experience.

2. a. Wilhelm Wundt (1904 revision of an earlier text, p. v) campaigning for a new, independent science of psychology.

3. b. William James (1890) commenting negatively on the structuralists' efforts to break consciousness into its elements and his view of consciousness as a continuously flowing stream.

Concept Check 1.2

1. b. B. F. Skinner (1971, p. 17) explaining why he believes that freedom is an illusion.

2. a. Sigmund Freud (1905, pp. 77–78) arguing that it is possible to probe into the unconscious depths of the mind.

3. c. Carl Rogers (1961, p. 27) commenting on others' assertion that he had an overly optimistic (Pollyannaish) view of human potential and discussing humans' basic drive toward personal growth.

Concept Check 1.3

1. c. Thomas and Chess's (1977) well-known New York Longitudinal Study is a landmark in developmental psychology.

2. a. Olds and Milner (1954) made this discovery by accident and thereby opened up a fascinating line of inquiry in physiological psychology.

3. e. Zuckerman (1971, 1979) pioneered the study of sensation seeking as a personality trait.

Concept Check 1.4

1. d. Industrial and organizational psychologists often strive to improve workers' productivity and morale.

2. c. One of the chief concerns of educational and school psychologists is achievement testing, which is intended to measure students' educational accomplishments.

3. a. Multiple personality disorder is a serious mental illness that is treated by clinical psychologists (and psychiatrists).

4. b. Though the work of counseling psychologists may overlap with that of clinical psychologists, more often their work focuses on the adjustment challenges that people face in everyday life, such as vocational decisions.

Concept Check 1.5

a. 2. Psychology is theoretically diverse.

b. 6. Heredity and environment jointly influence behavior.

c. 4. Behavior is determined by multiple causes.

d. 7. Our experience of the world is highly subjective.

Chapter 2
Concept Check 2.1

1. a. Formulate a testable hypothesis.

2. c. Collect the data.

3. d. Analyze the data and draw conclusions.

4. b. Select the research method and design the study.

5. e. Report the findings.

Concept Check 2.2

1. IV: Film violence (present versus absent).

DV: Heart rate and blood pressure (there are two DVs).

2. IV: Courtesy training (training versus no training).

DV: Number of customer complaints.

3. IV: Stimulus complexity (high versus low) and stimulus contrast (high versus low) (there are two IVs).

DV: Length of time spent staring at the stimuli.

4. IV: Group size (large versus small).

DV: Conformity.

Concept Check 2.3

1. b and e. The other three conclusions all equate correlation with causation.

2. a. Negative. As age increases, more people tend to have visual problems and acuity tends to decrease.

b. Positive. Studies show that highly educated people tend to earn higher incomes and that people with less education tend to earn lower incomes.

c. Negative. As shyness increases, the size of one's friendship network should decrease. However, research suggests that this inverse association may be weaker than widely believed.

Concept Check 2.4

1. d. Survey. You would distribute a survey to obtain information on subjects' social class, education, and attitudes about nuclear disarmament.

2. c. Case study. Using a case study approach, you could interview people with anxiety disorders, interview their parents, and examine their school records to look for similarities in childhood experiences. As a second choice, you might have people with anxiety disorders fill out a survey about their childhood experiences.

3. b. Naturalistic observation. To answer this question properly, you would want to observe baboons in their natural environment, without interference.

4. a. Experiment. To demonstrate a causal relationship, you would have to conduct an experiment. You would manipulate the presence or absence of food-related cues in controlled circumstances where subjects had an opportunity to eat some food, and monitor the amount eaten.

Concept Check 2.5

Methodological flaw	Study 1	Study 2
Sampling bias	✓	✓
Placebo effects	✓	___
Confounding of variables	✓	___
Distortions in self-report data	___	✓
Experimenter bias	✓	___

Explanations for Study 1. Sensory deprivation is an unusual kind of experience that may intrigue certain potential subjects, who may be more adventurous or more willing to take risks than the population at large. Using the first 80 students who sign up for this study may not yield a sample that is representative of the population. Assigning the first 40 subjects who sign up to the experimental group may confound these extraneous variables with the treatment (students who sign up most quickly may be the most adventurous). In announcing that he

will be examining the *detrimental* effects of sensory deprivation, the experimenter has created expectations in the subjects. These expectations could lead to placebo effects that have not been controlled for with a placebo group. The experimenter has also revealed that he has a bias about the outcome of the study. Since he supervises the treatments, he knows which subjects are in the experimental and control groups, thus aggravating potential problems with experimenter bias. For example, he might unintentionally give the control group subjects better instructions on how to do the pursuit-rotor task and thereby slant the study in favor of finding support for his hypothesis.

Explanations for Study 2. Sampling bias is a problem because the researcher has sampled only subjects from a low-income, inner-city neighborhood. A sample obtained in this way is not likely to be representative of the population at large. People are sensitive about the issue of racial prejudice, so distortions in self-report data are also likely. Many subjects may be swayed by social desirability bias and rate themselves as less prejudiced than they really are.

Chapter 3
Concept Check 3.1

1. d. Dendrite.

2. f. Myelin.

3. b. Neuron.

4. e. Axon.

5. a. Glia.

6. g. Terminal button.

7. h. Synapse.

Concept Check 3.2

1. d. GABA.

2. b. Norepinephrine.

3. e. Endorphins.

4. c. Dopamine.

5. a. Acetylcholine.

Concept Check 3.3

1. Left hemisphere damage, probably to Wernicke's area.

2. Deficit in dopamine synthesis in an area of the midbrain.

3. Deficit in acetylcholine synthesis and damage to the hippocampus.

4. Disturbance in dopamine activity.

Please note that neuropsychological assessment is not as simple as this introductory exercise may suggest. There are many possible causes of most disorders, and we discussed only a handful of leading causes for each.

Concept Check 3.4

1. Closer relatives; more distant relatives.

2. Identical twins; fraternal twins.

3. Biological parents; adoptive parents.

4. Genetic overlap or closeness; trait similarity.

Chapter 4
Concept Check 4.1

Dimension	Rods	Cones
Physical shape	Elongated	Stubby
Number in the retina	125 million	6.4 million
Area of the retina in which they are dominant receptor	Periphery	Center/fovea
Critical to color vision	No	Yes
Critical to peripheral vision	Yes	No
Sensitivity to dim light	Strong	Weak
Speed of dark adaptation	Slow	Rapid

Concept Check 4.2

	Trichromatic	Opponent process
Theory proposed by:	Young, Helmholtz	Hering
Can/can't account for complementary afterimages	can't	can
Explains first/later stage of color processing	first	later
Does/doesn't account for need for four terms to describe colors	doesn't	does

Concept Check 4.3

✓ **1.** Interposition. The arches in the front cut off part of the corridor behind them.

✓ **2.** Height in plane. The back of the corridor is higher on the horizontal plane than the front of the corridor is.

✓ **3.** Texture gradient. The more distant portions of the hallway are painted in less detail than the closer portions are.

✓ **4.** Relative size. The arches in the distance are smaller than those in the foreground.

✓ **5.** Light and shadow. Light shining in from the crossing corridor (it's coming from the left) contrasts with shadow elsewhere.

✓ **6.** Linear perspective. The lines of the corridor converge in the distance.

Concept Check 4.4

Dimension	Vision	Hearing
1. Stimulus	Light waves	Sound waves
2. Elements of stimulus and related perceptions	Wavelength/hue Amplitude/ brightness Purity/saturation	Frequency/pitch Amplitude/ loudness Purity/timbre
3. Receptors	Rods and cones	Hair cells
4. Location of receptors	Retina	Basilar membrane
5. Main location of processing in brain	Occipital lobe, visual cortex	Temporal lobe, auditory cortex

Concept Check 4.5

Dimension	Taste	Smell	Touch
Stimulus	Soluble chemicals in saliva	Volatile chemicals in air	Mechanical, thermal, and chemical energy due to external contact
Receptors	Clusters of taste cells	Olfactory cilia (hairlike structures)	Many (at least 6) types
Location of receptors	Taste buds on tongue	Upper area of nasal passages	Skin
Basic elements of perception	Sweet, sour, salty, bitter	No satisfactory classification scheme	Pressure, hot, cold, pain

Chapter 5
Concept Check 5.1

Characteristic	REM sleep	NREM sleep
Type of EEG activity	"Wide awake" brain waves, mostly beta	Varied, lots of delta waves
Eye movements	Rapid, lateral	Slow or absent
Dreaming	Frequent, vivid	Less frequent
Depth (difficulty in awakening)	Difficult to awaken	Varied, generally easier to awaken
Percentage of total sleep (in adults)	About 20%	About 80%
Increases or decreases (as percentage of sleep) during childhood	Percent decreases	Percent increases
Timing in sleep (dominates early or late)	Dominates later in cycle	Dominates early in cycle

Concept Check 5.2

1. Beta. Video games require alert information processing, which is associated with beta waves.

2. Alpha. Meditation involves relaxation, which is associated with alpha waves, and studies show increased alpha in meditators.

3. Theta. In stage 1 sleep, theta waves tend to be prevalent.

4. Beta. Nightmares are dreams, so you're probably in REM sleep, which paradoxically produces "wide awake" beta waves.

5. Beta. If you're a beginner, typing will be a "controlled process" requiring alert, focused attention, which should generate beta waves.

Concept Check 5.3

1. c. Stimulants.
2. d. Hallucinogens.
3. b. Sedatives.
4. f. Alcohol.
5. a. Narcotics.
6. e. Cannabis.

Chapter 6
Concept Check 6.1

1. CS: Fire in fireplace
   UCS: Pain from burn   CR/UCR: Fear

2. CS: Brake lights in rain
   UCS: Car accident   CR/UCR: Tensing up

3. CS: Sight of cat
   UCS: Cat dander   CR/UCR: Wheezing

Concept Check 6.2

1. d. Stimulus generalization.
2. a. Acquisition.
3. f. Higher-order conditioning.
4. e. Stimulus discrimination.
5. c. Spontaneous recovery.
6. b. Extinction.

Concept Check 6.3

1. FR. Each sale is a response and every third response earns reinforcement.

2. VI. A varied amount of time elapses before the response of doing yard work can earn reinforcement.

3. VR. Reinforcement occurs after a varied number of unreinforced casts (time is irrelevant; the more casts Martha makes, the more reinforcers she will receive).

4. CR. The designated response (reading a book) is reinforced (with a gold star) each and every time.

5. FI. A fixed time interval (3 years) has to elapse before Skip can earn a salary increase (the reinforcer).

Concept Check 6.4

1. Punishment.
2. Positive reinforcement.
3. Punishment.
4. Negative reinforcement (for Audrey); the dog is positively reinforced for its whining.
5. Negative reinforcement.
6. Extinction. When Edna's co-workers start to ignore her complaints, they are trying to extinguish the behavior (which had been positively reinforced when it won sympathy).

Concept Check 6.5

1. Classical conditioning. Marcia's blue windbreaker is a CS eliciting excitement in her dog.

2. Operant conditioning. Playing new songs leads to negative consequences (punishment), which weaken the tendency to play new songs. Playing

old songs leads to positive reinforcement, which gradually strengthens the tendency to play old songs.

3. Classical conditioning. The song was paired with the passion of new love so that it became a CS eliciting emotional, romantic feelings.

4. Both. Ralph's workplace is paired with criticism so that his workplace becomes a CS eliciting anxiety. Calling in sick is operant behavior that is strengthened through negative reinforcement (because it reduces anxiety).

Chapter 7
Concept Check 7.1

1. a. Semantic encoding.

2. d. Attention.

3. c. Visual imagery.

4. b. Elaboration.

Concept Check 7.2

Feature	Sensory memory	Short-term memory	Long-term memory
Encoding format	Copy of input	Largely phonemic	Largely semantic
Storage capacity	Large	Small (7 ± 2 chunks)	No known limit
Storage duration	¼ to 2 seconds	Up to 30 seconds	Minutes to years

Concept Check 7.3

1. Ineffective encoding due to lack of attention.

2. Retrieval failure due to motivated forgetting.

3. Proactive interference (previous learning of Joe Cocker's name interferes with new learning).

4. Retroactive interference (new learning of sociology interferes with older learning of history).

Concept Check 7.4

1. a. Atkinson and Shiffrin (1968).

2. c. Ebbinghaus (1885/1948).

3. b. Craik and Lockhart (1972).

4. d. Loftus (1979).

Concept Check 7.5

1. a. Declarative memory.

2. e. Long-term memory.

3. h. Sensory memory.

4. d. Implicit memory.

5. b. Episodic memory.

6. f. Procedural memory.

7. g. Semantic memory.

8. c. Explicit memory.

9. i. Short-term memory.

Chapter 8
Concept Check 8.1

1. d. Language is structured.

2. a. Language is symbolic.

3. c. Language is generative.

4. b. Language is semantic.

Concept Check 8.2

1. 2. One word is overextended to refer to a similar object.

2. 4. Words are combined into a sentence, but the rule for past tense is overgeneralized.

3. 3. Telegraphic sentence.

4. 5. Words are combined into a sentence, and past tense is used correctly.

5. 1. One word is used to refer to an entity.

Concept Check 8.3

1. Functional fixedness.

2. Forming subgoals.

3. Insight.

4. Searching for analogies.

5. Arrangement problem.

Concept Check 8.4

1. Elimination by aspects.

2. Availability heuristic.

3. Additive model.

Chapter 9
Concept Check 9.1

1. Test-retest reliability.

2. Criterion-related validity.

3. Content validity.

Concept Check 9.2

1. a. Galton (1869).

2. d. Wechsler (1958).

3. b. Binet and Simon (1948).

4. c. Terman (1916).

Concept Check 9.3

1. H. Given that the identical twins were reared apart, their greater similarity in comparison to fraternals reared together can only be due to heredity. This comparison is probably the most important piece of evidence supporting the genetic determination of IQ.

2. E. We tend to associate identical twins with evidence supporting heredity, but in this comparison genetic similarity is held constant since both sets of twins are identical. The only logical explanation for the greater similarity in identicals reared together is the effect of their being reared together (environment).

3. E. This comparison is similar to the previous one. Genetic similarity is held constant and a shared environment produces greater similarity than being reared apart.

4. B. This is nothing more than a quantification of Galton's original observation that intelligence runs in families. Since families share both genes and environment, either or both could be responsible for the observed correlation.

5. B. The similarity of adopted children to their biological parents can only be due to shared genes, and the similarity of adopted children to their foster parents can only be due to shared environment, so these correlations show the influence of both heredity and environment.

Concept Check 9.4

1. b. Gardner.

2. a. Galton.

3. c. Jensen.

4. d. Scarr.

5. e. Sternberg.

Chapter 10
Concept Check 10.1

	Relevant theory	Level of needs
1.	Drive theory (a deficit creates internal tension)	Love and belongingness needs
2.	Incentive theory (you're motivated by the triple bonus)	Safety and security needs
3.	Maslow's theory (interests reflect higher growth needs)	Cognitive and aesthetic needs
4.	Sociobiology (self-sacrifice to promote welfare of close kin)	Physiological needs

Concept Check 10.2

1. I. Early studies indicated that the VMH was a "stop eating" center, since artificially stimulating it curtails eating in rats while lesioning leads to overeating. Subsequent research indicates that the situation is somewhat more complicated; the VMH is not simply a "stop eating" center.

2. I. According to Mayer (1955, 1968), hunger increases when the amount of glucose in the blood decreases. Glucostats in the brain apparently monitor the uptake of glucose by cells in the body.

3. I. Insulin, a hormone produced by the pancreas, must be present for cells to extract glucose from the blood. If insulin is increased, more glucose is extracted, glucostats respond to the increase, and one experiences increased hunger.

4. D. Food preferences are learned; we tend to like what we are accustomed to eating. So no matter how delicious someone from another culture thinks some exotic delicacy is, you're not likely to be eager to eat it.

5. ?. Schachter and Gross (1968) found that obese people tend to snack when external cues indicate that it's dinnertime, while nonobese people tend not to, so they won't spoil their dinner.

6. I. Slochower, Kaplan, and Mann (1981) found that stress leads to increased eating in many people, although it could be stress-induced *arousal* that leads to eating, rather than stress itself.

Concept Check 10.3

1. d. Fear of failure.

2. c. Incentive value of success.

3. e. Perceived probability of failure.

4. a. Need for achievement.

Concept Check 10.4

2. James-Lange theory.

3. Schachter's two-factor theory.

4. Evolutionary theories.

Chapter 11
Concept Check 11.1

	Event	Stage	Organism	Time span
1.	Uterine implantation	germinal	zygote	0–2 weeks
2.	Muscle and bone begin to form	fetal	fetus	2 months to birth
3.	Vital organs and body systems begin to form	embryonic	embryo	2 weeks to 2 months

Concept Check 11.2

1. b. Animism is characteristic of the preoperational period.

2. c. Mastery of hierarchical classification occurs during the concrete operational period.

3. a. Lack of object permanence is characteristic of the sensorimotor period.

Concept Check 11.3

1. c. Commitment to personal ethics is characteristic of postconventional reasoning.

2. b. Concern about approval of others is characteristic of conventional reasoning.

3. a. Emphasis on positive or negative consequences is characteristic of preconventional reasoning.

Chapter 12
Concept Check 12.1

1. Regression.

2. Projection.

3. Reaction formation.

4. Repression.

5. Rationalization.

Concept Check 12.2

	Freud	Jung	Adler
1. Archetypes		✓	
2. Physical gratification	✓		
3. Striving for superiority			✓
4. Collective unconscious		✓	
5. Early childhood experiences	✓		✓
6. Dream analysis	✓	✓	
7. Birth order			✓
8. Unconscious determinants	✓	✓	

Concept Check 12.3

1. Bandura's observational learning. Sarah imitates a role model from television.

2. Maslow's need for self-actualization. Marilyn is striving to realize her fullest potential.

3. Freud's Oedipal complex. Johnny shows preference for his opposite-sex parent and emotional distance from his same-sex parent.

Concept Check 12.4

1. Maslow (1971, p. 36) commenting on the need for self-actualization.

2. Eysenck (1977, pp. 407–408) commenting on the biological roots of personality.

3. Freud (in Malcolm, 1980) commenting on the repression of sexuality.

Chapter 13
Concept Check 13.1

1. b. A choice between two unattractive options.

2. c. Weighing the positive and negative aspects of a single goal.

3. a. A choice between two attractive options.

Concept Check 13.2

1. a. Frustration due to delay.

2. d. Pressure to perform.

3. c. Change associated with leaving school and taking a new job.

4. a. Frustration due to loss of job.
c. Change in life circumstances.
d. Pressure to perform (in quickly obtaining new job).

Concept Check 13.3

Pathway 1: pituitary, ACTH, adrenal cortex, corticosteroids.

Pathway 2: hypothalamus, sympathetic division of the ANS, adrenal medulla, catecholamines.

Chapter 14
Concept Check 14.1

	Deviance	Maladaptive behavior	Personal distress
1. Alan		✓	
2. Monica			✓
3. Walter	✓		
4. Phyllis	✓	✓	✓

Concept Check 14.2

1. Obsessive-compulsive disorder (key symptoms: frequent rituals, ruminations about school).

2. Somatization disorder (key symptoms: history of physical complaints involving many different organ systems).

3. Conversion disorder (key symptoms: loss of function in single organ system).

Concept Check 14.3

1. Bipolar mood disorder, manic episode (key symptoms: extravagant plans, hyperactivity, reckless spending).

2. Paranoid schizophrenia (key symptoms: delusions of persecution and grandeur, along with deterioration of adaptive behavior).

3. Major depression (key symptoms: feelings of despair, low self-esteem, lack of energy).

Concept Check 14.4

	Anxiety disorders	Mood disorders	Schizophrenic disorders
Brain structure abnormalities			✓
Cognitive factors	✓	✓	
Communication deviance			✓
Conditioning	✓	✓	
Genetic predisposition	✓	✓	✓
Interpersonal factors		✓	✓
Neurochemical factors	✓	✓	✓
Observational learning	✓		
Stress	✓	✓	✓

Chapter 15

Concept Check 15.1

1. c **2.** a **3.** b

Concept Check 15.2

1. a. Systematic desensitization.

2. c. Aversion therapy.

3. b. Social skills training.

Concept Check 15.3

1. d **2.** b **3.** a **4.** c

Concept Check 15.4

1. c **2.** a **3.** b **4.** d **5.** b

Chapter 16

Concept Check 16.1

	Unstable	Stable
Internal	d	b
External	a	c

Concept Check 16.2

1. c. Fundamental attribution error (assuming that arriving late reflects personal qualities).

2. a. Illusory correlation effect (overestimating how often one has seen confirmations of the assertion that young, female professors get pregnant soon after being hired).

3. b. Stereotyping (assuming that all lawyers have certain traits).

4. d. Defensive attribution (derogating the victims of misfortune to minimize the apparent likelihood of a similar mishap).

Concept Check 16.3

1. *Target:* Cognitive component of attitudes (beliefs about program for regulating nursing homes).

Persuasion: Message factor (advice to use one-sided instead of two-sided arguments).

2. *Target:* Affective component of attitudes (feelings about candidate).

Persuasion: Source factor (advice on appearing likable, sincere, and compassionate).

3. *Target:* Behavioral component of attitudes (making contributions).

Persuasion: Receiver factor (considering audience's initial position regarding the candidate).

Concept Check 16.4

1. False. **2.** True. **3.** False. **4.** False.
5. True. **6.** False.

Appendix B

Statistical Methods

Empiricism depends on observation; precise observation depends on measurement; and measurement requires numbers. Thus, scientists routinely analyze numerical data to arrive at their conclusions. Over 2000 empirical studies are cited in this text, and all but a few of the simplest ones required a statistical analysis. ***Statistics* is the use of mathematics to organize, summarize, and interpret numerical data.** We discussed statistics briefly in Chapter 2, but in this Appendix we take a closer look.

To illustrate statistics in action, let's assume that we want to test a hypothesis that has generated quite an argument in your psychology class. The hypothesis is that college students who watch a great deal of television aren't as bright as those who watch TV infrequently. For the fun of it, your class decides to conduct a correlational study of itself, collecting survey and psychological test data. Your classmates all agree to respond to a short survey on their TV viewing habits. Because everyone at your school has had to take the Scholastic Aptitude Test (SAT), the class decides to use scores on the SAT verbal subtest as an index of how bright students are. All of them agree to allow the records office at the college to furnish their SAT scores to the professor, who replaces each student's name with a subject number (to protect students' right to privacy). Let's see how we could use statistics to analyze the data collected in our pilot study (a small, preliminary investigation).

Graphing Data

After collecting our data, our next step is to organize the data to get a quick overview of our numerical results. Let's assume that there are 20 students in your class, and when they estimate how many hours they spend per day watching TV, the results are as follows:

3	2	0	3	1
3	4	0	5	1
2	3	4	5	2
4	5	3	4	6

One of the simpler things that we can do to organize data is to create a ***frequency distribution*—an orderly arrangement of scores indicating the frequency of each score or group of scores.** Figure B.1(a) shows a frequency distribution for our data on TV viewing. The column on the left lists the possible scores (estimated hours of TV viewing) in order, and the column on the right lists the number of subjects with each score. Graphs can provide an even better overview of the data. One approach is to portray the data in a ***histo-***

Figure B.1. Graphing data. (a) Our raw data are tallied into a frequency distribution. **(b)** The same data are portrayed in a bar graph called a histogram. **(c)** A frequency polygon is plotted over the histogram. **(d)** The resultant frequency polygon is shown by itself.

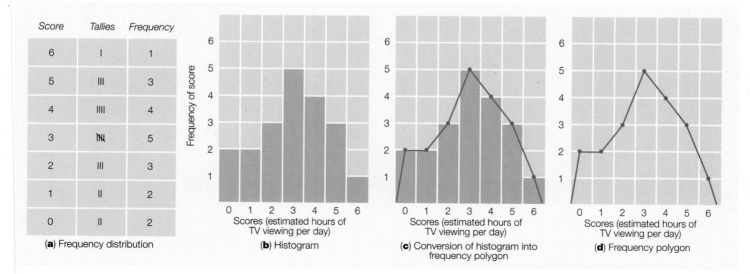

(a) Frequency distribution | (b) Histogram | (c) Conversion of histogram into frequency polygon | (d) Frequency polygon

gram, which is a bar graph that presents data from a frequency distribution. Such a histogram, summarizing our TV viewing data, is presented in Figure B.1(b).

Another widely used method of portraying data graphically is the *frequency polygon*—a line figure used to present data from a frequency distribution. Figures B.1(c) and B.1(d) show how our TV viewing data can be converted from a histogram to a frequency polygon. In both the bar graph and the line figure, the horizontal axis lists the possible scores and the vertical axis is used to indicate the frequency of each score. This use of the axes is nearly universal for frequency polygons, although sometimes it is reversed in histograms (the vertical axis lists possible scores, so the bars become horizontal).

Our graphs improve on the jumbled collection of scores that we started with, but *descriptive statistics*, **which are used to organize and summarize data**, provide some additional advantages. Let's see what the three measures of central tendency tell us about our data.

Measuring Central Tendency

In examining a set of data, it's routine to ask "What is a typical score in the distribution?" For instance, in this case we might compare the average amount of TV watching in our sample against national estimates, to determine whether our subjects appear to be representative of the population. The three measures of central tendency, the median, the mean, and the mode, give us indications regarding the typical score in a data set. As explained in Chapter 2, **the *median* is the score that falls in the center of a distribution, the *mean* is the arithmetic average of the scores,** and **the *mode* is the score that occurs most frequently.**

All three measures of central tendency are calculated for our TV viewing data in Figure B.2(a). As you can see, in this set of data, the mean, median, and mode all turn out to be the same score, which is 3. The correspondence among the three measures of central tendency seen in our TV viewing data is quite common, but there are situations in which the mean, median, and mode can yield very different estimates of central tendency. To illustrate, imagine that you're interviewing for a sales position at a company. Unbeknownst to you, the company's five salespeople earned the following incomes in the previous year: $20,000, $20,000, $25,000, $35,000, and $200,000. You ask how much the typical salesperson earns in a year.

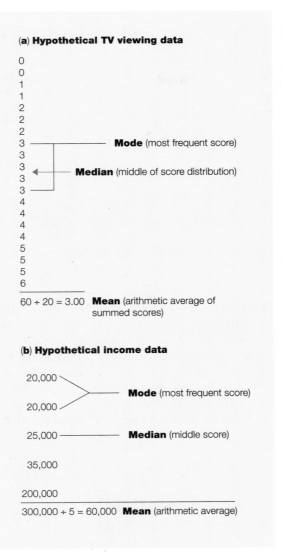

(a) Hypothetical TV viewing data

0
0
1
1
2
2
2
3 ——— **Mode** (most frequent score)
3
3 ◄— **Median** (middle of score distribution)
3
3
4
4
4
4
5
5
5
6

60 ÷ 20 = 3.00 **Mean** (arithmetic average of summed scores)

(b) Hypothetical income data

20,000
20,000 ——— **Mode** (most frequent score)
25,000 ——— **Median** (middle score)
35,000
200,000

300,000 ÷ 5 = 60,000 **Mean** (arithmetic average)

Figure B.2. Measures of central tendency. The mean, median, and mode usually converge, as in the case of our TV viewing data **(a)**. However, some data produce quite different values for mean, median, and mode, such as the invoice data in **(b)**.

The sales director proudly announces that her five salespeople earned a *mean* income of $60,000 last year. However, before you order that expensive, new sports car, you had better inquire about the *median* and *modal* income for the sales staff, which are shown in Figure B.2(b). In this case, one extreme score ($200,000) has inflated the mean, making it unrepresentative of the sales staff's earnings. In this instance, the median ($25,000) and the mode ($20,000) both provide better estimates of what you are likely to earn.

In general, the mean is the most useful measure of central tendency because additional statistical manipulations can be performed on it that are not possible with the median or mode. However, the mean is sensitive to extreme scores in a distribution, which can sometimes make the mean misleading. Thus, lack of agreement among the three measures of central tendency usually occurs when a few extreme scores pull the mean away from the

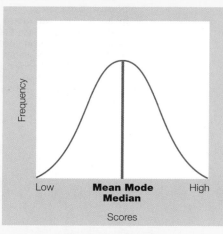

(a) Symmetrical distribution

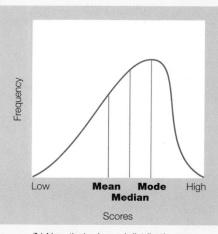

(b) Negatively skewed distribution

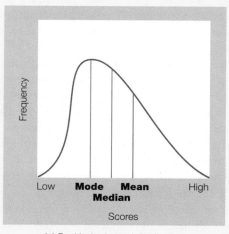

(c) Positively skewed distribution

Figure B.3. Measures of central tendency in skewed distributions. In a symmetrical distribution (**a**), the three measures of central tendency converge. However, in a negatively skewed distribution (**b**) or in a positively skewed distribution (**c**), the mean, median, and mode are pulled apart as shown here. Typically, in these situations the median provides the best index of central tendency.

center of the distribution, as shown in Figure B.3. The curves plotted in Figure B.3 are simply "smoothed out" frequency polygons based on data from many subjects. They show that when a distribution is symmetric, the measures of central tendency fall together, but this is not true in skewed or unbalanced distributions.

Figure B.3(b) shows a *negatively skewed distribution,* **in which most scores pile up at the high**

end of the scale (the negative skew refers to the direction in which the curve's "tail" points). **A** *positively skewed distribution,* **in which scores pile up at the low end of the scale,** is shown in Figure B.3(c). In both types of skewed distributions, a few extreme scores at one end pull the mean, and to a lesser degree the median, away from the mode. In these situations, the mean may be misleading and the median usually provides the best index of central tendency.

In any case, the measures of central tendency for our TV viewing data are reassuring, since they all agree and they fall reasonably close to national estimates regarding how much young adults watch TV (Huston & Wright, 1982). Given the small size of our group, this agreement with national norms doesn't *prove* that our sample is representative of the population, but at least there's no obvious reason to believe that they're unrepresentative.

Measuring Variability

Of course, everyone in our sample did not report identical TV viewing habits. Virtually all data sets are characterized by some variability. *Variability* **refers to how much the scores tend to vary or depart from the mean score.** For example, the distribution of golf scores for a mediocre, erratic golfer would be characterized by high variability, while scores for an equally mediocre but consistent golfer would show less variability.

The *standard deviation* **is an index of the amount of variability in a set of data.** It reflects the dispersion of scores in a distribution. This principle is portrayed graphically in Figure B.4, where the two distributions of golf scores have the same mean but the upper one has less variability

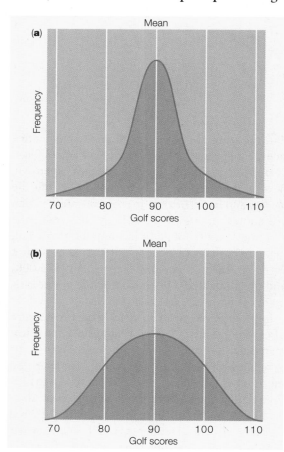

Figure B.4. The standard deviation and dispersion of data. Although both these distributions of golf scores have the same mean, their standard deviations will be different. In (**a**) the scores are bunched together and there is less variability than in (**b**), yielding a lower standard deviation for the data in distribution (**a**).

because the scores are "bunched up" in the center (for the consistent golfer). The distribution in Figure B.4(b) is characterized by more variability, as the erratic golfer's scores are more spread out. This distribution will yield a higher standard deviation than the distribution in Figure B.4(a).

The formula for calculating the standard deviation is shown in Figure B.5, where d stands for each score's deviation from the mean and Σ stands for summation. A step-by-step application of this formula to our TV viewing data, shown in Figure B.5, reveals that the standard deviation for our TV viewing data is 1.64. The standard deviation has a variety of uses. One of these uses will surface in the next section, where we discuss the normal distribution.

The Normal Distribution

The hypothesis in our study is that brighter students watch less TV than relatively dull students. To test this hypothesis, we're going to correlate TV viewing with SAT scores. But to make effective use of the SAT data, we need to understand what SAT scores mean, which brings us to the normal distribution.

The *normal distribution* **is a a symmetrical, bell-shaped curve that represents the pattern in which many human characteristics are dispersed in the population.** A great many physical qualities (for example, height, nose length, and running speed) and psychological traits (intelligence, spatial reasoning ability, introversion) are distributed in a manner that closely resembles this bell-shaped curve. When a trait is normally distributed, most scores fall near the center of the distribution (the mean) and the number of scores gradually declines as one moves away from the center in either direction. The normal distribution is *not* a law of nature. It's a mathematical function, or theoretical curve, that approximates the way nature seems to operate.

The normal distribution is the bedrock of the scoring system for most psychological tests, including the SAT. As we discuss in Chapter 9, psychological tests are *relative measures*; they assess how people score on a trait in comparison to other people. The normal distribution gives us a precise way to measure how people stack up in comparison to each other. The scores under the normal curve are dispersed in a fixed pattern, with the standard deviation serving as the unit of measurement, as shown in Figure B.6 on the next page. About 68% of the scores in the distribution fall within plus or minus 1 standard deviation of the

TV viewing score (X)	Deviation from mean (d)	Deviation squared (d^2)
0	−3	9
0	−3	9
1	−2	4
1	−2	4
2	−1	1
2	−1	1
2	−1	1
3	0	0
3	0	0
3	0	0
3	0	0
3	0	0
4	+1	1
4	+1	1
4	+1	1
4	+1	1
5	+2	4
5	+2	4
5	+2	4
N = 20 6	+3	9
$\Sigma X = 60$		$\Sigma d^2 = 54$

$$\text{Mean} = \frac{\Sigma X}{N} = \frac{60}{20} = 3.0$$

$$\text{Standard deviation} = \sqrt{\frac{\Sigma d^2}{N}} = \sqrt{\frac{54}{20}}$$

$$= \sqrt{2.70} = 1.64$$

Figure B.5. Steps in calculating the standard deviation. (1) Add the scores (ΣX) and divide by the number of scores (N) to calculate the mean (which comes out to 3.0 in this case). (2) Calculate each score's deviation from the mean by subtracting the mean from each score (the results are shown in the second column). (3) Square these deviations from the mean and total the results to obtain (Σd^2) as shown in the third column. (4) Insert the numbers for N and Σd^2 into the formula for the standard deviation and compute the results.

mean, while 95% of the scores fall within plus or minus 2 standard deviations of the mean. Given this fixed pattern, if you know the mean and standard deviation of a normally distributed trait, you can tell where any score falls in the distribution for the trait.

Although you may not have realized it, you probably have taken many tests in which the scoring system is based on the normal distribution. On the SAT, for instance, raw scores (the number of items correct on each subtest) are converted into standard scores that indicate where you fall in the normal distribution for the trait measured. In this conversion, the mean is set arbitrarily at 500 and the standard deviation at 100, as shown in Figure B.7 on the next page. Therefore, a score of 400 on the SAT verbal subtest means that you scored 1 standard deviation below the mean, while an SAT score of 600 indicates that you scored 1 standard deviation above the mean. Thus, SAT scores tell you how many standard deviations above or below the mean your score was. This system also provides the metric for IQ scales and many other types of psychological tests (see Chapter 9).

Test scores that place examinees in the normal distribution can always be converted to percentile scores, which are a little easier to interpret. **A**

Figure B.6. The normal distribution. Many characteristics are distributed in a pattern represented by this bell-shaped curve (each dot represents a case). The horizontal axis shows how far above or below the mean a score is (measured in plus or minus standard deviations). The vertical axis shows the number of cases obtaining each score. In a normal distribution, most cases fall near the center of the distribution, so that 68.26% of the cases fall within plus or minus 1 standard deviation of the mean. The number of cases gradually declines as one moves away from the mean in either direction, so that only 13.59% of the cases fall between 1 and 2 standard deviations above or below the mean, and even fewer cases (2.14%) fall between 2 and 3 standard deviations above or below the mean.

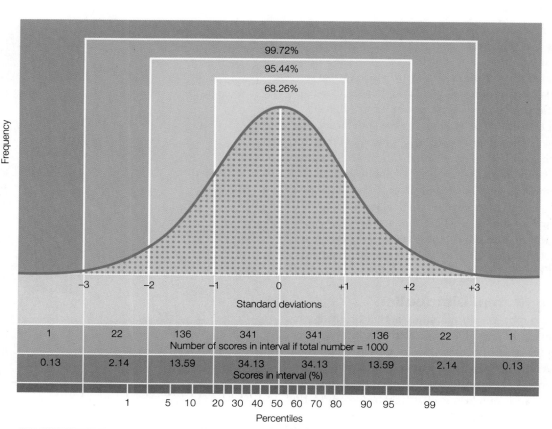

Figure B.7. The normal distribution and SAT scores. The normal distribution is the basis for the scoring system on many standardized tests. For example, on the Scholastic Aptitude Test (SAT), the mean is set at 500 and the standard deviation at 100. Hence, an SAT score tells you how many standard deviations above or below the mean you scored. For example, a score of 700 means you scored 2 standard deviations above the mean.

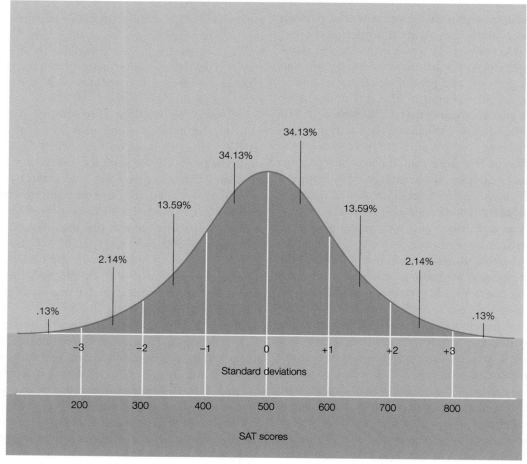

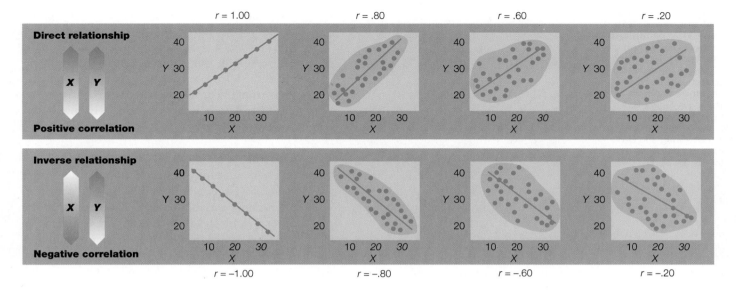

percentile score **indicates the percentage of people who score at or below the score you obtained.** For example, if you score at the 60th percentile, 60% of the people who take the test score the same or below you, while the remaining 40% score above you. There are tables available that permit us to convert any standard deviation placement in a normal distribution into a precise percentile score. Figure B.6 gives some percentile conversions for the normal curve.

Of course, not all distributions are normal. As we saw in Figure B.3, some distributions are skewed in one direction or the other. As an example, consider what would happen if a classroom exam were much too easy or much too hard. If the test were too easy, scores would be bunched up at the high end of the scale, as in Figure B.3(b). If the test were too hard, scores would be bunched up at the low end, as in Figure B.3(c).

Measuring Correlation

To determine whether TV viewing is related to SAT scores, we have to compute a *correlation coefficient*—**a numerical index of the degree of relationship that exists between two variables.** As discussed in Chapter 2, a *positive* correlation means that there is a *direct* relationship between two variables—say X and Y. This means that high scores on variable X are associated with high scores on variable Y and that low scores on X are associated with low scores on Y. A *negative* correlation indicates that there is an *inverse* relationship between two variables. This means that people who score high on variable X tend to score low on variable Y, whereas those who score low on X tend

to score high on Y. In our study, we hypothesized that as TV viewing increases, SAT scores will decrease, so we should expect a negative correlation between TV viewing and SAT scores.

The *magnitude* of a correlation coefficient indicates the *strength* of the association between two variables. This coefficient can vary between 0 and ±1.00. The coefficient is usually represented by the letter *r* (for example, *r* = .45). A coefficient near 0 tells us that there is no relationship between two variables. A coefficient of +1.00 or −1.00 indicates that there is a perfect, one-to-one correspondence between two variables. A perfect correlation is found only rarely when working with real data. The closer the coefficient is to either −1.00 or +1.00, the stronger the relationship is.

The direction and strength of correlations can be illustrated graphically in scatter diagrams. **A** *scatter diagram* **is a graph in which paired X and Y scores for each subject are plotted as single points.** Figure B.8 shows scatter diagrams for positive correlations in the upper half and for negative correlations in the bottom half. A perfect positive correlation and a perfect negative correlation are shown on the far left. When a correlation is perfect, the data points in the scatter diagram fall exactly in a straight line. However, positive and negative correlations yield lines slanted in the opposite direction because the lines map out opposite types of associations. Moving to the right in Figure B.8, you can see what happens when the magnitude of a correlation decreases. The data points scatter farther and farther from the straight line that would represent a perfect relationship.

What about our data relating TV viewing to

Figure B.8. Scatter diagrams of positive and negative correlations. Scatter diagrams plot paired X and Y scores as single points. Score plots slanted in the opposite direction result from positive (top row) as opposed to negative (bottom row) correlations. Moving across both rows (to the right), you can see that progressively weaker correlations result in more and more scattered plots of data points.

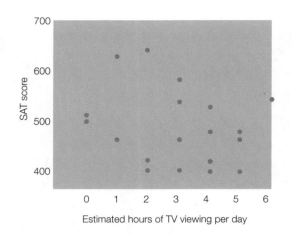

Figure B.9. Scatter diagram of the correlation between TV viewing and SAT scores. Our hypothetical data relating TV viewing to SAT scores are plotted in this scatter diagram. Compare it to the scatter diagrams seen in Figure B.8 and see whether you can estimate the correlation between TV viewing and SAT scores in our data (see the text for the answer).

Figure B.10. Computing a correlation coefficient. The calculations required to compute the Pearson product-moment coefficient of correlation are shown here. The formula looks intimidating, but it's just a matter of filling in the figures taken from the sums of the columns shown above the formula.

SAT scores? Figure B.9 shows a scatter diagram of these data. Having just learned about scatter diagrams, perhaps you can estimate the magnitude of the correlation between TV viewing and SAT scores. The scatter diagram of our data looks a lot like the one seen in the bottom right corner of Figure B.8, suggesting that the correlation will be in the vicinity of –.20.

The formula for computing the most widely used measure of correlation—the Pearson product-moment correlation—is shown in Figure B.10, along with the calculations for our data on TV viewing and SAT scores. The data yield a correla-

tion of $r = -.24$. This coefficient of correlation reveals that we have found a weak inverse association between TV viewing and performance on the SAT. Among our subjects, as TV viewing increases, SAT scores decrease, but the trend isn't very strong. We can get a better idea of how strong this correlation is by examining its predictive power.

Correlation and Prediction

As the magnitude of a correlation increases (gets closer to either –1.00 or +1.00), our ability to predict one variable based on knowledge of the other variable steadily increases. This relationship between the magnitude of a correlation and predictability can be quantified precisely. All we have to do is square the correlation coefficient (multiply it by itself) and this gives us the *coefficient of determination*, **the percentage of variation in one variable that can be predicted based on the other variable.** Thus, a correlation of .70 yields a coefficient of determination of .49 ($.70 \times .70 = .49$), indicating that variable X can account for 49% of the variation in variable Y. Figure B.11 shows how the coefficient of determination goes up as the magnitude of a correlation increases.

Unfortunately, a correlation of .24 doesn't give us much predictive power. We can account only for a little over 6% of the variation in variable Y. So, if we tried to predict individuals' SAT scores based on how much TV they watched, our predictions wouldn't be very accurate. Although a low correlation doesn't have much practical, predictive utility, it may still have theoretical value. Just knowing that there is a relationship between two variables can be theoretically interesting. However, we haven't yet addressed the question of whether our observed correlation is strong enough to support our hypothesis that there is a relationship between TV viewing and SAT scores. To make this judgment, we have to turn to inferential statistics and the process of hypothesis testing.

Hypothesis Testing

Inferential statistics go beyond the mere description of data. *Inferential statistics* are used to **interpret data and draw conclusions.** They permit researchers to decide whether their data support their hypotheses.

In Chapter 2, we showed how inferential statistics can be used to evaluate the results of an experiment; the same process can be applied to correlational data. In our study of TV viewing we hypothesized that we would find an inverse rela-

Subject number	TV viewing score (X)	X²	SAT score (Y)	Y²	XY
1	0	0	500	250,000	0
2	0	0	515	265,225	0
3	1	1	450	202,500	450
4	1	1	650	422,500	650
5	2	4	400	160,000	800
6	2	4	675	455,625	1350
7	2	4	425	180,625	850
8	3	9	400	160,000	1200
9	3	9	450	202,500	1350
10	3	9	500	250,000	1500
11	3	9	550	302,500	1650
12	3	9	600	360,000	1800
13	4	16	400	160,000	1600
14	4	16	425	180,625	1700
15	4	16	475	225,625	1900
16	4	16	525	275,625	2100
17	5	25	400	160,000	2000
18	5	25	450	202,500	2250
19	5	25	475	225,625	2375
20	6	36	550	302,500	3300
$N = 20$	$\Sigma X = 60$	$\Sigma X^2 = 234$	$\Sigma Y = 9815$	$\Sigma Y^2 = 4{,}943{,}975$	$\Sigma XY = 28{,}825$

Formula for Pearson product-moment correlation coefficient

$$r = \frac{(N)\Sigma XY - (\Sigma X)(\Sigma Y)}{\sqrt{[(N)\Sigma X^2 - (\Sigma X)^2][(N)\Sigma Y^2 - (\Sigma Y)^2]}}$$

$$= \frac{(20)(28{,}825) - (60)(9815)}{\sqrt{[(20)(234) - (60)^2][(20)(4{,}943{,}975) - (9815)^2]}}$$

$$= \frac{-12{,}400}{\sqrt{[1080][2{,}545{,}275]}}$$

$$= -.237$$

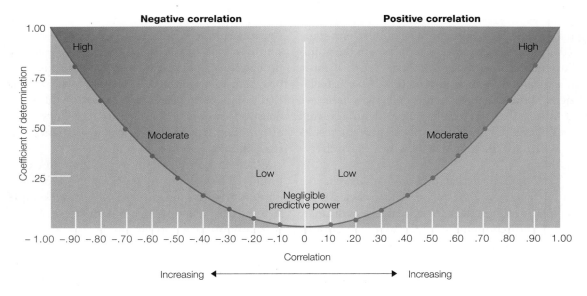

Figure B.11. Correlation and the coefficient of determination. The coefficient of determination is an index of a correlation's predictive power. As you can see, whether positive or negative, stronger correlations yield greater predictive power.

tionship between amount of TV watched and SAT scores. Sure enough, that's what we found. However, we have to ask ourselves a critical question: Is this observed correlation large enough to support our hypothesis, or might a correlation of this size have occurred by chance?

We have to ask a similar question nearly every time we conduct a study. Why? Because we are working only with a sample. In research, we observe a limited *sample* (in this case, 20 subjects) to draw conclusions about a much larger *population* (college students in general). There's always a possibility that if we drew a different sample from the population, the results might be different. Perhaps our results are unique to our sample and not generalizable to the larger population. If we were able to collect data on the entire population, we would not have to wrestle with this problem, but our dependence on a sample necessitates the use of inferential statistics to precisely evaluate the likelihood that our results are due to chance factors in sampling. Thus, inferential statistics are the key to making the inferential leap from the sample to the population (see Figure B.12).

Although it may seem backward, in hypothesis testing we formally test the *null* hypothesis. As applied to correlational data, the **null hypothesis is the assumption that there is no true relationship between the variables observed.** In our study, the null hypothesis is that there is no genuine association between TV viewing and SAT scores. We want to determine whether our results will permit us to *reject* the null hypothesis and thus conclude that our *research hypothesis* (that there *is* a relationship between the variables) has been supported. Why do we test directly the null hypoth-

esis instead of the research hypothesis? Because our probability calculations depend on assumptions tied to the null hypothesis. Specifically, we compute the probability of obtaining the results that we have observed if the null hypthesis is indeed true. The calculation of this probability hinges on a number of factors. A key factor is the amount of variability in the data, which is why the standard deviation is an important statistic.

Statistical Significance

When we reject the null hypothesis, we conclude that we have found *statistically significant* results. **Statistical significance is said to exist when the probability that the observed findings are due to chance is very low, usually less than 5**

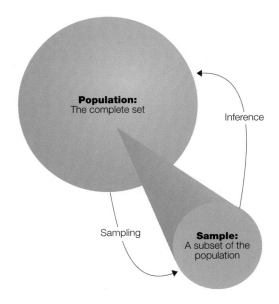

Figure B.12. The relationship between the population and the sample. In research, we are usually interested in a broad population, but we can observe only a small sample from the population. After making observations of our sample, we draw inferences about the population, based on the sample. This inferential process works well as long as the sample is reasonably representative of the population.

chances in 100. This means that if the null hypothesis is correct and we conduct our study 100 times, drawing a new sample from the population each time, we will get results such as those observed only 5 times out of 100. If our calculations allow us to reject the null hypothesis, we conclude that our results support our research hypothesis. Thus, statistically significant results typically are findings that *support* a research hypothesis.

The requirement that there be less than 5 chances in 100 that research results are due to chance is the *minimum* requirement for statistical significance. When this requirement is met, we say the results are significant at the .05 level. If researchers calculate that there is less than 1 chance in 100 that their results are due to chance factors in sampling, the results are significant at the .01 level. If there is less than a 1 in 1000 chance that findings are attributable to sampling error, the results are significant at the .001 level. Thus, there are several *levels* of significance that you may see cited in scientific articles.

Because we are only dealing in matters of probability, there is always the possibility that our decision to accept or reject the null hypothesis is wrong. The various significance levels indicate the probability of erroneously rejecting the null hypothesis (and inaccurately accepting the research hypothesis). At the .05 level of significance, there are 5 chances in 100 that we have made a mistake when we conclude that our results support our hypothesis, and at the .01 level of significance the chance of an erroneous conclusion is 1 in 100. Although researchers hold the probability of this type of error quite low, the probability is never zero. This is one of the reasons that competently executed studies of the same question can yield contradictory findings. The differences may be due to chance variations in sampling that can't be prevented.

What do we find when we evaluate our data linking TV viewing to students' SAT scores? The calculations indicate that, given our sample size and the variability in our data, the probability of obtaining a correlation of −.24 by chance is greater than 20%. That's not a high probability, but it's *not* low enough to reject the null hypothesis. Thus, our findings are not strong enough to allow us to conclude that we have supported our hypothesis.

Statistics and Empiricism

In summary, conclusions based on empirical research are a matter of probability, and there's always a possibility that the conclusions are wrong. However, two major strengths of the empirical approach are its precision and its intolerance of error. Scientists can give you precise estimates of the likelihood that their conclusions are wrong, and because they're intolerant of error, they hold this probability extremely low. It's their reliance on statistics that allows them to accomplish these goals.

Glossary

A

Absolute refractory period The minimum length of time after an action potential during which another action potential cannot begin.

Achievement motive The need to master difficult challenges, to outperform others, and to meet high standards of excellence.

Achievement tests Tests that gauge a person's mastery and knowledge of various subjects.

Acquired immune deficiency syndrome (AIDS) A disorder in which the immune system is gradually weakened and eventually disabled by the human immunodeficiency virus (HIV).

Acquisition The formation of a new conditioned response tendency.

Action potential A brief change in a neuron's electrical charge.

Additive color mixing Formation of colors by superimposing lights, putting more light in the mixture than exists in any one light by itself.

Adoption studies Research studies that assess hereditary influence by examining the resemblance between adopted children and both their biological and their adoptive parents.

Afferent nerve fibers Axons that carry information inward to the central nervous system from the periphery of the body.

Afterimage A visual image that persists after a stimulus is removed.

Age of viability The age at which a baby can survive in the event of a premature birth.

Aggression Any behavior that is intended to hurt someone, either physically or verbally.

Agonist A chemical that mimics the action of a neurotransmitter.

Agoraphobia A fear of going out to public places.

Alcohol A variety of beverages containing ethyl alcohol.

Altruism Selfless concern for the welfare of others that leads to helping behavior.

Amnesia A significant memory loss that is too extensive to be due to normal forgetting. See also *Anterograde amnesia, Psychogenic amnesia, Retrograde amnesia.*

Animism The belief that all things are living.

Antagonist A chemical that opposes the action of a neurotransmitter.

Antecedents In behavior modification, events that typically precede the target response.

Anterograde amnesia Loss of memories for events that occur after a head injury.

Antianxiety drugs Medications that relieve tension, apprehension, and nervousness.

Antidepressant drugs Medications that gradually elevate mood and help bring people out of a depression.

Antipsychotic drugs Medications used to gradually reduce psychotic symptoms, including hyperactivity, mental confusion, hallucinations, and delusions.

Anxiety disorders A class of disorders marked by feelings of excessive apprehension and anxiety.

Applied psychology The branch of psychology concerned with everyday, practical problems.

Approach-approach conflict A conflict situation in which a choice must be made between two attractive goals.

Approach-avoidance conflict A conflict situation in which a choice must be made about whether to pursue a single goal that has both attractive and unattractive aspects.

Aptitude tests Psychological tests used to assess talent for specific kinds of learning.

Archetypes According to Jung, emotionally charged images and thought forms that have universal meaning.

Attachment A close, emotional bond of affection between infants and their caregivers.

Attention Focusing awareness on a narrowed range of stimuli or events.

Attitudes Orientations that locate objects of thought on dimensions of judgment.

Attributions Inferences that people draw about the causes of events, others' behavior, and their own behavior.

Autonomic nervous system The system of nerves that connect to the heart, blood vessels, smooth muscles, and glands.

Availability heuristic Basing the estimated probability of an event on the ease with which relevant instances come to mind.

Aversion therapy A behavior therapy in which an aversive stimulus is paired with a stimulus that elicits an undesirable response.

Avoidance-avoidance conflict A conflict situation in which a choice must be made between two unattractive goals.

Avoidance learning Learning that has occurred when an organism engages in a response that prevents some aversive stimulation from occurring.

Axon A long, thin fiber that transmits signals away from the neuron cell body to other neurons, or to muscles or glands.

B

Basal metabolic rate The body's rate of energy output at rest after a 12-hour fast.

Baseline period In behavior modification, a span of time before the program begins, during which one systematically observes the target behavior.

Basilar membrane A structure that runs the length of the cochlea in the inner ear and holds the auditory receptors, called hair cells.

Behavior Any overt (observable) response or activity by an organism.

Behavior modification A systematic approach to changing behavior through the application of the principles of conditioning.

Behavior therapies Application of the principles of learning to direct efforts to change clients' maladaptive behaviors.

Behavioral contract A written agreement outlining a promise to adhere to the contingencies of a behavior modification program.

Behaviorism A theoretical orientation based on the premise that scientific psychology should study only observable behavior.

Belief perseverance The tendency to hang onto beliefs in the face of contradictory evidence.

Binocular cues Clues about distance based on the differing views of the two eyes.

Biological rhythms Periodic fluctuations in physiological functioning.

Biomedical therapies Physiological interventions intended to reduce symptoms associated with psychological disorders.

Biopsychosocial model A model of illness that holds that physical illness is caused by a complex interaction of biological, psychological, and sociocultural factors.

Bipolar mood disorders (formerly known as manic-depressive disorders) Mood disorders marked by the experience of both depressed and manic periods.

Bisexuals Persons who seek emotional-sexual relationships with members of either sex.

Blood-brain barrier A semipermeable membranelike mechanism that stops some chemicals from passing between the bloodstream and the brain.

Bystander effect A paradoxical social phenomenon in which people are less likely to provide needed help when they are in groups than when they are alone.

C

Cannabis The hemp plant from which marijuana, hashish, and THC are derived.

Case study An in-depth investigation of an individual subject.

Catastrophic thinking Unrealistically pessimistic appraisals of stress that exaggerate the magnitude of one's problems.

Catatonic schizophrenia A type of schizophrenia marked by striking motor disturbances, ranging from muscular rigidity to random motor activity.

Central nervous system (CNS) The brain and the spinal cord.

Centration The tendency to focus on just one feature of a problem, neglecting other important aspects.

Cephalocaudal trend The head-to-foot direction of motor development.

Cerebral cortex The convoluted outer layer of the cerebrum.

Cerebral hemispheres The right and left halves of the cerebrum.

Channel The medium through which a message is sent.

Chromosomes Threadlike strands of DNA (deoxyribonucleic acid) molecules that carry genetic information.

Chunk A group of familiar stimuli stored as a single unit.

Circadian rhythms The 24-hour biological cycles found in humans and many other species.

Classical conditioning A type of learning in which a neutral stimulus acquires the ability to evoke a response that was originally evoked by another stimulus.

Client-centered therapy An insight therapy that emphasizes providing a supportive emotional climate for clients, who play a major role in determining the pace and direction of their therapy.

Clinical psychologists Psychologists who specialize in the diagnosis and treatment of psychological disorders and everyday behavioral problems.

Clinical psychology The branch of psychology concerned with the diagnosis and treatment of psychological problems and disorders.

Cochlea The fluid-filled, coiled tunnel in the inner ear that contains the receptors for hearing.

Coefficient of determination The percent-age of variation in one variable that can be predicted based on the other variable.

Cognition The mental processes involved in acquiring knowledge.

Cognitive development Transitions in youngsters' patterns of thinking, including reasoning, remembering, and problem solving.

Cognitive dissonance A psychological state that exists when related cognitions are inconsistent.

Cognitive therapy An insight therapy that emphasizes recognizing and changing negative thoughts and maladaptive beliefs.

Collective unconscious According to Jung, a storehouse of latent memory traces inherited from people's ancestral past.

Collectivism Putting group goals ahead of personal goals and defining one's identity in terms of the groups one belongs to.

Color blindness Deficiency in the ability to distinguish among colors.

Companionate love Warm, trusting, tolerant affection for another whose life is deeply intertwined with one's own.

Compensation According to Adler, efforts to overcome imagined or real inferiorities by developing one's abilities.

Complementary colors Pairs of colors that produce gray tones when added together.

Compliance A type of conformity that occurs when people yield to social pressure in their public behavior, even though their private beliefs have not changed.

Concordance rate The percentage of twin pairs or other pairs of relatives that exhibit the same disorder.

Conditioned reinforcers. See *Secondary reinforcers.*

Conditioned response (CR) A learned reaction to a conditioned stimulus that occurs because of previous conditioning.

Conditioned stimulus (CS) A previously neutral stimulus that has, through conditioning, acquired the capacity to evoke a conditioned response.

Cones Specialized visual receptors that play a key role in daylight vision and color vision.

Confirmation bias The tendency to seek information that supports one's decisions and beliefs while ignoring disconfirming information.

Conflict A state that occurs when two or more incompatible motivations or behavioral impulses compete for expression.

Conformity The tendency for people to yield to real or imagined social pressure.

Confounding of variables A condition that exists whenever two variables are linked together in a way that makes it difficult to sort out their specific effects.

Conscious Whatever one is aware of at a particular point in time.

Consciousness One's awareness of internal and external stimuli.

Conservation Piaget's term for the awareness that physical quantities remain constant in spite of changes in their shape or appearance.

Consolidation A hypothetical process involving the gradual conversion of information into durable memory codes stored in long-term memory.

Construct validity The extent to which there is evidence that a test measures a particular hypothetical construct.

Constructive coping Relatively healthful efforts that people make to deal with stressful events.

Content validity The degree to which the content of a test is representative of the domain it's supposed to cover.

Continuous reinforcement Reinforcing every instance of a designated response.

Control group Subjects in a study who do not receive the special treatment given to the experimental group.

Convergent thinking Narrowing down a list of alternatives to converge on a single correct answer.

Conversion disorder A somatoform disorder characterized by a significant loss of physical function (with no apparent organic basis), usually in a single organ system.

Coping Active efforts to master, reduce, or tolerate the demands created by stress.

Corpus callosum The structure that connects the two cerebral hemispheres.

Correlation The extent to which two variables are related to each other.

Correlation coefficient A numerical index of the degree of relationship between two variables.

Counseling psychologists Psychologists who specialize in the treatment of everyday adjustment problems.

Creativity The generation of ideas that are original, novel, and useful.

Criterion-related validity Test validity that is estimated by correlating subjects' scores on a test with their scores on an independent criterion (another measure) of the trait assessed by the test.

Cross-sectional study A research study in which investigators compare groups of subjects of differing age who are observed at a single point in time.

Culture The widely shared customs, beliefs, values, norms, institutions, and other products of a community that are transmitted socially across generations.

Culture-bound disorders Abnormal syndromes found only in a few cultural groups.

Cumulative recorder A device that creates a graphic record of reinforcement and responding in a Skinner box as a function of time.

D

Dark adaptation The process in which the eyes become more sensitive to light in low illumination.

Data collection techniques Procedures for making empirical observations and measurements.

Decay theory The idea that forgetting occurs because memory traces fade with time.

Decision making The process of evaluating alternatives and making choices among them.

Declarative memory system Memory for factual information.

Defense mechanisms Largely unconscious reactions that protect a person from unpleasant emotions such as anxiety and guilt.

Defensive attribution The tendency to blame victims for their misfortune, so that one feels less likely to be victimized in a similar way.

Deinstitutionalization Transferring the treatment of mental illness from inpatient institutions to community-based facilities that emphasize outpatient care.

Delusions False beliefs that are maintained even though they are clearly out of touch with reality.

Dendrites Branchlike parts of a neuron that are specialized to receive information.

Dependent variable In an experiment, the variable that is thought to be affected by the manipulation of the independent variable.

Depressive disorders Mood disorders characterized by persistent feelings of sadness and despair and a loss of interest in previous sources of pleasure.

Depth perception Interpretation of visual cues that indicate how near or far away objects are.

Descriptive statistics Statistics that are used to organize and summarize data.

Development The sequence of age-related changes that occur as a person progresses from conception to death.

Developmental norms The average (median) age at which individuals display various behaviors and abilities.

Deviation IQ scores Scores that locate subjects precisely within the normal distribution, using the standard deviation as the unit of measurement.

Diagnosis Distinguishing one illness from another.

Discrimination Behaving differently, usually unfairly, toward the members of a group.

Discriminative stimuli Cues that influence operant behavior by indicating the probable consequences (reinforcement or non-reinforcement) of a response.

Disorganized schizophrenia A type of schizophrenia in which particularly severe deterioration of adaptive behavior is seen.

Displacement Diverting emotional feelings (usually anger) from their original source to a substitute target.

Display rules Cultural norms that regulate the appropriate expressions of emotions.

Dissociation A splitting off of mental processes into two separate, simultaneous streams of awareness.

Dissociative amnesia A sudden loss of memory for important personal information that is too extensive to be due to normal forgetting.

Dissociative disorders A class of disorders in which people lose contact with portions of their consciousness or memory, resulting in disruptions in their sense of identity.

Dissociative fugue A disorder in which people lose their memory for their entire lives along with their sense of personal identity.

Dissociative identity disorder. See *Multiple-personality disorder.*

Distal stimuli Stimuli that lie in the distance (that is, in the world outside the body).

Divergent thinking Trying to expand the range of alternatives by generating many possible solutions.

Double-blind procedure A research strategy in which neither subjects nor experimenters know which subjects are in the experimental or control groups.

Dream A mental experience during sleep that includes vivid visual images.

Dream analysis A psychoanalytic technique in which the therapist interprets the symbolic meaning of the client's dreams.

Drive An internal state of tension that motivates an organism to engage in activities that should reduce this tension.

Dual-coding theory Paivio's theory that memory is enhanced by forming both semantic and visual codes, since either can lead to recall.

E

Efferent nerve fibers Axons that carry information outward from the central nervous system to the periphery of the body.

Ego According to Freud, the decision-making component of personality that operates according to the reality principle.

Egocentrism A limited ability to share another person's viewpoint.

Elaboration Linking a stimulus to other information at the time of encoding.

Electrocardiograph (EKG) A device that records the contractions of the heart.

Electroconvulsive therapy (ECT) A biomedical treatment in which electric shock is used to produce a cortical seizure accompanied by convulsions.

Electroencephalograph (EEG) A device that monitors the electrical activity of the brain over time by means of recording electrodes attached to the surface of the scalp.

Electromyograph (EMG) A device that records muscular activity and tension.

Electrooculograph (EOG) A device that records eye movements.

Elicit To draw out or bring forth.

Embryonic stage The second stage of prenatal development, lasting from two weeks until the end of the second month.

Emit To send forth.

Emotion A subjective conscious experience (the cognitive component) accompanied by bodily arousal (the physiological component) and by characteristic overt expressions (the behavioral component).

Empiricism The premise that knowledge should be acquired through observation.

Encoding Forming a memory code.

Encoding specificity principle The idea that the value of a retrieval cue depends on how well it corresponds to the memory code.

Endocrine system A group of glands that secrete chemicals into the bloodstream that help control bodily functioning.

Endorphins The entire family of internally produced chemicals that resemble opiates in structure and effects.

Episodic memory system Chronological, or temporally dated, recollections of personal experiences.

Escape learning A type of learning in which an organism acquires a response that decreases or ends some aversive stimulation.

Etiology The apparent causation and developmental history of an illness.

Experiment A research method in which the investigator manipulates a variable under carefully controlled conditions and observes whether any changes occur in a second variable as a result.

Experimental group The subjects in a study who receive some special treatment in regard to the independent variable.

Experimenter bias A phenomenon that occurs when a researcher's expectations or preferences about the outcome of a study influence the results obtained.

Explicit memory Intentional recollection of previous experiences.

External attributions Ascribing the causes of behavior to situational demands and environmental constraints.

Extinction The gradual weakening and disappearance of a conditioned response tendency.

Extraneous variables Any variables other than the independent variable that seem likely to influence the dependent variable in a specific study.

Extraverts People who tend to be interested in the external world of people and things.

F

Family studies Scientific studies in which researchers assess hereditary influence by examining blood relatives to see how much they resemble each other on a specific trait.

Farsightedness A visual deficiency in which distant objects are seen clearly but close objects appear blurry.

Fast mapping The process by which children map a word onto an underlying concept after only one exposure to the word.

Feature analysis The process of detecting specific elements in visual input and assembling them into a more complex form.

Feature detectors Neurons that respond selectively to very specific features of more complex stimuli.

Fetal alcohol syndrome A collection of congenital (inborn) problems associated with excessive alcohol use during pregnancy.

Fetal stage The third stage of prenatal development, lasting from two months through birth.

Field dependence-independence Individuals' tendency to rely primarily on external versus internal frames of reference when orienting themselves in space.

Fight-or-flight response A physiological reaction to threat in which the autonomic nervous system mobilizes the organism for attacking (fight) or fleeing (flight) an enemy.

Fixation According to Freud, failure to move forward from one psychosexual stage to another as expected.

Fixed-interval (FI) schedule A reinforcement schedule in which the reinforcer is given for the first response that occurs after a fixed time interval has elapsed.

Fixed-ratio (FR) schedule A reinforcement schedule in which the reinforcer is given after a fixed number of nonreinforced responses.

Flashbulb memories Unusually vivid and detailed recollections of momentous events.

Forebrain The largest and most complex region of the brain, encompassing a variety of structures, including the thalamus, hypothalamus, limbic system, and cerebrum.

Forgetting curve A graph showing retention and forgetting over time.

Fovea A tiny spot in the center of the retina that contains only cones; visual acuity is greatest at this spot.

Framing How issues are posed or how choices are structured.

Free association A psychoanalytic technique in which clients spontaneously express their thoughts and feelings exactly as they occur, with as little censorship as possible.

Frequency distribution An orderly arrangement of scores indicating the frequency of each score or group of scores.

Frequency polygon A line figure used to present data from a frequency distribution.

Frustration The feeling that people experience in any situation in which their pursuit of some goal is thwarted.

Functional fixedness The tendency to perceive an item only in terms of its most common use.

Functionalism A school of psychology based on the belief that psychology should investigate the function or purpose of consciousness, rather than its structure.

Fundamental attribution error Observers' bias in favor of internal attributions in explaining others' behavior.

G

Galvanic skin response (GSR) An increase in the electrical conductivity of the skin that occurs when sweat glands increase their activity.

Gambler's fallacy The belief that the odds of a chance event increase if the event hasn't occurred recently.

Gender Culturally constructed distinctions between masculinity and femininity.

Gender differences Actual disparities between the sexes in typical behavior or average ability.

Gender roles Expectations about what is appropriate behavior for each sex.

Gender stereotypes Widely held beliefs about males' and females' abilities, personality traits, and social behavior.

General adaptation syndrome Selye's model of the body's stress response, consisting of three stages: alarm, resistance, and exhaustion.

Generalized anxiety disorder A psychological disorder marked by a chronic, high level of anxiety that is not tied to any specific threat.

Genes DNA segments that serve as the key functional units in hereditary transmission.

Genetic mapping The process of determining the location and chemical sequence of specific genes on specific chromosomes.

Germinal stage The first phase of prenatal development, encompassing the first two weeks after conception.

Glucose A simple sugar that is an important source of energy.

Glucostats Neurons sensitive to glucose in the surrounding fluid.

Group Two or more individuals who interact and are interdependent.

Group cohesiveness The strength of the liking relationships linking group members to each other and to the group itself.

Group polarization A phenomenon that occurs when group discussion strengthens a group's dominant point of view and produces a shift toward a more extreme decision in that direction.

Group therapy The simultaneous treatment of several or more clients in a group.

Groupthink A process in which members of a cohesive group emphasize concurrence at the expense of critical thinking in arriving at a decision.

Gustatory system The sensory system for taste.

H

Hallucinations Sensory perceptions that occur in the absence of a real, external stimulus, or gross distortions of perceptual input.

Hallucinogens A diverse group of drugs that have powerful effects on mental and emotional functioning, marked most prominently by distortions in sensory and perceptual experience.

Health psychology The subfield of psychology concerned with how psychosocial factors relate to the promotion and maintenance of health and with the causation, prevention, and treatment of illness.

Heritability ratio An estimate of the proportion of trait variability in a population that is determined by variations in genetic inheritance.

Heterosexuals Persons who seek emotional-sexual relationships with members of the other sex.

Heuristic A guiding principle or rule of thumb used in solving problems or making decisions.

Hierarchy of needs Maslow's systematic arrangement of needs according to priority, which assumes that basic needs must be met before less basic needs are aroused.

Higher-order conditioning A type of conditioning in which a conditioned stimulus functions as if it were an unconditioned stimulus.

Hindbrain The part of the brain that includes the cerebellum and two structures found in the lower part of the brainstem: the medulla and the pons.

Histogram A bar graph that presents data from a frequency distribution.

Holophrases Children's single-word utterances that appear to function like sentences.

Homeostasis A state of physiological equilibrium or stability.

Homosexuals Persons who seek emotional-sexual relationships with members of the same sex.

Hormones The chemical substances released by the endocrine glands.

Humanism A theoretical orientation that emphasizes the unique qualities of humans, especially their freedom and their potential for personal growth.

Hypnosis A systematic procedure that typically produces a heightened state of suggestibility.

Hypochondriasis A somatoform disorder characterized by excessive preoccupation with one's health and incessant worry about developing physical illnesses.

Hypothalamus A structure found near the

base of the forebrain that is involved in the regulation of basic biological needs.

Hypothesis A tentative statement about the relationship between two or more variables.

I

Id According to Freud, the primitive, instinctive component of personality that operates according to the pleasure principle.

Identical twins Twins that emerge from one zygote that splits for unknown reasons. Also called *Monozygotic twins.*

Identification Bolstering self-esteem by forming an imaginary or real alliance with some person or group.

Illusory correlation A misperception that occurs when people estimate that they have encountered more confirmations of an association between social traits than they have actually seen.

Immune response The body's defensive reaction to invasion by bacteria, viral agents, or other foreign substances.

Implicit memory Type of memory apparent when retention is exhibited on a task that does not require intentional remembering.

Impossible figures Objects that can be represented in two-dimensional pictures but cannot exist in three-dimensional space.

Incentive An external goal that has the capacity to motivate behavior.

Incongruence The degree of disparity between one's self-concept and one's actual experience.

Independent variable In an experiment, a condition or event that an experimenter varies in order to see its impact on another variable.

Individualism Putting personal goals ahead of group goals and defining one's identity in terms of personal attributes rather than group memberships.

Infant mortality The death rate in the first year of life per 1000 births.

Inferential statistics Statistics that are used to interpret data and draw conclusions.

Ingratiation A conscious effort to cultivate others' liking by complimenting them, agreeing with them, and doing them favors.

Ingroup The group that people belong to and identify with.

Insanity A legal status indicating that a person cannot be held responsible for his or her actions because of mental illness.

Insight In problem solving, the sudden discovery of the correct solution following incorrect attempts based primarily on trial and error.

Insight therapies Psychotherapy methods characterized by verbal interactions intended to enhance clients' self-knowledge and thus promote healthful changes in personality and behavior.

Insomnia Chronic problems in getting adequate sleep.

Insulin A hormone secreted by the pancreas that helps cells extract glucose from the blood.

Intelligence quotient (IQ) A child's mental age divided by chronological age, multiplied by 100.

Intelligence tests Psychological tests that measure general mental ability.

Interference theory The idea that people forget information because of competition from other material.

Intermittent reinforcement A reinforcement schedule in which a designated response is reinforced only some of the time.

Internal attributions Ascribing the causes of behavior to personal dispositions, traits, abilities, and feelings.

Interpersonal attraction Positive feelings toward another.

Interpretation In psychoanalysis, the therapist's attempts to explain the inner significance of the client's thoughts, feelings, memories, and behaviors.

Introspection Careful, systematic self-observation of one's own conscious experience.

Introverts People who tend to be preoccupied with the internal world of their own thoughts, feelings, and experiences.

Involuntary commitment A civil proceeding in which people are hospitalized in psychiatric facilities against their will.

Irreversibility The inability to envision reversing an action.

J

Journal A periodical that publishes technical and scholarly material, usually in a narrowly defined area of inquiry.

K

Kinesthetic system The sensory system that monitors the positions of the various parts of one's body.

L

Language A set of symbols that convey meaning, plus rules for combining those symbols, that can be used to generate an infinite variety of messages.

Language acquisition device (LAD) An innate mechanism or process that facilitates the learning of language.

Latent content According to Freud, the hidden or disguised meaning of the events in a dream.

Latitude of acceptance A range of potentially acceptable positions on an issue centered on one's initial attitude position.

Learned helplessness Passive behavior produced by exposure to unavoidable aversive events.

Learning A relatively durable change in behavior or knowledge that is due to experience.

Lens The transparent eye structure that focuses the light rays falling on the retina.

Levels-of-processing theory The theory holding that deeper levels of mental processing result in longer-lasting memory codes.

Lie detector. See *Polygraph.*

Life changes Any noticeable alterations in one's living circumstances that require readjustment.

Light adaptation The process whereby the eyes become less sensitive to light in high illumination.

Limbic system A loosely connected network of structures roughly located along the border between the cerebral cortex and deeper subcortical areas.

Linguistic relativity The hypothesis that one's language determines the nature of one's thought.

Link method Forming a mental image of items to be remembered in a way that links them together.

Lithium A chemical used to control mood swings in patients with bipolar mood disorders.

Long-term memory (LTM) An unlimited capacity store that can hold information over lengthy periods of time.

Longitudinal study A research study in which investigators observe one group of subjects repeatedly over a period of time.

M

Manifest content According to Freud, the plot of a dream at a surface level.

Matching hypothesis The idea that males and females of approximately equal physical attractiveness are likely to select each other as partners.

Maturation Development that reflects the gradual unfolding of one's genetic blueprint.

Mean The arithmetic average of the scores in a distribution.

Mean length of utterance (MLU) The average length of children's spoken statements (measured in phonemes).

Median The score that falls exactly in the center of a distribution of scores.

Medical model The view that it is useful to think of abnormal behavior as a disease.

Meditation A family of mental exercises in which a conscious attempt is made to focus attention in a nonanalytical way.

Menarche The first occurrence of menstruation.

Mental age In intelligence testing, a score that indicates that a child has displayed the mental ability typical of a child of that chronological (actual) age.

Mental hospital A medical institution specializing in providing inpatient care for psychological disorders.

Mental set Persisting in using problem-solving strategies that have worked in the past.

Message The information transmitted by a source.

Metalinguistic awareness The ability to reflect on the use of language.

Method of loci A mnemonic device that involves taking an imaginary walk along a familiar path where images of items to be remembered are associated with certain locations.

Midbrain The segment of the brain stem that lies between the hindbrain and the forebrain.

Mnemonic devices Strategies for enhancing memory.

Mode The score that occurs most frequently in a distribution.

Model A person whose behavior is observed by another.

Monocular cues Clues about distance based on the image in either eye alone.

Mood disorders A class of disorders marked by emotional disturbances of varied kinds that may spill over to disrupt physical, perceptual, social, and thought processes.

Morphemes The smallest units of meaning in a language.

Motivated forgetting Purposeful suppression of memories.

Motivation Goal-directed behavior.

Motor development The progression of muscular coordination required for physical activities.

Multiple-personality disorder A type of dissociative disorder characterized by the coexistence in one person of two or more largely complete, and usually very different, personalities.

Myelin sheath Insulating material, derived from glial cells, that encases some axons of neurons.

N

Narcotics (opiates) Drugs derived from opium that are capable of relieving pain.

Naturalistic observation A descriptive research method in which the researcher engages in careful, usually prolonged, observation of behavior without intervening directly with the subjects.

Nearsightedness A visual deficiency in which close objects are seen clearly but distant objects appear blurry.

Need for self-actualization The need to fulfill one's potential.

Negative reinforcement The strengthening of a response because it is followed by the removal of an aversive (unpleasant) stimulus.

Negatively skewed distribution A distribution in which most scores pile up at the high end of the scale.

Nerves Bundles of neuron fibers (axons) that are routed together in the peripheral nervous system.

Neuromodulators Chemicals that increase or decrease (modulate) the activity of specific neurotransmitters.

Neurons Individual cells in the nervous system that receive, integrate, and transmit information.

Neurotransmitters Chemicals that transmit information from one neuron to another.

Non-REM (NREM) sleep Sleep stages 1 through 4, which are marked by an absence of rapid eye movements, relatively little dreaming, and varied EEG activity.

Nonsense syllables Consonant-vowel-consonant arrangements that do not correspond to words.

Normal distribution A symmetrical, bell-shaped curve that represents the pattern in which many characteristics are dispersed in the population.

Null hypothesis In inferential statistics, the assumption that there is no true relationship between the variables being observed.

O

Obedience A form of compliance that occurs when people follow direct commands, usually from someone in a position of authority.

Object permanence Recognizing that objects continue to exist even when they are no longer visible.

Observational learning A type of learning that occurs when an organism's responding is influenced by the observation of others, who are called models.

Obsessive-compulsive disorder (OCD) A type of anxiety disorder marked by persistent, uncontrollable intrusions of unwanted thoughts (obsessions) and urges to engage in senseless rituals (compulsions).

Oedipal complex According to Freud, children's manifestation of erotically tinged desires for their opposite-sex parent, accompanied by feelings of hostility toward their same-sex parent.

Olfactory system The sensory system for smell.

Operant conditioning A form of learning in which voluntary responses come to be controlled by their consequences.

Operational definition A definition that describes the actions or operations that will be made to measure or control a variable.

Operations Internal transformations, manipulations, and reorganizations of mental structures.

Opiates. See *Narcotics.*

Optical illusion An apparently inexplicable discrepancy between the appearance of a visual stimulus and its physical reality.

Optimism A general tendency to expect good outcomes.

Outgroup People who are not part of the ingroup.

Overextensions Using a word incorrectly to describe a wider set of objects or actions than it is meant to.

Overlearning Continued rehearsal of material after one first appears to have mastered it.

Overregularization In children, incorrect generalization of grammatical rules to irregular cases where they do not apply.

P

Panic disorder A type of anxiety disorder characterized by recurrent attacks of overwhelming anxiety that usually occur suddenly and unexpectedly.

Paranoid schizophrenia A type of schizophrenia dominated by delusions of persecution along with delusions of grandeur.

Parasympathetic division The branch of the autonomic nervous system that generally conserves bodily resources.

Passionate love A complete absorption in another that includes tender sexual feelings and the agony and ecstasy of intense emotion.

Pavlovian conditioning. See *Classical conditioning.*

Percentile score A figure that indicates the percentage of people who score below the score one has obtained.

Perception The selection, organization, and interpretation of sensory input.

Perceptual constancy A tendency to experience a stable perception in the face of continually changing sensory input.

Perceptual hypothesis An inference about which distal stimuli could be responsible for the proximal stimuli sensed.

Perceptual set A readiness to perceive a stimulus in a particular way.

Performance evaluation Efforts to assess the quality of employees' work.

Peripheral nervous system All those nerves that lie outside the brain and spinal cord.

Person perception The process of forming impressions of others.

Personality An individual's unique constellation of consistent behavioral traits.

Personality tests Psychological tests that measure various aspects of personality, including motives, interests, values, and attitudes.

Personality trait A durable disposition to behave in a particular way in a variety of situations.

Phi phenomenon The illusion of movement created by presenting visual stimuli in rapid succession.

Phobic disorder A type of anxiety disorder marked by a persistent and irrational fear of an object or situation that presents no realistic danger.

Phonemes The smallest units of sound in a spoken language.

Physical dependence The condition that exists when a person must continue to take a drug to avoid withdrawal illness.

Pituitary gland The "master gland" of the endocrine system; it releases a great variety of hormones that fan out through the body, stimulating actions in the other endocrine glands.

Placebo effects The fact that subjects' expectations can lead them to experience some change even though they receive empty, fake, or ineffectual treatment.

Placenta A structure that allows oxygen and nutrients to pass into the fetus from the mother's bloodstream and bodily wastes to pass out to the mother.

Pleasure principle According to Freud, the principle upon which the id operates, demanding immediate gratification of its urges.

Polygenic traits Characteristics that are influenced by more than one pair of genes.

Polygraph A device that records autonomic fluctuations while a subject is questioned, in an effort to determine whether the subject is telling the truth.

Population The larger collection of animals or people from which a sample is drawn and that researchers want to generalize about.

Positive reinforcement Reinforcement that occurs when a response is strengthened because it is followed by the presentation of a rewarding stimulus.

Positively skewed distribution A distribution in which scores pile up at the low end of the scale.

Postsynaptic potential (PSP) A voltage change at the receptor site on a postsynaptic cell membrane.

Preconscious According to Freud, the level of awareness that contains material just beneath the surface of conscious awareness that can easily be retrieved.

Prejudice A negative attitude held toward members of a group.

Prenatal period The period from conception to birth, usually encompassing nine months of pregnancy.

Pressure Expectations or demands that one behave in a certain way.

Primacy effect The fact that items at the beginning of a list are recalled better than other items on the list.

Primary reinforcers Events that are inherently reinforcing because they satisfy biological needs.

Primary sex characteristics The sexual structures necessary for reproduction.

Proactive interference A memory problem that occurs when previously learned information interferes with the retention of new information.

Problem solving Active efforts to discover what must be done to achieve a goal that is not readily available.

Procedural memory system The repository of memories for actions, skills, and operations.

Prognosis A forecast about the probable course of an illness.

Projection Attributing one's own thoughts, feelings, or motives to another.

Projective tests Psychological tests that ask subjects to respond to vague, ambiguous stimuli in ways that may reveal the subjects' needs, feelings, and personality traits.

Proximal stimuli The stimulus energies that impinge directly on sensory receptors.

Proximity Geographic, residential, and other forms of spatial closeness.

Proximodistal trend The center-outward direction of motor development.

Psychiatrists Physicians who specialize in the diagnosis and treatment of psychological disorders.

Psychoactive drugs Chemical substances that modify mental, emotional, or behavioral functioning.

Psychoanalysis An insight therapy that emphasizes the recovery of unconscious conflicts, motives, and defenses through techniques such as free association and transference.

Psychoanalytic theory A theory developed by Freud that attempts to explain personality, motivation, and mental disorders by focusing on unconscious determinants of behavior.

Psychodynamic theories All the diverse theories descended from the work of Sigmund Freud that focus on unconscious mental forces.

Psychogenic amnesia A sudden loss of memory for important personal information that is too extensive to be due to normal forgetting.

Psychological dependence The condition that exists when a person must continue to take a drug in order to satisfy intense mental and emotional craving for the drug.

Psychological test A standardized measure of a sample of a person's behavior.

Psychology The science that studies behavior and the physiological and cognitive processes that underlie behavior, and the profession that applies the accumulated knowledge of this science to practical problems.

Psychopharmacotherapy The treatment of mental disorders with medication.

Psychosexual stages According to Freud, developmental periods with a characteristic sexual focus that leave their mark on adult personality.

Psychosomatic diseases Genuine physical ailments caused in part by psychological factors, especially emotional distress.

Puberty The stage during which sexual functions reach maturity, which marks the beginning of adolescence.

Pubescence The two-year span preceding puberty during which the changes leading to physical and sexual maturity take place.

Punishment An event that follows a response that weakens the tendency to make that response.

Pupil The opening in the center of the iris that helps regulate the amount of light passing into the rear chamber of the eye.

R

Random assignment of subjects The constitution of groups in a study such that all subjects have an equal chance of being assigned to any group or condition.

Rational-emotive therapy An approach to therapy that focuses on altering clients' patterns of irrational thinking to reduce maladaptive emotions and behavior.

Rationalization Creating false but plausible excuses to justify unacceptable behavior.

Reaction formation Behaving in a way that's exactly the opposite of one's true feelings.

Reaction range Genetically determined limits on IQ (or other traits).

Reality principle According to Freud, the principle on which the ego operates, which seeks to delay gratification of the id's urges until appropriate outlets and situations can be found.

Recall A measure of retention that requires subjects to reproduce information on their own without any cues.

Receiver The person to whom a message is sent.

Recency effect The fact that items near the end of a list are recalled better than other items on the list.

Receptive field of a visual cell The retinal area that, when stimulated, affects the firing of that cell.

Reciprocity Liking those who show that they like you.

Recognition A measure of retention that requires subjects to select previously learned information from an array of options.

Regression A reversion to immature patterns of behavior.

Rehearsal The process of repetitively verbalizing or thinking about information to be stored in memory.

Reinforcement An event following a response that strengthens an organism's tendency to make that response. See also *Negativce reinforcement; positive reinforcement.*

Reinforcement contingencies The circumstances or rules that determine whether responses lead to the presentation of reinforcers.

Relearning A measure of retention that requires a subject to memorize information a second time to determine how much time or effort is saved by having learned it before.

Reliability The measurement consistency of a test (or of other kinds of measurement techniques).

REM sleep A deep stage of sleep marked by rapid eye movements, high-frequency brain waves, and dreaming.

Replication The repetition of a study to see whether the earlier results are duplicated.

Representativeness heuristic Basing the estimated probability of an event on how similar it is to the typical prototype of that event.

Repression Keeping distressing thoughts and feelings buried in the unconscious.

Research methods Differing approaches to the observation, measurement, manipulation, and control of variables in empirical studies.

Resistance Largely unconscious defensive maneuvers a client uses to hinder the progress of therapy.

Resistance to extinction In operant conditioning, the phenomenon that occurs when an organism continues to make a response after delivery of the reinforcer for it has been terminated.

Resting potential The stable, negative charge of a neuron when it is inactive.

Retention The proportion of material retained (remembered).

Retina The neural tissue lining the inside back surface of the eye; it absorbs light, processes images, and sends visual information to the brain.

Retrieval Recovering information from memory stores.

Retroactive interference A memory problem that occurs when new information impairs the retention of previously learned information.

Retrograde amnesia Loss of memories for events that occurred prior to a head injury.

Reversible figure A drawing that is compatible with two different interpretations that can shift back and forth.

Risky decision making Making choices under conditions of uncertainty.

Rods Specialized visual receptors that play a key role in night vision and peripheral vision.

S

Sample The collection of subjects selected for observation in an empirical study.

Sampling bias A problem that occurs when a sample is not representative of the population from which it is drawn.

Scatter diagram A graph in which paired X and Y scores for each subject are plotted as single points.

Schedule of reinforcement A specific pattern of presentation of reinforcers over time.

Schema An organized cluster of knowledge about a particular object or sequence of events.

Schizophrenic disorders A class of psychological disorders marked by disturbances in thought that spill over to affect perceptual, social, and emotional processes.

Secondary (conditioned) reinforcers Stimulus events that acquire reinforcing qualities by being associated with primary reinforcers.

Secondary sex characteristics Physical features that distinguish one sex from the other but that are not essential for reproduction.

Sedatives Sleep-inducing drugs that tend to decrease central nervous system activation and behavioral activity.

Self-actualizing persons People with exceptionally healthy personalities, marked by continued personal growth.

Self-concept A collection of beliefs about one's own nature, unique qualities, and typical behavior.

Self-efficacy One's belief about one's ability to perform behaviors that should lead to expected outcomes.

Self-report inventories Personality tests that ask individuals to answer a series of questions about their characteristic behavior.

Self-serving bias The tendency to attribute one's successes to personal factors and one's failures to situational factors.

Semantic memory system General knowledge that is not tied to the time when the information was learned.

Semantic network A system of nodes representing concepts, joined together by pathways that link related concepts.

Senile dementia An abnormal deterioration in mental faculties seen in the elderly.

Sensation The stimulation of sense organs.

Sensory adaptation A gradual decline in sensitivity to prolonged stimulation.

Sensory memory The preservation of information in its original sensory form for a brief time, usually only a fraction of a second.

Separation anxiety Emotional distress seen in many infants when they are separated from people with whom they have formed an attachment.

Serial-position effect In memory tests, the fact that subjects show better recall for items at the beginning and end of a list than for items in the middle.

Set point A natural point of stability in body weight.

Sex The biologically based categories of male and female.

Sexual orientation A person's preference for emotional and sexual relationships with individuals of the same sex, the other sex, or either sex.

Shaping The reinforcement of closer and closer approximations of a desired response.

Short-term memory (STM) A limited-capacity store that can maintain unrehearsed information for about 20 to 30 seconds.

Skinner box A small enclosure in which an animal can make a specific response that is systematically recorded while the consequences of the response are controlled.

Slow-wave sleep Sleep stages 3 and 4, during which low-frequency delta waves become prominent in EEG recordings.

Social clock A person's notion of a developmental schedule that specifies what he or she should have accomplished by certain points in life.

Social desirability bias A tendency to give socially approved answers to questions about oneself.

Social loafing A reduction in effort by individuals when they work in groups as compared to when they work by themselves.

Social psychology The branch of psychology concerned with the way individuals' thoughts, feelings, and behaviors are influenced by others.

Social schemas Organized clusters of ideas about categories of social events and people.

Social skills training A behavior therapy designed to improve interpersonal skills that emphasizes modeling, behavioral rehearsal, and shaping.

Social support Various types of aid and succor provided by members of one's social networks.

Socialization The acquisition of the norms, roles, and behaviors expected of people in a particular society.

Sociobiology The study of the genetic and evolutionary basis of social behavior in all organisms, including humans.

Soma The cell body of a neuron; it contains the nucleus and much of the chemical machinery common to most cells.

Somatic nervous system The system of nerves that connect to voluntary skeletal muscles and to sensory receptors.

Somatization disorder A type of somatoform disorder marked by a history of diverse physical complaints that appear to be psychological in origin.

Somatoform disorders A class of psychological disorders involving physical ailments with no authentic organic basis that are due to psychological factors.

Source The person who sends a communication.

Source monitoring The process of making attributions about the origins of memories.

Source-monitoring error An error that occurs when a memory derived from one source is misattributed to another source.

Split-brain surgery A procedure in which the bundle of fibers that connects the cerebral hemispheres (the corpus callosum) is cut to reduce the severity of epileptic seizures.

Spontaneous recovery In classical conditioning, the reappearance of an extinguished response after a period of nonexposure to the conditioned stimulus.

SQ3R A study system designed to promote effective reading by means of five steps: survey, question, read, recite, and review.

Stage A developmental period during which characteristic patterns of behavior are exhibited and certain capacities become established.

Standard deviation An index of the amount of variability in a set of data.

Standardization The uniform procedures used in the administration and scoring of a test.

Statistical significance The condition that exists when the probability that the observed findings are due to chance is very low.

Statistics The use of mathematics to organize, summarize, and interpret numerical data. See also *Descriptive statistics, Inferential statistics.*

Stereotypes Widely held beliefs that people have certain characteristics because of their membership in a particular group.

Stimulants Drugs that tend to increase central nervous system activation and behavioral activity.

Stimulus Any detectable input from the environment.

Stimulus contiguity A temporal (time) association between two events.

Stimulus discrimination The phenomenon that occurs when an organism that has learned a response to a specific stimulus does *not* respond in the same way to stimuli that are similar to the original stimulus.

Stimulus generalization The phenomenon that occurs when an organism that has learned a response to a specific stimulus responds in the same way to new stimuli that are similar to the original stimulus.

Storage Maintaining encoded information in memory over time.

Stress Any circumstances that threaten or are perceived to threaten one's well-being and that thereby tax one's coping abilities.

Striving for superiority According to Adler, the universal drive to adapt, improve oneself, and master life's challenges.

Structuralism A school of psychology based on the notion that the task of psychology is to analyze consciousness into its basic elements and to investigate how these elements are related.

Subjects The persons or animals whose behavior is systematically observed in a study.

Subtractive color mixing Formation of colors by removing some wavelengths of light, leaving less light than was originally there.

Superego According to Freud, the moral component of personality that incorporates social standards about what represents right and wrong.

Survey A descriptive research method in which researchers use questionnaires or interviews to gather information about specific aspects of subjects' behavior.

Sympathetic division The branch of the autonomic nervous system that mobilizes the body's resources for emergencies.

Synapse A junction where information is transmitted from one neuron to another.

Synaptic cleft A microscopic gap between the terminal button of one neuron and the cell membrane of another neuron.

Syntax A system of rules that specify how words can be combined into phrases and sentences.

Systematic desensitization A behavior therapy used to reduce clients' anxiety responses through counterconditioning.

T

Tardive dyskinesia A neurological disorder marked by involuntary writhing and ticlike movements of the mouth, tongue, face, hands, or feet.

Telegraphic speech Speech that consists mainly of content words; articles, prepositions, and other less critical words are omitted.

Temperament An individual's characteristic mood, activity level, and emotional reactivity.

Terminal buttons Small knobs at the end of axons that secrete chemicals called neurotransmitters.

Test norms Standards that provide information about where a score on a psychological test ranks in relation to other scores on that test.

Test-retest reliability A type of reliability estimated by comparing subjects' scores on two administrations of a test.

Testwiseness The ability to use the characteristics and format of a cognitive test to maximize one's score.

Thalamus A structure in the forebrain through which all sensory information (except smell) must pass to get to the cerebral cortex.

Theory A system of interrelated ideas that is used to explain a set of observations.

Tip-of-the-tongue phenomenon A temporary inability to remember something accompanied by a feeling that it's just out of reach.

Token economy A system for doling out symbolic reinforcers that are exchanged later for a variety of genuine reinforcers.

Tolerance A progressive decrease in a person's responsiveness to a drug.

Transference In therapy, the phenomenon that occurs when clients start relating to their therapists in ways that mimic critical relationships in their lives.

Transvestism A sexual disorder in which a man achieves sexual arousal by dressing in women's clothing.

Trial In classical conditioning, any presentation of a stimulus or pair of stimuli.

Trial and error Trying possible solutions sequentially and discarding those that are in error until one works.

Twin studies A research design in which hereditary influence is assessed by comparing the resemblance of identical twins and fraternal twins with respect to a trait.

Type A personality A personality style characterized by (1) a strong competitive orientation, (2) impatience and time urgency, and (3) anger and hostility.

Type B personality A personality style marked by relatively relaxed, patient, easygoing, amicable behavior.

U

Unconditioned response (UCR) An unlearned reaction to an unconditioned stimulus that occurs without previous conditioning.

Unconditioned stimulus (UCS) A stimulus that evokes an unconditioned response without previous conditioning.

Unconscious According to Freud, thoughts, memories, and desires that are well below the surface of conscious awareness but that nonetheless exert great influence on behavior.

Undifferentiated schizophrenia A type of schizophrenia marked by idiosyncratic mixtures of schizophrenic symptoms.

V

Validity The ability of a test to measure what it was designed to measure.

Variability The extent to which the scores in a data set tend to vary from each other and from the mean.

Variable-interval (VI) schedule A reinforcement schedule in which the reinforcer is given for the first response after a variable time interval has elapsed.

Variable-ratio (VR) schedule A reinforcement schedule in which the reinforcer is given after a variable number of nonreinforced responses.

Variables Any measurable conditions, events, characteristics, or behaviors that are controlled or observed in a study.

Vestibular system The sensory system that responds to gravity and keeps people informed of their body's location in space.

Volley principle The theory holding that groups of auditory nerve fibers fire neural impulses in rapid succession, creating volleys of impulses.

Z

Zygote A one-celled organism formed by the union of a sperm and an egg.

References

Abou-Saleh, M. T. (1992). Lithium. In E. S. Paykel (Ed.), *Handbook of affective disorders* (2nd ed.). New York: Guilford Press.

Aboud, F. E. (1987). The development of ethnic self-identification and attitudes. In J. S. Phinney & M. J. Rotheram (Eds.), *Children's ethnic socialization: Pluralism and development*. Newbury Park, CA: Sage.

Abrams, R. (1992). *Electroconvulsive therapy*. New York: Oxford University Press.

Abramson, L. Y., Metalsky, G. I., & Alloy, L. B. (1989). Hopelessness depression: A theory-based subtype of depression. *Psychological Review, 96,* 358–372.

Abramson, L. Y., Seligman, M. E. P., & Teasdale, J. (1978). Learned helplessness in humans: Critique and reformulation. *Journal of Abnormal Psychology, 87,* 32–48.

Adams, H. E., & Cassidy, J. F. (1993). The classification of abnormal behavior: An overview. In P. B. Sutker & H. E. Adams (Eds.), *Comprehensive handbook of psychopathology* (2nd ed.). New York: Plenum.

Adams, J. L. (1980). *Conceptual blockbusting*. San Francisco: W. H. Freeman.

Adelmann, P. K., & Zajonc, R. B. (1989). Facial efference and the experience of emotion. *Annual Review of Psychology, 40,* 249–280.

Ader, R., & Cohen, N. (1981). Conditioned immunopharmacologic responses. In R. Ader (Ed.), *Psychoneuroimmunology*. New York: Academic Press.

Ader, R., & Cohen, N. (1984). Behavior and the immune system. In W. D. Gentry (Ed.), *Handbook of behavioral medicine*. New York: Guilford Press.

Ader, R., & Cohen, N. (1993). Psychoneuroimmunology: Conditioning and stress. *Annual Review of Psychology, 44,* 53–85.

Adler, A. (1917). *Study of organ inferiority and its psychical compensation*. New York: Nervous and Mental Diseases Publishing Co.

Adler, A. (1927). *Practice and theory of individual psychology*. New York: Harcourt, Brace & World.

Agnew, H. W., Webb, W. B., & Williams, R. L. (1964). The effects of stage 4 sleep deprivation. *Electroencephalography and Clinical Neurophysiology, 17,* 68–70.

Agnew, H. W., Webb, W. B., & Williams, R. L. (1967). Comparison of stage 4 and 1-REM sleep deprivation. *Perceptual and Motor Skills, 24,* 851–858.

Agnoli, F., & Krantz, D. H. (1989). Suppressing natural heuristics by formal instruction: The case of the conjunction fallacy. *Cognitive Psychology, 21,* 515–550.

Agras, W. S., & Berkowitz, R. (1988). Behavior therapy. In J. A. Talbott, R. E. Hales, & S. C. Yudofsky (Eds.), *The American Psychiatric Press textbook of psychiatry*. Washington, DC: American Psychiatric Press.

Ainsworth, M. D. S. (1979). Attachment as related to mother-infant interaction. In J. S. Rosenblatt,

R. A. Hinde, C. Beer, & M. Busnel (Eds.), *Advances in the study of behavior* (Vol. 9). New York: Academic Press.

Ainsworth, M. D. S., Blehar, M. C., Waters, E., & Wall, S. (1978). *Patterns of attachment: A psychological study of the strange situation*. Hillsdale, NJ: Erlbaum.

Albert, M. S. (1992). Alzheimer's disease: Cognitive aspects. In L. R. Squire (Ed.), *Encyclopedia of learning and memory*. New York: Macmillan.

Albert, M. S., & Moss, M. B. (1992). The assessment of memory disorders in patients with Alzheimer's disease. In L. R. Squire & N. Butters (Eds.), *Neuropsychology of memory* (2nd ed.). New York: Guilford Press.

Aldag, R. J., & Fuller, S. R. (1993). Beyond fiasco: A reappraisal of the groupthink phenomenon and a new model of group decision processes. *Psychological Bulletin, 113,* 533–552.

Alexander, C. N., Chandler, H. M., Langer, E. J., Newman, R. I., & Davies, J. L. (1989). Transcendental meditation, mindfulness, and longevity: An experimental study with the elderly. *Journal of Personality and Social Psychology, 57,* 950–964.

Alexander, C. N., Rainforth, M. V., & Gelderloos, P. (1991). Transcendental meditation, self actualization, and psychological health: A conceptual overview and statistical meta-analysis. *Journal of Social Behavior and Personality, 6*(5), 189–247.

Alexander, F. (1954). Psychoanalysis and psychotherapy. *Journal of the American Psychoanalytic Association, 2,* 722–733.

Alkon, D. L. (1989). Memory storage and neural systems. *Scientific American, 261,* 42–50.

Allen, S. J., Dawbarn, D., & Wilcock, G. K. (1988). Morphometric immunochemical analysis of neurons in the nucleus basalis of Meynert in Alzheimer's disease. *Brain Research, 454,* 275–281.

Allport, G. W. (1937). *Personality: A psychological interpretation*. New York: Holt.

Allport, G. W. (1961). *Pattern and growth in personality*. New York: Holt, Rinehart & Winston.

Altman, I. (1990). Centripetal and centrifugal trends in psychology. In L. Brickman & H. Ellis (Eds.), *Preparing psychologists for the 21st century: Proceedings of the National Conference on Graduate Education in Psychology*. Hillsdale, NJ: Erlbaum.

Amabile, T. M. (1983). *The social psychology of creativity*. New York: Springer-Verlag.

Amabile, T. M. (1990). Within you, without you: The social psychology of creativity, and beyond. In M. A. Runco & R. S. Albert (Eds.), *Theories of creativity*. Newbury Park, CA: Sage.

Amada, G. (1985). *A guide to psychotherapy*. Lanham, MD: Madison Books.

American Psychiatric Association. (1952). *Diagnostic and statistical manual of mental disorders*. Washington, DC: Author.

American Psychiatric Association. (1968). *Diagnostic and statistical manual of mental disorders* (2nd ed.). Washington, DC: Author.

American Psychiatric Association. (1980). *Diagnostic and statistical manual of mental disorders* (3rd ed.). Washington, DC: Author.

American Psychiatric Association. (1987). *Diagnostic and statistical manual of mental disorders* (3rd ed., rev.). Washington, DC: Author.

American Psychiatric Association. (1994). *Diagnostic and statistical manual of mental disorders* (4th ed.). Washington, DC: Author.

American Psychological Association. (1984). *Behavioral research with animals*. Washington, DC: Author.

American Psychological Association. (1992). Ethical principles of psychologists and code of conduct. *American Psychologist, 47,* 1597–1611.

American Psychological Association. (1993). *Profile of all APA members: 1993*. Washington, DC: Author.

Anand, B. K., & Brobeck, J. R. (1951). Hypothalamic control of food intake in rats and cats. *Yale Journal of Biology and Medicine, 24,* 123–140.

Anch, A. M., Browman, C. P., Mitler, M. M., & Walsh, J. K. (1988). *Sleep: A scientific perspective*. Englewood Cliffs, NJ: Prentice Hall.

Anderson, B. (1982). Test use today in elementary and secondary schools. In A. K. Wigdor & W. R. Garner (Eds.), *Ability testing: Uses, consequences and controversies*. Washington, DC: National Academy Press.

Anderson, B. F. (1980). *The complete thinker*. Englewood Cliffs, NJ: Prentice-Hall.

Anderson, K. J. (1990). Arousal and the inverted-U hypothesis: A critique of Neiss's "reconceptualizing arousal." *Psychological Bulletin, 107,* 96–100.

Anderson, S. M., & Klatzky, R. L. (1987). Traits and social stereotypes: Levels of categorization in person perception. *Journal of Personality and Social Psychology, 53,* 235–246.

Anderson, V. N. (1992). For whom is this world just? Sexual orientation and AIDS. *Journal of Applied Social Psychology, 22*(3), 248–259.

Andreasen, N. C. (1987). Creativity and mental illness: Prevalence rates in writers and their first-degree relatives. *American Journal of Psychiatry, 144,* 1288–1292.

Andreasen, N. C. (1988). Brain imaging: Applications in psychiatry. *Science, 239,* 1381–1388.

Andreasen, N. C. (1990). Positive and negative symptoms: Historical and conceptual aspects. In N. C. Andreasen (Ed.), *Modern problems of pharmacopsychiatry: Positive and negative symptoms and syndromes*. Basel: Karger.

Angoff, W. H. (1988). The nature-nurture debate, aptitudes, and group differences. *American Psychologist, 43*(9), 713–720.

Ansbacher, H. (1970, February). Alfred Adler, individual psychology. *Psychology Today*, pp. 42–44, 66.

Anthony, T., Copper, C., & Mullen, B. (1992). Cross-racial facial identification: A social cognitive integration. *Personality and Social Psychology Bulletin, 18,* 296–301.

Antill, J. K. (1987). Parents' beliefs and values about sex roles, sex differences, and sexuality: Their sources and implications. In P. Shaver & C. Hendrick (Eds.), *Sex and gender*. Newbury Park, CA: Sage.

Arkowitz, H. (1992). Integrative theories of therapy. In D. K. Freedheim (Ed.), *History of psychotherapy: A century of change*. Washington, DC: American Psychological Association.

Aron, A. (1988). The matching hypothesis reconsidered again: Comment on Kalick and Hamilton. *Journal of Personality and Social Psychology, 54,* 441–446.

Aronson, E. (1980). Large commitments for small rewards. In L. Festinger (Ed.), *Retrospections on social psychology*. New York: Oxford University Press.

Aronson, E., Brewer, M., & Carlsmith, J. M. (1985). Experimentation in social psychology. In G. Lindzey & E. Aronson (Eds.), *Handbook of social psychology* (3rd ed., Vol. 1). New York: Random House.

Aronson, E., & Mills, J. (1959). The effect of severity of initiation on liking for a group. *Journal of Abnormal and Social Psychology, 59,* 177–181.

Asch, S. E. (1951). Effects of group pressure on the modification and distortion of judgments. In H. Guetzkow (Ed.), *Groups, leadership and men*. Pittsburgh: Carnegie Press.

Asch, S. E. (1955). Opinions and social pressures. *Scientific American, 193*(5), 31–35.

Asch, S. E. (1956). Studies of independence and conformity: A minority of one against a unanimous majority. *Psychological Monographs, 70*(9, Whole No. 416).

Aschoff, J., & Wever, R. (1981). The circadian system of man. In J. Aschoff (Ed.), *Handbook of behavioral neurobiology: Vol. 4. Biological rhythms*. New York: Plenum.

Aserinsky, E., & Kleitman, N. (1953). Regularly occurring periods of eye mobility and concomitant phenomena during sleep. *Science, 118,* 273–274.

Aspinwall, L. G., & Taylor, S. E. (1992). Modeling cognitive adaptation: A longitudinal investigation of the impact of individual differences and coping on college adjustment and performance. *Journal of Personality and Social Psychology, 63,* 989–1003.

Asterita, M. F. (1985). *The physiology of stress*. New York: Human Sciences Press.

Atkinson, J. W. (1974). The mainsprings of achievement-oriented activity. In J. W. Atkinson & J. O. Raynor (Eds.), *Motivation and achievement*. New York: Wiley.

Atkinson, J. W. (1981). Studying personality in the context of an advanced motivational psychology. *American Psychologist, 36,* 117–128.

Atkinson, J. W. (1992). Motivational determinants of thematic apperception. In C. P. Smith (Ed.), *Motivation and personality: Handbook of thematic content analysis*. New York: Cambridge University Press.

Atkinson, J. W., & Birch, D. (1978). *Introduction to motivation*. New York: Van Nostrand.

Atkinson, J. W., & Litwin, G. H. (1960). Achievement motive and test anxiety conceived as motive to approach success and to avoid failure. *Journal of Abnormal and Social Psychology, 60,* 52–63.

Atkinson, R. C., & Shiffrin, R. M. (1968). Human memory: A proposed system and its control processes. In K. W. Spence & J. T. Spence (Eds.), *The psychology of learning and motivation* (Vol. 2). New York: Academic Press.

Atkinson, R. C., & Shiffrin, R. M. (1971). The control of short-term memory. *Scientific American, 225,* 82–90.

Austin, J. T., & Hanisch, K. A. (1990). Occupational attainment as a function of abilities and interests: A longitudinal analysis using Project TALENT data. *Journal of Applied Psychology, 75,* 77–86.

Averill, J. A. (1980). A constructivist view of emotion. In R. Plutchik & H. Kellerman (Eds.), *Emotion: Theory, research, and experience: Vol. 1. Theories of emotion*. New York: Academic Press.

Avery, D., & Winokur, G. (1978). Suicide, attempted suicide, and relapse rates in depression. *Archives of General Psychiatry, 35,* 749–753.

Axelrod, S., & Apsche, J. (1983). *The effects of punishment on human behavior*. New York: Academic Press.

Baars, B. J. (1986). *The cognitive revolution in psychology*. New York: Guilford Press.

Baddeley, A. D. (1976). *The psychology of memory*. New York: Basic Books.

Baddeley, A. D. (1989). The uses of working memory. In P. R. Soloman, G. R. Goethals, C. M. Kelley, & B. R. Stephens (Eds.), *Memory: Interdisciplinary approaches*. New York: Springer-Verlag.

Baddeley, A. D., & Hitch, G. (1974). Working memory. In G. H. Bower (Ed.), *The psychology of learning and motivation* (Vol. 8). New York: Academic Press.

Badia, P. (1990). Memories in sleep: Old and new. In R. R. Bootzin, J. F. Kihlstrom, & D. L. Schacter (Eds.), *Sleep and cognition*. Washington, DC: American Psychological Association.

Bahrick, H. P., Bahrick, P. C., & Wittlinger, R. P. (1975). Fifty years of memories of names and faces: A cross-sectional approach. *Journal of Experimental Psychology: General, 104,* 54–75.

Bailey, J. M., & Pillard, R. C. (1991). A genetic study of male homosexual orientation. *Archives of General Psychology, 48,* 1089–1097.

Bailey, J. M., Pillard, R. C., Neale, M. C. I., & Agyei, Y. (1993). Heritable factors influence sexual orientation in women. *Archives of General Psychiatry, 50,* 217–223.

Baillargeon, R., & DeVos, J. (1991). Object permanence in young infants: Further evidence. *Child Development, 62,* 1227–1246.

Bakan, P. (1971, August). The eyes have it. *Psychology Today,* pp. 64–69.

Baker, L. A., & Daniels, D. (1990). Nonshared environmental influences and personality differences in adult twins. *Journal of Personality and Social Psychology, 58,* 103–110.

Baker, S. W. (1980). Psychosexual differentiation in the human. *Biology of Reproduction, 22,* 61–72.

Balsam, P. D. (1988). Selection, representation, and equivalence of controlling stimuli. In R. C. Atkinson, R. J. Herrnstein, G. Lindzey, & R. D. Luce (Eds.), *Stevens' handbook of experimental psychology*. New York: Wiley.

Baltes, P. B., & Kliegl, R. (1992). Further testing of limits of cognitive plasticity: Negative age differences in a mnemonic skill are robust. *Developmental Psychology, 28,* 121–125.

Bandura, A. (1973). *Aggression: A social learning analysis*. Englewood Cliffs, NJ: Prentice-Hall.

Bandura, A. (1977). *Social learning theory*. Englewood Cliffs, NJ: Prentice-Hall.

Bandura, A. (1982). The psychology of chance encounters and life paths. *American Psychologist, 37,* 747–755.

Bandura, A. (1986). *Social foundations of thought and action: A social-cognitive theory*. Englewood Cliffs, NJ: Prentice-Hall.

Bandura, A. (1990). Perceived self-efficacy in the exercise of personal agency. *Journal of Applied Sport Psychology, 2*(2), 128–163.

Bandura, A. (1993). Perceived self-efficacy in cognitive development and functioning. *Educational Psychologist, 28*(2), 117–148.

Bandura, A., Ross, D., & Ross, S. A. (1963). Imitation of film-mediated aggressive models. *Journal of Abnormal and Social Psychology, 66,* 3–11.

Banks, W. P., & Krajicek, D. (1991). Perception. *Annual Review of Psychology, 42,* 305–331.

Barber, T. X. (1979). Suggested ("hypnotic") behavior: The trance paradigm versus an alternative paradigm. In E. Fromm & R. E. Shor (Eds.), *Hypnosis: Developments in research and new perspectives*. New York: Aldine.

Barber, T. X. (1986). Realities of stage hypnosis. In B. Zilbergeld, M. G. Edelstien, & D. L. Araoz (Eds.), *Hypnosis: Questions and answers*. New York: Norton.

Bard, P. (1934). On emotional experience after decortication with some remarks on theoretical views. *Psychological Review, 41,* 309–329.

Bar-Hillel, M. (1990). Back to base-rates. In R. M. Hogarth (Ed.), *Insights in decision making: A tribute to Hillel J. Einhorn*. Chicago: University of Chicago Press.

Barinaga, M. (1989). Manic depression gene put in limbo. *Science, 246,* 886–887.

Barlett, D. L., & Steele, J. B. (1979). *Empire: The life, legend and madness of Howard Hughes*. New York: Norton.

Barnett, P. A., & Gotlib, I. H. (1988). Psychosocial functioning and depression: Distinguishing among antecedents, concomitants, and consequences. *Psychological Bulletin, 104,* 97–126.

Baron, R. S., Cutrona, C. E., Hicklin, D., Russell, D. W., & Lubaroff, D. M. (1990). Social support and immune function among spouses of cancer patients. *Journal of Personality and Social Psychology, 59,* 344–352.

Barr, H. M., Streissguth, A. P., Darby, B. L., & Sampson, P. D. (1990). Prenatal exposure to alcohol, caffeine, tobacco, and aspirin: Effects on fine and gross motor performance in 4-year-old children. *Developmental Psychology, 26,* 339–348.

Barrett, D. (1988–1989). Dreams of death. *Omega, 19*(2), 95–101.

Barrett, G. V., & Depinet, R. L. (1991). A reconsideration of testing for competence rather than intelligence. *American Psychologist, 46,* 1012–1024.

Barrett, M. D. (1982). The holophrastic hypothesis: Conceptual and empirical issues. *Cognition, 11,* 47–76.

Barrett, M. D. (1989). Early language development. In A. Slater & G. Bremmer (Eds.), *Infant development*. London: Erlbaum.

Barron, F., & Harrington, D. M. (1981). Creativity, intelligence and personality. *Annual Review of Psychology, 32,* 439–476.

Barsky, A. J. (1988). The paradox of health. *New England Journal of Medicine, 318,* 414–418.

Barsky, A. J. (1989). Somatoform disorders. In H. I. Kaplan & B. J. Sadock (Eds.), *Comprehensive textbook of psychiatry/V*. Baltimore: Williams & Wilkins.

Barsky, A. J., Coeytaux, R. R., Sarnie, M. K., & Cleary, P. D. (1993). Hypochondriacal patients' beliefs about good health. *American Journal of Psychiatry, 150,* 1085–1090.

Barsky, A. J., Wyshak, G., & Klerman, G. L. (1990). The Somatosensory Amplification Scale and its relationship to hypochondriasis. *Journal of Psychiatry Research, 24,* 323–334.

Bartoshuk, L. M. (1968). Water taste in man. *Perception and Psychophysics, 3,* 69–72.

Bartoshuk, L. M. (1988). Taste. In R. C. Atkinson, R. J. Herrnstein, G. Lindzey, & R. D. Luce (Eds.), *Stevens' handbook of experimental psychology: Perception and motivation* (Vol. 1). New York: Wiley.

Bartoshuk, L. M. (1991). Taste, smell and pleasure. In R. C. Bolles (Ed.), *The hedonics of taste.* Hillsdale, NJ: Erlbaum.

Bartoshuk, L. M. (1993). The biological basis of food perception and acceptance. *Food Quality and Preference, 4,* 21–32.

Basbaum, A. I., & Fields, H. L. (1984). Endogenous pain control systems: Brainstem spinal pathways and endorphin circuitry. *Annual Review of Neuroscience, 7,* 309–338.

Bates, M. S., Edwards, W. T., & Anderson, K. O. (1993). Ethnocultural influences on variation in chronic pain perception. *Pain, 52*(1), 101–112.

Baumeister, R. F. (1989). The optimal margin of illusion. *Journal of Social and Clinical Psychology, 8,* 176–189.

Baumrind, D. (1964). Some thoughts on the ethics of reading Milgram's "Behavioral study of obedience." *American Psychologist, 19,* 421–423.

Baumrind, D. (1985). Research using intentional deception: Ethical issues revisited. *American Psychologist, 40,* 165–174.

Beahrs, J. O. (1983). Co-consciousness: A common denominator in hypnosis, multiple personality and normalcy. *American Journal of Clinical Hypnosis, 26*(2), 100–113.

Beck, A. T. (1976). *Cognitive therapy and the emotional disorders.* New York: International Universities Press.

Beck, A. T. (1987). Cognitive therapy. In J. K. Zeig (Ed.), *The evolution of psychotherapy.* New York: Brunner/Mazel.

Beck, A. T. (1988). Cognitive approaches to panic disorder: Theory and therapy. In S. Rachman & J. Maser (Eds.), *Panic: Psychological perspectives.* Hillsdale, NJ: Erlbaum.

Beck, A. T. (1991). Cognitive therapy: A 30-year retrospective. *American Psychologist, 46,* 368–375.

Beck, A. T., & Rush, A. J. (1989). Cognitive therapy. In H. I. Kaplan & B. J. Sadock (Eds.), *Comprehensive textbook of psychiatry/V.* Baltimore: Williams & Wilkins.

Becker, B. J. (1986). Influence again: An examination of reviews and studies of gender differences in social influence. In J. S. Hyde & M. C. Linn (Eds.), *The psychology of gender: Advances through meta-analysis.* Baltimore: Johns Hopkins University Press.

Becker, H. S. (1973). *Outsiders: Studies in the sociology of deviance.* New York: Free Press.

Becker, R. E. (1990). Social skills training. In A. S. Bellack & M. Hersen (Eds.), *Handbook of comparative treatments for adult disorders.* New York: Wiley.

Beecher, H. K. (1956). Relationship of significance of wound to pain experience. *Journal of the American Medical Association, 161,* 1609–1613.

Beilin, H. (1992). Piaget's enduring contribution to developmental psychology. *Developmental Psychology, 28,* 191–204.

Bekerian, D. A., & Bowers, J. M. (1983). Eyewitness testimony: Were we misled? *Journal of Experimental Psychology: Learning, Memory, and Cognition, 1,* 139–145.

Békésy, G. von. (1947). The variation of phase along the basilar membrane with sinusoidal vibrations. *Journal of the Acoustical Society of America, 19,* 452–460.

Bell, A. P., Weinberg, M. S., & Hammersmith, S. K. (1981). *Sexual preference: Its development in men and women.* Bloomington: Indiana University Press.

Bellisle, F. (1979). Human feeding behavior. *Neuroscience and Biobehavioral Reviews, 3,* 163–169.

Belsky, J. (1985). Exploring differences in marital change across the transition to parenthood: The role of violated expectations. *Journal of Marriage and the Family, 47,* 1037–1044.

Belsky, J. (1988). The "effects" of infant day care reconsidered. *Early Childhood Research Quarterly, 3,* 235–272.

Belsky, J. (1990). Infant day care, child development, and family policy. *Society, 27*(5), 10–12.

Belsky, J. (1992). Consequences of child care for children's development: A deconstructionist view. In A. Booth (Ed.), *Child care in the 1990s.* Hillsdale, NJ: Erlbaum.

Bem, S. L. (1985). Androgyny and gender schema theory: A conceptual and empirical integration. In T. B. Sonderegger (Ed.), *Nebraska symposium on motivation, 1984: Psychology and gender* (Vol. 32). Lincoln: University of Nebraska Press.

Benbow, C. P. (1988). Sex differences in mathematical reasoning ability in intellectually talented preadolescents: Their nature, effects, and possible causes. *Behavioral and Brain Sciences, 11,* 169–232.

Benjamin, L. T., Jr., Cavell, T. A., & Shallenberger, W. R., III. (1984). Staying with initial answers on objective tests: Is it a myth? *Teaching of Psychology, 11,* 133–141.

Bennett, H. L. (1993). The mind during surgery: The uncertain effects of anesthesia. *Advances, 9*(1), 5–16.

Benson, H. (1975). *The relaxation response.* New York: Morrow.

Benson, H., & Klipper, M. Z. (1988). *The relaxation response.* New York: Avon.

Berardo, D. H., Shehan, C. L., & Leslie, G. R. (1987). A residue of tradition: Jobs, careers, and spouses' time in housework. *Journal of Marriage and the Family, 49,* 381–390.

Berg, S. (1987). Intelligence and terminal decline. In G. L. Maddox & E. W. Busse (Eds.), *Aging: The universal human experience.* New York: Springer.

Berger, H. (1929). Über das elektrenkephalogramm des menschen. *Archiv für Psychiatrie und Nervenkrankheiten, 99,* 555–574.

Berger, T. W. (1984). Long-term potentiation of hippocampal synaptic transmission affects rate of behavioral learning. *Science, 224,* 627–630.

Berkowitz, L. (1969). The frustration-aggression hypothesis revisited. In L. Berkowitz (Ed.), *Roots of aggression: A re-examination of the frustration-aggression hypothesis.* New York: Atherton.

Berkowitz, L. (1989). Frustration-aggression hypothesis: Examination and reformulation. *Psychological Bulletin, 106,* 59–73.

Bernal, E. M. (1984). Bias in mental testing: Evidence for an alternative to the heredity-environment controversy. In C. R. Reynolds & R. T. Brown (Eds.), *Perspectives on bias in mental testing.* New York: Plenum.

Bernstein, I. L., & Meachum, C. L. (1990). Food aversion learning: Its impact on appetite. In E. D. Capaldi & T. L. Powley (Eds.), *Taste, experience, and feeding.* Washington, DC: American Psychological Association.

Berry, J. W. (1976). *Human ecology and cognitive style: Comparative studies in cultural and psychological adaptation.* New York: Sage/Halsted.

Berry, J. W. (1990). Cultural variations in cognitive style. In S. P. Wapner (Ed.), *Bio-psycho-social factors in cognitive style.* Hillsdale, NJ: Erlbaum.

Berry, J. W., Poortinga, Y., Segall, M., & Dasen, P. (1992). *Cross-cultural psychology.* New York: Cambridge University Press.

Berscheid, E. (1988). Some comments on love's anatomy: Or, whatever happened to old-fashioned lust. In R. J. Sternberg & M. L. Barnes (Eds.), *The psychology of love.* New Haven, CT: Yale University Press.

Berscheid, E., & Walster, E. (1978). *Interpersonal attraction.* Reading, MA: Addison-Wesley.

Betancourt, H., & Lopez, S. R. (1993). The study of culture, ethnicity, and race in American psychology. *American Psychologist, 48,* 629–637.

Beutler, L. E., Machado, P. P. P., & Neufeldt, S. A. (1994). Therapist variables. In A. E. Bergin & S. L. Garfield (Eds.), *Handbook of psychotherapy and behavior change* (4th ed.). New York: Wiley.

Biederman, I., Hilton, H. J., & Hummel, J. E. (1991). Pattern goodness and pattern recognition. In G. R. Lockhead & J. R. Pomerantz (Eds.), *The perception of structure.* Washington, DC: American Psychological Association.

Biener, L., & Abrams, D. B. (1991). The contemplation ladder: Validation of a measure of readiness to consider smoking cessation. *Health Psychology, 10,* 360–365.

Billings, A. G., Cronkite, R. C., & Moos, R. H. (1983). Social-environment factors in unipolar depression. *Journal of Abnormal Psychology, 92,* 119–133.

Binet, A. (1911). Nouvelle recherches sur la mesure du niveau intellectuel chez les enfants d'école. *L'Année Psychologique, 17,* 145–201.

Binet, A., & Simon, T. (1905). Méthodes nouvelles pour le diagnostic du niveau intellectuel des anormaux. *L'Année Psychologique, 11,* 191–244.

Binet, A., & Simon, T. (1908). Le développement de l'intelligence chez les enfants. *L'Année Psychologique, 14,* 1–94.

Binet, A., & Simon, T. (1905/1948). Upon the necessity of establishing a scientific diagnosis of inferior states of intelligence. In W. Dennis (Ed.), *Readings in the history of psychology.* New York: Appleton-Century-Crofts. (Original work published 1905)

Birch, L. L. (1987). The acquisition of food acceptance patterns in children. In R. A. Boakes, D. A. Popplewell, & M. J. Burton (Eds.), *Eating habits: Food, physiology and learned behaviour.* New York: Wiley.

Birch, L. L., McPhee, L., Sullivan, S., & Johnson, S. (1989). Conditioned meal initiation in young children. *Appetite, 13,* 105–113.

Black, D. W., & Winokur, G. (1990). Suicide and psychiatric diagnosis. In S. J. Blumenthal & D. J. Kupfer (Eds.), *Suicide over the life cycle: Risk factors, assessment, and treatment of suicidal patients.* Washington, DC: American Psychiatric Press.

Blair, S. L., & Johnson, M. P. (1992). Wives' perceptions of the fairness of the division of household labor: The intersection of housework and ideology. *Journal of Marriage and the Family, 54,* 570–581.

Blair, S. N., Kohl, H. W., Gordon, N. F., & Paffenbarger, R. S. (1992). How much physical activity is good for health? In G. S. Omenn, J. E. Fielding, & L. B. Lave (Eds.), *Annual review of public health* (Vol. 13). Palo Alto, CA: Annual Reviews.

Blair, S. N., Kohl, H. W., Paffenbarger, R. S., Clark, D. G., Cooper, K. H., & Gibbons, L. W. (1989). Physical fitness and all-cause mortality: A prospective study of healthy men and women. *Journal of the American Medical Association, 262,* 2395–2401.

Blakeslee, T. R. (1980). *The right brain.* Garden City, NY: Doubleday/Anchor.

Blanchard, F. A., Lilly, T., & Vaughn, L. A. (1991). Reducing the expression of racial prejudice. *Psychological Science, 2,* 101–105.

Blass, T. (1991). Understanding behavior in the Milgram obedience experiment: The role of personality, situations, and their interactions. *Journal of Personality and Social Psychology, 60,* 398–413.

Blau, Z. S. (1981). *Black children/white children: Competence, socialization and social structure.* New York: Free Press.

Blazer, D. G., Hughes, D., & George, L. K. (1987). Stressful life events and the onset of generalized anxiety syndrome. *American Journal of Psychiatry, 144,* 1178–1183.

Bleier, R. (1988). A decade of feminist critiques in the natural sciences. *Signs: Journal of Women in Culture and Society, 14,* 186–195.

Bleuler, E. (1911). *Dementia praecox or the group F schizophrenias.* New York: International Universities Press.

Bliwise, D. L. (1989). Normal aging. In M. H. Kryger, T. Roth, & W. C. Dement (Eds.), *Principles and practice of sleep medicine.* Philadelphia: Saunders.

Block, J. (1981). Some enduring and consequential structures of personality. In A. I. Rabins, J. Aronoff, A. Barclay & R. Zucker (Eds.), *Further explorations in personality.* New York: Wiley.

Block, J., & Dworkin, G. (1976). Heritability and inequality. In N. J. Block & G. Dworkin (Eds.), *The IQ controversy: critical readings.* New York: Pantheon.

Bloom, A. H. (1981). *The linguistic shaping of thought: A study of the impact of language on thinking in China and the West.* Hillsdale, NJ: Erlbaum.

Bloom, B. L. (1984). *Community mental health: A general introduction.* Pacific Grove, CA: Brooks/Cole.

Bloom, B. S. (Ed.). (1985). *Developing talent in young people.* New York: Ballantine.

Bloomfield, H. H., & Kory, R. B. (1976). *Happiness: The TM program, psychiatry, and enlightenment.* New York: Simon & Schuster.

Blum, K. (1984). *Handbook of abusable drugs.* New York: Gardner Press.

Boehm, A. E. (1985). Educational applications of intelligence testing. In B. B. Wolman (Ed.), *Handbook of intelligence: Theories, measurements, and applications.* New York: Wiley.

Bohannon, J. N., III, MacWhinney, B., & Snow, C. (1990). No negative evidence revisited: Beyond learnability or who has to prove what to whom. *Developmental Psychology, 26,* 221–226.

Bohannon, J. N., III, & Stanowicz, L. (1988). The issue of negative evidence: Adult responses to children's language errors. *Developmental Psychology, 24,* 684–689.

Bohannon, J. N., III, & Warren-Leubecker, A. (1989). Theoretical approaches to language acquisition. In J. Berko Gleason (Ed.), *The development of language.* Columbus, OH: Merrill.

Bolger, N. (1990). Coping as a personality process: A prospective study. *Journal of Personality and Social Psychology, 59,* 525–537.

Bolles, R. C. (1975). *Theory of motivation.* New York: Harper & Row.

Bonnet, M. H. (1982). Performance during sleep. In W. B. Webb (Ed.), *Biological rhythms, sleep and performance.* New York: Wiley.

Bonnet, M. H. (1991). Sleep deprivation. In M. Kryger, T. Roth, & W. C. Dement (Eds.), *Principles and practice of sleep medicine* (2nd ed.). Philadelphia: Saunders.

Bonnet, M. H. (1993). Deprivation, total: Behavioral effects. In M. A. Carskadon (Ed.), *Encyclopedia of sleep and dreaming.* New York: Macmillan.

Bootzin, R. R., Manber, R., Perlis, M. L., Salvio, M. A., & Wyatt, J. K. (1993). Sleep disorders. In P. B. Sutker & H. E. Adams (Eds.), *Comprehensive handbook of psychopathology* (2nd ed.). New York: Plenum.

Borbely, A. A. (1984). Sleep regulation: Outline of a model and its implications for depression. In A. A. Borbely & J. L. Valatx (Eds.), *Sleep mechanisms.* Berlin: Springer-Verlag.

Borbely, A. A. (1986). *Secrets of sleep.* New York: Basic Books.

Borbely, A. A., Achermann, P., Trachsel, L., & Tobler, I. (1989). Sleep initiation and initial sleep intensity: Interactions of homeostatic and circadian mechanisms. *Journal of Biological Rhythms, 4*(2), 149–160.

Bores-Rangel, E., Church, A. T., Szendre, D., & Reeves, C. (1990). Self-efficacy in relation to occupational consideration and academic performance in high school equivalency students. *Journal of Counseling Psychology, 37,* 407–418.

Bouchard, T. J., Jr., Lykken, D. T., McGue, M., Segal, N. L., & Tellegen, A. (1990). Sources of human psychological differences: The Minnesota study of twins reared apart. *Science, 250,* 223–228.

Bouchard, T. J., Jr., & McGue, M. (1981). Familial studies of intelligence: A review. *Science, 212,* 1055–1059.

Bouchard, T. J., Jr., & Segal, N. L. (1985). Environment and IQ. In B. B. Wolman (Ed.), *Handbook of intelligence: Theories, measurements and applications.* New York: Wiley.

Bourguignon, E. (1972). Dreams and altered states of consciousness in anthropological research. In F. L. K. Hsu (Ed.), *Psychological anthropology* (2nd ed.). Cambridge, MA: Schenkman.

Bower, G. H. (1970). Organizational factors in memory. *Cognitive Psychology, 1,* 18–46.

Bower, G. H., & Clark, M. C. (1969). Narrative stories as mediators of serial learning. *Psychonomic Science, 14,* 181–182.

Bower, G. H., Clark, M. C., Lesgold, A. M., & Winzenz, D. (1969). Hierarchical retrieval schemes in recall of categorized word lists. *Journal of Verbal Learning and Verbal Behavior, 8,* 323–343.

Bower, G. H., & Springston, F. (1970). Pauses as recoding points in letter series. *Journal of Experimental Psychology, 83,* 421–430.

Bowmaker, J. K., & Dartnall, H. J. A. (1980). Visual pigments of rods and cones in a human retina. *Journal of Physiology, 298,* 501–511.

Boynton, R. M. (1990). Human color perception. In K. N. Leibovic (Ed.), *Science of vision.* New York: Springer-Verlag.

Boynton, R. M., & Gordon, J. (1965). Bezold-Brucke hue shift measured by color naming technique. *Journal of the Optical Society of America, 55,* 78–86.

Boysson-Bardies, B., de Halle, P., Sagart, L., & Durand, C. (1989). A cross-linguistic investigation of vowel formants in babbling. *Journal of Child Language, 16,* 1–17.

Bradley, G. W. (1978). Self-serving biases in the attribution process: A re-examination of the fact or fiction question. *Journal of Personality and Social Psychology, 35,* 56–71.

Bradley, R. H. (1989). The use of the HOME inventory in longitudinal studies of child development. In M. H. Bornstein & N. A. Krasnegor (Eds.), *Stability and continuity in mental development: Behavioral and biological perspectives.* Hillsdale, NJ: Erlbaum.

Bradley, R. H., & Caldwell, B. M. (1980). The relation of home environment, cognitive competence and IQ among males and females. *Child Development, 51,* 1140–1148.

Bradshaw, J. L. (1989). *Hemispheric specialization and psychological function.* New York: Wiley.

Bram, S. (1985). Childlessness revisited: A longitudinal study of voluntarily childless couples, delayed parents, and parents. *Lifestyles: A Journal of Changing Patterns, 8*(1), 46–66.

Bray, G. A. (1986). Effects of obesity on health and happiness. In K. D. Brownell & J. P. Foreyt (Eds.), *Handbook of eating disorders: Physiology, psychology, and treatment of obesity, anorexia and bulimia.* New York: Basic Books.

Bray, G. A. (1990). Exercise and obesity. In C. Bouchard, R. J. Shephard, T. Stephens, J. R. Sutton, & B. D. McPherson (Eds.), *Exercise, fitness and health: A consensus of current knowledge.* Champaign, IL: Human Kinetics Books.

Breedlove, S. M. (1992). Sexual differentiation of the brain and behavior. In J. B. Becker, S. M. Breedlove, & D. Crews (Eds.), *Behavioral endocrinology.* Cambridge, MA: MIT Press.

Breggin, P. R. (1991). *Toxic psychiatry.* New York: St. Martin's Press.

Brehm, S. S. (1992). *Intimate relationships* (2nd ed.). New York: McGraw-Hill.

Breier, A., Buchanan, R. W., Kirkpatrick, B., Davis, O. R., Irish, D., Summerfelt, A., & Carpenter, W. T. (1994). Effects of clozapine on positive and negative symptoms in outpatients with schizophrenia. *American Journal of Psychiatry, 151,* 20–26.

Breland, K., & Breland, M. (1961). The misbehavior of organisms. *American Psychologist, 16,* 681–684.

Breland, K., & Breland, M. (1966). *Animal behavior.* New York: Macmillan.

Brent, D. A., & Kolko, D. J. (1990). The assessment and treatment of children and adolescents at risk for suicide. In S. J. Blumenthal & D. J. Kupfer (Eds.), *Suicide over the life cycle: Risk factors, assessment, and treatment of suicidal patients.* Washington, DC: American Psychiatric Press.

Bretherton, I. (1992). Attachment and bonding. In V. B. Van Hasselt & M. Hersen (Eds.), *Handbook of social development: A lifespan perspective.* New York: Plenum.

Bretl, D. J., & Cantor, J. (1988). The portrayal of

men and women in U.S. television commercials: A recent content analysis and trend over 15 years. *Sex Roles, 18*, 595–609.

Brett, J. F., Brief, A. P., Burke, M. J., George, J. M., & Webster, J. (1990). Negative affectivity and the reporting of stressful life events. *Health Psychology, 9*, 57–68.

Brewer, W. F., & Nakamura, G. V. (1984). The nature and function of schemas. In R. S. Wyer & T. K. Sroll (Eds.), *Handbook of social cognition.* Hillsdale, NJ: Erlbaum.

Brewer, W. F., & Treyens, J. C. (1981). Role of schemata in memory for places. *Cognitive Psychology, 13*, 207–230.

Briere, J., & Conte, J. R. (1993). Self-reported amnesia for abuse in adults molested as children. *Journal of Traumatic Stress, 6*(1), 21–31.

Briggs, S. R. (1989). The optimal level of measurement for personality constructs. In D. M. Buss & N. Cantor (Eds.), *Personality psychology: Recent trends and emerging directions.* New York: Springer.

Bringmann, W. G., & Balk, M. M. (1992). Another look at Wilhelm Wundt's publication record. *History of Psychology Newsletter, 24*(3/4), 50–66.

Brislin, R. (1993). *Understanding culture's influence on behavior.* Fort Worth: Harcourt Brace College Publishers.

Brobeck, J. R., Tepperman, T., & Long, C. N. (1943). Experimental hypothalamic hyperphagia in the albino rat. *Yale Journal of Biology and Medicine, 15*, 831–853.

Bromage, B. K., & Mayer, R. E. (1986). Quantitative and qualitative effects of repetition on learning from technical text. *Journal of Educational Psychology, 78*, 271–278.

Brooks-Gunn, J. (1991). Maturational timing variations in adolescent girls, antecedents of. In R. M. Lerner, A. C. Petersen, & J. Brooks-Gunn (Eds.), *Encyclopedia of adolescence.* New York: Garland.

Brooks-Gunn, J., & Reiter, E. O. (1990). The role of pubertal process. In S. S. Feldman & G. R. Elliot (Eds.), *At the threshold: The developing adolescent.* Cambridge, MA: Harvard University Press.

Browman, C. P., & Cartwright, R. D. (1980). The first-night effect on sleep and dreams. *Biological Psychiatry, 15*, 809–812.

Brown, A. S. (1991). A review of the tip-of-the-tongue experience. *Psychological Bulletin, 109*, 204–223.

Brown, J. D., & McGill, K. L. (1989). The cost of good fortune: When positive life events produce negative health consequences. *Journal of Personality and Social Psychology, 57*, 1103–1110.

Brown, J. D., & Rogers, R. J. (1991). Self-serving attributions: The role of physiological arousal. *Personality and Social Psychology Bulletin, 17*, 501–506.

Brown, M. (1974). Some determinants of persistence and initiation of achievement-related activities. In J. W. Atkinson & J. O. Raynor (Eds.), *Motivation and achievement.* Washington, DC: Halsted.

Brown, P., & Funk, S. C. (1986). Tardive dyskinesia: Barriers to the professional recognition of an iatrogenic disease. *Journal of Health and Social Behavior, 27*, 116–132.

Brown, R. (1973). *A first language: The early stages.* Cambridge: Harvard University Press.

Brown, R., & Hanlon, C. (1970). Derivational complexity and order of acquisition. In J. R. Hayes (Ed.), *Cognition and the development of language.* New York: Wiley.

Brown, R., & Kulik, J. (1977). Flashbulb memories. *Cognition, 5*, 73–99.

Brown, R., & McNeill, D. (1966). The "tip-of-the-tongue" phenomenon. *Journal of Verbal Learning and Verbal Behavior, 5*(4), 325–337.

Brown, R. T. (1989). Creativity: What are we to measure? In J. A. Glover, R. R. Ronning, & C. R. Reynolds (Eds.), *Handbook of creativity.* New York: Plenum.

Brownell, H. H., & Gardner, H. (1981). Hemisphere specialization: Definitions not incantations. *Behavioral and Brain Sciences, 4*, 64–65.

Brubaker, T. (1990). Families in later life: A burgeoning research area. *Journal of Marriage and the Family, 52*, 959–982.

Bruckner-Gordon, F., Gangi, B. K., & Wallman, G. U. (1988). *Making therapy work: Your guide to choosing, using, and ending therapy.* New York: Harper & Row.

Bruner, J. S. (1974). Concluding comments and summary of conference. In J. L. M. Dawson & W. J. Lonner (Eds.), *Readings in cross-cultural psychology.* Hong Kong: University of Hong Kong Press.

Bryden, M. P. (1982). *Laterality: Functional asymmetry in the intact brain.* New York: Academic Press.

Bryden, M. P. (1988). An overview of the dichotic listening procedure and its relation to cerebral organization. In K. Hugdahl (Ed.), *Handbook of dichotic listening.* Chichester, England: Wiley.

Buchsbaum, M. S. (1986). Functional imaging of the brain in psychiatry: Positron emission tomography. In P. A. Berger & H. K. H. Brodie (Eds.), *American handbook of psychiatry: Biological psychiatry* (2nd ed., Vol. 8). New York: Basic Books.

Buck, R. (1984). *The communication of emotion.* New York: Guilford Press.

Buda, M., & Tsuang, M. T. (1990). The epidemiology of suicide: Implications for clinical practice. In S. J. Blumenthal & D. J. Kupfer (Eds.), *Suicide over the life cycle: Risk factors, assessment, and treatment of suicidal patients.* Washington, DC: American Psychiatric Press.

Buhler, C., & Allen, M. (1972). *Introduction to humanistic psychology.* Pacific Grove, CA: Brooks/Cole.

Bullough, V. (1981). Age of menarche: A misunderstanding. *Science, 213*, 365–366.

Burger, J. M. (1986). Temporal effects on attributions: Actor and observer differences. *Social Cognition, 4*, 377–387.

Burger, J. M. (1993). *Personality.* Pacific Grove, CA: Brooks/Cole.

Buss, D. M. (1989). Sex differences in human mate preferences: Evolutionary hypotheses tested in 37 cultures. *Behavioral and Brain Sciences, 12*, 1–49.

Buss, D. M. (1994). Mate preferences in 37 cultures. In W. J. Lonner & R. S. Malpass (Eds.), *Psychology and culture.* Boston: Allyn & Bacon.

Bussey, K., & Bandura, A. (1984). Influence of gender constancy and social power on sex-linked modeling. *Journal of Personality and Social Psychology, 47*, 1292–1302.

Butcher, J. N. (1990). *The MMPI-2 in psychological treatment.* New York: Oxford University Press.

Butcher, J. N., & Keller, L. S. (1984). Objective personality assessment. In G. Goldstein & M. Hersen (Eds.), *Handbook of psychological assessment.* New York: Pergamon Press.

Butcher, J. N., Narikiyo, T., & Vitousek, K. B. (1993). Understanding abnormal behavior in cultural context. In P. B. Sutker & H. E. Adams (Eds.), *Comprehensive handbook of psychopathology.* New York: Plenum.

Buxton, C. E. (1985). American functionalism. In C. E. Buxton (Ed.), *Points of view in the modern history of psychology.* Orlando: Academic Press.

Buxton, M. N., Arkey, Y., Lagos, J., Deposito, F., Lowenthal, F., & Simring, S. (1981). Stress and platelet aggregation in hemophiliac children and their family members. *Research Communications in Psychology, Psychiatry and Behavior, 6*(1), 21–48.

Byrne, D. (1971). *The attraction paradigm.* New York: Academic Press.

Byrne, D., Clore, G. L., & Smeaton, G. (1986). The attraction hypothesis: Do similar attitudes affect anything? *Journal of Personality and Social Psychology, 51*, 1167–1170.

Byrne, D., & Murnen, S. K. (1988). Maintaining loving relationships. In R. J. Sternberg & M. L. Barnes (Eds.), *The psychology of love.* New Haven, CT: Yale University Press.

Cagen, R. H., & Rhein, L. D. (1980). Biochemical basis of recognition of taste and olfactory stimuli. In H. van der Starre (Ed.), *Olfaction and taste* (Vol. 7). London: IRL Press.

Cain, W. S. (1979). To know with the nose: Keys to odor identification. *Science, 203*, 467–470.

Cain, W. S. (1988). Olfaction. In R. C. Atkinson, R. J. Herrnstein, G. Lindzey, & R. D. Luce (Eds.), *Stevens' handbook of experimental psychology: Perception and motivation* (Vol. 1). New York: Wiley.

Calabrese, L. H. (1990). Exercise, immunity, cancer, and infection. In C. Bouchard, R. J. Shephard, T. Stephens, J. R. Sutton, & B. D. McPherson (Eds.), *Exercise, fitness, and health: A consensus of knowledge.* Champaign, IL: Human Kinetics Books.

Calev, A., Phil, D., Pass, H. L., Shapira, B., Fink, M., Tubi, N., & Lerer, B. (1993). ECT and memory. In C. E. Coffey (Ed.), *The clinical science of electroconvulsive therapy.* Washington, DC: American Psychiatric Press.

Cameron, L., Leventhal, E. A., & Leventhal, H. (1993). Symptom representations and affect as determinants of care seeking in a community-dwelling, adult sample population. *Health Psychology, 12*, 171–179.

Cameron, N. (1963). *Personality development and psychopathology.* Boston: Houghton Mifflin.

Campbell, J. (1971). *Hero with a thousand faces.* New York: Harcourt Brace Jovanovich.

Cannon, D. S., Baker, T. B., & Wehl, C. K. (1981). Emetic and electric shock alcohol aversion therapy: Six- and twelve-month followup. *Journal of Consulting and Clinical Psychology, 49*, 360–368.

Cannon, W. B. (1927). The James-Lange theory of emotions: A critical examination and an alternate theory. *American Journal of Psychology, 39*, 106–124.

Cannon, W. B. (1929). *Bodily changes in pain, hunger, fear and rage.* New York: Appleton.

Cannon, W. B. (1932). *The wisdom of the body.* New York: Norton.

Cannon, W. B., & Washburn, A. L. (1912). An explanation of hunger. *American Journal of Physiology, 29*, 444–454.

Capaldi, E. D., & VandenBos, G. R. (1991). Taste, food exposure, and eating behavior. *Hospital and Community Psychiatry, 42*(8), 787–789.

Capelli, C. A., Nakagawa, N., & Madden, C. M. (1990). How children understand sarcasm: The role of context and intonation. *Child Development, 61*, 1824–1841.

Carnegie, D. (1936). *How to win friends and influence people*. New York: Simon & Schuster.

Carpenter, W. T. (1992). The negative symptom challenge. *Archives of General Psychiatry, 49,* 236–237.

Carrington, P. (1987). Managing meditation in clinical practice. In M. A. West (Ed.), *The psychology of meditation*. Oxford: Clarendon Press.

Carroll, J. B. (1987). Jensen's mental chronometry: Some comments and questions. In S. Modgil & C. Modgil (Eds.), *Arthur Jensen: Consensus and controversy*. New York: Falmer Press.

Carskadon, M. A., & Dement, W. C. (1981). Cumulative effects of sleep restriction on daytime sleepiness. *Psychophysiology, 18,* 107–113.

Carson, R. C. (1991). Dilemmas in the pathway of the DSM-IV. *Journal of Abnormal Psychology, 100,* 302–307.

Carson, R. C., & Sanislow, C. A., III. (1993). The schizophrenias. In P. B. Sutker & H. E. Adams (Eds.), *Comprehensive handbook of psychopathology* (2nd ed.). New York: Plenum.

Cartwright, R. D. (1977). *Night life: Explorations in dreaming*. Englewood Cliffs, NJ: Prentice-Hall.

Cartwright, R. D., & Lamberg, L. (1992). *Crisis dreaming*. New York: HarperCollins.

Casey, R., & Rozin, P. (1989). Changing children's food preferences: Parent opinions. *Appetite, 12,* 171–182.

Caspi, A., Bolger, N., & Eckenrode, J. (1987). Linking person and context in the daily stress process. *Journal of Personality and Social Psychology, 52,* 184–195.

Castelloci, V. F. (1986). The chemical senses: Taste and smell. In E. R. Kandel & J. H. Schwartz (Eds.), *Principles of neural science*. New York: Elsevier.

Catalano, E. M. (1990). *Getting to sleep*. Oakland, CA: New Harbinger.

Catania, A. C. (1992). Reinforcement. In L. R. Squire (Ed.), *Encyclopedia of learning and memory*. New York: Macmillan.

Cattell, J. M. (1890). Mental tests and measurements. *Mind, 15,* 373–381.

Cattell, R. B. (1950). *Personality: A systematic, theoretical and factual study*. New York: McGraw-Hill.

Cattell, R. B. (1957). *Personality and motivation: Structure and measurement*. New York: Harcourt, Brace & World.

Cattell, R. B. (1965). *The scientific analysis of personality*. Baltimore: Penguin.

Cattell, R. B. (1966). *The scientific analysis of personality*. Chicago: Aldine.

Cattell, R. B. (1990). Advances in Cattellian personality theory. In L. A. Pervin (Ed.), *Handbook of personality: Theory and research*. New York: Guilford Press.

Cattell, R. B., Eber, H. W., & Tatsuoka, M. M. (1970). *Handbook of the Sixteen Personality Factor Questionnaire (16PF)*. Champaign, IL: Institute for Personality and Ability Testing.

Ceci, S. J. (1991). How much does schooling influence general intelligence and its cognitive components? A reassessment of the evidence. *Developmental Psychology, 27,* 703–722.

Ceci, S. J., & Bruck, M. (1993). Suggestibility of the child witness: A historical review and synthesis. *Psychological Bulletin, 113,* 403–439.

Ceci, S. J., & Liker, J. (1986). Academic and nonacademic intelligence: An experimental separation. In R. J. Sternberg & R. K. Wagner (Eds.),

Practical intelligence: Nature and origins of competence in the everyday world. Cambridge: Cambridge University Press.

Cerella, J. (1990). Aging and information-processing rate. In J. E. Birren & K. W. Schaie (Eds.), *Handbook of the psychology of aging* (3rd ed.). San Diego: Academic Press.

Cerletti, U., & Bini, L. (1938). Un nuevo metodo di shockterapie "L'elettro-shock." *Boll. Acad. Med. Roma, 64,* 136–138.

Chaiken, S. (1987). The heuristic model of persuasion. In M. P. Zanna, J. M. Olson, & C. P. Herman (Eds.), *Social influence: The Ontario symposium* (Vol. 5). Hillsdale, NJ: Erlbaum.

Chan, J. W. C., & Vernon, P. E. (1988). Individual differences among the peoples of China. In S. H. Irvine & J. W. Berry (Eds.), *Human abilities in cultural context*. New York: Cambridge University Press.

Chandra, R. K. (1991). Interactions between early nutrition and the immune system. In *Ciba Foundation Symposium No. 156*. Chichester, England: Wiley.

Charlesworth, W. R., & Kreutzer, M. A. (1973). Facial expression of infants and children. In P. Ekman (Ed.), *Darwin and facial expression*. New York: Academic Press.

Cheung, F. (1991). The use of mental health services by ethnic minorities. In H. F. Myers, P. Wohlford, L. P. Guzman, & R. Echemendia (Eds.), *Ethnic minority perspectives on clinical training and services in psychology*. Washington, DC: American Psychological Association.

Chiriboga, D. A. (1987). Personality in later life. In P. Silverman (Ed.), *The elderly as modern pioneers*. Bloomington: Indiana University Press.

Cholewiak, R., & Collins, A. (1991). Sensory and physiological bases of touch. In M. A. Heller & W. Schiff (Eds.), *The psychology of touch*. Hillsdale, NJ: Erlbaum.

Chomsky, N. (1957). *Syntactic structures*. The Hague: Mouton.

Chomsky, N. (1959). A review of B. F. Skinner's "Verbal Behavior." *Language, 35,* 26–58.

Chomsky, N. (1965). *Aspects of theory of syntax*. Cambridge, MA: MIT Press.

Chomsky, N. (1975). *Reflections on language*. New York: Pantheon.

Chomsky, N. (1986). *Knowledge of language: Its nature, origins, and use*. New York: Praeger.

Christensen, L. (1988). Deception in psychological research: When is its use justified? *Personality and Social Psychology Bulletin, 14,* 664–675.

Christianson, S. (1989). Flashbulb memories: Special, but not so special. *Memory & Cognition, 17,* 435–443.

Chumlea, W. C. (1982). Physical growth in adolescence. In B. B. Wolman (Ed.), *Handbook of developmental psychology*. Englewood Cliffs, NJ: Prentice-Hall.

Church, R. M. (1989). Theories of timing behavior. In S. P. Klein & R. R. Mowrer (Eds.), *Contemporary learning theories: Instrumental conditioning theory and the impact of biological constraints on learning*. Hillsdale, NJ: Erlbaum.

Cipolli, C., Baroncini, P., Fagioli, I., & Fumai, A. (1987). The thematic continuity of mental sleep experience in the same night. *Sleep, 10*(5), 473–479.

Clark, E. V. (1983). Meanings and concepts. In J. H. Flavell & E. M. Markman (Eds.), *Handbook of child psychology* (Vol. 3). New York: Wiley.

Clark, L. F. (1993). Stress and the cognitive-con-

versational benefits of social interaction. *Journal of Social and Clinical Psychology, 12,* 25–55.

Cloninger, C. R. (1989). Schizophrenia: Genetic etiological factors. In H. I. Kaplan & B. J. Sadock (Eds.), *Comprehensive textbook of psychiatry/V*. Baltimore: Williams & Wilkins.

Cohen, C. E. (1981). Person categories and social perception: Testing some boundaries of the processing effects of prior knowledge. *Journal of Personality and Social Psychology, 40,* 441–452.

Cohen, C. I., & Thompson, K. S. (1992). Homeless mentally ill or mentally ill homeless? *American Journal of Psychiatry, 149,* 816–823.

Cohen, D., & McCubbin, M. (1990). The political economy of tardive dyskinesia: Asymmetries in power and responsibility. *The Journal of Mind and Behavior, 11*(3/4), 465–488.

Cohen, S. (1980). *The substance abuse problem*. New York: Haworth Press.

Cohen, S. (1988). Psychosocial models of the role of social support in the etiology of physical disease. *Health Psychology, 7,* 269–297.

Cohen, S., & Hajioff, J. (1972). Life events and the onset of acute closed-angle glaucoma. *Journal of Psychosomatic Research, 16,* 335–341.

Cohen, S., & Lichtenstein, E. (1990). Perceived stress, quitting smoking, and smoking relapse. *Health Psychology, 9,* 466–478.

Cohen, S., Lichtenstein, E., Prochaska, J. O., Rossi, J. S., Gritz, E. R., Carr, C. R., Orleans, C. T., Schoenbach, V. J., Biener, L., Abrams, D., DiClemente, C., Curry, S., Marlatt, G. A., Cummings, K. M., Emont, S. L., Giovino, A., & Ossip-Klien, D. (1989). Debunking myths about self-quitting: Evidence from 10 prospective studies of persons who attempt to quit smoking by themselves. *American Psychologist, 44,* 1355–1365.

Cohen, S., & Syme, S. L. (Eds.). (1985). *Social support and health*. New York: Academic Press.

Cohen, S., Tyrrell, D. A. J., & Smith, A. P. (1993). Negative life events, perceived stress, negative affect, and susceptibility to the common cold. *Journal of Personality and Social Psychology, 64,* 131–140.

Colby, A., & Kohlberg, L. (1987). *The measurement of moral judgment* (Vols. 1–2). New York: Cambridge University Press.

Colby, A., Kohlberg, L., Gibbs, J., & Lieberman, M. (1983). A longitudinal study of moral development. *Monographs of the Society for Research in Child Development, 48*(1 & 2, Serial No. 200).

Cole, J. O., Goldberg, S. C., & Davis, J. M. (1966). Drugs in the treatment of psychosis. In P. Solomon (Ed.), *Psychiatric drugs*. New York: Grune & Stratton.

Cole, M. (1992). Culture in development. In M. H. Bornstein & M. E. Lamb (Eds.), *Developmental psychology: An advanced textbook* (3rd ed.). Hillsdale, NJ: Erlbaum.

Cole, M., Gay, J., Glick, J. A., Sharp, D. W. (1971). *The cultural context of learning and thinking: An exploration in experimental anthropology*. New York: Basic Books.

Cole, N. S. (1981). Bias in testing. *American Psychologist, 36,* 1067–1077.

Coleman, J. S., Campbell, E. O., Hobson, C. J., McPartland, J., Moody, A. M., Weinfield, F. D., & York, R. L. (1966). *Equality of educational opportunity*. Washington, DC: U.S. Government Printing Office.

Coleman, P. (1993). Overview of substance abuse. *Primary Care, 20*(1), 1–18.

Coleman, R. M. (1986). *Wide awake at 3:00 A.M.* New York: W. H. Freeman.

Coles, R. (1970). *Erik H. Erikson: The growth of his work*. Boston: Little, Brown.

Collins, A. M., & Loftus, E. F. (1975). A spreading activation theory of semantic processing. *Psychological Review, 82*, 407–428.

Collins, N. L., & Read, S. J. (1990). Adult attachment, working models, and relationship quality in dating couples. *Journal of Personality and Social Psychology, 58*, 644–663.

Colquhoun, W. P. (1984). Effects of personality on body temperature and mental efficiency following transmeridian flight. *Aviation, Space & Environmental Medicine, 55*(6), 493–496.

Colt, E. W., Wardlaw, S. L., & Frantz, A. G. (1981). The effect of running on plasma B-endorphin. *Life Sciences, 28*, 1637–1640.

Colwill, R. M. (1993). An associative analysis of instrumental learning. *Current Directions in Psychological Science, 2*(4), 111–116.

Conley, J. J. (1985). Longitudinal stability of personality traits: A multitrait-multimethod-multioccasion analysis. *Journal of Personality and Social Psychology, 49*, 1266–1282.

Conrad, R. (1964). Acoustic confusions in immediate memory. *British Journal of Psychology, 55*, 75–84.

Cook, M., & Mineka, S. (1989). Observational conditioning of fear to fear-relevant versus fear-irrelevant stimuli in rhesus monkeys. *Journal of Abnormal Psychology, 98*, 448–459.

Cooper, C. L. (1984). The social-psychological precursors to cancer. *Journal of Human Stress, 10*(1), 4–11.

Cooper, E. (1991). A critique of six measures for assessing creativity. *Journal of Creative Behavior, 25*(3), 194–204.

Cooper, J., & Fazio, R. H. (1984). A new look at dissonance theory. In L. Berkowitz (Ed.), *Advances in experimental social psychology* (Vol. 17). New York: Academic Press.

Cooper, J. R., Bloom, F. E., & Roth, R. H. (1991). *The biochemical basis of neuropharmacology* (6th ed.). New York: Oxford University Press.

Corballis, M. C. (1980). Laterality and myth. *American Psychologist, 35*, 284–295.

Corballis, M. C. (1991). *The lopsided ape*. New York: Oxford University Press.

Coren, S. (1989). Cross-cultural studies of visual illusions: The physiological confound. *Behavioral and Brain Sciences, 12*(1), 76–77.

Coren, S. (1992). *The left-hander syndrome: The causes and consequences of left-handedness*. New York: Free Press.

Coren, S., & Aks, D. J. (1990). Moon illusion in pictures: A multimechanism approach. *Journal of Experimental Psychology: Human Perception and Performance, 16*, 365–380.

Coren, S., & Girgus, J. S. (1978). *Seeing is deceiving: The psychology of visual illusions*. Hillsdale, NJ: Erlbaum.

Coren, S., & Ward, L. M. (1989). *Sensation and perception*. San Diego: Harcourt Brace Jovanovich.

Corkin, S. (1984). Lasting consequences of bilateral medial temporal lobectomy: Clinical course and experimental findings in H. M. *Seminars in Neurology, 4*, 249–259.

Coryell, W., & Winokur, G. (1992). Course and outcome. In E. S. Paykel (Ed.), *Handbook of affective disorders* (2nd ed.). New York: Guilford Press.

Costa, P. T., Jr., & McCrae, R. (1985). *NEO Personality Inventory*. Odessa, FL: Psychological Assessment Resources.

Costa, P. T., Jr., & McCrae, R. (1992). *Revised NEO Personality Inventory: NEO PI and NEO Five-Factor Inventory* (Professional Manual). Odessa, FL: Psychological Assessment Resources.

Costa, P. T., Jr., & McCrae, R. R. (1994). Set like plaster? Evidence for the stability of adult personality. In T. F. Heatherton & J. L. Weinberger (Eds.), *Can personality change?* Washington, DC: American Psychological Association.

Costello, C. C. (1982). Fears and phobias in women: A community study. *Journal of Abnormal Psychology, 91*, 280–286.

Cote, L., & Crutcher, M. D. (1991). The basal ganglia. In E. R. Kandel, J. H. Schwartz, & T. M. Jessell (Eds.), *Principles of neural science* (3rd ed.). New York: Elsevier.

Covi, L., & Primakoff, L. (1988). Cognitive group therapy. In A. J. Frances & R. E. Hales (Eds.), *Review of psychiatry: Volume 7*. Washington, DC: American Psychiatric Press.

Cowan, N. (1988). Evolving conceptions of memory storage, selective attention, and their mutual constraints within the human information-processing system. *Psychological Bulletin, 104*, 163–191.

Cowley, G. (1991, Summer). Children in peril [Special Issue]. *Newsweek*, pp. 18–21.

Cox, M. J., Owen, M. T., Henderson, V. K., & Margand, N. A. (1992). Prediction of infant-father and infant-mother attachment. *Developmental Psychology, 28*, 474–483.

Craik, F. I. M., & Lockhart, R. S. (1972). Levels of processing: A framework for memory research. *Journal of Verbal Learning and Verbal Behavior, 11*, 671–684.

Craik, F. I. M., & Tulving, E. (1975). Depth of processing and the retention of words in episodic memory. *Journal of Experimental Psychology: General, 104*, 268–294.

Crain, S. (1991). Language acquisition in the absence of experience. *Behavioral and Brain Sciences, 14*, 597–650.

Crane, P. T. (1985). Voluntary childlessness: Some notes on the decision making process. In D. B. Gutknecht & E. W. Butler (Eds.), *Family, self, and society: Emerging issues, alternatives, and interventions* (2nd ed.). New York: UPA.

Craufurd, D. I. O., Creed, F., & Jayson, M. D. (1990). Life events and psychological disturbance in patients with low-back pain. *Spine, 15*, 490–494.

Cravens, H. (1992). A scientific project locked in time: The Terman Genetic Studies of Genius, 1920s–1950s. *American Psychologist, 47*, 183–189.

Crawford, C. (1987). Sociobiology: Of what value to psychology? In C. Crawford, M. Smith, & D. Krebs (Eds.), *Sociobiology and psychology: Ideas, issues and applications*. Hillsdale, NJ: Erlbaum.

Creed, F. (1989). Appendectomy. In G. W. Brown & T. O. Harris (Eds.), *Life events and illness*. New York: Guilford Press.

Creed, F. (1993). Stress and psychosomatic disorders. In L. Goldberger & S. Breznitz (Eds.), *Handbook of stress: Theoretical and clinical aspects* (2nd ed.). New York: Free Press.

Crocker, J., & Luhtanen, R. (1990). Collective self-esteem and ingroup bias. *Journal of Personality and Social Psychology, 58*, 60–67.

Crockett, H. (1962). The achievement motive and differential occupational mobility in the United States. *American Sociological Review, 27*, 191–204.

Cross, C. K., & Hirschfeld, R. M. A. (1986). Epidemiology of disorders in adulthood: Suicide. In G. L. Klerman, M. M. Weissman, P. S. Appelbaum, & L. H. Roth (Eds.), *Psychiatry: Vol. 5. Social, epidemiologic, and legal psychiatry*. New York: Basic Books.

Crowe, R. R. (1988). Family and twin studies of panic disorders and agoraphobia. In R. Noyes, Jr., & G. D. Burrows (Eds.), *Handbook of anxiety: Biological, clinical, and cultural perspectives* (Vol. 1). Amsterdam: Elsevier.

Croyle, R. T., & Cooper, J. (1983). Dissonance arousal: Physiological evidence. *Journal of Personality and Social Psychology, 45*, 782–791.

Curran, D. K. (1987). *Adolescent suicidal behavior*. Washington: Hemisphere.

Cushman, P. (1992). Psychotherapy to 1992: A historically situated interpretation. In D. K. Freedheim (Ed.), *History of psychotherapy: A century of change*. Washington, DC: American Psychological Association.

Czeisler, C. A., Moore-Ede, M. C., & Coleman, R. M. (1982). Rotating shift work schedules that disrupt sleep are improved by applying circadian principles. *Science, 217*, 460–463.

Czeisler, C. A., Weitzman, E. D., Moore-Ede, M. C., Zimmerman, J. C., & Knauer, R. S. (1980). Human sleep: Its duration and organization depend on its circadian phase. *Science, 210*, 1264–1267.

Dallos, P. (1981). Cochlear physiology. *Annual Review of Psychology, 32*, 153–190.

Dana, R. H. (1993). *Multicultural assessment perspectives for professional psychology*. Boston: Allyn & Bacon.

D'Andrade, R. G. (1961). Anthropological studies of dreams. In F. Hsu (Ed.), *Psychological anthropology: Approaches to culture and personality*. Homewood, IL: Dorsey Press.

Danziger, K. (1990). *Constructing the subject: Historical origins of psychological research*. Cambridge, England: Cambridge University Press.

Darley, J. M., & Latané, B. (1968). Bystander intervention in emergencies: Diffusion of responsibility. *Journal of Personality and Social Psychology, 8*, 377–383.

Darwin, C. (1859). *On the origin of species*. London: Murray.

Darwin, C. (1871). *Descent of man*. London: Murray.

Darwin, C. (1872). *The expression of emotions in man and animals*. New York: Philosophical Library.

Dasen, P. R. (1994). Culture and cognitive development from a Piagetian perspective. In W. J. Lonner & R. Malpass (Eds.), *Psychology and culture*. Boston: Allyn & Bacon.

Davidson, J. (1976). Physiology of meditation and mystical states of consciousness. *Perspectives in Biology and Medicine, 19*, 345–380.

Davidson, J. R. T. (1992). Monoamine oxidase inhibitors. In E. S. Paykel (Ed.), *Handbook of affective disorders* (2nd ed.). New York: Guilford Press.

Davidson, N. (1988). *The failure of feminism*. Buffalo: Prometheus.

Davidson, R. J., & Cacioppo, J. T. (1992). New developments in the scientific study of emotion: An introduction to the special section. *Psychological Science, 3*, 21–22.

Davis, J. M. (1985). Antipsychotic drugs. In H. I. Kaplan & B. J. Sadock (Eds.), *Comprehensive textbook of psychiatry/IV*. Baltimore: Williams & Wilkins.

Davis, J. M., Barter, J. T., & Kane, J. M. (1989). Antipsychotic drugs. In H. I. Kaplan & B. J. Sadock

(Eds.), *Comprehensive textbook of psychiatry/V*. Baltimore: Williams & Wilkins.

Davis, J. M., & Glassman, A. H. (1989). Antidepressant drugs. In H. I. Kaplan & B. J. Sadock (Eds.), *Comprehensive textbook of psychiatry/V*. Baltimore: Williams & Wilkins.

Dawes, R. M. (1992). Why believe that for which there is no good evidence? *Issues in Child Abuse Accusations, 4*, 214–218.

Dawson, M. E., Hazlett, E. A., Filion, D. L., Neuchterlein, K. H., & Schell, A. M. (1993). Attention and schizophrenia: Impaired modulation of the startle reflex. *Journal of Abnormal Psychology, 102*, 633–641.

Day, R. H. (1965). Inappropriate constancy explanation of spatial distortions. *Nature, 207*, 891–893.

Deaux, K. (1984). From individual differences to social categories: Analysis of a decade's research on gender. *American Psychologist, 39*, 105–116.

Deaux, K. (1993). Commentary: Sorry, wrong number—A reply to Gentile's call. *Psychological Science, 4*, 125–126.

de Castro, J. M., & Brewer, E. M. (1992). The amount eaten in meals by humans is a power function of the number of people present. *Physiology and Behavior, 51*, 121–125.

Delgado, J. M. R. (1969). *Physical control of the mind.* New York: Harper & Row.

Delgado, P. L., Price, L. H., Heninger, G. R., & Charney, D. S. (1992). Neurochemistry. In E. S. Paykel (Ed.), *Handbook of affective disorders* (2nd ed.). New York: Guilford Press.

DeLongis, A., Folkman, S., & Lazarus, R. S. (1988). The impact of daily stress on health and mood: Psychological and social resources as mediators. *Journal of Personality and Social Psychology, 54*, 486–495.

Dement, W. C. (1978). *Some must watch while some must sleep.* New York: Norton.

Dement, W. C., & Kleitman, N. (1957). The relation of eye movements during sleep to dream activity: An objective method for the study of dreaming. *Journal of Experimental Psychology, 53*, 339–346.

Dement, W. C., & Wolpert, E. (1958). The relation of eye movements, bodily motility, and external stimuli to dream content. *Journal of Experimental Psychology, 53*, 543–553.

Demo, D. H. (1992). Parent-child relations: Assessing recent changes. *Journal of Marriage and the Family, 54*, 104–117.

Dennis, D. L., Buckner, J. C., Lipton, F. R., & Levine, I. S. (1991). A decade of research and services for homeless mentally ill persons: Where do we stand? *American Psychologist, 46*, 1129–1138.

Dennis, W. (1966). Age and creative productivity. *Journal of Gerontology, 21*(1), 1–8.

Deregowski, J. B. (1989). Real space and represented space: Cross-cultural perspectives. *Behavioral and Brain Sciences, 12*, 51–119.

Derogatis, L. R., & Coons, H. L. (1993). Self-report measures of stress. In L. Goldberger & S. Breznitz (Eds.), *Handbook of stress: Theoretical and clinical aspects* (2nd ed.). New York: Free Press.

DeValois, R. L., & Jacobs, G. H. (1984). Neural mechanisms of color vision. In I. Darian-Smith (Ed.), *The nervous system* (Vol. 3). Baltimore: Williams & Wilkins.

De Villiers, P. (1977). Choice in concurrent schedules and a quantitative formulation of the law of effect. In W. K. Honig & J. E. R. Staddon (Eds.), *Handbook of operant behavior*. Englewood Cliffs, NJ: Prentice-Hall.

Digman, J. M. (1990). Personality structure: Emergence of the five-factor model. *Annual Review of Psychology, 41*, 417–440.

Dillbeck, M. C., & Orme-Johnson, D. W. (1987). Physiological differences between transcendental meditation and rest. *American Psychologist, 42*, 879–881.

DiMatteo, M. R. (1991). *The psychology of health, illness, and medical care: An individual perspective.* Pacific Grove, CA: Brooks/Cole.

DiMatteo, M. R., & Friedman, H. S. (1982). *Social psychology and medicine.* Cambridge, MA: Oelgeschlager, Gunn & Hain.

Dinges, D. F. (1989). Napping patterns and effects in human adults. In D. F. Dinges & R. J. Broughton (Eds.), *Sleep and alertness: Chronobiological, behavioral, and medical aspects of napping.* New York: Raven.

Dinges, D. F., & Broughton, R. J. (1989). The significance of napping: A synthesis. In D. F. Dinges & R. J. Broughton (Eds.), *Sleep and alertness: Chronobiological, behavioral, and medical aspects of napping.* New York: Raven.

DiNicola, D. D., & DiMatteo, M. R. (1984). Practitioners, patients, and compliance with medical regimens: A social psychological perspective. In A. Baum, S. E. Taylor, & J. E. Singer (Eds.), *Handbook of psychology and health: Vol. 4. Social psychological aspects of health.* Hillsdale, NJ: Erlbaum.

Dion, K. K. (1986). Stereotyping based on physical attractiveness: Issues and conceptual perspectives. In C. P. Herman, M. P. Zanna, & E. T. Higgins (Eds.), *Appearance, stigma and social behavior: The Ontario symposium on personality and social psychology* (Vol. 3). Hillsdale, NJ: Erlbaum.

Dixon, N. F. (1980). Humor: A cognitive alternative to stress? In I. G. Sarason & C. D. Spielberger (Eds.), *Stress and anxiety* (Vol. 7). Washington, DC: Hemisphere.

Doerr, P., Pirke, K. M., Kockott, G., & Dittmor, F. (1976). Further studies on sex hormones in male homosexuals. *Archives of General Psychiatry, 33*, 611–614.

Dollaghan, C. (1985). Child meets word: "Fast mapping" in pre-school children. *Journal of Speech and Hearing Research, 28*, 449–454.

Dollard, J., Doob, L. W., Miller, N. E., Mowrer, O. H., & Sears, R. R. (1939). *Frustration and aggression.* New Haven, CT: Yale University Press.

Dollard, J., & Miller, N. E. (1950). *Personality and psychotherapy: An analysis in terms of learning, thinking and culture.* New York: McGraw-Hill.

Domjan, M. (1993). *The principles of learning and behavior.* Pacific Grove, CA: Brooks/Cole.

Donenberg, G. R., & Hoffman, L. W. (1988). Gender differences in moral development. *Sex Roles, 18*, 701–717.

Donlon, T. F. (Ed.). (1984). *The college board technical handbook for the Scholastic Aptitude Test and achievement tests.* New York: College Entrance Examination Board.

Donn, L. (1988). *Freud and Jung: Years of friendship, years of loss.* New York: Scribner's.

Dore, J. (1985). Holophrases revisited: Their logical development from dialog. In M. D. Barrett (Ed.), *Children's single-word speech.* Chichester, England: Wiley.

Dorner, G. (1988). Neuroendocrine response to estrogen and brain differentiation. *Archives of Sexual Behavior, 17*(1), 57–75.

Dovidio, J. F., & Gaertner, S. L. (1991). Changes in the expression of racial prejudice. In H. J. Knopke, R. J. Norrell, & R. W. Rogers (Eds.), *Opening doors: Perspectives in race relations in contemporary America.* Tuscaloosa: University of Alabama Press.

Drachman, D. A. (1986). Memory and cognitive function in normal aging. *Developmental Neuropsychology, 2*, 277–285.

Drake, R. E., Osher, F. C., & Wallach, M. A. (1991). Homelessness and dual diagnosis. *American Psychologist, 46*, 1149–1158.

Driskell, J. E., Willis, R. P., & Copper, C. (1992). Effect of overlearning on retention. *Journal of Applied Psychology, 77*(5), 615–622.

Duara, R. London, E. D., & Rapoport, S. I. (1985). Changes in structure and energy metabolism of the aging brain. In C. E. Finch & E. L. Schneider (Eds.), *Handbook of the biology of aging* (2nd ed.). New York: Van Nostrand Reinhold.

Duncan, B. L. (1976). Differential social perception and attribution of intergroup violence: Testing the lower limits of stereotyping of blacks. *Journal of Personality and Social Psychology, 34*, 590–598.

Duncan, P. D., Ritter, P. L., Dornbusch, S. M., Gross, R. T., & Carlsmith, J. M. (1985). The effects of pubertal timing on body image, school behavior, and deviance. *Youth and Adolescence, 14*, 227–235.

Dutton, D., & Aron, A. (1974). Some evidence for heightened sexual attraction under conditions of high anxiety. *Journal of Personality and Social Psychology, 30*, 510–517.

Dykman, B. M., Horowitz, L. M., Abramson, L. Y., & Usher, M. (1991). Schematic and situational determinants of depressed and nondepressed students' interpretation feedback. *Journal of Abnormal Psychology, 100*, 45–55.

Eagle, M. N., & Wolitzky, D. L. (1992). Psychoanalytic theories of psychotherapy. In D. K. Freedheim (Ed.), *History of psychotherapy: A century of change.* Washington, DC: American Psychological Association.

Eagly, A. H. (1987). *Sex differences in social behavior: A social-role interpretation.* Hillsdale, NJ: Erlbaum.

Eagly, A. H., Ashmore, R. D., Makhijani, M. G., & Longo, L. C. (1991). What is beautiful is good, but . . .: A meta-analytic review of research on the physical attractiveness stereotype. *Psychological Bulletin, 110*, 109–128.

Eagly, A. H., & Carli, L. L. (1981). Sex of researchers and sex-typed communications as determinants of sex differences in influenceability: A meta-analysis of social influence studies. *Psychological Bulletin, 90*, 1–20.

Eaton, W. W., Dryman, A., & Weissman, M. M. (1991). Panic and phobia. In L. N. Robins & D. A. Regier (Eds.), *Psychiatric disorders in America: The epidemiologic catchment area study.* New York: Free Press.

Ebbinghaus, H. (1885/1964). *Memory: A contribution to experimental psychology* (H. A. Ruger & E. R. Bussemius, Trans.). New York: Dover. (Original work published 1885)

Eccles, J. E. (1965). The synapse: *Scientific American, 212*, 56–66.

Edberg, P. (1990). Rorschach assessment. In A. Goldstein & M. Hersen (Eds.), *Handbook of psychological assessment.* New York: Pergamon Press.

Edelman, M. W. (1987). *Families in peril.* Cambridge, MA: Harvard University Press.

Edwards, B. (1989). *Drawing on the right side of the brain*. Los Angeles: J. P. Tarcher.

Efron, R. (1990). *The decline and fall of hemispheric specialization*. Hillsdale, NJ: Erlbaum.

Egan, K. J., Kogan, H. N., Garber, A., & Jarrett, M. (1983). The impact of psychological distress on the control of hypertension. *Journal of Human Stress*, 9(4), 4–10.

Ehlers, D. L., & Kupfer, D. J. (1989). Effects of age on delta and REM sleep parameters. *Electroencephalography & Clinical Neurophysiology*, 72(2), 118–125.

Ehrenberg, O., & Ehrenberg, M. (1986). *The psychotherapy maze*. Northvale, NJ: Aronson.

Eibl-Eibesfeldt, I. (1975). *Ethology: The biology of behavior*. New York: Holt, Rinehart & Winston.

Eich, E. (1990). Learning during sleep. In R. R. Bootzin, J. F. Kihlstrom, & D. L. Schacter (Eds.), *Sleep and cognition*. Washington, DC: American Psychological Association.

Einstein, G. O., Morris, J., & Smith, S. (1985). Note-taking, individual differences, and memory for lecture information. *Journal of Educational Psychology*, 77(5), 522–532.

Eisenberg, N., Miller, P. A., Shell, R., McNalley, S., & Shea, C. (1991). Prosocial development in adolescence: A longitudinal study. *Developmental Psychology*, 27, 849–857.

Eisler, R. M., & Ragsdale, K. (1992). Masculine gender role and midlife transition in men. In V. B. Van Hasselt & M. Hersen (Eds.), *Handbook of social development: A lifespan perspective*. New York: Plenum.

Ekman, P. (1972). Universals and cultural differences in facial expressions of emotion. In J. Cole (Ed.), *Nebraska symposium on motivation*. Lincoln: University of Nebraska Press.

Ekman, P. (1980). *The face of man*. New York: Garland Publishing.

Ekman, P. (1992). Facial expressions of emotion: New findings, new questions. *Psychological Science*, 3, 34–38.

Ekman, P. (1993). Facial expression and emotion. *American Psychologist*, 48, 384–392.

Ekman, P., & Friesen, W. V. (1975). *Unmasking the face*. Englewood Cliffs, NJ: Prentice-Hall.

Ekman, P., & Friesen, W. V. (1984). *Unmasking the face*. Palo Alto: Consulting Psychologists Press.

Ekman, P., Levenson, R. W., & Friesen, W. V. (1983). Autonomic nervous system activity distinguishes among emotions. *Science*, 221, 1208–1210.

Elias, M. F., Elias, J. W., & Elias, P. K. (1990). Biological and health influences on behavior. In J. E. Birren & K. W. Schaie (Eds.), *Handbook of the psychology of aging*. San Diego: Academic Press.

Ellard, K., Beaurepaire, J., Jones, M., Piper, D., & Tennant, C. (1990). Acute chronic stress in duodenal ulcer disease. *Gastroenterology*, 99, 1628–1632.

Elliott, C. S., & Archibald, R. B. (1989). Subjective framing and attitudes toward risk. *Journal of Economic Psychology*, 10, 321–328.

Elliott, E. (1989). Stress and illness. In S. Cheren (Ed.), *Psychosomatic medicine: Theory, physiology, and practice* (Vol. 1). Madison, CT: International Universities Press.

Elliott, G. R., & Barchas, J. D. (1986). Behavioral neurochemistry: The study of brain and behavior. In P. A. Berger & H. K. H. Brodie (Eds.), *American handbook of psychiatry: Biological psychiatry* (2nd ed., Vol. 8). New York: Basic Books.

Elliott, G. R., & Eisdorfer, C. (Eds.). (1982). *Stress and human health: Analysis and implications of research*. New York: Springer.

Ellis, A. (1962). *Reason and emotion in psychotherapy* (1st ed.) Seacaucus, NJ: Lyle Stuart.

Ellis, A. (1977). *Reason and emotion in psychotherapy*. Seacaucus, NJ: Lyle Stuart.

Ellis, A. (1985). *How to live with and without anger*. New York: Citadel Press.

Ellis, L., & Ames, M. A. (1987). Neurohormonal functioning and sexual orientation: A theory of homosexuality-heterosexuality. *Psychological Bulletin*, 101, 233–258.

Ellman, S. J., Spielman, A. J., Luck, D., Steiner, S. S., & Halperin, R. (1991). REM deprivation: A review. In S. J. Ellman & J. S. Antrobus (Eds.), *The mind in sleep: Psychology and psychophysiology* (2nd ed.). New York: Wiley.

Emmelkamp, P. M. G. (1994). Behavior therapy with adults. In A. E. Bergin & S. L. Garfield (Eds.), *Handbook of psychotherapy and behavior change* (4th ed.). New York: Wiley.

Emmelkamp, P. M. G., & Scholing, A. (1990). Behavioral treatment for simple and social phobias. In R. Noyes, Jr., M. Roth, & G. D. Burrows (Eds.), *Handbook of anxiety: The treatment of anxiety* (Vol. 4). Amsterdam: Elsevier.

Emmons, R. A., & King, L. A. (1988). Conflict among personal strivings: Immediate and long-term implications for psychological and physical well-being. *Journal of Personality and Social Psychology*, 54, 1040–1048.

Endler, N. S., & Parker, J. D. A. (1990). Multidimensional assessment of coping: A critical evaluation. *Journal of Personality and Social Psychology*, 58, 844–854.

English, J. T., & McCarrick, R. G. (1989). The economics of psychiatry. In H. I. Kaplan & B. J. Sadock (Eds.), *Comprehensive textbook of psychiatry/V* (Vol. 2). Baltimore: Williams & Wilkins.

Enright, J. T. (1980). *The timing of sleep and wakefulness*. New York: Springer.

Eppley, K., Abrams, A., & Shear, J. (1989). The differential effects of relaxation techniques on trait anxiety: A meta-analysis. *Journal of Clinical Psychology*, 45(6), 957–974.

Erdberg, P. (1990). Rorschach assessment. In G. Goldstein & M. Hersen (Eds.), *Handbook of psychological assessment* (2nd ed.). New York: Pergamon Press.

Erdle, S. (1990). Limitations of the heritability coefficient as an index of genetic and environmental influences on human behavior. *American Psychologist*, 45, 553–554.

Ericsson, K. A., & Polson, P. G. (1988). An experimental analysis of the mechanisms of a memory skill. *Journal of Experimental Psychology: Learning, Memory and Cognition*, 14, 305–316.

Erikson, E. (1963). *Childhood and society*. New York: Norton.

Erikson, E. (1968). *Identity: Youth and crisis*. New York: Norton.

Ernst, C., & Angst, J. (1983). Birth order: Its influence on personality. *Behavioral and Brain Sciences*, 10(1), 55.

Etaugh, C., & Liss, M. B. (1992). Home, school, and playroom: Training grounds for adult gender roles. *Sex Roles*, 26, 129–147.

Evans, C. E., & Haynes, R. B. (1990). Patient compliance. In R. E. Rakel (Ed.), *Textbook of family practice*. Philadelphia: Saunders.

Evans, R. L. (1981). New drug evaluations: Alprazolam. *Drug Intelligence and Clinical Pharmacy*, 15, 633–637.

Eysenck, H. J. (1959). Learning theory and behaviour therapy. *Journal of Mental Science*, 195, 61–75.

Eysenck, H. J. (1967). *The biological basis of personality*. Springfield, IL: Charles C Thomas.

Eysenck, H. J. (1977). *Crime and personality*. London: Routledge & Kegan Paul.

Eysenck, H. J. (1981). Is intelligence inherited? In H. J. Eysenck versus L. Kamin, *The intelligence controversy*. New York: Wiley.

Eysenck, H. J. (1982). *Personality, genetics and behavior: Selected papers*. New York: Praeger.

Eysenck, H. J. (1988). The concept of "intelligence": Useful or useless? *Intelligence*, 12(1), 1–16.

Eysenck, H. J. (1989). Discrimination reaction time and "g": A reply to Humphreys. *Intelligence*, 13(4), 325–326.

Eysenck, H. J. (1990a). Biological dimensions of personality. In L. A. Pervin (Ed.), *Handbook of personality: Theory and research*. New York: Guilford Press.

Eysenck, H. J. (1990b). *Decline and fall of the Freudian empire*. Washington, DC: Scott-Townsend.

Eysenck, H. J., & Eysenck, S. B. G. (1983). Recent advances in the cross-cultural study of personality. In J. N. Butcher & C. S. Spielberger (Eds.), *Advances in personality assessment* (Vol. 2). Hillsdale, NJ: Erlbaum.

Eysenck, H. J., & Kamin, L. (1981). *The intelligence controversy*. New York: Wiley.

Eysenck, M. W. (1984). *A handbook of cognitive psychology*. Hillsdale, NJ: Erlbaum.

Eysenck, M. W., Mogg, K., May, J., Richards, A., & Mathews, A. (1991). Bias in interpretation of ambiguous sentences related to threat in anxiety. *Journal of Abnormal Psychology*, 100, 144–150.

Fagley, N. S. (1987). Positional response bias in multiple-choice tests of learning: Its relation to testwiseness and guessing strategy. *Journal of Educational Psychology*, 79, 95–97.

Fagot, B. I., Hagan, R., Leinbach, M. D., & Kronsberg, S. (1985). Differential reactions to assertive and communicative acts of toddler boys and girls. *Child Development*, 56, 1499–1505.

Fagot, B. I., Leinbach, M. D., & O'Boyle, C. (1992). Gender labeling, gender stereotyping, and parenting behaviors. *Developmental Psychology*, 28, 225–230.

Fahey, P. J., & Gallagher-Allred, C. (1990). Nutrition. In R. E. Rakel (Ed.), *Textbook of family practice* (4th ed.). Philadelphia: Saunders.

Falbo, T., & Polit, D. F. (1986). Quantitative review of the only child literature: Research evidence and theory development. *Psychological Bulletin*, 100, 176–189.

Fancher, R. E. (1979). *Pioneers of psychology*. New York: Norton.

Fanselow, M. S. (1991). Analgesia as a response to aversive Pavlovian conditioned stimuli: Cognitive and emotional mediators. In M. R. Denny (Ed.), *Fear, avoidance and phobias*. Hillsdale, NJ: Erlbaum.

Faraday, A. (1974). *The dream game*. New York: Harper & Row.

Faravelli, C., & Pallanti, S. (1989). Recent life events and panic disorders. *American Journal of Psychiatry*, 146, 622–626.

Farrar, M. J. (1990). Discourse and the acquisition

of grammatical morphemes. *Journal of Child Language, 17,* 607–624.

Fava, G. A., Perini, G. I., Santonastaso, P., & Fornasa, C. V. (1989). Life events and psychological distress in dermatologic disorders: Psoriasis, chronic urticaria, and fungal infections. In T. W. Miller (Ed.), *Stressful life events.* Madison, CT: International Universities Press.

Featherstone, H. J., & Beitman, B. D. (1984). Marital migraine: A refractory daily headache. *Psychosomatics, 25*(1), 30–38.

Fechner, G. T. (1860). *Elemente der psychophysik* (Vol. 1). Leipzig: Breitkopf & Harterl.

Feder, H. H. (1984). Hormones and sexual behavior. *Annual Review of Psychology, 35,* 165–200.

Feeney, J. A., & Noller, P. (1990). Attachment style as a predictor of adult romantic relationships. *Journal of Personality and Social Psychology, 58,* 281–291.

Feingold, A. (1988a). Cognitive gender differences are disappearing. *American Psychologist, 43,* 95–103.

Feingold, A. (1988b). Matching for attractiveness in romantic partners and same-sex friends: A meta-analysis and theoretical critique. *Psychological Bulletin, 104,* 226–235.

Feingold, A. (1990). Gender differences in effects of physical attractiveness on romantic attraction: A comparison across five research paradigms. *Journal of Personality and Social Psychology, 59,* 981–993.

Feingold, A. (1992). Good-looking people are not what we think. *Psychological Bulletin, 111,* 304–341.

Feldman, D. H. (1988). Creativity: Dreams, insights, and transformations. In R. J. Sternberg (Ed.), *The nature of creativity: Contemporary psychological perspectives.* Cambridge: Cambridge University Press.

Fenwick, P. (1987). Meditation and the EEG. In M. A. West (Ed.), *The psychology of meditation.* Oxford: Clarendon Press.

Ferguson, N. B. L., & Keesey, R. E. (1975). Effect of a quinine-adulterated diet upon body-weight maintenance in male rats with ventromedial hypothalamic lesions. *Journal of Comparative and Physiological Psychology, 89,* 478–488.

Ferster, C. S., & Skinner, B. F. (1957). *Schedules of reinforcement.* New York: Appleton-Century-Crofts.

Festinger, L. (1957). *A theory of cognitive dissonance.* Stanford, CA: Stanford University Press.

Festinger, L., & Carlsmith, J. M. (1959). Cognitive consequences of forced compliance. *Journal of Abnormal and Social Psychology, 58,* 203–210.

Festinger, L., Schachter, S., & Back, K. (1950). *Social pressures in informal groups: A study of human factors in housing.* New York: Harper.

Fielding, J. E. (1985). Smoking: Health effects and control. *New England Journal of Medicine, 313,* 491–498, 555–561.

Fincham, F. D., & Bradbury, T. N. (1993). Marital satisfaction, depression, and attributions: A longitudinal analysis. *Journal of Personality and Social Psychology, 63,* 442–452.

Fine, R. (1990). *The history of psychoanalysis.* New York: Continuum.

Finer, B. (1980). Hypnosis and anaesthesia. In G. D. Burrows & L. Dennerstein (Eds.), *Handbook of hypnosis and psychosomatic medicine.* Amsterdam: Elsevier/North Holland Biomedical Press.

Fink, M. (1992). Electroconvulsive therapy. In E. S. Paykel (Ed.), *Handbook of affective disorders* (2nd ed.). New York: Guilford Press.

Finnegan, L. P., & Kandall, S. R. (1992). Maternal and neonatal effects of alcohol and drugs. In J. H. Lowinson, P. Ruiz, & R. B. Millman (Eds.), *Substance abuse: A comprehensive textbook.* Baltimore: Williams & Wilkins.

Fiore, M. C. (1992). Trends in cigarette smoking in the United States: The epidemiology of tobacco use. *Medical Clinics of North America, 76,* 289–303.

Fischer, P. J., & Breakey, W. R. (1991). The epidemiology of alcohol, drug, and mental disorders among homeless persons. *American Psychologist, 46,* 1115–1128.

Fischhoff, B. (1988). Judgment and decision making. In R. J. Sternberg & E. E. Smith (Eds.), *The psychology of human thought.* Cambridge: Cambridge University Press.

Fisher, S., & Greenberg, R. P. (1985). *The scientific credibility of Freud's theories and therapy.* New York: Columbia University Press.

Fishman, D. B., & Franks, C. M. (1992). Evolution and differentiation within behavior therapy: A theoretical epistemological review. In D. K. Freedheim (Ed.), *History of psychotherapy: A century of change.* Washington, DC: American Psychological Association.

Fiske, S. T., & Taylor, S. E. (1991). *Social cognition.* New York: McGraw-Hill.

Flavell, J. H. (1992). Cognitive development: Past, present, and future. *Developmental Psychology, 28,* 998–1005.

Fletcher, G. J. O., Fincham, F. D., Cramer, L., & Heron, N. (1987). The role of attributions in the development of dating relationships. *Journal of Personality and Social Psychology, 53,* 481–489.

Fletcher, G. J. O., & Ward, C. (1988). Attribution theory and processes: A cross-cultural perspective. In M. H. Bond (Ed.), *The cross-cultural challenge to social psychology.* Newbury Park, CA: Sage.

Folkins, C. H. & Sime, W. (1981). Physical fitness training and mental health. *American Psychologist, 36,* 373–389.

Forsyth, D. R. (1990). *An introduction to group dynamics.* Pacific Grove, CA: Brooks/Cole.

Forsyth, D. R., & McMillan, J. H. (1981). Attributions, affect, and expectations: A test of Weiner's three-dimensional model. *Journal of Educational Psychology, 73,* 393–403.

Forsyth, D. R., & Strong, S. R. (1986). The scientific study of counseling and psychotherapy: A unificationist view. *American Psychologist, 41,* 113–119.

Foulkes, D. (1985). *Dreaming: A cognitive-psychological analysis.* Hillsdale, NJ: Erlbaum.

Fowler, R. D. (1986, May). Howard Hughes: A psychological autopsy. *Psychology Today,* pp. 22–33.

Fowles, D. C. (1992). Schizophrenia: Diathesis-stress revisited. *Annual Review of Psychology, 43,* 303–336.

Fowles, D. C. (1993). A motivational theory of psychopathology. In W. Spaulding (Ed.), *Nebraska Symposium on Motivation: Integrated views of motivation, cognition and emotion* (Vol. 41). Lincoln: University of Nebraska Press.

Fozard, J. L. (1990). Vision and hearing in aging. In J. E. Birren & K. W. Schaie (Eds.), *Handbook of the psychology of aging* (3rd ed.). San Diego: Academic Press.

Frances, A. J., First, M. B., Widiger, T. A., Miele, G. M., Tilly, S. M., Davis, W. W., & Pincus, H. A. (1991). An A to Z guide to DSM-IV conundrums. *Journal of Abnormal Psychology, 100,* 407–412.

Frank, E. (1991). Interpersonal psychotherapy as a maintenance treatment for patients with recurrent depression. *Psychotherapy, 28,* 259–266.

Frank, G. (1983). *The Wechsler enterprise: An assessment of the development, structure and use of the Wechsler tests of intelligence.* New York: Pergamon Press.

Frank, J. D. (1961). *Persuasion and healing.* Baltimore: Johns Hopkins University Press.

Frank, L. K. (1939). Projective methods for the study of personality. *Journal of Psychology, 8,* 343–389.

Frank, L. R. (1990). Electroshock: Death, brain damage, memory loss, and brainwashing. *The Journal of Mind and Behavior, 11*(3/4), 489–512.

Frederiksen, N. (1986). Toward a broader conception of human intelligence. In R. J. Sternberg & R. K. Wagner (Eds.), *Practical intelligence: Nature and origins of competence in the everyday world.* Cambridge: Cambridge University Press.

Fremouw, W. J., de Perczel, M., & Ellis, T. E. (1990). *Suicide risk: Assessment and response guidelines.* New York: Pergamon Press.

Freud, S. (1900/1953). *The interpretation of dreams.* In J. Strachey (Ed.), *The standard edition of the complete psychological works of Sigmund Freud* (Vols. 4 and 5). London: Hogarth.

Freud, S. (1901/1960). *The psychopathology of everyday life.* In J. Strachey (Ed.), *The standard edition of the complete psychological works of Sigmund Freud* (Vol. 6). London: Hogarth.

Freud, S. (1905/1953). *Fragment of an analysis of a case of hysteria.* In J. Strachey (Ed.), *The standard edition of the complete psychological works of Sigmund Freud* (Vol. 7). London: Hogarth.

Freud, S. (1915/1959). Instincts and their vicissitudes. In E. Jones (Ed.), *The collected papers of Sigmund Freud* (Vol. 4). New York: Basic Books.

Freud, S. (1924). *A general introduction to psychoanalysis.* New York: Boni & Liveright.

Freud, S. (1933/1964). *New introductory lectures on psychoanalysis.* In J. Strachey (Ed.), *The standard edition of the complete psychological works of Sigmund Freud* (Vol. 22). London: Hogarth.

Freud, S. (1940). An outline of psychoanalysis. *International Journal of Psychoanalysis, 21,* 27–84.

Friedberg, J. (1976). *Shock treatment is not good for your brain.* San Francisco: Glide Publications.

Friedland, G. H., Saltzman, B. R., Rogers, M. F., Kahl, P. A., Lesser, M. L., Mayers, M. M., & Kelin, R. S. (1986). Lack of transmission of HTLV-III/LAV infection to household contacts of patients with AIDS or AIDS-related complex with oral candidiasis. *New England Journal of Medicine, 314,* 344–349.

Friedman, L. S., & Goodman, E. (1992). Adolescents at risk for HIV infection. *Primary Care, 19*(1), 171–190.

Friedman, M., & Rosenman, R. F. (1974). *Type A behavior and your heart.* New York: Knopf.

Friedmann, J., Globus, G., Huntley, A., Mullaney, D., Naitoh, P., & Johnson, L. (1977). Performance and mood during and after gradual sleep reduction. *Psychophysiology, 14,* 245–250.

Fries, H., Nillius, J., & Petersson, F. (1974). Epidemiology of secondary amenorrhea. *American Journal of Obstetrics and Gynecology, 118,* 473–479.

Froelicher, V. F. (1990). Exercise, fitness, and coronary heart disease. In C. Bouchard, R. J. Shephard, T. Stephens, J. R. Sutton, & B. D. McPherson (Eds.), *Exercise, fitness, and health: A* *consensus of current knowledge*. Champaign, IL: Human Kinetics Books.

Fromm, E. (1979). The nature of hypnosis and other altered states of consciousness: An ego-psychological theory. In E. Fromm & R. E. Shor (Eds.), *Hypnosis: Developments in research and new perspectives*. New York: Aldine.

Fuchs, R. M. (1984). Group therapy. In T. B. Karasu (Ed.), *The psychiatric therapies*. Washington, DC: American Psychiatric Association.

Furnham, A. (1986). Response bias, social desirability, and dissimulation. *Personality and Individual Differences, 7*, 385–400.

Furnham, A. F. (1984). Value systems and anomie in three cultures. *International Journal of Psychology, 19*, 565–579.

Furumoto, L. (1980). Mary Whiton Calkins (1863–1930). *Psychology of Women Quarterly, 5*, 55–68.

Furumoto, L., & Scarborough, E. (1986). Placing women in the history of psychology: The first American women psychologists. *American Psychologist, 41*, 35–42.

Gaito, J. (1976). Molecular psychobiology of memory: Its appearance, contributions, and decline. *Physiological Psychology, 4*, 476–484.

Galin, D. (1974). Implications for psychiatry of left and right cerebral specialization: A neuropsychological context for unconscious processes. *Archives of General Psychiatry, 31*, 572–583.

Galton, F. (1869). *Hereditary genius: An inquiry into its laws and consequences*. New York: Appleton.

Gantt, W. H. (1966). Conditional or conditioned, reflex or response? *Conditioned Reflex, 1*, 69–74.

Gantt, W. H. (1975, April 25). Unpublished lecture, Ohio State University. Cited in D. Hothersall, (1984), *History of psychology*. New York: Random House.

Garcia, J. (1989). Food for Tolman: Cognition and cathexis in concert. In T. Archer & L. G. Nilsson (Eds.), *Aversion, avoidance, and anxiety: Perspectives on aversively motivated behavior*. Hillsdale, NJ: Erlbaum.

Garcia, J., Clarke, J. C., & Hankins, W. G. (1973). Natural responses to scheduled rewards. In P. P. G. Bateson & P. Klopfer (Eds.), *Perspectives in ethology*. New York: Plenum.

Garcia, J., & Koelling, R. A. (1966). Learning with prolonged delay of reinforcement. *Psychonomic Science, 5*, 121–122.

Garcia, J., & Rusiniak, K. W. (1980). What the nose learns from the mouth. In D. Muller-Schwarze & R. M. Silverstein (Eds.), *Chemical signals*. New York: Plenum.

Garcia, M. E., Schmitz, J. M., & Doerfler, L. A. (1990). A fine-grained analysis of the role of self-efficacy in self-initiated attempts to quit smoking. *Journal of Consulting and Clinical Psychology, 58*, 317–322.

Gardner, E. (1975). *Fundamentals of neurology*. Philadelphia: Saunders.

Gardner, H. (1983). *Frames of mind: The theory of multiple intelligences*. New York: Basic Books.

Gardner, H. (1985). *The mind's new science: A history of the cognitive revolution*. New York: Basic Books.

Gardner, H., & Hatch, T. (1989). Multiple intelligences go to school: Educational implications of the theory of multiple intelligences. *Educational Researcher, 18*(8), 4–10.

Garfield, S. L. (1986). Problems in diagnostic classification. In T. Millon & G. L. Klerman (Eds.), *Contemporary directions in psychopathology: Toward the DSM-IV*. New York: Guilford Press.

Garfield, S. L. (1992). Major issues in psychotherapy research. In D. K. Freedheim (Ed.), *History of psychotherapy: A century of change*. Washington, DC: American Psychological Association.

Garfield, S. L. (1993). Methodological problems in clinical diagnosis. In P. B. Sutker & H. E. Adams (Eds.), *Comprehensive handbook of psychopathology* (2nd ed.). New York: Plenum.

Garfield, S. L., & Bergin, A. E. (1994). Introduction and historical overview. In A. E. Bergin & S. L. Garfield (Eds.), *Handbook of psychotherapy and behavior change* (4th ed.). New York: Wiley.

Garland, A. F., & Zigler, E. (1993). Adolescent suicide prevention: Current research and social policy implications. *American Psychologist, 48*(2), 169–182.

Garnets, L., & Kimmel, D. (1991). Lesbian and gay male dimensions in the psychological study of human diversity. In J. D. Goodchilds (Ed.), *Psychological perspectives on human diversity in America*. Washington, DC: American Psychological Association.

Garrett, V. D., Brantley, P. J., Jones, G. N., & McKnight, G. T. (1991). The relation between daily stress and Crohn's disease. *Journal of Behavioral Medicine, 14*(1), 87–96.

Garrow, J. S. (1986). Physiological aspects of obesity. In K. D. Brownell & J. P. Foreyt (Eds.), *Handbook of eating disorders: Physiology, psychology, and treatment of obesity, anorexia and bulimia*. New York: Basic Books.

Garvey, C. R. (1929). List of American psychology laboratories. *Psychological Bulletin, 26*, 652–660.

Gatewood, R., & Perloff, R. (1990). Testing and industrial application. In G. Goldstein & M. Hersen (Eds.), *Handbook of psychological assessment*. New York: Pergamon Press.

Gazzaniga, M. S. (1970). *The bisected brain*. New York: Appleton-Century-Crofts.

Gazzaniga, M. S., Bogen, J. E., & Sperry, R. W. (1965). Observations on visual perception after disconnexion of the cerebral hemispheres in man. *Brain, 88*, 221–236.

Gecas, V., & Seff, M. A. (1990). Families and adolescents: A review of the 1980s. *Journal of Marriage and the Family, 52*, 941–958.

Gelderloos, P., Walton, K. G., Orme-Johnson, D. W., & Alexander, C. N. (1991). Effectiveness of the Transcendental Meditation program in preventing and treating substance misuse: A review. *The International Journal of Addictions, 26*(3), 293–325.

Geller, J. L. (1992). A historical perspective on the role of state hospitals viewed from the era of the "revolving door." *American Journal of Psychiatry, 149*, 1526–1533.

Geller, L. (1982). The failure of self-actualization theory: A critique of Carl Rogers and Abraham Maslow. *Journal of Humanistic Psychology, 22*, 56–73.

Gentner, D. (1982). Why nouns are learned before verbs: Linguistic relativity versus natural partitioning. In S. A. Kuczaj, II (Ed.), *Language development: Vol. 2. Language, thought, and culture*. Hillsdale, NJ: Erlbaum.

Gentner, D. (1988). Metaphor as structure mapping: The relational shift. *Child Development, 59*, 47–59.

Gershon, E. S., Berrettini, W. H., & Goldin, L. R. (1989). Mood disorders: Genetic aspects. In H. I. Kaplan & B. J. Sadock (Eds.), *Comprehensive textbook of psychiatry/V*. Baltimore: Williams & Wilkins.

Geschwind, N., & Galaburda, A. M. (1987). *Cerebral lateralization: Biological mechanisms, associations, and pathology*. Cambridge, MA: MIT Press.

Ghez, C. (1991). The cerebellum. In E. R. Kandel, J. H. Schwartz, & T. M. Jessell (Eds.), *Principles of neural science* (3rd ed.). New York: Elsevier.

Ghiselli, E. E. (1966). *The validity of occupational aptitude tests*. New York: Wiley.

Ghiselli, E. E. (1973). The validity of aptitude tests in personnel selection. *Personnel Psychology, 26*, 461–477.

Giannini, A. J., & Miller, N. S. (1989). Drug abuse: A biopsychiatric model. *American Family Practice, 40*(5), 173–182.

Gibbs, N. (1990, October 8). Shameful bequests to the next generation. *Time*, pp. 42–48.

Gibson, H. B., & Heap, M. (1991). *Hypnosis in therapy*. Hillsdale, NJ: Erlbaum.

Gick, M. L., & Holyoak, K. (1980). Analogical problem solving. *Cognitive Psychology, 12*, 306–355.

Gigerenzer, G., Hoffrage, U., & Kleinbölting, H. (1991). Probabilistic mental models: A Brunswikian theory of confidence. *Psychological Review, 98*, 506–528.

Gilbert, C. D., & Wiesel, T. N. (1985). Intrinsic connectivity and receptive field properties in visual cortex. *Vision Research, 25*, 365–374.

Gilbert, D. T., Pelham, B. W., & Krull, D. S. (1988). On cognitive busyness: When person perceivers meet persons perceived. *Journal of Personality and Social Psychology, 54*, 733–739.

Gilder, G. (1986). *Men and marriage*. New York: Pelican.

Gilgen, A. R. (1982). *American psychology since World War II: A profile of the discipline*. Westport, CT: Greenwood Press.

Gillberg, M. (1984). The effects of two alternative timings of a one-hour nap on early morning performance. *Biological Psychology, 19*(1), 45–54.

Gilligan, C. (1982). *In a different voice: Psychological theory and women's development*. Cambridge, MA: Harvard University Press.

Gilligan, C., Hamner, T., & Lyons, N. (1990). *Making connections*. Cambridge: Harvard University Press.

Ginsburg, H. J., & Miller, S. M. (1982). Sex differences in children's risk-taking behavior. *Child Development, 53*, 426–428.

Glass, C. R., & Arnkoff, D. B. (1992). Behavior therapy. In D. K. Freedheim (Ed.), *History of psychotherapy: A century of change*. Washington, DC: American Psychological Association.

Gleason, J. B., & Ratner, N. B. (1993). Language development in children. In J. B. Gleason & N. B. Ratner (Eds.), *Psycholinguistics*. Fort Worth: Harcourt Brace Jovanovich.

Glenberg, A. M. (1992). Distributed practice effects. In L. R. Squire (Ed.), *Encyclopedia of learning and memory*. New York: Macmillan.

Glenn, N. D. (1990). Quantitative research on marital quality in the 1980s: A critical review. *Journal of Marriage and the Family, 52*, 818–831.

Gold, M. S. (1989). *Marijuana*. New York: Plenum.

Gold, M. S. (1992). Cocaine (and crack): Clinical aspects. In J. H. Lowinson, P. Ruiz, & R. B. Millman (Eds.), *Substance abuse: A comprehensive textbook* (2nd ed.). Baltimore: Williams & Wilkins.

Goldberg, H. (1983). *The new male-female relationship*. New York: Morrow.

Goldberg, L. R. (1993). The structure of phenotypic personality traits. *American Psychologist, 48,* 26–34.

Golden, C. J., Sawicki, R. F., & Franzen, M. D. (1990). Test construction. In G. Goldstein & M. Hersen (Eds.), *Handbook of psychological assessment.* New York: Pergamon Press.

Goldenberg, H. (1983). *Contemporary clinical psychology.* Pacific Grove, CA: Brooks/Cole.

Goldfield, B. A., & Reznick, J. S. (1990). Early lexical acquisition: Rate, content, and the vocabulary spurt. *Journal of Child Language, 17,* 171–183.

Goldfried, M. R., Greenberg, L. S., & Marmar, C. (1990). Individual psychotherapy: Process and outcome. *Annual Review of Psychology, 41,* 659–688.

Goldman, J., & Coté, L. (1991). Aging of the brain: Dementia of the Alzheimer's type. In E. R. Kandel, J. H. Schwartz, & T. M. Jessell (Eds.), *Principles of neural science* (3rd ed.). New York: Elsevier.

Goldmann, L. (1990). Cognitive processing and general anesthesia. In R. R. Bootzin, J. F. Kihlstrom, & D. L. Schacter (Eds.), *Sleep and cognition.* Washington, DC: American Psychological Association.

Goldstein, E. B. (1989). *Sensation and perception.* Belmont, CA: Wadsworth.

Goldstein, M. J. (1984). *Family factors that antedate the onset of schizophrenia and related disorders: The results of a fifteen-year prospective longitudinal study.* Paper presented at the Regional Symposium of the World Psychiatric Association Meeting, Helsinki, Finland.

Goldstein, W. M. (1990). Judgments of relative importance in decision making: Global vs. local interpretations of subjective weight. *Organizational Behavior and Human Decision Processes, 47,* 313–336.

Gonder-Frederick, L. A., Carter, W. R., Cox, D. J., & Clarke, W. L. (1990). Environmental stress and blood glucose change in insulin-dependent diabetes mellitus. *Health Psychology, 9,* 503–515.

Gonsiorek, J. C., & Weinrich, J. D. (1991). The definition and scope of sexual orientation. In J. C. Gonsiorek & J. D. Weinrich (Eds.), *Homosexuality: Research implications for public policy.* Newbury Park, CA: Sage.

Goodall, K. (1972, November). Field report: Shapers at work. *Psychology Today,* pp. 53–63, 132–138.

Goodenough, D. R. (1986). History of the field dependence construct. In M. Bertini, L. Pizzamiglio, & S. Wapner (Eds.), *Field dependence in psychological theory, research, and application.* Hillsdale, NJ: Erlbaum.

Goodenough, D. R. (1991). Dream recall: History and current status of the field. In S. J. Ellman & J. S. Antrobus (Eds.), *The mind in sleep: Psychology and psychophysiology* (2nd ed.). New York: Wiley.

Goodwin, C. J. (1991). Misportraying Pavlov's apparatus. *American Journal of Psychology, 104*(1), 135–141.

Goodwin, D. W. (1992). Alcohol: Clinical aspects. In J. H. Lowinson, P. Ruiz, & R. B. Millman (Eds.), *Substance abuse: A comprehensive textbook* (2nd ed.). Baltimore: Williams & Wilkins.

Goodwin, F. K., & Jamison, K. R. (1990). *Manic-depressive illness.* New York: Oxford University Press.

Gorman, J. M., & Davis, J. M. (1989). Antianxiety drugs. In H. I. Kaplan & B. J. Sadock (Eds.), *Comprehensive textbook of psychiatry/V.* Baltimore: Williams & Wilkins.

Gorman, M. E. (1989). Error, falsification and scientific inference: An experimental investigation. *Quarterly Journal of Experimental Psychology, 41*(2-A), 385–412.

Gottesman, I. I. (1991). *Schizophrenia genesis: The origins of madness.* New York: W. H. Freeman.

Gottesman, I. I. (1993). Origins of schizophrenia: Past as prologue. In R. Plomin & G. E. McClearn (Eds.), *Nature, nurture and psychology.* Washington, DC: American Psychological Association.

Gottfried, A. W. (1984). Home environment and early cognitive development: Integration, meta-analysis, and conclusions. In A. W. Gottfried (Ed.), *Home environment and early cognitive development: Longitudinal research.* Orlando: Academic Press.

Gould, R. L. (1975, February). Adult life stages: Growth toward self-tolerance. *Psychology Today,* pp. 74–78.

Gould, R. L. (1978). *Transformations: Growth and change in adult life.* New York: Simon & Schuster.

Gouras, P. (1991). Color vision. In E. R. Kandel, J. H. Schwartz, & T. M. Jessell (Eds.), *Principles of neural science* (3rd ed.). New York: Elsevier.

Gove, W. R. (1975). Labeling and mental illness: A critique. In W. R. Gove (Ed.), *The labeling of deviance: Evaluating a perspective.* New York: Halsted.

Graf, P., & Mandler, G. (1984). Activation makes words more accessible, but not necessarily more retrievable. *Journal of Verbal Learning and Verbal Behavior, 23,* 553–568.

Graff, H., & Stellar, E. (1962). Hyperphagia, obesity and finickiness. *Journal of Comparative and Physiological Psychology, 55,* 418–424.

Graham, J. R. (1990). *MMPI-2: Assessing personality and psychopathology.* New York: Oxford University Press.

Grant, I., McDonald, W. I., Patterson, T., & Trimble, M. R. (1989). Multiple sclerosis. In G. W. Brown & T. O. Harris (Eds.), *Life events and illness.* New York: Guilford Press.

Gray, D. S. (1989). Diagnosis and prevalence of obesity. *Medical Clinics of North America, 73,* 1–13.

Grebb, J. A., & Cancro, R. (1989). Schizophrenia: Clinical features. In H. I. Kaplan & B. J. Sadock (Eds.), *Comprehensive textbook of psychiatry/V.* Baltimore: Williams & Wilkins.

Green, D. W. (1990). Confirmation bias, problem-solving and cognitive models. In J. P. Caverni, J. M. Fabre, & M. Gonzalez (Eds.), *Cognitive biases.* Amsterdam: North-Holland.

Green., L. W., Tryon W. W., Marks, B., & Huryn, J. (1986). Periodontal disease as a function of life events stress. *Journal of Human Stress, 12*(1), 32–36.

Greenberg, J. S. (1990). *Comprehensive stress management.* Dubuque, IA: William C. Brown.

Greene, R. L. (1992). *Human memory: Paradigms and paradoxes.* Hillsdale, NJ: Erlbaum.

Greene, W. A., & Swisher, S. N. (1969). Psychological and somatic variables associated with the development and course of monozygotic twins discordant for leukemia. *Annals of the New York Academy of Sciences, 164,* 394–408.

Greenfield, P. M. & Smith, J. H. (1976). *The structure of communication in early language development.* New York: Academic Press.

Greeno, J. G. (1978). Nature of problem solving abilities. In W. K. Estes (Ed.), *Handbook of learning and cognitive processes* (Vol. 5). Hillsdale, NJ: Erlbaum.

Greenough, W. T. (1985). The possible role of experience-dependent synaptogenesis, or synapses on demand in the memory process. In N. M. Weinberger, J. L. McGaugh, & G. Lynch (Eds.), *Memory systems of the brain.* New York: Guilford Press.

Greenson, R. R. (1967). *The technique and practice of psychoanalysis* (Vol. 1). New York: International Universities Press.

Gregory, R. L. (1973). *Eye and brain.* New York: McGraw-Hill.

Gregory, R. L. (1978). *Eye and brain* (2nd ed.). New York: McGraw-Hill.

Griffith, R. M., Miyago, M., & Tago, A. (1958). The universality of typical dreams: Japanese vs. Americans. *American Anthropologist, 60,* 1173–1179.

Griggs, R. A., Jackson, S. L. & Napolitano, T. J. (1994). Brief introductory psychology textbooks: An objective analysis. *Teaching of Psychology, 21,* 136–140.

Grinker, J. A. (1982). Physiological and behavioral basis for human obesity. In D. W. Pfaff (Ed.), *The physiological mechanisms of motivation.* New York: Springer-Verlag.

Grinspoon, L., & Bakalar, J. B. (1992). Marihuana. In J. H. Lowinson, P. Ruiz, & R. B. Millman (Eds.), *Substance abuse: A comprehensive textbook* (2nd ed.). Baltimore: Williams & Wilkins.

Grob, G. N. (1983). Disease and environment in American history. In D. Mechanic (Ed.), *Handbook of health, health care, and the health professions.* New York: Free Press.

Grob, G. N. (1991). Origins of DSM-I: A study in appearance and reality. *American Journal of Psychiatry, 148,* 421–431.

Grossman, S. P. (1979). The biology of motivation. *Annual Review of Psychology, 30,* 209–242.

Grossman, S. P., Dacey, D., Halaris, A. E., Collier, T., & Routtenberg, A. (1978). Aphagia and adipsia after preferential destruction of nerve cell bodies in hypothalamus. *Science, 202,* 537–539.

Grossmann, K., Grossmann, K. E., Spangler, S., Suess, G., & Unzner, L. (1985). Maternal sensitivity and newborn orientation responses as related to quality of attachment in northern Germany. In I. Bretherton & E. Waters (Eds.), Growing points of attachment theory. *Monographs of the Society for Research for Child Development, 50,* (1–2, Serial No. 209).

Grossmann, K. E., & Grossmann, K. (1990). The wider concept of attachment in cross-cultural research. *Human Development, 33,* 31–47.

Grossmann, K. E., Grossmann, K., Huber, F., & Wartner, U. (1981). Children's behavior towards their mothers at 12 months and their fathers at 18 months in Ainsworth's Strange Situation. *International Journal of Behavioral Development, 4,* 157–181.

Grove, W. M., & Andreasen, N. C. (1992). Concepts, diagnosis and classification. In E. S. Paykel (Ed.), *Handbook of affective disorders* (2nd ed.). New York: Guilford Press.

Gruen, R. J. (1993). Stress and depression: Toward the development of integrative models. In L. Goldberger & S. Breznitz (Eds.), *Handbook of stress: Theoretical and clinical aspects.* New York: Free Press.

Grunberg, N. E., & Straub, R. O. (1992). The role of gender and taste class in the effects of stress on eating. *Health Psychology, 11,* 97–100.

Guenther, K. (1988). Mood and memory. In G. M. Davies & D. M. Thomson (Eds.), *Memory in context: Context in memory.* New York: Wiley.

Guilford, J. P. (1939). *General psychology.* Princeton, NJ: Van Nostrand Reinhold.

Guilford, J. P. (1959). Three faces of intellect. *American Psychologist, 14,* 469–479.

Gupta, G. R. (1992). Love, arranged marriage, and

the Indian social structure. In J. J. Macionis & N. V. Benokraitis (Eds.), *Seeing ourselves: Classic, contemporary and cross-cultural reading in sociology.* Englewood Cliffs, NJ: Prentice-Hall.

Gustavson, C. R., Kelly, D. J., Sweeney, M., & Garcia, J. (1976). Prey-lithium aversions I: Coyotes and wolves. *Behavioral Biology, 17,* 61–72.

Guyton, A. C. (1991). *Textbook of medical physiology.* Philadelphia: Saunders.

Haan, N. (1989). Personality at midlife. In S. Hunter & M. Sundel (Eds.), *Mid life myths: Issues, findings, and practice.* Newbury Park, CA: Sage.

Haan, N. (1993). The assessment of coping, defense, and stress. In L. Goldberger & S. Breznitz (Eds.), *Handbook of stress: Theoretical and clinical aspects* (2nd ed.). New York: Free Press.

Haensly, P. A., & Reynolds, C. R. (1989). Creativity and intelligence. In J. A. Glover, R. R. Ronning, & C. R. Reynolds (Eds.), *Handbook of creativity.* New York: Plenum.

Hagberg, J. M. (1990). Exercise, fitness, and hypertension. In C. Bouchard, R. J. Shephard, T. Stephens, J. R. Sutton, & B. D. McPherson (Eds.), *Exercise, fitness, and health: A consensus of current knowledge.* Champaign, IL: Human Kinetics Books.

Haglund, B., & Cnattingius, S. (1990). Cigarette smoking as a risk factor for sudden infant death syndrome: A population-based study. *American Journal of Public Health, 80,* 29–32.

Hales, D. (1987). *How to sleep like a baby.* New York: Ballantine.

Hall, C. S. (1966). *The meaning of dreams.* New York: McGraw-Hill.

Hall, C. S. (1979). The meaning of dreams. In D. Goleman & R. J. Davidson (Eds.), *Consciousness: Brain, states of awareness, and mysticism.* New York: Harper & Row.

Hall, C. S., & Nordby, V. J. (1972). *The individual and his dreams.* New York: Mentor.

Hall, C. S., & Van de Castle, R. L. (1966). *The content analysis of dreams.* New York: Appleton-Century-Crofts.

Hall, E. (1987). *Growing and changing: What the experts say.* New York: Random House.

Hall, G. S. (1904). *Adolescence.* New York: Appleton.

Hall, J. A. (1990). *Nonverbal sex differences: Communication accuracy and expressive style* (2nd ed.). Baltimore: Johns Hopkins University Press.

Hall, J. A., & Halberstadt, A. G. (1986). Smiling and gazing. In J. S. Hyde & M. C. Linn (Eds.), *The psychology of gender: Advances through meta-analysis.* Baltimore: Johns Hopkins University Press.

Hall, J. A., Roter, D. L., & Katz, N. R. (1988). Meta-analysis of correlates of provider behavior in medical encounters. *Medical Care, 26,* 1–19.

Halpern, D. F. (1984). *Thought and knowledge: An introduction to critical thinking.* Hillsdale, NJ: Erlbaum.

Halpern, D. F. (1989a). Things and pictures of things: Are perceptual processes invariant across cultures? *Behavioral and Brain Sciences, 12*(1), 84–85.

Halpern, D. F. (1989b). *Thought and knowledge: An introduction to critical thinking* (2nd ed.). Hillsdale, NJ: Erlbaum.

Halpern, D. F. (1992). *Sex differences in cognitive abilities.* Hillsdale, NJ: Erlbaum.

Hamer, D. H., Hu, S., Magnuson, V. L., Hu, N., & Pattatucci, A. M. L. (1993). A linkage between DNA markers on the X chromosome and male sexual orientation. *Science, 261,* 321–327.

Hamilton, D. L., & Sherman, S. J. (1989). Illusory

correlations: Implications for stereotype theory and research. In D. Bar-Tal, C. F. Graumann, A. W. Kruglanski, & W. Stroebe (Eds.), *Stereotyping and prejudice: Changing conceptions.* New York: Springer-Verlag.

Hamilton, W. D. (1970). Selfish and spiteful behavior in an evolutionary model. *Nature, 228,* 1218–1220.

Hansen, C. H., & Hansen, R. D. (1988). How rock music videos can change what is seen when boy meets girl: Priming stereotypic appraisal of social interactions. *Sex Roles, 19,* 287–316.

Hanshaw, J. B., Dudgeon, J. A., & Marshall, W. C. (1985). *Viral diseases of the fetus and newborn.* Philadelphia: Saunders.

Hanson, R. A. (1975). Consistency and stability of home environmental measures related to IQ. *Child Development, 46,* 470–480.

Harmsen, P., Rosengren, A., Tsipogianni, A., & Wilhelmsen, L. (1990). Risk factors for stroke in middle-aged men in Goteborg, Sweden. *Stroke, 21,* 23–29.

Harriman, L. C. (1986). Marital adjustment as related to personal and marital changes accompanying parenthood. *Family Relations, 35,* 233–239.

Harris, W. G. (1987). *Cary Grant: A touch of elegance.* New York: Doubleday.

Hartmann, E. (1973). *The functions of sleep.* New Haven, CT: Yale University Press.

Harvey, J. H., Town, J. P., & Yarkin, K. L. (1981). How fundamental is "the fundamental attribution error"? *Journal of Personality and Social Psychology, 40,* 346–349.

Hass, R. G. (1981). Effects of source characteristics on cognitive responses and persuasion. In R. E. Petty, T. M. Ostrom, & T. C. Brock (Eds.), *Cognitive responses in persuasion.* Hillsdale, NJ: Erlbaum.

Hastorf, A., & Cantril, H. (1954). They saw a game: A case study. *Journal of Abnormal and Social Psychology, 49,* 129–134.

Hatfield, E. (1988). Passionate and companionate love. In R. J. Sternberg & M. L. Barnes (Eds.), *The psychology of love.* New Haven, CT: Yale University Press.

Hatfield, E., & Rapson, R. L. (1993). *Love, sex, and intimacy: Their psychology, biology, and history.* New York: HarperCollins.

Hathaway, S. R., & McKinley, J. C. (1943). *Manual for the Minnesota Multiphasic Personality Inventory.* New York: Psychological Corporation.

Hauser, S. T., & Bowlds, M. K. (1990). Stress, coping, and adaptation. In S. S. Feldman & G. R. Feldman (Eds.), *At the threshold: The developing adolescent.* Cambridge, MA: Harvard University Press.

Hawton, K., Cole, D., O'Grady, J., & Osborn, M. (1982). Motivational aspects of deliberate self-positioning in adolescents. *British Journal of Psychiatry, 141,* 286–290.

Hazan, C., & Shaver, P. (1986). *Parental caregiving style questionnaire.* Unpublished questionnaire.

Hazan, C., & Shaver, P. (1987). Romantic love conceptualized as an attachment process. *Journal of Personality and Social Psychology, 52,* 511–524.

Hearst, E. (1979). One hundred years: Themes and perspectives. In E. Hearst (Ed.), *The first century of experimental psychology.* Hillsdale, NJ: Erlbaum.

Hearst, E. (1988). Fundamentals of learning and conditioning. In R. C. Atkinson, R. J. Herrnstein, G. Lindzey, & R. D. Luce (Eds.), *Stevens' handbook of experimental psychology.* New York: Wiley.

Heath, A. C., Kendler, K. S., Eaves, L. J., &

Martin, N. (1990). Evidence for genetic influences on sleep disturbance and sleep patterns in twins. *Sleep, 13,* 318–335.

Heath, R. G. (Ed.). (1964). *The role of pleasure in behavior.* New York: Harper & Row.

Heider, F. (1958). *The psychology of interpersonal relations.* New York: Wiley.

Hellige, J. B. (1990). Hemispheric asymmetry. *Annual Review of Psychology, 41,* 55–80.

Hellige, J. B. (1993). Unity of thought and action: Varieties of interaction between left and right cerebral hemispheres. *Current Directions in Psychological Science, 2*(1), 21–25.

Helmholtz, H. von. (1852). On the theory of compound colors. *Philosophical Magazine, 4,* 519–534.

Helmholtz, H. von. (1863). *On the sensations of tone as a physiological basis for the theory of music* (A. J. Ellis, Trans.). New York: Dover.

Helms, J. E. (1992). Why is there no study of cultural equivalence in standard cognitive ability testing? *American Psychologist, 47,* 1083–1101.

Helson, R., Mitchell, V., & Moane, G. (1984). Personality and patterns of adherence and nonadherence to the social clock. *Journal of Personality and Social Psychology, 46,* 1079–1096.

Helson, R., & Moane, G. (1987). Personality change in women from college to midlife. *Journal of Personality and Social Psychology, 53,* 176–186.

Helson, R., & Stewart, A. (1994). Personality change in adulthood. In T. F. Heatherton & J. L. Weinberger (Eds.), *Can personality change?* Washington, DC: American Psychological Association.

Hendrick, S. S., & Hendrick, C. (1992). *Liking, loving, and relating* (2nd ed.). Pacific Grove, CA: Brooks/Cole.

Henriksson, M. M., Aro, H. M., Marttunen, M. J., Heikkinen, M. E., Isometsae, E. T., Kuoppasalmi, K. I., & Loennqvist, J. K. (1993). Mental disorders and comorbidity in suicide. *American Journal of Psychiatry, 150,* 935–940.

Henry, K. R. (1984). Cochlear damage resulting from exposure to four different octave bands of noise at three different ages. *Behavioral Neuroscience, 1,* 107–117.

Hering, E. (1878). *Zür lehre vom lichtsinne.* Vienna: Gerold.

Herman, C. P., & Polivy, J. (1984). A boundary model for the regulation of eating. In A. B. Stunkard & E. Stellar (Eds.), *Eating and its disorders.* New York: Raven.

Herman, J. H. (1993). Color in dreams. In M. A. Carskadon (Ed.), *Encyclopedia of sleep and dreaming.* New York: Macmillan.

Hertzog, C., & Schaie, K. W. (1988). Stability and changes in adult intelligence: 2. Simultaneous analysis of longitudinal means and covariance structures. *Psychology and Aging, 3,* 122–130.

Heth, C. D., & Rescorla, R. A. (1973). Simultaneous and backward fear conditioning in the rat. *Journal of Comparative and Physiological Psychology, 82,* 434–443.

Hettich, P. I. (1992). *Learning skills for college and career.* Pacific Grove, CA: Brooks/Cole.

Hewstone, M. (1990). The "ultimate attribution error"? A review of the literature on intergroup causal attribution. *European Journal of Social Psychology, 20,* 311–335.

Hilgard, E. R. (1965). *Hypnotic susceptibility.* New York: Harcourt, Brace & World.

Hilgard, E. R. (1986). *Divided consciousness: Multiple* controls in human thought and action. New York: Wiley.

Hilgard, E. R. (1987). *Psychology in America: A historical survey.* San Diego: Harcourt Brace Jovanovich.

Hilliard, A. G., III. (1984). IQ testing as the emperor's new clothes: A critique of Jensen's *Bias in Mental Testing.* In C. R. Reynolds & R. T. Brown (Eds.), *Perspectives on bias in mental testing.* New York: Plenum.

Hillner, K. P. (1984). *History and systems of modern psychology: A conceptual approach.* New York: Gardner Press.

Hilton, J. L., Fein, S., & Miller, D. T. (1993). Suspicion and dispositional inference. *Personality and Social Psychology Bulletin, 19,* 501–512.

Hines, M. (1990). Gonadal hormones and human cognitive development. In J. Balthazart (Ed.), *Hormones, brain and behavior in vertebrates: 1. Sexual differentiation, neuroanatomical aspects, neurotransmitters and neuropeptides.* Basel: Karger.

Hintzman, D. L. (1990). Human learning and memory: Connections and dissociations. *Annual Review of Psychology, 41,* 109–139.

Hiroto, D. S., & Seligman, M. E. P. (1975). Generality of learned helplessness in man. *Journal of Personality and Social Psychology, 31,* 311–327.

Hirsch, J., Fried, S. K., Edens, N. K., & Leibel, R. L. (1989). The fat cell. *Medical Clinics of North America, 73,* 83–96.

Hirschfeld, R. M. A., & Davidson, L. (1988). Risk factors for suicide. In A. J. Frances & R. E. Hales (Eds.), *Review of psychiatry* (Vol. 7). Washington, DC: American Psychiatric Press.

Hobfoll, S. E., & Vaux, A. (1993). Social support: Resources and context. In L. Goldberger & S. Breznitz (Eds.), *Handbook of stress: Theoretical and clinical aspects* (2nd ed.). New York: Free Press.

Hobson, J. A. (1988). *The dreaming brain.* New York: Basic Books.

Hobson, J. A. (1989). *Sleep.* New York: Scientific American Library.

Hobson, J. A., & McCarley, R. W. (1977). The brain as a dream state generator: An activation-synthesis hypothesis of the dream process. *American Journal of Psychiatry, 134,* 1335–1348.

Hocevar, D., & Bachelor, P. (1989). A taxonomy and critique of measurements used in the study of creativity. In J. A. Glover, R. R. Ronning, & C. R. Reynolds (Eds.), *Handbook of creativity.* New York: Plenum.

Hochberg, J. (1988). Visual perception. In R. C. Atkinson, R. J. Herrnstein, G. Lindzey, & R. D. Luce (Eds.), *Stevens' handbook of experimental psychology* (2nd ed., Vol. 1). New York: Wiley.

Hodgkin, A. L., & Huxley, A. F. (1952). Currents carried by sodium and potassium ions through the membrane of the giant axon of Loligo. *Journal of Physiology, 116,* 449–472.

Hoebel, B. G. (1988). Neuroscience and motivation: Pathways and peptides that define motivational systems. In R. C. Atkinson, R. J. Herrnstein, G. Lindzey, & R. D. Luce (Eds.), *Stevens' handbook of experimental psychology* (2nd ed.). New York: Wiley.

Hoffman, C., Lau, I., & Johnson, D. R. (1986). The linguistic relativity of person cognition: An English-Chinese comparison. *Journal of Personality and Social Psychology, 51,* 1097–1105.

Hoffman, L. W. (1991). The influence of the family environment on personality: Accounting for sibling differences. *Psychological Bulletin, 110,* 187–203.

Hofstede, G. (1980). *Culture's consequences: International differences in work-related values.* Beverly Hills, CA: Sage.

Hofstede, G. (1983). Dimensions of national cultures in fifty countries and three regions. In J. Deregowski, S. Dzuirawiec, & R. Annis (Eds.), *Explications in cross-cultural psychology.* Lisse: Swets and Zeitlinger.

Hogarth, R. M. (1987). *Judgement and choice.* New York: Wiley.

Holahan, C. J., & Moos, R. H. (1985). Life stress and health: Personality, coping, and family support in stress resistance. *Journal of Personality and Social Psychology, 49,* 739–747.

Holahan, C. J., & Moos, R. H. (1990). Life stressors, resistance factors, and improved psychological functioning: An extension of the stress resistance paradigm. *Journal of Personality and Social Psychology, 58,* 909–917.

Holden, C. (1986, October). The rational optimist. *Psychology Today,* pp. 55–60.

Hollan, D. (1989). The personal use of dream beliefs in the Toraja Highlands. *Ethos, 17,* 166–186.

Hollander, E., Schiffman, E., Cohen, B., Rivera-Stein, M. A., Rosen, W., Gorman, J. M., Fyer, A. J., Papp, L., & Liebowitz, M. R. (1990). Signs of central nervous system dysfunction in obsessive-compulsive disorder. *Archives of General Psychiatry, 47,* 27–32.

Hollands, C. (1989). Trivial and questionable research on animals. In G. Langley (Ed.), *Animal experimentation: The consensus changes.* New York: Chapman & Hall.

Hollandsworth, J. G., Jr. (1990). *The physiology of psychological disorders: Schizophrenia, depression, anxiety, and substance abuse.* New York: Plenum.

Hollingworth, L. S. (1914). *Functional periodicity: An experimental study of the mental and motor abilities of women during menstruation.* New York: Teachers College, Columbia University.

Hollingworth, L. S. (1916). Sex differences in mental tests. *Psychological Bulletin, 13,* 377–383.

Hollon, S. D., & Beck, A. T. (1994). Cognitive and cognitive-behavioral therapies. In A. E. Bergin & S. L. Garfield (Eds.), *Handbook of psychotherapy and behavior change* (4th ed.). New York: Wiley.

Holmes, D. S. (1987). The influence of meditation versus rest on physiological arousal: A second examination. In M. A. West (Ed.), *The psychology of meditation.* Oxford: Clarendon Press.

Holmes, D. S. (1990). The evidence for repression: An examination of sixty years of research. In J. Singer (Ed.), *Repression and dissociation: Implications for personality, theory, psychopathology, and health.* Chicago: University of Chicago Press.

Holmes, T. H., & Rahe, R. H. (1967). The Social Readjustment Rating Scale. *Journal of Psychosomatic Research, 11,* 213–218.

Holt, R. R. (1993). Occupational stress. In L. Goldberger & S. Breznitz (Eds.), *Handbook of stress: Theoretical and clinical aspects* (2nd ed.). New York: Free Press.

Homma-True, R., Greene, B., Lopez, S. R., & Trimble, J. E. (1993). Ethnocultural diversity in clinical psychology. *The Clinical Psychologist, 46*(2), 50–63.

Honig, W. K., & Alsop, B. (1992). Operant behavior. In L. R. Squire (Ed.), *Encyclopedia of learning and memory.* New York: Macmillan.

Honts, C. R., & Perry, M. V. (1992). Polygraph

admissibility: Changes and challenges. *Law and Human Behavior, 16,* 357–379.

Hooper, J., & Teresi, D. (1986). *The 3-pound universe—The brain.* New York: Laurel.

Hopkins, B., & Westra, T. (1988). Maternal handling and motor development: An intracultural study. *Genetic, Social and General Psychology Monographs, 14,* 377–420.

Hopkins, B., & Westra, T. (1990). Motor development, maternal expectations, and the role of handling. *Infant Behavior and Development, 13,* 117–122.

Hopson, J. L. (1988, July/August). A pleasurable chemistry. *Psychology Today,* pp. 29–30, 32–33.

Horn, J. L. (1976). Human abilities: A review of research and theory in the early 1970s. *Annual Review of Psychology, 27,* 437–485.

Hornstein, G. A. (1992). The return of the repressed: Psychology's problematic relations with psychoanalysis, 1909–1960. *American Psychologist, 47,* 254–263.

Horowitz, F. D. (1992). John B. Watson's legacy: Learning and environment. *Developmental Psychology, 28,* 360–367.

Hothersall, D. (1984). *History of psychology.* New York: Random House.

House, J. S., Landis, K. R., & Umberson, D. (1988). Social relationships and health. *Science, 241,* 540–545.

Houston, B. K., Chesney, M. A., Black, G. W., Cates, D. S., & Hecker, M. H. L. (1992). Behavioral clusters and coronary heart disease. *Psychosomatic Medicine, 54,* 447–461.

Howard, A., Pion, G. M., Gottfredson, G. D., Flattau, P. E., Oskamp, S., Pfafflin, S. M., Bray, D. W., & Burstein, A. G. (1986). The changing face of American psychology: A report from the committee on employment and human resources. *American Psychologist, 41,* 1311–1327.

Howes, C., Phillips, D. A., & Whitebook, M. (1992). Thresholds of quality: Implications for the social development of children in center-based child care. *Child Development, 63,* 449–460.

Hubbard, T. L., Baird, J. C., & Ajmal, A. (1989). Different skills or different knowledge? *Behavioral and Brain Sciences, 12*(1), 86–87.

Hubel, D. H. (1979, September). The brain. *Scientific American,* pp. 38–47.

Hubel, D. H., & Wiesel, T. N. (1962). Receptive fields, binocular interaction and functional architecture in the cat's visual cortex. *Journal of Physiology, 160,* 106–154.

Hubel, D. H., & Wiesel, T. N. (1963). Receptive fields of cells in striate cortex of very young visually inexperienced kittens. *Journal of Neurophysiology, 26,* 994–1002.

Hubel, D. H., & Wiesel, T. N. (1979). Brain mechanisms of vision. In Scientific American (Eds.), *The brain.* San Franciso: W. H. Freeman.

Hudson, W. (1960). Pictorial depth perception in sub-cultural groups in Africa. *Journal of Social Psychology, 52,* 183–208.

Hudson, W. (1967). The study of the problem of pictorial perception among unacculturated groups. *International Journal of Psychology, 2,* 89–107.

Hughes, C. C. (1993). Culture in clinical psychiatry. In A. C. Gaw (Ed.), *Culture, ethnicity, and mental illness.* Washington, DC: American Psychiatric Press.

Hughes, J., Smith, T. W., Kosterlitz, H. W., Fothergill, L. A., Morgan, B. A., & Morris, H. R. (1975). Identification of two related pentapeptides from the brain with the potent opiate agonist activity. *Nature, 258,* 577–579.

Hull, C. L. (1943). *Principles of behavior.* New York: Appleton.

Hultsch, D. F., & Dixon, R. A. (1990). Learning and memory in aging. In J. E. Birren & K. W. Schaie (Eds.), *Handbook of the psychology of aging* (3rd ed.). San Diego: Academic Press.

Humphreys, M. S., Bain, J. D., & Pike, R. (1989). Different ways to cue a coherent memory system: A theory for episodic, semantic, and procedural tasks. *Psychological Review, 96,* 208–233.

Hunt, H. (1989). *The multiplicity of dreams: Memory, imagination and consciousness.* New Haven, CT: Yale University Press.

Hunt, J. M., Smith, M. F., & Kernan, J. B. (1985). The effects of expectancy disconfirmation and argument strength on message processing level: An application to personal selling. In E. C. Hirschman & M. B. Holbrook (Eds.), *Advances in consumer research* (Vol. 12). Provo, UT: Association for Consumer Research.

Hunt, M. (1974). *Sexual behavior in the 1970s.* Chicago: Playboy Press.

Hunt, W. A., & Matarazzo, J. D. (1982). Changing smoking behavior: A critique. In R. J. Gatchel, A. Baum, & J. E. Singer (Eds.), *Handbook of psychology and health: Vol. 1. Clinical psychology and behavioral medicine, overlapping disciplines.* Hillsdale, NJ: Erlbaum.

Hunter, J. E., & Hunter, R. F. (1984). Validity and utility of alternative predictors of job performance. *Psychological Bulletin, 96,* 72–98.

Hurvich, L. M. (1981). *Color vision.* Sunderland, MA: Sinnauer Associates.

Huston, A. C., & Wright, J. C. (1982). Effects of communications media on children. In C. B. Kopp & J. B. Krakow (Eds.), *The child: Development in a social context.* Reading, MA: Addison-Wesley.

Huston, A. C. (1983). Sex-typing. In P. H. Mussen (Ed.), *Handbook of child psychology* (4th ed., Vol. 4). New York: Wiley.

Huys, J., Evers-Kiebooms, G., & d'Ydewalle, G. (1990). Framing biases in genetic risk perception. In J. P. Caverni, J. M. Fabre, & M. Gonzalez (Eds.), *Cognitive biases.* Amsterdam: North-Holland.

Hyde, J. S. (1986). Gender differences in aggression. In J. S. Hyde & M. C. Linn (Eds.), *The psychology of gender differences: Advances through meta-analysis.* Baltimore: Johns Hopkins University Press.

Hyde, J. S., Fennema, E., & Lamon, S. J. (1990). Gender differences in mathematics performance: A meta-analysis. *Psychological Bulletin, 107,* 139–155.

Hyde, J. S., & Linn, M. C. (1988). Gender differences in verbal ability: A meta-analysis. *Psychological Bulletin, 104,* 53–69.

Ickovics, J. R., & Rodin, J. (1992). Women and AIDS in the United States: Epidemiology, natural history, and mediating mechanisms. *Health Psychology, 11,* 1–16.

Iezzi, A., & Adams, H. E. (1993). Somatoform and factitious disorders. In P. B. Sutker & H. E. Adams (Eds.), *Comprehensive handbook of psychopathology* (2nd ed.). New York: Plenum.

Ineichen, B. (1979). The social geography of marriage. In M. Cook & G. Wilson (Eds.), *Love and attraction.* New York: Pergamon.

Insko, C. A. (1965). Verbal reinforcement of attitudes. *Journal of Personality and Social Psychology, 2,* 621–623.

Irvine, S. H., & Berry, J. W. (1988). *Human abilities in cultural context.* New York: Cambridge University Press.

Isabella, R. A., & Belsky, J. (1991). Interactional synchrony and the origins of infant-mother attachment: A replication study. *Child Development, 62,* 373–384.

Isada, N. B., & Grossman, J. H., III. (1991). Perinatal infections. In S. G. Gabbe, J. R. Niebyl, & J. L. Simpson (Eds.), *Obstetrics: Normal and problem pregnancies.* New York: Churchill Livingstone.

Iwao, S. (1993). *The Japanese woman: Traditional image and changing reality.* New York: Free Press.

Iwawaki, S., & Vernon, P. E. (1988). Japanese abilities and achievements. In S. H. Irvine & J. W. Berry (Eds.), *Human abilities in cultural context.* New York: Cambridge University Press.

Izard, C. E. (1971). *The face of emotion.* New York: Appleton-Century-Crofts.

Izard, C. E. (1984). Emotion-cognition relationships and human development. In C. E. Izard, J. Kagan, & R. B. Zajonc (Eds.), *Emotions, cognition and behavior.* Cambridge, England: Cambridge University Press.

Izard, C. E. (1990). Facial expressions and the regulation of emotions. *Journal of Personality and Social Psychology, 58,* 487–498.

Izard, C. E. (1991). *The psychology of emotions.* New York: Plenum.

Jackson, D. N. (1973). Structured personality assessment. In B. B. Wolman (Ed.), *Handbook of general psychology.* Englewood Cliffs, NJ: Prentice-Hall.

Jackson, L. A., Sullivan, L. A., & Hodge, C. N. (1993). Stereotype effects on attributions, predictions, and evaluations: No two social judgments are quite alike. *Journal of Personality and Social Psychology, 65,* 69–84.

James, W. (1884). What is emotion. *Mind, 19,* 188–205.

James, W. (1890). *The principles of psychology.* New York: Holt.

James, W. (1902). *The varieties of religious experience.* New York: Modern Library.

Jamison, K. R. (1988). Manic-depressive illness and accomplishment: Creativity, leadership, and social class. In F. K. Goodwin & K. R. Jamison (Eds.), *Manic-depressive illness.* Oxford, England: Oxford University Press.

Jamison, K. R., Gerner, R. H., Hammen, C., & Padesky, C. (1980). Clouds and silver linings: Positive experiences associated with the primary affective disorders. *American Journal of Psychiatry, 137,* 198–202.

Jangid, R. K., Vyas, J. N., & Shukla, T. R. (1988). The effect of the Transcendental Meditation Programme on normal individuals. *Journal of Personality & Clinical Studies, 4*(1), 145–149.

Janis, I. L. (1958). *Psychological stress.* New York: Wiley.

Janis, I. L. (1972). *Victims of groupthink.* Boston: Houghton Mifflin.

Janis, I. L. (1973, January). Groupthink. *Yale Alumni Magazine,* pp. 16–19.

Janis, I. L. (1993). Decision making under stress. In L. Goldberger & S. Breznitz (Eds.), *Handbook of stress: Theoretical and clinical aspects* (2nd ed.). New York: Free Press.

Janis, I. L., & Mann, L. (1977). *Decision making: A psychological analysis of conflict, choice, and commitment.* New York: Free Press.

Jann, M. W., Jenike, M. A., & Lieberman, J. A. (1994). The new psychopharmaceuticals. *Patient Care, 28*(2), 47–61.

Janus, S. S., & Janus, C. L. (1993). *The Janus report on sexual behavior.* New York: Wiley.

Jaroff, L. (1993, November 29). Lies of the mind. *Time,* pp. 52–59.

Jarvik, M. E., & Schneider, N. G. (1992). Nicotine. In J. H. Lowinson, P. Ruiz, & R. B. Millman (Eds.), *Substance abuse: A comprehensive textbook* (2nd ed.). Baltimore: Williams & Wilkins.

Jefferson, J. W., & Greist, J. H. (1989). Lithium therapy. In H. I. Kaplan & B. J. Sadock (Eds.), *Comprehensive textbook of psychiatry/V.* Baltimore: Williams & Wilkins.

Jemmott, J. B., III, & Magloire, K. (1988). Academic stress, social support, and secretory immunoglobin A. *Journal of Personality and Social Psychology, 55,* 803–810.

Jenike, M. A., Baer, L., & Greist, J. H. (1990). Clomipramine versus fluoxetine in obsessive-compulsive disorder: A retrospective comparison of side effects and efficacy. *Journal of Clinical Psychopharmacology, 10*(2), 122–124.

Jenkins, J. G., & Dallenbach, K. M. (1924). Oblivescence during sleep and waking. *American Journal of Psychology, 35,* 605–612.

Jensen, A. R. (1969). How much can we boost IQ and scholastic achievement? *Harvard Educational Review, 39,* 1–23.

Jensen, A. R. (1980). *Bias in mental testing.* New York: Free Press.

Jensen, A. R. (1982). Reaction time and psychometric g. In H. J. Eysenck (Ed.), *A model for intelligence.* Springer-Verlag.

Jensen, A. R. (1987). Process differences and individual difference in some cognitive tasks. *Intelligence, 11,* 107–136.

Jensen, A. R. (1993a). Test validity: g versus "tacit knowledge." *Current Directions in Psychological Science, 2*(1), 9–10.

Jensen, A. R. (1993b). Why is reaction time correlated with psychometric g? *Current Directions in Psychological Science, 2*(2), 53–56.

John, O. P. (1990). The "big five" factor taxonomy: Dimensions of personality in the natural language and in questionnaires. In L. A. Pervin (Ed.), *Handbook of personality: Theory and research.* New York: Guilford Press.

Johnson, A. B. (1990). *Out of bedlam: The truth about deinstitutionalization.* New York: Basic Books.

Johnson, C., & Mullen, B. (1994). Evidence for the accessibility of paired distinctiveness in distinctiveness-based illusory correlation in stereotyping. *Personality and Social Psychology Bulletin, 20,* 65–70.

Johnson, D. (1990). Animal rights and human lives: Time for scientists to right the balance. *Psychological Science, 1,* 213–214.

Johnson, J. S., & Newport, E. L. (1989). Critical period effects in second language learning: The influence of maturational state on the acquisition of English as a second language. *Cognitive Psychology, 21,* 60–99.

Johnson, L. C. (1982). Sleep deprivation and performance. In W. B. Webb (Ed.), *Biological rhythms, sleep and performance.* New York: Wiley.

Johnson, L. C., Tepas, D. I., Colquhoun, W. P., & Colligan, M. J. (1981). *Biological rhythms, sleep and shift work.* New York: Spectrum.

Johnson, M. K., Hashtroudi, S., & Lindsay, D. S. (1993). Source monitoring. *Psychological Bulletin, 114,* 3–28.

Johnson, M. K., Springer, S. P., & Sternglanz, S. H. (1982). *How to succeed in college*. Los Altos, CA: William Kaufmann.

Johnston, W. A., & Dark, V. J. (1986). Selective attention. *Annual Review of Psychology, 37*, 43–75.

Johnston, W. A., & Heinz, S. P. (1978). Flexibility and capacity demands of attention. *Journal of Experimental Psychology: General, 107*, 420–435.

Jones, E. E. (1990). *Interpersonal perception*. New York: W. H. Freeman.

Jones, E. E., & Davis, K. E. (1965). From acts to dispositions: The attribution process in person perception. In L. Berkowitz (Ed.), *Advances in experimental social psychology* (Vol. 2). New York: Academic Press.

Jones, E. E., & Nisbett, R. E. (1971). The actor and the observer: Divergent perceptions of the causes of behavior. In E. E. Jones, D. E. Kanouse, H. H. Kelley, R. E. Nisbett, S. Valins, & B. Weiner (Eds.), *Attribution: Perceiving the causes of behavior.* Morristown, NJ: General Learning Press.

Jones, G. V. (1990). Misremembering a common object: When left is not right. *Memory & Cognition, 18*(2), 174–182.

Jones, J. S., & Oswald, I. (1968). Two cases of healthy insomnia. *Electroencephalography and Clinical Neurophysiology, 24*, 378–380.

Jones, R. A., & Brehm, J. W. (1970). Persuasiveness of one- and two-sided communications as a function of awareness there are two sides. *Journal of Experimental Social Psychology, 6*, 47–56.

Jordan, B. (1983). *Birth in four cultures*. Quebec, Canada: Eden Press.

Joseph, R. (1992). *The right brain and the unconscious*. New York: Plenum.

Jourard, S. M., & Landsman, T. (1980). *Healthy personality: An approach from the viewpoint of humanistic psychology*. New York: Macmillan.

Judd, C. M., & Park, B. (1988). Out-group homogeneity: Judgments of variability at the individual and group levels. *Journal of Personality and Social Psychology, 54*, 778–788.

Judd, C. M., Ryan, C. S., & Park, B. (1991). Accuracy in the judgment of in-group and out-group variability. *Journal of Personality and Social Psychology, 61*, 366–379.

Judd, L. L., McAdams, L. A., Budnick, B., & Braff, D. L. (1992). Sensory gating effects in schizophrenia: New results. *American Journal of Psychiatry, 149*, 488–493.

Julien, R. M. (1992). *A primer of drug action* (6th ed.). New York: W. H. Freeman.

Jung, C. G. (1917/1953). *On the psychology of the unconscious*. In H. Read, M. Fordham, & G. Adler (Eds.), *Collected works of C. G. Jung* (Vol. 7). Princeton, NJ: Princeton University Press.

Jung, C. G. (1921/1960). *Psychological types*. In H. Read, M. Fordham, & G. Adler (Eds.), *Collected works of C. G. Jung* (Vol. 6). Princeton, NJ: Princeton University Press.

Jung, C. G. (1933). *Modern man in search of a soul*. New York: Harcourt, Brace & World.

Kagan, J. (1969). Inadequate evidence and illogical conclusions. *Harvard Educational Review, 39*, 274–277.

Kagan, J., & Snidman, N. (1991). Temperamental factors in human development. *American Psychologist, 46*, 856–862.

Kahn, R. S., Davidson, M., Siever, L., Gabriel, S., Apter, S., & Davis, K. L. (1993). Serotonin function and treatment response to clozapine in schizo-phrenic patients. *American Journal of Psychiatry, 150*, 1337–1342.

Kahneman, D., & Tversky, A. (1982). Subjective probability: A judgment of representativeness. In D. Kahneman, P. Slovic, & A. Tversky (Eds.), *Judgment under uncertainty: Heuristics and biases*. Cambridge: Cambridge University Press.

Kahneman, D., & Tversky, A. (1984). Choices, values, and frames. *American Psychologist, 39*, 341–350.

Kail, R., & Hagen, J. W. (1982). Memory in childhood. In B. B. Wolman (Ed.), *Handbook of developmental psychology*. Englewood Cliffs, NJ: Prentice-Hall.

Kalant, H., & Kalant, O. J. (1979). Death in amphetamine users: Causes and rates. In D. E. Smith (Ed.), *Amphetamine use, misuse and abuse*. Boston: G. K. Hall.

Kalat, J. W. (1993). *Introduction to psychology*. Pacific Grove, CA: Brooks/Cole.

Kales, A., & Kales, J. D. (1984). *Evaluation and treatment of insomnia*. New York: Oxford University Press.

Kales, J. D., Kales, A., Bixler, E. O., Soldatos, C. R., Cadieux, R. J., Kashurba, G. J., & Vela-Bueno, A. (1984). Biopsychobehavioral correlates of insomnia: V. Clinical characteristics and behavioral correlates. *American Journal of Psychiatry, 141*, 1371–1376.

Kalick, S. M., & Hamilton, T. E., III. (1986). The matching hypothesis reexamined. *Journal of Personality and Social Psychology, 51*, 673–682.

Kalmuss, D., Davidson, A., & Cushman, L. (1992). Parenting expectations, experiences, and adjustment to parenthood: A test of the violated expectations framework. *Journal of Marriage and the Family, 52*, 516–526.

Kamen-Siegel, L., Rodin, J., Seligman, M. E. P., & Dwyer, J. (1991). Explanatory style and cell-mediated immunity in elderly men and women. *Health Psychology, 10*, 229–235.

Kamerman, S. B. (1993). International perspectives on child care policies and programs. *Pediatrics, 91*, 248–252.

Kamin, L. J. (1965). Temporal and intensity characteristics of the conditioned stimulus. In W. F. Prokasy (Ed.), *Classical conditioning*. New York: Appleton-Century-Crofts.

Kamin, L. J. (1981). Some historical facts about IQ testing. In H. J. Eysenck versus L. Kamin, *The intelligence controversy*. New York: Wiley.

Kamiya, J. (1969). Operant control of the EEG rhythm and some of its reported effects on consciousness. In C. T. Tart (Ed.), *Altered states of consciousness*. New York: Wiley.

Kandel, D. B. (1978). Similarity in real-life adolescent friendship pairs. *Journal of Personality and Social Psychology, 36*, 306–312.

Kandel, E. R. (1991). Disorders of thought: Schizophrenia. In E. R. Kandel, J. H. Schwartz, & T. M. Jessell (Eds.), *Principles of neural science* (3rd ed.). New York: Elsevier.

Kandel, E. R., & Jessell, T. M. (1991). Touch. In E. R. Kandel, J. H. Schwartz, & T. M. Jessell (Eds.), *Principles of neural science* (3rd ed.). New York: Elsevier.

Kandel, E. R., & Schwartz, J. H. (1991). Directly gated transmission at central synapses. In E. R. Kandel, J. H. Schwartz, & T. M. Jessell (Eds.), *Principles of neural science* (3rd ed.). New York: Elsevier.

Kanner, A. D., Coyne, J. C., Schaefer, C., & Lazarus, R. S. (1981). Comparison of two modes of stress measurement: Daily hassles and uplifts versus major life events. *Journal of Behavioral Medicine, 4*, 1–39.

Kanter, A. S. (1989). Homeless but not helpless: Legal issues in the care of homeless people with mental illness. *Journal of Social Issues, 45*(3), 91–104.

Kaplan, A. G. (1985). Female or male therapists for women patients: New formulations. *Psychiatry, 48*, 111–121.

Kaplan, H., & Dove, H. (1987). Infant development among the Ache of Eastern Paraguay. *Developmental Psychology, 23*, 190–198.

Kaplan, H. I. (1985). History of psychosomatic medicine. In H. I. Kaplan & B. J. Sadock (Eds.), *Comprehensive textbook of psychiatry/IV*. Baltimore: Williams & Wilkins.

Kaplan, H. I., & Sadock, B. J. (Eds.). (1993). *Comprehensive group psychotherapy*. Baltimore: Williams & Wilkins.

Kaplan, N. M. (1986). Dietary aspects of the treatment of hypertension. In L. Breslow, J. E. Fielding, & L. B. Lave (Eds.), *Annual review of public health* (Vol. 7). Palo Alto, CA: Annual Reviews.

Kaplan, R. M. (1985). The controversy related to the use of psychological tests. In B. B. Wolman (Ed.), *Handbook of intelligence: Theories, measurements, and applications*. New York: Wiley.

Kaplan, R. M., & Simon, H. J. (1990). Compliance in medical care: Reconsideration of self-predictions. *Annals of Behavioral Medicine, 12*, 66–71.

Karau, S. J., & Williams, K. D. (1993). Social loafing: A meta-analytic review and theoretical integration. *Journal of Personality and Social Psychology, 65*, 681–706.

Kardiner, A., & Linton, R. (1945). *The individual and his society*. New York: Columbia University Press.

Karno, M., & Golding, J. M. (1991). Obsessive compulsive disorder. In L. N. Robins & D. A. Regier (Eds.), *Psychiatric disorders in America: The epidemiologic catchment area study*. New York: Free Press.

Kashima, Y., & Triandis, H. C. (1986). The self-serving bias in attributions as a coping strategy: A cross-cultural study. *Journal of Cross-Cultural Psychology, 17*, 83–98.

Katz, L. J., & Slomka, G. T. (1990). Achievement testing. In G. Goldstein & M. Hersen (Eds.), *Handbook of psychological assessment*. New York: Pergamon Press.

Kaufman, L., & Rock, I. (1962). The moon illusion I. *Science, 136*, 953–961.

Kausler, D. H. (1985). Episodic memory: Memorizing performance. In N. Charness (Ed.), *Aging and human performance*. Chichester, England: Wiley.

Kavesh, L., & Lavin, C. (1988). *Tales from the front*. New York: Doubleday.

Kazdin, A. E. (1982). History of behavior modification. In A. S. Bellack, M. Hersen, & A. E. Kazdin (Eds.), *International handbook of behavior modification and behavior therapy*. New York: Plenum.

Kazdin, A. E. (1994). Methodology, design, and evaluation in psychotherapy research. In A. E. Bergin & S. L. Garfield (Eds.), *Handbook of psychotherapy and behavior change* (4th ed.). New York: Wiley.

Keesey, R. E. (1986). A set-point theory of obesity. In K. D. Brownell & J. P. Foreyt (Eds.), *Handbook of eating disorders: Physiology, psychology, and treatment of obesity, anorexia, and bulimia*. New York: Basic Books.

Keesey, R. E. (1988). The body-weight set point. *Postgraduate Medicine, 83*, 114–127.

Keesey, R. E., & Powley, T. L. (1975). Hypothalamic regulation of body weight. *American Scientist, 63*, 558–565.

Keesey, R. E., & Powley, T. L. (1986). The regulation of body weight. *Annual Review of Psychology, 37*, 109–133.

Keith, S. J., Regier, D. A., & Rae, D. S. (1991). Schizophrenic disorders. In L. N. Robins & D. A. Regier (Eds.), *Psychiatric disorders in America: The epidemiologic catchment area study.* New York: Free Press.

Keller, L. S., Butcher, J. N., & Slutske, W. S. (1990). Objective personality assessment. In G. Goldstein & M. Hersen (Eds.), *Handbook of psychological assessment.* New York: Pergamon Press.

Kelley, H. H. (1950). The warm-cold variable in first impressions of persons. *Journal of Personality, 18*, 431–439.

Kelley, H. H. (1967). Attributional theory in social psychology. *Nebraska Symposium on Motivation, 15*, 192–241.

Kelly, D. D. (1991). Sleep and dreaming. In E. R. Kandel, J. H. Schwartz, & T. M. Jessell (Eds.), *Principles of neural science* (3rd ed.). New York: Elsevier.

Kelly, J. P. (1991). The sense of balance. In E. R. Kandel, J. H. Schwartz, & T. M. Jessell (Eds.), *Principles of neural science* (3rd ed.). New York: Elsevier.

Kelman, H. C. (1967). Human use of human subjects: The problem of deception in social psychological experiments. *Psychological Bulletin, 67*, 1–11.

Kelman, H. C. (1982). Ethical issues in different social science methods. In T. L. Beauchamp, R. R. Faden, R. J. Wallace, Jr., & L. Walters (Eds.), *Ethical issues in social science research.* Baltimore: Johns Hopkins University Press.

Kendler, K. S., Neale, M. C., Kessler, R. C., Heath, A. C., & Eaves, L. J. (1992). Generalized anxiety disorder in women: A population-based twin study. *Archives of General Psychiatry, 49*, 267–272.

Kenrick, D. T. (1987). Gender, genes, and the social environment. In P. C. Shaver & C. Hendrick (Eds.), *Review of Personality and Social Psychology* (Vol. 8). Beverly Hills, CA: Sage.

Kenrick, D. T., & Funder, D. C. (1988). Profiting from controversy: Lessons from the person-situation debate. *American Psychologist, 43*, 23–34.

Kenrick, D. T., & Funder, D. C. (1991). The person-situation debate: Do personality traits really exist? In N. J. Derlega, B. A. Winstead, & W. H. Jones (Eds.), *Personality: Contemporary theory and research.* Chicago: Nelson-Hall.

Kenrick, D. T., & Stringfield, D. (1980). Personality traits and the eye of the beholder: Crossing some traditional philosophical boundaries in the search for consistency in all of the people. *Psychological Review, 87*, 88–104.

Keren, G. (1990). Cognitive aids and debiasing methods: Can cognitive pills cure cognitive ills? In J. P. Caverni, J. M. Fabre, & M. Gonzalez (Eds.), *Cognitive biases.* Amsterdam: North-Holland.

Khot, V., & Wyatt, R. J. (1991). Not all that moves is tardive dyskinesia. *American Journal of Psychiatry, 148*, 661–666.

Kiang, N. Y. S., & Peake, W. T. (1988). Physics and physiology of hearing. In R. C. Atkinson, R. J. Herrnstein, G. Lindzey, & R. D. Luce (Eds.), *Stevens' handbook of experimental psychology* (2nd ed., Vol. 1). New York: Wiley.

Kiecolt-Glaser, J. K., Garner, W., Speicher, C., Penn, G. M., Holliday, J., & Glaser, R. (1984). Psychosocial modifiers of immunocompetence in medical students. *Psychosomatic Medicine, 46*(1), 7–14.

Kiecolt-Glaser, J. K., Glaser, R., Williger, D., Stout, J., Messick, G., Sheppard, S., Ricker, D., Romisher, S. C., Briner, W., Bonnell, G., & Donnerberg, R. (1985). Psychosocial enhancement of immunocompetence in a geriatric population. *Health Psychology, 4*, 25–42.

Kiesler, C. A. (1982). Public and professional myths about mental hospitalization. *American Psychologist, 37*, 1232–1339.

Kiesler, C. A. (1991). Homelessness and public policy priorities. *American Psychologist, 46*, 1245–1252.

Kiesler, C. A. (1992). U.S. mental health policy: Doomed to fail. *American Psychologist, 47*, 1077–1082.

Kiesler, C. A. (1993). Mental health policy and mental hospitalization. *Current Directions in Psychological Science, 2*(3), 93–95.

Kiesling, R. (1983). Critique of Kiesler articles. *American Psychologist, 38*, 1127–1128.

Kihlstrom, J. F. (1985). Hypnosis. *Annual Review of Psychology, 36*, 385–418.

Kihlstrom, J. F. (1990). The psychological unconscious. In L. A. Pervin (Ed.), *Handbook of personality: Theory and research.* New York: Guilford Press.

Kihlstrom, J. F., Schacter, D. L., Cork, R. C., Hurt, C. A., & Behr, S. E. (1990). Implicit and explicit memory following surgical anesthesia. *Psychological Science, 1*, 303–306.

Kihlstrom, J. F., Tataryn, D. J., & Hoyt, I. P. (1993). Dissociative disorders. In P. B. Sutker & H. E. Adams (Eds.), *Comprehensive handbook of psychopathology* (2nd ed.). New York: Plenum.

Killeen, P. R. (1981). Learning as causal inference. In M. L. Commons & J. A. Nevin (Eds.), *Quantitative analyses of behavior: Vol. 1. Discriminative properties of reinforcement schedules.* Cambridge, MA: Ballinger.

Kimura, D. (1973). The asymmetry of the human brain. *Scientific American, 228*, 70–78.

Kimura, D. (1987). Are men's and women's brains really different? *Canadian Psychology, 28*, 133–147.

King, A. C., Taylor, C. B., & Haskell, W. L. (1993). Effects of differing intensities and formats of 12 months of exercise training on psychological outcomes in older adults. *Health Psychology, 12*, 292–300.

King, G. R., & Ellinwood, E. H. (1992). Amphetamines and other stimulants. In J. H. Lowinson, P. Ruiz, & R. B. Millman (Eds.), *Substance abuse: A comprehensive textbook* (2nd ed.). Baltimore: Williams & Wilkins.

Kinsbourne, M. (1980). If sex differences in brain lateralization exist, they have yet to be discovered. *Behavioral and Brain Sciences, 3*, 241–242.

Kinsbourne, M. (1982). Hemispheric specialization and the growth of human understanding. *American Psychologist, 37*, 411–420.

Kinsey, A. C., Pomeroy, W. B., & Martin, C. E. (1948). *Sexual behavior in the human male.* Philadelphia: Saunders.

Kinsey, A. C., Pomeroy, W. B., Martin, C. E., & Gebhard, P. H. (1953). *Sexual behavior in the human female.* Philadelphia: Saunders.

Kinsman, R. A., Dirks, J. F., & Jones, N. F. (1982). Psychomaintenance of chronic physical illness: Clinical assessment of personal styles affecting medical management. In T. Millon, C. Green, & R. Meagher (Eds.), *Handbook of clinical health psychology.* New York: Plenum.

Kirk, S. A., & Kutchins, H. (1992). *The selling of DSM: The rhetoric of science in psychiatry.* New York: Aldine de Gruyter.

Kissebah, A. H., Freedman, D. S., & Peiris, A. N. (1989). High risks of obesity. *Medical Clinics of North America, 73*, 111–138.

Kitson, G. C., & Sussman, M. B. (1982). Marital complaints, demographic characteristics, and symptoms of mental distress in divorce. *Journal of Marriage and the Family, 44*, 87–101.

Kittler, P. G., & Sucher, K. (1989). *Food and culture in America: A nutrition handbook.* New York: Van Nostrand Reinhold.

Klaus, M., & Kennell, J. (1982). *Parent-infant bonding.* St. Louis: C. V. Mosby.

Klayman, J., & Ha, Y-W. (1987). Confirmation, disconfirmation, and information in hypothesis testing. *Psychological Review, 94*, 211–228.

Klein, M. (1948). *Contributions to psychoanalysis.* London: Hogarth.

Kleinmuntz, B. (1980). *Essentials of abnormal psychology.* San Francisco: Harper & Row.

Kleinmuntz, B. (1985). *Personality and psychological assessment.* Malabar, FL: Robert E. Krieger.

Kleinmuntz, B., & Szucko, J. J. (1984). Lie detection in ancient and modern times: A call for contemporary scientific study. *American Psychologist, 39*, 766–776.

Klerman, E. B. (1993). Deprivation, selective: NREM sleep. In M. A. Carskadon (Ed.), *Encyclopedia of sleep and dreaming.* New York: Macmillan.

Klerman, G. L. (1990). Treatment of recurrent unipolar major depressive disorder. *Archives of General Psychiatry, 47*, 1158–1162.

Klerman, G. L., & Weissman, M. M. (1986). The interpersonal approach to understanding depression. In T. Millon & G. L. Klerman (Eds.), *Contemporary directions in psychopathology: Toward the DSM-IV.* New York: Guilford Press.

Klerman, G. L., Weissman, M. M., Markowitz, J. C., Glick, I., Wilner, P. J., Mason, B., & Shear, M. K. (1994). Medication and psychotherapy. In A. E. Bergin & S. L. Garfield (Eds.), *Handbook of psychotherapy and behavior change* (4th ed.). New York: Wiley.

Kline, D. W., & Schieber, F. (1985). Vision and aging. In J. E. Birren & K. W. Schaie (Eds.), *Handbook of the psychology of aging* (2nd ed.). New York: Van Nostrand Reinhold.

Kline, P. (1991). *Intelligence: The psychometric view.* New York: Routledge, Chapman, & Hall.

Kluckhohn, C., & Murray, H. A. (1948). *Personality in nature, society and culture.* New York: Knopf.

Kluegel, J. R. (1990). Trends in whites' explanations of the black-white gap in socioeconomic status. *American Sociological Review, 55*, 512–525.

Knittle, J. L., Merritt, R. J., Dixon-Shanies, D., Ginsberg-Fellner, F., Timmers, K. I., & Katz, D. P. (1981). Childhood obesity. In R. M. Suskind (Ed.), *Textbook of pediatric nutrition.* New York: Raven.

Knowles, J. B., Coulter, M., Wahnon, S., Reitz, W., & MacLean, A. W. (1990). Variation in process S: Effects on sleep continuity and architecture. *Sleep, 13*(2), 97–107.

Kogan, N. (1990). Personality and aging. In J. E. Birren & K. W. Schaie (Eds.), *Handbook of the psychology of aging.* San Diego: Academic Press.

Kohlberg, L. (1963). The development of children's orientations toward a moral order: I. Sequence in the development of moral thought. *Vita Humana, 6,* 11–33.

Kohlberg, L. (1964). Development of moral character and moral ideology. In L. W. Hoffman & M. L. Hoffman (Eds.), *Review of child development research* (Vol. 1). New York: Russell Sage Foundation.

Kohlberg, L. (1966). A cognitive-developmental analysis of children's sex-role concepts and attitudes. In E. E. Maccoby (Ed.), *The development of sex differences.* Stanford, CA: Stanford University Press.

Kohlberg, L. (1969). Stage and sequence: The cognitive-developmental approach to socialization. In D. A. Goslin (Ed.), *Handbook of socialization theory and research.* Chicago: Rand McNally.

Kohlberg, L. (1976). Moral stages and moralization: Cognitive-developmental approach. In T. Lickona (Ed.), *Moral development and behavior: Theory, research and social issues.* New York: Holt, Rinehart & Winston.

Kohlberg, L. (1981). *Essays on moral development* (Vol. 1). New York: Harper & Row.

Kohlberg, L. (1984). *Essays on moral development: Vol. 2. The psychology of moral development.* San Francisco: Harper & Row.

Kohut, H. (1971). *Analysis of the self.* New York: International Universities Press.

Kolb, B., & Whishaw, I. Q. (1990). *Fundamentals of human neuropsychology.* New York: W. H. Freeman.

Koob, G. F., & Bloom, F. E. (1988). Cellular and molecular mechanisms of drug dependence. *Science, 242,* 715–723.

Koranyi, E. K. (1989). Physiology of stress reviewed. In S. Cheren (Ed.), *Psychosomatic medicine: Theory, physiology, and practice* (Vol. 1). Madison, CT: International Universities Press.

Koriat, A., & Melkman, R. (1987). Depth of processing and memory organization. *Psychological Research, 49,* 183–188.

Kotovsky, K., Hayes, J. R., & Simon, H. A. (1985). Why are some problems hard? Evidence from Tower of Hanoi. *Cognitive Psychology, 17,* 248–294.

Kracke, W. (1991). Myths in dreams, thought in images: An Amazonian contribution to the psychoanalytic theory of primary process. In B. Tedlock (Ed.), *Dreaming: Anthropological and psychological interpretations.* Santa Fe, NM: School of American Research Press.

Kracke, W. (1992). Languages of dreaming: Anthropological approaches to the study of dreaming in other cultures. In J. Gackenback & A. Sheik (Eds.), *Dream images: A call to mental arms.* Amityville, NY: Baywood.

Krakauer, D., & Dallenbach, K. M. (1937). Gustatory adaptation to sweet, sour, and bitter. *American Journal of Psychology, 49,* 469–475.

Kravitz, D. A., & Martin, B. (1986). Ringelmann rediscovered: The original article. *Journal of Personality and Social Psychology, 50,* 936–941.

Krebs, D. (1987). The challenge of altruism in biology and psychology. In C. Crawford, M. Smith, & D. Krebs (Eds.), *Sociobiology and psychology: Ideas, issues and applications.* Hillsdale, NJ: Erlbaum.

Kribbs, N. B. (1993). Siesta. In M. A. Carskadon (Ed.), *Encyclopedia of sleep and dreaming.* New York: Macmillan.

Kripke, D. F., Simons, R. N., Garfunkel, L., & Hammond, C. (1979). Short and long sleep and sleeping pills: Is increased mortality associated? *Archives of General Psychiatry, 36,* 103–116.

Krueger, W. C. F. (1929). The effect of overlearning on retention. *Journal of Experimental Psychology, 12,* 71–78.

Kulick, A. R., Pope, H. G., & Keck, P. E. (1990). Lycanthropy and self-identification. *Journal of Nervous & Mental Disease, 178*(2), 134–137.

Lader, M. H. (1984). Antianxiety drugs. In T. B. Karasu (Ed.), *The psychiatric therapies.* Washington, DC: American Psychiatric Association.

Lader, M. H., & Herrington, R. (1990). *Biological treatments in psychiatry.* Oxford: Oxford University Press.

Laird, J. D. (1984). The real role of facial response in the experience of emotion: A reply to Tourangeau and Ellsworth, and others. *Journal of Personality and Social Psychology, 47,* 909–917.

Lakein, A. (1973). *How to get control of your time and your life.* New York: Peter H. Wyden.

Lamb, M. E. (1982). Parent-infant interaction, attachment and socioemotional development in infancy. In R. N. Emde & R. J. Harmon (Eds.), *The development of attachment and affiliative systems.* New York: Plenum.

Lamb, M. E. (Ed.). (1987). *The father's role: Cross-cultural perspectives.* Hillsdale, NJ: Erlbaum.

Lamb, M. E., Ketterlinus, R. D., & Fracasso, M. P. (1992). Parent-child relationships. In M. H. Bornstein & M. E. Lamb (Eds.), *Developmental psychology: An advanced textbook* (3rd ed.). Hillsdale, NJ: Erlbaum.

Lambert, M. J., & Bergin, A. E. (1992). Achievements and limitations of psychotherapy research. In D. K. Freedheim (Ed.), *History of psychotherapy: A century of change.* Washington, DC: American Psychological Association.

Lambert, M. J., & Bergin, A. E. (1994). The effectiveness of psychotherapy. In A. E. Bergin & S. L. Garfield (Eds.), *Handbook of psychotherapy and behavior change* (4th ed.). New York: Wiley.

Lambert, M. J., & Hill, C. E. (1994). Assessing psychotherapy outcomes and processes. In A. E. Bergin & S. L. Garfield (Eds.), *Handbook of psychotherapy and behavior change* (4th ed.). New York: Wiley.

Lampl, M., Veldhuis, J. D., & Johnson, M. L. (1992). Saltation and stasis: A model of human growth. *Science, 258,* 801–803.

Lange, C. (1885). One leuds beveegelser. In K. Dunlap (Ed.), *The emotions.* Baltimore: Williams & Wilkins.

LaRue, A., & Jarvik, L. F. (1982). Old age and biobehavioral changes. In B. B. Wolman (Ed.), *Handbook of developmental psychology.* Englewood Cliffs, NJ: Prentice-Hall.

Latané, B. (1981). The psychology of social impact. *American Psychologist, 36,* 343–356.

Latané, B., & Nida, S. A. (1981). Ten years of research on group size and helping. *Psychological Bulletin, 89,* 308–324.

Latané, B., Williams, K., & Harkins, S. (1979). Many hands make light the work: The causes and consequences of social loafing. *Journal of Personality and Social Psychology, 37,* 822–832.

Lattal, K. A. (1992). B. F. Skinner and psychology [Introduction to the Special Issue]. *American Psychologist, 27,* 1269–1272.

Lau, R. R. (1988). Beliefs about control and health behavior. In D. Gochman (Ed.), *Health behavior: Emerging research perspectives.* New York: Plenum.

Lauber, J. K. (1993). Public safety in transportation. In M. A. Carskadon (Ed.), *Encyclopedia of sleep and dreaming.* New York: Macmillan.

Laughlin, H. (1967). *The neuroses.* Washington, DC: Butterworth.

Laughlin, H. (1979). *The ego and its defenses.* New York: Aronson.

Lazarus, A. A., & Wilson, G. T. (1976). Behavior modification: Clinical and experimental perspectives. In B. B. Wolman (Ed.), *The therapist's handbook: Treatment methods of mental disorders.* New York: Van Nostrand Reinhold.

Lazarus, A. A. (1987). The need for technical eclecticism: Science, breadth, depth, and specificity. In J. K. Zeig (Ed.), *The evolution of psychology.* New York: Brunner/Mazel.

Lazarus, R. S. (1991). *Emotion and adaptation.* New York: Oxford University Press.

Lazarus, R. S. (1993). Why we should think of stress as a subset of emotion. In L. Goldberger & S. Breznitz (Eds.), *Handbook of stress: Theoretical and clinical aspects* (2nd ed.). New York: Free Press.

Lazarus, R. S., & Folkman, S. (1984). *Stress, appraisal and coping.* New York: Springer.

Leahey, T. H. (1987). *A history of psychology: Main currents in psychological thought* (2nd ed.). Englewood Cliffs, NJ: Prentice-Hall.

Leavitt, F. (1982). *Drugs and behavior.* New York: Wiley.

Leavy, R. L. (1983). Social support and psychological disorder: A review. *Journal of Community Psychology, 11,* 3–21.

LeBoeuf, M. (1980). *Imagineering.* New York: McGraw-Hill.

Leeper, R. W. (1935). A study of a neglected portion of the field of learning: The development of sensory organization. *Journal of Genetic Psychology, 46,* 41–75.

Leff, J., & Vaughn, C. (1981). The role of maintenance therapy and relatives' expressed emotion in relapse of schizophrenia: A two-year follow-up. *British Journal of Psychiatry, 139,* 102–104.

Leff, J., & Vaughn, C. (1985). *Expressed emotion in families.* New York: Guilford Press.

Legault, F., & Strayer, F. F. (1990). The emergence of sex-segregation in preschool peer groups. In F. F. Strayer (Ed.), *Social interaction and behavioral development during early childhood.* Montreal: La Maison D'Ethologie de Montreal.

Lehrer, P. M., & Woolfolk, R. L. (1984). Are stress reduction techniques interchangeable, or do they have specific effects? A review of the comparative empirical literature. In R. L. Woolfolk & P. M. Lehrer (Eds.), *Principles and practice of stress management.* New York: Guilford Press.

Leibovic, K. N. (1990). Vertebrate photoreceptors. In K. N. Leibovic (Ed.), *Science of vision.* New York: Springer-Verlag.

Le Magnen, J. (1990). A role for opiates in food reward and food addiction. In E. D. Capaldi & T. L. Powley (Eds.), *Taste, experience, and feeding.* Washington, DC: American Psychological Association.

Lennie, P., Trevarthen, C., Van Essen, D., & Wassle, H. (1990). Parallel processing of visual information. In L. Spillmann & J. S. Werner (Eds.), *Visual perception: The neurophysiological foundations.* San Diego: Academic Press.

Leo, J. (1987, January). Exploring the traits of twins. *Time,* p. 63.

Lester, B. M., Corwin, M. J., Sepkoski, C., Seifer, R., Peucker, M., McLaughlin, S., & Golub, H. L.

(1991). Neurobehavioral syndromes in cocaine-exposed newborn infants. *Child Development, 62*, 694–705.

LeVay, S. (1991). A difference in hypothalamic structure between heterosexual and homosexual men. *Science, 253*, 1034–1037.

Levenson, R. W. (1992). Autonomic nervous system differences among emotions. *Psychological Science, 3*, 23–27.

Levin, S., Yurgelun-Todd, D., & Craft, S. (1989). Contributions of clinical neuropsychology to the study of schizophrenia. *Journal of Abnormal Psychology, 98*, 341–356.

Levinson, D. J., with Darrow, C. M., Klein, E. G., Levinson, M. H., & McKee, B. (1978). *The seasons of a man's life.* New York: Knopf.

Levis, D. J. (1989). The case for a return to a two-factor theory of avoidance: The failure of non-fear interpretations. In S. B. Klein & R. R. Bowrer (Eds.), *Contemporary learning theories: Pavlovian conditioning and the status of traditional learning theory.* Hillsdale, NJ: Erlbaum.

Levy, J. (1985, May). Right brain, left brain: Fact or fiction. *Psychology Today*, pp. 38–44.

Levy, J., Trevarthen, C., & Sperry, R. W. (1972). Perception of bilateral chimeric figures following hemispheric disconnection. *Brain, 95*, 61–78.

Levy, S. M. (1985). *Behavior and cancer.* San Francisco: Jossey-Bass.

Lewin, K. (1935). *A dynamic theory of personality.* New York: McGraw-Hill.

Lewinsohn, P. M., Duncan, E. M., Stanton, A. K., & Hautzinger, M. (1986). Age at first onset for nonbipolar depression. *Journal of Abnormal Psychology, 95*, 378–383.

Lewinsohn, P. M., Hoberman, H., Teri, L., & Hautzinger, M. (1985). An integrative theory of depression. In S. Reiss & R. R. Bootzin (Eds.), *Theoretical issues in behavior therapy.* New York: Academic Press.

Lewinsohn, P. M., Rohde, P., Seeley, J. R., & Fischer, S. A. (1993). Age-cohort changes in the lifetime occurrence of depression and other mental disorders. *Journal of Abnormal Psychology, 102*, 110–120.

Lewis, D. O., Pincus, J. H., Feldman, M., Jackson, L., & Bard, B. (1986). Psychiatric, neurological, and psychoeducational characteristics of 15 death row inmates in the United States. *American Journal of Psychiatry, 143*, 838–845.

Lewis, J. M., Owen, M. T., & Cox, M. J. (1988). The transition to parenthood: III. Incorporation of the child into the family. *Family Process, 27*, 411–421.

Lewis, M., & Feiring, C. (1989). Infant, mother, and mother-infant interaction behavior and subsequent attachment. *Child Development, 60*, 831–837.

Lewis-Fernandez, R., & Kleinman, A. (1994). Culture, personality, and psychology. *Journal of Abnormal Psychology, 103*, 67–71.

Lewontin, R. C. (1976). Race and intelligence. In N. J. Block & G. Dworkin (Eds.), *The IQ controversy: Critical readings.* New York: Pantheon.

Lewontin, R. C., Rose, S., & Kamin, L. (1984). *Not in our genes: Biology, ideology and human nature.* New York: Pantheon.

Liberman, R. P., & Bedell, J. R. (1989). Behavior therapy. In H. I. Kaplan & B. J. Sadock (Eds.), *Comprehensive textbook of psychiatry/V.* Baltimore: Williams & Wilkins.

Liberman, R. P., Mueser, K. T., & DeRisi, W. J.

(1989). *Social skills training for psychiatric patients.* New York: Pergamon Press.

Libman, H. (1992). Pathogenesis, natural history, and classification of HIV infection. *Primary Care, 19*(1), 1–17.

Lichtenstein, E. (1980). *Psychotherapy: Approaches and applications.* Pacific Grove, CA: Brooks/Cole.

Lichtenstein, S., Fischhoff, B., & Phillips, L. D. (1982). Calibration of probabilities: The state of the art to 1980. In D. Kahneman, P. Slovic, & A. Tversky (Eds.), *Judgment under uncertainty: Heuristics and biases.* Cambridge: Cambridge University Press.

Lickey, M. E., & Gordon, B. (1991). *Medicine and mental illness: The use of drugs in psychiatry.* New York: W. H. Freeman.

Liebert, R. M., & Spiegler, M. D. (1990). *Personality: Strategies and issues.* Pacific Grove, CA: Brooks/Cole.

Lindgren, H. C. (1969). *The psychology of college success: A dynamic approach.* New York: Wiley.

Lindsay, D. S. (1993). Eyewitness suggestibility. *Current Directions in Psychological Science, 2*(3), 86–89.

Lindsay, D. S., & Johnson, M. K. (1989). The eyewitness suggestibility effects and memory for source. *Memory & Cognition, 17*, 349–358.

Lindsay, D. S., & Johnson, M. K. (1991). Recognition memory and source monitoring. *Bulletin of the Psychonomic Society, 29*, 203–205.

Lindsay, P. H., & Norman, D. A. (1977). *Human information processing.* New York: Academic Press.

Linn, M. C., & Hyde, J. S. (1989). Gender, mathematics, and science. *Educational Researcher, 18*(8), 17–19, 22–27.

Linn, M. C., & Petersen, A. C. (1986). A meta-analysis of gender differences in spatial ability: Implications for mathematics and science achievement. In J. S. Hyde & M. C. Linn (Eds.), *The psychology of gender: Advances through meta-analysis.* Baltimore: Johns Hopkins University Press.

Lippa, R. A. (1994). *Introduction to social psychology.* Pacific Grove, CA: Brooks/Cole.

Lipsey, M. W., & Wilson, D. B. (1993). The efficacy of psychological, educational, and behavioral treatment: Confirmation from meta-analysis. *American Psychologist, 48*, 1181–1209.

Litt, I. F., & Vaughan, V. C., III. (1992). Adolescence. In R. E. Behrman (Ed.), *Nelson textbook of pediatrics.* Philadelphia: Saunders.

Livingstone, M., & Hubel, D. (1988). Segregation of form, color, movement, and depth: Anatomy, physiology, and perception. *Science, 240*, 740–749.

Lloyd, M. A. (1985). *Adolescence.* New York: HarperCollins.

Locke, D. C. (1992). *Increasing multicultural understanding: A comprehensive model.* Newbury Park, CA: Sage.

Lockhart, R. S. (1992). Measurement of memory. In L. R. Squire (Ed.), *Encyclopedia of learning and memory.* New York: Macmillan.

Lockhart, R. S., & Craik, F. I. (1990). Levels of processing: A retrospective commentary on a framework for memory research. *Canadian Journal of Psychology, 44*(1), 87–112.

Locurto, C. (1990). The malleability of IQ as judged from adoption studies. *Intelligence, 14*, 275–292.

Locurto, C. (1991). *Sense and nonsense about IQ: The case for uniqueness.* New York: Praeger.

Loehlin, J. C. (1989). Partitioning environmental

and genetic contributions to behavioral development. *American Psychologist, 44*, 1285–1292.

Loehlin, J. C. (1992). *Genes and environment in personality development.* Newbury Park, CA: Sage.

Loftus, E. F. (1979). *Eyewitness testimony.* Cambridge, MA: Harvard University Press.

Loftus, E. F. (1992). When a lie becomes memory's truth: Memory distortion after exposure to misinformation. *Current Directions in Psychological Science, 1*, 121–123.

Loftus, E. F. (1993). The reality of repressed memories. *American Psychologist, 48*, 518–537.

Loftus, E. F., & Loftus, G. R. (1980). On the permanence of stored information in the human brain. *American Psychologist, 35*, 409–420.

Loftus, E. F., & Palmer, J. C. (1974). Reconstruction of automobile destruction: An example of the interaction between language and memory. *Journal of Verbal Learning and Verbal Behavior, 13*, 585–589.

Logue, A. W. (1991). *The psychology of eating and drinking* (2nd ed.). New York: W. H. Freeman.

Lohman, D. F. (1989). Human intelligence: An introduction to advances in theory and research. *Review of Educational Research, 59*(4), 333–373.

Longman, D. G., & Atkinson, R. H. (1991). *College learning and study skills.* St. Paul, MN: West.

Longstreth, L. E. (1984). Jensen's reaction-time investigations of intelligence: A critique. *Intelligence, 8*, 139–160.

Lubkin, I. M. (1990). Illness roles. In I. M. Lubkin (Ed.), *Chronic illness: Impact and interventions* (2nd ed.). Boston: Jones and Bartlett.

Luborsky, L., Singer, B., & Luborsky, L. (1975). Comparative studies of psychotherapies: Is it true that everyone has won and all must have prizes? *Archives of General Psychiatry, 32*, 995–1008.

Luchins, A. S. (1942). Mechanization in problem solving. *Psychological Monographs, 54*(6, Whole No. 248).

Lumsdaine, A., & Janis, I. (1953). Resistance to counterpropaganda presentation. *Public Opinion Quarterly, 17*, 311–318.

Lutz, C. (1987). Goals, events and understanding in Ifaluk emotion theory. In N. Quinn & D. Holland (Eds.), *Cultural models in language and thought.* Cambridge, England: Cambridge University Press.

Lykken, D. T. (1981). *A tremor in the blood: Uses and abuses of the lie detector.* New York: McGraw-Hill.

Lykken, D. T., McGue, M., Tellegen, A., & Bouchard, T. J., Jr. (1992). Emergenesis: Genetic traits that may not run in families. *American Psychologist, 47*, 1565–1577.

Lyness, S. A. (1993). Predictors of differences between Type A and Type B individuals in heart rate and blood pressure reactivity. *Psychological Bulletin, 114*, 266–295.

Lynn, R. (1987). The intelligence of the mongoloids: A psychometric, evolutionary and neurological theory. *Personality and Individual Differences, 8*, 813–844.

Lynn, R. (1991). Educational achievements of Asian Americans. *American Psychologist, 46*(8), 875–876.

Maccoby, E. E., & Jacklin, C. N. (1974). *The psychology of sex differences.* Stanford, CA: Stanford University Press.

Machung, A. (1989). Talking career, thinking job: Gender differences in career and family expectations of Berkeley seniors. *Family Studies, 15*, 35–58.

Mackenzie, B. (1984). Explaining race differences in IQ: The logic, the methodology, and the evidence. *American Psychologist, 39*, 1214–1233.

MacLean, P. D. (1954). Studies on limbic system ("viosceal brain") and their bearing on psychosomatic problems. In E. D. Wittkower & R. A. Cleghorn (Eds.), *Recent developments in psychosomatic medicine*. Philadelphia: Lippincott.

MacQueen, G., Marshall, J., Perdue, M., Siegel, S., & Bienenstock, J. (1989). Pavlovian conditioning of rat mucosal mast cells to secrete rat mast cell protease II. *Science, 243*, 83–86.

Macrae, C. N., Milne, A. B., & Bodenhausen, G. V. (1994). Stereotypes as energy-saving devices: A peek inside the cognitive toolbox. *Journal of Personality and Social Psychology, 66*, 37–47.

Maddi, S. R. (1989). *Personality theories: A comparative analysis*. Chicago, IL: Dorsey Press.

Madsen, K. B. (1968). *Theories of motivation*. Copenhagen: Munksgaard.

Madsen, K. B. (1973). Theories of motivation. In B. B. Wolman (Ed.), *Handbook of general psychology*. Englewood Cliffs, NJ: Prentice-Hall.

Maguire, W., Weisstein, N., & Klymenko, V. (1990). From visual structure to perceptual function. In K. N. Leibovic (Ed.), *Science of vision*. New York: Springer-Verlag.

Maier, N. R. F. (1931). Reasoning and learning. *Psychological Review, 38*, 332–346.

Main, D. M., & Main, E. K. (1991). Preterm birth. In S. G. Gabbe, J. R. Niebyl, & J. L. Simpson (Eds.), *Obstetrics: Normal and problem pregnancies*. New York: Churchill Livingstone.

Malcolm, J. (1980: Pt. 1, Nov. 24; Pt. 2, Dec. 1). The impossible profession. *The New Yorker*, pp. 55–133, 54–152.

Malina, R. M. (1990). Physical growth and performance during the transitional years (9–16). In R. Montemayor, G. R. Adams, & T. P. Gullotta (Eds.), *From childhood to adolescence: A transitional period?* Newbury Park, CA: Sage.

Malloy, M. H., Kao, T., & Lee, Y. J. (1992). Analyzing the effect of prenatal care on pregnancy outcome: A conditional approach. *American Journal of Public Health, 82*, 448–453.

Mandler, G. (1984). *Mind and body*. New York: Norton.

Mandler, G. (1989). Memory: Conscious and unconscious. In P. R. Soloman, G. R. Goethals, C. M. Kelley, & B. R. Stephens (Eds.), *Memory: Interdisciplinary approaches*. New York: Springer-Verlag.

Mandler, G. (1993). Thought, memory, and learning: Effects of emotional stress. In L. Goldberger & S. Breznitz (Eds.), *Handbook of stress: Theoretical and clinical aspects* (2nd ed.). New York: Free Press.

Mangelsdorf, S., Gunnar, M., Kestenbaum, R., Lang, S., & Andreas, D. (1990). Infant proneness-to-distress temperament, maternal personality, and mother-infant attachment: Associations and goodness of fit. *Child Development, 61*, 830–831.

Maratsos, M. (1983). Some current issues in the study of the acquisition of grammar. In J. H. Flavell & E. M. Markman (Eds.), *Handbook of child psychology* (Vol. 3). New York: Wiley.

Marcia, J. E. (1966). Development and validation of ego identity status. *Journal of Personality and Social Psychology, 3*, 551–558.

Marcia, J. E. (1980). Identity in adolescence. In J. Adelson (Ed.), *Handbook of adolescent psychology*. New York: Wiley.

Markowitsch, H. J., & Pritzel, M. (1985). The neuropathology of amnesia. *Progress in Neurobiology, 25*, 189–287.

Marks, I. M. (1987). *Fears, phobias, and rituals: Panic, anxiety, and their disorders*. New York: Oxford University Press.

Markus, H. R., & Kitayama, S. (1991). Culture and the self: Implications for cognition, emotion, and motivation. *Psychological Review, 98*, 224–253.

Marsella, A. J. (1979). Cross-cultural studies of mental disorders. In A. J. Marsella, R. Tharp, & T. Ciborowski (Eds.), *Perspectives in cross-cultural psychology*. New York: Academic Press.

Martin, C. L., & Halverson, C. F., Jr. (1987). The role of cognition in sex role acquisition. In D. B. Carter (Ed.), *Current conceptions of sex roles and sex typing: Theory and research*. New York: Praeger.

Martin, L. (1986). "Eskimo words for snow": A case study in the genesis and decay of an anthropological example. *American Psychologist, 88*, 418–423.

Martin, R. A., & Lefcourt, H. M. (1983). Sense of humor as a moderator of the relation between stressors and moods. *Journal of Personality and Social Psychology, 45*, 1313–1324.

Maser, J. D., Kaelber, C., & Weise, R. E. (1991). International use and attitudes toward DSM-III and DSM-III-R: Growing consensus in psychiatric classification. *Journal of Abnormal Psychology, 100*, 271–279.

Maslow, A. H. (1954). *Motivation and personality*. New York: Harper & Row.

Maslow, A. H. (1962). *Toward a psychology of being*. Princeton, NJ: Van Nostrand.

Maslow, A. H. (1968). *Toward a psychology of being*. New York: Van Nostrand.

Maslow, A. H. (1970). *Motivation and personality*. New York: Harper & Row.

Maslow, A. H. (1971). *Farther reaches of human nature*. New York: Viking Penguin.

Mason, J. W. (1975). A historical view of the stress field, Part II. *Journal of Human Stress, 1*, 22–36.

Masters, W. H., & Johnson, V. E. (1966). *Human sexual response*. Boston: Little, Brown.

Masters, W. H., & Johnson, V. E. (1970). *Human sexual inadequacy*. Boston: Little, Brown.

Matarazzo, J. D. (1992). Psychological testing and assessment in the 21st century. *American Psychologist, 47*, 1007–1018.

Matlin, M. W. (1989). *Cognition*. New York: Holt, Rinehart & Winston.

Matsumoto, D. (1994). *People: Psychology from a cultural perspective*. Pacific Grove, CA: Brooks/Cole.

Matthews, K. A. (1992). Myths and realities of the menopause. *Psychosomatic Medicine, 54*(1), 1–9.

Mayer, J. (1955). Regulation of energy intake and the body weight: The glucostatic theory and the lipostatic hypothesis. *Annals of the New York Academy of Science, 63*, 15–43.

Mayer, J. (1968). *Overweight: Causes and control*. Englewood Cliffs, NJ: Prentice-Hall.

Mays, V. M., & Albee, G. W. (1992). Psychotherapy and ethnic minorities. In D. K. Freedheim (Ed.), *History of psychotherapy: A century of change*. Washington, DC: American Psychological Association.

Mazur, J. E. (1993). Predicting the strength of a conditioned reinforcer: Effects of delay and uncertainty. *Current Directions in Psychological Science, 2*(3), 70–74.

McBride, P. E. (1992). The health consequences of smoking: Cardiovascular diseases. *Medical Clinics of North America, 76*, 333–353.

McCabe, A., & Lipscomb, T. J. (1988). Sex differences in children's verbal aggression. *Merrill-Palmer Quarterly, 34*, 389–401.

McCarty, D., Argeriou, M., Huebner, R. B., & Lubran, B. (1991). Alcoholism, drug abuse, and the homeless. *American Psychologist, 46*, 1139–1148.

McClearn, G. E., Plomin, R., Gora-Maslak, G., & Crabbe, J. C. (1991). The gene chase in behavioral science. *Psychological Science, 2*, 222–229.

McClelland, D. C. (1965). Achievement and entrepreneurship: A longitudinal study. *Journal of Personality and Social Psychology, 1*, 389–392.

McClelland, D. C. (1973). Testing for competence rather than for "intelligence." *American Psychologist, 28*, 1–14.

McClelland, D. C. (1975). *Power: The inner experience*. New York: Irvington.

McClelland, D. C. (1985). How motives, skills and values determine what people do. *American Psychologist, 40*, 812–825.

McClelland, D. C. (1987). Characteristics of successful entrepreneurs. *Journal of Creative Behavior, 3*, 219–233.

McClelland, D. C. (1993). Intelligence is not the best predictor of job performance. *Current Directions in Psychological Science, 2*(1), 5–6.

McClelland, D. C., Atkinson, J. W., Clark, R. A., & Lowell, E. L. (1953). *The achievement motive*. New York: Appleton-Century-Crofts.

McClelland, D. C., & Boyatzis, R. E. (1982). The leadership motive pattern and long-term success in management. *Journal of Applied Psychology, 67*, 737–743.

McClelland, D. C., & Koestner, R. (1992). The achievement motive. In C. P. Smith (Ed.), *Motivation and personality: Handbook of thematic content analysis*. New York: Cambridge University Press.

McCloskey, M., Wible, C. G., & Cohen, N. J. (1988). Is there a special flashbulb-memory mechanism? *Journal of Experimental Psychology: General, 117*, 171–181.

McConnell, J. V. (1962). Memory transfer through cannibalism in planarians. *Journal of Neuropsychiatry, 3*(Suppl. 1), 542–548.

McCrae, R. R. (1984). Situational determinants of coping responses: Loss, threat and challenge. *Journal of Personality and Social Psychology, 46*, 919–928.

McCrae, R. R., & Costa, P. T., Jr. (1984). *Emerging lives, enduring dispositions: Personality in adulthood*. Boston: Little, Brown.

McCrae, R. R., & Costa, P. T., Jr. (1985). Updating Norman's "adequate taxonomy": Intelligence and personality dimensions in natural language and in questionnaires. *Journal of Personality and Social Psychology, 49*, 710–721.

McCrae, R. R., & Costa, P. T., Jr. (1987). Validation of the five-factor model of personality across instruments and observers. *Journal of Personality and Social Psychology, 52*, 81–90.

McCrae R. R., & Costa, P. T., Jr. (1990). *Personality in adulthood*. New York: Guilford Press.

McDaniel, M. A., & Einstein, G. O. (1986). Bizarre imagery as an effective memory aid: The importance of distinctiveness. *Journal of Experimental Psychology: Learning, Memory & Cognition, 12*, 54–65.

McGaugh, J. L. (1989). Modulation of memory storage processes. In P. R. Soloman, G. R. Goethals, C. M. Kelley, & B. R. Stephens (Eds.), *Memory: Interdisciplinary approaches*. New York: Springer-Verlag.

McGaugh, J. L. (1992). Hormones and memory. In L. R. Squire (Ed.), *Encyclopedia of learning and memory*. New York: Macmillan.

McGeoch, J. A., & McDonald, W. T. (1931). Meaningful relation and retroactive inhibition. *American Journal of Psychology, 43*, 579–588.

McGinnies, E., & Ward, C. D. (1980). Better liked than right: Trustworthiness and expertise as factors in credibility. *Personality and Social Psychology Bulletin, 6*, 467–472.

McGlashan, T. H., & Fenton, W. S. (1992). The positive-negative distinction in schizophrenia: Review of natural history validators. *Archives of General Psychiatry, 49*, 63–72.

McGlashan, T. H., Mohr, D. C., Beutler, L. E., Engle, D., Shoham-Salomon, V., Bergan, J., Kaszniak, A. W., & Yost, E. B. (1990). Identification of patients at risk for nonresponse and negative outcome in psychotherapy. *Journal of Consulting and Clinical Psychology, 58*, 622–628.

McGue, M., Bouchard, T. J., Jr., Iacono, W. G., & Lykken, D. T. (1993). Behavioral genetics of cognitive ability: A life-span perspective. In R. Plomin & G. E. McClearn (Eds.), *Nature, nurture and psychology*. Washington, DC: American Psychological Association.

McGuire, T. R., & Haviland, J. M. (1985). Further considerations for behavior-genetic analysis of humans. *Journal of Personality and Social Psychology, 49*, 1434–1436.

McGuire, W. J. (1985). Attitudes and attitude change. In G. Lindzey & E. Aronson (Eds.), *Handbook of social psychology* (Vol. 2). New York: Random House.

McHale, S. M., Bartko, W. T., Crouter, A. C., & Perry-Jenkins, M. (1990). Children's housework and psychosocial functioning: The mediating effects of parents' sex-role behaviors and attitudes. *Child Development, 61*, 1413–1426.

McHugh, P. R., & Moran, T. H. (1985). The stomach: A conception of its dynamic role in satiety. *Progress in Psychobiology and Physiological Psychology*, pp. 197–232.

McIntosh, J. L. (1991). Epidemiology of suicide in the U.S. In A. A. Leenaars (Ed.), *Life span perspectives of suicide*. New York: Plenum.

McKean, K. (1985, June). Decisions, decisions. *Discover*, pp. 22–31.

McKenna, J. J. (1993). Co-sleeping. In M. A. Carskadon (Ed.), *Encyclopedia of sleep and dreaming*. New York: Macmillan.

McKhann, G. M. (1987). Multiple sclerosis. In G. Adelman (Ed.), *Encyclopedia of Neuroscience*. Boston: Birkhauser.

McKinlay, J. B., McKinlay, S. M., & Brambilla, D. (1987). The relative contributions of endocrine changes and social circumstances to depression in mid-aged women. *Journal of Health and Social Behavior, 28*(4), 345–363.

McNally, R. J. (1987). Preparedness and phobias: A review. *Psychological Bulletin, 101*, 283–303.

McNally, R. J. (1990). Psychological approaches to panic disorder: A review. *Psychological Bulletin, 108*, 403–419.

McNeill, D. (1970). *The acquisition of language: The study of developmental psycholinguistics*. New York: Harper & Row.

Mechanic, D. (1980). *Mental health and social policy*. Englewood Cliffs, NJ: Prentice-Hall.

Mednick, S. A., & Mednick, M. T. (1967). *Examiner's manual, Remote Associates Test*. Boston, MA: Houghton Mifflin.

Meehan, P. J., Lamb, J. A., Saltzman, L. E., & O'Carroll, P. W. (1992). Attempted suicide among young adults: Progress toward a meaningful estimate of prevalence. *American Journal of Psychiatry, 149*, 41–44.

Meeker, W. R. & Barber, T. X. (1971). Toward an explanation of stage hypnosis. *Journal of Abnormal Psychology, 77*, 61–70.

Meindl, J. R., & Lerner, M. J. (1984). Exacerbation of extreme responses to an out-group. *Journal of Personality and Social Psychology, 47*, 71–84.

Mellinger, G. D., Balter, M. B., & Uhlenhuth, E. H. (1985). Insomnia and its treatment: Prevalence and correlations. *Archives of General Psychiatry, 42*, 225–232.

Meltzoff, A. N., & Gopnik, A. (1989). On linking nonverbal imitation, representation, and language learning in the first two years of life. In G. E. Speidel & K. E. Nelson (Eds.), *The many faces of imitation in language learning*. New York: Springer-Verlag.

Melzack, R., & Wall, P. D. (1965). Pain mechanisms: A new theory. *Science, 150*, 971–979.

Melzack, R., & Wall, P. D. (1982). *The challenge of pain*. New York: Basic Books.

Mendelson, W. B. (1987). *Human sleep: Research and clinical care*. New York: Plenum.

Mendelson, W. B. (1990). Insomnia: The patient and the pill. In R. R. Bootzin, J. F. Kihlstrom, & D. L. Schacter (Eds.), *Sleep and cognition*. Washington, DC: American Psychological Association.

Mendelson, W. B. (1993). Sleeping pills. In M. A. Carskadon (Ed.), *Encyclopedia of sleep and dreaming*. New York: Macmillan.

Mentzer, R. L. (1982). Response biases in multiple-choice test item files. *Educational and Psychological Measurement, 42*, 437–448.

Mercer, J. R. (1975). Sociocultural factors in educational labeling. In M. J. Begab & S. A. Richardson (Eds.), *The mentally retarded and society: A social science perspective*. Baltimore: University Park Press.

Merckelbach, H., De Ruiter, C., Van Den Hout, M. A., & Hoekstra, R. (1989). Conditioning experiences and phobias. *Behavior Research and Therapy, 27*(6), 657–662.

Meredith, M. A., & Stein, B. E. (1983). Interactions among converging sensory inputs in the superior colliculus. *Science, 221*, 389–391.

Meyer, D. E., & Schvaneveldt, R. W. (1976). Meaning, memory structure, and mental processes. *Science, 192*, 27–33.

Meyer, R. G. (1992). *Practical clinical hypnosis: Techniques and applications*. New York: Lexington Books.

Middlebrooks, J. C., & Knudsen, E. I. (1984). A neural code for auditory space in the cat's superior colliculus. *The Journal of Neuroscience, 4*, 2621–2634.

Milgram, S. (1963). Behavioral study of obedience. *Journal of Abnormal and Social Psychology, 67*, 371–378.

Milgram, S. (1964). Issues in the study of obedience. *American Psychologist, 19*, 848–852.

Milgram, S. (1968). Reply to the critics. *International Journal of Psychiatry, 6*, 294–295.

Milgram, S. (1974). *Obedience to authority*. New York: Harper & Row.

Miller, A. G. (1986). *The obedience experiments: A case study of controversy in social science*. New York: Praeger.

Miller, G. A. (1956). The magical number seven, plus or minus two: Some limits on our capacity for processing information. *Psychological Review, 63*, 81–97.

Miller, G. A. (1991). *The science of words*. New York: Scientific American Library.

Miller, J. G. (1984). Culture and the development of everyday social explanation. *Journal of Personality and Social Psychology, 46*, 961–978.

Miller, N. E. (1941). The frustration-aggression hypothesis. *Psychological Review, 48*, 337–342.

Miller, N. E. (1944). Experimental studies of conflict. In J. M. Hunt (Ed.), *Personality and the behavior disorders* (Vol. 1). New York: Ronald.

Miller, N. E. (1959). Liberalization of basic S-R concepts: Extension to conflict behavior, motivation, and social learning. In S. Koch (Ed.), *Psychology: A study of a science* (Vol. 2). New York: McGraw-Hill.

Miller, N. E. (1985). The value of behavioral research on animals. *American Psychologist, 40*, 423–440.

Miller, P. H. (1989). *Theories of developmental psychology*. New York: W. H. Freeman.

Miller, P. M., & Fagley, N. S. (1991). The effects of framing, problem variations, and providing rationale on choice. *Personality and Social Psychology Bulletin, 17*(5), 517–522.

Miller, T. Q., Turner, C. W., Tindale, R. S., Posavac, E. J., & Dugoni, B. L. (1991). Reasons for the trend toward null findings in research on Type A behavior. *Psychological Bulletin, 110*, 469–485.

Millman, J., Bishop, C. H., & Ebel, R. (1965). An analysis of test-wiseness. *Educational and Psychological Measurement, 25*, 707–726.

Millstone, E. (1989). Methods and practices of animal experimentation. In G. Langley (Ed.), *Animal experimentation: The consensus changes*. New York: Chapman & Hall.

Mischel, W. (1961). Delay of gratification, need for achievement, and acquiescence in another culture. *Journal of Abnormal and Social Psychology, 62*, 543–552.

Mischel, W. (1968). *Personality and assessment*. New York: Wiley.

Mischel, W. (1973). Toward a cognitive social learning conceptualization of personality. *Psychological Review, 80*, 252–283.

Mischel, W. (1984). Convergences and challenges in the search for consistency. *American Psychologist, 39*, 351–364.

Mischel, W. (1990). Personality dispositions revisited and revised: A view after three decades. In L. A. Pervin (Ed.), *Handbook of personality: Theory and research*. New York: Guilford Press.

Mischel, W., & Mischel, H. N. (1976). A cognitive social learning approach to morality and self-regulation. In T. Lickona (Ed.), *Moral development and behavior: Theory, research and social issues*. New York: Holt, Rinehart & Winston.

Mishkin, M., & Appenzeller, T. (1987). The anatomy of memory. *Scientific American, 256*, 80–89.

Mishkin, M., Malamut, B., & Backevalier, J. (1984). Memories and habits: Two neural systems. In G. Lynch, J. L. McGaugh, & N. M. Weinberger (Eds.), *The neurobiology of learning and memory*. New York: Guilford Press.

Mitler, M. M. (1993). Public safety in the workplace. In M. A. Carskadon (Ed.), *Encyclopedia of sleep and dreaming*. New York: Macmillan.

Moates, D. R., & Schumacher, G. M. (1980). *An introduction to cognitive psychology*. Belmont, CA: Wadsworth.

Moghaddam, F. M., Taylor, D. M., & Wright,

S. C. (1993). *Social psychology in cross-cultural perspective*. New York: W. H. Freeman.

Moline, M. L. (1993). Jet lag. In M. A. Carskadon (Ed.), *Encyclopedia of sleep and dreaming*. New York: Macmillan.

Money, J., & Erhardt, A. A. (1972). *Man and woman, boy and girl: Differentiation and dimorphism of gender identity*. Baltimore: Johns Hopkins University Press.

Montemayor, R. (1986). Family variation in parent-adolescent storm and stress. *Journal of Adolescent Research, 1*, 15–31.

Moore, K. L., & Persaud, T. V. N. (1993). *Before we are born*. Philadelphia: Saunders.

Moore, R. Y. (1990). The circadian system and sleep-wake behavior. In J. Montplaisir & R. Godbout (Eds.), *Sleep and biological rhythms: Basic mechanisms and applications to psychiatry*. New York: Oxford University Press.

Moore-Ede, M. C., Sulzman, F. M., & Fuller, C. A. (1982). *The clocks that time us*. Cambridge, MA: Harvard University Press.

Moos, R. H., & Schaefer, J. A. (1993). Coping resources and processes: Current concepts and measures. In L. Goldberger & S. Breznitz (Eds.), *Handbook of stress: Theoretical and clinical aspects* (2nd ed.). New York: Free Press.

Morgan, C. D., & Murray, H. A. (1935). A method for investigating fantasies: The Thematic Apperception Test. *Archives of Neurology and Psychiatry, 34*, 289–306.

Morris, D. C. (1991, September). Cocaine heart disease. *Hospital Practice*, pp. 81–90.

Mortensen, M. E., Sever, L. E., & Oakley, G. P., Jr. (1991). Teratology and the epidemiology of birth defects. In S. G. Gabbe, J. R. Niebyl, & J. L. Simpson (Eds.), *Obstetrics: Normal and problem pregnancies*. New York: Churchill Livingstone.

Mott, S. R., Fazekas, N. F., & James, S. R. (1985). *Nursing care of children and families: A holistic approach*. Reading, MA: Addison-Wesley.

Mowrer, O. H. (1947). On the dual nature of learning: A reinterpretation of "conditioning" and "problem-solving." *Harvard Educational Review, 17*, 102–150.

Mozell, M. M., Smith, B. P., Smith P. E., Sullivan, R. L., & Swender, P. (1969). Nasal chemoreception in flavor identification. *Archives of Otolaryngology, 90*, 367–373.

Muldoon, M. F., Manuck, S. B., & Matthews, K. A. (1990). Effects of cholesterol lowering on mortality: A quantitative review of primary prevention trials. *British Medical Journal, 301*, 309–314.

Multon, K. D., Brown, S. D., & Lent, R. W. (1991). Relation of self-efficacy beliefs to academic outcomes: A meta-analytic investigation. *Journal of Counseling Psychology, 38*, 30–38.

Mumford, M. D., & Gustafson, S. B. (1988). Creativity syndrome: Integration, application, and innovation. *Psychological Bulletin, 103*, 27–43.

Murphy, J. M. (1976). Psychiatric labeling in cross-cultural perspective. *Science, 191*, 1019–1028.

Murray, H. A. (1938). *Explorations in personality*. New York: Oxford University Press.

Murstein, B. I., & Fontaine, P. A. (1993). The public's knowledge about psychologists and other mental health professionals. *American Psychologist, 48*, 839–845.

Myers, B. J. (1987). Mother-infant bonding as a critical period. In M. H. Bornstein (Ed.), *Sensitive periods in development: Interdisciplinary perspectives*. Hillsdale, NJ: Erlbaum.

Myers, D. G., & Lamm, H. (1976). The group polarization phenomenon. *Psychological Bulletin, 83*, 602–627.

Myerson, J., Hale, S., Wagstaff, D., Poon, L. W., & Smith, G. A. (1990). The information-loss model: A mathematical theory of age-related cognitive slowing. *Psychological Review, 97*, 475–487.

Nash, M. R. (1987). What, if anything, is regressed about hypnotic age regression? *Psychological Bulletin, 102*, 42–52.

Neale, M. A., & Northcraft, G. B. (1986). Experts, amateurs, and refrigerators: Comparing expert and amateur negotiators in a novel task. *Organizational Behavior and Human Decision Processes, 38*, 305–317.

Neely, J. H. (1989). Experimental dissociations and the episodic/semantic memory distinction. In H. L. Roediger, III, & F. I. M. Craik (Eds.), *Varieties of memory and consciousness*. Hillsdale, NJ: Erlbaum.

Neiss, R. (1988). Reconceptualizing arousal: Psychobiological states in motor performance. *Psychological Bulletin, 103*, 345–366.

Neiss, R. (1990). Ending arousal's reign of error: A reply to Anderson. *Psychological Bulletin, 107*, 101–105.

Neisser, U. (1967). *Cognitive psychology*. New York: Appleton-Century-Crofts.

Neisser, U., & Harsch, N. (1992). Phantom flashbulbs: False recollections of hearing the news about *Challenger*. In E. Winograd & U. Neisser (Eds.), *Affect and accuracy in recall: Studies of "flashbulb" memories*. New York: Cambridge University Press.

Nelson, T. O. (1978). Detecting small amounts of information in memory: Savings for nonrecognized items. *Journal of Experimental Psychology: Human Learning and Memory, 4*, 453–468.

Nemeth, C., & Chiles, C. (1988). Modelling courage: The role dissent in fostering independence. *European Journal of Social Psychology, 18*, 275–280.

Nemiah, J. C. (1985). Somatoform disorders. In H. I. Kaplan & B. J. Sadock (Eds.), *Comprehensive textbook of psychiatry/IV*. Baltimore: Williams & Wilkins.

Newcomb, P. A., & Carbone, P. P. (1992). The health consequences of smoking: Cancer. *Medical Clinics of North America, 76*, 305–331.

Newcombe, N., & Huttenlocher, J. (1992). Children's early ability to solve perspective-taking problems. *Developmental Psychology, 28*, 635–643.

Newell, A., Shaw, J. C., & Simon, H. A. (1958). Elements of a theory of human problem solving. *Psychological Review, 65*, 151–166.

Newsom, C., Favell, J. E., & Rincover, A. (1983). Side effects of punishment. In S. Axelrod & J. Apsche (Eds.), *The effects of punishment on human behavior*. New York: Academic Press.

Nezu, A. M., Nezu, C. M., & Blissett, S. E. (1988). Sense of humor as a moderator of the relation between stressful events and psychological distress: A prospective analysis. *Journal of Personality and Social Psychology, 54*, 520–525.

Nicholson, I. R., & Neufeld, R. W. J. (1993). Classification of the schizophrenias according to symptomatology: A two-factor model. *Journal of Abnormal Psychology, 102*, 259–270.

Nickerson, R. S., & Adams, M. J. (1979). Long-term memory for a common object. *Cognitive Psychology, 11*, 287–307.

Niebyl, J. R. (1991). Drugs in pregnancy and lactation. In S. G. Gabbe, J. R. Niebyl, & J. L. Simpson (Eds.), *Obstetrics: Normal and problem pregnancies*. New York: Churchill Livingstone.

Niijima, A. (1982). Glucose-sensitive afferent nerve fibers in the hepatic branch of the vagus nerve in the guinea pig. *Journal of Physiology, 332*, 315–323.

Nisbett, R. E. (1972). Hunger, obesity, and the ventromedial hypothalamus. *Psychological Review, 79*, 433–453.

Niswander, K. R. (1982). Prenatal care. In R. C. Benson (Ed.), *Current obstetric and gynecologic diagnosis and treatment*. Los Altos, CA: Lange Medical Publications.

Nolen-Hoeksema, S. (1990). *Sex differences in depression*. Stanford, CA: Stanford University Press.

Nolen-Hoeksema, S. (1991). Responses to depression and their effects on the duration of depressive episodes. *Journal of Abnormal Psychology, 100*, 569–582.

Norcross, J. C., & Goldfried, M. R. (Eds.). (1992). *Handbook of psychotherapy integration*. New York: Basic Books.

Norcross, J. C., & Prochaska, J. O. (1982). National survey of clinical psychologists: Affiliations and orientations. *Clinical Psychologist, 35*(3), 1, 4–6.

Norman, T. R., & Burrows, G. D. (1990). Buspirone for the treatment of generalized anxiety disorder. In R. Noyes, Jr., M. Roth, & G. D. Burrows (Eds.), *Handbook of anxiety: The treatment of anxiety* (Vol. 4). Amsterdam: Elsevier.

Novin, D., Robinson, B. A., Culbreth, L. A., & Tordoff, M. G. (1983). Is there a role for the liver in the control of food intake? *American Journal of Clinical Nutrition, 9*, 233–246.

Nowlis, D. P., & Kamiya, J. (1970). The control of electroencephalographic alpha rhythms through auditory feedback and the associated mental activity. *Psychophysiology, 6*, 476–484.

Noyes, R., Jr. (1988). Revision of the DSM-III classification of anxiety disorders. In R. Noyes, Jr., M. Roth, & G. D. Burrows (Eds.), *Handbook of anxiety: Classification, etiological factors and associated disturbances* (Vol. 2). Amsterdam: Elsevier.

Nunnally, J. C. (1982). The study of human change: Measurement, research strategies, and methods of analysis. In B. B. Wolman (Ed.), *Handbook of developmental psychology*. Englewood Cliffs, NJ: Prentice-Hall.

Nurnberger, J. I., & Zimmerman, J. (1970). Applied analysis of human behavior: An alternative to conventional motivational inferences and unconscious determination in therapeutic programming. *Behavior Therapy, 1*, 59–69.

Oakland, T., & Parmelee, R. (1985). Mental measurement of minority-group children. In B. B. Wolman (Ed.), *Handbook of intelligence: Theories, measurements, and applications*. New York: Wiley.

Ochse, R. (1990). *Before the gates of excellence: The determinants of creative genius*. Cambridge, England: Cambridge University Press.

Offer, D., Ostrov, E., Howard, K. I., & Atkinson, R. (1988). *The teenage world: Adolescents' self-image in ten countries*. New York: Plenum.

Ogilvie, R. D., & Wilkinson, R. T. (1988). Behavioral versus EEG-based monitoring of all-night sleep/wake patterns. *Sleep, 11*(2), 139–155.

Ogilvie, R. D., Wilkinson, R. T., & Allison, S. (1989). The detection of sleep onset: Behavioral, physiological, and subjective convergence. *Sleep, 12*(5), 458–474.

Öhman, A. (1979). Fear relevance, autonomic conditioning, and phobias: A laboratory model. In P. O.

Sjoden & S. Bates (Eds.), *Trends in behavior therapy*. New York: Academic Press.

Öhman, A., & Soares, J. J. F. (1993). On the automatic nature of phobic fear: Conditioned electrodermal responses to masked fear-relevant stimuli. *Journal of Abnormal Psychology, 102*, 121–132.

O'Keefe, D. J. (1990). *Persuasion: Theory and research*. Newbury Park, CA: Sage.

Olds, J. (1956). Pleasure centers in the brain. *Scientific American, 193*, 105–116.

Olds, J., & Milner, P. (1954). Positive reinforcement produced by electrical stimulation of the septal area and other regions of the rat brain. *Journal of Comparative and Physiological Psychology, 47*, 419–427.

Olds, M. E., & Fobes, J. L. (1981). The central basis of motivation: Intracranial self-stimulation studies. *Annual Review of Psychology, 32*, 523–574.

O'Leary, K. D., Kent, R. N., & Kanowitz, J. (1975). Shaping data collection congruent with experimental hypotheses. *Journal of Applied Behavior Analysis, 8*, 43–51.

Olsho, L. W., Harkins, S. W., & Lenhardt, M. L. (1985). Aging and the auditory system. In J. E. Birren & K. W. Schaie (Eds.), *Handbook of the psychology of aging* (2nd ed.). New York: Van Nostrand Reinhold.

Oomura, Y. (1976). Significance of glucose insulin and free fatty acid on the hypothalamic feeding and satiety neurons. In D. Novin, W. Wyrwicka, & G. Bray (Eds.), *Hunger: Basic mechanisms and clinical applications*. New York: Raven.

Orme-Johnson, D. W. (1987). Transcendental meditation and reduced health care utilization. *Psychosomatic Medicine, 49*, 493–507.

Orne, M. T. (1951). The mechanisms of hypnotic age regression: An experimental study. *Journal of Abnormal and Social Psychology, 46*, 213–225.

Orne, M. T., & Dinges, D. F. (1989). Hypnosis. In H. I. Kaplan & B. J. Sadock (Eds.), *Comprehensive textbook of psychiatry/V* (Vol. 2). Baltimore: Williams & Wilkins.

Orne, M. T., & Holland, C. C. (1968). On the ecological validity of laboratory deceptions. *International Journal of Psychiatry, 6*, 282–293.

Ornstein, R. E. (1977). *The psychology of consciousness*. New York: Harcourt Brace Jovanovich.

Oskamp, S. (1991). *Attitudes and opinions*. Englewood Cliffs, NJ: Prentice Hall.

Öst, L. (1987). Age of onset in different phobias. *Journal of Abnormal Psychology, 96*, 223–229.

Oswald, I. (1974). *Sleep*. Middlesex, NY: Penguin.

Paffenbarger, R. S., Hyde, R. T., & Wing, A. L. (1990). Physical activity and physical fitness as determinants of health and longevity. In C. Bouchard, R. J. Shephard, T. Stephens, J. R. Sutton, & B. D. McPherson (Eds.), *Exercise, fitness, and health: A consensus of current knowledge*. Champaign, IL: Human Kinetics Books.

Pagel, M. D., Smilkstein, G., Regen, H., & Montano, D. (1990). Psychosocial influences on new-born outcomes: A controlled prospective study. *Social Science Medicine, 30*, 597–604.

Paivio, A. (1969). Mental imagery in associative learning and memory. *Psychological Review, 76*, 241–263.

Paivio, A. (1986). *Mental representations: A dual coding approach*. New York: Oxford University Press.

Paivio, A., Smythe, P. E., & Yuille, J. C. (1968). Imagery versus meaningfulness of nouns in paired-associate learning. *Canadian Journal of Psychology, 22*, 427–441.

Palladino, J. J., & Carducci, B. J. (1984). Students' knowledge of sleep and dreams. *Teaching of Psychology, 11*, 189–191.

Panksepp, J. (1986). The neurochemistry of behavior. *Annual Review of Psychology, 37*, 77–107.

Parke, R. D. (1977). Some effects of punishment on children's behavior—revisited. In E. M. Hetherington & R. D. Parke (Eds.), *Contemporary readings in child psychology*. New York: McGraw-Hill.

Parke, R. D., & Slaby, R. G. (1983). The development of aggression. In E. M. Hetherington (Ed.), *Handbook of child psychology: Socialization, personality, and social development* (Vol. 4). New York: Wiley.

Parker, D. E. (1980). The vestibular apparatus. *Scientific American, 243*(5), 118–135.

Parker, G., & Hadzi-Pavlovic, D. (1990). Expressed emotion as a predictor of schizophrenic relapse: An analysis of aggregated data. *Psychological Medicine, 20*, 961–965.

Parks, T. E. (1984). Illusory figures: A (mostly) atheoretical review. *Psychological Bulletin, 95*, 282–300.

Parlee, M. B. (1973). The premenstrual syndrome. *Psychological Bulletin, 80*, 454–465.

Parlee, M. B. (1982). Changes in moods and activation levels during the menstrual cycle in experimentally naive subjects. *Psychology of Women Quarterly, 7*, 119–131.

Parsons, T. (1979). Definitions of health and illness in light of the American values and social structure. In E. G. Jaco (Ed.), *Patients, physicians and illness: A sourcebook in behavioral science and health*. New York: Free Press.

Patzer, G. L. (1985). *The physical attractiveness phenomena*. New York: Plenum.

Pauk, W. (1990). *How to study in college*. Boston: Houghton Mifflin.

Paul, S. M., Crawley, J. N., & Skolnick, P. (1986). The neurobiology of anxiety: The role of the GABA/benzodiazepine receptor complex. In P. A. Berger & H. K. H. Brodie (Eds.), *American handbook of psychiatry: Biological psychiatry* (2nd ed., Vol. 8). New York: Basic Books.

Paulhus, D. L. (1989). Socially desirable responding: Some new solutions to old problems. In D. M. Buss & N. Cantor (Eds.), *Personality psychology: Recent trends and emerging directions*. New York: Springer-Verlag.

Paulhus, D. L. (1991). Measurement and control of response bias. In J. P. Robinson, P. Shaver, & L. S. Wrightsman (Eds.), *Measures of personality and social psychological attitudes*. San Diego: Academic Press.

Paunonen, S. V., Jackson, D. N., Trzebinski, J., & Forsterling, F. (1992). Personality structure across cultures: A multimethod evaluation. *Journal of Personality and Social Psychology, 62*, 447–456.

Pavlov, I. P. (1906). The scientific investigation of psychical faculties or processes in the higher animals. *Science, 24*, 613–619.

Pavlov, I. P. (1927). *Conditioned reflexes* (G. V. Anrep, Trans.). London: Oxford University Press.

Paykel, E. S., & Cooper, Z. (1992). Life events and social stress. In E. S. Paykel (Ed.), *Handbook of affective disorders* (2nd ed.). New York: Guilford Press.

Payne, J. W. (1976). Task complexity and contingent processing in decision making: An information search and protocol analysis. *Organizational Behavior and Human Performance, 16*, 366–387.

Pearce, L. (1974). Duck! It's the new journalism. *New Times, 2*(10), 40–41.

Pearlman, C. A. (1982). Sleep structure variation and performance. In W. B. Webb (Ed.), *Biological rhythms, sleep and performance*. New York: Wiley.

Pease, D., & Gleason, J. B. (1985). Gaining meaning: Semantic development. In J. B. Gleason (Ed.), *The development of language*. Columbus: Charles E. Merrill.

Pedersen, N. L., Plomin, R., Nesselroade, J. R., & McClearn, G. E. (1992). A quantitative genetic analysis of cognitive abilities during the second half of the life span. *Psychological Science, 3*, 346–353.

Pedersen, P. (1994). A culture-centered approach to counseling. In W. J. Lonner & R. Malpass (Eds.), *Psychology and culture*. Boston: Allyn & Bacon.

Pennebaker, J. W. (1982). *The psychology of physical symptoms*. New York: Springer-Verlag.

Pennebaker, J. W. (1990). *Opening up: The healing power of confiding in others*. New York: Morrow.

Pennebaker, J. W., Colder, M., & Sharp, L. K. (1990). Accelerating the coping process. *Journal of Personality and Social Psychology, 58*, 528–537.

Pennebaker, J. W., Kiecolt-Glaser, J. K., & Glaser, R. (1988). Disclosure of traumas and immune function: Health implications for psychotherapy. *Journal of Consulting and Clinical Psychology, 56*, 239–245.

Perkins, D. V. (1982). The assessment of stress using life events scales. In L. Goldberger & S. Breznitz (Eds.), *Handbook of stress: Theoretical and clinical aspects*. New York: Free Press.

Perlman, M. D., & Kaufman, A. S. (1990). Assessment of child intelligence. In G. Goldstein & M. Hersen (Eds.), *Handbook of psychological assessment*. New York: Pergamon Press.

Perloff, R. M. (1993). *The dynamics of persuasion*. Hillsdale, NJ: Erlbaum.

Perone, M., Galizio, M., & Baron, A. (1988). The relevance of animal-based principles in the laboratory study of human operant conditioning. In G. Davey & C. Cullen (Eds.), *Human operant conditioning and behavior modification*. New York: Wiley.

Perris, C. (1992). Bipolar-unipolar distinction. In E. S. Paykel (Ed.), *Handbook of affective disorders*. New York: Guilford Press.

Perry, D. G., & Bussey, K. (1979). The social learning theory of sex differences: Imitation is alive and well. *Journal of Personality and Social Psychology, 37*, 1699–1712.

Perry, D. G., Kusel, S. J., & Perry, L. C. (1988). Victims of peer aggression. *Developmental Psychology, 24*, 807–814.

Perry, W., & Braff, D. L. (1994). Information-processing deficits and thought disorder in schizophrenia. *American Journal of Psychiatry, 151*, 363–367.

Pert, C. B., & Snyder, S. H. (1973). Opiate receptor: Demonstration in the nervous tissue. *Science, 179*, 1011–1014.

Pervin, L. A. (1994). Personality stability, personality change, and the question of process. In T. F. Heatherton & J. L. Weinberger (Eds.), *Can personality change?* Washington, DC: American Psychological Association.

Petersen, A. C. (1988). Adolescent development. *Annual Review of Psychology, 39*, 583–607.

Peterson, C., Seligman, M. E. P., & Vaillant, G. E. (1988). Pessimistic explanatory style is a risk factor for physical illness: A thirty-five-year longitudinal study. *Journal of Personality and Social Psychology, 55*, 23–27.

Peterson, L. R., & Peterson, M. J. (1959). Short-term retention of individual verbal items. *Journal of Experimental Psychology, 58,* 193–198.

Pettigrew, T. F. (1979). The ultimate attribution error: Extending Allport's analysis of prejudice. *Personality and Social Psychology Bulletin, 5,* 461–476.

Petty, R. E., & Cacioppo, J. T. (1979). Effects of forewarning of persuasive intent and involvement on cognitive responses and persuasion. *Personality and Social Psychology Bulletin, 5,* 173–176.

Petty, R. E., & Cacioppo, J. T. (1986). *Communication and persuasion: Central and peripheral routes to attitude change.* New York: Springer-Verlag.

Petty, R. E., Cacioppo, J. T., & Schumann, D. (1983). Central and peripheral routes to advertising effectiveness: The moderating role of involvement. *Journal of Consumer Research, 10,* 134–148.

Peyser, H. S. (1993). Stress, ethyl alcohol, and alcoholism. In L. Goldberger & S. Breznitz (Eds.), *Handbook of stress: Theoretical and clinical aspects* (2nd ed.). New York: Free Press.

Pfaffmann, C. (1951). Taste and smell. In S. S. Stevens (Ed.), *Handbook of experimental psychology.* New York: Wiley.

Pfaffmann, C. (1974). Specificity of the sweet receptors of the squirrel monkey. *Chemical Senses and Flavor, 1,* 61–67.

Pfaffmann, C. (1978). The vertebrate phylogeny, neural code, and integrative process of taste. In C. Carterette & M. P. Friedman (Eds.), *Handbook of perception* (Vol. 6A). New York: Academic Press.

Pfau, M., Kenski, H. C., Nitz, M., & Sorenson, J. (1990). Efficacy of inoculation strategies in promoting resistance to political attack messages: Application to direct mail. *Communication Monographs, 57,* 25–43.

Phillips, M. R., Wolf, A. S., & Coons, D. J. (1988). Psychiatry and the criminal justice system: Testing the myths. *American Journal of Psychiatry, 145,* 605–610.

Piaget, J. (1929). *The child's conception of the world.* New York: Harcourt, Brace.

Piaget, J. (1932). *The moral judgment of the child.* Glencoe, IL: Free Press.

Piaget, J. (1952). *The origins of intelligence in children.* New York: International Universities Press.

Piaget, J. (1954). *The construction of reality in the child.* New York: Basic Books.

Piaget, J. (1983). Piaget's theory. In P. H. Mussen (Ed.), *Handbook of child psychology* (Vol. 1). New York: Wiley.

Pilowsky, I. (1978). A general classification of abnormal illness behaviors. *British Journal of Psychology, 51,* 131–137.

Pinker, S. (1990). Language acquisition. In D. N. Osherson & H. Lasnik (Eds.), *Language: An invitation to cognitive science* (Vol. 1). Cambridge, MA: MIT Press.

Piotrowski, C., Sherry, D., & Keller, J. W. (1985). Psychodiagnostic test usage: A survey of the Society for Personality Assessment. *Journal of Personality Assessment, 49*(2), 115–119.

Piper, W. E. (1993). Group psychotherapy research. In H. I. Kaplan & B. J. Sadock (Eds.), *Comprehensive group psychotherapy.* Baltimore: Williams & Wilkins.

Pittman, F., III. (1994, January/Febuary). A buyer's guide to psychotherapy. *Psychology Today,* pp. 50–53, 74–81.

Plomin, R. (1990). *Nature and nurture: An introduction to human behavioral genetics.* Pacific Grove, CA: Brooks/Cole.

Plomin, R. (1993). Nature and nurture: Perspective and prospective. In R. Plomin & G. E. McClearn (Eds.), *Nature, nurture and psychology.* Washington, DC: American Psychological Association.

Plomin, R., Chipuer, H. M., & Loehlin, J. C. (1990). Behavioral genetics and personality. In L. A. Pervin (Ed.), *Handbook of personality: Theory and research.* New York: Guilford Press.

Plomin, R., & Daniels, D. (1987). Why are children in the same family so different from each other? *Behavioral and Brain Sciences, 10,* 1–16.

Plomin, R., & DeFries, J. C. (1980). Genetics and intelligence: Recent data. *Intelligence, 4,* 15–24.

Plomin, R., & Rende, R. (1991). Human behavioral genetics. *Annual Review of Psychology, 42,* 161–190.

Plutchik, R. (1980, February). A language for the emotions. *Psychology Today,* pp. 68–78.

Plutchik, R. (1984). Emotions: A general psychoevolutionary theory. In K. R. Scherer & P. Ekman (Eds.), *Approaches to emotion.* Hillsdale, NJ: Erlbaum.

Plutchik, R., Williams, M. H., Jerrett, I., Karasu, T. B., & Kane, C. (1978). Emotions, personality, and life stresses in asthma. *Journal of Psychosomatic Research, 22,* 425–431.

Polivy, J. (1981). On the induction of emotion in the laboratory: Discrete moods or multiple affective states? *Journal of Personality and Social Psychology, 41,* 803–817.

Pollack, R. H. (1989). Pictures, maybe; illusions, no. *Behavioral and Brain Sciences, 12*(1), 92–93.

Ponterotto, J. G., & Pedersen, P. B. (1993). *Preventing prejudice: A guide for counselors and educators.* Newbury Park, CA: Sage.

Pope, K. S., Keith-Spiegel, P., & Tabachnick, B. G. (1986). Sexual attraction to clients. *American Psychologist, 41,* 147–158.

Pope, M. K., & Smith, T. W. (1991). Cortisol excretion in high and low cynically hostile men. *Psychosomatic Medicine, 53*(4), 386–392.

Post, R. M. (1989). Mood disorders: Somatic treatment. In H. I. Kaplan & B. J. Sadock (Eds.), *Comprehensive textbook of psychiatry/V* (Vol. 2). Baltimore: Williams & Wilkins.

Postman, L. (1971). Transfer, interference and forgetting. In J. W. Kling & L. A. Riggs (Eds.), *Experimental psychology* (3rd ed.). New York: Holt, Rinehart & Winston.

Postman, L. (1985). Human learning and memory. In G. A. Kimble & K. Schlesinger (Eds.), *Topics in the history of psychology.* Hillsdale, NJ: Erlbaum.

Prentky, R. (1989). Creativity and psychopathology: Gambling at the seat of madness. In J. A. Glover, R. R. Ronning, & C. R. Reynolds (Eds.), *Handbook of creativity.* New York: Plenum.

Prince, G. (1978). Putting the other half to work. *Training: The Magazine of Human Resources Development, 15,* 57–61.

Prochaska, J. O. (1994). Strong and weak principles for progressing from precontemplation to action on the basis of twelve problem behaviors. *Health Psychology, 13,* 47–51.

Pruitt, D. G. (1971). Choice shifts in group discussion: An introductory review. *Journal of Personality and Social Psychology, 20,* 339–360.

Puente, A. E. (1990). Psychological assessment of minority group members. In G. Goldstein & M. Hersen (Eds.), *Handbook of psychological assessment.* New York: Pergamon Press.

Pugh, E. N., Jr. (1988). Vision: Physics and retinal physiology. In R. C. Atkinson, R. J. Herrnstein, G. Lindzey, & R. D. Luce (Eds.), *Stevens' handbook of experimental psychology* (Vol. 1). New York: Wiley.

Pullum, G. K. (1991). *The Great Eskimo vocabulary hoax.* Chicago: University of Chicago Press.

Quillin, P. (1987). *Healing nutrients.* New York: Random House.

Rabkin, J. G. (1993). Stress and psychiatric disorders. In L. Goldberger & S. Breznitz (Eds.), *Handbook of stress: Theoretical and clinical aspects* (2nd ed.). New York: Free Press.

Rachman, S. J. (1990). *Fear and courage.* New York: W. H. Freeman.

Rachman, S. J. (1992). Behavior therapy. In L. R. Squire (Ed.), *Encyclopedia of learning and memory.* New York: Macmillan.

Ragland, D. R., & Brand, R. J. (1988). Type A behavior and mortality from coronary heart disease. *The New England Journal of Medicine, 318*(2), 65–69.

Rahe, R. H., & Holmes, T. H. (1965). Social, psychologic, and psychophysiologic aspects of inguinal hernia. *Journal of Psychosomatic Research, 8,* 487–491.

Rajecki, D. W. (1990). *Attitudes.* Sunderland, MA: Sinnauer Associates.

Rapaport, K., & Burkhart, B. R. (1984). Personality and attitudinal characteristics of sexually coercive college males. *Journal of Abnormal Psychology, 93,* 216–221.

Rapee, R. M., & Barlow, D. H. (1993). Generalized anxiety disorder, panic disorder, and the phobias. In P. B. Sutker & H. E. Adams (Eds.), *Comprehensive handbook of psychopathology* (2nd ed.). New York: Plenum.

Raphael, K. G., Cloitre, M., & Dohrenwend, B. P. (1991). Problems of recall and misclassification with checklist methods of measuring stressful life events. *Health Psychology, 10,* 62–74.

Rapoport, J. L. (1989). The biology of obsessions and compulsions. *Scientific American, 260,* 82–89.

Rasmussen, T., & Milner, B. (1977). The role of early left brain injury in determining lateralization of cerebral speech functions. *Annals of the New York Academy of Sciences, 299,* 355–369.

Ratner, N. B., & Gleason, J. B. (1993). An introduction to psycholinguistics: What do language users know? In J. B. Gleason & N. B. Ratner (Eds.), *Psycholinguistics.* Fort Worth: Harcourt Brace Jovanovich.

Ray, O., & Ksir, C. (1990). *Drugs, society & human behavior.* St. Louis: Times Mirror/Mosby.

Raz, S. (1993). Structural cerebral pathology in schizophrenia: Regional or diffuse? *Journal of Abnormal Psychology, 102,* 445–452.

Read, C. R. (1991). Achievement and career choices: Comparisons of males and females. *Roeper Review, 13,* 188–193.

Read, J. D., & Bruce, D. (1982). Longitudinal tracking of difficult memory retrievals. *Cognitive Psychology, 14,* 280–300.

Ree, M. J., & Earles, J. A. (1992). Intelligence is the best predictor of job performance. *Current Directions in Psychological Science, 1,* 86–89.

Reed, J. G., & Baxter P. M. (1992). *Library use: A handbook for psychology.* Washington, DC: American Psychological Association.

Reed, S. K., Ernst, G. W., & Banerji, R. (1974).

The role of analogy in transfer between similar problem states. *Cognitive Psychology, 6,* 436–450.

Reese, H. W., & Rodeheaver, D. (1985). Problem solving and complex decision making. In J. E. Birren & K. W. Schaie (Eds.), *Handbook of the psychology of aging* (2nd ed.). New York: Van Nostrand Reinhold.

Regan, T. (1989). Ill-gotten gains. In G. Langley (Ed.), *Animal experimentation: The consensus changes.* New York: Chapman & Hall.

Regestein, Q. R., & Monk, T. H. (1991). Is the poor sleep of shift workers a disorder? *American Journal of Psychiatry, 148,* 1487–1493.

Rehm, L. P., & Tyndall, C. I. (1993). Mood disorders: Unipolar and bipolar. In P. B. Sutker & H. E. Adams (Eds.), *Comprehensive handbook of psychopathology* (2nd ed.). New York: Plenum.

Reich, P. A. (1986). *Language development.* Englewood Cliffs, NJ: Prentice-Hall.

Reid, R. L. (1991). Premenstrual syndrome. *The New England Journal of Medicine, 324*(17), 1208–1210.

Reinke, B. J., Ellicott, A. M., Harris, R. L., & Hancock, E. (1985). Timing of psychosocial changes in women's lives. *Human Development, 28,* 259–280.

Reisenzein, R. (1983). The Schachter theory of emotion: Two decades later. *Psychological Bulletin, 94,* 239–264.

Reiser, M. F. (1989). The future of psychoanalysis in academic psychiatry: Plain talk. *Psychoanalytic Quarterly, 58*(2), 185–209.

Reiss, S. (1991). Expectancy model of fear, anxiety and panic. *Clinical Psychology Review, 11,* 141–154.

Relman, A. (1982). Marijuana and health. *New England Journal of Medicine, 306*(10), 603–604.

Reschly, D. (1981). Psychological testing in educational classification and placement. *American Psychologist, 36,* 1094–1102.

Rescorla, R. A. (1978). Some implications of a cognitive perspective on Pavlovian conditioning. In S. H. Hulse, H. Fowler, & W. K. Honig (Eds.), *Cognitive processes in animal behavior.* Hillsdale, NJ: Erlbaum.

Rescorla, R. A. (1980). *Pavlovian second-order conditioning.* Hillsdale, NJ: Erlbaum.

Rescorla, R. A. (1987). A Pavlovian analysis of goal-directed behavior. *American Psychologist, 42,* 119–129.

Rescorla, R. A., & Solomon, R. L. (1967). Two-process learning theory: Relationships between Pavlovian conditioning and instrumental learning. *Psychological Review, 74,* 151–182.

Rescorla, R. A., & Wagner, A. R. (1972). A theory of Pavlovian conditioning: Variations in the effectiveness of reinforcement and nonreinforcement. In A. H. Black & W. F. Prokasky (Eds.), *Classical conditioning: II. Current research and theory.* New York: Appleton-Century-Crofts.

Rest, J. R. (1983). Morality. In P. H. Mussen (Ed.), *Handbook of child psychology* (4th ed., Vol. 3). New York: Wiley.

Rest, J. R. (1986). *Moral development: Advances in research and theory.* New York: Praeger.

Ricketts, W. (1984). Biological research on homosexuality: Ansell's cow or Occam's razor? *Journal of Homosexuality, 10,* 65–93.

Rietveld, W. J. (1985). Functional significance of the suprachiasmatic nucleus. In P. H. Redfern, I. C. Campbell, J. A. Davies, & K. F. Martin (Eds.), *Circadian rhythms in the central nervous system.* Deerfield Beach, FL: VCH.

Riley, L. R. (1987). *Psychology of language development: A primer.* Toronto: C. J. Hogrefe.

Rimm, D. C., & Cunningham, H. M. (1985). Behavior therapies. In S. J. Lynn & J. P. Garske (Eds.), *Contemporary psychotherapies: Models and methods.* Columbus, OH: Charles E. Merrill.

Roazen, P. (1976). *Erik H. Erikson: The power and limits of a vision.* New York: Free Press.

Robbins, D. (1971). Partial reinforcement: A selective review of the alleyway literature since 1960. *Psychological Bulletin, 76,* 415–431.

Roberts, P., & Newton, P. M. (1987). Levinsonian studies of women's adult development. *Psychology and Aging, 2,* 154–163.

Robins, C. J. (1988). Attributions and depression: Why is the literature so inconsistent? *Journal of Personality and Social Psychology, 54,* 880–889.

Robins, L. N., Locke, B. Z., & Regier, D. A. (1991). An overview of psychiatric disorders in America. In L. N. Robins & D. A. Regier (Eds.), *Psychiatric disorders in America: The epidemiologic catchment area study.* New York: Free Press.

Robins, L. N., & Regier, D. A. (Eds.). (1991). *Psychiatric disorders in America: The epidemiologic catchment area study.* New York: Free Press.

Robinson, F. P. (1970). *Effective study* (4th ed.). New York: Harper & Row.

Robinson, J. L., Kagan, J., Reznick, J. S., & Corley, R. (1992). The heritability of inhibited and uninhibited behavior: A twin study. *Developmental Psychology, 28,* 1030–1037.

Rock, I. (1986). The description and analysis of object and event perception. In K. R. Boff, L. Kaufman, & J. P. Thomas (Eds.), *Handbook of perception and human performance* (Vol. 2). New York: Wiley.

Rodin, J. (1978). Has the distinction between internal versus external control of feeding outlived its usefulness? In G. A. Bray (Ed.), *Recent advances in obesity research* (Vol. 2). London: Newman.

Rodin, J. (1981). Current status of the internal-external hypothesis for obesity: What went wrong? *American Psychologist, 36,* 361–372.

Rodin, J., Schank, D., & Striegel-Moore, R. H. (1989). Psychological features of obesity. *Medical Clinics of North America, 73,* 47–66.

Rodin, J., Wack, J., Ferrannini, E., & Defronzo, R. A. (1985). Effect of insulin and glucose on feeding behavior. *Metabolism, 34,* 826–831.

Roediger, H. L., III. (1980). Memory metaphors in cognitive psychology. *Memory & Cognition, 8,* 231–246.

Roediger, H. L., III. (1990). Implicit memory: Retention without remembering. *American Psychologist, 45,* 1043–1056.

Roediger, H. L., III, Weldon, M. S., & Challis, B. H. (1989). Explaining dissociations between implicit and explicit measures of retention: A processing account. In H. L. Roediger, III, & F. I. M. Craik (Eds.), *Varieties of memory and consciousness.* Hillsdale, NJ: Erlbaum.

Roffwarg, H. P., Muzio, J. N., & Dement, W. C. (1966). Ontogenetic development of the human sleep-dream cycle. *Science, 152,* 604–619.

Rogers, C. R. (1951). *Client-centered therapy: Its current practice, implications, and theory.* Boston: Houghton Mifflin.

Rogers, C. R. (1961). *On becoming a person: A therapist's view of psychotherapy.* Boston: Houghton Mifflin.

Rogers, C. R. (1980). *A way of being.* Boston: Houghton Mifflin.

Rogers, C. R. (1986). Client-centered therapy. In I. L. Kutash & A. Wolf (Eds.), *Psychotherapist's casebook.* San Francisco: Jossey-Bass.

Rogers, R. W. (1983). Cognitive and physiological processes in fear appeals and attitude change: A revised theory of protection motivation. In J. Cacioppo & R. Petty (Eds.), *Social psychophysiology.* New York: Guilford Press.

Rogoff, B. (1990). *Apprenticeship in thinking.* New York: Oxford University Press.

Role, L. W., & Kelly, J. P. (1991). The brain stem: Cranial nerve nuclei and the monoaminergic systems. In E. R. Kandel, J. H. Schwartz, & T. M. Jessell (Eds.), *Principles of neural science* (3rd ed.). New York: Elsevier.

Rollins, B., & Feldman, H. (1970). Marital satisfaction over the family life cycle. *Journal of Marriage and the Family, 32,* 20–28.

Rollman, G. B. (1991). Pain responsiveness. In M. A. Heller & W. Schiff (Eds.), *The psychology of touch.* Hillsdale, NJ: Erlbaum.

Roosa, M. W. (1988). The effect of age in the transition to parenthood: Are delayed childbearers a unique group? *Family Relations, 37,* 322–327.

Rosch, E. H. (1973). Natural categories. *Cognitive Psychology, 4,* 328–350.

Rose, S. P. R. (1992). Protein synthesis in long-term memory in vertebrates. In L. R. Squire (Ed.), *Encyclopedia of learning and memory.* New York: Macmillan.

Rosenbaum, J. F., Biederman, J., Bolduc, E. A., Hirschfeld, D. R., Faraone, S. V., & Kagan, J. (1992). Comorbidity of parental anxiety disorders as risk for childhood-onset anxiety in inhibited children. *American Journal of Psychiatry, 149,* 475–481.

Rosenbaum, M., Lakin, M., & Roback, H. B. (1992). Psychotherapy in groups. In D. K. Freedheim (Ed.), *History of psychotherapy: A century of change.* Washington, DC: American Psychological Association.

Rosenblith, J. F. (1992). *In the beginning: Development from conception to age two.* Newbury Park, CA: Sage.

Rosengren, A., Tibblin, G., & Wilhelmsen, L. (1991). Self-perceived psychological stress and incidence of coronary artery disease in middle-aged men. *American Journal of Cardiology, 68,* 1171–1175.

Rosenhan, D. L. (1973). On being sane in insane places. *Science, 179,* 250–258.

Rosenman, R. H. (1991). Type A behavior pattern and coronary heart disease: The hostility factor? *Stress Medicine, 7*(4), 245–253.

Rosenman, R. H. (1993). Relationships of the Type A behavior pattern with coronary heart disease. In L. Goldberger & S. Breznitz (Eds.), *Handbook of stress: Theoretical and clinical aspects* (2nd ed.). New York: Free Press.

Rosenthal, H. (1988). *Not with my life I don't: Preventing your suicide and that of others.* Muncie, IN: Accelerated Development.

Rosenthal, R. (1976). *Experimenter effects in behavioral research.* New York: Halsted.

Rosenthal, R., & Fode, K. L. (1963). Three experiments in experimenter bias. *Psychological Reports, 12,* 491–511.

Rosenzweig, S. (1985). Freud and experimental psychology: The emergence of idiodynamics. In S. Koch & D. E. Leary (Eds.), *A century of psychology as a science.* New York: McGraw-Hill.

Roskos-Ewoldsen, D. R., & Fazio, R. H. (1992). The accessibility of source likability as a determinant of persuasion. *Personality and Social Psychology Bulletin, 18*, 19–25.

Ross, B. (1991). William James: Spoiled child of American psychology. In G. A. Kimble, M. Wertheimer, & C. White (Eds.), *Portraits of pioneers in psychology*. Hillsdale, NJ: Erlbaum.

Ross, C. A., Anderson, G., Fleisher, W. P., & Norton, G. R. (1991). The frequency of multiple personality disorder among psychiatric inpatients. *American Journal of Psychiatry, 148*, 1717–1720.

Ross, C. A., Miller, S. D., Reagor, P., Bjornson, L., Fraser, G. A., & Anderson, G. (1990). Structured interview data on 102 cases of multiple personality disorder from four centers. *American Journal of Psychiatry, 147*, 596–601.

Ross, J., & Ferris, K. R. (1981). Interpersonal attraction and organizational outcome: A field experiment. *Administrative Science Quarterly, 26*, 617–632.

Ross, L. D. (1977). The intuitive psychologist and his shortcomings: Distortions in the attribution process. In L. Berkowitz (Ed.), *Advances in experimental social psychology* (Vol. 10). New York: Academic Press.

Ross, L. D., & Anderson, C. A. (1982). Shortcomings in the attribution process: On the origins and maintenance of erroneous social assessments. In D. Kahneman, P. Slovic, & A. Tversky (Eds.), *Judgement under uncertainty: Heuristics and biases*. Cambridge: Cambridge University Press.

Rossi, P. H. (1990). The old homeless and the new homelessness in historical perspective. *American Psychologist, 45*(8), 954–959.

Rothblum, E. D., Solomon, L. J., & Albee, G. W. (1986). A sociopolitical perspective of DSM-III. In T. Millon & G. L. Klerman (Eds.), *Contemporary directions in psychopathology: Toward the DSM-IV*. New York: Guilford Press.

Rotter, J. B. (1982). *The development and application of social learning theory*. New York: Praeger.

Roy, A. (1989). Suicide. In H. I. Kaplan & B. J. Sadock (Eds.), *Comprehensive textbook of psychiatry/V*. Baltimore: Williams & Wilkins.

Rozin, P. (1990). The importance of social factors in understanding the acquisition of food habits. In E. D. Capaldi & T. L. Powley (Eds.), *Taste, experience, and feeding*. Washington, DC: American Psychological Association.

Rubin, E. H., Zorumski, C. F., & Guze, S. B. (1986). Somatoform disorders. In T. Millon & G. L. Klerman (Eds.), *Contemporary directions in psychopathology: Toward the DSM-IV*. New York: Guilford Press.

Ruble, D. N., Fleming, A. S., Hackel, L. S., & Stangor, C. (1988). Changes in the marital relationship during the transition to first time motherhood: Effects of violated expectations concerning division of household labor. *Journal of Personality and Social Psychology, 55*, 78–87.

Ruble, T. L. (1983). Sex stereotypes: Issues of change in the 70s. *Sex Roles, 9*, 397–402.

Rubonis, A. V., & Bickman, L. (1991). Psychological impairment in the wake of disaster: The disaster-psychopathology relationship. *Psychological Bulletin, 109*, 384–399.

Rudorfer, M. V., & Goodwin, F. K. (1993). Introduction. In C. E. Coffey (Ed.), *The clinical science of electroconvulsive therapy*. Washington, DC: American Psychiatric Press.

Rundus, D. (1971). Analysis of rehearsal processes in free recall. *Journal of Experimental Psychology, 89*, 63–77.

Ruse, M. (1987). Sociobiology and knowledge: Is evolutionary epistemology a viable option? In C. Crawford, M. Smith, & D. Krebs (Eds.), *Sociobiology and psychology: Ideas, issues and applications*. Hillsdale, NJ: Erlbaum.

Rush, A. J. (1984). Cognitive therapy. In T. B. Karasu (Ed.), *The psychiatric therapies*. Washington, DC: American Psychiatric Press.

Rushton, J. P., Fulker, D. W., Neale, M. C., Nias, D. K. B., & Eysenck, H. J. (1986). Altruism and aggression: The heritability of individual differences. *Journal of Personality and Social Psychology, 50*, 1192–1198.

Russell, J. A. (1991). Culture and the categorization of emotions. *Psychological Bulletin, 110*, 426–450.

Russo, N. F., & Denmark, F. L. (1987). Contributions of women to psychology. *Annual Review of Psychology, 38*, 279–298.

Rutherford, W. (1886). A new theory of hearing. *Journal of Anatomy and Physiology, 21*, 166–168.

Rutter, M., Silberg, J., & Simonoff, E. (1993). Whither behavioral genetics?—A developmental psychopathological perspective. In R. Plomin & G. E. McClearn (Eds.), *Nature, nurture and psychology*. Washington, DC: American Psychological Association.

Rymer, R. (1989, March–April). Electroshock. *Hippocrates*, pp. 65–72.

Sachs, J. (1985). Prelinguistic development. In J. B. Gleason (Ed.), *The development of language*. Columbus: Charles E. Merrill.

Sacks, O. (1987). *The man who mistook his wife for a hat*. New York: Harper & Row.

Salthouse, T. A., & Babcock, R. L. (1991). Decomposing adult age differences in working memory. *Developmental Psychology, 27*, 763–776.

Salvendy, J. T. (1993). Selection and preparation of patients and organization of the group. In H. I. Kaplan & B. J. Sadock (Eds.), *Comprehensive group psychotherapy*. Baltimore: Williams & Wilkins.

Salzman, C. (1989). Treatment with antianxiety agents. In *Treatment of psychiatric disorders* (Vol. 3). Washington, DC: American Psychiatric Press.

Samelson, F. (1981). Struggle for scientific authority: The reception of Watson's behaviorism, 1913–1920. *Journal of the History of the Behavioral Sciences, 17*, 399–425.

Samet, J. M. (1992). The health benefits of smoking cessation. *Medical Clinics of North America, 76*, 399–414.

Sanderson, C., & Clarkin, J. F. (1994). Use of the NEO-PI personality dimensions in differential treatment planning. In P. T. Costa, Jr., & T. A. Widiger (Eds.), *Personality disorders and the five-factor model of personality*. Washington, DC: American Psychological Association.

Sanderson, W. C., & Barlow, D. H. (1990). A description of patients diagnosed with DSM-III-R generalized anxiety disorder. *Journal of Nervous and Mental Disease, 178*, 588–591.

Sandler, J. (1975). Aversion methods. In F. H. Kanfer & A. P. Goldstein (Eds.), *Helping people change: A textbook of methods*. New York: Pergamon Press.

Sapolsky, R. M. (1992). Neuroendocrinology and the stress-response. In J. B. Becker, S. M. Breedlove, & D. Crews (Eds.), *Behavioral Endocrinology*. Cambridge, MA: MIT Press.

Sarason, I. G., & Sarason, B. G. (1987). *Abnormal psychology: The problem of maladaptive behavior*. Englewood Cliffs, NJ: Prentice-Hall.

Sarnacki, R. E. (1979). An examination of test-wiseness in the cognitive domain. *Review of Educational Research, 49*, 252–279.

Sato, M. (1973). Gustatory receptor mechanism in mammals. *Advances in Biophysics, 4*, 103–152.

Saxe, G. N., van der Kolk, B. A., Berkowitz, R., Chinman, G., Hall, K., Lieberg, G., & Schwartz, J. (1993). Dissociative disorders in psychiatric inpatients. *American Journal of Psychiatry, 150*, 1037–1042.

Scarr, S. (1989). Protecting general intelligence: Constructs and consequences for interventions. In R. L. Linn (Ed.), *Intelligence: Measurement, theory, and public policy*. Urbana: University of Illinois Press.

Scarr, S., & Carter-Saltzman, L. (1979). Twin method: Defense of a critical assumption. *Behavior Genetics, 9*, 527–542.

Scarr, S., & Carter-Saltzman, L. (1982). Genetics and intelligence. In R. J. Sternberg (Ed.), *Handbook of human intelligence*. Cambridge, MA: Cambridge University Press.

Scarr, S., & Kidd, K. K. (1983). Developmental behavior genetics. In P. H. Mussen (Ed.), *Handbook of child psychology* (Vol. 2). New York: Wiley.

Scarr, S., Phillips, D., McCartney, K., & Abbott-Shim, M. (1993). Quality of child care as an aspect of family and child care policy in the United States. *Pediatrics, 91*, 182–188.

Scarr, S., & Weinberg, R. A. (1977). Intellectual similarities within families of both adopted and biological children. *Intelligence, 32*, 170–190.

Scarr, S., & Weinberg, R. A. (1983). The Minnesota adoption studies: Genetic differences and malleability. *Child Development, 54*, 260–267.

Schachter, S. (1959). *The psychology of affiliation*. Stanford, CA: Stanford University Press.

Schachter, S. (1964). The interaction of cognitive and physiological determinants of emotional state. In L. Berkowitz (Ed.), *Advances in experimental social psychology* (Vol. 1). New York: Academic Press.

Schachter, S. (1971). *Emotion, obesity and crime*. New York: Academic Press.

Schachter, S., & Gross, L. (1968). Manipulated time and eating behavior. *Journal of Personality and Social Psychology, 10*, 98–106.

Schachter, S., & Rodin, J. (1974). *Obese humans and rats*. Hillsdale, NJ: Erlbaum.

Schachter, S., & Singer, J. E. (1962). Cognitive, social and physiological determinants of emotional state. *Psychological Review, 69*, 379–399.

Schachter, S., & Singer, J. E. (1979). Comments on the Maslach and Marshall-Zimbardo experiments. *Journal of Personality and Social Psychology, 37*, 989–995.

Schacter, D. L. (1987). Implicit memory: History and current status. *Journal of Experimental Psychology: Learning, Memory and Cognition, 14*, 501–518.

Schacter, D. L. (1989). On the relation between memory and consciousness: Dissociable interactions and conscious experience. In H. L. Roediger, III, & F. I. M. Craik (Eds.), *Varieties of memory and consciousness*. Hillsdale, NJ: Erlbaum.

Schacter, D. L. (1992). Understanding implicit memory: A cognitive neuroscience approach. *American Psychologist, 47*, 559–569.

Schaeffer, M., Street, S., Singer, J., & Baum, A. (1988). Effects of control on the stress reactions of commuters. *Journal of Applied Social Psychology, 18,* 944–957.

Schaie, K. W. (1990). Intellectual development in adulthood. In J. E. Birren & K. W. Schaie (Eds.), *Handbook of the psychology of aging* (3rd ed.). San Diego: Academic Press.

Scharf, M. B., Mayleben, D. W., Kaffeman, M., Kvall, R., & Ochs, R. (1991). Dose response effects of zolpidem in normal geriatric subjects. *Journal of Clinical Psychiatry, 52,* 77–83.

Schau, C. G., & Scott, K. P. (1984). Impact of gender characteristics of instructional materials: An integration of the research literature. *Journal of Educational Psychology, 76,* 183–193.

Scheff, T. J. (1975). *Labeling madness.* Englewood Cliffs, NJ: Prentice-Hall.

Scheff, T. J. (1984). *Being mentally ill: A sociological theory.* New York: Aldine.

Scheidlinger, S. (1993). History of group psychotherapy. In H. I. Kaplan & B. J. Sadock (Eds.), *Comprehensive group psychotherapy.* Baltimore: Williams & Wilkins.

Scheier, M. F., & Carver, C. S. (1985). Optimism, coping and health: Assessment and implications of generalized expectancies. *Health Psychology, 4,* 219–247.

Scheier, M. F., & Carver, C. S. (1992). Effects of optimism on psychological and physical well-being: Theoretical overview and empirical update. *Cognitive Theory and Research, 16*(2), 201–228.

Scheier, M. F., Matthews, K. A., Owens, J. F., Magovern, G. J., Sr., Lefebvre, R. C., Abbott, R. A., & Carver, C. S. (1989). Dispositional optimism and recovery from coronary artery bypass surgery: The beneficial effects on physical and psychological well-being. *Journal of Personality and Social Psychology, 57,* 1024–1040.

Scheier, M. F., Weintraub, J. K., & Carver, C. S. (1986). Coping with stress: Divergent strategies of optimists and pessimists. *Journal of Personality and Social Psychology, 51,* 1257–1264.

Schiff, M., & Lewontin, R. (1986). *Education and class: The irrelevance of IQ genetic studies.* Oxford: Clarendon Press.

Schildkraut, J. J., Green, A. I., Mooney, J. J. (1985). Affective disorders: Biochemical aspects. In H. I. Kaplan & B. J. Sadock (Eds.), *Comprehensive textbook of psychiatry/IV.* Baltimore: Williams & Wilkins.

Schildkraut, J. J., Green, A. I., & Mooney, J. J. (1989). Mood disorders: Biochemical aspects. In H. I. Kaplan & B. J. Sadock (Eds.), *Comprehensive textbook of psychiatry/V.* Baltimore: Williams & Wilkins.

Schlenker, B. R. (1980). *Impression management: The self-concept, social identity, and interpersonal relations.* Pacific Grove, CA: Brooks/Cole.

Schlesinger, K. (1985). Behavioral genetics and the nature-nurture question. In G. A. Kimble & K. Schlesinger (Eds.), *Topics in the history of psychology* (Vol. 2). Hillsdale, NJ: Erlbaum.

Schlosberg, H. (1954). Three dimensions of emotion. *Psychological Review, 61,* 81–88.

Schuman, H., & Kalton, G. (1985). Survey methods. In G. Lindzey & E. Aronson (Eds.), *Handbook of social psychology* (3rd ed.). New York: Random House.

Schwartz, A. H., & Swartzburg, M. (1976). Hospital care. In B. B. Wolman (Ed.), *The therapist's handbook: Treatment methods of mental disorders.* New York: Van Nostrand Reinhold.

Schwartz, G. E. (1974, April). The facts on transcendental meditation, part II: TM relaxes some people and makes them feel better. *Psychology Today,* pp. 39–44.

Schwartz, S. H. (1990). Individualism-collectivism: Critique and proposed refinements. *Journal of Cross-Cultural Psychology, 21,* 139–157.

Scoville, W. B., & Milner, B. (1957). Loss of recent memory after bilateral hippocampal lesions. *Journal of Neurology, Neurosurgery & Psychiatry, 20,* 11–21.

Scull, A. (1990). Deinstitutionalization: Cycles of despair. *The Journal of Mind and Behavior, 11*(3/4), 301–312.

Sears, D. O. (1975). Political socialization. In F. I. Greenstein & N. W. Polsby (Eds.), *Handbook of political science* (Vol. 2). Reading, MA: Addison-Wesley.

Sears, D. O. (1986). College sophomores in the laboratory: Influences of a narrow data base on psychology's view of human nature. *Journal of Personality and Social Psychology, 51,* 515–530.

Sears, R. (1977). Sources of life satisfaction of the Terman gifted men. *American Psychologist, 32,* 119–128.

Seccombe, K. (1991). Assessing the costs and benefits of children: Gender comparisons among childfree husbands and wives. *Journal of Marriage and the Family, 53,* 191–202.

Segal, B. (1988). *Drugs and behavior.* New York: Gardner Press.

Segall, M. H., Campbell, D. T., Herskovits, M. J. (1966). *The influence of culture on visual perception.* Indianapolis: Bobbs-Merrill.

Segall, M. H., Dasen, P. R., Berry, J. W., & Poortinga, Y. H. (1990). *Human behavior in global perspective: An introduction to cross-cultural psychology.* New York: Pergamon Press.

Segrin, C., & Dillard, J. P. (1992). The interactional theory of depression: A meta-analysis of the research literature. *Journal of Social and Clinical Psychology, 11,* 43–70.

Sekuler, R., & Blake, R. (1990). *Perception.* New York: McGraw-Hill.

Seligman, M. E. P. (1971). Phobias and preparedness. *Behavior Therapy, 2,* 307–321.

Seligman, M. E. P. (1974). Depression and learned helplessness. In R. J. Friedman & M. M. Katz (Eds.), *The psychology of depression: Contemporary theory and research.* New York: Wiley.

Seligman, M. E. P. (1983). Learned helplessness. In E. Levitt, B. Rubin, & J. Brooks (Eds.), *Depression: Concepts, controversies and some new facts.* Hillsdale, NJ: Erlbaum.

Seligman, M. E. P. (1990). *Learned optimism.* New York: Pocket Books.

Seligman, M. E. P., & Hager, J. L. (1972, August). Biological boundaries of learning (The sauce béarnaise syndrome). *Psychology Today,* pp. 59–61, 84–87.

Seligman, M. E. P., & Johnston, J. C. (1973). A cognitive theory of avoidance learning. In F. J. McGuigan & D. B. Lumsden (Eds.), *Contemporary approaches to conditioning and learning.* Washington: V. H. Winston.

Selye, H. (1936). A syndrome produced by diverse nocuous agents. *Nature, 138,* 32.

Selye, H. (1956). *The stress of life.* New York: McGraw-Hill.

Selye, H. (1973). The evolution of the stress concept. *American Scientist, 61*(6), 672–699.

Selye, H. (1974). *Stress without distress.* New York: Lippincott.

Selye, H. (1982). History and present status of the stress concept. In L. Goldberger & S. Breznitz (Eds.), *Handbook of stress: Theoretical and clinical aspects.* New York: Free Press.

Shadish, W. R., Jr., Lurigio, A. J., & Lewis, D. A. (1989). After deinstitutionalization: The present and future of mental health long-term care policy. *Journal of Social Issues, 45*(3), 1–15.

Shafer, G., & Tversky, A. (1988). Languages and designs for probability judgement. In D. E. Bell, H. Raiffa, & A. Tversky (Eds.), *Decision making: Descriptive, normative, and prescriptive interactions.* New York: Cambridge University Press.

Shaffer, D. R. (1985). *Developmental psychology: Theory, research, and applications.* Pacific Grove, CA: Brooks/Cole.

Shaffer, D. R. (1989). *Developmental psychology: Childhood and adolescence.* Pacific Grove, CA: Brooks/Cole.

Shank, J. C. (1983). Disease incidence and prevalence. In R. B. Taylor (Ed.), *Family medicine: Principles and practice.* New York: Springer-Verlag.

Shapiro, D. H., Jr. (1984). Overview: Clinical and physiological comparison of meditation with other self-control strategies. In D. H. Shapiro, Jr., & R. N. Walsh (Eds.), *Meditation: Classic and contemporary perspectives.* New York: Aldine.

Shapiro, D. H., Jr. (1987). Implications of psychotherapy research for the study of meditation. In M. A. West (Ed.), *The psychology of meditation.* Oxford: Clarendon Press.

Shapiro, S., Skinner, E. A., Kessler, L. G., Von Korff, M., German, P. S., Tischler, G. L., Leaf, P. J., Benham, L., Cottler, L., & Regier, D. A. (1984). Utilization of health and mental health services. *Archives of General Psychiatry, 41,* 971–978.

Sharpe, D., Adair, J. G., & Roese, N. J. (1992). Twenty years of deception research: A decline in subjects' trust? *Personality and Social Psychology Bulletin, 18,* 585–590.

Shaver, P. R., & Hazan, C. (1993). Adult attachment: Theory and research. In W. Jones & D. Perlman (Eds.), *Advances in personal relationships* (Vol. 4). London: Jessica Kingsley.

Shaver, P. R., & Hazan, C. (1994). Attachment. In A. L. Weber & J. H. Harvey (Eds.), *Perspectives on close relationships.* Boston: Allyn & Bacon.

Shedler, J., Mayman, M., & Manis, M. (1993). The illusion of mental health. *American Psychologist, 48,* 1117–1131.

Sheehan, S. (1982). *Is there no place on earth for me?* Boston: Houghton Mifflin.

Shekelle, R. B., Hulley, S. B., Neaton, J. D., Billings, J. H., Borhani, N. O., Gerace, T. A., Jacobs, D. R., Lasser, N. L., Mittlemark, M. B., & Stamler, J. (1985). The MRFIT behavior pattern study: II. Type A behavior and incidence of coronary heart disease. *American Journal of Epidemiology, 122,* 559–570.

Shepard, R. N. (1990). *Mind sights.* New York: W. H. Freeman.

Sherif, M., & Hovland, C. I. (1961). *Social judgment: Assimilation and contrast effects in communication and attitude change.* New Haven, CT: Yale University Press.

Sherman, C. B. (1992). The health consequences of cigarette smoking: Pulmonary diseases. *Medical Clinics of North America, 76,* 355–375.

Sherman, M., & Key, C. B. (1932). The intelligence of isolated mountain children. *Child Development*, *3*, 279–290.

Shiffrin, R. M. (1988). Attention. In R. C. Atkinson, R. J. Herrnstein, G. Lindzey, & R. D. Luce (Eds.), *Stevens' handbook of experimental psychology* (Vol. 2). New York: Wiley.

Shimamura, A. P. (1992). Amnesia, organic. In L. R. Squire (Ed.), *Encyclopedia of learning and memory*. New York: Macmillan.

Shneidman, E. S. (1985). *At the point of no return*. New York: Wiley.

Shneidman, E. S., Farberow, N. L., & Litman, R. E. (Eds.). (1970). *The psychology of suicide*. New York: Science House.

Shweder, R. A., Mahapatra, M., & Miller, J. G. (1990). Culture and moral development. In J. W. Stigler, R. A. Shweder, & G. Herdt (Eds.), *Cultural psychology*. New York: Cambridge University Press.

Shweder, R. A., & Sullivan, M. A. (1993). Cultural psychology: Who needs it? *Annual Review of Psychology*, *44*, 497–523.

Sicard, G., & Holley, A. (1984). Receptor cell responses to odorants: Similarities and differences among odorants. *Brain Research*, *292*, 283–296.

Siegel, J. M., Johnson, J. H., & Sarason, I. G. (1979). Life changes and menstrual discomfort. *Journal of Human Stress*, *5*, 41–46.

Siegel, O. (1982). Personality development in adolescence. In B. B. Wolman, (Ed.), *Handbook of developmental psychology*. Englewood Cliffs, NJ: Prentice-Hall.

Siegel, S. (1983). Classical conditioning, drug tolerance, and drug dependence. In Y. Israel, F. B. Glaser, H. Kalant, R. E. Popham, W. Schmidt, & R. G. Smart (Eds.), *Research advances in alcohol and drug problems* (Vol. 7). New York: Plenum.

Siegel, S. (1989). Pharmacological conditioning and drug effects. In A. J. Goudie & M. W. Emmett-Oglesby (Eds.), *Psychoactive drugs: Tolerance and sensitization*. Clifton, NJ: Humana Press.

Siegler, R. S. (1986). *Children's thinking*. Englewood Cliffs, NJ: Prentice-Hall.

Siegler, R. S. (1991). *Children's thinking* (2nd ed.). Englewood Cliffs, NJ: Prentice-Hall.

Siegler, R. S. (1992). The other Alfred Binet. *Developmental Psychology*, *28*, 179–190.

Siegler, R. S. (1994). Cognitive variability: A key to understanding cognitive development. *Current Directions in Psychological Science*, *3*(1), 1–5.

Sigelman, C. K., & Shaffer, D. R. (1991). *Life-span human development*. Pacific Grove, CA: Brooks/Cole.

Signorielli, N. (1989). Television and conceptions about sex roles: Maintaining conventionality and the status quo. *Sex Roles*, *21*, 341–360.

Silverberg, S. B., Tennenbaum, D. L., & Jacob, T. (1992). Adolescence and family interaction. In V. B. Van Hasselt & M. Hersen (Eds.), *Handbook of social development: A lifespan perspective*. New York: Plenum.

Simmons, C. H., von Kolke, A., & Shimizu, H. (1986). Attitudes toward romantic love among American, German, and Japanese students. *Journal of Social Psychology*, *126*, 327–336.

Simon, G. E., & VonKorff, M. (1991). Somatization and psychiatric disorder in the NIMH epidemiologic catchment area study. *American Journal of Psychiatry*, *148*, 1494–1500.

Simon, H. A. (1957). *Models of man*. New York: Wiley.

Simon, H. A. (1974). How big is a chunk? *Science*, *183*, 482–488.

Simons, R. C., & Hughes, C. C. (1993). Culture-bound syndromes. In A. C. Gaw (Ed.), *Culture, ethnicity, and mental illness*. Washington, DC: American Psychiatric Press.

Simonton, D. K. (1990). Creativity and wisdom in aging. In J. E. Birren & K. W. Schaie (Eds.), *Handbook of the psychology of aging*. San Diego: Academic Press.

Simpson, J. A. (1990). Influence of attachment styles on romantic relationships. *Journal of Personality and Social Psychology*, *59*, 971–980.

Simpson, J. L. (1991). Fetal wastage. In S. G. Gabbe, J. R. Niebyl, & J. L. Simpson (Eds.), *Obstetrics: Normal and problem pregnancies*. New York: Churchill Livingstone.

Sinclair, D. (1981). *Mechanisms of cutaneous stimulation*. Oxford, England: Oxford University Press.

Singer, M. T., Wynne, L. C., & Toohey, M. L. (1978). Communication disorders and the families of schizophrenics. In L. C. Wynne, R. L. Cromwell, & S. Matthysse (Eds.), *The nature of schizophrenia: New approaches to research and treatment*. New York: Wiley Medical.

Sinha, D. (1983). Human assessment in the Indian context. In S. H. Irvine & J. W. Berry (Eds.), *Human assessment and cultural factors*. New York: Plenum.

Siscovick, D. S. (1990). Risks of exercising: Sudden cardiac death and injuries. In C. Bouchard, R. J. Shephard, T. Stephens, J. R. Sutton, & B. D. McPherson (Eds.), *Exercise, fitness, and health: A consensus of current knowledge*. Champaign, IL: Human Kinetics Books.

Siscovick, D. S., Weiss, N. S., Fletcher, R. H., & Lasky, T. (1984). The incidence of primary cardiac arrest during vigorous exercise. *New England Journal of Medicine*, *311*(14), 874–877.

Skinner, B. F. (1938). *The behavior of organisms*. New York: Appleton-Century-Crofts.

Skinner, B. F. (1953). *Science and human behavior*. New York: Macmillan.

Skinner, B. F. (1957). *Verbal behavior*. New York: Appleton-Century-Crofts.

Skinner, B. F. (1969). *Contingencies of reinforcement*. New York: Appleton-Century-Crofts.

Skinner, B. F. (1971). *Beyond freedom and dignity*. New York: Knopf.

Skinner, B. F. (1974). *About behaviorism*. New York: Knopf.

Skinner, B. F., Solomon, H. C., & Lindsley, O. R. (1953). *Studies in behavior therapy: Status report I*. Waltham, MA: Unpublished report, Metropolitan State Hospital.

Slamecka, N. J. (1985). Ebbinghaus: Some associations. *Journal of Experimental Psychology: Learning, Memory and Cognition*, *11*, 414–435.

Slaughter, M. (1990). The vertebrate retina. In K. N. Leibovic (Ed.), *Science of vision*. New York: Springer-Verlag.

Slavney, P. R. (1990). *Perspectives on hysteria*. Baltimore: Johns Hopkins University Press.

Slobin, D. I. (1985). *A cross linguistic study of language acquisition*. Hillsdale, NJ: Erlbaum.

Slochower, J., Kaplan, S. P., & Mann. L. (1981). The effects of life stress and weight on mood and eating. *Appetite*, *2*, 115–125.

Slovic, P. (1990). Choice. In D. N. Osherson & E. E. Smith (Eds.), *Thinking: An invitation to cognitive science* (Vol. 3). Cambridge, MA: MIT Press.

Slovic, P., Fischhoff, B., & Lichtenstein, S. (1982). Facts versus fears: Understanding perceived risk. In D. Kahneman, P. Slovic, & A. Tversky (Eds.), *Judg-*

ment under uncertainty: Heuristics and biases. Cambridge, England: Cambridge University Press.

Slovic, P., Lichtenstein, S., & Fischhoff, B. (1988). Decision making. In R. C. Atkinson, R. J. Herrnstein, G. Lindzey, & R. D. Luce (Eds.), *Stevens' handbook of experimental psychology* (Vol. 2). New York: Wiley.

Small, I. F., Small, J. G., & Milstein, V. (1986). Electroconvulsive therapy. In P. A. Berger & H. K. H. Brodie (Eds.), *American handbook of psychiatry: Biological psychiatry* (2nd ed., Vol. 8). New York: Basic Books.

Smilkstein, G. (1990). Psychosocial influences on health. In R. E. Rakel (Ed.), *Textbook of family practice*. Philadelphia: Saunders.

Smith, C. A., & Lazarus, R. S. (1993). Appraisal components, core relational themes, and the emotions. *Cognition and Emotion*, *7*, 233–269.

Smith, D. (1982). Trends in counseling and psychotherapy. *American Psychologist*, *37*, 802–809.

Smith, G. H., & Engel, R. (1968). Influence of a female model on perceived characteristics of an automobile. *Preceedings of the 76th Annual Convention of the American Psychological Association*, *3*, 681–682.

Smith, G. P., & Gibbs, J. (1992). The development and proof of the cholecystokinin hypothesis of satiety. In C. T. Dourish, S. J. Cooper, S. D. Iversen, & L. L. Iversen (Eds.), *Multiple cholecystokinin receptors in the CNS*. Oxford, England: Oxford University Press.

Smith, J. C. (1975). Meditation and psychotherapy: A review of the literature. *Psychological Bulletin*, *32*, 553–564.

Smith, J. C. (1993). *Understanding stress and coping*. New York: Macmillan.

Smith, M. L., & Glass, G. V. (1977). Meta-analysis of psychotherapy outcome studies. *American Psychologist*, *32*, 752–760.

Smith, M. L., Glass, G. V., & Miller, T. I. (1980). *The benefits of psychotherapy*. Baltimore: Johns Hopkins University Press.

Smith, P. B., & Bond, M. H. (1994). *Social psychology across cultures: Analysis and perspectives*. Boston: Allyn & Bacon.

Smith, S. (1988). Environmental context-dependent memory. In G. M. Davies & D. M. Thomson (Eds.), *Memory in context: Context in memory*. New York: Wiley.

Smith, T. W. (1991). *Ethnic images. GSS Topical Report No. 19*. Chicago: National Opinion Research Center.

Smith, T. W. (1992). Hostility and health: Current status of a psychosomatic hypothesis. *Health Psychology*, *11*, 139–150.

Smith, T. W., & Brown, P. C. (1991). Cynical hostility, attempts to exert social control, and cardiovascular reactivity in married couples. *Journal of Behavioral Medicine*, *14*(6), 581–592.

Snow, C. E. (1993). Bilingualism and second language acquisition. In J. B. Gleason & N. B. Ratner (Eds.), *Psycholinguistics*. Fort Worth: Harcourt Brace Jovanovich.

Snow, R. E. (1986). Individual differences in the design of educational programs. *American Psychologist*, *41*, 1029–1039.

Snyder, S. H. (1986). *Drugs and the brain*. New York: Scientific American Books.

Snyderman, M., & Rothman, S. (1987). Survey of expert opinion on intelligence and aptitude testing. *American Psychologist*, *42*, 137–144.

Sotiriou, P. E. (1993). *Integrating college study skills:*

Reasoning in reading, listening and writing. Belmont, CA: Wadsworth.

Spanos, N. P. (1986). Hypnotic behavior: A social-psychological interpretation of amnesia, analgesia, and "trance logic." *Behavioral & Brain Sciences, 9*(3), 449–467.

Spanos, N. P., Weekes, J. R., & Bertrand, L. D. (1985). Multiple personality: A social psychological perspective. *Journal of Abnormal Psychology, 94,* 362–376.

Sparks, D. L. (1988). Neural cartography: Sensory and motor maps in the superior colliculus. *Brain, Behavior and Evolution, 31,* 49–56.

Sperling, G. (1960). The information available in brief visual presentations. *Psychological Monographs, 74*(11, Whole No. 498).

Sperling, G. (1967). Successive approximations to a model for short-term memory. *Acta Psychologica, 27,* 285–292.

Sperry, R. W. (1982). Some effects of disconnecting the cerebral hemispheres. *Science, 217,* 1223–1226, 1250.

Spiegel, D., Cutcomb, S., Ren, C., & Pribram, K. (1985). Hypnotic hallucination alters evoked potentials. *Journal of Abnormal Psychology, 94,* 249–255.

Spiegel, D., & Spiegel, H. (1985). Hypnosis. In H. I. Kaplan & B. J. Sadock (Eds.), *Comprehensive textbook of psychiatry/IV.* Baltimore: Williams & Wilkins.

Spiegler, M. D., & Guevremont, D. C. (1993). *Contemporary behavior therapy.* Pacific Grove, CA: Brooks/Cole.

Spielberger, C. D., Johnson, E. H., Russell, S. F., Crane, R. J., Jacobs, G. A., & Worden, T. J. (1985). The experience and expression of anger. In M. A. Chesney, S. E. Goldston, & R. H. Rosenman (Eds.), *Anger and hostility in behavioral medicine.* New York: McGraw-Hill.

Spinweber, C. L. (1993). Gardner, Randy. In M. A. Carskadon (Ed.), *Encyclopedia of sleep and dreaming.* New York: Macmillan.

Sporakowski, M. J. (1988). A therapist's views on the consequences of change for the contemporary family. *Family Relations, 37,* 373–378.

Springer, S. P., & Deutsch, G. (1993). *Left brain, right brain* (4th ed.). New York: W. H. Freeman.

Squire, L. R. (1986). Mechanisms of memory. *Science, 232,* 1612–1619.

Squire, L. R. (1987). *Memory and brain.* New York: Oxford University Press.

Squire, L. R., & Cohen, N. J. (1984). Human memory and amnesia. In G. Lynch, J. L. McGaugh, & N. M. Weinberger (Eds.), *Neurobiology of learning and memory.* New York: Guilford Press.

Staats, A. W., & Staats, C. K. (1958). Attitudes established by classical conditioning. *Journal of Abnormal and Social Psychology, 57,* 37–40.

Staats, A. W., & Staats, C. K. (1963). *Complex human behavior.* New York: Holt, Rinehart & Winston.

Stalling, R. B. (1970). Personality similarity and evaluative meaning as conditioners of attraction. *Journal of Personality and Social Psychology, 14,* 77–82.

Stampi, C. (1989). Ultrashort sleep/wake patterns and sustained performance. In D. F. Dinges & R. J. Broughton (Eds.), *Sleep and alertness: Chronobiological, behavioral, and medical aspects of napping.* New York: Raven.

Stein, P. J. (1989). The diverse world of single adults. In J. M. Henslin (Ed.), *Marriage and family in a changing society* (3rd ed.). New York: Free Press.

Steinberg, L., Dornbusch, S. M., & Brown, B. B. (1992). Ethnic differences in adolescent achievement. *American Psychologist, 47,* 723–729.

Steinberg, L., & Silverberg, S. B. (1987). Influences on marital satisfaction during the middle stages of the family life cycle. *Journal of Marriage and the Family, 49,* 751–760.

Stekel, W. (1950). *Techniques of analytical psychotherapy.* New York: Liveright.

Stellar, E. (1954). The physiology of motivation. *Psychological Review, 61,* 5–22.

Stephan, W. G. (1989). A cognitive approach to stereotyping. In D. Bar-Tal, C. F. Graumann, A. W. Kruglanski, & W. Stroebe (Eds.), *Stereotyping and prejudice: Changing conceptions.* New York: Springer-Verlag.

Steriade, M., Ropert, N., Kitsikis, A., & Oakson, G. (1980). Ascending activating neuronal networks in midbrain reticular core and related rostral systems. In S. A. Hobson & A. M. Brazier (Eds.), *The reticular formation revisited: Specifying function for a nonspecific system.* New York: Raven.

Stern, W. (1914). *The psychological method of testing intelligence.* Baltimore: Warwick & York.

Sternberg, R. J. (1984). Toward a triarchic theory of intelligence. *Behavioral and Brain Sciences, 7,* 269–315.

Sternberg, R. J. (1985). *Beyond IQ: A triarchic theory of human intelligence.* New York: Cambridge University Press.

Sternberg, R. J. (1986). *Intelligence applied: Understanding and increasing your intellectual skills.* New York: Harcourt Brace Jovanovich.

Sternberg, R. J. (1988a). A three-facet model of creativity. In R. J. Sternberg (Ed.), *The nature of creativity: Contemporary psychological perspectives.* Cambridge, England: Cambridge University Press.

Sternberg, R. J. (1988b). *The triarchic mind: A new theory of human intelligence.* New York: Viking Press.

Sternberg, R. J. (1991). Theory-based testing of intellectual abilities: Rationale for the triarchic abilities test. In H. A. H. Rowe (Ed.), *Intelligence: Reconceptualization and measurement.* Hillsdale, NJ: Erlbaum.

Sternberg, R. J., Conway, B. E., Ketron, J. L., & Bernstein, M. (1981). People's conceptions of intelligence. *Journal of Personality and Social Psychology, 41,* 37–55.

Sternberg, R. J., & Lubart, T. I. (1992). Buy low and sell high: An investment approach to creativity. *Current Directions in Psychological Science, 1*(1), 1–5.

Sternberg, R. J., & Wagner, R. K. (1993). The *g*-ocentric view of intelligence and job performance is wrong. *Current Directions in Psychological Science, 2*(1), 1–5.

Stevens, S. S. (1955). The measurement of loudness. *Journal of the Acoustical Society of America, 27,* 815–819.

Stevenson, J. M. (1988). Suicide. In J. A. Talbott, R. E. Hales, & S. C. Yudofsky (Eds.), *The American Psychiatric Press textbook of psychiatry.* Washington, DC: American Psychiatric Press.

Stifter, C. A., & Fox, N. A. (1990). Infant reactivity: Physiological correlates of newborn and 5-month temperament. *Developmental Psychology, 26,* 582–588.

Stoddard, G. (1943). *The meaning of intelligence.* New York: Macmillan.

Stoll, A. L., Tohen, M., & Baldessarini, R. J. (1992). Increasing frequency of the diagnosis of obsessive-compulsive disorder. *American Journal of Psychiatry, 149,* 638–640.

Stone, A. A., Bovbjerg, D. H., Neale, J. M., Napoli, A., Valdimarsdottir, H., Cox, D., Hayden, F. G., & Gwaltney, J. M. (1992). Development of the common cold symptoms following experimental rhinovirus infection is related to prior stressful events. *Behavioral Medicine, 18,* 115–120.

Stone, L. (1977). *The family, sex and marriage in England 1500–1800.* New York: Harper & Row.

Stoner, J. A. F. (1961). *A comparison of individual and group decisions involving risk.* Unpublished master's thesis, Massachusetts Institute of Technology.

Streissguth, A. P., Barr, H. M., Sampson, P. D., Darby, B. L., & Martin, D. C. (1989). IQ at age 4 in relation to maternal alcohol use and smoking during pregnancy. *Developmental Psychology, 25,* 3–11.

Streissguth, A. P., Martin, D. C., Barr, H. M., Sandman, B. M., Kirchner, G. L., & Darby, B. L. (1984). Intrauterine alcohol and nicotine exposure: Attention and reaction time in 4-year-old children. *Developmental Psychology, 20,* 533–541.

Striegel-Moore, R., & Rodin, J. (1986). The influence of psychological variables in obesity. In K. D. Brownell & J. P. Foreyt (Eds.), *Handbook of eating disorders: Physiology, psychology, and treatment of obesity, anorexia and bulimia.* New York: Basic Books.

Strongman, K. T. (1978). *The psychology of emotion.* New York: Wiley.

Stumpf, H. (1993). The factor structure of the Personality Research Form: A cross-national evaluation. *Journal of Personality, 61,* 27–48.

Stunkard, A. J., Harris, J. R., Pederson, N. L., & McClearn, G. E. (1990). The body-mass index of twins who have been reared apart. *New England Journal of Medicine, 322,* 1483–1487.

Stunkard, A. J., Sorensen, T., Hanis, C., Teasdale, T. W., Chakraborty, R., Schull, W. J., & Schulsinger, F. (1986). An adoption study of human obesity. *New England Journal of Medicine, 314,* 193–198.

Sturgis, E. T. (1993). Obsessive-compulsive disorders. In P. B. Sutker & H. E. Adams (Eds.), *Comprehensive handbook of psychopathology* (2nd ed.). New York: Plenum.

Suddath, R. L., Christison, G. W., Torrey, E. F., Casanova, M. F., & Weinberger, D. R. (1990). Anatomical abnormalities in the brains of monozygotic twins discordant for schizophrenia. *The New England Journal of Medicine, 322*(12), 789–794.

Sue, S. (1991). Ethnicity and culture in psychological research and practice. In J. D. Goodchilds (Ed.), *Psychological perspectives on human diversity in America.* Washington, DC: American Psychological Association.

Sue, S., & Okazaki, S. (1990). Asian-American educational achievements: A phenomenon in search of an explanation. *American Psychologist, 45,* 913–920.

Sue, S., & Zane, N. (1987). The role of culture and cultural techniques in psychotherapy: A critique and reformulation. *American Psychologist, 42,* 37–45.

Sue, S., Zane, N., & Young, K. (1994). Research on psychotherapy with culturally diverse populations. In A. E. Bergin & S. L. Garfield (Eds.), *Handbook of psychotherapy and behavior change* (4th ed.). New York: Wiley.

Sulin, R. A., & Dooling, D. J. (1974). Intrusion of a thematic idea in retention of prose. *Journal of Experimental Psychology, 103,* 255–262.

Suls, J., & Marco, C. A. (1990). Relationship

between JAS- and FTAS-Type A behavior and Non-CHD illness: A prospective study controlling for negative affectivity. *Health Psychology, 9,* 479–492.

Super, C. M. (1976). Environmental effects on motor development: A case of African infant precocity. *Developmental Medicine and Child Neurology, 18,* 561–567.

Swartz, C. M. (1993). Clinical and laboratory predictors of ECT response. In C. E. Coffey (Ed.), *The clinical science of electroconvulsive therapy*. Washington, DC: American Psychiatric Press.

Sweeney, P. D., Anderson, K., & Bailey, S. (1986). Attributional style in depression: A meta-analytic review. *Journal of Personality and Social Psychology, 50,* 974–991.

Szasz, T. (1974). *The myth of mental illness*. New York: Harper & Row.

Szasz, T. (1990). Law and psychiatry: The problems that will not go away. *The Journal of Mind and Behavior, 11*(3/4), 557–564.

Tabakoff, B., & Hoffman, P. L. (1992). Alcohol: Neurobiology. In J. H. Lowinson, P. Ruiz, & R. B. Millman (Eds.), *Substance abuse: A comprehensive textbook* (2nd ed.). Baltimore: Williams & Wilkins.

Takahashi, K. (1986). Examining the Strange Situation procedure with Japanese mothers and 12-month-old infants. *Developmental Psychology, 19,* 184–191.

Takahashi, K. (1990). Are the key assumptions of the "Strange Situation" procedure universal? *Human Development, 33,* 23–30.

Tanner, J. M. (1978). *Fetus into man: Physical growth from conception to maturity*. Cambridge, MA: Harvard University Press.

Tart, C. T. (1988). From spontaneous event to lucidity: A review of attempts to consciously control nocturnal dreaming. In J. Gackenbach & S. LaBerge (Eds.), *Conscious mind, sleeping brain: Perspectives on lucid dreaming*. New York: Plenum.

Tavris, C. (1992). *The mismeasure of woman*. New York: Simon & Schuster.

Tavris, C., & Sadd, S. (1977). *The Redbook report on female sexuality*. New York: Delacorte.

Taylor, M., & Gelman, S. A. (1989). Incorporating new words into the lexicon: Preliminary evidence for language hierarchies in two-year-old children. *Child Development, 60,* 625–636.

Taylor, S. E. (1989). *Positive illusions: Creative self-deception and the healthy mind*. New York: Basic Books.

Tedlock, B. (1992). Zuni and Quiche dream sharing and interpreting. In B. Tedlock (Ed.), *Dreaming: Anthropological and psychological interpretations*. Santa Fe, NM: School of American Research Press.

Teicher, M. H., Glod, C., & Cole, J. O. (1990). Emergence of intense suicidal preoccupation during fluoxetine treatment. *American Journal of Psychiatry, 147,* 207–210.

Teitelbaum, P., & Epstein, A. (1962). The lateral hypothalamic syndrome: Recovery of feeding and drinking after lateral hypothalamic lesions. *Psychological Review, 69,* 74–90.

Tellegen, A., Lykken, D. T., Bouchard, T. J., Jr., Wilcox, K. J., Segal, N. L., & Rich, S. (1988). Personality similarity in twins reared apart and together. *Journal of Personality and Social Psychology, 54,* 1031–1039.

Temoshok, L., Sweet, D. M., & Zich, J. (1987). A three city comparison of the public's knowledge and attitudes about AIDS. *Psychology & Health, 1*(1), 43–60.

Tepas, D. I. (1982). Work/sleep time schedules and performance. In W. B. Webb (Ed.), *Biological rhythms, sleep and performance*. New York: Wiley.

Terman, L. M. (1916). *The measurement of intelligence*. Boston: Houghton-Mifflin.

Terman, L. M. (1922). The great conspiracy. *New Republic, 33,* 116–120.

Tesser, A., & Shaffer, D. R. (1990). Attitudes and attitude change. *Annual Review of Psychology, 41,* 479–523.

Tessier-Lavigne, M. (1991). Phototransduction and information processing in the retina. In E. R. Kandel, J. H. Schwartz, & T. M. Jessell (Eds.), *Principles of neural science* (3rd ed.). New York: Elsevier.

Tetlock, P. E., Peterson, R. S., McGuire, C., Chang, S., & Feld, P. (1992). Assessing political group dynamics: A test of the groupthink model. *Journal of Personality and Social Psychology, 63,* 403–425.

Teuber, M. (1974). Sources of ambiguity in the prints of Maurits C. Escher. *Scientific American, 231,* 90–104.

Thigpen, C. H., & Cleckley, H. M. (1984). On the incidence of multiple personality disorder: A brief communication. *International Journal of Clinical and Experimental Hypnosis, 32,* 63–66.

Thoma, S. J. (1986). Estimating gender differences in the comprehension and preference of moral issues. *Developmental Review, 6,* 165–180.

Thomas, A., & Chess, S. (1977). *Temperament and development*. New York: Brunner/Mazel.

Thomas, A., & Chess, S. (1989). Temperament and personality. In G. A. Kohnstamm, J. E. Bates, & M. K. Rothbart (Eds.), *Temperament in childhood*. New York: Wiley.

Thomas, A., Chess, S., & Birch, H. G. (1970). The origin of personality. *Scientific American, 223*(2), 102–109.

Thomas, D. R. (1992). Discrimination and generalization. In L. R. Squire (Ed.), *Encyclopedia of learning and memory*. New York: Macmillan.

Thomason, B. T., Brantkey, P. J., Jones, G. N., Dyer, H. R., & Morris, J. L. (1992). The relation between stress and disease activity in rheumatoid arthritis. *Journal of Behavioral Medicine, 15,* 215–220.

Thompson, D. A., & Campbell, R. G. (1977). Hunger in humans induced by 2-deoxy-D-glucose: Glucoprivic control of taste preference and food intake. *Science, 198,* 1065–1068.

Thompson, R. F. (1972). Sensory preconditioning. In R. F. Thompson & J. S. Voss (Eds.), *Topics in learning and performance*. New York: Academic Press.

Thompson, R. F. (1989). A model system approach to memory. In P. R. Solomon, G. R. Goethals, C. M. Kelley, & B. R. Stephens (Eds.), *Memory: Interdisciplinary approaches*. New York: Springer-Verlag.

Thorndyke, P. W. (1984). Applications of schema theory in cognitive research. In J. R. Anderson & S. M. Kosslyn (Eds.), *Tutorials in learning and memory*. San Francisco: W. H. Freeman.

Thorndyke, P. W., & Hayes-Roth, B. (1979). The use of schemata in the acquisition and transfer of knowledge. *Cognitive Psychology, 11,* 83–106.

Thornton, B. (1984). Defensive attribution of responsibility: Evidence for an arousal-based motivational bias. *Journal of Personality and Social Psychology, 46,* 721–734.

Thornton, B. (1992). Repression and its mediating influence on the defensive attribution of responsibility. *Journal of Research in Personality, 26,* 44–57.

Ting-Toomey, S. (1991). Intimacy expressions in three cultures: France, Japan and the United States. *International Journal of Intercultural Relations, 15,* 29–46.

Todd, J. T., & Morris, E. K. (1992). Case histories in the great power of steady misrepresentation. *American Psychologist, 47,* 1441–1453.

Tolman, E. C. (1922). A new formula for behaviorism. *Psychological Review, 29,* 44–53.

Tolman, E. C. (1932). *Purposive behavior in animals and men*. New York: Appleton-Century-Crofts.

Tomkins, S. S. (1980). Affect as amplification: Some modifications in theory. In R. Plutchik & H. Kellerman (Eds.), *Emotion: Theory, research and experience* (Vol. 1). New York: Academic Press.

Tomkins, S. S. (1991). *Affect, imagery, consciousness: 3. Anger and fear*. New York: Springer-Verlag.

Torsvall, L., Akerstedt, T., Gillander, K., & Knutsson, A. (1989). Sleep on the night shift: 24-hour EEG monitoring of spontaneous sleep/walk behavior. *Psychophysiology, 26*(3), 352–358.

Toufexis, A. (1990, December 17). Drowsy America. *Time*, pp. 78–85.

Toufexis, A. (1991, October 28). When can memories be trusted? *Time*, pp. 86–88.

Triandis, H. C. (1989). Self and social behavior in differing cultural contexts. *Psychological Review, 96,* 269–289.

Triandis, H. C. (1994). *Culture and social behavior*. New York: McGraw-Hill.

Trimble, J. E. (1988). Stereotypical images, American Indians, and prejudice. In P. A. Katz & D. A. Taylor (Eds.), *Eliminating racism: Profiles in controversy*. New York: Plenum.

Trope, Y., & Liberman, A. (1993). The use of trait conceptions to identify other people's behavior and to draw inferences about their personalities. *Personality and Social Psychology Bulletin, 19,* 553–562.

Tseng, W. S., Di, X., Ebata, K., Hsu, J., & Yuhua, C. (1986). Diagnostic pattern for neuroses in China, Japan, and the United States. *American Journal of Psychiatry, 43,* 1010–1014.

Tulving, E. (1985). How many memory systems are there? *American Psychologist, 40,* 385–398.

Tulving, E. (1986). What kind of a hypothesis is the distinction between episodic and semantic memory? *Journal of Experimental Psychology: Learning, Memory and Cognition, 12,* 307–311.

Tulving, E. (1987). Multiple memory systems and consciousness. *Human Neurobiology, 6*(2), 67–80.

Tulving, E. (1993). What is episodic memory? *Current Directions in Psychological Science, 2*(3), 67–70.

Tulving, E., & Psotka, J. (1971). Retroactive inhibition in free recall: Inaccessability of information available in the memory store. *Journal of Experimental Psychology, 87,* 1–8.

Tulving, E., & Schacter, D. L. (1990). Priming and human memory systems. *Science, 247,* 301–306.

Tulving, E., & Thomson, D. M. (1973). Encoding specificity and retrieval processes in episodic memory. *Psychological Review, 80,* 352–373.

Turkheimer, E. (1991). Individual and group differences in adoption studies of IQ. *Psychological Bulletin, 110,* 392–405.

Turkkan, J. S. (1989). Classical conditioning: The new hegemony. *Behavioral and Brain Sciences, 12,* 121–179.

Turnbull, W. W. (1979). Intelligence testing in the year 2000. In R. J. Sternberg & D. K. Detterman

(Eds.), *Human intelligence: Perspectives on its theory and measurement*. Norwood, NJ: Ablex.

Turner, M. E., Pratkanis, A. R., Probasco, P., & Leve, C. (1992). Threat, cohesion, and group effectiveness: Testing a social identity maintenance perspective on groupthink. *Journal of Personality and Social Psychology, 63*, 781–796.

Turner, S. M., McCann, B. S., Beidel, D. C., & Mezzich, J. E. (1986). DSM-III classification of the anxiety disorders: A psychometric study. *Journal of Abnormal Psychology, 95*, 168–172.

Tversky, A. (1972). Elimination by aspects: A theory of choice. *Psychological Review, 79*, 281–299.

Tversky, A., & Kahneman, D. (1971). Belief in the law of small numbers. *Psychological Bulletin, 76*, 105–110.

Tversky, A., & Kahneman, D. (1973). Availability: A heuristic for judging frequency and probability. *Cognitive Psychology, 5*, 207–232.

Tversky, A., & Kahneman, D. (1974). Judgments under uncertainty: Heuristics and biases. *Science, 185*, 1124–1131.

Tversky, A., & Kahneman, D. (1982). Judgment under uncertainty: Heuristics and biases. In D. Kahneman, P. Slovic, & A. Tversky (Eds.), *Judgment under uncertainty: Heuristics and biases*. New York: Cambridge University Press.

Tversky, A., & Kahneman, D. (1988). Rational choice and the framing of decisions. In D. E. Bell, H. Raiffa, & A. Tversky (Eds.), *Decision making: Descriptive, normative, and prescriptive interactions*. New York: Cambridge University Press.

Tversky, A., & Kahneman, D. (1991). Loss aversion in riskless choice: A reference-dependent model. *Quarterly Journal of Economics, 106*(4), 1039–1061.

Ulrich, R. E. (1991). Animal rights, animal wrongs and the question of balance. *Psychological Science, 2*, 197–201.

Underwood, B. J. (1961). Ten years of massed practice on distributed practice. *Psychological Review, 68*, 229–247.

Underwood, B. J. (1970). A breakdown of the total-time law in free-recall learning. *Journal of Verbal Learning and Verbal Behavior, 9*, 573–580.

Unger, R. K., & Crawford, M. (1993). Commentary: Sex and gender—The troubled relationship between terms and concepts. *Psychological Science, 4*, 122–124.

Upshaw, H. S. (1969). The personal reference scale: An approach to social judgment. In L. Berkowitz (Ed.), *Advances in experimental social psychology* (Vol. 4). New York: Academic Press.

U.S. Department of Health and Human Services. (1989). *Reducing the health consequences of smoking: 25 years of progress*. Rockville, MD: U.S. Government Printing Office.

U.S. Department of Health and Human Services. (1990). *The health benefits of smoking cessation: A report of the surgeon general*. Washington, DC: U.S. Government Printing Office.

Vaillant, G. E. (1992). *Ego mechanisms of defense: A guide for clinicians and researchers*. Washington, DC: American Psychiatric Press.

Vaillant, G. E. (1994). Ego mechanisms of defense and personality psychopathology. *Journal of Abnormal Psychology, 103*, 44–50.

Valenstein, E. S. (1973). *Brain control*. New York: Wiley.

Vallone, R. P., Griffin, D. W., Lin, S., & Ross, L. (1990). Overconfident prediction of future actions and outcomes by self and others. *Journal of Personality and Social Psychology, 58*, 582–592.

Vandenberg, S. G., & Vogler, G. P. (1985). Genetic determinants of intelligence. In B. B. Wolman (Ed.), *Handbook of intelligence: Theories, measurements, and applications*. New York: Wiley.

VandenBos, G. R., Cummings, N. A., & DeLeon, P. H. (1992). A century of psychotherapy: Economic and environmental influences. In D. K. Freedheim (Eds.), *History of psychotherapy: A century of change*. Washington, DC: American Psychological Association.

VanderPlate, C., Aral, S. O., & Magder, L. (1988). The relationship among genital herpes simplex virus, stress, and social support. *Health Psychology, 7*, 159–168.

van der Post, L. (1975). *Jung and the story of our time*. New York: Vintage Books.

van der Velde, F. W., van der Pligt, J., & Hooykaas, C. (1994). Perceiving AIDS-related risk: Accuracy as a function of differences in actual risk. *Health Psychology, 13*, 25–33.

Vane, J. R., & Motta, R. W. (1990). Group intelligence tests. In G. Goldstein & M. Hersen (Eds.), *Handbook of psychological assessment*. New York: Pergamon Press.

Van Houten, R. (1983). Punishment: From the animal laboratory to the applied setting. In S. Axelrod & J. Apsche (Eds.), *The effects of punishment on human behavior*. New York: Academic Press.

VanItallie, T. B. (1979). Obesity: Adverse effects on health and longevity. *American Journal of Clinical Nutrition, 32*, 2727.

Vaughn, B. E., Hinde-Stevenson, J., Waters, E., Kotsaftis, A., Lefever, G. B., Shouldice, A., Trudel, M., & Belsky, J. (1992). Attachment security and temperament in infancy and early childhood: Some conceptual clarifications. *Developmental Psychology, 28*, 463–473.

Ventura, J., Nuechterlein, K. H., Lukoff, D., & Hardesty, J. P. (1989). A prospective study of stressful life events and schizophrenic relapse. *Journal of Abnormal Psychology, 98*, 407–411.

Vernon, P. E. (1982). *The abilities and achievements of Orientals in North America*. New York: Academic Press.

Vierck, C. (1978). Somatosensory system. In R. B. Masterston (Ed.), *Handbook of sensory neurobiology*. New York: Plenum.

Vinogradov, S., & Yalom, I. D. (1988). Group therapy. In J. A. Talbott, R. E. Hales, & S. C. Yudofsky (Eds.), *The American Psychiatric Press textbook of psychiatry*. Washington, DC: American Psychiatric Press.

Vogt, T., Mullooly, J., Ernst, D., Pope, C., & Hollis, J. (1992). Social networks as predictors of ischemic heart disease, cancer, stroke and hypertension: Incidence, survival and mortality. *Journal of Clinical Epidemiology, 45*, 659–666.

Volkow, N. D., & Tancredi, L. R. (1991). Biological correlates of mental activity studied with PET. *American Journal of Psychiatry, 148*, 439–443.

Wade, P., & Bernstein, B. (1991). Culture sensitivity training and counselor's race: Effects on Black female client's perceptions and attrition. *Journal of Counseling Psychology, 38*, 9–15.

Wald, G. (1964). The receptors of human color vision. *Science, 145*, 1007–1017.

Walker, L. J. (1988). The development of moral reasoning. In R. Vasta (Ed.), *Annals of child development* (Vol. 5). Greenwich, CT: JAI Press.

Walker, L. J. (1989). A longitudinal study of moral reasoning. *Child Development, 60*, 157–166.

Walker, L. J. (1991). Sex differences in moral reasoning. In W. M. Kurtines & J. L. Gewirtz (Eds.), *Handbook of moral behavior and development* (Vol. 2). Hillsdale, NJ: Erlbaum.

Walker, L. J., & Taylor, J. H. (1991). Strange transitions in moral reasoning: A longitudinal study of developmental processes. *Developmental Psychology, 27*, 330–337.

Wallace, R. K., & Benson, H. (1972). The physiology of meditation. *Scientific American, 226*, 84–90.

Wallach, M. A. (1985). Creativity testing and giftedness. In F. D. Horowitz & M. O'Brien (Eds.), *The gifted and talented: Developmental perspectives*. Washington, DC: American Psychological Association.

Wallach, M. A., & Kogan, N. (1965). *Modes of thinking in young children*. New York: Holt, Rinehart & Winston.

Wallbott, H. G., & Scherer, K. R. (1988). How universal and specific is emotional experience? Evidence from 27 countries. In K. R. Scherer (Ed.), *Facets of emotions*. Hillsdale, NJ: Erlbaum.

Walraven, J., Enroth-Cugell, C., Hood, D. C., MacLeod, D. I. A., & Schnapf, J. L. (1990). The control of visual sensitivity: Receptoral and postreceptoral processes. In L. Spillmann & J. S. Werner (Eds.), *Visual perception: The neurophysiological foundations*. San Diego: Academic Press.

Walster, E., Aronson, V., Abrahams, D., & Rottmann, L. (1966). Importance of physical attractiveness in dating behavior. *Journal of Personality and Social Psychology, 4*, 508–516.

Walster, E., & Berscheid, E. (1974). A little bit about love: A minor essay on a major topic. In T. L. Huston (Ed.), *Foundations of interpersonal attraction*. New York: Academic Press.

Walter, T., & Siebert, A. (1990). *Student success: How to succeed in college and still have time for your friends*. Fort Worth: Holt, Rinehart & Winston.

Walters, C. C., & Grusec, J. E. (1977). *Punishment*. San Francisco: W. H. Freeman.

Wangensteen, O. H., & Carlson, A. J. (1931). Hunger sensation after total gastrectomy. *Proceedings of the Society for Experimental Biology, 28*, 545–547.

Wansell, G. (1983). *Haunted idol: The story of the real Cary Grant*. New York: Ballantine.

Warner, R. (1989). Deinstitutionalization: How did we get where we are? *Journal of Social Issues, 45*(3), 17–30.

Warrington, E. K., & Weiskrantz, L. (1970). Amnesic syndrome: Consolidation or retrieval? *Nature, 228*, 629–630.

Warwick, D. P. (1975, February). Social scientists ought to stop lying. *Psychology Today*, pp. 38, 40, 105–106.

Washburn, M. F. (1908). *The animal mind*. New York: MacMillan.

Watson, D. (1982). The actor and the observer: How are their perceptions of causality divergent? *Psychological Bulletin, 92*, 682–700.

Watson, D., & Pennebaker, J. W. (1989). Health complaints, stress, and distress: Exploring the central role of negative affectivity. *Psychological Review, 96*, 234–254.

Watson, D. L., & Tharp, R. G. (1989). *Self-directed behavior: Self-modification for personal adjustment* (5th ed.). Pacific Grove, CA: Brooks/Cole.

Watson, D. L., & Tharp, R. G. (1993). *Self-directed*

behavior: Self-modification for personal adjustment (6th ed.). Pacific Grove, CA: Brooks/Cole.

Watson, J. B. (1913). Psychology as the behaviorist views it. *Psychological Review, 20,* 158–177.

Watson, J. B. (1924). *Behaviorism.* New York: Norton.

Watson, J. B. (1930). *Behaviorism.* New York: Norton.

Watson, J. B., & Rayner, R. (1920). Conditioned emotional reactions. *Journal of Experimental Psychology, 3,* 1–14.

Weaver, R. C., & Rodnick, J. E. (1986). Type-A behavior: Clinical significance, evaluation, and management. *Journal of Family Practice, 23*(3), 255–261.

Webb, W. B. (1992a). Developmental aspects and a behavioral model of human sleep. In C. Stampi (Ed.), *Why we nap: Evolution, chronobiology, and functions of polyphasic and ultrashort sleep.* Boston: Birkhaeuser.

Webb, W. B. (1992b). *Sleep: The gentle tyrant.* Bolton, MA: Anker.

Webb, W. B., & Cartwright, R. D. (1978). Sleep and dreams. In M. R. Rosenzweig & L. W. Porter (Eds.), *Annual review of psychology* (Vol. 29). Palo Alto, CA: Annual Reviews.

Webb, W. B., & Dinges, D. F. (1989). Cultural perspectives on napping and the siesta. In D. F. Dinges & R. J. Broughton (Eds.), *Sleep and alertness: Chronobiological, behavioral, and medical aspects of napping.* New York: Raven.

Wechsler, D. (1939). *The measurement of adult intelligence.* Baltimore: Williams & Wilkins.

Wechsler, D. (1949). *Wechsler intelligence scale for children.* New York: Psychological Corporation.

Wechsler, D. (1955). *Manual, Wechsler adult intelligence scale.* New York: Psychological Corporation.

Wechsler, D. (1967). *Manual for the Wechsler preschool and primary scale of intelligence.* New York: Psychological Corporation.

Wechsler, D. (1981). *Manual for the Wechsler adult intelligence scale-revised.* New York: Psychological Corporation.

Wechsler, D. (1991). *WISC-III manual.* San Antonio, TX: Psychological Corporation.

Weinberg, R. A. (1989). Intelligence and IQ: Landmark issues and great debates. *American Psychologist, 44,* 98–104.

Weinberger, D. A. (1990). The construct validity of the repressive coping style. In J. L. Singer (Ed.), *Repression and dissociation.* Chicago: University of Chicago Press.

Weiner, B. (Ed.). (1974). *Achievement motivation and attribution theory.* Morristown, NJ: General Learning Press.

Weiner, B. (1980). *Human motivation.* New York: Holt, Rinehart & Winston.

Weiner, B., Frieze, I., Kukla, A., Reed, L., Rest, S., & Rosenbaum, R. M. (1972). Perceiving the causes of success and failure. In E. E. Jones, D. E. Kanouse, H. H. Kelley, R. E. Nisbett, S. Valins, & B. Weiner (Eds.), *Perceiving the causes of behavior.* Morristown, NJ: General Learning Press.

Weiner, H. (1978). Emotional factors. In S. C. Werner & S. H. Ingbar (Eds.), *The thyroid.* New York: Harper & Row.

Weiner, H. (1992). *Perturbing the organism: The biology of stressful experience.* Chicago: University of Chicago Press.

Weiner, R. D. (1984). Does electroconvulsive

therapy cause brain damage? *Behavioral and Brain Sciences, 7,* 1–22.

Weiner, R. D., & Coffey, C. E. (1988). Indications for use of electroconvulsive therapy. In A. J. Frances & R. E. Hales (Eds.), *Review of psychiatry* (Vol. 7). Washington, DC: American Psychiatric Press.

Weinstein, N. D. (1984). Why it won't happen to me: Perceptions of risk factors and susceptibility. *Health Psychology, 3,* 431–458.

Weinstein, N. D. (1989). Perceptions of personal susceptibility to harm. In V. M. Mays, G. W. Albee, & S. F. Schneider (Eds.), *Primary prevention of AIDS: Psychological approaches.* Newbury Park, CA: Sage.

Weisaeth, L. (1993). Disasters: Psychological and psychiatric aspects. In L. Goldberger & S. Breznitz (Eds.), *Handbook of stress: Theoretical and clinical aspects* (2nd ed.). New York: Free Press.

Weisberg, R. W. (1986). *Creativity: Genius and other myths.* New York: W. H. Freeman.

Weisberg, R. W. (1988). Problem solving and creativity. In R. J. Sternberg (Ed.), *The nature of creativity: Contemporary psychological perspectives.* Cambridge, England: Cambridge University Press.

Weissman, M. M., Bruce, M. L., Leaf, P. J., Florio, L. P., & Holzer, C., III. (1991). Affective disorders. In L. N. Robins & D. A. Regier (Eds.), *Psychiatric disorders in America: The epidemiologic catchment area study.* New York: Free Press.

Weisz, J. R., Rothbaum, F. M., & Blackburn, T. C. (1984). Standing out and standing in: The psychology of control in America and Japan. *American Psychologist, 39,* 955–969.

Weiten, W. (1984). Violation of selected item-construction principles in educational measurement. *Journal of Experimental Education, 51,* 46–50.

Weiten, W. (1988). Pressure as a form of stress and its relationship to psychological symptomatology. *Journal of Social and Clinical Psychology, 6*(1), 127–139.

Weiten, W., & Diamond, S. S. (1979). A critical review of the jury-simulation paradigm: The case of defendant characteristics. *Law and Human Behavior, 3,* 71–93.

Weiten, W., & Dixon, J. (1984, August). *Measurement of pressure as a form of stress.* Paper presented at the meeting of the American Psychological Association, Toronto, Ontario.

Weiten, W., & Wight, R. D. (1992). Portraits of a discipline: An examination of introductory psychology textbooks in America. In A. E. Puente, J. R. Matthews, & C. L. Brewer (Eds.), *Teaching psychology in America: A history.* Washington, DC: American Psychological Association.

Wekstein, L. (1979). *Handbook of suicidology.* New York: Brunner/Mazel.

Well, A. D., Pollatsek, A., & Boyce, S. J. (1990). Understanding the effects of sample size on the variability of the mean. *Organizational Behavior and Human Decision Processes, 47,* 289–312.

Welsh, D. K. (1993). Timing of sleep and wakefulness. In M. A. Carskadon (Ed.), *Encyclopedia of sleep and dreaming.* New York: Macmillan.

Wen, S. W., Goldenberg, R. L., Cutter, G. R., Hoffman, H. J., Cliver, S. P., Davis, R. O., & DuBard, M. B. (1990). Smoking, maternal age, fetal growth, and gestational age at delivery. *American Journal of Obstetrics and Gynecology, 162,* 53–58.

Wertheimer, M. (1912). Experimentelle studien über das sehen von bewegung. *Zeitschrift für Psychologie, 60,* 312–378.

Westen, D. (1990). Psychoanalytic approaches to personality. In L. A. Pervin (Ed.), *Handbook of personality: Theory and research.* New York: Guilford Press.

Wever, E. G., & Bray, C. W. (1937). The perception of low tones and the resonance-volley theory. *Journal of Psychology, 3,* 101–114.

Wever, R. A. (1979). *The circadian system of man: Results of experiments under temporal isolation.* New York: Springer-Verlag.

Wever, R. A. (1989). Light effects on human circadian rhythms: A review of recent andechs experiments. *Journal of Biological Rhythms, 4*(2), 161–185.

White, K. R. (1982). The relation between socioeconomic status and academic achievement. *Psychological Bulletin, 91,* 461–481.

White, P. A., & Younger, D. P. (1988). Differences in the ascription of transient internal states to self and other. *Journal of Experimental Psychology, 24,* 292–309.

Whorf, B. L. (1956). Science and linguistics. In J. B. Carroll (Ed.), *Language, thought and reality: Selected writings of Benjamin Lee Whorf.* Cambridge, MA: MIT Press.

Widiger, T. A., Frances, A. J., Pincus, H. A., Davis, W. W., & First, M. B. (1991). Toward an empirical classification for the DSM-IV. *Journal of Abnormal Psychology, 100,* 280–288.

Wielawski, I. (1991, October 3). Unlocking the secrets of memory. *Los Angeles Times,* p. 1.

Wiggins, J. S. (1992). Have model, will travel. *Journal of Personality, 60,* 527–532.

Wilcox, A. J., Weinberg, C. R., O'Connor, J. F., Baurd, D. D., Schlatterer, J. P., Canfield, R. E., Armstrong, E. G., & Nisula, B. C. (1988). Incidence of early loss of pregnancy. *New England Journal of Medicine, 319,* 189–194.

Wilder, D. A. (1981). Perceiving persons as a group: Categorization and intergroup relations. In D. L. Hamilton (Ed.), *Cognitive processing in stereotyping and intergroup behavior.* Hillsdale, NJ: Erlbaum.

Williams, B. A. (1988). Reinforcement, choice, and response strength. In R. C. Atkinson, R. J. Herrnstein, G. Lindzey, & R. D. Luce (Eds.), *Stevens' handbook of experimental psychology.* New York: Wiley.

Williams, C. D. (1959). The elimination of tantrum behavior by extinction procedures. *Journal of Abnormal and Social Psychology, 59,* 269.

Williams, M. H. (1992). Exploitation and inference: Mapping the damage from therapist-patient sexual involvement. *American Psychologist, 47,* 412–421.

Williams, N. A., & Deffenbacher, J. L. (1983). Life stress and chronic yeast infections. *Journal of Human Stress, 9*(1), 26–31.

Williams, R., Karacan, I., & Hursch, C. (1974). *EEG and human sleep.* New York: Wiley.

Williams, R. B., & Barefoot, J. C. (1988). Coronary-prone behavior: The emerging role of the hostility complex. In B. K. Houston & C. R. Snyder (Eds.), *Type A behavior pattern: Research, theory, and intervention.* New York: Wiley.

Williams, R. L., Dotson, W., Dow, P., & Williams, W. S. (1980). The war against testing: A current status report. *Journal of Negro Education, 49,* 263–273.

Willis, W. D. (1985). *The pain system. The neural basis of nociceptive transmission in the mammalian nervous system.* Basel: Karger.

Wilson, E. O. (1980). *Sociobiology*. Cambridge, MA: Harvard University Press.

Wilson, G. T. (1982). Alcohol and anxiety: Recent evidence on the tension reduction theory of alcohol use and abuse. In K. R. Blankstein & J. Polivy (Eds.), *Self-control and self-modification of emotional behavior*. New York: Plenum.

Wilson, M. (1993). DSM-III and the transformation of American psychiatry: A history. *American Journal of Psychiatry, 150*, 399–410.

Winfree, A. T. (1987). *The timing of biological clocks*. New York: Scientific American Library.

Wingerson, L. (1990). *Mapping our genes: The genome project and the future of medicine*. New York: Penguin.

Wingert, P., & Kantrowitz, B. (1990, Winter/Spring). The day care generation [Special Edition]. *Newsweek*, pp. 86–87, 89, 92.

Winograd, T. (1975). Frame representations and the declarative-procedural controversy. In D. Bobrow & A. Collins (Eds.), *Representation and understanding: Studies in cognitive science*. New York: Academic Press.

Winter, D. G. (1992). Content analysis of archival materials, personal documents, and everyday verbal productions. In C. P. Smith (Ed.), *Motivation and personality: Handbook of thematic content analysis*. New York: Cambridge University Press.

Wise, R. A., & Bozarth, M. A. (1987). A psychomotor stimulant theory of addiction. *Psychological Review, 94*, 469–492.

Wise, R. A., & Rompre, P. P. (1989). Brain dopamine and reward. *Annual Review of Psychology, 40*, 191–225.

Witkin, H. A. (1950). Individual differences in ease of perception of embedded figures. *Journal of Personality, 19*, 1–15.

Witkin, H. A., & Berry, J. W. (1975). Psychological differentiation in cross-cultural perspective. *Journal of Cross-Cultural Psychology, 6*, 4–87.

Witkin, H. A., Dyk, R. B., Paterson, H. F., Goodenough, D. R., & Karp, S. (1962). *Psychological differentiation*. New York: Wiley.

Witkin, H. A., & Goodenough, D. (1981). *Cognitive styles: Essence and origins*. New York: International Universities Press.

Witkin, H. A., Moore, C. A., Goodenough, D. R., & Cox, P. W. (1977). Field-dependent and field-independent cognitive styles and their educational implications. *Review of Educational Research*, 1–64.

Wittkower, E. D., & Warnes, H. (1984). Cultural aspects of psychotherapy. In J. E. Mezzich & C. E. Berganza (Eds.), *Culture and psychopathology*. New York: Columbia University Press.

Wixted, J. T., Bellack, A. S., & Hersen, M. (1990). Behavior therapy. In A. S. Bellack & M. Hersen (Eds.), *Handbook of comparative treatments for adult disorders*. New York: Wiley.

Wolf, R. M. (1965). The measurement of environments. In C. W. Harris (Ed.), *Proceedings of the 1964 invited conference on testing problems*. Princeton, NJ: Educational Testing Service.

Wolf, S., & Goodell, H. (1968). *Stress and disease*. Springfield, IL: Charles C Thomas.

Wolpe, J. (1958). *Psychotherapy by reciprocal inhibition*. Stanford, CA: Stanford University Press.

Wolpe, J. (1987). The promotion of scientific therapy: A long voyage. In J. K. Zeig (Ed.), *The evolution of psychotherapy*. New York: Brunner/Mazel.

Wolpe, J. (1990). *The practice of behavior therapy*. Elmsford, NY: Pergamon Press.

Wood, F., Ebert, V., & Kinsbourne, M. (1982). The episodic-semantic memory distinction in memory and amnesia: Clinical and experimental observations. In L. Cermak (Ed.), *Human memory and amnesia*. Hillsdale, NJ: Erlbaum.

Woolfolk, R. L. (1975). Psychophysiological correlates of meditation. *Archives of General Psychiatry, 32*, 1326–1333.

Woolfolk, R. L., & Richardson, F. C. (1978). *Stress, sanity and survival*. New York: Sovereign/Monarch.

Wundt, W. (1874/1904). *Principles of physiological psychology*. Leipzig: Engelmann.

Wyatt, R. J. (1985). Science and psychiatry. In H. I. Kaplan & B. J. Sadock (Eds.), *Comprehensive textbook of psychiatry/IV*. Baltimore: Williams & Wilkins.

Wyler, A. R., Masuda, M., & Holmes, T. H. (1971). Magnitude of life events and seriousness of illness. *Psychosomatic Medicine, 33*(2), 115–122.

Wyrwicka, W., & Dobrzecka, C. (1960). Relationship between feeding and satiation centers of the hypothalamus. *Science, 132*, 805–806.

Xiaghe, X., & Whyte, M. K. (1990). Love matches and arranged marriages: A Chinese replication. *Journal of Marriage and the Family, 52*, 709–722.

Yalom, I. D. (1985). *The theory and practice of group psychotherapy*. New York: Basic Books.

Yamamoto, J., Silva, J. A., Justice, L. R., Chang, C. Y., & Leong, G. B. (1993). Cross-cultural psychotherapy. In A. C. Gaw (Ed.), *Culture, ethnicity, and mental illness*. Washington, DC: American Psychiatric Press.

Yates, F. A. (1966). *The art of memory*. London: Routledge & Kegan Paul.

Yerkes, R. M., & Morgulis, S. (1909). The method of Pavlov in animal psychology. *Psychological Bulletin, 6*, 257–273.

Young, T. (1802). On the theory of light and colours. *Philosophical Transactions of the Royal Society of London, 92*, 12–48.

Zahn-Waxler, C., & Smith, K. D. (1992). The development of prosocial behavior. In V. B. Van Hasselt & M. Hersen (Eds.), *Handbook of social development: A lifespan perspective*. New York: Plenum.

Zajonc, R. B. (1980). Feeling and thinking: Preferences need no inferences. *American Psychologist, 35*, 151–175.

Zatzick, D. F., & Dimsdale, J. E. (1990). Cultural variations in response to painful stimuli. *Psychosomatic Medicine, 52*(5), 544–557.

Zechmeister, E. B., & Nyberg, S. E. (1982). *Human memory: An introduction to research and theory*. Pacific Grove, CA: Brooks/Cole.

Zeiler, M. (1977). Schedules of reinforcement: The controlling variables. In W. K. Honig & J. E. R. Staddon (Eds.), *Handbook of operant behavior*. Englewood Cliffs, NJ: Prentice-Hall.

Zenhausen, R. (1978). Imagery, cerebral dominance and style of thinking: A unified field model. *Bulletin of the Psychonomic Society, 12*, 381–384.

Zeskind, P. S., & Ramey, C. T. (1981). Preventing intellectual and interactional sequelae of fetal malnutrition: A longitudinal, transactional and synergistic approach to development. *Child Development, 52*, 213–218.

Zigler, E. F., & Gilman, E. (1993). Day care in America: What is needed? *Pediatrics, 91*, 175–178.

Zillmann, D. (1983). Transfer of excitation in emotional behavior. In J. T. Cacioppo & R. Petty (Eds.), *Social psychophysiology: A sourcebook*. New York: Guilford Press.

Zimmerman, I. L., & Woo-Sam, J. M. (1984). Intellectual assessment of children. In G. Goldstein & M. Hersen (Eds.), *Handbook of psychological assessment*. New York: Pergamon Press.

Zrenner, E., Abramov, I., Akita, M., Cowey, A., Livingstone, M., & Valberg, A. (1990). Color perception: Retina to cortex. In L. Spillman & J. S. Werner (Eds.), *Visual perception: The neurophysiological foundations*. San Diego: Academic Press.

Zubin, J. (1986). Implications of the vulnerability model for DSM-IV with special reference to schizophrenia. In T. Millon & G. L. Klerman (Eds.), *Contemporary directions in psychopathology: Toward the DSM-IV*. New York: Guilford Press.

Zuckerman, M. (1971). Dimensions of sensation seeking. *Journal of Consulting and Clinical Psychology, 36*, 45–52.

Zwislocki, J. J. (1981). Sound analysis in the ear: A history of discoveries. *American Scientist, 69*, 184–192.

Name Index

Erikson, E., 301–302, 311, 313–314
Ernst, C., 339
Ernst, G. W., 223
Etaugh, C., 326
Evans, C. E., 381
Evers-Kiebooms, G., 230
Eysenck, H. J., 253, 255, 339, 346–347, 348, 350, 352, 398, 399, 427
Eysenck, M. W., 219
Eysenck, S. B. G., 350

F

Fagley, N. S., 25, 230
Fagot, B. I., 325
Fahey, P. J., 378
Falbo, T., 339
Fancher, R. E., 152
Fanselow, M. S., 155
Faraday, A., 148
Faravelli, C., 399
Farberow, N. L., 415
Farrar, M. J., 218
Fava, G. A., 375
Favell, J. E., 170
Fazekas, N. F., 295
Fazio, R. Z., 458, 461
Featherstone, H. J., 375
Feeney, J. A., 456
Fein, S., 448
Feingold, A., 323, 446, 454
Feldman, D. H., 258
Feldman, H., 315
Fennema, E., 323
Fenton, W. S., 409
Fenwick, P., 139
Ferguson, N. B. L., 269
Ferris, K. R., 446
Ferster, C. S., 165
Festinger, L., 453, 459–460
Fieldling, J. E., 377
Fields, H. L., 113
Fincham, F. D., 453
Fine, R., 339
Finer, B., 137
Fink, M., 433
Finnegan, L. P., 294
Fiore, M. C., 377
Fischer, P. J., 438
Fischoff, B., 229, 233, 234
Fisher, S., 339
Fiske, S. T., 447
Flavell, J. H., 306
Fletcher, G. J. O., 452
Fobes, J. L., 70
Fode, K. L., 45
Folkins, C. H., 386
Fontaine, P. A., 420
Forsyth, D. R., 442, 451, 465
Foulkes, D., 148
Fowles, D. C., 397, 409, 410
Fox, N.A., 298
Fozard, J. L., 316
Fracasso, M. P., 299
Frances, A. J., 412
Frank, G., 242
Frank, J. D., 442
Frank, L. K., 358
Frank, L. R., 433, 434
Frantz, A. G., 62
Franzen, M. D., 239
Fredericksen, N., 256
Freedman, D. S., 286
Fremouw, W. J., 414, 415

Freud, S., 9, 11, 19, 121–122, 135, 148, 198, 264, 301, 330–337, 339, 351, 352, 363, 419, 422–424
Friedberg, J., 433
Friedland, G. H., 379
Friedman, H. S., 381
Friedman, L. S., 379
Friedman, M., 373
Friedmann, J., 146
Fries, H., 375
Friesen, W. V., 279
Froelicher, V. F., 378
Fuchs, R. M., 426
Fuller, S. R., 468
Funder, D. C., 343
Funk, S. C., 431
Furnham, A. F., 357, 456
Furomoto, L., 7

G

Gaertner, S. L., 470
Gaito, J., 201
Galaburda, A. M., 324
Galin, D., 80
Galizio, M., 167
Gallagher-Allred, C., 3, 78
Galton, F., 20, 241, 247
Gangi, B. K., 440
Gantt, W. H., 152
Garcia, J., 172–173
Garcia, M. E., 342
Gardner, E., 111
Gardner, H., 12, 82, 211, 256
Garfield, S. L., 393, 395, 426, 434
Garland, A. F., 310
Garnets, L., 273, 274
Garrett, V. D., 374, 375
Garrow, J. S., 287
Garvey, C. R., 5
Gatewood, R., 246
Gazzaniga, M. S., 13, 72, 73
Gecas, V., 315
Gelderloos, P., 139
Geller, J. L., 438
Geller, L., 267
Gelman, S. A., 215
Gentner, D., 215
George, L. K., 399
Gershon, E. S., 404
Geschwind, N., 324
Ghez, C., 66
Ghiselli, E., 246
Giannini, A. J., 143
Gibbs, J., 270
Gibbs, N., 295
Gibson, H. B., 136
Gibson, J. J., 32
Gick, M. L., 223
Gigerenzer, G., 234
Gilbert, C. D., 91
Gilbert, D. T., 450
Gilder, G., 326
Gilgen, A. R., 10
Gillberg, M., 146
Gilligan, C., 308, 309
Gilman, E., 300
Ginsburg, H., 39–40, 42
Girgus, J. S., 103
Glass, G. V., 427, 442
Glassman, A. H., 432
Gleason, J. B., 212, 213, 215
Glenberg, A. M., 206
Glenn, N. D., 314

Glod, C., 432
Goddard, H., 247, 254
Gold, M., 144
Goldberg, H., 326
Goldberg, L. R., 330
Goldberg, S. C., 431
Golden, C. J., 239
Goldenberg, H., 12
Goldfield, B. A., 215
Goldfried, M. R., 427, 434
Goldin, L. R., 404
Golding, J. M., 397
Goldman, J., 61
Goldmann, L., 122
Goldstein, E. B., 109
Goldstein, M. J., 410
Goldstein, W. M., 226
Gonder-Frederick, L. A., 375
Gonsiorek, J. C., 273
Goodall, K., 178
Goodell, H., 375
Goodenough, D. R., 148, 225
Goodman, E., 379
Goodwin, D., 144
Goodwin, D. W., 152
Goodwin, F. K., 404, 433
Gopnik, A., 218
Gordon, B., 430, 432
Gordon, J., 94
Gorman, J. M., 431
Gorman, M. E., 233
Gorn, G. J., 154
Gotlib, J. H., 406
Gottesman, I. I., 77, 409
Gottfried, A. W., 250
Gould, R. L., 312, 313
Gouras, P., 94
Gove, W. R., 390
Graf, P., 203
Graff, P., 269
Graham, J. R., 354
Grant, I., 375
Gray, D. S., 286
Grebb, J. A., 407
Green, A. I., 61, 405
Green, D. W., 233
Green, L. W., 374, 375
Greenberg, J. S., 386
Greenberg, L. S., 427
Greenberg, R. P., 339
Greene, B., 154
Greene, R. L., 191, 206
Greene, W. A., 375
Greenfield, P. M., 215
Greeno, J., 220
Greenough, W. T., 202
Greenson, R. R., 422
Gregory, R. L., 99, 103
Greist, J. H., 432
Griffth, R. M., 133
Grinker, J. A., 287
Grinspoon, L., 144
Grob, G. N., 361, 393
Gross, L., 271
Grossman, J. H., III, 294
Grossman, K., 300
Grossman, K. E., 300
Grossman, S. P., 68, 270
Grove, W. M., 403
Gruen, R. J., 364
Grunberg, N. E., 272, 371
Grusec, J. E., 170
Guenther, K., 199
Guevremont, D. C., 429

Guilford, J. P., 258
Gupta, G. R., 456
Gustavson, C. R., 173
Guyton, A. C., 88, 123
Guze, S. B., 399

H

Ha, Y. W., 233
Haan, N., 369
Hadzi-Pavlovic, D., 410
Haensly, P. A., 260
Hagberg, J. N., 378
Hager, J. L., 172
Haglund, B., 294
Halberstadt, A. G., 323
Hales, D., 147
Hall, C. S., 133, 134, 148
Hall, E., 251, 306
Hall, G. S., 6, 310
Hall, J. A., 323, 381
Halpern, D. F., 102, 224, 233, 323, 325
Halverson, C. F., Jr., 325
Hamer, D. H., 275
Hamilton, D. L., 471
Hamilton, T. E., III, 454
Hamilton, W. D., 263
Hammersmith, S. K., 273
Hamner, T., 309
Hanisch, K. A., 246
Hankins, W. G., 172
Hanlon, C., 217
Hansen, C. H., 326
Hansen, R. D., 326
Hanshaw, J. B., 295
Hanson, R. A., 250
Harkins, S., 466
Harkins, S. W., 316
Harmsen, P., 375
Harriman, L. C., 315
Harrington, D. M., 258, 260
Harris, W. G., 291
Harsch, N., 190
Hartmann, E., 132
Harvey, M., 450
Hashtroudi, S., 194
Haskell, W. L., 386
Hass, R. G., 457
Hastorf, A., 21
Hatch, T., 256
Hatfield, E., 454–455, 456
Hathaway, S. R., 354
Hauser, S. T., 311
Haviland, J. M., 349
Hayes, J. R., 223
Hayes-Roth, B., 207
Haynes, R. B., 381
Hazan, C., 299, 455–456
Heap, M., 136
Hearst, E., 156
Heath, A. C., 128
Heath, R. G., 70
Heider, F., 448–449
Heinz, S. P., 184
Hellige, J. B., 82
Helmholtz, H. von, 94, 108
Helms, J. E., 253
Helson, R., 312, 313
Hendrick, C., 454
Hendrick, S. S., 454
Henriksson, M. M., 414
Henry, K. R., 106
Hering, E., 94–95
Herrington, R., 431

Weisaeth, L., 362
Weisberg, R., 258
Weise, R. E., 395
Weiskrantz, L., 202
Weissman, M. M., 396, 403, 404
Weisstein, N., 92
Weisz, J. R., 452
Weiten, W., 6, 26, 37, 365
Wekstein, L., 415
Weldon, M. S., 203
Well, A. D., 233
Welsh, D. K., 124
Wen, S. W., 294
Wertheimer, M., 96
Westen, D., 339
Westra, T., 297
Wever, E. G., 109
Wever, R., 124, 125, 132
Whishaw, I. Q., 60, 63
White, K. R., 253
White, P. A., 450
Whitebook, M., 300
Whorf, B. L., 218
Whyte, M. K., 456
Wible, C. G., 190
Widiger, T. A., 393
Wielawski, I., 199
Wiesel, T., 70, 91–92, 96

Wiggins, J. S., 330
Wight, R. D., 6
Wilcock, G. K., 61
Wilcox, A. J., 293
Wilder, D. A., 472
Wilhelmsen, L., 375
Wilkinson, R. T., 122, 147
Williams, B. A., 167
Williams, C. D., 163
Williams, K. D., 466, 467
Williams, M. H., 441
Williams, N. A., 374, 375
Williams, R. B., 373
Williams, R. L., 128, 131
Williams, Robert L., 253
Willis, R. P., 206
Willis, W. D., 112
Wilson, D. B., 427
Wilson, E. O., 263
Wilson, G. T., 44, 141
Wilson, M., 393
Winfree, A. T., 124
Wing, A. L., 378, 386
Wingerson, L., 78
Wingert, P., 300
Winograd, T., 203

Winokur, G., 414, 415
Wise, R. A., 70
Witkin, H. A., 224–225
Wittkower, E. D., 434
Wittlinger, R. P., 195
Wixted, J. T., 429
Wolf, A. A., 411
Wolf, R. M., 253
Wolf, S., 375
Wolitzky, D. L., 422
Wolpe, J., 427, 428–429
Wolpert, E., 134
Wood, F., 204
Woolfolk, R. L., 139, 366, 385
Woo-Sam, J. M., 242, 245
Wright, J. C., 484
Wright, S. C., 20
Wundt, W., 4–5
Wyatt, R. J., 431, 437
Wyler, A. R., 30–32, 44
Wynne, L. C., 410
Wyrwicka, W., 269
Wyshak, G., 401

X
Xiaghe, X., 456

Y
Yalom, I. D., 426
Yamamoto, J., 435
Yarkin, K. L., 450
Yates, F. A., 206
Yerkes, R. M., 152
Young, K., 435
Young, T., 94
Younger, D. P., 450
Yuille, J. C., 186

Z
Zahn-Waxler, C., 309
Zajonc, R. B., 277
Zane, N., 435
Zatzick, D. F., 113
Zechmeister, E. B., 23, 206
Zeiler, M., 167
Zenhausen, R., 81
Zeskind, P. S., 294
Zich, J., 379
Zigler, E., 300, 310
Zillman, D., 283
Zimmernman, I. L., 242, 245
Zorumski, C. F., 399
Zrenner, E., 95
Zubin, J., 410
Zwislocki, J. J., 109

Subject Index

avoidance learning, 168–169
awareness, levels of, 121–122, 332–333
axons, 56, 57, 58, 63
    in optic nerve, 90

B

babbling, 214
babies. *See* infants
balance, sense of, 113–114
Bantu, 102
barbiturates, 140
basal metabolic rate, 287
baseline data, 178
basilar membrane, 108
Bay of Pigs, 467–468
beauty. *See* physical appearance
behavior, defined, 7
behavior modification, 178–180
behavior therapies, 420, 427–430, 439, 442
behavioral approach
    to attitude change, 459
    to language acquisition, 216–217
    to personality, 340–343, 352–353
behavioral contract, 180
behavioral genetics, 76–79, 346, 348–349
behavioral rehearsal, 429
behaviorism, 6–8, 9–10, 11, 340
belief perseverance, 233
bell-shaped curve, 244, 245, 485, 486
Bellini, Gentile and Giovanni, 115
belongingness needs, 267
beta waves, 122, 123
Beyond Freedom and Dignity (Skinner), 10
bias
    in attributions, 449–451, 471, 472
    experimenter, 44–45, 48
    sampling, 43
    self-serving, 451, 452
    social desirability, 44, 357
Big Five personality traits, 330, 348, 350, 356
binocular depth cues, 100
biofeedback, 121
biogenic amines, 61, 142–143
biological approach, 11, 13
    to personality, 346–349, 352–353
biological clocks, 124–125
biological needs, 266, 267
biological rhythms, 124–126
biomedical therapies, 420, 430–434, 439
biopsychosocial model, 361, 382
bipolar cells, 87, 90
bipolar disorders, 402–404, 432
birth defects, 293, 294
birth order, 339
bisexuality, 272, 273
blacks. *See* African Americans; minority groups
blind spot, 88
blood glucose level, 270
blood-brain barrier, 64
body language, 279
body temperature, 264, 265
bonding, mother-infant, 300
bounded rationality, 226
brain, 64
    abnormalities in, 409–410
    anatomy of, 66–72
    electrical activity in, 122–123, 126
    gender differences in, 324
    study of, 65–66
    visual pathways in, 90–91
brain-imaging techniques, 65–66
brain surgery, 70
brain waves, 121, 122–123, 126
brainstem, 66, 67
brightness, 86, 93

Broca's area, 71, 72
Buspar, 431
bystander effect, 465–466

C

caffeine, 147
cancer, 377, 378
cannabis, 140, 141, 142
Cannon-Bard theory, 282–283
Canseco twins, 77
case studies, 40–41, 42
cataracts, 88
catastrophic thinking, 383–384
catatonic schizophrenia, 408, 409
catecholamines, 368, 369
causation
    descriptive/correlational research and, 37, 39,
        42–43
    experimental method and, 36
    See also multifactorial causation
cell body, of neuron, 56
central nervous system (CNS), 63, 64. *See also*
    brain; spinal cord
central tendency, measures of, 483–484
centration, 304
cephalocaudal trend, 296
cerebellum, 66, 67, 68
cerebral cortex, 68, 70, 201
cerebral hemispheres, 70, 71–75
    gender differences in, 324–325
    specialization of, 71–75, 80–82
cerebrospinal fluid, 64
cerebrum, 67, 68, 70
Challenger spacecraft, 190
chance. *See* probability
change. *See* life changes
channels, communication, 457
chemical senses, 109–110
child abuse, 199–200
child-rearing, 315
    gender roles and, 326
    IQ and, 250–251
children, 319
    cognitive development in, 302–306
    decision to have, 314
    emotional development in, 299–301
    language development in, 214–216
    moral reasoning in, 307–308
    motor development in, 296–298
    personality development in, 301–302, 335–336
    sleep patterns in, 128–130
    social development in, 309
    temperament in, 298–299
China, 350, 452, 456
chloride ions, 57
choices, making, 226–230
cholecystokinin (CCK), 270
chromosomes, 76, 78, 292
chunking, 189
circadian rhythms, 124–126
Clark, Marcia, 82
class attendance, grades and, 24–25
classical conditioning, 151–160, 176–177, 271
    of anxiety disorders, 398
    of attitudes, 459
    aversion therapy and, 429
    basic processes in, 155–160
    in conjunction with operant conditioning, 169
    defined, 151
    distinguished from operant conditioning, 160
    in everyday life, 154–155
    observational learning and, 174, 341
    systematic desensitization and, 428
    terminology and procedures for, 153
claustrophobia, 396

client-centered therapy, 424–425, 439, 442
clinical diagnosis, use of tests for, 354
clinical psychologists, 40, 420–421
clinical psychology, 12, 15, 16
closure, 98
Clozaril, 432
co-sleeping, 130
cocaine, 141, 143, 144
cochlea, 107–108
Cochran, Johnny, 247
coefficient of determination, 488, 489
coercive sexual behavior, 41
cognition, 12, 211
cognitive appraisal, 277–278
cognitive approach
    to anxiety disorders, 398, 399
    to depression, 405–406
    to gender-role socialization, 325
    to intelligence, 255–256
    to language acquisition, 218
cognitive changes, with age, 316
cognitive development, 302–306, 318–321
    moral reasoning and, 308
cognitive dissonance, 460–461
cognitive psychology, 11, 12–13, 15, 16, 211–212
cognitive schemas. *See* schemas
cognitive skills, gender differences in, 323
cognitive style
    culture and, 224–225
    hemispheric differences in, 81, 82
cognitive therapy, 425–426, 442
cohesiveness, group, 468
collective unconscious, 337, 338
collectivism, 451–452, 456, 464–465
color blindness, 94, 95
color mixing, 93
color solid, 93
color terms, 219
color vision, 86, 89, 92–95
commitment, involuntary, 411–412
communication, persuasive, 457–458
communication deviance, 410
community mental health centers, 437, 440, 441
companionate love, 454–455
compensation, 338
complementary colors, 94
compliance, 463–464
compulsions, 396, 397
computerized tomography (CT), 65
concordance rates, 404, 409
concrete operational period, 303, 304–305
conditionability, 347
conditioned reinforcers, 165
conditioned response (CR), 153, 154, 155, 156,
    159
    extinction of, 156
    spontaneous recovery of, 156–157
conditioned stimulus (CS), 153, 154, 155, 156,
    158, 159, 172, 173
conditioning
    biological constraints on, 171–173
    cognitive processes in, 173–174
    defined, 151
    higher-order, 158–160
    See also classical conditioning; operant
        conditioning
cones, 87, 88–90, 95
confidence, in predictions, 234
confirmation bias, 233
conflict
    internal, 333
    types of, 3623–364
conformity, 462–463
    cultural differences in, 464–465
confounding of variables, 35

congruence, 344
Conner, Dennis, 263
conscious, 332
consciousness, 121–123
  as focus of psychology, 5, 6
  stream of, 6, 121
conservation, 304, 305
consistency, cross-situational, 342–343
consolidation, memory, 201
constancies, perceptual, 102–103
construct validity, 240
content validity, 239–240
context cues, 193
contiguity, stimulus, 156
contingencies, reinforcement, 161, 174, 179
continuity, perception and, 98
continuous reinforcement, 165
control, as research goal, 30
control group, 34, 36
convergence, 100
convergent thinking, 258
conversion disorder, 399, 400
coping, 369
  constructive, 372
  defensive, 371–372
  strategies for, 383–386
cornea, 87
coronary heart disease, 373–374
corpus callosum, 67, 70, 72, 324, 325
correlation, 37, 38–39, 487–488
  causation and, 39
  prediction and, 39, 488
  test reliability and, 239
correlation coefficient, 37, 38–39, 239, 487, 488
corticosteroids, 368, 369
Cosby, Bill, 458, 459
counseling, use of tests for, 354
counseling psychologists, 420–421
counseling psychology, 15, 16
counselors, 420, 421
counterattitudinal behavior, 460
counterconditioning, 428
counterfactual thinking, 219
coyotes, 172–173
CR. See conditioned response
crack cocaine, 141, 144
cramming, for exams, 206
creativity, 258–260
credibility, 457–458
criterion-related validity, 240
cross-sectional studies, 298
cross-situational consistency, 342–343
CS. See conditioned stimulus
CT (computerized-tomography) scans, 65
Cubists, 116–117
cultural disadvantage, 253
cultural diversity, 13–14
cultural groups, 13–14
culture
  abnormal behavior and, 412
  attachment and, 300–301
  attraction and, 456
  attributions and, 451–452
  cognitive style and, 224–225
  conformity and, 464–465
  defined, 19
  dreams and, 134–135
  elements of emotion and, 280–281
  influence of, 19-20
  IQ differences and, 252–254
  IQ testing and, 247
  language and, 218–219
  motor development and, 296–297
  optical illusions and, 104–105
  pain perception and, 112–113

  perception and, 100, 102, 114
  personality and, 349–350, 351
  psychotherapy and, 434–436
  sleep patterns and, 130
  taste preferences and, 110
  testing and, 257
culture-bound disorders, 412
cumulative deprivation hypothesis, 250
cumulative recorder, 161–162
curare, 61
cynical hostility, 374

D
Dali, Salvador, 117
Dani tribe, 218
dark adaptation, 89
data analysis, 31–32
data collection techniques, 31
database, of journal articles, 51
day care, 300
daydreaming, 147–148
decay theory, of forgetting, 196–197
decentration, 304
deception, in research, 46
decibels, 106
decision making, 226–230
  in groups, 467–469
  risky, 228–230, 232–234, 467
  strategies in, 226–227
declarative memory system, 203–204
defense mechanisms, 334–335, 371–372
defensive attribution, 450, 471
definition, operational, 30–31
deinstitutionalization, 437–438
delta waves, 122, 123, 126
delusions, 407–408
dendrites, 56
denial, 371, 372
dependence, drug, 142, 143
dependent variable, 33, 34, 36
depressants. See alcohol; narcotics; sedatives
depression, 402–403
  biological basis of, 61
  cognitive treatment for, 425
  creativity and, 260
  drug treatment for, 432
  shock therapy for, 433–434
  suicide and, 414
depressive disorder, 403
deprivation, environmental, 250, 253
depth perception, 100–102
description, as research goal, 29
descriptive/correlational research, 37–43
descriptive statistics, 483
determinism, 340
development, 291–292, 318–321
  defined, 292
  prenatal, 292–295
  See also specific types of development
developmental norms, 296
developmental psychology, 15, 16
deviance, as criteria for abnormality, 391
deviation IQ scores, 244–245
diagnosis, 331
Diagnostic and Statistical Manual of Mental Disorders, 393–395
dichromats, 94
diffusion of responsibility, 466
discipline, punishment used for, 169, 170
discrimination
  in classical conditioning, 158, 164
  in operant conditioning, 164
  prejudice and, 470, 471
discriminative stimuli, 164
disease, 361. See also physical illness

disorganized schizophrenia, 408
displacement, 334
display rules, 281
dissociation, 138
dissociative amnesia, 401–402
dissociative disorders, 401–402
dissociative fugue, 402
dissociative identity disorder, 402
dissonance theory, 459–461
distal stimuli, 98–99, 105
distance perception, 100–102
distress, as criteria for abnormality, 391
distribution. See normal distribution
divergent thinking, 258
diversity, cultural, 13–14
Dix, Dorothea, 436
dizygotic twins, 77
DNA, 76, 78
dopamine, 61, 68, 70, 142–143, 409, 432
double-blind procedures, 45
Doyle, Arthur Conan, 211
Dr. P, 85, 96
dream analysis, 422
dream interpretation, 148
dream recall, 148
dreaming, 133–136, 148
  culture and, 134–135
  REM periods and, 127, 128
  theories of, 135–136
drive theories, 264–265
drives, 10, 333
drowsiness, 131
drug dependence, 142, 143
drug overdose, 144
drug therapy, 430–433
  deinstitutionalization and, 438
drug use, during pregnancy, 294
drugs, psychoactive, 139–144
DSM-IV, 393–395
dual-coding theory, 186

E
ear, structure of, 107–108
eardrum, 107
eating behavior, 68, 264, 268–272, 286–288, 378
  culture and, 110
  stress and, 370, 371
eclecticism, in psychotherapy, 434, 442
ECT, 433–434
educational psychology, 15, 16
EEG (electroencephalograph), 121, 122–123, 126, 139
efferent nerve fibers, 63
effort justification, 460–461
ego, 331, 332, 333
egocentrism, 304
EKG (electrocardiograph), 123
elaboration, 185
elaboration likelihood model, 461
Elavil, 432
electrical stimulation of the brain (ESB), 65, 68, 69, 269
electrocardiograph (EKG), 123
electroconvulsive therapy (ECT), 433–434
electroencephalograph (EEG), 121, 122–123, 126, 139
electromyograph (EMG), 123
electrooculograph (EOG), 123
elicited responses, 153
elimination by aspects, 227
embryonic stage, 292, 293, 294
EMG (electromyograph), 123
emitted responses, 161
emotion(s)
  components of, 277–280

emotion(s) (*continued*)
culture and, 280–281
defined, 277
expressed, 410
motivation and, 277
primary, 284
regulation of, 69
in schizophrenia, 408
stress and, 366–367
theories of, 281–284
emotional development, in children, 299–301
emotional responses, conditioned, 154, 155
empathy, 424
empiricism, 17–18, 29, 47–48, 79, 231, 469, 490
empty nest, 315
encoding, 184–186
defined, 183
ineffective, 196
levels of processing for, 184–185
using mnemonics for, 207–208
encoding specificity principle, 198
endocrine system, 75–76
stress and, 368
See also hormones
endorphins, 62, 113, 155, 270
environment
gender differences and, 325–326
heredity and, 20–21, 79
intelligence and, 247–254
See also home environment; nature versus nurture
environmental deprivation, 250, 253
EOG (electrooculograph), 123
episodic memory system, 204–205
equilibrium
homeostatic, 264
sense of, 113–114
ESB. *See* electrical stimulation of the brain
escape learning, 168
Escher, M. C., 100, 117, 118
Eskimos, 218, 271, 281
essay tests, 196
esteem needs, 267
ethics, in research, 46–47, 48, 464
ethnic groups, 13
IQ differences in, 252–254
psychotherapy and, 434–436
stereotypes of, 447
See also culture
etiology, defined, 331
euphoria
in bipolar disorder, 404
drug-induced, 62, 141
evolution, 6
of emotion, 284
motivation and, 263–264
excitatory synapses, 59, 60, 61
exercise, 386
lack of, 378
exhaustion, stage of, 368
expectancy-value models, 265
expectations
drug effects and, 141
of experimenter, 45
person perception and, 447–448
subjects', 44
experience, subjectivity of, 141, 145, 205, 231, 382
experiment, defined, 33
experimental group, 34, 36
experimental psychology, 15, 16
experimental research, 33–37, 42
experimenter bias, 44–45
explicit memory, 202–203
expressed emotion, 410
external cues, for eating, 271–272, 286–287

extinction
of classical conditioned responses, 156, 164
of operantly conditioned responses, 162–163, 164
resistance to, 163
extraneous variables, 34–36
extraversion, 338, 347
eye, structure of, 87–90
eyewitness testimony, 194
Eysenck Personality Questionnaire, 350

F

facial expressions, 279–280
culture and, 280–281
facial-feedback hypothesis, 280
failure
attributions for, 449, 451, 471
fear of, 276–277
family, gender-role socialization in, 326
family environment, personality and, 349
family life cycle, 314, 315
family studies, 77, 248
fantasy, 371, 372
farsightedness, 88, 316
fast mapping, 215
fat cells, 288
fear
conditioned, 154, 157–158, 169, 398
of failure, 276–277
stress and, 366
fear appeals, 458
feature analysis, 96, 97
feature detectors, 92, 96, 97, 112,
feelings. *See* emotion(s)
females. *See* gender; women
fetal alcohol syndrome, 294
fetal stage, 292, 293, 294
field dependence-independence, 225, 226
fight-or-flight response, 64, 75, 278, 368
figure and ground, 97
findings, reporting of, 32
fitness, physical, 378, 386
five-factor model of personality, 330
fixation, 336
fixed-interval schedule, 166, 167
fixed-ratio schedule, 166
flashbulb memories, 190
flattery, 454
flatworms, 200–201
flavor, 110
food intake, 271, 272, 286–287
food preferences, 110
Fore tribe, 281
forebrain, 67, 68
forgetting, 195–200
encoding and, 184, 185, 196
measures of, 195–196
motivated, 198–199, 205, 334
reasons for, 196–199
forgetting curve, 195
form perception, 95–100
formal operational period, 303, 305–306
fovea, 87
framing, 230
fraternal twins, 77, 78, 248, 249, 348
free association, 422
free nerve endings, 112
free will, 10, 340
freebasing, 141
French Impressionists, 116
frequency
of brain waves, 122, 123
of sound waves, 106
frequency distributions, 482–483
frequency polygon, 482, 483, 484

frequency theory of pitch perception, 108, 109
Freudian slips, 9, 332
friendship, 453–454
frontal lobe, 71
frustration, 362, 366
frustration-aggression hypothesis, 369–370
fugue, dissociative, 402
functional fixedness, 221
functionalism, 5, 6
fundamental attribution error, 450, 452, 471

G

GABA, 61–62, 143, 397
galvanic skin response (GSR), 278
gambler's fallacy, 232
gambling, 166, 167, 229
gamma-aminobutyric acid (GABA), 61–62, 143, 397
ganglion cells, 87, 90, 95
Gardner, Randy, 130, 131
gate-control theory, 113
gay rights, 391, 392
gays, 273–274
AIDS and, 379
gender, 322
psychotherapy and, 441
gender differences, 322–326
in aggression, 309
biological origins of, 323–325
defined, 322
environmental origins of, 325–326
in mating priorities, 456
in moral reasoning, 308–309
in risk taking, 39–40, 42–43
in suicide, 414
gender-role socialization, 325–326
gender roles, 314, 325
gender stereotypes, 322, 323, 447, 471, 472
general adaptation syndrome, 367–368
generalization
in classical conditioning, 157–158, 164
in operant conditioning, 164
generalized anxiety disorder, 393, 395–396, 399
generativity versus self-absorption, 313–314
genes, 76, 78, 292
genetic mapping, 78–79
genetic overlap, 76, 248, 274, 404
genetic predisposition
to anxiety disorders, 397
to mood disorders, 404–405
to obesity, 287
genetic vulnerability
to mood disorders, 404
to schizophrenia, 409
genetics
basic principles of, 76–79
intelligence and, 248
sexual orientation and, 274
See also heredity
genital stage, 335, 336
Germany, 300
germinal stage, 293
Gestalt principles, 96–98, 117
Gestalt psychology, 8
glia, 55–56
glove anesthesia, 400
glucose, 270
glucostatic theory, 270
glucostats, 270
goals, of scientific approach, 29–30
gonadotropins, 75
gonads, 75
GPA, college admissions tests and, 39
Grant, Cary, 291
graphs, 482

posthypnotic suggestion, 137
postsynaptic neuron, 59
postsynaptic potential (PSP), 59, 60, 61
potassium ions, 57
power structure, in groups, 465
practice, distributed versus mass, 206
preconscious, 332
prediction
    correlation and, 39, 488
    as research goal, 29-30
predictions, confidence in, 234
predispositions. *See* genetic predisposition
preferences, learned, 271
pregnancy, 292-295
prejudice, 470, 471
premature birth, 294, 295
prenatal development, 292-295
    gender differences in, 324
    hormones and, 75
preoperational period, 303-304
preparedness, 398
pressure, 365-366
Pressure Inventory, 365
presynaptic neuron, 58-59
primacy effect, 190-191
primary colors, 94
primary-process thinking, 331, 332
primary reinforcers, 165
primary sex characteristics, 309
Principles of Psychology (James), 6
proactive interference, 198
probability, 232, 490
probability estimates, 229
problem solving, 219-226
    approaches to, 222-224
    barriers to, 220-222
    cross-cultural variations in, 224-225
    in formal operations, 306
problems, types of, 219-220
procedural memory system, 203-204
procrastination, 380
productivity
    in adulthood, 316, 317
    group, 466
prognosis, 331
projection, 334
projective tests, 275, 357-358
proximal stimuli, 99, 105
proximity
    attraction and, 453
    perception and, 97, 98
proximodistal trend, 296
Prozac, 432
pseudoforgetting, 196
psilocybin, 141
psyche, 4
psychiatric hospitals, 436-438
psychiatric nurses, 420, 421
psychiatrists, 420, 421, 441
psychoactive drugs, 140-144
psychoanalysis, 9, 419, 422-424, 439
psychoanalytic theory, 9, 11, 330-337
psychodiagnosis, 393-395
psychodynamic theories, 330-339, 352-353
psychodynamic therapies, 422-424, 442
Psychological Abstracts, 49-51
psychological disorders, 390, 391
    classification of, 393-395
    creativity and, 260
    culture and, 412, 434
    diagnoses of, 331, 332
    institutional treatment for, 436-439
    psychodynamic view of, 335
    suicide and, 414
    treatment of. *See* psychotherapy

See also specific disorders
psychological testing, 31, 237-240, 258-259, 485
    See also intelligence tests; personality tests
psychologists, 420-421
psychology
    defined, 4, 14
    diversity of, 3-4
    ethics in, 46-47, 48
    history of, 4-14
    number of studies in, 49
    as a profession, 12
    professional specialties in, 15, 16
    research areas in, 15, 16
    schools of, 5-6
    women in, 6, 7
    work settings for, 14, 15
psychometrics, 15, 16
psychopharmcotherapy, 430-433
psychosexual stages, 335-336
psychosocial development, 301-302, 311, 313-314
psychosomatic diseases, 373, 399
psychotherapy
    behavioral approaches to, 420, 427-430, 439, 442
    biomedical approaches to, 420, 430-434, 439
    blending approaches to, 434
    culture and, 434-436
    effectiveness of, 426-427, 430, 442
    elements of, 419-421
    finding services, 440-442
    group, 426
    influence of humanists on, 11
    insight approaches to, 421-427
    types of, 419-420, 442
psychoticism, 347
PsycINFO, 51, 52
PsycLIT, 51
puberty, 75-76, 309-310, 336
pubescence, 309
publishing, of findings, 32
Puck, Wolfgang, 260
punctuality, 20
punishment, 169-170, 180
    negative reinforcement and, 169, 170
    physical, 170, 171, 175
pupil, 87, 88

Q

questionnaires, 31, 41, 44
questions
    framing of, 229-230
    multiple-choice, 26, 196
    on IQ tests, 244
Quichua, 281

R

raccoons, training of, 171-172
racial prejudice, 470
random assignment, 35
ratio schedules, 166, 167
rational-emotive therapy, 383-384, 442
rationality, bounded, 226
rationalization, 334
reaction formation, 334
reaction range, 251
reaction time, 255
reading, SQ3R method for, 24
reality principle, 331, 332
reasoning. *See* decision making; moral reasoning; problem solving
recall, of dreams, 148
recall measures of retention, 195, 196
receiver, of persuasive messages, 457, 458
recency effect, 190-191
receptive fields

of visual cells, 90, 92
    for touch, 111-112
receptor sites, 58, 59, 60, 61, 405
receptors
    for hearing, 108, 109
    for skin senses, 111
    for smell, 111
    for taste, 109
    visual, 87-90
reciprocity, 454
recognition measures of retention, 195-196
reconstructive memories, 193-194, 205
reflexes, "psychic," 151-152, 153
refractory period, absolute, 57
regression, 334
rehearsal, 187-188, 189, 190, 193, 206
reinforcement, 160-161, 162, 163, 164-165
    choice of, 180
    defined, 160, 165
    delayed, 165
    in language development, 216
    negative, 167-168 169, 170, 179
    personality traits and, 341
    positive, 167, 179
    primary and secondary, 165
    schedules of, 165-167
    signal relations and, 173
reinforcement contingencies, 161, 342
relative size, 100, 101
relaxation, 148, 385, 428
relaxation response, 385
relaxation training, 139
relearning measures of retention, 196, 203
reliability, of tests, 238-239, 245
REM sleep, 126-127, 128, 129, 148
    deprivation of, 131-132
    dreaming and, 127, 128, 133
    need for, 132
Remote Association Test (RAT), 259
replication, of studies, 43
representative sample, 43-44
representativeness heuristic, 229, 232
repression, 199, 334
research, 354
    animal, 47
    deceptive, 46
    experimental, 8
    trends in, 12
research laboratories, 5
research methods, 29, 31, 33, 42
    descriptive/correlational, 37-43
    experimental, 33-37
resistance, to therapist, 423
resistance stage, 368
response-outcome (R-O) associations, 163
response rate, in operant conditioning, 161-162
response set, 357
response tendencies, 340
responses. *See* conditioned responses; unconditioned responses
responsibility, diffusion of, 466
resting potential, 57
retention
    interference and, 197-198, 206-207
    measures of, 195-196
reticular formation, 67, 68
retina, 87, 88-90
retinal disparity, 100
retrieval, memory, 183, 184, 192-195
retrieval cues, 192-193, 198, 207-208
retrieval failure, 198
retroactive interference, 198
retrograde amnesia, 201
reuptake, 59

stress (*continued*)
  emotional responses to, 366–367
  factors moderating impact of, 376–377
  managing, 383–386
  mood disorders and, 406
  nature of, 362–355
  of parenthood, 315
  physiological responses to, 367–369
  prolonged, 368
  schizophrenia and, 410–411
  task performance and, 367
  types of, 362–366
stress-vulnerability models, 413
structural encoding, 185
structuralism, 5–6
study habits, 22–24
subgoals, in problem solving, 222–223
subjective probability, 229
subjectivity, of experience, 21, 48
subjects
  deception of, 46
  defined, 31
  expectations of, 44
  experimental versus control, 34
  random assignment of, 35
  selection of, 43–44
substance P, 62
substance use disorders, 391
subtractive color mixing, 93
success
  achievement motivation and, 276
  attributions for, 449, 451, 471
  creativity and, 259
  IQ and, 246
suicide, 414–416
  adolescent, 310–311, 414
  prevention of, 415–416
suicide rates, 414
superego, 331, 332, 333, 334
superior colliculus, 90–91
superiority, striving for, 338–339
Surrealism, 117
surveys, 31, 41, 42, 44
sweat glands, 278
symbolism, in dreams, 148
symbols, 212, 338
sympathetic nervous system, 64, 368, 369
synapses, 56, 58–60
  drug effects and, 142–143
synaptic cleft, 58, 142
synaptic vesicles, 58, 59
synergistic drug effects, 143, 144
syntax, 214, 216
systematic desensitization, 428–429, 442

T

talent, 259
Tales from the Front (Kavesh & Lavin), 445, 447
tardive dyskinesia, 431
task performance, stress and, 367
taste, sense of, 109–110
taste aversions, 172–173, 271
taste buds, 109
taste preferences, 110, 271
TAT, 275, 357, 358
telegraphic speech, 215
television, gender-role socialization by, 326
Temiars, 130
temperament, 298–299
temperature, body, 124
temperature regulation, 265
temporal lobe, 70, 71, 108
terminal buttons, 56, 58
terminal drop, 316
test norms, 238

test-retest reliability, 238–239
test-taking strategies, 25–26
tests, psychological, 12, 237–240, 258–259
testwiseness, 25
texture gradients, 100, 101
thalamus, 67, 68, 69, 90–91, 108, 109, 109, 201
THC, 141
Thematic Apperception Test (TAT), 275, 357, 358
theoretical diversity, 18, 114, 145, 285, 351, 439
theory, 18
therapists, repressed memories controversy and, 200
therapy. *See* psychotherapy
theta waves, 122, 123, 139
thinking
  catastrophic, 383–384
  creative, 258
  negative, 425
  See also cognition; problem solving
Thorazine, 431
thought, language and, 218–219
timbre, 105, 106–107
time, perception of, 20
time management, 22–23
tip-of-the tongue phenomenon, 183, 192–193
titmouse, 174
toilet training, 336
token economies, 180
tolerance, drug, 142, 155
tongue, 109
Toraja, 135
Torriti, Jacopo, 115
touch, 111–113
toys, gender-typed, 326
traits. *See* personality traits
tranquilizers, 61–62, 430–431
transcendental meditation, 138
transference, in psychoanalysis, 423
trial, in conditioning, 153
trial and error, 222
triarchic theory of intelligence, 255
trichromatic theory, 93–94, 95
tricyclics, 405, 432
trust versus mistrust, 301
trustworthiness, 458
twin studies, 77–78, 248–249, 250, 274, 287, 346, 348, 404, 409
two-factor theory of emotion, 283
Type A personality, 373–374
Type B personality, 373

U

UCR. *See* unconditioned response
UCS. *See* unconditioned stimulus
ultraviolet spectrum, 87
uncertainty, 228
unconditional positive regard, 424
unconditioned response (UCR), 153
unconditioned stimulus (UCS), 153, 154, 155, 156, 158, 159, 172, 173
unconscious, 9, 18, 121, 122, 199, 332, 422–423
  collective, 337, 338
  personal, 337
undifferentiated schizophrenia, 408, 409
undoing, 371
unipolar disorders, 402, 403
University of Leipzig, 4
University of Minnesota Center for twin and Adoption Research, 346

V

validity
  of MMPI, 354–355
  of tests, 239–240, 245–246

Valium, 62, 430, 431, 432
value
  expected, 228–229
  of incentives, 265
variability, 484–485
variable-interval schedule, 166
variable-ratio schedule, 166, 167
variables, 30
  confounding of, 35
  dependent, 33, 34, 36
  extraneous, 34–36
  independent, 33–34, 36, 37
  manipulation of, 36, 37
  multiple, 36, 37
  ventricles, of brain, 410
ventromedial nucleus of hypothalamus (VMH), 269
Verbal Behavior (Skinner), 216
verifiability, 7
vestibular system, 113–114
Veterans Administration, 12
victims, blaming of, 450, 471
vision, 86–105
  color, 86, 89, 92–95
  declines with age, 316
visual acuity, 89
visual agnosia, 85
visual cortex, 70, 71, 90–92
visual fields, split brain and, 72–74
visual imagery, memory and, 185–186
visual-spatial tasks, 74
visual system, 86–105
vocabulary, children's, 215
vocational success, IQ scores and, 246
volley principle, 109
vulnerability, genetic, 404, 409

W

wavelength
  of light waves, 86, 87, 92–93
  of sound waves, 105, 106
Wechsler Adult Intelligence Scale (WAIS), 242, 243
weight problems, 286–288, 378
Wernicke's area, 71, 72
windigo, 412
wine tasting, 110
Winfrey, Oprah, 247
withdrawal illness, 143
women
  marital roles of, 314
  in psychology, 6, 7
  stereotypes of, 322, 323, 326
  suicide and, 414
  See also gender
words, 213, 214
work shifts, rotating, 125–126
working memory, 189, 193
World War I, 12
World War II, 12

X

Xanax, 430, 431

Y

Yoruba, 281

Z

Zollner illusion, 103
Zoloft, 432
Zulus, 104, 105
zygote, 292, 293

Credits

Photo Credits

Contents

xv: © Stephen Frisch/Stock, Boston; **xvi:** © Yves Forestier/Sygma; **xix:** © John Greim 1988/The Stock Shop; **xx:** John Markham/Bruce Coleman Ltd, London; **xxi:** AP/Wide World Photos; **xxii:** © Eugene Fisher/Gamma-Liaison Network; **xxiii:** Pool Reuters/Bettmann; **xxvi:** Reprinted by permission of the publishers from Henry A. Murray, *Thematic Apperception Test*, Cambridge, Mass.: Harvard University Press, Copyright © 1943 by the President and Fellows of Harvard College, © 1971 by Henry A. Murray; **xxvii:** © Tom McCarthy/Photo Edit; **xxviii:** © David Jeffrey/The Image Bank; **xxix:** © Zigy Kaluzy/Tony Stone Images; **xxx:** © Patti McConville/The Image Bank.

Chapter 1

3 (top left): © Stephen Frisch/Stock, Boston, (right) © Photo Edit, (bottom left) © James Wilson/Woodfin Camp & Associates; **7:** Archives of the History of American Psychology, University of Akron, Akron, Ohio; **15:** (top) © Charles Gupton/The Stock Market, (bottom) © Jeff Greenberg/Rainbow; **22:** © David Weintraub/Photo Researchers.

Chapter 2

40: Courtesy of Harvey Ginsburg, Ph.D., Southwest Texas State University; **45:** Courtesy of Robert Rosenthal; **46:** Yale University, courtesy of Neal Miller; **47:** © Yves Forestier/Sygma; **50:** Craig McClain.

Chapter 3

60: (left) © Terry Vine/Tony Stone Images, (bottom right) © Empics Ltd: Graham Chadwick/Woodfin Camp & Associates, (top right) © Les Stone/Sygma; **61:** © Dan McCoy/Rainbow; **62:** © 1991 Candace Pert; **65:** (left) © Alvis Upitis/The Image Bank, (right) © Dan McCoy/Rainbow; **66:** (top) © Dan McCoy/Rainbow, (bottom) Mallinckrodt Institute of Radiology/© 1989 Discover Magazine; **67:** © Manfred Kage/Peter Arnold, Inc.; **74:** Courtesy of Roger Sperry; **77:** (left) Courtesy of Leaf (Donruss), Lake Forest, IL, (right) Reproduced with the permission of and copyright 1991 by The Upper Deck Co.; **79:** Pennsylvania State University Center for Develop-

ment and Health Genetics; **82:** (left) © Tenneson/Gamma-Liaison Network, (right) Chun-Remote Pool/Sipa Press.

Chapter 4

85: © Diane Padys/FPG International; **88:** Craig McClain; **91:** © Ira Wyman/Sygma; **93:** BASF; **96:** Archives of the History of American Psychology, University of Akron, Akron, Ohio; **97:** © John David Fleck/Gamma-Liaison Network; **101:** (top left) © 1989 Floyd Holdman, (top right) © Gary Braasch, (center left) © Jeff Hunter/The Image Bank, (center right) © 1988 Bill Pogue, (bottom left) © Budge/Gamma Liaison Network, (bottom right) United States Department of Energy; **102:** Vincent van Gogh, *Hospital Corridor at Saint Remy* (1889), gouche and watercolor, $124^{1}/_{2} \times 18^{5}/_{8}"$ (61.3×47.3 cm), collection, The Museum of Modern Art, New York, Abby Aldrich Rockefeller Bequest; **104:** (left) © N. R. Rowan/The Image Works, (right) © Linda Bartlett/Photo Researchers, Inc.; **106:** © Jose A. Fernandez/Woodfin Camp & Associates; **109:** Yale School of Medicine; **110:** (left) © Danielle Pelligrini/Photo Researchers, Inc., (center) Guy Mary-Rousseliere, originally published in National Geographic Magazine, (right) © Malcolm Kirk; **115:** (top) *Maestro della cattura di Cristo, Cattura di Cristo*, parte centrale. Assisi, S. Francesco, Scala/Art Resource, (bottom) *Brera Predica di S. Marco Pinacoteca*, by Gentile e Giovanni Belini in Egitto, Scala/Art Resource, NY; **116:** (top) Georges Seurat, French, 1859–1891, *Sunday Afternoon on the Island of La Grand Jatte*, and detail, oil on canvas, 1884–1886, 207.6 × 308 cm., Helen Birch Bartlett Memorial Collection, 1926.224, © 1995 The Art Institute of Chicago, all rights reserved, (bottom) Pablo Picasso, *Violin and Grapes*, Ceret and Sorgues (spring–early fall 1912), oil on canvas, 20 × 24" (50.6 × 61cm), collection, The Museum of Modern Art, New York, Mrs. David M. Levy Bequest, Copyright ARS N.Y./SPADEM, 1912; **117:** Salvador Dali, *The Slave Market with the Disappearing Bust of Voltaire* (1940), Oil on canvas, $18^{1}/_{4} \times 25^{3}/_{8}$ inches. Collection of The Salvador Dali Museum, St. Petersburg, FL. Copyright © 1995 The Salvador Dali Museum, Inc. © 1995 Demart Pro Arte, Geneva/ARS, New York; **118:** Courtesy of Haags Gemeentemuseum, © 1961 M. C. Escher

Foundation, Baarn, Holland. All rights reserved.

Chapter 5

122: © Charles Gupton/The Stock Market; **123:** © John Greim 1988/The Stock Shop; **127:** Courtesy of William Dement; **130:** © Daemmrich/Stock, Boston; **131:** © Zefa/London/The Stock Market; **132:** Courtesy of Alexander Borbely; **134:** © Penny Tweedie/Tony Stone Images; **136:** Courtesy of Rosalind Cartwright, Rush Presbyterian St. Luke's Medical Center; **137:** (top) Courtesy of Theodore X. Barber, (bottom) AP/Wide World Photos; **138:** Courtesy of Ernest Hilgard, Stanford University; **144:** © Richard Sobol/Stock, Boston; **146:** © Topham/The Image Works.

Chapter 6

152: National Library of Medicine, Bethesda, Maryland; **155:** (top) Craig McClain, (bottom) © Pictor/Uniphoto; **158:** Archives of the History of American Psychology, University of Akron, Akron, Ohio; **160:** Courtesy of B. F. Skinner; **161:** © Richard Wood/Picture Cube; **163:** (left) Courtesy of Animal Behavior Enterprises, Inc., (right) © Elisabeth Weiland/Photo Researchers; **164:** © Hank Morgan/Rainbow; **166:** (top left) © Jeff Greenberg/Photo Edit, (top right) © Alain Keler/Sygma, (bottom left) © David Woods/The Stock Market, (bottom right) © Rick Dolye/Uniphoto; **173:** By permission of Dr. Carl Gustavson, photo courtesy of Prof. Stuart Ellins; **174:** John Markham/Bruce Coleman Ltd, London; **175:** (top) © Chip Henderson/Tony Stone Images, (bottom) Courtesy of Albert Bandura; **177:** (top left) By permission of Dr. Carl Gustavson, photo courtesy of Prof. Stuart Ellins, (top right) Archives of the History of American Psychology, (center left) © Elisabeth Weiland/Photo Researchers, (center right) © Alain Keler/Sygma, (bottom left) John Markham/Bruce Coleman Ltd, London, (bottom right) © Chip Henderson/Tony Stone Images.

Chapter 7

187: Marshall Cavendish Picture Library; **188:** Courtesy of George Miller; **190:** AP/Wide World Photos; **192:** Courtesy of William F. Brewer; **194:** Courtesy of Elizabeth Loftus; **195:** Wellcome Institute for the History of Medicine, London; **199:** (top) AP Photo/Mark Elias/Wide World Photos, (bottom) © Edward Ross/Sygma; **204:** (top) © Monkmeyer Press Photo, (bottom) Courtesy of Endel Tulving.

Chapter 8
211: Courtesy of Dr. Herbert Simon, Carnegie Mellon University; **216:** Wayne Weiten; **217:** Donna Coveney/MIT News Office; **218:** © Eugene Fisher/Gamma-Liaison Network; **226:** © Penny Tweedie/Woodfin Camp & Associates; **227:** (bottom) Craig McClain; **228:** (top left) © Tom McCarthy/Rainbow, (center left) AP Photo/Kathy Willens/Wide World Photos, (top right) Villard/238200/Sipa Press, (bottom) Craig McClain; **229:** (top) Edward W. Souza, News and Publication Service, Stanford University, (bottom) Courtesy of Daniel Kahneman.

Chapter 9
241: The Bettmann Archive; **242:** Archives of the History of American Psychology, University of Akron, Akron, Ohio; **247:** (left) Pool Reuters/Bettmann, (center) Reprinted with permission and courtesy of Harpo Productions, Inc., (right) © Tony Savino/Sygma; **251:** Courtesy of Sandra Scarr; **253:** Courtesy of Arthur R. Jensen; **254:** © 1991 David Hathcox, courtesy of Robert Sternberg; **260:** (left) © Bernard Gotfryd/Woodfin Camp & Associates, (center) Mark Adams/Gamma-Liaison Network, (right) Courtesy of Netscape Communications.

Chapter 10
263: (top) UPI/Bettmann, (bottom) Guy Gurney/*Sports Illustrated*; **264:** © Stephen J. Krasemann/DRK; **267:** Courtesy of Abraham Maslow, photo by William Carter; **271:** (top) © Steve Schleifer/Rainbow, (bottom) © John Eastcott/Vya Momatiuk/Woodfin Camp & Associates; **273:** © Jodi Buren/Woodfin Camp & Associates; **275:** Courtesy of David McClelland and Boston University Photo Services; **279:** (top) © David R. Frazier/Photo Researchers, (bottom) Dr. Paul Ekman, Human Interaction Laboratory, Langley Porter Institute; **280:** Copyright © 1975 Paul Ekman; **283:** (top) Courtesy of Stanley Schachter, (bottom) Courtesy of Donald G. Dutton, Department of Psychology, University of British Columbia; **287:** © Homor Sykes/Woodfin Camp & Associates.

Chapter 11
291: Archive Photos; **292:** (top left) © Science Source Photo/Photo Researchers, (bottom left) Science Source Photo/Photo Researchers, (right) © Cabisco/Visual Unlimited; **294:** Wayne Weiten; **297:** © Korner/AnthroPhoto; **299:** Erik Hesse; **301:** AP/Wide World Photos; **302:** © Michal

Heron/Woodfin Camp & Associates; **303:** Craig McClain; **305:** © Yves de Baines/Black Star; **307:** Harvard University Press Office; **313:** (left) AP/Wide World Photos, (right) Axel Koester/*Los Angeles Times*; **318:** © Dorothy Littell Greco/Stock, Boston; **319:** (left) © Network Productions/The Image Works, (right) © Bob Daemmrich/The Image Works; **320:** (left) © Bob Daemmrich/Tony Stone Images, (right) © Bob Daemmrich/The Image Works; **321:** (left) © Julie Marcotte/Tony Stone Images, (right) © Don Smetzer/Tony Stone Images; **325:** © Patti McConville/The Image Bank.

Chapter 12
330, 331: The Bettmann Archive; **337:** (top) Culver Pictures, Inc. (bottom) From *C. J. Jung Bild Und Wort*, © Walter-Verlag AG, Olten, Switzerland, 1977; **338:** (top) Culver Pictures, (bottom) © Sipa Press; **340:** Courtesy of B. F. Skinner; **341:** (top) © W. Hill/The Image Works, (bottom) Courtesy of Albert Bandura; **342:** Courtesy of Walter Mischel; **343:** Courtesy of Carl Rogers; **345:** Courtesy of Abraham Maslow; **347:** © Michael Nichols/Magnum Photos, Inc; **348:** Mark Gerson, FEIPP, London, courtesy of Hans J. Eysenck; **350:** © Cary Wolinsky/Stock, Boston; **351:** (top) Photo and Campus Services, University of Michigan, (bottom) Courtesy of Shinobu Kitayama; **352:** (from top to bottom) The Bettmann Archive, © Richard Wood/Picture Cube, © Zigy Kaluzny/Tony Stone Images, © Bob Daemmrich/Stock, Boston; **353:** (top to bottom) © Peter Southwick/Stock, Boston, © W. Hill/The Image Works, © Lawrence Migdale/Tony Stone Images; **357:** (top) Reprinted by permission of the publishers from Henry A. Murray, *Thematic Apperception Test*, Cambridge, Mass., Harvard University Press, Copyright © 1943 by the President and Fellows of Harvard College, © 1971 by Henry A. Murray, (bottom) © Mimi Forsyth/Monkmeyer Press Photo.

Chapter 13
362: Courtesy of Richard Lazerus; **367:** © Karsh/Woodfin Camp & Associates; **370:** © Tom McCarthy/The Picture Cube; **372:** Courtesy of Shelley E. Taylor; **374:** © Tom McCarthy/Photo Edit; **377:** © M. Bernsau/The Image Works; **380:** Steve Walag, University of California, Riverside; **381:** © Jeff Cadge/The Image Bank; **384:** Courtesy of Albert Ellis; **386:** © Bob Daemmrich/Stock, Boston.

Chapter 14
389: (left) Culver Pictures, Inc., (right) Detail from Di Benvenuto's *St. Catherine Exorcising Possessed Woman*, Denver Art Museum Collection; **390:** Joel Siegel, courtesy of Thomas Szasz; **391:** (top) © Rob Schoenbaum/Black Star, (bottom) © Peter

Menzel/Stock, Boston; **392:** © Sylvia Johnson/Woodfin Camp & Associates; **397:** (top) UPI/Bettmann, (bottom) AP/Wide World Photos; **407:** © David Jeffrey/The Image Bank; **409:** Courtesy of Nancy Andreasen; **411:** © Trippett/Sipa Press; **416:** © P. Chauvel/Sygma.

Chapter 15
419: (top) Mary Evans/Sigmund Freud Copyrights/Sulloway, (bottom) © Zigy Kaluzy/Tony Stone Images; **421:** © Sidney/Monkmeyer Press Photo; **422:** The Bettmann Archive; **424:** Courtesy of Carl Rogers; **425:** Courtesy of Aaron T. Beck; **426:** © Rick Brady/Uniphoto; **428:** Courtesy of Joseph Wolpe; **432:** Stuart Kenter & Associates; **433:** © James Wilson/Woodfin Camp & Associates; **435:** © Rhoda Sidney/Monkmeyer Press Photo; **436:** Culver Pictures, Inc, (inset) Detail of painting in Harrisburg State Hospital, photo by Ken Smith/LLR Collection; **441:** © Tom McCarthy.

Chapter 16
446: © Patti McConville/The Image Bank; **448:** Courtesy of the University of Kansas; **449:** © Eli Reed/Magnum Photos; **452:** © Dave Black; **453:** © Nancy Brown/The Image Bank; **454:** (top) Courtesy of Elaine Hatfield, (bottom) Courtesy of Ellen Berscheid; **459:** JELL-O is a registered trademark of Kraft General Foods, Inc. Reproduced with permission; **460:** © 1982 Karen Zebulon, courtesy of Leon Festinger; **463:** (top) Eric Kroll, (bottom) Photos copyright © 1965 by Stanley Milgram. From the film *Obedience*, distributed by The Pennsylvania State University. Reprinted by permission of Alexandra Milgram; **468:** © M. Attar/Sygma; **471:** © Robert E. Daemmrich/Tony Stone Images; **472:** © Bruce Ayers/Tony Stone Images.

Figure Credits

Chapter 1
Figure 1.4: Adapted from data from the American Psychological Association.
Figure 1.9: Adapted from a figure in *How to Succeed in College*, by M. K. Johnson, S. P. Springer, & S. H. Sternglanz. Copyright © 1982 by Crisp Publications, Inc., 1200 Hamilton Court, Menlo Park, CA 94025. Adapted by permission.
Figure 1.10: Adapted from *The Psychology of College Success: A Dymanic Approach*, by H. C. Lindgren, 1969. Copyright © 1969. Adapted by permission of H. C. Lindgren.
Figures 1.11 and 1.12: Adapted from "Staying with Initial Answers on Objection Tests: Is It a Myth?," by L. T. Benjamin, Jr., T. A. Cavell, & W. R. Shallenberger III, 1984, *Teaching of Psychology*, *II* (3), pp. 133–141. Copyright © 1984 by Lawrence

Erlbaum Associates, Inc. Adapted by permission;

Chapter 2
Table 2.2: Adapted from "Personality and Attitudinal Charactistics of Sexually Coercive College Males," by D. Rapaport and B. R. Burkhart, 1984, *Journal of Abnormal Psychology*, 93, (2), pp. 216–221. Copyright © 1984 by the American Psychological Association. Adapted by permission of the author.
Figure 2.11: Adapted from *Library Use: A Handbook for Psychology* (2nd ed.) by J. G. Reed and P. M. Baxter, p. 50, 1992. Copyright © 1992 by the American Psychological Association. Adapted by permission of the author.
Figures 2.12, 2.13: This material is reprinted with permission of the American Psychological Association, publisher of *Psychological Abstracts and the PsycINFO Database* (Copyright © 1967–1993) by the American Psychogical Association) and may not be reproduced without its prior consent.

Chapter 3
Figure 3.21: Based on data from "Behavioral Genetics of Cognitive Ability: A Life-Span Perspective," by M. McGue, T. J. Bouchard, W. G. Iacono, & D. T. Lykken, 1993. In R. Plomin & G. E. McClearn (Eds.), *Nature, Nurture and Psychology*. American Psychological Association. Extra version data based on *Genes and Environment in Personality Development*, by J. C. Loehlin, 1992. Sage Publications.
Figure 3.22: Cartoon courtesy of Roy Doty.
Figure 3.23: Reprinted by permission of The Putnam Publishing Group/Jeremy P. Tarcher, Inc. from *Drawing on the Right Side of the Brain* by Betty Edwards. Copyright © 1989 Betty Edwards.

Chapter 4
Figure 4.12: From *Introduction to Psychology* (2nd ed.), by James W. Kalat, p. 137. Copyright © 1990 by Wadsworth, Inc. Reproduced by permission.
Figure 4.24: Adapted by permission from an illustration by Ilil Arbel on page 83 of "Pictorial Perception and Culture," by Jan B. Deregowski in *Scientific American*, 227 (5) November 1972. Copyright © 1972 by Scientific American, Inc. All rights reserved.
Figure 4.29: Redrawn from *Mind Rights*, by R. N. Shepard, 1990, p. 144. Copyright © 1990 by Roger N. Shepard. Used by permission of W. H. Freeman and Company.
Figure 4.31: Table 5-3, adapted from *Introduction to Psychology* (9th ed.), by Rita L. Atkinson, Richard C. Atkinson, Edward F. Smith, and Ernest R. Hilgard, copyright © 1987 by Harcourt Brace and Company, reprinted by permission of the publisher.

Chapter 5
Figure 5.2: Adapted from *Wide Awake At 3 AM by Choice or by Chance*, by R. M. Coleman, 1986. W. H. Freeman & Company, Publishers. Copyright © 1986 by Richard M. Coleman. All rights reserved. Adapted by permission of the author.
Figure 5.5: From "Current Concepts: The Sleep Disorders," by P. Hauri, 1982. The Upjohn Company, Kalamazoo, Michigan. Used by permission.
Figure 5.7: Figure adapted from an updated revision of a figure in "Ontogenetic Development of Human Sleep Dream Cycle," by H. P. Roffwarg, J. N. Muzio, and W. C. Dement, 1966. *Science*, 152, 604–609. Copyright © 1966 by the American Association for the Advancement of Science. Adapted and revised by permission of the author.
Table 5.2: Figure from "The University of Typical Dreams: Japanese vs. Americans," by R. M. Griffith, O. Miyago, & A. Tago, 1958. *American Anthropologist*, 60, 1173–1179. Copyright © 1958 by the American Anthropological Association. Reproduced by permission of the American Anthropological Association from *American Anthropologist*, 60(6) pt. 1, December 1958. Not for further reproduction.
Table 5.3: Adapted from "The Personal Use of Dream Beliefs in the Toraja Highlands," by D. Hollan, 1989, *Ethos*, 17, 166–186. Copyright © 1989 by the American Anthropological Association. Reproduced by permission of the American Anthropological Association from *Ethos*, 17(2), June 1989. Not for further reproduction.
Figure 5.10: From Figure 4-6, adapted from *Hypnotic Susceptibility*, by Ernest R. Hilgard, 1965. Harcourt Brace and Company. Copyright 1965, renewed © 1993 by Ernest R. Hilgard. Used by permission of the author.
Figure 5.11: Based on an illustration on pg. 86 by Lorelle A. Raboni in *Scientific American*, 226, 85–90, February 1972, "The Physiology of Meditation," by R. K. Wallace and H. Bensen. Copyright © 1972 by Scientific American, Inc. All rights reserved.
Figure 5.13: Adapted from *Sleep, the Gentle Tyrant* (2nd ed.), by Wilse B. Webb, 1992. Copyright © 1992 by Anker Publishing Co., Bolton, MA. Adapted by permission.
Figure 5.14: Adapted from *How to Sleep Like a Baby* by Dianne Hales, p. 24. Copyright © 1987 by Dianne Hales. Reprinted by permission of Ballantine Books, a division of Random House, Inc.
Figure 5.16: Based on data from *Evaluation and Treatment of Insomnia*, by A. Kales and J. D. Kales, p. 95, 1984. Copyright © 1984 by Oxford University Press.

Chapter 6
Figure 6.1: Adapted from "The Method of Pavlov in Animal Psychology," by R. M. Yerkes and S. Morguluis, 1909, *Psychological Bulletin*, 6, 257–273. American Psychological Association.
Figure 6.21: Adapted from *Self-Directed Behavior: Self-Modification for Personal Adjustment*, by D. L. Watson and R. G. Tharp, 1989. Copyright © 1989 by Wadsworth , Inc. Adapted by permission of Brooks/Cole Publishing Company.

Chapter 7
Figure 7.1: From "Long-Term Memory for a Common Object," by R. S. Nickerson and M. J. Adams, 1979, *Cognitive Psychology*, 11, 287–307. Copyright © 1979 by Academic Press, Inc. Reprinted by permission.
Figure 7.8: Adapted from "Analysis of Rehearsal Processes in Free Recall," by D. Rundus, 1971, *Journal of Experimental Psychology*, 89, 63–77. Copyright © 1971 by the American Psychological Association. Adapted by permission of the author.
Figure 7.9: Adapted from "A Spreading Activation Theory of Semantic Processing," by A. M. Collins and E. Loftus, 1975, *Psychological Review*, 82, 407–428. Copyright © 1975 by the American Psychological Association. Adapted by permission of the author.
Figure 7.11: Based on "Reconstruction of Automobile Destruction: An Example of Interaction Between Language and Memory," by E. Loftus and J. C. Palmer, 1974, *Journal of Verbal Learning and Verbal Memory*, 13, 585–589.
Figure 7.16: From "Lies of the Mind," by Leon Jaroff, 1993, *Time Magazine*, November 29, 1993, p. 52. Copyright © 1993 Time, Inc. Reprinted by permission.
Figure 7.19: Data from "Quantitative and Qualitative Effects of Repetition on Learning from Technical Text," by B. K. Bromage and R. E. Mayer, 1986, *Journal of Educational Psychology*, 78 (4), 271–278. Copyright © 1986 by the American Psychological Association. Used by permission of the author.
Figure 7.20: Adapted from "A Breakdown of the Total-Time Law in Free-Recall Learning," by B. J. Underwood, 1970, *Journal of Verbal Learning and Verbal Behavior*, 9, 573–580. Copyright © 1970 by Academic Press, Inc. Adapted by permission.
Figure 7.21: Adapted from "Narrative Stories as Mediators of Serial Learning," by G. H. Bower and M. C. Clark, 1969, *Psychonomic Science*, 14, 181–182. Copyright © 1969 by the Psychonomic Society. Adapted by permission of the Psychonomic Society and the author.
Figure 7.22: Adapted from "Narrative Stories as Mediators of Serial Learning," by G. H. Bower and M. C. Clark, 1969, *Psychonomic Science*, 14, 181–182. Copyright © 1969 by the Psychonomic Society. Adapted by permission of the Psychonomic Society and the author.

Figure 7.23: Adapted from "Analysis of Mnemonic Device," by G. H. Bower, 1970, *American Scientist, 58*, Sept.–Oct., 496–499. Copyright © 1970 by the Scientific Research Society. Adapted by permission.

Chapter 8

Table 8.1: Adapted from *An Introduction to Cognitive Psychology*, by D. R. Moates and G. M. Schumacher. Copyright © 1980 by Wadsworth, Inc. Adapted by permission.
Figure 8.1: From *Child Development: A Topical Approach*, by A. Clarke-Stewart, S. Friedman, & J. Koch, 1985, p. 417. Copyright © 1985 by John Wiley & Sons, Inc. Reprinted by permission of John Wiley & Sons, Inc.
Figure 8.2: Adapted from *A First Language: The Early Stages*, by R. Brown, p. 55. Copyright © 1973 by the President and Fellows of Harvard College. Adapted by permission.
Figure 8.6: Adapted from "Classroom Experiments on Mental Set," by A. S. Luchins, 1942, *American Journal of Psychology, 1*(59), 295–298. Copyright © 1942 by University of Illinois Press. Adapted by permission.
Figure 8.7: From *Conceptual Blockbusting: A Guide to Better Ideas*, by J. L. Adams, pp. 17–18. Copyright © 1974 by James L. Adams. Used by permission of W. H. Freeman and Company.
Figure 8.8: Adapted from *Basic Psychology* (3rd ed.), by Howard H. Kendler, 1974, pp. 403–404. Copyright © 1974 The Benjamin-Cummings Publishing Co. Adapted by permission of Howard H. Kendler.
Figure 8.10: Adapted from "Classroom Experiments on Mental Set," by A. S. Luchins, 1942, *American Journal of Psychology, 1*(59), 295–298. Copyright © 1942 by University of Illinois Press. Adapted by permission.
Figure 8.11: From *Conceptual Blockbusting: A Guide to Better Ideas*, by J. L. Adams, pp. 17–18. Copyright © 1974 by James L. Adams. Used by permission of W. H. Freeman and Company.
Figure 8.12: Adapted from *Basic Psychology* (3rd ed.), by Howard H. Kendler, 1974, pp. 403–404. Copyright © 1974 The Benjamin-Cummings Publishing Co. Adapted by permission of Howard H. Kendler.
Figure 8.14: From "Field-Dependent and Field-Independent Cognitive Styles and Their Educational Implications," by H. A. Witkin, C. A. Moore, D. Goodenough, & P.W. Cox, 1977, *Review of Educational Research*, Winter 1977, pp. 1–164. Copyright © 1977 by the American Educational Research Association, Washington, D.C.

Chapter 9

Figure 9.6: Adapted from "People's Conceptions of Intelligence," by R. J. Sternberg, B. E. Conway, J. L. Keton, & M. Bernstein, 1981, *Journal of Personality and Social Psychology, 41*(1), p. 45. Copyright © 1981 by the American Psychological Association. Adapted by permission of the author.
Figure 9.7: Adapted from "Familial Studies of Intelligence: A Review," by T. J. Bouchard and M. McGue, 1981, *Science, 212*, 1055–1059. Copyright © 1981 by the American Association for the Advancement of Science. Adapted by permission of the author.
Figure 9.10: Based on *The Intelligence Controversy*, by H. J. Eysenck and L. Kamin, 1981. John Wiley & Sons, Inc.
Table 9.2: Adapted from "Multiple Intelligences Go to School: Educational Implications of the Theory of Multiple Intelligences," by H. Gardner, 1989, *Educational Researcher, 18*(8) 4–10. Copyright © 1989 American Educational Research Association.
Figure 9.12: Table adapted from *Cognition* by Margaret Matlin, copyright © 1983 by Holt Rinehart and Winston, Inc., reproduced by permission of the publisher.
Figure 9.13: From *Examiner's Manual: Remote Associates Test*, by Sarnoff and Martha Mednick, 1967. Houghton Mifflin Co. Copyright © 1967 by Sarnoff Mednick and Martha Mednick. Reprinted by permission of the author.

Chapter 10

Figure 10.8: Description reprinted by permission of David C. McClelland.
Figure 10.13: From *Unmasking the Face*, by Paul Ekman and W. V. Friesens. Consulting Psychological Press. Copyright © 1984, 1975 Paul Ekman. Reprinted by permission of Paul Ekman.
Figure 10.16: Adapted from art in "A Language for Emotions," by R. Plutchik, 1980, *Psychology Today, 13*(9), 68–78. Reprinted by permission from Psychology Today Magazine. Copyright © 1980 (Sussex Publishers, Inc.).
Figure 10.17: Adapted from "Obesity: Adverse Effects on Health and Longevity," by B. T. VanItallie, 1979, *American Journal of Clinical Nutrition, 32*, 2727. Copyright © 1979 by the American Society for Clinical Nutrition. Adapted by permission.

Chapter 11

Figure 11.1: Adapted from K. L. Moore and T. V. N. Persaud, *The Developing Human: Clinically Oriented Embryology* (5th ed.). Philadelphia. W. B. Saunders Co., 1993. Adapted by permission of the publisher and the author.
Figure 11.3: From a chart " Pay Now Or Pay Later," by Steve Hart in *Time Mazazine*, October 8, 1990, p. 45. Copyright © 1990 by Time Inc. Reproduced by permission.
Figure 11.6: Adapted from "Attachment," by P. R. Shaver and C. Hazan. In A. Weber and J. H. Harvey (Eds.), *Perspectives on Close Relationships*. Copyright © 1994 by Allyn and Bacon. Adapted by permission.
Table 11.2: Adapted from *Childhood and Society*, by Erik H. Erikson. Copyright 1950, © 1963 by W. W. Norton & Co. Inc., renewed 1978 , 1991 by by Erik H. Erikson. Reprinted by permission of W. W. Norton & Company, Inc.
Figure 11.9: Adapted from "The Development of Children's Orientations Toward a Moral Order: I. Sequence in the Development of Moral Thought," by L. Kohlberg, 1963, *Vita Humana 6*, 11–33. Copyright © 1963 by S. Karger Publishers, Inc. Basel. Adapted by permission.
Figure 11.12: Adapted from "Identity in Adolescence," by J. E. Marcia, 1980. In J. Adelson (Ed.) *Handbook of Adolescent Psychology*, pp. 159–210. Copyright © 1980 by John Wiley & Sons, Inc. Adapted by permission of John Wiley & Sons, Inc.
Figure 11.13: Adapted from "A Residue of Tradition: Job, Careers and Spouses," by Donna H. Berardo, Constance L. Shehan, & Gerald R. Leslie, *Journal of Marriage and the Family, 49* (May 1987), 381–390. Copyright © 1987 by the National Council on Family Relations, 3989 Central Avenue NE, Suite 550, Minneapolis, MN 55421. Adapted by permission.
Figure 11.14: Adapted from "Marital Satisfaction Across the Family Life Cycle," by Boyd C. Rollins and Harold Feldman, 1970, *Journal of Marriage and the Family, 32*, 20–28. Copyright © 1970 by the National Council on Family Relations, 3989 Central Avenue NE, Suite 550, Minneapolis, MN 55421. Adapted by permission.
Figure 11.15: Adapted data from "Creative Productivity Between the Ages of 20 and 80 Years," by W. Dennis, 1966, *Journal of Gerontology, 21*(1), 1–8. Copyright © 1966 by the Gerontological Society of America. Adapted by permission.
Table 11.5: Adapted from "Sex Stereotypes: Issues of Change in the 70s", by T. L. Ruble, 1983, *Sex Roles, 9*, 397–402. Copyright © 1983 Plenum Publishing Company. Adapted by permission.

Chapter 12

Table 12.1: From "Validation of the Five-Factor Model of Personality Across Instruments and Observers," by R. R. McCrea and P. T. Costa, 1987, *Journal of Personality and Social Psychology, 52*(1), 81–90. Data in public domain.
Figure 12.6: Adapted from *Personality: Theory, Research and Application*, by C. R. Potkay and B. Allen, 1986, p. 246. Brooks/Cole Publishing Co. Copyright © 1986 by C. Potkay and B. Allen. Adapted by permission of Bem Allen.
Figure 12.7: From H. J. Eysenck, *The Biological Basis of Personality* (1st ed.), p. 36,

1967. Courtesy of Charles C Thomas, Publisher, Springfield, IL.
Figure 12.8: Adapted from "Personality Similarity in Twins Reared Apart and Together," by A. Tellegen, D. T. Lykken, T. J. Bouchard, Jr., K. J. Wilcox, N. L. Segal, & S. Rich, 1988, *Journal of Personality and Social Psychology, 54*(6), 1031–1039. Copyright © 1988 by the American Psychological Association. Adapted by permission of the author.
Figure 12.9: Adapted from "Culture and the Self: Implications for Cognition, Emotion, and Motivation," by H. R. Markus and S. Kitayama, 1991, *Psychological Review, 98*, 224–253. Copyright © 1991 by the American Psychological Association. Adapted by permission.
Table 12.4: Adapted with permission from "Objective Personality Assessment," by L. S. Keller, J. N. Butcher, & W. S. Slutske, 1990. In G. Goldstein and M. Hersen (Eds.), *Handbook of Psychological Assessment*, pp. 345–386. Copyright © 1990. All rights reserved. Reprinted by permission of Allyn & Bacon.
Figure 12.11: From R. B. Cattell in *Psychology Today*, July 1973, pp. 40–46. Reprinted with permission from Psychology Today Magazine. Copyright © 1973 (Sussex Publishers, Inc.).

Chapter 13
Table 13.1: Adapted by permission from "The Social Readjustment Rating Scale," by T. H. Holmes and R. H. Rahe, 1967, *Journal of Psychosomatic Research, 11*, 213–218. Copyright © 1967 by Elsevier Science, Inc.
Figure 13.5: Adapted from *The Stress of Life*, by Hans Selye, 1956, p. 121. Copyright © 1956 by McGraw-Hill Book Company. Adapted by permission.
Table 13.2: Table adapted from *Abnormal Psychology and Modern Life* (8th ed.), by R. C. Carson, J. N. Butcher, & J. C. Coleman, 1988, pp. 64–65. Copyright © 1988 by Scott, Foresman and Company. Reprinted by permission of HarperCollins College Publishers.
Figure 13.9: Adapted from "Associative Learning Habit and Health Behavior," by W. A. Hunt, J. D. Matarazzo, S. M. Weiss, & W. D. Gentry, 1979, *Journal of Behavorial Medicine, 2*(2), 113. Copyright © 1979 by the Plenum Publishing Corporation. Adapted by permission.
Figure 13.10: Adapted from "A Three City Comparison of the Public's Knowledge and Attitudes About AIDS," by L. Temosho, D. M. Sweet, & J. Zich, 1987, *Psychology & Health, 1*(1), 43–60. Copyright © 1987 by Harwood Academic Publishers GmbH. Adapted by permission.
Figure 13.14: Text adapted from *The Relaxation Response*, pp. 14–15 by Herbert Benson and Miriam Z. Klipper. Copyright © 1975 by William Morrow & Company, Inc. By permission of William Morrow & Co., Inc.

Figure 13.15: Based on "Physical Fitness and All-Cause Mortality," by S. N. Blair, H. W. Kohl, R. S. Paffenbarger, D. G. Clark, K. H. Cooper, & L. W. Gibons, 1989, *Journal of the American Medical Association, 262*, 2395–2401. Copyright © 1989 by the American Medical Association. Use by permission.

Chapter 14
Figures 14.3, 14.4: Adapted with permission from *the Diagnostic and Statistical Manual of Mental Disorders* (4th ed.), 1994. Copyright © 1994 American Psychiatric Association
Figure 14.5: Adapted from "Panic and Phobia," by W. W. Eaton, A. Dryman, & M. M. Weissman. Adapted and reprinted with the permission of The Free Press, an imprint of Simon & Schuster from *Psychiatric Disorders in America: The Epidemiologic Catchmen Area Study* edited by Lee N. Robins and Darrel A. Regier. Copyright © 1991 by Lee N. Robins and Darrel A. Regier.
Table 14.2: From Sarason/Sarason, *Abnormal Psychology: The Problem of Maladaptive Behavior* (5th ed.). © 1987, p. 283. Reprinted by permission of Prentice-Hall, Inc., Englewood Cliffs, NJ.
Figure 14.10: From *Manic-Depressive Illness*, by Frederick K. Goodwin and Kay R. Jamison , p. 132. Copyright © 1990 by Oxford University Press., Inc. Reprinted by permission .
Figure 14.14: Data from "Clues to the Genetics and Neurobiology of Schizophrenia," by S. E. Nicol and I. I. Gottesman, 1983, *American Scientist, 71*, 398–404. Copyright © 1983 by Sigma Xi. Additional data from *Schizophrenia Genesis:The Origins of Madness*, by I. I. Gottesman, 1991. W. H. Freeman & Co.
Figure 14.16: Adapted from "Epidemiology of Suicide in the U.S.," by J. L. McIntosh, 1991. In A. A. Leenaars (Ed.), *Life Span Perspectives of Suicide*, p. 64. Copyright © 1991 by Plenum Publishing. Adapted by permission.
Figure 14.18: Adapted from "Suicide, Attempted Suicide and Relapse Rates in Depression," by D. Avery and G. Winokur, 1978, *Archives of General Psychiatry*, June, *35*, 749–753. Copyright © 1978 by the American Medical Association. Adapted by permission.

Chapter 15
Table 15.2: Adapted from *Cognitive Therapy and the Emotional Disorders*, by Aaron T. Beck, 1976, International Universities Press. Copyright © 1976 by Aaron T. Beck. Adapted by permission of the publisher.
Figure 15.1: From *Methods of Self-Change: An ABC Primer*, by K. E. Rudestam, 1980, pp. 42–43. Copyright © 1980 by Wadsworth, Inc. Reprinted by permission.

Figure 15.3: Data from *NIMH-PCS Collaborative Study I* and reported in "Drugs in the Treatment of Psychosis," by J. O. Cole, S. C. Goldberg, & J. M. Davis, 1966, 1985. In P. Solomon (Ed.), *Psychiatric Drugs*, Grune & Stratton. Data updated by J. M. Davis, 1985. Used by permission of John M. Davis.
Table 15.3: From "New Drug Evaluations: Alprazolam," by R. L. Evans, 1981, *Drug Intelligence and Clinical Pharmacy, 15*, 633–637. Copyright © 1981 by Harvey Whitney Books Company. Reprinted by permission.
Figure 15.8: Adapted from "Meta Analysis of Psychotherapy Outcome Series," by M. L. Smith and G. V. Glass, 1977, *American Psychologist, 32* (Sept.), 752–760. Copyright © 1977 by the American Psychological Association. Adapted by permission of the author.

Chapter 16
Page 445: Excerpt from: *Tales from the Front* by Cheryl Lavin and Laura Kavesh. Copyright © 1988 by Cheryl Lavin and Laura Kavesh. Used by permission of Doubleday, a division of Bantam Doubleday Dell Publishing Group, Inc.
Figure 16.2: Based on "Perceiving the Causes of Success and Failure," by B. Weiner, I. Friese, A. Kukla, L. Reed, & R. M. Rosenbaum, 1972. In E. E. Jones, D. E. Kanuouse, H. H. Kelley, R. E. Nisbett, S. Valins, & B. Weiner (Eds.) *Perceiving the Causes of Behavior*, 1972. General Learning Press. Used by permission of Dr. Bernard Weiner.
Figure 16.6: Adapted from *Introduction to Psychology*, by R. A. Lippa, 1994. Copyright © 1994 Brooks/Cole Publishing Company. Adapted by permission.
Figures 16.10, 16.11: From "Opinion and Social Pressure," by Solomon Asch, *Scientific American*, November 1955, from illustrations by Sara Love on pp. 32, 35. Copyright © 1955 by Scientific American, Inc. All rights reserved.
Figure 16.13: Data from "Bystander Intervention in Emergencies: Diffusion of Responsibility," by J. M. Darley and B. Latané, 1968, *Journal of Personality and Social Psychology, 8*, 377–383. American Psychological Association.
Figure 16.14: Data from "Many Hands Make Light the Work: The Causes and Consequences of Social Loafing," by B. Latané, K. Williams, & S. Harkins, 1979, *Journal of Personality and Social Psychology, 37*, 822–832. American Psychological Association.
Figure 16.16: Reprinted with permission of The Free Press, a division of Simon & Schuster, from *Decision Making: A Psychological Analysis of Conflict, Choice and Commitment*, p. 132, by Irving L. Janis and Leon Mann. Copyright © 1977 by The Free Press.

TO THE OWNER OF THIS BOOK:

I hope that I've been able to make this book likable. I'd like to learn your reactions to using this textbook. Only through your comments and the comments of others can I hope to improve the next edition of *Psychology: Themes and Variations, Briefer Version.*

School: _____

Your instructor's name: _____

1. What did you like most about *Psychology: Themes and Variations*? _____

_____

_____

2. What did you like least about the book? _____

_____

_____

3. Were all the chapters assigned for you to read?   Yes _____   No _____

    If not, which ones were omitted? _____

4. Did you use the Concept Checks?   Yes _____   No _____

    Were they helpful?   Yes _____   No _____

_____

_____

5. How interesting and informative were the Application sections? _____

_____

_____

6. How helpful were the themes in fostering an understanding of basic insights about psychology? _____

_____

_____

7. In the space below (or in a separate letter) please let me know what other comments about the book you'd like to make. (For example, did you like the Integrated Running Glossary?). I'd be delighted to hear from you!

_____

_____

_____

_____

Optional:

Your name: _____ Date: _____

May Brooks/Cole quote you, either in promotion for *Psychology: Themes and Variations, 3rd Edition, Briefer Version*, or in future publishing ventures?

Yes: _____ No: _____

Sincerely,

Wayne Weiten

FOLD HERE

BUSINESS REPLY MAIL
FIRST CLASS   PERMIT NO. 358   PACIFIC GROVE, CA

POSTAGE WILL BE PAID BY ADDRESSEE

ATT: *Wayne Weiten* _____

Brooks/Cole Publishing Company
511 Forest Lodge Road
Pacific Grove, California 93950-9968

NO POSTAGE
NECESSARY
IF MAILED
IN THE
UNITED STATES

FOLD HERE